Marketing Channels

A Management View

EIGHTH EDITION

BERT ROSENBLOOM

Drexel University

SOUTH-WESTERN
CENGAGE Learning·

Australia • Brazil • Japan • Korea • Mexico • Singapore • Spain • United Kingdom • United States

SOUTH-WESTERN
CENGAGE Learning·

Marketing Channels: A Management View, Eighth International Edition
Bert Rosenbloom

Vice President of Editorial, Business: Jack W. Calhoun

Editor-in-Chief: Melissa Acuña

Executive Editor: Michael Roche

Developmental Editor: Daniel Noguera

Editorial Assistant: Megan Fischer

Marketing Manager: Gretchen Swann

Marketing Coordinator: Leigh Smith

Senior Art Director: Stacy Jenkins Shirley

Senior Marketing Communications Manager: Jim Overly

Media Editor: John Rich

Manufacturing Planner: Ron Montgomery

Production Manager: D. Jean Buttrom

Content Project Management: PreMediaGlobal

Compositor: PreMediaGlobal

Permissions Acquisition Manager/Photo: Deanna Ettinger

Permissions Acquisition Manager/Text: Sam Marshall

Cover Designer: Patti Hudepohl

Cover Photo Credits:

    B/W Image: Getty Images/Hisham Ibrahim

    Color Image: Shutterstock Images/Lisa F. Young

Library of Congress Control Number: 2011940272

International Edition:

ISBN-13: 978-0-538-47760-4

ISBN-10: 0-538-47760-1

Cengage Learning International Offices

Asia
www.cengageasia.com
tel: (65) 6410 1200

Australia/New Zealand
www.cengage.com.au
tel: (61) 3 9685 4111

Brazil
www.cengage.com.br
tel: (55) 11 3665 9900

India
www.cengage.co.in
tel: (91) 11 4364 1111

Latin America
www.cengage.com.mx
tel: (52) 55 1500 6000

UK/Europe/Middle East/Africa
www.cengage.co.uk
tel: (44) 0 1264 332 424

Represented in Canada by Nelson Education, Ltd.
www.nelson.com
tel: (416) 752 9100/(800) 668 0671

Cengage Learning is a leading provider of customized learning solutions with office locations around the globe, including Singapore, the United Kingdom, Australia, Mexico, Brazil, and Japan. Locate your local office at: **www.cengage.com/global**

For product information: **www.cengage.com/international**
Visit your local office: **www.cengage.com/global**
Visit our corporate website: **www.cengage.com**

To
Pearl, Jack, Robyn, Staci, Jacob, and Anya

Brief Contents

Contents

PART 3   Managing the Marketing Channel

CHAPTER 9

CHAPTER 10

PART 5 Cases

Preface

Marketing channels provide the means through which the vast array of products and services from all over the globe are made available to hundreds of millions of customers seeking to buy those products and services in every country, city and town in the world. As we move into the second decade of the twenty-first century, new technologies coupled with globalization have dramatically transformed marketing channels as well as the expectations of customers served by marketing channels. Conventional "bricks and mortar" channels have not only been dramatically augmented by online channels but customers can also shop while literally being on the move from locations all over the globe with a laptop, iPhone, iPad or other device. This mobile commerce capability has been enhanced by the dramatic growth in social networking where more and more social networking sites now enable visitors to shop for products and services without having to leave those sites.

These developments have created a metamorphosis in marketing channels and customer expectations: Customers now expect, and marketing channels must now provide, high levels of choice to customers in what products and services are made available to them, how, when and where they wish to buy them. So, when it comes to which marketing channels customers will want access to in the twenty-first century, customer expectations are likely to drive an answer of "all of the above." If a consumer wants to be able to buy a product while on Facebook, an e-commerce channel embedded in the Facebook site will need to be there. If a customer wants to buy something using her smartphone while jogging, that channel must also be available. But when a different customer, or even the same customer, wants to visit a land-based store or browse though a paper catalog to buy something, that customer will still expect those "old fashioned" channels to be there as well.

This new multi-channel environment has broadened the task of channel strategy and management as we move beyond the first decade of the twenty-first century. The range of channel options available to the channel manager to make products and services conveniently available to channel-surfing customers is wider but the challenge of creating and managing an optimal channel mix has become greater. Channel managers must now not only understand the capabilities and limitations of conventional marketing channels but also the even greater challenge of how to integrate high-tech, electronic channels into conventional marketing channels to create a seamless customer experience. Although the "toolkit" available to channel managers to make products and services available to customers is now fuller, more knowledge and skill will be needed to use those tools effectively.

Features of the Eighth Edition

This eighth edition of *Marketing Channels: A Management View* has been revised to address the new multi-channel challenge of the twenty-first century. Throughout the book, new high-tech channel options such as mobile commerce (m-commerce) and channels associated with social networks (sometimes referred to as *s-commerce* or *f-commerce*, short for *Facebook commerce*), have been integrated into the various topical areas of channel management.

The integration of these new marketing channel options into the mainstream of marketing channel strategy and management is just part of the story of the eighth edition of *Marketing Channels: A Management View*. The text has been thoroughly revised to reflect changing economic, sociocultural, competitive, technological and legal phenomena as they impact marketing channels. This edition has also put even more stress on the growing importance of marketing channels as a strategic area of marketing management. The increased attention by companies and organizations across a broad spectrum of industries to view marketing channel strategy as a vital area for delivering customer value and creating sustainable competitive advantage has also been emphasized throughout the text.

This new edition focuses even more sharply on the need to view marketing channels as a strategic component of the marketing mix, along with the other strategic components of product, price, and promotion. The theme underlying every chapter stresses the need for the channel manager to understand how channel strategy can contribute to and be enhanced by the other strategic components of the marketing mix.

Every chapter of the eighth edition of *Marketing Channels: A Management View* has been carefully revised and updated to incorporate the latest thinking on marketing channels. New ideas and research findings from the academic literature have been blended with the most current insights from industry practice to provide cutting-edge coverage of all of the topics of marketing channels.

All of the Focus on Channels opening chapter vignettes are new in this edition and each chapter contains several new Channel Issues for Discussion mini-cases that reflect the most recent developments affecting marketing channels. Over a third of the Case Studies are new and they encompass a variety of topics in channels that were not covered in the cases they replace. Numerous new examples and vignettes have also been added to the chapters to illustrate concepts, using the most up-to-date material.

What has *not* changed through all eight editions of *Marketing Channels: A Management View* is the book's basic objective: *to provide a management focus and decision making framework to the field of marketing channels*. Theory, research and practice are covered thoroughly and blended into a discussion that stresses *decision making implications*. Also kept intact are the core features of the book that have been so well-received in previous editions. The organization of material within each chapter has been very carefully developed to keep the reader on target. The writing style stresses a clear, concise and interesting treatment of the subject and up-to-date examples and vignettes are employed abundantly in every chapter. Finally, the structure and pedagogy of the book have been carefully refined during the eight editions. Learning objectives, focused chapter-opening vignettes, precise organization and heading structure, end-of-chapter summaries, review questions, issues for discussion mini-cases at the end of each chapter and 25 full case studies at the back of the book, cross-referenced to the material in each chapter make the eighth edition of *Marketing Channels: A Management View* a truly user-friendly book.

Overview of the Eighth Edition

Part 1, Marketing Channel Systems, comprises four chapters that present the basic foundation of marketing channels concepts within a managerial framework. Chapter 1 presents the core concepts of marketing channels and has been revised to emphasize even more strongly the strategic importance of marketing channels in the larger field of marketing. Chapter 2 provides a detailed discussion of the channel participants, using the latest wholesale and retail census data available, and presents a detailed analysis of distribution tasks. Chapter 3 discusses the environment of marketing channels and the implications of environmental changes for marketing channel management. The discussion of economic, competitive, socio-cultural, technological and legal environments has been revised to reflect the latest developments in these areas. Chapter 4, dealing with behavioral processes in marketing channels, has been updated to incorporate relevant behavioral channel research conducted since publication of the previous edition.

Part 2, Developing the Marketing Channel, begins with a revised Chapter 5. This chapter provides a comprehensive discussion of strategy in marketing channels using a strategic framework for dealing with all of the key channel management decisions raised in subsequent chapters. Chapter 6 presents a thorough analysis of channel design. The seven-phase *channel design paradigm* used in the previous seven editions has been retained but some additional material and refinements have been added. Chapter 7 provides a detailed discussion of the last phase of channel design (selection of channel members) that incorporates some new illustrative material. Chapter 8, the last chapter in Part 2, deals with how various market dimensions influence channel design strategy and has been refined and updated where appropriate.

Part 3, Managing the Marketing Channel, comprising Chapters 9–14, deals with the administration of existing channels. Chapter 9 opens with a comprehensive analysis of the motivation of channel members. Along with updating and refinements, the revision of this chapter places emphasis on *strategic alliances and partnerships* for motivating channel members. Chapter 10, on product issues in channel management, has been revised to include still more emphasis on information gathering to monitor the product flow through the channel. The focus of Chapter 11 is on the interfaces between pricing and channel management. This chapter has been revised to update the material. Chapter 12, which discusses promotion through the marketing channel, has been updated to incorporate new research findings on push promotion strategies. Chapter 13 provides an overview of logistics in relation to channel management that addresses the newer emphasis on supply chain management and efficient consumer response. Chapter 14 presents an analysis of the issues involved in evaluating channel member performance. Appropriate updates and new references have been incorporated in this chapter.

Part 4, Additional Perspectives on Marketing Channels, contains the four final chapters of the textbook. Chapter 15, Electronic Marketing Channels, leads off this section with a comprehensive analysis of the role of Internet-based marketing channels. The chapter has been completely rewritten to reflect the metamorphosis that has occurred in E-commerce during the relatively short period since the last edition of the text was published. This chapter now also incorporates recent developments in mobile and so-cial-networking-based electronic marketing channels.

Chapter 16, which is new to this edition, presents a comprehensive analysis of business format franchise channels. Franchise terminology, trends in franchising, advantages and disadvantages of franchise channels, as well as implications for managing franchise channels are covered in this chapter. An appendix that reproduces the complete franchise contract for Dunkin' Donuts Inc. is included at the end of the chapter. Chapter 17, dealing with marketing channels for services, provides a concise overview of the characteristics of services as they relate to channel management. Chapter 18 presents an updated discussion of the key issues in international channel management.

Part 5 comprises 25 full case studies in a balanced mix of short, medium and long cases. Over one-third of the cases are new to this edition. A matrix relating the cases to relevant chapters can be found at the beginning of this part.

Supplementary Material

The eighth edition of *Marketing Channels: A Management View* is accompanied by answers to the review questions, commentaries on the issues for discussion, and a discussion of the cases, and a PowerPoint presentation, all of which can be found on the Web site at www.cengagebrain.com.

Acknowledgments

From the original edition of *Marketing Channels: A Management View* through this eighth edition, I have benefited greatly from the input of an outstanding group of reviewers. They have provided perspectives, insights and constructive criticisms that have been vital to the success of the book. I would therefore like to express my heartfelt thanks to the following colleagues who have participated in the review process on one or more of the editions of *Marketing Channels: A Management View.*

Boris W. Becker
Oregon State University

Thomas Belich
University of Minnesota

Stephanie Bibb
Chicago State University

William Black
University of Arizona–Tucson

Jerry Bradley
St. Joseph's University

Ernest Castillo
Fort Hays State University

M. Bixby Cooper
Michigan State University

Donald J. English, Jr.
St. Mary's College

S. Alton Erdem
University of Houston, Clear Lake

Nermin Eyboglu
Baruch College, City University of New York

Alan Flaschner
University of Toledo

J. Robert Foster
University of Texas at El Paso

Eugene H. Fox
Northeast Louisiana University

John Fraedrich
Southern Illinois University at Carbondale

David Glascoff
East Carolina University

Larry Gresham
Texas A&M University

Joseph Guiltinan
Notre Dame University

Jeffery Hittler
Indiana University

Stephen K. Keiser
University of Delaware

Keysok Kim
Baruch College, CUNY

Raymond W. Knab, Jr.
New York Institute of Technology

Ruth Krieger
Oklahoma State University

Charles W. Lamb, Jr.
Texas Christian University

Robert Loewer
San Jose State University

John Mather
Carnegie Mellon University

Donna T. Mayo
Middle Tennessee State University

Richard McFarland
Kansas State University

Joseph Miller
Indiana University

James Nall
Gardner-Webb University

Jacqueline Z. Nicholson
Westfield State College

James R. Ogden
Adams State College

Larry R. O'Neal
Stephen F. Austin State University

Nita Paden
Northern Arizona University

Richard L. Pinkerton
Cal State University, Fresno

Thomas G. Ponzurick
West Virginia University

J. R. Smith
Jackson State University

Casimir Raj
Saint Louis University

Tracy Tripp
Ithaca College

William Rhey
University of Tampa

Orville C. Walker, Jr.
University of Minnesota

Kenneth J. Rolnicki
Kellogg Community College

Kaylene C. Williams
University of Delaware

Rosalyn Rufer
Empire State College

Joyce A. Young
Indiana State University

Martin Schlissel
St. John's University

The staff at Cengage Learning South-Western also have my sincere appreciation for the high level of professionalism and skill they provided throughout the revision process of the eighth edition of *Marketing Channels: A Management View*. Mike Roche, Executive Acquisitions Editor, provided encouragement and advice that proved to be very helpful. Daniel Noguera, Developmental Editor, offered many ideas and suggestions for enhancing the manuscript. Jean Buttrom and Prashanth Kamavarapu, Production Editors, made sure that the myriad processes and details involved in the revision all fell into their proper places. PreMediaGlobal, Inc., provided excellent copy editing and the production expertise required to turn a rough manuscript into a polished textbook. Finally, Gretchen Swann, Marketing Manager, offered insights to promote the book effectively.

My research assistant Boryana Dimitrova deserves thanks for her help in the research for the eighth edition. Thanks are also due to Trina Larsen, head of the marketing department at Drexel University, for her encouragement during the revision process and for the support provided by Dean George Tesetsekos. I would also like to express my appreciation to the undergraduate and graduate students in my marketing channels classes at Drexel University who provided valuable input and feedback.

Finally, as with the earlier editions, my deepest thanks is reserved for my wife, Pearl, for her gracious and good-natured support throughout the long and arduous revision process.

Bert Rosenbloom
Philadelphia, Pa.,
September 2011

About the Author

Dr. Bert Rosenbloom holds the Rauth Chair in Marketing Management in the LeBow College of Business, at Drexel University. Before coming to Drexel, he served on the faculty of the City University of New York.

Dr. Rosenbloom is a leading expert on the management of marketing channels and distribution systems. *Marketing Channels: A Management View*, eighth edition is one of his twelve books. His book *Retail Marketing* (Random House), a pioneering text on the application of modern marketing methods to retail channels, has had a major impact on distribution throughout the U.S. and other countries around the world. Another of his books, *Marketing Functions and the Wholesaler Distributor* (Distribution Research and Education Foundation) has been acclaimed in the wholesaling sector for providing the industry with new concepts and analytical methods for increasing productivity in wholesale marketing channels.

Dr. Rosenbloom's research has been widely published in the major professional journals of marketing such as *Journal of Marketing, Journal of Retailing, Journal of the Academy of Marketing Science, Business Horizons, Industrial Marketing Management, Journal of Consumer Marketing, Journal of Personal Selling and Sales Management, Management Review, Long Range Planning, Psychology of Marketing, European Journal of Marketing* and numerous others. His research is also frequently presented at professional conferences of the American Marketing Association, Academy of Marketing Science, World Marketing Congress, Retail Research Society, Distribution Research and Education Foundation, Direct Selling Education Foundation, and many others in the United States, Western Europe, Eastern Europe, Asia, Australia, and New Zealand.

Dr. Rosenbloom served as the editor of the *Journal of Marketing Channels* and has served on the editorial boards of *Psychology & Marketing, Industrial Marketing Management*, the *Journal of Consumer Marketing, Journal of the Academy of Marketing Science*, and *Journal of International Consumer Marketing*, and on the ad hoc review boards of the *Journal of Marketing Research, Journal of Marketing* and *Journal of Retailing*. He also served as Academic Consulting Editor for the Random House series of books on marketing. In addition, he has served as the Vice President of the Philadelphia Chapter of the American Marketing Association, on the Board of Governors of the Academy of Marketing Science, and was awarded an Erskine Fellowship. He also served as President of the International Management Development Association.

As an active consultant, Dr. Rosenbloom has consulted for a broad range of industries in manufacturing, wholesaling, retailing, communications, services and real estate in the United States and abroad.

Dr. Rosenbloom is listed in *Who's Who in America, American Men and Women of Science* and *Who's Who in the World*.

Marketing Channels

PART 1

Marketing Channel Systems

CHAPTER 1

Marketing Channel Concepts

LEARNING OBJECTIVES

After reading this chapter, you should:

1. Realize that new Internet-based technologies have created a metamorphosis in marketing channels and distribution systems.

2. Recognize that today's customers expect more choices as to how, when, and where products and services are made available to them.

3. Be aware of the need for multi-channel strategies and structures to satisfy heightened customer expectations for channel choice.

4. Understand the definition of the marketing channel from a managerial perspective.

5. See how marketing channels relate to the other strategic variables in the marketing mix.

6. Know the flows in marketing channels and how they relate to channel management.

7. Understand the principles of specialization and division of labor as well as contactual efficiency in marketing channels.

8. Be familiar with the concepts of channel structure and ancillary structure and recognize the difference between them.

© Susan Van Etten

FOCUS ON CHANNELS

Amazon.com Has Become the Walmart of the Internet.
Now Walmart wants to be the Walmart of the Internet

When it comes to online channels of distribution, Amazon.com, with over $20 billion in annual sales, has been the overwhelming winner both in sales revenue and top-of-mind recognition. In fact, Amazon.com has become the ultimate icon for online shopping. Just about everybody in the world has heard of Amazon.com and a large portion of that vast audience has purchased something from the company. To say that Amazon.com has become the Walmart of the Internet is certainly not an overstatement, and if anything, might even be an understatement.

But will Amazon.com's domination of online channels of distribution continue into perpetuity? Not if Walmart can help it! Walmart, the world's largest retailer in conventional "bricks and mortar" retail channels is not about to let Amazon.com continue to dominate online channels without a pretty serious fight. In addition to rapidly building up its online channels for selling its own merchandise, Walmart has taken a page from Amazon.com's channel strategy playbook by offering merchandise from other retailers through Walmart's new virtual online mall called Walmart Marketplace. Over one million new items have been added to Walmart.com's product assortment from these outside sellers. And, just like Amazon.com's virtual mall, Walmart Marketplace will never see or touch the merchandise it sells because the affiliated retailers ship directly from their sites and handle all exchanges and returns while Walmart.com receives a commission on all product sales.

While imitation may be the sincerest form of flattery, does Walmart believe that its online channel sales might someday equal or surpass those of Amazon.com? Kerry Cooper, Walmart.com's chief marketing officer certainly thinks so: "Our vision is to make Walmart.com the most visited and valued online site."

If Mr. Cooper is right, someday Walmart, not Amazon.com, will be the Walmart of the Internet!

Source: Based on Miguel Bustillo and Geoffrey A. Fowler, "Wal-Mart Sets Outside Offerings In Online Mall," *Wall Street Journal* (September 1, 2009): B6.

We are now well into the second decade of the Twenty-First Century. As consumers in this era, we can still find all around us "bricks and mortar" stores, shopping centers, and malls. In fact, as we mentioned above, Walmart, the largest retailer in the world by sales volume, still derives most of its over $400 billion in revenue from its land-based stores.[1] Other giant retailers operating physical "big box" stores such as Home Depot, Staples, Best Buy, and numerous others are still here as well. So too are many other traditional marketing channel participants such as wholesalers and industrial distributors, manufacturer's representatives, and selling agents and brokers serving many industries while operating in the land-based world of physical facilities and legions of real people with "boots on the ground."

But the fact that these traditional marketing channels continue to exist and even thrive in the second decade of the Twenty-First Century does not change the fact that a great metamorphosis has occurred in this century that has profoundly altered the structure of marketing channels.[2] The emergence of Internet-based electronic commerce toward the end of the Twentieth Century was the seminal phenomenon[3] that set the stage for a host of new technologies, business models, and innovative firms that opened up a whole new world of possibilities for channels of distribution.[4] Indeed, it seems we cannot go through a single day without hearing about online commerce, mobile commerce, social networking, YouTube, Facebook, Twitter, Hulu, Skype, PayPal, the iPhone, iPad, cloud computing, "Cyber-Monday" instead of "Black Friday" and a host of other iconic terms and names associated with the digital age in which we live.

The implications of these and similar phenomena for marketing channel strategy and structure are just beginning to emerge.[5] One overriding implication, however, is already crystal clear: *customers now expect far more and better channel choices for gaining access to the vast array of products and services from all over the planet—how, where, and when they want them.*[6] From walking into a store to touching the screen on an iPhone while running to catch a plane, today's customer expects the buying experience to be simple, quick, and seamless. If it is not, a Tweet may soon be launched from the same iPhone to inform the unhappy customer's social network and whomever else is interested in hearing about the less-than-satisfactory buying experience.

Such heightened customer expectations for more and better ways to shop for products and services from around the globe have, in turn, created a formidable challenge for firms in the business of distributing those products and services: *High customer expectations not only need to be met, but exceeded, to provide the high-level shopping experience customers expect.*

It is through effective and efficient marketing channels that this challenge can be addressed. But in today's complex global environment, this is not an easy challenge to meet. Everyday, literally billions of people, as well as millions of industrial companies, businesses, institutions, and other organizations all over the world, need and want millions of different products and services. Somehow, this vast conglomeration must be sorted out and matched up so that customers get the goods and services when and where they are needed. This may involve shopping at a traditional retail store such as Gap to buy a sweater, downloading digitized music through an iPod or iPhone, downloading a book on a Kindle or an iPad, or even ordering the item the old-fashioned way by phone from one of the 17 billion paper catalogs still sent to customers annually in the United States alone.[7] In the business-to-business (B2B) sector, businesses may not only distribute through traditional industrial distributors, wholesalers, and manufacturers' representatives, but may also need the services of sophisticated online marketplaces such as Alibaba.com or online channel facilitators such as ChannelAdvisors.com.[8]

Most customers, especially in consumer markets, are unaware of the enormous effort involved in making such a tremendous array of products and services so conveniently available. They see only the end result of a host of strategies, plans, and actions that create new types of stores, distribution centers, services, and technologies that determine the structure and operation of marketing channels. Marketing channels in turn affect the lives of hundreds of millions of customers who rely on them to make the myriad products and services from around the globe so conveniently available.

In this book we go "behind the scenes" and take an in-depth look at marketing channels. We examine the nature of marketing channels, their importance in marketing, and how they evolve, develop, and change. We will focus especially on the role of strategy in marketing channels, as well as how they are designed, managed, and evaluated. Although, as alluded to earlier, much of the activity in marketing channels takes place behind the scenes, as we proceed through the text and peer into this background, a challenging and fascinating part of marketing will emerge.

The Multi-Channel Challenge

The expectations of today's customers both at the business-to-consumer (B2C) and business-to-business (B2B) levels, for high channel choice, flexibility, and an excellent buying experience is less likely to be satisfied by any one channel structure.[9] To meet these expanded customer expectations, a variety of different channels, often both land-based and Internet-based, is needed. Further, these multiple channels must be properly targeted to reach the appropriate customer segments and coordinated to make sure they mesh smoothly and complement, rather than undermine, each other. Needless to say, such effective multi-channel targeting and coordination does not happen by chance. Rather, close attention must be given to developing a multi-channel strategy that results in a set of marketing channels that makes products and services conveniently available to customers day in and day out, as well as for the long term.[10]

But the pursuit of an effective multi-channel strategy raises four key challenges that need to be addressed. These are briefly discussed here, but we will return to these issues[11] throughout the textbook.

1. Finding the optimal multi-channel mix
2. Creating multi-channel synergies

3. Avoiding multi-channel conflicts
4. Gaining a sustainable competitive advantage via multi-channel strategy

An Optimal Multi-Channel Mix

As alluded to earlier, Internet-based online channels have become a mainstream channel in the channel mixes of a vast number of firms that may also use several other channels such as:

- *Retail store channels*
- *Mail order channels*
- *Wholesale distributor channels*
- *Sales representative channels*
- *Call center channels*
- *Company sales force channels*
- *Vending machine channels*
- *Company-owned retail store channels*

For example, as shown in Figure 1.1, Apple Computer, Inc.'s multi-channel strategy employs a wide variety of channels to sell its iPhone, as well as other products including online, mobile phone service providers, wholesale clubs, mass merchandisers, consumer electronics stores, and its own retail stores. Hensen Natural Corporation, manufacturer of Monster Energy Drink and natural sodas and fruit drinks, relies on Coca-Cola Bottlers, a giant wholesale distributor, to gain access to multiple retail channels ranging from general mass merchandisers such as Walmart to vending machines and night clubs (See Figure 1.2).

FIGURE 1.1 iPhone Distribution Channel

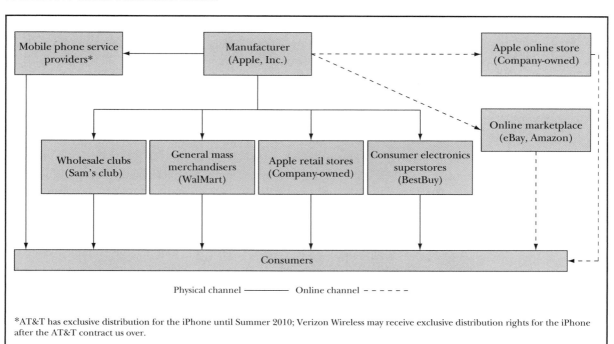

*AT&T has exclusive distribution for the iPhone until Summer 2010; Verizon Wireless may receive exclusive distribution rights for the iPhone after the AT&T contract us over.

FIGURE 1.2 Monster Energy Drink Distribution Channels

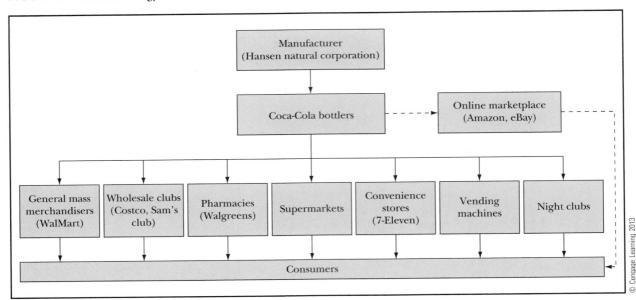

While a firm may use numerous channels in its multi-channel strategy, it is the quality of the channel mix rather than the quantity that is key in satisfying the firm's customer base.[12] In a very real sense, the firm's channel mix can be viewed as a **channel portfolio**, analogous to financial instruments in a conventional portfolio. So, just as a well-designed financial portfolio provides coverage across a range of investments to attain diversification, the well-designed channel portfolio would attempt to provide access to a range of customer segments while achieving channel diversification.

In future chapters, we will examine a number of ideas, concepts, and strategies that are important for developing a strong channel portfolio.

Multi-Channel Synergies

In the context of multi-channel strategy, synergy means using one channel to enhance the effectiveness and efficiency of other channels in the mix.[13] Using online channels to obtain information about a product before purchasing it in conventional "brick and mortar" channels is a common example of multi-channel synergy. Most customers buying new cars, for instance, use online channels to learn about product features, make comparisons to other brands, check on pricing, and find dealers before going to the auto-dealer channel to actually buy a car. Multi-channel synergies can also emerge when different channels in the mix "help each other out," and in doing so, create synergies that result in better customer service. This would occur, for example, when a customer confronted with a stockout from, say, a retail store channel is conveniently served by another channel from the mix. Consider, for example, Johnston and Murphy, a well-known manufacturer of men's shoes and apparel. The company sells its products through its own retail stores, independent retailers, a catalog mail order channel, and in recent years, via its online channel. If a Johnston and Murphy store does not have the particular shoe style or size when a customer comes in, the online channel "pinch hits" for the retail store channel by shipping the product directly to the customer's home at no charge to the customer and no effort on the customer's part because the store salesperson takes care of the online ordering process.

Creating such multi-channel synergies that satisfy or even delight customers by exceeding their expectations, while not always possible to achieve, is nevertheless a worthy aspiration to focus on when developing multi-channel strategies. We will have more to say on this topic later in the text.

Avoiding Multi-Channel Conflict

A major obstacle to developing successful multi-channel strategies is the emergence of conflict between different channels used for reaching the same customers. For example, if a manufacturer sells directly via its online channel or field sales force to the same customers served by independent distributors, the distributors may very well view the online and field salesforce channels as taking business away from their (independent distributor) channel. Thus, rather than viewing the multiple channel strategy as a means for providing more choice and flexibility to customers, it is viewed by the independent distributors as a zero-sum game: if one channel gains customers, then another channel must have lost customers.

Avoiding or at least mitigating such channel conflicts requires knowledge of the economic and behavioral factors that underlie marketing channels as well as astute channel strategy to attempt to "design out" or effectively manage such channel conflict. These topics will be treated in much greater depth later in the text.[14]

Sustainable Competitive Advantage and Multi-Channel Strategy

A **sustainable competitive advantage** is a competitive edge that cannot be quickly or easily copied by competitors.[15] In today's global competitive arena, gaining a sustainable competitive advantage by emphasizing the first three Ps of the marketing mix (product, price, and promotion) has become more difficult. With a few notable exceptions, product differences, whether based in design innovation, technological advances, quality, or brand identity, can be copied, matched, and even improved upon by competitors in a relatively short period of time. Similarly, a focus on low price as a means for attaining a sustainable competitive advantage may prove to be an even less-viable strategy today. There is always some country or region in the world where the product can be produced at a lower cost and then priced lower by competitors. Turning now to the third strategic arena of the marketing mix, promotion, this strategy may offer even less of a basis for gaining a sustainable competitive advantage than product and pricing strategy. Today, consumers are literally deluged with advertising and sales promotion messages both online (on Google alone advertisers spent over $22 billion in 2009) as well as through traditional media (over $125 billion). These huge expenditures have created a barrage of advertising and other forms of promotion to which consumers are exposed on a daily basis. This has created enormous clutter, which dramatically reduces the impact of promotional messages, regardless of how clever they are and in what media they are delivered, as literally thousands of messages knock each other out of the target audience's mind during very short periods of time. So, holding on to a competitive advantage through promotion for a substantial time period has become extremely difficult to do in the face of such intense clutter.

As a result of these developments, channel strategy and particularly multi-channel strategy have attracted increased attention as a means for gaining a sustainable competitive advantage. The main reason for this is that well-formulated channel strategies are more difficult for competitors to quickly copy. Developing effective channel strategies often requires a long-term commitment and significant amounts of investment in infrastructure and in the development of human skills. For example, Caterpillar's highly regarded world-wide channel system, based on well-capitalized megadealers, a supply chain that utilizes the most advanced information technology, and highly trained and motivated employees in the independent Caterpillar dealerships is not something that a competitor could copy and implement as quickly as it could copy a particular model of a Caterpillar earth moving machine.[16]

The Marketing Channel Defined

The concept of the marketing channel can be confusing. Often it is thought of as the route taken by a product as it moves from the producer to the consumer or other ultimate user. Some define it as the path taken by the title to goods as it moves through various agencies. Still others describe the marketing channel in terms of a loose coalition of business firms that have banded together for purposes of trade.

Much of the confusion stems from differing perspectives or viewpoints. The manufacturer, for example, may focus on the different intermediaries needed to get products to customers, so he might define the marketing channel in terms of the movement of the products through these various intermediaries. Intermediaries such as wholesalers or retailers who are expected to carry substantial inventories from various manufacturers and bear the risks associated with this function may view the flow of the title to the goods as the proper delineator of the marketing channel. Consumers may view the marketing channel as the collection of Web sites that they use when shopping online, or in the case of conventional channels, the stores they patronize. Finally, the researcher observing the marketing channel as it operates in the economic system may describe it in terms of its structural dimensions and efficiency of operation.

Given these differing perspectives, it is not possible to have a single definition of the marketing channel. In this text, we take a managerial decision-making viewpoint of the marketing channel as seen mainly through the eyes of marketing management, typically by producing and manufacturing firms. Thus, the marketing channel is viewed as one of the key marketing decision areas that marketing management must address. In this context, the **marketing channel** may be defined as:

> *the external contactual organization that management operates to achieve its distribution objectives.*

Four terms in this definition should be especially noted: *external, contactual organization, operates,* and *distribution objectives.*

The term **external** means that the marketing channel exists *outside* the firm. In other words, it is not part of a firm's internal organizational structure. Management of the marketing channel therefore involves the use of **interorganizational management**[17] (managing more that one firm) rather than **intraorganizational management** (managing one firm). It is important to keep this point in mind because many of the special problems and peculiarities of managing the marketing channel discussed later in the text stem from this external (interorganizational) structure.[18]

The term **contactual organization** refers to those firms or parties who are involved in negotiatory functions as a product or service moves from the producer to its ultimate user. Negotiatory functions consist of buying, selling, and transferring title to products or services. Consequently, only those firms or parties that engage in these functions are members of the marketing channel.[19] Other firms (usually referred to as *facilitating agencies*) such as transportation companies, public warehouses, banks, insurance companies, advertising agencies, and the like, that perform functions other than negotiatory, are excluded.[20] This distinction is not a matter of academic hairsplitting. The channel management problems involved when dealing with firms or parties performing negotiatory functions are often fundamentally different from those encountered when dealing with agencies that do not perform these functions. This will be apparent at many points as we proceed through the text.

The third term, **operates**, suggests involvement by management in the affairs of the channel. This involvement may range from the initial development of channel structure all the way to day-to-day management of the channel. When management operates the external contactual organization, it has made a decision not to let this organization run by itself. This does *not* mean that management can have total or even substantial control of the channel. In many cases, as we shall see in subsequent chapters, this is not possible. On the other hand, by operating the channel, management is acting to avoid unwitting control of *its* actions by the channel.[21]

Finally, **distribution objectives**, the fourth key term in the definition, means that management has certain distribution goals in mind. The marketing channel exists as a means for reaching these. The structure and management of the marketing channel are thus in part a function of a firm's distribution objectives. As these objectives change, variations in the external contactual organization and the way management attempts to operate it can also be expected to change. For example, when Dell Computer Corporation's distribution objectives changed from a focus primarily on B2B customers to include more emphasis on deeper penetration into the B2C market, Dell changed its channel structure to include retailers that provided a level of exposure and reach to consumers that had not been available from Dell's direct distribution channels.[22]

Use of the Term *Channel Manager*

Throughout this text we will generally be using the term **channel manager** to refer to anyone in a firm or organization who is involved in marketing channel decision making. In practice, relatively few firms or organizations actually have a single designated executive position called channel manager.[23] However, as shown in Figure 1.3, some major firms have executive positions where the duties are similar to those of the channel manager as defined here. The positions of "Channel Strategy Manager" at Advanced Micro Devices, Inc., "VP-Channel Manager" at McGraw-Hill and "Channel Marketing Manager" at Cisco Systems, Inc., Konica Minolta Business Solutions, and Newell Rubbermaid are perhaps the executive positions closest to the term channel manager as used in this text. More often, depending on the type of firm or organization and its size, many different executives are involved in making channel decisions. For large consumer goods manufacturers, for example, the vice president of marketing, general marketing manager, product manager, brand manager, and sales executive, such as the vice president of sales or the general sales manager, might be the key channel decision maker. In some franchise organizations, common in the fast-food and service fields, a middle management executive called "manager of franchisee relations" sometimes plays an important role in channel decision making along with top sales and marketing executives of the franchisor. In smaller businesses across a wide spectrum of both consumer and industrial products companies, most channel decisions will be handled by the owner/manager.

Given that so many different types and levels of managers are involved in channel decision making and that relatively few officially designated channel managers exist, we could have used a generic term such ash *decision maker* or *marketer* when referring to an

FIGURE 1.3 Channel
Management Job Titles
Used by Selected
U.S. Firms

Firm Name	Channel Management Job Title
Accenture	Sales Strategy and Channel Manager
Advanced Micro Devices, Inc.	Channel Strategy Manager
America Online	Channel Manager, Sales Operations
Assurant	Channel Development Manager
AT&T Wireless	Lead Channel Manager
Bank of America	VP, Channel Program Manager
Cisco Systems, Inc.	Channel Marketing Manager
Google, Inc.	Enterprise Channel Manager, Search
Honeywell International	Manager Channel Sales
Konica Minolta Business Solutions	Channel Marketing Manager
McAfee	Channel Marketing Manager
McGraw-Hill	VP-Channel Manager
Microsoft Corporation	Senior Channel and Communication Manager
Newell Rubbermaid	Channel Marketing Manager
Sallie Mae	Partner Channel Program Manager
Seagate Technology	Channel Programs Manager
SunGard	Channel Sales Manager
Symantec	Program Manager, Channel Readiness
T-Mobile	Senior Manager, Channel Strategy and Analysis

© Cengage Learning 2013

individual making channel decisions. However, we chose to use the term *channel manager* instead because it provides a sense of focus for referring to the important role of channel decision making within the firm. So, regardless of an individual's actual job title, when that person is involved in making channel decisions, he or she is filling the role of channel manager even though such a position may not formally exist on the firm's organization chart. In other words, anyone in the firm who is making channel decisions is, while involved in that activity, a channel manager.

Marketing Channels and Marketing Management Strategy

As alluded to in our discussion of gaining a sustainable competitive advantage earlier in this chapter, the classic marketing mix strategy model provides the framework for viewing the marketing channel from a marketing management perspective.[24] The marketing mix model portrays the marketing management process as a strategic blending of four controllable marketing variables (the marketing mix) to meet the demands of customers to which the firm wishes to appeal (the target markets) in light of internal and external uncontrollable variables. The basic marketing mix variables, often referred to as "The Four Ps," are product, price, promotion, and distribution (place). The external uncontrollable variables are such major environmental forces as the economy, sociocultural patterns of buyer behavior, competition, government, and technology; the nonmarketing functions of the firm constitute internal uncontrollable variables. Figure 1.4 shows a typical portrayal of the marketing mix strategy model. The major tasks of marketing management are to seek out potential target markets and to develop appropriate and coordinated product, price promotion, and distribution strategies to serve those markets in a competitive and dynamic environment.

FIGURE 1.4 Marketing Mix Strategy Model

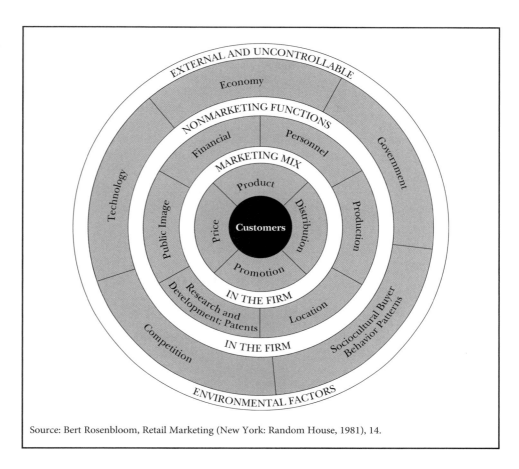

Source: Bert Rosenbloom, Retail Marketing (New York: Random House, 1981), 14.

Marketing **channel strategy**, one of the major strategic areas of marketing management, fits under the distribution (place) variable in the marketing mix. Management must develop and operate its marketing channels in such a way as to support and enhance the other strategic variables of the marketing mix in order to meet the demands of the firm's target markets.

The channel strategy employed by STIHL, Inc., the world's leading manufacturer of chain saws, and a major producer of other outdoor hand-held power equipment such as line trimmers, hedge trimmers, and blowers, illustrates the interrelationship between channel strategy and the other strategic variables of the marketing mix.

In terms of product strategy, STIHL, Inc. enjoys a reputation for making products of the highest quality. Its main manufacturing plant in Virginia Beach, Virginia is the largest and most advanced hand-held outdoor equipment design and engineering facility in the world.[25] STIHL's commitment to quality is enhanced by its emphasis on continuous product innovation and performance. The company also expects its products to be fuel efficient and environmentally responsible. This commitment to product quality and performance has resulted in a strong brand image for STIHL products among consumers and even competitors.

With regard to pricing strategy, in STIHL's marketing mix, the main focus is on value rather than low price. STIHL's culture reflects the "old fashioned" belief that you get what you pay for. So, while the company avoids using such terms as "higher priced" or "premium price," its pricing strategy is designed to reflect and support its superior products.

STIHL's promotional strategy is aimed at reinforcing the company's product quality and value pricing strategies. STIHL's Web site states that "Our Products Are Built to Perform" and offers detailed descriptions of a number of its leading products.[26]

The Web site also provides access to customer testimonials that stress the performance, durability, and value offered by STIHL products.

Turning now to the fourth strategic variable in STIHL's marketing mix, its channel strategy, the company has taken a novel approach but one that is consistent with the other three core strategies in the marketing mix: STIHL has chosen *not* to sell its products through the giant home improvement retailers, Home Depot and Lowe's. Indeed, STIHL makes it a point to announce to the world its refusal to deal with these mass merchandiser retail channels. On a regular basis, STIHL takes out whole-page advertisements in major newspapers such as *The Wall Street Journal*, boldly announcing its policy of avoiding the giant retailer channel (see Figure 1.5). It also airs

FIGURE 1.5
Advertisement in *The Wall Street Journal* by STIHL Announcing its Refusal to Deal with Lowe's or Home Depot

television ads with the same message. STIHL's channel strategy relies on selling its products through over 8,000 independent specialty retailers, all of whom have substantial product knowledge and the capability to service the product after it has been sold. Why has STIHL taken this unusual approach to its channel strategy by purposely and boldly avoiding Home Depot and Lowe's (as well as Sears and Walmart) even though these are the kinds of retailers that could make STIHL products available to tens of millions of customers? Peter Burton, senior vice president of sales at STIHL explains:

> *The big boxes are intimidating. They dictate guarantees and shift costly operational activities off their own backs and onto suppliers. And they expect their suppliers not just to hold down their prices but to consistently drop them annually. In short, the supplier [STIHL] is left helpless and increasingly profitless. If you sleep beside the 800-pound gorilla, you don't want to get caught underneath when it rolls over.*[27]

So, in essence, using the mass merchandise channels, while offering the opportunity for high volume sales would undermine STIHL's ability to control its own destiny. Product quality, pricing policies, and the promotional messages would all be ceded to the giant retailers. So too would the customer experience. Instead of providing customers with a full range of high-touch services and education required to make the right purchase, to use the product safely, and provide competent after-sale service, the mass merchants would focus on moving the products out the door in high volumes based on aggressive pricing.

By refusing to deal with the big box stores of the world and instead using a channel strategy that relies on thousands of relatively small independent retailers, STIHL has made its channel strategy the centerpiece of its marketing strategy and even its overall corporate strategy. This channel strategy has enabled STIHL to preserve and protect the core elements of what the company stands for: high quality and innovative products, priced to provide value to the customer, solid profitability for STIHL, and a real connection with its customers, not only before the sale but for many years after as well.

Channel Strategy versus Logistics Management

As pointed out earlier, channel strategy fits under the distribution variable of the marketing mix. Logistics management also fits under this variable—and the two components (channel strategy and logistics management) together comprise the distribution variable of the marketing mix, as illustrated in Figure 1.6.

Channel strategy and logistics management are closely related, but channel strategy is a much broader and more basic component than is logistics management. Channel strategy is concerned with the *entire process* of setting up and operating the contactual organization that is responsible for meeting the firm's distribution objectives. Logistics management, on the other hand, is more narrowly focused on providing product availability at the appropriate times and places in the marketing channel. Usually, channel strategy must already be formulated *before* logistics management can even be considered.

In recent years, the importance of building strategic relationships among channel members to enhance and facilitate the logistical process has been captured in the term "supply chain management" which recognizes that effective physical distribution involves more than 'mechanical' issues associated with transportation, storage, order processing, and inventory management. We will have more to say about this topic in Chapter 13.

An example from the STIHL case discussed earlier will help to clarify this point. STIHL needed to plan channel strategy to deal with such issues as the identification and selection of the appropriate dealers; how to motivate the dealers to promote its products; see that dealer sales personnel were properly trained to communicate the benefits

FIGURE 1.6
Marketing Mix
Strategic Variables with
Distribution Variable
Divided into Channel
and Logistics
Components

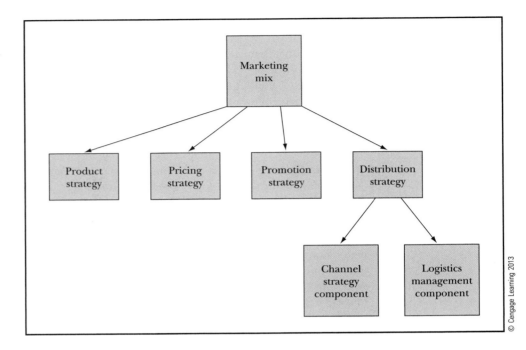

of STIHL products; sort out the various terms of the channel relationship such as credit, payment procedures, and inventory levels; determine what kinds and levels of promotional support would be provided; and many other factors. Continued contact between STIHL and its more than 8,000 independent dealers would also be needed to make sure that the channel strategy was actually being implemented and to resolve the inevitable problems that arise in the course of distributing products. So, only *after* this channel strategy had been developed and implemented through channel management would logistical management enter the picture. Obviously, if the dealers could not be convinced to carry and aggressively sell STIHL products, there would be little need for logistical management to provide for the delivery of the right quantities of the product at the right times and places.

Flows in Marketing Channels

When a marketing channel has been developed, a series of flows emerges. These flows provide the links that tie channel members and other agencies together in the distribution of goods and services.[28] From the standpoints of channel strategy and management, the most important of these flows are:

1. Product flow
2. Negotiation flow
3. Ownership flow
4. Information flow
5. Promotion flow

These flows can be illustrated by examining the flows associated with the channels of distribution for MillerCoors, the second largest brewery in the United States.[29] This is shown in Figure 1.7. The **product flow** refers to the actual physical movement of the product from the manufacturer (MillerCoors) through all of the parties who take physical possession of the product, from its point of production to final consumers. In the case of Coors beer, for example, the product comes from breweries and packaging plants

FIGURE 1.7 Five Flows in the Marketing Channel for Coors Beer

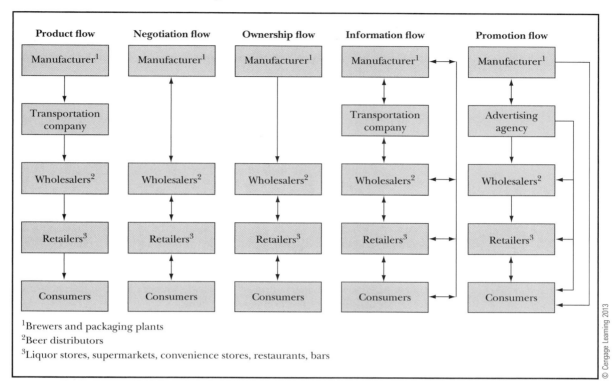

¹Brewers and packaging plants
²Beer distributors
³Liquor stores, supermarkets, convenience stores, restaurants, bars

in Colorado, Tennessee, and Virginia by way of company trucks or common carrier (transportation company) to beer distributors (wholesalers), who in turn shop the product (usually in their own trucks) to liquor stores, supermarkets, convenience stores, restaurants, and bars (retailers), where it is finally purchased by consumers.

The **negotiation flow** represents the interplay of the buying and selling functions associated with the transfer of title (right of ownership) to MillerCoors products. Notice in the figure that the transportation firm is not included in this flow because it does not participate in the negotiatory functions. Notice also that the arrows flow in *both* directions, indicating that negotiations involve a mutual exchange between buyers and sellers at all levels of the channel.

The **ownership flow** shows the movement of the title to the product as it is passed along from the manufacturer to final consumers. Here again, the transportation firm is not included because it does not take title to the product nor is it actively involved in facilitating the product's transfer. It is only involved in the transportation of the physical product itself.

Turning now to the **information flow**, we see that the transportation firm has reappeared in this flow and that all of the arrows showing the flow of information from the manufacturer to consumers are two-directional. All parties participate in the exchange of information, and the flow can be either up or down. For example, Coors may obtain information from the transportation company about its shipping schedule and rates, and the transportation company may in turn seek information from MillerCoors about when and in what quantities it plans to shop the product. The flow of information sometimes bypasses the transportation firm, as shown by the arrow leading from the manufacturer (at the right-hand side of the box) directly to the wholesalers, retailers, and consumers. This route of information flow occurs when the information sought does not concern the transportation company, such as details associated with the buying, selling, or promotion of MillerCoors products. For example, if the manufacturer makes available to beer distributors a special reduced price on, say, Coors Extra Gold beer, this information would be passed to the beer distributors directly and would not be of concern to the transportation firm.

Finally, the **promotion flow** refers to the flow of persuasive communication in the form of advertising, personal selling, sales promotion, and publicity. Here, a new component, the advertising agency, is included in the flow because the advertising agency is actively involved in providing and maintaining the promotion flow, especially the advertising element of promotion. The two-directional arrow connected by a line between the manufacturer and the advertising agency is meant to show that the manufacturer and advertising agency work together closely to develop promotional strategies. All other arrows show one-directional flow from the advertising agency or directly from the manufacturer to the other parties in the marketing channel.

The concept of channel flows provides another basis for distinguishing between channel strategy and logistics management. Earlier in this chapter we pointed out that channel strategy and management are broader components of distribution than logistics. In the context of the channel flows concept this follows because channel strategy and management involve planning for and managing *all* of the flows, whereas logistics is concerned almost exclusively with the management of the product flow.

Further, the concept of channel flows provides a good basis for separating channel members from nonmembers. Recall that in our definition of the marketing channel, only those parties who were engaged in the negotiatory functions of buying, selling and transferring title were considered to be members of the contactual organization (the marketing channel). From the standpoint of channel flows, then, only those parties who participate in the negotiation or ownership flows would be members of the marketing channel.

From a management standpoint, the concept of channel flows provides a useful framework for understanding the scope and complexity of channel management. By thinking in terms of the five flows, it becomes obvious that channel management involves much more than merely managing the physical product flow through the channel. The other flows (of negotiation, ownership, information, and promotion) must also be managed and coordinated effectively to achieve the firm's distribution objectives.[30] Indeed, much of the material in this text is concerned with channel management activities that involve these channel flows. Dealing with environmental changes and the behavioral dimensions of channels (topics treated in Chapters 3 and 4) certainly involves the information flow. Formulating channel strategies, designing the channel, and selecting the channel members (the topics of Chapters 5, 6, 7, and 8) are very much concerned with the negotiation, ownership, and information flows as well as the product flow. Motivating channel members (discussed in Chapter 9) is dependent on effective management of the information and promotion flows. Chapters 10, 11, 12, and 13 deal with the interfaces between channel management and management of the other variables in the marketing mix that require management and coordination of all of the flows. Finally, the evaluation of channel member performance (discussed in Chapter 14) is dependent almost entirely on effective management of the information flow.

From the perspective of channel management, the concept of flows in marketing channels helps to convey the dynamic nature of marketing channels. The word *flow* suggests movement or a fluid state, and indeed this is the nature of channels of distribution. Changes, both obvious and subtle, always seem to be occurring. New forms of distribution emerge, different types of intermediaries appear in the channel while others drop out, unusual competitive structures close off some avenues of distribution and open up others.[31] Changing patterns of buyer behavior and new forms of technology add yet another dimension of change. For example, MillerCoors information and promotional flows are now being augmented via Facebook and Twitter as messages flow from MillerCoors to fans and followers (MillerCoors customers) and vice versa.

Distribution through Intermediaries

A question asked since the time of ancient Greece is: Why do intermediaries so often stand between producers and the ultimate users of products? The question of the need for intermediaries in marketing channels has gained new currency in recent years with the rise of the Internet and online distribution channels. The term **disintermediation**, a fancy way of saying "eliminate the middleman," has become popular jargon in the business lexicon. The thinking underlying disintermediation is based on the awesome technological capacity of the Internet to connect everybody to everybody else, including all producers with final consumers. But so far, disintermediation has not occurred on a major scale. The fact that the Internet and the World Wide Web can connect hundreds of millions of people and institutions does not necessarily obviate the need for intermediaries. In fact, as we proceed through the text it will become apparent that technology, while important and as potent as the Internet, is not the only determinant of what role, if any, intermediaries will play in marketing channels. Economic considerations are also very important in determining whether intermediaries will appear in marketing channels, two of the most important of which are specialization/division of labor and contactual efficiency.

Specialization and Division of Labor

The first clear exposition of the **specialization and division of labor** principle is generally attributed to Adam Smith's classic book *The Wealth of Nations*, published in 1776. In this work, Smith cited an example from a pin factory. He noted that when the production operations necessary in the manufacture of pins were allocated among a group of workers so that each worker specialized in performing only one operation, a vast increase in output resulted over what was possible when this same number of workers individually performed all of the operations.

The logic of this principle has been well understood as it applies to a production setting. But this understanding is often lacking when specialization and division of labor is applied to a distribution situation, particularly when more than one firm is involved. Yet, whether applied to production or distribution, or within one firm or among several, the concept is fundamentally the same.[32] By breaking down a complex task into smaller, less complex ones and allocating them to parties who are specialists at performing them, much greater efficiency results. Figure 1.8 helps to illustrate this by comparing specialization and division of labor as applied to production versus distribution for a manufacturer of electric guitars. Though somewhat oversimplified, Figure 1.8 shows eight production tasks and seven distribution tasks involved in transforming wood and other components into an electric guitar, and then getting it to consumers. The eight production tasks have been allocated to various production stations in the factory, where workers who specialize in these tasks will perform them. On the right-hand side of Figure 1.8, various distribution tasks have been allocated among agents, wholesalers, and retailers, as well as the manufacturer and consumers.

The only difference in the application of the specialization and division of labor concept, as applied to production versus distribution in this figure, is that the production tasks have been allocated *intraorganizationally* whereas the distribution tasks have been allocated *interorganizationally*. Hence, just as the manufacturer's production manager should allocate production tasks on the basis of specialization and division of labor, so should the channel manager. Ideally he should allocate the distribution tasks to those

FIGURE 1.8
Specialization and Division of Labor Principle: Production versus Distribution for an Electric Guitar Manufacturer

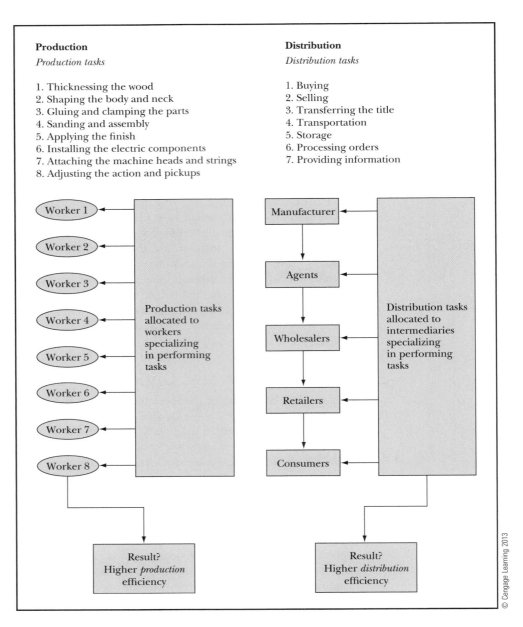

Production

Production tasks

1. Thicknessing the wood
2. Shaping the body and neck
3. Gluing and clamping the parts
4. Sanding and assembly
5. Applying the finish
6. Installing the electric components
7. Attaching the machine heads and strings
8. Adjusting the action and pickups

Distribution

Distribution tasks

1. Buying
2. Selling
3. Transferring the title
4. Transportation
5. Storage
6. Processing orders
7. Providing information

firms that can perform them most efficiently. His contactual organization would then reflect an optimal allocation of the distribution tasks. In reality, of course, this is not always possible. Nevertheless, by thinking in terms of the specialization and division of labor principle as applied to distribution, the channel manager will be better equipped at least to approach an optimal allocation of distribution tasks. In Chapter 6, on designing the marketing channel, we will deal with this issue in greater detail.

Contactual Efficiency

The second concept on which the framework for deciding whether to use intermediaries rests is contactual efficiency.[33] From the channel manager's viewpoint, **contactual efficiency** is the level of negotiation effort between sellers and buyers relative to

TABLE 1.1 EXAMPLE OF CONTACTUAL EFFICIENCY FOR THE GRANADA GUITAR COMPANY, DISTRIBUTING THROUGH RETAILERS ONLY

NEGOTIATION EFFORT (INPUTS)	ESTIMATED DOLLAR COSTS OF INPUTS	DISTRIBUTION OBJECTIVE (OUTPUT)	CONTACTUAL EFFICIENCY
1,500 sales visits 1,000 phone calls 10 magazine ads	@ $50 = $75,000 @ 3 = 3,000 @ 1,000 = 10,000 Total $88,000	Get 500 music stores to carry new guitar line.	Negotiation effort in dollar terms relative to achieving the distribution objective = $88,000

© Cengage Learning 2013

achieving a distribution objective. Thus, it is a relationship between an input (negotiation effort) and an output (the distribution objective). To illustrate this concept, consider the guitar manufacturer, hereafter referred to as Granada Guitar Company. Suppose Granada sets a distribution objective of getting 500 music stores to carry its new line of electric guitars. Assuming the firm were to deal directly with the retailers, the input would be the level of negotiation effort it expends in achieving the output—getting 500 music stores to carry the new line. To achieve this objective, Granada estimates it would need to have its sales force contact 2,500 stores, with many of these contacts requiring personal sales visits. Further, Granada believes it must use trade paper advertising to support the efforts of its salespeople. Management estimates it will take 1,500 sales calls, 1,000 telephone calls, and 10 trade magazine ads to finally achieve the objective. These figures are summarized in Table 1.1 along with some hypothetical estimates of dollar costs. Based on the figures shown in Table 1.1, Granada estimates it will cost $88,000 to achieve this particular distribution objective if it works through retailers only.

Suppose Granada goes on to consider adding wholesale intermediaries to its contactual organization. Granada believes that 25 wholesalers carrying the new line would be sufficient to get it accepted by the 500 retailers. Granada further estimates that it will take 100 personal sales calls on wholesalers, as well as 100 phone calls, to secure acceptance. However, Granada forecasts that double the advertising will be needed to support the salespeople (i.e., 20 magazine ads). These estimates are summarized in Table 1.2, which shows that the use of wholesalers provides a much higher level of contactual efficiency than if retailers alone were used. The reason for this is that the use of wholesalers has eliminated the need for direct contact with retailers, thereby greatly reducing the number of contacts needed.

TABLE 1.2 EXAMPLE OF CONTACTUAL EFFICIENCY FOR THE GRANADA GUITAR COMPANY, DISTRIBUTING THROUGH WHOLESALERS

NEGOTIATION EFFORT (INPUTS)	ESTIMATED DOLLAR COSTS OF INPUTS	DISTRIBUTION OBJECTIVE (OUTPUT)	CONTACTUAL EFFICIENCY
100 sales visits 100 phone calls 20 magazine ads	@ $50 = $5,000 @ 3 = 3,000 @ 1,000 = 20,000 Total $25,300	Get 500 music stores to carry new guitar line.	Negotiation effort in dollar terms relative to achieving the distribution objective = $25,300

© Cengage Learning 2013

FIGURE 1.9 How the
Introduction of an
Additional Intermediary Reduces the
Number of Contacts

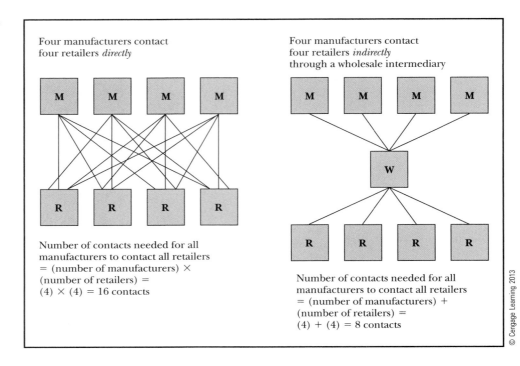

Four manufacturers contact
four retailers *directly*

Four manufacturers contact
four retailers *indirectly*
through a wholesale intermediary

Number of contacts needed for all
manufacturers to contact all retailers
= (number of manufacturers) ×
(number of retailers) =
(4) × (4) = 16 contacts

Number of contacts needed for all
manufacturers to contact all retailers
= (number of manufacturers) +
(number of retailers) =
(4) + (4) = 8 contacts

This example points to an important relationship between contactual efficiency and the use of intermediaries. *The use of additional intermediaries will often increase the level of contactual efficiency.* This principle is illustrated in Figure 1.9

This does not mean that considerations of contactual efficiency and specialization and division of labor are all that is needed to make a decision on intermediary usage. Many other variables (to be discussed in Part 2 of the text) must also be evaluated. But contactual efficiency and specialization and division of labor provide the channel manager with a basic framework for incorporating these other variables into decisions on the use of intermediaries.

Channel Structure

The concept of channel structure is one that often is not explicitly defined in the marketing literature. Perhaps the most typically discussed dimension is length—the number of levels of intermediaries in the channel (but as we shall see in Chapter 6, other dimensions of channel structure also exist).

When channel structure is presented, we typically see diagrams such as that shown in Figure 1.10. Or sometimes symbolic notations such as the following are used:

M → C	(two-level)	where A = Agent
M → R → C	(three-level)	C = Consumer
M → W → R → C	(four-level)	M = Manufacturer
M → A → W → R → C	(five-level)	R = Retailer
		W = Wholesaler

While these approaches do convey a general idea of the kinds of participants in the marketing channel and the levels at which they appear, they do not explicitly define channel structure. Moreover, they fail to suggest the relationship between channel structure and channel management.

FIGURE 1.10
A Typical Portrayal of Channel Structure for Consumer Goods

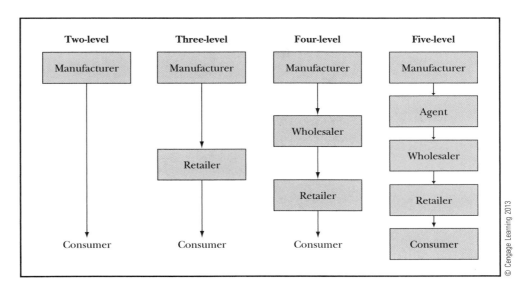

Our definition takes a managerial perspective by viewing **channel structure** as: *The group of channel members to which a set of distribution tasks has been allocated*. This definition suggests that in developing channel structure, the channel manager is faced with an *allocation decision*; that is, given a set of distribution tasks that must be performed to accomplish a firm's distribution objectives, the manager must decide how to allocate or structure the tasks. Thus, the structure of the channel will reflect the manner in which he or she has allocated these tasks among the members of the channel. For example, if after making the allocation decision the channel structure appears as M → W → R → C, this means that the channel manager has chosen to allocate the tasks to his or her own firm as well as to wholesalers, retailers, and consumers.

As we pointed out earlier in this chapter, in recent years the term **multi-channel strategy** has been heard with increasing frequency. This simply means that the firm has chosen to reach its customers through more than one channel. A multi-channel marketing strategy naturally results in a multi-channel structure because distribution tasks have been allocated among more than one channel structure. With the emergence of online sales channels toward the end of the Twentieth Century and the dramatic growth in online channels during the first decade of the Twenty-First Century, many firms have developed multi-channel strategies that include online channels. For example, the multi-channel structure used for Polo by Ralph Lauren apparel (shown in Figure 1.11), consists of sales through upscale department stores and specialty retailers, its own company stores, and online sales through its Web site, http://www. Polo.com. Sony Music Entertainment Inc., one of the largest recorded music companies in the world, uses a very broad array of channels in its multi-channel structure (see Figure 1.12). Using multiple-channel structures to reach consumers has become increasingly common in both consumer and business markets. In fact, firms that sell all of their products through a single-channel structure are the exception today rather than the rule. Most firms already have or soon will use a multi-channel strategy.[34] Figures 1.12–1.16 illustrate channel structures for a variety of products and services.

As discussed earlier, the primary paradigms for making the allocation decisions that result in various channel structures are specialization, division of labor, and contactual efficiency. Ideally the channel manager would like total control over the allocation of distribution tasks so that he or she could assign these tasks to the particular firms or

FIGURE 1.11
Marketing Channel Structure for Polo by Ralph Lauren Apparel

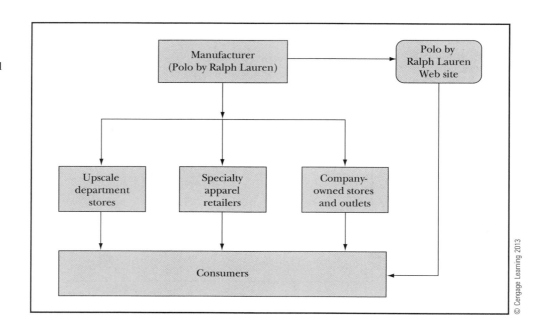

parties who are best suited to perform them. However, because the channel includes members that are independent firms, and because the channel is subject to environmental constraints, in reality the channel manager does not often have total control over the allocation of distribution tasks.[35]

In Part 2 of the text we will discuss the problems and constraints faced by the channel manager in attempting to develop an optimal channel structure.

FIGURE 1.12 Sony Music Distribution Channels

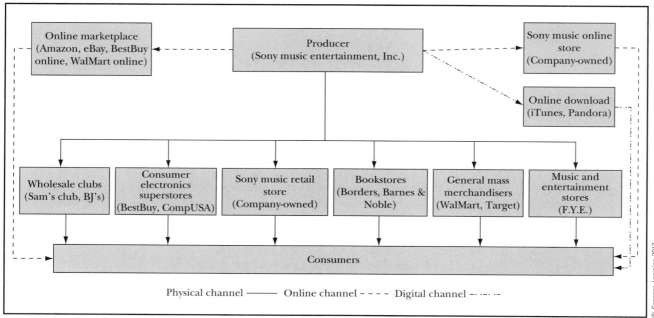

FIGURE 1.13
Marketing Channels for Consumer Electronics Products

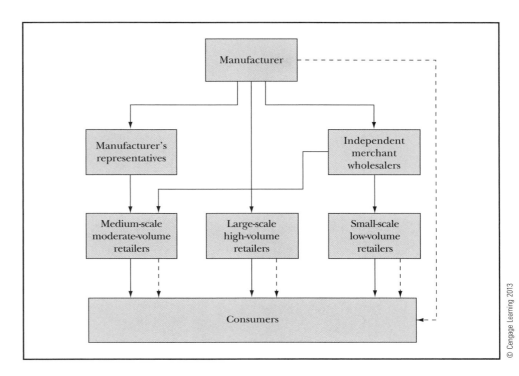

FIGURE 1.14 **Alternative Channel Structures for Business-to-Business Markets**

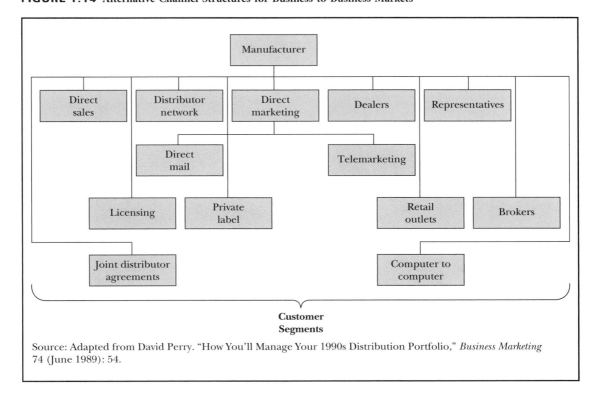

Source: Adapted from David Perry. "How You'll Manage Your 1990s Distribution Portfolio," *Business Marketing* 74 (June 1989): 54.

FIGURE 1.15
Channel Structure for eBay Showing Information/ Negotiation and Product Flows

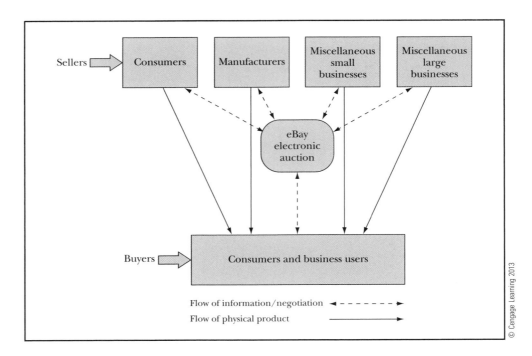

Ancillary Structure

We have defined the marketing channel as including only those participants who perform the negotiatory functions of buying, selling, and transferring title, and hence it follows that those who do *not* perform these functions are not members of the channel structure. We will consider these nonmember participants or facilitating agencies as belonging to the ancillary structure of the marketing channel. More specifically, we define

FIGURE 1.16
Marketing Channels for Services

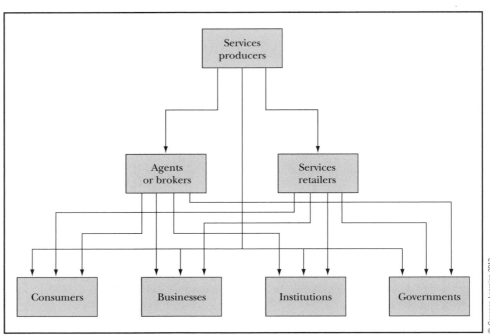

ancillary structure as: The group of institutions (facilitating agencies) that assists channel members in performing distribution tasks.

The basic decision facing the channel manager in attempting to develop ancillary structure is the same for developing channel structure; that is, he or she must attempt to allocat distribution tasks to those parties best suited to performing them. Because the channel manager is dealing with nonmember channel participants, however, the problems faced in developing and managing the ancillary structure are likely to be less complex than those encountered in developing (and managing) channel structures. This is because facilitating firms do not play a part in the channel decisions that ultimately control the distribution of goods and services to their target markets. Rather, the role of facilitating agencies comprising the ancillary structure is one of providing services to the channel members *after the basic channel decisions have already been made.*

The Black & Decker Corporation (B&D), one of the world's leading manufacturers of power tools, will serve as an example. B&D sells many of its industrial power tools through independent wholesalers (industrial distributors) who in turn sell these products to manufacturers, contractors, repair shops, schools, government agencies, and other industrial market segments. B&D's consumer power tools are sold through retailers such as hardware stores, home center stores, mass merchandisers, automotive stores, online retailers such as Amazon.com, and others who buy these products either directly from B&D or through wholesalers. For these marketing channels to operate efficiently, a number of nonnegotiatory tasks such as transportation, storage, insurance, financing, and advertising must be performed. In many cases, it is more advantageous for B&D, as well as its distributors and dealers, to "farm out" these tasks to facilitating agencies (the ancillary structure) rather than perform the tasks themselves. For instance, B&D uses common carriers to transport its power tools to industrial distributors, rather than maintaining its own fleet of trucks. Similarly, it relies on commercial insurance companies to protect against risks while the products are in transit, rather than attempting to self-insure. B&D also at times uses independent advertising agencies to promote its products rather than develop all of its advertising in-house. Wholesalers and retailers of B&D power tools also use facilitating agencies to perform some of these tasks rather than trying to undertake them alone.

In developing the ancillary structure to perform these tasks, the channel manager also deals with facilitating agencies who are outside of the channel decision-making process and who generally do not have as great a stake in the channel as do the channel members. Thus the trucking company that transports a load of power tools from a B&D manufacturing plant to an independent industrial distributor is concerned only with the relatively simple task of moving the products from point A to point B. Furthermore, the channel manager does not have to negotiate or deal with them on the same basis as channel members. For example, it is a formidable task for B&D to convince independent industrial distributors (channel members) to stock and enthusiastically promote its DeWalt line of power tools against the competition of other manufacturers such as Porter-Cable, Makita, or Ryobi. In developing channel structure, B&D is also faced with such difficult issues as the proper choice of channel members, how much of a role each will play in decision making, how control will be exercised, how performance will be evaluated, and many other issues to be discussed throughout this text.

Summary

After passing through the first decade of the Twenty-First Century, it has become clear that even though conventional channels are still very much in evidence, a metamorphosis has occurred in distribution channels driven by Internet-based online channels and many new technologies, business models, and innovative firms. While the implications of these developments for marketing channel strategy and management are just beginning to emerge, one implication is crystal clear: customers now expect far more and better choices for gaining access to the vast array of products and services from all over the globe—how, where, and when they want them.

To satisfy these heightened customer expectations for maximum channel choice and flexibility, more emphasis must be placed on multi-channel strategy and structure, particularly with regard to finding the optimal channel mix, creating multi-channel synergies, avoiding channel conflict, and gaining a sustainable comxpetitive advantage via channel strategy.

Although there are a number of ways to view marketing channels, a managerial viewpoint mainly from the perspective of producing and manufacturing firms is used in this text. In this context, the **marketing channel** is defined as *the external contactual organization that management operates to achieve its distribution objectives*. Only parties who perform the negotiatory functions of buying, selling, and transferring title are considered to be members of the marketing channel.

The basic marketing mix strategy model provides the framework for examining the marketing channel from a marketing management perspective. In this framework, marketing channel strategy and management fit under the distribution variable of the four basic strategic variables of the marketing mix (product, price, promotion, and distribution). The channel manager must develop and operate the external contactual organization (the marketing channel) in such a way as to support and enhance the other strategic variables of product, price, and promotion in the marketing mix in order to meet the demands of customers.

Channel strategy is a more basic and comprehensive component of distribution strategy than is logistics management. Channel strategy is concerned with the *entire process* of setting up and operating the contactual organization

that is responsible for meeting the firm's distribution objectives, whereas logistics management is more narrowly focused on providing product availability at the appropriate time and place in the marketing channel.

The links that tie channel members and other agencies together in the distribution of goods and services are referred to as **channel flows**. From a channel management standpoint, the most important of these flows are (1) product flow, (2) negotiation flow, (3) ownership flow, (4) information flow, and (5) promotion flow. The channel manager must effectively manage and coordinate all of these flows to achieve the firm's distribution objectives.

A basic decision facing the channel manager in the development of the marketing channel is whether to use intermediaries such as wholesalers and retailers in the contactual organization and whether facilitating agencies should also be used. The basis for making this decision rests on the two fundamental concepts of specialization and division of labor and contactual efficiency.

Channel structure refers to the group of channel members to which a set of distribution tasks has been allocated. In many cases, a particular firm might use a combination of different channel structures to implement its distribution strategy. This approach is now frequently referred to as a multi-channel structure, especially when one of the channel structures involves E-commerce via online sales in addition to conventional channels. **Ancillary structure** is the group of institutions and parties that assist channel members in performing distribution tasks. The channel manager would like to develop optimum channel and ancillary structures based on specialization, division of labor, and contactual efficiency. The ability to do so is limited, however, because the interorganizational setting in which the channel manager must operate reduces the capacity to control the independent channel members and facilitating agencies.

Review Questions

1. Why do customers expect more choice and flexibility as to how products and services are made available to them?

2. Multi-channel strategy that provides more choice to customers has become a virtual imperative today for more and more firms. What are some of the key challenges firms face in pursing a multi-channel strategy?

3. How does a management perspective of the marketing channel differ from some other views of the channel?

4. What is the distinction between interorganizational management and intraorganizational management?

5. Is management of the marketing channel the only instance of interorganizational management for a producing or manufacturing firm?

6. Operating the channel does not imply total control of the channel. Can you think of an example where the channel manager does not have total control of the channel but is still able to operate it?

7. Discuss the relationship between channel management and the marketing mix.

8. What is the difference between channel strategy and logistics management?

9. Identify the various flows in marketing channels and the direction of the flows. Why is the concept of channel flows useful for a better understanding of channel management?

10. Could the product flow operate independently from other channel flows?

11. Discuss the concept of specialization and division of labor as it applies to marketing channels.

12. Even though specialization and division of labor is the fundamental basis for allocating distribution tasks, can the channel manager make decisions about using intermediaries and facilitating agencies *solely* on that basis? Explain why or why not.

13. What is contactual efficiency? Can you think of examples of contactual efficiency that do not occur in a marketing channels context? If so, list.

14. Discuss the distinction between channel structure and ancillary structure.

15. Why is it so difficult for the channel manager to develop a truly optimal channel structure?

Channel Issues for Discussion

1. ROCKAUTO.COM is a leading online auto parts store that prides itself for offering a huge selection of auto parts, everyday low prices, fast shipping, and an easy-to-use Web site. Some ROCKAUTO.COM advertisements have even claimed that this online auto parts store is "head and shoulders" above any brick and mortar auto parts store. The company's slogan, "All The Parts Your Car Will Ever Need," suggests that customers have all the choice they could possibly want from ROCKAUTO.COM and that they need look no further than this online auto parts store to satisfy all their needs.

   Do you agree with ROCKAUTO.COM's claim? Might customers seeking auto parts need other channel options? Explain.

2. The TV reporter for a network news show is walking through a cornfield with a downtrodden-looking farmer in Iowa. As they continue through the field, the farmer comments: "My family and I have worked real hard over the years to produce a good crop, but we hardly get much of a price for it. But when I see how much they want for corn and just about any corn products in the supermarkets, I can't believe it. The consumer is paying a high price while I'm getting a very low price, so somebody must be making a lot of money in between." The reporter then turns to the camera and in a melodramatic style intones: "As you've just seen, we've talked with a farmer who, in spite of all his hard work, can hardly make a living. But you and I both know how high prices are in the supermarkets. Are we being ripped off by a bunch of middlemen?"

   Comment on the farmer's lament to the reporter and the reporter's remarks to the TV audience in light of the relevant channel concepts discussed in this chapter.

3. Growth in online retail sales has been outstripping conventional sales in retail stores. This online sales growth might be enhanced significantly by the latest online sales phenomenon of mobile commerce—shopping via mobile smart phones such as Apple's iPhone, Research in Motion's Blackberry, or Google's NexusOne. But so far, of the almost 50 million smart phone users that have access to the Internet, only about 7 million (under 15%) have actually bought something through their phones during the course of a year.

   Do you think mobile commerce via smart phone will grow rapidly in the future? Why or why not?

4. The dramatic growth in online sales in recent years has led many pundits to predict that mail order channels driven by paper catalogs would virtually disappear. But this has not happened. By the close of the first decade of the Twenty-First Century, over 17 billion catalogs were mailed to U.S. homes, which helped to produce over $700 billion in sales via this "old fashioned" channel of distribution.

   Why do you think such vast numbers of paper catalogs are still printed and mailed and such high levels of sales are still generated in mail order channels?

5. One of the major themes presented in this chapter is the need for choice as to how products and services are made available to customers. Thus, multi-channel strategies that provide a wide range of channels including an Internet-based online channel option have become imperative. Yet there are very successful firms that take a virtually opposite view by purposely limiting choice. A case in point is Edward Jones, a financial services company with the largest network of brokerage offices in the U.S.—more than 10,000 and still growing. Edward Jones has a Web site that its customers can visit but it does not offer its customers the option of trading online. Instead, all transactions must take place through an Edward Jones broker. Even with this single channel strategy, the company is still growing and is very profitable.

   Why do you think Edward Jones has been able to "buck the trend" toward multi-channel strategy that would include an online channel as a key option?

6. Susan Jensen, a marketing manager for a major consumer package goods manufacturer, is very upset with the sales results of the new oat bran cookies her company introduced three months ago. She believes that an important factor in the lackluster sales results is that too many supermarkets across the country were not featuring the product in giant end-of-aisle displays recommended by the manufacturer to evoke consumer impact and awareness. "I feel like hitting those store managers over the head for not featuring this product—if only I had more control over these guys," remarked a frustrated and angry Susan Jensen.

   Discuss the situation in the context of the definition of the marketing channel presented in the text.

References

1. Karen Talley, "Wal-Mart Ramps Up Online Efforts," *Wall Street Journal*, (April 7, 2010): B7A.

2. See for example: Spencer E. Ante, "At Amazon, Marketing is for Dummies," *Business Week* (September 28, 2009): 53–54.

3. Bert Rosenbloom, "The Ten Deadly Myths of E-Commerce," *Business Horizons*, (March–April) 2002): 61–66.

4. Jess Breven, "Justices to Test Patents for Business Methods," *Wall Street Journal*, (November 9, 2009): B1, B2.

5. See for example, Peter Grant and Nat Worden, "Behind Comcast Chief's Moves Are Fears About Internet Shift," *Wall Street Journal*, (October 2, 2009): A4.

6. Bert Rosenbloom, "Multi-Channel Strategy in Business-to-Business Markets: Prospect and Problems," *Industrial Marketing Management*, (January 2007): 4–9; Rajkumar Venkatesan, V. Kumar, and Nalini Ravishanker, "Multichannel Shopping: Causes and Consequences," *Journal of Marketing* (April 2007): 114–132.

7. Susan Snyder, "Web Not Yet the Answer to Costly College Textbooks," *Philadelphia Inquirer*, (February 8, 2010): A1, A8.

8. Aaron Beck, "Alibaba Profit Drops Amid Marketing Push," *Wall Street Journal*, (November 11, 2009): B6.

9. Joel El. Collier and Carol C. Bienstock, "How Do Customers Judge Quality in an E-Tailer?" *MIT Sloan Management Review*, (Fall 2006): 35–40; Phillip Kreindler and Copal Rajgura, "What B2B Customers Really Expect," *Harvard Business Review*, (August 2006); 22–24.

10. Bruce D. Weinberg, Salvatore Parise, and Patricia J. Guinan, "Multichannel Marketing, Mindset and Program Development," *Business Horizons*, (September–October 2007): 385–394.

11. Bert Rosenbloom, "Multichannel Strategy in Business-to-Business Markets: Prospects and Problems,": 5–7.

12. Sertain Kabadayi, Nermin Eyuboglu, and Gloria P. Thomas, "The Performance Implications of Designing Multiple Channels to Fit with Strategy and Environment," *Journal of Marketing*, (October 2007): 195–211.

13. For a related discussion, see: Stephanie M. Noble, David A. Griffith, and Marc G. Weingberger, "Consumer Derived Utilitarian Value and Channel Utilization in a Multi-Channel Retail Context," *Journal of Business Research*, (December 2005): 1643–1651.

14. Bert Rosenbloom, "Multi-Channel Strategy in Business-to-Business Markets: Prospects and Problems,": 7–8.

15. Michael Porter, Competitive Advantage: Creating and Sustaining Superior Performance. New York: Free Press, 1985.

16. Donald W. Fites, "Make Your Dealers Your Partners," *Harvard Business Review*, (March–April 1996): 84–85.

17. An in-depth discussion of the interorganizational point of view can be found in William Evan, "Toward a Theory of Inter-Organizational Relations," in *Distribution*

Channels: Behavioral Dimensions, ed. Louis W. Stern (New York: Houghton Mifflin, 1969), 73–89. See also R. L. Warren, "The Interorganizational Field as a Focus for Investigation," *Administrative Science Quarterly* 12 (December 1967): 396–419; and Gary L. Frazier, "Interorganizational Exchange Behavior in Marketing Channels: A Broadened Perspective," *Journal of Marketing* (Fall 1983): 68–78.

18. For a related discussion, see Daniel H. McQuiston, "A Conceptual Model for Building and Maintaining Relationships Between Manufacturers' Representatives and Their Principals," *Industrial Marketing Management* Vol. 30, 2001: 165–181.

19. This definition includes consumers or other final users as members of the marketing channel. See Kent L. Granzin, "The Consumption Unit as a Member of the Distribution Channel," in *Developments in Marketing Science,* Vol. XI, ed. Kenneth D. Bahn (Blacksburg, Va.: Academy of Marketing Science, 1988), 460–464.

20. This view is similar to that taken by Louis P. Bucklin, *Competition and Evolution in the Distributive Trades* (Englewood Cliffs, N.J.: Prentice-Hall, 1972), 9. For the original presentation of this concept, see Edmund D. McGarry, "The Contactual Function in Marketing," *Journal of Business,* (April 1951): 96–113.

21. For related discussions on the need for channel management, see Gary L. Frazier and Raymond C. Rody, "The Use of Influence Strategies in Interfirm Relationships in Industrial Product Channels," *Journal of Marketing* (January 1991): 52–69; and Peter R. Dickson, "Distributor Portfolio Analysis and the Channel Dependence Matrix: New Techniques for Understanding and Managing the Channel," *Journal of Marketing* (Summer 1983): 33–44. See also N. Mohan Reddy and Michael P. Marvin, "Developing a Manufacturer-Distributor Information Partnership," *Industrial Marketing Management* (May 1986): 157–163; and John T. Mentzer, "Managing Channel Relations in the 21st Century," *Journal of Business Logistics* 14, no. 1: 27–42.

22. For a related discussion see: Justin Scheck," H-P Plans to Fuse Printer, PC Units," *Wall Street Journal,* (September 30, 2009): B1.

23. Rolph E. Anderson, Rajiv Mehta, and Alan J. Dubinsky, "Will the Real Channel Manager Please Stand Up?" *Business Horizons*, (January–February 2003): 61–68; Donald W. Jackson, Jr., and Bruce J. Walker, "The Channels Manager: Marketing's Newest Aide?" *California Management Review* (Winter 1988): 52–58; and Bruce J. Walker, Janet E. Keith, and Donald W. Jackson, Jr., "The Channels Manager: Now, Soon or Never?" *Journal of the Academy of Marketing Science* (Summer 1985): 82–95.

24. For a review of the basic marketing mix strategy model, see Louis E. Boone and David Kurtz, *Contemporary Marketing,* 12th ed. (Fort Worth, Tex.: Dryden Press, 2009): Chapter 1.

25. Ken Waldron, "How Stihl Fulfilled Brand Promise of Superior Product, Customer Service," *Advertising Age*, (December 10, 2009): 1–3.

26. http://www.stihlusa.com/

27. "Thinking Outside the Box (stores): Stihl VP Talks Channel Strategy with Kellogg Students," http://www.kellogg.northwestern.edu/news_article/2008/peterburton.aspx.

28. The origin of the concept of flows in marketing channels is generally attributed to Roland S. Vaile, E.T. Grether, and Reavis Cox, *Marketing in the American Economy* (New York: Ronald Press, 1952): 113–129.

29. Eric Decker, "Miller Coors Merger Will Have Impact on Distributors," *Small Business Times*, Milwaukee (August 8, 2008): 1–2.

30. For a related discussion, see Frank V. Cespedes "Channel Management Is General Management," *California Management Review* (Fall 1988): 98–120; and Donald W. Jackson and Bruce J. Walker, "The Channels Manager: Marketing's Newest Aide?" *Business Horizons* (Winter 1980): 52–58.

31. Filipe Caelho and Chris Easingwood, "An Exploratory Study into the Drivers of Channel Change," *European Journal of Marketing*, (September–October 2008): 1005–1022.

32. The theoretical basis for this argument can be found in George J. Stigler, "The Division of Labor Is Limited by the Extent of the Market," *Journal of Political Economy* (June 1951): 185–193. For a more recent but related analysis, see Walter Zinn and Michael Levy, "Speculative Inventory Management: A Total Channel Perspective," *International Journal of Physical Distribution Management* 18, 5 (1988): 34–39.

33. The theoretical basis for contactual efficiency can be found in Wroe Alderson, "Factors Governing the Development of Marketing Channels," in *Marketing Channels for Manufactured Products,* ed. Richard M. Clewett (Homewood, Ill.: Irwin, 1954), 5–22.

34. Marcel van Birgelen, Ad de Jong, Ko de Ruyter, " Multi-Channel Service Retailing: The Effects of Channel Performance Satisfaction on Behavioral Intensions," *Journal of Retailing*, (Winter 2006): 367–377.

35. Kathleen Seiders, Leonard L. Berry, and Larry G. Gresham, "Attention Retailers! How Convenient Is Your Convenience Strategy?" *Sloan Management Review* (Spring 2000): 79–89.

CHAPTER 2

The Channel Participants

LEARNING OBJECTIVES

After reading this chapter you should:

1. Be familiar with the classification of the major participants in marketing channels.

2. Understand why producers and manufacturers often find it necessary to shift many of the distribution tasks to intermediaries.

3. Identify the major types of wholesalers as reflected in the *Census of Wholesale Trade*.

4. Be aware of major trends in wholesale structure, including patterns of size and concentration in wholesaling.

5. Recognize and explain the value of distribution tasks performed by the major types of wholesalers.

6. Appreciate the complexity of retail structure and be familiar with the different approaches used to classify retailers, including the classifications used by the *Census of Retail Trade*.

7. Know about major trends occurring in retail structure, especially with regard to size and concentration in retailing.

8. Have an overview of the distribution tasks performed by retailers.

9. Be cognizant of the retailer's changing role in the marketing channel.

10. Appreciate the role played by facilitating agencies in marketing channels.

© Wisniewska/Shutterstock

FOCUS ON CHANNELS

Add Another Middleman to the Channel and Things Will Really Get Moving—Like a Gazelle

You would think that adding another level of middleman to a channel of distribution would slow things down. Wouldn't products have to go through another "step" if an additional intermediary was added? Wouldn't this be bound to make the channel less efficient?

Well, just the opposite seems to be occurring in online channels of distribution for used electronic products based on the experience of Gazelle.com, a relative newcomer (founded in 2006), but already a major player in "re-commerce" (channels). Gazelle is a middleman that serves as an online specialty merchant wholesaler in re-commerce channels. But unlike eBay and numerous other online intermediaries, Gazelle actually buys, takes title to and physically holds used electronic goods. It obtains the used electronics such as iPods, laptops, cell phones, cameras, stereo speakers and other equipment from consumers who are looking to get rid of this stuff but don't want to go through the trouble of putting these items on eBay, Amazon or other sites that have become more complicated to use in recent years. Instead, Gazelle pays for used electronics upfront, regardless of whether the

goods end up selling. After a customer agrees to sell a product to Gazelle, the customer is provided with a free shipping label and packing material to mail it to Gazelle's fulfillment center in Boston, where the products are held in a warehouse. The used equipment is then photographed and listed in marketplaces such as eBay and Amazon, sold to wholesalers for global export or, in some cases, recycled.

Gazelle's system really gets things moving, according to Gazelle spokesperson Kristina Kennedy, who claims, "our [Gazelle's] biggest competitor is inertia." She's right, because in fact, only a tiny fraction of the $300 billion in used electronic equipment estimated to be in consumers' homes is sold via online channels each year simply because millions of consumers just-don't want to bother with selling online by themselves. But take away all of that hassle, as online intermediary Gazelle promises to do, and a lot more of that $300 billion of used electronic equipment will get moving as fast as, well, a gazelle!

Source: Based on Geoffrey A. Fowler, "Niche Sites Going After eBay," *Wall Street Journal*, December 9, 2009): B4.

The marketing channel was defined in the previous chapter as the external contactual organization that management operates to achieve its distribution objectives. We noted that the channel manager should use intermediaries in the channel based on the principles of specialization and division of labor as well as contactual efficiency. If the channel manager does a good job of allocating the distribution tasks among a well-chosen group of channel participants, the resulting channel structure should achieve the firm's distribution of objectives with a high level of effectiveness and efficiency.

In the present chapter we build on these concepts by discussing the various types of channel participants and the distribution tasks they perform. The information provided should help the channel manager to recognize the contributions that various intermediaries can make to marketing channels. With this knowledge, the channel manager can then make better decisions about who should participate in the firm's marketing channels.

An Overview of the Channel Participants

Figure 2.1 illustrates the basic dichotomy between channel membership based on performance or nonperformance of the negotiatory functions (buying, selling and transferring title). Participants who engage in these functions are linked together by the flows of negotiation or ownership (see Figure 1.7 in Chapter 1) and are therefore members of the contactual organization (the marketing channel).

The three basic divisions of the marketing channel depicted in Figure 2.1 are: (1) producers and manufacturers; (2) intermediaries and (3) final users. The latter two are broken down further into wholesale and retail intermediaries and consumer and industrial users, respectively. The final users, though technically members of the marketing channel because they are involved in negotiatory functions, from this point on will not be viewed as channel members in this text. In the context of the management perspective we are using, it is more appropriate to view final users as **target markets** that are served by the commercial subsystem of the channel. The **commercial channel** then, by definition, excludes final users. Thus, whenever the term *marketing channel* is mentioned in the remainder of the text, it is understood that we are referring to the commercial channel. Final users viewed as target markets are the subject of Chapter 8.

Since facilitating agencies do not perform negotiatory functions, they are not members of the channel. They do, however, participate in the operation of the channel by performing other functions. Six of the more common types of facilitating agencies are shown in Figure 2.1.

The structure of this chapter is derived from the diagram shown in Figure 2.1. We begin by discussing the commercial channel: producers, manufacturers and intermediaries. We then move to a discussion of the facilitating agencies.

Producers and Manufacturers

For the purpose of this text, producers and manufacturers consist of firms that are involved in extracting, growing or making products. This category includes those irms that the U.S. Bureau of the Census classifies under agriculture, forestry and fishing, mining, construction, manufacturing and some service industries.

The range of producing and manufacturing firms is enormous, both in terms of the diversity of goods and services produced and the size of the firms. It includes firms that

FIGURE 2.1 Classification of Channel Participants

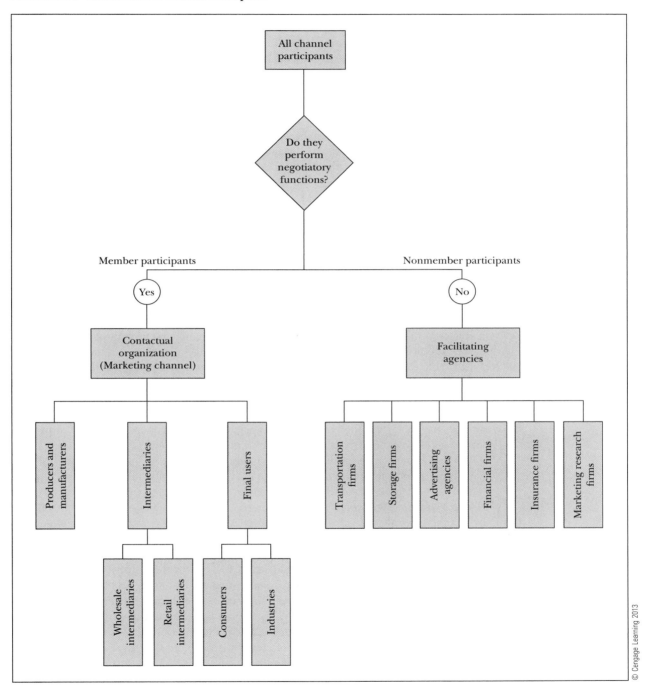

make everything from straight pins to jet planes and that vary in size from one-person operations to giant multinational corporations with many thousands of employees and multibillion-dollar sales volumes. But even with all this diversity, a thread of commonality runs through producing and manufacturing firms: all exist to offer products that satisfy the needs of customers. For the needs of those customers to be satisfied, products must be made available to customers when, where, and how they want them. Therefore, producing and manufacturing firms must ensure that their products are distributed to their intended markets. However, most producing and manufacturing firms, both large and small, are not in a favorable position to distribute their products directly to their final user markets.[1] They often lack the requisite expertise and economies of scale (and/or scope) to perform all of the tasks necessary to distribute their products effectively and efficiently to their final users.

With respect to expertise, many producers and manufacturers do not have nearly the level of expertise in distribution that they have attained in production or manufacturing. An electronics manufacturer may be operating at the leading edge of industry technology, yet know little about the best way to distribute its sophisticated products to its markets.[2] A drill bit manufacturer may make the finest products using the most advanced alloys, yet be quite naïve when it comes to the tasks necessary to distribute those products. A West Coast farm that grows the finest produce based on the latest developments in agricultural technology may know very little about how to make that produce available, in good condition and at low cost, to consumers on the East Coast. In short, expertise in production or manufacturing processes does not automatically translate into expertise in distribution.

Even for those producing and manufacturing firms that have or are capable of developing expertise in distribution, the economies of scale that are necessary for efficient production do not necessarily make for efficient distribution. To illustrate this point, consider a company such as Binney and Smith (B&S), the manufacturer of the famous Crayola Crayons. B&S is a relatively small manufacturer, but it is the world's foremost manufacturer of crayons. With sales totaling approximately 80 percent of the U.S. crayon market, the firm is able to manufacture crayons in huge quantities and has thus achieved considerable economies of scale in production. If one were to visualize the average total cost curve (ATC) for the production of crayons by B&S, it might appear as in Figure 2.2a. The figure shows that B&S, by producing at the output level of Q_1 is incurring a cost of C_1 per box of crayons produced. This is just about at the optimum point on the average cost curve. In other words, B&S is able to achieve economies of scale in production by spreading the firm's fixed cost over a great many crayons.

When it comes to performance of distribution tasks, however, such economies of scale may not be attainable. Suppose B&S were to attempt to distribute its crayons directly to the millions of consumers who use crayons. To provide adequate purchase convenience for these consumers, B&S would most likely need a large order processing facility to handle the volume of small, individual orders received. Moreover, B&S would need to maintain a huge inventory to meet demand, at least several separate warehouse locations around the country and would have to provide for transportation of the product to consumers.

The cost of setting up such an organization to perform these distribution tasks would be prohibitive. Indeed, it would be extremely unlikely that B&S could ever sell enough crayons to absorb these costs. If one were to visualize the average cost curve for the distribution of crayons directly to consumers by B&S, it might appear as in Figure 2.2b. When Figure 2.2b is compared to 2.2a, we can see that at the Q_1 level of boxes of crayons distributed, the cost of distribution per box of crayons is C_2. Note that this is not even close to the optimum point on the ATC curve and is much higher than the cost per box of crayons produced at the same level of output shown in Figure 2.2a. Thus, even though the Q_1 level was close to the optimum point on the average cost curve for the production of crayons (see Figure 2.2a), it does not even approach the optimum point on the average cost curve for distribution. In short, B&S would probably never be able to sell enough crayons to absorb the enormous fixed costs associated with the performance of the distribution tasks. However, by shifting the distribution tasks to other channel participants, such as wholesalers and/or retailers, B&S achieves substantial savings. The reason for this is that the

FIGURE 2.2
Hypothetical Average
Cost Curves for the
Production and
Distribution of
Crayons

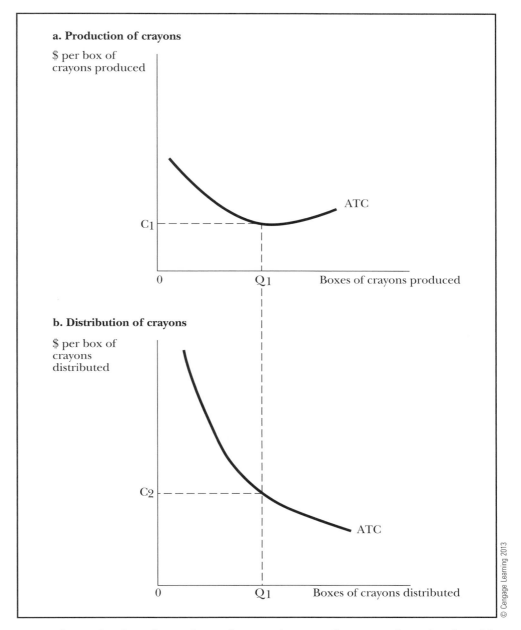

a. Production of crayons

$ per box of
crayons produced

C1

ATC

0   Q1   Boxes of crayons produced

b. Distribution of crayons

$ per box of
crayons
distributed

C2

ATC

0   Q1   Boxes of crayons distributed

© Cengage Learning 2013

intermediaries distribute the products of many other manufacturers and are therefore able to spread the high fixed costs of performing the distribution tasks over large quantities of diverse products, thus achieving *economies of scope* as well as *economies of scale* in distribution. This allows the intermediaries to operate closer to the optimum points on their average cost curves, which are often well below the corresponding points on manufacturers' average cost curves for distribution tasks.[3]

This example suggests the following generalization: *Producing and manufacturing firms often face high average costs for distribution tasks when they attempt to perform them by themselves.* This applies not only to small producers and manufacturers, but also to many large ones as well (even Microsoft, IBM and Procter and Gamble do not attempt to distribute all of their products to final customers). The scale economies that enable producers and manufacturers to operate at a low average cost for production processes are often absent in their performance of distribution tasks. Even the power of Internet-based e-commerce, which provides the technology for producers and manufacturers to be directly connected with final customers, could not overcome the underlying economic limitations often present with direct distribution. Disintermediation, which was expected to occur rapidly across numerous industries, did not materialize as expected.[4] Consequently, even in the high-tech age of e-commerce and the Internet, producing and manufacturing firms frequently search for channel members to whom they can shift some or all of the distribution tasks. Intermediaries at the wholesale and retail levels are the two basic types of institutions they can call upon to participate.

Intermediaries

Intermediaries, or middlemen, are independent businesses that assist producers and manufacturers (and final users) in the performance of negotiatory functions and other distribution tasks. Intermediaries thus participate in the negotiation and/or ownership flows (see the section titled "Flows in Marketing Channels" in Chapter 1). They operate at two basic levels: wholesale and retail.

Wholesale Intermediaries

Wholesalers consist of businesses that are engaged in selling goods for resale or business use to retail, industrial, commercial, institutional, professional or agricultural firms, as well as to other wholesalers. Also included are firms acting as agents or brokers in either buying goods for or selling them to such customers.[5]

Types and Kinds of Wholesalers   The most comprehensive and commonly used classification of wholesalers is that used by the *Census of Wholesale Trade*, published by the U.S. Department of Commerce every five years. This classification categorizes wholesalers into three major types:

1. Merchant wholesalers
2. Agents, brokers, and commission merchants
3. Manufacturers' sales branches and offices

Figure 2.3 provides a schematic diagram of these three types of wholesalers.

Merchant wholesalers are firms engaged primarily in buying, taking title to, usually storing and physically handling products in relatively large quantities. They then resell the products in smaller quantities to retailers, other wholesalers and to industrial, commercial or institutional concerns.. They go under many different names, such as wholesaler, jobber, distributor, industrial distributor, supply house, assembler, importer, exporter and others.

Agents, brokers, and commission merchants are also independent middlemen who do not, for all or most of their business, take title to the goods in which they deal. But they are actively involved in negotiatory functions of buying and selling while acting on behalf of their clients. They are usually compensated in the form of commissions on sales or purchases. Some of the more common types are known in their industries as manufacturers' agents, commission merchants, brokers, selling agents and import and export agents.

Manufacturers' sales branches and offices are owned and operated by manufacturers but are physically separated from manufacturing plants. They are used primarily for the purpose of distributing the manufacturer's own products at wholesale. Some have warehousing facilities where inventories are maintained, while others are merely sales offices. Some of them also sell allied and supplementary products purchased from other manufacturers.

FIGURE 2.3
Schematic Overview of
the Three Major Types
of Wholesalers

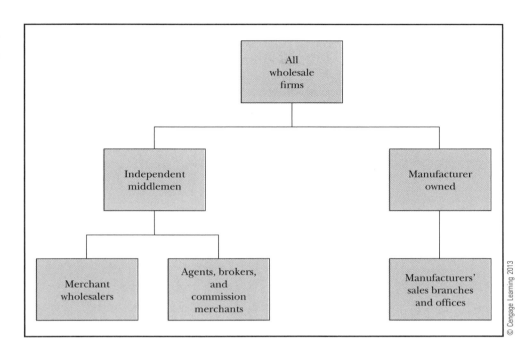

The *Census of Wholesale Trade* further classifies wholesalers by kind of business—of which there are 18 different categories. These kind-of-business groupings are shown in Table 2.1. For data gathering and reporting purposes, the *Census of Wholesale Trade* cross-classifies these kind-of-business groupings with the three major types of

TABLE 2.1 KIND-OF-BUSINESS GROUPINGS FOR WHOLESALERS

KIND-OF-BUSINESS GROUP	NAICS CODE
Durable Goods	
1. Motor vehicles and automotive parts and supplies	4231
2. Furniture and home furnishings	4232
3. Lumber and other construction materials	4233
4. Professional and commercial equipment and supplies	4234
5. Metals and minerals (except petroleum)	4235
6. Electrical goods	4236
7. Hardware, plumbing, heating equipment and supplies	4237
8. Machinery equipment and supplies	4238
9. Miscellaneous durable goods	4239
Nondurable Goods	
10. Paper and paper products	4241
11. Drugs, drug proprietaries, druggists' sundries	4242
12. Apparel, piece goods, notions	4243
13. Groceries and related products	4244
14. Farm products—raw materials	4245
15. Chemicals and allied products	4246
16. Petroleum and petroleum products	4247
17. Beer, wine, distilled alcoholic beverages	4248
18. Miscellaneous nondurable goods	4249

Source: U.S. Census Bureau, *Statistical Abstract of the United States: 2001* (121st edition) Washington, DC, 2001.

FIGURE 2.4
Wholesaler Sales (in millions of dollars) by Type of Wholesaler, 1992 and 2002

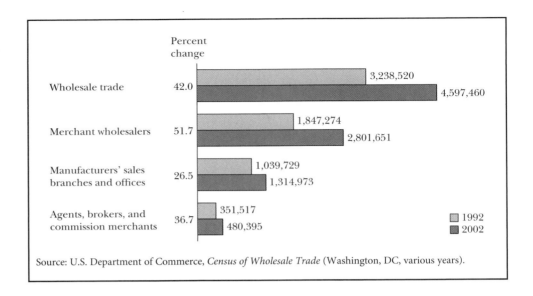

Source: U.S. Department of Commerce, *Census of Wholesale Trade* (Washington, DC, various years).

wholesalers. Hence data are available for the three types of wholesalers by various kind-of-business classifications for the United States as a whole and for many smaller geographical areas.

Structure and Trends in Wholesaling   The latest comprehensive *Census of Wholesale Trade* for which data are available, taken in 2002, showed that there were about 350,000 wholesaler firms and approximately 436,000 individual wholesale establishments, with combined total sales in excess of $4.6 trillion. A look at how this total breaks down among the categories of wholesalers reveals important trends in wholesaling for the decade between 1992 and 2002.

Figure 2.4 compares total sales of all wholesalers and sales broken down by the three major types of wholesalers for the years 1992 and 2002. Figure 2.5 compares the percentage of total sales for each of the three types of wholesalers for the same two years.

FIGURE 2.5
Percentage of Wholesaler Sales by Type of Wholesaler, 1992 and 2002

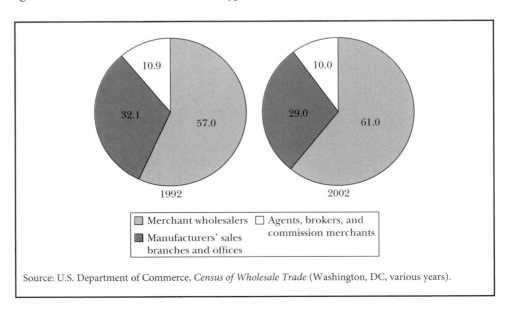

Source: U.S. Department of Commerce, *Census of Wholesale Trade* (Washington, DC, various years).

FIGURE 2.6
Percentage of
Wholesaler Sales by
Type of Wholesaler,
1948–2002

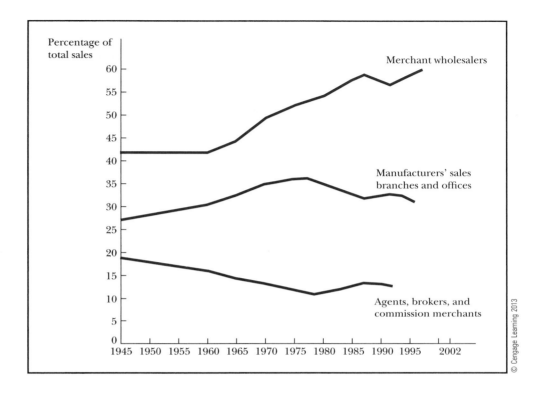

As shown in Figure 2.4, absolute sales of all three types of wholesalers increased substantially over this ten year period, although the percentage of increase varied somewhat. The largest increase (51.7%) was for merchant wholesalers. The smallest increase (26.5%) was for manufacturer sales branches and offices. The result as Figure 2.5 indicates, is that the percentage of total wholesale sales enjoyed by manufacturers' sales branches and offices decreased from 32.1 percent in 1992 to 29 percent in 2002, while the share of total wholesale sales of agents, brokers, and commission merchants slipped from 10.9 percent to 10 percent during that ten year period. The percentage of total wholesale sales of merchant wholesalers increased from 57 percent to 61 percent during that same period. This increase for merchant wholesalers represents a trend dating back to 1948 of steady growth in merchant wholesalers' percentage of wholesaler sales relative to manufacturers' sales branches and offices and agents, brokers and commission merchants.[6] This pattern of increase is shown in Figure 2.6.

Size and Concentration in Wholesaling Although wholesalers vary widely in size, the industry is still made up chiefly of small businesses. In terms of sales volume, many wholesalers are quite small, with almost 45 percent of all wholesale firms having annual sales of less than $1 million. Table 2.2 provides a further breakdown of wholesaler sales volume. As shown in the table, almost 87 percent of all wholesale firms reported total sales below $10 million, while under 6 percent had total sales of $25 million or more.

When size is measured in terms of number of employees per wholesale firm, the small size of most wholesalers is also quite evident. Table 2.3 shows this pattern. It is obvious from the table that relatively few wholesalers have large numbers of employees. Indeed, just over 2.3 percent had 100 or more employees, while over 50 percent had fewer than five employees. So, while there are some large—even giant—wholesalers, the majority, especially merchant wholesalers as well as agents and brokers, are still privately held, family-run businesses with small numbers of employees.[7]

TABLE 2.2 SALES VOLUME OF WHOLESALE FIRMS, 2002

ANNUAL SALES (IN MILLIONS OF DOLLARS)	NUMBER OF FIRMS	PERCENTAGE OF FIRMS
25 or over	15,781	5.3
10 but under 25	21,833	7.4
5 but under 10	27,316	9.3
2.5 but under 5	37,069	12.6
1.0 but under 2.5	60,615	20.5
Under 1	132,329	44.9
Total	295,003	100.0

Source: U.S. Department of Commerce, *Census of Wholesale Trade* (Washington, DC, 2002).

TABLE 2.3 NUMBERS OF EMPLOYEES IN WHOLESALE FIRMS, 2002

NUMBER OF EMPLOYEES	NUMBER OF FIRMS	PERCENTAGE OF FIRMS
100 or more	6,743	2.3
50 to 99	8,860	3.0
20 to 49	28,528	9.7
10 to 19	41,543	14.1
5 to 9	60,741	20.6
Less than 5	148,588	50.3
Total	295,003	100.0

Source: U.S. Department of Commerce, *Census of Wholesale Trade* (Washington, DC, 2002).

Economic concentration in terms of the percentage of total wholesale sales enjoyed by the largest firms is relatively low for merchant wholesalers as well as agents, brokers, and commission merchants, but significantly larger for manufacturers' sales branches and offices. As shown in Figure 2.7, the 50 largest merchant wholesalers and the 50 largest agents, brokers, and commission merchants accounted for less than 21 percent and under 28 percent of total sales respectively, while the 50 largest manufacturers' sales branches and offices accounted for almost 63 percent of total sales for this type of wholesaler. We should point out, however, that more consolidation is occurring among merchant wholesalers due to increasing numbers of mergers and acquisitions. Thus, both the average size of merchant wholesalers and the degree of concentration in the industry are increasing.

Distribution Tasks Performed by Merchant Wholesalers   Merchant wholesalers serve manufacturers as well as retailers and other customers. They have survived as intermediaries in the marketing channel because, as specialists in the performance of distribution tasks, they can operate at high levels of effectiveness and efficiency.[8]

Often the average cost curves for distribution tasks are lower for wholesalers, or they are able to operate closer to the optimum points on the curves than their suppliers.[9] Modern, well-managed merchant wholesalers are especially well suited for performing the following types of distribution tasks for producers and manufacturers:[10]

1. Providing market coverage
2. Making sales contacts
3. Holding inventory
4. Processing orders
5. Gathering market information
6. Offering customer support

FIGURE 2.7
Concentration of
Wholesale Sales (in
percent) by Type of
Wholesalers of Various
Sizes, 2002*

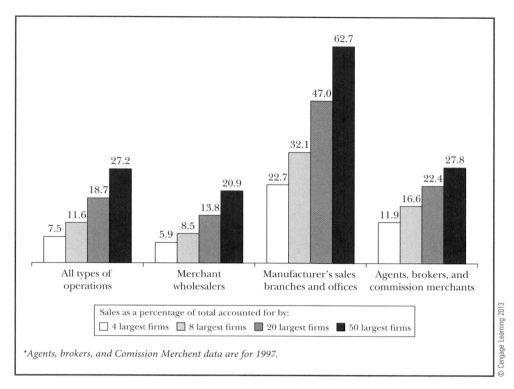

*Agents, brokers, and Comission Merchant data are for 1997.

© Cengage Learning 2013

Market coverage is provided by merchant wholesalers to manufacturers because the markets for the products of most manufacturers consist of many customers spread over large geographical areas. To have good market coverage so that their products are readily available to customers when needed, manufacturers often rely on merchant wholesalers to secure the necessary market coverage at reasonable cost. In the magazine industry, for example, the mass consolidation of magazine wholesalers from almost 3,000 to fewer than 50 in the past decade has publishers worried that their ability to reach small retail vendors in more remote markets will suffer.[11]

As Jackson and d'Amico point out in their study of merchant wholesalers serving industrial markets, "when large markets are dispersed geographically among several industries, and customers order frequently and require shorter lead times, distributors [merchant wholesalers] are more likely to be employed."[12] Table 2.4 shows the findings from their study, which compared the use of agents and merchant wholesalers by manufacturers selling industrial products. As shown in the table, 43 percent of the

TABLE 2.4 PERCENTAGE OF MANUFACTURERS' USE OF MERCHANT WHOLESALERS VERSUS AGENTS IN CONCENTRATED VERSUS DISPERSED MARKETS

	MARKET CHARACTERISTICS	
CHANNEL STRUCTURE[a]	CONCENTRATED[b]	DISPERSED[c]
Merchant wholesalers	57	43
Agents	78	22

[a]Based on 90 merchant wholesalers and 109 agents   [b]1 to 4 market centers   [c]5 to 10 market centers

Source: Adapted from Donald M. Jackson and Michael F. d'Amico, "Products and Markets Served by Distributors and Agents," *Industrial Marketing Management* 18 (February 1989): 29.

manufacturers operating in dispersed markets used merchant wholesalers, as compared to only 22 percent who used agents—a ratio of about two to one.

Sales contact is a valuable service provided by merchant wholesalers. For manufacturers, the cost of maintaining an outside sales force is high. If a manufacturer's product is sold to many customers over a large geographical area, the cost of covering the territory with its sales force can be prohibitive.[13] By using wholesalers to reach all or a significant portion of their customers, manufacturers may be able to substantially reduce the costs of outside sales contacts because their sales force would be calling on a relatively small number of wholesalers rather than a much larger number of customers.

The value of wholesalers in providing sales contact becomes even more apparent for manufacturers entering foreign markets. As Brown and Herring point out for the case of an American manufacturer attempting to sell its products in the U.K.:

> *The costs of setting up a U.K. sales operation are enormous: an office must be rented and equipped with all the necessary communication and data-processing equipment, staff must be recruited and trained (or relocated from America), the products must be marketed, and the potential customer base identified. There is a very large investment to be made, with no possibility of quick returns. A distributor, on the other hand, has all the infrastructure in place, knows the market, and should be able to provide sales very quickly.*[14]

Holding inventory is another crucial task performed by wholesalers for manufacturers. Merchant wholesalers take title to, and usually stock, the products of the manufacturers whom they represent. By doing so, they can reduce the manufacturers' financial burden and reduce some of the manufacturers' risk associated with holding large inventories. Moreover, by providing a ready outlet for manufacturers' products, wholesalers help manufacturers to better plan their production schedules. For example, Fort Howard Corporation, a paper products manufacturer, uses paper products wholesalers, such as Darter Inc. of University Park, Ill., to perform the inventory holding task. Fort Howard and Darter arranged a "partnership" agreement whereby Darter agrees to buy virtually all of its products from Fort Howard in exchange for favorable terms, including assured availability of products and faster deliveries. In exchange, Fort Howard has an assured high-volume outlet for its products as they come out of the factory and thus does not have to carry them in its own inventory.

Order processing performed by wholesalers is very helpful to manufacturers because many customers buy in small quantities. Yet manufacturers both large and small find it extremely inefficient to attempt to fill large numbers of small orders from thousands of customers. Many of the original dot-com firms engaged in e-commerce were undermined by the high fulfillment costs associated with thousands of small orders. For most of them, order processing costs were a major cause of their demise because the costs were very high relative to the value of the products being sold.[15] Wholesalers, on the other hand, are specifically geared to handle small orders from many customers. By carrying the products of many manufacturers, wholesalers' order processing costs can be absorbed by the sale of a broader array of products than that of a typical manufacturer. An outstanding example of a wholesaler that has achieved a very high level of expertise in performing the order-processing task is the McKesson Corporation, the world's largest wholesaler of pharmaceutical products. McKesson has always made order processing for its wide range of customers, including chains and independent retail drug stores, hospitals, food stores, and mass merchandisers, the keystone of its operation. Its distribution centers are highly automated with high-speed order-processing systems, flow racks with lighted displays that direct workers' order selection, special carousels that bring orders to order fillers, and conveyor systems that automatically route boxes to shipping points.

Few manufacturers can match McKesson's level of order processing in scale, sophistication, and efficiency.[16]

Gathering market information is another task of substantial benefit to manufacturers. Wholesalers are usually quite close to their customers geographically and in many cases have continuous contact through frequent sales calls. Hence, they are in a good position to learn about customers' product and service requirements. Such information, if passed on to manufacturers, can be valuable for product planning, pricing, and the development of competitive marketing strategy. For example, CDW Corporation, a leading distributor of information technology products and services to businesses, government and educational institutions, provides invaluable market information to hundreds of the manufacturers whose products it sells. CDW's technology specialists provide customers not only with the latest notebooks, desktops, printers, service, and storage devices but also with sophisticated technology solutions which, in turn, helps CDW's suppliers develop products that are targeted to customers' needs.[17]

Customer support is the final distribution task that wholesalers provide for manufacturers. Products may need to be exchanged or returned, or a customer may require setup, adjustment, repairs or technical assistance. For manufacturers to provide such services directly to large numbers of customers can be very costly. Instead, manufacturers can use wholesalers to assist them in providing these services to customers. This extra support by wholesalers, often referred to as **value added services**, plays a crucial role in making wholesalers vital members of the marketing channel from the standpoints of both the manufacturers who supply them and the customers to whom they sell. Consider the case of F.F. Despard located in Utica, N.Y. This wholesaler, specializing in cutting tools and abrasives products, puts a great deal of emphasis on customer support in the form of technical expertise. In fact, the company does not hire salespeople. Instead it employs *abrasives specialists* who are qualified to assist customers with a wide range of applications. This willingness on the part of F.F. Despard to provide this customer support has significantly lessened the burden on the abrasives manufacturers that supply this wholesaler.

In addition to performing the six distribution tasks for manufacturers merchant wholesalers are equally well suited to perform the following distribution tasks for their customers:[18]

1. Assuring product availability
2. Providing customer service
3. Extending credit and financial assistance
4. Offering assortment convenience
5. Breaking bulk
6. Helping customers with advice and technical support

Product availability, providing for the ready availability of products, is probably perhaps the most basic distribution task performed by wholesalers for customers. Because of the closeness of wholesalers to their customers and/or their sensitivity to customers' needs, they can provide a level of product availability that many manufacturers could not easily match. Consider what happened to Doug's TV, a retailer of television sets located in Beverly Hills, Fla. Doug's TV had been buying RCA brand television sets from Raybro Electronic Supplies, Inc., a local wholesaler. When RCA decided to drop Raybro and sell direct to retailers, Doug's TV found it faced serious product availability problems. Instead of two-day truck delivery, it now took a month to get TVs. To partially alleviate this problem, Doug's now has to place large orders, thus tying up more money in inventory.

Customer service is another valuable distribution task performed by wholesalers. Customers often require services such as delivery, repairs, or warranty work. By making these services available, wholesalers save their customers effort and expense.[19] For instance, Alco Standard Corporation, a large wholesaler of office products, provides repair services for customers' Ricoh, Canon and Sharp copy machines. Customers have found these services to be extremely convenient and helpful.[20]

Credit and financial assistance is provided by wholesalers in two ways. First, by extending open account credit to its customers on products sold, wholesalers allow customers to use products in their business before having to pay for them. Second, by stocking and providing ready availability for many of the items needed by their customers, wholesalers significantly reduce the financial inventory burden their customers would bear if they had to stock all the products themselves.

The case of Doug's TV, cited earlier in relation to product availability, also underscores the importance of wholesalers in providing credit and financial assistance. The wholesaler had let Doug's use favorable floor-plan financing terms on any size order, no matter how small. The manufacturer, on the other hand, allows such terms only on large orders.

Assortment convenience refers to the wholesaler's ability to bring together an assortment of products from a variety of manufacturers, greatly simplifying customers' ordering tasks.[21] Instead of having to order separately from dozens or even hundreds of manufacturers, customers can turn to one or a few general line or specialist wholesalers who can provide them with all or most of the products they need. For example, CDW, the giant wholesaler-distributor of information technology products mentioned earlier, fills thousands of orders for thousands of different products every day. In the process of doing so, it saves its customers enormous amounts of time and expense.

Breaking bulk is important because customers do not often need large quantities of products, or they may prefer to order only a small quantity at a time. Many manufacturers find it uneconomical to fill small orders and will establish minimum order requirements to discourage them. By buying large quantities from manufacturers and breaking down these "bulk" orders into smaller quantities, wholesalers provide customers with the ability to buy only the quantity they need. Here again, the case of CDW is instructive. While CDW handles huge orders for large corporations, government agencies, and institutions, most of its orders are relatively small. Many of these orders would be too small to be ordered directly from manufacturers because of minimum order requirements. CDW, however, buys in large quantities and then breaks them down into whatever amounts its customers wish to order.

Advice and technical support is the final distribution task wholesalers are called on to perform for their customers. Many products, even those that are not considered technical, may still require a certain amount of technical advice and assistance for proper use as well as advice on how they should be sold. Wholesalers, especially through a well-trained outside sales force, are able to provide this kind of technical and business assistance to customers. Ace Hardware Corporation, a large wholesaler based in Oak Brook, Ill., offers a good example of a wholesaler that is especially adept at providing its customers (mostly independent hardware retailers) with advice and technical support. Ace offers its dealers a wide range of help with inventory planning, advertising, store layout, customer service, computer applications and more.

Figure 2.8 provides a summary of the preceding discussion of the distribution tasks performed by merchant wholesalers. As shown in the figure, merchant wholesalers are placed between the set of six distribution tasks they perform for manufacturers and the six they perform for customers. The arrow leading down from the merchant wholesalers shows the result of performance of the distribution tasks: more effective and efficient marketing channels reflected in the margins received by merchant wholesalers. In effect, the margins earned by merchant wholesalers represent payment for services rendered by them and for value received by manufacturers and customers who bought the merchant wholesalers' most important product—*efficient performance of the distribution tasks.*

FIGURE 2.8
Distribution Tasks Performed by Merchant Wholesalers and Their Effect on the Marketing Channel

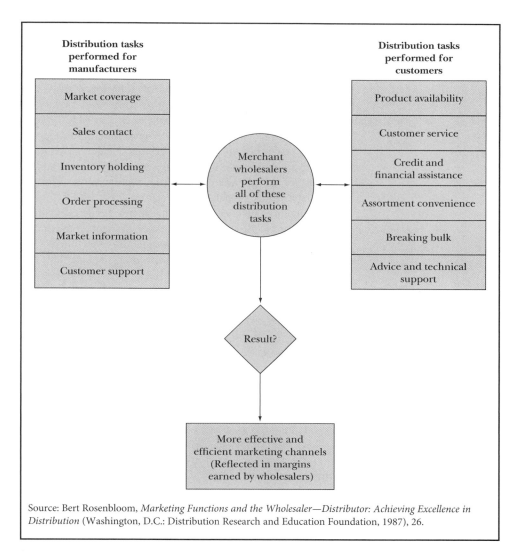

Source: Bert Rosenbloom, *Marketing Functions and the Wholesaler—Distributor: Achieving Excellence in Distribution* (Washington, D.C.: Distribution Research and Education Foundation, 1987), 26.

We should point out that not all merchant wholesalers in all lines of trade perform all of these distribution tasks all of the time. There are differences among merchant wholesalers in the extent to which they participate in the performance of distribution tasks. Many do perform all of the distribution tasks discussed here most of the time, or at least they attempt to. At the other end of the spectrum are some merchant wholesalers traditionally referred to in the marketing literature as **limited function wholesalers** who, though taking title to products, do not perform all of the distribution tasks discussed. For example, mail-order wholesalers do not provide sales contact through personal selling, cash-and-carry wholesalers do not extend credit, drop shippers do not carry inventory and rack jobbers generally do not provide much in the way of advice and technical support.

Distribution Tasks Performed by Agent Wholesalers As mentioned earlier in the chapter, agent wholesalers (defined by the *Census of Wholesale Trade* as agents, brokers, and commission merchants) do not take title to the products they sell. In addition, they do not perform as many distribution tasks as a typical merchant wholesaler.

Manufacturers' agents (also referred to as *manufacturers' representatives* or *reps*), for example, specialize mainly in performing the market coverage and sales contact distribution tasks for manufacturers. In effect, the manufacturers' agents substitute for the manufacturers' outside sales force. Thus, they are especially valuable to manufacturers who are not capable of fielding their own sales forces or to supplement the selling efforts of those manufacturers who do have their own sales forces but who find it uneconomical to use them for certain product categories or territories. Manufacturers' agents generally represent several manufacturers at the same time and operate in a wide range of product and service categories such as housewares, hardware, paint, chemicals, food-processing equipment, electronics and electrical components, steel and packaging. Services sold by manufacturers' agents include painting, plating services, machinery rebuilding, cleaning and a variety of business services.

Selling agents, another type of agent wholesaler, usually perform more distribution tasks than manufacturers' representatives. In fact, they may handle virtually the entire marketing and sales effort for the manufacturers they represent. Therefore, although selling agents usually do not physically hold inventory or take title to it, they may perform many, if not most, of the other distribution tasks such as providing market coverage, sales contact, order processing, marketing information, product availability, and customer services.

Although the basic marketing literature discusses manufacturers' agents and selling agents as though a clear and precise distinction exists between them, such a distinction is not usually made in practice. In fact, it is quite common to use terms such as *sales agent, selling agent, manufacturers' agent, manufacturers' representatives, reps,* or *export and import agents* interchangeably to refer to all types of agent wholesalers without any strict distinctions made about the degree to which they perform distribution tasks. Historical patterns of usage of terms in various trades arethe actual basis for referring to various types of agent wholesalers, rather than conceptual clarity or logic.

Brokers, the second major category of nontitle-taking wholesalers defined in the *Census of Wholesale Trade*, offer another example of the wide deviation between definitions based on the performance of distribution tasks presented in the marketing literature and performance in actual practice. In the marketing literature, the broker is usually defined as a go-between or a party who brings buyers and sellers together so that a transaction can becompleted. In the strictest definition sense, a broker performs only one distribution task—providing market information. Yet, in practice, some brokers may perform many, if not most, of the distribution tasks, so that for all practical purposes there is little to distinguish them from manufacturers' representatives or selling agents.

Consider the case of food brokers. A study by the National Food Brokers Association (NFBA) found that the overwhelming majority of food brokers perform a wide range of distribution tasks in marketing channels, which places them on par with manufacturers' representatives or selling agents. For example, many food brokers help manage marketing funds, recommend and execute trade promotions and even help create consumer promotion plans. Many are also involved with developing and executing the marketing programs of the manufacturers they represent. In so doing, they provide (in addition to market information) market coverage, sales contact, order processing, customer support and advice as well as product availability.[22] Figure 2.9 provides a further description of the services provided by food brokers.

Clearly, as Figure 2.9 indicates, the range of distribution tasks performed by food brokers places them well beyond the limited scope specified in the marketing textbook definition of brokers. Here again, the terminology used is more a function of historical accident than strict adherence. In fact, the term *food broker* is something of a misnomer because food brokers actually deal with many products besides food. While food brokers are not indicative of all brokers in other product categories, the role of brokers in

FIGURE 2.9
Distribution Tasks
Commonly Performed
by Food Brokers

Brokers provide a variety of specialized services that add value to the distribution process and help increase profits for their principals and customers. Brokers typically are engaged in one or more of the following:

- *Introducing their principals' new products to local market buyers.*
- *Regularly contacting retailers to ensure that a principal's products are in distribution and placed properly on the retail shelf.*
- *Coordinating with retailers to implement promotions, advertising campaigns, and couponing programs; to arrange in-store displays; and to conduct product demonstrations.*
- *Ensuring that a principal's products are ordered correctly, that shipments are received and priced correctly, and that unsalable items are credited and disposed of properly.*
- *In conjunction with their principals' marketing departments and customers, developing promotional programs for consumers in the local market.*
- *Through the use of advanced technologies, furnishing their principals with demographic data about consumer trends, product placement, marketing, and other information.*

Source: ASMC Foundation, "Specialized Services": *How Brokers Serve You* (Washington D.C., 1993) 2–3.
Copyright © ASMC Foundation. Reproduced by permission.

performing distribution tasks is generally expanding to the point that use of the word *broker* may understate the range of activities involved.

Finally, the third major category of agent wholesalers in the *Census of Wholesale Trade* is the **commission merchant**, who is of significance mainly in agricultural markets. Commission merchants perform a wide range of distribution tasks, including physically holding inventory (though not taking title), providing market coverage, sales contact, breaking bulk, credit and order processing. These distribution tasks are performed when commission merchants act on behalf of his or her principals (producers or manufacturers). Essentially, the commission merchant receives and warehouses products, helps locate buyers, makes sales, extends personal credit, processes orders and may arrange for delivery. After completing the sale and collecting money from buyers, the commission merchant remits it (less the commission for services supplied) to the principals, who sometimes remain anonymous to buyers.

What should be apparent from this discussion of distribution tasks performed by the various types of agent wholesalers is that generalizations about their roles in performing distribution tasks based on their "official" definitions can be misleading. A more meaningful way of determining just which distribution tasks are performed by which type of agent wholesaler is to look at the line of trade they are in or, better yet, the particular agent wholesaler in question. It may turn out that a broker in one line of trade performs a much wider array of distribution tasks than a manufacturers' representative in anotheror that a given selling agent does the same set of distribution tasks as a particular rep, broker or commission merchant.

Finally, regardless of whether the wholesaler in question is a merchant wholesaler or a so-called agent, broker or commission merchant, the wholesaler's participation in marketing channels is predicated on the performance of distribution tasks (services) that are desired by the manufacturers and customers.[23] Moreover, any of these wholesalers must be able to perform these distribution tasks more efficiently than either manufacturers or customers. With so many manufacturers and customers aggressively seeking ways to increase their productivity and reduce costs, they are taking a very hard look at the wholesaler's role in their marketing channels. Only those wholesalers who do an especially good job of performing distribution tasks at a very high level of efficiency are likely to remain in, let alone improve, their positions as viable members of the marketing channel.[24]

Retail Intermediaries

Retailers consist of business firms engaged primarily in selling merchandise for personal or household consumption and rendering services incidental to the sale of goods.

Kinds of Retailers   Retailers in the United States comprise an extremely complex and diverse conglomeration. They range in size from the so-called mom-and-pop neighborhood stores, with sales of less than $100,000 per year, to giant mass merchandise chains

---

TABLE 2.5 ALTERNATIVE BASES FOR CLASSIFYING RETAILERS

A. By Ownership of Establishment
1. Single-unit independent stores
2. Multiunit retail organizations
   a. chain stores
   b. branch stores
3. Manufacturer-owned retail outlets
4. Consumers' cooperative stores
5. Farmer-owned establishments
6. Company-owned stores (industrial stores) or commissaries
7. Government-operated stores (post exchanges, state liquor stores)
8. Public utility company stores (for sale of major appliances)

B. By Kind of Business (Merchandise Handled)
1. General merchandise group
   a. department stores
   b. dry goods, general merchandise stores
   c. general stores
   d. variety stores
2. Single-line stores (e.g., grocery, apparel, furniture)
3. Specialty stores (e.g., meat markets, lingerie shops, floor-covering stores)

C. By Size of Establishment
1. By number of employees
2. By annual sales volume

D. By Degree of Vertical Integration
1. Nonintegrated (retailing functions only)
2. Integrated with wholesaling functions
3. Integrated with manufacturing or other form-utility creation

E. By Type of Relationship with Other Business Organizations
1. Unaffiliated
2. Voluntarily affiliated with other retailers
   a. through wholesaler-sponsored voluntary chains
   b. through retailer cooperation
3. Affiliated with manufacturers by dealer franchises

F. By Method of Consumer Contact
1. Regular store
   a. leased department
2. Mail order
   a. by catalog selling
   b. by advertising in regular media
   c. by membership club plans
3. Household contacts
   a. by house-to-house canvassing
   b. by regular delivery route service
   c. by party plan selling
   d. Internet-based online sales

G. By Type of Location
1. Urban
   a. central business district
   b. secondary business district
   c. string street location
   d. neighborhood location
   e. controlled (planned) shopping center
   f. public market stalls
2. Small city
   a. downtown
   b. neighborhood
3. Rural stores
4. Roadside stands

H. By Type of Service Rendered
1. Full service
2. Limited service (cash-and-carry)
3. Self service

I. By Legal Form of Organization
1. Proprietorship
2. Partnership
3. Corporate
4. Special types

J. By Management Organizations or Operational Technique
1. Undifferentiated
2. Departmentalized

Source: Adapted from, Theodore N. Beckman, William R. Davidson, and W. Wayne Talarzyk, *Marketing*, 9th ed., (New York: Ronald Press, 1973), 239.

such as Walmart, with over $400 billion in annual sales. Methods of operation run from minimum service, spartan discount and outlet stores to elaborate operations with magnificent architecture in grand shopping malls. This category includes store retailers as well as nonstore retailers such as mail-order firms, direct selling (in-home) retailers, TV shopping show retailers and retailers operating on the Internet.[25] There are specialty retailers, broad-line department store retailers, giant superstore retailers, wholesale club retailers[26] factory outlet retailers as well as global, national, regional, and local retailers. The list can go on and on.

Over the years, a variety of classification schemes has been developed to help lend some order to this bewildering complexity. Table 2.5 outlines the most commonly used classification categories.

The most comprehensive and widely used approach to classifying retailers is that used by the *Census of Retail Trade*, which places all retailers into more than 50 kind-of-business classifications within 12 major groups. These major groups are shown in Table 2.6 in bold type with three-digit North American Industry Classification System (NAICS) codes. Most kind-of-business classifications used by the *Census of Retail Trade* are also listed in the table.

For data gathering and reporting purposes, the *Census of Retail Trade* cross-classifies these 12 major groups and the more specific kind-of-business categories with a variety of data, for the United States as a whole and for many smaller geographical areas as well.

Structure Trends in Retailing   As of 2002 (the most recent year for which data are available from the *Census of Retail Trade*), there were 1,114,637 retail establishments in the United States producing a sales volume of almost $3 trillion. When the previous census was taken in 1997 there were 1,118,447 retail establishments with a combined sales volume of almost $2.5 trillion. Given the decrease in number of establishments between 1997 and 2002 and the 20 percent increase in sales, the size of retail establishments measured by average sales volume per store must have increased significantly during those five years. This was indeed the case continuing a long-term trend dating back to 1948. As shown in Table 2.7, average sales for retail establishments were almost $2.7 million by 2002, up from $2.2 million in 1997. This is an increase of almost 23 percent.

This pattern of increasing total sales as well as average sales per retail establishment was consistent across all major kind-of-business groups between 1997 and 2002.

Concentration in Retailing   From the standpoint of economic concentration, retailing in the United States is increasingly dominated by large firms. In 2002, for example, large retailers (those with sales of $10 million or more) accounted for almost 80 percent of total retail sales, though they comprised just 4 percent of all retail firms. On the other hand, small retailers (those with sales of less than $1 million) accounted for 66 percent of all retail firms but less than 5 percent of total retail sales (see Figure 2.10).

The domination of retailing in the United States by large retailers is also evident in Figure 2.11, which shows that the 50 largest firms accounted for almost 39 percent of total retail sales in 2002. When one looks at particular kinds of retail businesses, the domination of large firms is even more striking. Figure 2.12, for example, shows four kinds of retailers where the four largest firms account for at least 72 percent of total sales in that category.

The preceding data shown up through Figure 2.12 only begin to convey the size and concentration of retailing. A more vivid picture emerges when the absolute size of

TABLE 2.6 TWELVE MAJOR KIND-OF-BUSINESS CLASSIFICATIONS USED IN THE *CENSUS OF RETAIL TRADE*

KIND OF BUSINESS	NAICS CODE	KIND OF BUSINESS	NAICS CODE
Retail trade	44–45	Gasoline stations	447
Motor vehicle & parts dealers	441	Gasoline stations with convenience stores	44711
Automobile dealers	4411	Other gasoline stations	44719
New car dealers	44111	**Clothing & clothing accessories stores**	448
Used car dealers	44112	Clothing stores	4481
Other motor vehicle dealers	4412	Mens clothing stores	44811
Recreational vehicle dealers	44121	Womens clothing stores	44812
Motorcycle, boat, & other motor		Childrens & infants clothing stores	44813
vehicle dealers	44122	Family clothing stores	44814
Automotive parts, accessories, & tire stores	4413	Clothing accessories stores	44815
Automotive parts & accessories stores	44131	Other clothing stores	44819
Tire dealers	44132	Shoe stores	4482
Furniture & home furnishings stores	442	Jewelry, luggage, & leather goods stores	4483
Furniture stores	4421	Jewelry stores	44831
Home furnishings stores	4422	Luggage & leather goods stores	44832
Floor covering stores	44221	**Sporting goods, hobby, book, & music stores**	451
Other home furnishings stores	44229	Sporting goods, hobby, & musical	
Electronics & appliance stores	443	instrument stores	4511
Appliance, television, & other		Sporting goods stores	45111
electronics stores	44311	Hobby, toy, & game stores	45112
Computer & software stores	44312	Sewing, needlework, & piece goods	
Camera & photographic supplies stores	44313	stores	45113
Building material & garden		Musical instrument & supplies stores	45114
equipment & supplies dealers	444	Book, periodical, & music stores	4512
Building material & supplies dealers	4441	Book stores & news dealers	45121
Home centers	44411	Prerecorded tape, compact disc,	
Paint & wallpaper stores	44412	& record stores	45122
Hardware stores	44413	**General merchandise stores**	452
Other building material dealers	44419	Department stores (incl. leased depts.)	4521
Lawn & garden equipment & supplies		Department stores (excl. leased depts.)	4521
stores	4442	Other general merchandise stores	4529
Outdoor power equipment stores	44421	Warehouse clubs & superstores	45291
Nursery & garden centers	44422	All other general merchandise stores	45299
Food & beverage stores	445	**Miscellaneous store retailers**	453
Grocery stores	4451	Florists	4531
Supermarkets & other grocery		Office supplies, stationery, & gift stores	4532
(except convenience) stores	44511	Office supplies & stationery stores	45321
Convenience stores	44512	Gift, novelty, & souvenir stores	45322
Specialty food stores	4452	Used merchandise stores	4533
Meat markets	44521	Other miscellaneous store retailers	4539
Fish & seafood markets	44522	Pet & pet supplies stores	45391
Fruit & vegetable markets	44523	Art dealers	45392
Other specialty food stores	44529	Manufactured (mobile) home dealers	45393
Beer, wine, & liquor stores	4453	All other miscellaneous store retailers	45399
Health & personal care stores	446	**Nonstore retailers**	454
Pharmacies & drug stores	44611	Electronic shopping & mail-order houses	4541
Cosmetics, beauty supplies, & perfume		Vending machine operators	4542
stores	44612	Direct selling establishments	4543
Optical goods stores	44613	Fuel dealers	45431
Other health & personal care stores	44619	Other direct selling establishments	45439

Source: U.S. Department of Commerce, Bureau of the Census, *1997 Economic Census, Retail Trade*, Series EC97R44A-US(RV) (Washington, D.C.: G.P.O., issued March 2000).

TABLE 2.7 TOTAL RETAIL SALES, NUMBER OF ESTABLISHMENTS, AND AVERAGE SALES PER ESTABLISHMENT, 1948–2002

YEAR	TOTAL (BILLIONS)	NUMBER OF STORES (MILLIONS)	AVERAGE SALES PER STORE
2002	$3,056.4	1.11	$2,742,000
1997	2,460.9	1.12	2,197,000
1992	1,894.1	1.53	1,242,000
1987	1,494.1	1.50	996,000
1982	1,038.2	1.42	731,000
1977	723.1	1.86	389,000
1972	470.8	1.91	246,000
1967	310.2	1.76	176,000
1963	244.2	1.71	143,000
1958	199.2	1.78	112,000
1948	130.5	1.77	74,000

Source: U.S. Department of Commerce, Bureau of the Census, *Census of Retail Trade* (Washington, D.C.: G.P.O., various years).

FIGURE 2.10
Percentage Distribution of Retail Firms and Sales by Size of Firms, 2002

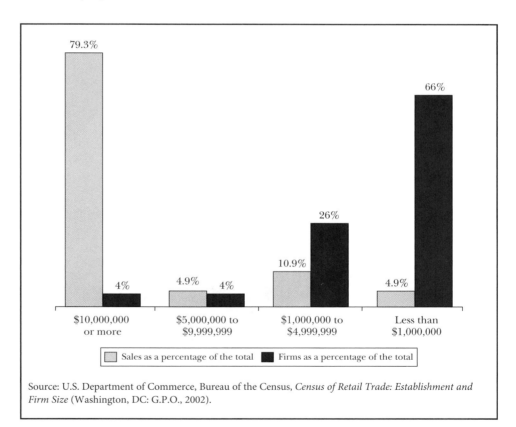

Source: U.S. Department of Commerce, Bureau of the Census, *Census of Retail Trade: Establishment and Firm Size* (Washington, DC: G.P.O., 2002).

retailers is considered. Table 2.8, for example, lists the 100 largest retailers in the United States, each of which has sales of at least $2 billion. Moreover, as shown in the table, each of the top 10 retailers had sales of more than $45 billion, the top five each produced sales of more than $60 billion, and the largest retailer (Walmart) achieved sales of over $400 billion!

FIGURE 2.11
Concentration of Sales among the Top 50 Retail Firms, 2002

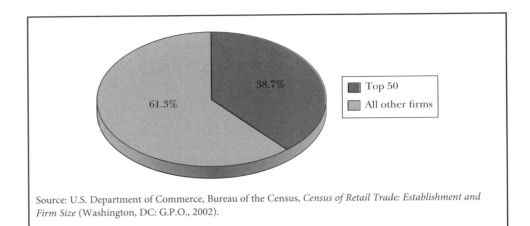

Source: U.S. Department of Commerce, Bureau of the Census, *Census of Retail Trade: Establishment and Firm Size* (Washington, DC: G.P.O., 2002).

FIGURE 2.12 Kinds of Retailers Where Largest Four Firms Account for at Least 50 Percent of Total Sales

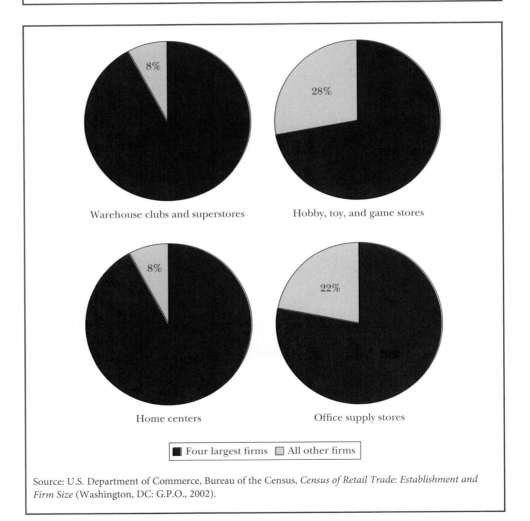

Source: U.S. Department of Commerce, Bureau of the Census, *Census of Retail Trade: Establishment and Firm Size* (Washington, DC: G.P.O., 2002).

Collectively in 2008, these 100 largest U.S. retailers had combined sales of almost one and three quarter trillion dollars ($1,732,317,025). This accounted for almost 44 percent of total estimated retail sales in the U.S. for that year.

TABLE 2.8 THE 100 LARGEST RETAILERS IN THE UNITED STATES, 2008

COMPANY/MAIN RETAIL SEGMENTS/FISCAL YEAR END	2008 REVENUES (000)	2007 REVENUES (000)	2008 PROFITS (000)	2007 PROFITS (000)	STORES 2008 *2007*
1. Wal-Mart Stores Inc, Bentonville, AR (SC, DS, WC, I, E) 1/31/09	$405,607,000	$378,476,000	$13,400,000	$12,731,000	7,873 *7,239*
2. The Kroger Co. Cincinnati, OH (S, CV, HS, SC) 1/31/09	76,000,000	70,235,000	1,249,000	1,181,000	3,550 *3,662*
3. Costco Issaquah, WA (WC, I, E) 8/31/08	72,483,020	64,400,155	1,282,725	1,082,772	512 *488*
4. The Home Depot† Atlanta, GA (HC, I) 2/1/09	71,288,000	77,349,000	2,312,000	4,210,000	2,274 *2,234*
5. Target Corp. Minneapolis; MN (DS, SC, E) 1/31/09	64,948,000	63,367,000	2,214,000	2,849,000	1,682 *1,591*
6. Walgreen Co. Deerfield, IL (DR) 8/31/08	59,034,000	53,762,000	2,157,000	2,041,000	6,934 *5,997*
7. CVS Caremark Corp.** Woonsocket, RI (DR) 12/31/08	48,989,900	45,086,500	3,483,700	2,691,300	6,923 *6,301*
8. Lowe's Cos. Mooresville, NC (HC, I) 1/30/09	48,230,000	48,283,000	2,195,000	2,809,000	1,649 *1,534*
9. Sears Holdings Hoffman Estates, IL (D, DS, C, I, E) 1/31/09	46,770,000	50,703,000	53,000	826,000	3,918 *3,847*
10. Best Buy Richfield, MN (HS, E, I,) 2/28/09	45,015,000	40,023,000	1,003,000	1,407,000	3,914 *1,314*
11. Safeway Pleasanton, CA (S, E, I) 1/3/09	$44,104,000	$42,286,000	$965,300	$888,400	1,739 *1,743*
12. Supervalu** Eden Prairie, MN (S) 2/28/09	34,664,000	34,341,000	−2,315,000	1,550,000	2,421 *2,474*
13. Rite Aid Camp Hill, PA (DR) 2/28/09	26,289,268	24,326,846	−2,915,420	−1,078,990	4,901 *5,059*
14. Macy's Cincinnati, OH (D.E.C) 1/31/09	24,892,000	26,313,000	−4,803,000	893,000	847 *853*
15. Publix Super Markets Lakeland, FL (S, CV) 2/27/09	24,109,584	23,193,590	1,089,770	1,183,925	993 *926*

†Continuing operations   *Estimate   **Retail operations only; operating income reported   ***Pro forma results

AS = Apparel Specialty	DS = Discount	HC = Home Center	SC = Supercenter	DNA = Does not apply
C = Catalog	DR = Drug Store	HS = Hard Lines Specialty	SH = Shoe Store	NA = Not available
CV = Convenience Store	E = Electronic	I = International	WC = Warehouse Wholesale Club	
D = Department	GM = General Merchandise	S = Supermarket		

TABLE 2.8 *(Continued)*

COMPANY/MAIN RETAIL SEGMENTS/FISCAL YEAR END	2008 REVENUES (000)	2007 REVENUES (000)	2008 PROFITS (000)	2007 PROFITS (000)	STORES 2008 *2007*
16. Staples Framingham, MA (HS, I, E) 1/31/09	23,083,775	19,372,682	805,264	995,670	2,218 *2,038*
17. Ahold USA** Chantilly, VA (S, E) 12/28/08	21,835,000	20,996,000	934,000	875,000	711 *705*
18. Delhaize America** Salisbury, NC (S) 12/31/08	19,222,000	18,293,000	996,321	957,511	1,594 *1,570*
19. Amazon.com Seattle, WA (E, I) 12/31/08	19,166,000	14,835,000	645,000	476,000	DNA DNA
20. TJX Cos. Framingham, MA (AS, HS, I) 1/31/09	18,999,505	18,336,726	880,617	771,750	2,652 *2,529*
21. J.C. Penney† Plano, TX (D, E, C) 1/31/09	18,486,000	19,860,000	567,000	1,105,000	1,093 *1,067*
22. Kohl's Department Stores Menomonee Falls, WI (D) 1/31/09	16,389,000	16,474,000	885,000	1,084,000	1,004 *929*
23. Alimentation Couche-Tard Laval, Quebec (CS) 4/26/09	15,781,100	15,370,000	3,900	189,300	5,443 *5,119*
24. 7-Eleven* Dallas, TX (CV) 12/31/08	15,000,000	12,800,000	NA	NA	5,680 *5,333*
25. Gap Inc. San Francisco, CA (AS, E, I) 1/31/09	14,526,000	15,763,000	967,000	833,000	3,149 *3,167*
26. H.E. Butt Grocery Co. San Antonio, TX (S.I) 10/31/08	14,500,000	13,500,000	NA	NA	338 *310*
27. Office Depot Delray Beach, FL (HS, I, E) 12/27/08	14,495,544	15,527,537	−1,478,938	395,615	1,429 *1,370*
28. Meijer* Grand Rapids, Ml (SC) 1/31/09	$13,900,000	$14,420,000	NA	NA	186 *181*
29. Toys "R" US Wayne, NJ (HS, I, E) 1/31/09	13,724,000	13,794,000	$218,000	$153,000	1,159 *1,560*
30. Military Exchange System Arlington, VA (GM) 1/31/09	12,725,592	12,400,000	NA	NA	4,028 *3,815*

†Continuing operations   *Estimate   **Retail operations only; operating income reported   ***Pro forma results

AS = Apparel Specialty   DS = Discount   HC = Home Center   SC = Supercenter   DNA = Does not apply
C = Catalog   DR = Drug Store   HS = Hard Lines Specialty   SH = Shoe Store   NA = Not available
CV = Convenience Store   E = Electronic   I = International   WC = Warehouse Wholesale Club
D = Department   GM = General Merchandise   S = Supermarket

TABLE 2.8 *(Continued)*

COMPANY/MAIN RETAIL SEGMENTS/FISCAL YEAR END	2008 REVENUES (000)	2007 REVENUES (000)	2008 PROFITS (000)	2007 PROFITS (000)	STORES 2008 *2007*
31. Dell Computer** Round Rock, TX (C, E) 1/30/09	11,529,000	10,378,000	143,000	2,000	DNA *DNA*
32. Dollar General Goodlettsville, TN (DS) 1/30/09	10,457,700	9,495,300	108,200	−12,800	8,362 *8,194*
33. 33.BJ's Wholesale Club Natick, MA (WC) 1/31/09	10,027,336	9,014,465	134,583	122,861	180 *177*
34. Apple** Cupertino, CA (HS, E, I) 9/27/08	9,655,000	6,611,000	NA	NA	247 *197*
35. A&P† Montvale, NJ (S) 2/28/09	9,516,186	6,401,130	−86,151	86,980	436 *447*
36. Limited Brands Columbus, OH (AS, C, E, I) 1/31/09	9,043,000	10,134,000	220,000	718,000	3,014 *2,926*
37. The Pantry Sanford, NC (CV) 9/25/08	8,995,626	6,911,163	31,783	26,732	1,653 *1,644*
38. GameStop Corp. Grapevine, TX (HS, I, E) 1/31/09	8,805,897	7,093,962	398,282	288,291	6,207 *5,264*
39. QuicTop* Tulsa, OK (CV) 4/30/09	8,700,000	8,400,000	NA	NA	501 *494*
40. Nordstorm Seattle (D, AS, C, E) 1/31/09	8,573,000	9,080,000	401,000	715,000	169 *156*
41. Office Max Naperville, IL (HS, E, I) 12/27/08	8,267,000	9,082,000	−1,657,900	207,400	1,022976
42. Menards* Eau Claire, WS (HC) 1/31/09	8,100,000	8,000,000	NA	NA	250 *235*
43. Liberty Media** Englewood Co (E, I, GM) 12/31/08	8,079,000	7,802,000	1,555,000	1,684,000	6 *6*
44. CDW Corp. Vernon Hills, IL (C. E) 12/31/08	8,071,000	8,145,000	NA	NA	DNA *DNA*
45. Giant Eagle* Pittsburgh, PA (S, CV) 6/30/09	8,000,000	7,100,000	NA	NA	366 *359*

†Continuing operations   *Estimate   **Retail operations only; operating income reported   ***Pro forma results

AS = Apparel Specialty   DS = Discount   HC = Home Center   SC = Supercenter   DNA = Does not apply
C = Catalog   DR = Drug Store   HS = Hard Lines Specialty   SH = Shoe Store   NA = Not available
CV = Convenience Store   E = Electronic   I = International   WC = Warehouse Wholesale Club
D = Department   GM = General Merchandise   S = Supermarket

TABLE 2.8 *(Continued)*

COMPANY/MAIN RETAIL SEGMENTS/FISCAL YEAR END	2008 REVENUES (000)	2007 REVENUES (000)	2008 PROFITS (000)	2007 PROFITS (000)	STORES 2008 *2007*
46. Whole Foods Market Austin, TX (S) 9/28/08	7,953,912	6,591,773	114,524	182,740	275 *276*
47. Winn-Dixie† Jacksonville, Fl (S) 6/25/08	$7,281,000	$7,201,000	$13,000	$280,000	521 *520*
48. Bed Bath & Beyond Union, NJ (HS) 2/28/09	7,208,340	7,048,942	425,123	562,808	1,037 *971*
49. Racetrac Patroleum* Smyrna GA (CV) 12/31/08	7,000,000	5,800,000	NA	NA	533 *525*
50. Dillard's Little Rock, AR (D) 1/31/09	6,988,440	7,370,806	−241,065	53,761	315 *326*
51. Family Dollar Stores Charlotte, NC (DS) 8/30/08	6,983,628	6,834,305	233,073	242,854	6,571 *6,430*
52. AutoZone Memphis, TN (HS, I) 8/30/08	6,522,706	6,169,804	641,606	595,672	4,240 *4,056*
53. Ross Stores Pleasanton, CA (AS) 1/31/09	6,486,139	5,975,212	305,441	261,051	956 *890*
54. Aldi* Batavia, IL (S) 1/31/09	6,250,000	6,000,000	NA	NA	1,000 *900*
55. Hy-Vee West Des Moines, IA (S, DR) 9/30/08	6,200,000	5,600,000	NA	NA	224 *224*
56. Trader Joe's* Monrovia, CA (S) 6/30/09	6,000,000	5,400,000	NA	NA	305 *297*
57. Defense Commissary Agency Fort Lee, VA (S) 9/30/08	5,813,245	5,537,505	NA	NA	273 *277*
58. Blockbuster Dallas (HS, I, E) 1/4/09	5,287,900	5,542,400	−374,100	−73,800	7,405 *7,830*
59. Foot Locker† New York, NY (SH, AS, I, E, C) 1/31/09	5,237,000	5,437,000	−79,000	43,000	3,641 *3,785*
60. Advance Auto Parts Roanoke, VA (HS) 1/3/09	5,142,255	4,844,404	238,038	238,317	3,368 *3,261*

†Continuing operations   *Estimate   **Retail operations only; operating income reported   ***Pro forma results

AS = Apparel Specialty	DS = Discount	HC = Home Center	SC = Supercenter	DNA = Does not apply
C = Catalog	DR = Drug Store	HS = Hard Lines Specialty	SH = Shoe Store	NA = Not available
CV = Convenience Store	E = Electronic	I = International	WC = Warehouse Wholesale Club	
D = Department	GM = General Merchandise	S = Supermarket		

TABLE 2.8 (Continued)

COMPANY/MAIN RETAIL SEGMENTS/FISCAL YEAR END	2008 REVENUES (000)	2007 REVENUES (000)	2008 PROFITS (000)	2007 PROFITS (000)	STORES 2008 2007
61. Barnes & Noble New York, NY (HS, E) 1/31/09	5,121,804	5,286,674	75,920	135,799	778 798
62. Save Mart* Modesto, CA (S) 3/31/09	5,100,000	4,600,000	NA	NA	245 248
63. PetSmart Phoenix, AZ (HS, E) 2/1/09	5,065,293	4,672,656	192,670	258,684	1,112 1,008
64. WaWa* Media, PA (CV) 12/31/08	5,050,000	5,000,000	NA	NA	569 576
65. Albertsons LLC* Boise, ID (S) 2/26/09	$5,000,000	$6,100,000	NA	NA	260 325
66. Sheetz Altoona, PA (CV) 9/30/08	4,900,000	3,900,000	NA	NA	350 339
67. Sherwin Williams** Cleveland, OH (HS,I) 12/31/08	4,830,000	4,955,000	647,900	766,000	3,346 3,325
68. Wegmans Food Markets Rochester, NY (S) 12/31/08	4,800,000	4,400,000	NA	NA	73 71
69. Casey's General Store Ankeny, IA (CV) 4/30/09	4,687,895	4,828,793	85,690	84,891	1,478 1,454
70. Big Lots Inc. Columbus, OH (DS) 1/31/09	4,645,283	4,656,302	151,547	158,461	1,339 1,353
71. Dollar Tree Chesapeake, VA (DS) 1/31/09	4,644,900	4,242,600	229,500	201,300	3,591 3,411
72. Nelman Marcus Group Dallas (D, C, HS, E) 8/2/08	4,600,500	4,390,100	142,800	111,900	69 60
73. Luxottica Group** Port Washington, NY (HS,I) 12/31/08	4,572,621	4,431,926	428,663	495,859	6,255 6,407
74. RadioShack Fort Worth, TX (HS, E, I) 12/31/08	4,224,500	4,251,700	192,400	236,800	6,752 6,670
75. Dick's Sporting Goods Pittsburgh, PA (HS) 12/31/08	4,130,128	3,888,422	−35,094	155,036	487 434
76. WinCo Foods* Boise, ID (S) 3/30/09	4,000,000	3,500,000	NA	NA	65 62

†Continuing operations   *Estimate   **Retail operations only; operating income reported   ***Pro forma results

AS = Apparel Specialty   DS = Discount   HC = Home Center   SC = Supercenter   DNA = Does not apply
C = Catalog   DR = Drug Store   HS = Hard Lines Specialty   SH = Shoe Store   NA = Not available
CV = Convenience Store   E = Electronic   I = International   WC = Warehouse Wholesale Club
D = Department   GM = General Merchandise   S = Supermarket

TABLE 2.8 (Continued)

COMPANY/MAIN RETAIL SEGMENTS/FISCAL YEAR END	2008 REVENUES (000)	2007 REVENUES (000)	2008 PROFITS (000)	2007 PROFITS (000)	STORES 2008 2007
77. Roundy's Milwaukee, WS (S) 12/31/08	4,000,000	4,000,000	NA	NA	152 153
78. Michaels Stores Irving, TX (HS, E) 1/31/09	3,817,000	3,862,000	−5,000	−32,000	1,170 1,129
79. Stater Bros. Markets San Bernardino, CA (S) 9/28/08	3,741,254	3,674,427	40,630	49,395	165 164
80. Harris-Teeter** Matthews, NC (S) 9/28/08	3,664,804	3,299,377	177,765	154,083	176 164
81. Bass Pro Shops* Springfield, MO (HS, E, C ,I) 12/31/08	3,600,000	3,200,000	NA	NA	54 49
82. O'Reily Automotive Springfield, MO (HS) 12/31/08	3,576,553	2,522,319	186,232	193,988	3,285 1,830
83. Burlington Coat Factory Warehouse Corp. Burlington, NJ (AS, HS) 5/30/09	$3,542,000	$3,393,000	NA	NA	433 397
84. Abercrombie & Fitch New Albany, OH (AS, C, E, I) 1/31/09	3,540,276	3,749,847	$272,255	$475,697	1,125 1,035
85. Belk Charlotte, NC (D) 1/31/09	3,499,423	3,824,803	−212,965	95,740	307 303
86. Raley's* West Sacramento, CA (S) 6/30/09	3,450,000	3,400,000	NA	NA	140 138
87. Collective Brands Topeka, KS (SH, I) 1/31/09	3,442,000	3,035,400	−68,700	42,700	4,877 4,892
88. Price Chopper/Golub Corp.* Schenectady, NY (S) 4/28/09	3,400,000	3,200,000	NA	NA	115 116
89. Williams Sonoma San Francisco (HS, E, C) 2/1/09	3,361,472	3,944,934	30,024	195,757	627 600
90. Borders Group Ann Arbor, MI (HS, I, E) 1/31/09	3,275,400	3,597,400	−186,700	−157,400	1,021 1,064
91. Ingles Markets Black Mountain, NC (S) 9/27/08	3,238,046	2,851,593	52,123	58,638	197 197

†Continuing operations　　*Estimate　　**Retail operations only; operating income reported　　***Pro forma results

AS = Apparel Specialty	DS = Discount	HC = Home Center	SC = Supercenter	DNA = Does not apply
C = Catalog	DR = Drug Store	HS = Hard Lines Specialty	SH = Shoe Store	NA = Not available
CV = Convenience Store	E = Electronic	I = International	WC = Warehouse Wholesale Club	
D = Department	GM = General Merchandise	S = Supermarket		

TABLE 2.8 *(Continued)*

COMPANY/MAIN RETAIL SEGMENTS/FISCAL YEAR END	2008 REVENUES (000)	2007 REVENUES (000)	2008 PROFITS (000)	2007 PROFITS (000)	STORES 2008 *2007*
92. Bon-Ton Stores York, PA (D) 1/31/09	3,225,415	3,468,569	−169,930	11,562	281 *280*
93. The Sports Authority Englewood, CO (HS, E) 1/28/09	3,160,000	3,000,000	NA	NA	462 *424*
94. Berkshire Hathaway** Omaha, NE (HS) 12/31/08	3,104,000	3,397,000	163,000	274,000	361 *379*
95. Ikea U.S.* Conshohocken, PA (HS, C, E) 8/31/08	3,100,000	2,700,000	NA	NA	34 *31*
96. Systemax Port Washington, NY (E, I, HS) 12/31/08	3,032,961	2,779,875	52,843	69,481	16 *0*
97. Saks Inc.† New York, NY (D. E) 1/31/09	3,029,743	3,224,076	−122,767	50,687	104 *102*
98. Tractor Supply Co. Brentwood, TN (GM) 12/27/08	3,007,949	2,703,212	81,930	96,241	855 *764*
99. Susser Holdings** Corpus Christi, TX (CV) 12/28/08	2,880,584	1,655,969	NA	NA	512 *504*
100. 100 HSN St. Petersburg, FL (E, I, C) 12/31/08	2,823,593	2,908,242	−2,390,888	164,804	DNA DNA

†Continuing operations   *Estimate   **Retail operations only; operating income reported   ***Pro forma results

AS = Apparel Specialty	DS = Discount	HC = Home Center	SC = Supercenter	DNA = Does not apply
C = Catalog	DR = Drug Store	HS = Hard Lines Specialty	SH = Shoe Store	NA = Not available
CV = Convenience Store	E = Electronic	I = International	WC = Warehouse Wholesale Club	
D = Department	GM = General Merchandise	S = Supermarket		

Source: Chain Store Age/Design Forum (August/September 2009): 20A–25A. Chain store age Copyright 2009 by LEBHAR-FRIEDMAN INC. Reproduced with permission of LEBHAR-FRIEDMAN INC via Copyright Clearance Center.

Online Sales in Retailing   Although we will address Internet-based online retail channels in much greater depth in Chapter 15 (Electronic Marketing Channels), a few basis facts are presented here to provide some perspective on the importance of online retail sales channels in the overall retail structure.

As of 2007, total online sales in the U.S. for all categories of goods totaled almost $127 billion. This accounted for almost 3.2 percent of total estimated retail sales in 2007 of close to $4 trillion.[27] Table 2.9 provides additional detail about online retail sales both in the aggregate and broken down by major kind-of-business classifications.

As can be seen from Table 2.9 in the kind-of-business categories dominated by retail stores, online sales as a percentage of total retail sales (except in the case of the Motor Vehicle and parts dealers) category, were under 3 percent of total sales in each category. However, in the nonstore retailers, especially the electronic shopping and mail-order houses sub-category, the percentages of online sales to total sales were well over 32

TABLE 2.9 RETAIL SALES TOTAL AND ONLINE BY KIND OF BUSINESS 2007

KIND OF BUSINESS	VALUE OF SALES (MIL. DOL.)		ONLINE AS PERCENT OF TOTAL SALES
	TOTAL	ONLINE	
Retail trade, total*	**3,994,823**	**126,697**	**3.2**
Motor vehicle and parts dealers	906,923	23,600	2.6
Furniture and home furnishings stores	115,349	796	0.7
Electronics and appliance stores	111,893	1,301	1.2
Food and beverage stores	559,625	1,022	0.2
Clothing and clothing accessories stores	221,097	2,115	1.0
Sporting goods, hobby, book, and music stores	86,906	1,686	1.9
Miscellaneous store retailers	117,447	1,963	1.7
Nonstore retailers	289,808	93,026	32.1
Electronic shopping and mail-order houses	199,199	88,915	44.6

*Includes other kinds of businesses not shown source:

Source: *Statistical Abstract of the United States: 2010* (129th Edition) Washington, D.C. 2009.: 646–647.

percent and close to 45 percent respectively. So, 2007 in the aggregate, online retail sales accounted for only 3.2 percent of total retail sales and several other major categories of conventional retailers, this percentage was even less. However retailers and Electronic shipping and mail-order houses accounted for a much larger portion of the total sales in their categories.

What is especially interesting to note for online sales is the growth that has occurred in less than a decade. In 1999, total online sales were just over $15 billion and accounted for about one-half of 1 percent of total retail sales. When compared with the 2007 sales data cited above, online sales increased by over 800 percent and by over 300 percent as a percentage of total retail sales!

Clearly retail sales via online channels of distribution have become a major and growing part of the channel structure serving consumers.[28] We will return to examine this trend and its implications in greater detail in Chapter 15.

Retailers' Growing Power in Marketing Channels

The power and influence of retailers in marketing channels have been growing. This trend follows three major developments: (1) increase in size and buying power; (2) application of advanced technologies and (3) use of modern marketing strategies.

As discussed earlier, the size of many retailers is increasing due to growth as well as to mergers, acquisitions and buyouts. Based on the data presented in Table 2.8, there is little question that many retailers are big—even huge—businesses. Because size translates into power, as retailers become larger, their capacity to influence the actions of other channel members (wholesalers and manufacturers) also becomes greater. All of the manufacturers who supply Walmart, for example, are considerably smaller than Walmart and are hardly in a position to exert a significant influence on Walmart's operating policies. On the contrary, because of Walmart's huge size and buying power, it is in a position to exert considerable influence on its suppliers. Indeed, in many cases, Walmart and other giant retailers can literally dictate the terms of sale they want to manufacturers. Macy's, the largest U.S. department store chain with over 800 stores, for example, is in such a powerful position that they can put the squeeze on suppliers to guarantee the department store's profits on the suppliers' products. If the products do not sell as well as expected and significant markdowns have to be taken, the manufacturers must agree to rebates or discounts on future orders to make up for lost profits. Toys R Us, the world's largest toy retailer with over $14 billion in sales, often gets shipments of hot, new toy products from the leading toy makers, such as Mattel, well in advance of smaller retailers. Home Depot, the world's largest home improvement retailer, has used its power to tell any of its suppliers that planned to sell their products online directly to consumers to drop that idea or be dropped by Home Depot. Such giant retailers with their enormous buying power, large market shares, and sophisticated managements have been referred to as **power retailers** and **category killers**, terms that convey the dominant positions these retailers enjoy.[29]

In short, Walmart, Home Depot, Macy's, Toys R Us, and virtually any of the multibillion-dollar retailers listed in Table 2.8, which in many cases are bigger than the manufacturers that supply them, have the capacity to assume dominant positions in the marketing channel.[30] This is especially the case for those kinds of retail businesses that are controlled by relatively few firms (refer again to Figure 2.12).

Growing size and concentration of retailers, as discussed on the foregoing pages, is the most fundamental reason for greater retailer power in marketing channels.[31] But two other factors are also important. The first is the increased application of advanced technology by retailers. The second is the growing emphasis by retailers on the use of modern marketing strategy.[32]

The many technological innovations of recent years have not gone unnoticed by retailers. Indeed, retailers have become astute followers and, more importantly, ardent users of many new technologies that have made them more sophisticated and demanding channel members. Giants such as Walmart, Home Depot, Target, Costco, Best Buy, Safeway, Amazon.com, and numerous others have become world-class in their use of information technology for inventory control and merchandise management as well as supply chain management.[33] But even the "smaller" retailers listed in the bottom 50 of the 100 largest retailers shown in Table 2.8 are using sophisticated information technology to spot slow-moving items and keep them off the shelf as well as to identify hot-selling merchandise so that it is available when and where customers want it. Many of these retailers have also been making better use of their scanner data for promotion and pricing decisions as well as to calculate profits on individual items through **direct product profitability (DPP) analysis**, shelf management, forecasting, and consumer shopping trip studies.

Perhaps the most exciting technological development being embraced by retailers is their growing use of the Internet to enhance the shopping experience of their customers. While the "pure-play" online retailers such as Amazon.com, which sells all of its product via the Internet, have gotten much of the attention in recent years,[34] another revolution is occurring in the way conventional retailers are integrating Internet-based e-commerce with their store and catalog operations. In fact, a new term called **threetailing** has emerged to describe this convergence of in-store, catalog, and online channels. Some retailers, such as JCPenney, are inviting their customers to come in (store), call in (catalog), or log on (online) to shop. Staples, the giant office superstore, has fully integrated its online capabilities with its retail operations so that customers can order online from the firm's extensive Web site and then pick up the product in the store. And if they want to return it, they can bring it back to the store.

These are, of course, just a small sample of the technologies being used by retailers, but they are indicative of the role of technology in increasing their capabilities and, in turn, their power in the marketing channel. We will examine technology as it affects marketing channels in greater detail in Chapter 3.

Turning now to retailers' growing emphasis on marketing, a fundamental change has been the evolution in thinking by leading retailers about the application of marketing strategy in a retail setting.[35] Retailers have traditionally been more supplier-(vendor) driven than market-driven. In recent years, however, more retailers are discovering the power of modern marketing methods for surviving and prospering in fiercely competitive retail markets. Indeed, some retailers now rival the best of the major U.S. consumer packaged goods manufacturers in the application of marketing strategies.

Consider, for example, the case of Kohl's, one of the fastest-growing discount department stores in the U.S. Kohl's has managed to differentiate itself from the pack by stressing a radically different store layout than its competitors. Kohl's uses what it refers to as a "racetrack" layout, designed to expose customers to the maximum amount of merchandise in the shortest time. Rather than walk up and down aisles, shoppers circle around the merchandise as they move through the store. Though they spend less time in the store, they buy more merchandise. This flies in the face of conventional retailing layout theory, which is based on the assumption that the more time customers spend in the store, the more merchandise they will purchase. All the manufacturers of the brand name apparel that Kohl's sells are eager to please this astute and fast-growing retailer.

Even relatively small retailers such as The Fresh Market, a family-owned supermarket chain, has become a force in upscale food marketing channels through adept use of marketing strategy. The Fresh Market has been recognized in the super-competitive supermarket arena as a leader in using market segmentation to zero in on its target market—educated high-income consumers in upscale neighborhoods. The Fresh Market's stores are typically 18,000 square feet (compared to the typical 40,000 square feet of U.S. supermarkets) and feature warm lighting, classical background music, and elegant décor to create the kind of shopping environment sought by the well-heeled market segment the store is targeting. The results have been spectacular. Fresh Market has enjoyed a same-store sales growth rate of over 9 percent, compared with the 2 percent rate of mass-market supermarkets. Even giant suppliers in the marketing channel have learned to respect the Fresh Market's considerable marketing expertise and are eager to get and keep their products on this posh supermarket's shelves.

To sum up, retailers in the United States and around the world[36] have become much larger and more concentrated, more technologically adept, and more sophisticated marketers. As a result, they have become far more powerful members of marketing channels in which they participate. In short, retailers are now the **gate-keepers** into consumer markets.[37]

From the suppliers' perspective, both at the producer and wholesaler levels, the implications of the retailers' new position are potentially ominous. To an increasing extent their basic marketing strategies in the areas of product planning and development, pricing and promotion will be constrained and even shaped by the considerable demands of a powerful retail sector. Suppliers that are not able to adjust to this new reality will have a difficult, if not impossible, task in gaining access to consumer markets.

Distribution Tasks Performed by Retailers

The role of retailers in performing distribution tasks is summarized very succinctly in a classic statement by Charles Y. Lazarus:

> *The role of the retailer in the distribution channel, regardless of his size or type, is to interpret the demands of his customers and to find and stock the goods these customers want, when they want them, and in the way they want them. This adds up to having the right assortments at the time customers are ready to buy.*[38]

Elaborating on Lazarus's list, we may specify the distribution tasks for which retailers are especially well suited, as follows:

1. Offering manpower and physical facilities that enable producers, manufacturers and wholesalers to have many points of contact with consumers close to their places of residence
2. Providing personal selling, advertising and display to aid in selling suppliers' products
3. Interpreting consumer demand and relaying this information back through the channel
4. Dividing large quantities into consumer-sized lots, thereby providing economies for supplies (by accepting relatively large shipments) and convenience for consumers
5. Offering storage, so that suppliers can have widely dispersed inventories of their products at low cost and enabling consumers to have close access to the products of producers, manufacturers and wholesalers
6. Removing substantial risk from the producer and manufacturer (or wholesaler) by ordering and accepting delivery in advance of the season

The level at which retailers perform these distribution tasks varies enormously across the spectrum of retailing, from an all-out effort to do everything to a bare bones level of doing little.

Nordstrom, a well-known chain of upscale department stores, is an excellent example of a retailer that puts forth all-out effort for its customers. In fact, this retailer has become famous for providing the highest level of service at the retail level. At Nordstrom, stocking the stores with highly desirable assortments of merchandise in impeccable surroundings and selling it through knowledgeable and helpful salespeople is only the beginning. Salespeople also gift wrap packages at no extra charge and sometimes drop off orders at customers' homes. Piano players serenade shoppers year-round. In Alaska, Nordstrom employees have been known to warm up cars while drivers spend a little more time shopping. There is even a story about a customer who got his money back on a tire even though Nordstrom does not sell tires! Nordstrom was simply attempting to live up to its "no questions asked" returns policy.

At the other end of the spectrum of retail service levels are off-price retailers such as Marshalls, an apparel chain that stocks an unpredictable assortment of merchandise in spartan surroundings and offers no personal service with long checkout lines. In the middle range are retailers such as Target, the chain of more than 1,500 discount department stores that has some of the ambience of upscale department stores and carries merchandise that is chic and fashionable, yet priced well below what conventional department stores charge. Although there is little sales help, store signage is excellent and wide aisles, attractive displays and short checkout lines create a different and better shopping experience than what customers would ordinarily expect from a discount mass merchandiser.

Then, of course, there are the so-called "pure-play" or Internet only retailers such as Amazon.com, Overstock.com, Furniture.com and many others that also perform distribution tasks. Even though these retailers sell only via online channels, they can and do provide excellent customer service by offering incredible selections of merchandise, thorough yet concise product descriptions and reviews, customized product assortments aimed at the particular interests of customers, as well as low prices and quick delivery. So, the fact that these retailers do not have physical facilities that customers can visit does not undermine their capacity to perform distribution tasks with a very high degree of effectiveness and efficiency.

In essence, each retail channel member makes its own decisions about how it will approach the performance of distribution tasks. But to remain a viable member of the marketing channel, each must offer something of value to its customers as well as its suppliers.[39] If it fails to do so, existing competitive retailers, other channel members or new forms of channel institutions will be only too happy to take its place in the marketing channel.[40]

The growing size of retailers, discussed earlier, has also affected the allocation of distribution tasks among channel members. Specifically, distribution tasks that were formerly the province of wholesalers or manufacturers have increasingly been taken over by the large-scale retailers. For example, most large chain store organizations and department stores have their own modern warehousing facilities enabling them to perform storage and order processing tasks very efficiently. This, in turn, has reduced their use of merchant wholesaler intermediaries to a marginal level. Voluntary associations of retailers,such as retailer cooperatives, wholesaler-initiated voluntary chains and franchise systems,have also grown. This enables many of these organizations to rival the scale economies of corporate chains.[41] Even single-unit independent retail stores have, on average, grown larger, utilized more modern facilities and equipment and performed distribution tasks more efficiently.

This poses a dilemma for the producer or manufacturer. On the one hand, the potential of retail intermediaries to perform distribution tasks effectively and efficiently has increased. But on the other hand, the larger scale of retailers has increased their power and independence; hence they are less easily influenced by the producer or manufacturer.[42] As a result, the channel manager in the producing or manufacturing firm will face both increased opportunities and greater difficulties in the course of using retailers in the channel of distribution, placing an especially high premium on effective channel management.

Facilitating Agencies

Facilitating Agencies are business firms that assist in the performance of distribution tasks other than buying, selling and transferring title. From the standpoint of the channel manager, they may be viewed as subcontractors to whom various distribution tasks can be *farmed out* based on the principle of specialization and division of labor. By properly allocating distribution tasks to facilitating agencies, the channel manager will have an ancillary structure that is an efficient mechanism for carrying out the firm's distribution objectives. Here are some of the more common types of facilitating agencies:

- *Transportation agencies include all firms offering transportation services on a public basis, such as United Parcel Service (UPS) and Federal Express as well as the U.S. Post Offices. Because of great economies of scale and scope, these and other common carriers are able to perform transportation services far more efficiently and cost-effectively than manufacturers, wholesalers or retailers.*
- *Storage agencies consist mainly of public warehouses that specialize in the storage of goods on a fee basis. Many of these firms provide great flexibility in performing the storage tasks. In some instances the goods of a channel member (producers, manufacturers, wholesalers or retailers) are not physically stored in the warehousing firm's facilities, but rather in the channel member's own facilities. Under this so-called field warehousing arrangement, the warehousing agency locks up the goods and issues a receipt, which often serves as collateral on a loan taken by the channel member.*
- *Order processing agencies are firms that specialize in order fulfillment tasks. They relieve manufacturers, wholesalers and retailers from some or all of the tasks of*

processing orders for shipment to customers. For example, Catalog Resources, Inc., based in Dover, Del., handles the order processing for the catalog sales of Laura Ashley, Caswell-Massey, Winterthur, and Hallmark cards, thus relieving these firms of the nuts and bolts involved in processing customers' orders themselves.

- *Third party logistics providers, sometimes referred to as "3PLs" or "TPLs," are firms that specialize in providing logistics services to companies or organizations that are not capable or who find it more convenient and efficient to let an outside firm perform most or all of the distribution tasks involved in supply chain management. Unlike more specialized firms or agencies that focus mainly on transportation, storage or order processing tasks, most third party logistics providers are capable of providing a broad range of logistical services that can be integrated and tailored to specific customer needs, including inventory management and control, material flows analysis, automated systems development, cross-docking systems design, freight forwarding, picking and packing and many others. One leading third party logistics provider, ELM Global Logistics, captures succinctly in its Web site description the range and depth of services 3PLs can offer:*

  > ELM is a Third Party Logistics Partner with distribution facilities totaling 1,000,000 square feet assisting companies with warehousing, physical distribution, and pick and pack requirements of all general merchandise. The range of services include cross-docking, repackaging, pick and pack services, computerized inventory, E.D.I. capabilities and short and long term storage.[43]

- *Advertising agencies offer the channel member expertise in developing promotion strategy. This can range from providing a small amount of assistance in writing an ad to complete design and execution of the advertising or promotional campaign.*
- *Financial agencies consist of firms such as banks, finance companies, and factors that specialize in discounting accounts receivable. Common to all of these firms is that they possess the financial resources and expertise that the channel manager often lacks.*
- *Insurance companies provide the channel manager with a means for shifting some of the risks inherent in any business venture, such as fire and theft losses, in-transit damage of goods and, in some cases, inclement weather.*
- *Marketing research firms have grown substantially in the past 20 years. Most large cities now have a number of marketing research firms offering a wide range of skills. The channel manager can call on these firms to provide information when his or her own firm lacks the necessary skills to obtain marketing information relevant to distribution.*

Summary

Many different types of parties participate in the marketing channel. Some are considered to be members while other participants are nonmembers. The former perform negotiatory functions and participate in the flows of negotiation and/or ownership, while the latter participants do not. Although final users (target markets) are members of the marketing channel, they are excluded from the commercial channel, which by definition excludes final users.

Producers and manufacturers consist of firms that are involved in extracting, growing or making products.

Though the range of types and sizes of producing and manufacturing firms is enormous, all are faced with the common task of distributing their products to their intended users. Many producers and manufacturers, however, lack the expertise and economies of scale and scope to distribute their products directly to their final users. Hence, in most cases, it is difficult and inefficient for manufacturers to distribute their products directly to final users. They often call on intermediaries at the wholesale and/or retail levels as well as facilitating agencies to share in the performance of the distribution tasks.

Wholesalers consist of businesses that are engaged in selling goods for resale or business use to retail, industrial, commercial, institutional, professional or agricultural firms or organizations as well as to other wholesalers. Wholesalers are classified into three basic types: (1) merchant wholesalers; (2) agents, brokers and commission merchants and (3) manufacturers' sales branches and offices. The first two are relatively small businesses and the level of economic concentration in wholesaling is generally low but it is increasing.

Merchant wholesalers are especially well suited for performing distribution tasks for producers or manufacturers such as providing market coverage, making sales contacts, holding inventory, processing orders, gathering market information and offering customer support. For their customers, merchant wholesalers are equally well suited to efficiently perform such distribution tasks as assuring product availability, providing customer service, extending credit and financial assistance, offering assortment convenience, breaking bulk and helping customers with advice and technical support.

As a rule, agent wholesalers do not perform as many distribution tasks as merchant wholesalers. However, the range of distribution task performance varies greatly. Moreover, the names given to various agent wholesalers—such as manufacturers' representative, selling agent, sales agent, rep, broker, and so on—are generally not accurate guides as to the level of distribution tasks performed by each category.

Retailers consist of businesses engaged primarily in selling merchandise for personal or household consumption and rendering services incidental to the sale of the goods. Retailers comprise an extremely diverse group in both type and size. The *Census of Retail Trade* classifies retailers into different kind-of-business

categories to provide some degree of order to this great diversity. Retail firms have been steadily growing larger over the past three decades and the level of economic concentration has become relatively high. Retailers are particularly well suited for performing such distribution tasks as:

- *Offering manpower and physical facilities that enable producers, manufacturers and wholesalers to have many points of contact with consumers*
- *Providing personal selling, advertising and display to sell suppliers' products*
- *Interpreting consumer demand and relaying it through the channel*
- *Dividing large quantities of products into consumer-sized lots*
- *Offering storage points close to points of consumer contact*
- *Reducing risks of producers, manufacturers and wholesalers by accepting delivery of merchandise in advance of the selling season*

As retailers, both land-based and online, continue to grow larger, more technologically sophisticated and begin to embrace modern marketing strategy, their role in the marketing channel will become an even more independent and dominant one. This will pose an increasing challenge to channel management in producing and manufacturing firms.

Facilitating agencies such as transportation companies, storage firms, order-processing firms, third party logistics providers, advertising agencies, financial institutions, insurers and marketing researchers, while not members of the marketing channel, are still called upon frequently by any or all of the channel members to help perform many different distribution tasks.

Review Questions

1. Explain the classification scheme of the channel participants shown in Figure 2.1.

2. Expertise and economies of scale in production do not necessarily translate into expertise and economies of scale and/or scope in distribution. Discuss this statement.

3. Why do you suppose the average costs of performing many distribution tasks are lower for intermediaries and facilitating agencies than for producers and manufacturers?

4. How does the *Census of Wholesale Trade* classify wholesale intermediaries?

5. Contrary to some predictions, wholesalers have not died out. What has happened to wholesalers in recent years?

6. Discuss the basic trends over the past 30 years with regard to total wholesale sales for (a) merchant wholesalers; (b) manufacturers' sales branches and offices and (c) agents, brokers and commission merchants.

7. Describe the distribution tasks that wholesalers are especially well suited for performing.

8. The average size of retail units (as measured by sales volume) has been increasing. What are some of the implications of this trend for channel management in producing and manufacturing firms?

9. What patterns seem to be emerging with respect to online retail sales vs. conventional retail sales since the first couple of years of the twenty-first century?

10. Describe the distribution tasks that retailers are especially well suited for performing.

11. Discuss retailers' growing power in the marketing channel in terms of the possible implications for channel management.

12. Identify and discuss several types of facilitating agencies and the role they play in channels of distribution.

Channel Issues for Discussion

1. Wrigley is the world's leading manufacturer of chewing gum, producing literally millions of packages of gum every day. It is a large, financially strong company whose manufacturing technology for producing gum is state-of-the-art. It sells its products to millions of gum-chewing consumers all over the United States and many other countries around the world. Still, Wrigley has never attempted to sell its chewing gum directly to consumers, but instead uses a wide variety of intermediaries at the wholesale and retail levels.

   Why do you suppose Wrigley has chosen to use intermediaries rather than sell direct to consumers? Explain the underlying economics of the company's policy.

2. The *Census of Wholesale Trade* and the *Census of Retail Trade* are published every five years by the Department of Commerce. The most recent census was taken in 2002 and the one before that was in 1997. However, the actual findings from the census are not made available until two and one-half to three years later. Thus, the findings from the 1997 census did not appear until 2000, and the 2002 census did not appear until the year 2005.

   How serious a problem do you think this is in terms of the timelines of information provided by the census?

3. W. W. Grainger, headquartered in Skokie, Ill., is one of the nation's largest wholesalers, with more than 600 branch locations. The company sells mainly industrial products such as electric motors, fans, blowers, air compressors, power transmission equipment along with thousands of

different components and replacement parts. Inventories and order processing are managed with advanced computer systems. Grainger buys products from about 2,000 manufacturers and resells them to almost one million customers. The principal means by which Grainger competes, according to the company's top management, is by offering such extras as wide availability of local stocks, outside salespeople, and customer service. Grainger has also put its complete catalog online so that customers have the option of visiting the company's Web site to place their orders.

   In a fundamental sense, is giant W. W. Grainger different from the host of mostly much smaller wholesalers in any other line of trade? Discuss in terms of the set of distribution tasks presented in the chapter.

4. Web fulfillment companies may start a new trend in online retailing. These firms allow conventional retailers to operate their online divisions without the expense and hassle of developing and running their own e-commerce operations. GSI Commerce, for example, handles Web site design, order fulfillment, and customer service for retailers who do not want to perform these distribution tasks themselves. Major retailers such as Dick's Sporting Goods, Modell's, QVC and Kmart have outsourced their online businesses to GSI Commerce. But as far as customers know, they are dealing only with the retailer when they visit the Web site. The Web fulfillment company stays completely behind the scenes. So, with almost no capital or human resources invested, retailers can still have a first-rate Web site as well as online sales and service capabilities. The catch

is that the Web fulfillment company gets to keep as much as 90 percent of online revenue. But on the other hand, the 10 percent that goes to the retailer is virtually pure profit.

Do arrangements such as these make sense? What are the advantages and disadvantages from the retailer's point of view?

5. Best Buy is by far the largest consumer electronics retailer in the world with sales of over $45 billion and almost 4,000 stores world wide. Best Buy enjoys tremendous power in the marketing channels within which it operates. All manufacturers and other suppliers providing products to Best Buy have to pay close attention to what this 1,000 pound gorilla of a retailer wants. But even when suppliers go out of their way to meet the demands of Best Buy, they are finding that the giant retailer could block them from getting their products to consumers because Best Buy may favor certain suppliers with which it can make especially attractive deals. In addition, Best Buy is increasing its emphasis on offering its own private brand products such as the thinnest laptop on the market and an all-electrical motorcycle.

Some of Best Buy's own products may even compete directly with famous supplier brands, such as Apple and Sony.

Why do you think Best Buy is flexing its muscles in the channel? Do you think this type of behavior is inevitable on the part of giant dominant retailers?

6. Jacobson Companies, headquartered in Des Moines, Iowa, describes itself on its Web site as a "can do" third party logistics company. The company is indicative of the new breed of logistics services firms that can do it all. If a company, whether a manufacturer, wholesaler, retailer or other type of firm, needs logistical help, they can find "one-stop shipping" for logistical services if they deal with 3PL firms. Along with the availability of an almost unlimited range of services, is the capability of many 3PLs to custom tailor the logistical services they provide to fit the particular needs of their clients.

Why do you think 3PLs have become such an important type of facilitating agency in market channels? Do you expect this trend to continue?

References

1. George J. Stigler, "The Division of Labor Is Limited by the Extent of the Market," *Journal of Political Economy* (June 1951): 185–193.

2. For an interesting case study related to this topic see: Ming-Hui Huang, "Eliminate the Middleman?" *Harvard Business Review* (March 2006): 33–43.

3. Bruce Mallen, "Functional Spin-Off: A Key to Anticipating Change in Distribution Structure," *Journal of Marketing* (July 1973): 18–25.

4. Bert Rosenbloom, "The Wholesaler's Role in the Marketing Channel: Disintermediation vs. Reintermediation," *The International Review of Distribution and Consumer Research* (September 2007): 327–339.

5. For some very interesting background on wholesaling, see Mushtaq Luqmani, Donna Goehle, Zahir A. Quraeshi, and Ugar Yavas, "Tracing the Development of Wholesaling Practice and Thought," *Journal of Marketing Channels* 1, no. 2 (1992): 75–77; see also William P. Danenburg, Russell L. Moncrief and William E. Taylor, *Introduction to Wholesale Distribution* (Englewood Cliffs, N.J.: Prentice-Hall, 1978).

6. For a related discussion on trends involving merchant wholesalers, see Stephen F. Pirog III and Michael F. Smith, "A Market-Orientation Approach to Identifying

Structural Change in Wholesaling," *Journal of Marketing Channels* (Winter 1996): 37.

7. For an extensive and in-depth look at wholesaling, see Robert F. Lusch et al., *Foundations of Wholesaling: A Strategic and Financial Chart Book* (Norman, Okla.: Distribution Research Program, College of Business Administration, 1996).

8. For a seminal discussion on this point see: Ronald D. Michman and Stanley D. Sibley, "Wholesaling: A Neglected Area," *Proceedings of the Annual Meeting of the Southern Marketing Association*, eds. David M. Klein and Allen E. Smith (Boca Raton, Fla.: Florida Atlantic University, 1985), 118–123.

9. *Facing the Forces of Change: The Road to Opportunity*, Washington, D.C., Distribution Research and Education Foundation, 2004.

10. Bert Rosenbloom, *Marketing Functions and the Wholesaler-Distributor: Achieving Excellence in Distribution* (Washington, D.C.: Research and Education Foundation, 1987), 17–28.

11. Mathew Rose, "Magazine Wholesaler Pressures Publishers, Adding to Their Woes," *Wall Street Journal* (March 5, 2001): A1, A6.

12. Donald M. Jackson and Michael F. d'Amico, "Products and Markets Served by Distributors and Agents," *Industrial Marketing Management* 18 (February 1989): 33.

13. James D. Hlavacek and Tommy J. McCuistion, "Industrial Distributors—When, Who, and How?" *Harvard Business Review* (March–April 1983): 96–101; James A. Narus, N. Mohan Reddy and George L. Pinchak, "Key Problems Facing Industrial Distributors," *Industrial Marketing Management* (August 1984): 139–147.

14. Reva Berman Brown and Richard Herring, "The Role of the Manufacturer's Distributor," *Industrial Marketing Management* 24 (October 1995): 285–295.

15. Bert Rosenbloom, "The Ten Deadly Myths of E-Commerce," *Business Horizons* (March–April 2002): 61–66.

16. Sharon L. Oswall and William R. Boulton, "Obtaining Industry Control: The Case of the Pharmaceutical Distribution Industry," *California Management Review* (Fall 1995): 139–162.

17. "Let's Get You Up to Date and Up to Speed," CDW advertisement in the *Wall Street Journal*, (August 17, 2009): R8.

18. Bert Rosenbloom, *Marketing Functions and the Wholesaler-Distributor: Achieving Excellence in Distribution* (Washington, D.C.: Distribution Research and Education Foundation, 1987), 17–28 Rosenbloom, Marketing Functions, 21–27.

19. For related discussion, see Eric Panitz, "Distribution Image and Marketing Strategy," *Industrial Marketing Management* (November 1988): 315–323.

20. Gautam Naik, "Pieces in Alco's Distribution Network Fall into Place," *Wall Street Journal* (November 13, 1992): B6.

21. Wroe Alderson, *Marketing Behavior and Executive Action* (Homewood, Ill.: Irwin, 1957).

22. Kate Murphy, "Food Brokers Are Bigger So Shelves Look Smaller," *The New York Times*, (September 2, 2004): 4.

23. For a related discussion see: Tim Hughes, "New Channels/Old Channels, Customer Management and Multi-Channels," *European Journal of Marketing*, Vol. 40, ½ 2006: 113–129.

24. Bert Rosenbloom, "The Wholesaler's Role in the Marketing Channel: Disintermediation vs. Reintermediation," *The International Review of Distribution and Consumer Research* (September 2007): 327–339 Bert Rosenbloom, "The Wholesalers' Role in the Marketing Channel,": 327–329.

25. See "Integrating Multiple Channels," *Chain Store Age* (August 2001): 24A–25A.

26. Sarah Skidmore, "Wholesale Clubs Grow as Supermarkets Slide," *Food Industry Writer*, (March 3, 2001): 1–2.

27. *Statistical Abstract of the United States: 2010*, (129th Edition) Washington, D.C.: 2009: 646–647.

28. Yet dramatic growth has also occurred in some types of small, land-based forms of retailing. A very interesting case in point is the growth of farmers markets. See for example: Lauren Etter, "Food for Thought: Do You Need Farmers for a Farmer's Market?" *Wall Street Journal*, (April 29, 2010): A1, A6.

29. Bert Rosenbloom and Diane Mollenkopf, "Dominant Buyers: Are They Changing the Wholesalers' Role in Marketing Channels?" *Journal of Marketing Channels* (Fall 1993): 73–89.

30. Some large retailers, however, are facing serious challenges. See, for example, "Department Stores Fight to Preserve Role That May Be Outdated," *Wall Street Journal*, (March 12, 2002): A1, A17.

31. For some possible exceptions to this pattern, see Roger R. Betancourt and David A. Goutschi, "Distribution Services and Economic Power in a Channel," *Journal of Retailing* (Fall 1998): 37–60; Kisum L. Aiwaldi, Norm Boria and Paul W. Farris, "Market Power and Performance: A Cross-Industry Analysis of Manufacturers and Retailers," *Journal of Retailing* (Fall 1995): 211–248; Paul R. Messinger and Chakravarthi Narasimhan, "Has Power Shifted in the Grocery Channel?" *Marketing Science* 14, no. 2: 189–223.

32. Bert Rosenbloom, "From Merchants to Marketers: Trends in U.S. Retailing for Europe to Watch," *THEXIS* (Spring 2001): 8–11.

33. Cliff Edwards, "Why Tech Bows to Best Buy," *Bloomberg Business Week*, (December 21, 2009): 48–54.

34. See Patricia B. Seybold, *Customers.com* (New York: Random House, 1998); John Hagel III and Marc Singer, *Net Worth* (Boston, MA: Harvard Business School Press, 1999).

35. Bert Rosenbloom and Marc Dupuis, "Low Price, Low Cost, High Service: A New Paradigm for Global Retailing?" *The International Review of Retail Distribution and Consumer Research* (April 1994): 149–158.

36. See for example: Carol Matlack, "A French Wal-Mart's Global Blitz," *Bloomberg Business Week*, (December 21, 2009): G4–G6.

37. Bert Rosenbloom and Diane Mollenkopf, "Dominant Buyers: Are They Changing the Wholesalers' Role in Marketing Channels?" *Journal of Marketing Channels* (Fall 1993): 73–89.

38. Charles Y. Lazarus, "The Retailer as a Link in the Distribution Channel," *Business Horizons* (February 1961): 95–98.

39. Joann Muller, "Attention Kmart: Find a Niche," *Business Week*, (February 4, 2002): 72.

40. See, for example, Roger Dickinson and Bixby Cooper, "The Emergence of Cost-Based Strategies in Retailing," *Journal of Marketing Channels* 2, (1992): 29–45. Also, for an excellent and comprehensive review of institutional changes in retailing, see Stephen Brown, "Institutional Change in Retailing: A Review and Synthesis," *European Journal of Marketing* 21(1987): 5–36.

41. See, for example, Carl Quintanilla, "Hardware Stores Try to Rattle Big Chains," *Wall Street Journal* (December 11, 1996): B1, B4.

42. Philip McVey, "Are Channels of Distribution What the Textbooks Say?" *Journal of Marketing* (January 1960): 61–65.

43. http://www.elmlogistics.com/about-us.html.

CHAPTER **3**

The Environment of Marketing Channels

LEARNING OBJECTIVES

After reading this chapter, you should:

1. Understand the impact of environment in a marketing channels context.
2. Be aware of some of the major economic forces affecting marketing channels.
3. Recognize that unusual economic conditions can have a dramatic impact on marketing channels.
4. Be cognizant of the international or global nature of the competitive environment as it affects marketing channels.
5. Be able to delineate the major types of competition in the context of marketing channel structure and strategy.
6. Appreciate some of the major sociocultural developments taking place with respect to their implications for marketing channels.
7. Be alert to rapid changes in technology and be sensitive to how such changes can affect marketing channels.
8. Gain a general knowledge of the basic antitrust laws as they apply to marketing channel strategy.
9. Be familiar with the key legal issues relating to marketing channels.

© Susan Van Etten

FOCUS ON CHANNELS

Say You Want a Revolution? Not if You're the Surviving Members of the Beatles

In the late 1960s, the Beatles released one of their most famous songs—"Revolution." The song was all about changing the world—not through destruction or war, but by people all over the planet doing good things to make the world a better place.

Today, millions of people think one of those revolutionary good things was the development of technology that allows music to be digitally downloaded from the Internet onto Apple iPods and other devices. Millions of songs are downloaded in this fashion every day all over the world, but not Beatles songs. Surviving Beatles, Paul McCartney and Ringo Star as well as the late John Lennon's widow, Yoko Ono, wanted to protect the integrity and mystique of Beatles music by controlling exactly how it is made available to Beatles fans. Distribution of Beatles music via electronic downloading technology is not consistent with this selective distribution objective. In short, if fans want Beatles music, they would have to acquire it through "old fashioned," low-tech channels that make the songs available only in the form of physical products, such as CDs, cassettes and records. In something of a bow to "modern" technology, fans could buy an extensive Beatles song collection with some video on a USB flash drive for $279. Another physical product containing Beatles music was also made available as part of a video game called "The Beatles Rock Band," which focused on the history of the band. But the music still had to be played through the game console and could not be downloaded or shared.

This "no-digital-download-channels-allowed" policy enforced by the surviving Beatles and their heirs was also vigorously supported by other rights holders, such as music company EMI and media giant Viacom.

So, for over a decade when it came to digitally downloaded Beatles' music, the answer from the surviving Beatles, as well as their heirs and stakeholders, was right there in the song "Revolution": *"Don't you know that you can count me out...."* But in November of 2010, Apple announced that Beatles music would soon be available for downloading via iTunes. Why the abrupt change in policy? Well, it seems that even the revolutionary Beatles could not ignore the technological revolution that hit the music industry.

Source: Based on: L. Gordon Crovitz, "Money Can't Buy Me Beatles," *Wall Street Journal*, (November 9, 2009): A17. Ethan Smith, "Apple Finally Snares Beatles," *Wall Street Journal*, (November 16, 2010): B1, B7.

Marketing channels operate in a continually changing environment.[1] So, the channel manager needs to be sensitive to the environment and the changes occurring to plan effective marketing channel strategies for addressing these changes successfully. To do so, the channel manager needs to understand the environ-mental factors that can affect marketing channel systems.

In this chapter, we examine the environment within which marketing channels operate in the context of the implications for channel strategy, structure and management.

The Marketing Channel and the Environment

The environment consists of myriad external, uncontrollable factors within which marketing channels exist. To give some order to this huge array of variables, we will categorize them in this chapter under the following five general headings:

1. Economic environment
2. Competitive environment
3. Sociocultural environment
4. Technological environment
5. Legal environment

This is not the only way to categorize environmental variables. Numerous other category systems (taxonomies) exist.[2] We have used this taxonomy simply because it provides a convenient and workable basis for discussing the environment of marketing channels. It should also be noted that the order in which the categories are listed and discussed does not imply any order of importance. For any given channel, the importance of particular environmental factors will vary in different situations and over time. As we proceed through this chapter, numerous examples of the diverse effects of environmental factors on different channels and at different times will be presented.

Before discussing each of these environmental categories and their possible effects on the marketing channel, a peculiarity of the influence of environment in a marketing channels context should be noted: because the marketing channel includes independent firms such as retailers and wholesalers, channel managers must also be concerned with the impact of the environment on these channel members. Further, because channel effectiveness is also influenced by the performance of nonmember participants, such as facilitating agencies, channel managers also need to take into account how the environment affects these nonmember participants. Thus, channel managers should analyze the impact of environment not only on their own firms and ultimate target markets, but also on the participants in the marketing channel. Figure 3.1 illustrates this by showing the environment affecting all channel participants and the target markets. The locus of channel management, (not necessarily) control, may lie in producing and manufacturing firms or in intermediary firms such as large wholesale or retailing organizations that are capable of administering the channel. The bracket at the bottom of the figure indicates that management's analysis of environmental effects should consider all of the channel participants.

This view of the impact of environment in a marketing channels context represents a key distinction between channel management and management of the other major variables in a firm's marketing mix (product, price and promotion). In short, when the channel manager considers environmental influences on channel strategy, he or she needs to look at the strategic implications not only for his or her own firm but for other channel participants that may be affected. It is not unusual for environmental forces such as an economic downturn or

FIGURE 3.1 The
**Impact of Environment
in a Marketing
Channels Context**

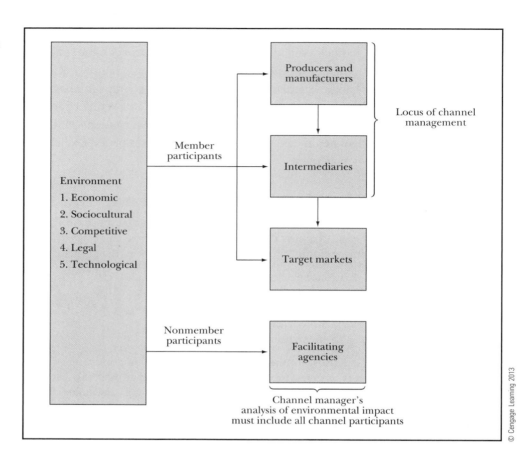

recession to be viewed differently by various members of the marketing channel.[3] Consider, for example, the impact of the recession that hit the U.S. economy in 2008 on U.S. automobile marketing channels. During the recession, auto dealers' sales slowed down drastically. One dealer, for instance, went from selling fifty cars per month to twelve per month.[4] This dealer, and numerous others throughout the country with similar sales declines, reacted to this severe economic downturn by cutting back drastically on expenditures in an attempt to hunker down and ride out the recession. But the auto manufacturers reacted to this bad economic environment in a very different way. Instead of empathizing with the plight of their dealers, "The Big Three" (GM, Ford, and Chrysler) auto makers viewed this recession as a strategic opportunity to get rid of poorly performing dealers. So, rather than expecting less from their dealers during this economic crisis, The Big Three demanded *more* from them. Those dealers that could not upgrade their facilities, hire more and better sales people and provide superior service were terminated by the hundreds. Thus, the same change in the environment, an economic recession, fostered very different strategic reactions from the automobile channel members: the auto dealers "pulled in their horns" while The Big Three auto manufacturers used the economic crisis to prune and streamline their marketing channels.

This extended view of environmental analysis, which includes all channel participants, should be kept in mind throughout this chapter and, for that matter, for the remainder of the text.

We now turn to a discussion of each of the major environmental categories. The discussion will focus on some of the key issues for each category and how they influence the marketing channel.

The Economic Environment

The economy is probably the most obvious and pervasive category of environmental variables affecting all members of the marketing channel. Hardly a day goes by without the state of the economy drawing the notice of consumers and executives in manufacturing, wholesaling and retailing firms. All of these parties must pay careful attention to what is happening in the economy. From a manufacturer raising capital for a long-term investment to a consumer buying a pound of coffee in the supermarket, all are affected by economic variables.

In a channel management context, economic factors are a critical determinant of channel member behavior and performance. The channel manager must therefore be aware of the influence of economic variables on the participants in the channels of distribution. In this section, we discuss several major economic phenomena in terms of their effects on various parties in the marketing channel and their implications for channel management.

Recession

While the official definition of a recession among professional economists is two consecutive quarters of decline in the Gross Domestic Product (GDP), any period in which the GDP is stagnant or increasing very slowly is often referred to as "recessionary" or at least as an "economic slowdown."

By the close of the 20th century, many pundits were talking about the "end of the business cycle" and a "new economy" where recessions would be a thing of the past. They argued that information technology was so good that businesses would be forewarned of any potential slowdowns in the economy and would be able to make the necessary adjustments, such as reducing inventories, so as to forestall the onset of a recession. By the dawning of the new millennium in 2000, and with the last recession of 1990–1991 almost a decade in the past, it looked as if the pundits would be right. Well, their hopes were short-lived, as the U.S. experienced not just one recession during the first decade of the twenty-first century, but two in the course of less than seven years; the recession of 2001–2002 and what has recently been referred to as the "Great Recession" of 2007–2008 which turned out to be the largest recession in terms of GDP decline and unemployment levels since the Great Depression of the 1930s. So, the business cycle with its periodic recessions, sometimes very severe ones, as well as economic slowdowns that fall short of a full-blown recession is still very much alive.

As a recessionary period unfolds, consumer spending, (especially for such durable goods as automobiles, major appliances and personal computers which consumers can postpone purchasing) usually slows down, sometimes drastically. But in the "Great Recession" of 2007–2008, not only did consumer spending decline drastically in housing, automobiles and just about everything else, but business investment also decreased substantially. This created what even technically trained economists were referring to as a "double whammy" decline in spending. Only a federal government stimulus bill that injected over $800 billion into the economy helped offset the dramatic declines in consumer and business spending.

All members of the marketing channel feel the effects of recession because sales volume levels and profitability fall significantly during recessions. During the "Great Recession" of 2007–2008, two out of The Big Three U.S. automakers went through bankruptcy in an effort to reorganize their cost structures to a point where they could be profitable at significantly lower sales levels.[5] As already mentioned earlier, hundreds of dealers were also terminated by GM and Chrysler in a quest to develop more efficient marketing channels for their cars, which consisted of fewer but larger and more efficient dealers.

Changes in consumer shopping behavior brought on by the recession also had a significant impact on virtually all participants in marketing channels, even for such basics as grocery products.[6] As consumers shifted to lower-priced products, manufacturers of famous national brands, such as H.J. Heinz Co., saw sales of even the most iconic products, such as Heinz Ketchup, decline as supermarkets responded to consumer demand for lower-priced products by stocking their shelves with more of their own brand products.[7] Even Starbucks, which had been viewed for many years as "recession proof," saw its sales decline substantially as consumers shifted to lower cost café latte-type coffee drinks from Dunkin Donuts and McDonalds or by making their own coffee at home.[8]

Given the greater price sensitivity on the part of consumers during recessionary periods, all channel members need to focus on delivering increased value, especially given the consumers' rapidly growing use of the Internet for shopping. Consumers searching Web sites to find special deals and coupons increased dramatically during the "Great Recession" of 2007–2008. According to comScore Media Metrix, a marketing research firm, EVERSAVE.com, a leading online coupon Web site, had some 8.6 million unique visitors to its Web site in November of 2008 looking for coupons on a huge range of products.[9] Manufacturers, distributors and retailers of those products trying to withstand the rigors of recessionary forces cannot ignore the growing ranks of Internet-savvy consumers searching for the best possible prices on products and services they are seeking during periods of economic decline or sluggishness.

Inflation

Over the past two decades, the rate of inflation as measured by the Consumer Price Index (CPI) has stayed well below 5 percent. In fact, as shown in Table 3.1, during the 19 year period from 1990–2009, the highest level reached by the CPI was 4.2 percent during 1990–1991 and the lowest point of −0.4 was reached in 2008–2009. The average CPI for the two decades was 2.7 percent. During the earlier decade of the 1980s, the CPI

TABLE 3.1 INFLATION RATES IN THE UNITED STATES AS MEASURED BY THE CONSUMER PRICE INDEX (CPI), 1990–2009

YEARS	ANNUAL CONSUMER PRICE INDEX INCREASES (PERCENT)
1990–1991	4.2
1991–1992	3.0
1992–1993	3.2
1993–1994	2.7
1994–1995	2.5
1995–1996	3.3
1996–1997	2.2
1997–1998	1.7
1998–1999	1.6
1999–2000	2.7
2000–2001	3.4
2001–2002	1.6
2002–2003	2.3
2003–2004	2.7
2004–2005	3.4
2005–2006	3.2
2006–2007	2.8
2007–2008	3.8
2008–2009	−0.4

was never higher than 5.6 percent with an average for the decade of 4.2 percent. Compared with the decade of the 1970s, when double-digit annual rates of inflation were common, inflation has been moderate to low for three decades. This long period of low inflation has led some economists to believe that high inflation is a phenomenon of the past and is not likely to return in the future.

Even though inflation rates have been relatively low for a considerable period of time, there is no guarantee that they will remain at such low levels in the future. Indeed, many mainstream economists argue that inflation rates could increase significantly if, for instance, the economy were to grow too rapidly, if the money supply were loosened excessively, or if a world crisis were to create energy shortages leading to spiraling energy prices. In light of these possibilities, it is prudent for the channel manager to become acquainted with the implications of higher inflation for marketing channel strategy.

The reactions of channel members at the wholesale and retail levels to high rates of inflation are in large measure determined by the reactions of consumers or other final users. Unfortunately, consumer reactions during inflationary periods are not easy to predict. High spending may continue even in the face of growing inflation, as consumers and other users follow a "buy now before the prices go higher" psychology. This, of course, further fuels the inflationary spiral. On the other hand, this psychology can be suddenly replaced by a "hold on to your money" frame of mind when users see a recession just around the corner. Paradoxically, such precipitous drop-offs in spending can help bring on and aggravate the very recession they fear.

In addition to the dramatic shifting in consumer spending that can occur during inflationary periods, many more subtle changes in consumer buying patterns may occur. For example, in the supermarket industry during inflationary periods, consumer buying patterns increasingly reflected such tactics as:

- *Going to the supermarket without bringing along extra money*
- *Putting items back before checking out*
- *Buying only the amount needed*
- *Buying less meat*
- *Stocking up on bargains*
- *Buying lower-quality brands*
- *Buying unplanned items only if they are on special sale*

Consumers also tend to "trade down" in terms of the stores they patronize during periods of high inflation. Stores such as Dollar General and Aldi that offer rock-bottom prices can take sales away even from discount giants Walmart and Target.[10] Finally, consumers surfing the Internet for bargains on both new and used merchandise offered on eBay and numerous other sites can be expected to increase as inflation undermines consumer purchasing power. Such patterns of consumer shopping behavior obviously reflect an attempt by consumers to cope with inflation.

From the perspective of the channel manager in the producing or manufacturing firm, such changes in consumer buying behavior should be viewed in the context of how they might affect channel member behavior and what the implications might be for channel strategy. For example, in the face of slower and more prudent consumer spending, retailers become increasingly cautious about what products they will handle. Moreover, because of higher interest rates, they generally try to reduce their inventory levels to the minimum. Finally, they will seek more special price deals from manufacturers and a higher level of promotional support. In the face of such increased channel member demands, an effective channel strategy must be developed to satisfy the channel members. Such a strategy might stress a change in emphasis on the manufacturer's product mix from higher-price to lower-price products. Scott Paper Co., for example, began offering lower-priced paper products to supermarkets so as not to lose shelf space in the face of strong price competition. Reducing the inventory burden on channel members through a streamlined product line, faster order processing and delivery and higher inventory turnover through stronger promotional support may also have to be incorporated into a channel strategy for meeting the demands of channel members who are attempting to operate profitably under the intense cost pressures imposed by inflation.

Deflation

Deflation on a wide scale resulting in a decline in prices across a broad spectrum of goods and services has not occurred in the United States since the Great Depression of the 1930s. If deflation similar to that experienced during the Depression were to occur in the future, the Consumer Price Index on which the data in Table 3.1 are based would show negative numbers rather than positive ones (a negative CPI was reported for just one year: 2008–2009).

Most economists do not expect a deflationary environment broad enough to cause a sustained decline in the Consumer Price Index to emerge in the foreseeable future. Nevertheless, inflation in recent years has become low enough (see Table 3.1) that such a development is not unthinkable. But what has already happened and what is very likely to continue in the future is deflation in certain sectors of the economy and in some product categories. Housing, automobiles, consumer electronics, computers, telecom equipment, some types of apparel, and many other commodities have experienced deflation recently. It is almost certain other sectors of the economy and other products will experience deflation in the future.[11]

Deflation, static prices or even very low rates of price increases can create serious channel management difficulties. The problem is one of trying to pass cost-induced price increases through the channel in the face of deflation or very low inflation rates. Why? Even with a very low inflation rate or with actual deflation in some sectors of the economy, manufacturers, wholesalers and retailers often face built-in cost pressures, such as higher energy costs, and especially from labor contracts that might have been negotiated several years earlier when the inflation rate was higher. But increasing prices to offset these cost pressures becomes very difficult when inflation is low because each member of the channel is highly sensitive to higher prices. Although it is relatively easy during periods of inflation to pass on price increases to the next level of the marketing channel all the way down to the final buyer, it becomes anything but easy when the inflation rate is low, and virtually impossible in a period of actual deflation.

Other Economic Issues

Recession, inflation and deflation are not the only variables in the economic environment. The federal budget deficit, the national debt, and the trade deficit, which have risen dramatically in recent years, are all of continuing concern as we move into the second decade of the twenty-first century. These phenomena are not bad in and of themselves, but they can aggravate recession and inflation. The budget deficit and the national debt make huge demands on capital and hence raise interest rates. This, in turn, adds to the level of inflation. The trade deficit, resulting from greater levels of imports than exports, can mean loss of jobs for U.S. workers, which can exacerbate recessionary forces by reducing the level of income.

Although the U.S. enjoyed very low interest rates by the second decade of the twenty-first century, there is no guarantee that high interest rates will not return. High interest rates can be a problem even when the inflation rate is moderate and the economy is not in a recession. This is particularly true of the **real interest rate**, which is the nominal rate of interest minus

TABLE 3.2 NOMINAL AND REAL INTEREST RATES COMPARED AT DIFFERENT RATES OF INFLATION		
NOMINAL INTEREST RATE (PERCENT)	INFLATION RATE	REAL INTEREST RATE
10	6	4
10	3	7

© Cengage Learning 2013

the inflation rate. Given the same nominal interest rate, the real interest rate will actually be *higher* when inflation is lower. This is illustrated in Table 3.2. At a nominal interest rate of 10 percent, when the inflation rate decreased from 6 to 3 percent, the real interest rate increased form 4 to 7 percent. What this means, of course, is that the true cost of borrowing money will actually increase when inflation moderates if nominal interest rates do not decrease sufficiently to offset the decrease in the inflation rate.

High interest rates can affect all members of the marketing channel. Even though consumers may be slow to recognize the effects of high real interest rates, eventually they catch on and their spending slows down. This, in turn, affects sales for retailers, wholesalers and manufacturers. Moreover, because manufacturers, wholesalers and retailers often need to borrow money, high real interest rates have a direct impact on their costs of doing business. So, even during what appear to be good economic conditions (when inflation is low and the economy is not in recession) high real interest rates can still cause problems by decreasing demand and increasing costs.

Another economic factor that can affect channel management, even in good economic times, is the value of the U.S. dollar relative to foreign currency. Ironically, a strong U.S. dollar can actually create channel management problems for U.S. manufacturers by making it more difficult to sell their products through channel members. When the value of the dollar is high, the price of U.S. products increases relative to foreign-made products because it takes more foreign dollars to buy U.S. products and fewer U.S. dollars to buy foreign goods. Hence, U.S. products can become less competitive. When this happens, it becomes much more difficult for U.S. manufacturers selling in international markets to move their products through overseas channels. But even in domestic channels, it becomes more difficult to move products because retailers and wholesalers find it attractive to buy more of the cheaper, foreign products.

In terms of the economic environment, then—regardless of the state of the economy, the channel manager needs to pay careful attention to the implications of economic factors on channel management. For even when "good times" are at hand, some subtle, even insidious, forces may create enough problems to make the "good times" look bad.

The Competitive Environment

Competition is always a critical factor to consider for all members of the marketing channel. This is especially the case in recent years as competition has become global in scope. No longer is it realistic for domestic firms to focus only on rivals within the boundaries of their own country. In addition, they need to pay close attention to existing and emerging competitors from all over the world. The terms *global marketplace, global arena* and *global competition* are not just international business jargon, but realistic descriptions of the competitive environment as it exists today in an increasing number of industries. Further, new technologies, especially those related to online commerce, discussed later in this chapter and in Chapter 15, have substantially changed the competitive landscape.

FIGURE 3.2 Types of Competition

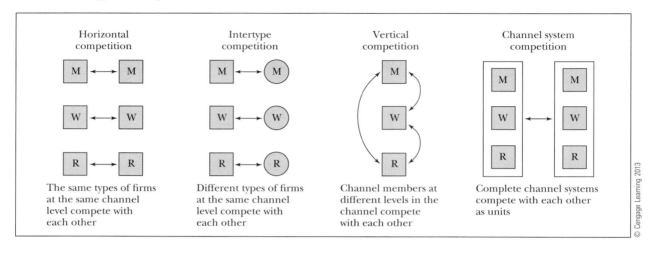

Types of Competition

Along with the broadened scope of competition and new forms of competition driven by new technologies, channel managers must also consider the major types of competition that can affect channel strategy. In particular, they need to focus on the following four types, depicted in Figure 3.2:[12]

1. Horizontal competition
2. Intertype competition
3. Vertical competition
4. Channel system competition[13]

Horizontal competition is competition between firms of the same type, For example, an automobile manufacturer versus another automobile manufacturer, a plumbing supply wholesaler versus another plumbing supply wholesaler, or one supermarket versus another. This is the most visible and frequently discussed form of competition. In economic theory, much of the treatment of competition deals with this horizontal type, although it is usually referred to simply as "competition," and often the firms involved are producers or manufacturers rather than wholesalers or retailers. The competitive battle between the giant consumer electronics retailers Best Buy and Circuit City is a recent, but likely to become classic, example of horizontal competition that resulted in the demise of one of the parties.[14] Both of these retailers sold similar products and operated in essentially the same format. Each operated hundreds of "big box" retail stores on a national scale emphasizing high sales volumes and low prices. But Best Buy proved to be the stronger competitor, ultimately resulting in Circuit City going out of business and closing its remaining 567 stores.

Intertype competition is competition between different types of firms at the same channel level, such as the off-price store versus the department store or the merchant wholesaler versus agents and brokers.[15] Also, in more recent years, intertype competition is reflected in online retailers competing with conventional store-based retailers. The intense competitive battle between online giant Amazon.com and the world's largest retailer, Walmart, is a case in point.[16] While total online sales account for less than 5 percent of total retail sales, Amazon (and other online retailers) believe that eventually online sales could account for 20 percent or more of total retail sales. Amazon's aggressive strategy of broadening its product line to compete in more product categories is aimed at taking a large chunk of that projected increase in market share for itself.

Intertype competition is also unfolding rapidly in the video retail business. For example, the still largest, though rapidly declining, conventional store-based video retailer Block-buster is being assaulted by competitors using other channels such as Netflix, which is heavily focused on mail order and online sales to distribute videos.[17] Meanwhile, on-demand movies and TV shows are increasingly being pushed by cable companies such as Comcast while Redbox's competitive channel relies on 22,000 vending machines, placed mainly in supermarkets and drugstores, to distribute videos.[18]

Obviously, such competitive dynamics associated with intertype competition can drastically alter the structure of marketing channels, even over relatively short periods of time.[19]

Vertical competition refers to competition between channel members at different levels in the channel, such as retailer versus wholesaler, wholesaler versus manufacturer or manufacturer versus retailer. Competition between manufacturers of national brands versus private brands (also referred to as private label) produced by retailers, which has been heating up in recent years, provides a good example of vertical competition.[20] National brand manufacturers have expended enormous resources developing and promoting their national brands in an effort to gain market share from competitive national brands and to help limit the penetration of private brands. But in recent years, private brands have been gaining market share at a significant pace.[21] By the latter part of the first decade of the twenty-first century, private brands were growing at a rate of 10 percent per year compared with national brand growth of only 4 percent per year. Macy's, one of the leading retailers emphasizing private brand merchandise, offers numerous brands that compete with the leading national brands, including ALFANT sportswear, intimate apparel, jewelry, shoes and accessories, *first impressions* clothing for newborns and infants, HOTEL COLLECTION luxury bedding, bath and mattresses, and Tools of the Trade cookware.[22] Home Depot offers numerous private brands, one of which (Hampton Bay electric fans) accounts for half of all fan sales in the United States. Home Depot's main competitor, Lowe's, also deals in numerous private brands such as Kobalt tools. In the food and drug field, private brands are also prevalent and growing. Safeway's O Organics cereal, for example, is aimed directly at taking market share from General Mills's iconic Cheerios.[23] Retailers love to sell their own brands not only because gross margins are higher, but because they can control their own destiny rather than be beholden to powerful manufacturers. Moreover, private brands that are available only from a particular retailer reduce price-focused comparison shopping by consumers because the products are available exclusively from that retailer. Finally, if consumers really like particular private label products, they may grow loyal to them and become steady repeat purchasers of those products. As competition between manufacturers and retailers intensifies, this vertical competition could become vertical conflict whereby one channel member acts to directly impede another channel member's attempt to achieve its objectives. This possible conflict aspect will be discussed in detail in Chapter 4.

Finally, **channel system competition** refers to complete channels competing with other complete channels. In order for channels to compete as complete units, they must be organized, cohesive organizations. Such channels have been referred to as **vertical marketing systems** and are classified into three types: (1) corporate; (2) contractual and (3) administered.[24] In **corporate channels**, production and marketing facilities are owned by the same company. Firestone Tire & Rubber Company and the Sherwin-Williams Co. are examples. In the **contractual channel**, independent channel members (producers or manufacturers, wholesalers, and retailers) are linked by a formal contractual agreement. Wholesaler-sponsored voluntary chains, retailer cooperatives, and franchise systems are the three major forms of contractual marketing systems. ServiStar in hardware, Independent Grocers' Alliance (IGA) in food, and Drug Guild are examples of such contractual marketing channels.

Business format franchising, where the franchisor not only provides the product to the franchisee, but the entire business format as well, is another type of contractual marketing system that has grown dramatically in recent years.[25] The most well-known examples of business format franchises are in the fast-food field with McDonalds being the largest. But business format franchise systems are common in many other fields as well. We will be discussing such franchise marketing channels in depth in Chapter 16.

Administered channel systems result from strong domination by one of the channel members, frequently a manufacturer, over the other members. This dominant position is a function of the leverage that the dominant channel member can achieve based on a monopoly of supply, special expertise, strong consumer acceptance of its products or other factors. Companies such as Scott, Ethan Allen, and Samsonite are examples of firms that operate administered marketing channels.

From the preceding discussion we can see that channel managers face a complex competitive environment. Not only do they have to think in terms of a broad global perspective of competition, they also need to worry about horizontal, intertype, vertical, and channel system competition. Fortunately, it is unlikely that they will face all of these types of competition simultaneously. Nevertheless, they should be sufficiently familiar with the four types to be able to recognize and distinguish among them.

Competitive Structure and Channel Management

From the producer's or manufacturer's standpoint, an understanding of competitive structure and the changes taking place in that structure are crucial for successful channel design and management.[26]

In designing the marketing channel, the channel manager needs to determine which kinds of distributors and/or dealers can provide the most efficient and effective distribution of the firm's products. But given that the competitive structure of distributors and dealers changes, sometimes rapidly, conventional ideas about the kinds of dealers or distributors that should sell particular products can quickly become obsolete. For example, it was not too long ago that most automotive parts and supplies were sold in automotive stores, sporting goods in sporting goods stores and hardware in hardware stores. In recent years, however, one can find all of these products in mass merchandisers, discount department stores, home center stores, warehouse clubs and even in many drugstores and supermarkets. And, of course, many of these products are available online from numerous types of firms operating on the Internet. Such **scrambled merchandising** (the selling of products through nontraditional outlets) has drastically changed the competitive landscape. Whereas once a manufacturer of auto parts, for example, would realistically think only in terms of designing a channel that used auto parts distributors and dealers, the options available have become much broader. The same is true for manufacturers of many other kinds of products. It seems that almost any type of store or other mode of sale, such as the mail or the Internet, can be an outlet for any kind of product. While this is not 100 percent true, it does suggest that conventional wisdom about who should sell what products does not hold in this new, competitive environment. One need only look at the wide variety of products being sold on the Internet to get a glimpse at how conventional wisdom about who should sell what and who competes against whom is being challenged.[27]

This changing competitive environment also means that producers and manufacturers attempting to manage marketing channels now face a more complex management task because they are dealing with more different types of channel members. For instance, the auto parts manufacturer that was accustomed to dealing mainly with independent auto parts stores now has to contend with mass merchandisers, home centers, drug chains, supermarkets, warehouse clubs and online distributors as well. Needless to say, the management policies and strategies for dealing with independent auto parts stores may not be effective in dealing with other kinds of channel members.

The foregoing discussion suggests that an understanding of the various types of competition affecting the channel provides the channel manager with a sharper focus to discern what is happening in the competitive environment. As we proceed through the text, we will deal with many types of decisions that the channel manager must face. Many of these decisions will require a consideration of the competitive environment faced by a firm or complete channel.

The Sociocultural Environment

The sociocultural environment pervades virtually all aspects of a society. Marketing channels (and particularly the structure of marketing channels) are therefore also influenced by the sociocultural environment within which they exist. Indeed, some channel analysts argue that this is a major force affecting channel structure.[28]

Over the past several decades, a number of studies in many countries around the world support this view. For example, Wadinambiaratchi studied channels for consumer goods in several developing countries as well as Japan, and found wide variations in channel structures, which he attributed to their different "social, psychological, cultural, and anthropological climates."[29] Figure 3.3 shows these variations in channel structure. A study of distribution channels in Great Britain and North America by Hall, Knapp and Winsten, others by Guirdham in Western Europe, Galbraith and Holton in Puerto Rico, Baker in tropical Africa and several more studies also lend support to this proposition.[30] Take, for example, the case of tropical Africa. In some of the countries, it is not unusual to find as many as ten levels of channel structure for imported consumer goods. Most of the very small retail intermediaries, often referred to as "mammy traders," deal in tiny quantities of products, such as a handful of salt, half a bar of soap or two to three cigarettes. Western observers, as well as some government officials in tropical African countries, are often appalled at this, believing it to be a highly irrational and inefficient channel structure. These observers, however, make the mistake of failing to consider the sociocultural context within which this channel structure exists. In actuality, the seemingly archaic channels with layer upon layer of tiny middlemen are quite rational when due allowance is made for the sociocultural factors involved. In terms of tropical Africa, these sociocultural factors include a wide geographic dispersion of the population, extremely limited consumer mobility and a necessary tradition of hand-to-mouth buying. Given these conditions, a modern Western-style supermarket would actually be highly irrational and inefficient.

Yet even in highly industrialized Japan, with some of the most advanced technology, marketing channels for many goods are very long and cumbersome with layers of middlemen and enormous numbers of tiny stores. Researchers who have examined Japanese marketing channel structure point to a number of sociocultural factors that tend to perpetuate such channels of distribution there.[31] One of these is the Japanese penchant for developing close business relationships among cooperating firms. This system is known as *keiretsu*. In the context of distribution, it links together a manufacturer and many wholesale and retail sales outlets. Such linkages protect the many small, inefficient distributors and retailers who participate in the *keiretsu* from competition from the larger, more efficient firms that are effectively kept out of the system. Several other sociocultural factors also contribute to the complex and inefficient channel structure in Japan. Some of the most frequently cited of these are (1) a societal attitude that favors small business, particularly small retailers, in the distributive sector of the economy; (2) the Japanese consumer's preference to shop in his or her own neighborhood; (3) a desire for fresh

FIGURE 3.3 Marketing Channel Structures in Developing Countries and Japan

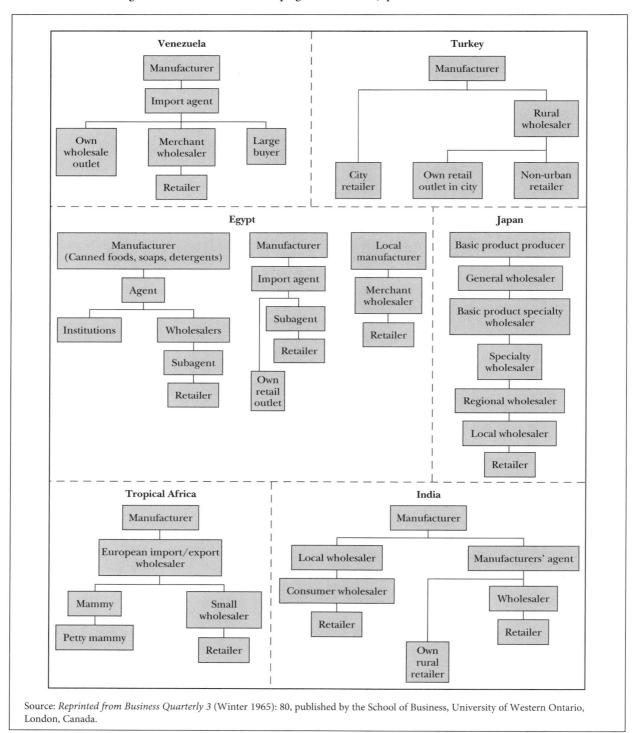

Source: *Reprinted from Business Quarterly 3* (Winter 1965): 80, published by the School of Business, University of Western Ontario, London, Canada.

food, good personal service and social contact during sales transactions; (4) a priority on maintaining low unemployment rates by encouraging the existence of many small stores where people can work and (5) a wish for "something to do" during retirement.[32] But these traditional channel structures are beginning to change as younger Japanese consumers, who have traveled and seen other cultures, are starting to demand more modern and efficient marketing channels in their own country.[33]

More recent studies of emerging countries such as Brazil, China, and India, as well as several Latin American countries also show that sociocultural factors specific to these countries have a significant influence on the structure of channel of distribution in these regions.[34]

So, the channel manager must be sensitive to the sociocultural environment in which marketing channels exist, whether they be in the U.S. or any other country around the globe.[35]

Other Sociocultural Forces

In recent years, several sociocultural phenomena have emerged that are not unique to any particular country or region. Rather, these are forces that already have and will continue to influence how marketing channels are designed and managed all over the world. Arguably, the most important of these sociocultural factors in terms of their relevance to marketing channels are:

1. Globalization
2. Consumer mobility and connectedness
3. Social networking
4. The Green Movement

Globalization—this term is most commonly used to describe the interconnectedness and interdependencies of countries around the world. In a business rather than a political context, globalization typically focuses on the vast and complex trade flows among countries and the international supply chains that make huge flows of products and services across national boundaries possible. Cooperative efforts by firms, such as Boeing, to utilize suppliers and fabricators from numerous countries to participate in the production of its most advanced aircrafts are also an important aspect of globalization. Further, globalization refers to the greatly increasing number of people who travel internationally. According to the United Nations World Tourism Organization (UNWTO), this number will exceed 1.5 billion annually by 2020.

But the concept of globalization also has a sociocultural dimension that transcends the physical flows of products and people across borders. Globalization can also be viewed as a frame-of-mind or outlook that is held by millions of consumers from all over the world.[36] It is an outlook that does not see the marketplace as limited to one or even a few countries, but rather as a much richer and exciting tapestry of numerous countries and cultures. Thus, the old adage about "the world being your marketplace" is no longer some trite expression, but a real expectation held by consumers exposed to the global marketplace. In short, consumers increasingly expect to have access to world-class products and services at the favorable prices global competition is supposed to foster. Such expectations are not limited only to consumers in the richest and most advanced countries. IKEA, the world-renowned Swedish retailer, found this out in its effort to penetrate the Russian market. Even after investing $4 billion and opening 11 stores, IKEA found that Russian "red tape" and corruption undermined its ability to deliver its hallmark, world-class experience to the Russian customer. The result was many unhappy, Russian consumers who kept money in their pockets rather than spending it in IKEA stores.[37]

So, the message of globalization for the channel manager is a straight forward one: *globalization has created world-class customer expectations that need to be satisfied through world-class channel strategy, design and management.* Although this message is simple, it is not easy. Rather, it is difficult to implement because of the many complexities and subtleties involved in developing and operating marketing channels that meet the requirements of the global arena. Much of the material in the forthcoming chapters of this book addresses the channel strategy and management issues associated with this challenge.

Mobility and Connectedness—To say that people do a great deal of running around today, whether for business or personal pursuits, is to state the obvious. To state that such mobility is increasingly taking place across greater distances is perhaps equally obvious in the U.S. and in other advanced economies around the world. Yet another clear observation is that this local, national and global movement is not at the cost of being out of touch. Today's highly mobile generation expects not only to cover a great deal of territory on a frequent basis, but to also be completely in touch with colleagues, friends and family in the process. Thus, a trade-off between mobility and contact is not acceptable. But more to the point, such a trade-off is not necessary thanks to the abundance of wireless networks, hundreds of millions of cell phones, the Internet and such new technologies as Skype.

This ability to constantly be on the move while still being able to stay in constant contact has not been lost on consumers. Indeed, buying products and services while literally running around has become a common expectation for consumers armed with laptops and smartphones all over the world. This phenomenon, which in recent years has generally been referred to as "mobile commerce" or simply m-commerce, while still accounting for just a tiny fraction of total retail sales (well under 1 percent), is expected to grow rapidly and become a mainstream and significant channel of distribution in the near future. So, in a literal sense, consumers will be able to buy virtually any product from virtually any place on the globe during the course of moving from one place to the next—possibly at great speed!

Here again, the channel strategy and design implications of this mobility and connectivity revolution are straightforward, but not easy to address. First, virtually all channel managers, regardless of what industries they operate in, will need to include m-commerce channels in their channel mixes simply because highly mobile and connected consumers expect to have such channels available to them. Second, channel managers will need to sort out the role that m-commerce channels will play in the multi-channel mix. Although the m-commerce channel is an important and growing one, it is not likely to completely replace retail store channels, catalog and mail order channels as well as PC-based online channels. Finally, channel managers will need to examine closely the potential and limitations of m-commerce channels. Although being able to sell products and services to consumers while they are in motion any place on the globe is a powerful channel option, there may also be limitations to this channel that will need to be recognized going forward.

Social Networking—This term refers to interaction in networks comprised of individuals or organizations that are linked together based on some type of common interest, such as friendship, beliefs, hobbies, professional pursuits, special knowledge and many others. Such social networks and the interactions among their participants, referred to in recent years as "social networking," are not a new phenomenon. In fact, social networks and social networking have existed for many decades. What is new, however, is the introduction in recent years of the Internet-based World Wide Web, which has enabled social networks and participants in such networks to increase exponentially so that literally millions, tens of millions, and, in some cases, even hundreds of millions of people can interact with each other via social networking sites. The largest of these is Facebook, with over 500 million registered users and still growing. Other leading general social networking Web sites include MySpace (130 million registered users) and Twitter (75 million registered users). More focused social networking sites have also garnered great numbers. One such site is LinkedIn (75 million registered users), which focuses specifically on business and professional networking. Classmates.com, with over 50 million registered users, specializes in school, college and military networking, while Buzz.net, with over 10 million registered users, specializes in music and pop culture. The 15 million registered users at Geni.com are interested mainly in sharing information about family relationships and genealogy. There are thousands of social networking sites in addition to these that range in size from multiple millions to just several hundred users.[38] Although these Web sites vary enormously in size and focus, they all have the same core function: enabling their users to communicate and share information with each other on a global scale at virtually any time of day or night.

In a business context, social networking has enabled millions of consumers to share information and opinions about products, services and firms they have dealt with or are considering dealing with. Moreover, many thousands of firms, from giant multinational corporations to small start-up businesses, are on social networking sites like Facebook and Twitter. These firms are constantly sharing information about new products, special events and promotions with users of the social network. JCPenney, for instance, uses Facebook and Twitter not only for customer product reviews and special offers, but also to communicate about new services the retailer will be offering. In 2010, JCPenney announced on both Web sites that it would soon be offering exclusive targeted promotions to shoppers with smartphones. Much smaller firms have also benefitted from social networking features. Consider, for instance, the case of Folbot Inc., a small manufacturer of kayaks located in Charleston, S.C. Folbot, which is on Twitter, uses this social network to zero in on potential customers who would probably be missed using conventional channels. David AvRutick, co-owner of Folbot, regularly searches Twitter for tweets that mention kayaking and then sends messages to the people who wrote them. One such message reached blogger Jackie Siddall after she posted a tweet that mentioned she wanted a kayak. After receiving the Twitter message from Mr. AvRutick about the incredible variety of kayaks offered by his firm, she ended up buying a $1,900 folding kayak from Folbot's e-commerce Web site.[39]

From a marketing channels perspective, social networking has not only empowered consumers to make much more informed decisions about the products they buy, the services they use and the firms they deal with through virtually limitless information sharing, but it has also enabled them to make better channel choices and made them more demanding about the channels they choose. Why? Because social networking enables consumers to share their experiences about channel choices. Good experiences and bad experiences associated with channel choices are quickly spread through the network. Moreover, because so much of the social networking that takes place is peer-to-peer (consumer-to-consumer), the credibility of the information received is higher than information shared business-to-consumer via social networking. Thus, if blogger Jackie Siddall, mentioned above, tweets that buying a kayak from Folbot's online channel was a terrific experience, this is likely to have a lot more credibility than if Folbot were to make the same claim on Twitter.

Just as social networking capability has empowered consumers to make more informed channel choices and fostered more demanding consumers, it has also equipped businesses at all levels of the channel with the capability to target potential customers that they could not have reached before and indeed may not have known about.

The Green Movement—This is a term that has often been used to refer to a focus on preserving the environment and human health. The philosophical roots of the Green Movement go back to the nineteenth century, but as we pass beyond the first decade of the twenty-first century, the Green Movement has assumed a very programmatic orientation. Much of the attention has been focused on possible adverse effects on human health and economic prosperity from such issues as climate change, pollution, chemicals and hormones in the food chain, the profligate use of resources and a number of other issues. *An Inconvenient Truth*, a film by former vice president of the United States, Al Gore, dramatically portrayed the horrendous effects of climate change on the future of the Earth and greatly heightened public awareness regarding climate change as well as the broader set of issues associated with the Green Movement. While these matters are controversial, even in the scientific community, there is no question that more attention is being given to Green Movement issues by the public at-large, businesses and government. In short, concern about the climate, pollution, the integrity of the food supply and the over-use of scarce resources is real and therefore cannot be ignored as a major social phenomenon of the twenty-first century.

What does this concern with Green issues have to do with marketing channel strategy and management? The answer is plenty. All members of marketing channels, including producers, wholesalers, agents, brokers and consumers, participate in activities that affect the environment and quality of life. Walmart, for example, estimated it could save 3,800 trees and 1,000 barrels of oil just by reducing unnecessary packing of just one product category: its private label toys. Further, Walmart purchased hybrid diesel-electric trucks and refrigeration trucks that use a small power unit for cooling, so the main engine can be turned off when the truck is stopped. The result? A 25 percent improvement in fuel efficiency for the Walmart truck fleet and an annual reduction of 400,000 tons of carbon dioxide emissions![40]

So, whether it focuses public attention on limiting the adverse effects of climate change or promoting the sale of more organic foods, the issues associated with the Green Movement provide tremendous opportunities as well as challenges to channel managers to be full participants in developing and managing marketing channels that will support the aspirations of the movement.[41]

The Technological Environment

Technology is the most continuously and rapidly changing aspect of the environment. Everyone could probably recite long lists of technological advances that have occurred in his or her lifetime or even just during the past decade. The widespread use of laptop computers, smartphones, GPS navigation systems, and electronic books are some of the most obvious examples.

In the face of this rapidly accelerating technology, the channel manager has to sort out those developments that are relevant to his or her own firm as well as the participants in the marketing channel and then determine how these changes might affect the channel participants.[42] This is not an easy task, nor one that can be precisely programmed. Technological changes, though continual, do not occur evenly or predictably over time.

While it is not possible to present a comprehensive list of technological developments impinging on the marketing channel, several are indicative of the kinds of advancements that should be watched carefully.

Electronic Data Interchange

Electronic data interchange (EDI) refers to the linking together of channel member information systems to provide real-time responses to communication between channel members. For example, a retailer's computerized inventory management system is connected with and monitored by the supplier's (manufacturer's or wholesaler's) computers. Ordering of merchandise can then take place automatically when the retailer's inventory level of that supplier's products reaches certain minimum reorder points. Thus, the retailer's computer orders the products from the manufacturer's or wholesaler's computers without human intervention or paperwork of any kind. The more sophisticated EDI systems can also forecast demand based on sales history. In this case, the manufacturer's or wholesaler's computers will initiate the order for the retailer by, in effect, predicting the quantity of items the retailer will need during a particular period. EDI systems can also be linked directly to production scheduling, allowing the factory's production to be determined by sales patterns taking place in retail outlets. In other words, the merchandise that is being sold on a given day in retail outlets all over the country will provide the information to guide the manufacturer's production process taking place on that same day. VF Corporation, the manufacturer of Lee and Wrangler brand jeans, used EDI to help unseat the famous Levi's as the jeans market share leader as measured in unit sales. According to retailers, Levi's was slow to in replenish stock. However, the quick response made possible by VF's sophisticated EDI technology enabled stores to replenish stock in two days, compared to two weeks or longer for Levi's.

The emergence of the Internet in recent years has enhanced the potential of EDI because the Internet enables firms to be connected and communicate in a fashion similar to EDI but with considerably less investment in computer hardware and software.[43] Thus, firms linked via the Internet will increasingly be able to enjoy the benefits associated with EDI at a "bargain basement" price.

There is little question that EDI technology enhances distribution efficiency, resulting in substantial benefit to all channel members as well as final customers. The manufacturer benefits through more accurate and timely production scheduling, while wholesalers and retailers save on order processing and inventory carrying costs. The final customer benefits from the reduced distribution costs made possible by EDI and by the higher probability of finding the particular items he or she is seeking on retailers' shelves.

The main negative is that the channel members must share information openly for the EDI system to work. So, for those channel members who feel they need control of what they believe to be sensitive or confidential information about the sales of their products, EDI can lose some of its appeal.

Scanners, Computerized Inventory Management, and Handheld Computers

Electronic scanning and computerized inventory management, enhanced by portable computers, cellular phone technology and the Internet, have created a new world in retailing and wholesaling. Not only has this technology drastically reduced the amount of labor and paperwork involved in inventory management, but it has also made a vast array of timely and valuable information available to managers, enabling them to make better merchandising decisions.[44] Information that might have taken weeks to obtain with a manual inventory system can be called up on the computer in seconds. Retailers and wholesalers of all sizes are now able to monitor the success or failure of products they handle much more closely than was possible just a few years ago. If a newly introduced product is not catching on, they know about it—and quickly. When the rate of sales growth of a successful product begins to slow down, they are able to spot this pattern at a very early stage. Products for which sales are stagnant, are not likely to be overlooked. On the other hand, hot-selling products can also be spotted quickly by retailers and wholesalers, and reordering can be just as fast. Thus the new technology is something of a mixed blessing for manufacturers. Quicker responses by retailers and wholesalers to fast-selling products can allow the manufacturer more time to plan ahead to increase production. But faster responses by these channel members to slow sellers can mean a sudden halt in orders as they use their up-to-the-minute, computer-generated inventory data to reduce their risk and protect their profit positions.

The system used by McKesson Drug Company, a giant drug wholesaler, provides a case in point. In its Delran, New Jersey warehouse, McKesson employees, called "robo-warehousemen," roam the aisles using portable computers to manage the inventory as it moves in and out of the warehouse. The computer, worn on the worker's waist, receives signals from a central computer telling him or her which merchandise needs to be gathered next. A message informing the worker where the merchandise is located appears on the computer screen that is strapped to the worker's arm. When the worker reaches the proper shelf, a laser scanner worn on the fingers is used to read each item. The computer then tallies all the merchandise, verifies that the correct number of items has been picked up and updates the master inventory. Another major uses of scanner-based inventory management is Frito-Lay, which owns over half of the $15 billion salty-snacks market. Virtually all of the company's 12,800 delivery people are equipped with handheld computers, enabling them to transmit sales and inventory data instantly back to headquarters when they visit stores on their routes. The effective use of this technology has played a major role in making Frito-Lay what competitors call an "invincible foe."

The Digital Revolution and Smartphones

The digital revolution is the term commonly used to describe the huge transformation that has taken place over the past three decades from analog and mechanical technology to digital technology. It is a revolution that is still continuing today. The most obvious and widespread manifestation of the digital revolution has been reflected in the massive growth of personal computing, the Internet, cell phone usage and, more recently, the downloading of music, movies as well as written materials, including entire books on E-books such as Amazon's Kindle, Barnes and Noble's Nook, and Apple's iPad.[45]

The digital revolution already has and will continue to have profound effects on channel structure and strategy.[46] This technology has made online shopping via the Internet a mainstream marketing channel in both B2C and B2B markets since the mid-1990s. Indeed, online channels continue to grow dramatically with sales in the hundreds of billions of dollars covering a vast array of different products and services and have become a part of the channel mix for the majority of firms at all levels of the channel, including the largest and smallest companies. The recent emergence of m-commerce, discussed earlier, was also made possible by the digital revolution.

The potential for channel managers to use this technology strategically to enhance the design and management of marketing channels is practically unlimited. Consider, for example, the potential of smartphones that have made the m-commerce channel possible. By 2010, shoppers had ordered over $2.2 billion of physical goods using smartphones. That is double the amount ordered in 2009 and five times more than in 2008![47] While this $2.2 billion is just a small fraction of the approximately $175 billion of total online sales in 2010, the rapid growth rate of m-commerce is almost certain to significantly increase its share of total online sales. Already, about 30 percent of retailers have commerce Web sites and many more will be adding such sites. The power of this technology to create a channel that offers an incredible level of flexibility and immediacy is compelling. Michelle Kelly, vice president of e-commerce for women's clothing retailer Lily Pulitzer, captures this capability succinctly:

> *I have a vision of a target consumer being at a party and thinking a friend's dress is gorgeous, looking it up on her phone and buying it!*[48]

Consider also James O'Brien, a 34-year-old senior Web developer who was on a trip to American Eagle Outfitters looking for a pair of jeans. When he found that the store was out of the style he wanted, while still in the store, he ordered the jeans on his iPhone. His explanation for using his iPhone?

> *"By the time I get home there's a good chance I'll forget about it."*[49]

It is not just fashion apparel retailers that have recognized the power of the mobile version of online commerce made possible by the smartphone and the digital revolution. The world's largest home improvement retailer, Home Depot, has gone all out to launch a state-of-the-art m-commerce site aimed at smartphone users and a special app for iPhone users to facilitate shopping on their m-commerce site. By 2014, Home Depot expects as much as 40 percent of the firm's total online sales to come from mobile phones.[50]

Channel managers can also use smartphone technology to "catch" consumers when they are near retail stores. For example, a start-up called Shopkick-Inc., has signed up Best Buy and Macy's as launch partners for a new kind of app for iPhones and Androids. The app detects when shoppers are in or near stores and then targets special offers and rewards for them. So, by taking advantage of smartphones' location-sensing capabilities as well as cameras that customers can use to scan bar codes on products, Shopkick's app is able to offer coupons or other special offers when shoppers are in a convenient position to buy.[51]

RFID

This acronym stands for *radio frequency identification*. This is a relatively new technology that uses a device called an RFID tag attached to a person or object, such as a product, that enables that person or product to be identified and tracked using radio waves.[52]

While there are many potential applications for RFID technology in the context of marketing channel management, the main application is believed to be in the area of inventory tracking, management of the supply chain and increasing the efficiency of the in-store buying process.

By implanting RFID chips or tags in or on a product, detailed information, including price, basic characteristics, date of manufacture, origin, and current location, can be recorded. The RFID tag can then transmit the information by radio waves to electronic readers, enabling products embedded with the chips to be scanned remotely and in bulk. Given this capability, RFID has the potential not only to dramatically enhance the effectiveness and efficiency of inventory control and supply chain but may offer an even more significant breakthrough: the elimination of checkout lines in retail stores by scanning shoppers' purchases as they are being made, rather than bringing the purchases to a checkout line. Some of the world's largest companies, including retailers Best Buy and Walmart, have been experimenting with RFID technology to assess its practicality and cost effectiveness. Although the jury is still out on these two questions and implementation of RFID on a large scale may be a decade or more away, the rewards are potentially great. As Robert Willett, Best Buy's chief information officer and chief of international operations, stated in a keynote address to RFID World Congress,[53]

> *the first store that removes checkouts all together will be the consumer champion forever and ever.*

So, RFID is a technology that channel managers will need to pay close attention to. While still in the early stages of development, if this technology proves to be scalable and cost effective, it has the potential to truly revolutionize not only inventory control in the supply chain, but the entire consumer in-store shopping process as well.

Cloud Computing

Cloud computing is an Internet-based technology that enables both large and small businesses and organizations to utilize highly sophisticated computer applications without having to have their own hardware, software, office computing space and staff.[54] Instead, by being part of the network, or "cloud," the user can access the computing capabilities needed on demand from a third- party provider via the Internet. By participating in the cloud, the client pays only for the computing services actually used, similar to paying utility bills. Another option is to pay for a subscription whereby the user agrees to purchase a fixed charge per time period, such as monthly. Given that the user of cloud computing services does not have to invest in the information technology needed to support sophisticated applications, including facilities and staff, the cost savings can be substantial. But even more important, because the third-party provider offers its services to numerous other clients, the economies of scale and scope provided by such **multi-tenancy** enables the cloud computing provider to develop powerful applications that would otherwise be feasible only for the largest customers to provide on their own. Given the advantages of cloud computing in terms of the powerful applications provided, its inherent cost advantages and the great flexibility it provides to users, this technology could revolutionize the information technology industry by making the need for individual firms to invest heavily in IT technology obsolete. Indeed, many of the world's leading IT technology companies, such as IBM, Hewlett Packard and Microsoft, see the revolutionary potential in cloud computing and are investing heavily in developing this technology.

From a marketing channels perspective, the capabilities provided by cloud computing mean that virtually any firm in the marketing channel regardless of size will find it feasible and cost effective to obtain the computing capabilities and expertise needed to develop and support whatever channel management applications they need, whether that involves managing distributor relationships, coordinating multiple channels or tracking products in the supply chain. Already, firms such as Salesforce.com and Amazon.com have taken leadership positions in offering cloud computing services that helped Dell Computer Corporation manage its global B2B channel network,. It also enabled Starbucks to operate an online community that captures ideas for enhancing the customer experience from Starbucks' vast world-wide customer base. Similarly, Amazon.com, which had developed a huge IT capability far beyond its own needs, has begun to offer cloud computing services to its affiliated merchants through its Amazon Web Service (AWS) division.[55] As a result, even small merchants that participate in the Amazon.com "cloud," can offer customers many of the sophisticated customer interfaces that the site has become famous for.

The Legal Environment

The legal environment refers to the set of laws that impact marketing channels. The legal structure resulting from these laws is not a static code. Rather, it is a continually evolving structure affected by changing values, norms, politics and precedents established through court cases. The varied and numerous court interpretations of laws impinging on channel management may appear to the channel manager to be a morass of legal hodgepodge. Fortunately, the marketing channel manager need not be an expert on the legal aspects of marketing channels. Nor should he or she aspire to such a position given the technical nature of the subject, as this would be a full-time job in itself. Only trained legal experts are in a position to deal competently with the legal complexities relevant to the marketing channel. Nevertheless, the channel manager still needs a general knowledge of some legislation pertaining to channels and familiarity with some of the legal issues relevant to channel management. This general background and awareness of the legal side of channel management will help the manager to communicate better with legal experts and perhaps help avoid potentially serious and costly legal problems that can arise in the management of marketing channels.

Legislation Affecting Marketing Channels

While there are many federal, state, local, and even international laws that can affect marketing channels, five pieces of federal legislation underlie most of the major channel management legal issues we will discuss later in this chapter. They are: (1) the Sherman Antitrust Act; (2) the Clayton Act; (3) the Federal Trade Commission Act; (4) the Robinson-Patman Act and (5) the Celler-Kefauver Act.

Sherman Antitrust Act   The Sherman Antitrust Act, passed in 1890, is the fundamental antimonopoly law of the United States. The philosophy underlying this piece of legislation is that public welfare is served best through competition. Thus, the act was aimed at prohibiting practices that would restrain competition in the marketplace. Section 1 of the Sherman Act forbids contracts or combinations that restrain interstate or foreign commerce. The act provides federal courts with the power to break up or dissolve monopolies and also provides for criminal penalties against individuals involved in the creation of illegal monopolies.

Clayton Act   The Clayton Act was passed in 1914 to strengthen the Sherman Antitrust Act. The Clayton Act supplements the Sherman Act by specifically prohibiting such practices as price discrimination, tying clauses, exclusive dealing, intercorporate stockholding and interlocking corporate directories among competing firms if these practices tend to substantially lessen competition or tend to create monopolies in any line of trade.

Federal Trade Commission Act   This act, also passed in 1914, established the Federal Trade Commission (FTC). The FTC, as a federal agency, was granted the power to investigate and enforce, through the use of injunctions, unfair methods of competition in interstate commerce. Such "unfair methods of competition" include not only those specifically stipulated in the Sherman and Clayton acts, but also any other practices that might be injurious to competition. Thus, the Federal Trade Commission Act significantly expanded the scope of the federal government in the regulation of interstate commerce.

Robinson-Patman Act   This act was passed in 1936 as an amendment to the Clayton Act. The Robinson-Patman Act was aimed at prohibiting a variety of forms of price discrimination that tended to lessen competition but which was inadequately covered by the Clayton Act.

Sections 2a and 2b of the act prohibit persons engaged in interstate commerce from discriminating in price or terms of sale for goods of like grade and quality if the effects of such discrimination are to substantially lessen competition or foster monopolies in any line of commerce. This act also bars the injury, destruction or prevention of competition with any person who either grants or knowingly receives the benefit of such discriminations, or with customers of either of them. The act does, however, allow for price differentials to different customers, under the following circumstances:

1. When the differentials in prices charged to different customers do not exceed the differences in the cost of manufacture, sale or delivery resulting from the differing methods or quantities in which such goods are sold or delivered to purchasers

2. When price changes that result in price differentials are necessary to meet changing market conditions, to avoid obsolescence of seasonal merchandise, to dispose of perishables, or to conduct legitimate closeout sales or court-imposed distress sales

3. When the price differentials quoted to selected customers are offered in good faith to meet competitors' prices and are not intended to injure competition

Section 2c of the act covers another form of price discrimination: unearned brokerage fees. Unearned brokerage fees are a device used by buyers to gain a lower price from the seller. Under this arrangement, a buyer would set up a fake brokerage firm that was actually part of its own organization and bill the seller for the "cost" of the brokerage fee. The desired result of this is to reduce the effective price paid by the buyer to the seller. Those buyers who did not set up such brokerage schemes would thus pay a higher price. Since those buyers who were able to set up such phony brokerage schemes were typically large-scale businesses, smaller businesses were at a significant disadvantage. Such practices were common before passage of the Robinson-Patman Act.

Sections 2d and 2e of the act cover what is perhaps the most nebulous area of price discrimination in marketing channels: promotional allowances and services. Promotional allowances and services refer to various forms of assistance from the seller to the buyer. These are often in the form of cooperative advertising allowances, payments for display of the suppliers' products, point-of-purchase materials, catalogs, display equipment, training programs, management assistance as well as a variety of other services (see Chapter 12). In order to offer such promotional allowances and services to customers legally, sellers must do so on a proportionally equal basis to all other customers distributing their products.

Celler-Kefauver Act   This act, passed in 1950, was an amendment to Section 7 of the Clayton Antitrust Act, which prohibited acquisitions or mergers that tended to lessen competition or create monopolies. The Celler-Kefauver Act broadened the scope of the Clayton Act so that the prohibitions against acquisitions and mergers that tended to lessen competition and foster monopolies as a result of horizontal mergers between firms would also apply to vertical mergers and acquisitions. Thus, the act is particularly relevant to situations involving vertical integration through acquisitions and mergers. In essence, such vertical integration is prohibited if it would substantially lessen competition or foster monopolies.

Legal Issues in Channel Management

Having discussed some of the basic federal legislation underlying the legal environment of marketing channels, we now turn our attention to some of the major legal issues in channel management that are affected by this legislation. What should be kept in mind as we proceed through our discussion of legal issues is the potential for conflict that exists between the objectives of an individual firm's channel management strategies and the interests of society at large. Thus, when a producer or manufacturer imposes vertical restrictions on its distributors or dealers (for example, by using exclusive dealing arrangements, territorial restrictions or price controls), such practices may be strategically sound for the firm imposing them but anticompetitive for society as a whole.

Dual Distribution   This term refers to the practice whereby a producer or manufacturer uses two or more different channel structures for distributing the same product to his target market. The selling of the same or similar products under different brand names for distribution through two or more channels is also a form of dual distribution.

Dual distribution, which in recent years is increasingly being referred to as **multichannel distribution**, is a frequent practice and not illegal per se under federal antitrust laws. Antitrust controversies have emerged, however, when a firm distributes through its own vertically integrated channel in competition with independent channel members at the wholesale or retail levels This is a common distribution arrangement in the marketing of petroleum products, tires, shoes, paint and drugs. Under such an arrangement, the manufacturer may gain an unfair competitive advantage by using company-owned outlets to undercut prices charged by independents. For example, automobile dealers have often complained about what they view as unfair competition from auto manufacturers when the manufacturers sell directly to large fleet buyers, such as auto rental companies. Dealers claim that the fleet buyers get a better price than they do. Hence, the fleet buyers attain an unfair competitive advantage in the new-and-used car markets when they sell many of these vehicles after a year of use at very attractive prices in the same local markets as the automobile dealers. Such practices make it very difficult for some independent dealers to compete and indeed may threaten their very existence. Carried to an extreme, a dominant manufacturer could gain a monopoly position by driving independent distributors or dealers out of business. In recent years, the courts have taken the position of requiring a manufacturer with a dominant role in a particular product line to seek to preserve the independent distributors or dealers of that product if such independent distributors or dealers exist. Dual distribution arrangements that work to eliminate the independent distributor or dealer are inconsistent with this position. Consequently, they may be viewed by the courts as having the potential to substantially lessen competition and may be in violation of the antitrust provisions of the Sherman and Clayton acts.

Exclusive Dealing   An exclusive dealing arrangement exists when a supplier requires its channel members to sell only its products or to refrain from selling products from directly competitive suppliers. The case of *Ben & Jerry's v. Häagen-Dazs* ice cream is a typical example of exclusive dealing. Häagen-Dazs stipulated that distributors selling its ice cream were not permitted to sell directly competitive brands, so that all of the distributors' attention would be focused on Häagen-Dazs. Ben & Jerry's argued, in a suit brought against Häagen-Dazs, that this policy severely limited its ability to compete with Häagen-Dazs because these distributors provided the main channel for getting Ben & Jerry's products into supermarket freezer cases. Without these distributors to carry its products, Ben & Jerry's claimed it would have no marketing channels for reaching consumers. Thus, the exclusive dealing policy that Häagen-Dazs was trying to implement represented an attempt to eliminate competition, argued Ben & Jerry.

With an exclusive dealing arrangement, the supplier gains a substantial degree of market protection from competitive products in the market areas covered by its channel members. If a channel member refuses to abide by this agreement, the supplier can cut off the channel member from selling its products.

Exclusive dealing arrangements are in violation of the antitrust provisions of the Clayton Act if their effect is to *substantially* lessen competition or foster monopolies. For example, Anheuser-Busch, the nation's largest brewer, was investigated by the Justice Department after the company launched a new channel strategy called "100% Share of Mind." This program is essentially an exclusive dealing policy because it seeks to get beer distributors to carry Anheuser products only. Products from other brewers, especially the small microbrewers and smaller national brands, cannot gain access to or are being forced off the shelves of the nation's 2,700 wholesale beer distributors. The Federal Trade Commission and the Justice Department also recently began investigating Apple to determine if an exclusive dealing policy employed by the company, involving applications developers for its iPhones, iPod Touches and iPads, would undermine competition. The concern is with Apple's stipulation that requires developers of applications for these mobile devices to use only Apple software tools to build their applications. Because Apple is such a dominant manufacturer, especially in the smartphone market where it has sold more than 100 million units, its exclusive dealing stipulation that allows application developers to use only Apple software may substantially lessen competition. By preventing other software tools from gaining access to tens of millions of Apple mobile devices, Apple ensures that only its own software will be used, even if competitors' software products are better and cost less.[56]

The substantiality test has usually been based on three conditions: (1) whether the exclusive arrangement excludes competitive products from a substantial share of the market (Justice Department guidelines stipulate that if a manufacturer has less than a 10 percent market share it will not bother pursuing the case); (2) whether the dollar amount involved is substantial and (3) whether the dispute is between large suppliers and a smaller distributor or dealer where the supplier's disparate economic power can be inherently coercive.[57] If any or all of these conditions exist, the exclusive dealing arrangement may be open to attack as anticompetitive under both the Sherman Act and the Federal Trade Commission Act.[58]

Full-Line Forcing   If a supplier requires channel members to carry a broad group of products (full line) in order to sell any particular products in the supplier's line this practice is often referred to as **full-line-forcing**. Full-line forcing is used to varying degrees in a wide range of industries. It represents, up to a point, a legitimate effort by the manufacturer to see that a broad range of its products is carried by channel members to discourage "cherry picking" of only the hottest items in the manufacturer's product line. The antitrust issue emerges when full-line forcing occurs to such an extent that it prevents other suppliers from selling competitive lines through channel members who are "loaded up" with the products of the supplier engaging in full-line forcing.

An example of full-line forcing that did step over the legal boundary involved Levi Strauss & Company. The Federal Trade Commission issued an injunction to cease and desist from the practice that Levi Strauss was using to force department and specialty stores to buy a broad range of apparel in order to obtain the hot-selling Levi's jeans. Much of this other apparel was not desirable merchandise that the retailers would have stocked of their own volition. Some of goods, for instance, consisted of clothing that had gone out of style. But the retailers were, in effect, forced to buy these products if they wanted access to the jeans, which constituted a very important merchandise category. The forced stocking of this other merchandise resulting from Levi's full-line forcing policy meant that the retailers had less capacity to stock apparel from other manufacturers. The effect was to lessen the competition to Levi Strauss from competing manufacturers by limiting available retailer shelf space. This, in turn, reduced consumer choice in the marketplace.

Price Discrimination   **Price discrimination**, which is covered specifically under the Robinson-Patman Act, refers to the practice whereby a supplier, either directly or indirectly, sells at different prices to the same class of channel members to the extent that such price differentials tend to lessen competition. For example, small independent book retailers represented by their trade association, the American Booksellers

Association, filed an antitrust lawsuit against major book publishers. The retailers allege that these publishers regularly favor giant chain stores with secret discounts and promotional deals that are not made available to smaller bookstores.

Discriminatory price differentials can take a variety of forms, some of which can be quite subtle. The classic case of the Simplicity Pattern Company illustrates just how subtle such price discrimination can be. The Federal Trade Commission charged the Simplicity Pattern Company with violating section 2e of the Robinson-Patman Act. The FTC argued that Simplicity, a manufacturer of sewing patterns, had practiced discrimination in offering promotional services to retailers. Specifically, Simplicity offered a large chain of retail variety stores free catalogs and display cases but did not offer them to small, independent fabric stores. The FTC found Simplicity guilty of violating section 2e of the Robinson-Patman Act. Simplicity appealed to the circuit court, which reversed the FTC's decision. On appeal by the FTC, the Supreme Court upheld the original FTC decision. In finding for the FTC, the court argued that since the variety stores and independent fabric stores were in competition, the granting of free catalogs and display cases was a discriminatory promotional allowance favoring the variety stores, resulting in a competitive disadvantage to the independents. Simplicity argued their motives for selling patterns were different. In the case of variety stores, the patterns were sold on a volume basis as an important merchandise item on which the stores intended to make a profit. For the fabric stores, however, patterns were sold on a limited basis as an accommodation to customers and thus were not a significant merchandise category on which the stores intended to make a profit. Simplicity argued that if the stores were not actually in competition, then the actions of Simplicity with respect to promotional allowances could not be viewed as impeding competition because such competition had never existed.

This case actually hinged on the competitive structure issue of whether the two types of stores were actually in competition with each other in the sale of sewing patterns. Subsequent observers of this case believe that if Simplicity had presented a better documented case for its argument of no competition between the variety and fabric stores, it may have won the case.

It is, of course, debatable as to whether the outcome would have been different if the competitive structure issue had simply been better articulated. But the case does bring up the kinds of subtle issues and interpretive difficulties that often emerge when dealing with the issues of price discrimination in channels of distribution as governed by the Robinson-Patman Act. It is no wonder that confusion and inconsistencies have been common in court interpretations involving the Robinson-Patman Act throughout its history. Consequently, accurate generalizations about whether specific channel pricing policies and practices constitute price discrimination are difficult to make.[59] A study by Norton Marks and Neely Inlow, however, found that the courts have focused mainly on more flagrant violations involving price discrimination.[60] Moreover, large firms (sales exceeding $1 billion) constituted almost 40 percent of the defendants, who came most frequently from the food, tobacco, oil, gas and petrochemical industries.

Price Maintenance   A supplier's attempt to control the prices charged by its channel members for the supplier's products is typically referred as **price maintenance** or **fair trade**. The supplier, in effect, dictates the prices charged by channel members to their customers. Thus, prices at which products are sold by channel members are not based on the discretion of the channel members in response to market forces, but rather on the requirements of the supplier. Such price maintenance arrangements can help manufacturers gain greater control over the distribution of their products.[61]

Strangely enough, this type of anticompetitive price fixing, which is really what such practices amount to, was exempted from federal antitrust legislation through passage of the Miller-Tydings Act in 1937 and the McGuire Act in 1952. These acts exempted retail price fixing by manufacturers in states that permitted vertical pricing arrangements between manufacturers and retailers. Such vertical price fixing agreements were typically referred to euphemistically as **fair trade laws**. Most states enacted various forms of these laws.

With the passage of the Consumer Goods Pricing Act in 1975, which repealed the Miller-Tydings and McGuire acts, the legal basis for exempting state fair trade laws from federal antitrust legislation no longer existed. Consequently, most state fair trade laws were no longer legal.

Although the demise of fair trade laws removed the legal underpinnings for the practice of price maintenance in the marketing channel, the practice has by no means disappeared. Many manufacturers still try to influence the prices charged by their channel members. They do so for a variety of reasons, such as to protect the image of their products, reduce the likelihood of price wars and provide channel members with sufficient profit margins to enable them to offer adequate pre- and post-sale service. Channel members who provide little service themselves and sell at low prices by feeding off the service provided by full-service channel members could be dropped as so-called **free riders**, as sometimes occurs when full-service channel members complain about the adverse effects of the low-price free riders on their businesses.[62]

Until recently, a manufacturer's dropping of price-cutting channel members was often viewed by the courts as being anticompetitive and as such in violation of the antitrust laws. But the precedent established by a recent Supreme Court decision may have swung the pendulum back in favor of allowing manufacturers to enforce price maintenance agreements with retailers.[63] In June of 2007, the Supreme Court issued a ruling involving Leegin Creative Leather Products Inc., a manufacturer of women's purses and accessories, and Kay's Kloset, a Dallas retailer, that could give manufacturers greater leeway in enforcing price maintenance policies whereby manufacturers stipulate to retailers the minimum price at which their products can be soldat retail. The court's ruling allows for such minimum pricing agreements to be examined on a case by case basis to determine if they are anticompetitive. In the case, Kay's Kloset filed a lawsuit against Leegin Creative Leather alleging that it was cut off from receiving Leegin products because it discounted its retail prices below the minimum price set by Leegin. The Supreme Court's 5-4 decision, written by Justice Anthony Kennedy, stated that minimum-pricing agreements between manufacturers and retailers are not necessarily anticompetitive and could actually benefit customers under certain circumstances. Justice Kennedy argued, for example, that such agreements could foster competition by providing retailers with enough profit to promote a brand or offer better service. Based on the precedent established by this Supreme Court decision, it would appear that any given manufacturer now has more freedom to set and enforce minimum pricing agreements with retailers as long as it can show that its particular price maintenance agreement with retailers is not anticompetitive.

Refusal to Deal   In general, suppliers may select whomever they want as channel members and **refuse to deal** with whomever they want. This right is based on the precedent established in a classic Supreme Court Case of 1919 (*United States v. Colgate and Company*) and is often referred to as the "Colgate doctrine." The court argued as follows:

> *The Sherman Act does not restrict the long recognized right of a trader or manufacturer engaged in an entirely private business, freely to exercise his own independent discretion as to the parties with whom he will deal. And, of course, he may announce in advance the circumstances under which he will refuse to deal.*

Thus, there are no legal barriers to sellers using their own criteria and judgment in the selection of channel members and announcing in advance the conditions under which they will refuse to deal.

In the case of existing channel members, however, there are legal restrictions on the seller's use of refusal to deal. Specifically, this practice cannot be used coercively to cut off channel members who will not conform to policies stipulated by the seller that may be illegal or in restraint of trade. Such would be the case, for example, if a manufacturer dropped a channel member who refused to abide by a set of specific prices or price ranges that were dictated by the manufacturer. Thus, even in light of the precedent established in the *Business Electronics v. Sharp Electronics* case, which allows suppliers much greater leeway in the use of price maintenance policies, the Sherman Act could still limit the manufacturer's freedom to drop a price-cutting channel member.

Resale Restrictions   When a manufacturer attempts to stipulate to whom channel members may resell the manufacturer's products and in what specific geographical market areas they may be sold he/she is engaging in the practice of **resale restrictions**.

Such restrictions can be very advantageous to both the manufacturer and the channel members. From the manufacturer's standpoint, the capacity to stipulate to whom products may be resold enables the manufacturer to retain and reserve certain accounts as **house accounts** (customers to whom the manufacturer sells directly) by prohibiting channel members from selling to those customers. Moreover, it enables the manufacturer to control the kinds of outlets from which final customers will buy. If, for example, a manufacturer that uses wholesalers wants only high-service retailers to sell its products, the manufacturer could specify the types of retailers to whom the wholesalers are permitted to sell. For example, Omega SA, a unit of Swatch Group Ltd. of Switzerland, was very upset when European distributors to whom it had sold its prestigious Omega watches resold them to an American distributor, who in turn sold them to the giant discount warehouse retailer Costco. Swatch believed that having Omega watches sold in Costco would undermine the high quality brand image of Omega watches, especially given that Costco heavily discounted watches to sell for $1,299 instead of Omega's suggested retail price of $1,999.[64] Further, by delineating the particular territories in which channel members are allowed to resell the manufacturer's products, the manufacturer can maintain a high degree of control over the distribution of products. From the channel members' standpoint, the territorial restrictions minimize **intrabrand competition** (competition between distributors selling the same branded product of a particular manufacturer) because each channel member is in effect given a "protected" geographical market area in which to sell the manufacturer's products. Other channel members selling the same products are then prohibited from selling in a geographical market area other than their own.

In deciding whether such restrictions constituted an illegal restraint of trade, the courts had used the so-called **rule of reason**. Under this rule, the courts weighed the intentions of the supplier and the effects of the supplier's resale restrictions on the market. If the restrictions were not intended and did not appear to result in a restraint of trade, they were generally allowed to stand.

In 1967, however, the landmark Supreme Court case of *United States v. Arnold Schwinn and Company* radically changed this rule of reason approach.[65] The Supreme Court ruled that under the Sherman Act, resale restrictions imposed by suppliers on their channel members are illegal per se. The court argued as follows:

Under the Sherman Act, it is unreasonable ... for a manufacturer to seek to restrict and confine areas or persons within which an article may be traded after the manufacturer has parted with dominion over it…. Once the manufacturer has parted with title and risk, he has parted with dominion over the product, and his effort thereafter to restrict territory or persons to whom the product may be transferred, whether by explicit agreement or by silent confirmation or understanding with the vendee, is per se a violation of Section I of the Sherman Act.

The effect of this ruling was to severely limit the legality of resale restrictions. Restrictive distribution policies, which had been practiced routinely by many firms for years, were now open to attack as violations of the Sherman Act. Yet some ten years earlier, in 1977, another landmark Supreme Court Case (*Continental TV Inc. et al. v. GTE Sylvania Inc.*) overturned the Schwinn case "per se" doctrine and essentially restored the rule of reason doctrine to govern the use of resale restrictions. The court ruled that resale restrictions are not necessarily anticompetitive if competition is viewed in a broader perspective. The court argued that resale restrictions can have "redeeming virtues" by promoting **interbrand competition** (competition between distributors in the sale of branded products of competing manufacturers), including fostering new companies and new products. Further, by inducing competent and aggressive retailers to undertake new efforts and offer special services and promotions, marketing efficiency can be improved and smaller firms can be aided in competing with larger ones. In sum, the court's position was that while resale restrictions might limit intrabrand competition, they could foster interbrand competition.

Even with the ruling in *GTE Sylvania*, however, the legality of resale restrictions is still up in the air. The court left the door open for antitrust action against resale restrictions if such resale restrictions have a "demonstrable economic effect."[66]

Tying Agreements   Agreements whereby a supplier sells a product to a channel member on condition that the channel member also purchase another product as well, or at least agrees not to purchase that product from any other supplier, are known as **tying agreements**. Full-line forcing, discussed earlier, is a special case of tying agreements.

Tying agreements put the supplier in a very advantageous position with respect to the channel members with whom the arrangement has been made. The supplier has a great deal of pricing leverage over the channel member since the channel member must accept tied products in order to obtain other products. In addition, the channel member is not free to purchase the tied products on the open market. In effect, the supplier is in a position to dictate the terms of sale. By far the most high-profile case of a tying arrangement that broke antitrust legislation involved Microsoft's Internet browser software. Microsoft tied or "comingled" its Internet Explorer browser software into its Windows operating system. So, computer manufacturers such as Compaq, Dell, Hewlett-Packard and IBM and virtually all other personal computer makers that used the Windows operating system (with the exception of Apple Macintosh) would have to take Microsoft's Internet Explorer. Because Microsoft's Windows operating system was used to run 95 percent of the world's PCs, it clearly had a monopoly in operating systems. By inextricably tying its Internet Explorer browser as a part of Windows, Microsoft had an unfair advantage over competitive browsers such as Netscape Communicator, which many experts argued was the originator of the point-and-click interface that made surfing the Internet so practical. Netscape argued in a lawsuit against Microsoft (which was later joined by the Federal Trade Commission and the Justice Department), that Microsoft's tie-in of Internet Explorer to Windows severely limited Netscape's ability to include its browser in PC operating systems. Indeed, Netscape argued and the Justice Department concurred that Microsoft did everything in its power to limit competition from Netscape, such as making it difficult to access Netscape via the Windows operating system even when the PC manufacturers included Netscape in the software bundle built into the PC.

After going through the courts for over three years, the Justice Department found that Microsoft was operating as a monopolist by tying its Internet Explorer browser so closely to Windows and was therefore in violation of antitrust laws.[67]

Vertical Integration   Firms that own and operates organizations at other levels of the distribution channel (for example, a manufacturer owning and operating its own wholesaling facilities and retail stores) are engaged in **vertical integration**. Vertical integration is practiced by a number of manufacturers in a variety of industries, such as Goodyear and Firestone in tires and Sherwin-Williams in paints.

Vertical integration can occur as a result of growth and evolution of the firm, whereby the firm decides to expand its organization to include wholesale and retail facilities. The reasons for doing so are often based on the firm's desire to gain scale economies and a high degree of control, which it believes vertical integration can offer. For example, Walt Disney Company bought Capital Cities/ABC Inc. in order to ensure a secure distribution system for the shows it produced.

However, vertical integration can also occurthrough acquisitions of and mergers with other firms at different levels of the channel. A manufacturer, for example, may acquire or merge with a wholesale or retailing organization.

Under the Celler-Kefauver amendment to the Sherman Act, such vertical integration by acquisition and merger is subject to antitrust action if the acquisitions or mergers tend to substantially lessen competition or foster monopoly. This can happen when the vertical integration occurs in a highly concentrated industry, thus eliminating an important source of supply to independent firms or significantly reducing the opportunity for competitive firms to reach the market. For example, a merger between Brown Shoe Company, a major shoe manufacturer, and Kinney Shoe Corporation, a former independent chain of retail shoe stores in the United States, was ruled illegal by the Supreme Court because the merger might have prevented other shoe manufacturers from selling through Kinney.[68]

Summary

Marketing channels develop and operate in a complex environment that is continually changing. Channel managers must therefore be sensitive to the environmental changes in order to plan effective marketing channel strategies for adapting to these changes successfully. To do so, they must have an understanding of the environment and how it can influence channel management.

While there are many ways to categorize the myriad of environmental variables, the following five-category taxonomy was used in this chapter: (1) economic environment; (2) competitive environment; (3) sociocultural environment; (4) technological environment and (5) legal environment.

When dealing with any or all of these environmental categories, channel managers need to consider the effects of environmental variables not only on their own firms and on their firms' target markets, but also on *all* the channel members and participants.

The economic environment is probably the most obvious and pervasive category of environmental variables affecting all members and participants in the channel. Especially important are the effects of recession, inflation and possible deflation; but even so-called normal economic conditions can create problems. The fundamental challenge confronting channel managers in the face of these economic developments is to help channel members weather difficult economic conditions. Advance planning to develop channel strategies for dealing with economic changes is the basis for successfully meeting this challenge.

The competitive environment must include global as well as domestic competition. Moreover, four major types of competition need to be addressed: (1) horizontal competition, where similar firms at the same level of the channel compete with each other; (2) intertype competition, where different types of firms at the same level of the channel compete; (3) vertical competition, where firms at different levels in the same channel compete with one another and (4) channel system competition, where entire channels compete with each other. Channel managers must watch all of these types of competition in order to determine how the competitive structure in which their channels operate is changing and what implications these changes may have for channel management strategy.

The sociocultural environment has an impact on marketing channels because the structure of marketing channels reflects the sociocultural environment in which they exist. So, channel managers must carefully observe changing sociocultural patterns in order to discern what implications these pattern changes will have for marketing channel strategy. Because of their profound influence in recent years, certain developments should be especially noted. These include: globalization, consumer mobility and connectedness, social networking and the Green movement.

The technological environment must be monitored carefully to evaluate the effects of technological changes

on marketing channels. Developments such as the Internet, computerized inventory management with handheld computers, EDI, the digital revolution, smartphones, RFID and cloud computing should be followed closely.

Finally, channel managers cannot ignore the legal environment, with its complex laws and continually changing precedents. While channel managers cannot be expected to be experts in the technicalities and nuances involved in the complex and changing legal environment affecting channel management, general knowledge and awareness of some of the basic laws and legal issues are needed. In particular, channel managers should be familiar with the basic provisions of the Sherman Act, Clayton Act, Federal Trade Commission Act, Robinson-Patman Act and the Celler-Kefauver Act. They should also understand how they affect such legal issues as: (1) dual distribution; (2) exclusive dealing; (3) full-line forcing; (4) price discrimination; (5) price maintenance; (6) refusal to deal; (7) resale restrictions; (8) tying agreements and (9) vertical integration through acquisitions and mergers.

Review Questions

1. How does the impact of the environment on channel strategy differ from other major strategy areas of the marketing mix?

2. In dealing with the effects of environment on channel strategy, the channel manager has a lot more to think about. Discuss this statement.

3. Discuss the fundamental channel management issues associated with recessionary, inflationary and deflationary periods in the economy.

4. Why might even "normal" economic conditions pose channel management problems?

5. Explain the four types of competition discussed in the chapter. Why is it important to recognize these different forms of competition?

6. Marketing channels reflect the sociocultural environments within which they exist. Explain this statement.

7. Discuss several major sociocultural forces that have emerged in recent years and how they have already affected marketing channel strategy and management and how they might do so in the future.

8. Technological changes, though continual, do not occur evenly or predictably over time. Discuss

the implications of this statement for channel management strategy.

9. Discuss the channel management implications of such technological developments as electronic scanners, high-tech point-of-sale displays, computerized inventory management systems, EDI, the digital revolution, smartphones, RFID and cloud computing.

10. What is the underlying philosophy of the Sherman Act with respect to the role of competition versus monopoly in promoting public welfare? Discuss.

11. Discuss the basic provisions of the (1) Sherman Antitrust Act; (2) Clayton Act; (3) Federal Trade Commission Act; (4) Robinson-Patman Act and (5) Celler-Kefauver Act.

12. Exclusive dealing, full-line forcing and tying agreements all have something in common. What is it? Discuss the antitrust implications of this common element.

13. Price maintenance, refusal to deal and resale restrictions all represent attempts by the supplier to exercise control over its channel members. What are the legal limits on the degree of control the

supplier can exercise through these three approaches?

14. Discuss the basic legal implications associated with the policies of dual distribution, price

discrimination and vertical integration through acquisitions and mergers.

Channel Issues for Discussion

1. James Johnson, vice president of marketing for a major manufacturer of fiberglass home insulation aimed at the DIY market, was elated after reading an article in *The Wall Street Journal* about the recent steep rise in energy prices. "This will be great for us. Our sales could double next season," he exclaimed to his general sales manager, Bill Allan, who had just walked into the office. "Tell your district sales managers to instruct their field salespeople to push home center retailers to double their inventory and floor space for home insulation," continued Johnson. Bill Allan dutifully responded, "I'll do it right away, but the last thing home centers are going to want is to stock up heavily on inventory when this energy price spiral might cause a recession."

Comment on this situation in terms of the different perspectives of the manufacturer and the retailers about this environmental development.

2. Almost 80 percent of chief financial officers at the 100 largest retailers say that too much inventory is the greatest risk factor to the viability of their businesses during recessionary periods. High inventories lead to heavy discounting when consumer demand is lacking. This, in turn, undermines gross margins. When demand is very weak, gross margins can disappear completely as retailers may be forced to liquidate slow moving merchandise at prices below their wholesale cost. Paradoxically, retailers also worry about having too *little* inventory to meet consumer demand and thus losing sales when consumers cannot find the products they are looking for on retailers' shelves. Hence, retailers attempting to manage their inventories during a recession often feel that when it comes to stocking their shelves, they are damned if they do and damned if they don't.

How might retailers deal with this inventory dilemma more effectively during recessionary periods? What might suppliers do to help retailers address this problem?

3. Home Depot, Toys "R" Us, Staples, Best Buy and many other giant retailers (often referred to as "category killers" or "big box" retailers because of their dominance in particular merchandise categories and the sheer physical size of the stores) are fierce competitors and are frequently accused of driving small retailers out of business. Observers who have witnessed this competitive struggle take place over the past decade say the reason that small retailers go out of business is that they "can't compete" with these giants. The verdict in most cases has been "no contest" between the retail giants and the little guys because the little guy so seldom wins or even gets to stay in business.

From a competitive standpoint, is such an outcome inevitable? Discuss. Is it really the "big guys" driving the "little guys" out of business or is there something more fundamental at work here?

4. When Circuit City, the world's second largest consumer electronics retailer went out of business in January of 2009, pundits thought most of Circuit City's business would be picked up by the largest consumer electronics retailer, Best Buy, as well as Walmart, which also sells a great deal of consumer electronics products. But the competitive landscape created by Circuit City's demise did not conform neatly to predictions. An Indianapolis-based regional chain of consumer electronics stores by the name of hhgregg decided to take a stab at competing with the giants on a national level. Hhgregg planned to open fifty stores in the very same markets Circuit City had operated in and, in some cases, even in former Circuit City stores. Hhgregg believes it can compete even with the huge Best Buy and Walmart by emphasizing high-end products and superior customer service provided by a highly trained sales force which is paid primarily on commission. Hhgregg believes that its more knowledgeable sales force, which receives almost 300 hours of training in its first year, covering over 500 different products sold in stores, will give it an edge in building a loyal customer base that its competitors will not be able to match.

Do you think hhgregg can compete with Best Buy and Walmart successfully as a relatively small consumer electronics retailer by offering a customer experience that is not available from the giants? Why or why not?

5. By 2009, social media services, such as Facebook and Twitter, had become a popular marketing tool for small businesses. In fact, almost 25 percent of firms with fewer than 100 employees were using social media for marketing purposes. This was more than double the percentage of the prior year. Many of these firms cite the ease of use and low cost of these social media as the main reason for using them for reaching out to and communicating with potential and existing customers.

How can the ability to communicate with customers via social media enhance channel management? Discuss.

6. Channels of distribution for books have gone through a metamorphosis in recent years with the emergence of e-books, such as Amazon's Kindle, Barnes & Noble's Nook, or Apple's iPad. Indeed, by mid-2010, Amazon.com reported that sales of books through its Kindle outnumbered its sales of hardcover books by a ratio of 180 e-books for every 100 hardcover books sold. Only paperback books still sold more units than

e-books. But the e-book channel continued to grow rapidly to account for close to 10 percent of total book sales by the end of 2010.

Do you think e-book channels will eventually totally replace conventional, physical book channels? Why or why not?

7. In mid-2009, a class action lawsuit was launched against Babies "R" Us, a division of Toys "R" Us, as well as five manufacturers from whom Babies "R" Us purchased baby products for resale in its stores. The suit alleges that Babies "R" Us and the supplying manufacturers conspired to fix prices on several products including strollers, high chairs, and car seats. The suit claims that between 2001 and 2006, over $500 million in merchandise produced by the five manufacturers and sold by Babies "R" Us was controlled by minimum pricing agreements. These sales amounted to between 10 to 50 percent of the five manufacturers' sales in the U.S. The lawsuit claims that the minimum pricing agreement was anticompetitive and resulted in consumers paying millions of dollars more for these baby products than they would have in the absence of such an agreement.

Discuss the possible strategic channel management advantages for both Babies "R" Us and the supplying manufacturers as a result of this price maintenance agreement versus the possible negative effects of the agreement on consumer welfare from a macro perspective.

References

1. See, for example, Ken Favaro, Tim Romberger, and David Meer, "Five Rules for Retailing in a Recession," *Harvard Business Review*, (April 2009): 64–72; Jon M. Hawes and Thomas L. Baker, "Type of Exchange and Environmental Uncertainty within a Marketing Channel," in *Proceedings of the Annual Educators' Conference of the American Marketing Association*, eds. Robert P. Leone and V. Kamar (Chicago: American Marketing Association, 1992), 496–500; Jeffrey C. Dilts, "Perceived Environmental Uncertainty and Perception of the Channel Relationship," in *Developments in Marketing Science, Proceedings of the Academy of Marketing Science*, Vol. XIV (Coral Gables, Fla.: Academy of Marketing Science, 1991), 96–99; F. Robert Dwyer and N. Ann Welsh, "Environmental Relationships of the International Political Economy of Marketing Channels," *Journal of Marketing Research* (November 1985): 397–414.

2. See, for example, Ravi S. Achrol, Torger Reve, and Louis W. Stern, "The Environment of Marketing Channel Dyads: A Framework for Comparative Analysis," *Journal of Marketing* (Fall 1983): 55–67.

3. Ken Favaro, Tim Romberger and David Meer, "Five Rules for Retailing in a Recession," *Harvard Business Review*, (April 2009): 67.

4. David Welch, "What Detroit Likes About the Crisis," *Business Week* (October 13, 2008): 78.

5. Finbarr O'Neill, "The Auto Industry's Comeback," *Wall Street Journal* (July 30, 2009): A17.

6. John Fine, "Why General Mills's Marketing Pays Off," *Business Week* (July 27, 2009): 67.

7. Timothy W. Martin and Ilan Brat, "Food Sellers Signal Weak Recovery," *Wall Street Journal* (February 26, 2010): B8.

8. Janet Adamy and Julie Jargon, "Starbucks Responds to Cost-Wary Market," *Wall Street Journal*, (March 19, 2010): B4.

9. "Coupon Clicking," *Marketing News* (January 30, 2009): 6.

10. Ann Zimmerman, "Dollar General Lays Bet On Opening New Stores," *Wall Street Journal* (May 14, 2010): B8.

11. Mary Ellen Lloyd, "Retailers Fret About Inventory Levels for Holidays," *Wall Street Journal* (September 30, 2009): B6.

12. These classifications of competition are based on the work of Joseph C. Palamountain, *The Politics of Distribution* (Cambridge, Mass.: Harvard University Press, 1955).

13. This mode of competition is derived from the work of Bert C. McCammon, "The Emergence and Growth of Contractually Integrated Channels in the American Economy," in *Marketing and Economic Development*, ed. P.D. Bennett (Chicago: American Marketing Association, 1965), 496–515.

14. Matthew Boyle, "A Contrarian Electronics Chain," *Business Week* (October 12, 2009): 66.

15. For additional background on intertype competition, see F. Robert Dwyer and Sejo Oh, "The Consequences of Intertype Competition on Retail and Interfirm Behavior," in *Proceedings of the Annual Educators' Conference of the American Marketing Association*, ed. Susan P. Douglas (Chicago: American Marketing Association, 1987): 23–28.

16. Geoffrey A. Fowler and Miguel Bustillo, "Wal-Mart, Amazon Gear Up for Holiday Battle," *Wall Street Journal* (October 19, 2009): B3.

17. "The Last Picture Show At Blockbuster?," *Bloomberg Businessweek* (April 5, 2010): 28.

18. Mike Spector, "Blockbuster Plots a Remake," *Wall Street Journal* (February 24, 2010): B1, B8.

19. See for example: Heather Todd, "Changing Channels," *Beverage World* (July 2003): 32–33.

20. Matthew Boyle, "Brand Killers," *Fortune* (April 11, 2003): 89–96.

21. John Jannarone, "Wal-Mart Spices Up Private Label," *Wall Street Journal* (February 6, 2010): B16.

22. http://www.macysine.comMacy/PrivateBrands.aspx.

23. Matthew Boyle, "Generics: Making Gains in the Shelf War," *Business Week* (November 10, 2008): 62.

24. Bert C. McCammon, "The Emergence and Growth of Contractually Integrated Channels in the American Economy," *Marketing and Economic Development* (Chicago: American Marketing Association, 1965), 498–504.

25. Anna Watson and Richard Johnson, "Managing the Franchisor-Franchisee Relationship: A Relationship Marketing Perspective," *Journal of Marketing Channels* (January–March 2010): 51–68.

26. For the most complete and thorough analysis of competitive structure and strategy, see Michael E. Porter, *Competitive Advantage: Creating and Sustaining Superior Performance* (New York: Free Press, 1985).

27. Martin Peers, "Rivals Explore Amazon's Territory," *Wall Street Journal* (January 7, 2010): C10.

28. Janeen Olsen and Kent L. Granzin, "Vertical Integration and Economic Development: An Empirical Investigation of Channel Integration" *Journal of Global Marketing* 7, no. 3 (1994): 7–39; Soumave Bandyopadhyay and Robert A. Robicheaux, "The Effects of Culture on Interfirm Communications," in *Proceedings of the Annual Educators' Conference of the American Marketing Association*, eds. Robert P. Leone and V. Kumar (Chicago: American Marketing Association, 1992), 100; and Janeen E. Olsen and Kent L. Granzin, "A Conceptualization of the Relationship between Economic Development and the Structure of Marketing Channels," in *Proceedings of the Annual Educators' Conference of the American Marketing Association*, eds. Russel Belk et al. (Chicago: American Marketing Association, 1987), 307–311. For an earlier but seminal discussion of this topic, see Jac L. Goldstucker, "The Influence of Culture on Channels of Distribution," in *Marketing and the New Science Planning*, ed. Robert L. King (Chicago: American Marketing Association, 1968), 468–473.

29. George Wadinambiaratchi, "Channels of Distribution in Developing Economies," *Business Quarterly* (Winter 1965): 74–82.

30. Margaret L. Hall, John Knapp and Christopher Winsten, *Distribution in Great Britain and North America* (London: Oxford University Press, 1961); Maureen Guirdham, *Marketing: The Management of Distribution Channels* (Oxford: Pergamon Press, 1972), 91–99; J. K. Galbraith and Richard H. Holton, *Marketing Efficiency in Puerto Rico* (Cambridge, Mass: Harvard University Press, 1955); Raymond W. Baker, "Marketing in Nigeria," *Journal of Marketing* 29 (July 1965): 40–48. Also see, for example, the selections in Reed Moyer and Stanley C. Hollander, eds., *Markets and Marketing in Developing Economies* (Chicago: American Marketing Association, 1968).

31. See, for example, Jeroen C. A. Potjes and Roy Thurik, "Japanese Supermarket Chains and Labor Costs—Part 2: A Comparison with French Variety Stores, Supermarkets and Hypermarkets," *Journal of Marketing Channels* 1, no. 3 (1992): 97–113.

32. Michael R. Czinkota and Jon Woronoff, *Japan's Market: The Distribution System* (New York: Praeger, 1986).

33. Juro Osawa, "Convenience Stores Score in Japan," *Wall Street Journal* (August 19, 2008): B2.

34. See for example: Mark D. Uncles, "Retail Change in China: Retrospect and Prospects," *The International Review of Retail Distribution and Consumer Research* (February 2010): 69–84; Guillermo D'Andrea, Belen Lopez-Aleman and Alejandro Stengel, "Why Small Retailers Endure in Latin America," *International Journal of Retail & Distribution Management*, (Vol. 34, No. 9 2006): 661–673.

35. Boryana Dimitrova and Bert Rosenbloom, "Standardization Versus Adaptation in Global Markets: Is Channel Strategy Different?" *Journal of Marketing Channels* (April-June 2010): 157–176.

36. See for example: Mark Cleveland, Michel Laroche and Nicolas Papdopoulos, "Cosmopolitanism, Consumer Ethnocentrism, and Materialism: An Eight-Country Study of Antecedents and Outcomes," *Journal of International Marketing* (17(1) 2009): 116–146; High M. Cannon and Attila Yaprak, "Will the Real-World Citizen Please Stand Up! The Many Faces of Cosmopolitan Consumer Behavior," *Journal of International Marketing* (10(4) 2002): 30–52.

37. Jason Bush, "IKEA in Russia: Enough is Enough," *Business Week* (July 13, 2009): 33.

38. See for example: http://en.wikipedia.org/wiki/ List_of_social_networking_Web_sites.

39. Sarah Needleman, "Entrepreneurs Question Value of Social Media," *Wall Street Journal* (March 16, 2010): B7.

40. Kee-hung Lai, T.C.E. Cheng and Ailie K.Y. Tang, "Green Retailing: Factors for Success," *California Management Review* (Winter 2010): 6–30.

41. See for example: Sushil Vachani and N. Craig Smith, "Socially Responsible Distribution: Distribution Strategies for Reaching the Bottom of the Pyramid," *California Management Review* (Winter, 2008): 52–84.

42. See for example: "The New Fundamentals: Technology's Impact on the Future of Marketing," *Bloomberg Businessweek* (March 1, 2010): 64–68.

43. For a related discussion, see Otis Port, "The Next Web," *Business Week* (March 4, 2002): 96–102.

44. For a related discussion, see: Karen Butner, "The Smarter Supply Chain of the Future," *Strategy and Leadership* (Vol. 38, No. 1 2010): 22–31.

45. Jeffrey A. Trachtenberg, "E-books Rewrite Bookselling," *Wall Street Journal* (May 21, 2010): A1, A2.

46. See for example, Jeffrey A. Trachtenberg, "Barnes & Noble Puts Faith in Digital Future," *Wall Street Journal* (February 24, 2010): B8.

47. Dana Mattioli, "Retailers Ring Up New Sales on Smartphones," *Wall Street Journal* (June 11, 2010): B7.

48. Ibid.

49. Ibid.

50. Ibid.

51. Geoffrey A. Fowler, "Retailers Reach Out on Cellphones," *Wall Street Journal* (April 21, 2010): B6.

52. "Radio-frequency identification," http://en.wikipedia.org/wik/Radiofrequency_identification.

53. Kris Hudson, "Best Buy Foresees Using RFID to Track Inventory," *Wall Street Journal* (April 4, 2007): B1.

54. "What is Cloud Computing?" http://www.salesforce.com/cloudcomputing/.

55. "Cloud Computing, What's in it for You?," *Wall Street Journal* (July 31, 2009): A18.

56. Thomas Catan and Yukari Iwatani Kane, "Apple Attracts Scrutiny from Regulators," *Wall Street Journal* (May 4, 2010): B4.

57. William L. Trombetta and Albert L. Page, "The Channel Control Issue under Scrutiny," *Journal of Retailing* (Summer 1978): 55; and "Easier Rules on Exclusive Dealing," *Business Week* (February 4, 1985): 40.

58. In some industries, exceptions to these provisions are often made. See Marianne M. Jennings, "Exclusive Distributorships in Soda Pop Industry Exempted from Antitrust Laws," *Marketing News* (January 23, 1981): 12.

59. For an analysis of some court cases and interpretations of price discrimination involving the Robinson-Patman Act, see Ray O. Werner, "Marketing and the Supreme Court in Transition 1982-1984," *Journal of Marketing* (Summer 1985): 99–101.

60. Norton E. Marks and Neely S. Inlow, "Price Discrimination and Its Impact on Small Business," *Journal of Consumer Marketing* (Winter 1988): 31–37.

61. See for example: Rene Sacasas, "Channel of Distribution Under Antitrust Statutes," *Journal of the Academy of Marketing Science*, (Fall 2006): 629–630.

62. For two excellent analyses of the issues involved in price maintenance, see Patrick J. Kaufmann, "Dealer Termination Agreements and Resale Price Maintenance: Implications of the Business Electronics Case and Proposed Amendment to the Sherman Act," *Journal of Retailing*, (Summer 1988): 113–124; and Mary Jane Sheffet and Debra L. Scammon, "Resale Price Maintenance: Is It Safe to Suggest Retail Prices?" *Journal of Marketing* (Fall 1985): 82–91.

63. Joseph Pereria, "Price Fixing Makes Comeback After Supreme Court Ruling," *Wall Street Journal* (August 18, 2008): A1, A12.

64. Brent Kendall, "Justices to Hear Retail Case," *Wall Street Journal* (April 20, 2010): B3.

65. *United States v. Arnold Schwinn and Company*, 388 U.S. 365(1967).

66. For an in-depth analysis of the territorial restriction issue based on empirical research, see Shantan Dutta, Jan B. Heide, and Mark Berger, "Vertical Territorial Restrictions and Public Policy: Theories and Industry Evidence," *Journal of Marketing* (October 1999): 121–134.

67. John R. Wilke, Rebecca Buckman, and Gary McWilliams, "Microsoft Lets PC Firms Remove Browser," *Wall Street Journal* (July 12, 2001): A3, A8.

68. Louis W. Stern and Adel I. El-Ansary, *Marketing Channels* (Englewood Cliffs, N.J.: Prentice-Hall, 1977), 344.

CHAPTER **4**

Behavioral Processes in Marketing Channels

LEARNING OBJECTIVES

After reading this chapter, you should:

1. Realize that the marketing channel can be viewed as a social system as well as an economic system.
2. Understand that behavioral processes such as conflict, power, role, and communication are inherent behavioral dimensions in marketing channels.
3. Be aware of how conflict emerges in marketing channels.
4. Know the major causes of channel conflict.
5. Be familiar with the effects of channel conflict.
6. Recognize the major issues involved in managing channel conflict.
7. Be familiar with the concept of power as it applies to the marketing channel.
8. Be aware of the basic research findings concerning the use of power.
9. Be alert to the concept and use of roles in marketing channels.
10. Have an appreciation for how behavioral processes can distort the flow of communications in marketing channels.

PRNewsFoto/Burger King Corporation

110

FOCUS ON CHANNELS

Burger King's One Dollar Whopper Junior Has Created a Grown-Up Power Struggle in the Marketing Channel

Burger King's franchisees want to have it their way when it comes to pricing the products they sell in their stores. To make their point about having this pricing power, the franchisees' national association representing a group of unhappy Burger King franchisees has filed a lawsuit in federal court claiming that the franchisor, Burger King, is dictating the maximum prices at which the franchisees can sell certain items on their menu. Of particular concern is the WHOPPER JR., which Burger King wants the franchisees to sell for $1 as part of its "Value Menu" of one-dollar items to satisfy a growing value-conscious consumer segment and to compete with McDonald's and Wendy's one-dollar offerings. Well, a number of the franchisees say that they are losing money when they sell the WHOPPER JR. for just $1 and resent being forced into this money-losing pricing strategy. But

Burger King argues that it needs to have the power to control prices, especially when such pricing power is necessary to respond to strategic competitive challenges by rival fast-food chains. Indeed, the future competitiveness and viability of the entire Burger King franchise system could be at stake. But the franchisees involved in the lawsuit don't buy this argument. They believe that the power to set their own prices in what they perceive to be their own best interests is a crucial part of maintaining their status as independent businesses.

So, it looks like the pricing battle over the WHOPPER JR. has created a whopper of a conflict in the channel between franchisor and franchisee that only the courts will be able to settle.

Source: Based on: Richard Gibson, "Burger King Franchisees Can't Have It Their Way," *Wall Street Journal* (January 21, 2010): B1, B5.

In Chapter 1 we defined the marketing channel from a managerial perspective and discussed channel structure in terms of the allocation of distribution tasks within the channel in accordance with the economic principles of specialization and division of labor as well as contactual efficiency. Chapters 2 and 3 discussed some of the background knowledge needed by the channel manager. Such fundamentals as the economic basis for the emergence of various channel participants, the characteristics of the participants, and the environmental constraints within which channel participants operate, were discussed.

In this chapter we turn to another kind of knowledge needed by the channel manager—a knowledge of the **behavioral dimensions** of the channel. An understanding of the behavioral dimensions of marketing channels is necessary because the marketing channel is not simply a rationally-ordered economic system devoid of social interactions and processes.[1] On the contrary, the marketing channel is very much a social system subject to the same behavioral processes characteristic of all social systems.[2] Consequently, understanding the behavioral processes occurring in marketing channels and having the ability to apply this knowledge in the development and management of the marketing channel, are important parts of the channel manager's job.[3]

The Marketing Channel as a Social System

A **social system** can be defined as:

> ... the system generated by any process of interaction on the sociocultural level, between two or more actors. The actor is either a concrete human individual (a person) or a collectivity.[4]

When these individuals or collectivities (firms or agencies) interact as members of the marketing channel, an **interorganizational social system** exists. The channel may no longer be viewed simply as an economic system affected solely by economic variables. Rather, the fundamental behavioral dimensions present in all social systems—such as conflict, power, role, and communications processes—come into play.[5]

In this chapter we discuss the behavioral processes of conflict, power,[6] role, and communication in a marketing channel's context. The emphasis will be on showing how these behavioral processes operate in the channel and on their importance to the channel manager in the development and management of the channel.

Conflict in the Marketing Channel

Much of the discussion throughout this text is based on an underlying assumption of trust, commitment, and cooperation among channel members, with an emphasis on building viable relationships to achieve distribution objectives. Indeed, channel strategy and management could not possibly be implemented effectively unless channel members trust each other, are able and willing to make a commitment to the channel relationship in terms of human and capital resources, and are willing to cooperate with each other.[7] But given that the marketing channel is a social system, there is no escaping the fundamental behavioral dimension inherent in all social systems—**conflict**. While there are many definitions of conflict, in the context of the marketing channel, conflict exists when a member of the marketing channel perceives that another member's actions impede the attainment of his or her goals. As Stern and Gorman state,

> *In any social system, when a component perceives the behavior of another component to be impeding the attainment of its goals or the effective performance of its instrumental behavior patterns, an atmosphere of frustration prevails. A state of conflict may, therefore, exist when two or more components of any given system of action, e.g., a channel of distribution, become objects of each other's frustration.*[8]

As an example of the emergence of conflict in marketing channels, consider the marketing channels for automobiles. The Big Three domestic auto manufacturers—GM, Ford, and Chrysler—are linked with independent dealers to form the marketing channels (and therefore social systems) for the distribution of U.S. automobiles. All three manufacturers record revenues and profits upon delivery of cars to the dealers. Hence, large inventories on dealer lots show up as favorable revenue, and profit results for manufacturers, so they relentlessly push dealers to order cars. But from the dealers' perspective, these large inventories are highly burdensome to finance when retail sales slow down. Such discrepancies between what is good for the manufacturers and what is good for the dealers have led to substantial conflict between the parties. The auto dealers perceive the manufacturers' behavior to be impeding their opportunity to control expenses, while the manufacturers view the dealers' resistance to carrying more cars as inhibiting their quest for sales and profit growth. Thus, manufacturers and auto dealers can become objects of each other's frustrations, especially during periods of slow retail auto sales.[9]

Conflict versus Competition

Conflict in the marketing channel should not be confused with competition, which also occurs in the channel.[10] Competition is behavior that is object-centered, indirect, and impersonal. Conflict, on the other hand, as shown in the preceding discussion is direct, personal, and opponent-centered behavior. Thus, in a conflict situation it is not the forces of the impersonal market that firms attempt to overcome, but other firms in the system with whom they are in conflict. Schmidt and Kochan make this distinction:

> *In the process of both competition and conflict the goals (of the various units) are perceived to be incompatible, and the units are striving respectively to attain these goals. In this context, competition occurs where, given incompatible goals, there is no interference with one another's attainment. The essential difference between competition and conflict is in the realm of interference or blocking activities.*[11]

Illustrations of the distinction between competition and conflict can be seen in food marketing. One form of competition between supermarket retailers and manufacturers is the so-called battle of private versus national brands. To call this a battle, struggle, or conflict is, in a stricter sense, a misnomer because what is actually taking place is competition. The attempts by manufacturers and supermarket retailers to gain wider acceptance of their respective brands is usually impersonal and market-centered. In other words, the parties are not engaged in direct blocking activities aimed at impeding each other's goals of increased consumer acceptance of their brands. Rather, for the most part, the parties compete in the consumer market. The level of consumer acceptance for the manufacturer's versus the retailer's brands thus becomes a function of consumer preference.

On the other hand, some of the behavior of manufacturers and supermarkets relating to grocery coupons belongs very much in the realm of conflict. The situation, which has led to conflict between manufacturers and supermarkets, is the practice of supermarkets' encouraging misredemption by consumers. In one extreme case, several food chains were involved in a "coupon war." Some of the stores were accepting any number of coupons regardless of what products were purchased. Some people cashed in coupons worth several hundred dollars. The manufacturers viewed this behavior by the supermarkets as an attempt to make a mockery of their intended objectives in the use of coupons. Consequently, heated conflicts resulted between the manufacturers and supermarkets over how many coupons the manufacturers would redeem.[12]

Causes of Channel Conflict

Although research suggests that the causes of channel conflict are quite diverse, in essence most can be placed into one or more of the following seven categories of underlying causes of channel conflict: role incongruities, resource scarcities, perceptual differences, expectational differences, decision domain disagreements, goal incompatibilities, and communication difficulties.

Role Incongruities   A role is a set of prescriptions that define what the behavior of position members (such as a member of a marketing channel) should be. Any given member of the marketing channel has a series of roles that he or she is expected to fulfill. For example, a franchisor is expected to provide extensive management assistance and promotional support to franchisees. In return, franchisees are expected to operate in strict accordance with the franchisor's standard operating procedures. If either the franchisor or franchisee deviates from the given role (for example, if the franchisee decides to institute some of his or her own policies), a conflict situation may result. We will discuss the concept of role as it applies to the marketing channel in greater depth later in this chapter.

Resource Scarcities   Sometimes conflict stems from a disagreement between channel members over the allocation of some valuable resources needed to achieve their respective goals. A common example of this is the allocation of retailers between a manufacturer and wholesalers. The retailers are viewed by both the manufacturer and the wholesaler as valuable resources necessary to achieve their distribution objectives. Frequently, the manufacturer will decide to keep some of the higher volume retailers as **house accounts** (stores to which the manufacturer will sell directly). This leads to objections by the wholesaler over what is considered to be an unfavorable allocation of this resource (the retailers). This kind of dispute often leads to conflict.

Another important example of resource scarcity as a cause of conflict involves site selections in franchised channels. In this case, the resource is the market in which particular franchisees operate. In any given market, existing franchisees serving that market can come into conflict with the franchisor if the franchisor establishes new franchisees in that market that could take business away from the existing franchisees. Some franchisees have gone so far as to initiate lawsuits to prevent franchisors from establishing new franchises outlets in what they perceive to be "their" market.[13]

Perceptual Differences   **Perception** refers to the way that an individual selects and interprets environmental stimuli. The way such stimuli are perceived, however, is often quite different from objective reality. In a marketing channel context, the various channel members may perceive the same stimuli but attach quite different interpretations to them.[14] A common example of this in the marketing channel is in the use of point-of-purchase (POP) displays. The manufacturer who provides these usually perceives POP as a valuable promotional tool needed to move products off a retailer's shelves.[15] The retailer, on the other hand, often perceives point-of-purchase material as useless junk that serves only to take up valuable floor space. A manufacturer of hardwood floors, for example, produced what it thought were beautiful four-color brochures illustrating the use of its floors in magnificent homes. These were meant to be given to customers at the point of purchase as a way of conveying the quality, beauty, and range of applications for the flooring. Several thousands of these brochures were sent to a major home center retailer along with a floor display. But rather than put the brochures with the display, the retailer used them mainly to crumple up as carton packing material for merchandise returns!

Expectational Differences   Various channel members have expectations about the behavior of other channel members. In practice, these expectations are predictions or forecasts concerning the future behaviors of other channel members.[16] Sometimes these forecasts turn out to be inaccurate, but the channel member who makes the forecast will take action based on the predicted outcomes. By doing so, a response behavior can be elicited from another channel member, that might not have occurred in the absence of the original action. In effect, a self-fulfilling prophecy is created. A case-in-point involved Aamco, the nation's largest transmission repair business. Extended warranties offered by auto manufacturers were expected to significantly reduce future transmission repair business for Aamco's franchisees. This expectation of reduced business led many of these franchisees to push for a reduction of franchise royalty fees from 9 percent to 5 percent and to an expansion of their territories. A bitter conflict ensued, with the parent Aamco arguing that it needed the higher royalty rates in order to advertise and promote more aggressively in the face of the expected reduced prospects for future transmission repair business.

Decision Domain Disagreements   Channel members explicitly or implicitly carve out for themselves an area of decision-making that they feel is exclusively theirs. In contractual channel systems, such as a franchise, these decision domains are quite explicit and are usually spelled out meticulously in the franchise contract. McDonald's, for example, has a detailed manual specifying the allocation of decision-making responsibilities between the franchisor and the franchisee. But in the more traditional, loosely-aligned channels comprised of independent firms, the decision domains are sometimes "up for grabs." Hence, conflicts can arise over which member has the right to make what decisions.

A traditional and pervasive example of this has been in the area of pricing decisions. Many retailers feel that pricing decisions are in their decision-making domain.[17] Some of the manufactures supplying these retailer, however, believe that they should have a say in price-making decisions.

The conflict between Burger King and its franchisees over pricing of the WHOPPER JR. discussed in the Focus item at the beginning of this chapter is a clear example of conflict caused by a decision domain disagreement involving price: Burger King believes that the decision to charge $1 for the WHOPPER JR. was in its decision domain while the franchisees suing Burger King believe this pricing decision should be in their domain.[18]

Goal Incompatibilities   Each member of the marketing channel has his or her own goals. When the goals of two or more of the members are incompatible—which happens often—conflict can result. A case-in-point of conflict in the channel caused by goal incompatibility can be seen in a conflict that emerged between Redbox, a company that offers $ 1-per-day DVD rentals through vending machines, and movie studios Universal and Fox.[19] Redbox's 18,000 DVD vending machines are located in major retailers such as Walmart, Kroger, and many others. Redbox has grown spectacularly by making current DVDs available to millions of consumers while they shop at the rock-bottom price of one dollar for a day's rental. Redbox's main goal is to continue to grow its highly successful vending machine-based DVD channel. To do so, Redbox needs to have plenty of current, low-priced DVDs available to stock its vending machines. But Universal and Fox believe that Redbox's pricing strategy of $1 rentals will undermine their goal of selling more of their DVDs at higher prices. Hence, both Universal and Fox have barred third-party distributors from supplying Redbox with videos produced by Universal and Fox Studios as early as other retailers get them. In response, Redbox launched a lawsuit against both Universal and Fox arguing that Universal and Fox Studios' action undermines Redbox's goal of making the widest possible selection of DVDs available to the largest number of consumers at the lowest possible prices through its vast network of in-store vending machines.

Communication Difficulties   Communication is the vehicle for all interactions among the channel members, whether such interactions are cooperative or conflicting.[20] A foul-up or breakdown in communications can quickly turn a cooperative relationship into a conflicting one. Consider the case of AlphaGraphics, a franchiser of printing services with more than 250 franchised outlets in the United States and abroad. Many of the franchisees were disgruntled due to what they felt was a lack of adequate support from the franchisor. The franchisees would send their royalty payments to AlphaGraphics and then receive virtually no information about how their money was being spent to help improve their businesses. Some of the franchisees were so irate that they sued the franchisor. AlphaGraphics claimed that it needed better information from the franchisees. For example, less than half of the franchisees were sending in the monthly financial statements requested by AlphaGraphics.

To resolve the conflict, AlphaGraphics completely revised its franchise contract with stipulations requiring much more openness about how the franchisor was spending the royalties paid by the franchisees, but also requiring the franchisees to provide detailed and timely financial data to AlphaGraphics.

Effects of Channel Conflict

The key question about the effects of conflict from the channel manager's point of view is how conflict affects channel efficiency. Does conflict reduce the efficiency with which distribution objectives are achieved? Can it increase efficiency? Might it not have any effect at all?[21] Before discussing these relationships we define more precisely what we mean by channel efficiency. **Channel efficiency** is:

> *The degree to which the total investment in the various inputs necessary to achieve a given distribution objective can be optimized in terms of outputs.*[22]

The greater the degree of optimization of inputs in carrying out a distribution objective, the higher the efficiency, and vice versa. These inputs can include anything necessary to achieve the distribution objective. For example, a manufacturer may set a distribution objective of getting 80 percent of its wholesalers to carry a new product line. Suppose that in an attempt to achieve this objective, the manufacturer encounters strong resistance from wholesalers, most of whom feel that they are already carrying too much inventory from this manufacturer. The resulting conflict could cause the manufacturer to direct its sales force to spend an extraordinary amount of time and effort to convince the reluctant wholesalers to carry the new line. In this example, extra input (time and effort of salespeople) would be needed to achieve the distribution objective, and this extra input could be measured in added costs.

Negative Effect—Reduced Efficiency   Figure 4.1 illustrates the most commonly-held belief about the effect of conflict on channel efficiency. It shows a negative relationship indicating that, as the level of conflict increases, channel efficiency declines.

An example of this relationship can be seen in situations such as the following: A large wholesaler (W) carries similar products from two manufacturers M_1 and M_2. At some point M_1 notices that the wholesaler has reduced purchases from him. M_1 is concerned about the reduction and makes a decision to attempt to regain the previous volume level from this wholesaler. A distribution objective has now been set by M_1 to regain the previous volume from W. The level of input that M_1 uses to achieve this objective will determine the level of channel efficiency achieved. Suppose M_1, after talking to W, learns that the latter is doing quite well with the products from M_2 and feels that

FIGURE 4.1
Conflict and Channel
Efficiency—Negative
Effect

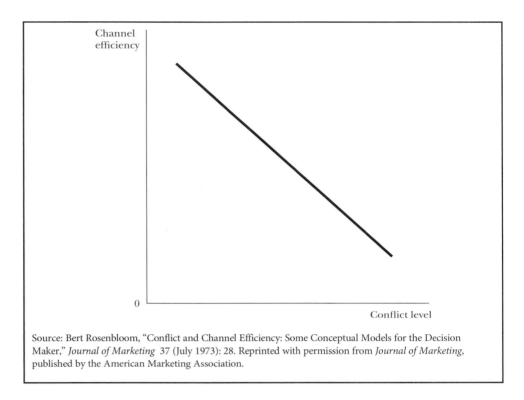

Source: Bert Rosenbloom, "Conflict and Channel Efficiency: Some Conceptual Models for the Decision Maker," *Journal of Marketing* 37 (July 1973): 28. Reprinted with permission from *Journal of Marketing*, published by the American Marketing Association.

he cannot carry more products from M_1. M_1 becomes angry and threatens W to cut off other product lines that W still purchases and finds very profitable. Yet suppose, as a reaction to the threats from M_1, W simply further reduces purchases from M_1. A conflict situation has now been created whose level continues to increase with each subsequent action of the two channel members. M_1 not only finds it necessary to devote more and more sales effort to get W to give in, but also increases advertising expenditures to create more consumer pull for added leverage on W to carry the new product line. It has now become increasingly difficult for M_1 to move products through the channel. That is, M_1 has to use higher levels of inputs (personal selling and advertising) to do so.

No Effect—Efficiency Remains Constant   Another possible relationship between conflict and channel efficiency is shown in Figure 4.2. In this relationship, the existence of conflict has caused no change in channel efficiency. Hence, the effect of conflict on input levels necessary to achieve distribution objectives is insignificant.

This type of relationship is thought to exist in channels that are characterized by a high level of dependency and commitment among the channel members. In other words, the parties to the conflict, consciously or unconsciously, are aware of the necessary nature of their relationship to one another. They feel that their need for each other to achieve their respective distribution objectives is so great that the conflict has no more than a superficial effect on their efficiency in operating the channel to achieve these objectives. In effect, the channel members learn to live with the conflict so that even in the face of hostilities and acrimony, channel efficiency is not affected.

Positive Effect—Efficiency Increased   Figure 4.3 shows a third possible effect of conflict on channel efficiency. Here conflict is shown to cause an increase in channel efficiency. An example will help to illustrate this possibility. A wholesaler finds that a manufacturer with whom a very profitable relationship had been enjoyed has decided

FIGURE 4.2
Conflict and Channel Efficiency—No Effect

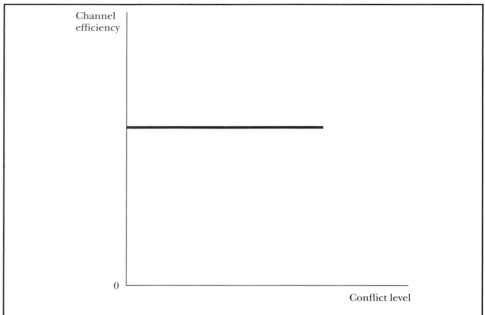

Source: Bert Rosenbloom, "Conflict and Channel Efficiency: Some Conceptual Models for the Decision Maker," *Journal of Marketing* 37 (July 1973): 28. Reprinted with permission from *Journal of Marketing*, published by the American Marketing Association.

FIGURE 4.3
Conflict and Channel Efficiency—Positive Effect

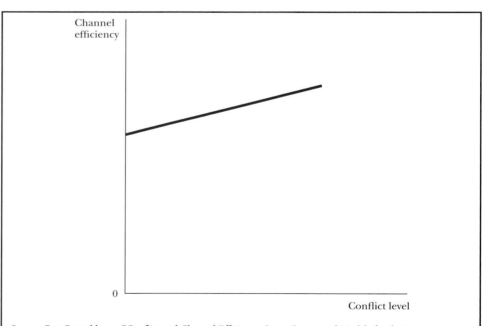

Source: Bert Rosenbloom, "Conflict and Channel Efficiency: Some Conceptual Models for the Decision Maker," *Journal of Marketing* 37 (July 1973): 29. Reprinted with permission from *Journal of Marketing*, published by the American Marketing Association.

to bypass the wholesaler with certain products and sell these directly to the retailers. The wholesaler at first reacts angrily toward the manufacturer's behavior. The seeds of conflict might develop further and ultimately lead to a conflict situation that could negatively affect channel efficiency for one or both of the parties to the conflict (see Figure 4.1). The conflict might, however, serve as an impetus for either or both of the channel members to reappraise their respective policies. For example, the wholesaler might overcome his or her anger and focus on his or her own performance and find it lacking. The wholesaler might find that the previous level of selling effort on behalf of some of the manufacturer's products was not as high as it could have been. Thus, he or she might view the manufacturer's behavior as justified under the circumstances and attempt to make some changes to do a more effective selling job.

The manufacturer might also reexamine the policies and find efforts in support of the wholesaler to be lacking. The manufacturer may decide that more special efforts and inducements are necessary to maintain the support of the wholesaler.

The result of this two-party reappraisal could be a reallocation of inputs based on the comparative advantages of each channel member for performing the distribution tasks necessary to achieve their respective distribution objectives. The reallocation of inputs between the two channel members stemming from the reappraisal could represent a better division of labor resulting in increased channel efficiency for one or possibly both channel members.[23]

Conflict and Channel Efficiency—General Curve   By combining the three models, a general curve showing the possible effects of conflict on channel efficiency results. This is shown in Figure 4.4.

FIGURE 4.4
Conflict and Channel Efficiency—General Curve

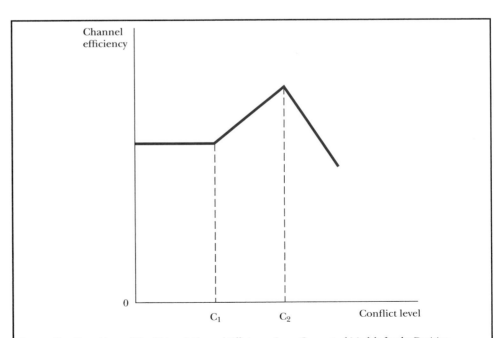

Source: Bert Rosenbloom, "Conflict and Channel Efficiency: Some Conceptual Models for the Decision Maker," *Journal of Marketing* 37 (July 1973): 29. Reprinted with permission from *Journal of Marketing*, published by the American Marketing Association.

In Figure 4.4 the level of conflict from 0 to C_1 suggests a tolerance range over which the conflict has no effect on channel efficiency. Over the range C_1C_2, the effect of conflict is positive, while beyond C_2, the effect is negative. The level C_2 in Figure 4.4 represents a threshold effect of conflict. Once the tolerance range is passed, the higher the level of conflict between C_1C_2, the greater the level of channel efficiency. Beyond C_2 (the threshold level), the greater the conflict level, the lower will be the level of channel efficiency.

Managing Channel Conflict

Our discussion on conflict in the marketing channel points to the following four generalizations:

1. Conflict is an inherent behavioral dimension in the marketing channel.
2. Given the numerous causes from which conflict may stem, it is a pervasive phenomenon in marketing channels.
3. Conflict can affect channel efficiency.
4. Various levels of conflict may have both negative and positive effects on channel efficiency, or possibly no effect.

The literature on the nature, causes, and effects of conflict in the marketing channel, though by no means definitive, does make a case for the significance of conflict in the channel. Although the channel manager does not have a set of precise principles or guidelines to refer to while attempting to manage conflict in the marketing channel, some approaches have been discussed in the literature. These will be discussed in terms of helping the manager (1) detect conflict or potential conflict, (2) appraise the possible effects of conflict, and (3) resolve channel conflict.

Detecting Channel Conflict   In practice, conflict is usually spotted after it is well-developed and obvious. This "after the fact" approach to the detection of channel conflict is unsatisfactory because the potentially negative effects of the conflict may have gotten a head start and may already be festering. So, it is better if the channel manager has some kind of "early warning system."

In what was perhaps the first study aimed at finding a method for early detection of channel conflict, Foster and Shuptrine suggest that a channel member can help spot potential conflict areas by surveying other channel members' perceptions of his or her performance.[24] The research on which their suggestion is based measured retailers' perceptions of wholesalers' and manufacturers' performances in five distribution-related tasks. In order to be of real value, however, the study noted that these perceptual measurements would have to be taken on a regular and continuing basis. Such regular surveys of channel members to help spot potential conflict are just as relevant today as they were when Foster and Shuptrine suggested this approach almost four decades ago. But today, with the availability of the Internet and widespread use of email, such surveys can be done much more quickly and easily electronically.

Surveys of channel members to identify areas of conflict can also be conducted by independent research firms. Not only might the outside research firm or consultant have greater expertise in designing and executing this type of study, but the independence of the outside party helps to avoid bias.

Surveys of channel members' perceptions of potential conflict areas can also be performed by outside parties such as trade associations or trade magazine publishers. *Industrial Distribution* magazine, for example, periodically conducts a comprehensive survey of manufacturer versus wholesaler perceptions about a wide variety of issues. Table 4.1 provides an excerpt from one of these studies.

TABLE 4.1 EXCERPT FROM *INDUSTRIAL DISTRIBUTION* MAGAZINE SURVEY OF MANUFACTURER VERSUS DISTRIBUTOR PERCEPTIONS ABOUT ADVANTAGES OF USING DISTRIBUTORS

ADVANTAGES OF SELLING THROUGH DISTRIBUTORS	PERCENTAGE OF RESPONDENTS PERCEIVING ADVANTAGE							
	TOTAL		MANUFACTURERS OF:			DISTRIBUTORS: NUMBER OF SUPPLIERS		
	MANUFAC-TURERS	DISTRI-BUTORS	COMMODI-TIES	NONCAPTIAL GOODS	CAPITAL EQUIPMENT	UP TO 25	25–100	100+
Wider market coverage and sales effort	72	66	72	69	68	65	66	69
Local, more frequent contact	54	60	54	44	64	64	59	53
Local inventory/ distributor warehouses	57	68	60	57	62	59	66	88
Distributor assumes credit risk	18	36	19	13	23	31	36	43
Distributor handles billing/invoicing	14	28	16	7	17	29	21	40
Manufacturers can ship in quantity	14	6	17	3	6	8	3	7
Distributor handles service/installations	9	28	8	18	17	38	25	19
Reduced sales expenses	24	29	25	15	19	33	28	22
Other	3	1	3	3	—	—	2	2

Source: "Manufacturer/Distributors Issues and Answers," *Industrial Distribution* Cahners Publishing Co. (March 1987): 48.

On the left-hand side of Table 4.1 are listed eight specific advantages of selling through distributors. The numbers to the right are the percentage of respondents (manufacturers and distributors) who perceived them as advantages. For instance, 72 percent of the manufacturers and 66 percent of the distributors agree that it is an advantage to use distributors to gain "wider market coverage and sales effort." Although this represents a difference in perception, it is not a very large one. Much larger discrepancies exist for "distributor assumes credit risk," where twice as many distributors (36 percent) saw this as an advantage of selling through distributors, as compared to only 18 percent of manufacturers. A similar disparity exists for "distributor handles billing/invoicing" (manufacturers 14 percent, distributors 28 percent). The greatest discrepancy in perception concerning the use of distributors is over the advantage of using distributors to "handle service/installations," where only 9 percent of the manufacturers saw this as an advantage as compared to 28 percent of the distributors.

Such discrepancies in perceptions on the part of manufacturers and distributors detected by studies such as these can be valuable in helping channel members to uncover areas of the relationship that might result in conflict.

The **marketing channel audit** offers another approach for uncovering potential conflict between channel members.[25] The term channel audit suggests a periodic and regular evaluation of key areas of the relationship of a given channel member with other members. In the process of appraising various areas of the relationship, potential conflicts are more likely to be detected. A case-in-point involved a large tire manufacturer who performed a marketing channel audit. One of the key areas evaluated was the manufacturer's promotional support for the retailers. A surprising finding in this area, and one that had the potential for generating conflict, involved the manufacturer's use of point-of-purchase promotional material. It turned out that the manufacturer's and the retailer's perceptions of the value of the POP material were very much at odds. The manufacturer perceived the material as an important and valuable dealer aid for helping the retailers sell to customers who had come into their stores. The retailers, on the other hand, perceived it as superfluous junk that did not help them solve their main promotional problem, which was how to get customers into the store in the first place! Thus, they felt that the manufacturer was letting them down by not providing promotional support where they *really* needed it. This perceptual difference (see the discussion earlier in this chapter on perceptual differences as a cause of conflict) over promotional strategy had planted the seeds of conflict. The advance warning provided by the channel audit, however, enabled the manufacturer to make appropriate changes and thus avoid the conflict.

Distributors' advisory councils or **channel members' committees** offer another approach to early detection of channel conflict. These groups consist of top management representatives of the manufacturer and key executives from a select group of distributors and/or dealers. Such groups meet on a regular basis to discuss a wide range of channel issues and strategies. Though not concerned primarily with channel conflict issues, these councils or committees provide a forum for exposing potential areas of conflict between channel members that might otherwise go unnoticed. The role of distributors' advisory councils or channel members' committees will be discussed in more detail in Chapter 9.

Appraising the Effect of Conflict   A growing body of literature has been emerging to assist the channel manager in developing methods for measuring conflict and its effects on channel efficiency. For example, Pruden, in one of the earliest attempts to measure conflict in a marketing channel setting, developed a scale for measuring the intensity of conflict between producers and distributors of building products.[26] Rosenberg and Stern investigated a channel for household durable goods and developed a scale for measuring the intensity of channel conflict associated with four different causes.[27] Pearson measured the intensity of conflict in a channel of distribution for grocery products and then attempted to relate this conflict measure to the performance of the channel.[28] Taking a somewhat different approach, Lusch measured channel conflict in terms of the frequency of disagreements between manufacturers and dealers in the automobile industry and related this conflict measure to dealer performance.[29] Using a conjoint measurement technique, Brown developed an approach for measuring the relative importance of conflict issues to the overall levels of conflict in a hypothetical channel conflict situation, and Brown and Day developed a method for measuring both the intensity and frequency of conflict in a channel for automobiles.[30] In one of the more recent studies, Laskey, Nicholls, and Roslow developed an index for measuring channel conflict comprised of five perceptual and five behavioral elements of channel conflict.[31] Though their study was conducted in the boat industry, the conflict index developed may have application to a wide range of industries. Several other studies dealing with conflict measurement in marketing channels also appear in the literature.[32]

The significance of this work is that it demonstrates that methods can be developed for measuring conflict in real-world marketing channels. While this work is still very much on the frontiers of marketing thought, it should *not* be dismissed by the channel manager as little more than so much esoterica suitable only for the academic. As more of this kind of research is done, the methods involved are likely to become more refined and applicable to a wider range of channels. Conceivably, in the future, such work may prove to be of real practical value to those responsible for channel management. For the present, most attempts to measure conflict and appraise its effects on channel efficiency will still be made at a conceptual level that relies on the manager's subjective judgment.

Resolving Conflict   When conflict exists in the channel, the channel manager should take action to resolve the conflict if it appears to be adversely affecting channel efficiency. A significant body of empirical work has emerged over the years to guide the channel manager in attempting to resolve channel conflict.

Rosenberg made several suggestions for dealing with channel conflict almost four decades ago that are just as relevant today.[33]

1. **A channel-wide committee** might be established for periodic evaluations of emerging problems related to conflict. Such a committee could function in a crisis management capacity by providing a forum for the diverse points of view of the various channel members. Rosenberg suggests that some committee members could be appointed as representatives by the manufacturer, while distributors and retailers could elect their own representatives to the committee.

2. **Joint goal-setting** by the committee (or some other vehicle)—that takes into account the goals and special capacities of the various channel members, the needs of consumers, and environmental constraints—would help to mitigate the effects of conflict. Even if it is not possible to develop joint goals that are in perfect harmony, the dialogue attendant to the attempt would in itself be beneficial to reducing conflict.

3. **A distribution executive** position might be created for each major firm in the channel.[34] The individual(s) filling this position would be responsible for exploring the firm's distribution-related problems. Further, this individual could try to make other executives in the firm more aware of the potential impact of conflict on the firm's efficiency. Finally, he or she could seek to identify the current shape of conflict issues in the channel.

Another approach for resolving channel conflict, suggested by Weigand and Wasson, is to have the parties involved submit to arbitration.[35] Weigand and Wasson point to the following five advantages of arbitration for resolving channel conflicts:

1. *Arbitration is fast.* The parties to a dispute can be quickly informed that a quarrel exists and told the time of a hearing. The evidence can then be heard by a panel and the decision rendered—all within a few weeks.

2. *Arbitration preserves secrecy.* Outside parties can be barred from the hearings. Decisions that are not matters of public record can be kept secret.

3. *Arbitration is less expensive than litigation.* There is an element of "corner-cutting" that takes place, that reduces the cost of a tolerable decision.

4. *Arbitration confronts problems in their incipient stage when they are easier to resolve.* The attitude can become: "We have a potential problem here; let us solve it before positions and options get too fixed."

5. *Arbitration often takes place before industry experts.* In many instances, the arbitrator or the arbitration panel is composed of those who know the industry and its practices. Some argue that this produces a fairer decision.

Zikmund and Catalanello propose using organizational development (OD) concepts and methods for resolving conflict in the marketing channel. Basically, this involves using behavioral scientists as consultants to develop educational strategies for helping channel members to cope with changes that may foster conflict.

Still another approach is offered by Dwyer and Walker. Based on behavioral laboratory research that simulated a channel environment, Dwyer and Walker argue that specialized bargaining and negotiation procedures might be fruitfully applied to the resolution of channel conflict.[36]

The research conducted by Schul, Pride, and Little mentioned earlier in this chapter produced findings suggesting that negative conflict can be reduced if the channel manager emphasizes a participative leadership style that attempts to reflect the needs and predispositions of the channel members.[37]

Research on conflict resolution, conducted by Dant and Schul in franchised channels for fast food, suggests that direct interaction between channel members that focuses on joint problem-solving can be effective in resolving conflict.[38] However, the authors also found that when the conflict involves high stakes, complexity, or major policy issues, and if the franchisee dependency level on the franchisor is high, resolution of the channel conflict is likely to require the intervention of an outside (third) party.

The feasibility and applicability of any of these approaches for resolving conflict will vary for different kinds of channels and under differing sets of circumstances.[39] For example, a relatively small manufacturing firm distributing through several relatively small wholesalers may find it somewhat impractical to set up a channel-wide committee or establish the position of distribution executive. A group of franchisees in conflict with their franchisor may feel that a resort to litigation in the courts would offer them a more powerful weapon than arbitration for resolving conflict. Face-to-face meetings may be effective when the number of channel members is small. However, recent research by Hibbard, Kumar, and Stern in a channel involving a Fortune 500 durables goods manufacturer selling through 1,200 independent dealers found that meeting to "work things out" through constructive discussion can actually *aggravate* rather than mitigate channel conflict.[40] Why? In a channel setting involving a one-to-many rather than a one-to-one relationship, it is nearly impossible for top management of the large manufacturer to engage in a constructive discussion with many hundreds of channel members. So, the job of conducting dialogue with the dealers must be relegated to lower-level representatives of the manufacturer who lack the authority to make the kind of policy changes that might resolve the conflict to the dealer's satisfaction. The result is frustration and potential exacerbation of the conflict because, from the dealers' perspective, the manufacturer is not engaging in serious dialogue.

What is more important than the specifics of any of these particular approaches is the underlying principle common in all of them. It may be stated as follows: *Timely action on the part of some party to the conflict is needed if the conflict is to be successfully resolved. Conversely, if conflict is simply "left alone," it is not likely to be successfully resolved and may get worse.* In short, channel conflict is not likely to go away by simply ignoring it. Rather, channel members must make an effort to resolve it.[41] Regardless of the specific approaches used in making that effort (with the possible exception of the one-to-many channel situation outlined in the Hibbard, Kumar, and Stern study), as long as they promote candid dialogue among the channel members and help to bring differences out in the open, they are likely to be beneficial for resolving conflict.[42] As in so many instances of conflict in realms other than that marketing channel, solutions involve some measure of compromise. But compromises are not possible without substantial dialogue between the parties to the conflict.[43] Thus, it is up to the channel manager to develop approaches for doing this, whether it is through arbitration, a channel-wide committee, organizational development, bargaining processes, or even a "peace conference" between channel members. This approach has been employed in the food industry between manufacturers and supermarkets. According to the Food Marketing Institute (FMI), the trade association for supermarkets, a formal peace treaty may well be the best way to resolve the ongoing conflicts between manufacturers and supermarkets over such issues as merchandising deals, pricing, terms of sales, slotting fees, and forward buying, that have been fraught with conflict.[44]

Power in the Marketing Channel

Numerous concepts of power exist in the literature. Dahl, for example, argues that "A has power over B to the extent that he can get B to do something that B would not otherwise do."[45] Miller and Butler argue that power simply refers to a person's ability to control the behavior of others.[46] Etziono views power as the capacity to overcome part or all of the resistance to change in the face of opposition.[47] Price suggests that the essence of power is the capacity to influence the behavior of others.[48]

As we can see from this discussion, there are numerous views on the concept of power. Yet there is a common theme running through all of them: power has to do with the capacity of one party to control or influence the behavior of another party or parties. Thus, when we use the term **power** in a marketing channel context we are referring to *the capacity of a particular channel member to control or influence the behavior of another channel member(s).* For example, when Hewlett-Packard Co. heard that Dell Computer Corp. was considering selling its own line of Dell printers, HP decided to drop Dell as a channel member.[49] Dell had been selling HP printers for more than eight years, often bundling them with package deals on Dell computers. HP apparently felt that its action might dissuade Dell from implementing its plan. But Dell paid little attention to HP's move because, as the world's largest PC maker at that time, it enjoyed a powerful position as a reseller of printers. Not only can Dell have printers made to sell under its own name, but other manufacturers such as Lexmark, Xerox Corp., and Seiko Epson Corp. were only too happy to continue selling printers through Dell.

The key to determining which channel members are likely to have the most power in any given situation lies in an understanding of the sources or bases of power available to the channel members.

Bases of Power for Channel Control

French and Raven define a **power base** as the source or root of the power that one party exercises over another. They delineate five such power bases: reward power, coercive power, legitimate power, referent power, and expert power.[50]

Reward Power   This source of power refers to the capacity of one channel member to reward another if the latter conforms to the influence of the former. This power base is present in virtually all channel systems. The rewards are usually manifested in the perceived or actual financial gains that channel members experience as a result of conforming to the wishes of another channel member. Channel members—whether at the producer, wholesaler, or retailer levels—will, in the longer run, remain viable members only if they can realize financial benefits form their channel membership.[51] There are exceptions to this general proposition when the channel relationship is based on contractual agreements that constrain the abilities of channel members to cease membership in an unprofitable channel. But even in this case, when the contract expires, the channel member who believes that the financial rewards from the channel have not been sufficient, is likely to leave the channel.

An example of a manufacturer's attempt to solicit channel members on the basis of reward power is shown in Figure 4.5, an advertisement that appeared in Discount Store News, a trade magazine that has widespread following among discount stores and mass merchandisers. The headline of the advertisement for the Hoover SteamVac Deluxe says "All Aboard." Later copy in the advertisement continues the train metaphor by saying, "You'll want to climb on for sales and profit, ... if you're not carrying SteamVac Deluxe with the attached tools, you could be left standing at the station." The manufacturer, Hoover, is holding out the reward of high sales and profits in an attempt to get retailers to carry this product. In the advertisement Hoover also promises additional rewards in

FIGURE 4.5 Trade Magazine Advertisement Illustrating the Use of Reward Power

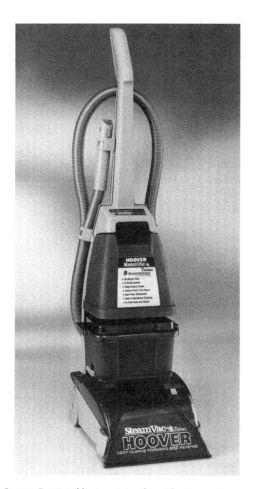

All Aboard.

Hoover® SteamVac™ Deluxe with on-board tools and 5-brush agitator.

It's been said that companies choose to lead, follow or get out of the way. Quite obviously Hoover chooses the first route.

SteamVac Deluxe with attached tools is one smart innovation to an already hot selling product line. You'll want to climb on for sales and profit, backed by a heavy year-round network TV campaign.

Look for SteamVac Deluxe on national TV.

So get on board. Because if you're not carrying SteamVac Deluxe with attached tools, you could be left standing in the station.

When it comes to supporting you, nobody does it like Hoover.

SPARC AWARDS
PARTNERSHIPS IN POWER RETAILING

NOBODY GETS THE DIRT LIKE HOOVER. NOBODY.™

© 1997 The Hoover Company

Source: *Reprinted by permission from The Hoover Co.*

the form of continuing promotional support to keep the product moving off retailers' shelves. Hoover's success in getting retailers to become channel members who will aggressively sell this product will depend heavily on the power to reward members for their services. If the manufacturer fails to convince the channel members that it is able to offer them sufficient rewards, the manufacturer's influence attempts in terms of getting channel member support and follow-through are unlikely to meet with much success.

Coercive Power   **Coercive power** is essentially the opposite of reward power. In this case a channel member's power over another is based on the expectation that the former will be able to punish the latter upon failure to conform to the former's influence attempts. Coercive power occurs frequently in channel relationships. Take, for example, the case of the Gallo Wine Co., the nation's largest manufacturer of wines. Gallo, which produces a huge variety of wines, used a form of full-line forcing (see Chapter 3) to coerce independent wine distributors to carry more than 40 different brands of its wine, even though most of the distributors did not want many of these brands. Given Gallo's great power, the distributors had little choice. Gallo simply would not sell the dealers its fast-moving, highly profitable wines unless they were willing to carry many of Gallo's slow moving and, in some cases, poor-quality wines as well. Most of the distributors could not afford to do without the better Gallo products, and so they were forced to acquiesce to Gallo's coercion. The situation became so onerous for the distributors that the Federal Trade Commission (FTC) stepped in and ordered Gallo to stop the practice.

In this example, Gallo's capacity to use coercive power stemmed from its great size and dominant position in the industry. It was thus able to exert very substantial pressure on its wholesalers to conform to its wishes. If they did not choose to behave as Gallo wanted them to, Gallo could cut them off with no significant loss to itself. This is typical of the operation of coercive power in the marketing channel. The firms that are able to use it are either large or in a very advantageous position—one resulting from a near-monopoly or a formal contractual status such as that enjoyed by many franchisors. In the absence of external constraints (such as government action if a law is violated, as in the case of Gallo), powerful channel members are in a position, at least in the short run, to dominate the weaker channel members, even to the extent of using threats and coercion.

We should point out that such powerful firms are not limited to producers or manufacturers. Wholesalers and retailers in a dominant position by virtue of their size or monopoly positions in particular trade areas may also resort to the use of coercive power. For example, Walmart, the world's largest retailer, has come under attack from manufacturers, wholesalers, and smaller retailers who claim that Walmart has used coercive power to enforce its channel policies. A case in point is Walmart's announcement that it would no longer buy through brokers and sales representatives but only direct from manufacturers. This announcement created such a stir that an organization, the Coalition of Americans to Save the Economy (CASE), was formed to combat Walmart's power play. Figure 4.6 shows an advertisement used by CASE to solicit members to fight back.

Legitimate Power   This power base stems from internalized norms in one channel member which dictate that another channel member has a legitimate right to influence the other, and that an obligation exists to accept the influence. In an intraorganizational system, as typified by a large business firm, legitimate power is pervasive and routinely accepted. Indeed, it would be extremely difficult for the organization to operate without it. At each level in the chain of command, the subordinate recognizes that his or her superior has a legitimate right to influence behavior and that the obligation exists to accept such influence. Thus, a salesperson reporting to a sales manager expects to take orders from the sales manager, who in turn takes orders from the vice president of marketing, and so on.

In an interorganizational system such as the marketing channel, on the other hand, legitimate power does not operate in the same fashion and is by no means a pervasive or well-accepted phenomenon. Given that many channels are comprised of independent business firms, there is no definite superior-subordinate relationship, and there are no clear-cut lines of authority or chains of command. It is only in contractually-linked

FIGURE 4.6
Advertisement
Complaining about the
Use of Coercive Power

Who loses when 'Power Buyers' dictate how products can be brought to market?

We all do!

Since late last year, Wal-Mart has systematically denied suppliers the right to use brokers and independent representatives to bring products to market. Suppliers who for years have used brokers as their cost-effective and efficient sales organizations are forced to give up the way they do business or lose access to Wal-Mart's retail empire.

Who loses by this type of power play? We all do.

Suppliers lose the right to choose their own sales representation—and potentially much more later on. Many small, entrepreneurial businesses—which create six out of 10 U.S. jobs—lose access to the very professionals who enable them to successfully compete. Retailers lose ground in their efforts to establish a "level playing field" of fair competition. Consumers lose the wide variety of retail formats and product offerings that keep the market vibrant and the local economy growing.

And, of course, brokers lose their livelihoods, not for lack of performance, but because of a unilateral dictate.

In fact, as many buyers and merchandisers will tell you, even the Power Buyer loses, as it struggles to perform the broker's function and thrust the higher sales cost on its suppliers.

CASE: Fighting for your rights

CASE is a recently formed non-profit coalition. Our mission is to preserve—through both education and advocacy—the right of suppliers to determine how they will bring products to the marketplace. Our goal is to maintain an open market in which everyone has an equal opportunity to compete.

If you share these goals and want to help, please call our toll-free hotline or mail in the coupon.

Because your rights are worth fighting for.

COALITION OF AMERICANS TO SAVE THE ECONOMY

Competition Keeps America Working

2233 Wisconsin Avenue, N.W., Suite 500, Washington, D.C. 20007

1-800-752-4111

YES, please send more information on CASE.

Name _____

Title _____ Phone _____

Address _____

City State _____ Zip _____

Retailer ☐   Supplier ☐   Broker Rep ☐

Source: Courtesy, Coalition of Americans to Save the Economy.

channels that anything approaching an organizational structure based on legitimate power exists. Consequently, for more loosely-aligned marketing channels, legitimate power is a virtually non-existent power base. A manufacturer selling through independent wholesalers, for example, cannot order the wholesaler to do something based on any legitimate power vested in the manufacturer that the wholesaler is obliged to accept. The manufacturer can, of course, offer inducements or use coercion (for example, threaten to drop the wholesaler) if the wholesaler refuses to comply with the manufacturer's influence attempt. But in these cases, the power bases involved would be reward and coercion, respectively, rather than a legitimate base.

In general then, the channel manager operating a loosely-aligned channel cannot rely on a legitimate power base to influence channel members. He or she must instead resort either to other power bases or to restructuring the channel into a more formal system such as a contractually-linked vertical system in an attempt to increase a legitimate power base.

Some of the strongest legitimate power bases are held by franchisors because legitimacy accrues to the franchisor through the franchise contract agreement with its franchisees. These contracts almost always spell out the specific rights and obligations of the parties. With few exceptions, the bulk of the legitimate power base is held by the franchisor rather than by the franchisees. For example, Southland Corporation, the franchisor of 7–11 Stores, has a contractual agreement with its franchisees that places Southland in a highly dominant position. Southland is entitled to 52 percent of its franchisees' gross profits. Southland also handles all of the franchisees' bookkeeping and sends them a monthly check for their net profits. If a franchisee's performance falls below a specified level, Southland can close down the franchisee with only 72 hours' notice.

Referent Power   When one channel member perceives his or her goals to be closely allied to, or congruent with, those of another member, a referent power base may exist. In other words, they may see each other as being in the same reference group. Hence, when this situation prevails, an attempt by one of the channel members to influence the behavior of the other is more likely to be seen by the latter as beneficial to the achievement of his or her own goals. For example, retailers or wholesalers who want to be identified as "leading," "high quality," or "prestigious" firms will use as their reference group those manufacturers whose products are consistent with the image they are attempting to project. This, in turn, gives those manufacturers a referent power base over the intermediaries who seek to sell their products. In the case of manufacturers who have very desirable products, the referent power base can be quite high, thus providing the manufacturers with substantial influence over channel members selling their products. See the advertisement in Figure 4.7 by Sylvan Learning Center, a franchisor of educational programs. The ad stresses the pride the company feels in being a world leader in supplementary education that has enhanced the lives of more than a million children. This advertisement, which appeared in the Wall Street Journal, was aimed not only at seeking new franchisees but also at reinforcing a sense of belonging and pride that Sylvan franchisees feel by being associated with a renowned educational organization.

Giant channel members such as Macy's, the world's largest department store chain, can also be influenced by referent power. To maintain and enhance its fashion image, which is crucial to Macy's competitive strategy to differentiate itself from discount mass merchandisers such as Walmart and Target, its shelves must be stocked with well-known national brands such as Polo by Ralph Lauren, Liz Claiborne, Jones Apparel Group, and many others.[52] Macy's is much larger than most of the manufacturers whose brands it sells and is thus capable of wielding substantial coercive power to force concessions on price and terms of sale from these manufacturers. Its inclination to exercise such power, however, is mitigated somewhat by its need to be associated with fashionable merchandise. So, in a very real sense the referent power available to manufacturers of well-known branded products can offset, at least to some degree, the coercive power available to giant retailers.

Expert Power   This base of power is derived from knowledge (or perception of knowledge) that one channel member attributes to another in some given area. In other

FIGURE 4.7
Advertisement Illustrating the Use of the Referent Power Base

Source: Courtesy of Sylvan Learning Centers.

words, one channel member's attempts to influence the other's behavior is based on superior expertise.

Expert power is quite common in the marketing channel. Many manufacturers provide retailers with management assistance relevant to various phases of the retailer's operations. Procter & Gamble's (P&G) Efficient Assortment Program, which helps retailers selling P&G products to carry the right assortments of P&G products to meet the particular needs of consumers in different markets with a minimum of excess inventory, is one such example. The program is advertised in trade publications such as *Discount Store News* to inform existing and potential channel members about the program. Retailers will often make changes based on the advice received out of respect for the expertise of the manufacturer or wholesaler who offers it.

In franchised channels, expertise is a crucial power base for the franchisor to influence franchisees. Though obviously the franchisor may also use other power bases, particularly legitimacy, the use of expert power is extremely important in gaining cooperative compliance from franchisees. The franchisees expect the franchisor to offer expertise on a regular and continuing basis. Indeed, one of the principal values of the franchise to the franchisee is the expertise of the franchisor in the particular line of business.[53] The advertisement for Dairy Queen shown in Figure 4.8, that appeared in the *Wall Street Journal*, stresses the expert power base with the headline "Franchise with Experience." This indicates to prospective franchisees that Dairy Queen knows what it is doing through the best teacher of all—experience. Franchisees that become a part of the Dairy Queen organization would therefore have the benefit of the kind of expertise that only the experience of a well-established franchise organization can provide.

FIGURE 4.8
Advertisement
Incorporating the
Expert Power Base in
a Franchised Channel

Source: "Dairy Queen", "DQ" and the ellipse logo are trademarks of American Dairy Queen Corp. Used with permission.

Expert advice can also flow up the channel from franchisee to franchisor because sometimes franchisees are in a position to "feel the pulse" of the consumer market better than the franchisor. Consider the case of Subway sandwich shops.[54] During the "Great Recession" of 2007-2008, the $5 footlong sandwich became a huge success. But it was a Subway franchisee not the franchisor that came up with the idea for the footlong. Stuart Frankel, the owner of two small Subway shops in Miami noticed that sales were slow on the weekends. He began to offer footlongs for $5 instead of the usual $6 and sales exploded by double digits! Within weeks, the $5 footlong became a big hit throughout the entire Subway franchise system. Apparently, Frankel's expertise, which in this case was his ability to "read the market," was lacking at franchisor, Subway's headquarters.

Using Power in the Marketing Channel

From the standpoint of the channel manager in the producing or manufacturing firm, power must be used to influence the behavior of the channel members toward helping the firm to achieve its distribution objectives.[55] Thus, the channel manager must use the available power bases in order to exercise power in the marketing channel. This raises two basic channel management issues: (1) Which power bases are available? and (2) Which base or bases should be used?

Identifying the Available Power Bases In most cases, dealing with the issue is straightforward because the power bases available to the channel manager at any given time can usually be readily identified. Generally, they are a function of the size of the producer or manufacturer relative to channel members, the organization of the channel, or a particular set of circumstances surrounding the channel relationship.[56]

With respect to size, typically a large producer or manufacturer dealing with relatively small channel members at the wholesale or retail levels has high reward and coercive power bases available and vice versa. On the other hand, giant retailers such as Home Depot, Walmart, and Amazon.com are larger than most of the manufacturers supplying them. Hence, such "power" or "dominant" retailers have high levels of reward and coercive power relative to the mostly smaller manufacturers from whom they buy. Such differences in the amount of power available to channel members (asymmetry) do not mean that the larger and more powerful channel member will automatically take advantage of its greater reward and coercive power bases.[57] It merely indicates that the potential for doing so exists.

In terms of channel organization, channels that are contractually linked, such as in a franchised system, provide the franchisor with a strong legal power base that derives from the contract. Conversely, conventional loosely-aligned channels offer the producer or manufacturer virtually no legal power base.

Finally, at any time in the channel relationship, circumstances may change, leading to an association with a particular power base.[58] For example, the expert power base may be available to the manufacturer in the early stages of the introduction of a new product because the manufacturer may be the only channel member who knows how to promote the product effectively. Consequently retailers may conform closely to the manufacturer's promotional "recommendations" because the manufacturer has the necessary expertise.

While there may be some situations where the availability of power bases may be difficult to identify, in most cases a careful appraisal of the basic channel relationship with respect to size and organizational structure of the channel, and any changing circumstances relevant to the channel relationship, will reveal the bases of power available.[59] For example, a study of food brokers and food wholesalers in channels of distribution for grocery products found that, at least in this particular channel, the amount of power of one channel member over another was not pervasive but related to specific issues and policy areas.[60] Similarly, an exploratory study involving retail florists supplied by wholesalers found that, due to the nature of the product, (an undifferentiated commodity), the amount of power available to any wholesaler is quite limited because the florists could easily buy similar flowers from a host of other wholesalers.[61]

Selecting and Using Appropriate Power Bases   Which bases should be used to exercise power in the marketing channel is a more difficult and complex issue for the channel manager to deal with than the previous issue of identifying the power bases available.[62] As Frazier and Antia point out:

> *Power can be used in a heavy-handed fashion to pressure channel members to take undesirable actions. No doubt, its use is contributing to worsened channel relationships in a variety of channel contexts. However, it is also important to recognize that power can be used to enhance the nature of relational exchange between channel members.*[63]

So, in order to use power to enhance, rather than inhibit, channel relationships, the channel manager needs to know how effective the various power bases are in influencing channel members to carry out the firm's distribution objectives, what possible reactions the channel members might have to the use of different power bases, and how the use of various power bases will affect the overall channel relationship. While there is as yet no definitive set of principles or guidelines for dealing with the issue of power base usage in the marketing channel, a growing body of analysis and empirical research has emerged to provide some useful insights into this issue.

A number of studies have focused on channel member reactions to the use of various power bases by the manufacturer and the effects that such usage may have on the overall channel relationship. Beier and Stern argue that noncoercive power bases are likely to lead to a higher level of satisfaction for the "weaker" channel members[64] Hunt and Nevin tested this hypothesis in franchised channels for fast foods.[65] Their findings do provide empirical support for the hypothesis. Based on these findings, Hunt and Nevin argue that, at least in a franchised channel, avoiding the use of coercive power by the franchisor is likely to yield the following results:

1. Franchisees are likely to have higher morale.
2. Franchisees are more likely to cooperate with the franchisor.
3. Franchisees are less likely to terminate their contracts.
4. Franchisees are less likely to file individual suits against the franchisor.
5. Franchisees are less likely to file class action suits.
6. Franchisees are less likely to seek protective legislation such as the "Franchise Full Disclosure Act" (1970).

A subsequent study by Lusch in franchised channels of distribution for automobiles reinforced Hunt and Nevin's findings.[66] The study found that the use of particular power bases by the manufacturers can have an impact on channel conflict. Specifically, it was found that the use of noncoercive bases of power (reward, legitimate, referent, and expert) tends to reduce channel conflict, whereas coercive power tends to increase conflict. Similar findings were also reported in a study of marketing channels for automobiles conducted by Brown and Frazier.[67]

In another study based on a simulated marketing channel comprised of graduate and undergraduate students, Dwyer found that reward, referent, legitimate, and expert power bases tend to promote a more cooperative channel relationship.[68] More recent studies also generally support this proposition. For example, Schul and Babakus, in a study involving 106 franchised real estate brokers representing the six major franchised real estate organizations doing business on a national basis, found that reward power tended to have a positive impact on the channel relationship while the use of coercive power had a negative impact.[69] Another study by Hunt, Mentzer, and Danes involving 67 manufacturers' representatives selling plumbing, heating, and air conditioning equipment in industrial markets found a statistically significant relationship between legitimate, referent, and expert power with the probability of channel members complying with an influence attempt based on these sources of power.[70]

In one of the few studies conducted outside the United States on power use in the marketing channel, Wilkinson investigated a channel of distribution for a major household durable product in Australia. The study found a direct relationship (though a weak one) between noncoercive bases of power and the degree of satisfaction of channel members with the channel relationship.[71]

In another study of marketing channels outside the United States, Johnson et al. examined how Japanese distributors of U.S.-manufactured consumer goods perceive the use of power sources by both themselves and their U.S. suppliers.[72] The study found that the Japanese relate differently to the use of power than is typical of Western cultures. For example, a U.S. channel participant attempting to influence a Japanese partner in a subtle, nonaggressive way by American standards may still be viewed as behaving in an overly aggressive manner by the Japanese. On the other hand, a U.S. channel member who seeks to make a point strongly with what is believed to be an aggressive use of power may not be taken seriously by Japanese channel members.

Finally, in a recent international study of marketing channels for beer in the People's Republic of China, Lee found that 95 indigenous beer distributors participating in the study had perceptions of power usage by their suppliers similar to those found for comparable distributors in Western marketing channels.[73] Specifically, the Chinese distributors divided power into aggressive and nonaggressive categories similar to the coercive and noncoercive dichotomy typical of Western distributors' perceptions of power employed by suppliers. Furthermore, as is the case in Western channels, the Chinese distributors were more satisfied with their suppliers when noncoercive (nonaggressive) power was used rather than coercive (aggressive) power. Indeed, the study found that the association between the use of noncoercive power and channel member (in this case, beer distributor) satisfaction was even greater in China than in the West.

Although no exact channel management implications on the use of power in the marketing channel can be gleaned from this research, several general inferences can be derived:

1. Some form of power must be exercised in order to influence channel member behavior.
2. The effectiveness of various power bases in influencing channel member behavior is probably situation-specific.[74] Depending on the particular structure of the channel

involved, the nature of the channel members, and the environmental context in which power is exercised, the effectiveness of the various power bases will vary.[75]

3. The exercise of power as well as how it is used can affect the degree of cooperation and conflict in the channel and can affect the levels of channel member satisfaction with the channel relationship.[76]

4. The use of coercive power appears to foster conflict and promote dissatisfaction to a greater degree than the other power bases.

5. The use of coercive power, especially in contractually-linked channels, can reduce the stability and viability of the channel and is likely to increase the probability that the coerced channel members will seek outside assistance (such as government action) to reduce the coercion.

While these generalizations should not be considered definitive, universal, or "carved in stone," they do offer the channel manager at least some degree of research-based guidance on the use of power in the marketing channel.[77] When coupled with sound managerial judgment, they may prove to be of real value in the development and management of the marketing channel.[78]

Role in the Marketing Channel

As with so many terms springing from behavioral sciences, there is a good deal of disagreement on the definition of role. The concept of role has been used to denote prescription, description, evaluation, and action. An acceptable definition of **role** for our purposes is:

A set of prescriptions defining what the behavior of a position member should be.[79]

In applying this definition to the marketing channel, Gill and Stern argue that the channel, when viewed as a social system, comprises a series of recognizable positions, with each organization (manufacturers, wholesalers, retailers) occupying one of these positions in the channel.[80] Each position has a set of socially defined prescriptions (roles) delineating what constitutes acceptable behavior for the occupants of these roles.[81] For example, a basic role prescription of the manufacturer's position may be to maximize the sales of his or her particular brand of product. The manufacturer is expected to compete with "social peers" (other manufacturers who are competitors) for market share. This role also prescribes aggressively promoting his or her brand to compete effectively. The role prescriptions of independent wholesalers, however, are likely to be quite different because the position occupied by the wholesaler will have a different set of prescriptions associated with it. For example, to the wholesaler, the product brand of this particular manufacturer may be just one of many sold. The wholesaler's role prescriptions are thus defined by his or her position as a wholesaler in competition with other wholesalers. This role may prescribe building sales with whatever brands are most heavily-demanded by retailers. If the manufacturer or wholesaler steps too far out of the prescribed role, conflict can result, which may adversely affect performance or even their survival. For example, if the wholesaler continues to carry a large stock of the manufacturer's brand even though similar products from several other manufacturers are more in demand at a given time, the wholesaler risks loss of sales volume and the loss of some retail accounts. On the other hand, the manufacturer could not "go along" with the wholesaler for an extended period of time if the latter were to stop buying from him or her and begin buying heavily from the other manufacturers for, clearly, this would serve to reduce the manufacturer's sales volume and market share.

Roles in the marketing channel do not necessarily stay the same. They can and do change over time. Developments in the automobile industry illustrate how the roles of channel members can change and therefore deviate from what had generally been perceived to be the normal or usual roles of the channel members.[82] Over the past two decades there has been substantial growth in "megadealers"—very large auto retailers carrying many different brands of cars. These large and powerful dealers are unhappy with the auto dealers' traditional role in the marketing channel because they feel they get little if any voice in the planning that's done by manufacturers. Many dealers want their role to expand and the megadealers have the power to make that happen. The dealers want this broader role in the channel to include being consulted on the decision-making process in product development, formulation of marketing strategies such as dealers' incentives, and being able to specify the provisions of warranty programs. Merely selling the cars that manufacturers decide to produce, in conformance with marketing strategies provided solely by the manufacturer, has become too narrow a role for an increasing number of automobile dealers.

As an example of how clearly defined roles help foster better understanding among channel members, consider the case of steel service centers. Steel service centers are a type of independent wholesaler operating in the industrial market. They buy steel in bulk from the major steel producers and often process it into various dimensions and forms. They maintain substantial inventories of these products, providing quick availability to their customers, usually manufacturers of such products as computers, small appliances, lighting fixtures, furniture, fire engines, restaurant and hotel equipment, air-conditioning systems, and many others. These steel service centers generally enjoy excellent relations with steel producers and their customers. One of the principal reasons for this, according to industry sources, is the clear understanding among the channel members of their respective roles.[83] For example, the role of steel producers as a direct supplier to smaller users has been decreasing because of rather high minimum order requirements (20 to 50 tons for some types of steel products). The steel producers saw in the steel service centers channel members who were ideally suited for filling the role of supplier to the smaller customers. The smaller customers in turn expected the steel service centers to provide processing such as cutting and shearing, storage, and the ability to deliver within short periods of time and in quantities smaller than the steel producers will handle. Though the "marriage" is not perfect, most indications are that these channel relationships are characterized by a very high level of understanding among the members of their respective roles.

In summary, a familiarity with the concept of role in the marketing channel fosters more extensive and sharper thinking about what is expected of each of the channel members. This is likely to promote the development of more congruent roles among channel members, which in turn should result in more cooperative and efficient channels.

From the channel manager's standpoint, the key value of the role concept is that it helps to describe and compare the expected behavior of channel members and provides insight into the constraints under which they operate. For example, the channel manager can use the concept of role to formulate such questions as the following:

1. What role do I expect a particular channel member to play in the channel?
2. What role is this member (potential or existing) expected to play by his or her peers (other firms of a similar type)?
3. Do my expectations for this member conflict with those of his or her peers?
4. What role does this member expect me to play?

By asking these kinds of questions about the roles of the various channel members, a clearer understanding of what part each is expected to play is more likely to emerge. This will help to minimize the confused and haphazard relationships that too often exist among channel members and thus reduce the possibility of role conflicts.[84]

Communication Process in the Marketing Channel

Communication has been described as "the glue that holds together a channel of distribution."[85] Communication provides the basis for sending and receiving information among the channel members and between the channel and its environment.[86] Communication activities undertaken by channel members create a flow of information within the channel, that is necessary for an efficient flow of products or services through the channel. Indeed, it is almost impossible to visualize an efficient product or service flow without an effective information flow.[87] Consequently, the channel manager must work to create and foster an effective flow of information within the channel. The approaches and methods used to do this will be discussed in detail in Chapters 9 and 12. Our purpose in introducing the subject of communication in the present chapter is to provide a backdrop for some of the behavioral problems attendant to communication in the marketing channel. A familiarity with the behavioral problems of channel communications is necessary if the channel manager is to avoid the pitfalls involved in attempting to create an effective information flow through the channel.

Behavioral Problems in Channel Communications

A pioneering study by Wittreich stands out as a landmark effort in pointing to the behavioral problems affecting communications in the marketing channel.[88] Although Wittreich's analysis deals specifically with the problems encountered by large corporate manufacturers attempting to communicate with relatively small independent retailers, his findings also provide insight for understanding behavioral communications problems in other channel structures; therefore, where appropriate, we have pointed to different kinds of channels to which his findings may also apply.

Wittreich delineates two basic behavioral problems that create communication difficulties between the manufacturer and small independent retailer in the channel structure: (1) differences in goals between manufacturers and their retailers, and (2) differences in the kinds of language they use to convey information.

Differing Goals   Corporate management in large manufacturing firms is characterized by a growth psychology. In corporate marketing strategy this translates into an aggressive effort to build sales volume. Those who participate in the marketing channel are thus expected to join whole-heartedly in this quest. On the other hand, this growth goal is not shared by the typical retail dealer. Rather, the small to medium-sized independent retailer is characterized by an essentially static psychology; that is, he or she is often satisfied with the existing level of business or, at the most, a modest and gradual expansion.

This difference in goals accounts for a large part of the communication problems in the marketing channel between large manufacturers and small retailers. To illustrate this, Wittreich cites the example of dealer incentives, which are widely used by manufacturers. Such incentives usually take the form of financial stimuli to the retailers to increase their sales volume. The volume discount is one such example, whereby an increasingly larger percentage discount on purchases is given to the dealer as volume increases. Manufacturers are frequently puzzled by their inability to communicate the benefits of these discounts effectively so that dealers will enthusiastically attempt to take advantage of them. Wittreich explains this communication problem as follows:

> *To understand such a puzzling point of view, we should recall ... that while management [of manufacturers] is characterized by the unrelenting surge of expansion, the*

dealer is often not the least bit interested in going beyond the level of business he has achieved. The latter, enjoying a good living as far as he is concerned, is not only satisfied to stay at his present level, but is annoyed at what he considers a supplier's "prodding" him into moving beyond that level. Furthermore, he not only resents such prodding, but considers it to be "unfair discrimination" in favor of dealers who are bigger than he is.[89]

Although this goal difference is presented in the context of large manufacturers distributing through relatively small retailers, the same problem may exist in other channel structures where one of the members is large and the others relatively small. Thus, it may hold for channels such as (1) a manufacturer distributing through small wholesalers, (2) a large wholesaler and small retailers, (3) a franchisor and comparatively small franchisees, and possibly others. Obviously, without empirical evidence, we cannot know this with any degree of certainty, but the extension of Wittreich's findings to other channel structures involving large and small members is certainly reasonable—particularly because the goal differences that Wittreich mentions are not a function of a particular kind of business such as manufacturer per se but rather appear to be closely related to the size of the firm and the philosophy of its management. A large wholesaler run by a professional management, for example, may have high growth goals that are inconsistent with those of the retailers through which the firm distributes.

With this in mind, the channel managers in large firms, whether producers, manufacturers, wholesalers, or service franchisors, should attempt to understand the goals of small channel members to learn whether they are much different from those of their own firms.

Language Differences   The other basic communication problem between the manufacturer and small retailer stems from the terminology or jargon used by professional corporate management in large manufacturing firms. Wittreich argues that although such language is well understood among professional managers, it is alien to the small retailer. To elucidate his point, he cites an example from the American brewing industry. Specifically, he asserts that the large brewers have a great deal of difficulty in communicating with small retail tavern owners.

> *The typical tavern owner is essentially not a businessman. He is not used to thinking in terms that are familiar to the businessman. To him "profit" is a high-falutin esoteric word used by wise guys who think they are better than he is. Being in business to "make money" he is more likely to respond to arguments or appeals which will help him do that than to arguments or appeals which are supposed to lead to "better profits." By the same token, talk about "merchandising" or "promotion" is likely to sail over his head. In order to get him to act, you have to speak to him in terms which are familiar and meaningful to him and which promise concrete rewards that he can grasp and understand.*[90]

Here again, Wittreich's argument may be applicable to other channel structures besides those consisting of a large manufacturer and small independent retailers to any channel structure characterized by a large corporate channel member dealing with significantly smaller channel members such as small wholesale distributors or franchisees. So, channel managers in large corporate organizations who distribute their products or services through smaller businesses need to make sure that they are speaking the "same language" in their channel communications.

Other Behavioral Problems in Channel Communications   Three other behavioral problems that can inhibit effective channel communications are those associated with perceptual differences among channel members, secretive behavior, and inadequate frequency of communication.

In the case of perceptual differences, channel members may perceive the same stimuli in different ways. One such difference, involving differing perception language, was discussed earlier in this chapter. Other perceptual differences, however, may distort communications and are not the result of differing perceptions of language. For example, such issues as delivery time may be perceived quite differently by various channel members.

One instance of this involved a manufacturer of a small portable hoist and a wholesaler with an exclusive franchise for the product. The manufacturer's first shipment to the wholesaler turned out to have 100 percent product defects. The wholesaler ended up having to take back every hoist sold. The manufacturer allowed the wholesaler to return the hoists and began work on correcting the defect. The manufacturer then became very cautious, wanting to be sure that the hoists were completely free of defects. This slowed up production, resulting in delivery times to the wholesaler of nine to ten months. The wholesaler complained bitterly to the manufacturer that customers were not willing to wait that long. The manufacturer's reaction was that if the wholesaler was not happy, it could easily find another wholesaler. The wholesaler's response was to sue the manufacturer for lost profits on orders not delivered on time. The manufacturer argued that under the circumstances, a delivery time of nine to ten months was reasonable. The wholesaler argued that a period of approximately 30 days was what is meant by a "reasonable" delivery time. The court found for the wholesaler, based on expert testimony that supported the wholesaler's perception of 30 days as a reasonable delivery time.

While this example involved the issue of delivery time, perceptual differences may occur among channel members on a wide variety of issues. It is therefore important that channel managers spell out such issues as delivery time, margin and discounts, return privilege, warranty provisions, and so forth, so that channel members have the same understanding as the manager. Channel managers must not mistakenly assume that "everybody knows" what a particular provision means or that "it is standard practice" in the industry. A little more care in this area is likely to make for more effective channel communications and minimize the possibilities of conflict and legal actions.

The tendency of channel members to behave in a secretive fashion can also inhibit effective channel communications, especially when this involves disclosure of a forthcoming promotional plan. Manufacturers are often reluctant to divulge many of the details of the plan to their channel members. By not divulging the plan before it is executed, the manufacturers fail to get potentially valuable feedback from middlemen on whether the plan will be appropriate, timely, and amenable to their support. Channel members also behave secretly because many of the participants in a given channel are also members of other competing channels. Thus the possibility of information leaks is high. Even though less effective coordination of efforts may result, the various channel members will often omit or distort information to guard against the transmittal of competitively sensitive information.[91]

We should point out that a certain amount of secrecy is often necessary in the channel. For example, in launching a major promotional campaign a firm frequently needs the element of surprise. By divulging the specifics of the campaign, the firm is more likely to lose this competitive advantage.

Unfortunately, there is no clear-cut answer as to when secrecy by channel members is a necessary form of behavior, and when it works to inhibit effective channel communications. Clearly, uniformly-high levels of secrecy under all circumstances are probably unnecessary. On the other hand, complete openness at all times is probably unwise. The channel manager must therefore decide the issue on an individual basis.

Finally, with regard to inadequate frequency of communication among channel members, a study by Mohr and Sohi in marketing channels for personal computers found that this could indeed inhibit effective channel communication. As the authors pointed out,

Infrequent communication may leave channel members feeling left out of the loop; downstream channel members may lack the necessary information to effectively merchandise and market a manufacturer's products. Hence, infrequent communication is associated with perceptions of lower communication quality.[92]

Although the authors caution about the generalizability of their findings (which were based on data from 125 computer retailers) to other channels, the association of infrequency of communication with lower quality of communication may well apply to a broad range of channels. This infrequency of communication problem appears to be exactly what happened to Chrysler Group LLC in its relationships with its 2,500 U.S. and international dealers.[93] Sergio Marchionne, the CEO of Italian auto maker Fiat also became the CEO of Chrysler when Fiat took over the bankrupt Chrysler in June of 2009. Yet, Marchionne did not directly communicate with the Chrysler dealers until September of 2010—well over a year since he became CEO of the merged organizations. Many of the dealers were upset and anxious about this lack of communications over such an extended period of time, especially given the tremendous turmoil created by the bankruptcy reorganization, the termination of hundreds of Chrysler dealers and the drastic decline in auto sales. Why had Marchionne taken so long to communicate with the dealers? He wanted to wait until his plans for new models were in place before communicating with the dealers. Apparently, he believed that keeping the dealers essentially in the dark for fourteen months until he had something exciting to communicate was preferable to communicating with the dealers when he had little of substance to share with them. But most of the dealers would rather have had more frequent communication from the CEO during such a trying time.

Summary

The marketing channel is characterized not only by economic processes but also by behavioral processes. The marketing channel may therefore be viewed as a social system affected by such behavioral dimensions as conflict, power, role, and communications processes. The channel manager needs knowledge of these behavioral dimensions as they operate in the marketing channel so that their effects can be incorporated into his or her decision making.

Conflict is an inherent behavioral dimension in marketing channels and is pervasive because it stems from many causes such as role incongruities, resource scarcities, perceptual differences, expectational differences, decision domain disagreements, goal incompatibilities, and communication difficulties. Conflict may have both negative and positive effects on channel efficiency, and in some cases no effect. The management of channel conflict involves three tasks: (1) detecting channel conflict, (2) appraising the effects of the conflict, and (3) resolving the conflict if it is having negative effects on channel efficiency. A variety of approaches can be used for detecting channel conflict, such as surveys of channel members' perceptions, channel audits, and distributors' advisory councils. The measurement of channel conflict has received considerable research attention, and a number of sophisticated methods now exist for measuring conflict and relating its effects to channel efficiency. While most of these methods have not been widely-used in practice, they can provide the channel manager with valuable insights for dealing with channel conflict. The resolution of conflict can be facilitated through the use of channel-wide committees, joint goal setting, distribution executives, arbitration, special organizations for gathering information, organizational development methods, specialized bargaining procedures, and joint problem solving. All of these approaches attempt to promote increased dialogue among the channel members in order to mitigate the effects of negative conflict.

Power is used in the marketing channel to influence the behavior of other channel members. Power is derived from five sources, or bases: (1) reward, (2) coercion, (3) legitimacy, (4) reference, and (5) expertise. The most fundamental and important issue facing the channel manager in the use if power in the marketing channel is deciding which power base or combination of power bases should be used to attain maximum influence over channel members, while at the same time avoiding conflict and promoting channel member satisfaction. This issue has received considerable research attention. The findings from this research can provide some guidance for using power in the marketing channel. Among the most important findings are that power effectiveness in the marketing channel appears to be situation-specific, that the use of power can affect the degree of cooperation and conflict in the channel and levels of channel member satisfaction, and that the use of coercive power appears to foster conflict and promote dissatisfaction to a greater degree than the other power bases.

Role, the set of prescriptions defining what the behavior of a position member should be, provides the channel manager with a basis for delineating what part he or she expects each channel member to play and what role the firm is expected to play in the marketing channel. By developing more congruent roles among the channel members, the channel manager is more likely to achieve a more effective and efficient marketing channel.

Communication flows within the channel are vital to the operation of the channel. However, behavioral problems such as divergent goals among channel members, language difficulties, perceptual differences, secretive behavior, and inadequate frequency of communication can cause distortions in the communications flow, which may reduce channel efficiency. The channel manager should therefore try to detect any behavioral problems that tend to inhibit the effective flow of information through the channel and resolve those problems before the communications process in the channel becomes seriously distorted.

Review Questions

1. A purely economic model of the marketing channel is inadequate. Explain.

2. Why does the channel manager need a familiarity with some of the behavioral processes occurring in the channel?

3. Discuss the distinction between conflict and competition in the marketing channel.

4. What are some of the underlying causes of conflict? Are these causes usually obvious? Are issues over which conflict may develop the same as the underlying causes?

5. Could more than one cause be associated with the development of conflict in the marketing channel?

6. Are the effects of conflict necessarily detrimental to channel efficiency? Explain.

7. How might conflict be a good thing in the marketing channel? Explain.

8. Discuss some of the means available to the channel manager for detecting channel conflict. Do you think they would be practical to use in the real world?

9. Discuss some of the approaches that the channel manager may use in attempting to manage conflict. Do all of these approaches share a common theme?

10. Why is it necessary to use power in the development and management of the channel?

11. What are the bases of power in the marketing channel? Is it possible to rank these bases according to their degree of effectiveness in influencing the behavior of another channel member before examining the particular set of circumstances or context of the influence attempt as it takes place in the channel?

12. How would a channel manager know which power bases are available?

13. Summarize what is known about the use of power in the marketing channel.

14. How can the channel manager use the concept of role to develop a more effective and efficient channel?

15. Discuss some of the behavioral problems that can "foul up" effective communications in the marketing channel.

Channel Issues for Discussion

1. Soon after the "Great Recession" of 2007–2008, food manufacturers and supermarkets got into what many industry observers describe as a pricing war. The supermarkets were upset because food manufacturers had been increasing the wholesale prices charged to supermarkets even though commodity prices and fuel costs to the manufacturers had been decreasing. The supermarkets felt caught in a profit squeeze because they could not pass on their higher costs to

price-sensitive consumers hurt by the recession. But the food manufacturers claimed they were in a profit bind as well because they were locked into contracts for commodities that were negotiated prior to the recession when prices were significantly higher. The conflict emerging from this pricing problem has caused some major supermarket chains to threaten to decrease shelf space allocated to national brands and to fill that space with more private brand products.

What do you think is the underlying cause of this conflict between the food manufacturers and supermarkets? How might it be resolved?

2. Bill Schwartz, the owner of Newvalue Supply, a medium-sized wholesaler of plumbing supplies, was furious. He had just gotten off the phone with the sales manager of Jefferson Industries, the manufacturer of a very profitable line of high-quality faucets that Newvalue had been selling for several years. "That SOB is now going to start selling the big home center accounts directly," fumed Bill Schwartz to his son Paul. "We've worked real hard to establish this line and then, when it finally gets going with some real volume, Jefferson wants to cut us out," he continued.

Discuss the possible underlying causes of the conflict that seems to be emerging in this situation.

3. Amoco, one of the nation's largest oil companies, has been forcing a number of its independent service stations to convert from full-service stations offering repair service to convenience stores or "gas only" stations. Thus the highly profitable repair part of the business will no longer be available to those station owners forced to convert. The franchised independent dealers have little choice but to give in to Amoco because the oil company typically owns the station's land and buildings and offers leases of only three years or less. This arrangement appears to vest all of the power with the producer and virtually none with the dealers.

Discuss this situation in light of the bases of power and the possible long-term effects on channel relationship.

4. "This is really out of bounds," remarked Lisa Johnston, the buyer of athletic footwear for a large chain of sporting goods stores. Ms. Johnston was referring to a new policy by Nike, the famous athletic shoe manufacturer, that required retailers

to place their orders six months in advance of delivery. "This is great for Nike because it enables them to plan their production effectively, but it makes life very difficult for us. Doesn't Nike know that retailing of athletic shoes is a fast-paced, highly competitive business? It's extremely hard to predict exactly what Nike shoes our customers will want that far in advance—and what about the other brands of athletic shoes we carry?" continued Ms. Johnston to an assistant buyer.

Does Nike understand the role of the retailer? Discuss.

5. In the summer of 2009, Walmart, the world's largest retailer, left no doubt about its enormous power in the marketing channel. Walmart announced to all manufacturers whose products it sells that they must adhere to Walmart's new "green" environmental initiative. The manufacturers must estimate and disclose the environmental costs of producing their products and then allow Walmart to use that information to develop a "green" rating system that will be disclosed to consumers on product labels. The cost of the "green" program will be borne entirely by the 100,000 Walmart suppliers. Although the program will take a number of years to fully implement, some parts of it may be in place by as early as mid-2011. Suppliers will not be able to opt out of this program. So all of them, from the largest to the smallest, will have to participate. If they do not, Walmart has made it clear that those suppliers will likely be dropped by the giant retailer.

What power base(s) appear to be in play in this situation? What do you think Walmart is trying to accomplish here by exercising its great power in the marketing channel?

6. As part of the U.S. government-initiated and -supervised bankruptcy reorganization of Chrysler Corp., almost 800 Chrysler dealerships were terminated. Many of those dealers felt that the forced closings by Chrysler of their businesses was grossly unfair and wanted to contest the closing either through arbitration or the courts. They could not do so, however, because the bankruptcy specifically prohibited arbitration or lawsuits against Chrysler. Indeed, one of the key reasons for pursuing the bankruptcy option was to gain protection from pushback from dealer lawsuits or arbitration actions. But the dealers

were able to lobby Congress to pass a law that would override bankruptcy protection and allow the dealers to pursue arbitration to stay in business as Chrysler dealers. Given the passage of the new law, many of the dealers looked to arbitration to keep their dealerships open.

Discuss the power shifting that seems to be occurring in the channel. Are there "good guys" and "bad guys" here? Explain in terms of the possible causes of the conflict and ensuing power struggle between Chrysler and its terminated dealers.

7. UPS Stores operate "pack and ship" stores on a franchise basis granted by the franchisor, UPS Inc. The stores not only provide pack and ship services but offer a variety of other products and services such as office supplies, copying, and notary services. The stores are also required by the franchisor to provide "drop off" services to customers. This refers to customers who do their own packing and then go online to purchase and pay for shipping labels directly from UPS. The customers then visit any UPS store to "drop off" their boxes at no charge to customers. UPS pays the UPS store $1 for each dropped off box. Many

of the UPS Stores franchisees do not like this policy. They argue that the online, direct-to-consumer channel is undermining the packing and shipping part of their business which accounts for the largest portion of their sales. Instead of bringing the items to be packed, weighed, and shipped at the UPS stores, customers can do this themselves. The UPS Stores franchisees argue that the $1 per box paid to them by UPS for drop-offs is not nearly enough to offset the lost revenue for its in-store packing and shipping. The franchisor sees the situation very differently. UPS argues that the drop-off policy helps to bring in new customers to UPS stores that would not have come before. This increased store traffic provides an opportunity for UPS Stores franchisees to sell these customers other products and services when they visit the stores. So, according to the franchisor, the drop-off program should be a net positive for franchisees.

Do you think the differing points of view between the franchisor UPS and the UPS Stores franchisees on the drop-off policy is a communications problem in the channel? Why or why not?

References

1. See, for example, F. Robert Dwyer, "Behavioral Dimensions in Marketing Channels," *Journal of Retailing* (Winter 1995): 329–330; Robert Dahlstrom and F. Robert Dwyer, "The Political Economy of Disribution Systems: A Review and Prospectus," *Journal of Marketing Channels* 2 no. 1,1992: 47–86; and Keun S. Lee, "A Framework of Channel Membership Involvement: Alienative, Calculative, and Moral Attitudinal Orientation," in *Developing in Marketing Science*, II ed. Kenneth D. Bahn (Blacksburg, Va: Academy of Marketing Science, 1988), 456–459.

2. For a seminal discussion of the marketing channel as a social system, see Louis W. Stern and Jay W. Brown, "Distribution Channels: A Social Systems Approach," in *Distribution Channels: Behavioral Dimensions*, ed. Louis W. Stern (New York: Houghton Mifflin, 1969), 6–19. See also Michael F. Foran and Anthony F. McGann, "A Scheme for Examining Marketing Channels as Social Systems," *Business Ideas and Facts* (Fall 1974): 51–54; Louis W. Stern and Torger Reve, "Distribution Channels as Political Economies: A Framework for Comparative Analysis," *Journal of Marketing* (Summer 1980): 52–64; James R. Brown and Sherman A. Timmins, "Substructural Dimensions of Interorganizational Relations in

Marketing Channels," *Journal of the Academy of Marketing Science* (Summer 1981): 163–173; Robert F. Lusch and James R. Brown, "Interdependency, Contracting, and Relational Behavior in Marketing Channels," *Journal of Marketing.* (October, 1996): 19–38.

3. For a related discussion see: Anna Watson and Richard Johnson, "Managing the Franchisor–Franchisee Relationship: A Relationship Marketing Perspective," *Journal of Marketing Channels* (January–March 2010): 51–68.

4. Talcott Parsons and Neil J. Smelser, *Economy and Society: A Study in the Integration of Economic and Social Theory* (New York: Free Press, 1956), 8.

5. Shelby D. Hunt, Nina M. Ray, and Van R. Wood, "Behavioral Dimensions of Channels of Distribution: Review and Synthesis," *Journal of the Academy of Marketing Science* (Summer 1985): 1–24.

6. For a seminal analysis of conflict and power in marketing channels, see John F. Gaski, "The Theory of Power and Conflict in Channels of Distribution," *Journal of Marketing* (Summer 1984): 9–29.

7. Russel P.J. Kingshott and Anthony Pecotich, "The Impact of Psychological Contracts on Trust and Commitment in Supplier-Distributor Relationships," *European Journal of Marketing* (Vol. 41, No. 9/10 2007):

1053–1072; Sunil Sahadev, "Economic Satisfaction and Relationship Commitment in Channels: The Role of Environmental Uncertainty, Collaboration Communication and Coordination Strategy," *European Journal of Marketing* (Vol. 42, No. 1/2 2008): 178–195; Rajiv Mehta, Trina Larsen, and Bert Rosenbloom, "The Influence of Leadership Style on Cooperation in Channels of Distribtution," *International Journal of Physical Distribution & Logistics Management* 26, no. 6 (1996): 32–59; Steven J. Skinner, Jule B. Gassenheimer, and Scott W. Kelley, "Cooperation in Supplier–Dealer Relations," *Journal of Retailing* (Summer 1992): 174–193.

8. Louis W. Stern and Ronald H. Gorman, "Conflict in Distribution Channels: An Exploration," in *Distribution Channels: Behavioral Dimensions*, ed. Louis W. Stern (New York: Houghton Mifflin, 1969), 156.

9. For a related discussion, see: Emily Maltby, "Chrysler Dealerships Fight Closings," *Wall Street Journal* (December 31, 2009): B2.

10. For a related discussion, see Rajiv P. Dant and Kent B. Monroe, "Dichotomy of Issue—Specific and Overall Perceptions: A New Paradigm for Channel Conflict and Cooperation Research," in *Philosophical and Radical Thought in Marketing*, eds. Fuat Firal et al. (Lexington, Mass: Lexington Books, 1988), 323–329.

11. Stuart M. Schmidt and Thomas A. Kochan, "Conflict: Toward Conceptual Clarity," *Administrative Science Quarterly* 17 (September 1972): 361. For further discussion on the distinction, see Louis W. Stern, Brian Sternthal, and C. Samuel Craig, "Managing Conflict in Distribution Channels: A Laboratory Study," *Journal of Marketing Research* (May 1973): 169–170.

12. Kate Zhao, "Retailers and Manufacturers Fight Coupon Fraud," *Wall Street Journal* (July 1, 2009): B5.

13. See Patrick J. Kaufmann and V. Kasturi Rangan, "A Model for Managing System Conflict During Franchise Expansion," *Journal of Retailing* (Summer 1990): 155–173.

14. Nan Zhou, Guijun Zhuang, and Leslie Sai-chung, "Perceptual Difference of Dependence and Its Impact on Conflict in Marketing Channels in China: An Empirical Study," *Industrial Marketing Management* (36, 2007): 309–321.

15. Cok Ouwerkerk, William Verbeke, Heino Hovingh, and Ed Peelen, "Retailers' and Manufacturers' Perceptions of the Temporary Display," *Journal of Marketing Channels* 6, no. 1 (1997): 1–16.

16. See, for example, J. Joseph Cronin, Jr., Steven J. Skinner, and L.W. Turley, "The Impact of Disconfirmed Expectations on Channel Conflict and Repurchase Intentions," in *Proceedings of the Annual Educators' Conference of the American Marketing Association*, ed. Robert F. Lusch et al. (Chicago: American Marketing Association, 1985), 172.

17. Timothy W. Martin, "CEO Denies Pricing War Between Grocers, Suppliers," *Wall Street Journal* (March 11, 2009): B3.

18. Richard Gibson, "Burger King Franchisees Can't Have It Their Way," *Wall Street Journal* (January 21, 2010): B1, B5.

19. "Hollywood vs. Redbox," *Business Week* (August 24 & 31, 2009): 038.

20. For an excellent discussion of the underlying theory of communicatins in marketing channels, see Jakki Mohr and John R. Nevin, "Communication Strategies in Marketing Channels: A Theoretical Perspective," *Journal of Marketing* (October 1990): 36–51.

21. For an excellent study related to these questions, see: Morys Z. Perry, "An Experimental Investigation of Conflict Response Behaviors and Performance Consequences in Manufacturer–Dealer Relationships: Do Issue Situations and Resolution Strategies Matter?," *Journal of Marketing Channels* (April–June 2009): 101–130; see also Kenneth A. Hunt, "The Relationship between Channel Conflict and Information Processing," *Journal of Retailing* (Winter 1995): 417–436.

22. Bert Rosenbloom, "Conflict and Channel Efficiency: Some Conceptual Models for the Decision Maker," *Journal of Marketing* (July 1973): 27.

23. For a related discussion, see Kathryn Frazer Winsted and Kenneth A. Hunt, "Functional Conflict in Channel Relationships," in *Proceedings of the Annual Educators' Conference of the American Marketing Association*, ed. Gary Frazier (Chicago: American Marketing Association, 1988), 244.

24. Robert J. Foster and Kelly F. Shuptrine, "Using Retailers' Perception of Channel Performance to Detect Potential Conflict," in *Proceedings of the American Marketing Association* (Chicago: American Marketing Association, August 1973), 110–123.

25. Reavis Cox and Thomas F. Schutte, "A Look at Channel Management," in *Proceedings of the American Marketing Association* (Chicago: American Marketing Association, August 1969): 99–105.

26. Henry O. Pruden, "Interorganizational Conflict, Linkage, and Exchange: A Study of Industrial Salesmen," *Academy of Management Journal* (September 1969): 339–350.

27. Larry J. Rosenberg and Louis W. Stern, "Conflict Measurement in the Distribution Channel," *Journal of Marketing Research* (November 1971): 437–442.

28. Michael M. Pearson, "The Conflict-Performance Assumption," *Journal of Purchasing* (February 1973): 57–69.

29. Robert F. Lusch, "Channel Conflict: Its Impact on Retailer Operating Performance," *Journal of Retailing* (Summer 1976): 3–12.

30. James R. Brown, "Toward Improved Measures of Distribution Channel Conflict," in *Proceedings of the Annual Educators' Conference of the American Marketing Association* (Chicago: American Marketing Association, 1977): 385–389; and James R. Brown and Ralph L. Day, "Measures of Manifest Conflict in Distribution Channels," *Journal of Marketing Research* (August 1981): 263–274.

31. Henry A. Laskey, J. A. F. Nicholls, and Sydney Roslow, "Management-Oriented Indices of Channel Conflict," *Journal of Marketing Channels* 2, no. 1 (1992): 87–103.

32. See, for example, Louis W. Stern, Brian Sternthal, and C. Samuel Craig, "Managing Conflict in Distribution Channels: A Laboratory Study," *Journal of Marketing Research* (May 1973): 169–179; Michael M. Pearson and John F. Monoky, "The Role of Conflict and Cooperation in Channel Performance," in *Proceedings of the Annual Educators' Conference of the American Marketing Association* (Chicago: American Marketing Association, 1976): 240–244; J. Stephen Kelly and J. Irwin Peters, "Vertical Conflict: A Comparative Analysis of Franchisees and Distributors," in *Proceedings of the Annual Educators' Conference of the American Marketing Association* (Chicago: American Marketing Association, 1977): 380–384; James R. Brown and Gary L. Frazier, "The Application of Channel Power: Effects and Connotations," in *Proceedings of the Annual Educators' Conference of the American Marketing Association* (Chicago: American Marketing Association, 1978): 266–270; and Michael Etgar, "Sources and Types of Intrachannel Conflict," *Journal of Retailing* (Spring 1979): 61–78.

33. Larry L. Rosenberg, "A New Approach to Distribution Conflict Management," *Business Horizons* (October 1974): 67–74.

34. For two related articles, see Bruce J. Walker, Janet E. Keith, and Donald W. Jackson, "The Channels Manager: Now, Soon or Never?" *Journal of the Academy of Marketing Science* (Summer 1985): 82–96; and Bert Rosenbloom, "The Influence of Manufacturer Organizational Structure on Marketing Channel Management," in *Proceedings of the Second World Marketing Congress* (Stirling, Scotland: University of Stirling, 1985): 733–744.

35. Robert E. Weigand and Hilda C. Wasson, "Arbitration in the Marketing Channel," *Business Horizons* (October 1974): 39–47.

36. Robert F. Dwyer and Orville C. Walker, Jr., "Bargaining in an Asymmetrical Power Structure," *Journal of Marketing* (Winter 1981): 104–115.

37. Schul, Pride, and Little, "The Impact of Channel Leadership," 23–27.

38. Rajiv P. Dant and Patrick L. Schul, "Conflict Resolution Processes in Contractual Channels of Distribution," *Journal of Marketing* (January 1992): 38–54.

39. See, for example, James R. Brown and Edward F. Fern, "Conflict in Marketing Channels: The Impact of Dual Distribution," in *Proceedings of the Sixth World Conference on Research in the Distributive Trades*, eds. Roy A. Thurik and Henk J. Gianotten (The Hague, Netherlands: Research Institute for Small and Medium-Sized Business, 1991), 349–356.

40. Jonathan D. Hibbard, Nirmalya Kumar, and Louis W. Stern, "Examining the Impact of Destructive Acts in Marketing Channel Relationships," *Journal of Marketing Research* (February 2001): 45–61.

41. George Balabanis, "Antecedents of Cooperation, Conflict and Relationship Longevity in an International Trade Intermediary's Supply Chain," *Journal of Global Marketing* 12, no. 2 (1998): 25–46.

42. For related discussion see: Morys Z. Perry, "An Experimental Investigation of Conflict Response Behaviors …" *Journal of Marketing Channels* (April–June 2009): 101–130.

43. For a related discussion see Nirmalya Kumar, "The Power of Trust in Manufacturer–Retailer Relationships," *Harvard Business Review* (November–December 1996): 92–96.

44. Howard Schlossberg, "Grocers Seek Peace Treaty in a War with Manufacturers," *Marketing News* (June 8, 1992): 16–17.

45. Robert A. Dahl, "The Concept of Power," *Behavioral Science* 2 (July 1957): 203–204.

46. Norman Miller and Donald Butler, "Social Power and Communication in Smaller Groups," *Behavioral Science* 14 (January 1969): 11.

47. Armitai W. Etzioni, *The Active Society* (New York: Free Press, 1968): 314.

48. James L. Price, *Organizational Effectiveness: An Inventory of Propositions* (Homewood, Ill: Irwin, 1969), 48.

49. Pui-Wing Tam, "Hewlett-Packard Discontinues Printer-Sales Deal with Dell," *Wall Street Journal* (July 24, 2002): B9.

50. John R. P. French and Bertram Raven, "The Bases of Social Power," in *Studies in Social Power*, ed. Dorwin Cartwright (Ann Arbor, Mich: University of Michigan, 1959), 612–613. Other power bases, such as information power, have also been discussed in the literature. See, for example, Nermin Eyuboglu and Osman A. Atac, "Informational Power: A Means for Increased Control in Channels of Distribution," *Psychology & Marketing* (Fall 1991): 197–213.

51. See for example: Paul Ziobro, "Burger King Franchisees Get to Keep Rebates," *Wall Street Journal* (February 3, 2010): B5.

52. Karen Talley, "Retailers, Suppliers Tussle," *Wall Street Journal* (February 11, 2009): B6A.

53. Anna Watson and Richard Johnson, "Managing the Franchisor–Franchisee Relationship: A Relationship Marketing Perspective," *Journal of Marketing Channels* (January–March 2010): 51–68.

54. Matthew Boyle, "The Accidental Hero," *Business Week* (November 16, 2009): 58–61.

55. James R. Brown, Anthony T. Cobb and Robert F. Lusch, "The Roles Played by Interorganizational Contracts and Justice in Marketing Channel Relationships," *Journal of Business Research* (59 2006): 166–175.

56. For a related discussion, see J. David Lichtenthal and Nermine Eyuboglu, "Channel Power in Business Markets: Structural Linkages," *Journal of Marketing Channels* 1, no. 1 (1991): 39–58; and Michael Etgar, "Channel Environment and Channel Leadership," *Journal of Marketing Research* (February 1977): 69–76.

57. See, for example, Keysuk Kim, "Interfirm Power and Coercive Influence Strategy in Industrial Channels of Distribution: A Contingency Perspective," *Proceedings of the American Marketing Association Summer Educators Conference* (Summer 1996): 384–385.

58. George H. Lucas and Larry G. Gresham, "Power, Conflict, Control, and the Application of Contingency Theory in Marketing Channels," *Journal of the Academy of Marketing Science* (Summer 1985): 27.

59. For a discussion of the research issues involved, see Gary L. Frazier, "On the Measurement of Interfirm Power in Channels of Distribution," *Journal of Marketing Research* (May 1983): 158–166.

60. Robert F. Lusch and Robert H. Ross, "The Nature of Power in a Marketing Channel," *Journal of the Academy of Marketing Science* (Summer 1985): 39–56.

61. Robert E. Krapfel and Robert Spekman, "Channel Power Sources, Satisfaction and Performance: An Exploration," in *Proceedings of the Annual Educators' Conference of the American Marketing Association* (Chicago: American Marketing Association, 1987): 30–34.

62. See, for example, Lynne Richardson and Thomas L. Powers, "Power Usage in the Channel: Perceptions by Personnel Level within the Organization," *Journal of Marketing Channels* 1, no. 4 (1992): 31–49; Jack J. Kasualis and Robert E. Spekman, "A Framework for the Use of Power," *European Journal of Marketing* (Fall 1980): 180–191. See also Nermine Eyuboglu and Nicholas M. Didow, "A Preliminary Test of the Applicability of Interdependence Theory in Explaining Power and Conflict in Distribution Channels," in *Proceedings of the Annual Educators' Conference of the American Marketing Association* (Chicago: American Marketing Association, 1987): 29.

63. Gary L. Frazier and Kersi D. Antia, "Exchange Relationships and Interfirm Power in Channels of Distribution," *Journal of the Academy of Marketing Science* (Fall 1995): 324.

64. Frederick J. Beier and Louis W. Stern, "Power in the Channel of Distribution, " in *Distribution Channels: Behavioral Dimensions* ed. Louis W. Stern (New York: Houghton Mifflin, 1969): 92–93.

65. Shelby D. Hunt and John R. Nevin, "Power in a Channel of Distribution: Sources and Consequences," *Journal of Marketing Research* (May 1974): 186–193.

66. Robert F. Lusch, "Sources of Power: Their Impact on Intrachannel Conflict," *Journal of Marketing Research* (November 1976): 382–390. For a critique of the methodology and findings of this study, see Michael Etgar, "Intrachannel Conflict and Use of Power," *Journal of Marketing Research* (May 1978): 273–274. For Lusch's reply to this critique, see Robert F. Lusch, "Intrachannel Conflict and Use of Power, A Reply," *Journal of Marketing Research* (May 1978): 275–276.

67. James R. Brown and Gary L. Frazier, "The Application of Channel Power: Its Effects and Connotations," *Proceedings of the Annual Educators' Conference of the American Marketing Association* (Chicago: American Marketing Association, 1978): 266–270.

68. Robert F. Dwyer, "Channel-Member Satisfaction: Laboratory Insights," *Journal of Retailing* (Summer 1980): 45–65.

69. Patrick L. Schul and Emin Babakus, "An Examination of the Interfirm Power–Conflict Relationship: The Intervening Role of the Channel Decision Structure," *Journal of Retailing* (Winter 1988): 381–404.

70. Kenneth A. Hunt, John T. Mentzer, and Jeffrey E. Danes, "The Effects of Power Sources on Compliance in a Channel of Distribution: A Casual Model," *Journal of Business Research* 15 (1987): 377–395. See also Robert F. Lusch and James R. Brown, "A Modified Model of Power in the Marketing Channel," *Journal of Marketing Research* (August 1982): 312–323; John F. Gaski and John R. Nevin, "The Differential Effects of Exercised and Unexercised Power Sources in a Marketing Channel," *Journal of Marketing Research* (May 1985): 135–142; and Donald A. Michie and Stanley D. Sibley, "Channel Member Satisfaction: Controversy Resolved," *Journal of the Academy of Marketing Science* (Spring 1985): 188–205.

71. Ian F. Wilkinson, "Power and Satisfaction in Distribution Channels," *Journal of Retailing* (Summer 1979): 79–94.

72. Jean L. Johnson, Tomoaki Sakano, Joseph A. Cote, and Naoto Onzo, "The Exercise of Interfirm Power and Its Repercussions in U.S.–Japanese Channel Relationships," *Journal of Marketing* (April 1993): 1–10.

73. Don Y. Lee, "Power, Conflict, and Satisfaction in IJV Supplier–Chinese Distributor Channels," *Journal of Business Research* 52 (2001): 149–160.

74. See, for example, Keysuk Kim, "On Interfirm Power, Channel Climate, and Solidarity in Industrial Distributor–Supplier Dyads," *Journal of the Academy of Marketing Science* 28, no. 3 (2000): 388–405.

75. For additional perspectives on this point, see Michael Etgar, "Differences in Use of Manufacturer Power in Conventional and Contractual Channels," *Journal of Retailing* (Winter 1978): 49–62.

76. For an excellent discussion of power in a marketing channels context that takes a very different perspective, see Frank V. Cespedes, "Channel Power: Suggestions for a Broadened Perspective," *Journal of Marketing Channels* 1, no. 3 (1992): 2–37. See also Charles L. Munson, Meir J. Rosenblatt, and Zehava Rosenblatt, "The Use and Abuse of Power in Supply Chains," *Business Horizons*, (January–February 1999): 55–65.

77. For some interesting findings on the use of power in industrial marketing channels, see Stanley D. Sibley and Donald A. Michie, "Distribution Performance and Power Sources," *Industrial Marketing Management* (February 1981): 59–65.

78. Experimental methods to examine the use of power in marketing channels can also be used as an aid to managerial judgment on using power effectively. See, for example, Kevin L. Webb and Nicholas M. Didow, "The Influence of Relative Power and Locus of Control on Channel Cooperation," *Journal of Marketing Channels* 4, no. 3/4 (1996): 71–94.

79. Bruce J. Biddle and Edwin J. Thomas, *Role Theory Concepts and Research* (New York: Wiley, 1966), 29.

80. Lynn E. Gill and Louis W. Stern, "Roles and Role Theory in Distribution Channel Systems," in *Distribution Channels: Behavioral Dimensions*. Louis W. Stern, ed. (Boston: Houghton Mifflin Co., 1969), 22–47.

81. See, for example, L. Joseph Cronin Jr., Thomas L. Baker, and Jon M. Hawes, "An Assessment of the Role Performance Measurement of Power-Dependency in Marketing Channels," *Journal of Business Research* 30 (1994): 201–210.

82. Finnbar O'Neil, "The Auto Industry's Comeback," *Wall Street Journal* (July 30, 2009): A17.

83. For additional perspective on this see: "Today's Metals Service Center Institute," http://www.msci.org/Description.aspx

84. For a related discussion, see Jule B. Gassenheimer, Roger J. Calantone, Judith M. Schmitz, and Robert A. Robicheaux, "Models of Channel Maintenance: What Is the Weaker Party to Do?" *Journal of Business Research* 30 (1994): 225–236.

85. Mohr and Nevin, "Communication Strategies in Marketing Channels," 36.

86. For an excellent article explaining how various types of channel relationships or "governance" influence channel communications, see Jakki J. Mohr, Robert J. Fisher, and John R. Nevin, "Collaborative Communication in Interfirm Integration and Control," *Journal of Marketing* (July 1996): 103–115.

87. Jakki J. Mohr and Ravipreet S. Sohi, "Communication Flows in Distribution Channels: Impact on Assessments of Communication Quality and Satisfaction," *Journal of Retailing* (Vol. 71 (4) 1995): 393–416.

88. Warren J. Wittreich, "Misunderstanding the Retailer," *Harvard Business Review* 40 (May–June 1962): 147–159.

89. Wittreich, "Misunderstanding the Retailer," 151.

90. Wittreich, "Musunderstanding the Retailer," 155.

91. For a related discussion see: Gary L. Frazier, Elliot Maltz, Kersi D. Antia and Aric Rindfleisch, "Distributor Sharing of Strategic Information with Suppliers," *Journal of Marketing* (July 2009): 31–43.

92. Jakki J. Mohr and Ravipreet S. Sohi, "Communication Flows in Distribution Channels: Impact on Assessments of Communication Quality and Satisfaction," 411.

93. Jeff Bennett, "Chrysler Dealers Get a Peek at Coming Models," *Wall Street Journal* (September 14, 2010): B3.

PART 2
Developing the Marketing Channel

CHAPTER **5**

Strategy in Marketing Channels

LEARNING OBJECTIVES

After reading this chapter, you should:

1. Understand the meaning of marketing channel strategy.
2. Be able to describe the six basic distribution decisions that most firms face.
3. Have an awareness of the potential for channel strategy to play a major role in overall corporate objectives.
4. Recognize the relationship of distribution to the other variables in the marketing mix and the role of channel strategy.
5. Be alerted to the conditions that tend to favor an emphasis on distribution strategy in developing the marketing mix.
6. Appreciate the role of channel strategy in creating a differential advantage through channel design.
7. Have a familiarity with the implications of the selection decision for channel strategy.
8. Know the key strategic decisions faced by the channel manager in the management of the marketing channel.
9. Understand the portfolio concept as it applies to motivating channel members.
10. Be aware of the main channel strategy issue involved in the evaluation of channel members.

FOCUS ON CHANNELS

Hollywood's Possible Abandonment of Its "Windowing" Distribution Strategy Could Throw Movie Theater Owners Out the Window

For many years, the major studios such as Disney, Paramount, Sony, Twentieth Century Fox, Universal, and others have used a channel strategy known as "windowing" in the movie industry to distribute movies to consumers. Under this strategy, new movies would first be shown only in movie theaters and then, usually four months later, they would be released through DVDs and cable. By delaying the release of movies through DVD and cable channels, a four-month "window" of opportunity is created for movie theaters as the exclusive distributors for newly released films. This distribution strategy also helped to maximize total revenue because delayed sales through DVD and cable channels would not cannibalize theater revenues because after the four-month window had passed, most movies would have completed their theater run.

But with the recent dramatic decline in DVD sales, the studios are considering an alternative to the windowing distribution strategy. The new strategy is called "premium video on demand." Basically, this involves enabling consumers to watch movies at home via DVD or cable within 30 days after theatrical release rather than the previous four-month waiting period. The studios are betting that consumers will be willing to pay a premium price for this service—as much as $20-$30 per movie. The studios also believe that this new premium video on demand distribution strategy is consistent with changes in consumer expectations because consumers have become accustomed to using a variety of devices to watch movies wherever and whenever they want. But there is a "fly" in the new distribution strategy "ointment": Theater owners hate it. They argue that the early home viewing option will hurt theater ticket sales because many movies would still be in theaters beyond the 30-day period. Some theater owners have even considered refusing to show movies that are offered early on DVDs and cable.

So, this new distribution strategy appears to offer a window of opportunity for studios; but, to theater owners, it looks like an open window through which they have been invited to commit suicide.

Source: Based On: Shira Ovide and Sam Schechner, "Hollywood Eyes Shortcut to TV," *Wall Street Journal* (May 22, 2010): A1, A4.

Having discussed basic marketing channel concepts and systems, the participants in marketing channels, the environment within which marketing channels operate, and behavioral processes in marketing channels in Part 1, we now turn our attention to the strategy side of marketing channels. This chapter presents a strategic framework for dealing with the key managerial decisions involved in marketing channels. Subsequent chapters in this part and later parts of the text are all related to the underlying strategic framework developed in this chapter. Hence this chapter is very important for getting the most out of the remainder of the text because it provides a strategic backdrop for most of the distribution channel management decisions discussed in later chapters.

Channel Strategy Defined

Kotler defines marketing strategy as "the broad principles by which the business unit expects to achieve its marketing objectives in a target market."[1] **Marketing channel strategy** can be viewed as a special case of the more general marketing strategy. Hence we can define marketing channel strategy as:

The broad principles by which the firm expects to achieve its distribution objectives for its target market(s).

This definition, though parallel to Kotler's definition of marketing strategy, is narrower because it focuses on the principles as guidelines for achieving the firm's distribution objectives rather than on general marketing objectives (which include product, price, and promotional objectives). Thus, marketing channel strategy is concerned with the *place* aspect of marketing strategy, while the other three Ps of the marketing mix address *product, price,* and *promotional* strategies.[2] As we shall see shortly, channel strategy, though relatively narrow in focus, may be of equal or more importance than the other strategic variables of the marketing mix, as well as of vital importance in the firm's overall objectives and strategies.[3]

To achieve their distribution objectives, most firms will have to address six basic distribution decisions:

1. What role should distribution play in the firm's overall objectives and strategies?
2. What role should distribution play in the marketing mix?
3. How should the firm's marketing channels be designed to achieve its distribution objectives?
4. What kinds of channel members should be selected to meet the firm's distribution objectives?
5. How can the marketing channel be managed to implement the firm's channel strategy and design effectively and efficiently on a continuing basis?
6. How can channel member performance be evaluated?

These six decisions are the "heart and soul" of distribution when viewed from a marketing channel management perspective.

The six basic distribution decisions can be dealt with on an ad hoc or "cross that bridge when you come to it" basis. But such an approach is shortsighted and can result in a "firefighting" mentality whereby distribution decisions are kept in the background until a crisis arises. Once the "fire" is put out, distribution decisions are returned to the background until the next crisis arises.[4] A sounder approach to dealing with distribution decisions is to formulate marketing channel strategy to provide the guiding principles for dealing with them. Such a strategic approach forces distribution decisions into the

FIGURE 5.1 Schematic Overview of Marketing Channel Strategy in Relation to Basic Distribution Decisions Covered in the Text

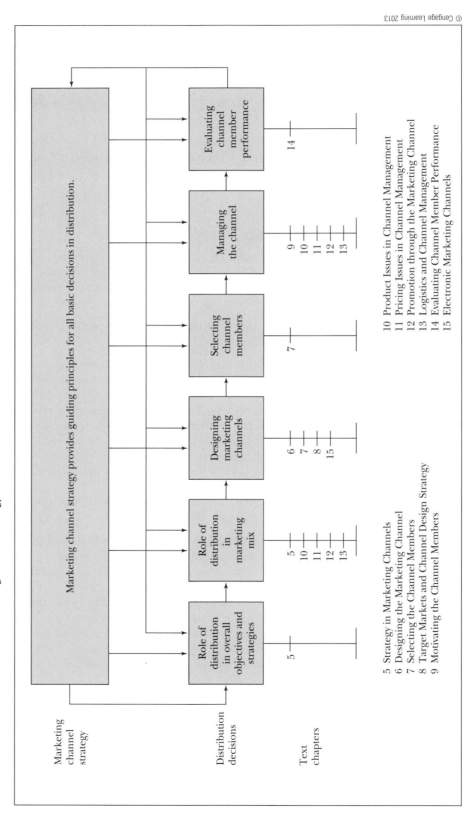

forefront of marketing strategy development and provides a set of guidelines for dealing with them on a *proactive* rather than reactive basis. Thus, management of distribution should, whenever possible, be guided by channel strategy. This is illustrated in Figure 5.1. The large rectangle at the top of this schematic overview represents the development of marketing channel strategy to provide the underlying guiding principles for addressing the six basic distribution decisions, which are shown as a series of squares. The vertical arrows leading from the marketing channel strategy rectangle are meant to convey this relationship. The horizontal arrows leading from each distribution decision to the next suggest the normal sequence of addressing the basic distribution decisions. The horizontal arrows at the left and right sides of the schematic overview convey the concept of feedback, both to prior distribution decisions and to strategy formulation. Finally, text chapters are indicated that focus primarily on each of the distribution decisions.

The rest of this chapter follows the framework shown in Figure 5.1 by discussing marketing channel strategy in relation to each of the six basic distribution decisions. Our purpose will not be to attempt to catalog all possible channel strategies, as there is a virtually unlimited range of strategies depending on the particular firm and circumstances involved. But we will provide an overview that shows the relationship between marketing channel strategy and the basic distribution decisions as well as conveys the importance of recognizing that relationship.

Marketing Channel Strategy and the Role of Distribution in Corporate Objectives and Strategy

The most fundamental distribution decision for any firm or organization to consider is the role that distribution is expected to play in a company's long-term overall objectives and strategies. More specifically, it has to decide whether the achievement of specific distribution objectives is crucial to the long-run success of the firm.[5] If the answer is yes, then the role of distribution should be considered at the highest management levels of the organization, including the president and even chairman of the board in large corporate organizational structures. Consider, for example, BMW, the internationally prestigious maker of high-performance luxury cars. BMW wants to revolutionize the way its automobiles are distributed in the United States. Rather than manufacturing automobiles ahead of time and placing them in dealer inventories, BMW has made a strategic decision that seeks to emulate the famous Dell Computer model by custom-building cars to order for each customer. BMW believes that this custom-made distribution strategy will not only save BMW and its dealers a great deal of money by reducing inventory carrying costs and rebates on cars that are not selling, but according to a J.D. Power & Associates survey, will result in more satisfied and loyal customers as well. At present, custom-ordered cars account for only 15 percent of BMW's sales in the U.S. But James O'Donnell, BMW's CEO, hopes to reach 40 percent by 2015. As an inducement to get more customers to buy their cars via custom orders, BMW will offer them unique choices of features and accessories and provide a video link of their cars "being born" at the factory.

Selling cars on a custom-made basis has been the Holy Grail of the auto industry for many years but so far, only BMW has taken the giant step to make it a core strategy of the company. If it is successful, O'Donnell believes that BMW's innovative distribution strategy will provide a key competitive advantage over other luxury brands by creating winners at all levels of the channel: BMW will build only cars that customers have committed to, dealers will reduce their costs, and customers will get exactly the cars they want.[6]

Given the potential importance of distribution, it should be considered in any strategic planning undertaken by the firm. This is illustrated in Figure 5.2. The diagram shows

FIGURE 5.2 The Strategic Planning Process and the Role of Distribution in the Firm

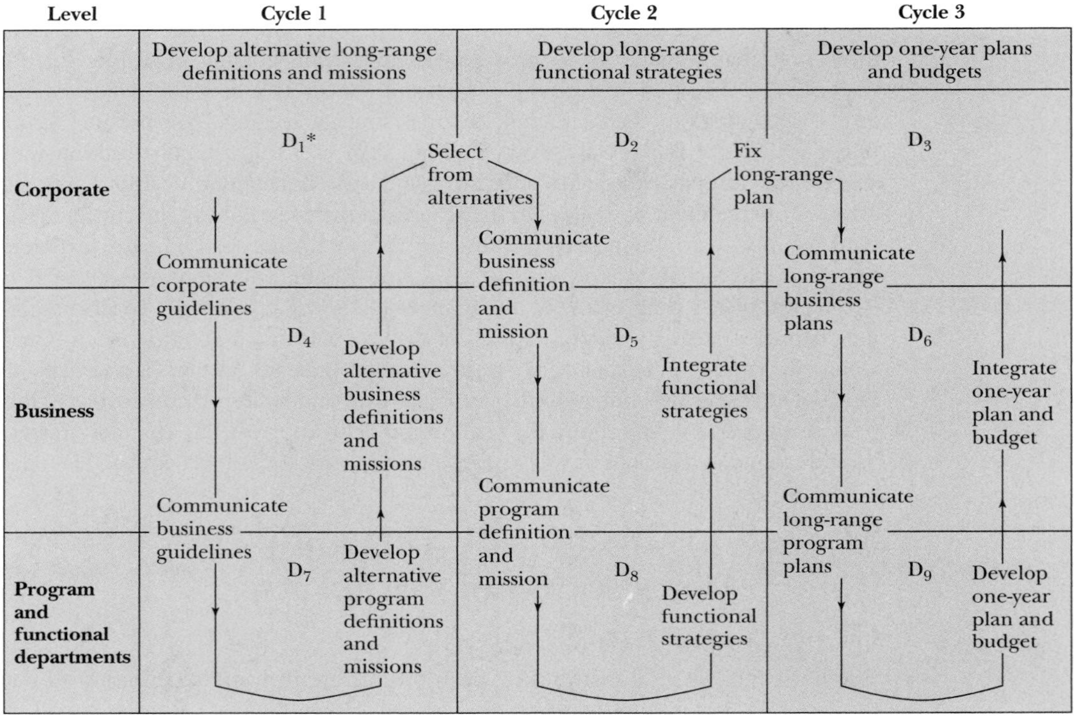

Level	Cycle 1	Cycle 2	Cycle 3
	Develop alternative long-range definitions and missions	Develop long-range functional strategies	Develop one-year plans and budgets
Corporate	D_1*	Select from alternatives → D_2	Fix long-range plan → D_3
	Communicate corporate guidelines	Communicate business definition and mission	Communicate long-range business plans
Business	D_4 Develop alternative business definitions and missions	D_5 Integrate functional strategies	D_6 Integrate one-year plan and budget
	Communicate business guidelines	Communicate program definition and mission	Communicate long-range program plans
Program and functional departments	D_7 Develop alternative program definitions and missions	D_8 Develop functional strategies	D_9 Develop one-year plan and budget

*D_1 to D_9 indicate order of appearance of the distribution issues in the cycles and levels of the strategic planning process; D_1 indicates earliest appearance while D_9 indicates last appearance.

Source: Adapted from Derek F. Abell and John S. Hammond, *Strategic Market Planning Problems and Analytical Approaches* (Englewood Cliffs, N.J.: Prentice-Hall, 1979), 451.

what Abell and Hammond refer to as a three-cycle strategic planning process.[7] Looking first at the corporate level, in cycle 1, planning is concerned with the management of fundamental and critical alternatives of defining the business and its future. In cycle 2, the definition of the business and its mission have already been determined and so the emphasis shifts to the formulation of functional strategies. In cycle 3, the focus shifts from long-range strategy to a short-term (usually one year) planning horizon—with the emphasis placed on detailed programming and budgeting. When this three-cycle planning process is undertaken in a large and diversified firm, all three levels will become involved in the strategic planning process: corporate, business, and program and functional departments. D_1 through D_9 indicate where and when the role of distribution would be addressed by firms having different priorities for distribution. The firm placing the highest priority on distribution would consider it in cycle 1 at the corporate level (D_1); the firm placing the lowest priority on distribution would address it in cycle 3 and only at the program and functional level (D_9). While Figure 5.2 is somewhat of an oversimplification of the interface between the role of distribution and the strategic planning process, it does convey the essential point—*the higher the priority given to distribution, the higher the level at which it should be considered in formulating the organization's overall objectives and strategies.*[8]

Determining the Priority Given to Distribution

The most famous and widely acclaimed management guru in the last one hundred years, Peter Drucker, had this to say about the importance of distribution:

Changes in distributive channels may not matter much to GNP and macroeconomics. But they should be a major concern to every business and industry … Everyone knows how fast technology is changing. Everyone knows about markets becoming global and about shifts in the work force and in demographics. But few people pay attention to changing distribution channels.[9]

Tom Peters, another famous management guru, makes a similar point about the importance of distribution in the firm:

Most firms make the mistake of paying too little attention to the somewhat attenuated members of their marketing team [marketing channel]. The [relatively few] companies that mind their distribution reap tangible rewards.[10]

The question of how much priority to place on distribution is one that can be answered only by the particular firm involved. If a firm's top management believes that distribution strategy is a core part of its corporate strategy for achieving its long-term goals, a high priority for, and a strong focus on distribution strategy become logical imperatives. The world's largest and best-known online retailer, Amazon.com, for example, from its founding almost two decades ago to today, has put enormous emphasis on distribution strategy. From the outset, Amazon.com's CEO, Jeff Bezos, decided to use a single, online channel strategy rather than a multi-channel strategy. But the single online channel strategy was the foundation of Amazon.com's business model. Amazon's online channel was designed to create an extraordinary customer experience by providing an easy and exciting customer interface, outstanding product selection, super efficient checkout, and quick delivery that few, if any, online or conventional competitors have been able to match.[11]

In contrast to Amazon.com, Apple CEO Steve Jobs made a strategic distribution decision soon after the start of the twenty-first century that involved the broadening of its channel mix to include the establishment of its own "bricks and mortar" retail stores. Jobs felt that in order to reach Apple's customers effectively and provide the kind of retail setting that would complement the exciting and innovative products Apple has become famous for, a chain of high quality retail stores designed to Apple's own specifications and located in the best shopping centers was needed. Apple's strategic decision to develop its company-owned retail store channel has played a vital role in Apple's outstanding growth and profitability in recent years not only because of the revenues and profits generated directly by the Apple stores, but by the showcase the stores provide for customers to see, touch, and try out new Apple products with the assistance of highly knowledgeable Apple employees in an exciting, high-tech atmosphere.[12]

In the service sector, financial services firm Edward Jones, with more than 10,000 physical brokerage offices blanketing the U.S., has placed tremendous emphasis on distribution strategy by deliberately maintaining its traditional channel structure that has served the firm for many decades. Even in the face of the technological revolution in financial services that has made online channels a dominant force for trading financial products, Edward Jones has steadfastly decided not to participate in the revolution. If an Edward Jones client wants to buy or sell stocks, bonds, mutual funds, or other financial instruments, he or she must do it through a local Edward Jones broker. So, while virtually all other large financial services firms have provided their clients with an online channel option, Edward Jones still offers only its "old fashioned" human broker channel.[13] Is Edward Jones "crazy" for sticking to this "outdated channel strategy?" Not according to the almost 7 million Edward

Jones clients who use it and J.D. Power & Associates that ranked Edward Jones as "Highest in Investor Satisfaction with Full Service Brokerage Firms." (See Figure 5.3).

Hewlett-Packard, now the world's largest PC manufacturer and a giant in the printer and IT services sector, makes it a point to emphasize the importance of distribution strategy to the firm's overall goals and objectives by setting off in italics the following statement in its annual report:[14]

> *If we fail to manage the distribution of our products and services properly, our revenue, gross margin and profitability could suffer.*

Numerous other companies across a wide range of industries have taken this message about the importance of distribution to heart. Battery manufacturer Rayovac Corp., for instance, in a quest to gain market share on its larger rivals, Duracell and Energizer, has

FIGURE 5.3
Excerpts from Edward Jones Web site Emphasizing Personal Contact Distribution Channel Strategy

placed the highest emphasis on gaining more penetration into mass merchandiser chan-nels, especially the world's largest retailer, Walmart Rayovac realizes that battery technol-ogy is essentially equal among the three major brands, so developing a channel strategy that will gain shelf space and thus reach larger numbers of consumers in the United States and abroad has become a top priority.[15]

WD-40, the ubiquitous lubricating product that is in 75 percent of all U.S. house-holds, has distribution at the heart of its corporate strategy to compete against such giants as 3M, DuPont, and GE, who have all unsuccessfully attempted to replace WD-40 with competing products. The main reason WD-40 has prevailed is that it places a great deal of attention on cultivating the broadest possible retail distribution channels. WD-40 is sold in every kind of retail outlet imaginable, and the company has paid extraordinary attention to keeping these diverse retailers happy with profitable deals, special merchandising campaigns, point-of-sale displays, and clever pricing strategies.

Giant consumer packaged goods manufacturer, Procter & Gamble Company, has placed tremendous emphasis on distribution, especially in terms of building strategic al-liances with giant retailers. Walmart accounts for more than 10 percent of P&G's domes-tic sales volume. To satisfy Walmart's demand for everyday low prices on P&G products, for special oversized packaging for its Sam's Clubs, and for many other demands, P&G has a whole team of executives living in Walmart's hometown of Bentonville, Arkansas, to cater to virtually every one of Walmart's wishes.

Many other examples of firms that place distribution at the heart of their corporate ob-jectives and strategies could also be cited. And, of course, there are many examples of firms that relegate distribution to a much lower priority. It is not possible to claim that those who look at distribution as a top management priority are right and those who do not are wrong. What is probably fair to say, however, is that to *automatically* dismiss dis-tribution as a decision area for top management concern in formulating corporate objec-tives and strategies limits the firm's ability to compete effectively in today's global markets.

Marketing Channel Strategy and the Marketing Mix

Whether or not the firm views distribution as worthy of top management concern when developing overall objectives and strategies, it must still deal with the issue of the role of distribution in the marketing mix. Developing a marketing mix of product, price, pro-motion, and distribution (place) strategies that meets the demands of the firm's target markets better than the competition is the essence of modern marketing management. This relationship between target market satisfaction and a firm's marketing mix can be represented as follows:

$$T_s = f(P_1, P_2, P_3, P_4)$$

where

T_s = degree of target market satisfaction

P_1 = product strategy

P_2 = pricing strategy

P_3 = promotional strategy

P_4 = place (distribution) strategy

The job of the marketing manager is to develop the right combination of the four Ps to provide and maintain the desired level of target market satisfactions (T_s). To do so, the marketing manger has to consider the possible contributions of each variable in meeting the demands of the target market.[16] Hence, the role of distribution must be considered along with the product, price, and promotion. This raises the question of how much emphasis should be placed on each strategic variable in the marketing mix. There is, of course, no general answer to this question. Each firm and each situation will vary and sometimes by a great deal. For example, a company in the pharmaceutical field with a new drug protected by a patent will derive much of its target market satisfaction (measured in terms of sales, profits, and market share) from its unique product. So, for the duration of the patent and assuming no competitive substitutes are available, the product variable will dominate its marketing mix. For a firm selling an undifferentiated commodity product such as standard computer chips, price will be the key variable in the marketing mix. Promotion, especially in the form of advertising, will tend to be the key variable in the marketing mix for companies such as cosmetics manufacturers, which rely on image to achieve market satisfaction. If the target market places a high level of emphasis on how a product is sold, how timely and conveniently it is made available, and where it is sold, distribution may be the leading variable in the marketing mix.

Yet, even if we acknowledge the wide range of variables in the marketing mix that any given firm might choose for strategic emphasis, a general case for stressing distribution strategy can still be made if any one of certain conditions prevails:

1. Distribution is the most relevant variable for satisfying target market demands.
2. Parity exists among competitors in the other three variables of the marketing mix.
3. A high degree of vulnerability exists because of competitors' neglect of distribution.
4. Distribution can enhance the firm by creating synergy from marketing channels.

The balance of this section is devoted to discussions of each of these conditions.

Distribution Relevance to Target Market Demand

Target market demand is, of course, the basis for developing an appropriate marketing mix. Hence, if customers in the firm's target market have demands that can be satisfied best through distribution strategy, this should be stressed in the firm's marketing mix.[17] In short, distribution becomes relevant because the target market wants it that way.[18]

As firms have become more oriented to target markets over the past two decades by listening more closely to their customers, the relevance of distribution has become apparent to an increasing number of companies because it plays such a key role in providing customer satisfaction. Why are marketing channels so closely linked to customer satisfaction? Because it is through distribution that the firm can provide the kinds and levels of service that make for satisfied customers. A case-in-point involved Volvo GM Heavy Truck Corporation.[19] Volvo GM dealers were losing business to competitors because of problems in providing prompt service. All too often dealers and the regional warehouses supplying them were out of stock of the parts needed for the repairs even though parts inventories at the dealerships and warehouses were increasing. Volvo GM knew the problem was caused by dealers' inability to predict the demand for parts and services accurately. But it was not until Volvo GM performed some careful market research that they understood the nature of the target market's demand for service. Specifically, Volvo GM found that customers use replacement parts in two distinctly different situations: scheduled maintenance and emergency roadside repairs. For the first situation, Volvo GM's existing distribution system worked well because customers' needs varied little, so the need for parts could be anticipated, ordered, and delivered on a regular basis. But in the second situation, the system was woefully inadequate because the demand for emergency repairs could not be predicted. So, no matter how much inventory was on warehouse and dealer shelves, key parts almost always seemed to be unavailable.

Having finally grasped the nature of the target market's demand for parts on an emergency basis, Volvo GM was able to develop a distribution strategy to meet the needs of its customers. Working with FedEx Logistics Services, Volvo GM set up a warehouse in Memphis, Tennessee, that stocked the full line of truck parts. Now when a dealer needs parts for emergency repairs, it simply calls a toll-free number or goes online to place an order and the parts are shipped out via air, often on the same day, and are available to dealers in the evening. Parts can also be delivered directly to a roadside repair site if need be. As is obvious, such a high level of customer service could be provided only through meticulous attention to distribution strategy and the superbly functioning marketing channel that resulted from such attention to target market needs.

Competitive Parity in Other Marketing Mix Variables

It is certainly no longer a secret that competition is increasingly fierce, especially since global competition has become the norm in so many industries. Consequently, more and more firms are competing with marketing mixes that are measured not only against those of strong domestic competitors but also against foreign ones. In such an intense competitive arena, it becomes increasingly difficult for a company to differentiate its marketing mix from that of the competition.[20] In the product area, the ability to maintain a lead in product innovation or quality is more difficult because of the rapidity of technology transfer across companies and national borders. With regard to the price variable, the capacity to maintain a pricing advantage is very limited due to the speed with which competitors can adjust their cost structures by moving their production facilities to lower-cost domestic or offshore locations. Marketing mix advantages based on promotion tend to be short-lived because novel or clever promotional messages quickly lose their appeal and are replaced by competitors' promotions that appear fresher.

Distribution, the fourth variable of the marketing mix, however, can offer a more favorable basis for developing competitive edge because advantages achieved in distribution are not as easily copied by competitors as the other three variables of the marketing mix. Why is this the case? Distribution advantages, if manifest in a superior marketing channel (rather than just the logistical aspects of distribution), are based on a combination of superior strategy, organization, and human capabilities. This is a combination not easily or quickly imitated by competitors. Consider, for example, the case of Caterpillar, Inc., the world leader in heavy earth-moving equipment. This firm has become famous not only for its excellent products, but perhaps even more so, for its outstanding distribution channel strategy. In what has now become a classic *Harvard Business Review* article, Donald Fites, a former Caterpillar CEO, captures succinctly the increasing need to consider distribution strategy as a means for overcoming competitive parity in other areas:

> *Engineering excellence, manufacturing efficiency, and quality are rapidly becoming givens: everyone is going to need them to be a player. Indeed, most companies deficient in these areas have already disappeared. That's one reason why I feel very bullish about my own company. We know how to do it [distribution strategy]. We have already built true partnerships with our dealers.*[21]

The "true partnerships with our dealers" that Fites refers to are not simply a logistical feat. Rather, they are dependent on carefully developed long-term channel strategy stressing the development of a superior group of dealers, a carefully managed interorganizational channel structure capable of responding quickly and flexibly, and a caliber of people in the channel system with the capacity to carry out the strategy. In short,

Caterpillar's partnerships with its dealers reflect its careful and thorough attention to relationship building with its dealer organization based on long-term trust, commitment, and cooperation between Caterpillar and its dealers. Matching this level of distribution capability confronts Caterpillar's competitors with a much greater challenge than simply matching its products, prices, and promotion. To duplicate Caterpillar's high-powered marketing channel would require long-term strategic changes, including relationship building[22] and human capital development. Obviously, this cannot be done easily or quickly. So, the moral of the story is that for those firms willing to expend the effort and resources, focusing on distribution as the main marketing mix variable on which to compete can be a fruitful strategy.

Distribution Neglect and Competitive Vulnerability

Neglect of distribution strategy by competitors provides an excellent opportunity for those companies who *are* willing to make the effort to develop distribution as a key strategic variable in the marketing mix. But to pursue this approach, the channel manager has to make a conscious effort to analyze target markets to determine if distribution has been neglected by competitors and whether vulnerabilities exist that can be exploited. Zappos.com, an online retailer of shoes, clothing, handbags, and accessories founded in 1999 and now generating sales in excess of a billion dollars, provides an excellent example of a firm that used innovative channel strategy to exploit competitor neglect of distribution strategy.[23] Zappos.com, which was acquired by Amazon.com in 2009 but still maintains its own identity and autonomy, has always stressed extraordinary service as the core of its corporate culture. The firm offers more than 1,200 brands, almost 3 million different products, free shipping, a one-year return policy, and 24-7 customer service by real people in its call center. All employees go through an intensive four-week training program not only to master all of the mechanics and details associated with providing excellent customer service, but also to absorb Zappos.com culture so that each employee becomes a living, breathing extension of the corporate culture. As a test of whether the employees can live up to this standard, CEO Tony Hsieh offers employees a buyout of $3,000 each after two weeks of training to anyone who wants to quit. Only one percent take him up on the offer. Zappos.com maintains its own warehouse and performs every aspect of its operations in-house to assure it can control the total customer experience.

Zappos.com has been able to bring its high-service online distribution channel to target customers who were dissatisfied by the limited selection and low levels of service provided by traditional bricks-and-mortar shoe stores, apparel, and accessories retailers. Many of these land-based retailers, for whatever reason, were unwilling or unable to provide the kind of customer experience that millions of consumers were seeking. When Zappos.com offered an alternative in the form of a direct online channel that provided superior product availability along with superb service, customers literally flocked to this new and better channel.

Distribution and Synergy for the Channel

As we have pointed out several times in this text, one of the difficulties of managing marketing channels is that it involves independent channel members—businesses that have their own objectives, policies, and strategies. Attempting to gain their cooperation so that they help the manufacturer to achieve its objectives and strategies is what makes interorganizational channel management such a challenge. Yet along with this challenge come opportunities, because a well-developed marketing channel comprised of the right channel members can provide synergy between the channel members that produces a superior distribution program. So in thinking about which variable to emphasize in the marketing mix, the potential for synergy in distribution should be considered.[24] By "hooking up" with the right kind of channel members, the marketing mix can be substantially strengthened to a degree not easily duplicated with the other variables. The most obvious example of this is when a channel member's reputation or prestige is stronger than the manufacturer's. By securing distribution of its products through such channel members at the wholesale or retail levels, the manufacturer immediately upgrades its own credibility. In effect, the manufacturer's products handled by famous retailers or well-established wholesalers become "anointed" as superior products to a degree beyond what the manufacturer could have accomplished on its own. This kind of synergy is exactly what NutriSystem, Inc., a maker of diet foods sold directly to consumers in various configurations that comprise the NutriSystem diet plan, hoped to gain by getting its products onto Walmart's shelves.[25] In late 2009, the company, based in Horsham, Pennsylvania, worked out a deal with Walmart to sell a specially developed "starter" version of the NutriSystem diet food products to sell for $148 at Walmart stores. Except for a much smaller scale relationship with Costco, prior to the Walmart relationship, NutriSystem had sold all of its products via telephone and online channels relying mainly on television commercials to promote its products to consumers. With the Walmart deal, NutriSystem hopes to gain much greater recognition and credibility for its diet products than it could achieve by continuing to sell its products only through direct to consumer channels. By convincing Walmart to carry its products, which will be sold in more than 3,200 Walmart stores, NutriSystem has received a defacto endorsement of its products by the world's largest and most powerful retailer.

Synergy through distribution goes well beyond the enhancement of the manufacturer's image. Strong and close working relationships between the manufacturer and channel members—which in recent years have been referred to increasingly as *distribution partnerships*, *partnering, strategic alliances,* or *networks*—can provide a substantial strategic advantage.[26] The previously discussed relationship between Procter & Gamble and Walmart is perhaps the most talked about strategic alliance of recent years. But many other such synergistic relationships have been established in a wide variety of industries.

In the industrial or business-to-business market, synergistic channel partnerships and alliances have also become popular. Motorola, for instance, as part of its Total Quality Management (TQM) program, has developed close, mutually beneficial relationships with suppliers through a program the company calls Suppliers Perceptions Measurement, which helps suppliers to meet Motorola's stringent quality and performance standards. The program has reduced the number of suppliers that Motorola deals with, but the relationships are closer and more mutually profitable.

Channel Strategy and Designing Marketing Channels

The subject of channel design, which involves the entire process of setting up a channel (or modifying an existing one), will be discussed in detail in Chapter 6 and continue into Chapters 7 and 8. It is a complex topic that requires several chapters to cover adequately.

Our purpose in introducing the topic of channel design in this chapter is limited to showing the relationship between channel strategy and channel design. This relationship is a straightforward one: *Channel strategy should guide channel design so as to help the firm attain a differential advantage.*

Differential Advantage and Channel Design

Differential advantage,[27] also called **sustainable competitive advantage**[28] in more recent years, refers to a firm's attainment of an advantageous position in the market relative to competitors—a place that enables it to use its particular strengths to satisfy customer demands better than its competitors on a long-term (sustainable) basis. The entire range of resources available to the firm and all of its major functional activities can contribute to the attempt to create a differential advantage. The level of capital, the quality of management and employees, and its overall production, financial, and marketing strategies all play a part.

Channel design, though just one component of this attempt to gain a differential advantage, can be a very important part.[29] Given that distribution is one of the major controllable variables of the marketing mix, it is no less important for the firm to seek a differential advantage in its channel design than in its product, pricing, and promotional strategies. Indeed, a differential advantage based on the design of a superior marketing channel can yield a formidable and long-term advantage because competitors cannot copy it easily.

Consider, again, the case of Caterpillar, a company whose channels of distribution are highly respected throughout the world. With a few exceptions, over the past 50 years Caterpillar has had one of the best financial track records in the heavy equipment industry or, for that matter, among all major U.S. corporations—even in the face of fierce competition from the Japanese.

What lies behind Caterpillar's success? While there are several factors that differentiate Caterpillar from competitors, the key ingredient of its success, as the company has stated many times, is a well-designed marketing channel system based on a superb dealer organization. The dealer network comprising the channel for most of Caterpillar's products consists of almost 200 domestic and overseas dealerships, all independently owned and relatively large. The average dealer's sales are well above $100 million and each has an average net worth in the millions. This financially strong and high-powered group of dealers has enabled Caterpillar to provide a level of product availability and service to its customers that is unrivaled in the industry. But this well-designed channel system that has given Caterpillar such a strong differential advantage is no accident. As discussed earlier in this chapter, over the years Caterpillar has placed great emphasis on building and nurturing its marketing channel system in a conscious effort to make it superior to the competition. One feature of the system, for example, is a computer network linking all dealers to the Morton, Illinois distribution center. This network enables dealers to order any part they need for delivery the next day in the United States and usually within 48 hours anywhere in the world. Caterpillar also conducts dozens of training programs for dealers both in the United States and abroad. Indeed, the company even conducts a course in Peoria, Illinois, to encourage dealers' children to remain in the business. As this example suggests, superior channel design can contribute significantly to a firm's quest to gain a differential advantage. Figure 5.4 shows an excerpt from Caterpillar's Web site that captures the importance Caterpillar attaches to its global dealer network.

Positioning the Channel to Gain Differential Advantage

In the channel manager's attempt to foster differential advantage through channel design, the concept of **channel position** can serve as a helpful guide. Narus and Anderson define a channel position as:

> *... the reputation a manufacturer acquires among distributors [channel members] for furnishing products, services, financial returns, programs, and systems that are in some way superior to those offered by competing manufacturers.*[30]

FIGURE 5.4 **Excerpt from Caterpillar Web site Stressing Importance of Dealer Network**

Channel positioning is what the firm does with its channel planning and decision making to attain the channel position. The key ingredient, according to Narus and Anderson, is to view the relationship with channel members as a *partnership* or *strategic alliance* that offers recognizable benefits to the manufacturer and channel members on a long-term basis. This is in contrast to typical short-term ad hoc incentive programs that are so common in many channel relationships and are really little more than short-term tactics rather than strategies. By thinking in terms of channel positioning, the channel manager takes a longer-term strategic view of channel design and is more likely to ask the question: How can I design the channel so that channel members will view my firm as having done a better job than the competitive manufacturers they represent? Lexus automobiles offers a good example of channel positioning by positioning its independent dealer channel as the best in the automobile industry.[31] This quest to position Lexus dealers as the best in the industry is stated explicitly in "THE LEXUS CONVENANT," which appears on the Lexus official Web site as the fourth commitment in the Covenant (see Figure 5.5). It reads as follows: "Lexus will have the finest dealer network in the industry." The next (fifth) Lexus commitment in the Covenant goes on to say: "Lexus will treat each customer as we would a guest in our home." In this channel positioning strategy, Lexus is clearly and purposefully setting the bar high for its dealer channel. Lexus expects its dealerships to be the best—no ifs, ands, or maybes. But even more to the point, this channel positioning strategy is also aimed at creating very high customer expectations for Lexus dealers. Indeed, Lexus is promising customers something well beyond what would normally be expected from an auto dealership: a customer experience that will "treat each customer as we would [treat] a guest in our home." Obviously, this is a tall order but one that Lexus takes very seriously. Indeed, right from the introduction of the Lexus brand in the late 1980s, prospective candidates for Lexus dealerships were evaluated as much on "soft" factors such as attitude toward the customer as on "hard" factors such as financial strength. By putting so much emphasis on the human dimension and people skills as part of the Lexus dealers' DNA, Lexus

FIGURE 5.5 Lexus Web site Showing THE LEXUS COVENANT

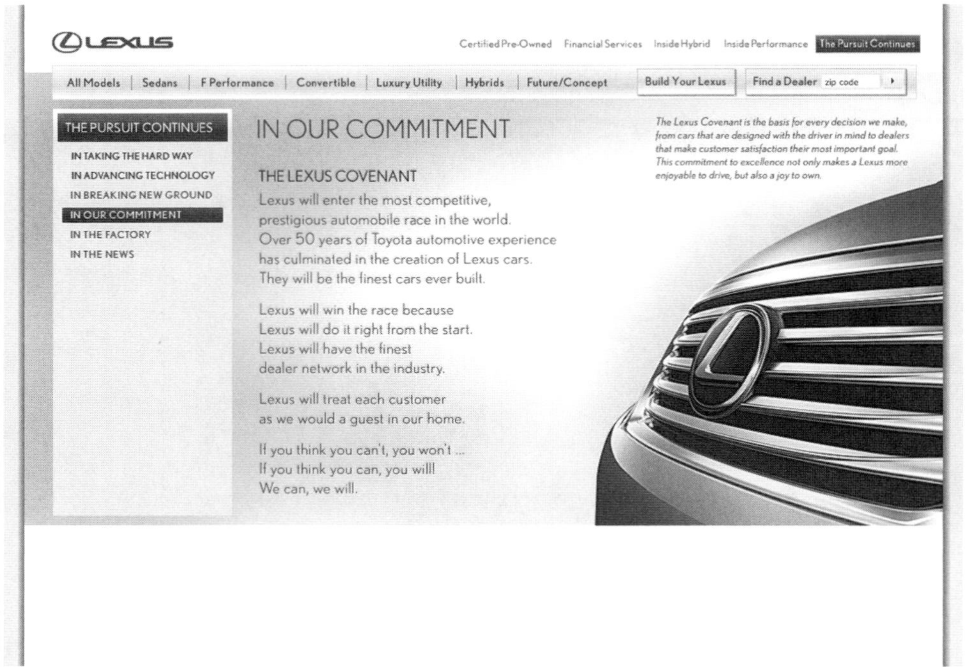

has won many awards over the years such as achieving the highest rating on the coveted J.D. Power Customer Service Index (CSI). But what is most important from a bottom line, competitive strategy standpoint is that Lexus has positioned its "best of breed" dealer channel as a key reason for buying a Lexus rather than another brand of luxury automobiles.

A well-positioned channel also means that the channel manager will have the confidence and support of the channel members in his or her attempt to gain a differential advantage. In short, a channel that is well-positioned with channel members should increase the manufacturer's chances of being well-positioned with final customers. The result could be the very differential advantage the manufacturer was seeking. Thus a good job of gaining the respect of channel members should result in the kind of channel position that improves the odds of attaining a real differential advantage with final customers because the channel members are positioned to be "cheerleaders" for the manufacturer who has attained the strong channel position.

Channel Strategy and the Selection of Channel Members

The selection of channel members is the final phase of channel design and is discussed comprehensively in Chapter 7. Our purpose in introducing the subject of channel member selection in this chapter is to show that this aspect of channel design also has a strategic dimension. In particular, the approach taken to channel member selection and the particular types of intermediaries chosen to become channel members should reflect the channel strategies the firm has developed to achieve its distribution objectives.[32] Moreover, the selection of channel members should be consistent with the firm's broader marketing objectives and strategies and may also need to reflect the objectives and strategies of the organization as a whole.[33] This follows because channel members, though independent businesses, are from the customers' perspective an extension of the manufacturer's own organization. Thus the types of middlemen selling the manufacturer's products ultimately reflect on the manufacturer. So, for example, a manufacturer that prides itself on providing prestigious products of the highest quality would have to be very careful about the kinds of channel members it chooses to sell its products. Rolex, for example, arguably the world's most prestigious watchmaker, takes extreme care in selecting only the most reputable retail dealers to sell its products. Rolex also advertises directly to customers in publications such as the Wall Street Journal to remind customers that only authorized Rolex jewelers can provide the superior selection, service, and warranty protection that customers purchasing such a prestigious product expect.

In contrast, if a manufacturer's products are "middle of the road" in quality and aimed at the mass market, its distribution strategy should stress broad coverage of the market. In this case, the types of channel members handling the product will be a much less sensitive issue. Bic Corporation, for example, manufacturer of the ubiquitous low-cost Bic ballpoint pens, stresses a channel member selection strategy that could be described as "open admissions" to virtually any intermediary who is capable of selling its products.

Between these extremes of world-class luxury products and the mundane 50-cent ballpoint pen are a host of other situations, involving both consumer and industrial products, in which channel member selection strategy is less obvious.[34] This is especially the case when channel member selection strategy also has to take into account long-term versus short-term trade-offs in sales, market share, and profits. In the toy industry, for example, toy manufacturers such as Mattel, Inc. are paying far more attention to channel member selection strategy by making exclusive dealing arrangements with certain retailers on particular toy items. In Mattel's famous Barbie doll line, for instance, Mattel is selling Barbie's younger sister Kelly only through Target stores. By selecting only one retail chain to carry certain products, manufacturers gain a higher degree of control over how the merchandise is marketed to final customers than if it were sold by many different retailers. Retailers like this arrangement because it eliminates direct competition for those products. Of course, the manufacturer also is taking a major risk by selecting only one retailer to sell products exclusively, because if the retailer does not perform up to expectations, no other retailers are available to take up the slack.

Channel Strategy and Managing the Marketing Channel

Channel management from the manufacturer's perspective involves all of the plans and actions taken by the manufacturer aimed at securing the cooperation of the channel members in achieving the manufacturer's distribution objectives.[35] This topic is discussed in depth in Chapters 9 through 13 in Part 3 of the text. Our purpose in introducing the topic of channel management here is limited to showing its relationship to channel strategy.

The channel manager attempting to plan and implement a program to gain the cooperation of channel members is faced with three strategic questions:

1. How close a relationship should be developed with the channel members?
2. How should the channel members be motivated to cooperate in achieving the manufacturer's distribution objectives?
3. How should the marketing mix be used to enhance channel member cooperation?

Closeness of Channel Relationships

In recent years a substantial body of literature has appeared arguing the need for closer relationships between manufacturers and channel members at the wholesale and/or retail levels. Only by developing close relationships, "partnerships," or strategic alliances can manufacturers and channel members work together to achieve high levels of effectiveness and efficiency in distribution, according to the argument. Indeed, the underlying philosophy of most of the literature on interorganizational channel management presupposes the need for close relationships between manufacturer and channel members.[36] Hardly any voices are heard from the other side of the argument—that of not stressing close channel relationships or even purposely keeping greater distance.[37] Does so much emphasis on one side and virtually none on the other mean that the "closeness is best" argument is right and the other is wrong? Actually, neither side is necessarily right or wrong.[38]

What should not be forgotten in this debate—or, more correctly, this one-sided argument—is that the question of how close a channel relationship any given manufacturer should develop with its channel members is really a question of strategy. If the channel manager believes that a close working relationship will help him or her do a better job of managing the channel and achieve the distribution objectives, then closeness should be emphasized. If, on the other hand, the channel manager believes that closeness is not necessary for effective management of the channel, then it is probably not necessary and indeed might even be wasteful of time, energy, and money. For a manufacturer of an undifferentiated commodity product sold through thousands of retailers, for example, it would most likely not be feasible to attempt to develop a close relationship with each retailer. Yet, if the manufacturer uses a relatively small group of wholesalers to reach those retailers, it may make a great deal of sense to establish a close relationship with the wholesalers.

Most of the examples cited in this chapter—including Caterpillar, BMW, Lexus, and NutriSystem did stress the need for close working relationships between the manufacturer and channel members. But this should not be taken to mean that this always or automatically should be the case. Bic, WD-40, and Rayovac, also cited in this chapter, could not possibly maintain close relationships with all of the retailers or even all of the wholesalers selling their products. It would be infeasible and uneconomical to do so. Consequently, each firm needs to examine the question of how close a relationship it will develop with its channel members.[39] Figure 5.6 helps to illustrate the channel strategy decision facing the channel manager by portraying it as a continuum. The relationship a manufacturer seeks with its channel members can range from very close, as with Caterpillar or Lexus and its dealers, to very loose, such as the relationship of Bic with, say, any given 7-Eleven store selling its ballpoint pens. In the middle might be the relationship between GM, Ford, or Chrysler and a typical auto dealer.[40]

As a rough strategic guide for dealing with the closeness question, the channel manager can relate it to the degree of distribution intensity that presumably would have been decided on while designing the channel. This, too, can be visualized as a continuum, as shown in Figure 5.7. The adjectives **intensive**, **selective**, and **exclusive**—used to describe the points on the continuum—are the traditional terms used in the marketing literature to indicate the number of channel members (at either the wholesale or the retail levels)

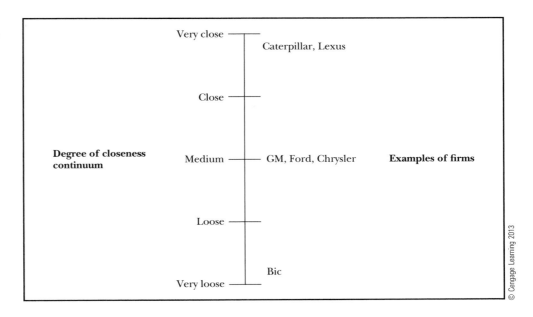

FIGURE 5.7
**Continuum of Intensity
of Distribution**

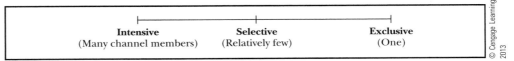

used by the manufacturer (see Chapter 6 under the heading "Intensity at the Various
Levels"). By combining the two continua from Figures 5.6 and 5.7, a graph portraying
the relationship between the degree of closeness and the distribution intensity can be
constructed, as shown in Figure 5.8. The figure shows a positive relationship between
distribution intensity and the degree of closeness in the channel relationship. This is
not meant to indicate a precise linear relationship. On the contrary, only a rough relationship is suggested to serve as a point of departure for dealing with the question of
how close a relationship should be developed between manufacturers and their channel
members. Figure 5.8 implies that, on average, with everything else being equal, if the
channel manager has designed a channel stressing intensive distribution he or she should
probably think in terms of a looser relationship with the many channel members involved than would be the case for the far fewer channel members involved in a more
selectively or exclusively designed channel.

Distribution intensity is not, of course, the only factor to consider in deciding how close
a relationship the manufacturer should develop with the channel members.[41] Many other
factors, such as markets being targeted, products, company policies, middlemen, environment, and behavioral dimensions can all play a role. These are discussed in detail in Chapter 6. But distribution intensity is probably as good a point as any to begin to deal with the
strategic question of how close a relationship to develop with channel members.

Motivation of Channel Members

The motivation of channel members is covered in detail in Chapter 9. There we discuss a
complete program for addressing this very important distribution decision. But, as we
have said throughout this chapter, when approaching any of the basic distribution decisions the channel manager should think in terms of the underlying channel strategy involved. When motivating channel members, the strategic challenge is to find the means

FIGURE 5.8
Relationship between Channel Closeness and Distribution Intensity

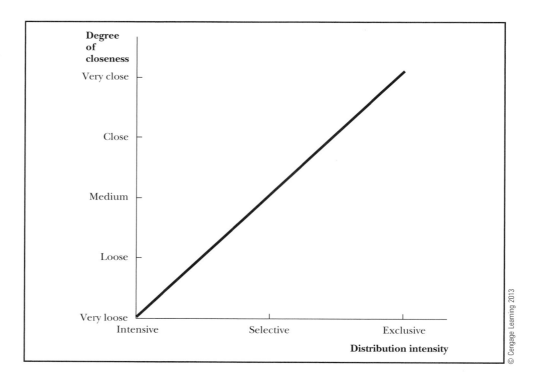

to secure strong channel member cooperation in achieving distribution objectives. Channel strategy in this context involves whatever ideas and plans the channel manager can devise to help achieve that result.[42] More specifically, it means putting together the right mix of tactics to motivate channel members. Table 5.1, for example, lists some of the most commonly used tactics for motivating channel members. As can be seen from the table, the list is very diverse, ranging from the "brute force" approach of **slotting allowances**[43]—a relatively recent term for the age-old practice of paying channel members to provide shelf space—all the way to the much more subtle approach of establishing distributor councils to provide a voice for channel members in decisions affecting the channel (see Chapter 9).

From the diverse array of channel tactics shown in Table 5.1 (along with many other possible ones not mentioned in the table), the channel manager must decide which to use to most effectively motivate the channel members. A systematic framework for doing this is presented in Chapter 9 so we will not deal with this decision framework here. What is appropriate at this point, however, is to discuss briefly a very general strategy that can help the channel manager to approach the question of motivating channel members in a more fruitful way. This general strategy is based on the concept of the portfolio—a concept that originated in the field of finance. Basically, the investor views the assorted investments he or she has as comprising a financial portfolio. Over time, the investor changes the mix of investments in the portfolio to achieve financial objectives via different strategies for each investment.

The portfolio concept has been borrowed by a number of other business areas including marketing. In product management, for example, the mix of products offered by a manufacturer can be portrayed as its **product portfolio**.[44] Consistent with the analogy to the financial portfolio, product management involves changing the mix of products and strategies to achieve marketing objectives usually specified in terms of sales, market share, and profits. The portfolio concept has also been applied in the context of marketing channels and is referred to as **distribution portfolio analysis (DPA)**.[45] While DPA

TABLE 5.1 MENU OF COMMON CHANNEL TACTICS FOR MOTIVATING CHANNEL MEMBERS

1. Pay higher "slotting allowances" (payment for shelf space) than competitive manufacturers.
2. Offer higher trade discounts (margins) to channel members than competitors offer.
3. Attempt to reward with higher margins those channel members performing more distribution tasks.
4. Offer channel members price-protected products by refusing to deal with price-cutting middlemen.*
5. Provide strong advertising and promotional support to channel members.
6. Provide a wider array of promotional allowances to channel members than competitors provide.
7. Make available to channel members more special deals and merchandising campaigns than do competitors.
8. Make available higher levels of cooperative advertising dollars than do competitors.
9. Make use of missionary salespeople to support channel members' sales efforts.
10. Develop an ideal balance between push and pull promotional strategies.
11. Protect channel members' sales through highly selective distribution.
12. Develop sales quotas for channel members based on analyses of their market potentials.
13. Offer channel members a "partnership" arrangement stressing mutual commitment and expectations.
14. Develop special licensing or franchising agreements to tighten the channel relationship.
15. Offer channel members an exclusive dealing arrangement.
16. Use dual distribution to foster interchannel rivalries.
17. Employ tying arrangements (including full-line forcing) to limit channel members' selling of competitive products.
18. Provide channel members with protected territories.
19. Provide channel members with high-quality, innovative, or distinctive products.
20. Emphasize product life cycle management to assure channel members of timely new product additions and deletions.
21. Assure guaranteed sales and unrestricted returns to channel members.
22. Provide sales training for channel members' salespeople.
23. Offer financial assistance to channel members.
24. Offer management assistance and training to channel members.
25. Provide channel members with superior logistical support.
26. Provide sophisticated on-line computer ordering for channel members.
27. Offer technical assistance and support for channel members.
28. Provide channel members with market research on their target markets.
29. Generate customer leads and pass them on to channel members.
30. Set up distributors' councils to provide channel members with more input into channel decision making.

*Refer to Chapter 3 for legal ramifications.

provides a comprehensive method for categorizing channel members, the essence of DPA is that it can help the channel manager to focus more insightfully on the channel members by viewing all of the channel structures and/or channel members as the portfolio. Each structure as well as defined groups of channel members are seen as particular "investments" within the portfolio.

Consider, for example, the channel structures shown in Figure 5.9. Taken together, these channel structures constitute the vertical portfolio of channel structures used by the manufacturer. These can be combined in a matrix showing a variety of possible channel structures and types of channel members, as illustrated in Figure 5.10. The different types and sizes of retailers, wholesalers, and manufacturers' representatives shown horizontally within the different vertical channel structures can each be viewed as a different investment instrument within the portfolio.

FIGURE 5.9
Vertical Profile of Different Channel Structures

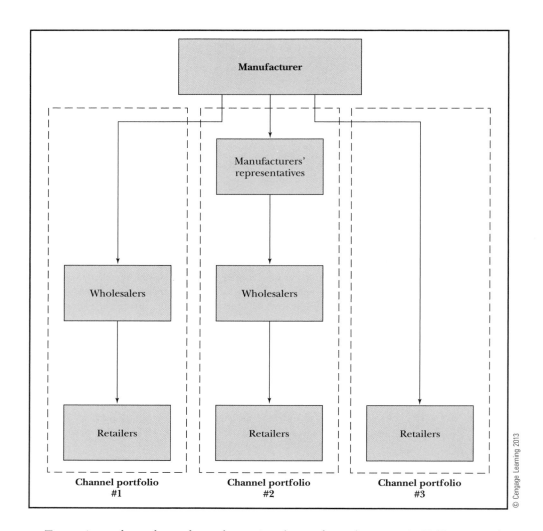

To motivate channel members, the tactics chosen from the menu in Table 5.1 might have to be varied for each category of channel member. Wholesalers, for example, might be highly motivated by a training program, whereas a high slotting allowance may be much closer to what mass merchandisers are seeking. The essential idea behind the portfolio approach to channel member motivation is that different types and sizes of channel members participating in various channel structures may respond differently to various motivation strategies. Some effort by the channel manager to group channel structures and members into a portfolio before launching a motivation program may prove to be helpful in targeting the appropriate motivation strategies.[46]

Although the channel portfolio concept provides a useful framework for determining which motivational approaches might be used for various classes of channel members, the channel manager should not lose sight of the final customer which, after all, is the real reason for developing an appropriate mix of channels and strategies in the portfolio. As Schoenbachler and Gordon point out in addressing this issue from the consumer perspective:

[Too often] the focus has been on the channel, how to improve the channel, and how to drive customers to the channel without offending other channel members. The focus should, however, be on the consumer rather than on the channel. The consumer or customer-centric focus encourages managers to develop and design channel alternatives that are successful and effective because they consider customer needs.[47]

FIGURE 5.10 Matrix of Vertical and Horizontal Portfolios of Channel Structures and Members

Vertical Channel Portfolio	Horizontal Channel Portfolio		
	Manufacturers' Representatives	Wholesalers	Retailers
Vertical channel portfolio #1		Large general line wholesalers	Small independent retailers
		Medium general line wholesalers	Mail order retailers
		Small general line wholesalers	
Vertical channel portfolio #2	Domestic representatives	Specialty wholesalers	Department stores
	Overseas representatives		Specialty stores
Vertical channel portfolio #3			Mass merchandisers
			Discount stores
			Specialty chains

© Cengage Learning 2013

Use of the Marketing Mix in Channel Management

Optimizing the marketing mix to meet the demands of the target market requires not only excellent strategy in each of the four strategic variables of the marketing mix, but also an understanding of the relationships or interfaces among them. Product strategy interfaces with pricing strategy, which in turn is related to promotional strategy, which further in turn is related to distribution strategy. This is illustrated in Figure 5.11.

What this means from a marketing mix standpoint is that plans and decisions made in one of the variables of the marketing mix have implications for the other variables. Thus, a decision to change the features of a product may require an increase in price, which in turn may require changes in promotion to explain the new product feature and justify the higher price. Finally, distribution could be affected because channel members selling the product may need to be informed about the changed product features. Furthermore, their attitudes toward selling the product in view of how its new price compares with competitive products might also have to be taken into account.

FIGURE 5.11
Interrelationships among the Four Strategic Variables of the Marketing Mix

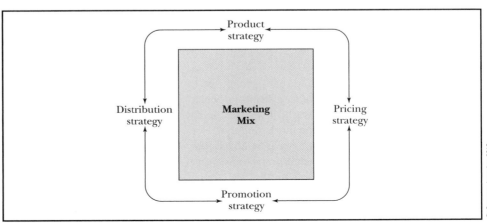

© Cengage Learning 2013

Ideally, effective marketing management would anticipate all of these interfaces and then formulate a marketing mix strategy for each variable in such a way that each would complement or reinforce the others. The result would be an optimum marketing mix with synergy achieved from an ideal blending of the four Ps to meet the demands of the target market.

In practice, of course, this ideal blending of the marketing mix is not possible. The real world is too complex and changes too quickly to allow that to happen very often. Nevertheless, the underlying strategic concept of developing synergy in the marketing mix by anticipating and incorporating interrelationships among the four Ps is still a worthwhile approach to managing the mix. Although a true optimum blending of the marketing mix may not be possible, a very effective one is attainable.

From the standpoint of distribution strategy and particularly of managing the marketing channel, the channel manager should keep the strategic concept of developing synergy clearly in mind. By doing so, the potential of the other Ps in the marketing mix for reinforcing rather than detracting from the management of the channel is more likely to be seen. This theme underlies all of the material presented in Chapters 10 through 13. These chapters discuss product, price, promotion, and logistics strategies as they interface with channel strategy and management.

Channel Strategy and the Evaluation of Channel Member Performance

The adage "the proof is in the pudding" is most apt when it comes to the evaluation of channel member performance because it is through this process that the channel manager should be able to obtain concrete evidence of how well the channel has been designed and managed.

The subject of channel member performance evaluation is covered in Chapter 14. There we discuss the distinction between day-to-day monitoring of channel member performance versus a longer-term approach of comprehensive performance evaluation that involves use of a variety of criteria and in some cases formal methods to gather and analyze the data needed to measure channel member performance.

At this point, we are concerned only with the underlying strategic significance of channel member performance evaluation, which in practice is concerned with one overriding question: *Have provisions been made in the design and management of the channel to assure that channel member performance will be evaluated effectively?* This question will direct the channel manager's attention toward viewing performance evaluation as an integral part of the development and management of the marketing channel rather than as an afterthought. This kind of approach to channel member performance evaluation can apply in virtually any industry, from a maker of luxury products such as Rolex watches to a producer of heavy earth-moving equipment such as Caterpillar.

Summary

Channel strategy refers to the broad principles by which the firm expects to achieve its distribution objectives for its target markets. As such, it focuses on the place variable of the four Ps of the marketing mix. Even though the focus of channel strategy is relatively narrow, it can have a major impact on, and be of great importance to, the firm's general marketing strategy as well as overall (corporate) objectives and strategies.

Channel strategy is relevant to all six of the basic distribution decisions faced by firms:

1. The role of distribution in the firm's overall objectives and strategies
2. The role of distribution in the marketing mix
3. The design of marketing channels
4. Selection of channel members

5. Management of the channel

6. Evaluation of channel member performance

If the role of distribution is considered vital to the firm's long-run success, then distribution strategy should be considered at the highest management levels in the organization and included in the strategic planning process.

With regard to the role of distribution in the marketing mix, a strong case for emphasizing distribution can be made if any of the following four conditions exist: (1) distribution is the most relevant variable in the marketing mix for satisfying target market demand; (2) competitive parity exists for the other marketing mix variables; (3) there is a high degree of competitive vulnerability because of neglect of distribution; or (4) distribution can create synergy.

In terms of the design of marketing channels, channel strategy should guide the design process in an attempt to gain a differential advantage for the firm through superior channel design. The channel manager should use the concept of channel positioning to position the channel so as to elicit the efforts of channel members as "cheerleaders" to attain a differential advantage for the manufacturer with final customers.

The selection of channel members should reflect the manufacturer's overall objectives and strategies as well as its marketing strategies in an effort to "hook up" only with channel members who are congruent with corporate objectives and are capable of implementing the strategies effectively and efficiently.

Managing the marketing channel calls for the channel manager to answer three strategic questions: How close a relationship should be developed with channel members? How should channel members be motivated? How should the marketing mix be used to enhance channel member cooperation?

Finally, when dealing with the sixth basic distribution decision—the evaluation of channel member performance—the channel manager must make sure that provisions have been made in the design and management of the channel to assure that channel member performance will be evaluated effectively.

Review Questions

1. How does channel strategy relate to marketing strategy?

2. Delineate and comment briefly on the six basic distribution decisions most firms will need to consider at one time or another.

3. Can a manufacturer automatically decide that distribution is of vital importance to the firm and should be an integral part of its strategic plan?

4. Should a firm automatically dismiss distribution in formulating its long-term corporate objectives and strategies?

5. Where does channel strategy "fit" into the marketing mix?

6. What clues should the channel manager look for in deciding how much emphasis to place on distribution as a key strategic variable in the marketing mix?

7. Explain the concept of synergy as it might apply to marketing channel strategy.

8. Discuss the concept of differential advantage as it relates to channel design strategy.

9. How does channel positioning relate to channel design and in turn to differential advantage via channel design?

10. Channel members viewed from the customers' perspective are an extension of the manufacturer's own organization. Do you agree or disagree? Explain.

11. Discuss the key strategic questions the channel manager faces when managing the marketing channel.

12. Identify the possible relationship between channel closeness and distribution intensity.

13. Discuss the portfolio concept as it applies to the motivation of channel members.

14. What is meant by "using the marketing mix" to gain the cooperation of channel members in implementing the manufacturer's channel strategy?

15. Discuss the underlying theme involved in channel strategy as it relates to the evaluation of channel member performances.

Channel Issues for Discussion

1. Although online sales channels have enjoyed tremendous growth over the past decade, a strategic disadvantage which could limit future growth potential is that of immediacy. For physical products ordered online, consumers do not have the same experience of taking the product with them immediately when they purchase it in a store. Rather, they must wait at least a day and sometimes several days. Recently, the world's largest online retailer, Amazon.com has attempted to mitigate the immediacy problem by offering same-day delivery in a number of major metropolitan areas. But the service is pricey—$17.99 per shipment plus $1.99 per pound of product weight. Now some traditional bricks and mortar retailers such as Nordstrom and the retail division of Jones Apparel Group Inc. think they have found a synergy that will provide a differential advantage over Amazon.com by using their retail stores as delivery centers for online operations. By doing so, these retailers believe they will be able to offer same-day service more efficiently and at lower cost than Amazon.com because, unlike Amazon.com, they have many stores very close to their customers.

   Do you think this synergy between the online and retail store channels available to traditional retailers that makes possible quicker and cheaper product delivery to consumers will provide a differential advantage to most retail store chains that also offer online sales channels?

2. Oakley Inc., based in Foothill Ranch, California, is best known as a manufacturer of high-end, avant-garde sunglasses, which it sells to the tune of over $300 million per year. It is also the company that donated sunglasses to all the miners rescued in the Chile mine disaster of 2010. About one third of those sales are made through the almost 2,000 stores of the Sunglass Hut chain of specialty retailers. The channel relationship between Oakley and Sunglass Hut has been a very good one. The slick Oakley sunglasses attract customers to Sunglass Hut, the margins are high, and Oakley has a channel partner through which it could sell literally tons of its sunglasses. But all this changed when Italian sunglass maker Luxoticca Group SA acquired the Sunglass Hut chain. Luxottica, which owns the famous brand, Ray-Ban, immediately cut back orders of Oakley products to be sold through Sunglass Hut stores to less than 20 percent of what they had been prior to the acquisition. Clearly, Luxottica wanted to move more of its own products through Sunglass Hut, and so in the future Sunglass Hut would have much less shelf space for Oakley products. Oakley's profit projections and stock prices dropped drastically on the news of this channel upheaval.

   Discuss Oakley's channel strategy from the possible downside of channel partnerships or strategic alliances that it had with Sunglass Hut. How might Oakley's channel strategy be changed to mitigate this kind of problem in the future?

3. Milwaukee is a famous name in industrial quality power tools. Its products are renowned for their rugged design and reliability. Most of its products are sold through wholesalers (industrial distributors) to a wide variety of power tool users including factories, contractors, mechanics, schools, government agencies, and many others. Milwaukee claims that almost 80 percent of its distributors have been associated with it for 25 years or more. Milwaukee describes itself as a consistent and reliable partner to distributors. The company says, "Our business succeeds when your business succeeds."

   Comment on this statement in terms of its possible implications for channel design, selection, management, and evaluation strategies.

4. Lincoln automobiles, the luxury car division of the Ford Motor Company, has fallen on hard times in recent years. Over the decade from 2000 to 2010, Lincoln fell from the top-selling luxury brand in the U.S. all the way down to number eight. Further, many consumers who buy luxury cars such as Lexus, BMW, Mercedes-Benz, and even Cadillac never consider purchasing a Lincoln product. Ford is now looking to revive and rejuvinate its Lincoln division to position it as a real competitor to the current foreign and domestic luxury cars. But Ford believes achieving this new upgraded position involves not just introducing better and more exciting cars; there is also a channel problem—too many Lincoln dealers and too few that have the kind of upscale facilities and service capabilities that can provide the kind of customer experience luxury automobile buyers expect. Ford estimates that it will

need to cut some 200 dealers from the current 1,200 and that many of the remaining dealers will have to spend something in the neighborhood of $2 million each to upgrade their dealerships.

Discuss the concept of the "customer experience" in terms of the role played by the product versus the channels through which it is sold.

5. Nespresso, a division of Nestle's SA, pioneered the development of the single serving coffee machine in 1986. By 2009, Nespresso had achieved sales of over $2.6 billion with double-digit growth projected for the next several years. The machines which have been imitated by more than twenty competitors, use a capsule or "pod" to make a single serving of coffee by pumping hot water through the pod under tremendous pressure. From the outset, Nespresso's business model was based on the sale of its exclusive coffee pods protected by many patents to generate most of the sales and profits for the company rather than on sales of the machines. The pod to coffee machine relationship is analogous to the cartridge and printer whereby the printer manufacturers rely on sales of print cartridges for the bulk of their revenues and profits. Nespresso recognized the extreme importance of maintaining the exclusivity and premium price of its coffee pods by stringently controlling their distribution channels. Consequently, Nespresso's coffee pods are sold only in its own stores, its online site, or by phone directly from Nespresso. Recently, competitors Sara Lee Corp. and Ethical Coffee Co., announced plans to introduce their own coffee capsules that will work in Nespresso machines. These capsules will be cheaper and more widely distributed than the Nespresso pods. Nespresso says it will take legal action if the competitors' products infringe on any of its patents.

Do you think Nespresso's distribution strategy based on tight control of the channels for its coffee pods can provide an effective means for dealing with the competition if the legal action fails to stop the competition from selling their Nespresso-compatible capsules? Why or why not?

6. For many years, Procter & Gamble, as well as the other giant consumer packaged goods manufacturers, used special deals and merchandising campaigns as the mainstay of their channel management strategy for dealing with channel members. Special discounts, allowances, slotting fees, coupons, payments for displays, and similar tactics were used abundantly to get retailers and wholesalers to push their products. The main problem with that approach to motivating channel members is that it can be very expensive for the manufacturer. It often requires higher costs for special packaging and handling, creates "peaks and valleys" in production, and increases the manufacturer's promotional costs. Moreover, from the consumer's point of view, the ups and downs in prices, when one week a box of Tide might sell for $3.79 and the next week for $7.79, fosters price sensitivity and erodes brand loyalty. In a fundamental break with this status quo approach to channel management, P&G offered its products to channel members at lower prices on an everyday and sustained basis. P&G believed this would reduce its own costs and enable channel members to pass on lower prices to consumers, also on an everyday basis.

What do you think of P&G's channel strategy? What are its possible strengths and weaknesses? Discuss from the standpoints of the manufacturer and the channel members.

7. The grocery business is one of the most competitive of all businesses, especially when it comes to getting a new product from a small manufacturer onto supermarket shelves. The typical supermarket carries about 30,000 different items, but some 15,000 new products are introduced each year. There is no way that all of these products will get on the shelves because there is limited space for such a host of new products. One method of helping the odds is for the manufacturer to pay slotting fees or pay-to-stay fees—in effect paying the retailers for the right to place the products on the retailers' shelves. But these fees can be very high, sometimes as much as $5,000 for four feet of shelf space per store per year.

Are "slotting fees" simply a way of life in highly competitive industries where the fight for shelf space is intense? Might there be other approaches? Discuss.

8. Movie studios are in something of a dilemma lately when it comes to planning their future channel strategy for distribution of their films. Electronic distribution is very profitable because, of the typical $4.99 cable companies charge consumers to rent a movie. The studios get to keep about 70 percent of that. DVDs are less profitable. The usual gross margin received by studios

on the sale of DVDs is about 30 percent. But there's a catch. Even though electronic channels for distributing movies are growing rapidly, "old fashioned" DVDs still account for approximately 70 percent of film profits. So, while electronic distribution holds great promise, especially given the expected growth potential for showing

movies on mobile devices such as smartphones, physical DVDs are still an important distribution channel for movies.

What kind of channel strategy would you recommend to the movie studios to deal with this challenge?

References

1. Philip Kotler, *Marketing Management Analysis, Planning Implementation and Control*, 6th ed. (Englewood Cliffs, N.J.: Prentice-Hall, 1988), 71.
2. For a comprehensive and in-depth treatment of marketing strategy see: David W. Cravens *Strategic Marketing* 5th edition. Chicago: Richard D. Irwin 1997.
3. For another perspective of channel strategy focusing on industrial channels, see Leonard J. Kistner, C. Anthony di Benedetto, and Sriraman Bhooraraghaven, "An Integrated Approach to the Development of Channel Strategy," *Industrial Marketing Management* 23 (1994): 315–322; see also Brent M. Wren, "Channel Structure and Strategic Choice in Marketing Channels," in *Enhancing Knowledge Development in Marketing: Proceedings of the Annual Educators' Conference of the American Marketing Association*, eds. Robert P. Leone and V. Kumar (Chicago: American Marketing Association, 1992), 529–535.
4. For a related discussion see: Joe Meyers, Evan Van Metre, and Andrew Pickersgill, "Steering Customers to the Right Channel," *McKinsey Quarterly* (October 2004): 1–6.
5. For additional in-depth discussion related to this issue, see Michael E. Porter, "Strategy and the Internet," *Harvard Business Review* (March 2001): 63–68.
6. Joann Muller, "The Bespoke Auto," *Forbes* (September 27, 2010): 96–98.
7. Derek F. Abell and John S. Hammond, *Strategic Market Planning Problems and Analytical Approaches* (Englewood Cliffs, N.J.: Prentice-Hall, 1979), 451.
8. For a related discussion see: Michael E. Porter, *Competitive Advantage: Creating and Sustaining Superior Performance* (New York: The Free Press, 1998).
9. Peter Drucker, "Manage by Walking around Outside," *Wall Street Journal* (May 11, 1990): A12.
10. Tom Peters, "Ignore Distribution Channels at Your Own Risk," *San Jose Mercury News* (February 13, 1986) 8G.
11. Spencer E. Ante, "At Amazon, Marketing is for Dummies," *Business Week* (September 28, 2009): 53–54.
12. Yukari Iwatani Kane and Ethan Smith, "Apple Sees New Money in Old Media," *Wall Street Journal* (January 21, 2010): B1, B2; Erick Schonfeld, "Apple's New Retail Strategy? Mini-Me," *Business Week* (November 2004): 44.
13. Susanne Craig, "For Edward D. Jones, Avoiding the Internet Is a Secret to Success," *Wall Street Journal* (August 8, 2001): A1, A4.
14. Hewlett-Packard Annual Report (2009): 23.
15. Robert Frank, "Rayovac to Buy Battery Business of Varta for about $262 million," *Wall Street Journal* (July 29, 2002): A6.
16. For a related discussion, see John T. Mentzer and Lisa R. Williams, "The Role of Logistics Leverage in Marketing Strategy," *Journal of Marketing Channels* 8, no. ¾ (2001): 29–47.
17. See, for example, "Integrating Multiple Channels," *Chain Store Age* (August 2001): 24A–25A.
18. For a related discussion see: Don Peppers and Martha Rogers, "Delivering a Smarter Multichannel Experience," *Sales and Marketing Management* (April 2007): 11–13.
19. James A. Narus and James C. Anderson, "Rethinking Distribution," *Harvard Business Review* (July–August 1996): 112–130.
20. See for example: Daisuke Wakabayashi, "Dell Unit Hunts for Cost Cuts," *Wall Street Journal* (April 28, 2010): B4.
21. Donald V. Fites, "Make Your Dealers Your Partners," *Harvard Business Review* (March–April 1996): 86.
22. For an insightful article dealing with the issue of relationship building in marketing channels, see John R. Nevin, "Relationship Marketing and Distribution Channels: Exploring Fundamental Issues," *Journal of the Academy of Marketing Science*, 23 no. 4 (1995): 327–334.
23. Paula Andruss, "Delivering Wow Through Service," *Marketing News* (October 15, 2008): 10.
24. See for example, Stacy Perman, "Multichannel Cross-Platform Synergy is Mega, Yo," *Business* 2.0 (August/September 2001): 164–165.
25. Reid Kanaley, "NutriSystem at Walmart," *Philadelphia Inquirer* (October 7, 2009): D1.
26. See, for example, "Forming Strategic Alliances between Suppliers and Distributors," *NeoBrief* (Issue 2, 1991): 1–5; James A. Narus and James C. Anderson, "Turn Your Industrial Distributors into Partners," *Harvard Business Review* (March-April 1986): 66–71; and James

C. Anderson and James A. Narus, "A Model of Distributor Firm and Manufacturer Firm Working Partnerships," *Journal of Marketing* (January 1990): 42–58.

27. Wroe Alderson, *Marketing Behavior and Executive Action* (Homewood, Ill: Irwin, 1957), 101–109. Also, for an excellent discussion of differential advantage from a marketing standpoint, see Victor J. Cook, Jr., "Marketing Strategy and Differential Advantage," *Journal of Marketing* (Spring 1983): 68–75.

28. Michael E. Porter, *Competitive Strategy: Techniques for Analyzing Industries and Competitors,* (New York: The Free Press, 1980).

29. For some additional perspective on this point, see Minakshi Trivedi, "Channel Selection: A Cost of Information Issue," *Journal of Marketing Channels* 4, no. 4 (1995): 1–13; and Hans Skytte, "How to Develop and Sustain Competitive Advantages through Interorganizational Relations between Retailers and Suppliers," in *Proceedings of the Sixth World Conference on Research in the Distributive Trades*, eds. Roy Thruik and Henk J. Gianotten (The Hague, Netherlands: Dutch Ministry of Economic Affairs, 1992), 133–140.

30. James A. Narus and James C. Anderson, "Strengthen Distributor Performance through Channel Positioning," *Sloan Management Review* (Winter 1988): 33.

31. "Creating the Lexus Customer Experience," *The Executive Issue*, (January 2009): 1–3.

32. For a related discussion presenting a method for helping to achieve this outcome, see Poh-Lin Yeoh and Roger J. Calantone, "An Application of the Analytical Hierarchy Process to International Marketing Selection of a Foreign Distributor," *Journal of Global Marketing*, 8, no. ¾ (1995): 39–65.

33. See, for example, Alexandra Peers and Nick Wingfield, "Sotheby's, eBay Team Up to Sell Fine Art Online," *Wall Street Journal* (January 31, 2002_: B8.

34. See for example: Miguel Bustillo and Nick Wingfield, "Best-Buy to Sell Green Vehicles," *Wall Street Journal* (July 6, 2009): B4.

35. For an excellent background article related to channel management, see Frank V. Cespedes and Raymond Corey, "Managing Multiple Channels," *Business Horizons* (July–August 1990): 67–77.

36. For an excellent discussion of this viewpoint in the context of industrial channels, see Jean L. Johnson, "Strategic Integration in Industrial Distribution Channels: Managing the Interfirm Relationship as a Strategic Asset," *Journal of the Academy of Marketing Science* (Winter 1999): 4–18.

37. For an insightful and candid article that does discuss the loosening or weakening of channel relationships, see

Gary L. Frazier and Kersi D. Antia, "Exchange Relationships and Interfirm Power in Channels of Distribution," *Journal of the Academy of Marketing Science* 23, no. 4 (1995): 321–326.

38. See, for example, James C. Anderson and James A. Narus, "Partnering as a Focused Market Strategy," *California Management Review* (Spring 1991): 95–113; and Jan R. Heide and George John, "Alliances in Industrial Purchasing: The Determinants of Joint Action in Buyer–Supplier Relationships," *Journal of Marketing Research* (February 1990): 24–36.

39. Kyle Cattani, Sebastian Heese, Wendell Gilland, and Jayashankar Swaminathan, "When Manufacturers Go Retail," *MIT Sloan Management Review* (Winter 2006): 9–11.

40. Jeff Bennett, "Some Chrysler Dealers See Un Problema in Fiat's Plan," *Wall Street Journal* (August 24, 2010): B1.

41. For a related discussion see: Geoffrey A. Fowler, Scott Morrison, and Sharon Terlep, "GM eBay End Online Sales Effort," *Wall Street Journal* (September 30, 2009): B2.

42. For a related discussion, see V. Kasturi Rangan and Jarkumar Ramchandran, "Integrating Distribution Strategy and Tactics: A Model and Application," *Management Science* (November 1991): 1377–1389.

43. For two excellent analyses of the role of slotting allowances in marketing channels, see J. Chris White, Lisa C. Troy, and R. Nicholas Gerlich, "The Role of Slotting Fees and Introductory Allowances in Retail Buyers' New Product Acceptance Decisions," *Journal of the Academy of Marketing Science* (Spring 2000,): 291–298; and Judy Siguaw, "Slotting Allowances: A New Variable in the Distribution Channel," in *Developments in Marketing Science, Volume XIV, Proceedings of the 15th Annual Conference of the Academy of Marketing Science*, ed. Robert L. King (Coral Gables, FL: Academy of Marketing Science, 1991), 91–100.

44. George S. Day, "Diagnosing the Product Portfolio," *Journal of Marketing* (April 1977): 29–38.

45. See, for example, David Perry, "How You'll Manage Your 1990s Distribution Portfolio," *Business Marketing* (June 1989): 52–56.

46. Peter R. Dickson, "Distributor Portfolio Analysis and the Channel Dependence Matrix: New Techniques for Understanding and Managing the Channel," *Journal of Marketing* (Summer 1983): 35–44.

47. Denise D. Schoenbachler and Geoffrey L. Gordon, "Multi-Channel Shopping: Understanding What Drives Channel Choice," *Journal of Consumer Marketing* 19, no. 1 (2002): 50.

CHAPTER 6

Designing Marketing Channels

LEARNING OBJECTIVES

After reading this chapter, you should:

1. Understand the meaning of channel design and the key distinguishing points associated with it.
2. Realize that channel design is a complex process.
3. Know the sequence of the channel design paradigm and understand the underlying logic of the sequence.
4. Recognize a variety of situations that might call for a channel design decision.
5. Be familiar with the concept of distribution objectives and the need for congruency with marketing and corporate objectives and strategies.
6. Be able to specify distribution tasks.
7. Recognize the three dimensions of channel structure and the strategic significance of each dimension.
8. Delineate the six basic categories of variables affecting channel structure.
9. Understand the concept of a heuristic in terms of its benefits and limitations in channel design.
10. Recognize the limitations of the channel manager's ability to choose an optimal channel structure.
11. Be familiar with the major approaches for choosing a channel structure.
12. Have an appreciation for the value of judgmental-heuristic approaches for choosing channel structures in the real world.

© OmniTerra Images

FOCUS ON CHANNELS

Google's Direct Channel Design for Its Smartphone Was Not Very Smart

Google, Inc. is one of the smartest and most successful companies in history. In less than a decade it became a global force as the unquestioned search engine leader with an advertising-based revenue model that generated billions of dollars in sales and extraordinary profits.

But even the best and brightest companies can make mistakes, and Google is no exception. In fact, the company made a big one when it designed its marketing channel for its Nexus One Smartphone. Google thought it could revolutionize the cell phone market by selling the phones directly to consumers online through its own web store with or without wireless contracts. But after only five months, Google announced it would be closing its web store. What caused the sudden shut down of Google's direct-to-customer channel structure? The same problem that mere mortal companies experience when they design the wrong channel: the channel failed to provide the kind of experience

customers were looking for. Most customers want a hands-on experience before buying a smartphone, and they also want a wide range of service plans to choose from that are clearly explained by a real person. The direct web store channel did not deliver these services, so sales turned out to be so bad that Google had no choice but to abandon its direct channel. Instead, Google announced in a blog post that it would be designing a different channel structure for the Nexus One that would use wireless carriers to make the phones available to consumers—the very same channel structure used by all competitive smartphone manufacturers.

So, if you Google the phrase "dumb channel design for smartphones," don't be surprised if the first result on the list to pop up contains the name of a company called Google!

Source: Based on Scott Morrison, "Google to Stop Online Sales of Nexus One Smartphones," *Wall Street Journal*, (May 17, 2010): B9.

The previous chapter examined marketing channel strategy in terms of the key distribution decisions that most firms face. As we pointed out, the first of these is to determine what role distribution should play in the firm's overall corporate objectives and strategies. The part distribution is expected to play among the four strategic areas of the marketing mix is the second major distribution decision. The third decision deals with the structure of the firm's marketing channels. To address this third major strategic distribution decision, the channel manager must get involved in the process of channel design, the subject of this chapter.

What Is Channel Design?

Use of the term *design* varies widely as it applies to the marketing channel. Some authors use the term as a noun to describe channel structure. Others use it to denote the formation of a new channel from scratch, while still others use it more broadly to include modifications to existing channels. Finally, design has also been used synonymously with the term *selection*, with no distinction made between the two.[1]

Such variations in usage can lead to confusion. So, before proceeding further, we will define more precisely what we mean by *design* as it applies to the marketing channel:

> **Channel design** *refers to decisions associated with developing new marketing channels where none had existed before, or to modifying existing channels.*

The first point to note in this definition is that channel design is presented as a decision faced by the marketer. In this sense channel design is similar to the other decision areas of the marketing mix, namely, product, price, and promotion. So, when viewed from a management perspective, the marketer must make decisions in each of these areas of the marketing mix.

A second point is that channel design is used in a broad sense to include either setting up channels from scratch or modifying existing channels. In fact, modification or redesign of existing channels, sometimes referred to in recent jargon as *reengineering* the marketing channel, is actually in practice a more common occurrence than setting up channels from scratch.[2]

Third, when used in its verb form, the term *design* implies that the marketer is consciously and actively allocating the distribution tasks in an attempt to develop an effective and efficient channel structure. The term is not used to refer to channel structures that have simply evolved.[3] In short, design means that management has taken a proactive role in developing the channel.

Fourth, *selection*, as we use the term refers to only one phase of channel design—the selection of the channel members.

Finally, the term *channel design* also has a strategic connotation because, as we pointed out in Chapter 5, channel design should be used as an integral part of the firm's attempt to gain a differential advantage or sustainable competitive advantage in the market.[4] Thus, using channel design as a strategic tool for gaining a differential advantage should be uppermost in the channel manager's thinking when designing marketing channels.

Who Engages in Channel Design?

Producers, manufacturers, wholesalers (consumer and industrial), and retailers all face channel design decisions. For retailers, however, channel design is viewed from a perspective opposite that of producers and manufacturers. Retailers look "up the channel" in an attempt to secure suppliers, rather than "down the channel" toward the market (as is the case for producers and manufacturers). Wholesale intermediaries face channel design decisions from both perspectives.

In this text we use the perspective of a firm (mainly producers, manufacturers, service providers, and franchisors) looking down the channel toward the market. Hence, we will discuss the topic of channel design from this perspective. This is not to minimize the importance of the other perspective. Indeed, it can be a very important problem for retailers (and for wholesalers and franchisees, as well). But an adequate treatment of the perspective of a firm looking up the channel is outside the scope of this text.[5]

A Paradigm of the Channel Design Decision

The channel design decision can be broken down into seven phases or steps:

1. Recognizing the need for a channel design decision
2. Setting and coordinating distribution objectives
3. Specifying distribution tasks

FIGURE 6.1

A Flowchart of the Channel Design Decision Paradigm

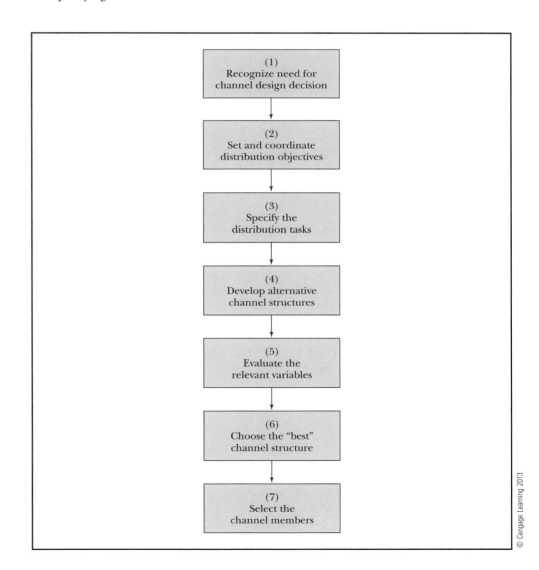

© Cengage Learning 2013

4. Developing possible alternative channel structures
5. Evaluating the variables affecting channel structure
6. Choosing the "best" channel structure
7. Selecting the channel members

These seven phases are shown schematically in Figure 6.1.

The organization of this chapter and of Chapter 7 follows this channel design paradigm. Each major section of this chapter focuses on one of the phases, from Phase 1 through Phase 6. Phase 7, the selection of channel members, is discussed separately in Chapter 7. Target markets, the most basic variable affecting channel design decisions, though discussed briefly in the present chapter, is of such importance that all of Chapter 8 (the last chapter in Part 2) is devoted to this topic.

Phase 1: Recognizing the Need for a Channel Design Decision

Many situations can indicate the need for a channel design decision.[6] Among them are the following:

1. Developing a new product or product line. If existing channels for other products are not suitable for the new product or product line, a new channel may have to be set up or the existing channels modified in some fashion.
2. Aiming an existing product at a new target market. A common example of this situation is a firm's introduction of a product in the consumer market after it has sold in the industrial market.
3. Making a major change in some other component of the marketing mix. For example, a new pricing policy emphasizing lower prices may require a shift to lower-price dealers such as discount mass merchandisers.
4. Establishing a new firm, either from scratch or as a result of mergers or acquisitions.
5. Adapting to changing intermediary policies that may inhibit the attainment of the firm's distribution objectives. For example, if intermediaries begin to emphasize their own private brands, then the manufacturer may want to add new distributors who will promote the company's products more enthusiastically.
6. Dealing with changes in availability of particular kinds of intermediaries. For example, French manufacturers of luxury goods such as Yves St. Laurent evening wear, Limoges china, and Christofle silverware faced channel design decisions in the U.S. market when the number of prestigious department stores was reduced as a result of the wave of acquisitions and mergers that occurred in the retail sector.
7. Opening up new geographic marketing areas (territories).
8. When technological advances make new channels possible, such as Internet-based online channels and smartphone technology that enabled mobile channels to emerge recently from a marginal to a major channel option.
9. Meeting the challenge of conflict or other behavioral problems.[7] For example, in some instances conflict may become so intense that it is not possible to resolve it without modifying the channel. A loss of power by a manufacturer to his or her distributors may also foster the need to design an entirely new channel.[8] Further, changing roles and communication difficulties may confront the marketer with channel design decisions (see Chapter 4).
10. Reviewing and evaluating. The regular periodic reviews and evaluations undertaken by a firm may point to the need for changes in the existing channels and possibly the need for new channels. (See Chapter 14).

This list, although by no means comprehensive, offers an overview of the more common conditions that may require the channel manager to make channel design decisions.[9] It is important to be familiar with this list because channel design decisions are not necessarily obvious, especially those involving modifications rather than the setting up of new channels.

Phase 2: Setting and Coordinating Distribution Objectives

Having recognized that a channel design decision is needed, the channel manager should try to develop a channel structure, whether from scratch or by modifying existing channels, that will help achieve the firm's distribution objectives effectively and efficiently. Yet quite often at this stage of the channel design decision, the firm's distribution objectives are not explicitly formulated, particularly because the changed conditions that created the need for channel design decisions (see previous section) might also have created the need for new or modified distribution objectives. It is important for the channel manager to evaluate carefully the firm's distribution objectives at this point to see if new ones are needed. An examination of the distribution objectives must also be made to see if they are coordinated with objectives and strategies in the other areas of the marketing mix (product, price and promotion), and with the overall objectives and strategies of the firm.

In order to set distribution objectives that are well coordinated with other marketing and firm objectives and strategies, the channel manager needs to perform three tasks:

1. Become familiar with the objectives and strategies in the other marketing mix areas and any other relevant objectives and strategies of the firm.
2. Set distribution objectives and state them explicitly.
3. Check to see if the distribution objectives set are congruent with marketing and other general objectives and strategies of the firm.

Each of these tasks will be treated individually in the discussion that follows.

Becoming familiar with Objectives and Strategies

Whomever is responsible for setting distribution objectives should also make an effort to learn which existing objectives and strategies in the firm may impinge on the distribution objectives to be set. In practice, often the same individual(s) who set(s) objectives for other components of the marketing mix will do so for distribution.[10] But even in this case, it is necessary to "think through" the interrelationships of the various marketing objectives and policies. Frito-Lay, maker of Doritos and Fritos and the world leader in salty snack foods, provides a good example of how even a giant, well-managed company can get off track when trying to relate distribution objectives to objectives and strategies in other areas of the marketing mix. The company puts great strategic emphasis on the freshness of its products—most of which have a very short shelf life. To meet its distribution objective for freshness, Frito-Lay designed a channel that uses almost 13,000 drivers/salespeople who deliver the product directly to grocery stores. Each driver/salesperson is equipped with state-of-the-art handheld personal computers to transmit sales and inventory data instantly back to headquarters. This "right to the store door" channel structure had become famous in the industry and is usually cited as the key competitive advantage in Frito-Lay's dominance of the salty snack market. Frito-Lay also tried the same channel structure for cookies and crackers—but with much less success. The reason? The strategic emphasis on freshness was not necessary for the longer shelf life of cookies and crackers. Hence the expense and added burden on the drivers/salespeople in attempting to meet the stringent distribution objective were not warranted for these products.

Setting Explicit Distribution Objectives

Distribution objectives are essentially statements describing the part that distribution is expected to play in achieving the firm's overall marketing and/or corporate objectives. Dell Computer, for example, which in recent years has sought to reinvigorate its growth by gaining more penetration in consumer markets on a global scale, states its distribution objective in its annual report as follows:

> Our growth strategy involves reaching more customers worldwide through new distribution channels such as consumer retail, expanding our relationships with value-added resellers, and augmenting select areas of our business through targeted acquisitions.[11]

Other examples of distribution objectives are as follows:

- *General Mills' decision to merge with Pillsbury was based heavily on General Mills's distribution objective, which sought to gain access to restaurants, school cafeterias, and vending machines by using Pillsbury's expertise in selling through those channels.*[12]
- *At the start of the new millennium, Apple Computer set a distribution objective to reach more consumers with what it refers to as the "Apple experience." So Apple developed a chain of its own retail stores to maximize its control over how its products would be presented to consumers at the retail level.*[13]
- *The Coca-Cola Co., based on a distribution objective seeking to broaden its penetration in the school and college markets, has used exclusive distribution contracts where schools or colleges agree to sell only Coca-Cola Company products. These exclusive contracts lock out competitors, and thereby help Coke achieve its distribution objective of gaining a high penetration rate in this market.*[14]
- *Amazon.com's overriding distribution objective from the outset for its exclusively online sales channel was to provide not just the best customer service but the best customer experience. Jeff Bezos, Amazon's founder and CEO sees an important distinction between these two terms:*[15]

> … customer service is a component of customer experience. Customer experience includes having the lowest price, having fast delivery, having it reliable enough so that you [the consumer] don't need to contact [anyone]. Then you save the customer service for those truly unusual situations.

So, Jeff Bezos's distribution objective for Amazon's online channel was, and still is, aimed not at "firefighting" particular customer problems via customer service, but to provide virtually all customers with a great shopping experience so that very few will require customer service involving human intervention.

Checking for Congruency

A congruency check in the context of channel design involves verifying that the distribution objectives do not conflict with objectives in the other areas of the marketing mix (product, price, and promotion) or with the overall marketing and general objectives and strategies of the company. In order to make such a check, it is important to examine the interrelationships and hierarchy of objectives and strategies in the firm. These are portrayed in Figure 6.2.

In the figure, objectives and strategies for the four components of the marketing mix are connected via two-way arrows. This is meant to convey the idea that these areas are interrelated. Hence, objectives and strategies pursued in any of these areas must generally be congruent with other areas. A high quality objective in the product area, for example, would most likely call for a pricing objective that would cover the probable higher costs of the

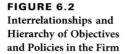

FIGURE 6.2
Interrelationships and Hierarchy of Objectives and Policies in the Firm

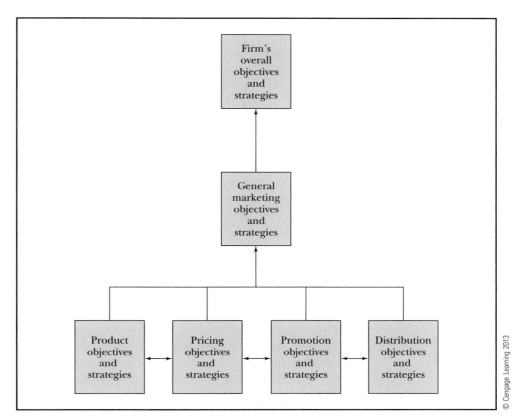

product and enhance its quality image. Promotional objectives would have to focus on communicating to the target market the superior quality of the product. At the same time, distribution objectives would need to be developed in terms of making the product conveniently available to that market in the types of outlets in which targeted consumers are likely to shop.

Figure 6.2 also suggests a hierarchy of objectives and strategies in the sense that objectives and strategies in each area of the marketing mix must also be congruent with higher-level marketing objectives and strategies. These in turn must be congruent with the even higher set of overall objectives and strategies in the firm.

Checking for congruency in this fashion is particularly important when setting distribution objectives because the distribution objectives can have a substantial long-term impact on the firm, especially if the distribution objective departs significantly from established objectives and strategies. Consider, for example, Starbucks's recent decision to distribute its Seattle's Best Coffee line through thousands of convenience stores, supermarkets, fast-food chains such as Burger King and Subway, and even in vending machines. Starbucks, which acquired Seattle's Best Coffee in 2003, had until 2010 sold the coffee mainly through the chain's own shops, Borders bookstores, and in about 2,500 supermarkets. Now with the new broad-based intensive distribution objective for Seattle's Best Coffee, which will use the slogan "Great Coffee Everywhere," Starbucks's hopes to reach many more potential customers who are not patronizing Starbucks's own coffee shops and at the same time compete against fast-food chains such as McDonald's, which has 30,000 restaurants in the U.S. selling premium coffee.[16] The danger posed by Starbucks's intensive distribution objective for Seattle's Best Coffee, however, is that it could cannibalize sales of Starbucks brand coffee. In addition, some coffee industry observers believe that such distribution through fast-food outlets, convenience stores, and vending machines could undermine not only the quality image of Seattle's Best Coffee, but the Starbucks brand itself. Only time will tell whether Starbucks's broadened distribution objective will be congruent with Starbucks's overall corporate objective of maintaining its image as the world's best coffee purveyor.

Phase 3: Specifying the Distribution Tasks

After distribution objectives have been set and coordinated, a number of distribution tasks (functions) must be performed if the distribution objectives are to be met. The channel manager should, therefore, specify explicitly the nature of these tasks.

Over the years, marketing scholars have discussed numerous lists of marketing tasks (functions).[17] These lists generally included such activities as buying, selling, communication, transportation, storage, risk taking, financing, breaking bulk, and others.[18] Such classifications of marketing functions, while useful to those seeking to explain the role of marketing in a macro context, are of little direct value to the channel manager operating in the individual firm. The job of the channel manager in outlining distribution functions or tasks is much more specific and situationally dependent. The kinds of tasks required to meet specific distribution objectives must be precisely stated. For example, a manufacturer of a consumer product such as, say, high-quality tennis racquets aimed at serious amateur tennis players would need to specify distribution tasks such as the following to make the racquets readily available to them:

1. Gather information on target market shopping patterns
2. Promote product availability in the target market
3. Maintain inventory storage to assure timely availability
4. Compile information about product features
5. Provide for hands-on tryout of product
6. Sell against competitive products
7. Process and fill specific customer orders
8. Transport the product
9. Arrange for credit provisions
10. Provide product warranty service
11. Provide repair and restringing service
12. Establish product return procedure

The specification of distribution tasks for products sold in industrial markets often has to be even more specifically stated than for consumer products. For example, a steel or metal producer whose distribution objectives call for dealing with a target market that contains many small customers would have such basic distribution tasks as selling, communication, transportation, storage, risk taking, and financing. But in addition, in order to serve the smaller customers, the producer would probably have to perform many more specialized tasks, such as the following:

1. Maintain readily available inventory (specified in terms of quantity and type)
2. Provide rapid delivery (specified in days or hours)
3. Offer credit
4. Provide emergency service
5. Supply semifabrication functions such as cutting, shearing, slotting, threading, pattern cutting, pattern rolling, rerolling, stretcher leveling, welding, grinding, forcing, and reaming
6. Include packaging and special handling
7. Provide technical assistance such as problem analysis, product selection, application, and end use product
8. Maintain market information

9. Offer storage space

10. Allow for absorption of size and grade obsolescence

11. Process orders and bill for many accounts

12. Offer return provisions

Though a number of these functions appear to be production rather than distribution tasks, when viewed in the context of being necessary to meet a particular distribution objective (such as dealing with smaller customers), they are indeed distribution tasks. The performance of these specialized tasks would be necessary because the distribution objective called for dealing with many small customers, and in most cases, small customers could not perform these tasks themselves. Consequently, the specific kinds of distribution tasks required are mainly a function of the distribution objectives that have been set, and, of course, the types of firms involved. For example, if the metal producer's distribution objective had called for dealing only with large customers, a number of the tasks could be eliminated or significantly reduced—particularly tasks 2, 4, 5, 6, 7, and 9.[19]

In specifying distribution tasks, it is especially important not to underestimate what is involved in making products and services conveniently available to final customers.[20] A substantial cause of the failures of so many dot-com, E-commerce firms in both business-to-consumer (B2C) and business-to-business (B2B) channels can be traced to grossly underestimating all of the distribution tasks needed to link firms efficiently with their customers.[21] Powerful Internet-based technologies and spectacular Web sites do not obviate the need to perform seemingly mundane distribution tasks such as picking, packing, stocking, and tracking thousands or even tens of thousands of orders received on a daily basis.[22] Indeed, Amazon.com found that it had to build a number of huge state-of-the-art warehouses and hire many hundreds of people to perform these seemingly "simple" distribution tasks.

Phase 4: Developing Possible Alternative Channel Structures

Having specified in detail the particular distribution tasks that need to be performed to achieve the distribution objectives, the channel manager should then consider alternative ways of allocating these tasks. Often, the channel manager will choose more than one channel structure in order to reach the target markets effectively and efficiently.[23] Kraft Foods Inc., for example, sells such products as its macaroni and cheese and Tombstone pizza, through supermarkets, wholesale food distributors, convenience stores, drugstore chains, mass merchandisers, and recently, through movie theaters via high-tech vending machines that heat up the products for immediate consumption by moviegoers.[24] Chapter 1 shows a variety of other multi-channel structures in diagrammatic format for several consumer product companies as well as for business-to-business and services distribution channels (see Figures 1.1, 1.2, 1.11, 1.12, 1.13, 1.14, 1.15, 1.16). But whether for single or multi-channel structures, business-to-business channels, or channels for services, the allocation alternatives (possible channel structures) should be in terms of the following three dimensions: (1) number of levels in the channel, (2) intensity at various levels, and (3) types of intermediaries at each level.

Number of Levels

The number of levels in a channel can range from two levels—which is the most direct (manufacturer → user)—up to five levels and occasionally even higher.

The number of alternatives that the channel manager can realistically consider for this structural dimension is often limited to no more than two or three choices. For example, it might be feasible to consider going direct (two-level), using one intermediary (three-level), or possibly two intermediaries (four-level). These limitations result from a variety of factors such as the particular industry practices, nature and size of the market, availability of intermediaries, and other variables (which we will discuss more fully in Phase 5). In some instances, this dimension of channel structure is the same for all manufacturers in the industry and may remain virtually fixed for long periods of time. In the domestic automobile industry, for instance, The Big Three auto manufacturers GM, Ford, and Chrysler all sell their cars through independent auto dealers, who in turn sell to final consumers. Even in the case of some so-called online auto sales, an independent auto dealer is still involved in the channel because the actual sale is made through a dealer. In other industries, the number of levels dimension is more flexible and subject to change in relatively short time periods. This has been particularly the case since the advent of online channels, which have enabled a wide variety of manufacturers of both consumer and industrial products to add the direct, two-level (manufacturer → user) channel to existing three-and four-level channel structures.

Intensity at the Various Levels

Intensity refers to the number of intermediaries at each level of the marketing channel. As we pointed out in Chapter 5, traditionally this dimension has been broken into three categories: (1) intensive, (2) selective, and (3) exclusive. **Intensive** (sometimes termed **saturation**) means that as many outlets as possible are used at each level of the channel. Many consumer convenience goods and industrial operating supplies fit this category. **Selective**, as the name suggests, means that not all possible intermediaries at a particular level are used, but rather that those included in the channel are carefully chosen. Consumer shopping goods are often in this category. **Exclusive** is actually a way of referring to a very highly-selective pattern of distribution. In this case only one intermediary in a particular market area is used. Specialty goods often fit into this category. Figure 6.3 illustrates the intensity of distribution dimension as it might apply to retail intermediaries. The figure shows that for a given market area (territory), a very high degree of selectivity or exclusive distribution corresponds to only one retailer in the territory. A lower degree of selectivity corresponds to a few retailers, while very low selectivity (or stated conversely, an intensive level of distribution) is associated with many retailers in the territory. The actual numbers involved will, of course, vary for different firms.

As we also discussed in Chapter 5, the intensity of distribution dimension is a very important aspect of channel structure because it is often a key factor in the firm's basic marketing strategy and will also reflect the firm's overall corporate objectives and strategies. A marketing strategy that seeks to blanket the market with a product requires a channel structure that stresses a very high level of distribution intensity. Wrigley chewing gum, for example, has used an intensive distribution channel structure throughout its history. It ships more than 1 million pounds of chewing gum per day to provide

FIGURE 6.3 Relationship between the Intensity of Distribution Dimension and Number of Retail Intermediaries Used in a Given Market Area

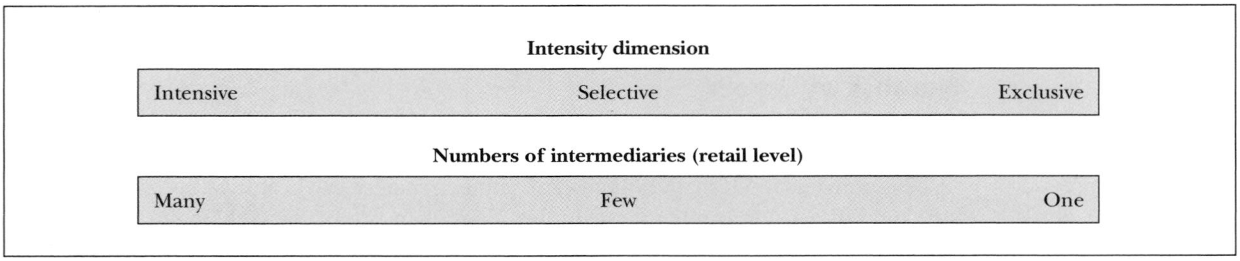

Intensity dimension		
Intensive	Selective	Exclusive

Numbers of intermediaries (retail level)		
Many	Few	One

ubiquitous availability of its products at virtually every conceivable outlet where consumers could buy chewing gum. A critical part of its channel structure is a vast network of independent wholesalers who are contacted by internally-based Wrigley telephone salespeople at least once per week. On the other hand, a marketing strategy that focuses on carefully chosen target markets, such as that used by Rolex watches, requires that a high degree of selectivity be built into the channel structure. In general, then, if a firm's basic marketing strategy emphasizes mass appeal for its products, it will most likely have to develop a channel structure that stresses intensive distribution, whereas a marketing strategy that stresses more narrow segmented marketing will probably call for a more selective channel structure.[25] Thus, as mentioned earlier, when Starbucks decided to pursue a mass market distribution objective for its Seattle's Best Coffee line, Starbucks shifted from a distribution intensity that was rather selective (a small number of its own stores, Borders book stores, and 2,500 supermarkets) to a much higher level of distribution intensity that included many thousands of fast-food restaurants, supermarkets, convenience stores, and vending machines.

Beyond this basic relationship with the firm's marketing strategy, the decision concerning degree of intensity is also often reflective of a firm's overall strategy for dealing with channel members (see the section titled "Channel Strategy and the Selection of Channel Members" in Chapter 5). Some firms like to choose their channel members or "partners" very carefully and then work closely with them in the distribution of the firm's products.[26] Other firms believe in selling through "almost anyone" and pay little attention to how the product is sold once it is in the hands of the firm's many channel members. Others are somewhere in between these two extremes. Thus, in considering the intensity dimension when designing the channel, the channel manager should carefully consider the firm's established strategies for dealing with intermediaries and try to stay within these guidelines.

Types of Intermediaries

The third dimension of channel structure deals with the particular types of intermediaries to be used (if any) at the various levels of the channel. In Chapter 2 we discussed different types of intermediaries available. Recall that there are many types listed in the *Census of Wholesale Trade* and the *Census of Retail Trade*. Unfortunately, there are many different names given to intermediaries, particularly those at the wholesale level, which were derived from the industry or trade long ago but which today convey little meaning about the services these firms offer.[27]

The channel manager should not overlook new types of intermediaries that have emerged, particularly electronic or online auction firms such as eBay or Amazon.com as possible sales outlets for consumer products. For industrial products sold in business-to-business markets, electronic marketplaces[28] such as Chemdex (chemical products), Converge.com (electronic components), and hundreds of others have emerged to serve B2B markets.[29]

The emphasis of the channel manager's analysis at this point should focus on the basic types of distribution tasks performed by these intermediaries.[30] For example, metal warehouse distributors, a type of industrial wholesaler, generally have the capability to perform all of the distribution tasks needed by metals producers in order for them to deal with smaller accounts.

Number of Possible Channel Structure Alternatives

Given that the channel manager should consider all three structural dimensions, (level, intensity, and type of intermediaries) in developing alternative channel structures, there are, in theory, a high number of possibilities. Consider the following: three levels, three degrees of intensity, five different types of intermediaries. The number of possible channel structures based on these three dimensions is:

$$3 \times 3 \times 5 = 45 \text{ possible structures}$$

Realistically, this number of alternative channel structures cannot usually be considered except when certain management science approaches are used (see Phase 6). Fortunately, in practice, the number of feasible alternatives for each dimension is often limited, so that it is seldom necessary to have more than a dozen alternative channel structures from which to choose. Usually, the number is considerably less than that.

Phase 5: Evaluating the Variables Affecting Channel Structure

Having laid out alternative channel structures, the channel manager should then evaluate a number of variables to determine how they are likely to influence various channel structures. Although there are a myriad of such variables, six basic categories are the most important:

1. Market variables
2. Product variables
3. Company variables
4. Intermediary variables
5. Environmental variables
6. Behavioral variables

In the course of discussing the variables in these categories, we will often cite a number of **heuristics** (rules of thumb) that relate these variables to channel structure. An example of one such heuristic is as follows:

> If a product is technically complex, the manufacturer should sell directly to its user instead of through intermediaries because of the need for liaison and technical advice, which intermediaries may not be equipped to provide.

Here a product variable (technical complexity) seemingly yields a simple prescription for channel structure. It would be nice if things were this simple, but usually this is *not* the case. Such heuristics, which are commonly mentioned in the marketing literature, are only crude guides to decision making. They should not be viewed as clear-cut prescriptions for choosing a particular channel structure. They are useful only to the extent that they offer some rough reflection of what would typically be expected given a particular condition, and thereby provide a point of departure for the analysis of different channel structures.

With this caveat in mind, we turn to a discussion of these six categories of variables and some of the related heuristics relevant to choosing channel structure.

Market Variables

Marketing management, including channel management, is based on the underlying philosophy of the classic marketing concept, which stresses customer (market) orientation. In developing and adapting the marketing mix, then, marketing managers should take their basic cues from the needs and wants of the target markets at which they are aiming. Hence, just as the products a firm offers, the prices it charges, and the promotional messages it employs should closely reflect the needs and wants of the target market, so too should the structure of its marketing channels.[31] Market variables are therefore the most fundamental to consider when designing a marketing channel. Indeed, market variables are of such importance in channel design that we have devoted an entire chapter to this topic (Chapter 8), where we discuss this topic in depth. So, in this section we will discuss market variables only briefly as they apply to channel design.

Four basic subcategories of market variables are particularly important in influencing channel structure. They are (1) market geography, (2) market size, (3) market density, and (4) market behavior.

Market Geography   Market geography refers to the geographical size of markets and their physical location and distance from the producer or manufacturer. From a channel design standpoint, the basic tasks that emerge when dealing with market geography are the development of a channel structure that adequately covers the markets in question and provides for an efficient flow of products to those markets.

An example of a popular heuristic for relating market geography to channel design is:

The greater the distance between the manufacturer and its markets, the higher the probability that the use of intermediaries will be less expensive than direct distribution.

This is often the case because the intermediaries buy in large quantities and then disperse the products in smaller quantities to final customers. For example, if a factory in China manufactured 10,000 toasters and then shipped them one at a time to final customers in the United States, handling and shipping costs would be vastly higher than if the factory shipped all 10,000 in one container load to a Walmart distribution center. The 10,000 toasters could then be distributed in lots of a hundred or so to individual Walmart stores for purchase by final consumers. So, having the retail intermediary, Walmart, in the channel reduces rather than increases distribution costs compared to a direct channel from distant manufacturer to consumer.

Market Size   The number of customers making up a market (consumer or industrial) determines the market size. From a channel design standpoint, the larger the number of individual customers, the larger the market size.

The usual operational measures of market size are the actual number of potential consumers or firms in the consumer and industrial markets, respectively. Dollar volume is typically not a good measure of market size because of the wide variations in dollar volume; that is, it is possible to have high dollar volumes from a small number of customers and vice versa. Only if dollar volume is highly correlated with the numbers of customers will it serve as a reliable measure of market size.

A general heuristic about market size relative to channel structure is:

If the market is large, the use of intermediaries is more likely to be needed because of the high transaction costs of serving large numbers of individual customers. Conversely, if the market is small, a firm is more likely to be able to avoid the use of intermediaries.

Market Density   The number of buying units (consumers or industrial firms) per unit of land area determines the density of the market. A market having 1,000 customers in an area of 100 square miles is more dense than one containing the same number of customers in an area of 500 square miles.

In general, the less dense the market, the more difficult and expensive is distribution. This is particularly true for the flow of goods to the market. Consequently, a typically cited heuristic for market density and channel structure is as follows:

The less dense the market, the more likely it is that intermediaries will be used. Stated conversely, the greater the density of the market, the higher the likelihood of eliminating intermediaries.

For example, a firm selling specialized industrial equipment such as drilling equipment for petroleum producers will have its market concentrated in a relatively small area in several states. On the other hand, a firm selling basic operating supplies such as oils and greases, abrasives, cleaning supplies, detergents, stationery supplies, and the like will find that its market is dispersed over a vast geographical area because there are so many potential users of these products. The possibility of designing a direct channel to serve such low-density markets is usually low because of the high costs involved in providing adequate service.

Market Behavior   Market behavior refers to the following four types of buying behaviors: (1) how customers buy, (2) when customers buy, (3) where customers buy, and (4) who does the buying.

Each of these patterns of buyer behavior may have a significant effect on channel structure.[32] Table 6.1 provides some examples. Here again we should keep in mind that the heuristics shown in Table 6.1 are merely rough indicators of what is typical. There are many exceptions to these heuristics under different sets of circumstances. The material in the table should be seen as providing illustrative examples only, and not as a source of reference for choosing channel structure. These market behaviors will be discussed in more detail in Chapter 8.

Product Variables

Product variables are another important category to consider in evaluating alternative channel structures.[33] Some of the most important product variables are bulk and weight, perishability, unit value, degree of standardization (custom-made versus standardized), technical versus nontechnical, newness, and prestige.

Bulk and Weight   Heavy and bulky products have very high handling and shipping costs relative to their value. The producers of such products should therefore attempt to minimize these costs by shipping only in large lots to the fewest possible points.

TABLE 6.1 EXAMPLES OF MARKET BUYING HABITS AND SOME CORRESPONDING HEURISTICS FOR CHANNEL STRUCTURE

BUYING HABITS	CORRESPONDING CHANNEL STRUCTURE HEURISTICS
How Customers typically buy in very small quantities.	Use long channels (perhaps several levels of intermediaries) to reach the market.
When Buying is highly seasonal.	Add intermediaries to the channel to perform the storage function, thereby reducing peaks and valleys in production.
Where Consumers increasingly tend to shop at home.	Eliminate wholesale and retail intermediaries and sell direct, via catalog or online.
Who Consumer market: Husband and wife are generally both involved in the purchase.	Distribute through retailers who successfully cater to both spouses.
Industrial market: Many individuals influence the purchasing decision.	Distribute directly for greater control of sales force to successfully reach all parties responsible for making purchase decisions.

© Cengage Learning 2013

Consequently, the channel structure for heavy and bulky products should, as a general rule, be as short as possible—usually direct from producer to user. The major exception to this occurs when customers buy in small quantities and need quick delivery. In this case it may be necessary to use some form of intermediary.

Of course, products that can be digitized such as many financial products, written material (including books) movies, and music have literally zero bulk or weight after being digitized. Hence, bulk and weight are not relevant factors to consider in the distribution of the digitizable versions of such products.

Perishablility   Products subject to rapid physical deterioration (such as fresh foods) and those that experience rapid fashion obsolescence are considered to be highly perishable. The sine qua non of channel design in this case is rapid movement of the product from production to its final user to minimize the risks attendant to high perishability. The following heuristic is appropriate:

> *When products are highly perishable, channel structures should be designed to provide for rapid delivery from producers to consumers.*

When producers and consumers are close, such channel structures can often be short. When greater distances are involved, however, the only practical and economical way to provide the necessary speed of delivery may be by using several intermediaries in the channel structure. Lettuce from California, for example, often goes through two levels of wholesalers before reaching retail stores and finally consumers.

Unit Value   In general, the lower the unit value of a product, the longer the channels should be. This is because the low unit value leaves a small margin for distribution costs. Such products as convenience goods in the consumer market and operating supplies in the industrial market typically use one or more intermediaries so that the costs of distribution can be shared by many other products that the intermediaries handle, thus creating economies of scale and scope. For example, it would be difficult to imagine the sale of a package of chewing gum directly from Wrigley to the consumer. Only by spreading the costs of distribution over the wide variety of products handled by wholesale or retail intermediaries is it possible to buy a package of chewing gum at retail for about 79 cents.

On the other hand, when the unit value of a product is high relative to its size and weight, as with fine jewelry, electronic products, luxury apparel, cosmetics, and other high unit value merchandise, direct distribution even over large distances is feasible because the handling and transportation costs are low relative to the value of the products. This high value to weight and size ratio is what enables Amazon.com to sell these products directly to consumers and even offer free shipping on orders over $25.

Degree of Standardization   In general, the influence of this product variable on channel structure is characterized by the relationship shown in Figure 6.4. Degree of standardization is shown on the horizontal axis as a continuum ranging from custom-made products to those that are identical. Channel length, on the vertical axis, is represented by the number of intermediaries, from none to several. Essentially, Figure 6.4 shows that custom-made products go directly from the producer to the user, but as products become more standardized, the opportunity to lengthen the channel by including intermediaries increases. For example, totally custom-made products such as industrial machinery very often are sold directly from the manufacturer to the user. Semi-custom products such as accessory equipment in the industrial market and furniture in the consumer market will often include one intermediary. On the other hand, highly standardized products such as operating supplies in the industrial market and convenience goods in the consumer market will frequently include more than one intermediary.

FIGURE 6.4
Relationship between
Degree of Product
Standardization and
Channel Length

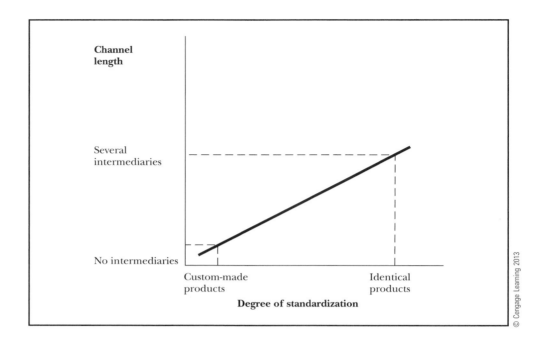

© Cengage Learning 2013

Technical versus Nontechnical   In the industrial market, a highly technical product will generally be distributed through a direct channel. The main reason for this is that the manufacturer needs sales and service people who are capable of communicating the product's technical features to potential customers who can provide continuing liaison, advice, and service after the sale is made. Even in consumer markets, products that are relatively technical, complex, or sophisticated such as home theater systems, high performance sports equipment, and more advanced personal computers are usually distributed through short channels for the same reasons.

Newness   Many new products in both consumer and industrial markets require extensive and aggressive promotion in the introductory stage to build demand. Usually, the longer the channel, the more difficult it is to achieve this kind of promotional effort from all of the channel members. Consequently, in the introductory stage, a shorter channel is generally viewed as an advantage for gaining product acceptance.[34] Further, the degree of selectivity also tends to be higher for new products because a more carefully selected group of intermediaries is more likely to provide more aggressive promotion.

Product Prestige   Prestigious products often associated with famous luxury brands such as Gucci, Rolex, Louis Vuitton, Mercedes-Benz, and many others need to maintain an aura of exclusivity and rareness that would be incompatible with mass market distribution channels. Hence, the channels for these products need to be designed to reinforce their prestigious aura by providing limited access to customers seeking to buy prestigious products.[35]

Company Variables

The most important company variables affecting channel design are (1) size, (2) financial capacity, (3) managerial expertise, and (4) objectives and strategies.

Size   In general, the range of options for different channel structures is a positive function of a firm's size. The power bases available to large firms—particularly those of reward, coercion, and expertise—enable them to exercise a substantial amount of power in the channel. This gives large firms a relatively high degree of flexibility in choosing channel structures compared to smaller firms. Consequently, the larger firm's capacity to develop channels that at least approach an optimal allocation of distribution tasks is typically higher than for smaller firms.

Financial Capacity   Generally, the greater the capital available to a company, the lower is its dependence of intermediaries. In order to sell directly to ultimate consumers or business users, a firm may need its own sales force and support services or retail stores, warehousing, and order processing capabilities. Larger firms are better able to bear the high cost of these facilities. There are, of course, exceptions to this pattern, particularly when direct mail-order channels or electronic channels utilizing the Internet are used. In both of these cases, even small firms with very limited financial capacities may find it feasible to sell directly to ultimate consumers (see Chapters 3 and 15).

Managerial Expertise   Some firms lack the managerial skills necessary to perform distribution tasks.[36] When this is the case, channel design must of necessity include the services of intermediaries, which may include wholesalers, manufacturers' representatives, selling agents, brokers, or others. Over time, as the firm's management gains experience, it may be feasible to change the structure to reduce the amount of reliance on intermediaries.

Objectives and Strategies   Marketing and general objectives and strategies (such as desire to exercise a high degree of control over the product and its service) may limit the use of intermediaries.[37] Further, such strategies as an emphasis on aggressive promotion and rapid reaction to changing market conditions will constrain the types of channel structures available to those firms employing such strategies.

Intermediary Variables

The key intermediary variables related to channel structure are (1) availability, (2) costs, and (3) the services offered.

Availability   In a number of cases, the availability of adequate intermediaries will influence channel structure. For example, lack of availability of appropriate intermediaries led Michael Dell, the founder of Dell Computer Corp., to design a direct mail-order channel that provided strong technical expertise as well as custom-designed personal computers. According to Michael Dell, existing retailers, both large and small, simply could not provide similar capabilities.

Cost   The cost of using intermediaries is always a consideration in choosing a channel structure. If the channel manager determines that the cost of using intermediaries is too high for the services performed, the channel structure is likely to minimize the use of intermediaries. Approaches for making this kind of decision will be discussed in Phase 6.

Services   The third variable, the services offered by intermediaries, is closely related to the selection of channel members (discussed in detail in the following chapter). Essentially this involves evaluating the services offered by particular intermediaries to see which ones can perform them most effectively at the lowest cost.[38] Consider, for example, Graybar Electric Co. Inc., a large electrical distributor serving the industrial business and government markets. Graybar invested tens of millions of dollars to install the mySAP.com E-business platform, which includes advanced capabilities in the areas of **customer relationship management (CRM)** and **supply chain management (SCM)**. Graybar made this investment in order to provide superior service to the manufacturers it represents (as well as the customers it serves).[39] So, rather than being "just another middleman" that manufacturers will seek to bypass, Graybar hopes this high level of service capability based on advanced technology will position this industrial distributor as an indispensable channel partner that will be eagerly courted by the best manufacturers.

Environmental Variables

As we pointed out in Chapter 3, environmental variables may affect all aspects of channel development and management. Economic, sociocultural,[40] competitive, technological, and legal environmental forces can have a significant impact on channel stunting and structure.[41] Indeed, as mentioned earlier in this chapter, the impact of environmental forces is one of the more common reasons for making channel design decisions.[42] Because Chapter 3 presented numerous examples of how the environment affects the channel, we need not go into detail here.

Behavioral Variables

When choosing a channel structure, the channel manager should review the behavioral variables discussed in Chapter 4. For example, developing more congruent roles for channel members can reduce a major cause of conflict. Giving more attention to the influence of behavioral problems that can distort communications (such as those discussed in Chapter 4) fosters a channel structure with a more effective communications flow. By keeping in mind the power bases available, the channel manager can help to ensure that the final choice of a channel structure is more likely to reflect a realistic basis for influencing channel members. For instance, a small, specialized manufacturer who decides to use large chain retailers in the channel structure is unlikely to be able to gain much influence or control if coercive power is used, yet he or she might very well be able to do so if expert power is stressed. A channel manager who needs a very high level of control to achieve distribution objectives may find that the legitimate power base (manifest in a strong franchise contract) should serve as the basis for channel structure. These and many other implications of behavioral variables may in particular instances be relevant for choosing an appropriate channel structure[43] (See Chapter 4).

Phase 6: Choosing the "Best" Channel Structure

In theory, the channel manager should choose an optimal channel structure that would offer the desired level of effectiveness in performing the distribution tasks at the lowest possible cost. If the firm's goal is to maximize its long-term profits, an optimal channel structure would be consistent with that goal.[44]

In reality, choosing an optimal channel structure, in the strictest sense of the term, is not possible, To do so would require the channel manager to have considered all possible alternative channel structures and to be able to calculate the exact payoffs associated with each alternative structure in terms of some criterion (usually profit). The channel manager would then choose the one alternative offering the highest payoff.[45]

Why is this not possible? First, as we pointed out in the section on Phase 4, management is not capable of knowing all the possible alternatives. The amount of information and time necessary to develop all possible alternative channel structures for achieving a particular distribution objective would be prohibitive. Moreover, even if management were willing to expend this time and effort, it would have no way of knowing when it had actually specified all of the possible alternatives.

Second, even if it were possible to specify all possible channel structures, precise methods do not exist for calculating the exact payoffs associated with each of the alternative structures. As we pointed out in the last section and in earlier chapters, the number of variables affecting the channel is legion and these variables are continually changing. Any method claiming to offer a means for calculating exact payoffs for each of the alternative channel structures would have to offer its user the ability to identify all relevant variables and tell precisely what effects each variable would have on the structure. Moreover, the method would also have to be capable of predicting the level and direction of change in all of the variables. Such a method or model is not a realistic possibility.

Nevertheless, even though no exact methods for choosing an optimal channel structure exist, some pioneering attempts at developing more exact methods do appear in the literature. We will discuss some of these briefly because they can provide insight for making good (if not optimal) choices of channel structure. Specifically, the approaches and methods that will be discussed can help to sharpen the channel manager's ability to evaluate variables affecting channel structure. Armed with this knowledge, the channel manager is then better prepared to choose channel structures that at least approach an optimal allocation of distribution tasks.

"Characteristics of Goods and Parallel Systems" Approach

First laid out in the late 1950s by Aspinwall, this approach places the main emphasis for choosing a channel structure on product variables[46] arguing that all products may be described in terms of the following five characteristics:

1. *Replacement rate*—the rate at which a good is purchased and consumed by users in order to provide the satisfaction a consumer expects from the product.
2. *Gross margin*—the difference between the laid-in cost and the final realized sales price. (This includes the sum of all gross margins as products move through the channel.)
3. *Adjustment*—services applied to goods in order to meet the exact needs of the consumer.
4. *Time of consumption*—the measured time of consumption during which the product gives up the utility desired.
5. *Searching time*—a measure of average time and distance from the retail store.

Aspinwall continues by presenting a method for classifying all products based on the degree to which they possess each of these characteristics. He does so by using an ingenious analogy to the color spectrum. Any product could be represented by its "shade" on this spectrum, which uses only three colors instead of the usual seven. As Table 6.2 shows, products with high replacement rates but low values for the other four characteristics are "red goods." Those products having medium values on all five characteristics are "orange goods," while those with a low replacement rate but higher values for the other four characteristics are "yellow goods." By visualizing a blending of these colors from red to yellow, with orange in between, an infinite gradation of values for products can be perceived.

Aspinwall argues that the channel structures used in the distribution (as well as promotion) of products are closely related to their "color" (that is, the degree to which they possess each of the five characteristics). For example, as the table shows, red products have a high replacement rate. The high frequency of purchase of red goods allows for a high degree of standardization and specialization in the performance of distribution tasks. This in turn creates the opportunity for more specialized marketing institutions to participate, resulting in long channels for red goods. Convenience goods in the consumer market and operating supplies in the industrial market fit this pattern.

TABLE 6.2 ASPINWALL'S "CHARACTERISTIC OF GOODS" THEORY COLOR CLASSIFICATION SCHEME

CHARACTERISTIC	COLOR CLASSIFICATION		
	RED GOODS	ORANGE GOODS	YELLOW GOODS
Replacement rate	High	Medium	Low
Gross margin	Low	Medium	High
Adjustment	Low	Medium	High
Time of consumption	Low	Medium	High
Searching time	Low	Medium	High

Source: W. Lazer and E.J. Kelly, *Managerial Marketing: Perspectives and Viewpoint*, rev. ed. (Homewood, Ill.: Richard D. Irwin, Inc. copyright 1962). Reproduced by permission of publisher.

Looking again at Table 6.2, we can see that yellow products are low in replacement rate but high in the other characteristics. This makes the performance of distribution tasks relatively expensive because of the lower opportunity for standardization and routinization compared to that of red goods. Custom-made products (such as a made-to-order suit, or industrial equipment specifically designed for its user's needs) are illustrative of yellow goods, which generally call for short channel structures.

Finally, we notice that orange goods rate a medium ranking on all five characteristics. These goods, though produced to standard specifications, will still require some degree of adjustment to adequately meet their user's needs. Automobiles and furniture are examples of orange products. The replacement rate for orange products is high enough to offer moderate opportunity for standardization and specialization. At least one intermediary is likely to enter the channel—for example, an automobile dealer buying from the manufacturer and selling to the consumer, or an industrial distributor operating between two manufacturers. Channel structures for orange goods tend to be medium in length; that is, generally containing at least one level of intermediary.

Figure 6.5 illustrates this parallel relationship between the characteristics of products and channel length. As the figure shows, the structure of the channel in terms of its length dimension parallels the characteristics of products.

Using Aspinwall's Approach   The chief value of Aspinwall's approach for the channel manager is that it provides a neat way of describing and relating a number of heuristics about how product characteristics might affect channel structure. Thus, the channel

FIGURE 6.5
Relationship between Product Characteristics and Length of Marketing Channels

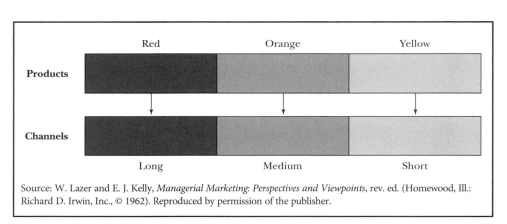

Source: W. Lazer and E. J. Kelly, *Managerial Marketing: Perspectives and Viewpoints*, rev. ed. (Homewood, Ill.: Richard D. Irwin, Inc., © 1962). Reproduced by permission of the publisher.

manager has a better handle on dealing with product variables. Rather than trying to enumerate many different product variables for each product, the channel manager can turn to Aspinwall's framework and describe virtually any product in terms of the five characteristics. Then, on the basis of judgment or by assigning numerical weights to each of the characteristics, the product may be classified as red, orange, or yellow.

The major problem with Aspinwall's approach is that it puts too much emphasis on product characteristics as the determinant of channel structure. It may become tempting to use this approach, while giving inadequate consideration to the other categories of variables that may important determinants of structure. Practical problems are also involved in getting the necessary information for developing appropriate measurements of the product characteristics.[47] For example, searching time is a particularly difficult type of information to obtain.

Financial Approach

Lambert offers another approach, developed in the 1960s, by arguing that the most important variables for choosing channel structure are financial:

> *Examination of the process of choosing a trade channel leads to the conclusion that the choice is determined primarily by financial rather than what are generally thought of as marketing considerations. This is shown to be the case regardless of whether the firm has adequate or limited financial resources to expand marketing operations. It is equally true whether the firm is contemplating shortening the channel, which requires more capital, or lengthening the channel, which will make funds formerly used in distribution available for other employment.[48]*

So, according to Lambert, choosing an appropriate channel structure is analogous to an investment decision of capital budgeting. Basically, this decision involves comparing estimated earnings on capital resulting from alternative channel structures in light of the cost of capital to determine the most profitable channel. Further, the use of capital for distribution must also be compared to the alternative of using the funds in manufacturing operations. Unless the firm can earn more than the cost of capital and the return that can be earned on the use of its funds in manufacturing, it should shift performance of marketing functions to intermediaries. More recently, Chu, et al. have taken a somewhat similar view to Lambert's financial approach to channel choice by developing a methodology for assessing the economic value of particular channel structures.[49] Using highly sophisticated structural modeling and policy simulation techniques to analyze channel structures in the personal computer industry, these researchers were able to provide economic rationales for decisions that PC manufacturers such as Dell, IBM, Toshiba, and others made with regard to the channel structures these firms chose.

Using the Financial Approach The financial approach serves as a useful reminder of the importance of financial variables in choosing a channel structure. Moreover, the perspective is appropriate because channel structure decisions are usually long-term ones compared with the other decision areas of the marketing mix. By viewing the channel as a long-term investment that must more than cover the cost of the capital invested in it and provide a better return than other alternative uses for capital (**opportunity cost**), the criteria for choosing a channel structure become more rigorous. The channel manager would then have to justify his or her choice of a channel structure based on these investment criteria.

The major problem with this approach lies in the difficulty of making it operational in a channel decision-making context. Regardless of the investment methods used (such as simple rate of return, or the more sophisticated discounted cash flow methods that take into account the present value of money), obtaining accurate estimates of future revenues and costs from alternative channel structures is very difficult. Indeed, forecasting future streams of revenues and costs even for capital goods such as buildings, machinery, and equipment for one firm is a tricky business often subject to huge errors. Given the number of variables that can affect channel relationships, especially when independent intermediaries are involved, the problem becomes far more difficult.[50]

Transaction Cost Analysis Approach

Transaction cost analysis (TCA), based on the work of Williamson,[51] has become the focus of much attention in the marketing channels literature.[52] TCA addresses the choice of marketing channel structure only in the most general case situation of choosing between the manufacturer performing all of the distribution tasks itself through vertical integration versus using independent intermediaries to perform some or most of the distribution tasks.

In the TCA approach, Williamson attempts to synthesize traditional economic analysis with behavioral concepts and research findings emerging from organizational behavior.

The main focus of TCA is on the cost of conducting the transactions necessary for a firm to accomplish its distribution tasks. Transaction costs are essentially the costs associated with performing tasks such as gathering information, negotiating, monitoring performance, and a variety of others.

In order for transactions to take place, **transaction-specific assets** are needed. These are the set of unique assets, both tangible and intangible, required to perform the distribution tasks. Specially designed store fixtures to display Polo (clothing) by Ralph Lauren would be an example of a tangible transaction-specific asset, while special knowledge and selling skills gained by salespeople to help project a high-quality fashion image of Polo apparel would be indicative of an intangible transaction-specific asset.

According to Williamson if asset specificity is high in the sense that these assets would require a high investment and have little or no value outside the channel for Polo products, then Polo would probably be better off doing everything itself and the company should choose a vertically integrated channel structure. Why? The reason Williamson would offer for this conclusion is based on his rather cynical view of human behavior in social systems; namely, he argues that people will behave **opportunistically**, which he defines as behavior that stresses "self-interest with guile." In other words, people in organizations are crafty and cunning enough to recognize when they are in the "driver's seat." Hence, if independent channel members control most or all of the transaction-specific assets, they will know they are virtually indispensable and will act accordingly. Consequently, they will demand terms that are skewed heavily toward their own self-interest, thereby increasing transaction costs for the manufacturer to uneconomic levels. The surest way to guard against this happening is for the manufacturer to keep the transaction-specific assets in-house where it can exercise much more control over them through the intraorganizational bureaucratic structure. On the other hand, if the transaction-specific asset situation is low, (there are many alternative uses for them), then the manufacturer does not have to worry about allocating them to independent channel members. If these channel members' demands become too self-serving, the assets can be easily transferred to another less-demanding group of channel members.

Using the TCA Approach   While an interesting approach to channel design in the academic marketing literature, TCA has some limitations from the standpoint of managerial usefulness.

First, it deals only with the most general channel structure dichotomy of vertical integration versus use of independent channel members. Thus it offers little insight into the range of possible channel structure choices for the majority of situations when vertical integration is not possible.

Second, the assumption of opportunistic behavior may not be an accurate reflection of behavior in marketing channels.[53] It seems to ignore cooperation, teamwork, partnership, and strategic alliance concepts prevalent in marketing channels,[54] and instead stresses an extreme form of self-interest by channel members.

Third, no real distinction is made between long-term and short-term issues in channel structure relationships. Many independent intermediaries may be willing to forego what Williamson refers to as opportunistic behavior to pursue a longer-term cooperative relationship. For example, a wholesaler or retailer given the opportunity to carry a hot-selling competitor's product may decide not to do so because it might jeopardize its long-term relationship with the manufacturer. Would this be opportunistic behavior or not? Williamson offers no basis for making such a distinction.

Fourth, the concept of asset specificity (transaction-specific assets) is very difficult to operationalize. Actually defining the set of transaction-specific assets and measuring its degree of transferability from one group of channel members to another are not feasible in many cases. Moreover, there are changes over time.

Last, but certainly not least, TCA is a one-dimensional, overly simplistic approach to choosing channel structure because it neglects most of the other relevant variables in channel choice (see Phase 5 in this chapter).

Management Science Approaches

It would certainly be desirable if the channel manager could take all possible channel structures, along with all the relevant variables, and "plug" these into a set of equations, which would then yield the optimal channel structure. Such an approach is possible in theory. In fact, some pioneering attempts have been made to use management science methods, such as operations research, simulation, and decision theory, in an effort to design optimal marketing channels.

For example, Balderston and Hoggatt developed a simulation model that was used to study the channel structures of the lumber industry on the West Coast.[55] The typical structure in this region is producer → wholesaler → retailer. The product flow is often drop-shipped in carload lots from the lumber producer to the retailer, with the wholesalers mainly performing information, risk-taking, and financing tasks. Balderston and Hoggatt were able to incorporate these features into their model, achieving a degree of realism sometimes lacking in simulation approaches. This simulation method may hold promise for more widespread applications to choosing channel structure, especially for those decisions that are too complex to handle mathematically (where only a limited number of alternatives and variables can be employed). Moreover, the approach has the added advantage of allowing the channel decision maker to "see what happens" as a result of the decisions by running the simulation model before actually executing the decisions in the real world.

Artle and Berglund developed a mathematical model that enables the user to calculate the costs of performing distribution tasks for alternative channel structures and then to select the one offering the lowest total cost and maximum profits.[56] Although their model dealt only with the personal selling tasks and with only two channel structure alternatives (producer → wholesaler → retailer, and producer → retailer), the method holds promise for applications to other distribution tasks and additional channel structure alternatives.

Alderson and Green show how Bayesian statistics can be applied to channel choice.[57] Their example addresses the decision of whether a firm using sales agents should change to its own sales force. This approach requires the channel manager to identify explicitly the various payoffs associated with different channel structures. The cost of information to help in making a decision is also incorporated into the analysis. Though the Bayesian approach appears to hold promise, its application to channel design decisions has been very limited. This may be due to the difficulty of obtaining accurate subjective probability estimates from decision makers, which are required in the Bayesian approach.

Baligh developed a comprehensive operations research model for structuring the problems of optimal channel choice.[58] His model allows for the determination of the combination of inputs that leads to channel control and therefore affects revenues and costs. The model thus provides a basis for incorporating the behavioral variable of power into formal mathematical frameworks.

Rangan provided a more sophisticated normative mathematical model that incorporates a number of basic distribution tasks such as holding inventory, providing credit, communicating product knowledge, order processing, and delivery.[59] The model also specifies the optimum channel structure in terms of length and intensity and includes specifications for levels of support for channel members. The model, which was testing in a large industrial firm, incorporates both hard financial data and judgment data from managers.

Moorthy constructed a mathematical model representing channel structure decisions faced by competing manufacturers with respect to using independent retailers (decentralization) versus developing their own channel structures (vertical integration) to reach their customers.[60]

In another approach, Rangan, Menezes, and Maier developed a method for choosing channel structures for new industrial products. The method focuses on product and market factors that influence channel choice. Eight so-called channel functions that need to be performed to satisfy industrial customer requirements are analyzed based on expert opinion in order to develop specific operational tasks that will need to be carried out via the channel. These functions are then combined through precisely specified consensus measurement procedure. The functional profile obtained is then "translated" into various channel structure alternatives, and the channel structure alternative yielding the highest profit is chosen.[61]

In still another approach, Atwong and Rosenbloom used the quantitative technique of correspondence analysis as a method for anticipating changes in channel structure through the shifting of marketing functions among channel members.[62] Their study examined the channel design decisions of 262 manufacturing companies in terms of how they allocated 12 marketing functions among wholesalers-distributors in marketing channels for a wide variety of products. The correspondence analysis provided a spatial map that enables channel managers to observe patterns of functional spin-off from manufacturers in the sample group to wholesaler-distributors. The results can provide insights to channel managers about emerging alternatives for allocating marketing functions among channel members when choosing channel structures.

Finally, in a very recent study, Shang et al. used what they refer to as a nonlinear mixed-integer programming model to develop a distribution channel structure for drug manufacturer, GlaxoSmithKline (GSK).[63] The model addresses the dual objectives of minimizing total distribution costs while improving customer service. The authors used their model to focus on five distribution related issues: (1) determining the optimal number of regional distribution centers GSK should use, (2) specifying the location of the centers in the U.S., (3) allocating retail stores and customers to the appropriate regional distribution centers, (4) estimating the total transportation costs and service levels under different scenarios, and (5) conducting a sensitivity analysis to assess the impact of changes on the distribution system. The authors report that the successful implementation of the model reduced total distribution costs for GSK by 6 percent per year and increased on-time delivery by over 40 percent.

Although the Shang et al. model dealt only with the logistical aspect of channel design, this approach may have the potential to be applied to a broader range of channel design issues in the future.

Using Management Science Approaches These approaches still need much more development before they are likely to find widespread application to channel choice. This is not to disparage such formalized approaches. On the contrary, in the future (under certain constrained conditions), they may be of real practical value. Even today such attempts should be encouraged because in the process of building formal models of channel choice decisions, the relevant variables and the relationships among them are made more explicit. But considering the state-of-the-art channel choice—for the present at least—will continue to be less formal, relying heavily on managerial judgment. These judgmental approaches are discussed in the next section.

Judgmental-Heuristic Approachs

As the name suggests, these approaches to choosing channel structure rely heavily on managerial judgment and heuristics, or rules of thumb. There are, however, variations in the degree of precision of judgmental-heuristic approaches. Some attempt to formalize the decision-making process to some degree, whereas others attempt to incorporate cost and revenue data. The three approaches below illustrate these variations in judgmental-heuristic approaches to choosing a channel.

Straight Qualitative Judgment Approach The qualitative approach is the crudest but, in practice, the most commonly used approach for choosing channel structures. Under this approach, the various alternative channel structures that have been generated are evaluated by management in terms of decision factors that are thought to be important. These may include such factors as short- and long-run cost and profit considerations, channel control issues, long-term growth potentials, and many others. Sometimes, however, these decision factors are not stated explicitly, and their relative importance is also not made clear. Nevertheless, an alternative is chosen that, in the opinion of management, best satisfies the various explicit or implicit decision factors.

As an example of this approach, consider the following: The Commodity Chemical Company has generated five channel alternatives (shown in Figure 6.6) for the distribution of its new swimming pool germicide product. If the straight quantitative judgment approach were to be used for choosing the "best" alternative, management would subjectively and qualitatively "weight" each of the alternatives in Figure 6.6 in terms of the decision factors it believes to be important. After considering the pros and cons of the five alternatives, management would then choose the alternative that in its judgment is the best one.[64]

Weighted Factor Score Approach A more refined version of the straight qualitative approach to choosing among channel alternatives is the **weighted factor approach** suggested by Kotler. This approach forces management to structure and quantify its judgments in choosing a channel alternative.[65] The approach consists of four basic steps:

1. The decision factors on which the channel choice will be based must be stated explicitly.
2. Weights are assigned to each of the decision factors in order to reflect their relative importance precisely in percentage terms.
3. Each channel alternative is rated on each of the decision factors, on a scale of 1 to 10.
4. The overall weighed factor score (the total score) is computed for each channel alternative by multiplying the factor weight (A) by the factor score (B).

FIGURE 6.6
Alternative Channels Proposed by the Commodity Chemical Company for Its New Pool Germicide Product

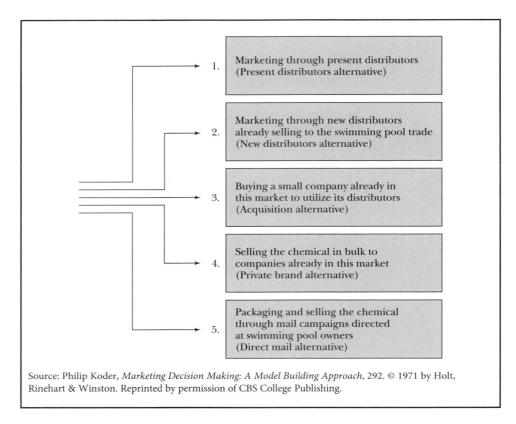

1. Marketing through present distributors (Present distributors alternative)

2. Marketing through new distributors already selling to the swimming pool trade (New distributors alternative)

3. Buying a small company already in this market to utilize its distributors (Acquisition alternative)

4. Selling the chemical in bulk to companies already in this market (Private brand alternative)

5. Packaging and selling the chemical through mail campaigns directed at swimming pool owners (Direct mail alternative)

Source: Philip Koder, *Marketing Decision Making: A Model Building Approach*, 292. © 1971 by Holt, Rinehart & Winston. Reprinted by permission of CBS College Publishing.

This procedure is illustrated in Table 6.3 for channel alternative 1 shown in Figure 6.6. Looking at the left-hand column of the table, we can see that the Commodity Chemical Company has stated five decision factors explicitly (step 1). The factor weights that have been assigned (step 2) are shown in the next column. The check marks

TABLE 6.3 WEIGHTED FACTOR SCORE METHOD APPLIED TO CHANNEL CHOICE: CHANNEL ALTERNATIVE 1

FACTOR	FACTOR WEIGHT (A)	FACTOR SCORE (B)											RATING (A × B)
		0	1	2	3	4	5	6	7	8	9	10	
1. Effectiveness in reaching swimming pool owners	15%				√								45
2. Amount of profit if this alternative works well	25%						√						125
3. Experience company will gain in consumer market	10%			√									20
4. Amount of investment involved (high score for low investment)	30%									√			240
5. Ability of company to cut short its losses	20%								√				140
	100%											Total score	570

Source: Adapted from, Philip Kotler, *Marketing Decision Making: A Model Building Approach*, 292. Copyright 1971 South-Western, a part of Cengage Learning, Inc. Reproduced by permission. www.cengage.com/permissions

represent management's ratings of channel alternative 1 on each of the decision factors (step 3). Finally, the factor weight (A) is multiplied by the factor score (B) for each decision factor and summed to arrive at the total score for channel alternative 1 (step 4).

This score of 570 is, in effect, a quantitative representation of management's judgment on the merits of this particular channel alternative. By repeating this procedure for each of the four remaining channel alternatives, five total scores will be available. Management would then be able to rank the five channel alternatives shown in Figure 6.6 in terms of their total scores. The one having the highest score would be the one judged best by management.

Distribution Costing Approach   Under this approach, estimates of costs and revenues for different channel alternatives are made, and the figures are compared to see how each alternative stacks up. Consider the following example that compares two channel structure alternatives: direct distribution (two-level structure) versus the use of distribution (three-level structure) by a manufacturer.[66]

Assume 6,000 potential customers, each one of whom requires a personal call by an outside salesperson every two weeks. If salespeople are able to make an average of six calls per day, each salesperson could then handle 60 customers. Given these figures, 100 outside salespeople would be needed by the manufacturer to serve the customer base.

Estimated Figures

100 salespeople @ $40,000	= $4,000,000
1 field sales manager per 10 salespeople @ $60,000 4 regions =	600,000
1 regional sales manager for each region @ $80,000 =	320,000
warehouse and office staff, inventory, interest on inventory, other overhead expenses =	5,000,000
Total costs for direct channel	$9,920,000

Assuming an average of 30 percent, gross margin on sales, the sales volume needed to cover these costs would be:

$$\$9,920,000 \div .30 = \$33,066,666$$

Suppose distributors were used with the following alternative trade margins offered by the manufacturer at the projected level of sales (rounded out to the nearest dollar):

If 20% then $33,066,666 × .20 = $6,613,333
If 15% then 33,066,666 × .15 = 4,960,000
If 10% then 33,066,666 × .10 = 3,306,667

Direct versus distributor cost comparison:

	20% Margin Assumption	15% Margin Assumption	10% Margin Assumption
Direct	$9,920,000	$9,920,000	$9,920,000
Distributor	6,613,333	4,960,000	3,306,667
Savings	$3,306,667	$4,960,000	$6,613,333

This is, of course, a simplified example. More elaborate and detailed versions of this kind of approach are discussed in the literature on distribution cost analysis.[67] Regardless of how elaborate or detailed the analysis, however, the basic theme of all such approaches stresses managerial judgment and estimations about what the costs and revenues of various channel structure alternatives are likely to be.[68]

Using Judgmental-Heuristic Approaches Regardless of which judgmental-heuristic approach is used, large doses of judgment, estimation, and even "guesstimation" are virtually unavoidable. To say otherwise is to imply that a greater degree of precision exists than is actually the case. For even with the weighted factor score or the distribution costing approaches, a large measure of managerial judgment is still needed to come up with the seemingly precise figures. This is not to say that the so-called judgmental-heuristic approaches are totally subjective. On the contrary, in some cases management's ability to make sharp judgments may be quite high and, if this is coupled with good empirical data on costs and revenues, highly satisfactory (though not optimal) channel choice decisions may be using judgmental-heuristic approaches.

Judgmental-heuristic approaches also enable the channel manager to readily incorporate nonfinancial criteria (decision factors) into channel choice decisions. Nonfinancial criteria such as the degree of control or goodwill available from a particular channel alternative may be of real importance.[69] If such criteria as control or goodwill are important considerations, judgmental-heuristic approaches offer the flexibility to include these in the decision. In the case of the straight qualitative judgment approach, this may be done implicitly, whereas in the weighted factor score approach, control or goodwill criteria can be used as explicit decision factors, and weights can be assigned to reflect their relative importance (see Table 6.3). Even with the distribution costing approach, nonfinancial factors such as control and goodwill may be applied after the fact. That is, once the cost and profit potentials for each channel alternative have been calculated, the channel manager may still make judgments about whether the channel alternative producing the highest financial return also meets control and goodwill criteria.

Summary

Channel design refers to those decisions associated with developing new marketing channels where none had existed before or to the modification of existing channels. Channel design is a very important aspect of the firm's overall marketing strategy because it can be a key factor in helping the firm gain a **differential advantage (sustainable competitive advantage)**.

Channel design can be viewed as a seven-phase process, referred to as the **channel design paradigm**. The first six phases were discussed in this chapter. The seventh phase is covered in the next chapter (Chapter 7).

Phase 1 involves recognizing the need for a channel design decision. While there are many situations in which the need to make channel design decisions is obvious (such as when a new product is being introduced), often the need is not so obvious. So, the channel manager must be alert to changing conditions, both internal and external, and determine whether such changes have implications for channel design.

Phase 2 is the setting and coordinating of distribution objectives. This involves making explicit statements describing the part that distribution is expected to play in reaching the firm's overall marketing objectives. Distribution objectives must be consistent or congruent with the firm's general marketing objectives and strategies as well as with its overall objectives and strategies. To assure that such congruency will be achieved, the channel manager must examine the firm's other objectives and strategies as they relate to the distribution objectives.

Phase 3 is the specification of the distribution tasks that will have to be performed in order to achieve the distribution objectives. The channel manager should be as specific as possible in delineating precisely the kinds of tasks that are involved.

Phase 4 consists of developing alternative channel structures. The channel structures should be specified in terms of three basic dimensions: (1) number of levels, (2) intensity at the various levels, and (3) the types of intermediaries to be used at each level.

Intensity can be intensive (as many intermediaries as possible), selective (fewer intermediaries carefully chosen), or exclusive (only one intermediary per market area). The intensity dimension should be carefully considered because it often reflects and is a crucial feature of the firm's basic marketing strategy, overall methods of operation, and image. The types of intermediaries to be used should also be carefully considered in light of availability of intermediaries and their capabilities for performing particular distribution tasks.

Phase 5 involves the evaluation of the variables affecting channel structure. Six major categories of variables need to be considered: (1) market variables, (2) product variables, (3) company variables, (4) intermediary variables, (5) environmental variables, and (6) behavioral variables. In relating these variables to channel structure, various heuristics (rules of thumb) are often used. While heuristics provide a useful shorthand approach for dealing with complex relationships, they should be considered only as a rough reflection of typical relationships and a starting point for a more thorough analysis. One category of variables, market variables, is so basic and important that we have devoted all of Chapter 8 to the topic.

Phase 6 is the choosing of the "best" channel structure for achieving the distribution objectives. It is not possible to choose a truly optimal channel in the strict sense of the term because the kinds of perfect information analysis and forecasting needed to do so are in most cases beyond the range of human capability. Nevertheless, approaches do exist for making good, if not optimal, channel choices. The "characteristics of goods and parallel systems" approach, the financial approach, the transaction cost analysis approach, and management science methods all help in this regard. Most channel choices, however, are still made on the basis of managerial judgment supplemented by heuristics and whatever data (even if imperfect) are available. Several variations of such judgmental-heuristic approaches to channel choice were discussed in this chapter.

Review Questions

1. Discuss the meaning of channel design in relation to such concepts as channel structure, selection, evolution of channels, and the allocation of distribution tasks.

2. Discuss the role of channel design in the quest to gain differential advantage.

3. In this chapter we discussed a number of conditions that may foster the need for channel design decisions. Name some others.

4. What is a distribution objective? What does it mean when we say that distribution objectives should be coordinated with other objectives and strategies of the firm?

5. Give an example of an incongruent distribution objective.

6. How do distribution tasks viewed from the perspective of the channel manager in a producing or manufacturing firm differ from the traditional lists of marketing functions?

7. Briefly describe the major categories of variables that should be considered when evaluating alternative channel structures.

8. Discuss the three dimensions of channel structure that should be considered in developing alternative channel structures.

9. Throughout our discussion of the many variables affecting channel choice, we cited a number of heuristics about how these variables are likely to influence channel structure. What useful purpose does this serve? What dangers does it hold?

10. Discuss the difficulties involved in attempting to choose an optimal channel structure.

11. Compare and contrast the so-called judgmental-heuristic approach to choosing a channel structure with any of the other approaches discussed in the chapter.

12. Does the "best" channel structure necessarily have to be the one offering the highest monetary payoff? Explain.

Channel Issues for Discussion

1. Best Buy Co., the largest consumer electronics retailer in the world, is famous for its giant 40,000 square-foot "big-box" stores. This channel has served Best Buy well over the years as consumers wandered through the giant product displays in the cavernous stores, and competitors such as Circuit City were literally driven out of business by Best Buy's dominant stores. But by

the end of the first decade of the Twenty-first century, Best Buy made a channel design decision that focused on adding a retail channel consisting of much smaller 3,000 square-foot stores to its large-store channel. The new smaller stores will be located in shopping malls as well as in urban downtown venues. Best Buy designed this new small-store channel structure mainly to do a better job of reaching the still-growing market for mobile phones, especially smartphones. These smaller stores will sell almost one hundred different phones as well as the services of nine carriers.

Do you think Best Buy's channel design decision is a good one? What other channel design options might Best Buy have pursued to accomplish its distribution objective?

2. Vending machines have existed as a mechanical channel for distributing a variety of products for many decades. Traditionally the typical products found in vending machines were soft drinks, candy, cigarettes, and snack foods. But in recent years the variety of products sold through vending machine channels has broadened dramatically. Consumers can now buy digital cameras, DVDs, iPods, baby diapers, and in Germany, even solid gold bars for which the price charged changes every two minutes with the ups and downs of the price of gold.

From a channel design standpoint, what do you see as the key variables to consider in determining whether vending machines could be a feasible channel choice for any given product of your choice?

3. Quaker Oats Co. made the most disastrous decision in the company's history when it acquired the Snapple Beverage Corp. After several years of horrible financial results, Quaker sold its Snapple division at a loss in excess of a billion dollars. What went wrong? Pundits point to several factors, especially the super-competitive nature of the soft drink market. But Quaker's lack of understanding of the channel structure for soft drinks certainly played a key role. Quaker had hoped to gain tremendous synergy by tying Snapple products to its highly successful Gatorade. But the typical distribution structure for Gatorade is from factory to retailers' warehouses, where individual stores then order what they need to keep their shelves stocked. Quaker knew this pattern well and was comfortable with it. By

contrast, Snapple is distributed directly to stores on trucks driven by independent distributors. Usually these distributors carry a variety of other branded soft drinks, so they would not devote undivided attention to Snapple products. Quaker either did not really understand this fundamental difference in channel structure or believed it could change it with relative ease. As it turned out, the company could not change the distribution structure of Snapple to mirror Gatorade.

Why do you think Quaker, a giant food products company with substantial resources, could not design a channel structure for Snapple that would parallel its channel for Gatorade?

4. Marketing channels should be designed to make products and services conveniently available to customers, how, when, and where they want them. This is exactly what several franchises such as Cousins Submarines Inc., Tasti D-Lite LLC frozen yogurt, and Toppers Pizza Inc. intend to do by changing their channel structures to include mobile channels consisting of fully equipped trucks and vans that can bring many of the products sold in their bricks and mortar stores right to customers where they work and play. How will potential customers know when and where these truck and van mini-restaurants will appear? Simple customers can track the whereabouts of the vendors by going to Facebook, Twitter, and FourSquare.

Do you think this type of mobile channel is just a novelty in fast-food channels or does it have the potential to be a major force for change in the channel structure of fast-food and other product and service distribution channels?

5. C.F. Martin & Company, located in Nazareth, Pennsylvania, is recognized by guitar enthusiasts as the manufacturer of the finest steel string acoustic guitars in the world. Martin is to guitars what Mercedes or even Rolls Royce is to automobiles in the minds of the target market at which the guitars are aimed—top-notch professional musicians and highly accomplished amateurs. After 150 years in the guitar business, Martin has decided to examine its approach to marketing comprehensively. As part of that process, the company has asked you, in your role as an independent marketing consultant, to set new distribution objectives.

What are some of the key issues you will need to address in carrying out your assignment?

6. Chrysler Group LLC. and Fiat SpA announced that they would partner to bring the subcompact Fiat 500 to be sold in the U.S. sometime in 2011. The Fiat 500 will be positioned as a direct competitor to BMW AG's Mini Cooper. The Fiat 500 will be sold through a select group of about 165 Chrysler dealers. The chosen dealers will also have the opportunity to sell the high-performance, luxury brand, Alfa Romeo, made by Fiat SpA, which will become available in 2012. But in order for the dealers to get the franchise to sell the Fiat 500 and Alfa Romeo cars, they will need to build special facilities including two separate showrooms for the cars. Each dealer will have to spend as much as $1 million to provide these separate facilities while also providing for staff to sell and service the cars. Both Chrysler and Fiat believe that for the Fiat 500 and Alfa Romeo brands to successfully penetrate the U.S. market, the channels through which they are sold must appear to consumers to be dedicated only to Fiat and Alfa Romeo rather than be mixed in with Chrysler, Dodge, and Jeep brands.

   Do you agree with Chrysler and Fiat's channel design strategy? Why or why not?

7. Giant pharmaceutical manufacturers such as Merck & Company and Pfizer have traditionally relied heavily on the doctor-to-patient channel to promote their products. In essence, this channel structure focuses attention on reaching doctors through extensive use of the drugmaker's outside salespeople, often referred to as "detailers," who call on medical professionals with plenty of free samples and other incentives such as expensive gifts, office supplies, and offers of free stays at plush resorts. But more powerful and knowledgeable buyers, especially the large hospitals and health maintenance organizations that are increasingly using MBAs rather than MDs to make decisions about what drug products they buy or prescribe, are threatening this channel. One industry observer, summing up the change, remarked that "schmoozing between salesman and doctor is being replaced by hard data and analysis presented to buying committees."

   How might such changes in buyer behavior affect the channel design decisions of the major pharmaceutical producers? Explain in terms of the relevant stages of the channel design paradigm.

References

1. See, for example, Allan J. Magrath and Kenneth G. Hardy, "Selecting Sales and Distribution Channels," *Industrial Marketing Management* 16 (August 1987): 273–278.

2. See for example: David Kesmodel, "Anheuser Weighs Change in Beer Sales, USB Says," *Wall Street Journal* (June 25, 2009): B3.

3. For a discussion of some of the problems associated with marketing channels that have been based on evolution rather than planning, see Douglas M. Lambert, *The Distribution Channels Decision* (New York: National Association of Accountants, 1978); Joseph P. Guiltinan, "Planned and Evolutionary Changes in Distribution Channels," *Journal of Retailing* (Summer 1974): 79–91; Michael D. Hutt and Thomas W. Speh, "Realigning Industrial Marketing Channels," *Industrial Marketing Management* (October 1982): 171–177; and John J. Withey, "Realities of Channel Dynamics: A Wholesaling Example," *Journal of the Academy of Marketing Science* (Summer 1985): 72–81.

4. Julia Chang, "Short-Term Buzz, Long-Term Strategy," *Sales and Marketing Management* (January 2007): 10.

5. For a discussion of some of these issues, see Hong Liu and Peter J. McGoldrick, "International Retail Sourcing: Trend, Nature, and Process" *Journal of International Marketing* 4, no. 4 (1996): 9–33; Janet Wagner, Richard Ettenson, and Jean Parrish, "Vendor Selection among Retail Buyers: An Analysis by Merchandise Division," *Journal of Retailing* (Spring 1989): 58–79; and David D. Shipley, "Resellers' Supplier Selection Criteria for Different Consumer Products," *European Journal of Marketing* 19 (1985): 26–36.

6. For an excellent study addressing this issue see: Filipe Coelho and Chris Easingwood, "An Exploratory Study into the Drivers of Channel Change," *European Journal of Marketing* Vol. 42, No. 9/10 2008: 1005–1022.

7. Nermin Eyuboglu and Sertan Kabadoyi, "Dealer-Manufacturer Alienation in a Multiple Channel System: The Moderating Effect of Structural Variables," *Journal of Marketing Channels* Vol. 12, No. 3, 2005: 5–26; Michael Harvey and Cheri Speier, "Developing an Inter-Organization Relational Marketing Perspective," *Journal of Marketing Channels* 7, no. 4 (2000): 23–44.

8. See, for example Lauranne Buchanan, "Vertical Trade Relationships: The Role of Dependence and Symmetry in

Attaining Organizational Goals," *Journal of Marketing Research* (February 1992): 65–75.

9. For some additional conditions, see Maureen Guirdham, *Marketing: The Management of Distribution Channels* (Oxford, U.K.: Pergamon Press, 1972), 129–130.

10. For a study of which executives in manufacturing firms are responsible for making channel design decisions, see Joe L. Welch, "An Investigation of Distribution Channel Selection Policies of U.S. Manufacturers," in *Proceedings of the Southeastern AIDS* (1976), 183–185; and Bruce J. Walker, Janet E. Keith, and Donald W. Jackson, "The Channels Manager: Now, Soon or Never?" *Journal of the Academy of Marketing Science* (Summer 1985): 82–96.

11. Dell Computer Corporation, Annual Report 2009: 4.

12. Julie Forster, "The Lucky Charm of Steve Sanger," *Business Week* (March 26, 2001): 75–76.

13. Pui-Wing Tam, "Apple Computer Tries Courting Retailers Again," *Wall Street Journal* (July 7, 2000): B1, B4.

14. Betsy McKay, "Coke Finds Its Exclusive School Contracts Aren't So Easily Given Up," *Wall Street Journal* (June 26, 2001): B1, B4.

15. Heather Green, "How Amazon Aims to Keep You Clicking," *Business Week* (March 2, 2009): 34.

16. Kevin Helliker, "Starbucks Targets Regular Joes," *Wall Street Journal* (May 12, 2010): B3.

17. For a recent example, see Robert D. Tamilia, Sylvain Senecal, and Gilles Corriveau, "Conventional Channels of Distribution and Electronic Intermediaries: A Functional Analysis," *Journal of Marketing Channels* 1, no. 3/4 (2002) 27–48.

18. See, for example, Bert Rosenbloom, *Marketing Functions and the Wholesaler-Distributor: Achieving Excellence in Distribution* (Washington D.C.: Distribution Research and Education Foundation, 1987). For some earlier analyses of marketing functions, see, for example, Franklin W. Ryan, "Functional Elements of Market Distribution," *Harvard Business Review* 13 (January 1935): 205–221; Edmund D. McGarry, "Some Functions of Marketing Reconsidered," in *Theory in Marketing*, eds. Revis Cox and Wroe Alderson (Homewood, Ill.: Irwin, 1950), 263–279; and John C. Naver and Ronald Savitt, *The Marketing Economy* (New York: Holt, Rinehart & Winston, 1971), 118–128.

19. For a related discussion dealing with manufacturers that sell in both industrial and consumer markets, see John A. Quelch, "Why Not Exploit Dual Marketing?" *Business Horizons* (January–February 1987): 52–60.

20. See, for example, Russel Adams, "Playboy Farms Out Business Duties," *Wall Street Journal* (November 24, 2009): B7.

21. Tamilia, Senecal, and Corriveau, "Conventional Channels of Distribution and Electronic Intermediaries," 31–39.

22. Jeanette Brown, Heather Green, and Wendy Zellner, "Shoppers Are Beating a Path to the Web," *Business Week* (December 24, 2001): 41.

23. "Integrating Multiple Channels," *Chain Store Age* (August 2001): 24A–25A.

24. Cathleen Egan, "Vending Machine Technology Matures, Offering Branded Food, Convenience," *Wall Street Journal* (December 13, 2001): B13.

25. For a very insightful analysis of the selectivity dimension, see Adam J. Fein and Erin Anderson, "Patterns of Credible Commitments: Territory and Brand Selectivity in Industrial Distribution Channels," *Journal of Marketing* (April 1997): 19–34.

26. James A. Narus and James C. Anderson, *Building Successful Working Partnerships* (Washington D.C.: Distribution Research and Education Foundation, 1987).

27. Bert Rosenbloom and Trina Larsen Andras, "Wholesalers as Global Marketers," *Journal of Marketing Channels*, Vol. 15, no. 4, 2008: 235–252.

28. Kim Cross, Marketplaces "That Work," *Business 2.0* (April 30, 2001): 38–40.

29. For an in-depth analysis of a related topic in B2B E-commerce, see C. M. Shashi and Bay O'Leary, "The Role of Internet Auctions in the Expansion of B2B Markets," *Industrial Marketing Management* 31(2002): 103–110.

30. For a related discussion, see Mini Hahn and Dae R. Chang, "An Extended Framework for Adjusting Channel Strategies in Industrial Markets," *Journal of Business and Industrial Marketing* (Spring 1992): 31–43.

31. Roland Moriority and Ursula Moran, "Managing Hybrid Marketing Systems," *Harvard Business Review* (November–December 1990): 146–155.

32. Jack Ewing, "Where Dell Sells with Brick and Mortar," *Business Week* (October 8, 2007): 78.

33. For a related discussion, see Paul D. Larson and Robert F. Lusch, "Functional Integration in Marketing Channels: A Determinant of Product Quality and Total Cost," *Journal of Marketing Channels* 2, no. 1 (1991): 1–28.

34. See: Maggie Gilmour, "Threadless: From Clicks to Bricks," *Business Week* (November 26, 2007): 84.

35. For a related discussion see: Elisabeth A. Sullivan, " H.O.G. Harley-Davidson Shows Brand Strength as It Navigates Down New Roads—and Picks Up More Female Riders Along the Way," *Marketing News* (November 1, 2008): 8.

36. For an insightful analysis of how this factor might apply in a start-up situation, see Wenyu Dou and David C.

Chou, "A Structural Analysis of Business-to-Business Digital Markets," *Industrial Marketing Management* 31 (2002): 172–174.

37. For an excellent discussion of this issue, see Frank V. Cespedes, "Control vs. Resources in Channel Design: Distribution Differences in One Industry," *Industrial Marketing Management* 17 (August 1988): 215–227.

38. Bert Rosenbloom and Trina L. Larsen, "How Foreign Firms View Their U.S. Distributors," *Industrial Marketing Management* (May 1992) 93–101.

39. Sean Callahan, "Distributors Far From Being Dead," *B to B* (April 19, 2002): *http://www.btobline.com/cgi-bin/article.pl?id=8551.*

40. See for example, Kartik N. Sheth, "India: Shopping with the Family," *McKinsey Quarterly*, no. 4, 2007: 74–75.

41. See, for example, Lonnie L. Ostrom, Craig Kelly, and Donald W. Jackson, "Vertical Territorial Restraints: Rules of Legality and Guidelines for Channel Design," *Journal of the Academy of Marketing Science* (Spring 1986): 1–6.

42. For an insightful article dealing with approaches for gaining an "early warning" about the impact of environment on marketing strategy, see Ronald D. Michman, "Why Forecast for the Long Term?" *Journal of Business Strategy* (September–October 1989): 36–40.

43. See Douglas W. LaBahn and Katrin R. Harich, "Sensitivity to National Business Culture: Effects on U.S. Mexican Channel Relationship Performance," *Journal of International Marketing* 5, no. 4 (1987): 29–51.

44. Patrick J. Kaufman, Richard M. Gordon, and James E. Owers, "Alternative Profitability Measures and Marketing Channel Structure: The Franchise Decision," *Journal of Business Research* 50 (2000): 217–224; A theoretical discussion related to this point can be found in Louis P. Bucklin, *A Theory of Distribution Channel Structure* (Berkeley: Institute of Business and Economic Research, University of California, 1966).

45. For a classic discussion of the limitations of the decision maker to operate optimally, see Herbert A. Simon, "Theories of Decision Making in Economic and Behavioral Sciences," *American Economic Review* 49 (June 1959): 253–283.

46. Leo Aspinwall, "The Characteristics of Goods and Parallel Systems Theories," in *Managerial Marketing*, eds. Eugene J. Kelly and William Lazer (Homewood, Ill.: Irwin, 1958), 434–450.

47. For a related discussion see Stefan Wuyts, Stefan Stremersch, Christophe Van Den Bulte and Philip Hans Franses, "Vertical Marketing Systems for Complex Products: A Triadic Perspective," *Journal of Marketing Research* (November 2004): 479–487.

48. Eugene W. Lambert, "Financial Considerations in Choosing a Marketing Channel," *MSU Business Topics* (Winter 1966): 17–26.

49. Junhong Chu, Pradeep K. Chintagunta, and Nautel J. Vilcassim, "Assessing the Economic Value of Distribution Channels: An Application to the Personal Computer Industry," *Journal of Marketing Research* (Febrary 2007): 29–41.

50. For another financial approach to channel choice, see Mary A. Higby, *An Evaluation of Alternative Channels of Distribution*, (East Lansing, Mich.: Graduate School of Business Administration, Michigan State University, 1977).

51. Oliver E. Williamson, *Markets and Hierarchies: Analysis and Antitrust Implications* (New York: Free Press, 1975).

52. See for example, Saul Klein, "Selection of International Marketing Channels," *Journal of Global Marketing* 4, no. 4 (1991): 21–37; and George John, "An Empirical Investigation of Some Antecedents of Opportunism in a Marketing Channel," *Journal of Marketing Research* (August 1984): 278–289; Erin Anderson, "The Salesperson as Outside Agent or Employee: A Transaction Cost Analysis," *Marketing Science* (Summer 1985): 234–254; F. Robert Dwyer and Sejo Oh, "A Transaction Cost Perspective on Vertical Contractual Structure and Interchannel Competitive Strategies," *Journal of Marketing* (April 1988): 21–34; and Saul Klein, Gary L. Frazier, and Victor J. Roth, "A Transaction Cost Analysis Model of Channel Integration in International Markets," *Journal of Marketing Research* (May 1990): 196–208.

53. See for example, Joost M.E. Pennings and Brian Wansink, "Channel Contract Behavior: The Role of Risk Attitudes, Risk Perceptions, and Channel Members' Market Structures," *Journal of Business*, Vol. 77, no. 4 (2004): 697–723.

54. For an excellent in-depth analysis related to this issue, see Ashwin W. Joshi and Rodney L. Stump, "The Contingent Effect of Specific Asset Investments on Joint Action in Manufacturer–Supplier Relationships: An Empirical Test on the Moderating Role of Reciprocal Asset Investments, Uncertainty, and Trust," *Journal of the Academy of Marketing Science* 27, no. 3 (1999): 291–305.

55. Fredrick E. Balderston and Austin C. Hoggatt, *Simulation of Market Processes* (Berkeley: Institute of Business and Economic Research, University of California, 1962), Chaps. 1–2.

56. Roland Artle and Sture Berglund, "A Note on Manufacturer's Choice of Distribution Channels," *Management Science* (July 1959): 460–471.

57. Wroe Alderson and Paul E. Green, "Bayesian Decision Theory in Channel Selection," in their text *Planning and Problem Solving in Marketing* (Homewood, Ill.: Irwin, 1964), 311–317.

58. Helmy H. Baligh, "A Theoretical Framework for Channel Choice," in *Marketing and Economic Development*, ed. Peter D. Bennett Chicago: American Marketing Association, 1965), 631–654.

59. V. Kasturi Rangan, "The Channel Design Decision: A Model and an Application," *Marketing Science* (Spring 1987): 156–174.

60. K. Sridhor Moorthy, "Strategic Decentralization in Channels," *Marketing Science* (Fall 1988): 335–355.

61. V. Kasturi Rangan, Melvyn A. J. Menezes, and E. P. Maier, "Channel Selection for New Industrial Products: A Framework, Method, and Application," *Journal of Marketing* (July 1992): 69–82.

62. Catherine T. Atwong and Bert Rosenbloom, "A Spatial Approach to Measuring Functional Spin-Offs in Marketing Channels," *Journal of Marketing Theory and Practice* (Fall 1995): 58–71.

63. Jennifer Shang, Tuba Pinar Yildirim, Panda Tadikamalla, Vikas Mittal, and Lawrence H. Brown, "Distribution Network Redesign for Marketing Competitiveness," *Journal of Marketing* (March 2009): 146–163.

64. This example is adapted from Philip Kotler, *Marketing Decision Making: A Model Building Approach* (New York: Holt, Rinehart & Winston, 1971), 291–293.

65. Kotler, *Marketing Decision Making*, 293.

66. This example is adapted from John M. Brion, *Marketing through the Wholesaler–Distributor Channel*, (Chicago: American Marketing Association, 1965), 5.

67. See, for example, D. R. Longman and M. Schiff, *Practical Distribution Cost Analysis* (Homewood, Ill.: Irwin, 1955); and Bruce Mallen and Stephen D. Silver, "Modern Marketing and the Accountant," *Cost and Management* 38 (February 1964): 75–85.

68. For a related discussion, see Frank Lynn, "The Changing Economics of Industrial Distribution," *Industrial Marketing Management* 21 (1992): 355–360.

69. For a related discussion, see John R. Nevin, "Relationship Marketing and Distribution Channels: Exploring Fundamental Issues," *Journal of the Academy of Marketing Science* 23, no. 4 (1995): 327–334.

CHAPTER **7**

Selecting the Channel Members

LEARNING OBJECTIVES

After reading this chapter, you should:

1. Have an appreciation for the importance of channel member selection.
2. Understand the relationship between channel member selection and distribution intensity.
3. Know the main sources for finding prospective channel members.
4. Be familiar with generalized lists of selection criteria.
5. Recognize the need for adapting selection criteria to the needs of particular firms.
6. Realize that channel member selection can be a two-way street.
7. Appreciate the need to offer incentives to prospective channel members to secure them as actual channel members.
8. Recognize the human side of channel member selection and the role of fair and friendly relationships in channels.

© J. Beam Photography

FOCUS ON CHANNELS

Exotic Mustard, Mayo and Salsa Aren't Just for Gourmet Shops Anymore

The U.S. condiment market, consisting mainly of mustards, mayonnaises and salsas, generated $5.6 billion in 2009 and is expected to reach $7 billion by 2015. What is driving such high sales growth for a seemingly peripheral product category? Industry observers say it's mainly due to 18- to 34-year-olds seeking more and more novel and exotic condiments such as lemon wasabi sauce, banana ketchup, whole-grain mustard, toasted garlic mayonnaises, fruit-flavored salsas and hundreds of other varieties. Such condiment mania has created what some condiment manufacturers describe as "the golden age of condiments." There seems to be no limit to the variety of different condiments consumers will chase after. Literally hundreds of new condiments are being brought to market each year mainly by family-owned small manufacturers such as Ohio-based Woeber's. Best known for its yellow and spicy brown mustards, Woeber's has added jalapeno, cranberry and wasabi flavored mustards as well as toasted garlic and cool dill mayonnaises to its product line.

Until recently, makers of such unusual and premium-priced products would select specialty retailers like Bristol Farms, a chain of 14 gourmet grocery stores in California, as the appropriate channel members to reach consumers. But not any more. The "big guys" from Walmart to Whole Foods and just about every other mainstream supermarket chain have become potential channel recruits for exotic condiments. Not only are these products profitable for the stores, but they also help attract the young, affluent 18-34 demographic that all stores crave.

So, at least for a little while, many small condiment manufacturers are in the driver's seat when it comes to selecting the supermarkets that will sell their products. After all, it's a lot more profitable for the supermarkets to attract customers with a hot salsa than with a hot price on a loss leader.

Source: Based on David Sax, "Spreading the Love," *Bloomberg BusinessWeek*, (October 11—October 17, 2010): 96–97.

When it comes to selecting employees, most firms are very careful. They may write job specifications, institute a broad-based search to find applicants and conduct a thorough screening and interviewing process before selecting people to join the firm. These companies go to such lengths because they recognize how important good employees are to the success of their businesses. The same holds true in the selection of channel members. Success in the marketplace requires strong channel members—those who can efficiently perform the distribution tasks necessary to implement the channel strategy. Thus the selection of channel members is a very important undertaking that should not be left to chance or haphazard methods.[1] In this chapter, we examine the kinds of issues the channel manager needs to address to make effective channel member selection decisions.

Channel Member Selection and Channel Design

The actual selection of firms that will become marketing channel members is the last phase of channel design (Phase 7; see Chapter 6). We should point out, however, that selection decisions are frequently necessary even when channel structure changes have not been made. That is, selection decisions may or may not be the result of channel design decisions. For example, suppose a firm needs more coverage in existing territories. Even though its channel structure remains the same in terms of length, intensity and types of intermediaries, the firm may need additional outlets to allow for growth. Another common reason for selection, independent of channel design decisions, is to replace channel members that have left the channel either voluntarily or otherwise.

Two other points about the relationship of channel design to selection should also be mentioned. First, an obvious point that is sometimes forgotten is that firms with a direct (manufacturer→user) channel structure do not have to worry about selection decisions. Because their allocation of the distribution tasks does not specify the use of intermediaries, they need not select any. Consequently, for firms that have chosen a direct channel structure as the best alternative, the channel design decision is a six-phase process.[2] Of course, if at a later point a firm decides to change its channel structure to include channel members, then selection becomes relevant.[3]

The second point deals with the relationship between the structural dimension of intensity (see Chapter 6 section on "Intensity at the Various Levels") and the selection of channel members. As a general rule, the greater the intensity of distribution, the less the emphasis on selection. As Pegram points out in his classic study of selection practices:

Such companies [those using intensive distribution] usually place their products in every logical outlet in an attempt to blanket the market and make their products universally available. They seldom exercise much discrimination in the selection of resellers other than ensuring that their credit is satisfactory. Often consumer items are largely "presold" through advertising, so that there is little concern over selection and choice of resellers is, practically speaking, nonexistent.[4]

Conversely, in referring to firms that emphasize more selective distribution, Pegram points to the need for a strong emphasis on the selection of channel members:

For these manufacturers [those with more selective distribution], distributor selection is critical, representing the juncture at which the manufacturer has greatest control and opportunity in the field for ensuring the marketing success of his products which move through resellers.[5]

At Goodyear's Tire and Rubber Co., for example, careful selection of channel members is given high priority. In its annual report, Goodyear explicitly addresses its channel selection philosophy:[6]

> ... our philosophy is simple and logical. We win with winners. We align with customers [dealers] who are outstanding. We then are focused intensely on building their businesses, not simply on selling tires. We have, by far, the best dealer network in the industry globally.

In general, then, if a channel has been structured to emphasize intensive distribution at the various levels, those intermediaries who are included as channel members are usually "selected" only to the extent that they have a reasonable probability of paying their bills.[7] On the other hand, if the channel structure stresses more selective distribution, the prospective members should be much more carefully scrutinized and selection decisions become more critical.[8] With these points in mind, we now turn our attention to the process of selecting channel members.

The Selection Process

The channel member selection process consists of the following three steps:

1. Finding prospective channel members
2. Applying selection criteria to determine the suitability of prospective channel members
3. Securing the prospective channel members as actual channel members

The remainder of this chapter follows this format, with each major section discussing one of these three steps.

Finding Prospective Channel Members

A wide variety of sources is available to help the channel manager find prospective channel members. The most important of these, listed in order of importance, are:

1. Field sales organization
2. Trade sources
3. Reseller inquiries
4. Customers
5. Advertising
6. Trade shows
7. Other sources

Field Sales Organization

For companies with their own sales force already calling on intermediaries at the wholesaler retail levels, these outside salespeople represent an excellent resource for finding new channel members.

Salespeople are in the best position to know potential channel members in their own territory. While making calls, they are often able to pick up information about intermediaries who are likely to be available. It is not unusual for a salesperson to be acquainted with the management and salespeople of major intermediaries in the same territory who are not representing his or her firm. The salesperson may even have prospective channel members lined up if the firm decides that its present channel members in that territory are to be changed or supplemented.

A potential problem in using the sales force to find prospective channel members is the possibility that the manufacturer may not adequately reward salespeople for their efforts in finding these potential channel members. If the manufacturer fails to take into account the time and effort expended in seeking out and establishing new contacts, but only rewards salespeople on sales volume for existing channel members, the sales force is not likely to spend much time finding new members. Thus, if the sales force is to be an effective resource for finding new channel members, the manufacturer must make it clear that salespeople will be properly rewarded for their efforts.[9]

Trade Sources

Trade sources such as trade associations, trade publications, directories, firms selling related or similar products, trade shows and the "grapevine" all are valuable sources of information about prospective intermediaries.

The National Association of Wholesaler-Distributors in Washington D.C. has a wealth of information about wholesalers and the National Retail Federation in New York offers a great deal of information regarding retail intermediaries.

The most specific sources of information in a particular industry are trade associations. Tables 7.1 and 7.2, for example, provide listings of a number of wholesale and retail trade associations. There are many others, but these two lists offer a general idea of

TABLE 7.1 SAMPLE LISTING OF WHOLESALE TRADE ASSOCIATIONS

- *American Machine Tool Distributors Association*
- *American Nursery & Landscaping Association*
- *American Veterinary Distributors Association*
- *Association of High Technology Distribution*
- *Appliance Parts Distributors Association Inc.*
- *Association of Pool & Spa Professionals (The)*
- *Automotive Aftermarket Industry Association*
- *Bicycle Product Suppliers Association*
- *Ceramic Tile Distributors Association*
- *Cooper & Brass Servicenter Association*
- *Food Marketing Institute*
- *Health Industry Distributors Association*
- *International Association of Plastics Distributors*
- *Material Handlers Equipment Distributors Association*
- *Metals Service Center Institute*
- *Motorcycle Industry Council*
- *National Association of Chemical Distributors*
- *National Association of Electrical Distributors*
- *National Association of Sporting Goods Wholesalers*
- *National Beer Wholesalers Association*
- *National Fastener Distributors Association*
- *National Grocers Association*
- *National Wood Flooring Association*
- *North American Building Material Distribution Association*
- *Pet Industry Distributors Association*
- *Petroleum Equipment Institute*
- *Professional Beauty Association*
- *Recreational Vehicle Aftermarket Association*
- *Safety Equipment Distributors Association Inc.*
- *Wine & Spirits Wholesalers of America Inc.*

Source: Compiled from: National Association of Wholesales Distributors, Member Association List at http://www.naw.org/about/assoclist.php (11/8/10).

> ### TABLE 7.2 SAMPLE LISTING OF RETAIL TRADE ASSOCIATIONS BY KIND OF BUSINESS

KIND OF BUSINESS	TRADE ASSOCIATION(S)
Building materials, hardware, and farm equipment dealers	National Retail Hardware Association (NRHA) National Lumber and Building Materials Dealers Association (NLBMDA)
General merchandise group	National Retail Merchants Association (NRMA) National Association of Variety Stores (NAVS) Mass Retailing Institute (MRI)
Food stores	National Association of Retail Grocers of the United States (NARGUS) National Association of Independent Food Retailers (NAIFR) National Association of Food Chains (NAFC) National Association of Convenience Stores (NACS) Supermarket Institute (SMI)
Automotive group	National Automobile Dealers Association (NADA) National Tire Dealers and Retreaders Association (NTDRA) Recreational Vehicle Dealers Association of North America (RVDA)
Apparel and accessory stores	Menswear Retailers of America (MRA) National Shoe Retailers Association (NSRA) Master Furriers Guild of America (MFGA)
Furniture, home furnishings, and equipment stores	National Home Furnishings Association (NHFA) National Appliance and Radio-TV Dealers Association (NARDA) National Association of Music Merchants (NAMM)
Drug and proprietary stores	National Association of Retail Druggists (NARD) National Association of Chain Drug Stores (NACDS)
Miscellaneous retail stores	Retail Jewelers of America (RJA) American Booksellers Association (ABA) Florists Transworld Delivery Association (FTDA) National Bicycle Dealers Association (NBDA)

Source: Reprinted from Bert Rosenbloom, "Retail Trade Associations as a Resource for Retailing Education," *Journal of Retailing* (Fall 1978): 55–56. Copyright © 1978, with permission from Elsevier.

the extent and scope of trade associations at the wholesale and retail levels. An excellent source for a listing of virtually all trade associations can be found in the *Encyclopedia of Associations*.[10]

Virtually all wholesale and retail trade associations as well as many sales and manufacturers' representative associations, now have Web site containing information that can be helpful for finding prospective channel members.[11] More and more associations are also on Facebook, Twitter and LinkedIn, which further enhances the usefulness of trade associations as a source for finding channel members by providing very timely information and the opportunity for dialogue.

Reseller Inquiries

Many firms learn about potential channel members through direct inquiries from intermediaries interested in handling their product line. For some manufacturers, this provides the main source of information about potential new channel members.

As would be expected, the firms receiving the highest numbers of inquiries from prospective channel members are the more prestigious ones in their respective industries. The 3M Company, for example, is deluged on a daily basis by hundreds of wholesalers, jobbers, industrial distributors and retailers that want to sell the latest products introduced by this company. For decades, 3M has been recognized as a leading innovator resulting in many highly successful new products that are eagerly sought by prospective 3M channel members.[12]

Customers

Some firms look to the customers of prospective intermediaries as a source of information. Manufacturers report that many customers are willing to give frank opinions about the intermediaries who call on them.

One of the best ways for the manufacturer to obtain information about potential intermediaries from customers is by conducting an informal or formal survey of their views of various distributors in their market areas. End users may well be able to provide insights about the strengths and weaknesses of prospective channel members from the customer point of view that the manufacturer could not obtain from its vantage point as a supplier.[13]

Advertising

Advertisements in trade magazines whether in hard copy or online, offer yet another approach to finding potential channel members. Figure 7.1, for example, shows an advertisement placed in *Beverage World*, a trade magazine available in both hard copy and digital versions. The advertisement is for Mike's Hard Lemonade, which as the name suggests, is lemonade fortified with alcohol.

This type of trade magazine advertising can generate a large number of inquiries from prospective channel members, thus providing a large pool from which to make selections.

FIGURE 7.1 Trade Magazine Advertisement Seeking Inquiries from Prospective Beverage Distributors

© Susan Van Etten

Trade Shows

Trade shows or conventions can be a very fruitful source for finding potential channel members. Many trade associations at both the wholesale and the retail levels hold annual conventions at which numerous wholesale or retail organizations in the particular trades are represented. By attending the convention, a manufacturer has access to a wide variety of potential channel members together in one place and time.[14] Such shows can be especially beneficial to small manufacturers, particularly in consumer products such as toys, gifts, hardware and sporting goods. They provide these manufacturers, who are often unknown in their industries, with a chance to meet face to face with many wholesalers and retailers who might be interested in carrying their products.

Other Sources

Some firms also find the following sources helpful for locating prospective intermediaries:

1. Chambers of commerce, banks and local real estate dealers
2. Classified telephone directories or the yellow pages
3. Direct-mail solicitations
4. Contacts from previous applications
5. Independent consultants
6. List brokers who sell lists of names of businesses[15]
7. Business databases
8. The Internet
9. Social networks such as Facebook, Twitter and LinkedIn.

Applying Selection Criteria

Having developed a list of prospective channel members, the next step is to appraise these prospects in light of selection criteria.

If a firm has not developed a set of criteria for selecting channel members, it should develop one. Several channel analysts have developed generalized lists of criteria. However, no list of criteria, no matter how carefully developed, is adequate for a firm under all conditions. Changing circumstances may require the firm to alter its emphasis; so the channel manager should be flexible in the use of selection criteria to allow for such conditions.

Generalized Lists of Criteria

Over a half century ago, in one of the first attempts to specify a set of selection criteria for choosing channel members, Brendel developed a list of 20 key questions for industrial firms to ask their prospective channel members.[16] Many of these questions are relevant for consumer products firms as well. Brendel's list of selection criteria, which has become a classic in marketing channels' literature, is as relevant today as it ever was. This list of 20 selection questions is as follows:

1. Does the distributor really want our line or is he or she after it because of the present-day shortages?
2. How well established is he or she?
3. What is his or her reputation among his or her customers?
4. What is his or her reputation among manufacturers?
5. Is he or she aggressive?
6. What other allied lines does the distributor handle?
7. What is the distributor's financial position?
8. Does he or she have the ability to discount his or her bills?
9. What is the size of his or her plant (facilities)?
10. Will he or she maintain an adequate inventory?
11. To what important customers does the distributor sell?

12. To which ones does he or she not sell?

13. Does the distributor maintain stable prices?

14. Does he or she provide yearly sales figures for the past five years?

15. What territory does the distributor actually cover with salespeople?

16. Are the distributor's salespeople trained?

17. How many field personnel does he or she have?

18. How many inside employees does he or she have?

19. Does the distributor believe in active cooperation, sales training and sales promotion?

20. What facilities does the distributor have for these activities?

Another set of criteria, proposed by Hlavacek and McCuistion, augments Brendel's list.[17] They argue that for technical products sold in the industrial market, manufacturers should select distributors who carry a small rather than large array of products. This follows because a lower number of products carried enables the distributor to focus more attention on a particular manufacturer's products. Hlavacek and McCuistion also suggest that the potential channel member's market coverage should be specified as a criterion not merely in terms of geographical coverage, but also in terms of **market segment coverage**. This term refers to whether or not the potential distributor deals with the specific market segments that the manufacturer is targeting, not simply whether the potential distributor happens to cover the geographical territories in which the manufacturer sells. Further, they also believe that financial capacity of the potential channel member, while important, should not be overemphasized because sometimes less well financed distributors are "hungrier" and more aggressive. The aggressiveness of a potential distributor is always a vital criterion. Even though Hlavacek and McCuistion's suggestions for selection criteria were presented in the context of manufacturers selling industrial products in industrial markets, these criteria may be applicable across a broader spectrum of channels.

Still another set of selection criteria is provided by Shipley based on a study of manufacturers in the United States and the United Kingdom.[18] The study reported on 12 criteria grouped under three basic categories: (1) sales and market factors; (2) product and service factors and (3) risk and uncertainty factors. These are shown in Table 7.3. The columns headed as "Percent" show the percentage of manufacturers in the study who mentioned a criterion as being used in their channel member selection decisions, while the columns headed "Rank" indicate the rank ordering. It is interesting to note the generally high degree of similarity in findings for the United States and the United Kingdom, suggesting that manufacturers in highly developed Western economies may tend to rely on similar selection criteria.

Based on a careful review of the international marketing literature relevant to selecting foreign distributors, Yeoh and Calantone identify six major categories of selection criteria: (1) commitment level; (2) financial strength; (3) marketing skills; (4) product-related factors; (5) planning abilities and (6) facilitating factors. They refer to these six factors as the "core competencies" that distributors must possess for effective representation in foreign markets.[19]

The most comprehensive and definitive list of channel member selection criteria, however, is still that offered over four decades ago by Pegram.[20] Like Shipley's list, Pegram's list is empirically based; but Pegram used a larger number and broader range of firms (more than 200 U.S. and Canadian manufacturers). Pegram divided the criteria into a number of categories. We will discuss 10 of these briefly in order to offer an overview of the kinds of criteria many firms find important to consider.

TABLE 7.3 FINDINGS OF SHIPLEY STUDY OF SELECTION CRITERIA USED BY MANUFACTURERS IN THE UNITED STATES AND THE UNITED KINGDOM	U.K. FIRMS N = 59		U.S. FIRMS N = 70	
	PERCENT	RANK	PERCENT	RANK
Sales and market factors				
Knowledge of the market	83	1	79	1
Market coverage	75	2	79	1
Number and quality of sales personnel	49	4	64	4
Frequency of sales calls	36	6	17	10
Product and service factors				
Knowledge of the product	47	5	30	6
Service and stocking facilities	20	10	23	8
Quality of service staff	11	11	27	7
Risk and uncertainty factors				
Enthusiasm for the product	61	3	50	5
Previous success	25	7	67	3
Costs involved	25	7	23	8
Extent of dealings with manufacturers' competitors	22	9	16	11
Executives' career histories	10	12	11	12
Others	5	13	9	13

Source: Reprinted from "Selection and Motivation of Distribution Intermediaries," by David B. Shipley, *Industrial marketing Management* (October 1984): 251. Copyright 1984, with permission from Elsevier.

Credit and Financial Condition   Nearly all of the manufacturers included in Pegram's study mentioned the investigation of credit and financial position of prospective intermediaries as vital. This was by far the most frequently used criterion for judging the acceptability of a prospective channel member.

Sales Strength   Most firms also mentioned the sales capacity of prospective intermediaries as a critical criterion. Some of the most commonly used measures of sales strength, particularly for wholesale intermediaries, are the quality of salespeople and, the actual number of salespeople employed. Manufacturers of more technical products are also concerned with the technical competence of the intermediary's salespeople.

Product Lines   Manufacturers were generally found to consider four aspects of the intermediary's product line: (1) *competitive* products; (2) *compatible* products; (3) *complementary* products and (4) *quality* of lines carried.

Manufacturers generally try to avoid, whenever possible, intermediaries who carry directly competitive product lines. Many of the intermediaries also share this view, particularly those who feel a sense of loyalty to their present suppliers. There are, of course, numerous exceptions to this "no directly competitive products" criterion.

Manufacturers typically prefer intermediaries who handle compatible products(any products that, by definition, do not directly compete with the manufacturer's line). Intermediaries who carry complementary products are looked upon favorably because, by carrying such products, they offer a better overall product mix to their customers. Finally, manufacturers generally seek intermediaries who carry product lines that are equal to or better than their own. Manufacturers do not want their products to be associated with inferior, unknown or "dog" lines if they can help it.

Reputation   Most manufacturers will flatly eliminate prospective intermediaries who do not enjoy a good reputation in their community. For retail intermediaries, store image is an especially critical component of the retailer's overall reputation. Hence, if the prospective retailer's image is not up to the standards the manufacturer is attempting to project for its products, this fact may be sufficient reason to avoid selecting that retailer as a channel member. Having the "wrong" kind of retailer selling its products can have serious adverse effects on the manufacturer's own reputation. Consequently, from a channel strategy perspective, the reputation of the distributors and retailers selling the manufacturer's product is one of the key strategic issues for the manufacturer to consider. The decision may require input from the highest levels in the organization, including the chairman of the board in certain cases.

Market Coverage   The adequacy of the intermediary in covering the geographical territory that the manufacturer would like to reach is known as **market coverage**. A further consideration is whether the prospective intermediary covers too much territory, which could lead to overlap of the coverage of existing intermediaries. Generally, manufacturers will attempt to get the best territorial coverage with a minimum of overlapping. This is an especially important consideration for a manufacturer using highly selective distribution.

Sales Performance   The main consideration here is whether the prospective intermediary can capture as much market share as the manufacturer expects. Often, the manufacturer will seek detailed sales performance data from prospective intermediaries to get a firsthand view of their effectiveness. If such direct evidence cannot be obtained, other sources include credit bureaus, competitive and noncompetitive distributors in the area, consumers of the manufacturer's products, customers of the distributor, other supplier firms and local trade people. Reports from these sources often give an indication of the intermediary's marketing performance history. Some manufacturers report that this is all they require to gain a sense of a prospective channel member's sales performance.

Management Succession   Many intermediaries are managed by the firm's owner and founder, many of whom, especially at the wholesale level, are independent, small businesses. Consequently, if the firm's principal dies, the continuity of management is left in doubt. The succession criterion is so important to Caterpillar, Inc., that the company has offered special seminars for many years to help persuade children of its existing distributors to carry on the business when their parents retire or pass away.[21]

Management Ability   Many manufacturers feel that a prospective channel member is not even worth considering if the quality of its management is poor. Therefore, this factor is of critical importance in choosing channel members.[22] Actually judging the quality of management is difficult because of the intangibles involved in making an evaluation. One of the key determinants is management's ability to organize, train and retain salespeople. In short, a good sales force is often indicative of good management.

Attitude   This criterion applies mainly to a prospective intermediary's aggressiveness, enthusiasm and initiative. These qualities are believed to be closely related to long-term success in handling the manufacturer's product. An evaluation of whether the prospective channel member has the "proper" attitude is generally a matter of managerial judgment because attitudes do not show up in black and white on financial statements.[23]

FIGURE 7.2 Key
Criteria to Consider
When Selecting
Channel Members

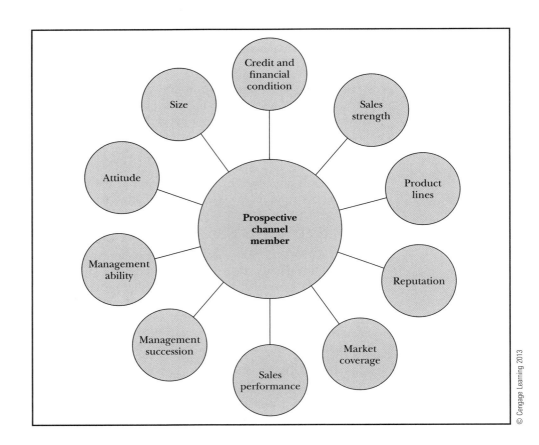

Size   Sometimes a prospective intermediary is judged on sheer size. The belief is that the larger the organization and sales volume, the larger the sales of the manufacturer's products. There are other reasons for considering large size as an important, positive criterion beyond this general belief. It is usually a safe assumption that large intermediaries are more successful, more profitable, better established and handle better product lines. Further, the large intermediary usually employs more salespeople (which leads to more exposure for the manufacturer's products) and is usually better equipped with offices, personnel and facilities than are small intermediaries.

Using Lists of Selection Criteria

While checklists such as those discussed above are not applicable to all firms under all conditions, they are still valuable because they help point to many of the key areas of consideration for selecting channel members. Even though each firm must develop its own specific set of selection criteria based on its own objectives and policies, such checklists provide a good starting point and can make this task easier. Moreover, the comprehensiveness of a firm's individualized list of selection criteria is likely to be greater if all of these general criteria are considered during its development. Figure 7.2 provides an overview visualization of the key criteria to consider when selecting channel members.

Securing the Channel Members

It is important to remember that the selection process is a two-way street. It is not only the producer or manufacturer who does the selecting, but also the intermediaries at both the wholesale and retail levels. Those who are large and well-established can be very selective about whom they represent.[24] Producers and manufacturers, except for those with truly extraordinary reputations and prestige, cannot expect quality intermediaries to stand in line to become channel members. Rather, most producers and manufacturers still need to do an effective selling job to secure the services of good intermediaries.

The channel manager in producing and manufacturing firms can use a number of specific incentives when attempting to secure channel members. All of these, however, should be aimed at conveying the firm's commitment to support prospective channel members so that these prospects are more likely to be successful with the line. In other words, the manufacturer or producer should make it clear to the prospective intermediary that the partnership will be mutually beneficial if each of the parties does the job. Pegram captures this point succinctly:

> *The keystone of many supplier sales policies is this concept: the supplier produces, the distributor sells and each is dependent upon the other. Together they form a team and teamwork is essential if the association is to prove mutually beneficial.*[25]

Now, more than four decades after Pegram made this observation, his words ring truer than ever. Partnerships or strategic alliances between manufacturers and intermediaries at the wholesale and/or retail levels based on mutual commitment and teamwork are not only popular, but have become the norm for relationships in many channels of distribution.[26]

Figure 7.3 captures this partnership concept in an advertisement in *DSN Retailing Today*, a trade magazine. The advertisement is aimed at securing retailers and distributors to sell Gillette products. The word "partnership" is used in the headline while the copy stresses the advantages of becoming a Gillette channel partner.

Specific Incentives for Securing Channel Members

Generally, the more specific the manufacturer can be in spelling out what kinds of support and assistance will be offered to channel members, the better. Prospective channel members want to know at the outset precisely "what is in it for them" if they decide to join the manufacturer's marketing channel.[27] While there are many possible incentives that the manufacturer might offer, most of them would fit within one of the following four areas: (1) good, profitable product line; (2) advertising and promotional support; (3) management assistance and (4) fair dealing policies and friendly relationships.

Product Line   At the heart of what the manufacturer has to offer is a good product line with strong sales and profit potential.[28] Indeed, if manufacturers can offer this, they may need to offer little else to secure all of the channel members they want. Obviously, manufacturers with well-known and highly respected products have a considerable advantage over lesser-known manufacturers. Thus, it is especially important for manufacturers whose products are not as well-known to do a good job of communicating the benefits of handling their products *from the channel member's point of view*. It is all too easy for manufacturers to get caught up in talking about how good their products are rather than stressing how effective their products can be in generating *sales and profits for the channel members*.

This emphasis on stressing the value of a good product line from channel members' perspective is illustrated in Figure 7.4, which shows a trade magazine advertisement for Snyder's, a pretzel manufacturer seeking to compete against much larger rivals Frito-Lay and Herr's. In the advertisement, Snyder's argues that the quality, variety and superior packaging of its products will not only sell well, but are also so desirable that consumers will view retailers carrying Snyder's pretzels as "destination" stores. The message Snyder's hopes retailers will glean from the advertisement is that their pretzels will serve as

FIGURE 7.3
Advertisement from the
Gillette Company
Stressing Advantages of
Becoming a Gillette
Channel Partner

Source: Courtesy, The Gillette Company.

a magnet to attract more customers These customers will then buy other products while in the stores, thus enhancing the retailers' sales and profits.

Advertising and Promotion Prospective intermediaries also look to manufacturers for promotional support.[29] In the consumer market, a strong program of national advertising is one of the most effective inducements to secure retail intermediaries. The manufacturer who can point to such a program gains almost immediate credibility in the eyes of prospective intermediaries in regards to the sales potential of the product line.

FIGURE 7.4
Advertisement in a Trade Magazine Stressing the Power of a Product Line to Attract More Customers to Retailers' Stores

Source: Courtesy, Snyder's of Hanover.

In the industrial market, a strong program of trade advertising offers a similar advantage. Additionally, in both the consumer and industrial markets, such factors as advertising allowances, cooperative advertising campaigns, point-of-purchase material and showroom displays indicate strong channel member support and serve as good inducements to prospective intermediaries to join the channel (see Chapter 12).

Management Assistance   Prospective channel members want to know whether the manufacturer is committed to helping them not only in the form of providing advertising and promotional support for selling the particular manufacturer's products, but also in going beyond this to help them do a better job of managing their businesses. Management assistance is good evidence of such a commitment. Management assistance can cover a wide range of areas, including training programs, financial analysis and planning, market analysis, inventory control procedures and promotional methods. The extent of such assistance varies widely depending on the type of channel relationship involved. A contractual channel relationship involving a comprehensive franchise agreement between the manufacturer and the channel members would generally be expected to provide for a much more comprehensive management assistance program than a conventional, loosely aligned channel relationship. But even in the latter situation, some form of management assistance is still possible and desirable. The "Your Category Management Partner" program offered to retailers and distributors by 3M provides an excellent example of management assistance at a level of sophistication that many retailers and distributors (even giant ones) might have difficulty doing on their own. This management assistance program is briefly outlined in Figure 7.5.

FIGURE 7.5
Brochure from the 3M Company Stressing Advantages of Becoming a 3M Channel Partner

Your Category Management Partner

3M's business analysis benefits are among the most extensive anywhere. The 3M business team approach is focused on solutions; 3M's insight into individual retail market dynamics helps drive sales, profits and market share for the retailer.

Among the major components of a 3M business analysis plan:

- Syndicated Data (Nielsen);
- Demographic Profiling (Market Metrics, Spectra);
- Planogram Financial Analysis.

SYNDICATED DATA identifies opportunities by analyzing account performance via market trends, market share and opportunity gap analysis.

DEMOGRAPHIC PROFILING provides a rational basis for consumer-focused micromarketing by isolating consumer demographics and preferences, calculating potential sales, and identifying competitive store interaction.

PLANOGRAM FINANCIAL ANALYSIS looks at product performance and sets benchmarks to directly address such critical shelf management issues as product variety vs. duplication and SKU turn/profit growth.

The bottom line: 3M business analysis capabilities are at the heart of a 3M-retailer category management partnership that aims at maximizing the potential of brands and their categories.

A World of Benefits

3M

What 3M Brings to The Table

- *Consumer-driven, innovative products*
- *Category-leading brands*
- *Higher margins and turns*
- *Unmatched consumer recognition*
- *Strong promotional opportunities*
- *Effective merchandising programs*
- *Consumer market insight*
- *Micro-marketing capabilities*

Source: Courtesy, 3M.

The figure shows an excerpt from a 3M brochure explaining the company's ability to provide a wide range of management assistance to its channel members. The bullet points on the right-hand side of the brochure highlight a number of the hard-hitting management assistance tools available to 3M's channel partners to help them achieve bottom-line results.

Fair Dealing and Friendly Relationship   As we pointed out in Chapter 4, marketing channel relationships are not mechanical or purely economic relationships lacking the "human element." Rather, a channel relationship is a relationship between organizations of people and, as such, is a social system subject to the same behavioral interactions and processes characteristic of all social systems. Channel members may like[30] or dislike, respect or disdain, suspect or fear each other. They may be cooperative or antagonistic, loyal or disloyal toward each other. In short, a marketing channel relationship is not only a business relationship but a human relationship as well.[31] Though the relationship may be couched in elaborate or formal agreements or even in legal contracts, the human, people-to-people element is never fully removed.[32] This fact should not be forgotten when attempting to secure channel members. Specifically, the manufacturer should convey to prospective channel members that he or she is genuinely interested in establishing a good relationship with prospective channel members built on the basis of trust and concern for their welfare, not only as business entities but as people as well.[33] In fact, some manufacturers even go so far as to refer to their channel members as their "family" of distributors or dealers. While this may be overstating the case, it does convey the manufacturer's belief in building a marketing channel that is based on more than dollars and cents.

This emphasis on fair dealing and friendly relationships should not, however, be expected to offset failings in the underlying economic or business bases of the channel relationship. Recent research has shown that interpersonal relationships, cordiality and even a genuine liking of channel members for each other are no substitute for substance in the form of competitive products, pricing and support programs.[34]

Summary

Just as the selection of good employees is critical to the success of a firm, so, too, is the selection of channel members because most firms need both to succeed in the marketplace.

The selection of channel members is the last (seventh) phase of channel design. Selection decisions can also be made independently of channel design decisions when new channel members are added to the channel or when those who have left are replaced. Only those manufacturers who sell directly to users are not faced with the selection of channel members.

In general, the more selective the intensity of distribution, the more emphasis the firm needs to place on selection and vice versa.

The selection process consists of three basic steps: (1) finding prospective channel members; (2) applying selection criteria to determine whether they are suitable and (3) securing the prospective members for the channel.

Finding prospective channel members generally poses few problems because many sources can be used for locating them: (1) the field sales organization; (2) trade sources; (3) reseller inquiries; (4) customers; (5) advertising, (6) trade shows and (7) other sources such as chambers of commerce, telephone directories, independent consultants, list brokers, databases and the Internet.

Applying selection criteria is a more difficult problem because no single list of criteria is appropriate for all firms. Each firm must develop its own list reflecting its particular objectives and policies. Moreover, these criteria must be flexible enough to allow for changing conditions. However, 10 general criteria are useful as a starting point for most firms to use when developing their own specialized set of selection criteria: (1) credit and financial condition; (2) sales strength; (3) product lines; (4) reputation; (5) market coverage; (6) sales performance; (7) management succession; (8) management ability; (9) attitude and (10) size.

Finally, securing the prospective members for the channel can be a challenge because, except in unusual cases, prospective channel members do not typically stand in line eagerly awaiting the manufacturer's call. Most manufacturers must therefore do an effective selling job to secure the services of quality channel members. Specific incentives can be used in the quest to

secure channel members: (1) providing a good, profitable product line; (2) offering advertising and promotional support; (3) providing management assistance and (4) assuring prospective channel members of fair dealing policies and a relationship built on trust and friendship. The channel manager should not, however, expect fair dealing and friendly relationships to offset deficiencies in the underlying economic basis of the channel relationship.

Review Questions

1. Are selection decisions always the result of changes in channel structure? Explain.

2. What is the relationship between intensity of distribution and the amount of emphasis given to selection?

3. Has a selection process really occurred in the case of very intensive distribution where all possible outlets are used in the channel design? Discuss.

4. Discuss several sources that the channel manager can use to help locate prospective channel members.

5. What is a potential problem with the use of the sales force as a means for finding prospective channel members?

6. Is it possible to develop a truly universal list of selection criteria for appraising prospective

channel members? What are some of the problems one might encounter in attempting to develop such a list?

7. Is Pegram's list of selection criteria descriptive or normative? Explain.

8. Briefly describe each of the 10 general criteria for selecting channel members that can be used as a starting point for developing more specialized lists of channel member selection criteria.

9. What are some of the specific incentives that the manufacturer can use to secure channel members?

10. In discussing the means available to secure prospective intermediaries as actual channel members, the chapter suggests that the offer of a "partnership" by the producer or manufacturer could serve as a strong inducement. What does this mean?

Channel Issues for Discussion

1. Apple, with its almost 300 company-owned stores, uses independent intermediaries, which it refers to as "third-party resellers." For its Mac computers, Apple is very careful about the intermediaries it selects to become members of its distribution channel. Once selected, Apple makes a substantial investment to enhance the capabilities of its chosen channel members to sell and service Apple products. Its "Apple Sales Consultant Program," for example, places Apple employees at selected channel members' stores to provide expertise on how to tell the Apple story and ensure a high-quality buying experience. The company also offers extensive training and support through what it refers to as its "Apple Premium Resellers Program" to selected channel members to help them develop high levels of customer service and product expertise. Apple strongly believes that providing high-quality sales

and after-sales support is critical for attracting new customers and retaining existing ones.

Do you think Apple's careful selection of channel members and its efforts to enable them to provide high-quality sales and service support are as important as Apple's unique products in creating a differential advantage for Apple?

2. Bill Harding, the national sales manager for a major appliance maker, realized that the company would have to add more wholesale distributors in at least a half-dozen major territories on the East Coast and in the Midwest to keep up with the growth in those markets. Bill knew he needed good distributors who were financially sound, with strong selling skills and offered high service capabilities. To zero in on these potential, new distributors, Harding decided to use the company's outside sales force covering those territories. He sent out memos to the district

sales managers, who in turn informed the field sales force to call on potential distributors in their territories and send back written reports. One month later, Harding was very disappointed with the lukewarm response he got. The reports he received were skimpy and superficial. Harding was a little befuddled with the situation because all of the salespeople who were asked to prospect for new accounts were high producers.

Why do you suppose Bill Harding did not get the enthusiastic response he wanted?

3. The Rust-Oleum Corporation is world-renowned for its anticorrosive coatings for virtually any application, for use on everything from heavy industrial equipment to consumer patio furniture. The company sells its industrial products through wholesalers (industrial distributors) and its consumer products through both wholesalers and retailers. Rust-Oleum has, for many years, talked about doing business with its channel members by the golden rule—"doing business together with sincerity, honesty and cooperation." The company is also fairly selective in its choice of distributors, limiting the number selected to the fewest possible needed to provide effective coverage of each market. In addition, Rust-Oleum makes it a point to say that it sells *through* the distributor, not just to him.

Given this approach to dealing with channel members, what criteria do you believe would be especially important for Rust-Oleum Corporation to emphasize in selecting prospective channel members?

4. John Paul Mitchell Systems, Inc., a manufacturer of specialized high-quality hair care products, has made it a policy to sell its products only through "hair care professionals." Only better beauty salons and specialty stores are selected by the company to represent its products. Yet somehow, Paul Mitchell products were being sold by Walmart stores in Texas. Upon hearing this, the company filed suit against Walmart, alleging that Walmart was selling substandard batches of Paul Mitchell products and had bought the products from a former Mitchell Systems supplier. The batch of products in question had been rejected by Paul Mitchell Systems because of poor quality and, therefore, should not have been made available for resale through *any* retailers, let alone Walmart. Mitchell Systems requested that the court issue a temporary restraining order that would forbid Walmart from selling the Paul Mitchell products.

Why did Mitchell Systems go to such lengths to prevent these products from being sold by Walmart? Discuss in terms of the channel member selection strategy apparently being used by the manufacturer.

5. New Balance has developed a strong reputation as a serious and leading manufacturer of high-performance and high-quality athletic footwear. Its use of technology to produce state-of-the-art running shoes and cross-trainers has earned the respect of many world-class athletes who rely on New Balance footwear to compete at the highest levels in their respective sports. So, it seemed strange to industry observers when New Balance's channel design strategy, implemented in the spring of 2009, chose Nine West shoe stores, a division of Jones Apparel Group Inc., to sell New Balance athletic footwear. What raised the eyebrows of the observers? The fit—not of the shoes, but of the two brands. Would Nine West, which is identified as a seller of fashionable women's shoes, undermine the brand image of New Balance as a maker of hard-core athletic shoes? Although the strategy is being tried on a limited basis in just 50 Nine West stores, if sales are good for the first six months, many additional Nine West stores will be added.

What do you see as the strategic rationale for New Balance selecting Nine West as a channel member to sell its high performance athletic footwear? Over the long run, do you think New Balance's channel member selection strategy will affect its product image?

6. Master Lock is perhaps the nation's best-known name in padlocks. Master Lock padlocks are sold intensively at the retail level through a wide range of stores, including hardware stores, home centers, automotive stores, bicycle shops (for bicycle padlocks), drugstores, supermarkets and many others. This wide retail network is supplied largely through wholesalers. Master Lock relies on wholesalers to provide the bulk of the sales and logistical support to the retail channel members. When retailers need help in ordering, stocking the right assortment, choosing point-of-purchase displays or advertising to consumers, Master Lock tells them to "ask your Master Lock distributor for all the advice and support you need."

Given that Master Lock expects its wholesale distributors to provide virtually all the support needed by retailers, what kind of support do you think the wholesaler distributors should expect from Master Lock?

References

1. See, for example, Eugene H. Fram, "We Can Do a Better Job of Selecting International Distributors," *Journal of Industrial Marketing* (Spring 1992): 61–70.

2. For a related discussion, see: Lawrence Delevingne, "Amway: Shining Up a Tarnished Name," *Business Week*, (August 11, 2008): 56.

3. See, for example, Greg Davis, "Dell Takes Top Honors in Server Category at Leading Channel Industry Awards," *CRN*, September, 9, 2010, http://community.dell.com/.

4. Roger Pegram, *Selecting and Evaluating Distributors* (New York: National Industrial Conference Board, 1965), 5.

5. Roger Pegram, *Selecting and Evaluating Distributors* (New York: National Industrial Conference Board, 1965), 3.

6. *Goodyear Tire & Rubber Company Annual Report 2009*, 5.

7. For an article related to this point, see Amy Merrick, "Kmart Suppliers Limit Risk in Case of Chapter 11 Filing," *Wall Street Journal*, (January 21, 2002): A4.

8. For a related analysis based on a mathematical model of the selection process, see V. Kasturi Rangan, Andris A. Zoltners and Robert J. Becker, "The Channel Intermediary Selection Decision: A Model and an Application," *Marketing Science* (September 1986): 1114–1122.

9. Thomas A. Stewart, "Leading Change from the Top," *Harvard Business Review*, (July-August 2006): 93–94.

10. *Encyclopedia of Associations* (Gale Research: 2009).

11. See for example, National Retail Federation (NRF), November, 11, 2010, http://www.nrf.com/modules.php? name=Pagestsp_id=146; National Association of Wholesaler Distributors (NAW), November 11, 2010, http://www.naw.org/about/aindex.php; Manufacturers' Agents National Association (MANA), http://www.manaonline.org.

12. *3M Company Annual Report 2009*, 5.

13. For a related discussion, see Richard N. Cordozo, Shannan H. Shipp and Kenneth J. Roering, "Proactive Strategic Partnerships: A New Business Markets Strategy," *Journal of Business and Industrial Marketing* (Winter 1992): 51–63.

14. Anna-Louise Jackson, "Must the Show Go On?" *Marketing News*, (April 15, 2009): 6.

15. See for example, *mailinglists direct*, November 11, 2010, http://www.mailing-lists-direct.com/.

16. Louis H. Brendel, "Where to Find and How to Choose Your Industrial Distributors," *Sales Management*, September 15, 1951.

17. James D. Hlavacek and Tommy J. McCuistion, "Industrial Distributors—When, Who, and How?" *Harvard Business Review* (March–April 1983): 96–101.

18. David D. Shipley, "Selection and Motivation of Distribution Intermediaries," *Industrial Marketing Management* (October 1984): 249–256.

19. Poh-Lin Yeoh and Rojer J. Calantone, "An Application of the Analytical Hierarchy Process to International Marketing: Selection of a Foreign Distributor," *Journal of Global Marketing* 8, no. 3/4 (1995): 39–65.

20. Roger Pegram, *Selecting and Evaluating Distributors* (New York: National Industrial Conference Board, 1965), 21–91.

21. Donald V. Fites, "Make Your Dealers Your Partners," *Harvard Business Review* (March–April 1996): 84–95.

22. Debbie Howell, "Fleming Takes Distribution Service to Next Level," *Retailing Today*, (November 5, 2001): 4.

23. Susan Berfield, "The New Star of Sellavision," *Bloomberg BusinessWeek*, (May 24–30): 60–63.

24. Janet Wagner, Richard Ettenson and Jean Parrish, "Vendor Selection Among Retail Buyers: An Analysis by Merchandise Division," *Journal of Retailing* (Spring 1989): 58–79.

25. Roger Pegram, *Selecting and Evaluating Distributors* (New York: National Industrial Conference Board, 1965), 100.

26. Rodolfo Vazquez, Victor Iglesias and Luis Ignacio Alvarez-Gonzalez, "Distribution Channel Relationships: The Conditions and Strategic Outcomes of Cooperation between Manufacturer and Distributor," *International Review of Retail Distribution and Consumer Research* (April 2005): 125–150; Sunil Sahadev, "Economic Satisfaction and Relationship Commitment in Channels," *European Journal of Marketing* Vol. 42 no. 1/2 (2008): 178–195.

27. Geoff Gordon, Roger Calantone and C.A. diBenedetto, "How Electrical Contractors Choose Distributors," *Industrial Marketing Management* 20 (1991): 29–42.

28. Mike Duff, "Supercenters Open Floodgates as Water Rises," *Retailing Today*, (October 10, 2002): 10.

29. Sridhar N. Ramaswami and Srini S. Srinivasan, "Analyzing the Impact of Promotions on Manufacturer and

Retailer Performance: A Framework for Cooperative Promotional Strategy," *Journal of Marketing Channels* 6no. 3/4 (1998): 131–145.

30. See, for example, Carolyn Y. Nicholson, Larry D. Compeau and Rajesh Sethi, "The Role of Interpersonal Liking in Building Trust in Long-Term Channel Relationships," *Journal of the Academy of Marketing Science* (Winter 2001): 3–15.

31. Russel P.J. Kingshott and Anthony Pecotich, "The Impact of Psychological Contracts on Trust and Commitment in Supplier–Distributor Relationships," *European Journal of Marketing* Vol. 41, no. 9/10 (2007): 1053–1072; Raymond A. Jussaume, Jr. and Patriya Tansuhaj, "Asian Variations in the Importance of Personal Attributes for Wholesaler Selection: Japanese and Thai Marketing Channels," *Journal of International Consumer Marketing* 3no. 3 (1991): 127–140.

32. For an interesting and insightful discussion relevant to establishing channel relationships, especially with regard to the issue of "fairness," see Roger Dickinson, "Negotiations in the Channel: The Negotiation Ratio," *Proceedings of the Sixth World Conference on Research in the Distributive Trades*, eds. Roy Thurik and Henk J. Giannotten (The Hague, Netherlands: Dutch Ministry of Economic Affairs, 1991), 261–266.

33. For a related discussion, see Jule B. Gassenheimer and Rosemary Ramsey, "The Impact of Dependence on Dealer Satisfaction: A Comparison of Reseller–Supplier Relationships," *Journal of Retailing* 70no. 3 (1994): 253–266.

34. Kenneth H. Wathne, Harold Biong and Jan B. Heide, "Choice of Supplier in Embedded Markets: Relationship and Marketing Program Effects," *Journal of Marketing* (April 2001): 54–66.

CHAPTER 8
Target Markets and Channel Design Strategy

LEARNING OBJECTIVES

After reading this chapter, you should:

1. Appreciate the importance of market variables as the most fundamental and significant variables to consider for channel design strategy.

2. Be familiar with the framework for market analysis and its four basic dimensions.

3. Recognize the importance of keeping track of changes in market geography as it might affect channel design strategy.

4. Know how market size relates to channel design strategy.

5. Grasp the concept of efficient congestion as it relates to market density.

6. Understand the meaning of market behavior in terms of the when, where, how and who shops for products and services.

7. Realize that any or all of the subdimensions of market behavior are subject to change.

8. Be cognizant of the implications of changes in market behavior on channel design strategy.

© OmniTerra Images

FOCUS ON CHANNELS

Do Farmers' Market Channels Have to Have Farmers?

In an ideal world where words and labels could be taken at face value, the term "farmers' market" would convey a straightforward meaning: a farmers' market is simply a marketing channel where local farmers sell their produce directly to consumers. But the real world is not this ideal world. In recent years, "farmers' market" has become a trendy term with quite a bit of cache in the grocery industry. It seems that more and more consumers have become interested in "fresh," "healthy," "natural" and "organic" foods. These attributes have come to be associated with farmers' markets. This association has not gone unnoticed by some big supermarket chains such as Safeway Inc. and Supervalue Inc. These giant retailers and others apparently view farmers' markets not as a particular type of marketing channel, but as a promotional device for attracting customers to their stores. Safeway Stores in Seattle, for example, put up signs saying "Farmers' Market" above produce displays in front of their stores and the Albertsons supermarkets division of Supervalue did the same thing in 200 stores in Washington, Oregon and Idaho. But the stands were not manned by local farmers and the origin of produce being sold was questionable. In fact, mangos on display in Washington were not only not locally grown (the Washington climate is not suitable), but may well have come from a foreign country!

Such loose usage of the term "farmers' market" by big conventional grocery retailers has sewn fear on the part of farmers groups such as the Farmers Market Coalition, a national trade group. They worry that the term will be diluted or even rendered meaningless if the big guys continue to encroach on the turf of the 6,000 plus real farmers' markets.

So, is the farmers' definition of "farmers' market" a reasonable one? They certainly think so. After all, when consumers go to a farmers' market, shouldn't they see farmers there?

Source: Based on Nick Wingfield and Ben Worthen, "Copy Farmers' Markets Reap a Crop of Complaints," *Wall Street Journal*, September 24, 2010: A3.

In Chapter 6, "Designing Marketing Channels," we pointed out that of all of the variables affecting the design of marketing channels, market variables are the most fundamental. This is because the needs and wants of the market being targeted by the channel manager should shape the design of the firm's marketing channels.[1] In other words, marketing channel design strategy should be **market-driven** so as to meet as closely as possible the demands of the firm's target markets (its customers). So, if customers expect to be able to shop online 24/7, shop while on the move via their smartphones, have movies and shows delivered via Hulu rather than conventional TV,[2] get a flu shot at a local mall rather than in a doctor's office[3] or have any of a myriad of other channel expectations, channel managers need to pay close attention so that their channel design strategies reflect the demands of the customers being targeted.[4] To do this successfully, the channel manager needs to be familiar with several dimensions of markets as they relate to the design of marketing channels.

In this chapter we examine these market dimensions in greater depth than we did in Chapter 6 and discuss their implications for various phases of the channel design process.

A Framework for Market Analysis

Markets, whether consumer or industrial, are complex. A myriad of factors may have to be considered in analyzing particular markets, so it is useful to have a framework to help provide some order to this complexity.

In this chapter, we use a framework consisting of four basic dimensions for discussing markets:

1. Market geography
2. Market size
3. Market density
4. Market behavior

This market framework is illustrated in Figure 8.1

The chapter is structured around these four basic dimensions. Each major section discusses one of the dimensions. The emphasis will be on showing how these market dimensions influence channel design strategy. The fourth dimension, market behavior, is the most complex. Accordingly, a larger portion of this chapter will be devoted to the market behavior dimension than to any of the other three dimensions.

FIGURE 8.1
A Framework for Analyzing Market Dimensions in Relation to Channel Design

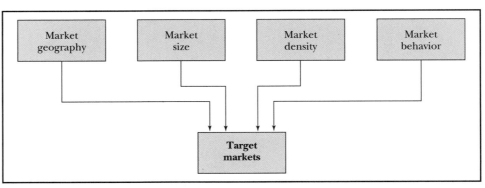

© Cengage Learning 2013

Market Geography and Channel Design Strategy

Market geography refers to the geographical extent of markets and where they are located. If the channel manager asks the questions "What do our markets look like geographically?" and "How distant are our markets?" the concern is with the market geography dimension.

The channel manager is charged with the task of evaluating market geography relative to channel structure to make sure that the structure is able to serve the markets effectively and efficiently. Changing market locations resulting from expanding geographical boundaries of existing markets or the opening up of new, more distant markets should signal the channel manager that modifications in channel structure may be needed. Starbucks, for example, has in recent years located coffee shops not only in every state in the U.S., but also all over the world, including many countries in Europe, Asia and South America. Starbucks is following in the footsteps of other firms such as McDonald's, Burger King and Kentucky Fried Chicken, which have been locating their restaurants throughout the world for many years. These firms have not let geographical distance stand in the way of reaching their target customers. Rather, they have developed and adapted their channel structures to serve these distant markets effectively and efficiently. In Chapter 18, which deals with global marketing channels, we will examine the issue in more detail.

Of course, another approach for dealing with distant markets in recent years is through Internet-based e-commerce channels. Given that the Internet provides worldwide reach electronically, geographical distance becomes less important, at least in theory. In practice, this has not been the case, especially for firms selling physical products that must be picked, packed and then shipped over great distances. Fulfillment, logistics and customer service still present challenges for both consumer and business markets even with the power of Internet technology.[5] We will return to this issue in greater depth in Chapter 15, which deals with electronic marketing channels and in Chapter 13 which focuses on logistics and supply chain management.

Locating Markets

As part of the firm's overall marketing strategy, the channel manager may be called on to delineate the geographical locations of target markets. Generally, this can be done in terms of one or more commonly accepted geographical units. The Bureau of the Census, for example, lists data for a number of geographical entities such as states, regions and divisions, counties, metropolitan statistical areas (MSAs), selected towns and townships and several other special-purpose designations. Table 8.1 provides definitions for these geographical entities. Postal ZIP codes are also useful for delineating markets geographically.

Some combination of these geographical entities typically serves as the basis for specifying the location of markets. Table 8.2 lists some useful sources for obtaining additional geographical market data.

More difficult than locating markets is keeping track of geographical changes in existing markets and forecasting such changes for the future. Given the increasing mobility of populations, the channel manager cannot expect market geography to remain stable for an extended time period.

In a global context, market geography has also changed dramatically in recent years. Most notably, countries in Southeast Asia as well as the former Eastern Bloc countries of Central and Eastern Europe have become key locations for emerging markets.

TABLE 8.1 GEOGRAPHICAL AREAS FOR WHICH CENSUS DATE ARE AVAILABLE

Geographic Terms and Definitions Used by U.S. Census Bureau

The Census Bureau produces population estimates for the Nation, the States, the District of Columbia, Puerto Rico, counties and equivalents, incorporated places, minor civil divisions, consolidated cities, census regions and divisions, and metropolitan areas.

Census Regions and Divisions

The Census Bureau delineates two sets of sub-national areas that are composed of states. This two-tiered system of areas consists of 9 census divisions nested in 4 census regions. The Northeast region includes the New England division: Connecticut, Maine, Massachusetts, New Hampshire, Rhode Island, and Vermont; and the Middle Atlantic division: New Jersey, New York, and Pennsylvania. The Midwest region includes the East North Central division: Illinois, Indiana, Michigan, Ohio, and Wisconsin; and the West North Central division: Iowa, Kansas, Minnesota, Missouri, Nebraska, North Dakota, and South Dakota. The South region includes the South Atlantic division: Delaware, District of Columbia, Florida, Georgia, Maryland, North Carolina, South Carolina, Virginia, West Virginia; the East South Central division: Alabama, Kentucky, Mississippi, and Tennessee; and the West South Central division: Arkansas, Louisiana, Oklahoma, and Texas. The West region includes the Mountain division: Arizona, Colorado, Idaho, Montana, Nevada, New Mexico, Utah, and Wyoming; and the Pacific division: Alaska, California, Hawaii, Oregon, and Washington.

Counties (and equivalents)

Counties are the primary legal divisions of most states. Most counties are functioning governmental units, whose powers and functions vary from state to state. In Louisiana, these primary divisions are known as parishes. In Alaska, the county equivalents consist of legally organized boroughs or "census areas" delineated for statistical purposes by the State of Alaska and the Census Bureau (since 1980). In four states (Maryland, Missouri, Nevada, and Virginia), one or more cities are independent of any county organization and thus constitute primary divisions of their states; the Census Bureau refers to these places as "independent cities" and treats them as the equivalents of counties for estimates purposes. The District of Columbia has no primary divisions and the entire area is considered to be the equivalent of a county. In Puerto Rico, municipios are the primary divisions and treated as county equivalents for estimates purposes. Legal changes to county boundaries or names are typically infrequent.

Minor Civil Divisions

Legally defined county subdivisions are referred to as minor civil divisions (MCDs.) MCDs are the primary divisions of a county. They comprise both governmentally functioning entities—that is, those with elected officials who provide services and raise revenues—and nonfunctioning entities that exist primarily for administrative purposes, such as election districts. Twenty-eight states and Puerto Rico have MCDs. However, the MCDs function as general purpose governmental units in all or part of only twenty states. Within these twenty states, PEP (Population Estimates Program) produces estimates for all governmentally functioning MCDs and for nonfunctioning MCDs in counties that contain at least one functioning MCD.

The legal powers and functions of MCDs vary from state to state. Most of the MCDs in twelve states (Connecticut, Maine, Massachusetts, Michigan, Minnesota, New Hampshire, New Jersey, New York, Pennsylvania, Rhode Island, Vermont, and Wisconsin) serve as general-purpose local governments. In the remaining eight states for which PEP produces MCD level estimates (Illinois, Indiana, Kansas, Missouri, Nebraska, North Dakota, Ohio, and South Dakota) the MCDs, for the most part, perform less of a governmental role and are less well known locally, even though they are active governmental units.

MCDs primarily are known as towns (in New England, New York, and Wisconsin), townships, and districts, but also include a variety of other entities. In Maine and New York, American Indian reservations are not part of any other MCD and therefore, the Census Bureau treats them as MCDs. PEP does not produce separate estimates for American Indian Reservations regardless of their MCD status. In some states, all or some incorporated places are subordinate to the MCDs in which they are located. Therefore, a place may be either independent of or dependent upon MCDs. In one state (Ohio), a multi-county place may be treated differently from county to county. No functioning MCDs exist in Puerto Rico.

Incorporated Places

The legal designations, powers, and functions of incorporated places vary from state to state. Incorporated places include cities, towns (except in New England, New York, and Wisconsin where the Census Bureau recognizes towns as MCDs for census purposes), boroughs (except in Alaska, where the Census Bureau recognizes boroughs as equivalents of counties, and New York, where the Census Bureau recognizes the five boroughs that constitute New York City as MCDs) and villages. Incorporated places can cross both county and MCD boundaries. When this occurs, the place name is followed by the designation "pt" (which stands for part). The PEP produces estimates of the unincorporated "balance of county" area for counties that are not entirely composed of incorporated places. Another way to understand this is to think of the "balance of county" as the county population minus the county population resident within incorporated places.

Consolidated Cities

Consolidated cities are a unit of government for which the functions of an incorporated place and its county or MCD have merged. The legal aspects of this action may result in both the primary incorporated place and the county or MCD

TABLE 8.1 *(Continued)*

continuing to exist as legal entities, even though the county or MCD performs few or no governmental functions. Where one or more other incorporated places within the consolidated government continue to function as separate governmental units, the primary incorporated place is referred to as a "consolidated city."

Estimates will be shown for consolidated cities and the consolidated city "balance," which is the consolidated city minus the semi-independent incorporated places located within the consolidated city. Consolidated cities include: Athens-Clark County, GA; Augusta-Richmond County, GA; Butte-Silver Bow, MT; Indianapolis, IN; Louisville-Jefferson County, KY;

Milford, CT; and Nashville-Davidson, TN. Estimates also are produced for the semi-independent places which together with the "balance record," sums to the entire territory of the consolidated city.

Metropolitan and Micropolitan Statistical Areas

The general concept of a metropolitan or micropolitan statistical area is that of a core area containing a substantial population nucleus, together with adjacent communities having a high degree of economic and social integration with that core. Metropolitan and micropolitan statistical areas comprise one or more entire counties. For more information see http://www.census.gov/population/www/estimates/aboutmetro.html

Source: U.S. Census Bureau, Population Division Washington, D.C.

Fortunately, channel managers are not required to measure, track and forecast these changes themselves. This is a job for experts in geography, demography, sociology and economics, and much of the data they generate is available from secondary sources. What is required of the channel manager, however, is an awareness of and sensitivity to changes in market geography reflected in the data and a willingness to examine their possible implications for channel design decisions.

TABLE 8.2 KEY PUBLISHED SOURCES FOR LOCATING MARKETS

SOURCE	DESCRIPTION
Census Bureau's *Metropolitan Map Series*	Published by U.S. Department of Commerce. Maps depicting all officially defined Standard Metropolitan Statistical Areas. Computerized version called *GBF/DIME* (Geographic Base File/Dual Independent Map Encoding) also available.
Commercial Atlas and Market Guide	Published by Rand McNally. Contains regional, state, and metropolitan area maps, as well as a vast amount of economic, transportation, communication, and population data. Also contains Canadian and world maps and information.
County and City Data Books	Published by U.S. Census Bureau. Convenient summary of statistics on the social and economic structure of counties and cities of the U.S.
Editor and Publisher Market Guide	Published by Editor and Publisher. Contains Market Guide Maps showing location of all U.S. and Canadian daily newspaper cities and metropolitan areas in the United States along with information on population, housing, industries, newspapers, and other data for each city and metropolitan area.
The Sourcebook of ZIP Codes	Published by ESRI Business Solutions (formerly CACI Marketing Systems). All residential and nonresidential ZIP codes. Spending potential indicated for 20 product/service categories; business date including total firms and total employees.

© Cengage Learning 2013

Market Size and Channel Design Strategy

The second dimension of the market framework, **market size**, refers to the number of buyers or potential buyers (consumer or industrial) in a given market.

Bucklin developed a model relating market size to channel structure, which provides some insight for using market size data.[6] Bucklin's model is shown in Figure 8.2. In the figure, the horizontal axis measures the number of buyers in the market with each buyer purchasing approximately the same number of units in each transaction. Cd is the cost of the direct channel, which is almost constant for each buyer. The slight downward slope is due to the likely existence of external marketplace economies for larger volumes (better marketplace facilities at a lower cost). On the other hand, the channel using intermediaries, Cm, shows high costs for a small market with a sharp decrease for larger volume. The high initial costs result from the extra handling and transaction costs necessary for the intermediary channel. At a low level of volume, any savings in concentration and dispersion are insufficient to offset these. But as volume increases and the cost of using intermediaries is spread over a larger number of buyers, costs decrease. When the market size reaches the point U_e in Figure 8.2, the cost of the intermediary structure is equal to the direct structure. As the market becomes even larger (to the right of U_e), the channel structure using intermediaries is lower in cost.

The insight provided by Bucklin's model into the possible relationship between market size and channel structure is of particular use to the channel manager in Phase 1 of the channel design decision (knowing when a channel design decision is needed). By keeping this theoretical model in mind, the channel manager seeing data on a changing market size is likely to be more sensitive to its implications for channel structure. For example, if market forecast data were to indicate a substantial increase

FIGURE 8.2 The Effect of Number of Buyers (U) on the Relative Cost of Direct Channel versus Middleman Channel

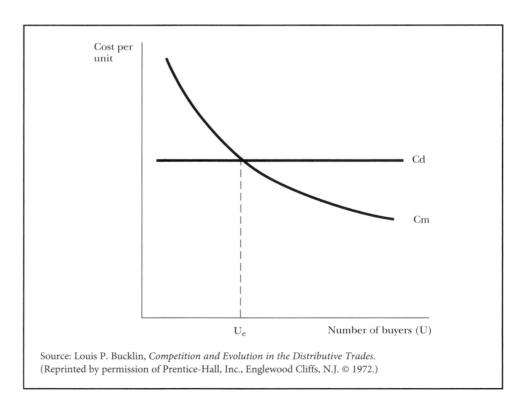

Source: Louis P. Bucklin, *Competition and Evolution in the Distributive Trades.* (Reprinted by permission of Prentice-Hall, Inc., Englewood Cliffs, N.J. © 1972.)

in the number of buyers in a particular market, questions such as the following should emerge:

1. Will the increase in the number of buyers increase or decrease the average cost of serving our buyers?
2. If an increase in average costs is likely, can our present channel structure be changed to reduce these costs before the market reaches its forecasted size?
3. If such structural changes could be made, would this yield a differential advantage to our firm?

The theory does not provide a clear-cut basis for answering these questions, so a large dose of judgment that takes into account the peculiarities of particular situations and other variables is still needed.[7] Take, for example, the case of the firm attempting to reach additional buyers in new territories. In this situation, a high, positive correlation between the market geography and the market size dimensions is very likely because the geographical size and the number of buyers are increasing together. Given this particular situation, the answer to question one could be that the increasing market size *will* increase the average cost of serving the buyers in the market. On the other hand, if the market size dimension is increasing while the market geography dimension remains constant (that is, if additional buyers are attracted within the present geographical territories), the effect on costs may be much less. Such growth in market size within an essentially fixed geographical market has enabled a very "old-fashioned" marketing channel—home delivery of milk—to make something of a comeback recently. Home delivery had, for many decades, been the dominant channel for milk. But by the early 1960s, this channel had virtually disappeared. Supermarkets and convenience stores became the preferred channels for most consumers. But with the recent demand for "fresh," "natural" and "organic" foods, some small dairies, such as Crescent Ridge Dairy Inc. in Sharon, Mass., have been able to position their locally produced milk sold in glass bottles and delivered directly to consumers' doorsteps as offering a superior customer experience. This positioning strategy, however, could only work if delivery costs could be kept under control. Fortunately, the growth in consumer demand for home delivery occurred within a stable geographical area in Sharon, Mass., so drivers could cover their territories quickly and efficiently.[8]

Market Density and Channel Design Strategy

Market density refers to the number of buyers or potential buyers per unit of geographical area. This market dimension should also be considered in channel design strategy because of its relationship to channel structure.

A useful concept that helps to illustrate the relationship is that of **efficient congestion.**[9] According to this concept, congested (high-density) markets can promote efficiency in the performance of several basic distribution tasks, particularly those of *transportation, storage, communication* and *negotiation.*

With respect to transportation and storage, a high geographical concentration of customers enables goods to be transported in large lots to the concentrated markets and stored in a relatively small number of inventories capable of adequately serving the compact markets. For markets characterized by low levels of density, smaller quantities of goods have to be transported and smaller inventories are needed.

In terms of communication and negotiation tasks, dense markets facilitate the flows of communication and negotiation.[10] This is especially true when face-to-face information and negotiation are necessary. For example, if a manufacturer's salesperson must call on 50 accounts, it will take much less sales time and effort to call on these accounts if they are located within an area of 100 square miles instead of 500.

The major strategic implication of this discussion is that the opportunity to achieve a relatively high level of customer access at low cost is higher in dense markets than in more dispersed ones. Consequently, manufacturers of a wide array of products including automobiles, consumer electronics, groceries, sporting goods, clothing, hardware and many others seek out distributors and retailers that operate in dense markets. Even though dense markets are most often located in major metropolitan areas and are the most competitive, the large number of customers in close proximity to huge assortments of products provides the greatest opportunity and highest level of efficiency. In short, high concentrations of customers foster marketing channels that make high concentrations of products available to those customers. Thus, customers benefit by having a vast array of products conveniently available to them at competitive prices. Channel members at the manufacturer, wholesaler and retailer levels, while often faced with intense competition in dense markets, have the offsetting advantage of the efficient congestion provided by high-density markets.

FIGURE 8.3 Typical Japanese Channel of Distribution for a Consumer Product

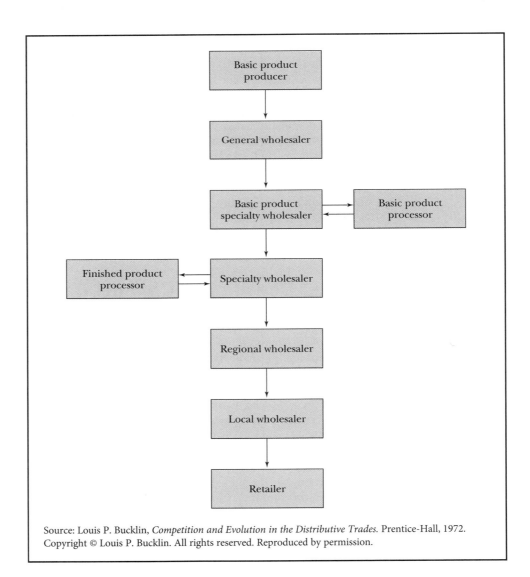

Source: Louis P. Bucklin, *Competition and Evolution in the Distributive Trades.* Prentice-Hall, 1972. Copyright © Louis P. Bucklin. All rights reserved. Reproduced by permission.

Although the relationship between dense markets and channel structure appears to be straightforward, the real world does not always conform to such neat implications. A case in point involves the Japanese market for consumer goods. Japan appears to have a market that is tailor-made for short channel structures. A huge population (almost half of that of the United States) is concentrated in an area only 4 percent as large as the United States. Yet channels are anything but short. Direct sales from the manufacturer to consumer are virtually unheard of, and a three-level structure (manufacturer → retailer → consumer) is almost as rare. Much more common are several levels of wholesalers intervening between the manufacturer and the retailer, resulting in channel structures of four or more levels (see Figure 8.3).[11]

The reason for such long channel structures even in the face of dense markets is the result of early Japanese sociocultural patterns. Historically, the long, complex channel structures grew from the early development of Japanese villages, which commonly distrusted each other. Many neutral middlemen were needed to sell goods from one village to the next. Then, as trading companies began to appear in the late nineteenth century, they became so prominent in buying and selling that many manufacturing companies never bothered to develop sales arms.

A channel manager unfamiliar with the Japanese culture would be in for a rude awakening if he or she eagerly eyed the dense Japanese market as the "perfect opportunity" for direct distribution based on efficient congestion. So, even though the concept of efficient congestion is a useful model for relating target market density to channel design strategy, it is certainly not a complete model. Other factors, even seemingly obscure ones,[12] such as the nuances of Japanese history and culture, can offset the ostensibly "hard" economic relationship between market density and channel structure.

Market Behavior and Channel Design Strategy

This fourth dimension, **market behavior**, consists of four subdimensions: *when the market buys, where the market buys, how the market buys and who buys.*

When Customers Buy

Neither consumer nor industrial markets buy products on a precisely predictable time schedule that remains constant per time period. Frequently there are seasonal, weekly and daily variations. Far more skis are sold to consumers in the winter than in the summer. Air conditioners, snow tires, antifreeze, eggnog, short-sleeve shirts and garden supplies are other obvious examples of products generally purchased seasonally.

Weekly and daily variations in buyer behavior are common at the retail level and vary across different trade areas throughout the country. In some areas, Wednesday may be the big shopping night, while in other areas it may be Thursday or Friday. Several shopping trends have followed a fairly similar pattern on a national basis, however, such as stores being open seven days a week and staying open later in the evening on all weekdays or even 24 hours a day. Many catalog mail-order firms offer customers the opportunity to shop 24 hours a day, seven days a week for 365 days a year. They provide this service in some cases with live operators, or if not, via voice mail, fax and, to an increasing extent, over the Internet.[13]

Shopping via the Internet during regular working hours has also become quite common in recent years. In fact, studies show that the peak period of the day for online shopping is 1 p.m. eastern standard time, while the slowest period is between the hours of 11 p.m. and 4 a.m. Online shopping activity then climbs rapidly in the early morning until the peak level is reached by the early afternoon (1 p.m.). The highest volume online shopping days of the week are Mondays and Tuesdays, while the weekend days of Saturday and Sunday show the lowest volume.[14]

Two important implications for the channel manager are related to this subdimension of when customers buy.

First, seasonal variations tend to create peaks and valleys in the manufacturer's production scheduling. Sometimes, hardly enough production capacity exists to meet demand, while at other times there is an excess capacity. Typically, the manufacturer would like to smooth out these peaks and valleys in production because this will usually lower average production costs. One way of attempting this is to produce in the off-season and maintain the products in inventory for the heavy selling season. But this can be a costly and potentially dangerous strategy if the manufacturer alone maintains the inventory. The costs attendant to carrying the inventory—such as those for storage, handling, insurance and financing (opportunity cost) plus the risk of lost, stolen and/or obsolete goods—can more than offset the production cost's savings from producing at a steady level. If, however, the manufacturer can get channel members to stock some of this inventory in the off-season, a portion of the costs and risks can be shifted to these channel members. But channel members do not like to buy in the off-season unless they are offered special inducements—particularly in the form of price concessions to compensate them for the added costs and risks involved. Only the most powerful manufacturer who enjoys a truly dominant position in the channel can achieve off-season sales without price inducements. For those manufacturers lacking this dominant position, price inducements are probably necessary. Consequently, manufacturers who experience wide seasonal variations in the purchase of their products should attempt to select channel members who are amenable to price inducements for off-season buying. In other words, a willingness to buy in the off-season (given price inducements) should be used as a criterion for selecting channel members.

The second implication of when customers buy as it affects channel design strategy is also of particular relevance in the selection phase of channel design. This is simply that the channel manager should attempt to *select channel members who are in tune with the changing patterns of when people buy.* In other words, the channel manager should try to avoid selecting channel members who are out of touch with the time demands of the markets they serve. For instance, some retailers continue to remain closed on Sundays, even though this has become the busiest shopping day for suburban consumers for many kinds of products. Many auto dealers for decades maintained hours for their service department that were extremely inconvenient for customers. Typically, they closed early on weekdays and were closed on Saturdays and Sundays. Some auto dealers are finally starting to offer more convenient service hours by staying open longer on weekdays and providing some Saturday hours.[15]

Including out-of-touch retailers in the channel could significantly hamper the manufacturer's competitive position in the markets served by such retailers. Similarly, in the industrial market, distributors who keep "bankers' hours" may not provide the best possible level of service to customers. This, in turn, can hurt the manufacturer's competitive position. Although some of these traditional "main street merchants" and "old-line distributors" still exist, their days are numbered. Their hours of operation reflect an attempt to make life convenient for *them* rather than their customers. So, regardless of their traditions, years in business and famous reputations, manufacturers seeking to make their products conveniently available to customers will rely on them less and less for reaching target markets.[16]

Where Customers Buy

The types of outlets from which customers choose to make their purchases and the location of those outlets should be an important driver of channel design strategy.[17] This subdimension is closely related to the market geography dimension discussed earlier in this chapter. This is because the types of outlets chosen by customers and their locations ultimately determine the actual geographic locations of the markets that the channel manager seeks to serve. Our focus in this section will be on briefly examining underlying behavioral patterns of buyers that affect market locations and, in turn, channel design.

Research on where consumers buy is often based on the assumption that they will behave so as to maximize their convenience in the selection of retail outlets. That is, the consumer is seen as engaged in balancing the desirability of near and distant retailers against the cost, time and energy that must be spent in overcoming distance. If this cost is too high for patronizing a distant store, the customer will seek one that is closer.[18] Finding a highly convenient location in terms of actual travel distance, driving or walking time or, in some cases, proximity to mass transit points has been a sine qua non of a good retail location.[19] This has been the case particularly for stores selling convenience goods, where intense competition is prevalent and a differential advantage based on non-price variables is difficult to achieve. Supermarkets, for example, have learned through market research and experience that a convenient location is of overwhelming importance in attracting consumer patronage. For retailers handling mainly shopping and specialty goods, such as department stores and specialty stores, a highly convenient location is also of great importance. However, some less prime locations may be offset by retailers who create differential advantages based on unusual merchandise, extraordinary varieties and assortments of merchandise, special services or other factors. In these cases, consumers may be willing to travel farther to gain access to these stores. In doing so they engage in trade-off behavior: forgoing some convenience for other factors offered by the more distant retailers.[20]

With the growth in online shopping as a major channel alternative in recent years, the location of retailers or other sellers is of little or no concern to customers who have chosen to use this channel choice. For these consumers, product selection, availability and price are the key factors that determine which online sellers will be chosen.

Even though there has been tremendous growth in consumer online sales during the first decade of the twenty-first century, from just a few billion dollars in 2000 to over $175 billion dollars by 2010, as a percentage of total retail sales, online sales still accounted for less than 4 percent of total retail sales through all channels. Thus, most consumer purchases are still made via conventional, land-based channels of distribution.[21]

So, while channel managers cannot afford to ignore electronic or online marketing channels, much of their attention still needs to be focused on changing patterns of where customers are shopping in the world of conventional channels. For example, far fewer customers are going to video stores, so literally thousands of video stores have closed over the last several years. The once mighty Blockbuster has filed for bankruptcy protection as consumers have moved to other channels including cable on demand, mail-order, iTunes downloads, Hulu, Netflix and vending machines.[22]

Consider also Walmart, the world's largest retailer. For decades, this giant retailer has been famous for big-box stores in the suburbs. Now it plans to open hundreds of much smaller stores in urban areas across the U.S. Why is Walmart doing this? Millions of consumers in urban areas, many of whom are in the lower income brackets, are looking for convenience. They want stores right in their neighborhoods that offer good selection and low prices. The high cost of gasoline has accelerated this demand.[23]

In the healthcare field, visiting retail pharmacies to get prescriptions filled is currently the channel of choice for millions of consumers. But this is a high-cost channel that pharmacy benefits management firms, such as St. Louis-based Express Scripts, are seeking to change. Express Scripts wants consumers to switch to mail-order channels for their recurring drug purchases.[24] Mail order suppliers can fill prescriptions through highly automated, large-scale, centralized pharmacies and provide a three-month supply rather than the one-month supply available from conventional retail pharmacies resulting in big cost savings. Will Express Scripts be successful in its quest to change the channels where millions of consumers get their prescriptions filled? Only time will tell, but early indications suggest that the company will get a positive response from consumers.[25]

Turning from healthcare to high-fashion channels, it seems that a large number of affluent consumers hurt by the Great Recession of 2008 now want to have more access to fashion merchandise from outlet stores. In fact, one major study found that 75 percent of consumers earning over $100,000 are favorably disposed to shopping at outlets.[26] The result? Famous retailers such as Bloomingdales, Lord & Taylor, Neiman Marcus Group, Saks Inc. and Nordstrom have all opened or will be opening outlet stores all over the country.

These are, of course, just a few examples of changes occurring in the channels where consumers shop. Numerous others are occurring and will continue to occur in the future. And these changes may not follow a predictable or obvious script, such as high-tech developments leading inevitably to high-tech channels. Reality tends to be more complicated than this. Indeed, as we mentioned earlier in this chapter, some really "old-fashioned" channels, such as farmers' markets and home delivery of milk by milkmen, can appear alongside the most modern, high-tech marketing channels!

How Customers Buy

Customer preferences reflected in purchase behavior indicate how the market buys (see Table 8.3 for examples). Each of the ten behaviors shown in the table can vary across different market segments and over time for any given product category. For example, with respect to food purchases, middle-income consumers who shop mainly in supermarkets buy in larger quantities than do lower-income consumers patronizing smaller neighborhood stores. More affluent consumers are also likely to demand more assistance from salespeople than less affluent consumers who are amenable to more self-service in many product categories. For almost all market segments, several of these patterns have been changing over time, such as the general shift to one-stop shopping, using credit and

---

TABLE 8.3 CONTRASTING BEHAVIORS RELATED TO HOW CUSTOMERS BUY AT THE CONSUMER LEVEL

1. Large quantities versus small quantities purchased in each transaction
2. Self-service versus assistance by salespeople
3. One-stop shopping versus buying from several stores
4. Impulse buying versus extensive decision making prior to purchase
5. Using cash versus credit
6. Shopping at home online or via catalog versus shopping at stores
7. Expending substantial effort through comparison shopping versus little effort
8. Demanding extensive service versus little service
9. Using smartphones to check prices and comparison shop while in-store versus using desk-top or laptop to comparison shop out-of-store.
10. Using self check out versus being checked out by store cashier.

© Cengage Learning 2013

debit cards instead of cash and making more use of the Internet for online shopping. For example, during the Christmas holiday season (the month between Thanksgiving and Christmas), online sales as a percentage of total retail sales more than doubled to over 8 percent from the just under 4 percent recorded for the entire year of 2010. Some observers believe that as more consumers have successful experiences using online channels during hectic holiday periods, they will develop more confidence in this channel option throughout the year, thus driving additional gains in the percentage of total retail sales going to online channels. The same pattern may also hold for mobile or m-commerce channels. While less than 5 percent of consumers had used smartphones or other mobile devices for shopping by the close of the first decade of the twenty-first century, significant growth is expected as consumers gain more experience and confidence in this channel and as sellers place more emphasis on using m-commerce channels in their channel portfolios.

Although there has been tremendous growth in online shopping in recent years, consumers still expect conventional channels to be readily available as well.[27] In fact, more and more consumers have become "channel surfers" because they shop in multiple channels—in a retailer's stores, from its catalogs and from its web site. Some industry observers have referred to this phenomenon as **threetailing** (in-store, catalog, online).[28]

Significant changes have also been occurring for specific segments of the market. For example, good personal selling at the retail level may be making a comeback, at least in the department and specialty store sectors. Such famous stores as Bloomingdale's, and Neiman Marcus have followed the lead of Nordstrom in meeting what appears to be increasing consumer demand for knowledgeable and helpful salespeople. At the same time, another segment of consumers is opting for membership in warehouse clubs such as Sam's Club, BJ's Wholesale and Costco, which stress Spartan surroundings and minimum service but low prices.[29]

Changing patterns of how consumers shop can also be seen in a phenomenon sometimes referred to as "**commando shopping**." The so-called commando shopper is one who visits stores advertising **loss-leaders** but instead of staying in the stores and buying additional products on which the stores make a significant profit margin, the commando shopper scoops up only the advertised loss-leader items and then immediately leaves the store. Such sophisticated (some might say ruthless) consumer shopping behavior defeats the purpose of one of the most important and time-honored promotional strategies used in retailing.

Sometimes a major change in how consumers shop is revealed through an innovation undertaken by a channel member that elicits a very favorable consumer response. Kohl's, a discount department store in the U.S. focusing heavily on brand-name apparel, is a good example of this. Kohl's uses its **racetrack layout** designed to expose customers to the maximum amount of merchandise in the shortest time. Rather than walking up and down aisles, shoppers circle around the merchandise as they move through the store. Though they spend less time in the store, they buy more merchandise.[30] This flies in the face of decades of retailing layout strategy, which has been predicated on the assumption that the more time customers spend in the store, the more merchandise they will purchase. So, retail store layouts have traditionally been designed as a maze of aisles and rows to keep customers "locked into" the store for as long as possible.[31] But the tremendous success of Kohl's circular, or racetrack, layout shows that customers appreciate the effort to make shopping quicker and easier, and they have rewarded the company by abandoning competitors and spending more of their dollars at Kohl's.

The changing nature of how customers buy means that the channel manager must be tuned in to what changes are likely to occur.[32] But the channel manager is also faced with an even more difficult problem—determining whether such changes are temporary or long-term. Because of the generally long-term nature of commitments among the channel members and often high costs of changing channels, the channel manager does not want to make substantial changes in the channel structure to respond to short-lived changes in buyer behavior. To do so is not only costly, but may also foster serious conflicts, which, in turn, may have adverse effects on channel performance and viability (see Chapter 4). Yet, if changes in how customers buy represent fundamental long-term patterns, prompt action in making channel design decisions to meet these changes can result in an important differential advantage to the firm, especially if the channel manager beats competitors to the punch in making the necessary channel design decisions.[33]

Who Buys

The subdimension of who does the buying has two aspects: (1) who makes the physical purchase and (2) who takes part in the buying decisions.

Who Makes the Purchases From a channel design standpoint, who actually buys the product can affect the type of retailers chosen in the consumer market[34] and may also influence the kinds of channel members used to serve industrial markets. For example, women traditionally shop in department stores far more heavily than men. Consequently, products that are known to be purchased mainly by men should not rely on department stores as the primary retail outlet. Product *purchase,* however, should not be confused with product *usage.* Many products used by men (such as shirts, ties, underwear, toiletries, jewelry and even some consumer electronics) are purchased for them by their wives or girlfriends in department stores. Care should therefore be taken to distinguish between who uses the product and who makes the actual purchase.

Some companies, such as Kimberly-Clark Corp., have gone to extraordinary lengths to help their channel members, such as Walgreen Co., Rite Aid Corp. and Family Dollar Stores Inc., to create retail channel environments that reflect the demands of who is doing the buying. Specifically, many of the customers patronizing these stores are over 65 years old and a significant segment of that group of older customers has physical limitations that can make a "normal" retailing environment challenging. To find out just how challenging, Todd Vang, a Walgreen's vice president, after going through a Kimberly-Clark training program, donned glasses that blurred his vision, placed unpopped popcorn in his shoes and taped his thumbs to his palms. He then went shopping in the store and after trying to find, reach up and pull down a can of soup, he quickly realized the difficulties that many over-60 customers encounter in a typical retail environment. To help make their stores more user-friendly for older adults, Walgreen's will spend between $30,000-$50,000 per store to put in call buttons near heavy merchandise, magnifying glasses on store shelves, change signage, provide smaller, more manageable shopping carts and numerous other tweaks.[35]

Another example of a firm going out of its way to adapt its channel design strategy to reflect who is doing the buying is British retail giant Tesco PLC. Before opening a chain of food stores on the west coast of the U.S., Tesco built a full-size prototype store inside a warehouse to create a realistic laboratory to observe first-hand the behavior patterns of consumers shopping in the particular kind of retail environment offered by Tesco's food stores, which are smaller than typical U.S. supermarkets but larger than convenience stores. Tesco's goal is "to design the perfect store for the American consumer in the 21st century."[36] The jury is still out on whether Tesco will achieve this objective, but the firm has certainly made a serious attempt to do so.

Understanding the behavior of consumers as they shop so that channel design strategy can better reflect what consumers are looking for is not limited to bricks and mortar channels. Consumers' shopping behavior online is being scrutinized extensively by such research firms as ATG, based in Cambridge, Mass. ATG uses an analytical technique referred to as "preference prediction" to help its clients create online shopping experiences that will be consistent with consumer online shopping behavior. By capturing data on the rapidity of mouse clicks, length of time consumers linger over product reviews, the different products they look at and a variety of other factors, ATG is able to derive insights about consumer shopping behaviors this can help sellers create online channel environments that can actually anticipate consumer preferences, almost as if the Web site had read the customer's mind![37]

Who Participates in the Buying Decision   The more difficult aspect to analyze than who actually makes the physical purchase is who *decides* to make the purchase in the first place. Indeed, this has been a topic of substantial research in the consumer behavior literature and in industrial marketing as well.

At the consumer level, the question of who takes part in the buying decision is usually in the context of a family unit. Influence on buying decisions revolves around the roles played by the husband, wife and, sometimes, the children. For example, a classic study of influence patterns in the purchase of men's clothing revealed that 61 percent of the men responding said women (wives or girlfriends or female friends) exerted a major influence on buying decisions and 20 percent reported some influence, while only 19 percent reported no influence.[38]

Best Buy Co., in an attempt to learn more about the role of females in buying decisions, has established what Best Buy calls "Women's Leadership Forums," loose-knit groups of female employees and customers that meet periodically all over the country. These groups hold discussions that help to identify the female perspective in the consumer decision process. For example, while Best Buy was well aware that the overwhelming majority of its customers are male, the reasons so many women were deciding not to shop at Best Buy were still a mystery. One insight that emerged from the Women's Leadership Forum sessions was the women's negative perception of Best Buy's merchandise presentation, particularly for major appliances. Women shoppers found Best Buy's penchant for simply lining up large quantities of appliances row upon row to be cold and sterile. The solution, which also emerged from the forums, was to redesign Best Buy showrooms to resemble kitchens. Appliance sales increased as more women decided to shop in the now more hospitable Best Buy showrooms.[39]

In the industrial market, it is not at all unusual to have several people in the buying firm involved in the purchase decision. This phenomenon is sometimes referred to as *multiple influences on the buying decision.* Webster and Wind refer to the sets of people who participate in industrial buying decisions and who are responsible for the consequences resulting from the decision as **buying centers.**[40] The buying center has six distinct roles that various individuals in the organization fill.[41]

1. *Users*—the members of the organization who will use the product or service. In many cases, the users initiate the buying proposal and help define the product specifications.
2. *Influencers*—people who influence the buying decision. They often help define specifications and also provide information for evaluating alternatives. Technical people are especially important as influencers.
3. *Deciders*—people who have the power to decide on product requirements and/or on suppliers.
4. *Approvers*—people who must authorize the proposed actions of deciders or buyers.
5. *Buyers*—people with formal authority for selecting the supplier and arranging the terms of purchase. Buyers may help shape product specifications, but they play their

major role in selecting vendors and negotiating. In more complex purchases, the buyers might include high-level executives as participants in the negotiations.

6. *Gatekeepers*—people who have the power to prevent sellers or information from reaching members of the buying center. For example, purchasing agents, receptionists and telephone operators may prevent salespeople from talking to users or deciders.

The task facing both the consumer and the industrial marketer is to make a careful evaluation of who is involved in making buying decisions so that they will be better able to target the influential parties.[42] The channel manager's role in this is to determine whether the planned or existing channel structure will inhibit or facilitate the firm's attempts to reach the more influential parties to buying decisions. Although there are no clear-cut methods for doing this, three heuristics provide some insight for examining channel structure and the capability to reach the influential parties to buying decisions.

First, as pointed out in earlier chapters, *as the channel becomes longer, the degree of control exercised by the manufacturer is lessened.* Consequently, the manufacturer's ability to oversee whether channel members are dealing with the more influential participants in purchasing decisions is also reduced. For example, if a product has gone through a four-level channel (M → W → R → C), the manufacturer can exercise little direct control to assure that the retailers' salespeople are focusing on the right family members at the point of purchase. Or, in the industrial market, a manufacturer selling through selling agents and industrial distributors may have limited ability to determine whether these channel members' salespeople are calling on the appropriate parties to buying decisions.

Second, as a corollary to the first heuristic, *as the intensity of distribution at each level of the channel becomes greater, the manufacturer's capacity to supervise the selling efforts of channel members becomes lower.*[43] Misdirected efforts by channel members as to who influences buying decisions are thus more difficult to detect and change than when more selective distribution exists at each level.

Third, *larger and more powerful channel members (such as Best Buy) are more difficult to influence than smaller, less powerful channel members.* So, for example, if an appliance manufacturer wanted Best Buy to change its merchandise presentation strategy to appeal more to the preferences of female shoppers, it needs to realize that getting the giant retailer to change is not likely to happen quickly or easily.

Other than heeding these three heuristics, the channel manager can help to assure the appropriateness of a channel structure for reaching the influential buying parties through explicit consideration of this issue when selecting channel members. By putting additional weight on the prospective channel members' management and sales force abilities to understand who influences buying decisions before they become channel members, subsequent problems in this regard can be reduced. While this was not cited explicitly as a specific criterion in the selection of intermediaries (see Chapter 7), it is implicit in the criteria of sales strength and management ability.

Summary

Market (customer) considerations are the key determinant of channel strategy and structure because when all is said and done, marketing channels must reflect the needs and wants of customers. In short, marketing channels must be customer-centric—reflecting how, when and where customers choose to acquire products and services as well as which customers make purchasing decisions and do the actual buying. Consequently, market variables are of fundamental importance in channel design decisions. The channel manager should attempt to analyze markets with a view toward gaining a sustainable competitive advantage through channel designs that serve those markets better than the competition.

In order to analyze markets effectively for channel design purposes, a framework consisting of four basic dimensions was used in this chapter. These are: (1) market geography, which deals with the physical location of markets and their distance from the producer or manufacturer; (2) market size, the number of buyers in a given market; (3) market density, the number of buyers per unit of geographical area and

(4) market behavior, which breaks down into four subdimensions of when, where and how the market buys as well as who buys.

The channel manager must attempt to understand how these dimensions and subdimensions operate in various markets and develop channel strategies and structures that will enable the firm to serve these markets effectively and efficiently. The channel manager must also be sensitive to changes in these dimensions and, if necessary, be able to make appropriate modifications in the channel structure to adapt to such changes.

Review Questions

1. The category of market variables was cited in Chapter 6 and the present chapter as one of fundamental importance to channel design. Explain why this is so.

2. Should market variables be examined before other variables when designing the channel? Explain.

3. In this chapter, a four-dimensional framework was used for analyzing markets in relation to channel design strategy. Define each of these dimensions.

4. In this chapter it was pointed out that market geography is subject to changes. Why should the channel manager be concerned with such changes?

5. If information indicates that the market size is increasing, what kinds of questions should this pose for the channel manager?

6. What is efficient congestion? How does this relate to market density? Is this relationship as straightforward as it seems?

7. The market behavior dimension was broken down into four subdimensions in this chapter. Define each of these subdimensions.

8. Discuss the major issues facing the channel manager with respect to where buyers make their purchases.

9. Identify any changing patterns of how consumers (or industrial buyers) purchase goods with which you are familiar. Trace the effects that these changes may have on the channel structure.

10. The subdimension of who participates in buying decisions may be of importance to the channel manager. Under what conditions might this be the case?

Channel Issues for Discussion

1. There is an old saying that predates the marketing concept by perhaps 100 years: "The customer is king." This is usually interpreted to mean that businesses should remember that the only reason they are in business is to serve the customer, because without customers there would be no business. This expression is seldom related to the design of marketing channels. Yet, in the long run, is it not the "customer king" who decrees the structure of the marketing channels that ultimately develop?

Do you agree or disagree? Discuss the statement using several examples for or against.

2. The number of consumers subscribing to cable television services in the U.S. had declined significantly by the end of the first decade of the twenty-first century. In the third quarter of 2010 alone, almost 120,000 consumers discontinued their cable subscriptions and the pace of decline is expected to not only continue, but to accelerate as well. This pattern of what some industry observers refer to as "cord-cutting" is being driven by a shift from cable to web-based channels provided by such firms as Hulu, Walt Disney, NBC, Universal and Netflix. Not only are the monthly subscription charges typically charged by these firms lower than those charged by

traditional cable companies, but the web-based channels also seem to fit better with modern consumer lifestyles.

What do you think is the cause of this dramatic shift from cable channels to web-based channels for delivery of home entertainment?

3. By the end of the first decade of the twenty-first century, the anti-junk food movement had really begun to take hold in the U.S. Of particular concern was the sale of junk food through vending machines in schools. The easy availability of salty snacks, candy and sodas made easily available from the machines provided a level of temptation that was just too enticing for many students to resist. But could vending machine channels that worked so effectively to sell junk food in schools work just as well for selling healthier foods? This is the question that Stonyfield Farm, a Londonderry, New Hampshire maker of organic yogurt, is seeking the answer to by putting health-food vending machines in a number of New England high schools. Stonyfield is betting that attractive displays of healthy snacks and the convenience provided by vending machines will prove to be just as effective in enticing students to buy healthy foods as they were in getting them to buy junk foods.

Do you think the vending machine channel will work for healthy foods as well as this channel worked to sell junk food to students? Why or why not?

4. Airports may be where the real action is in retailing. At least this is the impression one might get by observing some recent developments. Bloomingdale's was one of the first major retailers to open a branch in an airport when its clothing and gift boutique opened at JFK International Airport in New York. Now FAO Schwartz, a famous toy retailer, has opened branches in several airports, while McDonald's and Burger King are also moving in. A number of other major retailers may follow in airports throughout the United States.

Does this make sense? Discuss in terms of the relevant market dimensions that might underlie such developments.

5. Goya Foods Inc. produces and markets Hispanic foods sold mainly through supermarkets throughout the U.S., especially those that serve markets with large Hispanic populations. The company, based in Secaucus, New Jersey, has enjoyed strong sales growth in recent years. What is so different about the way Goya sells its wide range of food products, such as Spanish olive oil, beans, Caribbean fruit juices, soft drinks and desserts, is the company strategy for using shelf space in supermarkets: Goya displays all of its diverse food products together in one section rather than by category of product as is done for most food producers. Goya does this because the food brokers it uses to get placement for its products in the supermarkets have learned by working closely with store managers that this all-in-one section approach is consistent with how consumers shop. Some observers believe that Goya's shelf strategy causes the company to lose the so-called crossover market. That is, customers who are shopping for a particular product will not have the opportunity to compare the Goya product to competitors' products. But Goya is sticking to its guns, arguing that its store-within-a-store strategy has worked so well that it has never had to pay slotting fees to keep its products on store shelves.

If many of Goya's products represent high quality and excellent value, as the company claims, wouldn't a strategy of spreading the products all over the supermarket open up more opportunity for sales growth than confining all of Goya's products to one place in the store? Discuss.

6. For decades, giant big-box retailers like Walmart supercenters, Best Buy, Home Depot, Staples, Target and many others emphasized building bigger and bigger stores with broader assortments of merchandise and low prices to attract customers. But in recent years, customers pressed for time and having easy access to an extensive array of online channels are becoming frustrated with the difficulties of navigating their way through these giant retail stores, especially when they cannot find all of the items they have on their shopping lists. One study by Walmart, for example, found that an average shopper at a Walmart supercenter spends 21 minutes in the store but finds only 7 of the 10 items on her or his shopping list. There is growing concern among big-box retailers that the consumer's desire for a convenient and efficient shopping experience could undermine the big-box retail channel in the future.

Do you think that the days of giant, big-box retailers are numbered? Why or why not?

7. Avijit Mohan was really upset about the poor job the three department stores were doing with his line of fine brass products from India. "They just put the stuff out on the floor as though they were cheap trinkets that the customer buys on impulse. Don't they realize that this merchandise has to be sold by knowledgeable salespeople who can show the fine details, the artistic engraving and the hand hammering?" he remarked to his wife in frustration. "These are supposed to be top-notch retailers but they don't seem to know a thing about selling these products," he lamented.

Is Avijit Mohan being fair with his criticism? Discuss in terms of consumer buying patterns, the constraints on the department stores and Mohan's choice of channel structure to sell these products.

References

1. Lawrence G. Friedman, *Go To Market Strategy*, (Oxford: Butterworth-Heinemann, 2012); for an insightful study related to this point, see Thomas L. Baker, Penny M. Simpson and Judy A. Siguaw, "The Impact of Suppliers' Perceptions of Reseller Market Orientation on Key Relationship Constructs," *Journal of the Academy of Marketing Science* (Winter 1999): 50–77.

2. Matthew Garrahan, "Viewers Pull Plug on Cable TV," *Financial Times*, November 18, 2010: 17.

3. Timothy W. Martin, "Retailers Jocky to Market Swine-Flu Shots," *Wall Street Journal*, December 29, 2009: B1, B6.

4. Larry Kelly and Kyle Allen, "Crossing the Great Channel Divide," *Retailing Issues Letter* vol. 18, no. 2007: 1–6.

5. Thea Durfee and George Chen, "Should We E-?" *Journal of Business Strategy* (February 2002): 14–17.

6. Louis P. Bucklin, *Competition and Evolution in the Distributive Trades*, (Englewood Cliffs, N.J.: Prentice-Hall, 1972), pp. 17–18.

7. For an article that does provide insight into these and similar questions, see David J. Reibstein and Paul W. Farris, "Market Share and Distribution: A Generalization, a Speculation and Some Implications," *Marketing Science* vol. 14, no. 2 (1995): 190–202.

8. Gwendolyn Bounds, "Small Dairies Profit from a Resurgence of Home Deliveries," *Wall Street Journal*, May 15, 2007: B4.

9. Revis Cox, "Consumer Convenience and the Retail Structure of Cities," *Journal of Marketing* 23 (April 1959): 359–362; and Louis P. Bucklin, *A Theory of Distribution Channel Structure*, (Berkeley: University of California Press, 1966), 45.

10. Bucklin, *A Theory of Distribution Channel Structure*, 45.

11. For two excellent background works on Japanese marketing channels, see Yoshihiro Tajma, "Japan's Markets and Distribution System," *Journal of Marketing Channels* (Fall 1994): 3–16; and Michael R. Czinkota and Jon Woronoff, *Japan's Market: The Distribution System*, (New York: Praeger, 1986).

12. Boryana Dimitrova and Bert Rosenbloom, "Standardization Versus Adaptation in Global Markets: Is Channel Strategy Different?" *Journal of Marketing Channels* (April-June 2010): 157–176.

13. Chiquan Guo, "Competing in High-Growth Markets: The Case of E-Commerce," *Business Horizons* (March/April 2002): 77–83.

14. "Favorite U.S. Online Shopping Hours: Working Hours," (November 17, 2010). http://www.cybersource.com/news_ad_events/view.php?page_id=1524

15. For a related discussion, see: Finbarr O'Neill, "The Auto Industry's Comeback," *Wall Street Journal*, July 30, 2009: A17.

16. For a fascinating discussion related to the changing retailing scene and the social changes underlying them, see Stacy L. Wood, "Future Fantasies: A Social Change Perspective of Retailing in the 21st Century," *Journal of Retailing* 78 (2002): 78–83.

17. See for example: Utpal M. Dholakia, Barbara F. Kahn, Randy Reeves, Aric Rindfleisch, David Stewart and Earl Taylor, "Consumer Behavior in a Mulitchannel, Multimedia Retailing Environment," *Journal of Interactive Marketing* vol. 24 (2010): 86–95.

18. For a related discussion, see G. Roy Funkhouser and Richard Parker, "The Consumer Cost Matrix: A New Tool for Product, Service and Distribution Channel Design," *Journal of Consumer Marketing* (Summer 1986): 35–42.

19. Bert Rosenbloom, *Retail Marketing*, (New York: Random House, 1981), pp. 319–320.

20. Bert Rosenbloom, "The Trade Area Mix and Retailing Mix: A Retail Strategy Matrix," *Journal of Marketing* 40 (October 1976): 63–64.

21. U.S. Census Bureau "E-Stats," (May 27, 2010): 1–8. www.census.gov/estats

22. Jessie E. Vascellaro and Sam Schechner, "Slow Fade-Out for Video Stores," *Wall Street Journal*, September 30, 2010: A6.

23. Miguel Butillo, "Wal-Mart Plans Small, Urban Stores," *Wall Street Journal*, October 14, 2010: B1, B2.

24. Mathew Boyle, "Coaxing Patients Out of the Drugstore," *BusinessWeek*, July 27, 2009,: 58.

25. For an excellent study related to this issue, see: Rajasree K. Rajamma and Lou E. Pelton, "An Empirical Investigation of Consumers' Procurement of Pharmaceutical Products via Online Retail Channels," *Psychology and Marketing* (October 2009): 865–887.

26. Rachel Dodes, "Tony Retailers Hope Outlets Fuel Sales," *Wall Street Journal*, August 9, 2010: B7.

27. See for example: Ruby Roy Dholakia, Miao Zhao and Nikhilesh Dholakia, "Multichannel Retailing: A Case Study of Early Experiences," *Journal of Interactive Marketing* (Spring 2008): 63–74.

28. "Integrating Multiple Channels," *Chain Store Age* (August 2001): 24A.

29. Wendy Zellner, "Warehouse Clubs: When the Going Gets Tough," *Business Week*, July 16, 2002: 60.

30. Stephanie Anderson Forrest, "Don't Tell Kohl's There's a Slowdown," *Business Week* February 12, 2001: 62.

31. Bert Rosenbloom, "From Merchants to Marketers: Trends in U.S. Retailing for Europe to Watch," *Thexis* (Spring 2001): 8–11.

32. For an outstanding analysis of the role played by different forms of competition on channel structure, see Chip E. Miller, James Reardon and Denny McCorkle, "The Effects of Competition on Retail Structure: An Examination of Intratype, Intertype and Intercategory Competition," *Journal of Marketing* (October 1999): 107–120.

33. Joseph P. Guiltinan, "Planned and Evolutionary Changes in Distribution Channels," *Journal of Retailing* (Summer 1974): 79–91.

34. See, for example, E. W. Boatwright, J. Steven Kelly and William Haueisen, "Off-Price and Outlet Malls: A Profile of 'Heavy' Shoppers," *Proceedings of the Annual Educators' Conference of the American Marketing Association*, eds. Gary Frazier et al. (Chicago: American Marketing Association, 1988), pp. 237–241.

35. Ellen Byron, "Seeing Store Shelves Through Senior Eyes," *Wall Street Journal*, September 14, 2009: B1, B2.

36. Cecilie Rohwedder, "Tesco Studies Hard for U.S. Debut," *Wall Street Journal*, June 28, 2007: B1, B2.

37. Stephen Baker, "The Web Knows What You Want," *BusinessWeek*, July 27, 2009: 46–49.

38. Ronald D. Michman, "The Male Queue at the Checkout Counter," *Business Horizons* (May-June 1986): 51–55; Julie Flaherty "To Start a Men's Line, A Pitch to Women," *New York Times*, August 4, 2002: BU 5; for a fascinating study of consumer purchasing behavior for this product category in a foreign environment (Turkey), see Muge Arslan and Ercan Gegez, "Consumer Behavior in the Purchase of Men's Shirts: A Focus Group Research in the Turkish Market," paper presented at the *European Institute of Retailing and Services Science Annual Conference*, Heidelberg, Germany (August 16-19, 2002).

39. Miguel Bustillo and Mary Ellen Lloyd, "Best Buy Seeks Female Shoppers," *Wall Street Journal*, June 16, 2010: B5.

40. Frederick E. Webster, Jr. and Yoram Wind, *Organizational Buying Behavior*, (Englewood Cliffs, N.J.: Prentice Hall, 1972), 6.

41. Philip Kotler, *Marketing Management, Analysis, Planning, Implementation and Control*, 6th ed. (Englewood Cliffs, N.J.: Prentice-Hall, 1988), 213.

42. For an in-depth analysis related to this issue among industrial buyers, see Elizabeth J. Wilson, Gary L. Lilien and David T. Wilson, "Developing and Testing a Contingency Paradigm of Group Choice in Organizational Buying," *Journal of Marketing Research* (November 1991): 452–466.

43. For an article related to this issue, see Daniel C. Smith and Jan P. Owens, "Knowledge of Customers' Customers as a Basis of Sales Force Differentiation," *Journal of Personal Selling and Sales Management* (Summer 1995): 1–14.

PART **3**

Managing the Marketing Channel

CHAPTER 9

Motivating the Channel Members

LEARNING OBJECTIVES

After reading this chapter, you should:

1. Understand the definitions of channel management and motivation management in marketing channels.

2. Recognize the distinction between channel management decisions and channel design decisions.

3. Be familiar with the basic framework for motivating channel members.

4. Know the major means for learning about channel member needs and problems.

5. Understand the basic approaches for providing support for channel members.

6. Be aware of the underlying differences in the relationship implied in the three approaches for supporting channel members.

7. Be cognizant of the need to provide leadership in channels through the effective use of power.

8. Realize that there are significant limitations on the degree of channel control available to the channel manager in an interorganizational setting.

© OmniTerra Images

FOCUS ON CHANNELS

Looks like the Strategic Distribution Alliance between Starbucks and Kraft May Soon Stop Perking

Starbucks is best known for its chain of thousands of coffee shops located all over the globe. But Starbucks is also a major manufacturer of packaged coffee products sold outside of its coffee shops mainly in supermarkets. In fact, the packaged coffee products division of Starbucks has enjoyed dramatic growth over the last dozen years from $50 million in 1998 to over $500 million by 2010.

Starbucks has relied on a strategic alliance with Kraft Foods since 1998 to get its packaged coffee products onto grocery store shelves. The reason? Kraft has the distribution infrastructure and expertise needed to secure the retailer shelf space that Starbucks needs. The strategic alliance was set up so that Kraft would keep the revenues from retail sales of packaged coffee products and pay Starbucks a commission on sales.

Now, Starbucks wants to get out of its strategic alliance with Kraft, claiming that Kraft has not lived up to the terms of the alliance for such things as failing to create good store displays and not involving Starbucks in developing sales strategies.

Starbucks believes that substantial growth potential still exists for its packaged coffee products even as growth in its coffee shops has slowed. By breaking the alliance with Kraft, Starbucks hopes to gain more control and greater profit potential than by continuing the relationship. But there's a catch. Starbucks still does not have its own distribution infrastructure for reaching the retail grocery stores. So, Starbucks would either have to develop this capability from scratch or buy an existing system such as Kraft's or another company that has the kind of distribution clout needed to keep Starbucks's packaged coffee business perking.

Source: Based on John Jannarone, "Starbucks May Spill Kraft's Coffee," *Wall Street Journal* (November 29, 2010): C8.

In Part 2 of the text we opened with a discussion of the need for strategy in marketing channels (Chapter 5). We then presented a paradigm of the channel design process, including the selection of channel members with an extended analysis of target markets as they relate to channel design (Chapters 6, 7, and 8).

In this chapter we begin with the premise that a channel structure(s) with channel members capable of serving the target markets effectively and efficiently has already been developed. At this point, then, the channel manager needs to stress the *realization of this potential.*[1] Thus, managing the marketing channel becomes the main focus of attention. **Channel management** can be defined as *the administration of existing channels to secure the cooperation of channel members in achieving the firm's distribution objectives.* Three points should be particularly noted in this definition:

First, channel management deals with *existing* channels; that is we are assuming that the channel structure(s) has already been designed (or it has evolved) and that all of the members have been selected. Channel design decisions are therefore viewed as separate from channel management decisions. In practice, this distinction may be obscured at times. This is particularly the case when a channel management decision quickly lapses into a channel design decision. For example, a price incentive used to secure the cooperation of some channel members (channel management decision) may fail to do the job. This may result in management considering the possibility of changing to other types of channel members (channel design decision). Perhaps this distinction can be grasped best by thinking of channel design decisions as concerned with "setting up" the channel, whereas channel management deals with "running" what has already been set up.

The second point covers the phrase *secure the cooperation of channel members.* Implied in this is the notion that channel members do not automatically cooperate merely because they are members of the channel.[2] Rather, administrative actions are necessary to secure their cooperation.[3] If a producer, manufacturer, or franchisor enjoys substantial cooperation from channel members without having to administrate, this is not managing—it is simply a matter of being lucky.

Third, the term *distribution objectives*, although discussed in Chapter 6 with respect to channel design decisions, is equally relevant for channel management. Distribution objectives are statements describing the part that the distribution component of the marketing mix is expected to play in achieving the firm's overall marketing objectives. Carefully delineated distribution objectives are needed to guide the management of the channel.[4] Clearly, without knowing what the objectives are, it is difficult for the channel manager to know what direction to pursue in managing the channel.[5]

In this chapter we examine one of the most fundamental and important aspects of channel management—motivating channel members.[6] In the context of channel management, **motivation** refers to the actions taken by the manufacturer, producer or franchisor to foster channel member cooperation in implementing the distribution objectives. Our discussion is structured around the three basic facets involved in **motivation management** in the channel:

1. Finding out the needs and problems of channel members
2. Offering support to the channel members that is consistent with their needs and problems
3. Providing leadership through the effective use of power

Finding Out the Needs and Problems of Channel Members

Before the channel manager can successfully motivate channel members, an attempt must be made to learn what the members want from the channel relationship.[7] They may perceive needs and face problems quite different from those of the manufacturer.[8] McVey has pointed to these differences with several classic propositions that can be summarized as follows:

1. The middleman does not consider himself a "hired link in a chain forged by the manufacturer."
2. The middleman acts first and foremost as a purchasing agent for his customers, and only secondarily as a selling agent for suppliers. His interest is in selling *whatever products* his customers wish to buy from him.
3. The middleman views all the products he offers as a "family" of items that he sells as a packaged assortment to individual customers. He directs his selling efforts primarily at obtaining orders for the assortment, rather than for individual items.
4. Unless given some incentive to do so, the middleman will not maintain separate sales records of brands sold. Information that might be useful to manufacturers in product development, pricing, packaging, or promotion planning is "buried" in the middleman's own records, sometimes even purposely kept from suppliers.[9]

Implied in McVey's comments is the notion that manufacturers are often unaware of or insensitive to the needs and problems of their channel members. Consider, for example, the plight of Chrysler automobile dealers soon after the Chrysler Group LLC emerged from bankruptcy reorganization in late 2009. With no new models to sell, a very slow economy, and a reputation for questionable quality, dealer morale was at an all-time low. Many, if not most of the dealers felt like outcasts among the "fraternity" of auto dealerships. As one dealer in Wisconsin who wished not to be identified remarked:[10]

> I have people passing by my dealership
> like I'm not even here. Image is still
> everything in this business, and there is
> only so much I can do. Where's the help?

The help this dealer and most of his peers were asking for was a major advertising program by Chrysler Group LLC aimed at rebuilding the lowly image of Chrysler cars. They wanted a campaign that would mirror the one developed by General Motors Co., which had also recently emerged from bankruptcy, in which Chief Executive Edward E. Whitacre Jr. was shown walking through GM factories with an air of great confidence, touting the rebirth of GM.[11] But no such image rehabilitation program was planned for Chrysler. Chrysler's CEO Sergio Machionne decided to wait until Chrysler would have new products to introduce such as the Grand Cherokee several months hence before spending significant sums on advertising. But meanwhile, dealers felt they were being "hung out to dry" because

Chrysler seemed to be unaware of their need for some kind of morale booster to help get through the dark days until new models would appear in their showrooms.

This case points out the need for the channel manager to be sensitive to channel member needs and develop practical and effective approaches for finding out what problems channel members face as they attempt to survive and prosper in a highly competitive environment.[12] Even if Chrysler Group LLC felt that its strategy of waiting for new models to appear before launching a major advertising campaign was a sound one, it still could have done a better job of empathizing with the dealers' plight and made more of an effort to reassure them that their patience would be rewarded.

Approaches for Learning About Member Needs and Problems

All marketing channels have a flow of information running through them as part of the formal and informal communications systems that exist in the channel[13] (See the section "Flows in Marketing Channels" in Chapter 1). Figure 9.1 provides an overview of most of the major components that go into making up a typical channel communications system.

FIGURE 9.1 Model of a Channel Communications System

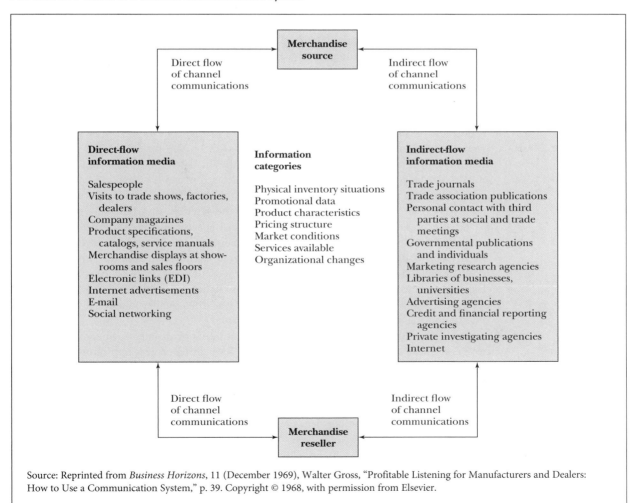

Source: Reprinted from *Business Horizons*, 11 (December 1969), Walter Gross, "Profitable Listening for Manufacturers and Dealers: How to Use a Communication System," p. 39. Copyright © 1968, with permission from Elsevier.

In recent years, the emergence of social networking sites such as Facebook, Twitter, LinkedIn, and many others can provide a great deal of additional information about channel member opinions, attitudes, and behaviors, which was not available before.[14] But the information provided by social networking communications processes, while abundant and potentially valuable, may still lack the kind of structure and focus required to obtain a good understanding of channel members' needs and problems. Consequently, the channel manager should not rely solely on the regular flow of information coming from the existing channel communications system for accurate and timely information on channel member needs and problems.[15] Rather, there is a need to go beyond the regular system and make use of one or all of the following four additional approaches for learning about channel member needs and problems: (1) research studies of channel members conducted by manufacturers, (2) research studies by outside parties, (3) marketing channel audits, and (4) distributor advisory councils.

Research Studies of Channel Members   While it has become common for manufacturers to conduct research studies dealing with their ultimate customers—to learn the kinds of products that customers want, what their brand preferences are, the kinds of shopping behaviors they engage in, and many other types of information—research studies of channel member needs and problems are rarer. Indeed, most manufacturers—even large and sophisticated ones—never conduct such research at all. Estimates indicate that less than 1 percent of manufacturers' research budgets is spent on channel member research.[16] This is unfortunate because sometimes research may be the only way to uncover subtle or hidden channel member needs or problems.[17] This is illustrated perfectly in the case of Loctite Corporation. Loctite is a well-known manufacturer of numerous adhesive and sealant products used in many different industries. The company sells most of its products through wholesale distributors who in turn sell to retailers as well as business and industrial customers. Loctite and its distributors were very much at odds over the sales job the distributors were doing with Loctite products. The company felt that the distributors did not care about selling the line because the distributors' salespeople almost never took along the Loctite product samples when making calls on customers. On the other hand, the distributors believed that Loctite Corporation was insensitive to their sales support needs because the samples, they felt, were not appropriate for use by salespeople. Loctite, believing that the samples were an excellent sales aid, was befuddled by the distributors' attitude. Finally, the quandary was solved when Loctite decided to do some research, which uncovered a simple explanation for the distributors' failure to use the Loctite samples. As it turned out, the Loctite product samples were designed to be carried in briefcases, but most of Loctite's distributors' salespeople did not carry briefcases! Once this was known, Loctite was quickly able to solve the problem by redesigning the samples, making them pocket-sized.[18]

As suggested by this example, certain types of needs or problems, though simple, may not be at all obvious. In such cases, a manufacturer-initiated research effort can be very useful in zeroing in on the problem.

Research Studies by Outside Parties   Research designed and executed by a third party who is not a member of the channel is sometimes necessary if complete and unbiased data on channel member needs and problems are to be obtained. The following examples[19] show how.

A mass-market clothing manufacturer made a costly discovery too late. The end-aisle display for use in retail stores was too large. Store managers said, "It will be left in the warehouse and eventually discarded." Unfortunately, it was only after making this costly and embarrassing mistake that the manufacturer used an outside research firm to perform a study of retailer space allocation plans so as to have an *objective* basis for designing future store displays.

A major top-shelf liquor manufacturer had been relying on its own sales force to "research" the effectiveness of its wholesale distributors. But the findings were at odds with sales data and retailer feedback. By using a third-party research firm to conduct in-depth interviews with retailers about their perceptions of the wholesalers, the manufacturer was able to get a truer picture of wholesaler performance. The results led to a major reorganization of the liquor manufacturer's marketing channels.

A fiber manufacturer supported its raw fiber product through trade advertising to top department and mass merchandise retailers. Although substantial funds were being spent, the effectiveness of the advertising in influencing the trade was questionable. An independent marketing research firm was finally called in to interview buyers and merchandise managers from 75 top chains and manufacturers using the fiber. The findings not only showed ways for improving the advertising message for higher impact on trade buyers, but also revealed that the targeting of the ads left much to be desired.

As these examples suggest, the use of outside parties to conduct research on channel member needs and problems provides higher assurance of objectivity. Further, for manufacturers who do not have marketing research departments or whose research capabilities are limited, the use of outside research firms offers manufacturers a level of expertise that is not available in their own organization.

Marketing Channel Audits   As with the periodic financial audit, which virtually all firms have performed, the channel manager can conduct a **marketing channel audit** periodically.[20] The basic thrust of this approach should be to gather data on how channel members perceive the manufacturer's marketing program and its component parts, where the relationships are strong and weak, and what is expected of the manufacturer to make the channel relationship viable and optimal. For example, the manufacturer may want to gather data from channel members on what their needs and problems are in areas such as:

1. Pricing policies, margins, and allowances
2. Extent and nature of the product line
3. New products and their marketing development through promotion
4. Servicing policies and procedures such as invoicing, order dating, shipping, warehousing, and others
5. Sales force performance in servicing the accounts

Further, the marketing channel audit should identify and define in detail the issues relevant to the manufacturer-wholesaler and/or manufacturer-retailer relationship. Calantone and Gassenheimer, for example, developed one of the most extensive inventories of channel issues available, based on a study in the office systems/furniture industry.[21] Their findings are shown in Table 9.1, where the specific issues are grouped into six overall areas that the authors found were crucial in the relationship between manufacturers and distributors. This list of basic areas and issues, while not meant to be universally applicable for all channel audits, nevertheless does provide an extensive checklist that can be helpful in the planning and development of any particular channel audit.[22]

Another point to note involves cross-referencing. Whatever areas and issues are chosen for a particular marketing channel audit, ideally they should be cross-tabulated or correlated as to kind of channel members, geographical location of channel members, sales volume levels achieved, and any other variables that might be relevant.

Finally, for the marketing channel audit to work effectively, it must be done on a periodic and regular basis so as to capture trends and patterns. Only in this way will it be possible to keep track of those issues that remain constant, those that dissipate, or

---

TABLE 9.1 GENERAL AREAS AND SPECIFIC ISSUES FOR CONSIDERATION IN A MARKETING CHANNEL AUDIT

1. Manufacturer's performance

Length of promised order cycle time for base line/in-stock products

Manufacturer's performance in meeting promised delivery dates

Availability of manufacturer sales reps to participate in customer calls and project bids

Overall manufacturing and finish quality of product relative to the price range involved

Continuity of system products over the extended time frame

Fees paid by manufacturer for reimbursement to dealer for local servicing of national/direct sales accounts

Fill rates on base line/in-stock items

Flexibility of credit policies to meet special situations

Advance notice on shipping delays

Advanced methods of ordering

Timely response to requests for assistance from manufacturer's sales representative

Accuracy of manufacturer in forecasting and committing to estimated shipping dates on contract/project orders

Formal training program by manufacturer in the area of facility management

Overall aesthetics and design of the product

Showroom layout planning assistance from manufacturer

Action on complaints related to order servicing and shipping

Ability to expedite and/or provide such service on product orders

Competitiveness of price

Inventory management counseling and assistance provided by manufacturer

Updated and current price data, specifications, and promotion materials provided by manufacturer

Formal sales training programs by manufacturer for dealer salespeople

Breadth of the product offering

Manufacturer's adherence to special shipping instructions

Accuracy in filling orders

After-the-sale follow-up by sales reps

Attention to details, from order placement to installation

Manufacturer's responsiveness to emergency/unusual needs

Computerized (CAD) floorplan/layout design services and/or assistance available from the manufacturer

2. Distributor's desire for autonomy in making its own decisions

Margins on sales to customer

Annual minimum volume quotas

Selection and breadth of the manufacturer's product line focused on

Acceptance and adoption of new products/lines developed or acquired by the manufacturer

Degree of independent/unsolicited participation by the manufacturer in selling new large accounts

Ability/freedom to select product lines from competing manufacturers

Procedures and techniques used to develop selling skills and account management for salespeople

3. Manufacturer's desire to influence the distributor's decision

Margins on sales to customer

Annual minimum volume quotas

Selection and breadth of the manufacturer's product line focused on

Acceptance and adoption of new products/lines developed or acquired by the manufacturer

Degree of independent/unsolicited participation by the manufacturer in selling new large accounts

Size, investment, and appearance of dealer showroom(s)

Ability/freedom to select product lines from competing manufacturers

Procedures and techniques used to develop selling skills and account management for salespeople

Ability/freedom to sell a manufacturer's products outside the implied/authorized sales territory

4. Manufacturer's use of power (pressure) to influence decision

Margins on sales to customer

Annual minimum volume quotas

Selection and breadth of the manufacturer's product line focused on

Acceptance and adoption of new products/lines developed or acquired by the manufacturer

Degree of independent/unsolicited participation by the manufacturer in selling new large accounts

Size, investment, and appearance of dealer showroom(s)

Ability/freedom to select product lines from competing manufacturers

Procedures and techniques used to develop selling skills and account management for salespeople

Ability/freedom to sell a manufacturer's products outside the implied/authorized sales territory

Order entry and communication methods used

5. Control relinquished to the manufacturer by the distributor

Margins on sales to customer

Annual minimum volume quotas

Selection and breadth of the manufacturer's product line focused on

Acceptance and adoption of new products/lines developed or acquired by the manufacturer

Degree of independent/unsolicited participation by the manufacturer in selling new large accounts

Ability/freedom to select product lines from competing manufacturers

TABLE 9.1 *(Continued)*

Ability/freedom to sell a manufacturer's products outside the implied/authorized sales territory	New product market opportunities through the manufacturer's local sales representative
6. Distributor's satisfaction with the working relationship	Sales growth potential from carrying the manufacturer's product line(s)
Profits generated from the manufacturer's product line(s)	Interest and concern the manufacturer has displayed in helping to accomplish dealer goals and objectives
Overall manner treated by the manufacturer's regional office or headquarters	The manufacturer's commitment to continuing overall marketing programs
Overall "sales support"/relationship with the manufacturer's local sales representative	Overall customer service levels provided by the manufacturer

Source: Adapted from Roger J. Calatone and Jule B. Gassenheimer, "Overcoming Basic Problems between Manufacturers and Distributors," *Industrial Marketing Management* 20 (1991): 218–219, Copyright 1991, with permission from Elsevier.

those that enlarge in scope.[23] Emerging issues are also more likely to be spotted if the audit is performed on a regular basis.

Distributor Advisory Councils Another effective approach for learning about channel member needs and problems is to set up a **distributor advisory council** (sometimes referred to as a **dealer advisory counsel** or **channel member committee**). These councils should consist of top management representatives from the manufacturer as well as representatives of the principals from the channel members. The top management people might consist of the vice president of marketing, general sales manager, and other top members of sales management. The distributor members should consist of a representative sample of distributors or dealers, such as 5 to 10 percent of the total. However, the total number should be limited to allow for full participation and exchange of dialogue by all parties present. In setting up a distributor advisory council, the normal procedure is to have cochairs—one elected by the members from the distributor group, and the other the top sales executive for the manufacturer.

Three significant benefits emerge from the use of a distributor advisory council.[24] First, it provides *recognition for the channel members*. Distributors or dealers, as do most other people, like to have a voice in planning what affects their own welfare. Channel members are therefore more likely to understand and support a manufacturer's actions if they have helped plan them. This gives distributors the feeling of being "in the know," which increases their sense of security and promotes greater identification with the interests of the manufacturer.

Second, the distributor advisory council provides a vehicle for *identifying and discussing mutual needs and problems* that are not transmitted through the regular channel information flow.

Third, the distributor advisory council results in an overall *improvement of channel communications*, which in turn helps the manufacturer to learn more about the needs and problems of channels members, and vice versa.

Anheuser-Busch (the world's largest beer producer) used a distributors' advisory group to gain insight into wholesalers' views on a controversial channel strategy initiative launched by the company. The beer distributors provided candid feedback about how they were reacting to Anheuser-Busch's program called "100 percent share of mind," which sought to have beer distributors focus mainly on Anheuser-Busch products while deemphasizing competitors' products. The giant beer manufacturer learned that there were considerable differences in perception about the nature of this channel strategy. In particular, a number of wholesalers were upset about losing the opportunity to sell competitors' "craft beers," which had become highly profitable for the wholesalers. Some of their concerns were assuaged when they learned via their representative on the council that the 100 percent share of mind program would be implemented on a *voluntary* basis and was not intended to be a mandate. When the wholesalers learned that they would get *incentives* to participate rather than intimidation, many of them viewed the program in a new cooperative light.[25]

Caterpillar, the giant industrial earth-moving equipment company, provides another case of a firm that uses its distributors' advisory council to learn about its dealers' views on a wide variety of dealer needs and problems. For example, at a meeting of the council, the dealers reported on a design flaw in a line of graders that could have caused the dealers serious problems in the form of injuries to their customers from banging their heads on a lid that was placed too low for proper servicing. Discussions in the council also revealed that the dealers would be better able to offer their customers the kind of rapid, high-quality service that Caterpillar was famous for by simply changing their inventory practices. Instead of ordering certain commonly needed parts that, no matter how quickly Caterpillar responded, inevitably involved delays, it was agreed that the dealers would henceforth always stock the full line of such parts, consisting mainly of relatively low-cost batteries and fan belts.[26]

So, whether the product involved ranges from beer[27] to industrial earth-moving equipment, the face-to-face dialogue and give and take provided by distributor advisory councils provide a valuable means for learning about channel member needs and problems.

Offering Support to Channel Members

Support for channel members refers to the producer or manufacturer's efforts in helping channel members to meet their needs and solve their problems. Such support should help to create a more highly motivated group of channel members.[28]

Unfortunately, support for channel members is all too often offered on a disorganized and ad hoc basis. When channel members appear to lack motivation they are "pumped up" with an extra price incentive, advertising allowance, dealer contest, or even a pep talk by the manufacturer.[29] Or, if they are having a problem in a particular area, the manufacturer may attempt to "patch it up" and hope that the problem will not come back again—at least for a little while.[30] Over four decades ago, McCammon made a penetrating comment on the inadequacy of this kind of approach to motivating channel members and it still rings true today:

> *Many programs [developed by the manufacturer] consist of hastily improvised trade deals, uninspired dealer contests, and unexamined discount structures … [and] this traditional attitude toward distributor programming is a luxury that no longer can be easily afforded.*[31]

So, as McCammon implies and more recent research supports,[32] the attainment of a highly motivated cooperating "team" of channel members in an interorganizational setting requires carefully planned programs.[33] Such programs for providing channel member support can generally be grouped into one of the following three categories: (1) **cooperative**, (2) **partnership or strategic alliance**, and (3) **distribution programming**. While all three of these approaches should emphasize careful planning, the level of sophistication and comprehensiveness of the approaches varies greatly. The cooperative approach represents the least sophisticated and comprehensive approach to channel member support, whereas distribution programming is the most sophisticated and comprehensive. The partnership or strategic alliance approach would generally fall somewhere between the other two.

Cooperative Arrangements

Cooperative arrangements between the manufacturer and channel members at the wholesale and retail levels have traditionally been used as the most common means of motivating channel members in conventional, loosely aligned channels. The types of cooperative arrangements or deals are quite diverse and are limited only by the creativity of the manufacturer distributor or retailer.[34] Table 9.2 lists 30 classic types of cooperative programs. Which of these is used and the specific arrangements or features involved vary widely across different industries. For example, cooperative advertising allowances, payments for interior displays, and coupon-handling allowances are offered extensively to retailers of consumer packaged goods such as supermarkets, drugstores, and mass merchandisers, while contests for salespeople and training programs are very popular at the wholesale level, especially among those selling industrial products.[35] Any of these cooperative programs that provide assistance to channel members must be offered on a nondiscriminatory basis to all channel members of the same class so as not to be in violation of the Robinson-Patman Act (see Chapter 3).

The underlying rationale of all such cooperative programs, from the manufacturer's point of view, is to provide incentives for getting extra effort from channel members in the promotion of products of the manufacturer offering the cooperative program. They do not always succeed in doing so, however. Many times the specific cooperative programs used do not meet channel member needs or they are poorly designed and executed.

TABLE 9.2 TYPICAL TYPES OF COOPERATIVE PROGRAMS PROVIDED BY MANUFACTURERS TO CHANNEL MEMBERS

1. Cooperative advertising allowances
2. Payments for interior displays, including shelf-extender, dump displays, "A" locations, aisle displays, etc.
3. Contests for buyers, salespeople, etc.
4. Allowances for a variety of warehousing functions
5. Payments for window display space, plus installation costs
6. Detail men who check inventory, put up stock, set up complete promotion, etc.
7. Demonstrators
8. Coupon-handling allowance
9. Free goods
10. Guaranteed sales
11. In-store and window display material
12. Local research work
13. Mail-in premium offers to customers
14. Preticketing
15. Automatic reorder systems
16. Delivery costs to individual stores of retailers or wholesalers
17. Studies of innumerable types, such as studies of merchandise management accounting
18. Liberal return privileges
19. Contributions to favorite charities for store personnel
20. Contributions to special anniversaries
21. Prizes, etc., to buyers when visiting showrooms—plus entertainment
22. Training salespeople
23. Payments for store fixtures
24. Payments for new store cost or improvements
25. An infinite variety of promotion allowances
26. Special payments for exclusive franchises
27. Payments of part of salary of salespeople
28. Time spent by manufacturer's salespeople in actual selling on retail floor or with distributors' field sales force
29. Inventory price adjustments
30. Store or distributor name mention in manufacturer's advertising

Source: Adapted from Edward B. Weiss, "How Much of a Retailer is the Manufacturer," *Advertising Age* 29, (July 21, 1958): 68. Copyright © 1958 by Crain Communications. Reproduced by permission.

Two cases help to illustrate the key features of cooperative programs that are indicative of unsuccessful and successful cooperative programs. The first involves a very large and famous consumer products manufacturer, Levi Strauss & Company; the second is a much smaller industrial products company, Warner Electric.

The cooperative program used by Levi Strauss & Company involved cooperative advertising. The program at first seemed straightforward. In return for retailers' featuring Levi products in their advertisements, the company would share the advertising costs with the retailers on an equal basis. But the "fine print" of the arrangement presented an entirely different story. To qualify for cost sharing with Levi, retailers had to submit published rate cards for newspapers or television. For all practical purposes this eliminated most small suburban and rural newspapers and such important retailer advertising media as flyers and circulars. Further, in order to participate in the program, retailers had to fill out a form so lengthy that it "would have required a Philadelphia lawyer to understand it," said one of Levi's chief competitors rather gleefully. Among those retailers that did subscribe to the program, many were not paid by Levi when they submitted their claims because they did not follow the exacting procedures laid down by Levi.[36]

The experience of Levi in its ill-conceived cooperative advertising program points out the most common problems that can befall not only cooperative advertising programs but many other cooperative programs as well. First, Levi did not *pay enough attention to the needs of its retailers* in the use of cooperative advertising. Such media as small local newspapers and handout circulars are an important form of advertising for many retailers. By effectively excluding these for reimbursement under the program, Levi was ignoring an important advertising need of its retailers. Second, by making the agreement so complicated and difficult to understand, Levi showed a *lack of sensitivity to the retailers' problems.* Specifically, retailers have enough to worry about in the day-to-day running of their businesses as they attempt to compete in a fiercely competitive environment. The last thing they need is more headaches in the form of complex and legalistic cooperative advertising arrangements. Finally, Levi's refusal to honor the retailers' claims because they were not submitted according to the "letter of the law" showed a *lack of trust* on the part of Levi toward its retailers.

Turning now to an example of a well-conceived and executed cooperative program, consider the one instituted by Warner Electric to motivate its industrial distributors.[37] The cooperative program in the form of a sales contest was instituted by Warner during the heart of a recession. The program, called "Sweep" (Sell Warner—Earn Extra Profit), was aimed at getting Warner's distributors to sell to customers of Warner's competitors.

The distributors' salespeople received bonuses ranging from $10 to $50 from Warner each time they identified a prospect that was buying from a competitor. Warner also gave a 5 percent bonus to salespeople who closed a sale of $1,000 or more to a new customer. For the distributors' principals (owners), Warner held a "Sweep" stakes by offering free inventory. "Sweep" stakes chances were awarded in proportion to the number of new prospects or sales closed by their salespeople. The first-place winner received $25,000 in Warner merchandise and the second-place winner got $10,000 worth.

The program was operated from mid-July through December. Paperwork was kept to a minimum and the rules were simple so that everyone satisfying the program's requirements was appropriately rewarded. The five-month program, which elicited the participation of all of Warner's distributors, identified more than 750 new customers and produced more than $5 million in new business. The program also took the distributors' attention away from the recession and helped them focus on selling.

In contrast to Levi's program, Warner's program reflected the best features of a good cooperative program. It *focused on channel member needs and problems* by providing a welcome sales stimulus as well as monetary rewards during a difficult recessionary period. It was also *simple and straightforward*, with no complex rules and procedures to follow. Finally, it conveyed a clear *sense of mutual benefit* because even though it was unabashedly designed to push a particular manufacturer's products, it offered immediate and tangible rewards for the distributors who participated.

Partnerships and Strategic Alliances

Terms such as *distribution partnerships, channel partners, distributor partners, dealer partners*, and *strategic alliances* have been appearing with increasing frequency in the marketing channels literature[38] as well as the trade press in recent years.[39] What these terms are referring to is a type of channel relationship that goes beyond the ad hoc, on-again/off-again interactions typical of traditional cooperative relationships between the manufacturer and its channel members. **Partnerships** or **strategic alliances** instead stress a *continuing and mutually supportive relationship*[40] between the manufacturer and its channel members in an effort to provide a more highly motivated team, network, or alliance of channel partners.[41] The traditional "us-against-them" mentality is replaced with a new, cooperative perception of "us" in an effective channel partnership or strategic alliance. In describing these types of interfirm relationships in marketing channels, Johnson argues that channel members become strategically integrated in the process:

> *At the most fundamental level, strategic integration between firms begins when the relationship becomes important. The firm in the relationship has an explicit and acknowledged stake in the other's success because the other plays a role in the firm's own strategic picture.*[42]

Consider, for example, Home Depot's channel partnership arrangement with LG Electronics Inc.[43] By the middle of the first decade of the twenty-first century, Home Depot was seeking to dramatically increase its market penetration for major appliances to compete more successfully against Lowe's and Sears, which had a longer history and more experience with major appliances. Home Depot believed that the best way to make a bigger impact in this product category was to emphasize quick delivery. So, Home Depot looked to its channel partner LG Electronics to support its strategic focus on quick customer delivery. Specifically, Home Depot wanted to guarantee customers that if they ordered LG appliances from Home Depot, the machines would be delivered to their homes within 48 hours. To meet this delivery specification, LG spent millions of dollars to establish warehouses at a dozen key locations throughout the U.S. and set up a nationwide computer network and call centers. In six months, LG was able to meet Home Depot's 48-hour customer delivery specifications.

Another good example of a channel partnership or strategic alliance can be seen in Dell Inc.'s Registered Partner program which Dell established when it made the strategic channel design decision to use intermediaries to augment its direct distribution channel by the middle of the first decade of the twenty-first century.[44] In exchange for aggressively selling Dell products to the tune of $9 billion in annual sales, Dell Registered Partners get to use Dell's logo, receive enhanced post-sale support, numerous financing options, access to Dell's partner Web site for online ordering, white papers on industry trends, a comprehensive set of marketing materials, and a variety of other forms of support from Dell.

The concept of partnerships (or strategic alliances) in marketing channels is not new. Indeed, these kinds of relationships have existed for decades in some marketing channels. Black & Decker, for example, in its industrial power tool division, has employed such approaches since the mid-1960s. The statement of policy shown in Figure 9.2

FIGURE 9.2 Black & Decker Corporation's Statement of Policy toward Channel Members

A STATEMENT OF POLICY

INDUSTRIAL DIVISION

It is our firm belief that Black & Decker and its duly Authorized Distributors have fundamental obligations to each other. We believe that mutually profitable operations depend upon mutual acceptance of these obligations as outlined.

WHAT DISTRIBUTORS CAN EXPECT FROM BLACK & DECKER

1. **Selective Distribution:**
   - Appointed on the basis of power tool potential in each marketing area
   - Adequate to insure penetration of all markets for our products
   - Selected in accordance with the terms of this "Statement of Policy"
2. **Specialized Field Sales Assistance Through:**
   - The largest, best-trained field sales organization in the industry
   - Product and market training for Distributor's sales organization by means of effective sales meetings, power tool clinic sessions and joint sales calls in the field
   - Availability of market potential information to assist Distributor's sales planning
   - Assistance in the maintenance of a well balanced and current power tool and accessory inventory
3. **Healthy Profit Opportunities Through:**
   - Equitable profit margins on power tools and accessories
   - Assured inventory turnover
   - Maintaining an orderly market
   - Refusal to deal with Distributors who do not feel that the sales policies we suggest are based upon sound business judgment
4. **Aggressive Advertising and Sales Promotion Through:**
   - The best-known brand name in the industry
   - The largest and best program of national advertising, direct mail assistance and display materials in the power tool field
5. **Leadership ch and Development Through:**
   - The broadest, most complete line in the industry
   - Continued leadership in product performance, value, styling and innovation
6. **Leadership in Manufacturing From:**
   - The largest, most modern plants in the industry
   - Unparalleled quality control standards
   - Thorough testing of all products before shipment
7. **Nation-wide Network of Factory-operated Service Facilities Which:**
   - Offer prompt, expert repair service at reasonable cost
   - Stock genuine Black & Decker replacement parts
8. **The Famous Black & Decker Guarantee Which:**
   - Protects the purchaser against defective material or workmanship for the life of the product

WHAT BLACK & DECKER EXPECTS FROM DISTRIBUTORS

1. **Effective Sales Results Through:**
   - An aggressive sales organization, knowledgeable in the application and selling of Black & Decker products
   - Effective sales management focus on our line
   - Adequate penetration of the potential market for our products in the Distributor's normal trading area
   - Cooperation with Black & Decker's field sales personnel in developing sales programs, meetings and work schedules designed to build sales performance
2. **Vigorous Promotional Activity Through:**
   - Imaginative advertising, direct mail activity, displays and catalog coverage of the Black & Decker line
3. **Protection of Black & Decker's Brand Name and Reputation By:**
   - Following the sales policies recommended by the company
   - Restricting sales to the Distributor's normal trading area
   - Discouraging the sale of Black & Decker products through non-authorized sales organizations, so that the customer will receive maximum service after purchase.
   - Abstaining from marketing practices that, in any way, damage the reputation of the company or its products
4. **Maintenance of an Adequate Inventory By:**
   - Stocking tools and accessories of a variety and quantity commensurate with markets served and the highest standards of customer service. ("Adequate Inventory" shall be a matter of agreement between each Distributor and the appropriate Black & Decker sales representative.)
5. **Provision of Those Other Services and Functions Which Characterize a Good Distributor, Such As:**
   - Extending credit to the user
   - Following up customer inquiries
   - Rendering prompt delivery from local stocks
   - Making available prompt technical services to customers
   - Keeping informed on market conditions

With this STATEMENT OF POLICY, we reaffirm our belief in the economic soundness of the Distributor, our resolve continually to improve and diversify the products we offer and, through Distributor channels, to cultivate an ever-widening market for Black & Decker products.

THE BLACK & DECKER MANUFACTURING COMPANY

President

Chairman of the Board

Source: Roger M. Pegram, *Selecting and Evaluating Distributors* (New York: The Conference Board, Business Policy Study No. 116, 1965): 114. Reproduced with permission from The Conference Board, Inc. Business Cycle Indicators (2010). © 2010, The Conference Board, Inc.

reflects the essence of the partnership approach in spelling out the expectations for mutual commitment between Black & Decker and its distributors. Moreover, over three decades ago, Webster, in a seminal study of industrial distributors, described the relationship between a number of the distributors and manufacturers he studied as being indicative of this partnership approach.[45] The partnerships, Webster observed, were not partnerships in the legal sense of the term, but rather were a way of describing a supportive relationship between channel members based on a careful delineation of their mutual roles in the channel. He states:

> *The idea of a partnership remains essential; when the manufacturer turns to the distributor for added help, he does not give up his own responsibility for effective marketing, nor can he expect the distributor to respond positively to all suggestions. Rather, he assumes new responsibilities for making the distributor more effective—through programs of product development, careful pricing, promotional support, technical assistance, order servicing, and through training programs for the distributors' salespeople and management.*[46]

Webster points to three basic phases in the development of a "partnership" arrangement between channel members. First, if it has not already been done, an explicit statement of policies should be made by the manufacturer in such areas as product availability, technical support, pricing, and any other relevant areas. (Figure 9.2, as noted earlier, shows such a statement of policy for the Black & Decker Corporation.) This having been done, the roles of the channel members can then be more precisely defined in terms of the tasks they will be expected to perform and the compensation they will receive for doing so.

The second phase is an assessment of all existing distributors as to their capabilities for fulfilling their roles. The approaches suggested for determining channel member needs and problems discussed earlier in this chapter can be applied with equal effectiveness for appraising channel members' strengths and weaknesses. The manufacturer should pay particular attention to helping distributors overcome any weaknesses by developing specific programs in these areas. For example, if a distributor has an inadequately trained sales force, the manufacturer might develop a training program aimed at improving the skills of the distributor's salespeople. If a particular channel member is having problems controlling inventory, the manufacturer might attempt to offer expertise in this area. In short, the manufacturer's support programs should be clearly and sharply focused on the distributors' areas of greatest need.[47]

Third, the manufacturer should continually appraise the appropriateness of the policies that guide the relationship with channel members. In the face of a rapidly changing environment (see Chapter 3), no set of channel policies can remain static for very long.[48]

Partnerships or strategic alliances aimed at building more highly-motivated channel members have become increasingly common in a wide range of industries. At the retail level, Procter & Gamble and Walmart have built what is perhaps the most talked about strategic alliance in the consumer package goods industry by emphasizing close working relationships, including having P&G executives permanently on-site at Walmart's headquarters in Bentonville, Arkansas, to stay closely in touch with Walmart's top management. A sophisticated Electronic Data Interchange (EDI) system also provides a highly efficient means for assuring availability of P&G products in all 7,500 domestic and foreign Walmart stores. Walmart has also developed a very successful partnership with the Coca-Cola Company (see Figure 9.3).

FIGURE 9.3 Advertisement in a Trade Magazine for a Marketing Channel Strategic Alliance

Source: Courtesy of the Coca~Cola Company.

FIGURE 9.4
Basic Principles for Building Successful Channel Partnerships

Principle	Description
Both partners should gain from the relationship.	Structure relationships for win-win outcomes so both partners can prosper.
Each party should be treated with respect.	Focus should be on understanding the culture of each partner (not just their assets), and all commitments should be honored.
Promise only what can be delivered.	Partners should be honest in establishing expectations.
Specific objectives should be defined before the relationship is firmly established.	Problems will inevitably arise if the relationship drifts along aimlessly.
Striving for long-term commitment is important to both parties.	Some actions may be required that do not immediately benefit the partners but will be beneficial in the long term.
Each side should take the time to understand the other partner's culture.	Understand each other's needs, learn about "inner workings," and appreciate different vantage points used.
Each side should develop champions of the relationship.	Each firm should appoint a main contact who is responsible for working with the partner.
Lines of communication should be kept open.	Both partners must feel comfortable raising and discussing difficult issues before they turn into major conflicts.
The best decision is one made together.	Unilateral decisions should be avoided; forcing a partner to accept a decision fosters mistrust.
Preserve the continuity of the relationship.	Turnover of key employees in partner firms can be detrimental to the viability of the partnership, so managing to ensure smooth transition is crucial.

Source: Adapted from Frank K. Sonnenberg, "Partnering: Entering the Age of Cooperation," 51–52, *Journal of Business Strategy* (May–June 1992). Reprinted by permission from Emerald Group Publishing Limited.

In more recent years, Webster's basic guidelines for establishing partnerships among channel members have been expanded and refined, so that now a more complete set of principles—such as those developed by Sonnenberg[49] as summarized in Figure 9.4—can be used as guidelines for establishing partnerships or strategic alliances in marketing channels.

Even more recently, Adobor and McMullen have used the term *e-alliances* to describe strategic alliances formed primarily as a part of an E-commerce strategy.[50] They argue that because of the dynamic and volatile environment of E-commerce relationships, channel members need to pay especially close attention to such issues as well-defined exit strategies, short-term commitment, the swift development of trust, and ease of management. Figure 9.5 provides a more detailed overview of the kinds if issues that need to be addressed in e-alliances. Moen, a leading manufacturer of high-end kitchen and bathroom faucets, provides an example of an e-alliance. Moen is extending the e-alliance it had established with its suppliers to its wholesalers, through whom Moen makes 50 percent of its sales. This e-alliance enabled Moen to reduce product development time from 24 months to 16 months by using the Internet

FIGURE 9.5 Guidelines for Establishing E-Alliances

Dimension	E-alliance Management Guidelines
Goals and objectives	• Clear goals will make the job of managing the alliance relatively easy. • E-alliances should be focused on specific items. • A narrow and well-defined purpose will be an asset.
Protecting interests	• Contractual provisions must be explicit and cover as much as possible. • The contract should spell out the responsibility and authority of each partner. • Majority ownership typically confers commensurate authority. • Shared management is a means of control. But this makes for organizational complexity, and the difficulties of managing the alliance may be greater than when one partner makes most of the decisions. In such cases, decide how control and decision-making will be shared.
Trust	• Trust is important, but environmental uncertainty and time pressure mean that one either trusts quickly or perhaps never at all. • Competence and reliability in task performance is very important to the swift development of trust. • Joint investments can serve to buttress trust creation.
Multiple relations	• In selecting allies, try to minimize risk and maximize returns. • Use the organizing form to diversify risk; mix informal and more integrated forms to diversify risk in multiple alliances. • Ally with some established firms and some start-ups as a way to diversify risk and protect your interests.
Exit strategy	• Clearly define the exit strategy; it may offer the best protection in a volatile environment. • Consider the conditions under which each partner can opt out of the deal. • Consider how assets and liabilities will be disposed of in the event of collapse. • Determine the dispute resolution mechanisms ahead of time. • How the relationship ends has important implications for your reputation.
Structure	• Simplicity of design is a virtue. • Structure alliances to reduce task and organizational complexity. • Again, clarity of goals in the alliance can be very helpful here. • Set goals that are complementary with your partner's goals.
Commitment	• Single, serial, or contingent relationships are preferable to open-ended ones. • Short-term commitment seems preferable in view of the volatility of the environment. • Pursue projects in phases.

Source: Reprinted from *Business Horizons* (March–April 2002), Henry Adobor and Ronald S. McMullen, "Strategic Partnering in E-Commerce: Guidelines for Managing Alliances," p. 75, Copyright © 2002, with permission from Elsevier.

rather than fax and conventional mail for design and engineering collaboration with several dozen suppliers. By electronically integrating ordering, inventory, and sales data with wholesalers via the Internet, Moen seeks to match the success it achieved on the supply side of the channel on the sales side of the channel. The partnership helped Moen attain not only greater efficiency and speed but a dramatic reduction in order errors, which had been running as high as 40 percent from the wholesalers' use of fax orders.[51]

In the industrial sector, Caterpillar, which has been mentioned on several previous occasions in this text, is known around the world for the quality of the relationships it has built with its dealers over many decades.[52] Caterpillar summarizes the essence of its philosophy succinctly in a few simple paragraphs in a pamphlet titled *Caterpillar Code of Worldwide Business Conduct and Operating Principles:*

Relationships with Dealers

Caterpillar dealers have often been described as one of the world's best distribution systems and source of the company's marketing strength. It is our intent to maintain independently owned dealers wherever satisfactory results are—or can be—achieved. We seek close, long-lasting relationships with such dealers.

We support dealers with a worldwide network of corporate parts facilities. We provide a wide range of assistance to dealers to help assure high quality support for Caterpillar products.

Caterpillar dealership agreements embody our commitment to fair competitive practices, and reflect customs and laws of various countries where Caterpillar products are sold. Our obligations under these agreements are to be observed scrupulously.[53]

The Rust-Oleum Corporation, which sells both consumer and industrial products, provides another example of a firm that stresses a partnership approach in dealing with its distributors. Rust-Oleum has been especially adept at developing programs based on a sensitivity to distributor needs along with a working-together theme in all of the company's efforts to motivate its distributors. The Rust-Oleum Partners-in-Profit program—which offers deferred payments, special advertising allowances, and other assistance that helps distributors reduce their inventory burden and increase profits on a continuing basis—is a good example of this type of partnership approach to supporting channel members. Figure 9.6 shows the cover from the brochure explaining the program to distributors.

FIGURE 9.6 Cover from Rust-Oleum Corporation Brochure Describing a Partnership Program for Distributors

Source: Courtesy of Rust-Oleum Corporation, Vernon Hills, IL 60601.

Finally, Alcoa (Aluminum Company of America) has also been acclaimed in the industrial market for developing sophisticated partnerships with its distributors—cooperative efforts that go to extraordinary lengths, not only in dealing with the broad principles for creating successful partnerships (as outlined in Figure 9.4), but also in attending to even the smallest details of the relationship. The following situation related by Ron Kregarise, a senior Alcoa executive, shows just how Alcoa's partnership with its channel members is focused on the details of the operation:

> *Sometimes, when a distributor stacks the skids, they don't stack the skid with a package ticket on the outside. We only put a package ticket on one end, so the forklift driver can have a difficult time isolating and identifying a particular skid that their internal paperwork requires. Why not put a package ticket at both ends so that when a guy stacks it, it doesn't matter which way he stacks it, he can always see what the package number is. It is not a big thing, but it makes it easier for the customer to do business with Alcoa rather than our competitors, and there are a number of similar examples. We call them groundball singles or bunts, rather than home runs.*[54]

So, channel partnerships or strategic alliances can involve "home runs"—such as the direct linking of channel members with the manufacturer through electronic data interchange (EDI), such as the example of Procter & Gamble and Walmart, Rust-Oleum, or Caterpillar—or, the "groundball singles" of paying attention to the myriad details of channel member needs and problems, such as Alcoa's placement of an additional package ticket. Just as in baseball, the development of winning channel partnerships and alliances often involves combining home runs and singles with many other aspects of the game.

Distribution Programming

The most comprehensive approach for achieving a highly motivated channel team is that of **distribution programming**. Distribution programming goes beyond the typical partnership or strategic alliance because it deals with virtually all aspects of the channel relationship. McCammon, who pioneered the concept of distribution programming, defines it as *a comprehensive set of policies for the promotion of a product through the channel.*[55]

The essence of this approach is the development of a planned, professionally managed channel. The program is developed as a joint effort between the manufacturer and the channel members to incorporate the needs of both. If done well, the program should offer all channel members the advantages of a vertically integrated channel while at the same time allowing them to maintain their status as independent business firms. Automobile manufacturer BMW (Bayerische Motorren Werke), for example, developed a distribution programming approach with its independent auto dealers to meet the challenge of selling the large numbers of used BMW's on dealers' lots.[56] The popularity of leasing new luxury cars instead of buying them creates a huge quantity of preowned (used) late-model cars when the leases expire after two to three years. The challenge for BMW and its dealers was how to sell this glut of off-lease BMWs efficiently and profitably. BMW's answer was the development of the "Certified Preowned" used vehicle program. This is a carefully and thoroughly programmed approach to recycling these cars so that BMW, its dealers, and consumers are all happy with the arrangement. From the $20 million that BMW spends annually on TV advertising to support the program, to special financing arrangements, meticulous mechanical inspections of each vehicle by the dealers to BMW's specifications, and special warranty provisions covering consumers for six years or 100,000 miles, virtually every detail in the Certified Preowned Program has been anticipated and built into the program. So, BMW dealers literally do not have to think about how to go about selling off-lease cars because BMW's distribution programming approach has worked out all the strategy and tactics down to the last detail.

The first step in developing a comprehensive distribution program is an analysis by the manufacturer of marketing objectives and the kinds and levels of support needed from channel members to achieve these objectives.[57] Further, the manufacturer must ascertain the needs and problem areas of channel members (see previous sections of this chapter for methods of doing this). Table 9.3 outlines some of the major areas that should be included in the analysis for both the manufacturer and the channel members.

After this analysis has been completed, the specific channel policies can be formulated. There are a myriad of possible channel policies that the manufacturer may use,

TABLE 9.3 A FRAME OF REFERENCE FOR DISTRIBUTION PROGRAMMING

Manufacturer's Marketing Goals

Based on a careful analysis of:
Corporate capability
Competition
Demand
Cost–volume relationships
Legal considerations
Reseller capability and stated in terms of:
Sales (dollars and units)
Market share
Contribution to overhead
Rate of return on investment
Customer attitude, preference, and "readiness-to-buy" indices

Manufacturer's Channel Requirements

Reseller support needed to achieve marketing goals stated in terms of:
Coverage ratio
Amount and location of display space
Level and composition of inventory investment
Service capability and standards
Advertising, sales promotion, and personal selling support
Market development activities

Retailer's Requirements

Compensation expected for required support stated in terms of:
Managerial aspirations
Trade preferences
Financial goals
Rate of inventory turnover
Rate of return on investment
Gross margin (dollars and percent)
Contribution to overhead (dollars and percent)
Gross margin and contribution to overhead per dollar invested in inventory
Gross margin and contribution to overhead per unit of space
Nonfinancial goals

Distribution Policies

Price concessions
Financial assistance
Protective provisions

Source: From *Vertical Marketing Systems*, ed. Louis P. Bucklin, p. 33. Scott, Foresman, 1970. Copyright © Louis P. Bucklin. All rights reserved. Reproduced by permission.

depending on the type of industry involved, the nature of the channel members involved, and past practices in the channel. Nevertheless, virtually all of the policy options available can be categorized into three major groups:

1. Those offering price concessions to channel members
2. Those offering financial assistance
3. Those offering some kind of protection for channel members

Table 9.4 lists a number of the more frequently encountered policy options in each category.

With a comprehensive list of possible channel policy options such as that shown in Table 9.4, together with the analyses of the manufacturer's goals and the needs and problems of channel members, a programmed merchandising agreement can be developed for the channel members. An outline of such an agreement is shown in Table 9.5. Finally, Table 9.6 contrasts a conventional channel relationship with one characterized by a distribution programming arrangement.

TABLE 9.4 EXAMPLES OF CHANNEL POLICY OPTIONS

I. "Price" Concessions

    A. Discount Structure:
        trade (functional) discounts
        quantity discounts
        cash discounts
        anticipation allowances
        free goods
        prepaid freight
        new product, display, and advertising
          allowances (without performance
          requirements)
        seasonal discounts
        mixed carload privilege
        drop shipping privilege
        trade deals

    B. Discount Substitutes:
        display materials
        premarked merchandise
        inventory control programs
        catalogs and sales promotion
          literature
        training programs
        shelf-stocking programs
        advertising matrices
        management consulting services
        merchandising programs
        sales "spiffs"
        technical assistance
        payment of sales personnel
          and demonstrator salaries
        promotional and advertising
          allowances (with performance
          requirements)

II. Financial Assistance

    A. Conventional Lending Arrangements:
        term loans
        inventory floor plans
        notes payable financing
        accounts payable financing
        installment financing of fixtures and equipment
        lease and note guarantee programs
        accounts receivable financing

    B. Extended Dating:
        E.O.M. dating
        seasonal dating
        R.O.G. dating
        "extra" dating
        postdating

III. Protective Provisions

    A. Price Protection:
        premarked merchandise
        "franchise" pricing
        agency agreements

    B. Inventory Protection:
        consignment selling
        memorandum selling
        liberal returns allowances
        rebate programs
        reorder guarantees
        guaranteed support of sales events
        maintenance of "spot" stocks and fast delivery

    C. Territorial Protection:
        selective distribution
        exclusive distribution

TABLE 9.5 OUTLINE OF A PROGRAMMED MERCHANDISING AGREEMENT

1. **Merchandising Goals**
   a. Planned sales
   b. Planned initial markup percentage
   c. Planned reductions, including planned markdown, shortages, and discounts
   d. Planned gross margin
   e. Planned expense ratio (optional)
   f. Planned profit margin (optional)

2. **Inventory Plan**
   a. Planned rate of inventory turnover
   b. Planned merchandise assortments, including basic or model stock plans
   c. Formalized "never out" lists
   d. Desired mix of promotional versus regular merchandise

3. **Merchandise Presentation Plan**
   a. Recommended store fixtures
   b. Space allocation plan
   c. Visual merchandising plan
   d. Needed promotional materials, including point-of-purchase displays, consumer literature, and price signs

4. **Personal Selling Plan**
   a. Recommended sales presentations
   b. Sales training plan
   c. Special incentive arrangements, including "spiffs," salespeople's contests, and related activities

5. **Advertising and Sales Promotion Plan**
   a. Advertising and sales promotion budget
   b. Media schedule
   c. Copy themes for major campaigns and promotions
   d. Special sales events

6. **Responsibilities and Due Dates**
   a. Supplier's responsibilities in connection with the plan
   b. Retailer's responsibilities in connection with the plan

Source: From *Vertical Marketing Systems*, ed. Louis P. Bucklin, p. 33. Scott, Foresman, 1970. Copyright © Louis P. Bucklin. All rights reserved. Reproduced by permission.

TABLE 9.6 COMPARISON OF CHARACTERISTICS OF SUPPLIER/RETAILER RELATIONSHIPS IN A CONVENTIONAL CHANNEL VERSUS A PROGRAMMED SYSTEM

CHARACTERISTIC	CONVENTIONAL CHANNEL	PROGRAMMED SYSTEM
Nature of contacts	Negotiations on an individual order basis	Advance joint planning for an extended time period
Information considered	Supplier sales presentation	Retailer's merchandising data
Supplier participants	Supplier's territorial salesperson	Salesperson and major regional or headquarters executive
Retailer participants	Buyer	Various executives, perhaps top management
Retailer's goals	Sales gain and percent markup	Programmed total profitability
Supplier's goals	Big order on each call	Continuing profitable relationship
Nature of performance evaluation	Event centered; primarily related to sales volume and other short-term performance criteria	Specific performance criteria written into the program

Source: Reprinted with permission from *Marketing News*, published by the American Marketing Association, Ronald L. Ernst, "Distribution Channel 'Detente' Benefits Suppliers, Retailers, and Consumers."

Ethan Allen Interiors Inc., a leading manufacturer of furniture and home furnishings, is a good example of a firm that stresses the distribution programming approach to supporting its channel members. Ethan Allen's retail network consists of almost 300 stores in the United States and several foreign countries. About half of these stores are company-owned while the rest are independent. But, except for the ownership, virtually no differences exist in the strategy and operations of the company-owned and independent retailers. All of the management and marketing strategies and operations of Ethan Allen's independent retailers have been precisely programmed by Ethan Allen to conform with its approach to the sale of home furnishings. The Ethan Allen program specifies that retailers carry no competing products from other manufacturers. The furniture styles, almost all of which are manufactured by Ethan Allen, are also kept stable for years, and most items are open stock so that customers can add additional pieces at later dates. Ethan Allen also controls the outside and inside appearance of the stores, from architecture to layout, lighting to display, closely. The company programs even the method of selling the furniture. It usually consists of visits to the home by the store's "designers" (Ethan Allen does not use the term salespeople), who help customers select furniture and accessories according to a decorating plan prepared by the designer. Most advertising, special events, promotions, and sales are also developed and administered by Ethan Allen rather than by the independent retailers. The company also sends retailers' salespeople (designers) to Ethan Allen College. At the "college"—a series of special training sessions—they learn not only about home decorating techniques, but also, and perhaps more important, about the Ethan Allen "way of doing things." The program is designed to build a sense of teamwork between Ethan Allen and its independent retailers in an effort to "turn customers into clients" and thereby foster long-term relationships with the kind of repeat sales that are less sensitive to economic slowdowns and price-slashing competitors.

This programmed approach to channel member support has created a distinct niche for Ethan Allen in the fiercely competitive furniture market. Rather than competing on price, as is so common in the home furnishings industry, Ethan Allen retailers—thanks to the company's carefully programmed approach—are able to compete on the basis of quality, service, and customer assistance while achieving better-than-average gross margin and net profits in the process.

Distribution programming is also the approach used in many franchised channels, especially in the service sector.[58] McDonald's in fast food, Holiday Inn in hotels, and Century 21 in real estate, for example have highly-developed distribution programs for motivating their franchise channel members. Indeed, virtually every facet down to the smallest operational detail is preprogrammed for the franchisees. McDonald's, for instance, specifies exactly how a McDonald's restaurant should be designed and precisely what it can and cannot have in it (vending machines and telephones, for example, are specifically prohibited). Similarly, Holiday Inn has an exact set of policies and standards that each franchisee must live up to when offering lodging services to the public; and Century 21 has a set of services and an approach to selling real estate that must be followed by all individual agencies franchised by Century 21. Such rigorous distribution programs developed within the framework of a formal franchise contract result in a very closely knit, highly controlled form of distribution. Such arrangements go well beyond the partnership approach, to the higher level of leader (the franchisor) and followers (the franchisees). We will examine these issues in greater detail in Chapter 16, Franchise Marketing Channels.

Providing Leadership to Motivate Channel Members

Even if the channel manager has developed an excellent system for learning about channel members' needs and problems, and no matter what approach is used to support them, control must still be exercised through effective leadership on a continuing basis to attain a well-motivated team of channel members.[59]

Seldom is it possible for the channel manager to achieve total control, no matter how much power underlies his or her leadership attempts.[60] This state would exist only if the channel manager were able to predict all events related to the channel with perfect accuracy, and achieve the desired outcomes at all times. For the most part, this is a theoretical state not achievable in the reality of an interorganizational system such as the marketing channel. Over four decades ago, Little explained succinctly the problems of achieving high levels of control and leadership in this interorganizational setting:

> *Because firms are loosely arranged, the advantages of central direction are in large measure missing. The absence of single ownership, or close contractual agreements, means that the benefits of a formal power (superior, subordinate) base are not realized. The reward and penalty system is not as precise and is less easily effected. Similarly, overall planning for the entire system is uncoordinated and the perspective necessary to maximize total system effort is diffused. Less recognition of common goals by various member firms in the channel, as compared to a formally structured organization, is also probable.*[61]

As Little points out, the interorganizational setting of the marketing channel creates a set of conditions that makes strong leadership more difficult to achieve. This is particularly the case in channels that have evolved as a group of loosely-aligned firms. But even in channels that have been designed to foster a higher degree of control, such as those based on contractual commitments or distribution programming, the special circumstances attendant to interorganizational systems discussed by Little do not completely disappear. Thus, even though the basis for control through strong leadership is significantly greater in formally-structured or contractual channels, such as in franchised channels, it does not often equal the level achieved in an intraorganizational setting.[62] This is not meant to suggest that the channel manager cannot hope to exercise a high level of leadership in an effort to motivate independent channel members.[63] Rather, we are simply pointing out that, in attempting to do so, the channel manager will face a more difficult set of problems. But even in the difficult context of the marketing channel, effective leadership of channel members can produce good results.

The award-winning channel management program used by Cisco Systems, the world's largest manufacturer of high-tech networking products such as routers, switches, and products for integrating voice, videos, data, and security systems in computer networks helps to show the important role of leadership in the motivation of channel members.[64] While Cisco Systems uses a variety of channels to reach its tens of thousands of final customers, one of its most important channels, accounting for over $30 billion in sales, is what Cisco refers to as its "value-add channel resellers" or VARs. The VARs are channel members that go well beyond the mere reselling of Cisco products. Rather, the VARs develop close relationships with customers to learn about their networking needs, integrate hardware and software and develop customized solutions to solve customer problems. Often the VARs will utilize third-party products if they offer better and more economical alternatives to Cisco products. VARs can also provide planning assistance, design, installation, support, remote monitoring, and provide network management assistance.

Because these VAR channel partners provide such an extraordinary level of high-value services to final customers, typical volume-based incentive programs whereby channel members are rewarded essentially based on how much sales volume they produce are not an effective basis for motivating this class of channel members. Why? Because a volume-based incentive system whereby the more of the manufacturer's products the channel member sells, the higher the discount offered to the VAR, does not recognize the extraordinary effort and expense incurred by the VARs in providing an array of high-value services to final customers.

Cisco Systems' approach to managing its VAR channel recognized early on the shortcomings of the volume-based incentive system. By the dawn of the twenty-first century, Cisco's enlightened channel leadership produced an incentive system that provided equal rewards to channel members having similar capabilities to provide high-value services to final customers regardless of how much Cisco product each sold. Specifically, channel partners would be compensated with incentives tied to various types of value-added behavior by transaction as opposed to rewards based on total volume of Cisco products resold by the channel partner.

To make this value-based model work, Cisco provides broad and intensive leadership by offering training, an extensive Cisco certification program, and by establishing performance targets on a variety of metrics including end-user satisfaction, level of VAR investment, as well as VAR profitability.

As alluded to earlier, Cisco's superior channel leadership has resulted in several industry awards including the VAR Annual Report Card (ARC) for eight consecutive years, the Computer Reseller News (CRN) Channel Champions award over the same eight-year period, and perhaps the most important accolade of all—adoption of much of Cisco's channel management model by Microsoft!

Summary

Even when the marketing channel has been carefully designed to reflect a near optimum allocation of the distribution tasks, strong cooperation from the channel members cannot be expected as a matter of course. Rather, channel management—the administration of existing channels to secure the cooperation of channel members in achieving the firm's distribution objectives—is necessary.

A fundamental part of channel management is that of motivating the channel members to perform their tasks effectively and efficiently. In order to motivate channel members successfully, the channel manager must deal with three major facets of motivation management in the channel: (1) learning about the needs and problems of channel members, (2) developing programs to support their needs and helping them to deal with their particular problem areas, and (3) providing leadership.

Finding out the needs and problems of channel members is not a matter of happenstance. The channel manager cannot rely solely on existing channel communication systems to yield all of the relevant information concerning channel member needs and problems. Rather, at times the channel manager must look beyond the regular flow of information in the channel to gather the necessary data by using such approaches as (1) research studies of channel members conducted by the firm, (2) research studies by outside parties to assure objectivity, (3) periodic marketing channel audits, and (4) distributor advisory councils.

Once the channel manager has the necessary information on channel member needs and problems, support programs must be developed to address them. Good support programs require careful planning. Ad hoc, piecemeal, or "quick fix" approaches to channel member support are becoming increasingly unacceptable to channel members.

Planned approaches to channel member support can generally be grouped into one of three categories: (1) cooperative arrangements, (2) partnerships or strategic alliances, and (3) distribution programming.

The cooperative approach is the least sophisticated and comprehensive approach to channel member support. Basically, the manufacturer and the channel members agree on a series of cooperative activities such as cooperative advertising, promotional allowances, or incentive programs. If the cooperative program offered by the manufacturer is on target in terms of meeting channel member needs and problems, and if it is carefully planned and supervised, it can be an effective means for motivating channel members.

The partnership (or strategic alliance) concept is a more sophisticated and comprehensive approach to channel member motivation. Essentially, partnerships or strategic alliances are based on a careful delineation of the mutual roles of the manufacturer and the channel members—that is, the kinds of commitments that the manufacturer expects from the channel members and the kinds of support that the channel members can expect from the manufacturer. The idea underlying such a relationship is mutual support between manufacturer and channel members in order to create a well-organized team effort in the distribution of the manufacturer's products. If well-

developed and well-executed, the partnership or strategic alliance approach can provide an excellent basis for motivating channel members.

Finally, distribution programming offers the most sophisticated and comprehensive approach to channel member motivation. Distribution programming involves the development of a comprehensive plan for managing the marketing channel. Key areas of the relationship between manufacturer and channel members are studied and a comprehensive channel management plan is developed to cover all of those areas. Typically, such programs are initiated and directed by the manufacturer, but channel members at the wholesale or retail levels can also initiate and direct distribution programming arrangements.

Regardless of which approach the channel manager uses to motivate channel members, leadership must still be exercised on a continuing basis if the motivation programs are to operate effectively and viably. In attempting to exercise such leadership, however, the channel manager must remember to deal with several significant challenges characteristic of the interorganizational setting of the marketing channel. Among these are (1) the looseness of the organization of the many channel systems, (2) a proclivity by channel members to avoid central direction, (3) lack of single ownership, and (4) no clear demarcation of a super-subordinate relationship.

Review Questions

1. Discuss the distinction between channel management and channel design.

2. Even if a marketing channel has been carefully designed in such a way that its structure reflects a near-optimal allocation of distribution tasks, the channel cannot be expected to "run" by itself. Discuss this statement.

3. An effective information flow in the channel is all that is needed to inform the channel manager of the needs and problems of channel members. Do you agree or disagree? Discuss.

4. What are some of the major sources of interaction that exist in the typical channel communications system?

5. Discuss the major features of the four approaches for finding out about channel member needs and problems discussed in this chapter.

6. Compare and contrast the major features of cooperative arrangements, partnerships and strategic alliances, and distribution programming as approaches for motivating channel members.

7. Discuss the differences between a conventional channel and a channel based on a distribution programming arrangement.

8. Discuss the concept of leadership as it applies to motivating channel members.

9. What are some of the problems faced by the channel manager in attempting to exercise leadership to motivate channel members in the interorganizational setting of the marketing channel?

10. What particular facets of the Cisco Systems case indicate effective leadership in motivating the firm's channel members?

Channel Issues for Discussion

1. Steinway & Sons has manufactured the world's best pianos for well over a century. Steinway sells its pianos in the U.S. through less than 75 carefully selected dealers. The quality of Steinway pianos is unquestionably very high, but for a time Steinway's management of its channel could make no such quality claim. It seems that Steinway was not sufficiently aware of its dealers' problems including low profit margins on the pianos, slow-moving inventory, and high costs associated with supplying Steinway pianos to performers (a service all dealers were expected to provide). Indeed, Steinway's main focus was on getting its dealers to stock more inventory, upgrade their showrooms, and hire more salespeople. Steinway's answer for dealing with this manufacturer/dealer disconnect was to send its president and CEO out on the road for half a year to visit the dealers in person so as to learn first-hand about their needs and problems.

   What do you think of Steinway's approach for learning about its channel members' needs and problems? Is there a better way to do this? Would Steinway's approach be feasible for other companies? Explain.

2. The ubiquitous Bic razors, cigarette lighters, and, of course, ballpoint pens are sold by more than 100,000 supermarkets, drugstores, and other mass merchandisers in the United States. Bic Corporation has traditionally relied on large numbers of mass marketers to sell these products.

   Can Bic Corporation be "partners" with each of the 100,000 retailers selling these products? Explain why or why not?

3. Harley-Davidson Inc. is one of the world's most well recognized companies because of its famous motorcycles—often referred to as "Hogs" by bike enthusiasts. During most of the 1990s, Harley motorbikes were in short supply, so Harley's 600 independent dealers had no trouble moving the bikes out the door almost as soon as they arrived from the factory—often at prices higher than the sticker price. But by 2001, just around the 100th anniversary of Harley-Davidson, things began to slow down, reflecting the stagnant economy. Bikes were not rolling out of the dealer showrooms as fast, and in fact, inventories in dealerships all over the country were starting to grow even though some of the bikes were offered at substantial discounts. Yet even in the face of slowing sales to consumers, Harley-Davidson was able to show an annual sales increase of over 25 percent. How was this possible? Harley was booking shipments of the bikes to dealers as if they were final sales to customers. Many of the dealers were very unhappy with this practice, often referring to it as "channel stuffing"—loading up the dealers with inventory that outstrips final customer demand to give the appearance of sales growth.

   Are the dealers just being "crybabies" in accusing Harley-Davidson of channel stuffing? Is this just one-way channel partnership with the dealers being fair-weather friends? Discuss.

4. Mary Robinson, vice president of marketing for a famous men's dress shirt manufacturer, had spent three months working on the in-store promotional campaign to be used for the new all-cotton, easy-care shirt line. The campaign stressed an unusual point-of-purchase fixture: a life-sized cardboard figure wearing one of the actual shirts. Department stores and specialty stores were expected to use this display to attract customers' attention to the new line by featuring it prominently. Robinson had played a major role in creating this dealer promotion and was rather proud of it. The campaign had now been going on for six weeks and she was anxiously awaiting the report prepared by the company's marketing research department, due that afternoon. She just knew it would be laudatory. In fact, however, most of the retailers thought the campaign was a disaster—especially the life-sized cardboard sign that many of them did not have the space to display. And even if they did, they added, they thought it would be gauche to do so.

   Can Mary be sure that the research report that will be on her desk that afternoon will fully and accurately convey the retailers' opinions? Discuss.

5. For decades, McDonald's was almost universally admired as the leader in the fast-food industry.

Its franchise system was the envy of virtually all the other fast-food chains. But at the start of the new millennium, problems that had been festering during the late 1990s began not only to undermine McDonald's enviable reputation but also to hit the top and bottom lines. Same-store sales fell off by as much as 10 percent for many units and net profits went down even more. Ironically, a major cause of the problem McDonald's was experiencing resulted from an attempt to improve its products. McDonald's and many of its franchisees made a huge investment in kitchen technology to enable the restaurant to custom-make food to individual customer orders so it would be fresher and tastier than the premade products kept hot under warming lights. But the new approach, which McDonald's called "Made for You," slowed down service dramatically. This in turn created a "chain reaction" of unhappy customers as well as employees who felt frustrated at not being able to meet customers' demands for speedier service. Moreover, the employees felt abused when customers complained to them. McDonald's claims the franchisees have not learned how to use the new kitchen technology properly, while the franchisees say the new technology is flawed and poorly-designed.

What do *you* think is going on here? Does McDonald's really understand the needs and problems of its franchisees? Was the support in the form of an attempt to provide a better product for the customer misdirected? Discuss.

6. GTE's Sylvania Lighting Division introduced "Prestige Partnership," a program aimed at helping its 2,200 distributors do a more effective job of marketing Sylvania products. In particular, the program will help the distributors locate market segments for which Sylvania products are especially well suited. Through a database called Sylvania Source, detailed data will be provided on the names, addresses, and phone numbers of businesses, as well as the names of the individuals in charge of ordering lighting products, the annual sales potentials of the customers, and the number of lighting fixtures each customer has. Sylvania and its distributors also do a road show with a "Lightmobile" created by Sylvania to provide customers with a mobile

educational program on lighting applications. All this augments Sylvania's "Techniques for Better Lighting" information kit, which the distributors make available to final customers. The partnership has been wholeheartedly embraced by distributors, according to Sylvania, and has motivated them to become better marketers of Sylvania products.

Why do you think Sylvania's partnership program is effective? Discuss from the standpoint of the distributors' needs and problems. Does the partnership program suggest effective leadership on Sylvania's part? Explain.

7. FilmDistrict, a newly-formed film studio and distributor worked out a deal with Netflix, Inc. to stream new movies over the Internet just a few months after they are released on DVDs. Under the terms of the agreement, new movies from FilmDistrict will be licensed exclusively to Netflix instead of appearing on premium cable channels. Industry observers believe this deal reflects the new realities of changing channels for movies from theaters, home videos, and cable pay TV to online streaming. Netflix also has a similar deal with Relativity Media, the movie company that financed the highly-acclaimed boxing movie, *The Fighter*.

Given the rapid and dramatic changes occurring in film distribution channels, how might partnerships or alliances such as that between Netflix and FilmDistrict be helpful to either firm in managing their distribution channels?

8. Toyota Motor Corporation took extraordinary care in developing the channel and selecting the dealers for its Lexus luxury cars. The attention to detail in setting up the channel for the Lexus is reminiscent of the kind of care Toyota gives to the building of its cars. In fact, standards for the dealerships cover such minute details as setting specifications for doorknob designs and the grade of rice paper for *sohji* screens used to decorate the dealerships. It would seem that everything had been so carefully planned that the Lexus dealerships should virtually run themselves.

Comment on this situation in terms of the need for channel management and the motivation of channel members.

References

1. For an excellent overview and analysis of the major themes underlying channel management, see Gary L. Frazier, "Organizing and Managing Channels of Distribution," *Journal of the Academy of Marketing Science* (Spring 1999): 226–240.

2. For a related discussion, see: Margarida Duarte and Gary Davies, "Trust as a Mediator of Channel Power," *Journal of Marketing Channels* (Vol. 11, nos. 2/3 2004): 77–102; Jan B. Heide, "Interorganizational Governance in Marketing Channels," *Journal of Marketing* (January 1994): 71–85.

3. Melina Parker, Kerrie Bridson, and Jody Evans, "Motivations for Developing Direct Trade Relationships," *International Journal of Retail & Distribution Management* (Vol. 34, no. 2/3 2006): 121–134; Steven J. Skinner, Julie B. Gassenheimer, and Scott W. Kelley, "Cooperation in Supplier–Dealer Relations," *Journal of Retailing* (Summer 1992): 174–193; Deborah Salmond and Robert Spekman, "Collaboration as a Mode of Managing Long-Term Buyer–Seller Relationships," in *Proceedings of the Annual Educators' Conference of the American Marketing Association*, eds. Terrence Shimp et al. (Chicago: American Marketing Association, 1986), 162–166; and William T. Ross, "Managing Marketing Channel Relationships," Working Paper No. 85–106 (Cambridge, Mass: Marketing Science Institute, July 1985): 1–17.

4. Julie G. Gassenheimer, Roger J. Calantone, and Joseph I. Scully, "Supplier Involvement and Dealer Satisfaction: Implications for Enhancing Channel Relationships," *Journal of Business and Industrial Marketing* 10, no. 2 f(1995): 7–19.

5. Janice M. Payan and John R. Nevin, "Influence Strategy Efficacy in Supplier–Distributor Relationships," *Journal of Business Research* (Vol. 59, 2006): 457–467; Richard Lee Miller, William F. Lewis, and L. Paul Merenski, "A Value Exchange Model for the Channel of Distribution: Implications for Management and Research," *Journal of the Academy of Marketing Science* (Fall 1985): 2–4.

6. Lester E. Goodman and Paul A. Dion, "The Determinants of Commitment in the Distributor–Manufacturer Relationship," *Industrial Marketing Management* 30 (2001): 287–300.

7. For a related discussion, see Nermine Eyuboglu, "Securing Marketing Support from Channel Members: Insights from an Empirical Study," in *Proceedings of the Sixth Bi-Annual World Marketing Congress*, eds. M. Joseph Sirgy, Kenneth D. Bahn, and Tunc Erem (Blacksburg, Va.: Academy of Marketing Science, 1993), 140–145; David Shipley, "What British Distributors Dislike about Manufacturers," *Industrial Marketing Management* (May 1987): 153–162; and Patrick L. Shul, Taylor E. Little Jr., and William M. Pride, "Channel Climate: Its Impact on Channel Members' Satisfaction," *Journal of Retailing* (Summer 1985): 9–38.

8. James A. Narus, N. Mohan Reddy, and George L. Pinchak, "Key Problems Facing Industrial Distributors," *Industrial Marketing Management* (August 1984): 139–147; and James C. Anderson and James A. Narus, "A Model of the Distributor's Perspective of Distributor–Manufacturer Working Relationships," *Journal of Marketing* 48 (Fall 1984): 62–74.

9. Phillip McVey, "Are Channels of Distribution What the Textbooks Say?" *Journal of Marketing* 24 (January 1960): 61–65.

10. Jeff Bennett, "Chrysler Ads Aim to Rebuild Image," *Wall Street Journal* (June 9, 2010): B1.

11. John D. Stoll, "GM Plans a Return to Car Leasing," *Wall Street Journal* (July 29, 2010): B1.

12. For a related discussion, see Judy A. Siguaw, Penny M. Simpson, and Thomas L. Baker, "Effects of Supplier Market Orientation on Distributor Market Orientation and the Channel Relationship: The Distributor Perspective," *Journal of Marketing* (July 1998): 99–111.

13. See Kenneth A. Hunt and Cathy Hartman, "Attribution Theory in Channels of Distribution: Extensions and Applications," in *Developments in Marketing Science, Proceedings of the Annual Conference of the Academy of Marketing Science*, ed. Kenneth D. Bahn (Academy of Marketing Science, 1988), 465–469; and Gary L. Frazier and Jagdish N. Sheth, "An Attitude-Behavior Framework for Distribution Channel Management," *Journal of Marketing* 49 (Summer 1985): 38–48.

14. For an excellent analysis of the socio-psychological factors underlying channel relationships see: W. Bruce Wrenn and John J. Withey, "Modes of Social Interaction Between Organizations: A Social-Psychological Explanation of Relationships Between Channel Dyads," *Journal of Marketing Channels* (Vol. 11, no. 4, 2004): 43–59.

15. For a related discussion, see J. Thomas M. Hult, Ann-Christine M. Hult, and Bryan A. Lukas, "Creating Shared Vision in the Marketing Channel Network," *Journal of Marketing Channels* 5, no. 3/4; (1996): 1–18.

16. Gerald Meyers, "Trade Buyers Are Influential but Underresearched," *Marketing News* (February 1, 1988): 12.

17. See for example: Joseph F. Kovar, "VARs to Dell: Good Start, Now Here's What We Want," *AVAYA* (May 18, 2007): 1–4.

18. Ellen M. Kleinberg, "Improving Distributor Relations: Communications Solves Most Problems," *Industrial Marketing* (February 1981): 72.

19. Meyers, "Trade Buyers Are Influential but Underresearched," 120.

20. Revis Cox, Thomas F. Schutte, and Kendrik S. Few, "Toward the Analysis of Trade Channel Perception," in *Combined Proceedings 1971 Spring and Fall Conference of the American Marketing Association*, ed. Fred C. Allvine (Chicago: American Marketing Association, 1972), 189–193.

21. Roger J. Calantone and Jule B. Gassenheimer, "Overcoming Basic Problems between Manufacturers and Distributors," *Industrial Marketing Management* 20 (1991): 215–221.

22. For perspective on a type of marketing channel audit referred to as "Relationship Appraisal," see Stuart A. Hanmen-Lloyd, "Relationship Appraisal: A Route to Improved Reseller Channel Performance," *Industrial Marketing Management* 25 (1996): 173–185.

23. For an in-depth analysis of issues that might emerge, particularly in the context of opportunistic behavior by channel members, see Kenneth H. Wathne and Jan B. Heide, "Opportunism in Interfirm Relationships: Forms, Outcomes, and Solutions," *Journal of Marketing* (October 2000): 36–51.

24. Gene L. Bego, "Joint Benefits of a Distributor Council," in *Building a Sound Distributor Organization* (New York: National Industrial Conference Board, 1964), 44–49.

25. Maxim Lenderman, "Mind Games: Anheuser-Busch Wants Its Wholesaler's Whole Attention," *Beverage World* (September 1996): 70–74.

26. Donald V. Fites, "Make Your Dealers Your Partners," *Harvard Business Review* (March–April 1996): 84–95.

27. For a very interesting study involving channel relationships in the brewing industry, see Lynne D. Richardson and Robert A. Robicheaux, "Supplier's Desire to Influence Related to Perceived Use of Power and Performance," *Journal of Business Research* 25 (1992): 243–250.

28. Other crucial factors can affect such an outcome, however; see Kirti Sawhney Celly and Gary L. Frazier, "Outcome-Based and Behavior-Based Coordination Effects in Channel Relationships," *Journal of Marketing Research* (May 1996): 200–210.

29. Sholnn Freeman, "Chrysler's Chief Takes to the Road to Rev Up Dealers," *Wall Street Journal* (November 12, 2003): B2.

30. See, for example, Janet E. Keith, Donald W. Jackson, Jr., and Lawrence A. Crosby, "Effects of Alternative Types of Influence Strategies under Different Channel Dependency Structures," *Journal of Marketing* 54 (July 1990): 30–41; Erin Anderson, Leonard M. Lodish, and Barton A. Weitz, "Resource Allocation Behavior in Conventional Channels," *Journal of Marketing Research*

(February 1987): 85–97; J. Joseph Cronin, Jr., and Michael H. Morris, "Satisfying Customer Expectations: The Effect on Conflict and Repurchase Intentions in Industrial Marketing Channels," *Journal of the Academy of Marketing Science* (Winter 1989): 41–49; and Gary L. Frazier and John O. Summers, "Interfirm Influence Strategies and Their Application within Distribution Channels," *Journal of Marketing* 48 (Summer 1984): 43–55.

31. Bert C. McCammon, Jr., "Perspectives of Distribution Programming," in *Vertical Marketing Systems*, ed. Louis P. Bucklin (Glenview, Ill.: Scott, Foresman, 1970), 32.

32. See for example: Stefan Wuyts and Inge Geyskens, "The Formation of Buyer–Supplier Relationships: Detailed Contract Drafting and Close Partners Selection," *Journal of Marketing* (October 2005): 103–117; Ignacio Rodriguez del Bosque Rodriguez, Jesus Callado Agudo, and Hector San Martin Gutierrez, "Determinants of Economic and Social Satisfaction in Manufacturer–Distributor Relationships," *Industrial Marketing Management* (Vol. 35 2006): 666–675.

33. See, for example, Bruce J. Walker, Janet E. Keith, and Donald W. Jackson, Jr., "The Channels Manager: Now, Soon, or Never?" *Journal of the Academy of Marketing Science* (Summer 1985): 82–96; Reinhard H. Schmidt and Gerd Wagner, "Risk Distribution and Bonding Mechanisms in Industrial Marketing," *Journal of Business Research* 13 (1985): 421–433; James R. Moore and Donald W. Eckrich, "Marketing Channels from a Manufacturer's Perspective: Are They Really Managed?" in *Marketing: 1776–1976 and Beyond*, ed. Kenneth L. Bernhardt (Chicago: American Marketing Association, 1976), 248–255; and Philip B. Schary and Boris W. Becker, "Distribution as a Decision System," in *Combined Proceedings*, 1972 Spring and Fall Conference of the American Marketing Association, eds. Boris W. Becker and Helmut Becker (Chicago: American Marketing Association, 1973), 310–314.

34. John Fine, "Bargain—Rate Buzz," *Business Week* (February 9, 2009): 65–66.

35. For a related discussion, see James E. Zemanek, Jr., "Manufacturer Influence versus Manufacturer Salesperson Influence over the Industrial Distributor," *Industrial Marketing Management* 26 (1997): 59–66.

36. "Levi Strauss: A Touch of Fashion—and a Dash of Humility," *Business Week* (October 24, 1983): 85, 88.

37. Cynthia R. Milsap, "Conquering the Distributor Incentive Blues," *Business Marketing* (November 1985): 122–125.4.

38. See, for example, Henry Adobor and Ronald S. McMullen, "Strategic Partnering in E-Commerce:

Guidelines for Managing Alliances," *Business Horizons* (March–April 2002): 67–76; Louis P. Bucklin and Sanjit Sengupta, "Organizing Successful Co-Marketing Alliances," *Journal of Marketing* 57 (April 1993): 32–46; Bill Dowling, "How to Form Lasting Partnerships," *Industrial Distribution* (June 15, 1992): 75; Bert Rosenbloom, "Motivating Your International Channel Partners," *Business Horizons* (March–April 1990): 53–57; James C. Anderson and James A. Narus, "A Model of Distributor Firm and Manufacturer Firm Working Partnerships," *Journal of Marketing* 54 (January 1990): 42–58; Rajagopalan Sethuraman, James C. Anderson, and James A. Narus, "Partnership Advantage and Its Determinants in Distributor and Manufacturer Working Relationships," *Journal of Business Research* 17 (1988): 327–347; and N. Mohan Reddy and Michael P. Marvin, "Developing a Manufacturer–Distributor Information Partnership," *Industrial Marketing Management* 15 (1986): 157–163.

39. "Apple's Big Partner: iPhone and Wal-Mart," *Business Week* (January 12, 2009): 6; "To Boost Buying Power, Wal-Mart Woos Partners," *Bloomberg Businessweek* (October 11-17, 2010): 36; Mary Ellen Lloyd, "Radio Shack, Verizon Link Up at Sam's Club," *Wall Street Journal* (October 7, 2009): B5B.

40. For an insightful analysis of relationships, partnership, and strategic alliances, see Ashwin W. Joshi, "Long-term Relationships, Partnershps, and Strategic Alliances: A Contingency Theory of Relationship Marketing," *Journal of Marketing Channels* 4 no. 3 (1995): 75–94.

41. For an excellent in-depth research study related to this point, see Erin Anderson and Barton Weitz, "The Use of Pledges to Build and Sustain Commitment in Distribution Channels," *Journal of Marketing Research* 29 (February 1992): 18–24; Also, for an excellent discussion of strategic alliances as a competitive advantage, see James E. Ricks, "Benefits of Domestic Vertical and Horizontal Strategic Alliances," *Journal of Business and Industrial Marketing* 8 no. 4 (1993): 52–57.

42. Jean L. Johnson, "Strategic Integration in Industrial Distribution Channels: Managing the Interfirm Relationship as a Strategic Asset," *Journal of the Academy of Marketing Science* (Winter 1999): 5.

43. Moon Ihlwan and Brian Grow, "Red-Hot White Goods," *Business Week* (October 30, 2006): 48.

44. "Dell Announces Channel Program Details," http//www.phonesplusmag.com/ (Posted on: 12/05/2007).

45. Frederick E. Webster, Jr., "The Role of the Industrial Distributor," *Journal of Marketing* 40 (July 1976): 10–16.

46. Webster, "The Role of the Industrial Distributor," 15.

47. Bert Rosenbloom, "Motivating Independent Distribution Channel Members," *Industrial Marketing Management* (August 1978): 275–281.

48. For an excellent empirical study of environment as one of the key factors affecting supplier/distributor relationships, see Kirti Sawhney Celly and Gary L. Frazier, " Outcome-Based and Behavior-Based Coordination Efforts in Channel Relationships," *Journal of Marketing Research* (May 1996): 200–210.

49. Frank K. Sonnenberg, "Partnering: Entering the Age of Cooperation," *Journal of Business Strategy* (May–June 1992): 51–52.

50. Adobor and McMullen, "Strategic Partnering in E-Commerce," 67.

51. Faith Keenan, "Opening the Spigot," *Business Week@biz* (June 4, 2001): EB17–EB20.

52. Martin Gierke, "Caterpillar Dealer Identity: Customer Loyalty and an Extraordinary Partnership," *Design Management Review* (Winter 2006): 55–61.

53. *Caterpillar Code of Worldwide Business Conduct and Operating Principles*, (Peoria, Ill: Caterpillar Inc. 1992), 6.

54. From B. G. Yovovich, "Partnering at Its Best," *Business Marketing* (March 1992): 36–37.

55. McCammon, "Perspectives in Distribution Programming," 43.

56. Joseph B. White, "Certified Used Cars Star in BMW Ads," *Wall Street Journal* (February 12, 2002): B9.

57. For a related discussion, see Keysuk Kim, "On the Effects of Customer Conditions on Distributor Commitment and Supplier Commitment in Industrial Channels of Distribution," *Journal of Business Research* 51 (2001): 87–99.

58. See for example: Thomas Burkle and Thorsten Posselt, "Franchising as a Plural System: A Risk-Based Explanation," *Journal of Retailing* (Vol. 84, no. 1, 2008): 39–47.

59. For three excellent analyses of leadership and control in marketing channels, see Retha A. Price, "An Investigation of Path-Goal Leadership Theory in Marketing Channels," *Journal of Retailing* (Fall 1991): 339–361; Timothy R. Barnett and Danny R. Arnold, "Justification and Application of Path-Goal Contingency Leadership Theory to Marketing Channel Leadership," *Journal of Business Research* 19 (1989): 283–292; and John B. English and Danny R. Arnold, "An Overview of Channel Control and Control Antecedents," in *Proceedings of the Winter Educators' Conference of the American Marketing Association*, ed. Russel A. Belk (Chicago: American Marketing Association, 1987), 301–306.

60. Adel I. El-Ansary and Robert A. Robicheaux, "A Theory of Channel Control: Revisited," *Journal of Marketing* 38 (January 1974): 2.

61. Robert W. Little, "The Marketing Channel: Who Should Lead This Extra-Corporate Organization," *Journal of Marketing* 34 (January 1970): 32.

62. For a related discussion, see Patrick L. Shul, "An investigation of Path-Goal Leadership Theory and Its Impact on Intrachannel Conflict and Satisfaction," *Journal of the Academy of Marketing Science* (Winter 1987): 42–52.

63. For some alternative approaches to exercising leadership in the channel, see Rajiv Mehta, Trina Larsen, and Bert Rosenbloom, "The Influence of Leadership Style on Co-operation in Channels of Distribution," *International Journal of Physical Ditribution & Logistics Management* 26, no. 6 (1996): 32–59.

64. The material related to Cisco Systems in this section is based on: Kirthi Kalyanam and Surinder Brar, "From Volume to Value: Managing the Value-Add Reseller Channel at Cisco Systems," *California Management Review* (Fall 2009): 94–119.

CHAPTER **10**

Product Issues in Channel Management

LEARNING OBJECTIVES

After reading this chapter you should:

1. Understand the concept of marketing mix variables as resources for channel management.

2. Realize that there are many potential interfaces between product management and channel management.

3. Recognize the most basic interfaces between new product planning and channel management.

4. Know the implications of each stage of the product life cycle for channel management.

5. Be aware of the relationship between strategic product management and channel management.

6. Be cognizant of how product differentiation, product positioning, product line expansion and contraction, trading up and trading down and product brand strategy relate to channel management.

7. Appreciate the role of marketing channels in providing product service.

© OmniTerra Images

FOCUS ON CHANNELS

Can Amazon.com Get Manufacturers to Shrink the Amount of Shrink-Wrapped Product Packaging They Produce?

Shrink-wrapped packaging has become a ubiquitous fact of life for a huge variety of consumer products. Some of this packaging is of the "bullet-proof" hard, clear plastic type that is literally impregnable unless one has a box cutter, knife or heavy-duty shears handy. And even with these implements, the job of getting the product out from under the tough plastic can be difficult and dangerous. In fact, over 6,000 people each year go to emergency rooms from injuries suffered while opening these hard plastic packages. Further, to add insult to injury, this hard plastic, along with the softer kind, is bad for the environment. About 15 percent of the refuse Americans send to landfills is from product packaging, and the plastic component of this mass of trash (both hard and soft) can take up to 600 years to degrade!

One giant retailer, Amazon.com, has decided to do something about the plastic packaging problem by using its clout with the manufacturers whose products it sells to get them to change their ways. Amazon's clout comes not only from its size, with over $35 billion in annual sales, but also from the feedback it gets from its millions of online customers. Many of them have complained to Amazon in no uncertain terms about the problems they've had with product packaging, especially the hard plastic type. Amazon has shared these customer complaints with such mega manufacturers as Procter & Gamble and Philips Electronics, and plans to broaden this information sharing to include many other manufacturers.

So, Amazon.com, with the support of its customers, is already influencing an important part of manufacturers' product planning and development decisions—how products are packaged—and plans to continue to do so. In short, Amazon has signaled the manufacturers to shrink the amount of shrink-wrap or face shrinking shelf space at Amazon!

Source: Based on "Scuttle Shrink-Wrap," *Philadelphia Inquirer*, September 11, 2010: A8.

In the previous chapter, we discussed the motivation of channel members as a fundamental element of channel management. But channel management (the administration of existing channels to secure the cooperation of channel members in achieving the firm's distribution objectives) involves more than just motivation management. Even a comprehensive and carefully planned motivation program will not assure the channel manager of a highly cooperative channel team operating at its peak level of effectiveness and efficiency. Rather, the channel manager who aspires to attain this level of channel performance must also be skilled at using the elements of the marketing mix to facilitate the administration of the channel. As we pointed out in Chapter 5 in our discussion of channel strategy, the channel manager needs to use the firm's product, pricing, promotion and logistics variables to their maximum effect in securing cooperation from channel members.[1] In this context, these marketing mix variables may be viewed as *resources*; how these resources are used will affect the performance of channel members either by facilitating or inhibiting their performance. The channel manager would, of course, like to use the marketing mix so as to achieve the former as often as possible. In order to do this, however, the channel manager needs to understand how the other marketing mix variables interface with the channel variable, and what the implications for these interfaces are for channel management. He or she would then be in a better position to coordinate all four strategic components of the marketing mix to create the synergy needed to best meet the needs of customers. Although the term *synergy* has been overused in recent years as applying to too many business situations, synergy in the context of channel management is apropos. Indeed, it should be the theme underlying all of the channel manager's efforts to manage marketing channels effectively and efficiently. In very practical terms, this means that the channel manager should always be asking the question: *How can I blend the strategic components of the marketing mix to best advantage in the management of the marketing channel?*

In this chapter, we discuss some of the interfaces of the product variable with the channel variable of the marketing mix and some of the implications for channel management. Chapters 11 and 12 deal with price and promotion as they interface with channel management, while Chapter 13 examines interfaces between logistics and channel management.

Many potential interfaces exist between product management and channel management.[2] Though it is not possible to deal with all of these in this chapter, we will discuss a sufficient number of examples to provide an overall idea of some of the more basic relationships and implications. Our purpose in this section is not to present a comprehensive inventory of possible product-channel management interfaces, but rather to develop a sense of awareness on the part of the channel manager about the impact of product decisions on channel management decisions.

The discussion and examples presented are organized around three major areas of product management:

1. New product planning and development
2. The product life cycle
3. Strategic product management

New Product Planning and Channel Management

The development of new products is a challenge faced by virtually all producers and manufacturers serving both consumer and industrial markets. New technologies, changing customer preferences and competitive forces all contribute to the need to introduce new products.[3] Yet the success rate for new products is low. Consumer package goods companies launch more than 45,000 new products each year, yet about 75 percent of those products will fail in less than two years, even with heavy national advertising. Moreover, many of the two-year survivors will fail well within five years of their introduction, such that new product failure rates of 90 percent are not unusual. Given such high rates of new product failure, manufacturers need to do a better job of new product planning and development if they hope to reduce these high rates.[4]

Achieving success for new products is dependent on many factors, such as the innovativeness and quality of the product itself, its price, how effectively it is promoted,[5] the nature of customer demand, competitive factors, timing and many others.[6] One of these other factors is the degree of support a new product receives from independent channel members.[7] Without a high level of cooperation from the channel members, it is much more difficult to gain market acceptance for a new product.[8] It is therefore crucial for the channel manager to analyze the possible channel implications in the planning and development of new products. The focus of this analysis should be on what can be done in the planning and development stage to promote a higher level of cooperation from the channel members in gaining a successful market for the product.[9] Although there are many possible issues that the channel manager may consider, depending on the type of industry and the particular circumstances involved, the following five issues are frequently important for a wide range of channels:

1. What input, if any, can channel members provide for new product planning?
2. What has been done to assure that new products will be acceptable to the channel members?
3. Do the new products fit into the present channel members' assortments?
4. Will any special education or training be necessary to prepare the channel members to sell the new products effectively?
5. Will the product cause the channel members any special problems?

Encouraging Channel Member Input for New Product Planning

One way of promoting increased enthusiasm and acceptance for new products by channel members is by obtaining some input from them for new product planning. This input may range from soliciting ideas for new products during the idea-generating stage of new product planning all the way to getting feedback from selected channel members during the test-marketing or commercialization stage. Henkel Consumer Adhesives, the largest maker of the well-known product Duck Tape, is a perfect example of a manufacturer that put input for a new product from one of its channel members to good use.[10] In this case, the channel member was mighty Walmart, the world's largest retailer, through whom Henkel Consumer Adhesives had been selling its "plain vanilla" (silver) Duck Tape for many years. It seems Walmart noticed that lots of kids were coming in to buy Duck Tape for their skateboards and other extreme sports equipment. Walmart kept hearing that these kids wanted to get the tape in fun colors. Walmart, which has been known to give new product ideas to such giant manufacturers as Procter & Gamble, got this information back to Henkel. The manufacturer wasted no time in developing a new line of neon-colored tapes. These tapes have been tremendous sellers and big profit makers for both Henkel and Walmart.

Input for new product planning by channel members does not necessarily involve the basic product itself or even minor features of the product. In fact, input on the size of the product or on packaging changes may be all that is needed to enhance channel member cooperation. A number of consumer packaged goods manufacturers, for example, have responded to suggestions by warehouse clubs, such as Sam's Club and Costco, that products be packaged in special larger sizes and multiple packages that conform better to their high-volume merchandising strategy. Further, as pointed out in the "Focus on Channels" vignette at the beginning of this chapter, giant channel member Amazon.com made its desire for manufacturers to produce more consumer-friendly and environmentally-friendly packaging in no uncertain terms.

Seeking input from channel members for new product planning, however, may require that the manufacturer keep channel members informed about new product plans. Many manufacturers are very sensitive about their new product plans for competitive reasons and are reluctant to divulge them to channel members until the last moment before the product is introduced. In some cases, this type of secretive behavior may be justified. But if competitive considerations do not require such secrecy, the manufacturer has little to lose and much to gain by seeking input from, and sharing new product plans with, channel members. Channel members are more likely to enthusiastically support new products that they have played a part in developing.

Fostering Channel Member Acceptance of New Products

For a new product to be successful it must, of course, be accepted by the final users—whether they are industrial customers or final customers. But success is also dependent upon acceptance of the new product by channel members through whom it passes in reaching final customers.[11]

However, whereas final users are most concerned about how the product will perform when *used*, channel members are much more interested in how the *product will sell, whether it will be easy to stock and display* and, most important, whether it will be *profitable.*[12]

Looking first at the issue of salability of a new product, the key factor here is the perceptions of channel members. Specifically, they have to believe that they can sell the product or they are not going to be enthusiastic about carrying it. Take, for example, what has been going on recently in the food industry. The real standout new products in this industry belong to the so-called organic food category, which is enjoying dramatic growth.[13] Everything from fresh fruits and vegetables to breakfast cereals and even ketchup that are naturally grown and produced without chemical fertilizers, artificial ingredients or additives of any kind are in great demand by consumers. While sales of conventional products are barely growing at 1 percent per year, sales of many organic foods are increasing at double digit levels. At Whole Foods Market Inc., the largest natural food retailer in the U.S., products are practically jumping off the shelves as more and more consumers turn to organic foods. But the new organic products that are moving so quickly at Whole Foods as well as at the special "natural foods" departments in supermarket giants, such as Kroger Co. and Safeway Inc., are not those produced by huge manufacturers such as General Mills, Quaker Oats, Kraft Foods Inc. and H.J. Heinz Co. Instead, most of the products are from small, little-known producers such as Eden Foods, Fantastic Foods, Purity Foods, Rising Moon, Small Planet Foods and many others. These companies are producing organic versions of a huge range of foods from organic apples to organic zucchini and everything in between, including beverages, breads, cereals, pastas, soups and frozen meals. Why the preference for the little guys over the big guys by both the natural food chains and supermarkets? In a word: *credibility*. These retailers do not believe that the big, old-line food manufacturers that have used artificial ingredients and additives so abundantly in their products are really serious and capable of producing good organic products that will be acceptable to their customers.[14]

In getting channel members to accept new products, the issue of ease of stocking and display has become more important than ever as more and more new products compete for shelf space.[15] Figure 10.1, which shows square watermelons first developed by Japanese farmers, is an outstanding example of producers going out of their way to address the shelf space concerns of retailers by making it easier and more efficient for retailers to stock and display this popular but bulky and cumbersome fruit. With the same objective in mind but for a very different product, Procter & Gamble Company redesigned the bottle for its Ivory shampoo from a teardrop shape to a tall cylinder, which saved retailers 29 cents per case in handling and storage costs. P&G also repackaged its Pringles potato chips in a new "supersize" can, replacing the two smaller cans wrapped in plastic, which consumed more shelf space. This saved retailers over 90 cents per case. Thus, even giant manufacturers such as Procter & Gamble (which for many years had a reputation for being arrogant and heavy-handed toward its channel members) are paying more attention to channel members' stocking and display requirements.

FIGURE 10.1 Square Watermelons Ease Retailer Stocking and Display Problems

© AP Photo/Kyoto

Finally, the importance of the profitability potential of new products for channel members cannot be overstated. Retailers have been overwhelmed with new products. In the product categories of personal care and household products, 85 percent of sales were generated by less than 8 percent of the products, according to Paine Webber Group. Complicated product lines and pricing also create huge headaches for retailers as they try to sort out how much products are actually costing them amid frequent specials, rebates and discounts. A study by Anderson Consulting, for example, found that as a result of such complexities, an incredible 38 percent of all grocery invoices (where such special deals are most common) contained errors.[16] As a result of these experiences, retailers have become hyper-skeptical, even cynical, about the profitability potential of the barrage of new products offered to them. Thus, the opportunity for manufacturers to "slip something by" retailers or have an unprofitable product get "lost in the shuffle" has become increasingly difficult. Retailers, and to an increasing extent wholesalers as well, recognize that the only real asset they have to sell is shelf space.[17] Hence they are not going to allow this precious space to be clogged by a proliferation of unprofitable products.

Fitting the New Product into Channel Member Assortments

The particular mix of products carried by any given channel member is his **assortment**. All of the products carried by a supermarket, department store, home-improvement store, plumbing supply wholesaler and so on constitute assortments of products they handle and depend on to generate sales. Thus, a channel member's assortment is analogous to a manufacturer's **product mix** (all products that the manufacturer produces).

When a manufacturer develops a new product, it is adding to its product mix. Presumably, during the development of the new product some consideration has been given to how well the new product fits into the product mix from the standpoints of both production and marketing. In short, the manufacturer has probably evaluated whether the capacity exists to manufacture and market the product efficiently. A key consideration on the marketing side of this evaluation should be whether existing channel members will view the new product as an appropriate one to add to *their* assortments.

In recent years, product proliferation by manufacturers has become perhaps the most challenging issue for channel members attempting to manage their product assortments. Over a period of several decades, manufacturers had grown accustomed to launching not only more different products, but also to making incremental variations of their popular existing products to keep their brands visible to consumers and maintain shelf space on channel members' shelves. While a wide variety of manufacturers pursued this product proliferation strategy, it has been particularly evident in the food and consumer packaged goods (CPG) industries. By 2008, almost 47,000 products were on a typical food retailer's shelves—an increase of more than 50 percent since 1996. In the broader product category of CPG, new product introductions (including feature and size variations) had soared to 47,113 by 2008—more than double the amount introduced a decade earlier.[18] Thus, retailer assortments were bulging with huge varieties of products. A typical Target store, for example, carried 88 kinds of Pantene shampoos, conditioners and styling products! At Jewel supermarket, many dozens of toothpastes line the shelves. For Colgate alone, the products include TarterProtection, Whitening, Sparkling White, Max White, Whitening with Oxygen Bubbles and Total Whitening—some of which are available in several different sizes! In the cookie aisle of Jewel, more than a dozen versions of Oreo cookies line the shelves.[19] Even in apparel, the iconic brand Burberry has not escaped the product proliferation bandwagon. Best known for its famous trench coat, Burberry also makes 6,000 different clothing products each year![20]

Such product proliferation has created unwieldy and inefficient product assortments for more and more retailers. Apparently, following the belief that in product assortment management, less is more, some major retailers have made a conscious and concerted effort to prune their merchandise assortments to more manageable sizes not only to reduce their inventory and administrative costs, but to simplify the consumer decision process as well.[21] For example, Walgreen Co. has cut the number of superglues it carries from 25 to 11. Walmart Stores Inc. reduced the 24 different tape measures it offered to 4 and Kroger Co. is testing the feasibility of a 30 percent cut in the variety of breakfast cereals it stocks. Even Burberry has decided to reduce the number of different products it offers each year to 4,200 from 6,000—almost one-third less.

Retailer pushback against product proliferation by manufacturers appears to be an important trend rather than a fleeting, temporary phenomenon. Large and powerful retailers that often dominate the channel are relentlessly seeking to drive down costs and enhance efficiency.[22] Moreover, as the "buying agents" for their customers rather than "selling agents" for manufacturers, it is the retailers, who take their cues from their customers rather than manufacturers, that decide which products to add and which to delete from their merchandise assortments. For the foreseeable future, it appears that assortment management by retailers will be skewed more toward product deletions than product additions. Manufacturers and other suppliers cannot ignore this more stringent retailer stance toward assortment management. New products, especially variations of existing products masquerading as new products, will have to jump considerably higher hurdles before they will be added to retailer product assortments.

Educating Channel Members about New Products

It is not unusual for channel members to need special education or training provided by the manufacturer in order to sell new products successfully. The type and level of special education will, of course, vary depending on the type of industry involved and the technical complexity of the product. A fairly complex piece of industrial equipment, for example, may require many hours of instruction by the manufacturer to train the channel members in the product's use and the special features to emphasize in sales presentations. On the other hand, a simple, consumer packaged good may require no more than a few minutes of advice on the proper display of the product. Between these two extremes are many variations in the educational requirements for new products. But it is well worth the effort for channel managers to investigate the possible educational requirements of new products as they are being developed. This will enable them to plan the educational programs that may be needed by the channel members, rather than having to throw them together hastily after the products are sitting on channel members' shelves.

Consider, for example, the situation that faced Hyde Athletic Industries, the manufacturer of a running shoe called the Saucony Jazz 300. This extremely lightweight running shoe had developed a loyal following among women runners when they began commuting to work in comfortable running shoes. But Hyde had never explained the shoe's benefit to retailers, hence it remained an obscure product carried only in a limited number of stores. Then the shoe was rated number one by *Consumer Reports* in overall quality and performance, surpassing well-known and much larger rivals such as Nike, Reebok and Etonic. Moreover, priced at under $70, this American-made athletic shoe was also rated a "best buy" by *Consumer Reports*. The favorable publicity generated by the *Consumer Reports* article made some major sporting goods retailers, who had formerly scoffed at this unknown brand, finally take notice. Demand suddenly increased dramatically as savvy consumers carrying the magazine article charged into stores asking for the

Saucony Jazz 300. Unfortunately, the boost given to the product from the *Consumer Reports* article basically amounted to just a short-term blip. In the face of massive advertising by Nike and the other well-known brands, the Saucony Jazz would soon be forgotten. A retailer education program that builds on the impetus created by the *Consumer Reports* article is what knowledgeable observers believe Hyde needed to sustain the success of the Saucony Jazz 300 and future Hyde products. Because *Consumer Reports* results cannot be used in advertising, retailers' salespeople would have to be educated to tell the Hyde quality story to consumers. In short, this is a case where a little dealer education might have gone a long way in keeping Hyde products on retailers' shelves.

Making Sure New Products Are Trouble-Free

No channel member wants to take on a new product that will cause trouble.[23] This applies to channel problems that may arise while the product is still in the channel member's inventory as well as to those that may appear soon after the product is sold to a customer. Most channel members have enough problems to deal with in running their businesses without taking on new products that add to their problems. For example, Home Depot, the nation's largest home center chain, is very demanding about the new products it will accept from manufacturers—even down to what seem to be trivial details. Home Depot has insisted that some manufacturers of light fixtures and gas grills rewrite assembly-and-use instructions that it found too difficult to read. It has even insisted that manufacturers put labels with bar codes on bulky and hard-to-handle items, such as sheets of plywood and wood dowels, to make for easier stocking and customer checkout.

A more substantial problem with a new product, which has emerged as a classic example of how new product problems can create problems for channel members, involved Jaguar automobiles when it introduced the X-Type model to the U.S. market in 2001. At the time, Jaguar Cars Ltd. was owned by the Ford Motor Company. Ford developed the new X-Type Jaguar at a lower price point that Ford hoped would dramatically increase penetration of the Jaguar brand in the U.S. This $30,000 entry-level luxury car, or "baby Jag," as it was called, was meant to compete with the Mercedes-Benz C-Class and BMW 3-Series, which were positioned as entry-level luxury cars in the same price range. But Ford, looking to the X-Type to quickly grow Jaguar sales, produced the X-Type in large numbers (90,000 in 2001) and built it on the chassis of the much cheaper Ford Mondeo compact. The result of this overly aggressive growth strategy led to two serious problems not only for Jaguar, but also for Ford's independent Jaguar dealers. First, the large numbers and oversupply of the X-Type, the "baby Jags," undermined the exclusive prestige image of the overall line of Jaguar, automobiles. This had serious repercussions for Jaguar dealers because they depend heavily on the high-level luxury image of Jaguar to compete against the other luxury car brands. Second, in the rush to get the X-Type to market, Ford was careless about quality. The result was higher warranty costs and a drop of 17 notches in the 2001 J.D. Power & Associates, Inc. initial quality survey to 19th place for Jaguar cars. Future sales values not only for the X-Type, but for all Jaguar models were adversely affected by the tarnished image and quality glitches associated with the Jaguar. Unfortunately, Jaguar dealers could not escape the negative consequences of Ford's careless new product strategy in the launch of the X-Type Jaguar.

As these examples suggest, problems with new products can range from being a nuisance that makes it more difficult for the channel members to stock and sell the product, as in the case of Home Depot, all the way to more serious flaws that can undermine the brand equity that channel members, such as Jaguar dealers, rely on to attract customers.

While it is not possible to prevent all problems with new products, extra care in new product planning may help turn up defects before new products begin flowing through the channel and into the hands of customers. Clearly, avoiding such problems is crucial to maintaining a strong and highly motivated team of channel members.[24]

The Product Life Cycle and Channel Management

The **product life cycle (PLC)** is a model for describing the states through which a product passes. The PLC has been discussed extensively in the marketing literature and is almost always presented in the basic marketing texts,[25] so we need not go into detail here. We will, however, briefly review the four stages to provide a sharper focus for our forthcoming discussion on the implications of the product life cycle for channel management.

Figure 10.2 is a typical portrayal of the product life cycle model. As the figure shows, a product typically follows a curve, which can be divided into four basic stages: *introduction, growth, maturity and decline*. The introductory stage is one of slow growth as the product begins to gain a foothold in the market. Profits, as shown by the profit curve in Figure 10.2, are nonexistent or very low during this stage due to the high costs of introducing the product in the market. The growth stage is marked by rapid market acceptance and relatively high profits, as shown by the steeper, upward slopes of the sales and profit curves during this stage. Maturity is characterized by a decreasing rate of sales growth (the slope of the curve is less steep) as the market becomes more highly saturated. Profits tend to peak and then decline during the maturity stage because of the heavy selling costs necessary for the product to hold its own against competition. Finally, decline occurs when sales decrease absolutely and profits plummet quickly to the zero point.

Not all products pass through this life cycle; there are many exceptions and variations. Moreover, the stages may not be nearly as distinct as those shown in Figure 10.2 and the time during which a product completes its cycle may vary greatly, from under one year in some cases to several decades in others.

Despite such variations, the PLC is still useful as a framework for developing marketing strategies during the different stages. Since this text is concerned with the channel variable, our focus on discussing the product life cycle will be on the strategic implications of each of the stages of the PLC for channel management. Figure 10.3 shows the major channel management implications of the four stages of the product life cycle, each of which will be discussed in more detail.

FIGURE 10.2 The Product Life Cycle

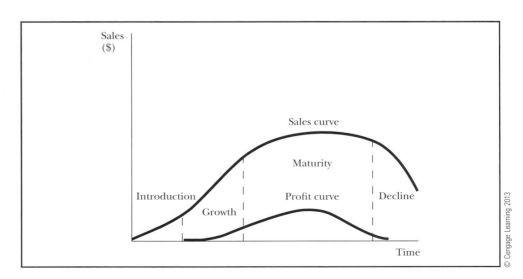

© Cengage Learning 2013

FIGURE 10.3 Stages of the Product Life Cycle and Their Implications for Channel Management

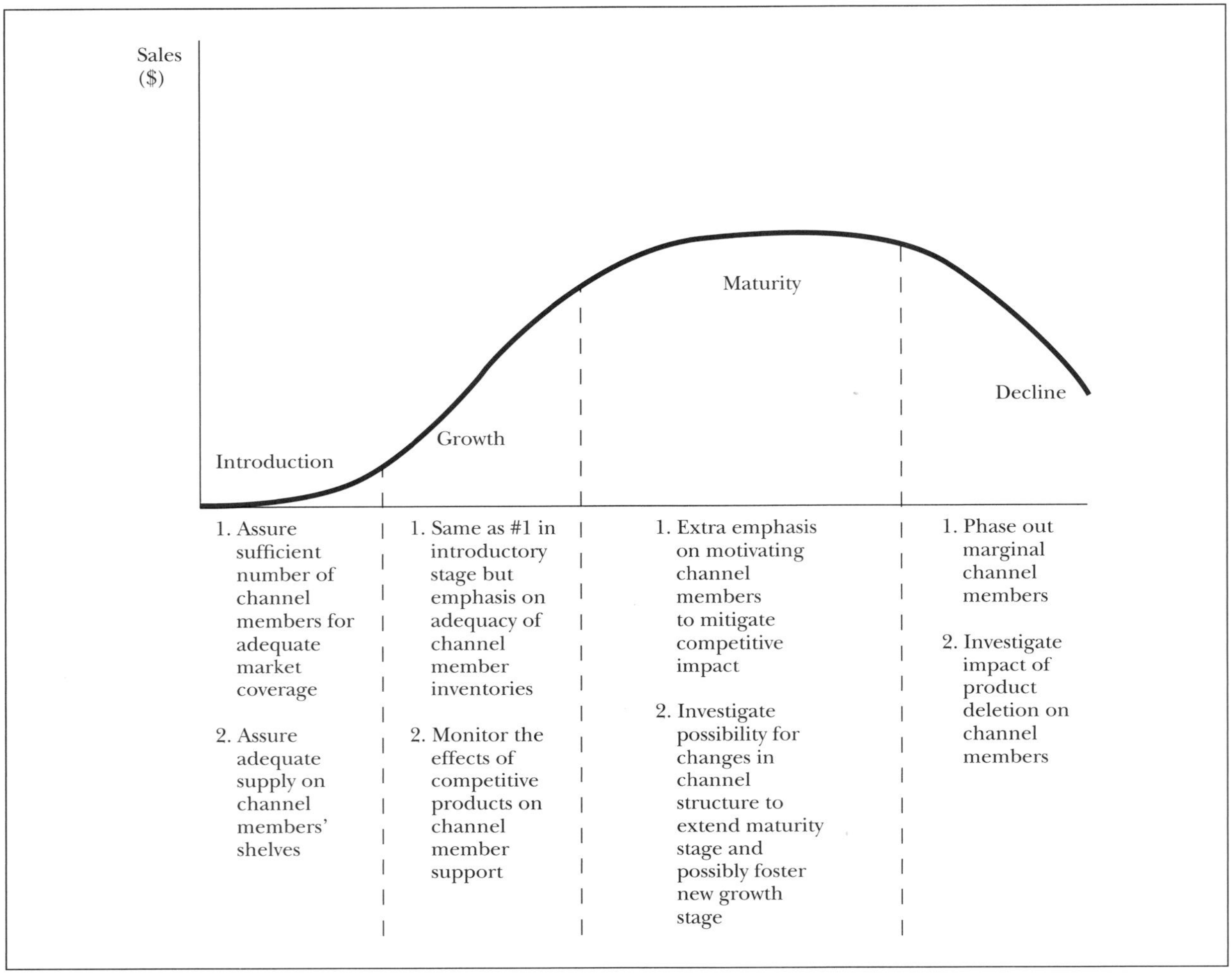

Sales ($)

Introduction | Growth | Maturity | Decline

1. Assure sufficient number of channel members for adequate market coverage

2. Assure adequate supply on channel members' shelves

1. Same as #1 in introductory stage but emphasis on adequacy of channel member inventories

2. Monitor the effects of competitive products on channel member support

1. Extra emphasis on motivating channel members to mitigate competitive impact

2. Investigate possibility for changes in channel structure to extend maturity stage and possibly foster new growth stage

1. Phase out marginal channel members

2. Investigate impact of product deletion on channel members

© Cengage Learning 2013

The Introductory Stage and Channel Management

During the introductory stage, strong promotional efforts are needed to launch the product. This often entails heavy expenses for advertising and other forms of promotion. All this is for naught, however, if the product is not readily available at the final point of purchase. Thus, during the introductory stage, it is imperative for the channel manager to assure that channel members can provide adequate market coverage for the product.[26] This is not a simple task—a good deal of planning and coordination are necessary to provide adequate market coverage at the final point of sale. Breakdowns in planning and coordination are common. For example, Nabisco Foods significantly underestimated the demand for one of the products in its SnackWell's line of low-fat cookies and crackers. The product in question, Devil's Food Cookie Cakes, was in extremely short supply from the moment it was introduced. Supermarket managers from coast to coast could not get nearly enough of the cookies, so Nabisco was forced to allocate very limited supply among as many supermarkets as possible. In most cases, the tiny shipments were sold out within hours or even minutes of being received as shoppers rushed to snap them up.

One might argue in this case that Nabisco faced a rather "good" problem here because consumer demand for the cookies was much greater than the supply, so all it needed to do was produce more cookies to make everybody happy. Unfortunately, the technology involved in producing Devil's Food Cookie Cakes is complex and it requires significant lead time to set up additional manufacturing facilities to produce them in larger quantities. In the meantime, many of the supermarkets were disgruntled with the shortage because their customers were unhappy about it and the shelf space dedicated to this product remained empty much of the time. If not corrected in a reasonable time through a significant increase in supply, such shortage-plagued product introductions can undermine the future of a potentially spectacularly successful product.

For products that can be digitized and delivered electronically online, such as books, making sure that sufficient market coverage is available to satisfy consumer demand in the introductory stage of the PLC can be significantly enhanced. A case in point involves the well-known author John Grisham's latest novel, *The Confession*, which was introduced in both hardcover and e-book versions simultaneously in the fall of 2010. The publisher, Random House, and the author were delighted with the results: in the first week, e-book sales reached 70,000 compared to about 200,000 hard cover books.[27] At Amazon.com, the Kindle e-book edition actually outsold the hardcover edition during the first week. Grisham, who at first opposed the simultaneous introduction of e-books with hardbound books, fearing the e-books channel would cannibalize hardcover sales, now believes that the combination of traditional and electronic channels provided a level of market coverage that actually increased total book sales. Whether electronic and physical versions of products sold simultaneously to provide broad market coverage during the introductory stage of the product life cycle results in higher total sales or just divides a given level of sales between the two channels remains to be seen. But when this option is available, it is probably likely that, at least in the near future, more and more firms will use both channels simultaneously in an effort to maximize sales.

The Growth Stage and Channel Management

As the product enters the growth stage, rapid market growth begins. In order to help sustain this growth, the channel manager faces two important challenges in channel management:

1. To ensure that product availability provided to the market by channel members is adequate so as not to inhibit growth.
2. To carefully monitor channel member actions with respect to competitive products already handled by them and keep an eye out for potential competitors who are attempting to "break into" the channel.

The problem of making sure that the product is available to the market becomes a more difficult one to deal with as the product shifts out of the introductory stage into the stage of rapid growth. This is particularly true for consumer products sold to mass markets through numerous wholesale and retail channel members. Yet dealing with this problem effectively can mean the difference between success or failure in sustaining market acceptance for the product. An observation made by Luck a generation ago is even more relevant today:

> *Wholesalers and retailers play major roles in the market success of products which they distribute. Relatively small shifts in shelf facings, out-of-stocks, displays, and other dealer support may produce favorable or dangerous trends.*[28]

The approach for dealing with this problem is through *monitoring* the product flow as it moves through the channel. Formal and systematic reporting procedures are necessary, however, for effective monitoring. While some manufacturers may be able to develop their own reporting systems (relying on sales analysis data, reports from their field sales force and estimates made by their own research departments), a growing number are turning to specialized independent marketing research firms such as ACNielsen, SymphonyIRIGroup and others to provide this kind of information.[29]

The second problem, monitoring the channel members' actions with respect to competitive products, is at least of equal importance to monitoring one's own products. The high sales enjoyed by a product during its growth stage are bound to attract competitors who are eager to grab a "piece of the action." In many cases, these competitors' products will find a place on the shelves of a manufacturer's channel members. Consequently, a manufacturer must fight competitors for the channel members' support to sustain the growth of the firm's product. In a classic analysis of the product life cycle, Levitt argues that the key to dealing with this kind of competition in the growth stage lies in the anticipation of competitive actions and the pre-planning of appropriate strategy during the previous stage of the product life cycle. He states:

> *At each stage in a product's life cycle, each management decision must consider the competitive requirements of the next stage. Thus a decision to establish a strong branding policy during the market growth stage might help to insulate the brand against strong price competition later.*[30]

One well-known manufacturer that has been especially adept at keeping its products on retailers' shelves against continuing onslaughts from competitors is Polo Ralph Lauren Corp.[31] This firm has managed to maintain its dominant position by providing a range of brands that appeal to different levels of retailers. They range from Polo Ralph Lauren Corp.'s most luxurious and super premium-priced apparel sold under the "Black Label" logo, featuring $250 shirts and $3,000 suede jackets, to the "Chaps" brand that includes men's dress shirts at $30 sold at discount retailers such as Kohl's Corp. The "American Living" label offers even lower priced apparel sold at JCPenney, while the middle upper-end brand, "Polo by Ralph Lauren," products are sold at such retailers as Macy's, Bloomingdales and Lord & Taylor. Polo Ralph Lauren Corp. also offers several other brands such as "RRL," "RLX," "Polo Sport" and "Rugby." While the price range of brands from "Black Label" to "American Living" is wide, all of the brands enjoy a luxury image that retailers at all levels find difficult to resist. So, while competitors such as Calvin Klein, Jones of New York and a host of others, including retailers' own private label merchandise, keep trying to knock Polo Ralph Lauren brands off retailers' shelves, so far they have enjoyed only limited success in doing so. Retailers have reserved a significant amount of shelf space for Polo Ralph Lauren Corp. products, not because they think Mr. Ralph Lauren is an interesting character, but because his products from top to bottom convey an image of luxury and style that brings customers into their stores and keeps them coming back year after year. This constant attention to product management so as to stay at least one step ahead of competitors has enabled Polo Ralph Lauren Corp. to remain in the growth stage of the PLC for over four decades!

The Maturity Stage and Channel Management

The slow growth or saturation characteristic of the maturity stage suggests two strategic emphases for channel management:

1. Extra emphasis should be put on making sure the product remains desirable for channel members.
2. At the same time, possible changes in channel structure, particularly the selection of different types of intermediaries, should be investigated to forestall the decline stage and possibly create a new growth stage.

In the face of slower growth or near-saturation, the sales and turnover rate for the product will decline for many of the channel members. In response to this, they may reduce or totally stop ordering the product. Some will have special sales or closeouts to get rid of the product as quickly as possible, fearing the possibility of being "stuck" with a product that nobody wants. In order to lessen the severity of this pattern of channel member behavior, the channel manager must take steps to make the product more attractive to channel members. The most direct tactics for doing this are those that will increase the profit potential of the product and reduce the risks associated with handling it. Such tactics as extra trade discounts, advertising allowances, special package deal discounts and more liberal return policies are appropriate. Consideration must be given, of course, to whether such stopgap measures are profitable and in the manufacturer's long-run interest.

A more comprehensive and long-term channel strategy for the maturity stage is to change the channel structure through which the product is distributed. In some cases this may lead to a renewed growth stage for the product. Consider, for example, the case of Woolite. Woolite was sold for years only in department stores. Then American Home Products, the manufacturer, introduced the product in food stores to gain access to mass markets. Nothing else was changed. Woolite was still the same product, with the same package and the same product features. Yet sales tripled after the first year! The reason? Consumers found it easier and more convenient to buy Woolite through the new channels and so started using it much more often.

While the channel manager should not necessarily attempt to change channels for a product as a matter of course in the maturity stage, an investigation of this possibility is probably well worth the effort. Indeed, given the widespread acceptance of online channels in recent years, channel design decisions that place mature products into online channels may provide some extra longevity or even foster renewed growth. This is exactly what happened to Kiwi Shoe polish, a sleepy, 100-year-old brand, when Kiwi decided to make its products available online, both from its own Web site and through numerous other online sellers just after the start of the new millennium.[32] Helped along by the additional exposure provided by the online channel, sales of Kiwi products, which had been virtually stagnant, increased at an annual rate of over 4 percent and reached $310 million by 2007.

The Decline Stage and Channel Management

Barring a dramatic turnaround, which occasionally does occur, rapid decline can occur when a product is in the decline stage.[33] Given this situation, the channel manager should focus attention on two channel implications:

1. Can marginal outlets be phased out quickly to avoid further profit erosion?
2. Will dropping the product cause an adverse reaction on the part of existing channel members?

Even when a product has reached the decline stage, a substantial number of channel members may still be carrying it. Many of them will be low-volume, however, often ordering the product in very small quantities. The high-volume channel members, for the most part, will already have dropped the product. This leaves the channel manager with a high-cost, low-volume channel for the product, which further erodes an already deteriorating profit picture. Thus the channel manager should consider whether the very-low-volume outlets should be phased out. Basically, this requires an analysis of the revenues produced by each outlet, weighed against the cost of servicing each of them. This procedure will be discussed in more detail in Chapter 14 (Evaluating Channel Member Performance).

The second issue of possible adverse reactions by channel members when a manufacturer drops a declining product has been discussed in a classic article by Alexander:

Products are often associated in the marketing process. The sale of one is helped by the presence of another in the product mix. When elimination of a product forces a customer who buys all or a large part of his requirements of a group of profitable items from the firm to turn to another supplier for his needs of the dropped product, he might shift some or all of his other patronage as well. Accordingly, it is sometimes wise for management to retain in its mix a no-profit item, in order to hold sales volume of highly profitable products. But this should not be done blindly without analysis.[34]

Unfortunately, the procedure for making this kind of analysis is not clear-cut. Nevertheless, Alexander does sketch out the basic guidelines that should be used in such an analysis:

When this marketing interdependence exists in a deletion problem, the decision maker should seek to discover the customers who buy the sick [product in the decline stage] product; what other items in the mix they buy; in what quantities; and how much profit they contribute …

… Marketing research may be conducted to discover the extent to which the customer purchases of profitable items actually are associated with that of the sick product. Although the results may not be precise, they may supply an order-of-magnitude idea of the interlocking patronage situation.[35]

Obvious examples of products that have been in the decline stage in recent years include floppy discs, CDs, typewriters, liquid paper, 35mm cameras, film, landline telephones and dial-up Internet service. But even with the dramatic decline of these products, there are still significant numbers of customers who, for one reason or another, want to buy them. So, channel managers cannot completely abandon the channels that make these declining products available to those customers.

Strategic Product Management and Channel Management

Strategic management of the product line is a challenge faced by virtually all manufacturers. No product line can be simply left alone to remain fixed in time—certainly not if it is to remain a viable and profitable product line.

Successful product strategies depend on a variety of factors such as the quality, innovativeness or technological sophistication of the products themselves, the power of the brand, the capabilities of the managers charged with overseeing the product line, the financial capacity and willingness of the firm to provide the promotional support often necessary to implement product strategies and several other factors. One of these other factors, and a frequently overlooked one, is the role played by channel members in implementing product strategies.[36] Since most manufacturers do not market their products directly to their final users, they will at some point have to call on their channel members to implement the product strategies formulated by manufacturers. Thus, the success of the manufacturer's product strategies is at least to some extent, and sometimes to a very great extent, dependent upon the effectiveness of the channel members in carrying out the manufacturer's product strategies. This interface between product strategy and channel management will be discussed for several different product strategies.

Product Differentiation and Channel Management

Product differentiation is probably the most widely used product strategy. In essence, product differentiation represents the manufacturer's attempt to portray a product or products as being different from competitive products and, therefore, more desirable to purchase even though the price may be higher.

Product differentiation is not necessarily based on differences in physical characteristics. It can also be created by putting different names on products, packaging them differently, using certain advertising appeals, selling them through different stores or some combination of these factors. The real key to creating a differentiated product is to get the consumer to *perceive* a significant difference. As long as this happens, it makes little difference whether or not the product is physically identical to another product. Conversely, if the consumer does not perceive such a difference, the fact that the product is physically different is inconsequential. Thus, product differentiation is not so much a matter of making a product that is physically different as it is getting consumers to *see* a difference.

The task of conveying this difference is not always just the manufacturer's job. Channel members may also be called upon to help create a differentiated product. The kinds of stores the product is sold in, the way it is displayed and sold and the services provided can be critical in creating a differentiated product.[37] Consider, for example, gourmet cookware maker All-Clad Metalcrafters LLC. All-Clad makes some of the world's finest and most expensive pots and pans. Made in Cannonsburg, Pa., a 10-inch fry pan sells for as much as $125 and a top-of-the-line stockpot can cost over $400.[38] The cookware is manufactured to a very high standard using a patented process of sandwiching different metals, such as aluminum or copper, with stainless steel to foster optimum heat distribution, durability and beauty. All-Clad is aimed at consumers who want something special in their cookware, not only in its functional performance, but also in the image and cachet projected by displaying such gourmet cookware in their kitchens. All-Clad sells only through upscale retailers such as Bloomingdale's and Williams-Sonoma, who sell at full price. All-Clad refers to this channel strategy as "skimming"—selling only through top-tier retailers while specifically avoiding middle-of-the-road stores such as Kohl's or discounters such as Target or Walmart. Even though these discount chains are enjoying the fastest growth and are dominating the market, All-Clad believes that its product differentiation strategy would be quickly undermined if its products were to appear on the shelves of retailers that do not project the same sense of quality, style and prestige that All-Clad has worked so hard to create.

While All-Clad has been very successful in using retailers to implement its product differentiation strategy for its cookware, Maytag was not so successful in doing so for its dishwashers. Maytag, which enjoyed a superior quality image for its washing machines, attempted to differentiate its dishwashers on the same basis—better quality than competitive products. According to objective tests conducted by *Consumer Reports*, Maytag's dishwashers were better than competitive brands; the Maytag' dishwasher's unique washing mechanism, designed and patented by the company, resulted in a top rating. The outward appearance of the Maytag dishwashers, however, was not much different from competitive dishwashers costing considerably less than Maytag. Indeed, the Maytag dishwashers looked more like the low end of the competitive lines. Thus, for Maytag's product differentiation strategy to work, consumers would have to learn the "inside story" of Maytag's superior quality through a combination of advertising and especially strong selling by the retailer at the point of sale. Unfortunately, Maytag simply assumed that the superior quality of the Maytag dishwasher would be recognized by consumers and hence the dishwashers would "sell themselves" at the retail level. This did not happen, however, because Maytag had not adequately developed a channel management program to support its product strategy for dishwashers. Advertising was not intensive enough to pre-sell the product through the creation of the same superior quality image Maytag enjoyed for washing machines. But the greatest shortcoming was that Maytag made no special effort to train or induce retail salespeople to communicate the quality of Maytag dishwashers to consumers. Without these retail "cheerleaders," Maytag was just another "face" in the crowd of dishwashers.

The successful implementation of a product differentiation strategy for All-Clad and Maytag's failure are traceable to two different approaches to channel management. All-Clad selected the kind of quality retailers needed to help make its pots and pans special. Maytag, on the other hand, paid little attention to providing strong advertising support or to training and inducing retail salespeople to promote Maytag's superior quality.

Two channel management implications for product differentiation strategy can be derived from the foregoing. First, when product differentiation strategy is affected by *who* will be selling the product, the channel manager should try to select and help develop channel members who "fit" the product's image. Second, when product differentiation strategy is influenced by *how* the product is sold at retail, the channel manager should provide retailers with the kind of support and assistance needed to properly present the product.

Product Positioning and Channel Management

Product positioning is another widely used product strategy. Basically, product positioning refers to a manufacturer's attempt to have consumers perceive products in a particular way relative to competitive products. If this is accomplished, the product is then "positioned" in consumers' minds as an alternative to other products that they currently use. For example, Source Perrier, the French manufacturer of Perrier bottled mineral water, was able to position the product in the U.S. market as being an alternative to liquor and soft drinks. Orange juice producers engaged in a major promotional campaign to position orange juice as an alternative to soft drinks. The dairy industry conducted a similar campaign aimed at positioning milk as an alternative to many soft drinks, while 7-Up tried to position its product as an alternative to cola drinks. Such product positioning strategy is not limited to beverages; the strategy is also employed in a wide range of other product categories from chewing tobacco (as an alternative to cigarettes) to mobile homes (as an alternative to regular homes).

As with product differentiation, product positioning can also be heavily focused on the particular brand of a product and in fact may be inextricably tied to the brand. Hence, BMW's successful positioning as the ultimate driving machine, or Gatorade's as the thirst-quenching sports drink, are arguably as much a function of the brand names involved as the physical attributes of the products.

While successful product positioning strategy depends upon many factors, the types of stores selling the product and how they display and promote it can be very important. For Perrier to be positioned as an alternative to soft drinks, it was necessary for the product to be sold in supermarkets and displayed en masse in the same aisle as soft drinks. But gaining and maintaining this supermarket shelf space was by no means automatic. Perrier had to put together a channel management program to recruit independent soft drink bottlers and beer distributors throughout the United States to distribute Perrier water to the supermarkets, set up displays and continually restock the markets rapidly as the product moved off the shelves. Without this mass distribution approach to support the product positioning strategy, Perrier water might well have remained in its previous position as an obscure, expensive mineral water sold only in dusty corners of out-of-the-way gourmet shops. Instead, Perrier's channel strategy not only fostered huge growth for its own product, but also was crucial in positioning bottled water as a new multibillion-dollar category for supermarkets throughout the United States.

The tremendous success of Starbucks Corp.'s instant coffee, called Via, is an especially good example of how channel strategy needs to work in tandem with product strategy to implement a product positioning strategy successfully. Via was rolled out to all Starbucks stores in the U.S. and Canada in September of 2009.[39] For many decades, instant coffee was viewed by serious coffee drinkers as an inferior product compared to fresh-brewed coffee. Instant coffee was something sold in supermarkets to unsophisticated consumers who were seeking convenience and low price and cared little about taste. Thus, Starbucks faced a major challenge when it sought to position its Via instant coffee as a high quality product that, as shown in Figure 10.4, Starbucks advertised as "instant coffee that tastes as delicious as our brewed." How did Starbucks hope to accomplish this feat? First, Starbucks distributed Via coffee only in its own stores creating an instant "halo effect" for Via instant coffee. This association provided instant credibility for Via. After all, Starbucks claims that it sells the finest coffee in the world, so why would it jeopardize its reputation and brand equity by offering a product that did not measure up to Starbuck's quality standards? Second, Starbucks used its stores to offer consumers a "taste

FIGURE 10.4 Newspaper Advertisement for Starbucks Instant Coffee

Courtesy of Susan Van Etten

challenge." From October 2 to October 5, 2009, Starbucks challenged customers to come into its stores for a taste test and, regardless of their opinion, receive a free cup of coffee. In effect, Starbucks was putting its coffee where its "mouth" was. Finally, Starbucks trained all of its baristas to say good things about Via, talk it up and promote it as a product that would enable customers to enjoy Starbucks coffee even when they could not make it to a Starbucks store, thus reinforcing the tag line of the advertisement (see Figure 10.4), "never be without great coffee." After the introduction of Via, Starbucks' same-store sales increased significantly for the first time in several quarters due almost entirely to additional sales volume generated by Via.

Starbuck's successful product positioning strategy depended heavily on leveraging the power of its retail store channel to quickly and effectively create a new perception for instant coffee. Rather than introduce Starbucks instant coffee into supermarket channels, the logical channel for instant coffee, Starbucks chose the much bolder but riskier strategy of selling instant coffee in its stores right alongside its venerated fresh-brewed, "hand-made" coffee.

Product Line Expansion/Contraction and Channel Management

At one time or another, most manufacturers find it necessary to expand or contract their product lines.[40] In fact, they often engage in both processes simultaneously by adding products even as they drop others that are at the end of their life cycle or that are selling too poorly to continue offering.

Such **product line expansion and pruning strategies** can create problems in dealing with channel members because it is very difficult to find a "perfect" blend of products in the line that will satisfy all channel members.[41] When the product line is expanded, some of the channel members may complain about product proliferation, which increases their inventory costs and complicates their selling job (see previous discussion pp. 298–299). When products are dropped from the line, other channel members (or even the same ones who complained about the proliferation of products) may carp about losing products for which they still have plenty of customers.

With regard to product proliferation, a few figures are instructive:

- *Procter & Gamble Co. at one time had 31 varieties of its Head & Shoulders shampoo and 52 different versions of Crest toothpaste.*
- *Consumer product companies launch almost 50,000 new items each year.*
- *Nabisco offers 8,000 different varieties of baked goods.*
- *Some 25 percent of the 47,000 items in a typical supermarket sell less than one item per month.*

Studies have shown that such product proliferation does not result in higher sales but rather in *lower* sales by confusing consumers[42] and making it more difficult for channel members to keep shelves stocked with so many items.

So, from a channel management standpoint, product line expansion and pruning strategies present the manufacturer with a delicate balancing act when attempting to gain channel member support for reshaped product lines. Moreover, with the growing emphasis by channel members (especially giant retailers) on **category management**— that is, the management of product categories as business units, customizing them on a store-by-store basis to more precisely meet customer needs—the demands made on manufacturers by channel members to have the right mix of products are becoming greater than ever.[43] While there are no simple, clear-cut approaches for always having the right mix of products to satisfy ever more demanding channel members, several points are worth considering when dealing with the interface between product line expansion and contraction and channel strategy. First, although a manufacturer obviously must be the master of its own product line and be free to change it in what is believed to be its best interests, it makes sense to incorporate channel member views whenever possible. Often, this may require little more than seeking the opinion of some key accounts about prospective product line additions and deletions. Second, the manufacturer should attempt to explain to channel members the rationale underlying product line expansion or deletion strategies. While they might not be completely satisfied with the explanation, it can still go a long way toward removing the confusion and mystery that often surround such moves. Finally, the manufacturer should try to provide adequate advance notice of significant product line changes to channel members to allow them sufficient time to prepare for such changes.

Trading Down, Trading Up and Channel Management

Closely related to product line expansion and contraction strategies are the product strategies of trading down and trading up. **Trading down** refers to adding lower-priced products or a different product line to a product mix than had typically been offered in the past. **Trading up** is essentially the opposite—adding products or a product line that are substantially more expensive than other products in the line or mix. Trading down is the manufacturer's attempt to use product strategy to appeal to the low end of the market, while trading up is the use of product strategy to reach the high end of the market. Accordingly, trading down and trading up are also often referred to as going "down market" or "up market," respectively.

Trading down and trading up can be high-risk strategies because they may reflect profound departures from the company's normal base of operations. The manufacturer may now face (1) new markets about which it may know very little; (2) new competitors it has not faced before and (3) quite possibly new channel members and/or new problems with existing channel members. Because our focus in this chapter is on the channel management implications of product strategy, we will look at the third issue—the channel management problems associated with trading up and trading down. Basically, there are two problems to consider.

The first and most basic question is whether existing channel members provide adequate coverage of the high-end or low-end market segments to which the trade-up or trade-down product is aimed. If they do not, new channel members will have to be added and/or the basic design of the channel may have to be changed. This is exactly what Levi Strauss & Co. faced in its trade-down strategy when the company introduced its new Levi Strauss Signature brand of lower-priced jeans.[44] To achieve the kind of mass-market coverage needed to grow the new Signature jeans line, Levi's decided to use the discount mass merchandiser Walmart as its main channel of distribution. Walmart would enable Levi's to reach the large numbers of consumers seeking a lower-priced version of the famous-name jeans. Levi's believed that this channel strategy was absolutely essential to achieve high market penetration for the new low-priced line. The existing channel members that Levi's relied on to sell its classic "red tab" jeans, consisting of traditional department stores and specialty stores, simply did not have the market coverage in the lower end of the market to successfully implement Levi's trade-down product strategy.

The second channel management problem faced by the manufacturer when trading up or down is a more subtle and perhaps more difficult one. It may be stated as follows: Will the channel members have confidence in the manufacturer's ability to successfully market the trade-up or trade-down product? Channel members, whether at the wholesale or retail level, develop certain perceptions about the kinds of products with which particular manufacturers are associated. When a particular manufacturer that has been perceived as a supplier of "good, solid mid-priced products" suddenly introduces a much more expensive or a much cheaper product, doubts are likely to arise among the channel members about whether the manufacturer is "out of its depth" or really "knows what it is doing" with its trade-up or trade-down strategy. Giant retailers such as Walmart, for example, reflected this view when Royal Appliance Manufacturing Company tried a trade-up strategy with its Dirt Devil vacuum cleaner. The original product, a lightweight hand-held vacuum cleaner with a revolving brush, had been spectacularly successful. Selling for about $40, the powerful, little red vacuum cleaner practically rolled off retailers' shelves. But after less than two years, Royal decided to add a much more expensive upright version of the Dirt Devil, which was to sell for $139. This product would now go head-to-head with other upright models, including those of the more established Hoover Company, which dominated the market in upright vacuum cleaners. Understandably, retailers were skeptical about Royal's chances for competing with Hoover. At first, heavy advertising by Royal helped its higher-priced Dirt Devil to gain what appeared to be an initial foothold. But before the $139 Dirt Devil had established itself as a viable product, Royal introduced another upright model for $99, which cannibalized sales from the higher-priced machine and hurt retailers' margins. This convinced the already skeptical retailers that Royal was in over its head, and lack of retailer confidence in Royal's trade-up product strategy contributed to the lackluster sales of the higher-priced upright Dirt Devils, which never approached the sales success of the original product.

Product Brand Strategy and Channel Management

Most manufacturers have several options when considering **product brand strategies**. They might sell all their products (1) under one national brand; (2) under several national brands (a "family" of brands); (3) under private brands or (4) under both national and private brands. Manufacturers also have further options within these four. For example, a national brand manufacturer may decide to sell only certain product lines or models of its brands through particular types of channel members. Goodyear, for example, uses different model designations for the tires it sells through mass merchandisers and smaller independent dealers so that these channel members do not appear to be in direct competition with each other.

Any of these options may, at certain times, pose channel management problems.[45] But it is the fourth option, selling under both national and private brands, that presents the most difficult channel management problems because when the manufacturer sells under both national and private brands, direct competition with channel members may result. In other words, the final users of the product have the choice of buying the manufacturer's brand (national brand) or the channel member's brand (private brand), both of which are produced by the same manufacturer. Whirlpool, for example, sells under its own Whirlpool national brand through independent distributors and dealers. It also serves as a major supplier for Sears' private brand, Kenmore. Borden, one of the largest makers of national brand coffee creamers (Cremora), Scott Paper, with the second largest nation brand paper towel (Viva) and Union Carbide, with its leading national brand Glad Bags, all manufacture other versions of these products for private or so-called no-name generic brand sales. A host of other consumer goods manufacturers across a wide spectrum of industries also engage in similar brand strategies. Indeed, such dual distribution strategies are becoming increasingly common as national brand manufacturers seek to make use of excess production capacity and compete against private brand products made for large chain retailers by nonnational brand manufacturers.

But such competition between manufacturers and channel members fostered by this dual national and private brand product strategy can create serious problems between the manufacturer and its channel members if the competition becomes too direct. Consider, for example, the case of a well-known liquor manufacturer that sold its liquor products both under its own national brand and under many private labels. One of its major channel members, a large chain of liquor stores in New York, sold this manufacturer's products under both the national brand and its own label (private brand). Even though the national and private brands might have come from the very same barrel, the private brand liquor sold for considerably less than the national brand. As more and more of the store's customers realized the products were the same, they bought more of the private brand and less of the national brand. Indeed, it was only around the Christmas season when customers were buying liquor as gifts that sales of the national brand picked up. The manufacturer was now in the unenviable position of having created a "monster" in the form of a widely accepted private brand liquor that could have serious negative consequences for the long-term viability of its own national brand product.[46]

When a manufacturer pursues a brand strategy that is based on both national and private brands, it has to expect that somewhere down the road it may run into the competitive problem of too much direct competition between the national and private brand versions of its products. Hence, the channel management implications of this type of brand strategy need to be addressed. The manufacturer should at least attempt to delineate some of the possible distribution scenarios associated with selling under both national and private brands. For example: Will there be any cases where the *same* distributors or dealers will sell both the national and private brand versions of the product? Will those distributors or dealers who sell the national brand version of the product compete in the same geographic markets as those selling the private brand version? How are distributors or dealers likely to react to these types of situations should they arise?

Some attention paid to such channel issues *before* embarking on a dual national and private brand strategy will help alert the manufacturer to the need for setting clear channel management policies to guide dual brand strategies.[47] Examples of such polices are (1) not selling both the national and private brand versions of these products to the same channel members; (2) selling the national and private brand versions of the product in different geographical territories so they are less likely to compete in the same market areas and (3) making the products physically different enough so that even if the first two policies are not feasible, the direct competition between the national and private brand versions of the product will be minimized.[48]

Product Service Strategy and Channel Management

Many products in both the consumer and industrial spheres require service after the sale. Thus, manufacturers of these products should make some provisions for after-sale service, either by offering it directly at the factory, through their own network of service centers, through channel members, through authorized independent service centers or by some combination of these organizations.[49] Unfortunately, with a few notable exceptions such as STIHL Inc., the world's leading manufacturer of hand-held power equipment discussed extensively in Chapter 1, the provision for product service has too often been overlooked by manufacturers as a strategic issue in product management, especially among consumer goods manufacturers. Service has been relegated to a secondary position in product strategy planning or, even worse, has been considered as an afterthought or minor detail in product management. It is no wonder, then, that consumers often express great dissatisfaction with the availability and quality of after-sale service for a wide range of consumer products.

Such poor product service reflects a shortcoming not only in product management, but also in channel management because it is the job of the marketing channel to make the necessary service available to the final end user along with the product. A marketing channel that provides for effective and efficient delivery of the product is still not fully effective or efficient if it does not provide for product service.

If good product service is to be provided by the channel, however, the manufacturer must view the issue of product service as a basic strategic issue in product management *and* channel management. Indeed, the appeal of the product can be significantly enhanced through a strong service image if the manufacturer has developed a strong service capability in the channel. Lexus, for example, whose overall channel strategy was discussed at some length in Chapter 5, has developed and nurtured a reputation for providing outstanding service for owners of its luxury cars. Customers not only get quick and easy appointments for service at authorized Lexus dealerships, but are also provided with loaner cars at no charge. But even more important is the attentiveness and sensitivity to customer satisfaction provided by Lexus dealers' service departments. If a customer is concerned about what might appear to be a tiny, virtually unnoticeable scratch on an interior panel, the dealer will in all likelihood be authorized by Lexus to replace the entire panel. If a hardly audible squeak bothers a customer, a dealer mechanic will be directed to spend whatever time is necessary to get rid of it. This emphasis on service excellence by the Lexus dealer network has become inextricably tied to the product. Thus, the brand equity enjoyed by Lexus is supported not only by the superior quality of the product itself, but by the extraordinary service provided by Lexus dealers as well.

Attaining such channel member support is not a matter of good luck. The manufacturer who expects strong cooperation from channel members in providing service must make it clear to channel members that service is an important part of the overall product strategy and incentives must be provided for the channel members to cooperate in the service program.

Summary

Effective channel management requires that the channel manager be aware of how channel management interfaces with the other variables of the marketing mix: product, price, promotion and logistics. The channel manager should view the firm's strategies in each of these marketing mix areas as resources that can be employed for improving the firm's channel management strategies.

In this chapter, the first of these strategic interfaces—product management and channel management—was discussed. Three basic areas of product management as it interfaces with channel management were considered: (1) new product planning and development; (2) the product life cycle and (3) strategic product management.

With respect to new product planning and development, the channel manger should be concerned with such basic product channel management issues as: (1) obtaining channel member input into new product

planning; (2) promoting channel member acceptance of new products; (3) fitting new products into channel member assortments; (4) educating channel members about new products and (5) making sure new products are as trouble-free as possible. Care and attention given to these issues can go a long way toward improving the probability of success for new products.

The product life-cycle implications for channel management must also be understood by the channel manager if channel management is to be used effectively to enhance the life cycle of a product. During the introductory stage of the life cycle, the channel manager must ensure that a sufficient number of channel members is available for adequate market coverage. As the product moves into the growth stage, the adequacy of channel member coverage must be reinforced and the effects of competitive products on channel member support should be carefully monitored. As the product moves through the growth stage and into the maturity stage, extra emphasis should be placed on motivating channel members to help mitigate the impact of competitive products and the possibility of changing the channel structure to extend the maturity stage or to help create a new growth stage should be investigated. Finally, as the product enters the decline stage, marginal channel members should be phased out and the impact of the deletion of the product from the manufacturer's product line should be investigated.

Strategic management of the product line is a task faced by virtually all manufacturers if the product line is to remain viable and profitable. A number of basic strategies can be pursued in the strategic management of the product. Among the most important of these for a wide variety of manufacturers are: (1) product differentiation strategy; (2) product positioning strategy; (3) product line expansion and contraction strategies; (4) trading-up and trading-down strategies; (5) product brand strategies and (6) product service strategy. The channel manager must understand the interrelationships of these product strategies with channel management strategies and attempt to use channel management to support the successful implementation of these product strategies.

Review Questions

1. The product, price, promotion and logistics variables may be viewed by the channel manager as resources in helping secure a higher level of channel member cooperation. Discuss the statement.

2. Discuss the importance of gaining channel member support in building market acceptance for a new product.

3. Is it practical to elicit channel member input into the manufacturer's product planning and development process? What problems might this create?

4. Fitting new products to the channel members' assortments may sometimes be a problem. When might this be the case?

5. Discuss the product life cycle stages and the basic implications of each stage for channel management.

6. Under which conditions might a seemingly simple product deletion decision create possible adverse reactions on the part of channel members?

7. Discuss the relationship between strategic product management and channel management. Is one of these areas more important than the other? Explain.

8. Explain the role played by channel management in the implementation of product differentiation and product positioning strategies.

9. What are some of the channel management problems that can arise when pursuing product line expansion and contraction strategies, trading-up and trading-down strategies and a product brand strategy that uses both national and private brands?

10. Discuss the role of the marketing channel in providing after-sale service.

Channel Issues for Discussion

1. With the widespread use of e-books, such as Amazon.com's Kindle, book publishers are faced with a tough channel decision: should they introduce the conventional hardcover and the e-book versions simultaneously or delay release to the e-book channel until after the hardcover has had a chance to generate sales through the conventional channels? HarperCollins, the publisher of former vice presidential candidate Sarah Palin's book, *Going Rogue: An American Life*, opted for the delay strategy. The publisher chose to wait over a month after the release of the hardcover before making the book available via e-book. The publisher had produced 1.5 million copies of the hardcover version, which were available for sale in book stores and online in mid-November. But the e-book version was not made available until December 26, the day after Christmas. Apparently HarperCollins was worried about the e-book cannibalizing sales from the hardcover version.

Do you think HarperCollins made the right channel decision? Why or why not?

2. RadioShack, with over 6,500 locations worldwide, has been struggling for a number of years with an image of being "old-fashioned" or "out of touch" with new technologies. RadioShack was viewed by tech-savvy consumers as a place to buy

odds-and-ends electrical items, such as adaptors and cables, but not the place to buy smartphones. But by the latter part of the first decade of the twenty-first century, RadioShack, which started to refer to itself in advertisements as "The Shack," began selling what is arguably the most iconic example of high-tech, cool products—the Apple iPhone. Apple Inc., which is known for being very selective about who qualifies to sell its products, nevertheless decided to let RadioShack sell the iPhone.

Why do you think Apple decided to use RadioShack as a channel member for selling iPhones? Do you think the product life cycle played a role in Apple's decision?

3. Toddler University Inc. is the name of a shoe company that makes children's footwear. The company grew from almost nothing to sales exceeding $25 million. The secret of Toddler University's success, according to some industry observers, is a unique product design that can drastically reduce retailers' inventory requirements. In regular children's shoes, there are 11 sizes and 5 widths—so, to have a complete selection, retailers would have to stock 55 pairs of shoes for each particular model. But Toddler University has patented a shoe that allows the use of a one-width shoe with five shoe inserts of varying widths, thus drastically reducing the retailer's inventory requirements.

Comment on this development in light of what you believe to be the relevant product strategy and channel management strategy interface.

4. Procter & Gamble has become so concerned about the proliferation of private-label products that it has taken the extraordinary step of suing one of its own channel members that sells private labels as well as large volumes of P&G products. The firm in question, F&M Distributors Inc., operates over 100 drug stores. P&G claims that F&M's private-label merchandise is designed and packaged to look almost identical to famous brand P&G products, such as Pantene Pro-V, Head & Shoulders, Secret, Sure and Noxema. P&G not only wants F&M to discontinue the sale of such copycat, private-label products, but seeks damages as well. P&G had initiated similar suits before against private-label imitators, but the targets of those lawsuits had been manufacturers of private-label merchandise rather than

distributors of P&G products. Industry observers think P&G is taking quite a risk in suing its own channel members because they are unlikely to be enthusiastic sellers of P&G products after being sued by P&G.

What seems to be going on here in terms of private versus national brand competition and the role of independent distributors? Do you believe P&G is acting wisely in suing one of its own channel members? Explain why or why not.

5. Expensive sunglasses, ranging in price from $50 to $200 or even higher in some cases, have become quite the rage. Ray-Ban, one of the leaders of the pricey sunglasses phenomenon, was joined by numerous other manufacturers, such as Oakley Inc., which specializes in expensive sunglasses for skiers, motor bikers, water sports participants and basketball players, and Gargoyles Performance Eyewear, which makes a wide range of sunglasses ranging in price from $85 to $190. Such variety and high prices reflect a product positioning strategy that has transformed sunglasses from an essentially utilitarian product to an important fashion item associated with upscale, sports-oriented, glamorous lifestyles.

What role do retailers play in pulling off this new product positioning strategy with sunglasses? Discuss.

6. Even famous and iconic Fortune 100 companies sometimes manufacture defective products that end up on the shelves of thousands of retailers. This is what happened to Johnson & Johnson, one of the world's leading manufacturers of patent medicines. In 2009, J&J withdrew from retailer shelves significant quantities of some of its best-known and successful products such as Motrin, Tylenol, Benadryl, Rolaids, St. Joseph aspirin and others. Consumers complained about a musty, mildew-like odor that could cause nausea, stomach pain or diarrhea.

Given that even the largest and most highly respected companies such as J&J can, at times, produce defective products that make their way through retail channels all the way to the consumer, should channel members view such incidents as inevitable? Discuss.

7. Private-label products sell in supermarkets typically for about 10 to 20 percent less than national brands, yet the profit margins realized by supermarkets are usually about 10 to 15 percent higher than for national brands—so, supermarkets like

private-label brands. But in recent years, there has been a tendency for supermarkets to upgrade their private brands to compete more directly with high-price premium national brands on quality. Several supermarkets, for example, have

developed their own version of the Dove super-premium ice cream bar. Some observers believe that such trading-up of private-label products will undermine their appeal.

Do you agree or disagree? Explain why.

References

1. For a related discussion, see Boonghee Yoo, Naveen Donthu and Sungho Lee, "An Examination of Selected Marketing Mix Elements and Brand Equity," *Journal of the Academy of Marketing Science* (Spring 2000): 195–211.

2. See, for example, J. Miguel Villas-Boas, "Product Line Design for a Distribution Channel," *Marketing Science* 17, no. 2 (1998): 156–169.

3. For an excellent article on this issue, see Gerald G. Udell and Linda S. Pettijohn, "A Retailer's View of Industrial Innovation: An Interview with David Glass, CEO of Wal-Mart Stores Inc.," *Journal of Product Innovation Management* 8 (1991): 231–239.

4. For a related discussion, see: Barry Berman, "Products, Products Everywhere," *MIT Sloan Management Review* (August 2010): 1–3.

5. Wujin Chu, "Demand Signaling and Screening in Channels of Distribution," *Marketing Science* (Fall 1992): 327–347.

6. See, for example: R. Nicholas Gerlich, Rockney G. Walters and Oliver P. Heil, "Factors Affecting Retailer Acceptance of New Packaged Goods," *Journal of Food Products Marketing* (September 1994): 65–92.

7. Lan Luo, P.K. Kannan and Brian T. Ratchford, "New Product Development Under Channel Acceptance," *Marketing Science* (March-April 2007): 149–163.

8. For an analysis of how early or pioneer products fare against later entrants with new products, see: Frank H. Alpert, Michael A. Kamins and John L. Graham, "An Examination of Reseller Buyer Attitudes toward Order of Brand Entry," *Journal of Marketing* (July 1992): 25–37.

9. Eilene Zimmerman, "Getting Your Product Onto Retail Shelves," *New York Times*, October 21, 2010: B8; Elizabeth J. Wilson and Arch G. Woodside, "Marketing New Products with Distributors," *Industrial Marketing Management* 21 (1992): 15–21.

10. Ellen Neuborne, "The World's Largest Focus Group," *Business 2.0* (October 2002): 58–59.

11. For an insightful analysis related to this point, see: Frederick E. Webster, Jr., "Understanding the Relationships Among Brands, Consumers and Resellers," *Journal of the Academy of Marketing Science* (Winter 2000): 17–23.

12. For a related discussion, see: Vithala R. Rao and Edward W. McLaughlin, "Modeling the Decision to Add New Products by Channel Intermediaries," *Journal of Marketing* 53 (January 1989): 80–88.

13. Tom Craig, "Health Food Is No Longer a 4-Letter Word," *Retailing Today*, October 7, 2002: 15.

14. Kevin Helliker, "In Natural Foods, A Big Name's No Big Help," *Wall Street Journal*, June 7, 2002: B1, B4.

15. Betsy McKay, "Thinking Inside the Box Helps Soda Makers Boost Sales," *Wall Street Journal*, August 2, 2002: B1, B3.

16. Zachary Schiller, Greg Burns and Karen Lowry Miller, "Make It Simple," *Wall Street Journal*, September 9, 1996: 98.

17. Simon Harper, Amit Kapoor, John Potter and Laura Thompson, "The Missing Metric: Measuring Shelf Space Profitability," Booz Allen Hamilton, *Perspective Report* 2007: 1–5.

18. Ilan Brat, Ellen Byron and Ann Zimmerman, "Retailers Cut Back on Variety, Once the Spice of Marketing," *Wall Street Journal*, June 26, 2009: A1, A12.

19. Brat, Byron and Zimmerman, "Retailers Cut Back on Variety," A12.

20. Cecilie Rohwedder, "Burberry CEO Retrenches: Fewer Items, Faster Delivery," *Wall Street Journal*, May 24, 2007: B1, B3.

21. For an excellent study of how retailer assortment decisions affect consumers, see: D. Eric Boyd and Kenneth D. Baha, "When Do Large Product Assortments Benefit Consumers? An Information Processing Perspective," *Journal of Retailing* co. 85, no. 3 2009: 288–297.

22. Fabio Musso, "Innovation in Marketing Channels," *SYMPHONYA* vol. no. 1 (2010): 4–7.

23. See, for example: Sharon Terlep and Mariko Sanchanta, "Focus Now Turns to Toyota's Fix," *Wall Street Journal*, February 2, 2010: B1, B2.

24. For two excellent articles on product liability as it affects channel members, see: David Griffith, James Kenderdine and Fred Morgan, "Intermediate Sellers: Wholesalers Liability for Defective Products," *Journal of Marketing Channels* 3 (1993): 47–71; and Karl A. Boedecker and Fred W. Morgan, "The Channel Implications of Product

Liability Developments," *Journal of Retailing* (Winter 1980): 59–72.

25. See, for example: Louis E. Boone and David L. Kurtz, *Contemporary Marketing* 14 edition. Cengage Learning 2009.

26. See, for example: Nickolas Nickolaus, "Marketing New Products with Industrial Distributors," *Industrial Marketing Management* 19 (1990): 287–299.

27. Jeffrey A. Trachtenberg, "Same Day E-Book Sales Propel Grisham's Thriller," *Wall Street Journal*, November 9, 2010: B10.

28. David J. Luck, "Interfaces of a Product Manager," *Journal of Marketing* 33 (October 1969): 33.

29. "The Nielsen Co.," *Marketing News*, August 15, 2008: H6–H9; for some alternative monitoring procedures, see: V. Kanti Prasad, Wayne R. Casper and Robert J. Schiefter, "Alternatives to the Traditional Retail Stores Audit: A Field Study," *Journal of Marketing* 48 (Winter 1984): 54–61.

30. Theodore Levitt, "Exploit the Product Life Cycle," *Harvard Business Review* (November-December 1965): 91.

31. Teri Agins, "Polo's High-Stakes Balancing Act," *Wall Street Journal*, May 31, 2007: B1, B5.

32. Julie Jargon, "Kiwi Goes Beyond Shine in Effort to Step Up Sales," *Wall Street Journal*, December 20, 2007: B1, B2.

33. For an excellent discussion of the product deletion process, see George J. Avlontis, "Product Elimination Decision Making: Does Formality Matter?" *Journal of Marketing* 49 (Winter 1985): 41–52.

34. R. S. Alexander, "The Death and Burial of 'Sick' Products," *Journal of Marketing* 28 (April 1964): 5. See also: Joseph P. Guiltinan, "Risk-Aversive Pricing Policies: Problems and Alternatives," *Journal of Marketing* 40 (January 1976): 11.

35. Alexander, "Death and Burial of 'Sick' Products," 5–6.

36. Bert Rosenbloom, "Better Product Strategy through Alert Channel Management," *Journal of Consumer Marketing* (Fall 1984): 71–80.

37. For a related discussion, see: John A. Quelch, "Marketing the Premium Product," *Business Horizons* (May-June 1987): 38–45.

38. Timothy Aeppel, "Cookware Heavyweights," *Wall Street Journal*, June 21, 2002: B1, B4.

39. Julie Jargon, "Starbucks Growth Revives, Perked by Via," *Wall Street Journal*, January 21, 2010: B7.

40. See: Avlonitis, "Product Elimination Decision Making," 41–45.

41. For a related discussion, see: Pallavi Gogoi, "Why Avon is Going Hollywood," *Business Week*, July 28, 2008: 58.

42. See, for example: Peter Boatwright and Joseph C. Nunes, "Reducing Assortment: An Attribute-Based Approach," *Journal of Marketing* (July 2001): 50–63.

43. Suman Basuroy, Murali K. Mantrala and Rockney G. Walters, "The Impact of Category Management on Retail Prices and Performance: Theory and Evidence," *Journal of Marketing* (October 2001): 16–32.

44. Emily Scardino, "Wal-Mart Tapped to Host Levi's Coming Out Party," *Retailing Today*, November 11, 2002: 1, 11.

45. See, for example: Phillip Parker, "Befriending the Private Label," *Harvard Business Review* (February 2006): 61–62; Steve Hamm, "Rivals Say HP is Using Hardball Tactics," *Business Week*, February 19, 2007: 48–49.

46. Robert E. Weigand, "Fit Products and Channels to Your Market," *Harvard Business Review* (January-February 1977): 104.

47. Monica Gomez Suarez, "Shelf Space Assigned to Store and National Brands," *International Journal of Retail & Distribution Management* vol. 33, no. 1 (2005): 858–878.

48. For a related analysis, see: Javier Oubina, Natalia Rubio and Maria Jesus Yague, "Strategic Management of Store Brands: An Analysis from the Manufacturer's Perspective," *International Journal of Retail & Distribution Management* vol. 34, no. 10 (2006): 742–760.

49. For one of the most comprehensive approaches manufacturers can use to address the product service issue, see: Edward Feitzinger and Hau L. Lee, "Mass Customization at Hewlett-Packard: The Power of Postponement," *Harvard Business Review* (January-February 1997): 116–121.

CHAPTER 11
Pricing Issues in Channel Management

LEARNING OBJECTIVES

After reading this chapter you should:

1. Be aware of the importance of pricing issues in marketing channel management.
2. Understand the "anatomy" of channel pricing structure and the pervasiveness of its influence in channel pricing strategy.
3. Recognize the channel manager's role in influencing the firm's pricing strategy.
4. Know the basic guidelines for developing effective channel pricing strategy.
5. Realize that these guidelines are not simple prescriptions for channel pricing strategy.
6. Be cognizant of some of the most basic and recurring issues in channel pricing policies.

FOCUS ON CHANNELS

Will Smartphone Wielding Consumers Armed with Powerful Apps Control Channel Pricing Strategy?

Who will control channel pricing strategy as we move into the second decade of the twenty-first century? Will it be famous-name manufacturers, global wholesale distributors or giant powerful retailers? Actually, none of the above. It looks like the consumer is the party to watch, particularly consumers "armed" with smartphones and the apps that provide them with virtually perfect price transparency at any time and any place. One such consumer is 25-year-old Tri Tang who went into action with his Android smartphone, equipped with TheFind app while shopping in a Best Buy store. After spotting the perfect gift for his girlfriend, a Garmin global positioning system priced at $184.85, instead of taking the unit off the shelf and putting it in his shopping cart, he drew his Android phone. Downloading TheFind app, Mr. Tang typed in the model number and was able to instantly compare the Best Buy price with prices offered by other retailers. Within seconds he learned that Amazon.com offered the same model for $106.75 with no tax and free shipping. Mr. Tang then used his Android to order the Garmin GPS from Amazon.com while standing in the aisle of Best Buy right next to the Garmin display!

Mr. Tang's use of TheFind app was not very unusual. In fact, that app had been downloaded over 400,000 times even though it had been out for just four weeks. A somewhat similar app, called RedLaser, which enables shoppers to use mobile phone cameras to scan bar codes for price comparisons had been downloaded over six million times after having been out for just over one year.

So, as more and more consumers use these apps to scrutinize prices while at the point of purchase, the "point of purchase" may well become a misnomer because not much purchasing will take place there. Instead, armed with these price checking smart phone apps, the "point of purchase" could devolve into the place where consumers make it a point to check the best price!

Source: Based on Miguel Bustillo and Ann Zimmerman, "Phone-Wielding Shoppers Strike Fear into Retailers," *Wall Street Journal*, December 16, 2010: A1, A19.

Studies of top-level marketing executives have found that pricing decisions cause them more concern than any other strategic marketing decision area, including new product introductions, promotion and changing patterns of distribution. Such top executive concern over pricing strategy is not surprising because pricing, perhaps more than any other marketing mix variable, is seen as having a direct link to the firm's bottom line.[1]

Strangely, however, pricing has received less attention in marketing literature than most other marketing issues. Moreover, of the marketing literature that does deal with pricing, most of it focuses on pricing strategy as it relates to the firm's ultimate target markets. Pricing strategy *as it relates to channel management* has received even less attention.[2] Yet many potential interfaces exist between pricing strategy and channel management,[3] a number of which we will discuss during the course of this chapter. Before getting into the specifics of these interfaces, it is important to be familiar with the underlying structure, or anatomy, of channel pricing because virtually all of the issues in channel pricing discussed in this chapter are in one way or another related to this channel pricing structure.

Anatomy of Channel Pricing Structure

Pricing in the marketing channel can be thought of as analogous to who gets what "piece of the pie." That is, participants at the various levels in the channel each want a part of the total price (the price paid by the final buyer) sufficient to cover their costs and provide a desired level of profit. To illustrate this, consider the diagram shown in Figure 11.1, which shows the channel pricing structure for a set of guitar strings with a list price of $10.00. The figure shows the costs, prices charged and gross margins received by each channel participant. The structure is based on a discount to the consumer of 25 percent off list price, a trade discount of 50 percent off list price for the retailer and 66 percent off list price for the wholesaler. Thus, the consumer is able to buy the strings for $7.50, the retailer is able to buy them for $5.00 while the wholesaler is able to buy them for $3.40. It is assumed that the manufacturer was able to produce the strings for $2.50. The final price of $7.50 paid by the consumer, representing a 25 percent discount off the list price of the strings, is based on the assumption that the retailer most likely has to sell them at a discount in order to meet the competitive situation in its local market.

The dollar gross margins shown on the right-hand side of Figure 11.1, in effect, represent payment for services rendered by each channel participant. The $2.50 received by the retailer, for example, is compensation for performing all of the distribution tasks necessary to make the guitar strings conveniently available to professional and amateur musicians. The $1.60 gross margin received by the wholesaler presumably is payment for its performance of the distribution tasks involved in making the strings available to retailers in the relatively small quantities desired. Finally, the $0.90 received by the manufacturer should remunerate it for the distribution tasks involved in making the strings available in large quantities to the wholesaler. Figure 11.2 provides a summary of the financial data shown in Figure 11.1 along with gross margin percentages for the various channel participants.

The trade discounts and gross margins shown in Figures 11.1 and 11.2 are typical for this industry and this particular product category. For other industries and product categories, these numbers will, of course, vary widely. But the underlying concept is the same—*each channel participant wants a price that provides a gross margin sufficient to*

FIGURE 11.1 Anatomy of Channel Pricing Structure for a Set of Guitar Strings with a List Price of $10.00

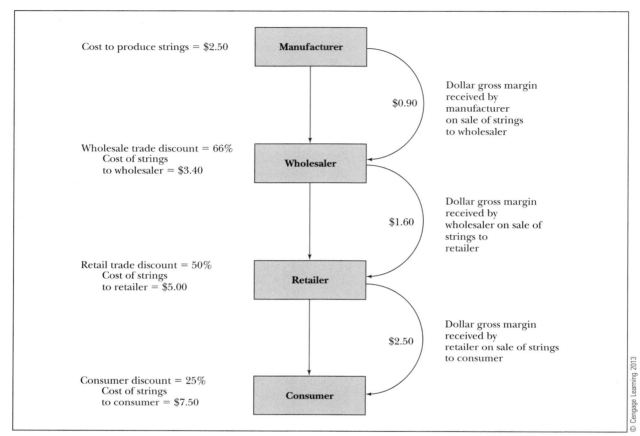

FIGURE 11.2 Schedule of Channel Pricing Structure for a Set of Guitar Strings with a List Price of $10.00

Channel Participant	Trade Discount	Cost	Dollar Markup	Gross Margin on Selling Price	Gross Margin on Cost
			Pricing Data		
Manufacturer		$2.50	$0.90	(1) 26.5%	(2) 36.0%
Wholesaler	66%	$3.40	$1.60	(3) 32.0%	(4) 47.1%
Retailer	50%	$5.00	$2.50	(5) 33.3%	(6) 50.0%
Consumer	25%	$7.50			

Retail discount offered by retailer based on competitive conditions. (Strictly speaking, this is not officially a trade discount.)

Notes: (1) Dollar markup/selling price to wholesaler (wholesaler's cost) = 0.90/3.40 = 26.5%

(2) Dollar markup/manufacturer's cost of producing = 0.90/2.50 = 36.0%

(3) Dollar markup/selling price to retailer (retailer's cost) = 1.60/5.00 = 32.0%

(4) Dollar markup/wholesaler's cost = 1.60/3.40 = 47.1%

(5) Dollar markup/selling price to consumer (consumer's cost) = 2.50/7.50 = 33.3%

(6) Dollar markup/retailer's cost = 2.50/5.00 = 50.0%

cover its expenses and provide a contribution to profit. Thus, a channel member will only carry a product—whether guitar strings or a personal computer—if the margin provided is sufficient to cover the costs of stocking and selling it with something left for profit. While this generalization may not hold for all products at all times, it does hold for *most* products at *most* times, especially in the long run.

The channel manager in a manufacturing firm must always be cognizant of the "golden rule" of channel pricing when developing pricing strategy. We may state it as follows:

It is not enough to base pricing decisions only on the market, internal cost considerations and competitive factors. Rather, for those firms using independent channel members, explicit consideration of how pricing decisions affect channel member behavior is an important part of pricing strategy.

Therefore, pricing decisions have a substantial impact on channel member performance. Specifically, if channel members perceive the manufacturer's pricing strategy as congruent with their own interests, they are more likely to provide a higher level of cooperation.[4] If, on the other hand, the manufacturer's pricing decisions reflect a lack of awareness of channel member needs or appear to work against them, a much lower level of cooperation, or even conflict, is the more likely result. Thus, the major challenge facing the channel manager in the area of pricing is to help foster pricing strategies that promote channel member cooperation and minimize conflict. Those responsible for managing the channel must play a role in the manufacturer's pricing decisions by focusing on the channel considerations attendant to pricing decisions.

Figure 11.3 helps to illustrate this role. As the figure shows, the channel manager's attention should be on the channel considerations involved in making pricing decisions. In other words, the channel manager must analyze and think through the channel implications of pricing decisions. Take, for example, a manufacturer's decision to cut the price of a product. The channel members may have many possible reactions to this decision—some may be positive while others may be averse to the manufacturer's point of view.

FIGURE 11.3 The Channel Manager's Role in the Manufacturer's Pricing Decisions

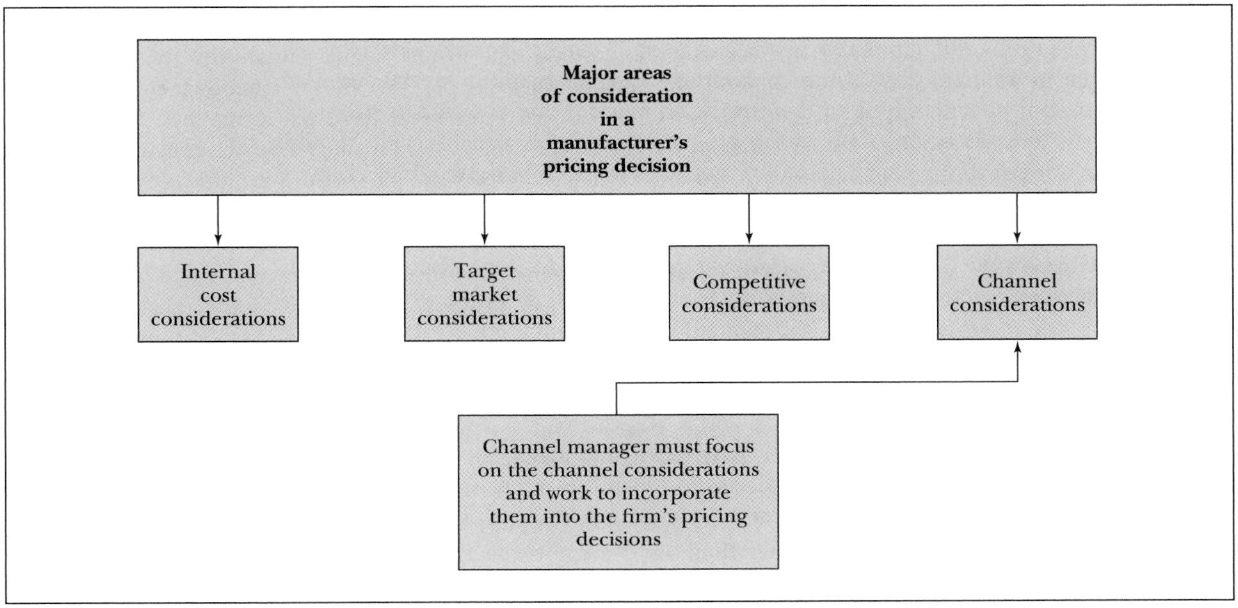

TABLE 11.1 POSSIBLE REACTIONS OF CHANNEL MEMBERS TO A MANUFACTURER-INITIATED PRICE CUT

1. They may expect the price cut to increase their sales volume and profitability.
2. They may become reluctant to deal with the product because of the possible effect of the price cut on the product's quality image.
3. They may be concerned about the price cut on the images of their own firms because their customers may associate them with handling low-priced, mediocre merchandise.
4. They may resent the reduction in their margins, which may result from the price cut.
5. They may be concerned about the loss in value of their existing inventories of the product after the price cut.
6. They may feel threatened by the possible proliferation of price cutting on the product by their competitors.
7. They may resent the loss of stability engendered by the price cut.
8. They may be leery of what this price cut portends for the future pricing policies of the manufacturer.

Source: Reprinted by permission of the publisher, from Alfred R. Oxenfeldt, *Pricing Strategies* (New York: AMACOM, 1975), 227, © 1975 by AMACOM, a division of American Management Association.

Table 11.1 lists some of the more common possible reactions of channel members to a manufacturer's decision to reduce prices to the ultimate buyer. As the table indicates, channel members may have many possible reactions.

Consider, for example, when McDonald's Corp. tested a $1.00 pricing strategy for all fountain soft drinks sold in McDonald's stores regardless of size. This represented a substantial price reduction from the $1.39 that McDonald's franchisees typically charged for larger size drinks.[5] McDonald's believed this price cutting strategy, if implemented by its franchisees, would produce a very positive outcome. McDonald's research suggested that the "$1.00 regardless of size soft drink strategy" would attract many new customers not only from competitive fast-food restaurants, but from customers who patronize convenience stores such as 7-Eleven. The franchisor also believed that the strategy would increase store traffic that, in turn, would lead to additional sales from other items on the menu. Further, McDonald's felt that given the very high margins on fountain soft drinks, estimated to be about 90 percent, the price cut would not damage franchisee profitability. But significant numbers of franchisees did not agree with McDonald's positive view. Rather, they worried that discounting soft drinks would undermine their strategy of using the high margins to help compensate for low margin items, such as those on McDonald's $1.00 "Value Menu." Some franchisees were also concerned that the soda discounts could cut into McCafe coffee drink sales. Finally, there was considerable worry about competitive reactions, particularly if similar price cuts were made by competitive fast-food chains that could drive down the margins on soft drinks permanently.

It is the channel manager's job to find out about such channel member views and to appraise their effects on channel member performance. In practice, this kind of evaluation would not usually be conducted as a distinct and separate project. That is, an evaluation of how the manufacturer's existing or proposed pricing strategies influence channel member behavior would normally be included as part of the general evaluation of channel member needs and problems discussed in Chapter 9. Pricing strategies that are at odds with channel member needs may be brought up at distributor advisory council meetings, emerge as part of the findings from a survey of channel members or a marketing channel audit or possibly be conveyed as feedback in the regular flow of channel communications. But because of the importance of pricing strategy in influencing channel member cooperation, the channel manager should be extra sensitive and pay particular attention to channel member views about pricing strategy. Whenever possible, the channel manager should attempt to have channel members' viewpoints on pricing issues included as an integral part of the manufacturer's price-making process.[6] If this is done successfully, many of the problems that may arise after pricing decisions have taken effect can be anticipated and hopefully avoided.[7] With this background on pricing strategy and channel management interfaces in mind, we now turn our attention to some specific guidelines for dealing with pricing issues and their implications for channel management.

Guidelines for Developing Effective Channel Pricing Strategies

The guidelines presented here offer some general prescriptions on how to formulate pricing strategies that will help to promote channel member cooperation and minimize conflict.[8] Obviously, there is no guarantee that even scrupulous adherence to these guidelines will ensure this result. In fact, there are sure to be many particular circumstances and situations where some of these guidelines will not apply or will be irrelevant. Nevertheless, these guidelines are worthy of study because they do provide a basic framework and benchmark for pricing decisions that incorporate channel considerations. The guidelines are as follows:

1. Each efficient reseller must obtain unit profit margins in excess of unit operating costs.
2. Each class of reseller margins should vary in rough proportion to the cost of the functions the reseller performs.
3. At all points in the vertical chain (channel levels), prices charged must be in line with those charged for comparable rival brands.
4. Special distribution arrangements (variations in functions performed or departures from the usual flow of merchandise) should be accompanied by corresponding variations in financial arrangements.
5. Margins allowed to any type of reseller must conform to the conventional percentage norms unless a very strong case can be made for departing from the norms.
6. Variations in margins on individual models and styles of a line are permissible and expected. They must, however, vary around the conventional margin for the trade.
7. A price structure should contain offerings at the chief price points where such price points exist.
8. A manufacturer's price structure must reflect variations in the attractiveness of individual product offerings.

Each of these guidelines will be discussed in some detail.

Profit Margins

Clearly, the channel members need margins that are more than adequate to cover the costs associated with handling a particular product. Tables 11.2 and 11.3 provide examples of retailer and wholesaler margins and other operating data. While this guideline may be relaxed at times, as in the case of products needed to fill out assortments or used for special promotions such as **loss leaders**, this is the exception rather than the rule. As we noted earlier (see Figures 11.1 and 11.2), channel members generally will not carry, let alone enthusiastically support, products whose margins are inadequate to cover their costs and provide room for profit. This applies particularly over the long term. In fact, even those manufacturers with an exceptionally strong consumer franchise

TABLE 11.2 MARGINS AND OTHER OPERATING DATA OF SELECTED RETAILERS

TYPE OF RETAILER	GROSS MARGIN	OPERATING EXPENSES	NET PROFIT BEFORE TAXES
Department stores	39.6%	36.6%	1.3%
Drugstores	25.8	23.8	1.3
Fuel oil	16.5	14.2	2.1
Furniture	46.0	45.5	0.7
Gasoline service stations	9.5	8.3	1.2
Groceries and meats	37.9	33.5	3.2
Household appliances	33.5	30.8	2.9
Liquor	24.9	20.6	3.6
Mobile homes	30.3	32.5	1.9
Sporting goods	36.5	33.6	0.7
Vending machines	47.0	44.7	1.6

Note: All figures are shown as a percentage of sales.

Source: Compiled from *Annual Statement Studies* (Robert Morris Associates, 2010).

TABLE 11.3 MARGINS AND OTHER OPERATING DATA OF SELECTED WHOLESALERS

TYPE OF WHOLESALER	GROSS MARGIN	OPERATING EXPENSES	NET PROFIT BEFORE TAXES
Chemicals	20.6%	16.4%	9.2%
Dairy products	18.2	15.1	2.7
Drugs	33.9	26.4	5.5
Frozen foods	15.3	12.8	1.7
Furniture	28.2	27.6	−0.2
Grain	9.4	6.5	3.0
Groceries	18.3	16.1	2.5
Jewelry	29.3	28.4	−0.3
Petroleum products	6.8	5.2	1.4
Sporting goods	28.9	25.0	1.7
Tobacco and tobacco products	11.2	6.8	3.7
Wine, liquor, and beer	25.6	20.6	4.6

Note: All figures are shown as a percentage of sales.

Source: Compiled from *Annual Statement Studies* (Robert Morris Associates, 2010).

who can virtually dictate to their channel members will eventually lose their support. Over time, those channel members who feel that the manufacturer is not allowing them sufficient margins are likely to seek out other suppliers or establish and promote their own private brands.[9]

In a classic analysis of pricing in marketing channels, Warshaw underscores this proposition by arguing that manufacturers are, in reality, "buying" distribution services through the margins they offer. If these margins are not equal to the prices sought by intermediaries, in the long run the manufacturer will not be able to buy their services in a competitive environment. Warshaw states this viewpoint as follows:

> *Viewing the problem as one of buying distribution can be useful in developing effective pricing policies.... The concept of buying distribution emphasizes the fact that the price paid to gain channel support must reflect not only the marketing job performed by the channel, but also the competitive environment in which the channel operates.*[10]

Thus, the channel manager should be involved in a continuous review of channel member margin structures to determine if they are adequate. Particular attention should also be paid to changes in the competitive environment that are likely to influence channel member perceptions of the existing margin structures.

Different Classes of Resellers

Ideally, the channel manager would like to set margins so that they would vary in direct proportion to functions performed by different classes of channel members.[11] In reality, however, few manufacturers have the power or cost accounting data to set margins in strict accordance with this guideline. Margins at the wholesale and retail levels and for various types of agent intermediaries are typically governed by strong traditions that permeate the industry. Precipitous downward deviations from these norms are feasible only for the most powerful manufacturers. Nevertheless, periodic reviews of the margin structures available to different classes of channel members should be made, with a view toward making gradual changes if warranted. Oxenfeldt suggests that questions such as the following be posed in this review:

1. Do channel members hold inventories?
2. Do they make purchases in large or small quantities?
3. Do they provide repair services?
4. Do they extend credit to customers?
5. Do they deliver?
6. Do they help train the customers' sales force?

Of course, many other questions might also be posed. But the main point of periodically reviewing channel member services in relation to the margins granted them is to find out whether there are any major inequities that are creating problems in the ranks of particular classes of channel members. Giant home improvement retailers such as Home Depot and Lowe's, for example, demand and expect to get from manufacturers prices that are as low or often lower than those received from wholesalers that buy from those same manufacturers. Thus, even though Home Depot, Lowe's and similar giant retail chains are technically called "retailers," they buy in such large quantities and perform so many wholesaler functions, including warehousing, order processing and shipment to their individual stores, that except for the name, they are in reality giant wholesalers as well as retailers. Consequently, these "retailers" feel they are more than entitled to the lowest prices available to wholesalers. In fact, if such discount levels are not made available, these retailers are very likely to deemphasize the products of those manufacturers and may even drop them altogether.

Rival Brands

Differentials in the margins available to channel members carrying competitive brands should be kept within tolerable limits. If a particular manufacturer's brand is at a clear disadvantage given the margin a channel member can obtain from it relative to another brand (and this cannot be offset by higher volumes), the channel member will not devote much effort to promoting it.

The practical question facing the channel manager attempting to apply this guideline is: What levels of margin differentials are within tolerable limits? Unfortunately, there is no straightforward answer to this question. Significant variations in margins may be quite tolerable in some cases but not in others. A manufacturer that is well entrenched in many consumer electronics products, such as Sony, can depend on its mass advertising and sales promotion to establish strong consumer preference to pull its products through the channel. At the retail level, promotion by the retailer in the form of local advertising and strong personal selling are relatively minor factors in achieving high sales of Sony products. Accordingly, relatively low margins granted to the retailer are feasible. On the other hand, a smaller, specialized manufacturer, such as Magnavox, has to concentrate its distribution through fewer, more carefully selected and aggressive retailers who can draw customers to themselves with strong local advertising and personal selling. A manufacturer in this position will have to offer larger margins to its retailers to cover the higher costs associated with a more aggressive selling effort.

Channel managers, then, should attempt to weigh any margin differentials between their own and competitive brands in terms of what kind of support their firms offer and what level of support they expect from channel members. If this relationship is found to differ significantly from the competition, differentials in margins should be examined in terms of these differences.

Special Pricing Deals

Special pricing deals offered by a manufacturer to channel members can take many forms including higher discounts, rebates, free goods, enhanced quantity discounts, and others. The purpose behind such special pricing offers is, of course, to stimulate sales of the manufacturer's product during the period of special pricing promotion. In recent years, however, special price promotions have often become the norm in terms of channel member expectations. Thus, channel members come to view these price deals not as "special" or temporary, but rather the normal state of affairs. As such, channel members expect the manufacturer to regularly and continually offer special pricing deals.

From the standpoint of the manufacturer, such channel member expectations can create not only channel pricing problems, but can also undermine brand equity if relentless price cutting becomes associated with the brand. This is exactly the type of situation that Diageo PLC, the world's largest distiller, faced when it pursued more aggressive pricing deals for some of its famous brand liquors.[12] On one of its most popular products, Captain Morgan Parrot Bay Rum, Diageo offered a price promotion and rebate that enhanced distributor and retailer sales volume and significantly lowered prices to consumers on the popular rum. But as CEO John McDonell of rival distiller Patron Spirits International, the maker of Patron tequila, which has avoided such price-cutting deals remarked:

> *"The major suppliers have conditioned the consumers and retailers that there is going to be major deals."*[13]

So, the channel manager is faced with a tough balancing act when it comes to offering special pricing deals. Aggressive pricing may be needed at times such as during economic slowdowns, which is what motivated Diageo PLC's aggressive pricing deals. But, if offered too frequently, channel members may come to expect such deals as a matter of course. Further, as alluded to above, frequent price cutting can undermine the brand equity of famous products, even for such popular ones as Captain Morgan rum.

Conventional Norms in Margins

Oxenfeldt points to the almost universal tendency of channel members to expect margins to meet generally accepted norms:

> *In most trades, resellers have come to regard some particular percentage margin as normal, fair, and proper. They may not obtain that margin on most of the items they sell; even when it is indeed a typical margin, they may not receive it all of the time.... But although the conventional margin may not be an economic reality in the marketplace, it may nevertheless strongly influence the reaction of resellers to the lines they are offered. Failure of a reseller to be "allowed" the conventional margin may create major resentment that results in resellers' giving limited sales support to a brand.*[14]

This strong commitment among channel members to what they consider to be the normal, fair or proper margin makes it very difficult for the manufacturer to deviate from the conventional margin structures. This does not suggest, however, that the manufacturer must slavishly adhere to the norms. As pointed out in the previous sections, exceptions are possible if they can be justified in the eyes of the channel members. What may be viewed as quite reasonable by the manufacturer, however, may be seen quite differently by the channel members.[15] It is the job of the channel manager to attempt to explain to the channel members any margin changes that deviate downward from the norm. While this will not, of course, guarantee that the channel members will support the change, it will at least convey to them the manufacturer's reasons for taking the action. Goodyear Tire & Rubber Co., for example, decided to raise prices to some of its largest distributors after learning that these distributors were undercutting the prices Goodyear charged smaller distributors. The prices Goodyear had been charging its large distributors were so low that the distributors would buy tires in huge quantities and then resell them to smaller distributors outside their own areas. Even with transportation costs added, the prices offered to the small distributors were lower than what Goodyear was charging. Many of the large distributors showed their displeasure with Goodyear's price increase by cutting back orders, but Goodyear stuck to its guns. By closing the gap between prices charged to large and small distributors, Goodyear's revenue per tire actually increased. Goodyear made no attempt to disguise its new pricing policy. Distributors were put on notice that Goodyear's price increase was needed to discourage large distributors from undercutting Goodyear's sales to small distributors.[16]

Margin Variation on Models

Variations in margins on individual models and styles in a product line are common. Manufacturers frequently include in the product line items whose main purpose is to build traffic in the retailers' stores or to serve as "door openers" for wholesalers' field sales forces. These products (often referred to as **promotional products**) are usually the lowest priced in the line and yield relatively low margins for both the manufacturer and channel members. Fortunately, channel members are often amenable to accepting the lower margins associated with these products so long as they are convinced of the promotional value of the product in building patronage. For example, automobile manufacturers frequently advertise "stripped-down" versions of various models at low prices. The strategy behind this is to build traffic in the dealer showroom. With this increased traffic, the dealers have greater opportunity to trade up the prospective buyer to a higher-priced model or to sell optional equipment for the stripped-down promotional model. The margins on the higher-priced models and on the options added to the stripped-down promotional car are significantly higher.

Margins on products in the line that are significantly below the norm and that are not intended as promotional products are much more difficult to justify in the eyes of the channel members. Channel members are therefore far less likely to promote these products with enthusiasm. Indeed, among the so-called deadwood items in a product line, a high proportion are likely to be those that offer low margins to channel members and lack promotional appeal. As a general rule, then, the channel manager should attempt to influence product line pricing so as to use low-margin products for promotional purposes whenever possible.

Price Points

Price points are specific prices, usually at the retail level, at which consumers expect to find products. In some cases certain price points may become entrenched so that consumers almost always expect to find products at those points. Price points can exist for items of very low unit value, such as the McDonald's "Value Menu" McDouble $1.00 cheeseburger and its competitive counterpart, the Whopper Jr., offered by Burger King, all the way to luxury products of very high unit value, such as the over $75,000 Mercedes Benz S Class, BMW 7 series, Jaguar XJ and several others. Between these two extremes are price points such as the under $500 laptop computer,[17] the under $10.00 price for e-book downloads of popular best sellers or 46-inch flat screen TVs for under $1,000. Price points move up or down over time as a result of inflation and changing technology. So, while inflation has dramatically increased the price point for a cup of coffee, advances in electronics have drastically lowered the price points for personal computers, flat-screen TVs and most other consumer electronic products.

The channel manager needs to be aware of the price points at which channel members expect to offer products and help to assure that such products are available to the channel members. Not having products to sell at popular price points can deprive channel members of significant sales simply because they lack products that fit these price points. This holds whether the product in question is a $1.00 cheeseburger at a fast-food restaurant or an $80,000 luxury sedan at a prestigious auto dealership. Indeed, one of the luxury auto makers, BMW, has made it a core strategy to assure its dealers have cars at virtually all of the price points for upscale automobiles, from near luxury 100 Series and 300 Series cars all the way to six-figure 800 Series ultra luxury cars.

Product Variations

When a manufacturer attaches prices to the various models within a given product line, it should be careful to associate price differences with differences in product features.[18] If the price differences are not closely associated with visible or identified product features, the channel members will have a more difficult selling job. For example, a sporting goods retailer handling a line of five models of tennis rackets would like to have an easy "handle" in the form of specific product features that salespeople can use to explain price differences to customers. If, for example, the product differences between the $100 and $150 models are not made explicit, the retailer is likely to take the course of least resistance—selling mainly the lower-priced model or whichever model in the line is easiest to sell. A little extra care by the manufacturer in thinking about the pricing of the product line *from the channel members' perspective* can mitigate this kind of pricing problem.

Other Issues in Channel Pricing

The guidelines for channel pricing just discussed deal with a wide range of channel pricing issues. Yet the channel manager is likely to face other channel pricing issues that require more specific and detailed attention. Six of the most important of these are discussed in the remainder of this chapter.

Exercising Control in Channel Pricing

As stated earlier in this chapter, the manufacturer's pricing strategies often require channel member support and cooperation if they are to be implemented effectively. But, as we have also pointed out throughout this text, channel members have minds of their own and often want to do things their own way. This is especially true when it comes to pricing. Of all of the elements of the marketing mix, channel members typically view pricing as the area that is most in their domain.[19] They may defer to the manufacturer's claim to know how the product should be manufactured, promoted and even distributed; but when it comes to pricing, channel members believe that they know best and should therefore be free to pursue their own pricing strategies.[20] As long as the manufacturer's pricing policies do not infringe on the channel members' pricing freedom, there is no problem. But as soon as the manufacturer seeks to exercise some control over channel members' pricing strategies, channel members may feel that the manufacturer has stepped out of its proper boundary.

Yet, from the manufacturer's point of view, some of the most important pricing strategies may call for having some degree of control over the channel members' pricing policies.[21] For example, a manufacturer may want to use pricing strategy to help maintain the quality image of its products and, hence, does not want channel members cutting prices significantly. Or a manufacturer may believe, as many do, that "stable" prices are in the best, long-run interest of the firm and its channel members because price cutting can lead to fierce price wars that create havoc for the manufacturer and channel members. Even though outright dictating by the manufacturer of the selling price that channel members can charge their customers may violate antitrust legislation, many manufacturers still attempt to influence channel members to conform to their pricing policies. In attempting to do so, however, the manufacturer is faced with the difficult and delicate task of enforcing pricing policies without alienating channel members, while still staying within the boundaries of antitrust legislation. Needless to say, this is not easy to do—as Stride Rite Corporation found out the hard way when it was ordered to pay over $7 million in an antitrust settlement. The case stemmed from Stride Rite's attempt to coerce retailers to sell six styles of its Keds women's athletic shoes at suggested retail prices specified by Stride Rite. Shipments were curtailed or cut off if the retailers did not comply with Stride Rite's pricing policy.

Although there is no surefire way to avoid the problem Stride Rite encountered when it tried to exercise pricing control in its marketing channels, several guidelines can be offered.

First, any type of coercive approaches to controlling channel member pricing policies should probably be ruled out. Not only are they likely to increase the probability of alienating the channel members, but they may be illegal as well.

Second, encroachment by the manufacturer into the domain of channel member pricing policies should be undertaken only if the manufacturer believes that it is in his or her vital, long-term strategic interest to do so. Such a pricing strategy should never be taken lightly or applied in circumstances that are not of crucial importance.

Finally, if the manufacturer does feel that it is necessary to exercise some control over channel member pricing policies, an attempt should be made to do so through what might be called "friendly persuasion." ScottsMirical-Gro Company strategy for influencing channel member pricing policies is the model for this kind of approach. A leading manufacturer of lawn-care products, Scotts has a long-standing policy of having dealers maintain the manufacturer's "suggested" prices. The company expects all of its dealers to conform to that policy. But rather than attempting to use coercion, Scotts is able to attain its pricing objectives by persuading dealers that the suggested prices are in their own self-interest. Scotts argues that the company's suggested retail prices are necessary to provide dealers with adequate margins to cover the high levels of service they are expected to offer, such as providing ample stocks and assortments of Scotts products, adequate safety stock and a high degree of personal attention and counseling for lawn-care customers. Thus, Scotts' approach is to build a strong case for its pricing strategy and then let the dealers decide for themselves whether they want to conform to Scotts' pricing policies. Scotts has also avoided other potential pricing problems by selling only certain product lines to discount mass merchants, while reserving others for sale only through more service-oriented independent retailers.

Changing Price Policies

Another important channel pricing issue that the manufacturer is almost sure to face at one time or another is dealing with channel member reactions to major changes in the manufacturer's pricing policies and related terms of sale. Almost certainly, a time will come when the manufacturer feels it necessary to make major changes in these two areas. The need might spring from cost pressures, competitive factors or a variety of other external developments beyond the manufacturer's control.[22] But regardless of the cause, major changes in the manufacturer's pricing policies are bound to affect channel members.

Typically, channel members become very uneasy when they hear about significant changes in manufacturer pricing policies or terms of sale. Channel members become accustomed to dealing with the manufacturer based on a particular set of pricing policies that may have existed in basically the same form for a long period of time. Indeed, their own pricing strategies may be closely tied to the existing pricing policies of the manufacturer.[23] Hence, any change in the status quo becomes a cause for concern, especially when the manufacturer's price policy changes appear to be aimed at toughening channel pricing policies or related terms of sale.

The celebrated pricing strategy change undertaken by Procter & Gamble provides a case in point. P&G decided to offer fewer "special" discount deals on the sale of its products to retailers and instead have consistently lower wholesale prices. Thus, retailers could offer consumers everyday low prices on P&G products rather than on-again/off-again promotions that tend to undermine consumer brand loyalty and encourage consumers to "bounce" from shelf to shelf seeking whatever brand happens to be on sale or offers the highest discount coupon. Moreover, P&G also hoped to smooth out the peaks and valleys in demand associated with the old pricing strategy, which wreaked havoc on production and distribution scheduling. But retailer reactions to P&G's changed pricing strategy have been mixed. Some welcome it, but many others feel the pricing strategy limits their promotional and merchandising flexibility and may even reduce their profits. Studies undertaken at the University of Chicago suggest that the retailers' concerns may be well grounded because findings from the study show that grocery retailers offering everyday low prices are not as profitable as those using traditional promotional pricing strategies. If further research continues to reflect this pattern and if retailer experience confirms the outcome of lower profits associated with the everyday low-pricing strategy, P&G and other manufacturers pushing retailers to pursue this strategy may be faced with many disgruntled retailers who will be more than eager to promote competitors' products that are priced the old-fashioned way.[24]

With regard to changing terms of sale, a development in the apparel industry underscores how such changes can heighten tensions in the channel. The terms of sale in question here are what is typically referred to in the industry as **markdown money**. Essentially, markdown money is a payment by an apparel maker to the retailer, usually a department store, to help offset the money the retailers lose when items do not sell at full price. The specific terms of just how much markdown money the manufacturer will pay to the retailer to offset price reductions and the time frame involved are negotiated between manufacturer and department store. Sometimes these agreements are verbal rather than written in a formal contract. But the basic concept of markdown money is always the same: retailers expect manufacturers to absorb a significant portion of the markdowns taken by retailers on the manufacturers' products. This practice has existed for decades in the apparel business. But in recent years, some apparel manufacturers, such as Nicole Miller Ltd., have refused to pay markdown money. Another apparel manufacturer, Michael Kors, has launched a multi-million dollar lawsuit against Saks Fifth Avenue aimed at what it alleges are unfair practices involving markdown money.[25] Such challenges to this decades-old practice have thrown the industry into turmoil. Other apparel makers, such as Jones Apparel Group, Liz Claiborne Inc., Tommy Hilfiger Corp. and Polo Ralph Lauren Corp., have become confused as to how to proceed in their relationships with department stores given the uncertain future of markdown money. On the one hand, all of these manufacturers want to get as much of their new products as possible into the major retailers. By offering generous amounts of markdown money, retailer risk is reduced, hence they will stock more of the manufacturer's products. However, because a competitive manufacturer, such as Nicole Miller, has refused to pay markdown money and another competitor, Michael Kors, had launched a lawsuit, the future viability of markdown money may be in jeopardy.

From a channel management perspective, such uncertainty over the future of terms of sale that have been in place for decades can be unsettling. Whether such changes in terms of sale deal with markdown money or other terms, such as return privileges, financing arrangements or delivery provisions, the channel manager needs to determine whether the old ways of doing business can continue or whether new terms can and should be put in place.

Passing Price Increases through the Channel

Price increases by manufacturers are virtually inevitable and during inflationary periods in the economy they become steeper and more frequent. So long as each channel member is able to pass along manufacturer-initiated price increases to the next channel member, and ultimately to the final user, the price increase issue is not too worrisome. But when increased prices cannot be totally passed through the channel and channel members have to begin absorbing some or all of the price increases by cutting into *their* margins, price increases become a critical issue. Take, for example, the case of Japanese auto manufacturers. By the end of the first decade of the twenty-first century, the value of the U.S. dollar was decreasing significantly relative to the Japanese yen. Dealers selling Japanese cars were forced to either absorb the higher wholesale costs for the cars or raise prices, which could adversely affect their sales in the highly competitive U.S. auto market. The same dilemma also faced many supermarket chains during this time period as a result of rapidly increasing commodity processes that resulted in higher wholesale prices on many grocery products.[26] Here again, the supermarkets either had to raise prices or absorb at least some of the cost themselves. Given the ultra-competitive retail food market, many supermarkets felt they had little choice but to absorb, rather than pass on to consumers, a substantial portion of their higher costs even though this adversely affected their bottom lines. Needless to say, the supermarkets were not pleased with food manufacturers that did not share but simply passed on to retailers the burden of absorbing the higher costs.

In addition to the direct monetary difficulties arising from nontransferable price increases, another possible problem is the ill will that they can create as each channel member blames the next for the price increases. Unfortunately, such price increases are too often simply passed along in rote fashion by the manufacturer (and other channel members) before other possible alternatives or strategies that could help mitigate the effects of the price increase are given adequate consideration. Such alternatives and strategies include the following:

First, before passing on a price increase, manufacturers could give more thought to the long- and short-term implications of going through with the price increase versus attempting to hold the line on prices to the greatest extent possible. There may be cases where the short-term negative effects on the manufacturer's profits of holding the line on prices are more than offset by the long-term benefits, such as a more loyal and viable team of channel members. Most of the major Japanese auto manufacturers, for instance, did in fact attempt to hold the line on prices by absorbing some of the increased costs associated with the rising value of the yen. But this became increasingly difficult to do without drastically eroding their profits over the longer run.

Second, if passing on the price increase is unavoidable, the manufacturer should do whatever possible to mitigate the negative effects of the increase on channel members. This is what giant beer maker, Anheuser-Busch InBev did soon after it raised beer prices in the U.S. in 2009 right after the "Great Recession of 2008." The price increase of over 4 percent at a time when overall consumer prices in the U.S. were down 2.1 percent upset retailers who believed that if they passed on the price increase to final customers, their sales volume would suffer. To help offset the price increase and prop up its retailers' sales, Anheuser-Busch InBev began offering rebates on a number of its products and introduced more special promotions on its lower-priced brands.[27]

In addition to rebates and other price-related strategies for mitigating the effects of price increases on channel members, other solutions include offering financial assistance, more liberal payment terms and special deals, such as allowing the channel members to buy before the price increase goes into effect.

Finally, the manufacturer could change its strategies in the other areas of the marketing mix, particularly product strategy, to help offset the effects of price increases. For example, the product could be improved so that at least the channel members would have a "handle" for justifying the price increase to their customers on the basis of more value in the product. Conversely, the product could be downgraded, not necessarily from a quality standpoint, but in terms of reduction in certain features and accessories that may not be vital to the appeal and performance of the product.[28] Such a stripped-down version of the product selling at a lower price may be quite preferable to the "fancier" version at a significantly higher price. Another, although rather controversial, product strategy to offset higher costs is to reduce the size of the package. Instead of the package containing one pound, for example, it could be reduced to 14 ounces. Many food and packaged goods manufacturers have pursued this strategy in recent years as an alternative to raising prices.

Dual Channel Pricing

If the manufacturer uses a dual channel structure that provides for direct sales by the manufacturer to final customers as well as sales through independent channel members for the same products, careful attention needs to be paid to the pricing strategy used by the manufacturer.[29]

Although manufacturers selling their products directly to customers in seeming competition with their independent channel members is certainly not a new phenomenon, the tremendous growth of online channels in recent years has created another major pathway for manufacturers to reach consumers directly.[30] Long before online channels emerged, the appropriate pricing strategy for manufacturers selling their products directly to consumers as well as through independent resellers was to never sell at prices lower than those charged by the independent channel members. It is even better if the manufacturer charges a higher price than the independent channel members when the final customer seeks to buy through the manufacturer-direct channel. By pricing higher for the direct channel, the manufacturer, rather than the retailer, will be at a competitive disadvantage. This channel pricing strategy prescription holds just as strongly today in an age of high-tech online and mobile channels as it did several decades ago when the only direct-to-consumer channels for manufacturers were via mail order and door-to-door.[31] But then as now, manufacturers that set prices below those charged by their channel members not only undermine the channel relationship but set the stage for a complete breakup. Channel members are typically already resentful when manufacturers sell direct at equal or higher prices than those offered by channel members. If manufacturers become so audacious as to sell at *lower prices*, channel members are likely to "go ballistic" by dropping the offending manufacturers' products as quickly as possible.

So, the channel manager needs to pay careful attention to make sure that multi-channel pricing strategies pursued by his or her firm do not undermine channel member sales and profit potential.

Using Price Incentives in the Channel

Pricing strategy is frequently used by manufacturers as a promotional tool. A wide range of pricing devices is used to carry out such pricing strategy, including special deals, seasonal discounts, rebates,[32] price reductions, coupons, two for the price of one and a variety of others. The purpose of such promotional pricing is, of course, to increase the sales and market share of the product of the manufacturer that is offering the special prices.[33] Among manufacturers of consumer packaged goods, price promotions, particularly coupons, have become so common and widespread that many consumers regard them as a "birthright" to which they are entitled when they buy the product. The vast array of coupons available online has further increased consumer expectations for coupons to be provided for virtually any product purchased.

Such enthusiasm for promotional pricing strategies shown by consumers is not always shared by channel members, however. Retailers, especially supermarkets, drug chains and mass merchandisers, often complain about the headaches and nuisance involved in handling millions of coupons, making sure products that are supposed to be specially reduced actually reflect this when placed on store shelves and following up on the many details involved in taking advantage of special pricing deals offered by so many different manufacturers. Thus, from the manufacturer's point of view, gaining strong retailer acceptance and follow-through on pricing promotions can be a problem.

Part of the problem can be solved merely by making pricing promotions as simple and straightforward as possible, so that channel members can participate with a minimum of time and effort.[34] The more significant problem underlying some price promotions, however, stems from the *differing price elasticities of consumers versus retailers* (or wholesalers)—that is, consumers' responses to price reductions may differ significantly from those of retailers.[35] What consumers might perceive as an attractive price reduction may be perceived by retailers as insignificant and unworthy of the extra effort and risk involved (for instance, if extra inventory has to be purchased). Five or six cents off on a bar of soap may be sufficient to increase consumer demand for the product, but the corresponding price incentive offered to retailers for participating in the price promotion may not be sufficient to stimulate *their* desire to be fully involved in the deal. The extra few cents in gross margin available to the retailer for participating may not compensate the store sufficiently for the higher inventory and handling costs involved as well as the extra display or shelf space that is often called for in such promotions. Consequently, the stores often participate in promotions but follow through only halfheartedly on key aspects of the promotional deal, such as providing extra display space, stocking the product on more prominent shelf facings and featuring the product in its advertising. When this happens, the manufacturer does not obtain the full impact of its promotional pricing strategy because low retailer acceptance and follow-through undermine the stimulative effects of the strategy. Further, many retailers as well as wholesalers will take advantage of manufacturers' promotions by engaging in **forward buying**. In this case, the channel members load up on the discounted products featured in the promotion, but pass on the lower price for just a portion of the amount purchased to their customers. The rest is held in inventory by retailers for sale at the regular price after the promotion has run its course. This practice defeats the purpose of the manufacturer's promotion, which assumes that the channel members will pass on all of the discounted merchandise to build sales and market share for the products in question.

The solution to the problem of getting better mileage out of manufacturer-initiated price promotions begins with recognition on the part of the manufacturer of the differing price elasticities between consumers and retailers. Price promotion strategies should be designed to be *at least as attractive to retailers as they are to consumers.* Manufacturers may give a great deal of thought to how much of a price incentive they need to offer to stimulate consumer demand through a price promotion. But if manufacturers expect strong retailer support for their price promotions, they also need to make a similar effort to determine just how much of a price incentive they need to offer retailers (or wholesalers) in order to secure it.[36] Even with such efforts, however, in highly competitive markets, such as those for consumer packaged goods, retailers and wholesalers will often take advantage of price promotions so as to maximize *their* profit potential whether or not it helps the manufacturer or the final consumer.

Dealing with the Gray Market and Free Riding

Two of the most troublesome developments affecting the pricing policies and strategies of many manufacturers of branded products are the gray market and the related phenomenon of free riding.

The **gray market** refers to the sale, usually at low prices, of brand-name products by unauthorized distributors or dealers.[37] Sometimes the origin of the products is overseas manufacturers, such as those in Japan, Europe or China. At other times, they may be produced by a domestic manufacturer in the United States, ostensibly for sale overseas, or by a U.S. subsidiary abroad. In any case, if these domestic or imported products are sold in the United States by distributors or dealers who were not officially authorized by the manufacturer to sell the products, such goods become part of the gray market.[38] The diversity of products sold in the gray market is also quite broad, including automobiles such as the BMW, luxury clothing and accessories, personal computers, Nikon cameras, Duracell batteries and even Opium, the world's best-selling perfume.[39]

Free riding is a term used to describe the behavior of distributors and dealers who offer low prices but little, if any, services, to customers. By undercutting the prices charged by distributors or dealers who display a full selection of the products and provide information, sales assistance and after-sale service, the discounters get a "free ride" from the services provided by the higher-priced, full-service distributors and dealers. Thus, for example, a customer seeking a Nikon Coolpix P7000 Digital Camera may go to a full-service Nikon dealer, see a wide selection of models and lenses, have the camera's operation explained by a knowledgeable salesperson and be able to handle and try the product; but then, when it comes to actually purchasing the product, that customer may buy the product at a significantly lower price from an online retailer. In such a case, the full-service dealer did everything but make the sale, which went instead to the lower-priced online dealer who got a "free ride" from the efforts of the full service dealer.

The gray market and the free riding phenomenon are related in that often products sold by free riders are gray market products, although this is by no means always the case.

Gray markets and free riding can both be of serious concern to the manufacturers of the products involved if these practices are widespread enough to disrupt the manufacturers' ability to manage their marketing channels. Specifically, authorized channel members who are providing the level of service the manufacturer is seeking in the sale of its products will be very unhappy if they are being undercut by unauthorized distributors, dealers selling gray market products or even authorized channel members who are "giving the products away." Some of these unhappy channel members may drop the product and seek out other manufacturers who have been less affected by the gray market and free riders. Others may retaliate by "footballing" the product—making disparaging remarks about a product in order to sell a competitor's product. Still others may pursue the "if you can't beat 'em, join 'em" approach and become gray market sellers and/or free riders themselves.

Any and all of these channel member responses to the gray market and free riding may not be in the manufacturer's long-run interest and indeed could be highly detrimental. Unfortunately, there is no obvious or easy solution to the problems associated with the gray market or free riding. With regard to the manufacturer's pricing strategy, it may be a violation of antitrust law if the manufacturer uses coercion to dictate the prices charged by channel members (see Chapter 3) and, of course, the manufacturer can exercise even less control over the pricing practices of unauthorized distributors and dealers. With respect to keeping products out of the gray market, the manufacturer can stop selling to channel members who resell the products to unauthorized distributors or dealers. But with so many potential sources for products that are manufactured and distributed in so many countries around the world and given the proliferation of online gray market sellers, even this strong measure may have only a limited effect.[40] So, in the short run, manufacturers attempting to maintain the price of their products in the face of the gray market and free riding are likely to experience only limited success. But in the longer run, channel design decisions that result in more closely controlled channels and selective distribution (see Chapters 5, 6 and 7) as well as changing buyer preferences (such as a desire for more service) may help to limit the growth of the gray market and free riding.[41]

Summary

Pricing strategy should incorporate not only internal cost, target market and competitive considerations, but channel considerations as well. The channel considerations, however, are often given the least attention in the manufacturer's pricing strategy and are sometimes almost overlooked completely. This is unfortunate because pricing strategy can have a substantial impact on channel member behavior. Specifically, if channel members perceive the manufacturer's pricing strategy as congruent with their own interests, they are more likely to provide a higher level of cooperation. If, on the other hand, the manufacturer's approach to pricing reflects a lack of awareness of channel members' needs or appears to work against them, a much lower level of cooperation, or even conflict, is the more

likely result. So the major challenge facing the channel manager in the area of pricing is to foster pricing strategies that promote channel member cooperation and minimize conflict.

The channel manager needs to be familiar with the anatomy of channel pricing in order to understand that each channel member needs to be adequately compensated for the part it plays in performing the distribution tasks. In effect, then, the channel manager is buying distribution when the services of channel members are sought.

In developing pricing strategies, the manufacturer should pay particular attention to the following eight guidelines: (1) profit margins made available to channel members should be adequate to cover costs and provide for reasonable profits; (2) margins offered to different classes of channel members should vary in rough proportion to the functions they perform; (3) margins available to channel members on the manufacturer's products should be competitive with those of rival brands; (4) special arrangements between the manufacturer and channel members that result in either an increase or decrease in services rendered should be reflected in the margins available to channel members; (5) whenever possible, the manufacturer should try to conform to conventional norms for margins in the trade; (6) variations in margins on different models or styles of the manufacturer's products should be logical and usually not too far off the conventional margin in the trade; (7) if price points exist at the wholesale and/or retail levels, they should be recognized and products should be priced so as to meet those price points and (8) variations in prices by a manufacturer for different products in its line should, whenever possible, be associated with visible or identifiable differences in product features to help channel members do a more effective selling job.

The chapter also discussed six major pricing issues that the manufacturer is likely to face at one time or another.

The first of these dealt with pricing control in the channel. In general, if a manufacturer seeks to exercise control over channel member pricing policies, it should avoid using coercion and instead use "friendly persuasion" approaches that allow channel members to decide for themselves if they want to conform to the manufacturer's pricing policies.

The second pricing issue dealt with the impact of major price policy changes on channel member behavior. Whenever possible, the channel manager should

attempt to predict channel member reactions to these changes *before* they are undertaken.

The third issue concerned the passing of price increases through the channel. When channel members cannot pass on price increases, they must absorb the increases themselves. This results not only in severe financial difficulties in some cases, but in a great deal of ill will as well. Manufacturers should often make more of an effort to consider other options or strategies to mitigate the negative effects of such price increases on channel members.

The fourth issue in channel pricing dealt with the use of price incentives. While some incentives produce strong stimulative effects on consumer demand for the manufacturer's products, the price elasticity underlying consumer reaction may not be the same for channel members. Hence channel members may respond much less enthusiastically to the price promotion. Thus, manufacturers should attempt to make price incentives at least as attractive to channel members as they are to consumers if they expect to get strong channel member support.

The fifth issue dealt with pricing in duel channels. The manufacturer should price products sold directly at equal or higher prices than those sold through independent channel members.

The sixth issue concerned the problems created for the manufacturer's pricing strategies and policies by the gray market and free riding. While there are no easy or short-term answers to these problems, in the longer run, more tightly controlled channels featuring selective distribution along with changes in buyer preferences toward more service may limit the growth of both the gray market and free riding.

Review Questions

1. The basic factors to consider in developing pricing strategies are market variables, internal cost and competitive forces. Do you agree or disagree? Explain.

2. What should be the role of the channel manager in formulating the manufacturer's pricing policies and strategies?

3. Explain the concept of "buying distribution services" as it applies to channel pricing strategy.

4. How might different classes of channel members, rival brands and special arrangements between the manufacturer and channel members affect pricing strategies?

5. What is meant by conventional norms in margins? How does this concept affect channel pricing policy?

6. Discuss the issues involved in channel pricing to account for margin variations on different models in a product line, price points and product variations.

7. Discuss the problems associated with the manufacturer's attempt to exercise price control in the channel. How should the manufacturer deal with these problems?

8. Why might major changes in the manufacturer's pricing policies or terms of sale create havoc for

the channel members? How might the manufacturer mitigate the negative effects of such changes?

9. Discuss some alternative strategies available to the manufacturer contemplating the passing of price increases through the channel.

10. What is the underlying factor responsible for possible differing reactions of consumers versus channel members to a manufacturer-initiated price incentive? Explain.

11. Why is participation in the gray market attractive to many distributors and dealers? Discuss.

12. Free riding, though profitable for some types of dealers, can be detrimental for manufacturers, full-service dealers and even consumers. Do you agree or disagree? Explain.

Channel Issues for Discussion

1. Apple CEO Steve Jobs has been quoted as saying: "We don't know how to build a sub-$500 computer that is not a piece of junk." Job's disdain for the under $500 price point for personal computers reflects his belief that price should not be the driver of product developments. Through much of its history, Apple has pursued a premium pricing strategy to complement its reputation for offering more innovative and superior products. So, even if Apple resellers were to clamor for Apple to offer lower-priced computers (as well as other products) to compete at price points that Apple is missing, Apple is likely to say no.

   Discuss Apple's pricing strategy in terms of its future implications for the company's channel strategy.

2. A sales representative from a wholesaler of sporting goods called on a sporting goods retailer in the middle of the summer. The salesman was particularly fond of the new line of exercise equipment from a major manufacturer his company was now carrying. He went through his presentation of showing pictures, leaflets and catalogs for about 20 minutes. Finally, the store owner held up his hand as if to say "wait a minute" and said, "What's the bottom line? How much can I make on this stuff? Normally we get 50 percent off list price on these products and I see from your catalog that most of your merchandise offers that. But the market around here is very competitive. Stores discount this stuff like crazy. I need 35 percent gross margin to pay my expenses and make a profit. How can I be sure this merchandise will measure up?"

   What would be your response to the store owner? Present an argument that would address his concerns on gross margins.

3. Amazon.com became the world's largest e-book seller by offering new best selling books for a fixed price of $9.99 regardless of the fame and popularity of the author or the prestige of the publisher. But some publishers have balked at Amazon's e-book pricing strategy. They believe that over time, the $9.99 price will create a ceiling for consumer price perception about the value of new books. If consumers believe new books from famed authors and top publishers are worth no more than $9.99, the publishers' ability to price their products at what they believe them to be worth will be undermined or destroyed completely. In early 2010, five publishers, including Macmillan, one of the largest and most prestigious book publishers, refused to offer their books through Amazon's Kindle e-books and instead decided to distribute their e-book list through Apple's iPad, which allows the publisher to set the price. Some of the e-books distributed through Apple will be priced at $14.99.

   Who do you think should control the pricing of e-book best sellers in the marketing channel? Why?

4. Tina Anderson talked to knowledgeable salespeople about the pros and cons of a variety of cameras, discussed the various features and handled the cameras to see how they felt while at the Camera Store, a full-service camera shop at a regional shopping mall. She decided to buy a Konica Minolta DiMAGE X50. But she did not buy it from the Camera Store. Instead she said thank you very much to the salesperson and left the store. She went over to the Starbucks across the street, ordered a tall frappuccino and, while sipping the drink, ordered the Konica Minolta DiMAGE X50 using her Apple iPhone to find the lowest price online seller. Three days later, the camera was delivered by UPS to Tina's home. Tina was delighted—she had saved $60 and the camera was exactly the same one she had tried

out in the Camera Store. Tina could not have cared less whether the online dealer was authorized to sell Konica Minolta cameras.

Discuss this situation from the point of view of Tina Anderson, the Camera Store, the online dealer and the manufacturer.

5. Anheuser-Busch InBev and MillerCoors LLC control about 80 percent of the U.S. beer market. Most of the beer distributed by both companies is sold through independent beer distributors who, in turn, sell the beer to retailers, restaurants and bars. Anheuser-Busch InBev, which had been acquired by Belgium-based brewer InBev in mid-2008, soon after embarked on a cost-cutting

program. One key cost focus was distributor margins: Anheuser-Busch distributors received about $1.00 for each case of Budweiser distributed to retail channel members compared to $.85 paid by MillerCoors to distributors. By eliminating that 15 cent difference in margin, Anheuser-Busch InBev estimated it could save about $200 million per year! But Anheuser-Busch distributors, many of whom had decades-old relationships with the brewer, would not be happy with the lower margins.

Should Anheuser-Busch InBev proceed with the margin cut? Why or why not?

References

1. See: David Shipley and Elizabeth Bourdon, "Distributor Pricing in Very Competitive Markets," *Industrial Marketing Management* (1990): 215–224; and William B. Wagner, "Changing Industrial Buyer-Seller Pricing Concerns," *Industrial Marketing Management* (1981): 109–117.
2. Some notable exceptions include: Cenk Kocas and Jonathan D. Bohlman, "Segmented Switches and Retailer Pricing Strategies," *Journal of Marketing* (May 2008): 124–142; Rajeev K. Tyagi, "Do Strategic Conclusions Depend on How Price is Defined in Models of Distribution Channels?" *Journal of Marketing Research* (May 2005): 228–232; Garesh Iyer, "Coordinating Channels Under Price and Nonprice Competition," *Marketing Science* 17, no. 4 (1998): 338–355; S. Chan Choi, "Price Competition in a Duopoly Common Retailer Channel," *Journal of Retailing* 72, no. 2 (1996): 117–134; Charles A. Ingene and Mark E. Parry, "Coordination and Manufacturer Profit Maximization: The Multiple Retailer Channel," *Journal of Retailing* 71, no. 2 (1995): 129–151; and Rockney G. Walters and Scott B. MacKenzie, "A Structural Equations Analysis of the Impact of Price Promotions on Store Performance," *Journal of Marketing Research* (February 1988): 51–63.
3. See, for example: Sudheer Gupta and Richard Loulou, "Process Innovation, Product Differentiation and Channel Structure: Strategic Incentives in a Duopoly," *Marketing Science* 17, no. 4 (1998): 301–316; and Gerald E. Smith, Meera P. Venkatraman and Lawrence H. Wortzel, "Strategic Marketing Fit in Manufacturer-Retailer Relationships: Price Leaders versus Merchandise Differentiators," *Journal of Retailing* 71, no. 3 (1995): 297–315.
4. For a related discussion, see: Wujin Chu and Preyas S. Desai, "Channel Coordination Mechanisms for Customer Satisfaction," *Marketing Science* 14, no. 4 (1995): 343–359.
5. Paul Ziobro, "McDonald's Bets Pricing At $1 Will Heat Up Summer Sales," *Wall Street Journal*, March 18, 2010: B6.
6. For another approach in which the sales force might be utilized for this purpose, see: P. Ronald Stephenson, William L. Cron and Gary L. Frazier, "Delegating Pricing Authority to Sales Force: The Effects on Sales and Profit Performance," *Journal of Marketing* (Spring 1979): 21–28.
7. For a related discussion, see: Christopher Farrell and Zachary Schiller, "Stuck, How Companies Cope When They Can't Raise Prices," *BusinessWeek*, November 15, 1993: 146–155.
8. Alfred R. Oxenfeldt, *Pricing Strategies* (New York: AMACOM, a division of American Management Association, 1975), 140.
9. For a related discussion, see Robert Berner and Stephanie Anderson, "Wal-Mart is Eating Everybody's Lunch," *BusinessWeek*, April 15, 2002: 43.
10. Martin R. Warshaw, "Pricing to Gain Wholesalers' Selling Support," *Journal of Marketing* (July 1962): 50–51.
11. Sumee Choi and Anna S. Mattila, "Perceived Fairness of Price Differences Across Channels: The Moderating Role of Price Frame and Norm Perceptions," *Journal of Marketing Theory and Practice* (Winter 2009): 27–47; Joseph P. Guiltinan, "The Price Bundling of Services: A Normative Framework," *Journal of Marketing* (April 1987): 74–85.
12. David Kesmodel, "Liquor Discounts Become Bad Habit for Spirit Makers," *Wall Street Journal*, February 25, 2010: B1.
13. Kesmodel, "Liquor Discounts Become Bad Habit," B1.

14. Oxenfeldt, *Pricing Strategies*, 144.

15. Bert Rosenbloom and Paul R. Warshaw, "Perceptions of Wholesaler Functional Role Prescriptions in Marketing Channels," *European Journal of Marketing* no. 2 (1989): 31–46.

16. Timothy Aeppel, "After Cost Cutting Companies Turn Toward Price Rises," *Wall Street Journal*, September 18, 2002: A1, A12.

17. For a related discussion, see: Stephan Wildstrom, "The Stubborn Luxury of Apple," *BusinessWeek*, November 23, 2009: 82.

18. Oxenfeldt, *Pricing Strategies*, 145.

19. See the discussion in Chapter 4 on decision domain disagreements as a cause of conflict.

20. For an insightful article related to the issue of which channel member should make pricing decisions, see: Jospeh Kamen, "Price Filtering: Restricting Price Deals to Those Least Likely to Buy Without Them," *Journal of Consumer Marketing* (Summer 1989): 37–43.

21. For a related discussion, see: Rajiv K. Sinha, Fernando S. Machado and Collin Sellman, "Don't Think Twice, It's All Right: Music of Piracy and Pricing in a DRM-Free Environment," *Journal of Marketing* (March 2010): 40–54.

22. See, for example, Kent B.Monroe and Adris A. Zoltners, "Pricing the Product Line During Periods of Scarcity," *Journal of Marketing* (Summer 1979): 49–49.

23. For a related discussion, see: David Shipley and Leslie Davies, "The Role and Burden Allocation of Credit in Distribution Channels," *Journal of Marketing Channels* (1991): 3–22.

24. For an excellent, in-depth study related to this issue, see: Kusum L. Ailawadi, Donald R. Lehmann and Scott A. Neslin, "Market Response to a Major Policy Change in the Marketing Mix: Learning from Procter & Gamble's Value Pricing Strategy," *Journal of Marketing* (January 2001): 44–61.

25. Ellen Byron and Teri Agins, "Probing Price Tags," *Wall Street Journal*, May 13, 2005: B1, B2.

26. Cecillie Rohwedder, Aaron O. Patrick and Timothy W. Martin, "Big Grocer Pulls Unilever Items Over Pricing," *Wall Street Journal*, February 11, 2009: B1, B5.

27. Dean Foust, "Looks Like a Beer Brawl," *BusinessWeek*, July 28, 2008: 52; David Kesmodel, "Beer Makes Plain More Price Boosts," *Wall Street Journal*, August 26, 2009: B1.

28. See, for example: "Microsoft's Aggressive New Pricing Strategy," *BusinessWeek*, July 27, 2009: 51.

29. For an in-depth analysis of this pricing strategy, see: Ruiliang Yan, "Pricing Strategy for Companies with Mixed Online and Traditional Retailing Distribution Markets," *Journal of Product and Brand Management* vol. 17, no. 1 (2008): 48–56.

30. Bert Rosenbloom, "Multi-Channel Strategy in Business-to-Business Markets: Prospects and Problems," *Industrial Marketing Management* (January 2007): 4–9.

31. Kyle Cattani and Hans Sebastian, "When Manufacturers Go Retail," *Sloan Management Review* (Winter 2006): 8–10.

32. See, for example: "Sholnn Freeman and Joseph B. White, "GM to Roll Out Cash-Rebate Sales Drive," *Wall Street Journal*, January 3, 2002: A3.

33. For an excellent study of how such special price deals operate to increase consumer purchases, see: Robert C. Blattberg, Gary D. Eppen and Joshua Lieberman, "A Theoretical and Empirical Evaluation of Price Deals for Consumer Non-durables," *Journal of Marketing* (Winter 1981): 116–129.

34. For a related discussion, see: Amy Merrick, "Retailers Try to Get Leg Up on Markdowns with New Software," *Wall Street Journal*, August 7, 2001: A1, A6.

35. For an article related to price elasticities, see: Gerard J. Tellis, "The Price Elasticity of Selective Demand: A Meta-Analysis of Econometric Models of Sales," *Journal of Marketing Research* (November 1988): 331–341.

36. See, for example: Justin Scheck, "H-P Wields Clout to Undercut PC Rivals," *Wall Street Journal*, September 24, 2009: B1.

37. For a thorough background article on the gray market, see: James Cross, James Stephans and Robert E. Benjamin, "Gray Markets: A Legal Review and Public Policy Perspective," *Journal of Public Policy and Marketing* (1990): 183–194.

38. See Larry S. Lowe and Kevin McCrohan, "Gray Markets in the United States," *Journal of Consumer Marketing* (Winter 1988): 41–45.

39. Dale F. Duhan and Mary Jane Sheffet, "Gray Markets and the Legal Status of Parallel Importation," *Journal of Marketing* (July 1988): 75–83; and James M. Maskulka and Melissa O'Neal, "Gray Market Consumers: New Channel Captains?" in *Proceedings of the Winter Educators' Conference of the American Marketing Association*, eds. Russel Belk et al. (Chicago: American Marketing Association, 1987), 1–4.

40. For some additional perspectives on dealing with the gray market, see Larry S. Lowe and Kevin F. McCrohan, "Minimize the Impact of the Gray Market," *Journal of Business Strategy* (November–December 1989): 47–50.

41. Mary Jane Sheffet and Debra L. Scammon, "Resale Price Maintenance: Is It Safe to Suggest Retail Prices?" *Journal of Marketing* (Fall 1985): 89–90.

CHAPTER 12

Promotion through the Marketing Channel

LEARNING OBJECTIVES

After reading this chapter you should:

1. Recognize that reseller (channel member) support is one of the major tools of the manufacturer's promotional mix.
2. Understand the distinction between pull and push promotional strategies.
3. Realize that push promotional strategies are being used with increasing frequency and account for more dollars than pull promotions.
4. View promotion through channel members as a major form of channel strategy rather than mere tactical actions to get channel members to sell more products.
5. Know about the major findings from research on push promotions.
6. Be familiar with the basic types of push promotions that require channel member support.
7. Know the four types of "kinder and gentler" push promotional strategies.
8. Have a feel for the pros and cons of the various promotional strategies in the context of gaining channel member support.

Courtesy of Susan Van Etten

FOCUS ON CHANNELS

For Max Factor, the Key to Growth is Less U.S. Retailer Shelf Space

That's right, Max Factor, one of the legendary names in cosmetics has decided to leave the shelves of U.S. retailers for greener shelf spaces abroad, especially in England and Russia. Max Factor, which has been owned by Procter & Gamble Company since 1991, already generates most of its annual $1.2 billion in sales from foreign retailers. While its products can still be found on the shelves of some 8,000 U.S. retailers, the brand's shelf space is dwarfed by P&G's other famous cosmetics line, Cover Girl, which is sold in 50,000 stores in the U.S. But after 2010, Max Factor will rapidly disappear from U.S. stores. Why did this happen? Basically, U.S. retailer shelf space was not big enough for both P&G cosmetic brands. Giant mass market U.S. retailers looking to reduce costs and control product proliferation in already cluttered beauty aisles, were not willing to give more shelf space to Max Factor products. Not unless they were offered big promotional incentives from P&G to do so. But P&G was not about to throw a lot of trade promotion money at mass merchandisers, supermarkets, and drug chains to promote the Max Factor brand. P&G has made it a policy in recent years to avoid such trade promotion in favor of strong national advertising to build long-term brand equity and value. P&G reasoned that targeting the Max Factor brand to foreign markets where retailer power and demands are often less intense made strategic sense. P&G could focus on brand building to create a strong franchise among consumers for Max Factor cosmetics rather than get caught up in constantly having to offer special deals and merchandizing campaigns to dominant U.S retailers.

So, sometimes less is more, whether this involves using fewer cosmetics to make a face more beautiful, or less trade promotion to make a product more desirable.

Source: Based on Ellen Byron, "Max Factor Kisses America Goodbye," *Wall Street Journal* (June 5, 2009): B1.

The previous two chapters dealt with the first two components of the marketing mix, product strategy, and pricing strategy, as they interface with channel management. In this chapter we turn our attention to the third major component of the marketing mix, promotion strategy, as it interfaces with channel management.

The term **promotion** has been used as shorthand for referring to all of the persuasive communications activities employed by businesses and other organizations. These include advertising, personal selling, publicity, sales promotion, sponsorship, point-of-purchase communications, and in more recent years the use of social networking sites such as Facebook and Twitter to promote products and services. Increasingly, marketers are using the term **integrated marketing communications** instead of the term promotion to refer to the systematic use of several or all of these tools in a coordinated effort to achieve maximum promotional impact.[1] For example, Absolut vodka is not only heavily advertised in magazines, but also advertised on Facebook where superstar rapper and businessman Jay-Z serves as a spokesman for Absolut vodka. A mini documentary about Jay-Z on YouTube and slick point-of-purchase display materials in liquor stores complete the integrated promotion program.

Because most products and services are not sold directly to final customers, the promotion programs undertaken by producers, manufacturers, franchisors, and service creators need the assistance and support of channel members to be successful.[2] Even the most sophisticated promotional program that integrates advertising, personal selling, sales promotion, and publicity will not do the job unless it receives strong channel member cooperation and follow-through.[3] But, as we have emphasized throughout this text, because the channel members are independent businesses, the degree of control the manufacturer can exercise over how products are sold once they are in the hands of the channel members is limited. Thus, the effectiveness of the overall promotional strategy depends on *how successful the manufacturer is in securing cooperation from independent channel members in implementing the promotional strategy.*[4]

Some manufacturers rely almost entirely on promotion in the form of advertising to their target markets to "pull" their products through the channel and hence indirectly secure channel member cooperation. The belief underlying this so-called **pull strategy** is that by building strong consumer (or industrial user) demand for a product, the manufacturer will force channel members to automatically promote the manufacturer's product because it is in their obvious self-interest to do so.[5]

While there is a good deal of merit in pull strategy, in the long run it is often insufficient by itself to secure strong channel member promotional support. Rather, the manufacturer also needs to work directly with the channel members to develop viable channel member promotional support.[6] An approach referred to as **push strategy**, requires more direct involvement by the manufacturer with channel members in the use of promotional strategies.[7] Although *push strategy* has come to be an accepted term, it is something of a misnomer because it implies that the manufacturer is forcing promotion programs on channel members. Actually, the real concept underlying the push strategy should be one of *mutual effort and cooperation* between the manufacturer and channel members in the development and implementation of promotional strategies.[8] In this sense, then, the manufacturer does not push channel members into promoting its product, but instead seeks their participation and cooperation to provide effective promotional strategies that will be mutually beneficial to the manufacturer and the channel members.[9] Figure 12.1 illustrates the pull and push approaches to promotional strategy.

No inherent conflict exists between the two approaches, and in fact they are often used together very successfully. Many companies, such as Kellogg, Coca Cola, Kraft, and Campbell Soup, spend heavily on both types of promotion.[10] Despite some notable exceptions—such as Procter & Gamble's widely-discussed effort to dramatically reduce its emphasis on push promotions (see Focus item at the beginning of this chapter), the overall trend in promotional emphasis has been toward push promotion rather than pull.[11] Given the increasing size and power of retailers and wholesalers (see Chapter 2), this pattern is not surprising. Indeed, studies show that about 50 percent of every dollar spent on promotion goes for push type promotions.[12] Moreover, each year in the grocery field alone, 15,000 new products vie for shelf space—yet there is room on the shelves for only 5 percent of this number. To increase the odds of success, manufacturers are forced to spend huge sums on various push promotions to make their products attractive to retailers. Obviously, retailers (and to an increasing extent wholesale channel members as well) are not content to be merely conduits through which giant manufacturers using massive national advertising can smoothly send their products to the final customer.

FIGURE 12.1 Pull versus Push Promotional Strategies

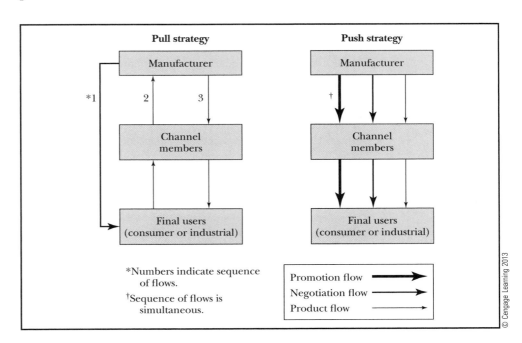

© Cengage Learning 2013

In this chapter we discuss a variety of promotional strategies that emphasize the push approach to promotion and hence call for substantial channel member participation. The success of these promotional strategies is influenced greatly by the degree of cooperation the channel manager can secure from the channel members in implementing these strategies.[13]

Basic Push Promotion Strategies in Marketing Channels

A wide variety of push promotion strategies call for the involvement of channel members in the promotion of the manufacturer's products. Before discussing these, however, we should reemphasize an important point discussed in Chapter 9 (Motivating the Channel Members). In general, any marketing mix strategies calling for channel member cooperation should not be haphazard one-shot, quick-fix approaches. Rather, strategies that involve channel members stand a higher probability of being favorably received by the channel members when they are *part of an overall program of manufacturer support of channel member needs*.[14] Distribution programming and the partnerships/strategic alliances discussed earlier in this text (see, in particular, Chapter 9) can be valuable in this regard. Essentially, the manufacturer must establish a comprehensive approach for providing support to channel members if their cooperation in the promotion of products is expected. A growing body of research on push promotion conducted over several decades lends empirical support to this proposition.[15]

Promotional strategies emphasizing the push approach initiated by the manufacturer but requiring channel member support and follow-through can take many forms. Most, however, can be placed into one of the following seven categories: cooperative advertising, promotional allowances, slotting fees, displays and selling aids, in-store promotions, contests and incentives, and special deals and merchandising campaigns.

Cooperative Advertising

One of the most pervasive forms of promotional assistance offered by manufacturers to channel members is that of cooperative advertising.[16] For example, *Advertising Age* estimates that in just one quarter of 2009, manufacturers selling products through Walmart provided close to $100 million in cooperative advertising money to Walmart and many additional millions of dollars to other large retailers such as Target, Walgreens, and CVS in that same quarter.[17]

Although there are many variations, one of the most common is sharing in the cost on a 50-50 basis up to some percentage of the retailer's purchases from the manufacturer. If, for example, a channel member made purchases of $100,000 from the manufacturer, the amount of advertising funds available to the retailer would be $3,000 if the maximum allowance was 3 percent of purchases.

Manufacturers usually want to exercise at least some level of control over all or part of a cooperative advertising campaign. Quite often advertising format suggestions or even completely prepared advertisements for newspapers, magazines, or broadcast media are supplied by manufacturers. Figure 12.2 shows some prepared newspaper advertisements offered by FRAM/Autolite to its dealers.

For the manufacturer, the effectiveness of cooperative advertising as a promotional strategy depends heavily on the level of support offered by the channel members. Specifically, the channel members must (1) have a sufficient inventory of the advertised product, (2) offer adequate point-of-purchase display, and (3) provide personal

FIGURE 12.2
Sample Prepared Newspaper Advertisements for FRAM/Autolite Dealers

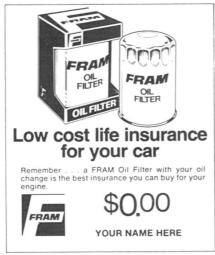

Source: Courtesy of FRAM Corporation.

selling support if required. Getting this kind of support, however, requires careful administration of the cooperative program by the manufacturer.[18] Lack of careful administration may result in poor channel member follow-through or even outright abuses, which are common. One common ploy of retailers has been around for years. A retailer buys newspaper space at the lower local linage rate but bills the manufacturer for its share at the higher national rate, pocketing the difference. In fact, some retailers (particularly department stores) have been known to finance entire advertising expenses for particular departments by billing the supplier at the higher rate.

Abuses are also common among food retailers, where cooperative advertising dollars (often referred to as "case allowances") sometimes are not entirely used to advertise only the sponsoring manufacturer's products but are instead added directly to the store's profits or even used to advertise the store's own private-brand merchandise. To avoid such abuses, some manufacturers have developed formal and carefully administered cooperative advertising programs that require clear-cut proof that cooperative advertising money provided to channel members was properly and effectively spent. Figure 12.3 illustrates co-op requirements for a program developed by FRAM/Autolite.

FIGURE 12.3
FRAM/Autolite
Requirements for
Cooperative
Advertisement
Reimbursements

CO-OP PROOF

GENERAL GUIDELINES

Advertising that conforms to the following guidelines may be coordinated locally without prior approval from Fram national headquarters:

1. Approved advertising is defined as newspaper, newspaper inserts, broadcast (TV or Radio), signs (painted or ordered from Fram), direct mail and billboards.

   Magazine advertising requires prior approval from Providence.

2. Advertisements must give customers a reason to buy Fram/Autolite products (benefit, price, etc.) and a specific retail location where purchase may be made.

3. The amount of an advertisement Mutual Fund will pay:

   A. The Mutual Fund will pay for the portion of the space/time of an advertisement devoted to the sale of Fram/Autolite products plus 33% of that portion for Fram's share of signature and heading. Payment will not exceed 100% of the total cost.

   B. In no case will Mutual Fund payments exceed the amount of current Mutual Fund accruals.

4. **Production costs are excluded from reimbursement.** Also excluded from these funds are cash awards, yearbooks, programs, matchbooks, labels, stationery, handouts and advertising specialties. Check with our representative for categories not mentioned in this policy.

5. Mutual Funds will pay only net local advertising rates, less all discounts and rebates.

6. Claims must be submitted within sixty (60) days after expenses have been incurred. Claims not submitted within this time period will not be reimbursable under the Fram/Autolite Mutual Fund Program.

_____

All claims should be handled
through the local Fram
representative

REQUIREMENTS FOR NEWSPAPER ADVERTISING

A. Single Insertions:
   An original full tear sheet* of the Fram/Autolite ad, plus a copy of the newspaper invoice.

B. Multiple Insertions (same ad in different newspapers):
   1. An original single full tear sheet.*
   2. A list of newspapers including:
      a. The exact date the ad ran.
      b. Size/space devoted to Fram/Autolite products.
      c. The net local rate for each newspaper involved.
      d. This list must be signed by a principal of the claiming distributorship.

C. Newspaper Inserts:
   1. An original of the insert.
   2. A copy of the printing bill.
   3. A copy of the insertion invoice.

D. Unpaid Circulation (Shoppers Guide, Pennysaver):
   1. A full copy of Pennysaver or Shoppers Guide.
   2. A copy of the publisher's invoice.
   3. A copy of the current rate card.

E. The use of a logo only is not acceptable. Advertising must give a reason to buy.

REQUIREMENTS FOR OUTDOOR SIGNS

Erection and wiring are reimbursable. Where the proposed sign costs will exceed $1,500, an advance layout of the proposed sign and two vendor quotes must be submitted to Fram/Autolite Headquarters by your local Fram/Autolite representative before work is authorized.

To receive reimbursement for billboards:
A. Affidavit of Performance
B. Picture of the billboard
C. Vendor invoice

To receive reimbursement for signs:
A. Vendor invoice
B. A photo of the entire sign

*Full tear sheet means a tear sheet that shows the entire ad, the name and date of the newspaper.

Source: Courtesy of FRAM Corporation.

While effective administration by the manufacturer is necessary to avoid abuses and to help secure cooperation from the channel members in a cooperative advertising program, the channel manager must also be sensitive to the channel members' primary concern about this kind of promotional assistance. Specifically, channel members often feel that the ads the manufacturer wants them to run put a disproportional emphasis on the manufacturer's particular products and not enough on patronage appeals. If this is the case, a channel member is likely to be reluctant in supporting the program and may also feel justified in engaging in abuses.

Promotional Allowances

The most typical strategy used for promotional allowances is to offer the channel member a direct cash payment or a certain percentage of the purchases on particular products. The allowances are offered to encourage retailers to buy more of the manufacturer's products, to give the products more prominent shelf space, to feature the products in special floor or end-of-aisle displays, or to engage in other similar promotional activity.

Promotional allowances offered by manufacturers to retailers have increased in recent years not only because giant and powerful retailers have become more demanding, but these big retailers, especially food and consumer packaged goods (CPG) retailers, recognize that consumers hurt by the "Great Recession" of 2007-2008, are eager to find good deals. So, retailers expect manufacturers to provide an abundance of promotional incentives to pass on to consumers. This, of course, can be expensive. McKinsey & Company estimates that promotional allowances can easily amount to 5 percent of sales.[19] Given the high cost of promotional allowances, more manufacturers are conducting research, sometimes on their own but more often by hiring outside consulting firms such as SymphonyIRIGroup to determine whether they are getting their money's worth in terms of retailer cooperation and follow-through. Consultants such as SymphonyIRIGroup have developed extensive and sophisticated methods for measuring the effects of all types of promotional programs.[20] But such measurements are still taken after the fact. If a manufacturer wants to do something up front to enhance channel member support and follow-through, the most positive step to take is to make sure that the promotional allowance program is consistent with channel member needs.[21]

This has been the guiding philosophy, for instance, of Curtice-Burns Foods, Inc., a food processor that has been able to compete with the giants of the food industry by emphasizing promotional allowances instead of more costly national advertising. Curtice-Burns has always made sure that its promotional programs work to the channel members' benefit. For example, when Curtice-Burns ran a supermarket promotion for its pie fillings, it was not only generous in offering promotional allowances to the supermarkets but also went a step beyond by arranging the in-store displays in such a way as to also promote the supermarkets' private brands of complementary baking ingredients. Thus Curtice-Burns gave retailers an opportunity to add to sales and profits. Such extra measures of effort and caring in the use of promotional allowances can go a long way toward securing channel member support for a promotion. Indeed, in an arena usually characterized by a plethora of half-hearted, stale, and cliché promotions, those that show a little imagination can be real standouts.

Slotting Fees

Slotting fees or **slotting allowances** are payments (either in cash or merchandise) by manufacturers to persuade channel members, especially retailers, to stock, display, and support new products.[22]

Although slotting fees are really just another form of promotional allowance, we discuss them here as a separate category because they have become such an important and controversial form of promotion in marketing channels. In the grocery industry, where slotting fees are most commonly used, manufacturers spend some $9 billion per year on this type of promotion. Slotting fees are also becoming more popular in other product categories, such as over-the-counter drugs, home improvement products, automotive parts, books, magazines, tobacco, apparel, and others.[23]

Slotting fees are one of the most controversial forms of push promotion because manufacturers and retailers have such different views on them. Manufacturers often view slotting fees as a way of increasing retailer market power by forcing manufacturers to pay large sums of money to get their new products onto retailers' shelves. Moreover, many manufacturers believe that slotting fees discriminate against manufacturers, particularly smaller ones, who do not have the resources to pay high slotting fees. Retailers, on the other hand, typically view slotting fees as a way of compensating them for the risks they bear when taking on new products that may not sell well and as fair compensation for their efforts in promoting and selling the new products. Further they argue, slotting fees can serve as a screening device by providing an advance signal of which new products are likely to do well because, the reasoning goes, manufacturers would not be willing to pay high slotting fees on "dog" products. However, research conducted by Bloom, Gundlach, and Cannon involving more than 800 managers of grocery manufacturers, retailers, and wholesalers found that in practice neither manufacturers nor retailers viewed slotting fees as an effective predictor of how well products would sell.[24]

The controversy over slotting fees has grown so intense that it has attracted the attention of some members of Congress, the Federal Trade Commission (FTC), and the General Accounting Office (GAO). Their investigations have focused on whether this aggressive promotional practice violates antitrust laws and whether slotting fees may in some cases amount to a form of payola, which is usually illegal. Some critics also claim that slotting fees result in higher prices to consumers because manufacturers build the cost of the slotting fees they expect to pay into the price of new products.[25] Supporters of slotting fees take the opposite viewpoint, arguing that the fees actually lower prices paid by consumers because the payments made to retailers in the form of slotting fees get passed on to the consumer in the form of lower prices.[26] But in the study by Bloom, Gundlach, and Cannon cited earlier, the findings show that neither manufacturers nor retailers believe that slotting allowances result in lower retail prices.

From the viewpoint of the channel manager, particularly in a grocery manufacturing or producing firm, slotting fees must be viewed as a reality that is not likely to go away anytime soon.[27] Moreover, as mentioned earlier in this section, slotting fees already have spread to other product categories, and this broadening trend is likely to continue as retailers become even larger and more powerful. Slotting fees may well become the most dominant form of promotional allowance demanded by large-scale retailers in many lines of trade. What can the channel manager do in the face of retailer power to demand high slotting fees to sell manufacturers' new products? While admitting that serious conflict over slotting allowances exists between manufacturers and retailers, based on their study, Bloom, Gundlach, and Cannon actually offer a bit of optimism and some concrete suggestions for fostering cooperation in the use of slotting allowances:

Conflict [over slotting allowances] could be addressed through joint sponsorship [between manufacturers and retailers] of research on the effects of slotting fees on (1) manufacturer-retailer relations, (2) retailer assortments, (3) allocation of manufacturer marketing budgets, (4) manufacturers' distribution decisions, and (5) the ability of goods to get to market . . . Interactions on these topics could provide each side an opportunity to understand the other's perspective better.[28]

In essence, then, rather than just wishing slotting fees would go away or approaching them as a necessary evil, the channel manager, by attempting to work with retailers, may discover areas of commonality leading to slotting fee arrangements that create more win-win, rather than win-lose, situations.[29]

Displays and Selling Aids

Displays and selling aids include all kinds of special racks, shelving, platforms, signs, promotion kits, and specially designed in-store displays both large and small, including interactive electronic devices used by retailers to promote the sale of products to customers while they are in the stores. Often these displays and selling aids are referred to in the trade as **POP (point-of-purchase)** displays. Billions of dollars are spent each year on POP displays and many of them are developed by manufacturers and supplied to retailers in an effort to get retailers to use the POP materials to promote their products.

Displays and selling aids can be highly effective[30] but quite often manufacturers have difficulty getting retailers to use these materials.[31] Consequently, as discussed earlier, special incentives in the form of promotional allowances are often necessary to encourage their use. The reason is that channel members are usually flooded with such promotional material to the point that it is simply thrown away or never even opened. For example, the average supermarket at any given time is faced with 1,000 items offered on promotions but has the capacity to set up only about 50 end-of-aisle displays each week. Along with this problem of overabundance, there is also sometimes a failure on the part of the manufacturer to take the time to demonstrate the usefulness of this material to channel members. A wide disparity of perceived usefulness of such materials often exists between the manufacturer and channel members. Thus the channel manager must make an effort to see whether the firm's selling aids and displays are serving any useful purpose or whether they are more of a bother than a help.

Figure 12.4 shows a carefully thought out and well-designed display of the Evergreen & Ivy candle line offered by Hannas, a manufacturer of candles. The display is intended for use in department stores, specialty stores, mass merchandisers, drug store chains, and supermarkets. The display has several features that are likely to appeal to such retail channel members and hence enhance the prospect that it will be used effectively. First, it can be used by virtually any kind of retailer that sells candles. Second, it takes a product that comes in many different sizes that would be unwieldy to stock and show properly on retailers' regular shelving and puts them all in an attractive dedicated display fixture. Third, empty slots for candles that need restocking can be easily spotted. Fourth, it takes up a minimum of floor space while still being interesting and attractive. Finally, this display encourages the channel members to stock the full line of Evergreen & Ivy candles, because it is designed as a unified platform that creates the impression of a candle boutique—in effect a candle store within the larger store environment.

Even the most effective in-store displays must take account of changing patterns of consumer behavior that can be influenced by changing economic conditions. For example, during and soon after the "Great Recession" of 2007–2008, studies conducted by Envirosell, a highly regarded consulting firm specializing in in-store displays, noticed several changes in shoppers' behavior as they came in contact with store displays:[32]

FIGURE 12.4 An Example of a Well-Designed In-store Display

Source: Courtesy, Hanna's Candle Co.

- *The average amount of time shoppers spend in store aisles increased by about 20 percent.*
- *Shoppers spent more time reading labels and seemed to be studying them more carefully.*
- *Shoppers were more frequently discarding items in other store locations rather than bringing them to the checkout line.*
- *Shoppers seemed to stress more over making product choices while stopped at store displays, especially when the choice involved a higher priced product.*

The CEO and founder of Envirosell, Paco Underhill, believes that retail displays and point of purchase materials need to address such changing shopper demands to be effective. As an example of a firm doing a good job of adapting their displays to be more in tune with shoppers, Underhill points to Whole Foods' approach to in-store displays that "talk to the shopper." For instance, a large sign in the fish department over the Red Kale and Rainbow Chard reads "Why Buy Organic?". The sign then goes on to explain the benefits of organic fish. In the produce department, a sign is stuck directly in with Russian Banana fingerling potatoes that reads, "How cute are these?" Underhill explains the rationale behind these Whole Foods displays as follows:[33]

> It's [the organic fish sign] meant to make shoppers feel they're buying something valuable, maybe doing something virtuous. These [the Russian Banana fingerling potatoes] are more expensive than Idaho potatoes, so they're trying to find creative ways of getting you to trade up or trying something new.

So, in an age when personal selling by real people has virtually disappeared from many retail stores, displays and selling aids that connect with shoppers even in the face of significant changes in shopper behavior have become more important than ever. Manufacturers and other suppliers that want retailers to vigorously promote their products will have to pay more attention to developing more effective displays and selling aids.

In-store Promotion Events

Most in-store promotions are short-term events designed to create added interest and excitement for the manufacturer's products. Store visits by famous chefs representing manufacturers, such as Emeril Lagasse for his line of cookware manufactured by All-Clad to conduct gourmet cooking demonstrations, and store appearances by Derek Jeter promoting Nike products are examples of popular in-store promotions.[34]

Some promotions have attempted to be more unusual and dramatic. Coca-Cola company, for example, in what has now become a famous case of an imaginative and exciting in-store promotion, entombed a popular Kansas City disc jockey in a mountain of Coke cases at a supermarket and had him broadcast an appeal to "Buy me out!" A few hours later the store was a shambles—but the DJ was free and Coke had pulled off one of the most spectacular promotions in its history.

A more subtle and genteel form of in-store promotion—one that has gained increased popularity in recent years—is the **trunk show**, which is used mainly by better apparel, shoe, and jewelry manufacturers. As the name suggests, the manufacturer visits the retail store, carrying a "trunk" of some of its latest and best products. A gala party or event is usually put on as part of these promotions to get customers in a buying mood. This format worked successfully, for example, at Barneys, one of the world's largest clothing retailers in New York City, at a trunk show put on by Oxford Clothes, a prestigious men's suit manufacturer.

Still another form of "in-store" (on-site) promotion becoming increasingly popular is the use of samples, a $1.2 billion industry that is growing rapidly.[35] But instead of giving out samples in stores, they are distributed to consumers in situations that maximize the product's appeal. So, for example, Dove body wash, deodorant, and face cloths were handed out in Bally's Fitness Clubs; Dr. Scholl's gave its blister treatment cushions to runners at the Chicago Marathon; and Starbucks Corp. offered its frozen Frappuccino bars in Union Square in New York on a day when the temperature reached over 90 degrees. Industry experts predict that this kind of contextual or situational sampling will become increasingly popular because it is more focused and thus has more impact. So, just setting up a table in a supermarket and handing out samples is no longer enough. Steve Sickinger, senior vice president of sales at Sunflow Group, Inc., a promotional services firm, argues that marketers need to be more imaginative today:

> The traditional delivery vehicles [for samples] are becoming passé. The more you want to reach a specific target, the more clever you have to become.[36]

Regardless of the form of the in-store (or out-of-store) promotion, whether blatant and crass or sophisticated and subtle, the key issue for the channel manager is whether the *retailers perceive benefits from it*. Few retailers will be enthusiastic about cooperating with a manufacturer's in-store promotional event unless doing so yields specific benefits in the form of direct sales and profit increases and/or increased recognition for their stores. Thus the planning of a successful in-store promotion should always include considerations of the potential benefits for the retailers involved.

As manufacturers continue to compete even more intensely to get their products into retail stores and keep them there, the role of in-store promotions should grow. One sign of this trend is the emergence of specialized firms that organize samplings and demonstrations at stores.

Contests and Incentives

Contests and incentives sponsored by manufacturers to stimulate channel member sales efforts for their products are another popular form of promotion. Here again, as is the case with so many types of push promotions, contests and incentives can take many forms and are limited only with the imagination. A novel sales contest sponsored by Apple Computer, for example, offered the top-producing dealer salespeople the use of a pearl-white Porsche for one year and $3,000 in cash to cover gas and other expenses. While the Apple contest used a car and cash as incentives, the range of incentives used in such promotions can be very broad, including all types of merchandise, travel, or even gourmet steaks, as shown in Figure 12.5.

Sometimes the impact of a contest or incentive promotion can be increased by tying it to some major event at the local, state, national, or even international level. This is what 3M did in an incentive campaign involving industrial distributors selling its occupational health and safety products (which ranged from a 12-cent disposable respirator to $500 pieces of safety equipment). 3M used the Olympic games as the focal point for a distributor sales contest that involved prizes ranging from sweatshirts bearing the Olympics logo to major travel awards. Using significant events such as the Olympics can enhance the meaning and excitement of contests and incentives for channel member salespeople. These events can add glamour and emotional impact, such as the competitive spirit and patriotism associated with the Olympic games.

Contests and incentives should not be developed hastily, however, because they can be among the most difficult forms of promotional assistance to administer without creating ill will and conflict on the part of channel members. This is because some of the contests and incentives developed by the manufacturer can foster behavior by the channel members' salespeople that is potentially detrimental to the channel members. For example, a manufacturer may offer a series of trips to exotic places to the highest volume salespeople employed by the wholesale or retail channel members, or may offer **push money (PM)** directly to channel member salespeople for pushing certain products. From the standpoint of the channel members, however, these or similar programs may be seen as conflicting with their (channel members') objectives. Specifically, a wholesaler or retailer with a long-established reputation for offering customers the products they desire does not want its salespeople to pressure these customers into buying products that may not serve their needs as well but will help the salesperson win a contest.

So, in the development of any contest or incentive program, the manufacturer should go out of its way to determine the views of channel members toward such forms of promotion. The potential conflict that can be avoided by doing so is likely to be well worth the effort.

FIGURE 12.5
Example of Novel
Product Used for
Incentive Promotion

Why an Omaha Steaks Incentive Program?

It Motivates! It activates.
It stimulates

And best of all . . . it keeps on working! After you introduce your Omaha
Steaks incentive program . . . just remember to stand clear of the door!

Watch Your Sales Team Sell!
Your sales team will climb over each
other to get out and sell their way to a
delicious steak award. Omaha Steaks
Incentive Programs kindle that spark
of desire! They trigger everyone's fantasies of elegant dining and casual,
carefree living. Here are incentives
your people can share with family and
friends. The appeal is powerful. Universal!

With Beef . . . Glorious Beef
But don't kid yourself! You'd better use
the best. You want beef that's going to
melt in their mouth.

Only the best corn-fed, naturally aged,
closely trimmed, Midwestern beef is
selected by Omaha Steaks. USDA in-
spected Prime and Top Choice cuts.
The steaks are perfectly wrapped for
freshness, insta-frozen and packaged
in handsome, impressive, full-color
boxes.

**And Flexible Programs . . .
Priced Right for You**
Omaha Steaks gourmet food awards
fit any type of program:

• Straight Incentives
• Custom-designed Contests
• Plateau Programs
• 810 Programs (Steak Bucks)
• Gift Certificates

An effective program can be tailored to
your budget . . . and you'll be amazed at
the number of quality services included in your package!

For Every Use
Need a sales incentive? A dealer incentive? A consumer premium? Employee awards? Business gifts? You
name it . . . you can have it . . . with next
to no work on your part!

We'll Handle All the Details
We'll take the orders. Keep the inventories. Do the packing. Handle the
shipping. We'll take care of placing
your greeting in each package, too.

*Mouthwatering steaks will motivate
and stimulate your sales team.*

Call Right Away Today . . .
TOLL FREE 1-800-228-2480.
(In Nebraska, Call COLLECT
0-402-397-9314.)
One of our knowledgeable Incentive
Specialist will answer all your ques-
tions. Be sure to ask about our steak
sampler package!

Let's Motivate!
Let's Activate!
Let's Stimulate!

Omaha Steaks
International®
Dept. 4313, P.O. Box 3300
Omaha, Nebraska 68103

Source: Courtesy, Omaha Steaks International. Jim Krantz photo.

Special Promotional Deals and Merchandising Campaigns

Special promotional deals and merchandising campaigns comprise a catch-all category. It
includes a variety of push type promotional deals such as discounts to channel members
to encourage them to order more products, favorable offers to consumers to foster larger
purchases (for example, buy one and get one free), percentage or cents-off offers, rebates,

coupons, prizes, and premium offers. These kinds of trade promotions are especially popular in grocery and drug product categories but have also become common for consumer electronics, home improvement products, and apparel.

Promotional deals and merchandising campaigns may overlap one or more of the six promotional strategies previously discussed. For example, a promotional deal on a cereal product may require the retailer to use a special display to feature the cereal prominently in the store in exchange for a promotional allowance.

Promotional deals and merchandising campaigns have been very heavily used in recent years. For example, some 60 percent of supermarket sales were estimated to involve items that were put on deals, and as much as 90 percent of soft-drink products were sold on deals.

The fact that special deals and merchandising campaigns are in such widespread use does not mean that most manufacturers are happy with them. On the contrary, a great deal of concern exists about their value as a promotional tool.[37] Indeed, research has shown that these kinds of trade deals can (1) erode consumer brand loyalty, (2) foster deal-to-deal purchasing by channel members, (3) fail to provide pass-through saving for consumers, and (4) encourage the diverting of merchandise to other retailers and wholesalers instead of being sold at discount to consumers. Even more worrisome for manufacturers, special deals have increased the already fierce competition for channel members' shelf space. Thus, manufacturers find themselves having to offer more and more inducements in the deals to meet the competition to keep their products on stores' shelves.[38] Finally, and perhaps most worrisome of all, are the increased costs of special deals and merchandising campaigns. As the "ante" keeps increasing in terms of what channel members are demanding, so do the manufacturers' costs of meeting these demands.

Nevertheless, an entire "culture" built on promotional deals and merchandising campaigns has become the norm in consumer packaged goods' channels. This culture, in which manufacturers induce retailers and wholesalers to buy far more products than they can sell in a reasonable period, is usually referred to as **trade loading**, **forward buying**, or **channel stuffing.** The result is that at any given time, $75 to $100 billion of merchandise is in the channel, stacked up in retailer and wholesaler warehouses as well as in trucks or railcars. This gridlock of excess inventory slows down the distribution process, so that it takes an average of 84 days for a product to travel from factory floor to retail shelf. It is estimated that only 30 percent of the trade promotion discounts offered by manufacturers are actually passed through to consumers in the form of lower prices. Of the remaining 70 percent, 35 percent is lost in inefficiencies and the other 35 percent goes directly into retailers' and wholesalers' pockets.[39]

Figure 12.6 provides an illustration of what typically happens in promotional deals involving trade loading.

Unfortunately, there is no simple solution to the problems created by such promotional deals. As we pointed out previously in this chapter and earlier in this text, retailers are becoming larger and more powerful. Hence they have the capacity to be very aggressive and demanding in regard to special deals and merchandising campaigns. They expect, and are able to get, very favorable terms. Manufacturers such as Procter & Gamble, which are attempting to escape from this deal treadmill by reemphasizing product brand development through renewed stress on advertising to build consumer brand loyalty, face a tough challenge. However, the availability of social media sites in recent years, especially Facebook and Twitter, that enable manufacturers to communicate more directly with consumers may help to offset the demands of powerful retailers' constant pushing for more special deals. Kraft Foods, for example, has developed advertising campaigns specifically for Facebook for three of its most popular products: Wheat Thins crackers, Oreo cookies, and Crystal Light flavored beverage.[40] Pepsi Co. has

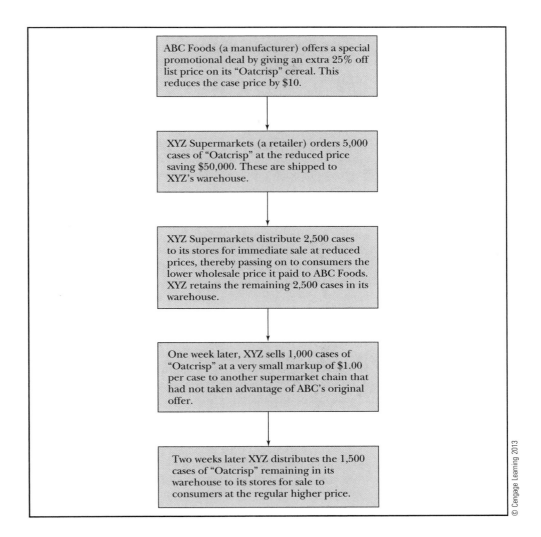

ABC Foods (a manufacturer) offers a special promotional deal by giving an extra 25% off list price on its "Oatcrisp" cereal. This reduces the case price by $10.

XYZ Supermarkets (a retailer) orders 5,000 cases of "Oatcrisp" at the reduced price saving $50,000. These are shipped to XYZ's warehouse.

XYZ Supermarkets distribute 2,500 cases to its stores for immediate sale at reduced prices, thereby passing on to consumers the lower wholesale price it paid to ABC Foods. XYZ retains the remaining 2,500 cases in its warehouse.

One week later, XYZ sells 1,000 cases of "Oatcrisp" at a very small markup of $1.00 per case to another supermarket chain that had not taken advantage of ABC's original offer.

Two weeks later XYZ distributes the 1,500 cases of "Oatcrisp" remaining in its warehouse to its stores for sale to consumers at the regular higher price.

© Cengage Learning 2013

followed a similar path by developing special Facebook advertising campaigns for its Mountain Dew soft drink[41] and Procter & Gamble has designed campaigns for its Olay skincare products, Tide detergent and Ivory Soap for YouTube, Twitter, and Facebook.[42] All of these manufacturers believe that connecting directly with consumers via social media helps to reinforce the value of their brands and fosters brand loyalty. Strong consumer loyalty can serve as an antidote to intense price-oriented retailer promotions that seek to get consumers to buy any brand product that happens to be on deal at a given time.

"Kinder and Gentler" Push Promotion Strategies in Marketing Channels

The seven promotional strategies discussed in the previous section are straightforward, hard-hitting promotions, unabashedly aimed at getting channel members to push a particular manufacturer's products rather than the competitors'. Nothing about these strategies is ambiguous or subtle.

Other promotional strategies, whose ultimate purpose is also to get channel members to push a particular manufacturer's products, stress doing so using more finesse, subtlety, and a more circuitous route. We refer to these as "kinder and gentler" push promotions. The most important of these are training programs, quota specification, missionary selling, and trade shows.

Training Programs

Training programs aimed at improving the performance of channel members' salespeople can be one of the most effective strategies for building channel member promotional cooperation. Such programs can demonstrate in a highly visible way the manufacturer's commitment to helping channel members in an area in which many of them need help. At both the wholesale and retail levels, the day-to-day pressures of doing business leave little room for much in the way of sales training. This is particularly true for many smaller wholesalers and retailers. But even for the larger ones who have their own programs, the manufacturer's assistance in this area provides a valuable supplement and helps to offset the cost of the program.

To be effective, however, manufacturer-sponsored training programs for channel member salespeople must be planned to meet the particular needs of the channel members and must be implemented in a manner that is acceptable to them. Because there are some important differences, we will discuss this topic separately for channel members at the wholesale and retail levels.

Wholesale Level Training Programs Training programs at the wholesale level should be aimed at helping the wholesaler's salespeople in three major areas: (1) their knowledge of the manufacturer's particular product, (2) their selling techniques, and (3) their skill in counseling the customers they call on.

The first area is the most obvious one for emphasis from the manufacturer's point of view. Sometimes, however, product training is overemphasized at the expense of the other two areas. In fact, many organizations spend 75 to 100 percent of their education budgets on product knowledge, leaving the other areas virtually untouched.

More attention, therefore, needs to be given to the second area of selling skills, and even more to the third area of counseling customers. Topics covered should include listening skills, trust-building and tension-reducing skills, feedback skills, skills in selling to difficult types of people, how to protect an image of excellence, and knowing when and how to sell features and/or benefits. This suggests that training programs that are more subtle about their bottom-line objective (those that spend less time extolling the virtues of the sponsoring manufacturer's product) may, paradoxically, be more effective in actually attaining the objective of preferential treatment from the distributors.

Retail Level Training Programs Training programs aimed at retail salespeople are useful mainly for products that still need a significant level of personal sales assistance. Stores operating mainly on a self-service basis have little need for sales training.

The area of sales training needed at the retail level basically parallels the first two at the wholesale level: (1) product knowledge and (2) selling technique. The third area, counseling, also exists but in a much more limited sense. The type of counseling the retail salesperson offers to customers would cover product usage and would not, of course, deal with such issues as how the customer can promote the product or provide management assistance.

Poor personal selling at the retail level has become almost legendary. The reasons for this are too numerous to mention here. Certainly, the poor quality of retail selling cannot be blamed to any great extent on inadequate manufacturer training programs—retailers are far more guilty in this regard. Nevertheless, the manufacturer can help to improve the performance of retail salespeople by offering or providing support for training programs aimed at specific and limited objectives. Consider, for example, studies of retail salespeople in consumer electronics stores conducted by McKinsey & Company. The consultants found that 86 percent of the time, salespeople failed to ask to close the sale and very few of these salespeople were familiar with or followed the four classic stages of the selling process of: (1) open, (2) ask for needs, (3) demonstrate, and (4) close.[43] McKinsey believes that providing training to retail salespeople whether in consumer electronics stores or other types of stores so that salespeople learn the basics of the selling process is highly feasible and profitable. Why? Because McKinsey's research shows that as many as 40 percent of customers entering stores are still undecided about what to buy. Hence, these shoppers are open to persuasion by retail salespeople. A better trained salesforce can help assure that the shopper will actually become a buyer, has a better chance of upselling the customer to higher-priced, more profitable merchandise, and is more capable of cross-selling customers related product accessories. So, manufacturers that want their products to be sold by more capable retail salespeople should think very seriously about providing assistance and support for retailer sales training programs.

Quota Specification

The sales volumes that manufacturers specify for channel members to generate during a certain time period are called **sales quotas**. They are viewed as a promotional strategy because manufacturers set quotas in the belief that they will spur channel members on to greater effort in return for rewards offered for reaching or exceeding quotas. Sales quotas have been used extensively in the domestic automotive industry to foster aggressive dealer selling. Dealer rebates or **hold backs** computed as a percentage of total sales are given to dealers who attain the quotas specified by the auto manufacturer. These can amount to a substantial sum and can make a major difference in the dealers' overall profit picture for the period.

Sales quotas if used properly can be an effective promotional strategy for improving channel member promotional support. The key to using quotas properly, however, lies in the context in which they are presented to the channel members. If they are presented in a coercive fashion, they may produce ill will and conflict rather than support (as would occur, for instance, if the manufacturer set a quota without consulting the channel members and then held it up as something to be attained—or else). Further, if the manufacturer's line does not make up an important part of the channel member's product mix, the channel member may simply ignore the quota. On the other hand, if quotas are developed in conjunction with the channel members, and if they are presented in the context of *providing information on the sales potentials* in the channel members' territories, they can be a positive force in fostering channel member support.

The approach to setting quotas used by Black & Decker in its consumer products division is indicative of this latter approach. Sales quotas are assigned at the beginning of the year to key wholesalers. These quotas are closely related to market penetration goals that Black & Decker's marketing department establishes for specific territories involved, and these are then submitted to the distributors for approval. Any differences are worked out between the distributors and Black & Decker's field sales management.

Missionary Selling

The term **missionary selling** was first used to describe the activities of manufacturers' salespeople who were sent specifically to convince distributors that they should handle the manufacturer's new products. Because they were attempting to "convert" distributors away from competitors' products and toward their own, they were called "missionary salesmen." Today the term is usually applied to any of the manufacturer's salespeople who are specifically assigned to supplement the selling activities of channel members.

In the consumer goods industries, missionary salespeople (sometimes called detail salespeople) may be called upon to perform any of the following activities:

- *Checking wholesale and retail inventory levels*
- *Calling on retailers to inform them of products*
- *Helping to arrange window and in-store displays*
- *Answering the wholesalers' and retailers' questions and providing advice and training*
- *Trying to promote goodwill*
- *Taking orders for merchandise*

In addition to these tasks, missionary salespeople may do regular selling as well. For many years in the cosmetics and fragrance industries, manufacturers' missionary salespeople have been put directly on the sales floor to supplement retailers' own sales staffs. In recent years this practice has also caught on in the apparel field. Manufacturers such as Liz Claiborne Inc., Evan Picone Inc., and J.H. Collectibles are very active in supplying their own salespeople to help retailers sell. Liz Claiborne, for example, uses its own salespeople in a number of department stores, and Evan Picone makes extensive use of "rotators"—missionary salespeople who visit retail stores. These manufacturers report sales increases of 20 to 40 percent in stores where they have placed their own salespeople.

In the business-to-business market, missionary salespeople are also a valuable tool. Among other things, they are often involved in such activities as the following:

- *Training distributor salespeople*
- *Accompanying distributor salespeople on sales calls to assist their selling efforts*
- *Taking initial orders for new products from the final user*
- *Providing technical assistance*
- *Helping distributors' salespeople to close sales, especially those who require technical knowledge beyond the scope of the distributors' salespeople*

The use of missionary salespeople in building channel member promotional support is a double-edged sword. On the positive side, missionary selling is a useful promotional strategy when the channel members lack the sales capacity or competence to handle tasks assigned to them by the manufacturer, and when the channel members *desire* this kind of assistance.

On the negative side, however, are several problems. First, using missionary salespeople is expensive, particularly in the business-to-business market because it requires a highly-educated, specially-trained sales force, often with engineering and graduate degrees, and these are usually the highest-paid salespeople. Even in the retail sector, missionary selling can increase costs. A second problem is that missionary selling can lead to conflicts in the channel, which may occur when missionary salespeople begin performing many of the channel members' tasks. The channel member, for example, may perceive this to mean that the manufacturer is on the verge of bypassing him or her altogether and as a result may reduce the level of promotional support given to the manufacturer. A final problem is that some channel members view missionary salespeople as bothersome because they take up too much of the time of their own sales force. This is particularly the case when the products of a manufacturer who uses missionary salespeople play only a small part in the channel member's product mix.

With the foregoing potential problems in mind, the channel manager must therefore pay careful attention to the attitudes of channel members toward the use of missionary salespeople. They can be an expensive mistake if their use fosters conflict rather than increases promotional cooperation from the channel members.

Trade Shows

Trade shows are usually annual events organized by associations in particular industries, ranging from toys to heavy industrial equipment. While some trade shows may include only manufacturers, wholesalers, or retailers, most shows have representatives at all three levels of the channel plus an assortment of manufacturers' representatives, agents, brokers, and facilitating agencies. The focal point of trade shows for any given manufacturer, wholesaler, or retail participant is the exhibit booth at which the firm displays its products and presents its promotional message to attendees as well as to representatives of the media, who often come to trade shows.

The main objective of participating in a trade show (aside from making sales) is to attain the maximum impact and gain the widest recognition for the firm's products—especially new products—and thus to enhance the firm's recognition and respect among its relevant publics. So, for example, a manufacturer of musical instruments that sells its products through wholesalers and retailers would be interested in impressing not only conference attendees representing the wholesalers and retailers who already carry this manufacturer's products but also those who do not carry them now but may be convinced to do so in the future.

From the standpoint of the manufacturer, using trade shows as a promotional strategy for motivating channel members can be very worthwhile. First, it provides an opportunity to sell existing and new channel members (who are often represented in large numbers at the show) substantial quantities of products they might not have bought in the absence of the hype and hoopla that are characteristic of trade shows. Second, it provides an opportunity to show channel members new products, strategies, and promotional programs on a face-to-face basis. Third, it offers a chance to socialize with channel members in ways that might not be possible in the course of regular business relationships. For example, the manufacturer may have a number of its top executives present at the show to talk with wholesalers and/or retailers that sell its products. Finally, and perhaps most important from a long-run channel promotional strategy standpoint, a strong presence and impact made by the manufacturer—especially if it seems to shine above other competing manufacturers at the show—can create a sense of pride and belonging in the channel members that sell its products. The channel members thus see themselves as being a part of a winning team that leads the industry. Consequently, the manufacturer has an opportunity to strengthen its referent power base (see Chapter 4) if it does a good job at trade shows. The payoff from this outcome can provide a long-term differential advantage for the manufacturer in the form of a more prideful and committed group of channel members.

Summary

One of the major tools the manufacturer uses for implementing an integrated promotional program is selling support by channel members. While some manufacturers feel that they can rely mainly on promotion to their target markets to "pull" their products through the channel, in most cases this is not enough. Direct involvement, or "pushing" by the manufacturer in a joint approach to promotion with channel members is usually also needed to develop an effective and viable promotional program. Because channel members are independent businesses, however, the degree of control the manufacturer can exercise over how its products are promoted is significantly reduced once they are in the hands of the channel members. Consequently, a manufacturer must carefully administer promotional strategies involving channel members to help assure a high degree of channel member cooperation in the promotion of its products.

Research shows that merely offering more monetary incentives on an ad hoc basis is not sufficient to secure promotional cooperation from channel members. Rather, the manufacturer needs to carefully evaluate the needs of the channel members and attempt to incorporate them in its push promotion as part of a comprehensive channel promotion strategy.

Push promotional strategies involving channel members can be placed into seven general categories: (1) cooperative advertising, (2) promotional allowances, (3) slotting fees, (4) displays and selling aids, (5) instore promotions, (6) contests and incentives, (7) special deals and merchandising campaigns.

In addition to these seven straightforward push promotion strategies, there are several other more subtle ones, four of which were discussed in this chapter under the heading of "kinder and gentler" push promotions. These are (1) training programs, (2) quota specification, (3) missionary selling, and (4) trade shows.

Training programs are more common for wholesale channel members than for retail. But in either case, the training programs should not be narrowly confined to

being merely a "sales pitch" for the particular manufacturer's product. Rather, training programs worthy of the name should help the channel members not only to sell more of the particular manufacturer's products but to improve their overall businesses as well.

Manufacturers often use quotas as a device to increase channel members' sales efforts. The key to using such sales quotas successfully is to present them in a constructive and informative manner rather than in a coercive way.

Missionary salespeople are employed by the manufacturer to help focus channel members' attention on the manufacturer's products and to assist the channel members in their selling efforts. The use of missionary salespeople can be very effective if the channel members want the help that is offered, if the missionary salespeople do not take up too much of the channel members' time, and if they do not divert too much of the channel members' salespeople's time from other products.

Trade shows at which manufacturers have a chance to exhibit their products and to show off the caliber of their organizations provide an opportunity to interact with channel members and also foster excitement and a sense of pride in channel members who carry the manufacturers' products.

Review Questions

1. Explain the rationale for including selling support by resellers in a distribution channel as a major tool for implementing promotional strategy.

2. Why is the success of a manufacturer's overall promotional strategy dependent to a significant extent on channel member cooperation?

3. Regardless of the specific promotional strategies that the manufacturer uses, a higher level of channel member cooperation is more likely to be gained if these strategies are part of an overall program of channel member support. Discuss this statement.

4. Discuss the pros and cons of following promotional strategies from the manufacturer's and channel member's viewpoints: (a) cooperative advertising, (b) promotional allowances, (c) slotting fees, (d) displays and selling aids, (e) in-store promotions, (f) contests and incentives, and (g) special deals and merchandising campaigns.

5. Because the manufacturer's major objective in instituting a training program for channel member salespeople is to get them to give preferential treatment to the firm's products, the manufacturer should design training programs that are, in effect, "commercials" for its particular products. Discuss the validity of this statement.

6. Should coercive power be the basis for developing a sales quota program for channel members?

7. How might the use of missionary salespeople foster conflict rather than cooperation in the channel?

8. Discuss the rationale for using trade shows as a basis for obtaining promotional support from channel members.

Channel Issues for Discussion

1. In November of 2010, Lowe's, the nation's second largest home improvement retailer, ran a day-after-Thanksgiving Black Friday promotion using Facebook. Lowe's picked out several items that were offered at incredibly low prices (typically 90% off). Then the heavily discounted

merchandise was offered to Lowe's' Facebook fans and was limited to the first 100 consumers that checked out with the items at Lowes.com. Lowe's believed that offering this new "give-away" via Facebook would create a lot of buzz, which in turn would accelerate the growth of Lowe's' fans on Facebook. These Facebook fans, Lowe's hoped, would not only stay in touch but would be more inclined to become loyal Lowe's customers because the regular and continuous interaction with the home improvement retailer via Facebook would evolve into a real relationship between Lowe's and its Facebook fans rather than just a retailer selling home improvement products to customers.

If you were the manufacturer of any of the items used in Lowe's' Facebook promotion, what might you be worried about with regard to Lowe's' Facebook promotional strategy? Do you think the worry is justified? Discuss.

2. "I just can't get these guys to feature our new fresh pasta products the way they should," remarked Alice DeMarco, a product manager for a major manufacturer that had ventured into the new growth field of fresh refrigerated foods. Fresh pasta was to be one of the company's key products in its effort to build the fresh food product category. The "guys" DeMarco referred to were store managers for a regional supermarket chain. They were not using the manufacturer's carefully planned display with special signs to feature the fresh pasta. Instead, they had simply stacked up the pasta in the refrigerator case next to the eggs and milk in most of the stores. This had been going on for more than five weeks, and the new fresh pasta line had not done well. DeMarco blamed the poor results on lack of retailer promotion support.

Discuss the situation in terms of the need to obtain channel member support and follow-through in push promotions.

3. Sales through department stores account for about one-third of the $170 billion world market for cosmetics. One of the major reasons— perhaps the *most* important reason—for department stores' ability to hold their own in the sale of cosmetics despite heavy competition from mass merchandisers, supermarkets, and drug chains is their use of trained salespeople

(cosmeticians) who are able to provide personal attention and advice to customers.

Might this same approach to promotion work for a wider range of products, even in the face of the long-term trend toward mass self-service selling and away from personal selling at the retail level? Discuss.

4. Push type promotions are not limited to the supermarket or the Chevrolet dealer. Some manufacturers of "highbrow" products also do their share of push promotion. For instance, Steinway & Sons, the almost 150-year-old manufacturer of fine concert pianos, has had a policy for many years of placing its pianos free of charge in selected concert halls, music schools, and recording studios to promote the product. Not long ago, Yamaha, a Japanese competitor, developed a similar promotion. This struck a sour note with Steinway, whose reaction was anything but highbrow. Its dealers were told in no uncertain terms not to participate in the Yamaha promotion, and Steinway cut off the franchise of one major dealer to serve as an example.

Discuss this development in terms of the notion of "kinder and gentler" promotions. Given the general nature of promotion and what it seeks to accomplish, can there really be such a thing as "kinder and gentler" promotions?

5. Retail carpet dealers are in an industry that is deluged with manufacturers' push promotions on an almost daily basis, making it difficult for any particular carpet manufacturer to attract retailers' attention with promotional programs. So when Mohawk Industries, one of the largest U.S. carpet manufacturers, launched a sales incentive program to push its DuPont Stainmaster carpets, it focused directly on the retailers' salespeople. To initially attract their attention, Mohawk developed a customized rock CD labeled Mohawk Rocks and a poster that explained the details of the program. The actual awards for meeting specified levels of sales of the Stainmaster carpets were in the form of merchandise and free travel—typical perks for such programs. But the response to this incentive campaign was unusually high. Mohawk believes that the CD and poster provided a special touch that helped to make this essentially standard manufacturer sales incentive promotional campaign stand out from the crowd. Many salespeople, after glancing at

the poster, could not resist giving a listen to the CD, and once they did, Mohawk's promotion made it onto their "radar screens."

Discuss the challenge of making sales contests and incentives aimed at channel members interesting and attractive enough to achieve a high level of participation.

6. Aris Isotoner, a division of Sara Lee Corporation, is one of the world's largest manufacturers of gloves. It was the first company to put gloves in boxes and its four-way stretch fabric, which enables it to offer one-size-fits-all for most of its products, has made it unique in the industry. But what makes this company even more unusual is that it does 75 percent of its annual sales in just five weeks—the period from Thanksgiving to Christmas. The company has learned from experience that point-of-purchase display is the key to capitalizing on this brief window of sales opportunity, because this five-week period is when store traffic is highest and when impulse buying is at its peak. Thus, Aris Isotoner puts most of its promotional emphasis on designing and getting retailers to use POP displays. For example, one of its newest display units, costing about $200 each,

uses all neutral colors so as to blend with any retailer's décor.

Why do you think Aris Isotoner has been so successful in employing POP as its key promotional tool in a retail environment that is often hostile to POP?

7. Gillette, now a division of Procter & Gamble, has developed its own iPhone application called "uArt." This app enables consumers to upload a picture of themselves and then use the Gillette Fusion razor (your finger that shows up as a Fusion razor on the iPhone screen) to virtually shave and then create many facial hairstyles and see the results of the various looks on the iPhone screen. Gillette believes that reaching customers and potential customers via an entertaining but potentially useful iPhone app is not just a cute app that its customers "will get a kick out of," but has become a necessary part of its promotional mix to stay connected with its customer base, especially its younger customers.

Do you agree with Gillette's position? Why or why not? How might Gillette's iPhone app promotional strategy affect retailers selling Gillette products?

References

1. Terence A. Shimp, *Advertising Promotion and Other Aspects of Integrated Marketing Communications* 7th ed. Mason, Ohio: South-Western/Cengage Learning 2010.

2. See for example: Flora F. Gu, Namwoon Kim, David K. Tse, and Danny T. Wang, "Managing Distributors' Changing Motivations Over the Course of a Joint Program," *Journal of Marketing* (September 2010): 32–47.

3. Sang Yong Kim and Richard Staelin, "Manufacturer Allowances and Retailer Pass-Through Rates in a Competitive Environment," *Marketing Science* 18, no. 1 (1999): 59–76.

4. For a related study, see: Norris Bruce, Preyas S. Desai, and Richard Staelin, "The Better They Are, the More They Give: Trade Promotions of Consumer Durables," *Journal of Marketing Research* (February 2005): 54–66.

5. For an analysis that models aspects of the pull promotional process, see Eitan Gerstner and James D. Hess, "Pull Promotions and Channels Coordination," *Marketing Science* (Winter 1995): 43–60.

6. Kasum Ailawadi, Paul W. Farris, and Ervin Shames, "Trade Promotion: Essential to Selling Through Resellers," *Sloan Management Review* (No. 1, 1999): 83–92.

7. Michael Levy, John Webster, and Roger A. Kerin, "Formulating Push Marketing Strategies: A Method and Application," *Journal of Marketing* (Winter 1983): 25–34; and Michael Levy and George W. Jones, "The Effect on Sales of Changes in a Push Marketing Strategy in a Marketing Channel Context," *Journal of the Academy of Marketing Science* (Winter 1984): 85–88.

8. For a related discussion, see James R. Brown and Sherman A. Timmins, "Substructural Dimensions of Interorganizational Relations in Marketing Channels," *Journal of the Academy of Marketing Science* (Summer 1981): 168–169.

9. For some insightful background on this relationship, see Donald R. Glover, "Distributor Attitudes toward Manufacturer-Sponsored Promotions," *Industrial Marketing Management* (1991): 241–249.

10. Robert Berner, "Can Procter & Gamble Clean Up Its Act?" *Business Week* (March 12, 2000): 80–83.

11. For a related discussion see: David Kesmodel, "To Trump Small Brewers, Beer Makers Get Crafty," *Wall Street Journal* (October 26, 2007): B1, B3.

12. *Cox Direct 20th Annual Survey of Promotional Practices* (Largo, Florida: Cox Direct, 2000), 40.

13. For an excellent article that deals with the key psychological dimensions underlying this relationship, see Nermin Eyuboglu and Andreas Buja, "Dynamics of Channel Negotiations: Contention and Reciprocity," *Psychology and Marketing* (February 1993): 47–65.

14. Miguel I. Gomez, Vithala R. Rao, and Edward W. McLaughlin, "Empirical Analysis of Budget and Allocation of Trade Promotions in the U.S. Supermarket Industry," *Journal of Marketing Research* (August 2007): 410–424.

15. Xavier Dreze and David R. Bell, "Creating Win-Win Trade Promotions: Theory and Empirical Analysis of Scan-Back Trade Deals," *Marketing Science* (Winter 2003): 16–39; Kasum L. Ailawadi, "The Retail Power-Performance Conundrum: What Have We Learned?" *Journal of Retailing* (Autumn 2001): 299–318; Jack J. Kasulis, Fred W. Morgan, David E. Griffiths, and James M. Kenderdine, "Managing Trade Promotions in the Context of Market Power," *Journal of the Academy of Marketing Science* (Summer 1999): 320–332; Phillip Nerrillo and Dawn Iocobucci, "Trade Promotions, a Call for a More Rational Approach," *Business Horizons* (July-August 1995): 75–76; Ajay Bhasin, Roger Dickinson, Christine G. Hauri, and William A. Robinson, "Promotion Investments That Keep Paying Off," *Journal of Consumer Marketing* (Winter 1989): 31–36; Ronald C. Curhan and Robert J. Kopp, "Obtaining Retailer Support for Trade Deals: Key Success Factors," *Journal of Advertising Research* (December 1987-January 1988): 51–60.

16. For an excellent article dealing with key issues in cooperative advertising, see Sydney Roslow, Henry A. Laskey, and J. A. F. Nicholls, "Enigma of Cooperative Advertising," *Journal of Business and Industrial Marketing* 8, no. 2 (1993): 70–79.

17. Jack Neff, "Wal-Mart Ups the Ante with Brand Co-op Ads—In More Ways Than One," *Advertising Age* (November 30, 2009): 1–3.

18. For a related discussion, see Debbie Howell "Popularity of Ethnic Cuisine Improves Positioning at Mass," *DSN Retailing Today* (July 7, 2002): 21.

19. Tanja Randery, Bill Caesar, and Mike Longman, "Achieving Channel Excellence," McKinsey & Company Marketing Practice Report (June 2002): 3.

20. See for example: "The Next Generation of Shopper Marketing" *Time and Trend Report*. SymphonyIRIGroup 2010.

21. Rockney G. Walters, "An Empirical Investigation into Retailer Response to Manufacturer Trade Promotions," *Journal of Retailing* (Summer 1989): 253–272.

22. For an excellent background, overview and analysis of slotting fees see: Gregory T. Gundlach, "Slotting Fees—Fees Charged by Grocery Retailers for Shelf Space: Are They Stifling Competition?" Statement made before the California State Senate Standing Committee on Business, Professions and Economic Development (February 9, 2005): 1–12.

23. Paul N. Bloom, Gregory T. Gundlach, and Joseph P. Cannon, "Slotting Allowances and Fees: Schools of Thought and Views of Practicing Managers," *Journal of Marketing* (April 2000): 92.

24. Bloom, Gundlach, and Cannon, "Slotting Fees," 92–108.

25. John L. Stanton, "Slotting Allowances: Short Term Gains and Long-Term Negative Effects on Retailers and Consumers," *International Journal of Retail & Distribution Management* Vol. 34, No. 3, 2006: 187–197.

26. For a related analysis that views slotting fees as a form of shelf space "insurance" paid to the retailer that can improve efficiency, see: Timothy J. Richards and Paul M. Patterson, "Slotting Allowances as Real Options: An Alternative Explanation," *Journal of Business* Vol. 77, No. 2 (2004): 675–696.

27. For an insightful analysis of the role of slotting fees, see J. Chris White, Lisa C. Troy, and R. Nicholas Gerlich, "The Role of Slotting Fees and Introductory Allowances in Retail Buyers' New Product Acceptance Decisions," *Journal of the Academy of Marketing Science* (Spring 2000): 291–298.

28. Bloom, Gundlach, and Cannon, "Slotting Allowances and Fees," 106.

29. Richards and Patterson, "Slotting Allowances as Real Options:" 691–693.

30. In fact, research has shown that even in the absence of consumer price incentives, in-store promotion can be effective; see J. Jeffrey Unman and Leigh McAllister, "A Retailer Promotion Policy Model Considering Promotion Signal Sensitivity," *Marketing Science* (Fall 1993): 339–356.

31. See, for example, Coy Ouwarkerk, William Verbeke, Heinz Hovingh, and Ed Peelen, "Retailers' and Manufacturers' Perceptions of the Temporary Display," *Journal of Marketing Channels* 6, no. 1 (1997): 1–16.

32. Susan Berfield, "Getting the Most Out of Every Shopper," *Business Week* (January 9, 2000): 45–46.

33. Berfield, "Getting the Most Out of Every Shopper," 46.

34. Stanley Holmes and Christine Tierney, "How Nike Got Its Game Back," *Business Week* (November 4, 2002): 129–131.

35. Geoffrey A. Fowler, "When Free Samples Became Saviors," *Wall Street Journal* (August 14, 2001): B1, B4.

36. Fowler, "When Free Samples Became Saviors," B1.

37. Jack J. Kasulis, Fred W. Morgan, David E. Griffith, and James M. Kenderdine, "Managing Trade Promotions in the Context of Market Power," *Journal of the Academy of Marketing Science* (Summer 1999): 320–332.

38. See for example: Ann Zimmerman and Anita Raghavan, "Special Deals for Distributors Draw Scrutiny," *Wall Street Journal* (November 7, 2003): B1, B5.

39. Dean Foust, "Coke: The Cost of Babying Bottlers," *Business Week* (December 9, 2002): 93–94.

40. Sara Ines Calderon, "Kraft Foods Focuses Messaging on Facebook," *Inside Facebook* (July 5, 2010): 1–6.

41. Christopher Heine, "Mountain Dew, J.C. Penney Run Display Ads with Facebook," *Click Z* (October 15, 2010): 1.

42. Dan Sewell, "Procter & Gamble Embraces Social Media for Promotion," *Greenbay Press* Gazatte.com (December 17, 2010): 1–2, http://www.greenbaypressgazatte.com/fdcp/?

43. Josh Leibowotz, "Rediscovering the Art of Selling," *McKinsey Quarterly* (October 2010): 117–119.

CHAPTER **13**

Logistics and Channel Management

LEARNING OBJECTIVES

After reading this chapter you should:

1. Be familiar with the definition of logistics, or physical distribution.
2. Have an awareness of the recent supply chain management emphasis of logistics.
3. Be aware of the role of logistics in the firm.
4. Understand the systems concept and the total cost approach as they apply to logistics.
5. Know the major components of any logistics system.
6. Recognize that the output of a logistics system is good customer service.
7. Be cognizant of the distinction between logistics management and channel management.
8. Have an overview of four key interfaces between channel management and logistics management.

© Ryan Pyle/Corbis

FOCUS ON CHANNELS

Who Says Logistics Can't Be Fashionable?

Not Zara, the Spanish fashion apparel specialty chain that may soon overtake Gap for the title of the world's largest clothing retailer. Zara thinks logistics is *very* fashionable because without the company's innovative and high-powered logistical system, Zara's ability to have up-to-the-minute fashion apparel in its network of stores all over the world would not be possible. In fact, Zara's command of logistics is so good that designs can move from sketch pad to finished product in stores all over the world in just two weeks! This "fast fashion" system has made Zara the envy of just about every other major apparel chain. The global retailer always seems to have the latest trendy fashions in its stores before its competitors and doesn't often get stuck with big batches of out-of-fashion merchandise that have to be heavily discounted.

How does Zara do it? The answer can be stated in three words: logistics, logistics, logistics! Because Zara's business model is all about having the latest fashions available in its global network of stores in the right quantities and sizes, Zara's supply chain must be ultra-fast and super flexible to make this happen. So, an intense focus on logistics permeates the company's corporate culture. Store managers are trained to monitor what's selling and to spot new fashion trends every day and immediately report this information to headquarters. Over half of Zara's merchandise is produced in relatively high cost factories in Spain, Portugal and Mexico rather than much lower cost Asian factories. But by doing so, Zara saves a great deal of time and shipping costs are lower. Zara's factories operate on the just-in-time inventory system developed in cooperation with Toyota Motors, the world leader in JIT. So, inventory costs are minimized. All warehousing is centralized in Spain so no complex coordination of warehouses in different countries is needed. Zara's order cycle time from its Spanish warehouses? Just 24 hours for stores in Europe and no more than 48 hours for stores in the Americas and Asia. This speedy delivery is made possible by using air shipments. It's more expensive but inventory carrying costs are lower and there is little risk of being stuck with big quantities of out-of-season merchandise.

So, while Zara is always a hit on fashion runways, the runways that tie its logistics system together are what make Zara's apparel an even bigger hit in its stores.

Source: Based on: Kerry Capell, "Zara Thrives By Breaking All the Rules," *BusinessWeek*, October 20, 2008: 66.

In this chapter we turn our attention to the fourth major element needed to foster a cooperative team of channel members—an effective and efficient logistics system. **Logistics**, also often referred to as **physical distribution** (PD), has many definitions, but most share the same underlying theme expressed in Kotler's classic definition, which defines logistics as "Planning, implementing, and controlling the physical flows of materials and final goods from points of origin to points of use to meet customers' needs at a profit."[1] In more recent years, with the growing emphasis on marketing channels cooperating in partnerships and strategic alliances (see Chapter 9), the term **supply chain management** (SCM) has come into common usage to describe logistical systems that emphasize close cooperation and comprehensive interorganizational management to integrate the logistical operations of the different firms into the channel.[2] Although a detailed discussion of the differences between what might be referred to as the "traditional" approach to logistics and the supply chain management approach is beyond the scope of this chapter, Table 13.1 provides an overview of the key distinctions. In any case, whether one chooses to use the term *physical distribution, logistics, supply chain management* or an even newer term being used by some authors, *demand chain planning*,[3] the underlying principle emphasized throughout this text is the building of strong cooperation among channel members through effective interorganizational management.[4]

Overviews of logistics appear in many basic marketing textbooks[5] and excellent, comprehensive treatments of the subject can be found in textbooks dealing exclusively with logistics management.[6] Here we will be concerned mainly with several important interfaces between logistics management and channel management. An awareness of these interfaces is necessary if the channel manager is to play a part in shaping the firm's logistics strategy so that it is more likely to foster channel member cooperation rather than conflict.[7] First, however, we will briefly review several basic aspects of logistics: the role of logistics in channel management, logistics systems, costs and components as well as customer service as the output of the logistics system.

The Role of Logistics

Even the most carefully designed and managed marketing channel must rely on logistics to actually make products available to customers. The movement of the right amount of the right products to the right place at the right time—a commonly heard description of what logistics is supposed to do—is more than a catchy phrase. It is, in fact, the essence of the role of logistics in the marketing channel.

Getting the right amount of the right products to the right place at the right time, especially in a global environment, is obviously no simple or inexpensive job. On the contrary, global markets, with their diversity of customer segments spread over vast geographic areas, can make the task of logistics complex and expensive.[8] In fact, the field has become so complex and sophisticated that a multibillion-dollar industry referred to as **third-party logistics providers** (sometimes referred to as **3PLs**) has emerged during the past two decades.[9] These firms specialize in performing most or all of the logistical tasks that manufacturers or other channel members would normally perform themselves.

TABLE 13.1 COMPARISON OF TRADITIONAL AND SUPPLY CHAIN APPROACHES TO THE MANAGEMENT OF LOGISTICS

	APPROACH	
ELEMENT	TRADITIONAL	SUPPLY CHAIN
Inventory management approach	Independent efforts	Joint reduction in channel inventories
Total cost approach	Minimize firm costs	Channel-wide cost efficiencies
Time horizon	Short-term	Long-term
Amount of information sharing and monitoring	Limited to needs of current transaction	As required for planning and monitoring processes
Amount of coordination of multiple levels in the channel	Single contact for the transaction between channel pairs	Multiple contacts between levels in firms and levels in channel
Joint planning	Transaction-based	Ongoing
Compatibility of corporate philosophies	Not relevant	Compatible at least for key relationships
Breadth of supplier base	Large to increase competition and spread risk	Small to increase coordination
Channel leadership	Not needed	Needed for coordination focus
Amount of sharing risks and rewards	Each on its own	Risks and rewards shared over the long term
Speed of operations, information, and inventory flows	"Warehouse" orientation (storage, safety stock) interrupted by barriers to flows; localized to channel pairs	"Distribution center" orientation (inventory velocity) interconnecting flows; JIT Quick Response across the channel

Source: Martha C. Cooper and Lisa M. Ellram, "Characteristics of Supply Chain Management and Implication for Purchasing and Logistics Strategy," *The International Journal of Logistics Management* 4, no. 2 (1993): 16. Copyright © 1993 by Emerald Group Publishing Limited. All rights reserved. Reproduced by permission.

As specialists in logistics, companies such as Strategic Distribution Inc. (SDI), which focus on maintenance, repair and operating supplies (MRO), are able to provide superior service at lower cost than the firms who hire them. Here is how SDI describes the logistical services it offers to its clients on its Web site:

> Our end goal is to help you cut costs up and down your supply chain. But our approach focuses on solutions, not products. We deliver the technology and processes that give you the power to manage. We dig deep into the mundane details of MRO—through stacks of work orders, hundreds of suppliers, and thousands of SKUs—and uncover opportunities to help you save.[10]

While still accounting for less than 8 percent of the roughly $1.6 trillion spent on logistics by all firms in the United States, 3PLs have been growing rapidly (see Figure 13.1). Third-party logistics providers, or 3PLs, have also become a major force on a global scale. Total revenues in 2009 from all the countries around the world in which they operated amounted to over $507 billion. Moreover, the total amount spent on logistics by all firms and organizations in the world is estimated to be over $6.6 trillion in 2009![11]

Thus, logistics is a gigantic industry that pervades virtually all firms all over the globe. It is no wonder then that this important marketing component has been receiving increased attention that has led to significant innovations in logistics. The grocery industry, for example, has launched a massive effort to improve the logistics of food distribution from farm to consumer. The initiative, referred to in the industry as **Efficient Consumer Response (ECR)**, seeks to provide consumers with better service and more value through the cooperation of all firms in the supply chain. In the process, the industry hopes to save over $30 billion annually in logistical costs, creating a win-win situation of lower prices for consumers and stronger profits for all channel members in the food industry. Substantial progress has already been made toward implementing ECR in the food industry, but perhaps even more impressive is the fact that the ECR concept is spreading to numerous other industries.[12]

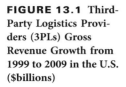

FIGURE 13.1 Third-Party Logistics Providers (3PLs) Gross Revenue Growth from 1999 to 2009 in the U.S. ($billions)

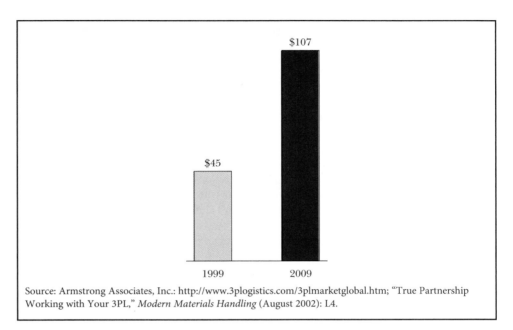

Source: Armstrong Associates, Inc.: http://www.3plogistics.com/3plmarketglobal.htm; "True Partnership Working with Your 3PL," *Modern Materials Handling* (August 2002): L4.

So, logistics—getting the right amount of the right products to the right place at the right time at the lowest possible cost to the customer (whether captured in new, perhaps more exciting, terms such as supply chain management and Efficient Consumer Response or in the traditional "plain vanilla" term "logistics")—unquestionably plays a crucial role in channel management.

Logistics Systems, Components and Costs

Prior to World War II, logistics was equated mainly with transportation. Hence the field was narrowly defined in terms of the activities involved in shipping and receiving products and was given relatively little management attention. But during World War II, developments in military logistics required to move vast amounts of supplies to the European and Pacific war theaters demonstrated the importance of logistics in winning the war. Of particular note was the emergence of the **systems concept** for dealing with logistical problems; that is, more attention was paid to the various factors involved in the logistical process and the interrelationships among them. Rather than being thought of as separate and distinct from one another, such factors as transportation, materials handling, inventory control, warehousing and packaging of goods were seen as interrelated components of a system. Thus, decisions or actions affecting one component could have implications for other components of the logistical system. For example, a faster mode of transportation for moving a quantity of supplies from point A to point B could result in a lower level of inventory needed at point B, which in turn could result in a smaller warehouse required. Or conversely, a slower mode of transport for shipping products from point A to B might well mean that a larger inventory and a larger warehouse would be needed at point B because of the slower rate of resupply.

This concept of logistics as a system has served as the foundation of modern logistics management.[13] In essence, those in charge of managing logistics seek to find the optimum combination of basic logistics components (transportation, materials handling, order processing, inventory control, warehousing and packaging) to meet customer service demands.

In a commercial or profit-making context—which, of course, involves most business situations—the logistics manager also attempts to achieve the desired level of customer service at the lowest cost by applying the **total cost approach**. This concept is a logical extension of the systems concept because it addresses *all* the costs of logistics together, rather than the separate costs of individual components, and seeks to minimize the total cost. Consequently, when designing a logistics system, a company must examine the cost of each component and how it affects other components. For instance, a faster mode of transport from point A to point B might increase transportation costs. But, since the inventory levels and warehouse needed at point B would be smaller (because the faster transportation mode allows for quicker resupply), the inventory carrying costs and warehouse costs will be lower. These savings in costs may be more than enough to offset the higher transportation costs. So, from the standpoint of the *total cost of the logistics system*, the increase in transportation costs for the faster mode of transport may well result in a *lower total cost* for logistics.

The use of the systems concept and the total cost approach to manage logistics is shown in Figure 13.2. This figure suggests that all basic components of the system are related and that the systems concept and the total cost approach provide the guiding principles for blending the components so as to provide the types and levels of services desired by customers at the lowest total cost for the logistics system as a whole.[14]

Each of the components of the logistics system will now be briefly considered.

FIGURE 13.2 View of Logistics Management Based on the Systems Concept and the Total Cost Approach

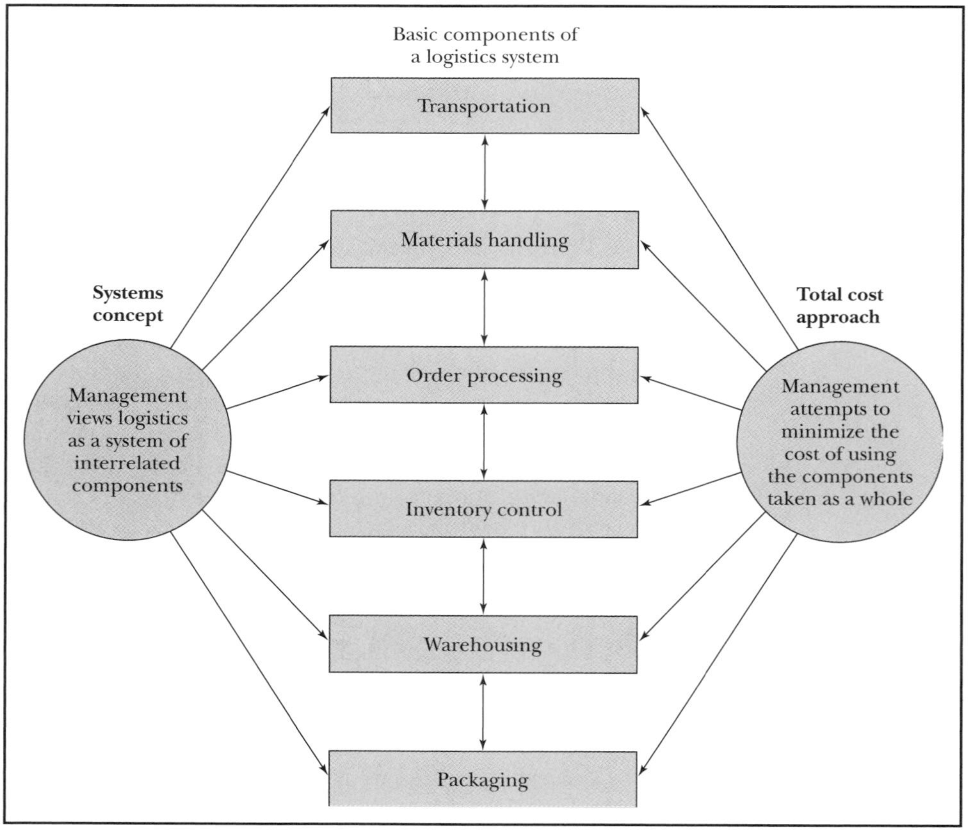

Transportation

Transportation is the most fundamental and obviously necessary component of any logistics system, for clearly, in the case of physical products that must be moved from one location to another, a transaction cannot be completed until transportation has occurred. Transportation is also quite often the component accounting for the highest percentage of the total cost of logistics. So, controlling or, better yet, cutting transportation costs has become a top priority in the logistics industry. Indeed, in a meticulous effort to reduce transportation costs, the world's largest freight transportation company, UPS, has studied literally every step in the transportation process. Among the numerous cost-cutting measures UPS initiated based on the findings of the study was to tell their truck drivers to avoid left turns whenever possible because they take longer to make than right-hand turns![15]

From a logistics management standpoint, the overriding issue facing the firm is choosing the optimum mode of transportation to meet customer service demands. This can be a very complex and technical task because there are so many considerations. A few of these are:

1. Should the firm use its own carriers or common carriers?[16]
2. What are the different rates available?
3. What specific transportation services are offered?
4. How reliable are various common carriers?
5. What modes of transport are competitors using?

Moreover, if the systems concept and total cost approach are applied, the logistics manager must think in terms of how the transportation component interacts with and affects the total cost of logistics.[17] Such decisions require specialized knowledge and expertise not only of logistics systems, but also of the specialized needs of the industry involved and of the latest technologies available.[18] For example, Rand McNally offers a variety of software called *MileMaker®*, described as:

> the industry-standard rating and routing solution for the commercial trucking marketplace. MileMaker® software contains the only electronic version of the Household Goods Carriers' Bureau (HHG) Mileage Guide data. HHG miles and routes give both carriers and shippers consistent, accurate mileages that simplify rate negotiations, make it easier and faster to analyze freight rates, reduce costs associated with electronic rating, and streamline audit process. MileMaker® software also includes Practical Miles, a calculation of the shortest time route between two points, which allows for estimation of arrival time.[19]

Logistics managers must keep abreast of such developments in transportation and have the expertise to take advantage of them to enhance their transportation performance.

Materials Handling

Materials handling encompasses the range of activities and equipment involved in the placement and movement of products in storage areas. Issues that must be addressed when designing materials handling systems include how to minimize the distances products are moved within the warehouse during the course of receiving, storage and shipping; what kinds of mechanical equipment (such as conveyor belts, cranes and forklifts) should be used and how to make the best use of labor when receiving, handling and shipping products. For example, the growing use of **cross-docking** (sometimes referred to as *flow-through distribution*) has significantly enhanced materials handling efficiency. In cross-docking, products from an arriving truck are not stored in a warehouse and then picked later to fill orders. Rather, the merchandise is immediately moved across the receiving dock to other trucks for immediate delivery to stores. This eliminates the need to pick stored products at a later time. In short, products are moved straight from receiving to shipping.

But designing efficient materials handling processes such as cross-docking can involve highly technical and sophisticated engineering analyses. This, of course, requires special knowledge and expertise that go far beyond the scope of this text and is really a job for specialists in the design of materials handling systems. What is appropriate to mention here, however, is that materials handling can be a critically important part of a logistics system. Procter & Gamble, for example, has research that shows that cross-docking can reduce distributors' per-case handling costs by as much as two-thirds, cutting 35 to 45 cents of a distributor's average cost of 60 to 70 cents per case to deliver products to a store.[20]

Order Processing

The task of filling customer orders may at first appear to be a minor part of logistics and a rather routine activity that does not require a great deal of thought to do well. In fact, order processing is often a key component of logistics and developing an efficient order processing system can be far from routine.

The importance of order processing in logistics lies in its relationships with **order cycle time**, which is the time between when an order is placed and when it is received by the customer. If order processing is cumbersome and inefficient, it can slow down the order cycle time considerably. It can even increase transportation costs if a faster mode of transportation must be used to make up for the slow order processing time.

"Routine" order processing may actually be the result of a great deal of planning, capital investment and training of people. When many thousands of orders are received on a daily basis, filling the orders quickly and accurately can be a challenging task. This is the case at many large firms, including W. W. Grainger Inc., one of the world's leading business-to-business distributors of equipment, components and supplies with more than 1.8 million commercial, industrial, contractor and institutional customers in 153 countries around the world. Grainger has more than 600 distribution centers and carries over 900,000 different products, all of which are sold through its regular catalog or online. Grainger receives more than 115,000 individual orders per day via phone, fax or online.[21] To process this vast array of daily orders accurately and efficiently, the company has developed a state-of-the-art satellite communications system that links all of its distributors, allows its customers to link their Web site to Grainger's and provides instant access to the nearest Grainger distributor location. In many cases, Grainger's order processing is so efficient that an order can be filled and delivered the same day it was placed. This quick and efficient order processing throughout the entire Grainger distributor network is absolutely essential to Grainger's core mission of providing rapid and reliable product availability to its million-plus customers throughout the U.S. and abroad.

The planning, design and management of such sophisticated order processing systems are hardly routine. Indeed, in the hospital supply industry where medical and surgical supplies account for some 750,000 different products, developing a modern order processing system is a nightmarish challenge because there is no standard nomenclature for all these different products. Confusion and costly mix-ups have caused large numbers of errors and hundreds of thousands of returns for credit.[22]

Inventory Control

Inventory control refers to the firm's attempt to hold the lowest level of inventory that will still enable it to meet customer demand. This is a never-ending battle that all firms face. It is a critically important one as well. Inventory carrying costs—including the costs of financing, insurance, storage and lost, damaged and stolen goods—on average can amount to approximately 25 percent of the value of the inventory per year. For some types of merchandise, such as perishable goods or fashion merchandise, carrying costs can be considerably higher. Yet without inventory to meet customer demand on a regular and timely basis, a firm could not stay in business for very long.

Ideally, a firm wants to keep inventory at the lowest possible level and, at the same time, place orders for goods in large quantities because placing the fewest possible orders enables the firm to minimize ordering costs.[23] Unfortunately, there is a conflict between these two objectives. Average inventory carrying costs rise in direct proportion to the level of the inventory, while average ordering costs decrease in rough proportion to the size of the order. Thus, a trade-off must be made between these two costs to find the optimum levels for both. This point, usually referred to as the **economic order quantity (EOQ)**, occurs at the point at which total costs (inventory carrying costs plus ordering costs) are lowest, as illustrated in Figure 13.3. As the figure shows, the logistics manager must constantly aspire to achieve the lowest total cost by balancing inventory carrying and ordering costs.

One firm that has done a good job of controlling its inventory is Corning Consumer Products Co., a unit of Corning Inc. Having the right quantities and design patterns on Corelle dinnerware had become a huge problem because it was so difficult to predict consumer buying patterns, especially around Christmas. To solve the problem, Corning developed a sophisticated inventory control system. A key feature of the system is the requirement that Corning keep a major portion of its Corelle dinnerware undecorated until it gets up-to-the-minute sales data from retailers. Soon after the system was installed, it saved the company from a disastrous mistake. A week after a giant retail chain launched a special on 12-piece dinnerware sets, the computer-based forecasting model (a crucial part of the inventory control system) predicted that the promotion would be a flop. Corning quickly warned another retailer to cancel its order for 160,000

FIGURE 13.3 Economic Order Quantity (EOQ) Model

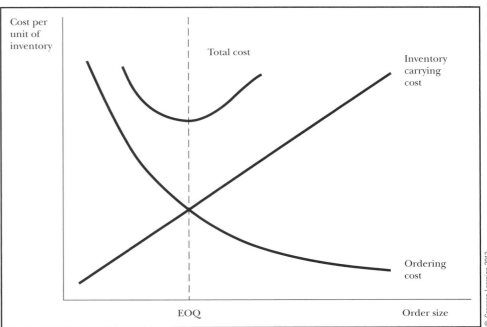

© Cengage Learning 2013

of these sets. Then, the unfinished dishes were decorated in another, more popular design and shipped out—all in less than two weeks. Corning expects this more flexible inventory control system to reduce the amount of time inventory stays in the warehouse by half, thus sharply increasing turnover.

The battle to control inventory costs is one that firms—even some of the world's largest and most sophisticated ones—can never seem to outgrow. A case in point is Walmart Stores Inc. Almost universally regarded as a leader in rigorous, high-tech inventory management, Walmart recently experienced inventory control problems when its 2010 fourth quarter inventory unexpectedly increased by 11 percent over the previous year. What caused Walmart's inventory bulge? Analysts think Walmart was overly optimistic in forecasting an increase in same-store sales for the quarter. In actuality, same-store sales *decreased* by 1.8 percent, leaving Walmart with considerable excess inventory.[24]

Warehousing

The warehousing or storage component of a logistics system is concerned with the holding of products until they are ready to be sold. Warehousing can actually be one of the more complex components of a logistics system because, quite often, warehousing options entail several key decisions, each of which can be difficult and complex to deal with. The most basic of these decisions are (1) the location of warehouse facilities; (2) the number of warehousing units; (3) the size of units; (4) the design of units, including layout and internal systems and (5) the questions of ownership.

A discussion of each of these areas is far beyond the scope of this text. Moreover, successful decisions in each of the areas requires careful planning and analyses and may require input from experts in such fields as location analysis, real estate, operations research and industrial engineering, in addition to logistics management. What can be said at this point, however, is that warehousing can be an important component of a logistics system because it is so closely linked to the ability of firms to provide high levels of customer service. For example, with the growth of the Internet as a major consumer shopping channel, far more shipments of *eaches*—single items as opposed to product lots—have created massive numbers of *onesie* transactions in which only a single item is purchased. Moreover, consumers expect these single items to be delivered very quickly. Experts in the warehousing industry think that such demands by Internet shoppers *increase* rather than decrease the need for warehousing. Why? Because many Internet retailers are just "storefronts" with no inventory on hand. They rely on numerous well-located and efficient warehouses—either their own or third party—to provide the level of product availability demanded by Internet shoppers.

But even when it comes to conventional "land based" distribution, the importance of good warehouses in creating an efficient logistics system cannot be overstated. Whirlpool Corp., one of the world's leading appliance manufacturers, finally became a believer in the importance of warehousing after struggling for decades with a hodgepodge of old warehouses, transport depots, factory distribution centers and numerous temporary buildings used to handle overflows of appliances. Retailers often had to wait five to ten days to receive an order. In 2006, Whirlpool launched a four-year, $600 million program to upgrade its warehouse facilities. Instead of the existing 41 outdated warehouse sites, Whirlpool replaced them with 10 new regional distribution centers. The result? Retailers now can receive orders in 48–72 hours even though Whirlpool has *reduced* its average inventory level by $250 million a year, while increases in efficiency have saved the company $100 million in annual warehouse expenses![25]

Packaging

Packaging and the costs associated with the packaging of products are relevant as a component of the logistics system because packaging can affect the other components of the system, and vice versa. For example, the type of transport used can affect packaging and packing costs. In the case of airfreight, for instance, packaging costs are usually reduced because risks of damage are generally lower than if rail or truck were used. Materials handling and order processing procedures and costs can also be affected by packaging because well-designed packaging can help to increase efficiencies in these components of the logistics system. Effective packaging can also help control inventory carrying costs by reducing product damage. Further, warehouse space and thus costs can be saved if packaging is designed to be space efficient.

Here again, a detailed discussion is well beyond the scope of this chapter. Packaging design is a highly specialized area within the field of industrial design. For example, Whirlpool Corp., in an effort to reduce millions of dollars in annual losses from dents and dings in appliances occurring during handling and shipping, has launched a major packaging redesign initiative. The company has assembled a team of engineers in the U.S. and India and provided them with a $400,000 supercomputer to see if it is possible to design packaging for major appliances that will significantly reduce shipping and handling related damage. Whirlpool hopes the program will result in $3.00 of savings for every dollar spent.[26]

So, the point to be made here is that packaging is far more than a promotional device for fostering product differentiation and attracting consumer attention. Packaging has an important logistics dimension that can make a significant difference in the effectiveness and efficiency of the logistics system.[27] Indeed, a product in distinctive and effective packaging will have even more appeal if it is also easy to handle, stacks up with no problem and takes minimum space on the channel members' shelves.

The Output of the Logistics System: Customer Service and Competitive Advantage

Johnson et al. capture succinctly the meaning and importance of customer service in the context of logistics:

> Customer service is the collection of activities performed in filling orders and keeping customers happy or creating in the customer's mind the perception of an organization that is easy to do business with.[28]

Over the years, logistics researchers and practitioners have given a great deal of thought to the kinds of services that can be provided by a logistics system.[29] A number of attempts have been made to define and enumerate these services and to measure performance in terms of what logistics experts refer to as **service standards**. Heskett, Galskowsky and Ivie, for example, stress the following nine categories of logistics service standards:

1. Time from order receipt to order shipment
2. Order size and assortment constraints
3. Percentage of items out of stock
4. Percentage of orders filled accurately
5. Percentage of orders filled within a given number of days from receipt of the order
6. Percentage of orders filled
7. Percentage of customer orders that arrive in good condition

8. Order cycle time (time from order placement to order delivery)

9. Ease and flexibility of order placement[30]

These logistics service standards are usually quantified in some fashion and then the firm's actual performance is measured against these standards. For example, the first standard—time from order receipt to order shipment—might be set at 24 hours for 90 percent of all orders received. So, for every 100 orders received, the firm must have 90 of the orders processed and shipped within 24 hours to meet the standard. The second service standard in the list might be set in terms of some minimum quantity of products, for example, certain restrictions might be placed on mixing the various products unless specified minimum requirements of each are ordered. A steel producer, for example, might set the minimum order for various gauges of sheet metal at two tons; so, for a customer to order several gauges in a single order, a certain combined minimum tonnage might have to be met. The third standard—percentage of items out of stock, or **stockouts**—is almost always set in terms of percent of items ordered during a given period that cannot be filled from inventory. Thus, if a manufacturer wants to fill 95 percent of the items ordered, its stockout percentage can be no higher than 5 percent to meet the standard. The other six service standards in the list can be quantified and used in a similar fashion.

LaLonde describes customer service in terms of the six key elements:[31]

1. Product availability

2. Order cycle time

3. Distribution system flexibility

4. Distribution system information

5. Distribution system malfunction

6. Postsale product support

Mentzer, Gomes and Krapfel list 26 different measures of customer service based on an extensive review of the literature.[32] These are shown in Table 13.2.

Finally, Bowersox and Closs distill what they refer to as "Basic Service Capability" into three categories: (1) availability; (2) operational performance and (3) reliability. Each of these service capability categories is defined in Table 13.3.

Regardless of the particular services provided by the logistics system, the key issue is not how many or which firm offers the most but whether the services offered are targeted at *real customer needs*.[33] If the output of the firm's logistics system is simply a

TABLE 13.2 INVENTORY OF LOGISTICS CUSTOMER SERVICE

1. Order processing time	14. Claims response
2. Order assembly time	15. Billing procedures
3. Delivery time	16. Average order cycle time
4. Inventory reliability	17. Order cycle time variability
5. Order size constraints	18. Rush service
6. Consolidation allowed	19. Availability
7. Consistency	20. Competent technical representatives
8. Frequency of sales visits	21. Equipment demonstrations
9. Ordering convenience	22. Availability of published material
10. Order progress information	23. Accuracy in filling orders
11. Inventory backup during promotions	24. Terms of sale
12. Invoice format	25. Protective packaging
13. Physical condition of goods	26. Cooperation

TABLE 13.3 LOGISTICAL SERVICE STANDARDS COMPRISING BASIC SERVICE CAPABILITY

BASIC SERVICE CAPABILITY	DESCRIPTION	MEASURES
Availability	Capacity to have inventory when it is desired to customers	Stockout frequency Fill rate Orders shipped complete
Operational performance	Expected performance outcome of logistical system	Speed Consistency Flexibility Malfunction recovery
Reliability	Ability to comply with planned levels of inventory availability and performance	Measurement variables[1] Measurement units[2] Measurement base[3]

[1] Those specified in logistics service program.
[2] Physical unit measures that can be tracked such as cases, units, weight, etc.
[3] Level of aggregation such as overall system, product line, customer segments, etc.

Source: With kind permission from Springer Science+Business Media: Journal of the Academy of Marketing Science, excerpted from "Physical Distribution Service: A Fundamental Marketing Concept?", Winter 1989, p. 55, John T. Mentzer, Roger Gomes, and Robert F. Krapfel, Jr.

host of high-cost services that customers do not recognize as being of significant value, then the real output is not customer service but expensive lost motion.

Recently, Ketchen et al. have argued that the output of a firm's logistical system or supply chain should not only be aimed at providing superior customer service, but should also be seen as a core dimension of a firm's competitive strategy. In short, logistics or supply chain management should serve as a key dimension for creating a differential advantage for the firm. Ketchen et al. refer to this more strategic view of supply chain management as "best value supply chains."[34] They go on to contrast their concept of best value supply chains with what they refer to as "typical supply chains" in terms of eight key issues associated with supply chain management. This is shown in Table 13.4. The table also includes suggestions for transitioning from typical supply chain to best value supply chain as well as examples of companies that, in Ketchen et al.'s opinion, have already adopted the best value supply chains concept.

Although basing a firm's strategic competitive advantage mainly on superior supply chain management may not be suitable for all firms, the best value supply chain concept does serve to highlight the importance of logistics. And, at least for *some* firms, it suggests that the output of the logistical system can be measured not only in terms of excellent customer service, but also in terms of the effectiveness of the firm's competitive strategy.

Four Key Areas of Interface between Logistics and Channel Management

In Chapter 1 we discussed the relationship of channel strategy and management to logistics management. We pointed out that logistics management is *subsidiary* to the larger area of channel management. In other words, channel management is a broader, more comprehensive element of distribution strategy than is logistics management. Channel management is involved with the administration of *all* of the major channel flows (product, negotiation, ownership, information and promotion), whereas logistics is concerned mainly with the product flow. But, we also noted in Chapter 1 that logistics management and channel management are very closely linked and interdependent[35] because a well-designed and administered marketing channel cannot exist without an efficient flow of

TABLE 13.4 FROM TYPICAL TO BEST VALUE SUPPLY CHAINS

ISSUE	TYPICAL SUPPLY CHAINS	BEST VALUE SUPPLY CHAINS	KEY TO MAKING THE TRANSITION TO A BEST VALUE APPROACH	EXAMPLE COMPANY
Approach to supply chain management	Supply chains *support* strategy by ensuring the needed flow of goods and services	Firms should leverage strategic supply chain management, agility, adaptability, and alignment to *create* competitive advantages	Executives must view supply chains as a strategic weapon rather than as a cost center	*Zara* keeps pace with and creates transient fads in the fashion industry through very rapid product development and distribution
Agility	Moderate capacity to react to changes	Good capacity to anticipate and react to changes	Executives must devise a company-specific approach to managing the costs of buffers	*Raytheon Technical Services Company* locates an executive office nearby key customers
Adaptability	Focus on efficiency through the use of discrete supply chains	Maintain overlapping supply chains to ensure customer service	Executives must be willing to accept the added expense of duplication	Based on customer's needs, *Computer Science Corporation* positions some inventory close to customer locations while other items are warehoused centrally
Alignment	Supply chain members sometimes forced to choose between their own interest and the chain's interest	A rising tide lifts all boats—the interests of supply chain members are consistent with each other	Executives must view problems from the supply chain level of analysis rather than the firm level	When a supplier's suggestion saves *R.R. Donnelly* money, the firm splits the savings with the supplier
Strategic sourcing	Involve suppliers later in the product development process / Monitor internal processes	Involve suppliers early in product development and throughout / Monitor performance end-to-end	Sourcing managers must adopt a holistic, "big picture" view of their role in the company	Aerospace firms such as *Northrup Grumman* create product development alliances years in advance of government proposals for new aircraft
Logistics management	Treat logistics as a transportation mechanism	Treat logistics as a strategic inventory mechanism	Finding the ideal balance of speed, quality, cost, and flexibility within distribution systems	*Dell Computers* revolutionized the personal computer business through by-passing retailers and distributing directly to customers
Supply chain information systems	Participants have data at the same time or after a product's movement	Participants have data prior to a product's movement	Information systems must be created that allow data sharing across supply chain participants while protecting each firm's proprietary data	*Wal-Mart* uses satellite technology, radio frequency identification (RFID), and Global Positioning Systems to track inventory in real time
Relationship management	Moderate success at matching nature of relationship to the task	Effectively match nature of relationship to the task	Recognizing that most supply chain relationships should be managed through contracts, not rich partnerships	*Wendy's* carefully examined its 225 suppliers to identify less than 40 that were candidates for collaboration

Source: Reprinted from *Business Horizons*, V. 51, David J. Ketchen, Jr., William Rebarick, G. Thomas, M. Hult, and David Meyer, "Best Value Supply Chains: A Key Competitive Weapon for the 2st Century," p. 238, Copyright 2008, with permission from Elsevier.

products to the channel members and final target markets in the right quantities and at the right times and places. In short, channel management and logistics management work together to provide effective and efficient distribution. But such meshing of channel management and logistics management requires good coordination. This especially applies to four major interfaces between channel management and logistics management:

1. Defining the kinds of logistics service standards that channel members want
2. Making sure that the proposed logistics program designed by the manufacturer meets channel member service standards
3. Selling channel members on the logistics program
4. Monitoring the results of the logistics program once it has been instituted

These are portrayed in a sequential format in Figure 13.4. The remainder of this chapter discusses each of these areas of logistics in the channel management interface.

Defining Logistics Service Standards

In general, the higher the service standards offered by the manufacturer, the higher the costs will be. While well-designed logistics systems and modern technology can keep these costs under control, it is usually not possible to completely escape the trade-off of higher costs for higher service standards.

A manufacturer or other channel member must cover the costs either indirectly in the price it charges for products or by passing them along to channel members in the form of service charges. In either case, there is little point in offering logistics services that channel members do not want or higher levels of service than they desire. Types or levels of logistics service that go beyond real channel member demands simply increase costs for channel members without providing any desired benefits. Thus, the key issue facing the channel manager with respect to defining logistics service standards is *to determine precisely the types and levels of logistics service desired by the channel members.* To deal with this issue effectively, the channel manager needs to obtain the channel members' views about what kinds of service standards *they* want *before* the manufacturer develops a logistics program.

FIGURE 13.4 Interfaces between Logistics and Channel Management, Viewed Sequentially

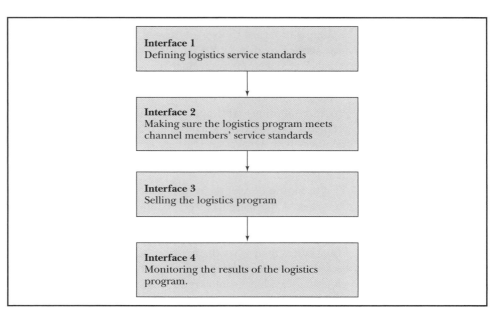

Source: With kind permission from Springer Science+Business Media: *Journal of the Academy of Marketing Science,* "Measuring physical distribution service quality," 25:1, 1997, p. 41, Beinstock et al.

Unfortunately, managers often do not really know in an objective sense what customers want with regard to service standards; but all too often managers *think* they do. As Bowersox points out:

> *All top managers "feel" they know what customers want. But fewer than one out of five companies establish rigid customer service standards, or systematically digest feedback to improve operations.*[36]

Although, as Bowersox's comments suggest, fewer than 20 percent of firms make a "systematic" attempt to find out the service standard needs of their customers. Approaches and methods for doing so have been discussed in the literature for many years.

More than four decades ago, Hutchinson and Stolle suggested the use of survey research to find out what kinds of service standards channel members are seeking[37]— whether, for example, they want shorter order cycle times, EDI systems for computer-to-computer ordering, high degrees of flexibility in ordering procedures or other specific logistics services. Such surveys can help the channel manager to find out whether channel members would be willing to pay (for instance, through larger orders or higher prices) for improved logistics service. Finally, surveys can provide information from the channel members about the service levels of competitors. Such data will be useful for pinpointing areas where logistics can be used to gain a competitive advantage.

More recently, substantial progress has been made in research-based methods for learning about what service standards are important for customers. A notable example of such progress is an approach developed by Bienstock, Mentzer and Bird that provides management with a valid, reliable and practical measurement instrument for assessing perceptions of logistical service quality.[38] The research, based on a broad sample of industrial customers, including manufacturers, government agencies, health care providers, wholesalers, a telecommunications company and several other industries, provided important insights into how industrial customers perceive service quality. Specifically, it was found that three key factors—*timelines* of deliveries, *availability* of products and *condition* of products—significantly influence purchasing managers' perceptions of the quality of logistical service, with timeliness being the most important of the three. Thus, manufacturers now have empirically based findings on what industrial customers are seeking with regard to logistics service, or what the authors refer to as **physical distribution service quality (PDSQ)**. Moreover, the questionnaire used in the study provides valuable guidance for individual firms seeking to develop their own questionnaires for assessing PDSQ. The questionnaire is shown in Figure 13.5.

Finally, instead of (or along with) surveys of channel members or prospective program offerings, the approaches for learning about channel member needs and problems discussed in Chapter 9 may be used. In this case, the desires of channel members with respect to logistics service standards could be included as part of the general effort to find out about channel member needs and problems in areas other than logistics.

In sum, the development of logistics service standards should not be based solely on the views of the manufacturer; channel members' views should also be incorporated. If this is done, the set of logistics service standards developed by the manufacturer is much more likely to reflect the kinds and levels of service that the channel members *actually want*, rather than what the manufacturer may *think* they want. Since the channel members, in one way or another, pay for the logistics services offered by manufacturers, they should at least have some say in what they are getting for their money.

FIGURE 13.5 Questionnaire Used to Measure Logistics Service Quality

---

Logistics Service Questionnaire

This questionnaire asks you some questions about the physical distribution service you receive from your suppliers. For this questionnaire, physical distribution service is defined as all the activities that are involved in the physical delivery of products from a supplier to your company. In answering all the questions in this questionnaire, please think about the product you purchase most often.

Global Quality Items

Q1. The quality of this supplier's physical distribution service is

1	2	3	4	5	6	7
Very poor						Excellent

Q2. Rate the overall quality of the physical distribution service you receive from this supplier by circling one of the numbers below from 1 to 7, with 1 being the lowest rating and 7 being the highest rating.

1	2	3	4	5	6	7
Lowest						Highest

Purchase Intentions Items

B1. The likelihood of my firm purchasing from this supplier again is

1	2	3	4	5	6	7
Very low						Very high

B2. My firm has no plans to purchase from this supplier again in the future.

1	2	3	4	5	6	7
Strongly disagree						Strongly agree

What are the annual sales in dollars for your company?
_____.

What are the total assets in dollars for your company?
_____.

How many employees does your company have?
_____.

Is your company primarily a

____ Manufacturer   ____ Mining company
____ Wholesaler   ____ Financial institution
____ Market research company ____ Publisher
____ Advertising company   ____ Retailer
____ Health care company   ____ Telecommunications
____ Government agency   company
____ Other (please specify) _____

Expectations

Enter a number to the right of each feature of physical distribution service, indicating whether you think suppliers in general should offer the feature; that is, whether you feel it is reasonable to expect a supplier to offer the feature. (Values range from 1, strongly disagree, to 7, strongly agree.)

Timeliness Items

Literature should be available concerning delivery procedures.
Literature should be available concerning delivery options.
Suppliers should comply with the customer's choice of transportation mode or carrier.
Order placement procedures should be flexible.
Order placement procedures should be convenient.
Order communication time should be short.
Response to backorders should be consistent.
Backorder times should be short.
Suppliers should be able to respond to rush orders.
Transportation times should be consistent.
Products ordered should be delivered on time.
All orders should be delivered on time.
The time between placing and receiving an order should be short.
Delivery should be rapid.
The time between placing and receiving an order should be consistent.
The time it takes my supplier to put my order together should be consistent.
The time between my supplier receiving and shipping my order should be short.
The time it takes my supplier to put my order together should be short.

Availability Items

Invoices should be easy to understand.
Suppliers should unpack and stock my order in my warehouse.
Suppliers should demonstrate equipment or products prior to order placement.
Literature concerning product assortment should be available.
Suppliers should not impose maximum-order size constraints.
Minimum-order size constraints should not be imposed.
Suppliers should not impose order assortment constraints.
Order status information should be readily available.
Invoices should match purchase orders.

FIGURE 13.5 *(continued)*

Inventory should be carried at numerous locations.
Return procedures should be convenient.
Billing procedures should be accurate.
Inventory should be consistent.
A wide assortment of products should be available.
Orders should be available in inventory when ordered.
Suppliers should have inventory available near my facility.
If suppliers are notified of possible increases in upcoming orders, they should maintain extra inventory.
Products ordered should be available in inventory.
Products should consistently be available in inventory.

Condition Items
Suppliers should be responsible for disposing of packing or shipping containers.
Competent technical support should be provided.
Orders should be protectively packaged.
All orders should be delivered undamaged.
All orders should be accurate (i.e., items ordered should arrive, not unordered items).
All products should be delivered undamaged.
Orders should be packaged conveniently.

Perceived Performance
This question concerns the physical distribution service performance of a specific supplier. For this question, please think about your primary, secondary, and third most often used supplier for the product you most often purchase and indicate the extent to which you agree or disagree that the performance you receive from this supplier possesses each feature below.

Timeliness Items
Literature concerning delivery procedures is available.
Literature is available concerning delivery options.
This supplier complies with the customer's choice of transportation mode or carrier.
Order placement procedures are flexible.
Order placement procedures are convenient.
Backorder times are short.
Order communication time is short.
Order communication time is consistent.
Response to backorders is consistent.
This supplier is able to respond to rush orders.
Transportation times are consistent.
Products ordered are delivered on time.
All orders are delivered on time.
The time between placing and receiving an order is short.

Delivery is rapid.
The time between placing and receiving an order is consistent.
The time it takes my supplier to put my order together is consistent.
The time between my supplier receiving and shipping my order is short.
The time it takes my supplier to put my order together is short.

Availability Items
Invoices are easy to understand.
This supplier unpacks and stocks my order in my warehouse.
This supplier demonstrates equipment or products prior to order placement.
Literature concerning product assortment is available.
This supplier does not impose maximum-order size constraints.
Minimum-order size constraints are not imposed.
This supplier does not impose order assortment constraints.
Order status information is readily available.
Invoices from this supplier match purchase orders.
Inventory is at numerous locations.
Return procedures are convenient.
Billing procedures are accurate.
Inventory is consistent.
A wide assortment of products is available.
Orders are available in inventory when ordered.
This supplier has inventory available near my facility.
If this supplier is notified of possible increases in upcoming orders, extra inventory is maintained.
Products ordered are available in inventory.
Products are consistently available in inventory.

Condition Items
This supplier disposes of packing or shipping containers.
This supplier provides competent technical support.
Orders are protectively packaged.
All orders are delivered undamaged.
All orders are accurate (i.e., items ordered should arrive, not unordered items).
All products are delivered undamaged.
Orders are packaged conveniently.

What is your job title?_____.

In what state is your office located? _____.

Source: With kind permission from Springer Science+Business Media: *Journal of the Academy of Marketing Science*, adapted from "Measuring physical distribution service quality," 25:1, 1997, p. 41–43, Beinstock et al.

Evaluating the Logistics Program

A logistics program may be offered to channel members as a separate entity or may be included as a major component of the manufacturer's overall approach for supporting channel member needs. If the latter is the case, the logistics program may, for example, be the key feature of a channel "partnership" or strategic alliance,[39] or it may play an important role in a comprehensive distribution programming agreement (see Chapter 9).

In practice, the actual design would be done by experts in the field of logistics: either internal staff on the manufacturer's payroll or outside consultants, such as the Garr Consulting Group. This type of organization has the breadth and depth of expertise required to design complex, modern logistical systems. Nevertheless, the channel manager should still play a role to ensure that the program does indeed meet the channel members' service requirements. Fortunately, this does not require a high level of expertise in the technical aspects of logistics design. It *does*, however, require the channel manager to have a clear understanding of the *objectives* of the logistics program. In short, it is the channel manager's job to make sure that the program the experts prepare is really what the channel members want, for it is all too possible to have a sophisticated logistics program incorporating the latest technical advances and still be far off the mark in terms of meeting channel member needs—a situation that does little to foster channel member support.

Consider what happened to the Gillette Company, maker of the world's largest-selling brand of razor blades and safety razors. Gillette was faced with a staggering assortment of changes in its operations. Among these were diversification into a broad range of toiletry products, a shift of its main distribution channels from drug chains and more intense competition from competitors. Gillette sought to get "one up" on the competition in providing logistics service to its thousands of channel members by emphasizing speedy deliveries of its new blades. The logistics program designed to accomplish this was dependent upon the fastest mode of transport—airfreight. But it turned out that the cost of airfreight-based logistics service was too high. Both Gillette and many of its channel members were unhappy about the high costs and resulting lower profit margins. Gillette quickly dropped this program and developed one based on the use of lower-cost surface transport.

Inadequate evaluation of a logistics system can lead to horrendous problems in business-to-business markets as well. This is especially the case when so-called "killer software apps" (high-tech software for synchronizing the supply chain) do not live up to over-hyped expectations. The experience of Solectron Corp., the world's largest electronics manufacturer, recently acquired by Flextronics International Ltd., provides a case in point.[40] Early in the new millennium, most of Solectron's major customers, including Cisco, Ericsson and Lucent, forecast tremendous growth in demand for wireless phones and networking equipment. Solectron did not really believe these rosy forecasts but nevertheless went ahead and produced at maximum capacity based on assurances from its big customers, whom it viewed as its strategic channel partners, that they would pay for any excess inventory in the supply chain. But it soon became clear that the predicted high sales growth would fall drastically off the mark, so Solectron's customers cut their orders dramatically. But by this point it was too late for Solectron to stop the orders it had placed for materials and components for its 4,000 suppliers. The result? Solectron was stuck with almost $5 billion of excess inventory. The intricate supply chain utilizing the latest software to link Solectron's computers to its suppliers and customers proved to be of little value in the face of bad forecasting. In fact, the closely linked computer-to-computer supply chain actually created something of a domino effect that exacerbated the inventory buildup problem because the original inaccurate forecast permeated the entire supply chain.

So, no matter how high tech and exciting a logistics system may appear, the channel manager still needs to assess what can realistically be expected as well as what might happen if something goes wrong.

Selling the Channel Members on the Logistics Program

Regardless of how good a manufacturer perceives its logistics program to be, it still must convince channel members of its value.[41] Stewart made this point succinctly in the seminal discussion of this topic:

> *A word of caution! Changes in [physical] distribution must be palatable to the company's customers [channel members]. Changes which provide cost benefits only to the manufacturer without corresponding benefits to customers may be more difficult to implement than those that offer incentives to customers to change.[42]*

Stewart went on to suggest several types of appeals that, if emphasized by the manufacturer in attempting to sell the logistics program, may help the manufacturer to be more convincing. They are as relevant today as ever. Manufacturers should emphasize that a new logistics program can foster:[43]

1. Fewer out-of-stock occurrences.
2. Reduced channel member inventories.
3. Increased manufacturer support for channel members.

Minimizing Out-of-Stock Occurrences   By minimizing out-of-stock occurrences through an improved logistics program, sales lost by the channel members will be reduced. Walmart has become legendary for its almost religious zeal in reducing the number of stockouts; in fact, its success in reducing stockouts has played a major role in the company's spectacular success. Manufacturers who seek to sell their products through Walmart know that they must meet Walmart's stringent standards for keeping the giant retailer's shelves consistently stocked. Thus, if a manufacturer can convince channel members that the new logistics system will indeed help them achieve this result, it has a very potent argument for gaining an enthusiastic reception for the program. Indeed, reducing the problem of stockouts is probably the strongest appeal that can be presented to channel members because it is such a bottom-line factor. The out-of-stock issue, for example, is what one leading logistics consulting firm, the Garr Consulting Group mentioned earlier, has used in trade magazine advertisements to attract the attention of clients and promote Garr's value in reengineering their logistics system to reduce stockouts (see Figure 13.6).

Of course, this must actually be the case. The new logistics program must be capable of achieving this result. False, misleading or exaggerated promises made about a new logistics program, if not borne out when the system is put into operation, are likely to create conflict rather than enhance channel member cooperation. No matter how enthusiastic the channel manager may be about the benefits of a reengineered logistical system, overselling it to channel members should be avoided.

Computer-to-computer ordering arrangements and Electronic Data Interchange (EDI) are good examples of systems that *do* appear to be living up to the benefits promised. Now widely used, these systems have revolutionized traditional ordering practices and drastically reduced out-of-stock occurrences. Rather than having to write an order, phone it in and wait for confirmation, a channel member simply inputs the order on a computer terminal and it is electronically transferred to the manufacturer's computer

FIGURE 13.6 Trade Magazine Advertisement by Consulting Firm Stressing the Value of Reducing Stockouts

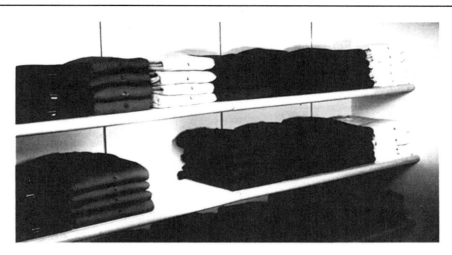

Out-of-Stock is Out of the Question.

An out-of stock position in today's retail market is unacceptable. Likewise, an over-stock position is equally unacceptable. Both problems represent significant challenges in the supply chain. It's how well you get the product to your customer that distinguishes your position in the marketplace today

In the current atmosphere of shrinking margins, retailers must reexamine the way in which they manage their inventory and bring goods from vendors to their stores *just in time*. The Garr Consulting Group's "total system perspective" has helped organizations use innovative logistics management

techniques to rethink how they manage inventory flow: through the integration of merchandising, logistics and store operations. This may involve implementing a new technology or reengineering a current operational system.   But ultimately, the goal is the same: to satisfy the customer's highest demands at the lowest possible cost.

This is why Garr works with you every step of the way . . . to provide comprehensive planning and implementation that will sustain improved performance and hold down operating costs. So that you being less than the best is out of the question.

Garr–using innovative solutions to solve business problems

— THE —
GARR
CONSULTING
GROUP

404-955-6142
1240 Powers Ferry Road, Marietta, GA 30067

Merchandising Planning • Inventory Management • Long-Range Planning • Facility Design
Transportation Modeling • Staff Scheduling • Store Operations • Performance Incentives

Source: Courtesy of the Garr Consulting Group, Marrietta, Georgia.

system almost instantaneously. The order could also pass through a third party (facilitating agency) with time-sharing capabilities. Such an "electronic mailbox system" enables orders to be stored until the manufacturer's computer is ready to accept them. Once the order is received by the manufacturer, products are picked from inventory, delivery documents are prepared, a common carrier is notified to pick up the order and an invoice and bill of lading are issued. Most systems also make adjustments to invoices, confirm orders, provide shipping advice and present information on new products, price changes and promotional programs. In the most advanced computer-to-computer ordering systems, the supplier's computer does not wait for orders to come in from customers but takes the initiative by interrogating the customer's computer to check inventory levels. If the customer is low on any items, the supplier's computer automatically places an order for the customer.

In recent years, the availability of the Internet and networked personal computers has substantially lowered the cost of computer-to-computer ordering systems. Instead of having to invest in large mainframe computers and the specialized programs and training often needed for older EDI systems, small businesses can now use their desktop PCs and the Internet to achieve results that in the past required far more expensive and dedicated EDI infrastructure.

Reducing Channel Member Inventory Requirements   A well-designed and responsive logistics program can mean shortened channel member order cycles, which in turn can mean the channel members can carry lower inventories. To the extent that a manufacturer can develop such a logistics program to a greater degree than its competitors, the possibility exists for channel members to gain an economic advantage by doing more of their business with this particular manufacturer. The **kanban,** or **just-in-time (JIT),** system of inventory management developed by the Japanese automotive industry is perhaps the most talked about example of a logistics innovation that can have spectacular effects in terms of reducing inventory requirements. The principle of JIT is to have only enough inventory on hand to meet immediate production needs with no reserve stock. In this way, manufacturers receive parts and materials "just in time" to meet the day's manufacturing quota with virtually no extra.[44] But the JIT approach depends on excellent cooperation between the manufacturer and its suppliers and also on a superbly designed and executed logistics system.[45] If done well, though, the results can be dramatic because inventory costs can be reduced by tremendous amounts, sometimes well over 50 percent.

While the just-in-time system has been associated mainly with manufacturers, and particularly the automotive industry, it has a much wider potential application. Indeed, knowledgeable observers believe it could apply to virtually any industry and all types and levels of channel relationships.[46] Moreover, the system may well set the pace, or even become the norm, for what is expected from efficient logistics systems—perfection in the flow of any type of goods from vendor to purchaser. Hence firms that are unable to keep up with this pace may well find themselves at a serious competitive disadvantage.

The global fashion apparel retailer Zara, discussed in the "Focus on Channels" vignette at the beginning of this chapter, is an outstanding example of a firm employing JIT to put its competitors at a disadvantage. As we pointed out, the up-to-the-minute fashions appearing in Zara retail stores all over the world would not be possible without the use of a logistics program based on JIT. Furthermore, as an added bonus, inventory levels at Zara stores and the costs associated with carrying inventory are substantially lower than those of competitors that do not have JIT-based logistical systems in place.

Strengthening the Manufacturer-Channel Member Relationship   A carefully designed logistics program aimed at improving service to the channel members can serve as one of the most tangible signs of the manufacturer's concern and commitment to the channel members' success. In presenting a proposed logistics program to the channel members, the channel manager should emphasize that the program was conceived to help them (the channel members) to be more successful. When presented in this light, a newly proposed logistics program can be a potent marketing tool for building channel member support. Indeed, the role of better logistics management in strengthening the overall marketing efforts of channel members is growing in importance. It offers manufacturers who can make use of logistics management for this purpose an increasingly powerful tool for building channel member support and loyalty through partnerships or strategic alliances focused on superior logistical performance. As Bowersox points out:

> *For companies satisfied with logistics partnerships a common factor overrides all others in a recognition that this business activity is an important part of marketing strategy. Product, promotion, and price are the traditional competitive ingredients, while time and place competencies have taken a back seat. That relative neglect is changing. Those companies forming alliances are seeking to exploit their logistical competencies—not weaknesses.[47]*

As these comments suggest, improved logistics management offers great potential as a strategic marketing tool. But it will offer even greater potential to manufacturers who are able to extend their superior logistics capabilities to help channel members improve *their* logistics and marketing capabilities as well.

Monitoring the Logistics System

Over three decades ago, while referring to the need to continually monitor a logistics system, Weeks coined a rule, which he calls the Great Physical Distribution Management Paradox (GPDMP). This rule applies today more than ever:

> *Any given PD strategy, carefully thought out, wholeheartedly accepted, honestly implemented, thoroughly debugged and scrupulously maintained, will be hopelessly inappropriate five years later.[48]*

Weeks's GPDMP rule points out the difficult problem of keeping logistics systems—even well-designed, up-to-date ones—consistent with channel member needs. Logistics systems, once put into place, cannot be simply left alone with the expectation that they will continue to work well and meet channel member needs indefinitely. Rather, logistics systems must be continuously monitored, both in terms of how successfully they are performing for the manufacturer and, just as important, how well they are meeting changing channel member needs.[49] Thus, as part of an overall attempt to learn about the needs and problems of channel members (see Chapter 9), the channel manager should continually monitor the channel members' reactions to logistics programs. The principal objectives of such monitoring are to appraise channel members' responses to the program and to find out whether modifications are needed.

The most effective way of monitoring channel member reactions is to conduct a survey of a sample of channel members. If the number of channel members is small, it may be feasible to include all of them. The survey dealing with the logistics program may be conducted as part of an overall marketing channel audit (see Chapters 9 and 14), or separately. In either case, the key areas of customer service at which the logistics program was aimed should be examined. The manufacturer must be careful, however, to follow through by actually making improvements in those areas of logistics service that channel members feel are deficient. According to a seminal study of channel member responses to such logistics surveys, channel member satisfaction with the manufacturer's logistics program tends to *decrease* when channel members who pointed out deficiencies see no subsequent attempts to remedy the deficiencies.[50]

In a sense, then, logistics surveys may open a Pandora's box by focusing channel members' attention on the manufacturer's logistics program and making them more sensitive to its shortcomings. To close the box successfully, the manufacturer must make it clear to channel members that it intends to take prompt and effective action to overcome any shortcomings in the logistics program. A manufacturer is more likely to take such actions if it views the logistics program as an *integral part* of the overall marketing program.

Summary

Logistics, or the synonymous term *physical distribution*, involves planning, implementing and controlling the physical flows of materials and final goods from points of origin to points of use to meet customers' needs at a profit. In recent years, the term *supply chain management* has been used to describe logistics systems characterized by strong cooperation among channel members in partnerships and strategic alliances to gain efficiencies and thereby lower the total cost of logistics while improving customer service.

The basic role of logistics is to get the right amount of the right products to the right place at the right time. Logistics is also a huge area in terms of its pervasiveness and level of expenditure, which amounts to over $6.4 trillion by all firms and organizations in the world.

Any logistics system consists of six basic components: (1) transportation; (2) materials handling; (3) order processing; (4) inventory control; (5) warehousing and (6) packaging. The modern view of logistics management is based on the systems concept and the total cost approach, which stress the interrelationships of each of the components and the total costs of all of the components taken together. The output of a logistics system should be effective and efficient service that is accurately targeted to customer needs and in some cases an important component for gaining a competitive advantage.

Channel management interfaces with logistics management in at least four areas: (1) defining channel member service standards; (2) making sure a proposed logistics program meets those standards; (3) selling the program to the channel members and (4) monitoring the program once instituted to determine if it continues to meet channel members' service needs.

With regard to the first interface, the key issue facing the channel manager is to determine precisely what types and levels of logistics service are desired by the channel members. Separate surveys of channel members or surveys conducted as part of an overall effort to learn about channel members' needs and problems (see Chapter 9) offer an effective approach for dealing with this issue.

The second interface calls for a careful analysis of the logistics service program from the *channel members'* perspective to see if it actually meets the needs it was designed to serve. Many logistics systems, though modern and sophisticated from the manufacturer's viewpoint, may still be inadequate from the channel members' standpoint.

The main task posed by the third interface is for the manufacturer to convince the channel members of the value of the system and thereby secure their cooperation and support in implementing the program. No matter how good a manufacturer thinks the logistics program is, it should not assume that the program will sell itself. Channel members must be convinced of its value. If the manufacturer can convince channel members that the logistics program will help to (1) minimize out-of-stock occurrences; (2) reduce channel member inventory requirements and (3) strengthen the manufacturer-channel member relationship in a way that benefits the channel members, the manufacturer has a potent set of appeals for selling the logistics program to the channel members. Of course, the logistics system must actually be able to deliver on these promises.

Finally, interface four focuses on the need to monitor a logistics program that has been put in place. No matter how well designed and well implemented the system is, over time channel members' changing needs and problems are sure to create shortcomings in the logistics system. Careful monitoring of the system should help to spot such deficiencies before they become severe enough to significantly endanger the effectiveness and efficiency of the logistics program and, even more important, before they undermine the relationship between the manufacturer and the channel members.

Review Questions

1. Logistics is much more than simply shipping products to customers. Explain.

2. Discuss the key distinctions between the "traditional" approach to logistics and the more recent supply chain management emphasis.

3. What is the essential role of logistics in the channel? Explain.

4. Discuss the systems concept and the total cost approach as they apply to logistics management.

5. Briefly describe the basic components of any logistics system.

6. What is the key issue involved in measuring the output of the logistics system? How does this

relate to logistics service standards and gaining a competitive advantage?

7. Discuss the relationship between channel management and logistics management. Is one of these areas more important than the other? Explain why or why not.

8. Identify and discuss the four major areas of interface between channel management and logistics management.

9. Why is the task of defining logistics service standards for channel members a channel management issue as well as a logistics issue?

10. What role should be played by the channel manager in the design of a logistics program for the channel members?

11. Why might it be necessary to sell the channel members on a proposed logistics program? What kinds of appeals might be used?

12. Computer-to-computer ordering systems and EDI have dramatically improved ordering efficiency. What might be the danger in uncritically accepting this statement? Discuss.

13. Discuss how the just-in-time inventory (JIT) system works. Why has this development had such a profound effect on logistics and channel management?

14. Logistics programs in recent years have incorporated many sophisticated developments closely associated with computer technology. Some of these logistics programs have been described in the literature in very optimistic terms, to say the least. Discuss the implications of this statement in terms of channel member expectations for proposed logistics programs and how these expectations might affect their evaluations of the programs after they have been instituted.

Channel Issues for Discussion

1. Barnes & Noble introduced its electronic book reader, the Nook, in mid-October 2009. Within days it became Barnes & Noble's fastest selling product. In fact, sales were so good that Barnes & Noble announced in mid-November that customers ordering the Nook would not receive it until the first week of January at the earliest. So, a huge number of customers looking forward to receiving or giving the Nook for Christmas would be disappointed. Barnes & Noble's explanation for the shortfall was that it had underestimated demand and could not ramp up production in time to meet holiday demand.

   Is Barnes & Noble's failure to have a sufficient inventory of Nooks to meet demand a supply chain problem? Why or why not? Discuss.

2. Timberland Company is one of the world's best-known manufacturers of casual shoes and sports boots. For many years the company's logistical system was geared to large orders. Hence priority was given to major department stores and retail chains that purchased in large quantities. But market reports were indicating that consumers were shopping in increasing numbers at small independent retailers and boutiques for the kinds of shoes and boots sold by Timberland. So, the problem facing Timberland was how to service the large numbers of small retailers with their

tiny orders while still maintaining high levels of efficiency and low order processing costs. To meet this challenge, Timberland reengineered its logistical system by using modern scanning equipment to control inventory, track merchandise and handle all paperwork automatically.

   Does this situation represent an interface between channel management and logistics management? Explain.

3. U.S. Jaguar dealers used to wait at least one week to receive parts from England. Parts were shipped in bulk by Jaguar to a U.S. warehouse where they were split up, repackaged and then shipped to individual dealers. Working closely with Federal Express, Jaguar initiated a new logistics system that shortened the time by four days. Under the new system, dealers order a part directly from Jaguar in England and the part is then air expressed via Federal Express. The time between order placement and receipt at the dealership is no longer than three days.

   Comment on the change in Jaguar's logistics system in terms of its relevance for providing customer service and the possible trade-offs in higher costs.

4. East Coast Auto Supply, a distributor of auto parts located in the New England area, received much of its inventory of rebuilt auto parts from a

Los Angeles wholesaler that imports the remanufactured parts from several Asian countries where labor costs are low. East Coast Auto Supply received most of its shipments by truck, which generally took a week to ten days to arrive. One day, an airfreight company sales representative called on the firm to attempt to sell it on the use of airfreight. José Menedez, the owner of East Coast, did not wait for the sales pitch. Instead he wanted to get right to the "bottom line" by asking the sales representative for the cost per ton to ship goods by airfreight. After learning the cost, Menedez laughed and told the airfreight representative to "get out of the office." It was more than double what East Coast paid for truck transportation.

Might Menedez have been too hasty in throwing the airfreight sales representative out of the office? Explain.

5. Farouk Systems Inc. is a manufacturer of high quality, hand-held hair care products such as hair dryers, hair irons and professional quality shampoos and hair colorings. The company has annual sales volume in excess of $1 billion and sells its products in over 100 countries. But what is unusual about this company is that in spite of its vast and diversified customer base spanning much of the globe, all of Farouk Systems manufacturing is done in the U.S. at a large factory in Houston, Texas. The company had done some manufacturing in China but decided to discontinue this overseas manufacturing to consolidate all manufacturing in Houston. Farouk Systems believes that not only will product quality be enhanced by not outsourcing production, but inventory costs will be substantially less than if products were produced in multiple overseas locations.

Do you agree with Farouk Systems's strategy? Can you make a case for confining production to just one home plant even though products must be supplied to customers in over one hundred countries around the world?

6. Cross-docking, or *flow-through distribution*, which eliminates storage in the warehouse and the subsequent need to pick stock to fill orders, can dramatically reduce labor and inventory carrying costs. The concept seems simple enough: Instead of unloading merchandise and putting it into the warehouse, just move it across the loading docks to other trucks and send the merchandise on to its intended final destination. Nothing to it.

Is cross-docking really so simple? What are some of the complicating factors that make this seemingly simple concept challenging to implement?

7. Walmart is contacting all of the manufacturers that supply its more than 4,000 U.S. stores with a logistics proposition: The world's largest retailer wants to use its own fleet of trucks to pick up products directly from manufacturers and deliver the merchandise to Walmart's stores. In short, Walmart's truck fleet would replace manufacturers' or common carriers' trucks. By doing so, Walmart believes it will enjoy substantial cost savings while allowing manufacturers to concentrate on what they do best—making products rather than managing logistical systems. Walmart, with about 6,500 trucks and over 50,000 trailers, believes it has the capacity to implement this new logistical program.

Do you think Walmart's logistical initiative is a good idea? Why or why not? Explain.

8. OfficeMax, with about 900 stores and annual sales of just under $10 billion, is the number two player in the office supply superstore channel. Holding first and third place are Staples and Office Depot. Even though OfficeMax has locations that are as good as or superior to those of its rivals, the same or better merchandise and prices and equally friendly and competent staff, it has lagged in logistical efficiency, especially in the area of inventory management. For most of its over two decade history, OfficeMax had vendors ship products directly to individual stores. This resulted in inefficient order size levels, high shipping and order processing costs, and, worst of all, frequent stockouts because orders often came from distant manufacturers. OfficeMax's response was to build three giant distribution centers to which virtually all of OfficeMax's suppliers would ship their products. The three distribution centers would then redistribute the products to all of the company's 900 stores. The result is that 95 percent of all merchandise flows through the three giant distribution centers before going to the stores.

Discuss the logistical rationale for this two-step flow of merchandise: from manufacturer to distribution centers and then to stores. Doesn't it seem counterintuitive that an extra step in the chain of distribution would increase efficiency? Explain.

References

1. Philip Kotler, *Marketing Management Analysis, Planning, Implementation, and Control*, 9th ed. (Upper Saddle River, N.J.: Prentice-Hall, 1997), 591.

2. See, for example: John T. Mentzer, Theodore P. Stark and Terry L. Esper, "Supply Chain Management and Its Relationship to Logistics, Marketing, Production, and Operations Management," *Journal of Business Logistics* 29, no. 1 (2008): 31–46; Rakesh Niraj, Mahendra Gupta and Chakravarthi Narasimhan, "Customer Profitability in a Supply Chain," *Journal of Marketing* (July 2001): 1–16; George Balabanis, "Antecedents of Cooperation, Conflict, and Relationship Longevity in an International Trade Intermediary's Supply Chain," *Journal of Global Marketing* 12, no. 2 (1998): 25–46; Tom Davis, "Effective Supply Chain Management," *Sloan Management Review* (Summer 1993): 35–46; and Joseph R. Carter and Bruce G. Ferrin, "The Impact of Transportation Costs on Supply Chain Management" *Journal of Business Logistics* 16, no. 1 (1995): 189–212.

3. Philip Kotler, *Marketing Management*, 11th ed. (Upper Saddle River, N.J.: Prentice-Hall 2003), 551.

4. The term *supply chain management* is often used to describe the entire distribution process from raw materials to final customer. Here the term is used in the narrower sense of distribution of finished products from manufacturer to final customers, but with an emphasis on interfirm cooperation, efficiency and cost reduction. Jospeh L. Cavinato, "A Total Cost/Value Model for Supply Chain Competitiveness," *Journal of Business Logistics* 13, no. 2 (1992): 285–301.

5. See, for example: Louis E. Boone and David L. Kurtz, *Contemporary Marketing*, 14th ed. Chapter 13. (South-Western, 2010).

6. See, for example: John J. Coyle, C. John Langley, Brian Gibson, Robert A. Novak and Edward J. Bardi, *Supply Chain Management: A Logistics Perspective*, 8th ed. (South-Western, 2009).

7. For a related discussion, see: Martin Hingley, "Relationship Development in the UK Fresh Product Supply Chain," *Journal of Marketing Channels* 12, no. 1 (2004): 27–50.

8. Brian D. Neureuther and George Kenyon, "Mitigating Supply Chain Vulnerability," *Journal of Marketing Channels* (July-September 2009): 245–263; Kathryn E. Stecke and Sanjay Kumar, "Sources of Supply Chain Disruptions, Factors That Breed Vulnerability and Mitigating Strategies," *Journal of Marketing Channels* (July-September 2009): 193–226.

9. "A True Partnership: Working with Your 3PL," *Modern Materials Handling* (August 2002): L3–L12.

10. "*SDI: The Power to Cut Costs Up and Down Your MRO Supply Chain*," http://www.sdi.com/company/company_index.html.

11. Armstrong Associates Inc. Web site, "*Global 3PL Market Size Estimates*," Armstrong Associates Inc.: http://www.3plogistics.com/3PLmarketGlobal.htm.

12. See, for example: Ritu Lohtia, "Frank" Tian Xie and Ramesh Subramaniam, "Efficient Consumer Response in Japan Industry Concerns, Current Status, Benefits, and Barriers to Implementation," *Journal of Business Research* 57 (2004): 306–311.

13. Nikolaos Papavassiliou, Emilios Archontoulis, Dheeraj Sharma and Annie Liu, "Total System Integration and Distribution Channels: An Exploratory Investigation of a Market Setting in Greece," *Journal of Marketing Channels* 13, no. 2 (2005): 29–50.

14. For an excellent example of the implementation of these concepts, see: John J. Burbridge, Jr., "The Implementation of a Distribution Plan: A Case Study," *International Journal of Physical Distribution and Materials Management* 1 (1987): 28–38.

15. Mary Jane Credeur, "Squeezing More Green Out of Brown," *Bloomburg Business Week* (September 20-26, 2010): 43.

16. Chris Burrett, Carol Wolf, and Mathew Boyle, "Why Walmart Wants to Take the Driver's Seat," *Bloomburg Business Week*, May 31-June 6, 2010: 17–18.

17. See, for example: Rick Brooks, "Package Carriers Deliver Bad News to Shippers: Heap of Higher Fees," *Wall Street Journal*, January 3, 2002: B1, B3.

18. See, for example: "Transportation Upgrade Boots Productivity," *Grocery Distribution* (September/October 1997): 28–32.

19. Rand McNally Software, http://trucking.randmcnally.com/rmc/tdm/products/MileMaker/tdmMMIndex.jsp?BV_Ses.

20. Carol Casper, "Flow-Through: Mirage or Reality?" *Food Logistics* (October/November 1997): 44–58.

21. http://pressroom.graomger.com/phoenix.zhtml?c=194987?+p=irol-factsheet (2/28/2011).

22. Rhonda L. Rundle, "Hospital Cost Cutters Push Use of Scanners to Track Inventories," *Wall Street Journal*, June 10, 1997: A1, A8.

23. For a related discussion, see: Yan Dong, Venkatesh Shankar and Martin Dresner, "Efficient Replenishment in the Distribution Channel," *Journal of Retailing* 83, no. 3 (2007): 253–278.

24. Miguel Bustillo, "Walmart's Slump Persists," *Wall Street Journal*, February 23, 2011: B3.

25. Joe Barrett, "Whirlpool Cleans Up Its Delivery Act," *Wall Street Journal*, September 23, 2009: B1, B2.

26. Ilan Brat, "As Costs Rise, Whirlpool Makes a Dent in Dings," *Wall Street Journal*, July 30, 2007: B1, B2.

27. See, for example: Diana Twede and Robb Clark, "Supply Chain Issues in Reusable Packaging," *Journal of Marketing Channels* 12, no. 1 (2004): 7–26.

28. James C. Johnson, Donald F. Wood, Daniel L. Wardlow and Paul R. Murphy, Jr., *Contemporary Logistics*, 7th ed. (Upper Saddle River, N.J.: Prentice-Hall, 1998), 108.

29. See, for example: Arnold Malz and Elliot Malz, "Customer Service in the Distributor Channel—Empirical Findings," *Journal of Business Logistics* 19, no. 2 (1998): 103–129; and Patricia J. Daugherty, Theodore P. Stank and Alexander E. Ellinger, "Leveraging Logistics Service on Market Share," *Journal of Business Logistics* 19, no. 2 (1998): 35–49.

30. James L. Heskett, Nicholas A. Galskowsky and Robert M. Ivie, *Business Logistics*, 2nd ed. (New York: Ronald Press, 1973), 250–251. For a more comprehensive and thorough discussion of logistics service, see Martin Christopher, Philip Schary and Tage Skjott-Larsen, *Customer Service and Distribution Strategy*, (New York: Wiley, 1979).

31. Bernard J. LaLonde, *The Distribution Handbook* (New York: Free Press, 1985), 244.

32. John T. Mentzer, Roger Gomes and Robert E. Krapfel, Jr., "Physical Distribution Service: A Fundamental Marketing Concept?" *Journal of the Academy of Marketing Science* (Winter 1989): 53–62.

33. For a related discussion, see: Carol C. Bienstock, John T. Mentzer and Monroe Murphy Bird, "Measuring Physical Distribution Service Quality," *Journal of the Academy of Marketing Science* (Winter 1997): 31–44.

34. David J. Ketchen, Jr., William Rebarick, G. Thomas Hult and David Meyer, "Best Value Supply Chains: A Key Competitive Weapon for the 21st Century," *Business Horizons* 51 (2008): 235–243.

35. Alexander E. Ellinger, Scott B. Keller and John P. Hensen, "Bridging the Divide between Logistics and Marketing: Facilitating Collaborative Behavior," *Journal of Business Logistics* 27, no. 2 (2006): 1–27.

36. Donald J. Bowersox, "The Strategic Benefit of Logistics Alliances," *Harvard Business Review* (July-August 1990): 40.

37. William M. Hutchinson and John F. Stolle, "How to Manage Customer Service," *Harvard Business Review* (November-December 1968): 85–96.

38. Beinstock, Mentzer, and Bird, "Measuring Physical Distribution Service Quality," 31–44.

39. For an insightful article related to this topic, see Walfried Lassar and Walter Zinn, "Informal Channel Relationships in Logistics," *Journal of Business Logistics* 16, no. 1 (1995): 81–106.

40. Pete Engardio, "Why the Supply Chain Broke Down," *BusinessWeek*, March 19, 2000: 41.

41. For a related discussion, see: Daniel C. Bello, Ritu Lohtia and Vanita Sangtani, "An Institutional Analysis of Supply Chain Innovations in Global Marketing Channels," *Industrial Marketing Management* 33 (2004): 57–64.

42. Wendell M. Stewart, "Physical Distribution: Key to Improved Volume and Profits," *Journal of Marketing* (January 1965): 70.

43. Stewart, "Physical Distribution," 68.

44. Faye W. Gilbert, Joyce A. Young and Charles R. O'Neal, "Buyer-Seller Relationships in Just-in-Time Purchasing Environments," *Journal of Business Research* 29 (1994): 111–120.

45. Steve McDaniel, Joseph G. Ornsby and Alicia B. Gresham, "The Effects of JIT on Distribution," *Industrial Marketing Management* (1992): 145–149.

46. L. Joseph Rosenberg and David P. Campbell, "Just-in-Time Inventory Control: A Subset of Channel Management," *Journal of the Academy of Marketing Science* (Summer 1985): 124–133.

47. Bowersox, "The Strategic Benefits of Logistics Alliances," 40.

48. Jonathan Weeks, "Planning for Physical Distribution," *Long Range Planning* (June 1977): 65.

49. For a related discussion, see Rick Brooks, "Air Shippers Hurt by Penny-Pinchers, Better Ground Service," *Wall Street Journal* (July 15, 2002): B1, B6

50. William D. Perreault, Jr., and Frederick A. Russ, "Physical Distribution Service in Industrial Purchase Decision," *Journal of Marketing* (April 1976): 10.

CHAPTER **14**

Evaluating Channel Member Performance

LEARNING OBJECTIVES

After reading this chapter you should:

1. Recognize the importance of evaluating channel member performance.
2. Be familiar with the factors that limit the scope and frequency of evaluations.
3. Understand the difference between performance evaluation and day-to-day monitoring.
4. Know the basic format for a channel member performance audit.
5. Be aware of the key criteria used in the channel member performance audit.
6. Have knowledge of the three basic approaches for applying performance criteria.
7. Realize that corrective actions are sometimes necessary to improve channel member performance and that they are preferable to the termination of channel members.

© toddmedia/iStockphoto.com

FOCUS ON CHANNELS

If Dealers Don't Measure Up, They Get Dear John Letters Instead of John Deere Tractors

John Deere tractors and other farm equipment are famous the world over. Deere & Co., the manufacturer of the iconic green tractors, dates all the way back to 1837 when John Deere founded the company by inventing a new type of plow that helped to revolutionize American farming. Today, the company is a corporate giant with annual sales of more than $26 billion.

Deere & Co. sells its tractors and farm equipment through almost 3000 independent dealers. These dealers vary widely in size from the large dealer groups with multiple locations generating sales in excess of $100 million to "small," single location dealers with annual sales of about $5 million. Many dealers have been selling Deere products for decades or even generations and take great pride in having helped to make Deere & Co. the powerhouse manufacturer it has become. Indeed, it was not unusual for dealers to refer to their relationship with Deere as being part of the family.

Well, CEO Robert Lane, a former banker, has come to view the marketing channel relationship in a very different light. Says Lane:

For years we talked about Deere as a family. The fact is we are not a family. What we are is a high-performance team ... If someone [a dealer] is not pulling their weight, you're not on the high-performance team anymore.

To stay on the high-performance team, dealers not only need to achieve targeted levels of sales volume in their territories, but must also be capable of providing excellent technical service to their customers to keep customers' Deere equipment running and have the kind of sophisticated logistical programs to assure that parts will be readily available when customers need them.

Unfortunately, not all of the dealers are capable of meeting this standard. So, these dealers will not be receiving any more John Deere tractors to sell in their stores. What they get instead are Dear John letters!

Source: Based on Ilan Brat and Timothy Aeppel, "Why Deere is Weeding Out Dealers Even as Farms Boom," *Wall Street Journal*, August 14, 2007: A1, A10.

No well-managed firm could operate successfully in the long run without periodically evaluating the performance of its employees. The same holds true for the firm's channel members because the success of the firm in meeting its objectives also depends on how well the firm's independent channel members perform.[1] Thus, the evaluation of channel member performance is just as important as the evaluation of employees working within the firm. The only differences are that in evaluating channel members, the channel manager is dealing with independent business firms rather than employees and the setting of the evaluation process is interorganizational rather than intraorganizational.

In this chapter, we will discuss the evaluation of channel member performance in the interorganizational setting of the marketing channel. Our emphasis will be on pointing out appropriate criteria for performance evaluation and on the application of these criteria for measuring channel member performance.

Before proceeding, however, we briefly discuss two important background issues related to channel member performance evaluation. These are: (1) factors affecting the scope and frequency of evaluations and (2) the distinction between monitoring channel member performance and comprehensive performance evaluation.

Factors Affecting Scope and Frequency of Evaluations

Four factors affect the scope and frequency of channel member evaluations: (1) degree of the manufacturer's control over the channel members; (2) relative importance of the channel members; (3) nature of the product and (4) number of channel members.[2]

Degree of Control

The degree of control a producer, manufacturer or franchisor has over its channel members plays a major role in determining the scope and frequency of its evaluations. If control is based on strong contractual agreements with channel members,[3] the channel manager is in a position to demand a great deal of information on channel member performance on virtually every aspect of the channel members' operations (sometimes including data on personal finances). Further, manufacturers enjoying strong acceptance for their products or a dominant market position have a great deal of leverage over the channel members. This makes it much easier for channel managers to request—and get—extensive channel member performance data that enable them to conduct more comprehensive evaluations.

On the other hand, a manufacturer that lacks strong market acceptance for its products and strong channel control based on contractual commitments can exert much less control over channel members. Further, many channel members will not view the manufacturer's particular brand of products as of great importance to them because the products in question may account for only a very small percentage of the channel member's sales. Consequently, they are less likely to be willing to take the time and trouble necessary to provide the manufacturer with comprehensive performance data for a full-scale channel member evaluation.

Importance of Channel Members

For the manufacturer who sells all of its output through intermediaries, the evaluation of channel members is likely to be much more comprehensive than for manufacturers who rely less on intermediaries. This is because the firm's success in the market is so directly dependent on the channel members' performance.[4] A manufacturer of major appliances that markets its entire output through distributors and dealers, for example, is likely to perform a careful and thorough evaluation of these channel members because they provide the only access to the company's final markets. On the other hand, a tire manufacturer that uses its own company-owned retail stores to market the major portion of its products and relies on independent automotive stores for only a small percentage of its sales may very well perform only a cursory evaluation of these dealers.

Nature of the Product

Generally, the more complex the product is, the broader the scope of the evaluation and vice versa. For example, a manufacturer of high-volume products of low unit value requiring little after-sale servicing may settle for routine sales data as the basis for an evaluation of channel members. On the other hand, a channel member handling an expensive and complex machine tool requiring a high degree of after-sale service is likely to be scrutinized by the manufacturer over a much broader range of criteria related to ultimate target market satisfaction. Further, for products of very high unit value, the gain or loss of a single order is important to the manufacturer. In such cases, the channel manager is likely to evaluate the channel member's performance very carefully, particularly if an order has been lost.

Number of Channel Members

For the manufacturer using intensive distribution, channel member evaluation may be little more than a cursory "once over lightly" look at current sales figures.[5] Some manufacturers find it necessary to use an "evaluation by exception" process whereby a more thorough evaluation is reserved only for those channel members who show sales figures that are unusually out of line.

At the other extreme, manufacturers using highly selective distribution find that their close working relationships with their channel members gives them access to a broad range of data enabling them to conduct very comprehensive performance evaluations.[6]

Performance Evaluation versus Day-to-Day Monitoring

In his seminal study of channel member evaluations by manufacturers, Pegram identified two basic types of evaluation approaches:

> *Though not always clearly separated in practice, two different types of distributor evaluations are in evidence in the procedures of participating manufacturers: (a) appraisals designed to assist management in maintaining current operating control of distributors' efforts, insofar as the sale of the company's products is concerned; and (b) overall performance reviews designed to give management a complete and, hopefully, objective analysis of each distributor's operations.[7]*

The first type of evaluation is basically a routine, day-to-day monitoring of performance of the channel members based almost exclusively on sales criteria. Billings of sales to the channel members, reflected in standard sales analysis reports (such as from scanner data), can furnish the basic information needed for this kind of evaluation.

Pegram describes the other type of channel member evaluation as follows:

> *The second type of evaluation is concerned less with short-term guidance of that part of the company's sales program carried out by distributors than with an overall appraisal*

of each distributor's conformance to the manufacturer's ideal or established standard for outlets representing him.[8]

This second approach is a much broader evaluation procedure that usually involves a number of criteria besides sales.[9] As an example of this more comprehensive approach to channel member evaluation, consider the case of well-known paint manufacturer Glidden. Glidden sells a large portion of its paints through giant home improvement retailer Home Depot. But in recent years, sales and market share for the paint company dropped substantially. One Glidden senior marketing executive remarked that Glidden was "really just existing."[10] In a major effort to turn things around, Glidden launched an extensive review of its marketing strategy including an in-depth evaluation of its Home Depot channel. In the evaluation process, Glidden found a subtle but critical flaw in the way its products were being sold by Home Depot. Do-it-yourself consumers strolling down the aisles at Home Depot were intimidated when they were expected to make paint choices for their homes from two-inch square paint chips provided by Home Depot at the point of purchase. Many customers simply walked away. Glidden's solution to the problem? Redesign its Web site to allow customers to electronically paint simulated rooms, so consumers could confidently make paint color decisions before going to the store. So, instead of Home Depot having to try to sell Glidden paints with tiny paint chips at the point of purchase, Glidden took over much of the selling task by using its Web site to pre-sell consumers before they entered Home Depot stores. The results were dramatic. Sales of Glidden paint at Home Depot increased by 50 percent year-over-year![11]

This kind of comprehensive and in-depth evaluation that enabled Glidden to uncover a seemingly minor but critical problem in its home center channel is the type of evaluation process we will be examining in the chapter. To clearly distinguish this approach from the day-to-day monitoring of channel member sales performance, the second and more comprehensive approach will be referred to as a *channel member performance audit*.

Channel Member Performance Audit

The **channel member performance audit** is a periodic and comprehensive review of channel member performance.[12] The audit may be done for one, several or all of the channel members at the wholesale and/or retail levels. The frequency of the audit varies, but seldom is it done more frequently than once per year per channel member.

The channel member performance audit consists of three phases: (1) developing criteria for measuring channel member performance; (2) periodically evaluating the channel members' performance against the criteria and (3) recommending corrective actions to reduce the number of inadequate performances. Figure 14.1 provides a schematic overview of the channel member performance audit; the process is discussed in the remainder of this chapter.

Developing Criteria

Many possible criteria for measuring channel member performance can be used. A study conducted by Spriggs in the heavy truck industry, for example, used 34 criteria for evaluating dealer performance.[13] These are shown in Table 14.1. But most manufacturers use a combination of the following: (1) sales performance of channel members; (2) inventory maintained by channel members; (3) selling capabilities of channel members; (4) customer service and technical support capabilities of channel members; (5) attitudes of channel members; (6) competition faced by channel members and (7) general growth prospects of the channel members.[14]

FIGURE 14.1
Channel Member
Performance Audit

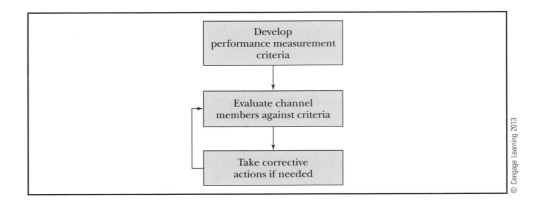

© Cengage Learning 2013

Sales Performance   Sales performance is unquestionably the most important and commonly used criterion for evaluating channel member performance. Indeed, if the channel member's sales performance is not adequate, there may be little else that matters.

In examining the channel member's sales performance, the channel manager should be careful to distinguish between (1) the sales of the manufacturer to the channel member and (2) the channel member's sales of the manufacturer's products to customers. These may be substantially different during a given period. Only when turnover is very rapid, as in the case of perishables, do manufacturer-to-channel member sales offer a reliable measure of the channel member's current sales volume. Whenever possible, the channel manager should attempt to get sales data from the channel members on their

TABLE 14.1 THIRTY-FOUR PERFORMANCE MEASURES USED IN STUDY OF CHANNEL MEMBER PERFORMANCE IN THE HEAVY TRUCK INDUSTRY

OUTCOME-BASED MEASURES	BEHAVIOR-BASED MEASURES
1. Volume ($), total dealership	17. Service department
2. Profit, total dealership	18. Warranty claims processing
3. Sales margins	19. Buildings/facilities
4. Inventory turnover	20. Office systems
5. Market share	21. Employee incentive plans
6. Customer satisfaction	22. Coverage of trade area
7. Sales expenses	23. Product knowledge/salespersons
8. Return on investment	24. Selling skills/salespersons
9. Inventory expense	25. Dealership financial plan
10. Overall customer service level	26. Dealership business plan
11. Volume (units) by product type	27. Advtg./promo. program
12. Volume ($) per salesperson	28. No. of customer complaints
13. Volume ($) to quota	29. Buyer credit management
14. Profit, by supplier	30. Sales forecast—accuracy
15. Volume ($) by product type	31. Sales calls—total no.
16. Profit by product type	32. Calls—current customers
	33. Calls—noncustomers
	34. Number of product demos

Source: Adapted from Mark T. Spriggs, "A Framework for More Valid Measures of Channel Member Performance," *Journal of Retailing* 70, no. 4 (1994): 335.

sales of the manufacturer's products to *their* customers. The manufacturer's ability to get this information, however, is dependent upon the degree of control exerted over channel members. In a contractual channel where the channel members are franchisees, the manufacturer may have a legal right to such information by virtue of the franchise contract. For example, the Southland Corporation, which franchises 7-11 stores, demands and gets detailed sales information from each of its franchised store units whenever it asks for it.[15]

On the other hand, in traditional, loosely aligned channels, the manufacturer's ability to obtain sales data may be quite limited. In this case, the manufacturer must use data on sales to the channel members as the best approximation of current channel member sales.

Regardless of which of these two types of sales data is used, the channel manager should evaluate sales data in terms of the following: (1) comparisons of the channel member's current sales to historical sales; (2) cross comparisons of a member's sales with those of other channel members and (3) comparisons of the channel member's sales with predetermined quotas (if quotas were assigned).

In the case of historical comparisons, the channel manager should look for both total figures and specific figures by product line if such data are available. The more detailed the data are, the better, because the higher level of detail provided in breakdowns by product lines helps the channel manager to spot changing patterns of sales for his or her product line. Figure 14.2, for example, shows a form used by the ARO Corporation, a manufacturer of tool and hoist products, to evaluate the historical sales performance of its distributors. This form provides categories for both total sales and sales by particular product. A graphical format, which gives a pictorial representation of historical sales patterns, is also provided.

Comparisons of sales among the channel members are also a critical measure of channel member performance because it is quite common for a small number of the channel members to account for a major portion of the sales. One frequently cited ratio is that about 20 percent of channel members account for 80 to 85 percent of sales. Figure 14.3 illustrates this pattern. Often, this pattern results in a disproportionately high level of marketing costs relative to the sales generated by the low-performing channel members, with a resultant negative effect on the manufacturer's profit picture. Cross comparisons of channel members' sales performances, made on a regular basis, help to reveal these adverse patterns more readily.[16]

Finally, if the manufacturer has set sales quotas for channel members, it should evaluate the channel member's actual sales performance in comparison with the quota. If the quota has been broken down by product lines, channel member performance for each category should also be examined. Further, when comparing the channel member's sales performance versus the quota, the channel manager should not only look at the ratio itself, but also consider it in light of the performances turned in by other channel members on quota attainments. If the quota attainment ratio is generally low for a majority of the channel members, the problem is more likely to be an unrealistically high quota rather than poor channel member performance.

Inventory Maintenance Maintaining an adequate level of inventory is another major indicator of channel member performance. Essentially, the manufacturer wants the channel member to live up to the inventory stocking requirements specified in the original agreement between the manufacturer and the channel member.[17] Some of these agreements are quite formal and are manifest in a dealer or distributor contract between the manufacturer and channel members. An individualized schedule of inventory requirements is usually worked out between the manufacturer and the channel member based

FIGURE 14.2 Form for Evaluating Channel Member Sales Performance

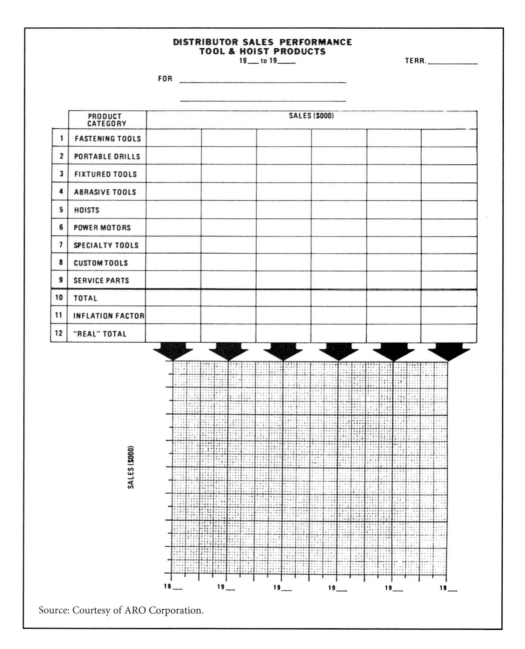

Source: Courtesy of ARO Corporation.

on the sales potential estimated for the territory. The channel member is then expected to abide by this agreement and is evaluated accordingly. Failure by the channel member to live up to the agreement is often viewed as a serious matter by the manufacturer.

Even if agreements on channel member inventories were not originally formalized in a contract, maintenance of inventory is still an important criterion for evaluation. However, in the absence of the formal contract, the manufacturer has less recourse to take action against channel members whose performance is inadequate in this area. Thus, if the manufacturer puts a great deal of weight on inventory maintenance as a criterion of channel member performance, an attempt should be made to include this in a formal agreement with the prospective channel member during the selection phase of channel

FIGURE 14.3 Small
Percentage of Channel
Members Accounting
for Major Portion of
Sales

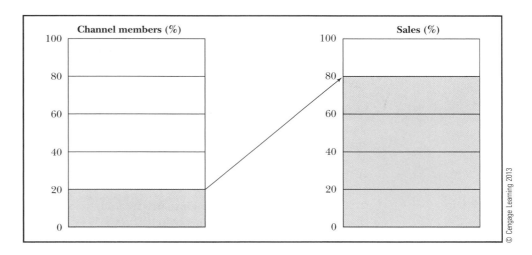

design. Of course, many small and less dominant manufacturers lack the power to get potential channel members to agree to strict inventory stocking requirements.

Actually checking on the level of inventory maintained by the channel member may range from being simple to very difficult. When manufacturers deal with a small number of channel members at the wholesale level, a check of inventory levels can often be done by the field sales force as part of the regular sales calls. For manufacturers selling through a large number of wholesale and/or retail channel members, as in the case of consumer packaged goods, the job can be much more formidable. It may even require the use of outside market research firms that offer a specialized inventory monitoring service, such as the A.C. Nielsen Company. However, regardless of whether manufacturers check the channel members' inventories themselves or have it done by an outside firm, they should, at a minimum, consider such inventory-related questions as those shown in Table 14.2.

Selling Capabilities   While channel members' overall sales performances offer a general idea of their sales capabilities, many manufacturers also believe it is worthwhile to evaluate channel members' sales capabilities more directly by appraising their salespeople. This is particularly the case for channel members at the wholesale level. If individual sales records for channel members' salespeople can be obtained, the manufacturer has an excellent source of information. These individual ratings enable the manufacturer to discern patterns of sales performance and to develop an overall sales capability rating for

TABLE 14.2 KEY QUESTIONS FOR EVALUATING CHANNEL MEMBER INVENTORY PERFORMANCE

1. What is the total level of the channel member's inventory?
2. How much shelf or floor space is being devoted to the inventory?
3. How much shelf or floor space is being provided relative to competitors' inventory?
4. What is the breakdown by particular products in units and dollars?
5. How do these figures compare with the channel member's estimated purchases of related and competitive lines?
6. What is the condition of the inventory and inventory facilities?
7. How much old stock is on hand and what efforts have been made to move it?
8. How adequate is the channel member's inventory control and record-keeping system?

each channel member, which can then be used for cross comparisons among channel members. Obtaining such information, however, is often a problem because many channel members do not want to reveal or go to the trouble of providing this information to the manufacturer.[18]

Assuming the channel members are willing to provide the information, the manufacturer should pay particular attention to such factors as: (1) the number of salespeople the channel member assigns to the manufacturer's product line; (2) the technical knowledge and competence of the channel member's salespeople and (3) salesperson interest in the manufacturer's products.

The number of salespeople that the channel member is willing to assign to the manufacturer's line provides insight into the exposure and market coverage the manufacturer's products are getting.

Technical knowledge and competence are usually appraised on a judgment basis ranging from excellent to poor. Some manufacturers, however, have developed a quantitative rating by using the amount of extra sales time requested by a channel member as a proxy measure of technical knowledge and competence. The relationship is viewed as being an inverse one—the more extra help requested, the lower the level of competence, and vice versa. Whatever the method used, the most useful data result from evaluating the pattern over time. If the channel member's salespeople appear to be growing weaker in technical expertise, this may ultimately be reflected adversely in future sales performance data.

With respect to interest of salespeople, measures that the manufacturer can use include: (1) attendance at manufacturer sponsored schools, seminars and clinics; (2) reports from the channel member's customers and (3) the opinions of the manufacturer's field sales force. A declining level of interest on the part of the channel member's salespeople may well reflect a declining interest on the part of the channel member's top management. If this is the case, the future performance of the channel member is almost sure to be lower.

Customer Service and Technical Support Capabilities   For channel members whose customers require substantial levels of customer service and/or technical support, the capacity of channel members to provide such capabilities can be a very important evaluative criterion. As mentioned in the Focus on Channels vignette at the beginning of this chapter, for example, Deere & Co. made the ability of its dealers to provide high quality service and technical support to its customers a crucial criterion for evaluating its dealers.[19] So much so, in fact, that a dealer's inability to meet Deere's standards was grounds for termination of the dealer. Deere's rationale for putting so much weight on dealer service and technical support capabilities? Deere's final customers, most of whom are in the agricultural sector, count on their tractors and other farm equipment to keep going 24/7 to survive in this intensely competitive business. Only dealers committed to mastering new technologies, as well as maintaining efficient supply chains and having the capabilities to provide rapid response to customers' needs, would be able to meet Deere's high performance expectations.

Attitudes of Channel Members   The importance of favorable channel member attitudes toward the manufacturer and its product line should not be underestimated as criteria that can eventually affect sales performance.[20] Unfortunately, in practice, channel member attitudes are usually not evaluated unless their sales performance is unsatisfactory. As Pegram pointed out in his pioneering study of channel member performance evaluation:

So long as distributor sales are going well, attitudes in themselves may not be closely examined on the assumption that interest and cooperation are probably at acceptable levels. It is when the performance of the distributor account falls short of that expected by the supplier that the latter is apt to start looking into attitudinal factors that may underlie the poor showing.[21]

The problem with this approach to the evaluation of channel member attitudes is, of course, that attitudinal problems are addressed only *after* they have contributed to poor performance as reflected in sales data. In order to spot negative channel member attitudes *before* they affect performance, attitudes should be evaluated independently of sales data. All of the approaches to learning about channel member needs and problems discussed in Chapter 9, such as formal research studies by the manufacturer, channel audits and distributor advisory councils, can be useful for assessing channel member attitudes. Finally, though it is less satisfactory than the more formal approaches, the channel manager can use informal feedback from the sales force and the grapevine to keep track of channel member attitudes.

Competition The channel manager should consider two types of competition when evaluating channel member performance: (1) competition from other intermediaries and (2) competition from other product lines carried by the manufacturer's own channel members.

An evaluation of a channel member's performance relative to competition from other intermediaries in the same territory or trade area serves two purposes. First, it helps to put the channel member's performance in perspective; that is, by seeing how a particular channel member stacks up against the competition, the other performance criteria become more meaningful. For example, a particular channel member may have been evaluated as having done poorly on sales volume. However, if it turns out that the territory is characterized by an extraordinary level of competition, that channel member's performance may be seen in quite a different light. Indeed, it may be viewed as excellent under the circumstances. Some manufacturers, in fact, will go out of their way to provide extra support to those channel members who are faced with extraordinary competition.

Second, comparative information can be very useful in the event that the manufacturer decides to expand coverage by adding new channel members or if it becomes necessary to replace existing ones. While precise and detailed figures on the performance of competitors are difficult to obtain, general information and rank data can often be provided by the manufacturer's salespeople and sales management. Often, this involves simply asking the manufacturer's salespeople, district sales manager or other sales management personnel to list, in order of importance, competitors of the manufacturer's channel members in particular markets.

The second type of competition, that from competitive lines carried by the manufacturer's own channel members, must also be evaluated very carefully. The main question to evaluate here is, of course, the relative support offered by the channel member for the manufacturer's products versus the competition. If the channel member is putting too much support behind the competition and too little on the manufacturer's products, this will usually be reflected in other performance criteria evaluated by the manufacturer—particularly sales criteria. However, there is frequently a lag between the channel member's switch to an emphasis on competitive products and the resulting lowered sales figures. By spotting this change in emphasis early, the channel manager is in a better position to take appropriate measures *before* the channel member's actions are reflected in sales figures.

General Growth Prospects This final criterion focuses on the future prospects for channel member performance. The basic questions that the manufacturer should seek to answer in this type of evaluation are listed in Table 14.3. In periodically evaluating most or all channel members in terms of the growth prospect questions presented in

TABLE 14.3 KEY QUESTIONS FOR EVALUATING CHANNEL MEMBER GROWTH PROSPECTS

1. Does the channel member's past performance indicate that sales of the manufacturer's products are likely to keep pace with those projected for the channel member's region, district, or trade area?
2. Has the channel member's overall performance been in keeping with the general level of business activity in the area?
3. Is the channel member's organization expanding or showing signs of improvement in facilities, capitalization, inventory maintained, and quality of lines represented?
4. Are the channel member's personnel not only growing in number but also becoming more highly qualified?
5. Is the channel member, and with it the manufacturer's representation in the area, likely to some day be in jeopardy because of the channel member's management, age, health, or succession arrangements?
6. Does the channel member have the adaptability and the overall capacity to meet market expansions that may occur in its area?
7. What are the channel member's estimates of its own medium- and long-range outlooks?

Source: Compiled from Roger Pegram, *Selecting and Evaluating Distributors*, Business Policy Study No. 116 (New York: National Industrial Conference Board, 1965), 127–128.

this table, the channel manager will gain a valuable overall view of the total channel system. This will provide useful information for formulating realistic objectives for the coming years and particularly for projecting the role of the channel members in the company's future marketing strategies.

Other Criteria Although the seven criteria just discussed are the most commonly used and provide most of the evaluation information needed by manufacturers, other criteria are also used in some cases (see Table 14.1). The most important of these are: (1) financial status of channel members;[22] (2) their character and reputation; (3) the quality of service offered by channel members to *their* customers; (4) the physical facilities of channel members and, finally, (5) channel member satisfaction.

The financial status of channel members is normally carefully considered in the selection of channel members and, if channel members have been paying their bills promptly, there is usually little need for further evaluation. In the face of changing economic and competitive conditions, however, a channel member's financial status can change significantly. Some manufacturers attempt to make regular reviews of their channel members' financial position to obtain an early warning of any possible financial deterioration that might adversely affect the manufacturer at a later date.

The character and reputation of channel members are also usually considered carefully before channel members are selected.[23] Changes can occur over time, however, especially if there has been a change in ownership or if major changes have occurred in a channel member's operating policies. If such developments have taken place for particular channel members, it may be wise for the manufacturer to investigate whether there has been any substantial change in these channel members' reputations. This can usually be done most effectively by talking with some of the channel members' customers.

The quality of service offered by channel members is ultimately reflected in their sales performance.[24] If their service level is inadequate, their customers will, in the long run, seek out other suppliers. But in the short run, declines in channel members' service levels may not show up in sales performance data because the channel members' customers may not as yet have found alternative sources of supply. Thus, if it is suspected that particular channel members may be slipping in providing service to their customers, the manufacturer should investigate this problem before it shows up in decreased channel member sales performance.

For certain categories of products, particularly luxury goods sold by retail-level channel members, the quality of the physical facilities of the channel member can be a very important evaluative criterion. In general, the manufacturer of the luxury product in question expects its channel members to provide a level of atmospherics and ambiance commensurate with the quality of the product. For example, the Lincoln division of the Ford Motor Company wants its dealers to significantly upgrade their showrooms and service facilities to project an image that will be on par with Lexus, BMW and Mercedes dealerships. Ford believes that having high level dealership facilities is absolutely essential to support the new line of luxury cars Lincoln will be introducing. Those dealers that cannot or will not make the substantial investment required to meet Lincoln's new standard face a high probability of being dropped by Lincoln.[25]

Finally, another, perhaps more subtle, evaluation criterion being considered in recent years, at least in the more academic studies of channel member evaluation, is channel member satisfaction. This criterion has been labeled as belonging in the realm of "social satisfaction" rather than the "economic satisfaction" that channel members desire from the channel relationship. But as Geyskens and Steenkamp point out, economic and social satisfaction of channel members may be related:

> *Understanding this distinction between "economic satisfaction" and "social satisfaction" is important because a channel member's activities may produce economic satisfaction with its counterpart while undermining the counterpart's social satisfaction, or vice versa.*[26]

The contrasts between evaluating channel members' social satisfaction, which deals with personal contacts and interactions among channel members, and the more straightforward "dollars and cents" issues associated with economic satisfaction are illustrated in Table 14.4.

Applying Performance Criteria

Having developed a set of criteria for channel member performance evaluation, the channel manager must evaluate the channel members in terms of these criteria. There are essentially three approaches that may be used: (1) separate performance evaluations on one or more criteria; (2) multiple criteria combined informally to evaluate overall

TABLE 14.4 ISSUES ASSOCIATED WITH ECONOMIC SATISFACTION VS. SOCIAL SATISFACTION OF CHANNEL MEMBERS

ECONOMIC SATISFACTION	SOCIAL SATISFACTION
1. My relationship with this supplier has provided me with a dominant and profitable market position in my sales area.	1. The working relationship of my firm with this supplier is characterized by feelings of hostility.
2. My relationship with this supplier is very attractive with respect to discounts.	2. This supplier expresses criticism tactfully.
3. I am very pleased with my decision to distribute the supplier's products since their high quality increases customer traffic.	3. Interactions between my firm and this supplier are characterized by mutual respect.
4. The marketing policy of this supplier helps me to get my work done effectively.	4. This supplier leaves me in the dark about things I ought to know.
5. This supplier provides me with marketing and selling support of high quality.	5. This supplier refuses to explain the reasons for its policies.

Source: Adapted from Inge Geyskens and Jan-Benedict E. M. Steenkamp, "Economic and Social Satisfaction: Measurement and Relevance to Marketing Channel Relationships," *Journal of Retailing* 76, no. 1 (2000): 21.

performance qualitatively or (3) multiple criteria combined formally to arrive at a quantitative index of overall performance.

Separate Performance Evaluations   Separate performance evaluations measure channel member performance against one or more of the criteria discussed in the previous section. No attempt is made, however, to combine these performance measures either formally or informally to arrive at an overall picture of performance.

This approach is most commonly used when the number of channel members is very large (as is often the case when intensive distribution is used by the manufacturer) and when the criteria employed are limited to no more than sales performance, inventory maintenance and, possibly, selling capabilities. This approach to channel member evaluation is portrayed in Table 14.5.

As shown in Table 14.5, the operational measures used to evaluate performance are applied separately. Consequently, when this approach is used, the evaluation consists of little more than a review of each channel member's performance on the relevant criteria. The main advantage of this approach is that it is simple and fast once the necessary data on channel member performance has been gathered.

A significant disadvantage, however, is that this separate approach offers little insight into overall performance. This is especially true when a channel member's performance is uneven across criteria. For example, it is quite possible for a channel member to show good sales performance but at the same time have a low inventory to sales ratio. This may mean that the channel member has been able to carry a relatively low level of inventory to achieve high sales volume. In effect, the channel member may be using the manufacturer as a "warehouse" by carrying as little inventory as possible and making many small orders. While this situation may be acceptable in the short run, in the long run such channel member behavior is bound to show up in either lower sales as competitive activity increases in the territory or inordinate high costs to the manufacturer for servicing this account.

Multiple Criteria Combined Informally   The multiple criteria approach represents a step forward from separate evaluations of performance criteria in that an attempt is made to combine the various criteria into an overall judgment about channel member performance. However, the various performance measures within and among each of the criteria categories are combined only in an informal and qualitative manner; that is, the relative importance or weights assigned to each of the performance measures are not

TABLE 14.5 CHANNEL MEMBER PERFORMANCE EVALUATION USING CRITERIA SEPARATELY

CRITERION	FREQUENTLY USED OPERATIONAL PERFORMANCE MEASURES	PROCEDURE FOR COMBINING MEASURES
Sales performance	Gross sales Sales growth over time Sales made/sales quota Market share	No attempt made to combine the operational performance measures within or among the criteria categories
Inventory maintenance	Average inventory maintained Inventory/sales Inventory turnover	
Selling capabilities	Total number of salespeople Salespeople assigned to manufacturer's product	

© Cengage Learning 2013

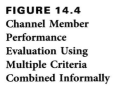

FIGURE 14.4
**Channel Member
Performance
Evaluation Using
Multiple Criteria
Combined Informally**

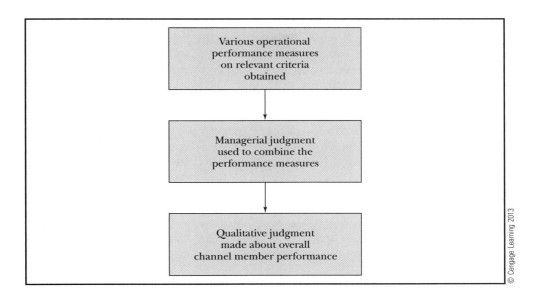

made explicit and no formal quantitative index of overall performance is computed. This approach, which some may refer to as a "black box" type, is portrayed in Figure 14.4.

The major advantages of this approach to evaluating channel member performance are its simplicity and flexibility. It is simple in the sense that no further formal procedures are necessary to combine the particular performance measures on the various criteria once they have been obtained. The channel manager can assign weights and "add" these on the basis of subjective judgment derived from experience. Flexibility exists in this approach because the weights assigned to each criterion can reflect their changing relative importance.

Three major problems are associated with this approach, however. The first involves trade-offs in performance ratings. When a channel member has done well in terms of some criteria but less so on others, the absence of formal weighting procedures for each criterion can lead to highly arbitrary overall performance ratings. A second, closely related problem is that of making performance comparisons among channel members. If the relative weights assigned to each criterion are not the same for each channel member, then comparisons of performance ratings among channel members are not valid. Finally, this approach still does not offer a single quantitative index reflecting overall performance.

Multiple Criteria Combined Formally   A formal rating system using multiple criteria enables the channel manager to arrive at an overall quantitative performance rating for each channel member. The channel members can then be evaluated in terms of this overall performance rating.[27] This approach consists of the following five steps:

1. Criteria and associated operational measures are decided on.
2. Weights are assigned to each of the criteria to reflect their relative importance.
3. Each channel member being evaluated is then rated on each of the criteria on a scale of 0 to 10.
4. The score on each criterion is multiplied by the weight for that criterion. This yields weighted criterion ratings.
5. The weighted criterion ratings are summed to yield the overall performance rating (index) for each channel member.

This method is illustrated in Table 14.6.

If more than one operational measure is used to represent each criterion category, weights may be assigned to each of the measures and the scoring done on each of the measures. Total scores for each criterion are then added together to arrive at the overall performance score. This is shown in Table 14.7 for the sales criterion. Four operational measures used with the sales criterion receiving a weighting of .50.

The major advantages of this approach are that the weights are assigned to the criteria and the associated operational performance measures are made explicit and an overall quantitative index of performance is obtained. Thus, the major disadvantages associated with the informal approach to combining criteria are resolved. On the other hand, if several criteria categories are used along with several operational measures per criterion, the method can become cumbersome. Nevertheless, the overall performance index produced by this method enables the channel manager to analyze overall channel member performance in a number of useful ways. For example, the overall performance scores for each channel member can be ranked as shown in Table 14.8 or perhaps arranged in a frequency distribution as illustrated in Table 14.9.

There are also many other ways of summarizing these overall rating scores, depending upon the information the channel manager needs. For example, the channel manager may be interested in: (1) the mean, median or modal scores; (2) various ranges and/or

TABLE 14.6 WEIGHTED CRITERIA METHOD FOR EVALUATING CHANNEL MEMBER PERFORMANCE

CRITERIA	(A) CRITERIA WEIGHTS	(B) CRITERIA SCORES 0 1 2 3 4 5 6 7 8 9 10	(A × B) WEIGHTED SCORES
1. Sales performance	.50	✓ (7)	3.50
2. Inventory maintenance	.20	✓ (5)	1.00
3. Selling capabilities	.15	✓ (6)	0.90
4. Attitudes	.10	✓ (4)	0.40
5. Growth prospects	.05	✓ (3)	0.15
	1.00	Overall performance rating	5.95

© Cengage Learning 2013

TABLE 14.7 WEIGHTED CRITERIA METHOD FOR EVALUATING CHANNEL MEMBER PERFORMANCE USING SEVERAL MEASURES PER CRITERION

CRITERIA AND ASSOCIATED OPERATIONAL MEASURES	(A) WEIGHTS	(B) SCORES 0 1 2 3 4 5 6 7 8 9 10	(A × B) WEIGHTED SCORES
1. Sales performance			
a. Gross sales	.20	✓ (6)	1.20
b. Sales growth	.15	✓ (7)	1.05
c. Sales made/sales quota	.10	✓ (4)	0.40
d. Market share	.05	✓ (8)	0.40
Total score for sales criterion			3.05
Total scores for each of the other criteria added			XX
Overall performance rating			XX

© Cengage Learning 2013

TABLE 14.8 HYPOTHETICAL RANKING OF TEN CHANNEL MEMBERS USING THE WEIGHTED CRITERIA METHOD

CHANNEL MEMBER	OVERALL PERFORMANCE RATING SCORE	RANK
A	6.72	1
B	6.31	2
C	6.00	3
D	5.95	4
E	5.20	5
F	4.97	6
G	4.25	7
H	3.87	8
I	3.01	9
J	2.56	10

© Cengage Learning 2013

TABLE 14.9 HYPOTHETICAL FREQUENCY DISTRIBUTION OF 500 CHANNEL MEMBERS' OVERALL PERFORMANCE RATINGS

OVERALL PERFORMANCE RATING RANGE CATEGORIES	NUMBER OF CHANNEL MEMBERS
8–10[a]	40
6 but less than 8	63
4 but less than 6	234
2 but less than 4	111
Below 2	52
Total	500

[a]Highest possible overall rating

© Cengage Learning 2013

cross tabulations of the overall scores by the size of channel member; (3) type of outlet (at the wholesale or the retail level) or (4) geographic territories.[28]

Recommending Corrective Actions

In general, manufacturers should try to recommend corrective actions to improve the performance of channel members who are not meeting minimum performance standards. Terminations of these channel members should be used only as a last resort.[29]

If corrective actions aimed at rehabilitation rather than termination are contemplated, the channel manager should attempt to find out why these channel members have performed poorly.[30] In order to do this, however, a special effort must be made to learn about the needs and problems of poorly performing channel members to pinpoint the reasons for failure. These may range from basic management inadequacies on the part of the channel members to insufficient support of the channel members by the manufacturer. Indeed, both kinds of problems may exist.[31] To find out, the channel manager must carefully analyze the channel members' needs and problems. We discussed this in Chapter 9 and need only recap the major points briefly here. First, the channel manager cannot expect to obtain adequate information about channel member needs and problems by passively waiting to receive the information. Rather, the channel manager must develop concrete and practical approaches aimed at actively seeking information on channel member needs and problems.[32] Examples of these approaches include (1) building a formal channel communications network; (2) conducting marketing channel audits; (3) forming distributor advisory councils and (4) utilizing research conducted by outside parties (all of which we discussed in Chapter 9).[33] Second, programs of channel member support must be congruent with channel member needs and problems. For example, the poor performance of a particular channel member may be traced to a poorly trained sales force. If this is the case, the keystone feature of any rehabilitation program developed by the manufacturer should stress training of the channel member's salespeople. Third, the manufacturer must exercise leadership through the skillful use of power (see Chapters 4 and 9). In the context of a corrective program to improve the effectiveness of a poorly performing channel member, the use of coercive power may have to be carefully avoided even though it may appear to offer quick, short-term results. Finally, the constraints imposed by the interorganizational setting of the marketing channel (see Chapter 9) must be understood if the channel manager expects to achieve a positive channel member response to the rehabilitation program. If the foregoing principles are followed, the probability of having a successful corrective program for poorly performing channel members is likely to be higher.

Summary

The success of the firm using independent channel members to serve its target markets is dependent upon effective and efficient performance from its channel members. The evaluation of channel member performance is therefore an important part of channel management.

The scope and frequency of channel member performance evaluations are affected by (1) the degree of the manufacturer's control over the channel members; (2) the relative importance of channel members; (3) the nature of the product and (4) the number of channel members involved.

The evaluation of channel members can be done on a routine, day-to-day basis whereby the evaluation consists essentially of monitoring channel members' sales. But to evaluate channel members thoroughly and effectively, the channel manager must not only monitor day-to-day performance, but also periodically conduct a channel member performance audit. Such an audit consists of three basic phases: (1) developing appropriate criteria for evaluating performance; (2) applying the criteria to measure performance and (3) recommending corrective actions to reduce the number of poorly performing channel members.

While many criteria can be used to evaluate channel member performance, the most basic and important of these are: (1) sales performance of channel members to *their* customers; (2) the level of inventory maintained by channel members; (3) channel members' selling capabilities; (4) customer service and technical support capabilities of channel members; (5) attitudes of

channel members; (6) the way channel members deal with competitive product lines and competitors and (7) the general growth prospects of channel members. Other criteria, including the physical facilities of channel members and the social satisfaction of channel members, may also need to be considered.

The application of these criteria to evaluate channel member performance can be approached in basically three ways: (1) separate performance evaluations on one or more criteria; (2) multiple criteria combined informally and (3) multiple criteria combined formally to arrive at a quantitative index. With separate performance evaluations, channel member performance is measured against one or more of the criteria, but no attempt is made to combine these performance measures either formally or informally to arrive at an overall measure of performance. The multiple criteria approach represents a step forward from separate evaluations in that an attempt is made to combine the various criteria into an overall judgment about channel member performance. Combining the various performance measures is done, however, only in an informal and qualitative manner. Finally, multiple criteria are combined formally through a weighting procedure and an overall quantitative index of channel member performance is derived. This is the most sophisticated approach for measuring channel member performance.

Corrective action should be taken for those channel members who do not meet minimum performance standards. In order to develop the right kinds of corrective actions, the channel manager should attempt to uncover channel member problems that may underlie the performance problems and try to help the channel member to solve these problems.

Review Questions

1. Explain why the evaluation of channel member performance is (or is not) just as important as the evaluation of employees working within the firms.

2. Discuss the major factors affecting the scope and frequency of channel member performance evaluations.

3. Discuss the distinction between channel member performance evaluation and day-to-day monitoring of channel member performance. Is this distinction always clear-cut in practice? Explain why or why not.

4. Are sales *to* the channel member during a given period typically a good measure of the sales made *by* the channel member during the period? Discuss.

5. What kinds of sales data should the channel manager try to obtain to measure sales performance? What kinds of information are provided by these data?

6. Why should the channel manager be concerned about the failure of channel members to live up to inventory stocking agreements?

7. The only real measure of a channel member's selling capabilities is the sales achieved for the manufacturer's product. Do you agree or disagree? Discuss.

8. Discuss the rationale for including customer service and technical support capabilities of channel members as performance criteria.

9. What kinds of questions should the channel manager seek to answer in appraising the general growth prospects of channel members?

10. Discuss the pros and cons of the three major approaches for applying performance evaluation criteria to measure channel member performance.

Channel Issues for Discussion

1. Southland's 7-11 stores consist mostly of independent franchisees. Even though the franchisees are independent businesses, Southland is able to get detailed performance data on all phases of their operations on a daily basis. Franchisees that do not measure up to Southland's performance standards can be terminated on 72 hours' notice.

   Why do you think Southland is able to wield such strong control over information gathering from its 7-11 franchisees?

2. Black & Decker's industrial products division requires its distributors to maintain an adequate inventory by stocking tools and accessories of a variety and quantity commensurate with markets served and the highest standards of customer service. The exact quantity and variety of products carried by each distributor is based on an agreement made between the distributor and the appropriate Black & Decker sales representative.

   Discuss Black & Decker's approach to inventory stocking. What problems do you see in securing compliance from the channel members?

3. Applying performance criteria can be difficult because so many factors may be involved and may change over time. Moreover, some performance criteria may apply differentially to particular channel members in varying circumstances.

   Given these difficulties, is it possible to have truly fair and equitable performance criteria to evaluate channel member performance?

4. Midas Inc., best known for its automobile muffler repair business, provides its products and services through hundreds of franchised dealers throughout the U.S. Although Midas offers other auto services, such as brake replacement and suspension system repair, mufflers still account for the majority of the firm's sales. Perhaps the most important reason for this is Midas's famous lifetime warranty on its mufflers. Consumers who have their muffler replaced at a Midas dealer are entitled to a free replacement if anything goes wrong or even if the muffler wears out for as long as the customer owns the car. Midas has traditionally relied on the honor system where the dealer's word alone was sufficient to get credit

from Midas for muffler replacements under the warranty. But Midas wants to change this system to a more stringent one requiring dealers to return the replaced mufflers to verify that they are indeed defective or worn out. The dealers are up in arms about the new policy because they think it will limit their flexibility in dealing with *their* customers and thereby undermine goodwill.

What do you think might have triggered Midas's new policy? Do you think the new policy will affect dealer behavior? If so, how?

5. Holiday Inn, a division of Inter Continental Hotels Group PLC, recently terminated 700 Holiday Inn franchise channel members. According to Holiday Inn, these channel members failed to meet Holiday Inn's minimum standards. Over the years, the channel members did not make

regular renovations and they were not willing to make the necessary investments in upgrades, such as new bedding, bathroom fixtures and other improvements, that would help to position Holiday Inn as a more upscale chain of hotels. Many of the channel members felt blindsided by what they saw as the franchisor's stringent requirements and rigorous enforcement. Some of the franchisees had been associated with Holiday Inn for decades and felt that they had been loyal and productive channel members. They questioned the fairness of Holiday Inn's negative evaluation of their performance.

Do you think Holiday Inn's termination of so many channel members was "fair"? Discuss from the point of view of the franchisor (Holiday Inn) and the franchisees (channel members).

References

1. Mark T. Spriggs, "A Framework for More Valid Measures of Channel Member Performance," *Journal of Retailing* vol. 70, No. 4 (1994): 327–343; E. Raymond Corey, Frank V. Cespedes and V. Kasturi Rangan, *Going to Market* (Boston: Harvard Business School Press, 1989), pp. 94–96.
2. Roger Pegram, *Selecting and Evaluating Distributors* (New York: Industrial Conference Board, 1965), pp. 103–104.
3. For a related discussion, see: Kersi D. Antia and Gary L. Frazier, "The Severity of Contract Enforcement in Interfirm Channel Relationships," *Journal of Marketing* (October 2001): 67–88.
4. For an excellent study of such dependency in relation to performance in franchised channels, see: M. Christine Lewis and Douglas M. Lambert, "A Model of Channel Member Performance, Dependence, and Satisfaction," *Journal of Retailing* (Summer 1991): 202–225.
5. J. Joseph Cronin, Jr. and Scott Kelley, "An Investigation of the Impact of Marketing Strategies in Determining Retail Profit Performance," in *Marketing: The Next Decade*, eds. D. M. Klein and A. E. Smith, *Proceedings of the Southern Marketing Association* (1985): 251–254.
6. See Manohar U. Kalwani and Narakesari Narayandas, "Long-Term Manufacturer-Supplier Relationships: Do They Pay Off for Supplier Firms?" *Journal of Marketing* (January 1995): 1–16.
7. Pegram, *Selecting and Evaluating Distributors*, 109.
8. Pegram, *Selecting and Evaluating Distributors*.
9. For a related discussion, see: Jacques Bughin, Amy Guggenheim and Marc Singer, "How Poor Metrics Undermine Digital Marketing," *McKinsey Quarterly* vol. 1 (2009): 106–107.
10. Hilary Masell Oswald, "Brand Remodel," *Marketing News*, (March 30, 2011): 8.
11. Oswald, "Brand Remodel," 8.
12. For related discussions, see: Michael C. Mayo, "A Framework for Evaluating Performance in Channels of Distribution," in *Marketing in an Environment of Change*, ed. Robert L. King, *Proceedings of the Southern Marketing Association* (1986): 207–210. See also: William G. Brown and E. D. Reiten, "Auditing Distribution Channels," *Journal of Marketing* (July 1978): 38–41; and Peter R. Dickson, "Distributor Portfolio Analysis and the Channel Dependence Matrix: New Techniques for Understanding and Managing the Channel," *Journal of Marketing* (Summer 1983): 35–44.
13. Spriggs, "A Framework for More Valid Measures of Channel Member Performance," pp. 327–340.
14. Pegram, *Selecting and Evaluating Distributors*, pp. 109–125.
15. Norihike Shirouzu and John Bognell, "7-Eleven Operators Resist Systems to Monitor Managers," *Wall Street Journal*, June 16, 1997: B1, B3.
16. For a related discussion, see: Tim Young, "How to Cook Up a Successful Sales Channel," *X-Sells*, February, 17, 2005, http://www.techmor.com/ManagingthePartner Relationship.htm: 1–3.

17. For a view of the relationship from the channel member's perspective, see: Joel Dreyfuss, "Shaping Up Your Suppliers," *Fortune*, April 10, 1989: 116–122.

18. See, for example: James L. Haverty, "The Information Flow and Its Impact Upon Channel Performance in the Food Industry," in *Developments in Marketing Science*, ed. N. Malholtra (Miami, Fla.: Academy of Marketing Science, 1986), pp. 6–11.

19. Ilan Brat and Timothy Aeppel, "Why Deere is Weeding Out Dealers Even as Farms Boom," *Wall Street Journal*, August 14, 2007: A1, A10.

20. For a related discussion, see: Robert A. Ping, Jr., "Does Satisfaction Moderate the Association between Alternative Attractiveness and Exit Intention in a Marketing Channel?" *Journal of the Academy of Marketing Science* 22, no. 4 (1994): 364–371.

21. Pegram, *Selecting and Evaluating Distributors*, 123.

22. Gwen Moran, "When Money is Due," *Entrepreneur* (March 2011): 68.

23. See, for example: Cyndee Miller, "Nordstrom Is Tops in Survey," *Marketing News*, February 15, 1993: 12.

24. "Empire Builders," *Businessweek.com*, May 14, 2001: EB28.

25. Matthew Dolan and Jeff Bennett, "Lincoln Dealers Will Shrink," *Wall Street Journal*, October 6, 2010: B3.

26. Inge Geyskens and Jan-Benedict E. M. Steenkamp, "Economic and Social Satisfaction: Measurement and Relevance to Marketing Channel Relationships," *Journal of Retailing* 76, no. 1 (2000): 11–12.

27. This approach is adapted from the Weighted Factor Score Method. See Philip Kotler, *Marketing Decision Making: A Model Building Approach* (New York: Hold, Rinehart & Winston, 1968), pp. 293–294.

28. For additional perspective on the weighted factor score approach to channel member evaluation, see: John W. Cebrowski, "Managing Expectations to Enhance Distribution Program Success," *Journal of Business and Industrial Marketing* 9, no. 1 (1994): 17–23.

29. For a somewhat contrary viewpoint to this recommendation, see: Robert A. Ping, Jr., "Unexplored Antecedents of Exiting in a Marketing Channel," *Journal of Retailing* 75, no. 2 (1999): 218–241.

30. See, for example: Robert A. Ping Jr., "Exploring Antecedents of Exiting a Marketing Channel," *Journal of Retailing* (Summer 1999): 218–241; Robert Ping and F. Robert Dwyer, "Relationship Termination in Marketing Channels," eds. Gary Frazier et al. *Proceedings of the Educators' Conference of the American Marketing Association* (Chicago: American Marketing Association, 1988), 245–250.

31. Paul D. Ellis, "Factors Affecting the Termination Propensity of Inter-firm Relationships," *European Journal of Marketing* vol. 40, no. 11/12 (2006): 1169–1177.

32. For an illustrative example, see: "Retailers Rank Supplier Services," *Lawn and Garden Marketing* (January 1987): 8–11.

33. Patricia E. Moody, "Customer Supplier Integration: Why Being an Excellent Customer Counts," *Business Horizons* (July–August 1992): 52–57.

PART 4

Additional Perspectives on Marketing Channels

CHAPTER **15**

Electronic Marketing Channels

LEARNING OBJECTIVES

After reading this chapter you should:

1. Recognize that electronic marketing channels have become an everyday reality.
2. Understand and be able to define what is meant by electronic marketing channels.
3. Appreciate the difference between use of the Internet for information gathering versus true Internet-based interactive shopping.
4. Realize that electronic marketing channels can result in both disintermediation and reintermediation in channel structure.
5. Know the limitations of the Internet in terms of product flow and order fulfillment.
6. Be familiar with developments and trends in electronic marketing channels.
7. Be cognizant of the key implications of electronic marketing channels for the six major decision areas of marketing channel strategy.

© Susan Van Etten

FOCUS ON CHANNELS

Electronic Channels Meet Traditional Channels at L.L. Bean

L.L. Bean is the quintessential example of a retailer steeped in tradition. From its middle-of-the-road products such as chinos and duck shoes to its paper catalogs and focus on personal service, the 98-year-old company stands as a bastion of old-fashioned retailing in a sea of technological change.

Well, things are not always what they seem. In fact, L.L. Bean has become a pretty tech-savvy retailer that has not only embraced e-commerce technology for selling products online but has managed to integrate the new technology with the best features of its traditional retail channels. While L.L. Bean's vice president for customer satisfaction, Terry Sutton, would probably blush if the word "synergy" were used to describe the marriage of high-tech channels with the company's traditional high-touch retailing model, the term is certainly apropos. L.L. Bean's Web site makes placing orders as intuitive as Amazon.com's site, package tracking is state-of-the-art, and the site enables customers to rate and review all products sold by the company. But this sophisticated e-commerce channel is greatly enhanced by L.L. Bean's people-to-people dimension. All online shoppers can chat with a knowledgeable call center agent through instant messaging and e-mail. Or, if they prefer, through a "click and call" feature that prompts a help call from an L.L. Bean employee within two minutes for any online shopper who wants more information.

It's no wonder then, that for the first time, L.L. Bean's online sales topped catalog sales in 2010. By ordering online, customers get the best of both worlds—the speed and efficiency of e-commerce supported by personalized service from knowledgeable and friendly L.L. Bean employees.

So, it looks like L.L. Bean's traditional and electronic channels go together just as well as one of the company's button-down shirts and a pair of its chino pants!

Source: Based on: Michael Arndt, "L.L. Bean Follows Its Shoppers to the Web," *Bloomberg Business Week* (March 1, 2010): 43.

Throughout previous chapters in this text we have touched on technology as it affects marketing channels in numerous instances. Clearly, technology, particularly as it relates to the Internet, personal computers, and smartphones, has had a major impact on the design and management of marketing channels. But as we move into the second decade of the twenty-first century, the role of the Internet-based technologies in marketing channels is likely to grow substantially.[1] Although most of the radical predictions of the late twentieth century that Internet-based e-commerce would "change everything" and that online shopping would replace virtually all "brick and mortar" stores have not come true (and probably never will),[2] online shopping has become an everyday reality for hundreds of millions of customers from all over the world. Shopping via the Internet is now a mainstream marketing channel that, while not replacing store or mail-order channels, exists alongside them as another major channel choice for consumers.[3]

In addition, shopping online while on the move via smartphones and other hand-held devices has become an increasingly common occurrence during the last several years.[4] While such **mobile commerce** or **m-commerce**, as this electronic channel is typically referred to, is still in its infancy, this channel is expected to grow rapidly as consumers become more comfortable with this mode of shopping. Still another form of electronic channel is beginning to emerge on social media sites such as Facebook, Twitter, MySpace, LinkedIn and numerous others. While the use of social media as another form of electronic marketing channel is so far just a small blip on the "radar screen," some products and services have already begun to be bought and sold on social media sites and many more are sure to follow.[5]

In this chapter we examine the still-emerging topic of electronic marketing channels. Specifically, we discuss the meaning of electronic marketing channels, their structure, developments, and trends, as well as advantages and disadvantages of these channels. Finally, we consider the implications of electronic marketing channels for channel strategy and management.

Electronic Marketing Channels Defined

As is common when new technologies arrive on the scene, many new terms also appear, and a whole new set of jargon often develops. Moreover, the various terms used may not have precise meanings and in any case, the meanings are frequently interpreted differently by various constituencies.[6]

Such is the case with the term we have used as the title of this chapter—"electronic marketing channels." Other similar terms appearing in the marketing literature, in the popular business press, and in practice include electronic commerce (E-commerce), doing business on the World Wide Web, Internet commerce or Internet shopping, shopping online, shopping in Cyberspace, Web shopping, virtual shopping, electronic distribution, or just plain online shopping. Moreover, with the recent emergence of mobile electronic channels and the extension of electronic channels into social networking sites, more terms related to electronic marketing channels have appeared such as mobile e-commerce, mobile commerce, (or just m-commerce), social commerce, s-commerce, social referral marketing, and f-commerce (short for Facebook commerce). This list, though long, is by no means comprehensive. Additional terms, variations, or combinations of the above terms could also be added to this list. Needless to say, so many terms and usages lead to confusion. Hence we will try here to define electronic marketing channels as clearly as possible, although we make no claims to a precise or exacting definition. **Electronic marketing channels** as we are using the term here can be defined as

> *the use of the Internet to make products and services available so that the target market with access to computers or other enabling devices can shop and complete the transaction for purchase via interactive electronic means.*

Several points need to be made to clarify this definition. First, the term *available* as used in the definition does not imply physical availability of the product over the Internet. Although it is true that some products and services such as printed matter, music, and movies can be digitized for electronic delivery,[7] physical products and services cannot be transported over the Internet.[8] As we shall see later in this chapter, this obvious but often forgotten fact has very important implications for the role of the Internet as a marketing channel.

Second, the term *other enabling devices* includes all other technologies that provide access to the Internet besides desktop and laptop computers including smartphones, personal digital assistants (PDAs), Web-enabled televisions and e-readers such as Amazon.com's Kindle, Barnes & Noble's Nook, and the Apple iPad.

Finally, the completion of the transaction through *interactive electronic means* is used to convey the idea of "stepping over the line" from merely using the Internet as a kind of electronic mail-order catalog. Thus, if customers who browse a firm's products at its Web site or Facebook page still have to use the telephone or go to a store to buy those products, all that has really changed from conventional channels is that the seller's products appear on a computer or perhaps smartphone screen rather than in print or television screen.

Structure of Electronic Marketing Channels

Electronic marketing channels have been portrayed in numerous articles on the subject as a whole new paradigm for distribution channels, a very different kind of "animal" that will profoundly reshape marketing channel structure.[9] Some have seen electronic marketing channels as ringing the death knell for the "middleman." After all, the argument goes, who needs all these retailers, wholesalers, brokers, and so on, when producers and consumers all over the world can be linked directly to each other via the Internet?[10]

How much of this predicted radical transformation of channel structure is hype and how much is based on reality? To gain some insight into this question, we need to take a more in-depth look at channel structure in terms of three key phenomena:

- *Disintermediation versus reintermediation*
- *The information flow versus the product flow*
- *Virtual channel structure versus physical channel structure*

Disintermediation versus Reintermediation

Recall from Chapter 1 that channel structure was defined as "the group of channel members to which a set of distribution tasks has been allocated." Often such an allocation of the distribution tasks includes retailers and/or wholesalers as well as other middlemen in the marketing channel who help producers and final customers to perform all of the distribution tasks needed to make products and services conveniently available.

As noted earlier, given that the Internet has the capacity to link producers and final customers directly to each other electronically, there has been much discussion about the demise of intermediaries in the channel. In fact, an important sounding piece of jargon has emerged to describe this process—**disintermediation**.[11] According to the concept of disintermediation, intermediaries become superfluous because producers gain exposure to vast numbers of customers in cyberspace. All they need to do so is have a Web site. Then millions of customers with access to the Internet can search for and contact producers directly to buy electronically. In such a scenario, who needs middlemen? So, the inexorable process of disintermediation is bound to occur.

But reality has not conformed to the theory of disintermediation. In fact, some of the most popular and frequently mentioned examples of Internet firms that supposedly show the disintermediation process in action are examples of **reintermediation**—shifting, changing, or adding middlemen to the channel.[12]

Amazon.com, for example, the largest and best-known e-commerce company in the world, is very much a middleman. In fact, it is a retailer that uses the Internet rather than stores or mail-order catalogs to sell to its customers. But Amazon.com still buys most of the products it sells from numerous manufacturers (and sometimes from wholesalers) and then resells this merchandise, which it stocks in its own warehouses, over the Internet to final customers. This channel is depicted in Figure 15.1. As the figure shows, disintermediation—in the sense that the retailer is removed from the channel and manufacturers sell directly to consumers—has not occurred. Rather, what has actually happened is reintermediation in the form of an online retailer (Amazon.com) that augments and in some cases replaces conventional store and/or catalog retailers as another type of intermediary in the marketing channel.

Consider another e-commerce firm, Autobytel, Inc., arguably the best-known firm "selling" cars over the Internet.[13] Do consumers really *buy* cars on the Internet? Actually they still buy the cars from regular auto dealers, with Autobytel and similar firms serving as a broker between auto dealers and consumers. This is illustrated in Figure 15.2. Although the broker does not take title to the car or physically handle it, he is still part of the channel because he facilitates the transfer of title by bringing seller (auto dealer) and buyer (the consumer) together to complete a transaction.

FIGURE 15.1 Amazon.com as a Cyber Middleman in an Electronic Marketing Channel

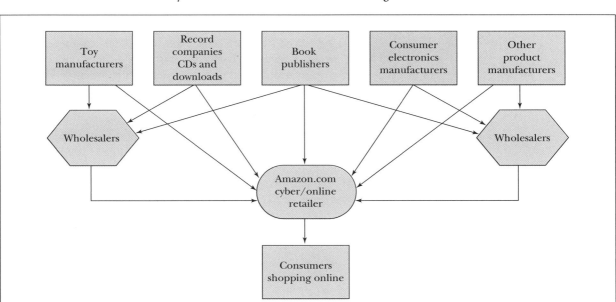

FIGURE 15.2
Conventional and Internet Auto Channel Structure

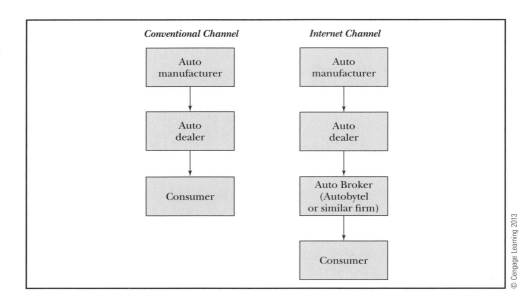

Consumers do not directly pay for the services of Autobytel when they visit its Web site (Autobytel.com) to gather information on cars and dealers. Rather, the dealers pay monthly fees for referrals of consumers who visit the Web site. Dealers then contact consumers either by e-mail, telephone, fax, or conventional mail with their best offers.

Both consumers and auto dealers who have used this channel like the arrangement. The car buyers have access to a vast array of information and choice of dealers via the Internet and the dealers have access to a much wider customer base and lower selling costs because they can reduce advertising costs and sales commissions.

Here again, Autobytel's appearance in the marketing channel is an example of reintermediation rather than disintermediation. In fact, in this case, reintermediation involved the *lengthening* of the channel rather than the shortening of automobile channels because an extra level, Autobytel, was added to the channel structure.

Finally, consider the case of Peapod, Inc., the pioneer in online grocery shopping.[14] Online shoppers visit Peapod's Web site from which they can order from a list of over 8,000 grocery and other products. After receiving the customer's order online, Peapod employees in Peapod's own warehouses, pick, pack, and deliver the orders to customers' homes. Peapod does not obtain the products it sells directly from manufactures. Instead, Peapod buys the products stocked in its warehouses in bulk from supermarket chains, Stop & Shop and Giant with whom it has developed a strategic alliance. So, in effect, these supermarkets serve as "wholesalers" between manufacturers and Peapod. Customers pay delivery charges ranging from $9.95 for orders under $100 to $6.95 for orders of $100 and over. Peapod keeps all of the consumer fees and commissions—the supermarkets benefit from the extra sales volume generated.

Here again, the Internet-based electronic marketing channel structure is an example of reintermediation rather than disintermediation. Figure 15.3 shows this pattern. Peapod, in effect, becomes another level of retailer in the channel between the supermarket and the consumer. Thus Peapod goes well beyond the broker role of Autobytel discussed earlier because it actually physically stocks, handles and transports the products.

So far, shopping for groceries on the Internet has accounted for just a tiny fraction of grocery sales. Peapod, which has been around since the late 1980s, operates in limited, densely populated communities in just twelve states and serves a total of just

FIGURE 15.3
Conventional versus
Internet-Based Channel
for Groceries

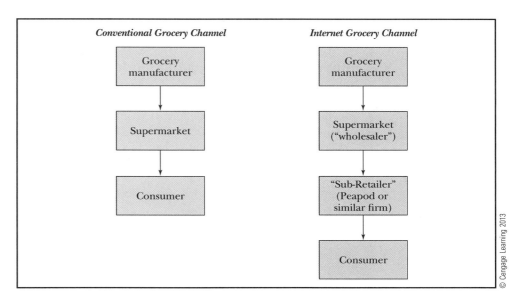

350,000 customers. While still growing, Peapod and other online grocers will probably never overtake in-store grocery channels. The reality of electronic marketing channels for groceries as currently configured creates an additional step in channel structure that undermines the efficiency of the supermarket over the old-fashioned corner grocery store that it replaced. Why? Because in terms of the allocation of distribution tasks, the small grocer has in effect reappeared in the form of Peapod and similar firms that in turn use the supermarket in the same way as the little grocery store used to use the wholesaler. Peapod even provides delivery—just as the corner grocery store used to. This can result in high costs for distribution, especially when customers are dispersed over larger geographical areas typical of many suburban communities in the U.S. The cost of delivering many relatively small orders to widely dispersed customers can be substantial. When this high delivery cost is added to the order processing costs involved in picking and packing each order by paid employees rather than for "free" by customers strolling through supermarkets processing their own orders via self service, such costs can be prohibitive. The thin margins on many grocery products may not be sufficient to offset these costs even when the delivery charge is added on.

Disintermediation versus Reintermediation—The Verdict   Even though all three examples cited illustrate reintermediation rather than disintermediation from the emergence of Internet-based electronic marketing channels, this does *not* mean that reintermediation has definitely prevailed or that electronic marketing channels will predominantly foster reintermediation rather than disintermediation. After all, dramatic examples of disintermediation can also be cited. In the travel industry, for example, huge numbers of conventional travel agents have been disintermediated from travel channels. But even in this case, such disintermediation has been accompanied by reintermediation with the emergence of online travel agents such as Priceline.com, Hotwire, Orbitz, Travelocity, Expedia, and many others.

Whether the Internet fosters more disintermediation than reintermediation or vice versa over the long run remains to be seen.[15] What we can say at this point, however, is that the Internet, no matter how technologically sophisticated it becomes or how much it is hyped, does not repeal the laws of economics as they relate to channel structure: *Efficiency in the performance of distribution tasks is what ultimately determines what form channel structure will take.* The next section addresses this point more fully.

Information Flow versus the Product Flow

In the first chapter of this text, we discussed a series of five flows that occur in the marketing channel: (1) product flow, (2) negotiation flow, (3) ownership flow, (4) information flow, and (5) promotion flow. It is important to keep these flows in mind when examining the effects of the Internet on marketing channel structure. Specifically, the Internet can be superbly efficient at handling the last four flows but is incapable of handling the first one. Why? Because flows 2, 3, 4, and 5 consist of electrons of information that can be digitized rapidly and then moved over the Internet at the speed of light. But the physical product flow (which also includes many services, such as auto repairs) cannot be digitized and hence is processed much more slowly, often by humans, and moves from sellers to buyers even in the best-case scenario at no greater speed than that of a jet plane. This is perhaps one of the most frequently forgotten limitations of the Internet when used as an electronic marketing channel: *The physical product flow cannot be conveyed over the Internet.* Thus, the distribution tasks that require time and place utilities such as transportation, storage, and order processing must be done by other means. Quite often these other means involve people, warehouses, dollies, pallets, trucks, trains, or airplanes.[16] In short, despite the awesome speed and information flow over the Internet, the actual *fulfillment* of transactions between buyers and sellers still mostly takes place the "old-fashioned" way. For example, in the case of Amazon.com cited earlier, the Internet efficiently conveys information and promotion about all products sold by the firm. Negotiation, at least in the simplest sense of consumers agreeing to the price listed, can be conducted on the Internet, and transfer of ownership occurs over the Internet when consumers place their orders because title to merchandise is electronically transferred. But to actually get products into the hands of customers via the product flow requires Amazon to perform the distribution tasks of storage, handling, shipping, and transportation.[17] In fact, Amazon has more than 31,000 employees, most of whom are involved in performing the distribution tasks necessary to fulfill orders for physical products. And, during the Christmas holiday season, Amazon hires more than 15,000 temporary employees, most of whom will be working in the "back office" picking, packing, and shipping products that comprise the physical flow of products to customers all over the world.[18]

What can be concluded from the above discussion is that electronic marketing channels based on the Internet are not "complete" marketing channels because they cannot handle the crucial physical product flow. Yet it is the product flow upon which all of the other flows are based. Clearly, there would be little need for the other flows in the absence of the product flow.

This inherent limitation of the Internet when used as a marketing channel means there are also limits as to how much of a role it will play in the distribution of goods and services.

Virtual Channel Structure versus Conventional Channel Structure

What are the limits of electronic marketing channels in terms of providing the type of channel structure needed to satisfy customer demands? Specifically, can the virtual channel structure created on the Internet provide a substitute for physical structure, such as stores and shopping malls that are so much a part of conventional channel structure?

Perhaps the answer is "yes" for certain segments of customers and "no" for others. Or the answer might be "yes" or "no" within the same segments for different products and services. For example, many auto dealers using Autobytel or similar online brokers believe most customers will still want to visit auto dealerships to test drive the car and "smell the leather" of the upholstery. Many consumers, even some of those who buy books online from Amazon.com, still like to visit retail book superstores such as Barnes & Noble to browse the displays, enjoy the ambience, and have a cappuccino. Even ardent users of Peapod's Internet grocery shopping service may still appreciate the selection and immediacy provided by a visit to the supermarket. Moreover, there are numerous every-day consumer needs that cannot be satisfied by the virtual structure of electronic market-ing channels, such as getting a haircut, filling your car with gasoline, having your clothes cleaned, grabbing a quick hamburger, or actually trying on a suit or dress before deciding to buy it.

So, it is probably safe to say that for the foreseeable future, customer demands for real rather than virtual stores, malls, and service facilities, assure that the major portion of the channel structure will still be made up of bricks and mortar rather than Web sites in cyberspace. But what is also apparent, as we have pointed out on several occasions throughout this book, is that customers want maximum choice in marketing channels. It's not "either/or" but rather "in addition to" that more and more customers are de-manding.[19] So, channel managers will need to provide multiple channel structures con-sisting of a mix of the real and virtual.[20] Further, as we have also pointed out earlier, even within the virtual or online channel, more customers expect additional choice in the form of being able to use their smartphones for mobile or m-commerce,[21] and some customers are demanding an electronic channel option on social networking sites such as Facebook, MySpace, and Twitter.

Developments and Trends in Electronic Marketing Channels

Online shopping via electronic marketing channels has grown dramatically from about $25 billion in annual sales at the beginning of the twenty-first century to over 175 billion by 2010.[22] Moreover, as shown in Table 15.1, online sales are expected to continue to grow substantially over the next several years to $279 billion by 2015. While the pace of growth in online sales during this period is expected to drop from a high of 12.1 percent in 2010 to 7.7 percent annual growth in 2015, this rate of sales growth is still more than three times greater than the 2.5 percent annual sales growth predicted for sales made through conventional retail channels. This much higher rate of growth in retail sales via electronic channels compared with sales through conventional channels will increase the percentage of online sales relative to total retail sales. This pattern is

TABLE 15.1 TOTAL ONLINE RETAIL SALES 2009–2015

YEAR	ONLINE SALES (BILLIONS OF DOLLARS)	PERCENT INCREASE
2009	157	
2010	176	12.1
2011	*197	11.9
2012	*218	10.7
2013	*240	10.1
2014	*259	7.9
2015	*279	7.7

*projection.

Source: Compiled from Forrester Research data.

TABLE 15.2 ONLINE SALES AS A PERCENTAGE OF TOTAL RETAIL SALES 2009–2012

YEAR	ONLINE SALES AS PERCENT OF TOTAL SALES
2009	8.0
2010	8.0
2011	*9.0
2012	*10.0
2013	*10.0
2014	*11.0
2015	*11.0

*projections.

Source: Compiled from Forrester Research data.

depicted in Table 15.2, which shows an increase in online sales as a percentage of total retail sales from 8 percent in 2009 to 11 percent by 2015. This represents a projected increase of 24 percent over the six year time period.

The range of products consumers buy through online channels is fairly diverse. Table 15.3, for example, shows some of the most popular product categories sold through online channels in recent years. As shown, the highest sales were in the apparel, accessories, footwear and jewelry category, followed by computer hardware and software. Sales in the double digit billions of dollars also occurred and are expected to continue for the product categories of books, music and videos; consumer electronics; and grocery and pet food.

Another way of capturing the extent and pervasiveness of online shopping is to look at the number and percentage of households shopping online. This is depicted in Table 15.4. As shown, by 2009 almost 53 million households had engaged in online shopping, which represents over two thirds of all Internet capable households. This

TABLE 15.3 ONLINE RETAIL SALES FOR SELECTED PRODUCT CATEGORIES (2009–2012)

PRODUCT CATEGORY	TOTAL SALES (BILLIONS OF DOLLARS)			
	2009	2010	*2011	*2012
Computer hardware and software	28.9	30.8	32.6	34.1
Consumer electronics	11.5	12.8	14.2	15.5
Books, music and videos	12.3	13.4	14.4	15.3
Tickets	7.2	7.7	8.1	8.6
Consumer health	6.3	7.2	8.2	9.1
Apparel, accessories, footwear and jewelry	31.1	34.4	37.6	40.7
Grocery and pet food	10.9	12.8	14.8	16.8
Toys and video games	6.5	6.8	7.0	7.9
Sporting goods	3.1	3.4	3.7	3.9
Flowers and specialty gifts	5.4	5.9	6.4	6.8
Office products	5.7	6.3	6.6	7.1

*projections.

Source: Compiled from Forrester Research data.

TABLE 15.4 ONLINE SHOPPING USAGE BY HOUSEHOLD 2009-2012

YEARS	INTERNET HOUSEHOLDS (MILLIONS)	NUMBER OF HOUSE-HOLDS SHOPPING ONLINE (MILLIONS)	PERCENT OF INTERNET HOUSEHOLDS SHOPPING ONLINE
2009	78.0	52.7	67.6
2010	79.1	53.6	67.8
*2011	80.5	54.6	67.8
*2012	81.6	55.3	67.8

*projections.

Source: Compiled from *DMA 2010 Statistical Fact Book*. New York: Direct Marketing Association, 2009.

TABLE 15.5 AGE RANGE OF ONLINE SHOPPERS 2009

AGE RANGE	PERCENTAGE
18–32	30
33–44	23
45–54	22
55–63	13
64–72	7
73 and above	5
Total	100

Source: Compiled from Pew Research Center data 2010.

TABLE 15.6 INCOME LEVELS OF ONLINE SHOPPERS 2010

INCOME RANGE	PERCENTAGE
Under $50,000	23
$50,000–$99,999	42
Over $100,000	35
Total	100

Source: Compiled from State of the U.S. Online Retail Economy in Q4 2010, ComScore Inc. (February 2011): 11.

already very high penetration level is expected to grow modestly to 55.3 million households by 2012, representing 67.8 percent of Internet capable households.

Online marketing channels are utilized by consumers of all ages and income levels as shown in Tables 15.5 and 15.6. But there are some significant differences in spending associated with age and income level. As shown in Table 15.5, the largest percentage of online shoppers (30 percent) are between the ages of 18 and 32, while the smallest percentage of online shoppers is in the age 73 and above category. Further, Table 15.5 also suggests an inverse correlation between age and online shopping because as age level increases, the percentage of online shoppers decreases. This pattern appears to lend support to the notion that younger consumers are more tech-savvy and hence more prone to use high-tech electronic marketing channels than their older counterparts.

With regard to income level, Table 15.6 shows that the highest percentage of shoppers using online channels has incomes between $50,000 and $99,999, while the lowest percentage has incomes under $50,000. Unlike the relationship between age and online shopping patterns, there is no obvious correlation here between income and online shopping. Although there appears to be some positive correlation over the income range of under $50,000 through $99,999, when income rises to over $100,000 the percentage of online shoppers *decreases* significantly. So, after what appears to be a threshold level of $100,000, the relationship between income and online shopping becomes an inverse one. No obvious explanation for this pattern can be offered here. It may be that the opportunity cost of time makes high-income consumers less inclined to use their valuable time for online shopping excursions. For the lower income group (under $50,000), the smaller percentage of online shopping could be explained by less personal computer ownership, lower availability of high speed Internet access in their homes, and smaller disposable incomes.

In sum, with sales through online channels in the hundreds of billions of dollars, strong growth in sales expected well into the future, and online channels being used by consumers of all ages and income levels, there is little doubt that online sales via Internet-based electronic channels have become a major, and viable channel option for tens of millions of consumers.[23]

Mobile Electronic Channels

Mobile commerce or m-commerce alluded to previously in this text on several occasions refers to electronic marketing channels that enable consumers to conveniently shop online from virtually any location or while on the move. This capability has existed for almost two decades via the laptop computer, which, at least in theory, provides the portability consumers need to engage in m-commerce. But it was the appearance of smartphones less than a decade ago that really increased interest in m-commerce as a potentially important marketing channel. The extreme portability, convenience, and multi-functionality of smartphones provide an ideal platform for consumers to shop from virtually any location or literally while on the run. At the same time, from the standpoint of sellers seeking to satisfy consumers' desire for choice as to how products and services are made available to them, smartphones offer the technology to provide electronic channels that can effectively target consumers wherever they are and even if they are in motion.[24] Moreover, consumers in increasing numbers are recognizing and using their smartphones not only to purchase products but to do research on products, find coupons, and compare prices. Numerous smartphone applications (apps) have already appeared and continue to emerge which have enhanced the potential of m-commerce to become a major marketing channel (see Figure 15.4 for some examples).

Although m-commerce sales via smartphones had reached approximately $2 billion by 2010, they accounted for only about one percent of total online sales that year. But growth has been very strong. Sales in 2010 were twice the level of 2009 and five times 2008 m-commerce sales. Future growth in m-commerce sales is expected to continue but not at the torrid pace of the 2008 to 2010 period.

As shown in Table 15.7, the types of products purchased via m-commerce channels have been focused on just a few major categories with the largest being digital content for mobile phones. But as consumers become more comfortable with using their smartphones for shopping, the range of products purchased is likely to increase substantially.

According to studies done by A.C. Nielson, only about 7 percent of smartphone owners had used their phones to purchase products in 2009. This low penetration level can be viewed as a positive for the growth of m-commerce because it suggests that there is still plenty of room to grow. On the other hand, the low penetration level could instead be signaling that even at this early stage in the development of m-commerce channels there may be problems or obstacles that need to be addressed before smartphone-based m-commerce can reach its full potential. Table 15.8, which lists reasons consumers give

FIGURE 15.4
Examples of Popular Smartphone Apps for M-Commerce Channels

Name of App	What it does
SHOPSAVVY	Allows consumers to comparison shop by scanning product bar codes with camera phone and then finds lowest price online and at nearby store retailers. Consumers can also complete purchase.
YOWZA	Uses GPS to determine shopper's location then delivers coupons to nearby stores that can be used by shopper.
RETREVOQ	Uses text and tweets to offer information to shoppers about consumer electronics products they are considering. Gives advice on price, whether or not item is a good buy and provides link to online product reviews.
FASTMALL	Provides interactive maps of malls, quickest route to stores, where food vendors are located, where shopper's car is parked, nearest restroom location. Also helps shoppers find coupons.
THEFIND	Shoppers can check which stores carry the products they are seeking, where the stores are located, and can compare prices of nearby retailers and online retailers.
GROCERYIQ	Enables consumers to create grocery lists, organize them, access coupons, and share lists with others. Shoppers can also take photos of bar codes to add items to their lists and create lists of frequently or previously purchased items.

Source: Natalie Zmuda, "An App for That, Too: How Mobile is Changing Shopping," *Advertising Age* (March 1, 2010). Copyright © 2010 by Crain Communications. Reproduced by permission.

TABLE 15.7 TYPES OF PRODUCTS BOUGHT BY CONSUMERS USING SMARTPHONES FOR ONLINE SHOPPING IN 2009

PRODUCT	PERCENT OF SMARTPHONE SHOPPERS BUYING PRODUCTS
Digital content for mobile phones	58
Consumer electronics	51
Computers and related equipment	37
Books	36
Clothing	31
Jewelry and watches	20
Other	6

Source: Compiled from *DMA 2010 Statistical Fact Book*. New York: Dink Marketing Association, 2010, p. 101.

TABLE 15.8 REASONS CONSUMERS GIVE FOR NOT PURCHASING USING SMARTPHONES

REASONS	PERCENT
Purchasing process take too much time	38
Transactions difficult to complete	28
Products are difficult to find	17
Concerns about credit card security	15
Other	24

Source: Compiled from *DMA 2010 Statistical Fact Book*. New York: Direct Marketing Association, 2010, p. 101.

for *not* using smartphones to purchase products, suggests that some hurdles still lay in the path of this channel.

In sum, the m-commerce component of electronic marketing channels based on smartphone technology is already an established marketing channel. While still small in sales volume and so far limited to only a few product categories, the potential of m-commerce is high. As smartphone penetration levels increase and as more smartphone users get over some of the obstacles to using them for shopping, m-commerce could become a major channel of distribution in the not-so-distant future.

Electronic Channels on Social Network Sites

Social networking, a phenomenon discussed earlier in this text (see Chapter 3), has become a major and pervasive force in the U.S. and many countries around the globe.[25] By 2009, almost half of all Americans had a Facebook or MySpace account. And, among younger Americans, age 18 to 33, almost three-fourths were registered with Facebook or MySpace (see Table 15.9).

So far, most consumers have used social networking sites such as Facebook, MySpace, Twitter, and many others as essentially a high-tech communications medium to share their ideas, opinions, and activities with friends and for a wide range of applications such as those shown in Table 15.10. But as can be seen from Table 15.10, 18 percent of 18 to 24 year olds claim to have used social networking sites for shopping. This suggests that businesses that already have a substantial presence on social networks to communicate with consumers will need to seriously consider adding e-commerce capabilities to these social networking sites. Some have already done so. Delta, for example, enables visitors to its Facebook page to buy tickets from a "ticket window" without having to go to Delta's regular Web site. So far, Delta is the only airline to offer an electronic channel on Facebook but others are likely to follow. Indeed, with the majority of businesses both large and small already using social networking to communicate with their customers, the logical next step would be to provide the electronic marketing channels needed to actually *sell* their products and services to customers directly on social

TABLE 15.9 DEMOGRAPHICS OF SOCIAL NETWORK USERS

DEMOGRAPHICS	HAVE A FACEBOOK OR MYSPACE ACCOUNT (PERCENT)
18–33	74
34–44	47
45–54	41
55 and older	24
GENDER	
Male	45
Female	52
EDUCATION	
High school or less	40
Some college	55
College graduate or more	52
ALL AMERICANS	48

Source: Compiled from *DMA 2010 Statistical Fact Book.* New York: Direct Marketing Association, 2010.

TABLE 15.10 APPLICATIONS USED BY 18–24 YEAR OLDS ON SOCIAL NETWORKS	
APPLICATIONS	**PERCENT**
Photos	89
Games	53
Entertainment	51
News	32
Weather	29
Travel	27
Sports	22
Shopping	18
Food	14
Others	53

Source: Natalie Zmuda, "An App for That, Too: How Mobile is Changing Shopping," Advertising Age (March 1, 2010). Copyright © 2010 by Crain Communications. Reproduced by permission.

networking sites.[26] So, the availability of electronic marketing channels on the social networking sites of businesses may well become an integral feature on most of these sites in the near future.

Advantages and Disadvantages of Electronic Marketing Channels

The data presented in the previous section show that electronic marketing channels have become a major channel option for millions of consumers and businesses to buy and sell hundreds of billions of dollars worth of goods and services online. The data also show that the mobile version of electronic channels, typically referred to as m-commerce, has become an established and rapidly growing channel option. Finally, although just beginning to emerge, electronic channels embedded in social networking sites have become a reality that could enjoy spectacular growth in the next few years. In this section we examine several key advantages and disadvantages of electronic marketing channels.

Advantages of Electronic Marketing Channels

Five advantages of electronic marketing channels are frequently mentioned for online shopping via electronic marketing channels.

- *Global scope and reach*
- *Convenience/rapid transaction processing*
- *Information processing efficiency and flexibility*
- *Data-based management and relationship capabilities*
- *Lower sales and distribution costs*

Global Scope and Reach   Internet-based electronic marketing channels enable buyers and sellers with access to the Internet to connect with each other on a global scale. Businesses from the very large to the very small can set up a Web site and/or social networking site with e-commerce capabilities and deal with customers literally half a world away or just across town. Furthermore, even if the seller does not have a Web site or social networking site, she/he can use an online auction such as eBay to sell to customers.

So, from both the demand and supply sides of the global market, electronic marketing channels including those associated with m-commerce and those embedded in social networking sites, provide a platform for global (as well as local) commerce at a level of effectiveness, convenience, and timeliness that is not matched by conventional channels.[27]

Convenience/Rapid Transaction Processing From research conducted about online shopping, convenience is the most important reason offered by consumers for shopping online.[28] When compared to shopping in retail stores, which usually entails driving to a store or mall, parking, walking, finding sales help, and waiting in checkout lines to complete the transaction, shopping via electronic marketing channels offers greater convenience. This is especially the case now that m-commerce and shopping without having to leave a social networking site have been added to the electronic channel mix. Obviously, the capabilities provided by smartphones and other hand-held electronic devices to shop online from almost any location or while traveling from one place to another, add tremendous convenience for consumers. And, the capacity to shop while on social networking sites enhances the already high level of convenience available to consumers.[29] Even venerable old firms such as Brooks Brothers, Avon, and as mentioned earlier, Delta, have recognized the potential of enabling their customers to shop on the popular social networking site Facebook by offering customers the convenience of electronic marketing channels right on Facebook.

Information-Processing Efficiency and Flexibility From both the customers' and sellers' perspectives, electronic marketing channels provide the potential for great efficiency and flexibility. The most obvious information advantage provided by sellers to customers is the vast array of content on the Internet. Consumers can visit hundreds of thousands of Web sites, which often provide substantial amounts of information in an attractive and useful format. Online shoppers can also take advantage of a variety of tools and specialized Web sites to compare prices, gather specialized information, obtain coupons, and search for special deals (See Table 15.11).

TABLE 15.11 ONLINE TOOLS AND WEB SITES CONSUMERS USE TO FIND DEALS (2009)

ONLINE TOOLS AND WEB SITES	PERCENT USING
Search engines	59
Coupon Web sites	29
Price comparison Web sites	27
E-mail newsletters	25
Advertisements	24
Bargain-tracking Web sites	14
Shopping-themed social networks	5
Blogs	5
Price protection Web sites	4
Widgets or toolbar price drop alerts	2
Others	11
Any of the above	86

Source: Compiled from *DMA 2010 Statistical Fact Book*: New York: Direct Marketing Association 2010.

The potential of sellers to create, and customers to use, sophisticated screening and sorting capabilities provides great flexibility in the use of product information.[30] Customers interested in buying, say, low-salt soups, or tires with certain performance characteristics and tread wear, or airline tickets to Paris for less than $500, can get such information immediately, provided online sellers or service providers have prepared such information.

At the most advanced level, a high degree of customization along with a high level of interactivity is possible via electronic marketing channels.[31] For example, Land's End offers a program on its Web site called My Virtual Model™. With this technology, a consumer can create a customized 3-D model by providing critical measurements that are then applied to the individual's personal Virtual Model. The result, according to Land's End, is practically a "mirror image" of the customer. Once the Virtual Model is created, the customer can use it to "try on" items and outfits and see how they will look. These images can be stored and recalled for later reference. Once created, the consumer's Virtual Model can also be used at other apparel Web sites in the My Virtual Model network and can be e-mailed to friends and family.[32]

Data-Based Management and Relationship Enhancement   The technology underlying electronic marketing channels enables firms to target customers efficiently on both a large and small scale, including niches or microsegments of a very small group of customers with similar demands.[33] Even **one-to-one marketing**, where the seller adapts its offerings to meet the unique needs of a single consumer, is feasible via Internet-based online shopping.[34] Still a further potential advantage of the Internet is the ability to track customer visits to the firm's Web site or social networking site and develop a continuing dialogue and relationship over time. Such electronic tagging of customer visits, known as *cookies*, can be a powerful marketing tool if linked to demographic and psychographic data that customers have provided through prior purchases, registration, or online surveys.[35] By using e-mail addresses to reach carefully targeted customers who have expressed interest in a firm's products or services, a continuing electronic dialogue or relationship can be built. Of course, such customer targeting and relationship building needs to be done on a very selective basis to avoid the Internet equivalent of junk mail by bombarding consumers with unsolicited e-mails, or **spam** in Internet jargon.[36]

Lower Sales and Distribution Costs   In theory, the use of electronic marketing channels can reduce sales and distribution costs by making it possible to perform distribution tasks more efficiently than through conventional channels. For example, if the Internet can provide information customers need more cost effectively than television or magazine advertising or face-to-face communication from salespeople, sales costs can be reduced. If the use of the Internet as a marketing channel enables a firm to centralize its inventory in a single location from which it can process and ship orders at lower cost than by spreading its inventory out in numerous retail store locations, then indeed electronic marketing channels may reduce the cost of distribution.

We should reemphasize that such potential cost savings from the use of electronic marketing channels would not *necessarily* be from "eliminating middlemen" in the channel through disintermediation. As we discussed earlier in this chapter, electronic marketing channels in some cases may contain *more* rather than fewer middlemen in the channel structure. The real question is: *Which combination of organizations comprising the channel structure, whether conventional or electronic, can perform the distribution tasks demanded by customers at the lowest cost?*

Although the superiority of electronic marketing channels over conventional channels as a means of reducing sales and distribution costs has not yet been proven, the *potential* of electronic marketing channels for reducing these costs can be glimpsed in the anecdotal evidence from particular firms that have realized substantial cost savings. For example, auto dealers who have used the Internet to "sell" cars have saved on advertising and sales commissions.[37] Online retailers such as Wine.com, which sells wines over the Internet (See Figure 15.5), have helped small vineyards reduce the costs of sales and distribution by completely taking over these functions and using the Internet exclusively to market the wines all over the world. Perhaps the biggest Internet success story to date for sales and distribution costs savings is Dell Computer Corporation, which sells over

FIGURE 15.5 Home Page from Web Site of Wine.com

$50 million per day online and has managed to do so at lower cost than its rivals using conventional channels.

Disadvantages of Electronic Marketing Channels

We now turn our attention to four disadvantages of electronic marketing channels:

- *Lack of contact with actual products and delayed possession*
- *Fulfillment logistics not at Internet speed or efficiency*
- *Clutter for both buyers and sellers*
- *Nonpurchase motives for shopping not addressed*

No Contact with Product and Delayed Possession   In theory, almost any product and many services can be sold online. But in reality that is open to question. Despite the high-tech nature of electronic marketing channels, the same limitations experienced by low-tech mail-order channels apply. Namely, consumers have no direct contact with products—they cannot see, touch, feel, smell, or try on the actual products sold on the Internet.[38] Moreover, products cannot be demonstrated or tried out, which is very important in the case of automobiles, audio equipment, sporting goods, and many other product categories requiring a relatively high level of consumer contact. Further, the ambience of shopping in stores that many consumers consider an integral part of the shopping experience is missing in cyberspace. Finally, the instant gratification of buying the product and then possessing it immediately is not available through electronic marketing channels.

These same disadvantages have plagued mail-order channels for over a century and have been largely responsible for limiting mail-order sales to less than 5 percent of total retail sales in the United States. Although electronic marketing channels offer a new technology for shopping, this technology does not overcome the inherent problems of no product contact and no immediacy of possession.

Fulfillment and Logistics Lag   We discussed the fulfillment and logistics problem previously in this chapter so we need not go into great detail here. Essentially, what needs to be remembered is that the Internet *processes and transports electrons, not physical products.* Hence order fulfillment and logistics must still be performed. Warehouses, inventory, stock picking, order processing, packing, and shipping do not disappear simply because consumers use the Internet to buy a product. Moreover, the processing and shipping of many small orders, often one unit at a time, is expensive from both an order-processing and a transportation standpoint. In the case of products of low unit value, such costs may account for a high proportion of the retail price of the product.

So, with the exception of products that can be "delivered" electronically—mainly music, written materials, tickets, reservations, and financial investments—the majority of products and many services require logistical fulfillment capabilities that the Internet cannot provide. Tedlow captures this point succinctly in referring to the short shrift so often given to the logistical dimension of electronic marketing channels:

> *The problems of logistics are often finessed by interactive-home-shopping enthusiasts. Shoppers have to come into actual possession of the items they purchase. How is that to be accomplished?*[39]

How indeed? If electronic marketing channels are to reach their full potential, whatever that may be, more attention will need to be focused on the "old-fashioned" nuts-and-bolts logistics challenges.

Web Clutter   Literally millions of sellers at all levels of the channel from manufacturers to retailers have established Web sites and/or social networking sites making clutter a real problem in cyberspace.

From the demand (consumer) side, even with the help of powerful general search engines such as Google, Yahoo, Bing, and Ask as well as specialized shopping engines such as Shopping.com, TheFind, PriceGrabber, Shopzilla, bizrate and others, online shoppers still face a bewildering array of possible online choices. Navigating this "sea" of options popping up on the computer or smartphone screen can be challenging for all but the most experienced and tech-savvy online shoppers.

On the supply (sellers) side, standing out from the vast crowd of other sellers' Web or social networking sites is a major problem for all but the very largest and most powerful online sellers who have strong name recognition and the money to pay for heavy online and offline advertising to avoid getting lost in the shuffle.[40] Furthermore, large sellers are more likely to have the capacity to pay for **search engine optimization** that results in prominent placement on top search engines. So, even though small sellers can set up Web sites or social networking sites with electronic channels capable of reaching customers all over the globe with relative ease and at a modest cost, getting *noticed* by potential customers on the Web is still more a matter of powerful promotion than powerful technology.

Ignores Personal and Social Shopping Motives   In a classic article titled "Why Do People Shop?" Tauber provided some very insightful observations.[41] He found that people do not shop simply to make purchases. Rather the desire to make a purchase is just one part of a complex set of personal and social motives for shopping. Personal motives for shopping include the need to play the role of shopper, diversion from the routine of daily life, self-gratification, learning about new trends, physical activity, and sensory stimulation. Social motives for shopping include gaining social experience outside the home, communication with others having similar interests, peer group attraction, status and authority, and for some shoppers, the pleasure of bargaining.

Evidence from later studies as well as a vast amount of accumulated experience over the decades has validated Tauber's findings. The impact of these findings on new methods and technologies that claim to offer consumers greater convenience at the cost of not satisfying these other personal and social motives is important. Indeed, Tauber's words from almost four decades ago may be prophetic in defining the limits of online shopping.

> If the shopping process offers benefits other than exposure to products, then retail innovations that attempt to reduce "shopping effort" (vending machines, mail order or home delivery) may have a dire future for some product categories.[42]

Tauber, of course, did not mention the Internet as a "retail innovation" because it did not yet exist. But had it existed, he surely would have mentioned it because the same analysis he applied to other convenience-based approaches to shopping would also apply to online shopping: It fails to satisfy most of the consumer's motives for shopping.

Implications for Marketing Channel Strategy and Management

In Chapter 5 of this text, we discussed six strategic distribution decisions that many firms and virtually all manufacturers must address in order to meet their distribution objectives. Electronic marketing channels, though they bring an exciting technological dimension to marketing channel systems, do not fundamentally alter these six decision areas. The channel manager still needs to consider each one as he/she did before the advent of Internet-based marketing channels. But now there is more to think about because the channel manager needs to include electronic marketing channels among the myriad other issues already under consideration.

In the following sections, we take a brief look at some of the implications that electronic marketing channels raise for each of the six decision areas. Our purpose in doing so is not to provide an inventory of relevant considerations because, given the relative newness of electronic marketing channels, many of these have not as yet been identified. So, our discussion will be limited to pointing out just a few factors that seem to be relevant in each of the six marketing channel decision areas.

Objectives and Strategies of the Firm and Electronic Marketing Channels

In deciding what role distribution will play in the firm's overall objectives and strategies, companies undoubtedly have a broader range of options with electronic marketing channels added to the mix. But this new channel option has also made the planning and decision-making process more complex because a whole new "bag of tricks" has become available.

Probably the most basic issue the channel manager will need to consider is whether Internet-based channels fundamentally affect the firm's decision about the priority it will give to distribution strategy. If, for example, a firm believes it can be successful by becoming a pure-play online seller by using the Internet as its only channel for reaching customers, it will obviously need to give an extremely high priority to distribution strategy. Amazon.com, mentioned several times earlier in this chapter, is a clear example of this because the primary basis of its quest to gain a sustainable competitive advantage is through exclusive use of the Internet as its channel for reaching customers.

Whether distribution strategy in general and electronic marketing channels in particular should play a key role in a firm's overall objectives and strategy is, of course, an issue that can only be addressed by a firm's management. For some firms, distribution strategy and electronic marketing channels may not be seen as playing a key role. But what is virtually certain is that few firms will be able to ignore this issue going forward.

Role of Electronic Marketing Channels in the Marketing Mix

The need to blend the four Ps of the marketing mix—product, price, promotion, and place—to satisfy the demands of the target market is still the fundamental paradigm of modern marketing management, with or without electronic marketing channels including the mobile and social networking versions of these channels. Electronic marketing channels made possible by the Internet, however, may change the blend of the marketing mix. Specifically, the fourth P, place (distribution), may assume a larger role relative to the other three variables for more and more firms. Why? Because the Internet, with its vast capacity to convey information, may reduce the potency of the first three Ps as a basis for gaining a sustainable competitive advantage. If increasingly powerful Internet search engines and intensive communications among consumers via social networks can provide a level of information flow that approaches the theoretical ideal that economists refer to as "perfect information," it will be more difficult for firms to differentiate products based on consumer ignorance of product attributes. If pricing information is widely available on the Internet from price comparison sites and consumers regularly sharing price information with their friends and followers on Facebook and Twitter, then no firm will have a pricing advantage because customers will know about all prevailing prices.[43] Furthermore, with regard to the promotion variable in the marketing mix, the widespread sharing of information among consumers on social networks can dilute the power of the promotional messages presented by firms. Why? Because information shared consumer-to-consumer, (sometimes referred to as peer-to-peer), has a higher credibility factor than company-sponsored promotional messages. In short, consumer-to-consumer information sharing about products and services is more believable than firm-to-consumer promotional messages.

Channel Design and Electronic Marketing Channels

The seven-phase channel design paradigm presented in Chapter 6 as a framework for setting up new channels or modifying existing channels does not change in any fundamental sense with the emergence of electronic marketing channels. This relatively new technology should, however, alert the channel manager to the additional channel structure options available based on the Internet.[44] This is especially relevant in Phase 1, recognizing the need to make channel design decisions; Phase 4, developing possible channel alternatives; and Phase 6, choosing the best channel structure. For example, the channel manager might find that large segments of the customers that buy her/his company's products are active on leading social networks such as Facebook, MySpace, Twitter, and Linkedin. Given that information, the channel manager probably should give serious consideration as to whether electronic channels should be developed to make the company's products available to customers through those social networking sites. Whether the firm is a corporate giant such as IBM, which decided to emulate Dell Computer's successful use of the Internet to sell computer equipment, or a small start-up company, channel design decisions *must* now consider electronic marketing channels in the channel mix. Indeed as we have pointed out on numerous occasions throughout this text, customers are *demanding* more channel choices because today's consumers are not one-dimensional in their shopping behavior. They want options that fit their particular needs, circumstances, and situations.[45] A consumer who usually loves to shop in stores in order to see, touch, and try out merchandise may nevertheless purchase online if pressed for time. On the other hand, a consumer who delights in online shopping may, around the Christmas season, temporarily abandon her computer to get into the spirit and excitement of the holiday shopping in stores and malls,[46] and then use her smartphone while in the stores and malls to find the best deals. Another consumer, relaxing on the weekend in front of the fireplace while having a drink with a loved one, may leisurely thumb through a catalog and place an order via cell phone—having had enough of looking at a computer screen during the work week. Still another consumer may be on the beach wishing he had a better pair of sunglasses. So, he uses his smartphone to visit Ray-Ban's Facebook page just to get some information but is delighted to learn that he can buy the sunglasses on that site if he chooses. After text messaging a few friends for their opinions about Ray-Ban Sunglasses he orders them from Ray-Ban's Facebook page.

So, the challenge for the channel manager is to provide "channel-surfing" consumers with whatever channels or combination of channels they desire. Consequently, developing an effective multichannel marketing strategy has become a crucial goal of channel design.

This same argument also holds in industrial or business-to-business (B2B) markets, where more and more firms are demanding that *all* suppliers provide Internet-based channels as an option.

Channel Member Selection and Electronic Marketing Channels

It is key to recognize that, despite the Internet, channel member selection will remain an important decision for most producers and manufacturers. Our discussion earlier in this chapter on disintermediation versus reintermediation shows that electronic marketing channels do not necessarily result in a reduction in the number of channel intermediaries, and in fact, often the opposite is true—more intermediaries appear in electronic marketing channels. Consequently, the need to select prospective channel members carefully will remain an important part of channel decision making. Moreover, in the new multichannel environment discussed at many points throughout this text, conventional marketing channels will continue to exist right alongside electronic channels. Thus, the channel manager will still face selection decisions for conventional channel members. But the selection decision may be further complicated by the need to avoid conflict with conventional channel members, who may feel that electronic marketing channels could take business away from them. So, this issue may well have to be addressed carefully and thoroughly during the selection phase of channel design.

Channel Management and Electronic Marketing Channels

What is important to keep in mind about the implications of electronic marketing channels for channel management decisions is that channel management is likely to be *more* challenging and complex rather than less as a result of this technology. The fact that Internet technology underlies electronic marketing channels does not mean that channel management can move to "automatic pilot" mode. The fundamental issues of motivating channel members, building cooperation, managing conflict, and coordinating elements of the marketing mix to meet the firm's distribution objectives will still require the full attention of the channel manager. In fact, greater attention will be needed because, as we have pointed out many times, in most cases electronic marketing channels will be just one among several different marketing channel structures rather than the only one. Hence, given this multichannel challenge, the channel manager will not only have to deal with managing conventional channels where familiar territory may create a relatively high comfort level, but also with the new and less familiar electronic marketing channels where the comfort level is likely to be lower.[47]

Evaluation and Electronic Marketing Channels

Even with the widespread acceptance of electronic marketing channels including m-commerce and s-commerce (sales through electronic channels on social networking sites) channels, the principles of channel member performance evaluation and even the key criteria discussed in Chapter 14 are still relevant. Metrics dealing with channel member sales, sales growth, inventory levels, customer service capabilities, attitudes, profit margins,[48] and numerous others are often needed to measure performance. Early hyperbole about the Internet "changing everything" to the point that "conventional," "brick and mortar," "land-based," or "legacy" evaluation metrics had become obsolete to be replaced by new cyberspace Internet or e-commerce metrics such as "eyeballs," "site hits," and "bounce rates" has been largely discredited. While it is true that some new metrics were needed to better capture buying patterns associated with electronic marketing channels, this does not mean that the "old" metrics are no longer relevant. For example, the metric of store traffic to measure the volume of customers entering conventional retail stores by a manufacturer using retailers to sell his products may need to be supplemented by the number of "hits" on the Web sites of cyberspace retailers carrying the manufacturer's products. But the core *concept* underlying the metrics of store traffic or site hits is essentially the same: it is a measure of the volume of customers visiting the store or visiting the Web site.

While a detailed discussion of the possible new metrics needed to evaluate channel members operating in cyberspace is beyond the scope of this chapter, Figure 15.6 provides a brief overview of ten of the key metrics that have been widely used in e-commerce.

FIGURE 15.6
Ten Metrics Every
E-Commerce Site
Should Monitor

1. **New Visitor Conversion Rate:** Most etailers rarely differentiate between their new and return visitor conversion rates. By isolating the new visitor conversion rate, you'll be able to see a clearer picture of what's happening when first time visitors land on your site from search engines or other ad campaigns.
2. **Return Visitor Conversion Rate:** Unfortunately, not everyone buys on the first visit. The next best thing, however, is getting them back to your site. By analyzing your return visitor conversion rate, you'll see how likely you are to convert your return traffic. Most likely, you'll find that your return visitor conversion rate is the higher of the two.
3. **Pageviews/Visit:** Pageviews per visit can reflect how well your site engages your audience. An increasing number of pageviews per visit can indicate that your content is interesting, therefore visitors are spending more time browsing it. However, a high pageviews per visit metric can also indicate unecessarily complicated processes such as checkout or product browsing.
4. **Items/Order:** If your site has a suggested product feature to encourage add-ons, you would benefit by tracking how many items you sell per order.
5. **Average Order Value:** While your target average order value will vary greatly based on your industry, it would be wise to monitor this metric over time. Ideally, you'd like to see a year over year increase.
6. **Landing Page Bounce Rates:** A bounce occurs when a visitor visits a page on your site, and immediately clicks away and goes no further. High bounce rates can be caused by a number of factors including excessive loading times, irrelevant content, unnactractive site design, etc. Be sure to monitor your bounce rates on all your important entry pages including your home page and any Search Engine Optimization (SEO) or Pay Per Click (PPC) landing pages.
7. **Landing Page Load Times:** As mentioned above, excessive page load time can wreak havoc on your bounce rates. Monitor your page load times on different connection speeds with a free tool from WebSiteOptimization.com
8. **Traffic Sources:** Google analytics breaks visit sources into 3 categories: Direct visits (from typing your URL directly), Search engines visits (both SEO and PPC), and referring sites (any other sites linking to yours). Obviously, the percentage of visits from each of these sources will vary for every site. However, as your brand grows, you'd like to see more visits coming from direct URL entry. These tend to convert better.
9. **Orders Per Customer Per Year:** Come up with a calculation of how many times a customer orders per given time period. This serves as a good tool for determining how much you can afford to spend on marketing or re-marketing.
10. **Shopping Cart/Checkout Abandonment Rate:** Measure what percentage of visitors abandon the shopping process at each step in your checkout. For example, how many abandon after adding an item to the cart? After entering shipping & billing info? After entering credit card info? Too high of an abandonment rate could signal a serious checkout problem.

Source: Justin Palmer, "10 Metrics Every eCommerce Site Should Monitor." Palmer Web Marketing, 2010. Copyright © 2010 by Palmer Web Marketing. Reproduced by permission.

The salient point to remember with regard to the area of channel member evaluation is that regardless of the technologies underlying a particular type of channel, the channel manager needs to focus on metrics that are relevant to the particular channel or channel mix that she/he needs to use to accomplish the distribution objectives. If that involves the e-metric of **Shopping Cart/Checkout Abandonment Rate** (see Figure 15.6) and/or the bricks and mortar metric **inventory maintenance** (see Chapter 14) then those are the metrics that should be used regardless of whether one of those metrics may be viewed as "new age" and the other as "yesterday's news."

Summary

Electronic marketing channels (including mobile and social networking versions) have become a mainstream channel choice for consumers and an important channel option for many firms. While the dramatic forecasts of about a decade ago that the "Internet would change everything" by virtually eliminating "bricks and mortar" stores and shopping malls have not come to pass, online shopping has taken its place as a viable marketing channel alongside conventional "land-based" channels.

To qualify as electronic marketing channels, the customer and seller must be able to use the Internet to interact with each other and complete the transaction. Although many pundits have predicted that electronic marketing channels would eliminate most middlemen from the channel structure (disintermediation) because the need for intermediaries becomes superfluous given the capabilities of the Internet, so far this has not happened. In fact, there are numerous examples of reintermediation where new types of intermediaries appear in the channel, sometimes adding to the number of levels in the channel structure. This pattern appears to be more common than disintermediation in electronic marketing channels. Why has this occurred? Because in spite of the power of Internet technology, the laws of economics have not been repealed. The number and types of intermediaries that appear in the channel are still determined by which or what combination of channel members can perform the distribution tasks most effectively and efficiently.

Online shopping by consumers has grown from virtually nothing in the mid-1990s to over $175 billion by 2010, accounting for approximately 8 percent of total retail sales. Millions of people have engaged in online shopping to purchase a wide array of products. Growth in online sales are expected to outpace conventional retail sales over the next several years and m-commerce and s-commerce sales will grow even faster.

Advantages associated with electronic marketing channels include (1) global scope and reach, (2) convenience/rapid transaction processing, (3) information processing efficiency and flexibility, (4) data-based management and relationship capabilities, and (5) lower sales and distribution costs.

Disadvantages of using the Internet as a channel include (1) lack of contact with actual products and delayed possession; (2) fulfillment logistics not at Internet speed and efficiency; (3) clutter on the Internet, and (4) nonpurchase motives for shopping not addressed.

The emergence of electronic commerce has implications for all of the major decision areas of marketing channel strategy and management but does not fundamentally alter the decision areas themselves. However, the existence of viable online channels along with conventional channels means that the channel manager must now deal with the increasing complexity and additional challenges emerging from this new multichannel environment.

Review Questions

1. What was meant by the claim that the "Internet changes everything?"

2. Define the meaning and key points in the definition of "electronic marketing channels" and discuss the key points in the definition.

3. Does the fact that a customer uses the Internet to buy a product or service mean that he or she is using an electronic marketing channel? Explain.

4. Explain the concepts of disintermediation and reintermediation.

5. Will the increasing use of electronic marketing channels necessarily result in more disintermediation? Explain.

6. Why has the use of the Internet as a marketing channel resulted in reintermediation in the channel structure for a number of well-known firms?

7. Discuss the five flows in marketing channels and how these relate to the use of the Internet as an electronic marketing channel.

8. From the standpoint of customer demand, can virtual channel structure usually replace physical channel structure? Explain.

9. Based on the survey data discussed in this chapter, what have been some key developments and trends in electronic marketing channels as they have affected consumers?

10. What are the key advantages of electronic marketing channels?

11. What are the key disadvantages of electronic marketing channels?

12. Discuss some implications of electronic marketing channels for the major areas of channel decision-making.

13. Have electronic marketing channels fundamentally changed marketing channel strategy and management? Discuss.

Channel Issues for Discussion

1. The Internet electronically links many thousands of manufacturers to millions of consumers, thereby eliminating the need for middlemen in the twenty-first century. Who needs intermediaries if customers can go online and manufacturers all have Web site that can be visited by customers from literally all corners of the earth? Shopping trips, malls, stores, indeed, the bricks and mortar of current channel structure will eventually become obsolete—a relic of earlier centuries.

   Do you agree or disagree with this scenario? Discuss.

2. Maytag Corp. is famous for what are arguably the best washing machines and dishwashers in the world. The brand recognition and brand equity levels of Maytag products among consumers are among the highest of any consumer product. About 400,000 consumers visit Maytag's Web site each month. But surprisingly, Maytag does not sell its products directly to consumers via its Web site. Rather, Maytag uses about 10,000 bricks and mortar retail stores. The visitor to Maytag's Web site can examine a huge range of Maytag appliances and get detailed product information. Site visitors can even select the items they want and electronically place them in a shopping cart. But consumers do not actually complete purchases from Maytag directly. Instead, consumers are asked for their zip codes, and Maytag's specialized software directs them to the nearest independent retailers. They can then complete the purchase from the dealer online and arrange delivery or visit the store in person. Maytag likes this arrangement very much because, according to Maytag, it keeps its independent dealers happy and lowers its distribution costs.

   What do you think about Maytag's electronic marketing channel strategy? Is Maytag "missing the boat" by not selling directly to the vast numbers of consumers who visit its Web site every month? Discuss.

3. Office Depot has almost 1,000 office superstores and a giant catalog of office supplies that it offers via mail order. Yet Office Depot also enables its customers to shop on the Internet. Its Web site offers virtually all of the products Office Depot carries in its stores and catalog and guarantees next-day delivery to most locations in the United States with no delivery charge on orders over $50. Online order tracking is available, and customized ordering, which takes into account the historical patterns of an individual customer's product purchases, is also a feature of Office Depot's Internet-based channel.

   What do you see as the advantages of Office Depot's multichannel strategy? Are there any disadvantages?

4. Online channels provide consumers with 24/7 access to a vast array of products and services that can be ordered at any time at the leisure of the online shopper. But online channels can also be used to create a sense of urgency for customers to buy immediately or lose out on wonderful bargains they will never see again. This "buy now or lose out" sense of urgency is the concept behind online "flash sales" where merchandise is offered at heavy discounts but is available only for a very short time. Flash sales seem to be especially potent for selling luxury and high fashion merchandise online that is virtually never discounted in conventional retail stores. Such online flash sales are the mainstay of online fashion retailers such as HauteLook Inc., Gilt Groupe, and RueLaLa, but this model is also spreading to the online divisions of such fashionable and famous luxury retailers as Saks Inc.,

Neiman Marcus Group, and Nordstrom, which recently bought HauteLook.

Do you think flash sales channels are a "flash in the pan" or a viable long-term electronic channel? Why or why not?

5. One of the potentially powerful advantages of m-commerce is the ability of sellers to target offers to consumers when they are in close proximity to the seller. This is made possible based on smartphone technology that tracks the exact geographical locations of their users. For example, if a consumer is near a Staples Office Superstore, a text message can be automatically sent to the consumer's smartphone about a special offer on, say, print cartridges and paper. The technology that has made such m-commerce-based proximity marketing possible was developed by startups such as ShopKick, Where, and Loopt, as well as by giants such as AT&T's ShopAlerts. Although available to anyone with a smartphone, the proximity alerts will only be sent to consumers who have signed up for the program.

Do you think this type of m-commerce is an important channel option for consumers and sellers? Why or why not?

6. 1-800 Flowers.com has been on Facebook almost from the first day the social networking site appeared. The online flower retailer uses Facebook to keep in touch with its many customers and to establish a forum to foster a continued dialogue with customers and potential customers. But by the middle of 2009, 1-800 Flowers.com added a shopping tab to its Facebook page that allows visitors to browse and purchase flowers without having to leave the Facebook social networking site. 1-800 Flowers.com believes that embedding an electronic marketing channel on its Facebook page adds value to the customer experience by making it more convenient for customers to buy flowers online.

Do you see any possible downside to adding electronic marketing channels to social networking sites? Discuss.

References

1. Erick Schonfeld, "Forrester: Online Retail Sales Will Grow to $250 Billion by 2014," http://techcrunch.com/2010/03/08/forrester-forecast-online-retail-sales-will-grow-to-250-billion-by-2014/ (4/8/2011).

2. For in-depth background on this topic see: David E. Williams, "The Evolution of e-tailing," *International Review of Retail Distribution and Consumer Research* (July 2009): 219–249.

3. Devon S. Johnson, "Beyond Trail: Consumer Assimilation of Electronic Channels," *Journal of Interactive Marketing* (Spring 2008): 28–44.

4. Olga Kharif, "M-commerce's Big Moment," *Bloomberg Business Week* (October 11, 2009): 101–102.

5. See for example: Paula Andruss, "Social Shopping," *Marketing News* (January 2, 2011): 11, 21.

6. Pallab Paul, "Marketing on the Internet," *Journal of Consumer Marketing* 13, no. 4 (1996): 27–39.

7. Michelle Kung and Geoffrey A. Fowler, "Warner Likes Facebook Rentals," *Wall Street Journal* (March 9, 2011): B4.

8. For an excellent discussion related to this point, see Steven E. Salkin, "Debunking the Myths of the Internet," *Warehousing Management* (October 1997): 29–32.

9. See, for example, Richard W. Oliver, "The Seven Laws of E-Commerce Strategy," *Journal of Business Strategy* (September-October 2000): 8–10.

10. Joshua D. Libresco, "Internet Commerce Threatens Intermediaries," *Marketing News* (November 24, 1997): 11; Robert Benjamin and Rolf Wigand, "Electronic Markets and Virtual Value Chains on the Information Superhighway," *Sloan Management Review* (Winter 1995): 62–72; Debra Spar and Jeffrey J. Bussgang, "The Net," *Harvard Business Review* (May–June 1996): 125–133.

11. See, for example, David Bank, "Middlemen Find Ways to Survive Cyberspace Shopping," *Wall Street Journal* (December 12, 1996): B6.

12. Philip Anderson and Erin Anderson, "The New E-Commerce Intermediaries," *MIT Sloan Management Review* (Summer 2002): 53–62.

13. Autobytel/.com:http://www.autobytal.com/

14. PEAPOD LLC Corporate Fact Sheet, http://www.peapod.com/corpiafo/companyFachSheet.jhtm/.

15. See for example: Nanette Byrnes, "More Chicks at the Bricks," *Business Week* (December 17, 2007): 50–52.

16. Salkin, "Debunking the Myths," 30.

17. Robert D. Hof, "Amazon: We've Never Said We Had to Do It All," *Business Week* (October 15, 2001): 53.

18. Emily Fredrix, "Amazon.com to Hire Thousands to Fill Orders," http:finance.yahoo.com/news/Amazon-to-hire-thousands-apf-407345135.html?x=0 (11/13/2010).

19. For a related discussion see: Amit Basu and Steve Muylle, "How to Plan E-Business Initiatives in Established Companies," *MIT Sloan Management Review* (Fall 2007): 28–36

20. Tony Hsieh, "Getting a Foothold Online," *Wall Street Journal* (June 7, 2010): A17.

21. Natalie Zmuda, "An App for That, Too: How Mobile is Changing Shopping," *Advertising Age* (March 1, 2010): 1–4.

22. Scott Morrison and Geoffrey A. Fowler, "EBay Pushes into Amazon Turf," *Wall Street Journal* (April 29, 2011): B1.

23. For an in-depth analyses related to this topic see: V. Kumar and Rajkumar Venkatesan, "Who Are the Multichannel Shoppers and How Do They Perform? Correlates of Multichannel Shopping Behavior," *Journal of Interactive Marketing* (Spring 2005): 44–62.

24. Brad Stone, "The Retailer's Clever Little Helper," *Bloomberg Business Week* (August 30, 2010): 31–32.

25. Andreas M. Kaplan and Michael Haenlein, "Users of the World Unite! The Challenges and Opportunities of Social Media," *Business Horizons* Vol. 53 (2010): 59–68.

26. See for example: Brad Stone, "Sell Your Friends," *Bloomberg Business Week* (October 3, 2010): 64–68.

27. Christopher Grosso, "What's Working Online," *McKinsey Quarterly* Issue 3 (2005): 18–20.

28. "The Consumer Online," *Stores* (January 1998, Sec. 2): 8.

29. Sarah Shannon and Olga Kharif, "Flipping Friends into Customers," *Bloomberg Business Week* (February 21, 2010): 22–23.

30. Joseph Alba, John Lynch, Barton Weitz, Chris Janiszewski, Richard Lutz, Alan Sawyer, and Stacy Wood, "Interactive Home Shopping: Consumer, Retailer, and Manufacturer Incentives to Participate in Electronic Marketplaces," *Journal of Marketing* (July 1997): 38–53.

31. Karen M. Kroll, "E-Shoppers Make a Memory with Customization Feature," *Stores* (December 2002): 62–63.

32. For another version of this type of online customization, see "Brooks Brothers Body Scan," *Business 2.0* (January 23, 2001): 24.

33. See for example: Jane Porter, "Bargain Bin Luxe Online," *Business Week* (November 3, 2008): 55.

34. Aaron Grossman, "One-to-One: Net Marketing Opportunities Can Heighten Customer Loyalty, Satisfaction," *Marketing News* (January 19, 1998): 13.

35. Jessica E. Vascellaro, "Online Retailers Are Watching You," *Wall Street Journal* (November 28, 2006): D1, D3.

36. Kenneth Leung, "Marketing with Electronic Mail Without Spam," *Marketing News* (January 18, 1998): 11.

37. Kevin Helliker, "Americans Renew Their Love for Cars—Online," *Wall Street Journal* (August 27, 2009): D1., D6.

38. For an excellent and in-depth analysis related to these issues see: Rajasree K. Rajamma, Audhesh K. Paswan, and Muhammed M. Hossain, "Why Do Shoppers Abandon Shopping Carts? Perceived Waiting Time, Risk, and Transaction Inconvenience," *Journal of Product and Brand Management* Vol. 18, No. 3 (200):188–197.

39. Richard S. Tedlow, "Roadkill on the Information Superhighway," *Harvard Business Review* (November–December 1996): 165.

40. For related discussion see: Elisabeth A. Sullivan, "Virtually Satisfied Easily Navigable Web sites that Deliver the Sought-After Info Win With Consumers," *Marketing News* (October 15, 2008): 8.

41. Edward M. Tauber, "Why Do People Shop?" *Journal of Marketing* (October 1972): 46–49.

42. Tauber, "Why Do People Shop," 49.

43. For an in-depth discussion related to these issues see: Dhruv Grewal, Ramkumar Janakiraman, Kirthi Kallyanam, P. K. Kannam, Brian Ratchford, Reo Song, and Stephen Tolerico, "Strategic Online and Offline Retail Pricing: A Review and Research Agenda," *Journal of Interactive Marketing* Vol. 24 (2010): v138–154.

44. For an excellent analysis of whether adding an Internet channel option adds value to the firm, see Inge Geyskens, Katrijin Gielens, and Marnik G. Dekimpe, "The Market Valuation of Internet Channel Additions," *Journal of Marketing* (April 2002): 102–119.

45. Linda C. Ireland, "Channel Integration Strategies," *Target Marketing* (September 2002): 34–43.

46. For a different view see: Ann Zimmerman, "Gift Shoppers Flocked to the Web," *Wall Street Journal* (December 24, 2010): B1, B2.

47. For a related discussion, see Eugene H. Fram, "E-Commerce Survivors: Finding Value Amid Broken Dreams," *Business Horizons* (July-August 2003): 15–20.

48. Julia Angwin, "Latest Dot-Com Fad Is a Bit Old-Fashioned: It's Called Profitability," *Wall Street Journal* (August 14, 2001): A1, A6.

CHAPTER **16**

Franchise Marketing Channels

LEARNING OBJECTIVES

After reading this chapter you should:

1. Realize that franchise channels are a particular type of marketing channel.
2. Be familiar with some key franchise jargon.
3. Recognize the scope and importance of franchise channels.
4. Understand the rationale underlying franchise channels.
5. Know about the downsides associated with franchise channels.
6. Appreciate the different perspectives of franchisor and franchisee with regard to the rationale and downsides of franchise channels.
7. Be cognizant of the channel management implications of franchise channels.

PRNewFoto/Burger King Corporation

445

FOCUS ON CHANNELS

A Loss Leader is a Good Thing Says the Franchisor.
No, It's a Bad Thing Say the Franchisees.

Franchisors and their franchise channel members are supposed to work together to create win-win results for the franchisor and the franchisee. Most of the franchisor's revenue comes from royalties—a percentage cut of franchisee sales paid by the franchisees to the franchisor. The higher the sales for franchisees, the higher the revenue from royalty payments paid to the franchisor. So, shouldn't both franchisor and franchisee be happy about this arrangement? The franchisor has an incentive to help the franchisees increase their sales because this will result in higher royalties and the franchisees pay more in royalties only if their sales increase.

Well, the real world of franchising is not so pat. Franchisees are concerned about *how* the franchisor helps them attain higher sales. If the franchisor's strategy involves actions that franchisees believe will hurt their profits, they can get very upset. This is exactly what happened when franchisor Burger King directed its franchisees to reduce the price of its Double Cheeseburger to just $1.00 during the Great Recession of 2008. Burger King believed this $1.00 double cheeseburger would be "just what the doctor ordered" to stimulate sales during bad economic times. Burger King argued that the bargain burger would attract customers who would then buy other items such as fries and soft drinks where margins are higher. Many of the franchisees didn't see it that way. They believed the $1.00 Double Cheeseburger was not a *loss-leader* that would generate additional sales of other menu items but simply a *loser* that undermined their profits.

Acting on behalf of many disgruntled franchisees, the Burger King National Franchisee Association launched a lawsuit in November of 2009. But a federal district court dismissed the lawsuit finding that the franchisor, Burger King, needed broad discretion to develop competitive marketing strategies—even ones that franchisees believed are detrimental to them. Needless to say, the Burger King franchisees were not happy with the ruling and filed a motion for the court to reconsider. The case is still pending.

Regardless of the final outcome of the case, the $1.00 Double Cheeseburger which most consumers think tastes great, has left a bad taste in the mouths of a lot of Burger King franchisees.

Source: Based on Richard Gibson, "Franchisee v. Franchisor," *Wall Street Journal* (February 14, 2011): R3.

Franchise Marketing Channels

In previous chapters we have examined a wide variety of issues associated with channel strategy, design, management, and evaluation. We have also discussed core marketing channel concepts, the environment within which marketing channels operate and behavioral processes in marketing channels. In the preceding Chapter 15, we also addressed the newly emerging and rapidly growing area of electronic marketing channels.

In this chapter, we turn our attention to another important and growing channel type within the larger field of marketing channels—**franchise marketing channels**. Although franchise marketing channels are not as new on the scene as electronic marketing channels, franchise channels have played and continue to play a huge and growing role in making products and services conveniently available to tens of millions of consumers.[1] Although a franchise channel is just a particular type of marketing channel, franchise channels often present peculiarities and challenges that vary significantly from conventional channels in terms of the nature of the relationship between channel members and the operation of the channel.[2] These variations from conventional marketing channels will become apparent as we proceed through this chapter. The chapter is organized around the following topics:

- *Franchise channel concepts and terminology*
- *Scope and importance of franchise channels*
- *Rationale for franchise channels*
- *Downsides of franchise channels*
- *Channel management implications of franchise channels*

Franchise Channels Concepts and Terminology

As mentioned above, although franchise channels of distribution are just a special type of marketing channel, several concepts and terms have emerged to identify and describe various aspects of franchise channels.[3] It is important that these concepts and terms be clearly understood because, in a very real sense, they are the language of franchising. These concepts and terms are discussed below.

Franchise

In the most general sense, a **franchise** is a legal agreement between two independent parties whereby one of those parties grants a license to the other party to sell a trademarked product or service. The party who owns the trademarked product or service is the franchisor while the party granted the right to sell the product or service is the franchisee. There are two different types of franchises: a **product distribution franchise** and a **business format franchise.**[4]

Product Distribution Franchise This type of franchise represents the original concept of a franchise described above. That is, the franchisor licenses its trademarked product (or service) to franchisees who then have the right to sell the franchisor's products or services. In this type of franchise, the franchisor provides relatively little in the way of management and marketing assistance to the franchisees. Essentially, as the term product distribution franchise suggests, the franchisees get the legal right to sell the franchisor's products and little else. Product distribution franchises are predominantly found in automobile, petroleum, and soft drink channels. For example, GM, Ford, Chrysler, and most foreign automobile manufacturers use product distribution franchises that grant independent automobile dealers the right to sell their cars. ExxonMobile and the other major oil companies as well as the Coca Cola and Pepsi use the same system to sell their products through independent service stations and bottlers.

Business Format Franchise   In this type of franchise, not only does the franchisor license the franchisee to sell the franchisor's trademarked product or service, but the franchisor also provides the complete system or format for operating the business. This typically includes training, marketing strategy, logos, promotion management systems, financial control procedures, quality control standards, and anything else needed to set up and manage the franchisee's business. Often the components of the business format are written up in detail and supplied to the franchisee in the form of an operating manual which can be hundreds of pages in length. A close working relationship and frequent communication between franchisor and franchisees are also usually part of a business format franchise.[5] This type of franchise is common in a variety of franchise distribution channels (see Figure 16.1).

In recent years, it has become customary to refer to a business format franchise simply as a franchise because it is by far the more common type of franchise. So, unless otherwise specified, when the term franchise is used in this text, it is understood that we are referring to the business format category of franchise.

Franchise Channel Structure

Arrangements between franchisor and franchisee are generally structured in two ways: a **single-unit franchise** or a **multi-unit franchise**.

Single-Unit-Franchise   In this type of structure, the franchisor grants the franchisee the right to own and operate one unit. This is the most common and simplest form of franchise channel structure. If the franchisee is successful with a single unit and then

FIGURE 16.1
Examples of Companies Operating Business Format Franchise Marketing Channels in Various Industries

Automotive Services	AAMCO Transmission Meineke Discount Mufflers Midas International
Convenience Stores	APlus Family Mart 7-Eleven
Health & Beauty	Cost Cutters Family Hair Care Jenny Craig International The Zoo Health Club
Lodging	Aloha Hotels Budget Hotels Marriot Hotels
Cleaning and Maintenance	Furniture Medic Merry Maids Service Master
Real Estate	Century 21 Caldwell Banker RE/MAX International
Restaurants	McDonalds Pizza Hut Taco Bell
Retailing	Athlete's Foot GNC Radio Shack

© Cengage Learning 2013

decides to buy one or more additional units, this is still considered to be a single-unit channel structure but with additional units added.

Multi-Unit-Franchise   Under this structure, the franchisor grants the franchisee the right to own and operate more than one unit at the outset of the relationship. This multi-unit franchise structure can be achieved through an area development franchise or a master franchise agreement.[6] With an area development franchise, the franchisee is granted the right to open more than one unit during a certain time period and within a specified geographic area. For example, a business service franchisee may agree to open six units within three years from the date of the agreement in the city of Los Angeles.

A multi-unit franchise structure based on a master franchise agreement provides more rights and flexibility to the franchisee than would be the case if an area development franchise were used.[7] Here, along with the right to open a certain number of units in a specified territory, the master franchisee also has the right to sell franchises to prospective franchisees in the defined territory. These franchisees are usually referred to as **sub-franchisees**. The master franchisee may also assume many of the tasks normally provided by the franchisor such as providing training and management assistance. In return the master franchisee may receive fees and royalties from the sub-franchisees.

Franchising

Franchising, although often referred to as an industry or type of business, is actually a method of distribution that utilizes franchise marketing channels to make products and especially services available to customers. As already mentioned above, in a marketing channel based on a business format franchise, franchisor and franchisee are legally linked together in a relationship that goes well beyond just the right to sell a product or service. Thus, franchise marketing channels are more closely knit than conventional channels and the relationship among channel members is broader and more encompassing.[8] As we shall see later in this chapter, this can have both advantages and disadvantages for franchisors and franchisees. Further, the tighter more comprehensive relationship characteristic of franchise marketing channels can present the channel manager with challenges that are different from those encountered in conventional, loosely aligned channels.[9]

Franchise Fee

A franchise fee is typically a one-time flat fee paid by the franchisee to the franchisor usually when the franchisee signs the franchise contract. Depending on the type of franchise involved, this fee can range from a few thousand dollars to well over a million dollars or more. The franchise fee does not necessarily pay for physical assets needed to operate the franchise. Often, the fee or a substantial part of the fee is a "pay to play" payment that compensates the franchisor for providing the franchisee with the right to use the franchisor's business model.

Royalty Fee

Most franchisees are required to pay a regular and continuous royalty fee to the franchisor for as long as they hold the franchise.[10] Usually, this fee is set by the franchisor based on a percentage of the franchisee's gross sales although that is not always the case. In some instances the royalty fee may be a fixed amount of money paid by the franchisee to the franchisor regardless of franchisee sales. When royalty rates are based on sales, the franchisor's royalties from franchisees will vary in direct proportion to the franchisee's sales. Although the percentage of sales method for paying a royalty fee has the advantage of automatically adjusting to changing franchisee revenues, the fixed method provides both franchisee and franchisor with more certainty about how much franchisees will pay and franchisors will receive.

Scope and Importance of Franchise Channels

Franchise marketing channels play a huge role in the distribution system of the United States. By the mid point of the first decade of the twenty-first century, the total output of franchise channels measured in dollars was almost $881 billion per year accounting for 4.4 percent of the private-sector output of the United States. The franchise distribution system is composed of over 909,000 franchise business establishments that provide more than 11 million jobs or 8.1 percent of the private-sector workforce. The payroll produced by franchise channels is almost $279 billion or 5.3 percent of all private-sector payrolls in the United States.[11] Table 16.1 provides additional metrics on franchise channels segmented by product distribution franchises and business format franchises.

Franchise distribution channels are prevalent across a wide range of businesses. Table 16.2, for example, shows sales and number of establishments for business format franchises across ten different industries.

TABLE 16.1 SALES, ESTABLISHMENTS, JOBS, AND PAYROLL FOR FRANCHISED DISTRIBUTION CHANNELS IN 2005

	PRODUCT DISTRIBUTION FRANCHISES	BUSINESS FORMAT FRANCHISES	TOTAL
Sales	215.6 billion (24.5%)	665.3 billion (75.5%)	880.9 billion
Establishments	135,817 (14.9%)	773,436 (85.1%)	909,253
Jobs	2,011,938 (18.2%)	9,017,267 (81.8%)	11,029,205
Payroll	71.7 billion (25.7%)	206.9 billion (74.3%)	278.6 billion

Source: Compiled from: "The Economic Impact of Franchised Businesses," International Franchise Association Educational Foundation: White Paper (January 31, 2008): 3.

TABLE 16.2 BUSINESS FORMAT FRANCHISE SALES AND ESTABLISHMENTS FOR TEN INDUSTRIES IN 2005

INDUSTRIES	SALES (BILLIONS$)	ESTABLISHMENTS
Automotive	25.3	35,616
Business Services	151.0	193,063
Commercial & Residential Services	32.9	54,495
Food (Retail)	47.0	61,039
Lodging	48.0	30,014
Personal Services	96.1	76,824
Quick Service Restaurants	152.1	167,578
Real Estate	26.2	33,900
Retail Products and Services	36.5	78,621
Table/Full Service Restaurants	50.4	42,285
Total	665.6	773,435

Source: Compiled from: "The Economic Impact of Franchised Businesses," International Franchise Association Educational Foundation: White Paper (January 31, 2008): 4–6.

FIGURE 16.2 Number of Jobs Provided by Major Economic Sectors 2005

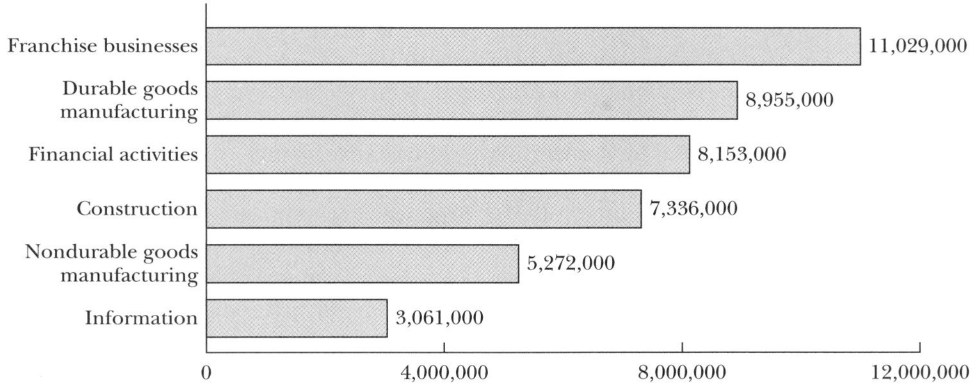

Source: *Compiled from: Matthew Shay, "Economic Impact of Franchised Businesses: Volume 2. IFA Franchising (March 12, 2008): 2. www. buildingopportunities.com.*

Another way of gaining perspective on the scope and importance of franchising is to compare the number of jobs provided by franchise businesses relative to other major sectors of the economy. This is done in Figure 16.2. As shown in the Figure, the 11,029,000 jobs provided by franchised businesses is significantly larger than the 8,995,000 jobs in the next largest category, durable goods manufacturing and well above the number of jobs in several other major economic sectors.

Franchising and franchise channels continue to grow dramatically. In 2010, the U.S. Department of Commerce estimated that one out of every two businesses in the United States operated under some form of franchise system. Moreover, the breadth of different kinds of franchises has also continued to increase with more than 300 types of businesses involved in franchising. This growth in size and scope of franchising is expected to continue well into the future. In fact, by the beginning of the second decade of the twenty-first century, a new franchise outlet was opening every five minutes of each working day!

Franchising and franchise channels are not limited to the United States. More than 400 U.S.-based franchise companies operate internationally and more than 100 foreign franchise firms have operations in the U.S. Finally, franchising and franchise channels exist and are growing in every developed country in the world.[12]

Rationale for Franchise Marketing Channels

From the franchisor's point of view, three major reasons have traditionally been cited for distributing via franchise channels: (1) capital advantages, (2) potential to reduce distribution costs, and (3) the possible high level of managerial motivation fostered by franchising.[13]

Capital advantages are often cited as *the* most important reason for adopting franchised distribution. The acquisition of funds through franchising does not dilute ownership in the business to the same degree as does equity financing through the sale of securities to the public. Further, it does not create the indebtedness attendant to borrowing, which may be too burdensome for the firm to carry. Many franchise companies, have thus been able to use the initial fees paid by their franchisees as a major source of working capital. Obtaining capital through the sale of franchises also offers the franchisor a high level of flexibility in the use of capital, and the capital accumulation can be accomplished rapidly.[14] For example, the franchisor is able to use capital collected from new franchisees for national advertising, franchisee training, and other areas of operations. On the other hand, if the firm opts to obtain capital through borrowing or the sale of securities, certain provisions often limit management discretion in the use of funds.

The potential for franchising to reduce distribution costs is particularly important for the firm whose main channel alternative consists of establishing its own network of company-owned outlets. If the firm were to rely on distribution through company-owned branch units or stores, it would be burdened with fixed overhead expenses that would have to be met regardless of the sales volume achieved. The high costs of maintaining company-owned business operations in many different locations would have to be borne solely by the firm. By using a franchise channel, however, members would assume much of this overhead cost and would also pay for the right to market the firm's products or services. Such royalties must be paid on the franchisee's gross sales—regardless of whether the franchise is making any profit.[15]

With respect to managerial motivation, franchisees as independent business people are more likely than salaried employees to work hard at developing their markets. Further, the franchisee is often better motivated to accomplishment than a company employee because of his or her self-image as a local businessperson who is important in the community.

From the perspective of the potential franchisee, franchising has several important appeals. First, the amount of uncertainty involved in going into business is reduced with a franchise. Presumably, the particular business approach being offered by the franchisor has been successfully tested. Second, the franchisor in many cases offers a well-known trademarked product or service, which is likely to already have a high level of consumer acceptance. Third, as shown in Figure 16.3, many franchisors offer initial and continuing assistance to their franchisees, including site selection, market surveys, merchandising assistance, operating manuals, advertising, accounting, and many others. Indeed, the extensive services offered by the franchisor are often cited as the main reason for the franchisee's willingness to buy a franchise.[16] Fourth, in many cases franchising enables an individual to enter a business that would be prohibitively expensive if he or she tried to go it alone. Being a member of a franchised system may enable the individual to get financial assistance directly from the franchisor, or may put the individual in a better position to secure funds from other sources, if it is a respected franchise. Finally, some

FIGURE 16.3
Typical Initial and Continuing Assistance Offered By Franchisors to Franchisees

Initial Assistance	Continuing Assistance
Facility design and layout	Advertising
Franchisee employee training	Auditing and record keeping
Franchisee fee financing	Centralized purchasing
Lease negotiation	Field supervision
Management training	Franchisee employee training
Marketing surveys and site selection	Group insurance plans
Operating manuals	Market research
	Merchandising and promotional materials
	Quality control inspections

© Cengage Learning 2013

prospective franchisees decide to join a franchise organization because the prospects for making adequate returns in a relatively short period of time are often higher than is the case for independent businesses.[17]

The advantages of franchising have made it a very attractive choice for entrepreneurs who want to be in business for themselves, yet be part of a structured system that enhances their chances for success. This has made franchising particularly appealing to former executives and managers who have lost their jobs as a result of corporate downsizing in recent years.

Some Downsides of Franchise Channels

Although franchise marketing channels offer both franchisors and franchisees some very substantial benefits over conventional channels, there are also some downsides associated with franchise marketing channels. These are discussed below from the standpoints of the franchisor and franchisee.

Downsides for the Franchisor

A franchisor seeking to develop and operate a franchise marketing channel faces at least three potential downside risks compared to conventional channels.

First, franchise channels can limit the flexibility of the franchisor. As discussed earlier, the essence of the modern business format franchise is its programmed business model or format that addresses all areas of the business from advertising to management systems, training, and just about everything else needed to create and sustain the whole "package" that constitutes a franchise. While it is well recognized that this business format drastically reduces the flexibility of the franchisee, what is sometimes forgotten is it also *reduces the flexibility of the franchisor.* The franchisor that has created and developed the business format which is then sold to franchisees creates a set of expectations on the part of franchisees that they expect to remain relatively stable over time.[18] In other words, franchisees have literally bought into the franchisor's concept and mode of operation for which they have paid a franchise fee and continuing royalties. In return, the franchisees expect the franchisor to stay true to the model they "signed up for." If any change is made by the franchisor that might have a negative impact on the franchisees, the franchisees may believe they have not only a right to know about it but also a right to veto the change. For example, as mentioned in the Focus on Channels Vignette at the beginning of this chapter, when franchisor Burger King introduced its $1.00 Double Cheeseburger, many Burger King franchisees felt Burger King was deviating from the original model that allowed Burger King franchisees, rather than the franchisor, to set the price.[19] Consequently number of Burger King franchisees, (supported by their national franchisee association)[20] believing that they were losing money on the $1.00 cheeseburger, launched a lawsuit to prevent franchisor Burger King from deviating from the original terms of its agreement. Such conflicts over what franchisors may believe is strategic flexibility needed to deal with changing market or competitive circumstances, may be seen by franchisees as unwarranted deviations from what the franchisor had originally agreed to.

A second potential downside of franchise channels from the franchisor's point of view, is overly high expectations on the part of franchisees. Compared to prospective channel members in conventional channels, franchise channel members tend to have higher expectations in terms of the support and assistance they will receive from the franchisor.[21] High expectations on the part of franchisees about what franchisors will do for them "goes with the territory" of business format franchising. After all, the franchisees reason, the franchisor has developed a business model or format that presumably is valuable enough to charge a substantial fee and collect royalties from franchisees. So, it is reasonable for franchisees to expect something significant in return from the franchisor.[22] However, it is not unusual for franchisees to expect too much from the franchisor, especially in terms of assurances or guarantees of success. While very few franchisors ever explicitly offer such guarantees to franchisees, this does not stop franchisees from having unrealistic expectations. Indeed, numerous lawsuits initiated by franchisees against franchisors stem from "misunderstandings" about franchisee expectations.[23]

Finally, another potential downside to franchise channels from the franchisor's point of view is the increased regulatory scrutiny the franchisor is exposed to. Franchisors are regulated by federal and state laws that require franchisors to provide prospective franchisees with disclosure information that delineates the nature of the franchise and the franchisor-franchisee relationship in detail.[24] One major document required by the Federal Trade Commission that must be provided to prospective franchisees is the **Uniform Franchise Offering Circular (UFOC).** This document provides detailed information to the franchisees about the franchisor including the following:

- *Financial statements*
- *Key staff qualifications*
- *Management experience in franchising*
- *Fees and royalties*
- *Territorial rights*
- *Responsibilities of the franchisor to the franchisee*
- *Contact information for other franchisees in the system*
- *Copy of the actual franchise agreement*

Fourteen states require that the franchisor register their UFOCs with the state before conducting any franchising activity in the state. Further, UFOCs are subject to the so-called "ten-day-rule" which means that upon receiving the UFOC, franchisees have a 10-business day cooling-off-period before they are allowed to sign a franchise agreement.

In addition to the UFOC, all franchisees are legally linked to the franchisor by a contract usually referred to as the **franchise agreement.** This document typically includes the following provisions:

- *Use of trademarks*
- *Territory*
- *Rights and obligations*
- *Standards, procedures, training, assistance, advertising, etc.*
- *Duration of the franchise*
- *Payments to be made by franchisee or franchisor*
- *Termination and transfer rights*

So, compared with conventional, loosely aligned channels, the regulatory environment for franchise channels is more intense. For firms that seek the maximum freedom to develop and manage their marketing channels, franchise channels may not meet their needs.

Downsides for the Franchisee

From the franchisee's point of view, three potential downside risks are often associated with franchise channels.

The first of these is the limited independence of the franchisee. Many franchisors are fond of saying that franchising provides the opportunity to "*go into business for yourself, but not by yourself.*" Although this statement captures the essence of the principal upside rationale for the franchisee to participate in a franchise channel, it also hints at the principal drawback—*the lack of independence afforded by franchising.* The pre-packaged and programmed nature of business format franchising usually provides very little room for deviation from the prescribed program dictated by the franchisor. If the franchisee wants to do things her or his own way there is little leeway to do so in a typical franchise channel. So, for prospective franchisees who have an entrepreneurial flair, and who are creative and independent, becoming a franchisee in a modern business format franchise channel may lead to frustration rather than satisfaction.[25]

A second potential downside for franchisees participating as channel members in franchise channels is the obligation of franchisees to provide a percentage of their gross revenues to the franchisor as royalty payments. This obligation is a continuing one that lasts for as long as the franchise agreement is in effect, regardless of whether the franchisee makes a profit or not. Franchisees who have limited or no profits may come to resent the relentless demands made on them to constantly pay royalties to the franchisor even when times are bad. Indeed, some of these franchisees may believe that the reason they are not profitable is because of what they perceive to be the high royalties they have to pay to the franchisor. And, to add insult to injury, franchisees may also be required to pay a percentage of their revenue to the franchisor to pay for advertising expenses incurred by the franchisor.[26] This can create even greater resentment against the franchisor. Thus, for channel members who want more control over how the revenue they generate from their own efforts is allocated and spent, franchise distribution may not be an appropriate channel in which to participate.

A third potential problem for the franchisee with franchise distribution channels, is what can be described as a negative halo effect. A franchisee is part of a larger system that may contain dozens, hundreds, or even thousands of other franchisees. The image and reputation of the franchise accrues to each franchisee in the channel. If a few or even one member of the franchise system generates negative publicity, all franchisees in the system may suffer. If, for instance, a fast food franchise in, say, a suburb of Los Angeles experiences a problem with food poisoning that gets picked up as a story on Yahoo, the negative publicity can damage the reputation and business of all the franchisees. Further, sometimes the franchisor may be the target of negative publicity that can hurt the franchisees. This is what happened to Taco Bell when it was accused in a customer-rights class-action lawsuit of false advertising, concerning the percentage of pure beef in the fillings of its tacos. Although the allegations proved to be false, Taco Bell felt compelled to spend millions of dollars on advertising and public relations to try to counteract the negative publicity generated by the lawsuit. The lawsuit was dropped after a short time but the possible adverse effects on individual Taco Bell franchisees of what turned out to be a smear campaign will probably never be known.

Channel Management Implications of Franchise Channels

As we pointed out at the beginning of this chapter, franchise channels are just a particular type of marketing channel. But in franchise channels, the channel participants are closely linked together via a legal contract and the strategy, operations, and activities of the franchise channel members are comprehensively programmed by the franchisor. This strategic and tactical direction of franchisees by the franchisor can affect the relationship between participants in franchise channels in ways that are somewhat different from conventional channels. Such differences can have implications for the management of franchise channels. In the following sections we examine some of these channel management implications.

Channel Design and Franchise Channels

In the process of designing the marketing channel, the channel manager seeking to develop a channel that offers a high degree of control will almost certainly have to consider the franchise channel model as one of the alternatives under consideration. This proposition assumes, of course, that a business format franchise channel would be a reasonable channel choice given the industry involved and/or the products and services being offered. If, for example, the firm is selling heavy industrial machinery to a target market that consists mainly of manufacturers, the business format franchise model is not likely to be a realistic or feasible channel option. Or, on the other end of the spectrum, a consumer packaged goods manufacturer such as Procter & Gamble is not likely to consider using a franchise channel instead of the vast network of supermarkets, drugstores, and mass merchandisers channels used to make its vast family of brands available to millions of consumers all over the world. However, Procter & Gamble *did* decide to use franchise channels to establish several service businesses that are leveraged off of two of Procter & Gamble's most famous brands—Mr. Clean and Tide. The Mr. Clean brand is the name used for a Mr. Clean Car Wash franchise and Tide for a Tide Dry Cleaners franchise (see Figures 16.4 and 16.5). Procter & Gamble, through its wholly-owned subsidiary Agile Pursuits Franchising, Inc., decided to use the franchise channel model for these new service businesses to maintain a high degree of control over the channel members. Because the franchisees are providing car washes and dry cleaning services under these world-famous Procter & Gamble brands (Mr. Clean and Tide), the company wants to make sure that the brand equity of those famous brands is preserved and enhanced by maintaining a high degree of control over the quality of the services provided.

So, whether a firm is a giant global corporation such as Procter & Gamble or a smaller manufacturer or supplier, the relationship between channel design and control has to be considered. Although the highest level of control can be achieved by designing a vertically integrated channel where all of the stores or other points of contact with customers are company-owned and operated, in many cases, this is not feasible, economically and operationally. Moreover, as discussed earlier in this chapter, the capital costs of establishing a large domestic or global network of wholly-owned stores may be prohibitive. Further, as we also pointed out earlier, company stores managed by employees rather than independent stores run by entrepreneurs, may lack the motivation needed to build and sustain the business. Thus, the channel manager pursuing a channel design strategy that seeks to build a high level of control into the channel but that still relies on independent highly motivated channel members will almost always have to consider the franchise channel option.

Selection of Franchise Channel Members

In a franchise channel of distribution the selection of channel members poses a peculiar, even paradoxical challenge for the franchisor. Specifically, the franchisor wants prospective franchisees that are highly motivated and entrepreneurial yet not so independent and creative that they want to do things their own way rather than the franchisor's way. Independence and creativity, which are typically viewed as positive and desirable personality traits of entrepreneurs, can actually undermine the business model of franchising. Why? Because the success of franchise channels relies on conformance by the franchisee to a rigid program and business format developed by the franchisor. If the franchisee deviates from the prescribed format, the result is more likely to produce a negative outcome rather than a positive one. While the franchisor's model may not be a perfect one, usually a great deal of thought, planning, and experience have gone into its development. Changes to the model by well-meaning, independent-minded

FIGURE 16.4
Advertisement by
Procter & Gamble
Seeking Franchisees for
Mr. Clean Car Wash

Source: Courtesy of Procter & Gamble. Used by permission.

franchisees, although they may have some merit, may still have to be carefully vetted by the franchisor to see whether the franchisee's new ideas will be consistent with the established model. But independent and creative franchisees are likely to become frustrated and even angry with what they may perceive to be the franchisor's slow, plodding, and bureaucratic behavior if it does not respond soon and favorably to the franchisee's ideas.

Consequently, franchisors need to select franchisees who possess a good balance between independence and creativity on the one hand and capacity to take direction on the other. Fortunately, there are substantial numbers of prospective franchisees who have this balance. Their independence is satisfied by the fact that they are able to own their own business and their creativity can be expressed but within the boundaries of the business format prescribed by the franchisor. But, finding and recruiting prospective

FIGURE 16.5
Advertisement by
Procter & Gamble
Seeking Franchisees for
Mr. Tide Dry Cleaners

Source: Courtesy of Procter & Gamble. Used by permission.

franchisees with this kind of balance means that franchisors have to devote considerable time and effort to the selection process. Some franchisors have their own in-house staffs and have developed their own psychological personality profiles to identify ideal franchisees. Other franchisors rely on outside consultants to help in the selection process.[27]

In sum then, the selection of prospective franchise channel members who have the capacity to become successful franchisees has to go beyond the usual "hard", objective selection criteria such as financial strength and experience to include the psychological and personality traits that fit the franchise model.

Motivation of Franchisees

The motivation of franchise channel members differs somewhat from the motivation of channel members in conventional channels. As pointed out in Chapter 9, the motivation of channel members consists of three basic phases: (1) finding out the needs and problems of channel members, (2) offering support and assistance that is consistent with those needs and problems, and (3) providing leadership on a continuing basis. Although this basic framework still holds for motivating franchise channel members, the emphasis and focus change because of the programmed approach used in business format franchising. In particular, the cooperative and partnership approaches commonly used to support and assist channel members in conventional channels (see Chapter 9), have less of a role to play in franchise channels. Rather, the programmed approach to providing channel member support and assistance is the option used in most modern franchises. Further, the leadership role in franchise channels not only definitively resides with the franchisor but the intensity of leadership tends to be higher in franchise channels than in conventional channels.[28] In short, the franchisor's program (business format) provides the foundation for motivating the franchisees because it specifies the overall concept, strategy, and operational procedures which, if followed closely by franchisees, should increase the odds of franchisee success. Thus, much of the franchisor's role in providing leadership involves convincing the franchisees to adhere to the plan and in supervising its implementation.[29]

This seeming one-way flow of direction from franchisor to franchisee does not mean that franchisors should be insensitive to franchisee needs and problems and that they should not make an effort to find out what their needs and problems are. On the contrary, knowing the issues and challenges that franchisees are facing is still important but the franchisor's response to the feedback it receives from franchisees cannot typically be as flexible and far reaching as would be the case in conventional channels. This is because the franchisor's responses are constrained by the programmed business format and franchise agreement that defines the nature of the franchise and the nature of the relationship between the franchisor and franchisee. So, the degree of freedom that franchisors have to adjust their policies to better align with changing needs and problems of franchisees is likely to be lower in franchise channels than in conventional marketing channels. The channel manager faced with the task of motivating franchise channel members needs to be aware of this systemic constraint on her or his capacity to react to franchisee needs and problems. For example, a franchisee may complain about certain provisions of the programmed business model (format) such as a requirement to follow certain accounting procedures or a contractual obligation such as the royalty rate paid by the franchisee to the franchisor. Upon learning this, the franchisor is not likely to be able to quickly change policies, strategies, and contractual obligations to satisfy the demands of the dissatisfied franchisee. While it may appear to be insensitive for the franchisor to ignore the concerns or demands of the disgruntled franchisee, if the franchisee's demands are inconsistent with or violate the business model and/or contractual agreement, the franchisor has little choice but to point out honestly the limitations imposed by the business format and franchise contract. The franchisees may not be happy with this, but they are likely to be even less happy if the franchisor makes promises to them that cannot be fulfilled while still staying within the parameters of the business model and franchise agreement.

Managing the Marketing Mix in Franchise Channels

In Chapters 10-13 we examined a number of interfaces between channel management and the other strategic variables in the marketing mix: product strategy, pricing strategy, promotion strategy, and logistical strategy. The underlying theme of our discussion was that the channel manager should attempt to manage the firm's marketing channels so that the other variables in the marketing mix will help to support and enhance channel strategy rather than undermine it.

This same theme holds for channel management in franchise channels. However, because of the nature of modern franchising that, in effect, pre-packages the marketing mix into a programmed format that franchisees are legally obligated to follow, the implementation of marketing mix management in franchise channels is different at least in degree from conventional channels. Specifically, it tends to be less fluid and flexible. Product, pricing, promotion, and logistics strategies in franchise channels can, of course, be changed over time but not as easily or quickly as in conventional channels. Consider for example, what happened to Thomas Sergio, a franchisee in an upscale wine-bistro franchise chain called the Grape when he wanted to offer his customers lower price wines than the typical $15.00 per glass wines specified by the franchisor. The franchisor did not oblige because the product and pricing strategies used in the Grape's business model were based on premium wines and premium prices.[30] While it is possible that if enough franchisees in the chain were experiencing the same problem as franchisee

Thomas Sergio, the franchisor might be willing to adapt its product and pricing strategies, such a change could not be made easily or quickly. In the case of the Grape, the franchisor believed and perhaps justifiably so, that the introduction of lower-priced wines might undermine the premium image of the franchise.

Consider also the case of Quiznos, a franchise chain of sandwich shops whose business format is aimed at positioning Quiznos as a cut above the better-known and much larger Subway franchise. To support its one notch up positioning strategy, Quiznos priced its sandwiches higher than Subway's. But when the Great Recession of 2008 took hold, customers wanted lower prices. Quiznos did respond with a $4.00 Toastly Torpedo and a $3.00 Toasty Bullet as well as a $5.00 sandwich, soup, or salad combo, but not in time to rescue several hundred franchisees that for too long lacked the kind of products and prices needed to survive in a recessionary environment.[31] Quiznos reprogramming of its marketing mix to better support its franchisees did occur, but not quickly enough to satisfy not only the franchisees that went out of business but many of the remaining 4,000 whose profits were hurt by what they perceived, fairly or unfairly, to be Quiznos' tardy changes in its product and pricing strategies to better support the franchisees.

In sum, managing the marketing mix in franchise channels presents the channel manager with a dilemma. On the one hand, he or she would like to quickly adapt product, price, promotion, and logistics strategies in ways that would help franchisees. But, on the other hand, the channel manager is constrained with regard to the actions that can be taken by the relatively fixed strategic framework prescribed by the franchise business format.[32] While there is no pat answer to this dilemma, a sensible approach is for the channel manager to "push the envelope" in managing the marketing mix to help franchisees as long as such action does not undermine the core elements of the business format.

Evaluating Franchisee Performance

In Chapter 14, where we examined the evaluation of channel member performance in detail, we noted four factors that affect the scope and frequency of evaluations:

- *Degree of control*
- *Importance of channel members*
- *Nature of the product*
- *Number of channel members*

In franchise channels, it is the first two factors that are especially relevant.

With regard to the first factor, degree of control, the generally high level of control that the franchisor has over the franchisee enables the franchisor to request and receive a great deal of performance data from the franchisees on a regular and frequent basis. Sometimes, such as in the case of 7-11 convenience stores, detailed financial data from 7-11 franchisees must be provided to the franchisor on a daily basis.[33] Franchisors also often require franchisees to allow the franchisor to observe, onsite, the franchisee's performance on such criteria as cleanliness of facilities, maintenance, adequacy of staffing, adherence to prescribed operating hours, employee training procedures, and numerous other criteria.

In most cases, the franchisor's right to franchisee performance data and the authority to conduct onsite evaluations of franchisees is specified in the franchise agreement. Such contractually mandated franchisor access to franchisee performance information contrasts sharply with conventional channels where channel members are under no such contractual obligation to provide performance data and allow onsite visits.

If properly managed, the high degree of control by the franchisor that provides for a guaranteed, detailed, and regular flow of performance information from franchisee to franchisor can be beneficial for both parties. For the franchisor, the transparency and timeliness provided by the prompt and regular flow of information about franchisee performance can provide an early warning of problems and offer insight for taking timely corrective actions. For the franchisees, knowing that the franchisor has access to an extensive range of information about their performance, can motivate them to adhere to performance standards that might not have occurred to the same degree in the absence of the contractual requirement. For this happy outcome to occur, however, the performance evaluation process needs to be conducted in a non-threatening and unobtrusive manner.[34] So, rather than franchisors emphasizing sanctions if performance expectations are not met, they should instead stress the value of abundant performance information for making positive improvements in performance.

Turning now to the second factor affecting the scope and frequency of evaluations, the importance of channel members, in franchise channels. The relationship here is straightforward: Because the franchisees are the sole source of the franchisor's revenues and provide all of the contact points for customers, each and every franchisee is important. While obviously very large franchisees may be viewed as more important in terms of revenue generation than very small franchisees in the system, this does not change the fact that *all* of the franchisees make a contribution to the franchisor's revenue stream through the royalties they pay. In addition, each franchisee, regardless of size, "carries the banner" of the franchisor.[35] That is, it is the franchisees that present the franchisor's offering to customers. If any of the franchisees do not live up to performance expectations, the image or brand equity of the franchise can be seriously undermined. In the long run, this can be even more important than the revenue generated by the franchisees because a damaged franchise brand eventually will be reflected in lower growth opportunities as well as diminished revenue and profit in the future.[36] So, the critical importance of each franchisee to the franchisor mandates that the franchisor pay a great deal of attention to franchisee performance evaluation.

Summary

Franchise marketing channels, although just a particular type of marketing channel, can present issues and challenges that differ from conventional channels. This is particularly the case for business format franchise channels thay go well beyond the original franchise concept of having a license to sell a particular brand of product or service. In a business format franchise, the franchisor grants the franchisee not only the right to sell the product or service but specifies the entire program for developing and operating the business. This may include such components as building design, marketing strategy, management processes, training, accounting systems, and numerous others.

Franchising has its own "language" including such terms as franchise, product distribution franchise, business format franchise, single-unit-franchise, multi-unit-franchise, franchise fee, royalty, franchise agreement, and UFOC (uniform franchise offering circular). To avoid confusion, it is important for the channel manager to be familiar with these basic franchise concepts and terms.

Franchise marketing channels play a huge role in the distribution system of the United States (and many other countries around the world). In the U.S., sales through franchise channels approached $900 billion and more than 900,000 franchise establishments participated in the system. Franchise channels also accounted for more than eleven million jobs.

A strong argument or rationale can be made for the existence of franchise marketing channels based on several fundamental factors. From the franchisor's perspective these are: (1) capital advantages, (2) potential to reduce distribution costs, and (3) superior managerial motivation of franchisees. From the franchisee's perspective, franchising offers: (1) reduced uncertainty, (2) a well-known trademarked product or service, (3) assistance and service provided by the franchisor, (4) lower cost of entry, and (5) faster opportunity to earn profits.

There are also some potential downsides to franchise channels. For the franchisor these include: (1) limited flexibility, (2) high franchisee expectations, and (3) increased regulatory scrutiny. Downsides for the franchisee include: (1) limited independence, (2) continuous royalty payments to the franchisor, and (3) a possible negative halo effect.

The special nature of franchise channels can have important implications for channel management. At the channel design stage, franchise channels offer the channel manager the opportunity to "build in" a high level of control. In the selection process, the channel manager faces the paradox of choosing highly motivated franchisees but ones that will not want to do things their own way. In the motivation of franchise channel members, the channel manager is confronted with constraints in

reacting to franchisee needs and problems because of the relatively fixed nature of the programmed business format of the franchise. In the management of the marketing mix, the pre-packaged nature of the marketing mix limits the channel manager's ability to react quickly to changing conditions facing the franchisees. Finally, with regard to evaluation of franchisee performance, the high degree of control of the franchisor over franchisees afforded by the franchise contract, and the importance of each franchisee in the system enables the channel manager to exert considerable leverage for gathering information on franchisee performance.

Review Questions

1. Franchise channels are just a particular type of marketing channel. Discuss this statement.
2. What is the difference between a product distribution franchise and a business format franchise?
3. Discuss the channel structure of a single-unit franchise versus a multi-unit franchise.
4. Is a franchise fee the same thing as a royalty fee? Discuss.
5. How important are franchise channels in terms of sales, jobs, and payroll generated?
6. Discuss the outlook for growth in franchise channels in the United States.
7. Discuss the rationale for franchising from the franchisor's and franchisee's point of view.
8. Are there some downsides to franchise channels? What are they from the perspectives of franchisor and franchisee?
9. What key implication does the channel manager need to think about with regard to franchise channels when designing marketing channels?
10. Discuss the paradox the channel manager faces when selecting prospective channel members for franchise channels.
11. How might the motivation of franchise channel members differ compared with conventional channels?
12. Of the three basic approaches to motivating channel members, which is most appropriate for use in franchise channels? Why?
13. Discuss how the channel manager's "hands are tied" when managing the marketing mix in franchise channels.
14. What key factors affect the evaluation of channel member performance?
15. What is the caveat the channel manager should be aware of when evaluating the performance of franchise channel members?

Channel Issues for Discussion

1. Snap-on Tools is the franchisor for a unique business format franchise that uses franchisees in mobile vans to sell high quality tools and equipment to professional mechanics. The franchisees bring the tools and equipment to the mechanics at their worksites so that the mechanics do not lose time shopping for tools. One of the features of the business format is Snap-on prescribing the level and variety of inventory to be carried by the franchisees. Snap-on argues that it has the knowledge and experience needed to assure that

each franchisee has the optimum inventory mix. Many of the franchisees, however, claim that the territories they serve are diverse and have different customer needs. So they can become loaded down with inventory that they cannot sell if they rely on Snap-on to specify their inventories. This dispute over the control of franchisee inventory has created a conflict that resulted in some franchisees launching lawsuits against the franchisor.

Discuss the issue of inventory determination from the franchisor's and the franchisee's points of view. Do you think that specifying the franchisees' inventory mix is a crucial component of the business format?

2. 7-Eleven, Inc. operates the world's largest convenience store retailer franchise. In business for over eight decades, 7-Eleven has thousands of stores all over the world and boasts that it has an instantly recognizable, world-famous trademark. Yet 7-Eleven says that it can provide prospective franchisees with the opportunity to own a true neighborhood business. 7-Eleven believes that its ordering system, POS scanning system, and other technologies enable franchisees to have customized product assortments that reflect the localized needs and preferences of customers. Thus, franchisees can always have the products customers want whenever they step into a local store. 7-Eleven also promises to prepare its franchisees for success by providing initial and ongoing training, financial assistance, payroll services, twice-a-week consulting services and other support.

   Does 7-Eleven's model live up to the statement often heard in franchising circles that: "Franchising lets you go into business for yourself but not by yourself?" Discuss.

3. The Federal Trade Commission in a pamphlet it publishes entitled, *Buying a Franchise A Consumer Guide*, points out that when people buy a franchise they often get to sell goods and services that have instant name recognition. The FTC also says that prospective franchisees should expect to receive training and support that can help them succeed. But the agency then adds the following caveat: "But purchasing a franchise is like every other investment: there's no guarantee of success."

   Although success is not guaranteed, what advantages does franchising offer to a prospective franchisee over a conventional business?

4. Jose Fernandez recently became a franchisee in the Cartridge World franchise. Cartridge World specializes in selling replacement cartridges for printers and fax machine cartridges. Jose was pleased to be one of the almost 1700 franchisees in the Cartridge

World franchise (the world's largest toner replacement franchise). Although he had paid a franchise fee of $30,000 to Cartridge World and invested almost $140,000 to start up his franchise, he was confident that the future would be good. Cartridge World had been in business for almost 15 years and the fact that so many franchisees had been established during that time gave him the feeling of being part of a large and strong organization. Further, he thought there would always be a need for print cartridges simply because print cartridges always run out of ink and have to be refilled or replaced. The only thing that really concerned Jose was the 6 percent royalty he had to pay to Cartridge World on all of his sales. Competition from other toner replacement franchises, Cartridge Depot and Rapid Refill was growing and big name cartridge manufacturers such as Hewlett Packard were getting more aggressive. Jose wondered if he could continue to pay the 6 percent royalty in the long run if increased price competition squeezed his margins.

   How might Cartridge World address the concerns of Jose Fernandez? Are there limitations on Cartridge World's capacity to respond? Explain.

5. H&R Block is by far the largest franchisor of tax preparation services with over 4,500 franchisees. Startup costs range from about $35,000 to $100,000 and there is no franchise fee. But the royalty rate on all revenues generated by the franchisees is 30 percent—one of the highest rates in franchising for any type of franchise business. H&R Block franchisees are not permitted to operate from home or even in kiosks in stores and malls. Instead, they must operate from a store or office format. Franchisees receive substantial training from H&R Block based on the expertise and systems developed by H&R Block over half a century.

   Is H&R Block's royalty rate too high? Why or why not? Discuss in terms of what support the franchisor offers to the franchisee, the nature of the service provided by the franchisee, and the franchisee's obligations to the franchisor.

References

1. Julie Bennett, "By the Numbers," *Entrepreneur* (January 2001): 114.
2. For a related discussion see: Jacques Boulay, "The Role of Contract, Information Systems and Norms in the Governance of Franchise Systems," *International Journal of Retail and Distribution Management* Vol. 38, No. 9 (2010): 662–676.

3. See for example: "Frequently Asked Questions about Franchising," International Franchise Association Report: http://www.franchise.org/taq.aspx (11/17/10): 19.

4. Barbara Beshel, "An Introduction to Franchising," Pepsico. Foundation; The Money Institute http://themoneyinstitute2000.com: 1–5.

5. Anna Watson and Richard Johnson, "Managing the Franchisor-Franchisee Relationship: A Relationship Marketing Perspective," *Journal of Marketing Channels*, (January-March 2010): 51–68.

6. Anne Marie Doherty and Nicholas Alexander, "Power and Control in International Retail Franchising," *European Journal of Marketing*, Vol 40, No. 11/12 (2006): 1292–1316.

7. Dildar Hussain and Josef Windspanger, "Multi-Unit Ownership Strategy in Franchising: Development of an Integrated Model," *Journal of Marketing Channels*, (January-March 2010): 3–32; Patrick J. Kaufmann, Naveen Donthu, Charles M. Brooks, "An Illustrative Application of Multi-Unit Franchise Expansion in a Local Retail Market," *Journal of Marketing Channels* Vol. 14, No. 4 (2007): 85–106.

8. Richard Gibson, "The Franchise Decision," *Wall Street Journal* (May 11, 2009): R9.

9. Surinder Tikoo, "Franchisor Use of Influence and Conflict in a Business Format Franchise System," *International Journal of Retail & Distribution Management* Vol. 33m No.5 (2005): 329–342.

10. For an excellent analysis of franchisee failure see: Steven R. Holmberg and Kathryn Boe Morgan, "Retail Marketing Channel Franchise Failure: A Strategic Management Perspective and Longitudinal Analysis," *Journal of Marketing Channels* Vol. 11, No. 2/3 (2004): 55–76.

11. "The Economic Impact of Franchised Businesses," Vol. II While Paper prepared by Price Waterhouse Coopers for the International Franchise Association Education Foundation (January 31, 2008): 1–6.

12. For related discussions see: John F. Preble and Richard C. Hoffman, "Strategies for Business Format Franchisors to Expand into Global Markets," *Journal of Marketing Channels*, Vol. 13, No. 3 (2006): 29–50; Anne Marie Doherty, "Support Mechanisms in International Retail Franchise Networks," *International Journal of Retail & Distribution Management*, Vol. 35, No. 10 (2007): 781–802.

13. Patrick McGuire, "Franchise Distribution Report No. 523, New York: The Conference Board, 1971: 2–3.

14. Anna Watson, "Small Business Growth Through Franchising: A Qualitative Investigation," *Journal of Marketing Channels*, Vol. 15, No. 1 (2008): 3–20.

15. For a related discussion see: Marko Grunhagen, Richard L. Flight, and David J. Boggs, "Franchising During Times of Economic Recession: A Longitudinal Analysis of Automotive Service Franchises," *Journal of Marketing Channels*, (January-March 2011): 57–77.

16. Tarique Hossain, "Franchisor's Cumulative Franchising Experience and Its Impact on Franchising Management Strategies," *Journal of Marketing Channels* Vol. 15, No. 1, (2008): 43–69.

17. For related studies see: John E. Clarkin, "Channel Changes: An Examination of Ownership Changes in Franchise Firms," *Journal of Marketing Channels*, Vol. 15, No. 1, (2008): 23–42; Jeffrey S. Bracker and John N. Pearson, "The Input of Franchising on the Financial Performance of Small Firms," *Journal of the Academy of Marketing Science* (Winter 1986): 10–17.

18. Yu-An, Ian Phau, and Raymond W.K. Chen, "Conceptualizing the Franchise System Quality (SSQ) Matrix: An Exploratory Study," *Journal of Marketing Channels* Vol. 14, No. 4 (2007): 41–64.

19. Richard Gibson, "Have It Whose Way?" *Wall Street Journal* (May 17, 2010): R6, R7.

20. For an excellent analysis of franchisee associations see: Benjamin Lawrence and Patrick J. Kaufmann, "Franchisee Associations: Strategic Focus or Response to Franchisor Opportunism," *Journal of Marketing Channels* (April-June 2010): 137–156.

21. Stephen Bennett, Lorelle Frazer, and Scott Weaven, "What Prospective Franchisees Are Seeking," *Journal of Marketing Channels* (January-March 2010): 69–87.

22. Elisabeth A. Sullivan, "Going the Distance," *Marketing News* (July 30, 2009): 8.

23. For a related discussion see: Victoria Bordonaba-Juste and Yolanda Polo-Redondo, "The Effect of Relationship Marketing Strategy on Franchise Channels: Evidence from Spanish Franchisees," *Journal of Marketing Channels* Vol. 15, No. 1 (2008): 71–91.

24. See for example: Frank H. Wadsworth and K. Chris Cox, "Identifying Risky Franchises," *Journal of Marketing Channels* (January-March 2011): 43–55.

25. See for example: Emily Maltby, "Want to Buy a Franchise? The Requirements Went Up," *Wall Street Journal* (November 15, 2010): R9.

26. Richard Gibson, "Curves Closes Clubs as Stamina Runs Out," *Wall Street Journal* (July 7, 2007): B1, B2.

27. "Testing Psyches of Future Franchisees," *Wall Street Journal* (May 20, 1988): 27.

28. For another perspective on this issue see: Darin W. White, "The Impact of Marketing Strategy Creation Style

on the Formation of a Climate of Trust in a Retail Franchise Setting," *European Journal of Marketing* Vol. 44, No. 1/2 (2010): 162–179.

29. See for example: Richard Gibson, "Package Deal," *Wall Street Journal* (May 8, 2008): R13.

30. Rob Johnson, "Dreams Come True or Not," *Wall Street Journal* (May 16, 2011): R6.

31. Michael Arndt, "Damn! Torpedoes Get Quiznos Back on Track" *Bloomberg Business Week* (January 25, 2010): 54–55.

32. For a related discussion see: Raymond Flandez, "A Look at High-Performance Franchisees," *Wall Street Journal* (February 12, 2008): B5.

33. Norrihiko Shirouzu and John Bognell, "7-Eleven Operators Resist System to Monitor Managers," *Wall Street Journal* (June 16, 1997): B3.

34. Chiharu Ishida and James R. Brown, "The Crowding Out Effects of Monitoring in Franchise Relationships: The Mediating Role of Relational Solidarity," *Journal of Marketing Channels* (January-March 2011): 19–41.

35. Anna-Louise Jackson, "Chicago Franchise Systems," *Marketing News* (February 28, 2009): 8.

36. For a related discussion see: Julian Ming-Sung Cheng, Julia Ying-Chao Lin, Hill H-J Tu and Nina S-H Wu, "Toward a Stage Model of International Franchise System Development: The Experience of Firms from Taiwan," *Journal of Marketing Channels* Vol. 14, No. 4 (2007): 65–83.

Dunkin' Donuts Incorporated Franchise Agreement

Parties

This Agreement, dated _____,
20 _____ is made by and between DUNKIN'
DONUTS INCORPORATED, a Delaware corporation
having its principal place of business in Randolph,
Massachusetts (hereinafter referred to as "DUNKIN'
DONUTS"), and the following individuals or entity (hereinafter referred to collectively as "FRANCHISEE"):

_____

_____

Introduction

DUNKIN' DONUTS, as the result of the expenditure of
time, effort and money, has acquired experience and skill
in the development, opening and operating of shops and
distribution outlets involving the production, merchandising and sale of donuts and other related products utilizing a specially designed building or facility with
specially developed equipment, equipment layouts, interior and exterior accessories, identification schemes, products, management programs, standards, distribution
and delivery methods, specifications and proprietary
marks and information, all of which are referred to in
this Agreement as the "DUNKIN' DONUTS SYSTEM."

DUNKIN' DONUTS has developed and used and
continues to use and control the usage of, in connection with its business and the business of its DUNKIN'
DONUTS franchisees, certain proprietary interests, trademarks, service marks and trade names, including
"DUNKIN' DONUTS," which is registered as a trademark on the Principal Register of the United States
Patent Office (the "PROPRIETARY MARKS"), to

identify for the public the source of goods and services
marketed thereunder and to represent to the public
high and uniform standards of quality, cleanliness, appearance and service.

FRANCHISEE, being cognizant of the distinctive and
valuable significance to the public of all of the foregoing, desires to make use of the trademark "DUNKIN'
DONUTS," and to enjoy the benefits of that mark, the
other PROPRIETARY MARKS and the DUNKIN' DO-
NUTS SYSTEM.

FRANCHISEE understands the importance of DUN-
KIN' DONUTS' high and uniform standards of quality,
cleanliness, appearance and service to the value of the
DUNKIN' DONUTS SYSTEM and the necessity of
opening and operating FRANCHISEE's DUNKIN'
DONUTS SHOP in conformity with the DUNKIN'
DONUTS SYSTEM and in accordance with DUNKIN'
DONUTS' standards and specifications.

Grant of the Franchise

In recognition of all the above, the parties agree as
follows:

1. A. DUNKIN' DONUTS hereby grants to FRAN-
CHISEE during the term hereof and FRANCHISEE ac-
cepts a franchise to operate a donut shop utilizing the
DUNKIN' DONUTS SYSTEM in accordance with the
terms, covenants and conditions of this Agreement, at
one location only, situated at

_____

(No.) (Street) (City or Town) (State) (Zip Code)

(the "DUNKIN' DONUTS SHOP" or the "SHOP"). The
term of this Agreement shall extend twenty (20) years
from the date the SHOP opens (or, in the case of an

existing shop, originally opened) to serve the general public, or until _____, whichever is sooner. This franchise includes the right to use, in connection therewith and at the agreed location, the trademark "DUNKIN' DONUTS," along with other PROPRIETARY MARKS owned and utilized by DUNKIN' DONUTS in connection with other DUNKIN' DONUTS shops, and the right to use the DUNKIN' DONUTS SYSTEM including confidential and valuable information which now exists or may be acquired hereafter and set forth in DUNKIN' DONUTS' operating manuals or otherwise disclosed to DUNKIN' DONUTS franchisees.

1. B. For a new DUNKIN' DONUTS SHOP where the location is to be developed by FRANCHISEE, this franchise is granted to FRANCHISEE subject to (and shall become effective only upon compliance with) the terms, covenants, and conditions of the DUNKIN' DONUTS FRANCHISE OWNER DEVELOPMENT AGREEMENT executed concurrently herewith by DUNKIN' DONUTS and FRANCHISEE.

1. C. This Agreement shall automatically expire upon the earlier expiration of any lease relating to the FRANCHISEE's occupancy of the DUNKIN' DONUTS SHOP.

1. D. FRANCHISEE and all partners and shareholders of FRANCHISEE represent and warrant to DUNKIN' DONUTS that each individual is a United States citizen or a lawful resident alien of the United States, that each corporation is and shall remain duly organized and in good standing during the term of this Agreement, and that all financial and other information which FRANCHISEE has provided to DUNKIN' DONUTS in connection with FRANCHISEE's application for this DUNKIN' DONUTS franchise is true and accurate.

Initial Services Furnished by DUNKIN' DONUTS

2. DUNKIN' DONUTS agrees:

2. A. For a new DUNKIN' DONUTS SHOP where the location is to be developed by DUNKIN' DONUTS, to use reasonable efforts (i) to acquire control of the real estate for the term of this Agreement, and (ii) to cause the DUNKIN' DONUTS SHOP thereon to be constructed, subject to the regulations of all governmental authorities having jurisdiction, and to thereupon lease the DUNKIN' DONUTS SHOP either directly or through a subsidiary to FRANCHISEE. In the event DUNKIN' DONUTS is unable to lease the DUNKIN' DONUTS SHOP to FRANCHISEE, FRANCHISEE shall have the option to terminate this Agreement and obtain a refund of the INITIAL FRANCHISE FEE paid to DUNKIN' DONUTS or to accept a substitute location should one be proposed to FRANCHISEE by DUNKIN' DONUTS;

2. B. For a new DUNKIN' DONUTS SHOP where the location is to be developed by FRANCHISEE, to approve the location if it meets the standards employed by DUNKIN' DONUTS in selecting other locations at the time; and to provide FRANCHISEE with one copy of the standard plans and specifications for a DUNKIN' DONUTS shop;

2. C. To make available the specifications and/or requirements for the equipment to be utilized in the DUNKIN' DONUTS SHOP;

2. D. To make available to FRANCHISEE and FRANCHISEE's designated representative, prior to the opening of the DUNKIN' DONUTS SHOP, a training program at the DUNKIN' DONUTS University Corporate Training Center (DDU) with respect to the operation of the DUNKIN' DONUTS SYSTEM;

2. E. To provide operating procedures to assist FRANCHISEE in complying with DUNKIN' DONUTS' standard methods of record keeping, controls, staffing and training requirements, and production methods, and in developing approved sources of supply;

2. F. To make available to FRANCHISEE assistance, based on the experience and judgment of DUNKIN' DONUTS, in the preopening, opening and initial operation of the DUNKIN' DONUTS SHOP and in conforming to the requirements of the DUNKIN' DONUTS SYSTEM; and

2. G. To prepare and coordinate the Grand Opening Promotional Advertising Program (or such other advertising program as DUNKIN' DONUTS may specify) for the initial opening of the DUNKIN' DONUTS SHOP.

Continuing Services Furnished by DUNKIN' DONUTS

3. DUNKIN' DONUTS agrees:

3. A. To maintain a continuing advisory relationship with FRANCHISEE, including consultation in the areas of marketing, merchandising and general business operations;

3. B. To provide operating manuals to FRANCHISEE, which contain the standards, specifications, procedures and techniques of the DUNKIN' DONUTS SYSTEM, and to revise, from time to time, the content of the manuals to incorporate new developments regarding standards, specifications, procedures and techniques.

3. C. To continue its efforts to maintain high and uniform standards of quality, cleanliness, appearance and service at all DUNKIN' DONUTS shops, thus protecting and enhancing the reputation of DUNKIN' DONUTS and the demand for the products of the DUNKIN' DONUTS SYSTEM and, to that end, to make reasonable efforts to disseminate its standards and specifications to potential suppliers of FRANCHISEE upon the written request of FRANCHISEE;

3. D. To review for approval all proposed advertising and promotional materials relating to FRANCHISEE's DUNKIN' DONUTS operations prepared by FRANCHISEE for use in local advertising; and

3. E. To administer The DUNKIN' DONUTS Franchise Owners Advertising and Sales Promotion Fund (the "Fund") and to direct the development of all advertising and promotional programs. One-fifth of FRANCHISEE's 5% advertising contribution (1% of the GROSS SALES of the SHOP) will be utilized, at the discretion of DUNKIN' DONUTS, to provide for the administrative expenses of the Fund and for programs designed to increase sales and enhance and further develop the public reputation and image of DUNKIN' DONUTS and the DUNKIN' DONUTS SYSTEM. The balance, including any interest earned by the Fund, will be used for advertising and related expenses. Contributions to the Fund in excess of 5% of GROSS SALES shall be used in accordance with the programs to which they relate. The content of all advertising, as well as the media in which the advertising is to be placed and the advertising area, shall be at the discretion of DUNKIN' DONUTS. Upon request, DUNKIN' DONUTS will provide FRANCHISEE a statement of receipts and disbursements of the Fund, prepared by an independent certified public accountant, for each fiscal year of the Fund.

Payments: Initial Franchise Fee

4. FRANCHISEE agrees:

4. A. For a new DUNKIN' DONUTS SHOP where the location is developed by DUNKIN' DONUTS, FRANCHISEE shall pay to DUNKIN' DONUTS _____ Dollars ($__) representing the INITIAL FRANCHISE FEE, payable as follows: Five Thousand Dollars ($5,000.00) upon the execution of this Agreement; Ten Thousand Dollars ($10,000.00) upon execution of the LEASE OF DUNKIN' DONUTS SHOP and the remaining unpaid balance prior to attendance by FRANCHISEE or FRANCHISEE's designated representative at the DUNKIN' DONUTS training course or

thirty (30) days prior to the scheduled opening of the DUNKIN' DONUTS SHOP, whichever date is earlier.

4. B. For a new DUNKIN' DONUTS SHOP where the location is developed by FRANCHISEE, FRANCHISEE shall pay to DUNKIN' DONUTS _____ Dollars ($__) representing the INITIAL FRANCHISE FEE, payable as follows: Four Thousand Dollars ($4,000.00) upon the execution of this Agreement; and the remaining unpaid balance upon written approval by DUNKIN' DONUTS of FRANCHISEE's location for the DUNKIN' DONUTS SHOP. If the DUNKIN' DONUTS SHOP is not open to serve the general public within fifteen (15) months from the date of this Agreement, the INITIAL FRANCHISE FEE shall be increased to the then current INITIAL FRANCHISE FEE, which shall be payable to DUNKIN' DONUTS upon demand, unless DUNKIN' DONUTS elects to terminate this Agreement.

Refunds

4. C. At any time prior to the time that the second payment required under the terms of Paragraphs 4.A or 4.B of this Agreement becomes due, FRANCHISEE may, by written notice, terminate this Agreement. In that event, DUNKIN' DONUTS will return the initial installment paid upon execution of this Agreement, less a charge of Two Thousand Dollars ($2,000.00) to compensate DUNKIN' DONUTS for assistance rendered to FRANCHISEE to the date of termination. Franchise fees are not otherwise refundable.

Grand Opening

4. D. FRANCHISEE shall pay to the Fund Three Thousand Dollars ($3,000.00), which shall be nonrefundable after the DUNKIN' DONUTS SHOP commences operation, for a Grand Opening Promotional Advertising Program (or such other advertising program as DUNKIN' DONUTS may specify). Payment shall be made in full prior to attendance by FRANCHISEE or FRANCHISEE's designated representative at the DUNKIN' DONUTS training course or thirty (30) days prior to the scheduled opening of the DUNKIN' DONUTS SHOP, whichever date is earlier.

Continuing Franchise Fees

4. E. FRANCHISEE shall pay to DUNKIN' DONUTS at Post Office Box 294, Randolph, Massachusetts 02368 (or such other address as DUNKIN' DONUTS shall from time to time give to FRANCHISEE in writing), on or before Thursday of each week, a sum equal to four and nine-tenths percent (4.9%) of

the GROSS SALES of the DUNKIN' DONUTS SHOP for the seven (7) day period ending at the close of business on the preceding Saturday. The term "GROSS SALES" in this Agreement shall include all sales made by FRANCHISEE pursuant to this Agreement, but shall not include the sale of cigarettes, sales taxes or similar taxes.

Advertising

4. F. FRANCHISEE shall pay to the Fund at the same time, for the same seven (7) day period, in the same manner as, and in addition to, the payments provided for under Paragraph 4.E. of this Agreement, 5% of the GROSS SALES of the DUNKIN' DONUTS SHOP (excluding wholesale sales to accounts approved in writing, in advance, by DUNKIN' DONUTS). In addition, FRANCHISEE shall participate in and make additional payments to the Fund with respect to all advertising, marketing and other DUNKIN' DONUTS programs which from time to time are supported by a majority of producing DUNKIN' DONUTS SHOPS in the market in which the DUNKIN' DONUTS SHOP is located with respect to local programs, and in the Continental United States, with respect to national programs. DUNKIN' DONUTS reserves the right in its sole and absolute discretion to designate or change the composition of shops included in the base for purposes of determining a majority. FRANCHISEE shall have complete discretion as to the prices he charges for products sold in the DUNKIN' DONUTS SHOP. Nothing herein shall be construed to require FRANCHISEE to establish prices in accordance with programs supported by the majority of shops.

Covenants of the Franchise

5. FRANCHISEE understands and acknowledges that every detail of the DUNKIN' DONUTS SYSTEM is important to DUNKIN' DONUTS, to FRANCHISEE and to other DUNKIN' DONUTS franchisees in order to develop and maintain high and uniform standards of quality, cleanliness, appearance, service, facilities, products and techniques to increase the demand for DUNKIN' DONUTS products and to protect and enhance the reputation and goodwill of DUNKIN' DONUTS. Accordingly, FRANCHISEE agrees to: devote full time, energy and effort to the management and operation of the DUNKIN' DONUTS SHOP; obtain from DUNKIN' DONUTS prior written approval of all wholesale accounts; use best efforts to maximize sales of the DUNKIN' DONUTS SHOP; ensure accurate

reporting of GROSS SALES to DUNKIN' DONUTS; and implement all procedures recommended by DUNKIN' DONUTS to minimize employee theft. FRANCHISEE further agrees that employee theft shall not relieve FRANCHISEE of the obligation to make all payments to DUNKIN' DONUTS based on GROSS SALES pursuant to Paragraph 4 of this Agreement and that accurate reporting of GROSS SALES includes ringing all sales in the cash register at the time the product is delivered to the purchaser including without limitation retail, wholesale, bulk discount sales and sales for which payment may be deferred.

FRANCHISEE also agrees:

5. A. To use all materials, ingredients, supplies, paper goods, uniforms, fixtures, furnishings, signs, equipment, methods of exterior and interior design and construction and methods of product preparation and delivery prescribed by or which conform with DUNKIN' DONUTS' standards and specifications and to carry out the business covered by this Agreement in accordance with the operational standards and specifications established by DUNKIN' DONUTS and set forth in DUNKIN' DONUTS' operating manuals and other documents as they presently exist or shall exist in the future or as may be otherwise disclosed to DUNKIN' DONUTS' franchisees from time to time.

5. B. To refrain from using or selling any products, materials, ingredients, supplies, paper goods, uniforms, fixtures, furnishings, signs, equipment and methods of product preparation, merchandising, and delivery which do not meet DUNKIN' DONUTS' standards and specifications.

5. C. To offer for sale only such products as shall be expressly approved for sale at the DUNKIN' DONUTS SHOP in writing in advance by DUNKIN' DONUTS and to offer for sale all products that have been designated as approved by DUNKIN' DONUTS.

5. D. To maintain at all times a sufficient supply of approved products.

5. E. To purchase all food products, supplies, equipment and materials required for the operation of the DUNKIN' DONUTS SHOP from suppliers who demonstrate, to the reasonable satisfaction of DUNKIN' DONUTS, the ability to meet all of DUNKIN' DONUTS' standards and specifications for such items; who possess adequate capacity and facilities to supply FRANCHISEE'S needs in the quantities, at the times and with the reliability requisite to an efficient operation and who have been approved, in writing, by

DUNKIN' DONUTS. Prior to purchasing any items from any supplier not previously approved by DUNKIN' DONUTS, FRANCHISEE shall submit to DUNKIN' DONUTS a written request for approval of the supplier. DUNKIN' DONUTS may require that samples from the supplier be delivered to DUNKIN' DONUTS or to a designated independent testing laboratory for testing prior to approval and use. A charge not to exceed the actual cost of the test shall be made by DUNKIN' DONUTS and shall be paid by FRANCHISEE; provided, however, the cost of the first test requested by FRANCHISEE in any calendar year shall be borne by DUNKIN' DONUTS.

Shop Maintenance

5. F. To maintain, at FRANCHISEE's expense, at all times, the interior and exterior of the DUNKIN' DONUTS SHOP and all fixtures, furnishings, signs and equipment in the highest degree of cleanliness, orderliness, sanitation and repair, as reasonably required by DUNKIN' DONUTS, and to make no material alteration, addition, replacement or improvement in, or to, the interior or exterior (including the parking lot and landscaped areas) of the DUNKIN' DONUTS SHOP without the prior written consent of DUNKIN' DONUTS.

Staffing and Training

5. G. To manage the DUNKIN' DONUTS SHOP at all times with at least two (2) individuals, one of whom must be the FRANCHISEE or partner or shareholder of FRANCHISEE. Both individuals must have successfully completed the DUNKIN' DONUTS training program at DDU. Both individuals must have literacy and fluency in the English language sufficient, in the good faith opinion of DUNKIN' DONUTS, to satisfactorily complete training at DDU and to communicate with employees, customers, and suppliers of DUNKIN' DONUTS. In the event FRANCHISEE applies for and receives approval to develop or purchase an additional DUNKIN' DONUTS shop, DUNKIN' DONUTS requires that the additional shop be managed by at least one DDU trained individual approved by DUNKIN' DONUTS.

5. G.1. To ensure that all employees are trained in accordance with DUNKIN' DONUTS in-shop training procedures. Also, FRANCHISEE shall ensure that the manager and all employees whose duties include customer service have sufficient fluency in the English language to adequately meet the public in the DUNKIN' DONUTS SHOP.

5. G.2. To attend and to require those employed in the DUNKIN' DONUTS SHOP to attend such further training as DUNKIN' DONUTS shall from time to time reasonably require.

Training Costs

5. G.3. To pay the cost of training materials, salaries, accommodations and travel expenses, if any, of FRANCHISEE or any other individual employed in the DUNKIN' DONUTS SHOP. FRANCHISEE will also bear the cost of in-shop training programs. The cost of presenting the DDU training program will be borne by DUNKIN' DONUTS.

Books, Records and Reports

5. H. To keep full, complete and accurate books and accounts in accordance with generally accepted accounting principles and in the form and manner prescribed below or as may be further prescribed by DUNKIN' DONUTS from time to time.

5. H.1. To submit to DUNKIN' DONUTS, on or before Thursday of each week, on an approved form, a signed statement of GROSS SALES for the seven (7) day period ending at the close of business on the preceding Saturday along with all monies required to be paid under Paragraphs 4.E. and 4.F. of this Agreement.

5. H.2. To submit to DUNKIN' DONUTS, on or before the twentieth (20th) day of each month, on an approved form, a profit and loss statement of the DUNKIN' DONUTS SHOP for the preceding calendar or fiscal month prepared in accordance with generally accepted accounting principles.

5. H.3. To submit to DUNKIN' DONUTS, within thirty (30) days after the close of each six (6) month period, commencing with the opening of the DUNKIN' DONUTS SHOP, on an approved form, a profit and loss statement for the six (6) month period and a balance sheet (including a statement of retained earnings or partnership account) as of the end of the period. Annual financial statements must be certified by an independent certified public accountant or such other independent public accountant as may be acceptable to DUNKIN' DONUTS.

5. H.4. To submit to DUNKIN' DONUTS such other periodic forms and reports as may be prescribed and at the times prescribed by DUNKIN' DONUTS.

5. H.5. To preserve for a period of not less than three (3) years during the term of this Agreement and for not less than three (3) years following the term of

this Agreement, in the English language, all accounting records and supporting documents relating to the FRANCHISEE's operations under this Agreement, or any lease with DUNKIN' DONUTS or its subsidiary, including but not limited to:

a. daily cash reports;
b. cash receipts journal and general ledger;
c. cash disbursements journal and weekly payroll register;
d. monthly bank statements, and daily deposit slips and canceled checks;
e. all tax returns;
f. supplier's invoices (paid and unpaid);
g. dated cash register tapes (detailed and summary);
h. semi-annual balance sheets and monthly profit and loss statements;
i. daily production, throwaway and finishing records and weekly inventories;
j. records of promotion and coupon redemptions;
k. records of all wholesale accounts (prior written approval of wholesale accounts by DUNKIN' DONUTS is required); and
l. such other records as DUNKIN' DONUTS may from time to time request.

Registers

5. I. FRANCHISEE shall record all sales on a cash register, the make, model and serial number of which has been individually approved in writing by DUNKIN' DONUTS; such cash register shall contain a device that will record accumulated sales and cannot be turned back or reset, and a back-up power system for memory storage in the event of power loss.

Insurance

5. J. FRANCHISEE shall procure, before the commencement of business, and maintain in full force and effect during the entire term of this Agreement, at FRANCHISEE's sole expense, an insurance policy or policies protecting the FRANCHISEE and DUNKIN' DONUTS, and their directors and employees, against any loss, liability or expense whatsoever from, without limitation, fire, personal injury, theft, death, property damage or otherwise, arising or occurring upon or in connection with the DUNKIN' DONUTS SHOP or by reason of FRANCHISEE's operation or occupancy of the DUNKIN' DONUTS SHOP. Such policy or policies shall include comprehensive general liability insurance, including but not limited to, product, contractual, and owned and non-owned vehicle liability coverages, with a single limit of one million

dollars ($1,000,000) (or such higher limits as DUNKIN' DONUTS, in its sole and absolute discretion, may from time to time require, and as may be required under the terms of any lease for the DUNKIN' DONUTS SHOP) for bodily injury and property damage combined, "All Risk" property damage insurance, including without limitation flood and earthquake protection, for the full replacement cost value of the DUNKIN' DONUTS SHOP and the contents thereof, plate glass insurance and boiler insurance, if applicable, and such statutory insurance as may be required in the state in which the DUNKIN' DONUTS SHOP is located. All insurance afforded by the policies required under the terms of this Paragraph shall:

1. Be written in the names of FRANCHISEE, DUNKIN' DONUTS, and any other parties as directed by DUNKIN' DONUTS, as their respective interest may appear;
2. Be written by insurance companies acceptable to DUNKIN' DONUTS;
3. Contain provisions denying to the insurer acquisition by subrogation of rights of recovery against any party named;
4. Contain the provision that cancellation or alteration cannot be made without at least thirty (30) days written notice to any party named; and
5. Not be limited in any way by reason of any insurance which may be maintained by DUNKIN' DONUTS or any party named.

During the term of this Agreement, FRANCHISEE shall promptly (but in no event later than ten (10) days after any such policy becomes effective or such payment is due) furnish DUNKIN' DONUTS with duplicate originals of all insurance policies, including renewal and replacement policies, together with evidence that the premiums therefor have been paid. If at any time FRANCHISEE fails to comply with the provisions of this Paragraph 5.J., DUNKIN' DONUTS, in addition to all other remedies available, shall have the option (but shall not be required) to obtain such insurance with respect to the DUNKIN' DONUTS SHOP, and keep the same in effect. FRANCHISEE shall thereupon pay DUNKIN' DONUTS when and as billed for the costs of the premiums therefor. Maintenance of insurance and the performance by FRANCHISEE of the obligations under this Paragraph shall not relieve FRANCHISEE of liability under the indemnity provisions set forth in this Agreement.

Continuous Operation

5. K. If all conditions precedent to the opening of the DUNKIN' DONUTS SHOP have been satisfied, FRANCHISEE shall promptly open the DUNKIN' DONUTS SHOP to the general public as soon as construction and equipping the DUNKIN' DONUTS SHOP are substantially complete. FRANCHISEE shall thereafter keep the DUNKIN' DONUTS SHOP open and in normal operation 24 hours a day on all days except Christmas and Thanksgiving unless prior written approval is obtained from DUNKIN' DONUTS or unless DUNKIN' DONUTS otherwise directs in writing. FRANCHISEE shall operate the DUNKIN' DONUTS SHOP so as to maximize GROSS SALES and maintain all standards of the DUNKIN' DONUTS SYSTEM.

Advertising Approval

5. L. FRANCHISEE shall submit all advertising and promotional materials prepared for use in local areas to DUNKIN' DONUTS prior to use. In the event written disapproval of the advertising and promotional material is not received by FRANCHISEE from DUNKIN' DONUTS within fifteen (15) days from the date such material is received by DUNKIN' DONUTS, said materials shall be deemed approved unless and until subsequently disapproved.

Company-Developed Real Estate

5. M. In the event DUNKIN' DONUTS develops a new shop and leases the DUNKIN' DONUTS SHOP to FRANCHISEE, FRANCHISEE agrees to enter into a LEASE OF DUNKIN' DONUTS SHOP with, at DUNKIN' DONUTS' option, DUNKIN' DONUTS or its rental subsidiary. FRANCHISEE recognizes that, in the event DUNKIN' DONUTS or its subsidiary leases the DUNKIN' DONUTS SHOP to FRANCHISEE, rent payable under the lease will include additional compensation to DUNKIN' DONUTS or its subsidiary for the acquisition, by purchase or lease, or otherwise, of the DUNKIN' DONUTS SHOP. In the event, during the term of this Agreement or any extension thereof, FRANCHISEE directly or indirectly acquires ownership or control of the property, FRANCHISEE also agrees to grant to DUNKIN' DONUTS, under its standard LEASE OPTION AGREEMENT, the option to acquire the location in the event of default by FRANCHISEE under this Agreement or in the event of FRANCHISEE'S default under any lease or mortgage relating to the premises.

Franchisee-Developed Real Estate

5. N. For a new DUNKIN' DONUTS SHOP where the location is to be developed by FRANCHISEE, FRANCHISEE agrees to develop the DUNKIN' DONUTS SHOP in accordance with plans, specifications, documentation and procedures approved in writing by DUNKIN' DONUTS; to purchase and install in the DUNKIN' DONUTS SHOP fixtures, furnishings, equipment, signs and materials from suppliers which have been approved by DUNKIN' DONUTS; to cause the DUNKIN' DONUTS SHOP to open to the public within fifteen (15) months from the date of this Agreement, and to grant to DUNKIN' DONUTS the option to acquire the location in the event of default by FRANCHISEE under this Agreement or in the event of FRANCHISEE'S default under any lease or mortgage relating to the premises. FRANCHISEE also agrees to execute, concurrently with the execution of this Agreement, but before permitting construction to begin on the DUNKIN' DONUTS SHOP, DUNKIN' DONUTS' FRANCHISE OWNER DEVELOPMENT AGREEMENT and DUNKIN' DONUTS' LEASE OPTION AGREEMENT (with attachments) duly executed in recordable form by FRANCHISEE and the landowner of the premises.

Remodel

5. O. FRANCHISEE agrees to renovate and remodel the interior and exterior of the DUNKIN' DONUTS SHOP (including but not limited to fixtures, furnishings, signs and equipment) no later than the tenth (10th) anniversary of the original opening date of the DUNKIN' DONUTS SHOP to the then current design for shops of comparable age and condition. The nature and scope of renovation and remodeling shall be as then generally required by DUNKIN' DONUTS for shops of comparable age and condition.

Cross-Guarantee

5. P. In the event FRANCHISEE, or any partner or shareholder thereof, holds any interest in a DUNKIN' DONUTS franchise other than the DUNKIN' DONUTS SHOP, FRANCHISEE and the partners and shareholders of FRANCHISEE who own an interest in any other franchise(s) agree to execute concurrently with this Agreement DUNKIN' DONUTS' AGREEMENT OF CROSS-GUARANTEE to DUNKIN' DONUTS for the payment of fees, rents and other obligations for each franchise in which FRANCHISEE

or any partner or shareholder thereof holds or acquires any interest.

Compliance with Regulations

5. Q. FRANCHISEE agrees to comply promptly with all applicable laws, rules, regulations, ordinances and orders of public authorities including, but not limited to, Government Agencies, Board of Fire Underwriters and other similar organizations. The term "Government Agencies" shall include without limitation all governmental units, however designated, which address health, safety, sanitation, environmental or other issues affecting operations of the DUNKIN' DONUTS SHOP.

5. R. FRANCHISEE agrees to submit to DUNKIN' DONUTS promptly upon receipt thereof, copies of all customer complaints and notices and communications from Government Agencies and hereby authorizes Government Agencies to provide directly to DUNKIN' DONUTS copies of all such notices and communications.

Personal Guarantees

5. S. FRANCHISEE agrees to enter into this Agreement and the various other agreements with DUNKIN' DONUTS as an individual, individuals, general partnership or corporation provided that all individuals, general partners, officers, shareholders and directors (if a corporation) will be required to personally guarantee full payment and performance of FRANCHISEE'S money and other obligations under this Agreement and any lease for the premises with DUNKIN' DONUTS or its subsidiary.

5. S.1. If FRANCHISEE is a corporation, said corporation must be in compliance with the requirements applicable to corporations set forth in paragraph 10.C. hereof;

5. S.2. FRANCHISEE may not be a limited partnership, trust or other entity not specifically authorized herein.

Certain Rights of DUNKIN' DONUTS

6. A. In order to preserve the validity and integrity of the PROPRIETARY MARKS and to assure that the standards and specifications of the DUNKIN' DONUTS SYSTEM are properly employed in the operation of the DUNKIN' DONUTS SHOP, DUNKIN' DONUTS, or its agents, shall have the right, at all times, to enter and inspect the DUNKIN' DONUTS SHOP and the right to select materials, ingredients, products, supplies, paper goods, uniforms, fixtures, furnishings, signs and equipment for evaluation purposes

to assure that these items conform to the standards and specifications of the DUNKIN' DONUTS SYSTEM. DUNKIN' DONUTS may require FRANCHISEE to remove any item which does not conform with applicable standards and specifications. DUNKIN' DONUTS may remove or destroy at FRANCHISEE's expense any item which does not conform to applicable standards and specifications.

6. B. If, within twenty-four (24) hours following written notice by DUNKIN' DONUTS requesting the correction of an unhealthy, unsanitary or unclean condition, or within thirty (30) days following written notice by DUNKIN' DONUTS requesting repairs, alterations or painting of the DUNKIN' DONUTS SHOP, FRANCHISEE has not corrected the condition or completed the repairs, alterations or painting, DUNKIN' DONUTS may, without being guilty of, or liable for, trespass or tort and without prejudice to any other rights or remedies, enter the DUNKIN' DONUTS SHOP and cause the repairs, alterations or painting to be completed, or the condition to be corrected, at the expense of FRANCHISEE.

6. C. DUNKIN' DONUTS' representatives shall have the right to examine FRANCHISEE's original books, records and supporting documents at reasonable times and to perform such tests and analyses as it deems appropriate to verify GROSS SALES. If an examination reveals that the GROSS SALES reported by FRANCHISEE to DUNKIN' DONUTS are less than the GROSS SALES ascertained by the examination, then FRANCHISEE shall immediately pay to DUNKIN' DONUTS any amounts owing to DUNKIN' DONUTS and the Fund and DUNKIN' DONUTS' rental subsidiary based upon the corrected GROSS SALES. All examinations shall be at the expense of DUNKIN' DONUTS; however, if an examination results from FRANCHISEE's failure to prepare, deliver or preserve statements or records required by Paragraph 5.H. of this Agreement, or results in the discovery of a discrepancy in the GROSS SALES reported by FRANCHISEE, FRANCHISEE shall pay, or reimburse DUNKIN' DONUTS for any and all expenses connected with the examination, including, but not limited to, reasonable accounting and legal fees, the unpaid amounts owed to DUNKIN' DONUTS, its rental subsidiary and the Fund, and interest thereon from the date payment was due at 18% per annum or the highest permissible rate. Such payments will be without prejudice to any other remedies DUNKIN' DONUTS may have under this Agreement, including the right to

terminate, without opportunity to cure, in the case of intentional underreporting of GROSS SALES.

6. D. FRANCHISEE and all partners and shareholders of FRANCHISEE shall, upon the request of DUNKIN' DONUTS in connection with the examination of FRANCHISEE's books and records under Paragraph 6.C. of this Agreement, provide DUNKIN' DONUTS' representatives with personal federal and state tax returns, bank statements (including deposit slips and cancelled checks) and such other documents and information as DUNKIN' DONUTS may in its sole discretion request in connection with DUNKIN' DONUTS' efforts to verify GROSS SALES reported to DUNKIN' DONUTS under this Agreement or any LEASE OF DUNKIN' DONUTS SHOP. Personal tax returns and financial data unrelated to the franchise business need not be provided by any partner or shareholder of FRANCHISEE who has not been active in the business and, in addition, has not directly or indirectly owned or controlled at least a majority interest in the franchise or any LEASE OF DUNKIN' DONUTS SHOP, alone or in conjunction with any other family member or related entity.

6. E. FRANCHISEE hereby grants DUNKIN' DONUTS the irrevocable right to inspect the records of all suppliers, distributors, group purchasing programs, distribution centers, and other third parties supplying food products, supplies, equipment and materials to FRANCHISEE and hereby irrevocably authorizes such parties to release such records to DUNKIN' DONUTS.

Proprietary Marks

7. A. FRANCHISEE acknowledges that "DUNKIN' DONUTS" is a registered trademark, that said mark has been and is being used by DUNKIN' DONUTS and by its franchisees and licensees, that said mark, together with the other PROPRIETARY MARKS, presently owned by DUNKIN' DONUTS or which may be acquired in the future, constitutes part of the DUNKIN' DONUTS SYSTEM and that valuable goodwill is associated with and attached to said mark and the other PROPRIETARY MARKS, FRANCHISEE agrees to use said mark and the other PROPRIETARY MARKS only in the manner and to the extent specifically licensed by this Agreement. FRANCHISEE further agrees that any unauthorized use or continued use after the termination of this Agreement shall constitute irreparable harm subject to injunctive relief.

7. A.1. FRANCHISEE understands that FRANCHISEE's license to use any or all of the PROPRIETARY MARKS is non-exclusive and relates solely to the location set forth in Paragraph 1.A. of this Agreement. FRANCHISEE further acknowledges that DUNKIN' DONUTS, in its sole discretion, has the right to operate or franchise other DUNKIN' DONUTS SHOPS and sales outlets under, and to grant other licenses in, and to, any or all of the PROPRIETARY MARKS, in each case at such locations and on such terms and conditions as DUNKIN' DONUTS deems acceptable.

7. A.2. FRANCHISEE agrees that, during the term of this Agreement and after the expiration or termination thereof, FRANCHISEE shall not directly or indirectly contest or aid in contesting the validity or ownership of the PROPRIETARY MARKS.

7. A.3. FRANCHISEE agrees to notify DUNKIN' DONUTS promptly of any litigation instituted by FRANCHISEE, or by any person, firm or corporation against FRANCHISEE, relating to the PROPRIETARY MARKS. In the event DUNKIN' DONUTS undertakes the defense or prosecution of any such litigation, FRANCHISEE agrees to execute any and all documents and do such acts and things as may, in the opinion of counsel for DUNKIN' DONUTS, be necessary to carry out such defense or prosecution.

7. B. It is expressly recognized that any and all goodwill associated with the PROPRIETARY MARKS, including any goodwill which might be deemed to have arisen through FRANCHISEE's activities, inures directly and exclusively to the benefit of DUNKIN' DONUTS.

7. C. FRANCHISEE shall operate, advertise and promote the DUNKIN' DONUTS SHOP under the name "DUNKIN' DONUTS," with no accompanying words or symbols of any nature, except as may be otherwise required by law. FRANCHISEE shall not use, as part of its corporate or other business name, any PROPRIETARY MARKS used by DUNKIN' DONUTS, including, but not limited to, "DUNKIN' DONUTS," "DUNKIN," "DUNK" or any form or variations thereof which, in the judgment of DUNKIN' DONUTS, is likely to cause third parties to be confused or mistaken with respect to the separate identities of DUNKIN' DONUTS and FRANCHISEE.

Restrictions on the FRANCHISEE'S Activities

8. A. During the term of this Agreement or any extension thereof, and for a period of two (2) years thereafter, regardless of the cause of termination, neither FRANCHISEE, nor any partner, if FRANCHISEE is a partnership, nor any shareholder, if FRANCHISEE is a corporation, shall, except with respect to the ownership

or operation by the FRANCHISEE of additional licensed DUNKIN' DONUTS shops:

8. A.1. Divert or attempt to divert any business or customer of the DUNKIN' DONUTS SHOP to any competitor, by direct or indirect inducement or otherwise, or do or perform, directly or indirectly, any other act injurious or prejudicial to the goodwill associated with DUNKIN' DONUTS' PROPRIETARY MARKS and the DUNKIN' DONUTS SYSTEM;

8. A.2. Employ or seek to employ any person who is at that time employed by DUNKIN' DONUTS or by any other DUNKIN' DONUTS franchisee, or otherwise directly or indirectly induce such person to leave such employment;

8. A.3. Own, maintain, engage in, be employed by, or have any interest in any other business which sells or offers to sell any product of a type offered by a DUNKIN' DONUTS SHOP; provided that, during the two (2) year period following expiration or termination of this Agreement only, the provisions of this subparagraph 3, shall not apply to another business located more than five (5) miles from the DUNKIN' DONUTS SHOP or from any other DUNKIN' DONUTS SHOP. Either party to this Agreement, upon notice in writing to the other, shall have the right to have determined whether said five (5) mile radius is a reasonable restriction on FRANCHISEE's activities during said two (2) year period by requesting that the matter be submitted to arbitration in accordance with the rules of the American Arbitration Association then applicable for commercial disputes. In such event, each party shall select one arbitrator and the two shall select a third and the decision of the arbitrators shall be final and binding upon the parties. FRANCHISEE further agrees that, in the event arbitration is requested, FRANCHISEE will engage in no competitive activities pending resolution of the dispute; or

8. A.4. Communicate or divulge to, or use for the benefit of, any other person, persons, partnership, association or corporation any information or knowledge concerning the methods of constructing, equipping or operating a DUNKIN' DONUTS SHOP and all other information or knowledge which DUNKIN' DONUTS deems confidential which may be communicated to FRANCHISEE, or of which FRANCHISEE may be apprised by virtue of FRANCHISEE's operation under the terms of this Agreement. FRANCHISEE shall divulge such confidential information only to such of its employees as must have access to it in order to operate the licensed business. Any and all information, knowledge and know-how including, without limitation, drawings, materials, specifications, techniques, and other data, which DUNKIN' DONUTS designates as confidential shall be deemed confidential for purposes of this Agreement. DUNKIN' DONUTS shall have the non-exclusive right to use and incorporate in the DUNKIN' DONUTS SYSTEM, for the benefit of itself and other franchisees of the DUNKIN' DONUTS SYSTEM, any modifications, changes, and improvements developed or discovered by FRANCHISEE or FRANCHISEE's employees or agents in connection with the licensed business, without any liability or obligation to the developer thereof.

8. B. The covenants contained in this Paragraph 8 shall be construed as severable and independent and shall be interpreted and applied consistently with the requirements of reasonableness and equity. If all or any portion of a covenant in this Paragraph 8 is held unreasonable or unenforceable by a court or agency having valid jurisdiction in a decision to which DUNKIN' DONUTS is a party, FRANCHISEE expressly agrees to be bound by any lesser covenant included within the terms of such greater covenant that imposes the maximum duty permitted by law, as if the lesser covenant were separately stated in, and made a part of, this Paragraph.

8. C. FRANCHISEE understands and acknowledges that DUNKIN' DONUTS shall have the right, in its sole discretion, to reduce the scope of any covenant set forth in this Paragraph 8, or of any portion or portions thereof, without FRANCHISEE's consent, and FRANCHISEE agrees to comply forthwith with any covenant as modified, which shall be fully enforceable, the provisions of Paragraphs 14.A. and/or 15 of this Agreement notwithstanding.

8. D. FRANCHISEE agrees that the existence of any claims against DUNKIN' DONUTS, whether or not arising from this Agreement, shall not constitute a defense to the enforcement by DUNKIN' DONUTS of the covenants in this Paragraph 8.

8. E. FRANCHISEE acknowledges that FRANCHISEE's violation of the terms of this Paragraph 8 would result in irreparable injury to DUNKIN' DONUTS for which no adequate remedy at law may be available, and FRANCHISEE accordingly consents to the issuance of an injunction prohibiting any conduct by FRANCHISEE in violation of the terms of this Paragraph 8.

Default

9. A. FRANCHISEE shall be in default under this Agreement:

9. A.1. If FRANCHISEE shall become insolvent or make an assignment for the benefit of creditors, or if a

petition in bankruptcy is filed by FRANCHISEE, or such a petition is filed against and consented to by FRANCHISEE, or is not dismissed within thirty (30) days, or if FRANCHISEE is adjudicated a bankrupt, or if a bill in equity or other proceeding for the appointment of a receiver of FRANCHISEE or other custodian for FRANCHISEE's business or assets is filed and is consented to by FRANCHISEE or is not dismissed within thirty (30) days, or a receiver or other custodian is appointed, or if proceedings for composition with creditors under any state or federal law should be instituted by or against FRANCHISEE or if the real or personal property of FRANCHISEE shall be sold at levy thereupon by any sheriff, marshal or constable.

9. A.2. If FRANCHISEE fails to comply with any law, regulation, order or DUNKIN' DONUTS standard relating to health, sanitation or safety; or if FRANCHISEE ceases to operate, but does not abandon, the DUNKIN' DONUTS SHOP for a period of forty-eight (48) hours without the prior written consent of DUNKIN' DONUTS.

9. A.3. If FRANCHISEE fails, refuses, or neglects to pay when due to DUNKIN' DONUTS any monies owing to DUNKIN' DONUTS or to the Fund.

9. A.4. If FRANCHISEE fails to comply with any of FRANCHISEE's obligations under this Agreement not otherwise set forth in Paragraph 9 of this Agreement; or if FRANCHISEE fails to carry out in all respects its obligations under any lease for the DUNKIN' DONUTS SHOP, or under any mortgage, equipment agreement, promissory note, conditional sales contract or other contract materially affecting the DUNKIN' DONUTS SHOP to which the FRANCHISEE is a party or by which FRANCHISEE is bound, whether or not DUNKIN' DONUTS is a party thereto.

9. A.5. If FRANCHISEE abandons the DUNKIN' DONUTS SHOP; or if FRANCHISEE intentionally underreports GROSS SALES or falsifies financial data; or if FRANCHISEE's lease for the DUNKIN' DONUTS SHOP with DUNKIN' DONUTS or a subsidiary of DUNKIN' DONUTS is terminated or expires.

Cure Period

9. B. Except as otherwise provided in Paragraph 9 of this Agreement, FRANCHISEE shall have the right to cure FRANCHISEE's default under this Agreement within the applicable period set forth below, following written notice of default from DUNKIN' DONUTS. In the event that a statute in the state wherein the DUNKIN' DONUTS SHOP is located requires a cure period for the

applicable default which is longer than the cure period specified below, the statutory cure period shall apply.

9. B.1. A twenty-four (24) hour cure period shall apply to the violation of any law, regulation, order or DUNKIN' DONUTS standard relating to health, sanitation or safety; or if the FRANCHISEE ceases to operate, but does not abandon; the DUNKIN' DONUTS SHOP for a period of forty-eight (48) hours without the prior written consent of DUNKIN' DONUTS.

9. B.2. A seven (7) day cure period shall apply if FRANCHISEE fails, refuses, or neglects to pay when due to DUNKIN' DONUTS any monies owing to DUNKIN' DONUTS or to the Fund, or if FRANCHISEE fails to maintain the insurance coverage set forth in Paragraph 5.J. of this Agreement.

9. B.3. A thirty (30) day cure period shall apply if FRANCHISEE fails to comply with any of FRANCHISEE's obligations under this Agreement, unless otherwise specified in Paragraph 9 of this Agreement, or if FRANCHISEE fails to carry out in all respects its obligations under any lease for the DUNKIN' DONUTS SHOP, or under any mortgage, equipment agreement, promissory note, conditional sales contract or other contract materially affecting the DUNKIN' DONUTS SHOP to which FRANCHISEE is a party or by which the FRANCHISEE is bound, whether or not DUNKIN' DONUTS is a party thereto.

No Cure Period

9. B.4. No cure period shall be available if FRANCHISEE abandons the DUNKIN' DONUTS SHOP; or if FRANCHISEE intentionally underreports GROSS SALES or falsifies financial data; or if FRANCHISEE's lease for the DUNKIN' DONUTS SHOP with DUNKIN' DONUTS or a subsidiary of DUNKIN' DONUTS is terminated or expires.

Interest and Costs

9. C.1 If FRANCHISEE fails to remit when due any payments required under this Agreement, FRANCHISEE agrees to pay all collection costs, reasonable attorney's fees and interest on the unpaid amounts at 18% per annum or the highest permissible rate, in addition to the unpaid amounts.

9. C.2. If FRANCHISEE fails to cure a default, following notice, within the applicable time period set forth in subparagraph 9.B., or if this Agreement is terminated, FRANCHISEE shall pay to DUNKIN' DONUTS all damages, costs and expenses, including

without limitation interest at 18% per annum, or the highest permissible rate, and reasonable attorneys' fees, incurred by DUNKIN' DONUTS as a result of any such default or termination; and said interest and all damages, costs and expenses, including reasonable attorney's fees, may be included in and form a part of the judgment awarded to DUNKIN' DONUTS in any proceedings brought by DUNKIN' DONUTS against FRANCHISEE. Continued use by FRANCHISEE of DUNKIN' DONUTS' trademarks, trade names, PROPRIETARY MARKS, and service marks after termination of this Agreement shall constitute willful trademark infringement by FRANCHISEE. Nothing in this Agreement shall preclude DUNKIN' DONUTS from seeking any remedy under federal or state law for willful trademark infringement, including without limitation treble damages and injunctive relief.

Termination

9. D. Except as set forth in Paragraph 9.E., if FRANCHISEE fails to cure to DUNKIN' DONUTS satisfaction within the applicable period following notice from DUNKIN' DONUTS, DUNKIN' DONUTS may, in addition to all other remedies at law or in equity or as otherwise set forth in this Agreement, immediately terminate this Agreement. Except as set forth in Paragraph 9.E., such termination shall be effective immediately upon receipt of a written notice of termination from DUNKIN' DONUTS.

9. E. This Agreement shall immediately terminate upon the occurrence of any event set forth in Paragraph 9.A.1., without opportunity to cure or notice of termination.

9. F. Upon any termination or expiration of this Agreement:

9. F.1. FRANCHISEE shall promptly pay to DUNKIN' DONUTS all sums owing or accrued prior to such termination or expiration from FRANCHISEE to DUNKIN' DONUTS, the Fund, and DUNKIN' DONUTS' rental subsidiary. Said sums shall also include interest of 18% per annum or the highest permissible rate and any damages, costs and expenses, including reasonable attorney's fees incurred by DUNKIN' DONUTS by reason of default on the part of FRANCHISEE.

9. F.2. FRANCHISEE shall immediately cease to use, by advertising or in any other manner whatsoever, any methods associated with the name "DUNKIN' DONUTS," any or all of the PROPRIETARY MARKS and any other trade secrets, confidential information, operating manuals, slogans, signs, symbols or devices

forming part of the DUNKIN' DONUTS SYSTEM or otherwise used in connection with the operation of the DUNKIN' DONUTS SHOP. FRANCHISEE agrees that any unauthorized use or continued use after the termination of this Agreement shall constitute irreparable harm subject to injunctive relief.

9. F.3. FRANCHISEE shall immediately return to DUNKIN' DONUTS all operating manuals, plans, specifications and other materials containing information prepared by DUNKIN' DONUTS and relative to the operation of a DUNKIN' DONUTS SHOP, and

9. F.4. FRANCHISEE shall continue to comply with, for the period specified therein, Paragraph 8, of this Agreement.

9. G. No right or remedy herein conferred upon or reserved to DUNKIN' DONUTS is exclusive of any other right or remedy herein, or by law or equity provided or permitted, but each shall be cumulative of every other right or remedy given hereunder.

Transfer of Interest

10. A. This Agreement shall inure to the benefit of the successors and assigns of DUNKIN' DONUTS. DUNKIN' DONUTS shall have the right to assign its rights under this Agreement to any person, persons, partnership, association or corporation, provided that the transferee agrees in writing to assume all obligations undertaken by DUNKIN' DONUTS herein and FRANCHISEE receives a statement from both DUNKIN' DONUTS and its transferee to that effect. Upon such assignment and assumption, DUNKIN' DONUTS shall be under no further obligation hereunder, except for accrued liabilities, if any.

10. B. Except as hereinafter provided, neither FRANCHISEE, nor any partner, if FRANCHISEE is a partnership, nor any shareholder, if FRANCHISEE is a corporation, without DUNKIN' DONUTS' prior written consent, shall, by operation of law or otherwise, sell, assign, transfer, convey, give away, pledge, mortgage or otherwise encumber to any person, persons, partnership, association or corporation, any interest in this Agreement, or any interest in the franchise granted hereby, or any interest in any proprietorship, partnership or corporation which owns any interest in the franchise, nor offer, permit or suffer the same. Any purported assignment or transfer not having the prior written consent of DUNKIN' DONUTS shall be null and void and shall constitute default hereunder. Any proposed transfer must meet all the requirements of

DUNKIN' DONUTS including, but not limited to those set forth in Paragraph 10.C. and the following:

10. B.1. FRANCHISEE shall have operated the DUNKIN' DONUTS SHOP for a period of six (6) months prior to the proposed transfer.

10. B.2. The sales price of the interest to be conveyed shall not be so high, in the good faith judgment of DUNKIN' DONUTS, as to jeopardize the ability of the transferee to maintain, operate and promote the DUNKIN' DONUTS SHOP properly and meet his financial obligations to DUNKIN' DONUTS, third party suppliers and creditors. This provision shall not create any liability on the part of DUNKIN' DONUTS to the transferee in the event that DUNKIN' DONUTS approves the transfer and the transferee experiences financial difficulties.

10. B.3. The transferee may not be a limited partnership, trust or other entity not specifically authorized herein;

10. B.4. All accrued money obligations of FRANCHISEE to DUNKIN' DONUTS, the Fund, DUNKIN' DONUTS' rental subsidiary, and obligations of FRANCHISEE which DUNKIN' DONUTS has guaranteed, liens, deferred rent and all other obligations under the LEASE OF DUNKIN' DONUTS SHOP, if any, shall have been satisfied prior to assignment or transfer.

10. B.5. The DUNKIN' DONUTS SHOP, including equipment, signs, building, improvements, interior and exterior, shall be in good operating condition and repair and in compliance with DUNKIN' DONUTS then current standards, including without limitation replacements and additions.

10. B.6. FRANCHISEE and any transferee hereby agree not to assert any security interest, lien, claim or right now or hereafter in this franchise, the franchise granted to the transferee, or lease for the DUNKIN' DONUTS SHOP and further agree that any security interest, lien, claim or right asserted with respect to any personal property at the above location shall not include any after-acquired property and shall be subject, junior and subordinate to any security interest, lien, claim or right now or hereafter asserted by DUNKIN' DONUTS, its successors or assigns.

10. B.7. In the event the transferee, or any partner or shareholder thereof, holds any interest in a DUNKIN' DONUTS franchise other than the DUNKIN' DONUTS SHOP, the transferee and the partners and shareholders thereof who own an interest in other DUNKIN' DONUTS franchise(s) shall execute DUNKIN' DONUTS' AGREEMENT OF CROSS-GUARANTEE to DUNKIN' DONUTS for the payment of fees, rents and other obligations for each DUNKIN' DONUTS franchise(s) in which the transferee or any partner or shareholder thereof holds or acquires any interest.

10. C. DUNKIN' DONUTS shall not unreasonably withhold its consent to any transfer referred to in Paragraph 10.B. of this Agreement when requested, provided, however:

10. C.1. If FRANCHISEE is an individual or partnership and desires to assign and transfer this Agreement to a corporation:

a. Said transferee corporation shall be newly organized and its charter shall provide that its activities are confined exclusively to operating DUNKIN' DONUTS shops as licensed under this Agreement.

b. FRANCHISEE or, if FRANCHISEE is a partnership, the partners licensed herein to operate the franchise shall be the owner or owners of the majority stock interest of the transferee corporation.

c. FRANCHISEE or, if FRANCHISEE is a partnership, one of the partners licensed herein to operate the franchise shall be the principal executive officer of the corporation.

d. The transferee corporation and all shareholders of transferee corporation shall enter into a written assignment, under seal, in a form satisfactory to DUNKIN' DONUTS, with the transferee corporation assuming all of the FRANCHISEE's obligations under this Agreement.

e. All shareholders of the transferee corporation shall enter into a written agreement, in a form satisfactory to DUNKIN' DONUTS, jointly and severally guaranteeing the full payment and performance of the transferee corporation's obligations to DUNKIN' DONUTS.

f. Each stock certificate of the transferee corporation shall have conspicuously endorsed upon it a statement that it is held subject to, and that further assignment or transfer thereof is subject to, all restrictions imposed upon transfers by this Agreement; and

g. No new shares of common or preferred voting stock in the transferee corporation shall be issued to any person, persons, partnership, association or corporation without obtaining DUNKIN' DONUTS' prior written consent, which shall not unreasonably be withheld.

Transfer of Control

10. C.2. If a transfer, alone or together with other previous, simultaneous or proposed transfers, whether

related or unrelated, would have the effect of transferring an interest of fifty percent (50%) or more in the franchise licensed herein, or the entity holding such franchise, to someone other than an original signatory of this Agreement:

a. The transferee and each partner and shareholder of transferee must be a United States citizen or lawful resident alien of the United States and shall be of good moral character and reputation and shall have a good credit rating and business qualifications reasonably acceptable to DUNKIN' DONUTS. Such qualifications include, without limitation, literacy and fluency in the English language sufficient, in the good faith opinion of DUNKIN' DONUTS, to communicate with employees, customers, and suppliers of DUNKIN' DONUTS and to satisfactorily complete training at DDU. FRANCHISEE shall provide DUNKIN' DONUTS with such information as DUNKIN' DONUTS may require to make such determination concerning each such proposed transferee;

b. The transferee must designate two managers for the DUNKIN' DONUTS SHOP, one of whom must be a transferee or a partner or shareholder of the transferee. Prior to the transfer, both managers must successfully complete the DUNKIN' DONUTS training course then in effect for franchisees;

c. The transferee, including all shareholders and partners of the transferee, shall jointly and severally execute, on DUNKIN' DONUTS' then current forms, a Franchise Agreement and any other standard ancillary agreement, including without limitation a priority payment agreement, if applicable, with DUNKIN' DONUTS. The priority in payment agreement will provide, among other things, that if the transferee is unable at any time to make payments to the transferor for the purchase of the DUNKIN' DONUTS SHOP and to DUNKIN' DONUTS and/or its rental subsidiary under the Franchise Agreement and Lease, that payments to DUNKIN' DONUTS, the Fund, and DUNKIN' DONUTS' rental subsidiary will have priority. With respect to the then-current Franchisee Agreement, no greater percentages of the GROSS SALES than those required by Paragraphs 4.E. and 4.F. shall be required.

d. The transferor, and all individuals proposing to transfer an interest in the franchise, shall execute a general release under seal of all claims against DUNKIN' DONUTS and a priority in payment agreement, if applicable.

e. Unless a longer period is agreed upon by DUNKIN' DONUTS and the transferee, the term of the Franchise Agreement required pursuant to this subparagraph shall be for the unexpired term of this Agreement. Except in the instance that a period longer than the unexpired term of this Agreement is agreed upon by DUNKIN' DONUTS, transferee shall pay no INITIAL FRANCHISE FEE as provided in Paragraph 4 of this Agreement.

f. If transferee is a corporation:

(1) Each stock certificate of the transferee corporation shall have conspicuously endorsed upon it a statement that it is held subject to, and that further assignment or transfer thereof is subject to, all restrictions imposed upon transfers by this Agreement;

(2) No new shares of common or preferred voting stock in the transferee corporation shall be issued to any person, persons, partnership, association or corporation without obtaining DUNKIN' DONUTS' prior written consent; and

(3) All shareholders of the transferee corporation shall enter into a written agreement, in a form satisfactory to DUNKIN' DONUTS, jointly and severally guaranteeing the full payment and performance of the transferee corporation's obligations to DUNKIN' DONUTS.

Transfer Fee

g. FRANCHISEE shall have fully paid and satisfied all of FRANCHISEE's obligations to DUNKIN' DONUTS, the Fund, and DUNKIN' DONUTS' rental subsidiary and DUNKIN' DONUTS shall have been paid a Transfer Fee equal to the greater of Four Thousand Dollars ($4,000.00), increased by 5% compounded annually during the term of this Agreement and any renewal period, or:

(1) 5% of the Adjusted Sales Price of the DUNKIN' DONUTS SHOP if the sale takes place within three (3) years after the date on which FRANCHISEE opened the SHOP to the public (as a new shop), or the date on which FRANCHISEE acquired the SHOP (as a previously operated shop); or

(2) 3% of the Adjusted Sales Price of the DUNKIN' DONUTS SHOP if the sale takes place after three (3) years from the date on which FRANCHISEE opened the SHOP to the public (as a new shop), or the date on which FRANCHISEE acquired the SHOP (as a previously operated shop).

The Adjusted Sales Price shall include, without limitation, cash, assumption of debt, equipment lease obligations, and deferred financing and amounts allocated to property of every kind, nature and description: furniture, fixtures, signs, equipment, supplies and inventory; excluding only amounts reasonably allocated to land and building if owned by FRANCHISEE. It is intended that all consideration to be paid to FRANCHISEE, or for the benefit of FRANCHISEE, however designated and whether or not included in the Contract of Sale shall be deemed part of the Adjusted Sales Price including, but not by way of limitation, amounts allocated to a covenant not to compete or personal service agreement.

The Adjusted Sales Price shall be the Sales Price to be received by FRANCHISEE upon transfer of the DUNKIN' DONUTS SHOP less the amount paid by FRANCHISEE for the DUNKIN' DONUTS SHOP if purchased from another franchisee or from DUNKIN' DONUTS as a previously operated shop. No adjustment shall be made for amounts paid in connection with the development of a new DUNKIN' DONUTS shop.

DUNKIN' DONUTS will waive the five percent (5%) or three percent (3%) fee but not the fixed fee of $4,000 (subject to increase) in connection with transfer of the DUNKIN' DONUTS SHOP to FRANCHISEE'S spouse or one or more of FRANCHISEE'S children provided that, in DUNKIN' DONUTS' good faith opinion, FRANCHISEE has been in full compliance with the terms of all agreements with DUNKIN' DONUTS and its rental subsidiary. However, the Franchise Agreement issued to the spouse and/or children will be on the then-current form in use at the time of transfer including the then-current Transfer Fee provision.

For purposes of determining the correct Transfer Fee, DUNKIN' DONUTS reserves the right to reallocate amounts which FRANCHISEE and the transferee have allocated to land, building, equipment, covenant against competition, personal service agreement, or otherwise if, in the good faith opinion of DUNKIN' DONUTS, the allocation of the parties is unreasonable in relation to the value of the franchised business. If DUNKIN' DONUTS purchases the DUNKIN' DONUTS SHOP from FRANCHISEE by exercise of its right of first refusal under subparagraph 10.F. hereof, the Transfer Fee shall be payable by FRANCHISEE to DUNKIN' DONUTS as if FRANCHISEE had sold the franchised business to a third party.

h. Upon compliance with the aforesaid conditions and DUNKIN' DONUTS' approval of the transfer, FRANCHISEE and any shareholders or partners participating in said transfer shall, to the extent of the interest so transferred, thereupon be relieved of further obligations under the terms of this Agreement, except that FRANCHISEE and any former shareholders or partners of FRANCHISEE shall remain obligated for FRANCHISEE's money obligations under Paragraph 4., through the date of sale, and under the restrictive covenants contained in Paragraph 8., after the date of sale.

Transfer of Less than Control

10. C.3. If a transfer would have the effect of transferring an interest of forty-nine percent (49%) or less in the franchise licensed herein, or the entity holding such franchise, to someone other than an original signatory of this Agreement:

a. The transferee and each partner and shareholder of transferee must be a United States citizen or lawful resident alien of the United States and shall be of good moral character and reputation and shall have a good credit rating and business qualifications reasonably acceptable to DUNKIN' DONUTS. FRANCHISEE shall provide DUNKIN' DONUTS with such information as DUNKIN' DONUTS may require to make such determination concerning each such proposed transferee;

b. The transferee must designate two managers for the DUNKIN' DONUTS SHOP, one of whom must be a transferee or a partner or shareholder of the transferee. Prior to the transfer, both managers must successfully complete the DUNKIN' DONUTS training course then in effect for franchisees;

c. The transferee, including all shareholders and partners of the transferee, shall jointly and severally execute this Agreement and any other standard ancillary agreement, including without limitation a priority payment agreement, if applicable, with DUNKIN' DONUTS. The priority in payment agreement will provide, among other things, that if the transferee is unable at any time to make payments to the transferor for the purchase of the DUNKIN' DONUTS SHOP and to DUNKIN' DONUTS and/or its rental subsidiary under the Franchise Agreement and Lease, that payments to DUNKIN' DONUTS, the Fund, and DUNKIN' DONUTS' rental subsidiary will have priority.

d. The transferor and all individuals proposing to transfer an interest in the franchise, shall execute a general release under seal of all claims against DUNKIN' DONUTS and a priority in payment agreement, if applicable.

e. If transferee is a corporation:

(1) Each stock certificate of the transferee corporation shall have conspicuously endorsed upon it a statement that it is held subject to, and that further assignment or transfer thereof is subject to, all restrictions imposed upon transfers by this Agreement;

(2) No new shares of common or preferred voting stock in the transferee corporation shall be issued to any person, persons, partnership, association or corporation without obtaining DUNKIN' DONUTS' prior written consent; and

(3) All shareholders of the transferee corporation shall enter into a written agreement, in a form satisfactory to DUNKIN' DONUTS, jointly and severally guaranteeing the full payment and performance of the transferee corporation's obligations to DUNKIN' DONUTS.

f. Upon compliance with the aforesaid conditions and DUNKIN' DONUTS' approval of the transfer, FRANCHISEE and any shareholders or partners participating in said transfer shall, to the extent of the interest so transferred, thereupon be relieved of further obligations under the terms of this Agreement, except that FRANCHISEE and any former shareholders or partners of FRANCHISEE shall remain obligated for FRANCHISEE's money obligations under Paragraph 4., through the date of sale, and under the restrictive covenants contained in Paragraph 8., after the date of sale.

Transfer on Death

10. D. In the event of the death of FRANCHISEE, or any partner or shareholder thereof at any time during the term of this Agreement, the legal representative of FRANCHISEE, partner or shareholder, together with all surviving partners or shareholders, if any, jointly, shall, within three (3) months of such event apply, in writing, for the right to transfer the franchise, or the interest of the deceased partner or shareholder in such franchise, to such person or persons as the legal representative may specify. Such transfer shall be approved by DUNKIN' DONUTS upon the fulfillment of all of the conditions set forth in Paragraph 10.C.2. or 10.C.3. (as applicable) of this Agreement, except that no transfer fee shall be required if the transferee is a beneficiary or heir of FRANCHISEE.

10. E. If the legal representative and all surviving partners or shareholders, if any, do not comply with the aforesaid provisions of Paragraph 10. or do not propose a transferee acceptable to DUNKIN' DONUTS under the

standards set forth in Paragraph 10.C.2. and 10.C.3., all rights licensed to FRANCHISEE under this Agreement shall terminate forthwith and automatically revert to DUNKIN' DONUTS. DUNKIN' DONUTS shall have the right and option, exercisable upon such termination, to purchase all furniture, fixtures, signs, equipment and other chattels at a price to be agreed upon by the parties or, if no agreement as to price is reached by the parties, at such price as may be determined by a qualified appraiser, approved by both parties, such approval not to be unreasonably withheld. DUNKIN' DONUTS shall give notice of its intent to exercise said option no later than twenty-one (21) days prior to termination.

Right of First Refusal

10. F. If FRANCHISEE, or any shareholder or partner thereof, has received and desires to accept a signed, bona fide written offer from a third party to purchase FRANCHISEE's franchise or shareholder's or partner's interest in the franchise, FRANCHISEE or such shareholder or partner shall notify and provide DUNKIN' DONUTS with a copy of such offer, and DUNKIN' DONUTS shall have the right and option, exercisable within forty-five (45) days after its receipt of a copy of the offer to purchase FRANCHISEE'S franchise, or such shareholder's or partner's interest in the franchise, on the same terms and conditions as offered by said third party. DUNKIN' DONUTS' exercise of its right to purchase FRANCHISEE's franchise hereunder shall not relieve FRANCHISEE of its transfer fee obligation to DUNKIN' DONUTS under Paragraph 10.C.2.g. Should DUNKIN' DONUTS not exercise this option and the terms of the unaccepted offer be altered, DUNKIN' DONUTS shall, in each instance, be notified of the changed offer and shall again have forty-five (45) days to purchase on the altered terms. Should DUNKIN' DONUTS not exercise this option and the terms of the unaccepted offer be altered, DUNKIN' DONUTS shall, in each instance, be notified of the changed offer and shall again have forty-five (45) days to purchase on the altered terms. Should DUNKIN' DONUTS not exercise this option, the terms of Paragraph 10.C.2. and 10.C.3. (as applicable) shall apply to any transfer which may be contemplated.

Relationship of Parties

11. A. This Agreement does not constitute FRANCHISEE an agent, legal representative, joint venturer, partner, employee or servant of DUNKIN' DONUTS or its subsidiary for any purpose whatsoever; and it is

deemed understood between the parties hereto that FRANCHISEE shall be an independent contractor and is in no way authorized to make any contract, agreement, warranty or representation on behalf of DUNKIN' DONUTS or its subsidiary or to create any obligation, express or implied, on behalf of DUNKIN' DONUTS or its subsidiary. The parties agree that this Agreement does not create a fiduciary relationship between DUNKIN' DONUTS or its subsidiary and FRANCHISEE.

11. B. Under no circumstances shall DUNKIN' DONUTS or FRANCHISEE be liable for any act, omission, debt or any other obligation of the other. Each party shall indemnify and save the other harmless against any such claim and the cost of defending against such claims arising directly or indirectly from, or as a result of, or in connection with, FRANCHISEE's operation of the DUNKIN' DONUTS SHOP.

Non-Waiver

12. No failure of DUNKIN' DONUTS to exercise any power reserved to it hereunder, or to insist upon strict compliance by FRANCHISEE with any obligation or condition hereunder, and no custom or practice of the parties in variance with the terms hereof, shall constitute a waiver of DUNKIN' DONUTS' right to demand strict compliance with the terms hereof. Waiver by DUNKIN' DONUTS of any particular default by FRANCHISEE shall not affect or impair DUNKIN' DONUTS' right in respect to any subsequent default of the same or of a different nature; nor shall any delay, waiver, forbearance or omission of DUNKIN' DONUTS to exercise any power or rights arising out of any breach or default by FRANCHISEE of any of the terms, provisions or covenants hereof affect or impair DUNKIN' DONUTS' rights, nor shall such constitute a waiver by DUNKIN' DONUTS of any right hereunder or of the right to declare any subsequent breach or default. Subsequent acceptance by DUNKIN' DONUTS of the payments due to it hereunder shall not be deemed to be a waiver by DUNKIN' DONUTS of any preceding breach by FRANCHISEE of any terms, covenants or conditions of this Agreement. Acceptance by DUNKIN' DONUTS of payments due it hereunder from any person or entity other than FRANCHISEE shall be deemed to be acceptance from such person or entity as an agent of FRANCHISEE and not as recognition of such person or entity as an assignee or successor to FRANCHISEE.

Notices

13. All notices hereunder by DUNKIN' DONUTS to FRANCHISEE shall at DUNKIN' DONUTS' option be personally delivered or sent by telecopier, or prepaid private courier, or certified mail to the FRANCHISEE at the address set forth below or at such other address as FRANCHISEE may from time to time give notice of to DUNKIN' DONUTS. All notices hereunder by FRANCHISEE to DUNKIN' DONUTS shall be sent by certified mail to DUNKIN' DONUTS INCORPORATED, Post Office Box 317, Randolph, Massachusetts 02368, Attn: Senior Vice President and General Counsel or at such other address as DUNKIN' DONUTS may from time to time give notice of to FRANCHISEE.

To FRANCHISEE: _____

Entire Agreement

14. A. This Agreement, and the documents referred to herein shall be the entire, full and complete agreement between DUNKIN' DONUTS and FRANCHISEE concerning the subject matter hereof, and supersedes all prior agreements, no other representation having induced FRANCHISEE to execute this Agreement; and there are no representations, inducements, promises or agreements, oral or otherwise, between the parties not embodied herein, which are of any force or effect with reference to this Agreement or otherwise. No amendment, change or variance from this Agreement shall be binding on either party unless executed in writing.

14. B. The success of the business venture contemplated to be undertaken by FRANCHISEE by virtue of this Agreement is speculative and depends, to a large extent, upon the ability of FRANCHISEE as an independent businessman, as well as other factors. DUNKIN' DONUTS does not make any representations or warranty as to the potential success of the business venture contemplated hereby. FRANCHISEE acknowledges that it has entered into this Agreement after making an independent investigation of DUNKIN' DONUTS' operations, and not upon any representation as to profits which FRANCHISEE in particular might be expected to realize, nor has anyone made any other representation which is not expressly set forth herein, to induce FRANCHISEE to accept this franchise and execute this Agreement.

14. C. Captions, paragraph and subparagraph designations and section headings are included in this Agreement for convenience only, and in no way do they define, limit, construe or describe the scope or intent of the respective parts of this Agreement.

Severability

15. Each section, part, term and provision of this Agreement shall be considered severable, and if, for

any reason, any section, part, term or provision herein is determined to be invalid and contrary to, or in conflict with, any existing or future law or regulation of a court or agency having valid jurisdiction, such shall not impair the operation or affect the remaining portions, sections, parts, terms or provisions of this Agreement, and the latter will continue to be given full force and effect and bind the parties hereto; and said invalid section, part, term or provision shall be deemed not to be a part of this Agreement.

Applicable Law

16. A. This Agreement shall be interpreted, construed and governed by the laws of the Commonwealth of Massachusetts.

16. B. Nothing herein contained shall bar the right of either party to obtain injunctive relief against threatened conduct that will cause loss or damages, under the usual equity rules, including the applicable rules for obtaining preliminary injunctions.

IN WITNESS WHEREOF the parties hereto, intending to be legally bound hereby, have duly executed, sealed and delivered this Agreement in triplicate the day and year first written above. FRANCHISEE acknowledges receipt of this Franchise Agreement, together with any amendments, at least five (5) days prior to the date hereof.

ATTEST/WITNESS:

_____ FRANCHISEE

_____ By _____

_____ FRANCHISEE

_____ FRANCHISEE

_____ FRANCHISEE

ATTEST: FRANCHISEE
DUNKIN' DONUTS INCORPORATED FRANCHISOR

_____ By _____
Secretary   Vice President

PERSONAL GUARANTEE OF OFFICERS, SHAREHOLDERS AND DIRECTORS OF A CORPORATION

We, the undersigned officers, directors and/or shareholders of one hundred (100%) percent of the original issue of capital stock of _____ a corporation organized under the laws of the state of [_____] waiving demand and notice, hereby, jointly and severally, personally guarantee the full payment of the corporation's money obligations under Paragraph 4, and performance of the corporation's other obligations under this Franchise Agreement, including Paragraph 8 in its entirety relative to the restrictions on the activities of FRANCHISEE and personally agree that said Paragraphs shall be binding on each of us personally, as if each of us were FRANCHISEE.

The undersigned, jointly and severally, agree that DUNKIN' DONUTS may, without notice to or consent of the undersigned, (a) extend, in whole or in part, the time for payment of the corporation's money obligations under Paragraph 4; (b) modify, with the consent of the corporation, its money or other obligations hereunder; and/or (c) settle, waive or compromise any claim of DUNKIN' DONUTS against FRANCHISEE or any of the undersigned, all without in any way affecting the personal guarantee of the undersigned.

This Guarantee is intended to take effect as a sealed instrument.

Signed in the presence of:

_____ Witness   _____ Individually

_____ Witness   _____ Individually

_____ Witness   _____ Individually

_____ Witness   _____ Individually

_____ Witness   _____ Individually

CHAPTER 17

Marketing Channels for Services

LEARNING OBJECTIVES

After reading this chapter you should:

1. Recognize the importance of services as a major and rapidly growing sector of the U.S. economy.
2. Realize that the basic objectives of both product marketing and service marketing are the same.
3. Understand the five characteristics of services that distinguish them from products.
4. Know how marketing channels can be instrumental in tangibilizing services.
5. Be cognizant of the problems presented by the inseparability of services and the difficulties of standardizing services for channel design and management.
6. Be sensitive to the need for customer involvement in many services.
7. Have an awareness of how the perishability of services affects channel strategy, design and management.
8. Be familiar with some additional perspectives on marketing channels for services so as to recognize possible relationships between services and marketing channels.

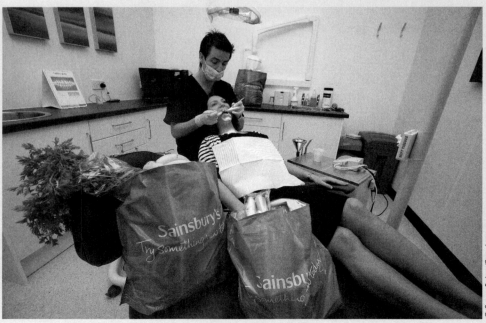

© George Furlong/Getty Images

FOCUS ON CHANNELS

Dental Services in a Supermarket?

For well over half a century supermarkets have provided the main marketing channel for making food available to customers in developed countries all over the world. Over the years, supermarkets have been adding more and more general merchandise items such as cookware, light bulbs, magazines, greeting cards, and many other items to help offset the low margins on most grocery items and to make more efficient use of space. Some supermarkets have also added services, such as bank branches to the mix. But one particular supermarket chain, British giant Sainsbury's, has decided to push the envelope of diversification much farther along by providing dental services in one of its supermarkets in Manchester. While still in the trial stage, if this supermarket channel for providing dental care catches on, Sainsbury's plans to open at least 50 more dental offices in supermarkets all over England.

The prototype dental office in the Manchester supermarket will be run by a local dentist, and the office will be open to service clients during regular store hours including evenings and weekends. The fees charged will be comparable to or less than those charged by Britain's national health service. A dental check-up, for example, will cost the equivalent of $29 U.S.

Sainsbury's doesn't think its supermarket-based marketing channel for delivering dental services will make going to the dentist fun but it can certainly make it more convenient. But will having a dental office in the same store as the candy aisle encourage consumers to put less of those sugary items in their shopping carts? Hardly likely. The British are famous for their sweet tooth. So, even if customers filling their shopping carts with sweets means more fillings in their teeth, they won't have to go very far to find a dentist!

Source: Based on: Ali McConnon, "Root Canal? Try Aisle Five," *Business Week* (October 13, 2008): 16.

The array of services used by consumers is phenomenally diverse, ranging from brain surgery to shoe shines.[1] In between these extremes are services provided by hotels, auto repair shops, barbers, house painters, bankers, entertainers, insurance agencies and thousands of others.

A great deal of attention has been focused on services in recent years because they account for a major part of the economy.[2] The service sector of the U.S. economy is more than twice the size of the manufacturing sector. Moreover, service sector firms account for about two-thirds of gross domestic product and employ more than four out of every five private sector workers in the United States[3]

Given the tremendous and growing importance of services, the attention being given to marketing them is not surprising.[4] Any organization or individual offering a service stands a better chance of being successful if the services offered are targeted to meet customer demand and presented to customers so as to maximize their appeal. In terms of meeting these two basic objectives—that is, being in tune with customer demand and enhancing customer appeal—the marketing of services is the same as the marketing of products. However, because services differ from products in several significant ways, the *approach* and *emphasis* used in the marketing of services are often different.[5] The difference can apply to all four of the basic strategic components of the marketing mix: product strategy, price strategy, promotional strategy and distribution strategy.[6]

Throughout this text our emphasis, of course, has been on the distribution component of the marketing mix. Hence, our discussion in this chapter will focus specifically on the role of distribution in the marketing of services. After discussing the key characteristics of services that distinguish them from products, we will examine how marketing channel strategy, design and management relate to each of these special characteristics of services and will then discuss some additional perspectives on the relationship between services and marketing channels.

Special Characteristics of Services

Five characteristics distinguishing services from products have been emphasized in the literature of services marketing. These are (1) the intangibility of services, (2) the inseparability of services from service providers, (3) the difficulty of standardizing services, (4) the high degree of customer involvement in services, and (5) the perishability of services.

Intangibility of Services

In general, services are much less tangible than physical products. An automobile is a visible product that the consumer can see, touch, sit in and drive. Services, such as insurance on the automobile or a tune-up of the engine, while not unnoticed by the consumer, do not have the same degree of tangibility. Consumers are likely to have much more definite impressions and preferences about particular automobiles than they do about auto insurance and tune-ups. Moreover, from the producer's point of view, it is probably easier to differentiate one brand of automobile from another through product features, style, or performance characteristics than it is to differentiate auto insurance or tune-up services. Style, visible features, and performance characteristics are not available to the service producer to nearly the same degree as they are to the producer of products.

Inseparability of Services

When a manufacturer produces a product, whether it is a jumbo jet or a toothpick, a physical entity is created that exists apart from the manufacturer itself. In a very real sense, the product has a "life" or a "personality" of its own on which it can be judged by the potential customer completely apart from the firm that produced it. By contrast, most services are inextricably tied to the providers of the service, and the services produced do not exist as physical entities in and of themselves. Thus the service provided by a dentist is the direct result of the training and skill of that particular dentist. The work does not exist apart from him or her. The same could be said for a house painter, airline pilot, lawyer or marriage counselor. Although some of their results may possess a degree of tangibility—the filling in a tooth, the paint on the house, the completed flight and so on—the services provided in all of these cases are still much more closely tied to the service providers than would be the case for the anonymous workers who make products.[7]

Difficulty of Standardization

A primary hallmark of products manufactured by an advanced industrial society is the high degree of standardization. The consumer buying a manufacturer's product expects that his or her product will be the same as the thousands or even millions of others of the same model.

In the production of services, however, achieving the levels of standardization so common in mass-produced products is much more difficult. Because so many services are people-intensive and, as we pointed out earlier, are inextricably tied to the people providing them, the variability associated with the human element is much more likely to creep into the production of services than into the production of products. In fact, even the same person providing a service can show substantial variability from one performance to the next during time period of as little as an hour. A hairstylist, for example, may provide three or four haircuts in the course of one hour that vary in quality based on the stylist's mood or degree of concentration. While a reasonably high degree of standardization may be possible for routine or simple services, such as the quick oil changes pioneered by Jiffy Lube or automatic car washes that rely mainly on machines rather than people, high-level services such as medical care, legal advice, computer systems design and maintenance, and all the others that rely on large doses of human skill are difficult if not impossible to standardize to the same degree as products.

Customer Involvement in Services

Except in the case of custom-made products, consumers do not as individuals play much of a role in determining the nature of the products manufactured for them. A consumer buying a can of Campbell's chicken noodle soup has not specified the characteristics of the product. Essentially, the consumer is involved only with the consumption of the product, not its creation.

In contrast, involvement by the consumer in the production of a service is often greater than for a product. For example, an accounting firm will often make extensive use of client input regarding what the client is looking for in the service. Even the services provided by fast-food restaurants may allow choices, such as whether the customer wants a hamburger with or without onions, mustard, lettuce, tomatoes, and pickles.

Perishability of Services

Services cannot be produced ahead of or in anticipation of customer needs and then stored in inventory until purchased. A rock concert given in a stadium with 60,000 seats that sells only 50,000 tickets cannot save the 10,000 unsold seats to sell at another time. The 10,000 unsold seats are lost for all time.[8] Similarly, unsold airline seats, hotel stays, and TV or radio air time for advertising are far more perishable than even such delicate products as vegetables, fruits or avant-garde fashions. These products can be inventoried for a short time if care is used, and may still have some salvage value even if not in peak condition or up-to-the-minute style. But the unsold services cannot be stored even for a few minutes and the salvage value of an unsold service is zero.

Implications of Service Characteristics for Channel Management

The special characteristics of services just discussed are not simply academic distinctions that can be pointed out and then forgotten. On the contrary, in many cases these special characteristics have significant implications for all areas of marketing management, including channel management, especially the formulation of channel strategy, designing the channel, managing the channel, and in some cases evaluating channel member performance.[9] Table 17.1, for example, lists a number of implications for services offered at the retail level.

In this section we will discuss some of the major implications for channel management of each of the five special service characteristics. Our purpose is not to be exhaustive but rather to provide some illustrative examples to foster a measure of sensitivity to the potential relationships between the characteristics of services and the management of marketing channels.[10]

Intangibility and Channel Management

The intangibility of services, which as we pointed out earlier makes them more difficult to differentiate than products, requires marketers to be more imaginative in order to successfully distinguish their services from those of competitors. From a marketing mix standpoint, the service producer can attempt to use product strategy to make the service more tangible—that is, by attempting to associate the service with some image or object, it can be made more concrete. The pair of hands used by Allstate Insurance with its motto "You're in good hands with Allstate" is an attempt to embody the concept of security provided by its insurance services. The bars of soap, shampoo and shoe-shine cloths offered by hotels to their customers are an attempt to use objects as a tangible manifestation of the careful attention given to customers' every need. Price and promotion can also be used to represent the service in a more material form. A high price for a service can convey quality, or an advertisement might help potential customers visualize the service in a more tangible way. For instance, ads used by plastic surgeons showing women or men with perfect figures imply that the service will do the same for new clients.

How a service is actually offered to customers—that is, the marketing channels through which it is sold—can provide the most direct and potent basis for tangibilizing the service and hence can create a stronger basis for differentiating it from competitors' services,[11] because the customer is directly exposed to and experiences the service provided by the channel. Consider the case of Residence Inn by Marriott. This division of Marriott Corporation specializes in providing accommodations on a long-term basis; that is, from five days to six months or even longer. The key to selling this service,

TABLE 17.1 IMPLICATIONS FOR SERVICE RETAILING IN SEVEN MANAGEMENT AREAS

SERVICES AS COMPARED TO GOODS	MANAGERIAL CHANGES NEEDED FOR SERVICES RETAILING
A. Measuring Performance	
Capital expenditures vary widely for different services.	Return on net worth may not be the most important measurement of the value of a service to the retailer.
Little or no inventories are required to offer services.	Turnover, markdown controls, and other goods-related controls are not appropriate.
Labor costs are higher.	Profit after labor costs replaces the gross margin of goods retailing.
Some services support the sale of goods.	Sales-supporting services should be evaluated differently from revenue-producing services.
Cost accounting is more important.	Job-specific records will be required to assess the profitability of each sale.
B. Store Organization	
Supervision is more specialized.	Separate management for service areas will be required.
Search for service employees is more specific.	Nontraditional sources for identification of employees must be used.
Employee turnover is lower.	Frequent salary and performance reviews must be carried out.
Pay is higher for skilled craftspeople than for merchandising personnel.	Pay levels will need to be adjusted upward over periods of longevity for service employees.
C. Service Production	
Involvement in manufacturing of the service is greater.	Production skills will need to be obtained by supervisors.
Emphasis on quality control is greater.	Supervisors must be able to assess the quality of a service performed for a customer.
Need to monitor consumer satisfaction is greater.	Research with prior customers is needed to measure their satisfaction with the service.
Need to refine scheduling of employees is greater.	Maximizing the service employees' time requires matching consumer purchasing to ability to produce the service.
Quality must be consistent among all outlets.	Standards for consistency of the service must be established and continually evaluated; central training may be required for craft workers in multiple branch operations.
D. Pricing	
Services vary in cost; therefore, pricing is more difficult.	Prices may be quoted within a range instead of an exact figure before the purchase.
More difficulties occur in price competition or promotion based on price.	Services should be promoted on the basis of criteria other than price.
E. Sales Promotion	
Value is more difficult for consumers to determine.	Consumers need to be convinced of value through personal selling.
Service availability is difficult to display within store.	In-store signing or a service center is required to notify customers of service availability.
Visual presentation is more important.	Before-and-after photographs may be possible with some services. Testimonials may be possible with other services.
Cross-selling with goods is important.	A quota or bonus for goods salespersons who suggest services will lead to increased service selling.
Catalog advertising is more difficult.	Conditions for the sale and away-from-the-store performance must be specified.
F. Complaints	
Returning a service is more difficult.	Policies must be established for adjusting the service purchased with a dissatisfied customer.
A customer is more sensitive about services involving the person.	Specific guarantees and policies about adjustments must be established; new types of insurance must be added to cover liabilities.
G. Controls	
Opportunity to steal customers is greater.	Employee assurance of loyalty must be established. Protection of store loyalty must be obtained.

Source: This was adapted from J. Patrick Kelly and William R. George, "Strategic Management Issues for the Retailing of Services," *Journal of Retailing* (June 1982): 40–43, Copyright © 1982 by Elsevier. Reproduced by permission.

according to company officials, is to provide a kind of hotel service different from that typically offered by hotels used to providing accommodations for stays of two or three days. In particular, a "homey" atmosphere conveys to customers the feeling that they are *living* at Residence Inns rather than simply staying there. To accomplish this, the division has designed a variety of service delivery features to foster the feeling of being at home. For example, all accommodations are suites of several rooms with furnishings that include sofas and chairs, rather than single or double rooms with beds. These suites provide about 20 percent more space than rooms offered even by luxury hotels. All of the suites have full-service kitchens complete with pots, pans and dishes so that residents can cook a meal just as if they were at home. Residence Inns even offer a grocery shopping service whereby residents can leave a grocery list at the front desk in the morning and find the kitchen shelves and the refrigerator stocked by the time they return in the evening. To complete the homelike environment, many of the suites have fully operating fireplaces. Yet even with all these "homey" amenities, Residence-Inn by Marriott still offers all of the features needed to conduct business including high speed Internet service in all suites as well as a complete business center at all locations.

Clearly, the Residence Inn division recognizes the importance of creating tangible benefits for customers through careful attention to how service is presented to customers at the end point of the marketing channel.

Inseparability and Channel Management

Because services do not exist apart from the provider of the service, the service and the channel providing it are virtually inseparable. When consumers go to an automobile service station to get an oil change, or to the bank to make a deposit, or to the dry cleaner to have shirts laundered, the channels with which they interact are the manifestations of the service provided. All aspects of the marketing channel with which the consumer comes in contact are thus a reflection of the quality of the service.

This can include a host of factors. For example, important aspects of the physical facilities include access, parking, external signs, appearance of the building exterior, and the interior décor, lighting, climate control, fixtures, and cleanliness. Consider, for example, a fitness center that is easy to reach, has convenient parking, a well-manicured exterior lawn, up-to-date and well-maintained fitness equipment, quality carpeting, indirect lighting and is immaculately clean. Contrast this with another fitness center that is difficult to get to, offers few parking spaces, and has an ugly exterior. Inside, the equipment looks old and poorly maintained, the lighting is harsh, and the place looks and feels grimy. Obviously, consumer perceptions about the quality of service offered by the two fitness centers are likely to be very different.

Perhaps even more important than physical facilities are the people who come into direct contact with customers. If the staff at the more upscale fitness center is not knowledgeable, appears distant, and insensitive to client concerns, the initial favorable impression given by the good physical facilities could be very quickly undermined. On the other hand, even the more downscale fitness center with its inferior physical facilities could be offset at least to some degree by a staff that is knowledgeable, friendly, and goes out of its way to be helpful to clients. Of course, the best situation is one in which both facilities and people are at a level that will reflect on the service in the most positive way possible.

The importance of these physical and human factors cannot be overemphasized. At the point of contact between customer and service provider, the service and the channel *are the same thing* from the standpoint of consumer perceptions.[12] When an air traveler has to stand in a long line to check in, steps into a plane that is dirty, and is treated poorly by the flight attendants, no amount of clever image-building advertising by the airline about the quality of its service is likely to counteract the negative experience.[13]

So, in making services available to customers through marketing channels, the inseparability of services from the provider means that the service provider does not have the "safety net" available to the product manufacturer, whereby the product itself can make up for poor distribution. If the channel does not do its job well, the service will not be received well by the customer.[14]

Difficulty of Standardization and Channel Management

Any provider of services who achieves a level of service capable of satisfying its target customers would like to be able to duplicate that performance throughout all of its units at any given time as well as to repeat the performance over time. Holiday Inns Inc. captured this concept perfectly with its famous slogan, "The best surprise is no surprise." This means that its goal is to provide a consistent level of service at all of its hotels, anywhere in the world, so that customers will never be surprised by variations in service from one hotel to the next. Holiday Inns defines its service in terms of a set of standards that all of its units are required to meet.

Although attaining absolute perfection in the standardization of services is a theoretical ideal not achievable in the real world, organizations can still attempt to achieve the maximum possible consistency so as to at least approach that ideal. For multiple-unit service organizations when the units are independently owned, as in a franchise organization, it is through effective channel management that the ideal of perfect service standardization is pursued. However, getting each independent business unit to deliver a consistent level of service is somewhat analogous to the product manufacturer attempting to obtain all-out selling effort and support for its products from all of its channel members. This is a formidable challenge in the case of product marketing; it is even more so in a services marketing context because of the high human element so often involved in providing services. Thus, even though a franchisor can require its franchisees to build virtually identical outlets all over the country or even around the world, to get them to *behave* the same way in every outlet is much more difficult. Some may be more capable than others, some may be more or less highly motivated, and some will have different opinions from the franchisor about how their businesses should be run. Such divergencies can be a help or a hindrance in providing service to customers, depending on whether the franchisees' wavering from the franchisor's standards results in better or poorer service.

Customer Involvement and Channel Management

While not true for all services, many services do require a fair degree of involvement by the customer. Obvious examples include the services of barbers, fitness clubs, tax preparers, home decorators, and health care providers. Their services generally require input from the customer in order to be performed successfully.

A channel designed to provide these and other services requiring customer input should attempt to facilitate customer involvement. For example, astute salons provide plenty of mirrors for customers to see what is going on as their hair is being cut, and stylists make a special effort to seek customers' views on how they would like their hair cut. Modern fitness clubs often do individual workups to assess each customer's overall physical condition and then provide computerized fitness programs of weight and aerobic exercises to improve the customer's fitness level. In the field of healthcare, firms such as Healthpoint Technologies, Inc. have developed machines for providing basic healthcare services to consumers while they are shopping, exercising, or working. One of the company's machines called the Vita-Stat (see Figure 17.1) provides accurate blood pressure, weight and other health information such as heart rate and 30-day average blood pressure readings. This and other models can be placed in many different kinds of

FIGURE 17.1
Vita-Stat Machine for Do-It-Yourself Healthcare Diagnostics Service Channels

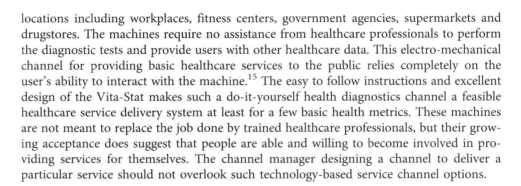

Model 90555

Vita-Stat's/E Model 90555 is a blood pressure, weight and health information center.

Health tracking...

- *Data retention capability allows computerized tracking of readings.*
- *Stores up to 20 readings using confidential identification and PIN.*
- *Optional built-in printer provides hardcopy record.*

Informative...

- *Measures blood pressure, heart rate and weight.*
- *Calculates 30-day average blood pressure.*
- *Library of health topics covers high blood pressure, diet, weight and exercise.*

User friendly...

- *Full color interactive display monitor indicates level of hypertension in graphical format.*
- *Swing-out locking seat for easy wheelchair access.*
- *All measurments taken in the seated position.*

Vita-Stat Æ blood pressure monitors are designed to meet the special needs of environments with high ambient noise and high volume. They are widely used in workplace wellness centers, health clinics, hospital outreach programs, military recreation centers and governmental agencies.

locations including workplaces, fitness centers, government agencies, supermarkets and drugstores. The machines require no assistance from healthcare professionals to perform the diagnostic tests and provide users with other healthcare data. This electro-mechanical channel for providing basic healthcare services to the public relies completely on the user's ability to interact with the machine.[15] The easy to follow instructions and excellent design of the Vita-Stat makes such a do-it-yourself health diagnostics channel a feasible healthcare service delivery system at least for a few basic health metrics. These machines are not meant to replace the job done by trained healthcare professionals, but their growing acceptance does suggest that people are able and willing to become involved in providing services for themselves. The channel manager designing a channel to deliver a particular service should not overlook such technology-based service channel options.

Perishability of Services and Channel Management

The main implication of the perishability of services for channel management is straightforward: The channel should be designed to maximize the sale of a service during its limited exposure to the target market. The reason, as mentioned earlier, is that unsold services cannot be packed up and put away to sell on another day, as is the case with most products. Thus maximum exposure even to the point of overkill is the watchword in developing channels for services—whether the services involve seats on an airliner, beds in a hospital, tickets to a concert, or appointments with the dentist or beautician. In short, the channel must be designed so as to connect as efficiently as possible those providing the service with those desiring to obtain it. The specific channel structure needed to accomplish this will, of course vary depending on the nature of the service being offered. For example, even with the dramatic growth of Internet-based online ticket sales, airlines still make extensive use of independent travel agents in their channel structures to maximize the exposure of their service to the traveling public. For example, even with the heavy emphasis by the airline and hotel industries to sell tickets and lodging directly to consumers via the Internet, they still make extensive use of indirect channels to maximize sales. Online travel agencies such as Priceline.com, Hotwire, Orbitz, Expedia, Travelocity, and numerous others are used extensively to reach more customers and even "old-fashioned," land-based travel agents still play an important role in the channels used by airlines and hotels.[16] In the broader travel and leisure industry including airlines, hotels, cruises, and tour operators, multiple channels that use both online and traditional travel agents are still employed extensively. Even for business travel, online and conventional travel agents participate extensively in business-to-business channels for business travel. Indeed, in recent years, many in-house, corporate travel departments have been replaced by online travel agencies. For example, ORBITZ FOR BUSINESS, a division of online travel agency ORBITZ, offers an extensive array of services for the business travel market via its online channels.

Additional Perspectives on Marketing Channels for Services

The preceding discussion focused on what are generally recognized as the key distinguishing characteristics of services and some basic implications of these distinctions for channel management.

We now turn our attention to some additional characteristics of services marketing that, though perhaps not as generally recognized as the five already discussed, are nevertheless important in developing and operating marketing channels for services.

Shorter Channels

As a general rule, marketing channels for services tend to be shorter than channels for products. In many cases the service channel is direct from service provider to user, as shown in Figure 17.2. In fact, this channel structure is typical of most small, independent service providers across a wide spectrum of services. Doctors, dentists, lawyers, accountants, barbers, auto mechanics, architects, shoe repairers, dry cleaners and a host of other independent professional and business people use the channel structure shown in the figure.

Given the absence of intermediaries in these direct structures, the channel management issues associated with interorganizational management discussed throughout this text do not arise.[17] Thus the direct structure eliminates the challenge of designing an appropriate channel structure in terms of length, intensity and type of intermediaries at each level (see Chapter 6); the selection of intermediaries (see Chapter 7); and the need to motivate intermediaries to do an effective job of selling the product (see Chapter 9). Nevertheless, all of the target market issues associated with channel design (see Chapter 8) must be faced. These issues include where to locate service facilities (market geography), how large the facilities should be to meet demand (market size), and whether sufficient numbers of customers will be within range of the service (market density), as well as when, where, how, and who will use the services (market behavior). Manufacturers design channels that use intermediaries at the wholesale and/or retail levels. Service producers, who are, in effect, manufacturers and retailers combined, have to address these issues

FIGURE 17.2
**Typical Channel
Structure Length for
Service Channel**

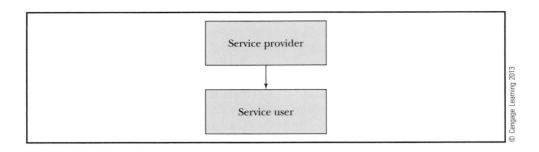

© Cengage Learning 2013

themselves.[18] Thus, independent service providers must still design channels at the retail level that make their services conveniently available to their target markets.[19]

Large-scale service providers offering a wide variety of services may have short channel structures even though they have many outlets. This is the case when the units are company owned rather than independent businesses. Here again, the issues associated with interorganizational management of independent intermediaries are not a consideration. Consider, for example, the case of Charles Schwab & Company, the nation's largest and best-known discount brokerage house. Schwab has more than 300 company-owned retail brokerage offices located in major markets throughout the United States as well as a branch in Puerto Rico and London. All of the people in these offices are Schwab employees subject to the direct authority and control of the home office. Interorganizational management is not needed. Like small independent service providers, however, large service organizations with many units still face all of the issues associated with designing channels to meet the needs of target markets.[20] In a large-scale organization serving many diverse market locations, this is, of course, a much more complicated task than would be the case for the single unit service provider that is no different in concept. In the case of Schwab, for example, even though all of the branches are company-owned, the challenge of making sure that the branches are providing high levels of service to clients still needs to be met. Further, coordinating the different channels used by Schwab to reach its customers also needs to be addressed. Clients can walk into one of Schwab's branch offices, talk to a Schwab representative by phone, log onto Schwab's Web site or utilize Schwab's newest mobile channel via iPhone or Android smartphones.[21] Regardless of which channel or channels clients decide to use, assuring a good client experience in each channel and a "seamless" experience across channels still requires effective channel management even though Schwab's channels have no independent intermediaries.

Franchise Channels

When channels involving the use of independent intermediaries are used in providing services, they often are franchise channels stressing the **business format** approach to franchising (see Chapter 16). As we discussed in Chapter 16, this form of franchising is characterized by a close business relationship between franchisor and franchisee that includes not only the product, service, and trademark, but the entire business format itself, including marketing strategy, training, merchandising management, operating manuals and standards, quality control and continuing two-way communications. Such franchised channels exist for a wide range of services, including real estate sales, automotive repairs, lodging, recreation, rentals, educational services, restaurants, dry cleaning, business services and even hospitals.[22]

The widespread use of business format franchises in many marketing channels for services is not surprising. It represents an attempt to deal with one of the main characteristic problems of providing services, as mentioned earlier—the difficulty of standardizing services. By using business format franchising as the underlying basis of the channel relationship, a service provider has the potential to reap the benefits of both the scale economies of a large organization and the entrepreneurial drive and motivation associated with independently owned businesses, while still attaining the degree of control necessary to foster standardization in services offered by the independent franchise units.[23] Indeed, the essence of modern business format franchising is a complete framework and set of specifications that the franchisor provides for operating the business. Consequently, when franchisees sign up with a franchisor they are not expected to provide a service their way but rather the franchisor's way, as spelled out in the formal franchise contract and under close supervision by the franchisor.

In essence, then, franchising offers a powerful tool for overcoming the problem of service standardization in large multiunit service organizations when the units are independently owned.[24] As we pointed out earlier, the ideal of perfect standardization of services among all units is not totally achievable in practice. Even with the most ironclad franchise agreements and intense supervision, the franchisor cannot totally control inconsistencies based on human differences and changing circumstances.[25] Nevertheless, for the firm seeking to provide almost any kind of service at a high (though not perfect) level of consistency on a large scale, franchising may provide the best opportunity to do so.

Customization of Services

Products made to fit individualized customer needs are relatively rare in consumer markets and even in industrial markets. Although there are numerous exceptions, most products are not custom-made but rather are mass-produced to meet the needs of relatively large market segments. Even when choice is involved, as in selecting the colors and options for an automobile, the range of choice is based on an established set of options that is still relatively restrictive.

Among services, however, many of them provide for a high degree of customization. Some of the most highly customized services are listed in Table 17.2. Indeed, for many of the services listed, it is possible for the consumer to receive a service that is unique.

The need for a high degree of customization in some services makes it more difficult to design and operate channels, which normally rely on standardized, routine, and repetitive processes to operate efficiently. Major changes or even nuances required in providing custom services demand individual planning, special efforts, and frequent changes, all of which slow down the system and in some cases undermine its core business model. This is what happened to Hyatt Legal Services, a company that attempted to create a

---

TABLE 17.2 EXAMPLES OF SERVICES THAT CAN BE HIGHLY CUSTOMIZED

Legal services
Health care/surgery
Architectural design
Executive search
Real estate sales
Taxi service
Hairstyling
Plumbing/air conditioning
Education (tutorials)
Telephone service
Hotel services
Retail banking
Fine restaurant service

Source: Based on Christopher H. Lovelock, *Services Marketing* (Englewood Cliffs, N.J.: Prentice-Hall, 1984), 56.

dramatically different channel for providing legal services to the public. Using the business format franchise model, Hyatt recruited franchisees and opened more than 200 offices in shopping centers all over the country that concentrated on routine legal matters such as simple wills and uncontested divorces and charged low standardized fees. But after just a few years, Hyatt Legal Services was forced to close most of the shopping center franchisee offices and retrench into a network affiliation of lawyers called Hyatt Legal Plans.[26] Why did Hyatt Legal Services franchise channel strategy for providing legal services to the mass market fail? The rigid business format franchise model did not work for legal services that deviated from the standardized and routine matters that the channel was designed to serve. So, when more complex legal matters arose, Hyatt Legal Services franchisees were not able to deal with them even though fees were potentially much higher. The new organization, which was purchased and became a subsidiary of the Metlife Company, uses a less formal affiliation structure utilizing independent law offices throughout the country that enables Hyatt Legal Plans to offer a higher degree of flexibility in providing legal services to clients with lower overhead costs.

So, for services requiring a high degree of customization, small-scale channels consisting of local independent service providers are likely to continue to play a major role.

Channel Flows

Marketing channels for products comprise a series of flows, as we pointed out in Chapter 1. The most obvious is the physical flow of the products themselves. But with most services there is no flow of products through the channel. The flows that "carry" the service through the channel are those of information, negotiation, and promotion. Thus, the variables related to the product flow in designing and managing a channel—such as product bulk and weight, unit value, and degree of technicality (see Chapter 6)—do not have to be addressed. This can simplify the design and management of marketing channels significantly because, in many cases, the flows of information, negotiation, and promotion can be handled electronically. However, the channel manager still has to remember that just because a service *can* be delivered via electronic channels does not mean that it *should* be delivered through those channels. Although anything that can be digitized can be delivered through the customers' desktop or laptop computer, tablet computer, or smartphone, the channel manager should not lose sight of the fact that ultimately it is *consumer preferences in the marketplace* that determine the type of channel structure that emerges. The huge growth in music downloads, electronic books, streaming and on demand videos, online banking, and numerous other technology-based innovations of recent years all could not have taken place unless consumers *chose* to make use of these electronic channels. So, the fact that most services do not involve a physical product flow does not mean that the channel manager should automatically attempt to use electronic channels to make all or most services available to customers. Many customers may still prefer "old-fashioned," people intensive channels for certain types of services.[27] For example, a recent study conducted by American Express found that 90 percent of customers preferred to talk to real people on the telephone when they need customer service.[28]

Summary

A huge range and diversity of services is provided by the American economy. The service sector is now more than twice the size of the manufacturing sector. In other words, more and more of what is produced by the economy is in the form of services rather than goods.

In recent years, the marketing discipline has focused increasing attention on the marketing of services because, just as is the case with products, services must be in tune with customer demand and presented so as to maximize their appeal. The approach and emphasis used in the marketing of services, however, are often different from the marketing of products. These differences stem from several generally recognizable characteristics of services that distinguish them from products. These are (1) the intangibility of services, (2) the inseparability of services from the service providers, (3) the difficulties of standardizing services, (4) the high degree of customer involvement in many services, and (5) the perishability of services.

From a general marketing management standpoint, all of these special characteristics of services have implications for managing the four major strategic components of the marketing mix. In fact, the implications for channel strategy and management are often even more important for distribution than the other components of the marketing mix because services are so

directly connected with service providers at the end point of the channel. Hence, from the customer's point of view, the service and the service provider are often one and the same. So, making services readily available to customers when and where they want them through well-designed and well-managed marketing channels is critically important to service marketers.

Along with the five generally recognized distinguishing characteristics of services, the channel manager should also be familiar with several other important perspectives on services, including the implications for channel management of shorter channels, the widespread use of franchising, the relatively high degree of customization in many services, and the lack of a product flow for services.

Review Questions

1. Why has in increasing amount of attention been given to services marketing in recent years?

2. Which basic marketing objectives are the same for both products and services?

3. Briefly discuss the five generally acknowledged distinguishing characteristics of services in terms of contrasts between services and products.

4. What role can marketing channels play in helping the service provider to tangibilize the service? How does this relate to the other strategic components of the marketing mix?

5. Does the inseparability of services from their providers make it more difficult or easier to market services as opposed to products?

6. Discuss the problem of standardizing services as it relates to channel design and management.

7. Should customer involvement in providing services be avoided if at all possible in the design

and management of the channel to deliver the service? Discuss.

8. What is the key implication of the perishability of services for channel design? Explain.

9. Do the generally shorter channels used to distribute services usually make it more or less complicated to design marketing channels? Why?

10. Discuss the role of business format franchising in providing services on a consistent or standardized basis.

11. How does the need for customization in many services tend to reduce the efficiency and cost advantages of large-scale channels?

12. Does the lack of a product flow alter the design and management of marketing channels for services as compared to marketing channels designed by manufacturers? Explain.

Channel Issues for Discussion

1. Firms of all sizes have developed many kinds of social-networking tools, instant messaging programs, and text messaging systems to deal with customer service inquiries. But a recent survey by American Express Co. found that almost 90 percent of the respondents said they still want their inquiries handled by real customer service representatives in real time over the "old-fashioned" telephone.

In light of all the new technology available to customers, why do you think they still prefer the old-fashioned telephone-based service channel? Discuss.

2. House calls by doctors is a type of medical service that has all but disappeared. But it may be making a comeback. A medical firm in Seattle called Carewa has started to send doctors to the homes of Microsoft employees who are covered by

Microsoft's medical insurance program. Micro-soft decided that the house call program made good economic sense, because the cost of a house call at about $150 is one-tenth the cost of a $1,500 emergency room visit. And, because most emergency room visits are not made for real medical emergencies but for non-life-threatening medical problems such as ear infections and the flu, house calls could be safely substituted for emergency room visits. Moreover, house calls enable doctors to examine patients in their own surroundings, which might provide valuable clues related to the patient's condition. Moreover, by not having to leave their houses, patients will not spread germs in emergency rooms.

Do you think channels for medical services that provide for "home delivery" will become an important trend? Why or why not?

3. OpenTable.com Inc., with more than 13,000 participating restaurants, is the market leader in online restaurant reservations service providers. Restaurants pay a monthly fee as well as $1.00 per head for reservations made by diners through OpenTable.com. But OpenTable also charges 25 cents per head even if diners make reservations through the restaurants' own Web sites. By making reservations through OpenTable, diners also earn points that can be redeemed for discount coupons. But there may be a problem with this seemingly straightforward deal between OpenTable and restaurants using its services. Some diners claim that if they make their reservations through OpenTable, the restaurants retaliate for the extra cost involved by seating diners at inferior table locations and by providing poor service. OpenTable denies this.

Why would restaurants unhappy with the deal being offered to them by OpenTable take out their frustration on diners? Discuss.

4. Late one Thursday afternoon George Mitchell went to the airline ticket counter of a major carrier that had recently launched an ad campaign challenging customers to "find out how

good we really are." Mitchell needed to reschedule his flight in order to reach a client by 9:00 Friday morning. Not only did Mitchell wait 20 minutes in a long line, but the ticket agent was not very sympathetic. After what seemed like a great deal of haggling, he was reticketed for an earlier flight. When he reached the departure gate he learned that this flight would be more than an hour late. Finally, climbing into the plane and taking his seat in the business-class section, Mitchell was ready to relax. He could not unwind, however, because of several small, crying children traveling with their parents in the first-class section. (They were travelling free on frequent flier awards, Mitchell assumed.) The flight attendants in the business-class section had made themselves scarce. Mitchell remarked under his breath that indeed he did find out how good the airline really was.

Comment on Mitchell's experience in terms of the role of the service provider delivering the service at the end point of the marketing channel.

5. Automated teller machines (ATMs) and, more recently, online banking, were thought to provide such a valuable service alternative that customers would need far fewer personal banking services with human tellers in traditional bank branches. In short, these new technologies were supposed to reduce drastically the number of bank tellers and branches. But things did not work out that way. Between 1995 and 2005 the number of bank branches grew from 50,000 to 70,000, an increase of 40 percent. The number of tellers to staff the branches also increased in roughly the same proportion during this decade. This happened despite the fact that the number of banking firms actually decreased dramatically from 10,000 to less than 8,000 during that same period.

What do you think is going on here? Why do you think so many consumers still demand "old-fashioned" bank branches and tellers in spite of new technological alternatives? Discuss.

References

1. See for example: Willa Plank, "One-Way Car Rentals," *Wall Street Journal* (October 14, 2010): D4.
2. Leonard L. Berry, *On Great Service: A Framework for Action* (New York: The Free Press, 1995); and Christopher H. Lovelock, *Service Marketing, Text, Cases and Readings*, 2nd ed. (Englewood Cliffs, N.J.: Prentice-Hall, 1993).
3. Justin Lahart, "Service Sector Expand," *Wall Street Journal* (October 6, 2010): A4.

4. See Raymond P. Fisk, Stephen W. Brown, and Mary Jo Bitner, "Tracking the Evolution of the Services Marketing Literature," *Journal of Retailing* (Spring 1993): 61–103; Sak Onkvisit and John J. Shaw, "Service Marketing: Image, Branding, and Competition," *Business Horizons* (January-February 1989): 13–18; Betsy D. Gelb, Samuel V. Smith, and Gabriel M. Gelb, "Service Marketing Lessons from the Professionals," *Business Horizons* (September-October 1988): 29–34; and J. Patrick Kelly and William R. George, "Strategic Management Issues for the Retailing of Services," *Journal of Retailing* (Summer 1982): 26–43.

5. Leonard L. Berry, "Services Marketing Is Different," in Christopher H. Lovelock, *Services Marketing* (Englewood Cliffs, N.J.: Prentice-Hall, 1984), 29–37.

6. For a related discussion see: Caroline Wiertz, Ko de Ruyter, Cherie Keen, and Sandra Streukens, "Cooperating for Service Excellence in Multichannel Service Systems: An Empirical Assessment," *Journal of Business Research* Vol. 57 (2004): 424–436.

7. For a related discussion, see Syed Saad Andeleeb and Amiya K. Basu, "Technical Complexity and Consumer Knowledge as Moderators of Service Quality Evaluation in the Automobile Service Industry," *Journal of Retailing* 70, 4 (1994): 367–381.

8. Ethan Smith, "Promoter Crowds Ticketmaster," *Wall Street Journal* (February 3, 2011): B1.

9. See, for example, Donald H. Light, "A Guide for New Distribution Channel Strategies for Service Firms," *Journal of Business Strategy* (Summer 1986): 56–64; Stephen J. Gould, "Macrodynamic Trends in Health Care: A Distribution and Retailing Perspective," *Health Care Management Review* (Spring 1988): 15–22; and Charles W. Lamb Jr., and John L. Crompton, "Distribution Decisions for Public Services," *Journal of the Academy of Marketing Science* (Summer 1985): 107–122.

10. For an excellent study related to this point, see Rajiv P. Dant, James R. Lumpkin, and Mohammed Y.A. Rawwas, "Sources of Generalized Versus Issue-Specific Dis/Satisfaction in Service Channels of Distribution: A Review and Comparative Investigation," *Journal of Business Research* 42 (May 1998): 7–23.

11. For a related discussion see: Ronald Grove, "Hulu's Tough Choices," *Business Week* (December 7, 2009): 28.

12. For an excellent discussion related to this issue see: Zhi Wang and Stuart Horsburgh, "Linking Network Coherence to Service Performance: Modeling Airline Strategic Alliances," *Journal of Marketing Channels* Vol. 14, No. 3 (2009): 51–79.

13. Holman W. Jenkins Jr., "The Airlines Discover Content," *Wall Street Journal* (January 21, 2011): A11.

14. See for example: Bruce Schoenfeld, "A Different Kind of Connection," *Entrepreneur* (June 2011): 24.

15. http://www.medscreening.com/vitastat.html (May 25, 2011).

16. Tom Belden, "A Return Trip to Travel Agents," *Philadelphia Enquirer* (July 10, 2007): D1, D6.

17. For a very interesting analysis of a novel service channel that *does* use intermediaries see: Joyce A. Young, "The IndyCar Series: A Marketing Channels Perspective," *International Journal of Sport Management and Marketing* Vol. 8, No. 1/2 (2010): 57–72.

18. For a related discussion, see Gregory D. Upah, "Mass Marketing in Service Retailing: A Review and Synthesis of Major Methods," *Journal of Retailing* (Fall 1980): 59–76.

19. Pamela D. Morrison and John H. Roberts, "Matching Electronic Distribution Channels to Product Characteristics: The Role of Congruence in Consideration Set Formation," *Journal of Business Research* 41, 3 (1998): 223–229.

20. See: Rajasree K. Rajamma, "Services Purchased at Brick and Mortar Versus Online Stores, and Shopping Motivation," *Journal of Services Marketing* Vol. 21, No. 3 (2007): 200–212.

21. For a related discussion see: Amy Feldman, "Buddy, Can You E-Mail Me 100 Bucks?" *Business Week* (November 23, 2009): 68.

22. Julie Bennett, "Dry Cleaning to Dog Walking: Franchises Help People Transform Their Lives," *Wall Street Journal* (February 11, 2002): B7.

23. For an excellent discussion related to this point, see James C. Cross and Bruce J. Walker, "Service Marketing and Franchising: A Practical Business Marriage," *Business Horizons* (November-December 1987): 50–58.

24. Ownership patterns tend to change over time, however. See Francine Lafontaine and Patrick J. Kaufmann, "The Evolution of Ownership Patterns in Franchise Systems," *Journal of Retailing* 70, 2 (1994): 97–113.

25. Patricia M. Doney, James M. Barry and Russell Abratt, "Trust Determinants and Outcomes in Global B2B Services," *European Journal of Marketing* Vol. 41, No. 9/10 (2007): 1096–1116.

26. http://www.legalplans.com/brisk.html (May 27, 2011).

27. Irene C.L. Ng, "Establishing a Service Channel: A Transaction Cost Analysis of a Channel Contract Between a Cruise Line and a Tour Operator," *Journal of Services Marketing* Vol. 21, No. 1 (2007): 4–14.

28. Joe Light, "With Customer Service, Real Person Trumps Text," *Wall Street Journal* (April 25, 2011): B7.

CHAPTER **18**
International Channel Perspectives

LEARNING OBJECTIVES

After reading this chapter you should:

1. Recognize the need to consider marketing channels from an international perspective.
2. Have an appreciation for the broader and more complex environment within which international marketing channels operate.
3. Be familiar with key environmental factors affecting international marketing channels.
4. Understand the behavioral aspects as they influence international channels.
5. Know how to approach the design of marketing channels from an international perspective.
6. Be cognizant of the various channel structures associated with international marketing channels.
7. Be aware of the major facets in motivating channel members from an international viewpoint.
8. Realize that exercising leadership in international marketing channels is often more difficult than in domestic marketing channels.

© AP Photo/Imaginechina

FOCUS ON CHANNELS

Cadillac Wants to Become the Cadillac of Automobile Channels in China

During the first three quarters of the twentieth century, the name Cadillac stood for world-class quality. In fact, "Cadillac" became so synonymous with quality that the name could be applied to virtually any product or service simply by adding the word "The" before the Cadillac name and then identifying the product or service. So, the very best refrigerator could be described as "The Cadillac of refrigerators" or the best hotel as "The Cadillac of hotels," etc. Well, during the last quarter of the twentieth century, the quality of Cadillac cars slipped and so did the name's association with quality. But by the end of the first decade of the twenty-first century, Cadillac had made a big comeback. Cadillac was on a path to produce automobiles that will not only live up to the quality image of the Cadillac name in its glory days, but to once again make the name synonymous with quality.

General Motors is counting on this Cadillac brand renaissance to compete with Audi, BMW and Mercedes in China by developing superior automobile channels. GM believes that to compete with the European trio that holds a 77 percent market share to Cadillac's 3 percent, it will need more than just equally good cars. Cadillac will also need the world's best auto dealers that can provide the growing number of affluent Chinese luxury car buyers with an unequaled customer experience. And this is exactly what Cadillac has done in its 39 mainland dealerships. Showroom attendants greet visitors in an elegantly designed polished glass entrance. Fine cigars and Napa Valley wines are offered at a black-marble bar. Luxurious VIP rooms with leather sofas are available for deal making while a mini-museum exhibit and film capture the famous pedigree of Cadillac's 110-year history. Hu Ming, a 44-year-old entrepreneur who visited a Cadillac auto dealer in Beijing was impressed enough to plunk down $65,000 for a Cadillac SLS. Says Hu:

Everything gave me the feeling I was a VIP. The décor is very different from other brands. The place has an American style.

So, by selling Cadillacs in "The Cadillac of automobile dealers," GM is betting that there will be a lot more Hu Mings buying Cadillacs.

Source: Based on Dexter Roberts, "Cadillac Floors It in China," *Business Week* (June 4, 2007): 52.

Slower growth in domestic markets and fierce foreign competition are making the need for international operations an inescapable reality for more and more companies.[1] Channel strategy, as one of the key elements of the marketing mix, will therefore need to focus increasingly on the international dimension of channel management.[2]

In this chapter, we examine some of the key channel issues discussed earlier in the text, but we will now consider them exclusively from an international perspective. Our purpose is not to provide comprehensive and detailed coverage of the international aspects of channel management, as this would be far beyond the scope of this chapter. Moreover, a substantial body of excellent international marketing literature relevant to the topic is already available for more in-depth study.[3] Our discussion will be limited to highlighting some of the key considerations that the channel manager should address if the firm's marketing channels extend into international markets. Hopefully, this will help him or her develop an awareness of the international side of channel management as well as an appreciation for the need to seek further knowledge when faced with international channel decisions.

Specifically, we will focus on the following major topic areas from an international perspective:

- *Environment of international channel management*
- *Behavioral processes in international channels*
- *Designing international channels*
- *Motivating international channel members*

Environment of International Channel Management

In Chapter 3 we described the environment as consisting of all external uncontrollable factors within which the marketing channel exists. The major categories of environmental variables discussed were economic, competitive, sociocultural, technological and legal. The channel was viewed as an **open system** that interacts with and adapts to its environment by changing the structure and processes of its components.

All of these concepts still apply when an international perspective is taken. The only difference is that when the channel extends into the international arena, the environment becomes larger and more complex because the firm is attempting to adapt its channels not only to the national environment but to the relevant international environment as well.[4] Consequently, even though the basic concepts of channel strategy and management remain the same, the channel manager is faced with more unknowns and greater complexity.[5]

To develop and manage channels successfully in foreign environments, the channel manager needs to be aware of, and sensitive to, the environmental differences in the countries involved and how these differences affect channel strategy.[6] Obviously, it is not possible for us to go into a treatise on environmental differences among countries. What we can do, however, is present a few illustrative examples of environmental factors associated with several foreign countries to show how they can influence marketing channel strategy. Our discussion will be structured around the five major categories of environmental variables discussed in Chapter 3.

Economic Factors and International Channels

All of the economic conditions occurring in the domestic environment can occur in foreign environments as well. Indeed, the changes can be much more dramatic. For example, whereas high inflation occurring in the United States during the first decade of the twenty-first century meant anything above 3 percent per year, in a number of countries in Asia, Eastern Europe and South America, inflation rates in the double digits were not uncommon.

Recessions in the United States are also usually paralleled in many foreign countries, especially in Western Europe and Asia, and they are often more severe. Deflation, which has occurred in some sectors of the U.S. economy such as housing, computers, consumer electronics, apparel and major appliances, occurred on a much wider scale in Asian countries such as Indonesia, Malaysia, Taiwan, Thailand, South Korea and especially in Japan.

Fluctuations in foreign currency exchange rates can also drastically affect all phases of a U.S. firm's strategy in international markets as the dollar becomes stronger or weaker against foreign currencies. A strong dollar weakens the competitiveness of American products in foreign markets, while a weak dollar can make them more attractive because it makes U.S. products sold overseas more affordable to foreign consumers.[7]

For example, the U.S. dollar, which had been strong relative to the euro early in the twenty-first century, had fallen sharply by the end of the decade. So, instead of the $.85 it took to buy one euro in 2000, by 2011, it took $1.45 to purchase one euro.

Many economists as well as U.S. manufacturers exporting products to Europe viewed this fall in the dollar as a positive development. They believed it would make U.S. products cheaper in the European markets and would help to limit exports from those countries to the United States because the relatively weak dollar would make those products more expensive.

While any of these economic variables can affect all elements of the marketing mix, foreign channel strategy may pose even more problems because relationships with foreign channel members may be affected.[8]

Competitive Environment and International Channels

Competitive structure in foreign countries can be quite different from that in the United States. The free market of the United States is less evident in other highly developed Western countries; and in many less-developed countries, free and open competition hardly exists.[9] Hence, the channel structure will have to adapt to variations in competitive structures among many different countries.

Consider, for example, how Kodak approached this issue when it introduced its Ektaprint copier-duplicator line into the European market. Kodak's European marketing region encompassed an area that included eighteen countries and 400 million people with many different languages, cultures and currencies. The market Kodak was aiming for in all of the European countries was defined as "the mid-to high-volume office copier-duplicator segment." But it seemed that everyone else was also competing for that same market—other well-known American firms such as IBM and Xerox as well as European and Japanese firms. This resulted in a highly complex competitive structure across the 18 countries involved.

In order to deal with this complex competitive structure, Kodak established thirteen separate marketing companies, each with its own management and marketing channels specifically designed for the territory to be served. These individual management and channel systems enabled Kodak to position itself strongly against the diverse competition it faced because they made it possible for Kodak to provide superior levels of product availability and customer service in each of the different foreign markets.

Sociocultural Environment and International Channels

Differences in sociocultural factors across different countries are an important fact of life in international marketing.[10] Cultural values, norms of behavior, attitudes and perceptions vary enormously around the world. A very significant portion of the international marketing literature has focused on these differences in an attempt to enlighten international marketing managers. Unfortunately, many mistakes and major blunders have been made by both large and small U.S. firms that have ventured into international markets without even a rudimentary understanding of the different sociocultural factors they were facing.[11]

Although here again differences in sociocultural factors can influence all elements of the marketing mix, the channel variable is especially sensitive because it often involves more person-to-person or organization-to-organization contact than the other variables. Hence, the firm has to be especially careful to pay attention to sociocultural differences in the development of international channel relationships.[12] For example, Ben & Jerry's Homemade Holdings, Inc., the famous U.S.-based gourmet ice cream maker, had a rude awakening when it entered the Russian market. Ben & Jerry's decided to use licensing arrangements with independent Russian entrepreneurs to establish ice cream parlors in several Russian cities. Ben & Jerry's was surprised, to say the least, by the different business culture in Russia. American-style efficiency and results orientation were not characteristic of the Russian culture, which was just emerging from decades of Soviet Communism, an environment that had stifled initiative and did not reward efficiency. So, Ben & Jerry's had to deal with a variety of culturally based business problems such as indifference to on-time delivery of products to stores, a seemingly built-in unfriendly attitude toward customer service, and distributors in monopoly positions with links to organized crime. This cultural environment was quite a contrast to the largely straightforward genteel business culture Ben & Jerry's had been used to in the United States. It took Ben & Jerry's about four years to get the Russian venture up and running at a level that could show modest profits.

Technological Environment and International Channels

The level of technology and rate of technological change in foreign environments is another factor that can affect channel strategy.[13] In some countries, especially the less developed ones in Asia, Latin America and Africa, communications and transportation technology is relatively primitive, whereas in the more advanced countries of Western Europe and Japan, technology often matches or even surpasses that of the United States. Seven & I Holdings Co. of Japan, the Japanese company that controls 7-Eleven stores in Japan, for example, has become a world leader in the use of information systems to manage distribution and merchandising in its almost 13,000 stores in Japan. 7-Eleven Japan uses its computerized store operations support system to send orders to suppliers via the headquarters central computer. The company can precisely plan delivery schedules for all the stores, which helps suppliers to substantially reduce the frequency of visits and lowers costs. Given such precisely planned schedules, suppliers are then expected to deliver in specified quantities on specified dates to conform with 7-Eleven Japan's program. If they do not meet the schedule, the suppliers must pay 7-Eleven Japan the lost opportunity costs of the undelivered products. Such advanced technology puts tremendous pressure on suppliers to develop technologies of their own that will enable them to meet the rigorous demands of the company. Those who cannot do so, whether they be domestic or foreign, will not be able to continue to do business with 7-Eleven Japan. Thus, just as leading U.S. retailers such as Walmart and Home Depot have forced suppliers to meet the technological demands required to supply these retail giants, so too have foreign retailers and distributors raised the bar.

Legal/Political Environment and International Channels

In Chapter 3 we discussed at some length the legal environment as it affects channel strategy in the United States. In the international sphere, a U.S. firm seeking to establish channels of distribution in foreign countries can face a wide array of complex and burdensome government regulations, policies, and political pressures that can make even what might appear to be the simplest of arrangements for securing distribution very difficult and complicated. The obvious legal factors such as tariffs, import restrictions, quotas, and other government regulations affecting the distribution of foreign products within the countries in question may be just the tip of the iceberg. Highly specific, obscure, and even downright strange regulations and prohibitions can make it very difficult to establish foreign distribution.

Japan provides a case in point.[14] Indeed, sometimes in Japan rules and regulations are not even written down. This is what International Game Technologies (IGT), an American manufacturer of slot machines, found out when it attempted to sell its machines there.[15] IGT's one-armed bandits dominate most markets around the world, but it sold none in the huge Japanese market that accounts for two-thirds of the world market. IGT launched a full-scale effort to break into the Japanese market—but it hit a stone wall when it found out it could not even get a copy of Japan's rules and specifications for gambling machines. Unlike the United States and other developed countries, in Japan such formal written guidelines do not exist. Instead, the country's National Policy Agency decides which products are acceptable based on informal, unwritten "understandings." Hence, no one fully knows what the rules are or precisely what the Japanese bureaucrats want. IGT had to file specifications for its slot machines more than twenty times before it could even get to the testing stage, to see if they were acceptable to the Japanese bureaucrats. And once they were tested, IGT had to go back to the drawing board many more times in an attempt to meet the elusive standards. It took more than a year to make the modifications needed to finally get to the starting line for selling the machines in Japan.

Such government actions (which some knowledgeable observers of the Japanese scene say result from political pressure by Japanese companies that feel threatened by imports) are hardly conducive to establishing strong relationships between American manufacturers and Japanese distributors.[16] Similar situations occur in many other countries all over the world. Thus, the firm seeking to establish effective channels in foreign markets needs to investigate the legal environment of each country very carefully in an attempt to determine how the various regulations could conceivably affect channel strategy.[17]

Behavioral Processes in International Channels

Chapter 4 discussed the important part that behavioral dimensions play in marketing channel systems. In order to avoid negative conflict, use power effectively, and establish good communications, the channel manager must understand the behavioral aspects of channel systems. The behavioral side can be even more important in foreign channels than in domestic channels because cultural patterns in a number of countries often place more emphasis on person-to-person relationships than is typical in the United States.[18] In Japan and China for example, the ability to establish personal relationships and even friendships with channel members is crucial to securing their support at the wholesale or retail levels.

The experience of Bose Corporation provides a classic illustration. Bose is well known in the United States as a manufacturer of audio speakers of outstanding quality and technical superiority. In an effort to build international distribution, Bose attempted to break into the Japanese market. The results were disastrous. Over a three-year period, despite intense efforts, the company sold fewer than a hundred sets of speakers in Japan and had no choice but to pull out of the country. The reason? Reflecting some years later on what went wrong, the company's founder, Amar Bose, identified the key problem as the failure of his marketing people to establish close personal ties with their Japanese distributor. As Bose would eventually realize, Japan is an intensely relationship-oriented society. Personal connections are the very essence of doing business *nihonshiki* (Japanese-style). Such personal relationships, if they had not already been established through old school ties and family friendships, can be developed only through long hours of social contact and even late-night drinking bouts.

Bose's export sales staff did not take the necessary time, face-to-face, to convince its Japanese distributor of the advantages of Bose's unique direct/reflecting audio technology that bounces sound waves off walls rather than sending them directly toward the listener. Unconvinced (and perhaps somewhat untrusting of a company that had not paid its "social relationship dues"), the Japanese distributor took it upon itself to "improve" the sound by removing one of the essential components. This produced a sound quality that Bose acoustical engineers described as "simply terrible" and, in retrospect, it is no wonder that so few Japanese audiophiles bought the product.

Bose's failure to secure effective distribution in Japan because of its lack of understanding of the behavioral side of Japanese marketing channels is not, of course, unique to this company or country.[19] Numerous other American firms have failed in Japan and in many other countries for the same reason. So, whether the firm is attempting to design and manage channels in the United States, Japan, or any other country in the world, the need to consider the behavioral dimensions of channel relationships is always important—and in some countries, as in Japan, absolutely critical.

Designing International Channels

Although presented mainly in a domestic setting, the design of distribution channels discussed in Chapters 6 and 7 (in terms of the seven-phase channel design paradigm) also applies to the international scene.

The first phase, recognizing that a channel design decision must be made, can be viewed from national and/or international perspectives.[20] For example, if the firm is seeking new markets for its products (a common reason for facing channel design decisions), the new markets might be located in the United States or overseas. In both cases, the firm may have to either design entirely new channels or modify existing ones to reach the markets.[21]

Setting and coordinating distribution objectives, Phase 2 of channel design, also applies equally to national and international situations. If the firm's distribution objectives specify reaching overseas markets, then the design of the channel will need to reflect this fact.[22]

Phase 3 of channel design, the specification of distribution tasks, also holds for both national and international channel design decisions. In either case, the firm must examine carefully the kinds of tasks that need to be performed to successfully meet the firm's distribution objectives.[23]

The development of alternative channel structures, Phase 4 of the channel design paradigm, however, takes a different twist when international alternatives are considered.

This is because a different set of channel structure alternatives will need to be considered for international distribution that would not usually be relevant if channels were being designed only for domestic distribution. These channel structure alternatives are determined by the particular approaches to international marketing involvement that the firm seeks.[24] These range from occasional or casual exporting all the way to extensive foreign production and marketing. Figure 18.1 portrays the various approaches. Our discussion will focus only on the approaches associated with production in the home (U.S.) market. Foreign production entails corporate-level strategic considerations that go far beyond the scope of channel design.

Indirect Exporting

The term **indirect exporting** means that a firm sells products in foreign markets but does not have any special division within its organization or make any significant effort at international marketing. In effect, the firm is a domestic marketer that exports some of its products. Following are the four most common approaches for indirect exporting.

Casual Exporting The firm that just wants to "get its feet wet" in selling its products overseas might occasionally export a small portion of its products. Indeed, the firm may not even be fully aware that some of its products are going overseas because regular domestic customers, especially those in the industrial market, may be buying the products in the United States and shipping them to their foreign operations. Unsolicited orders from foreign countries, many of which may be made online, may also account

FIGURE 18.1 Alternative Approaches for Foreign Market Entry

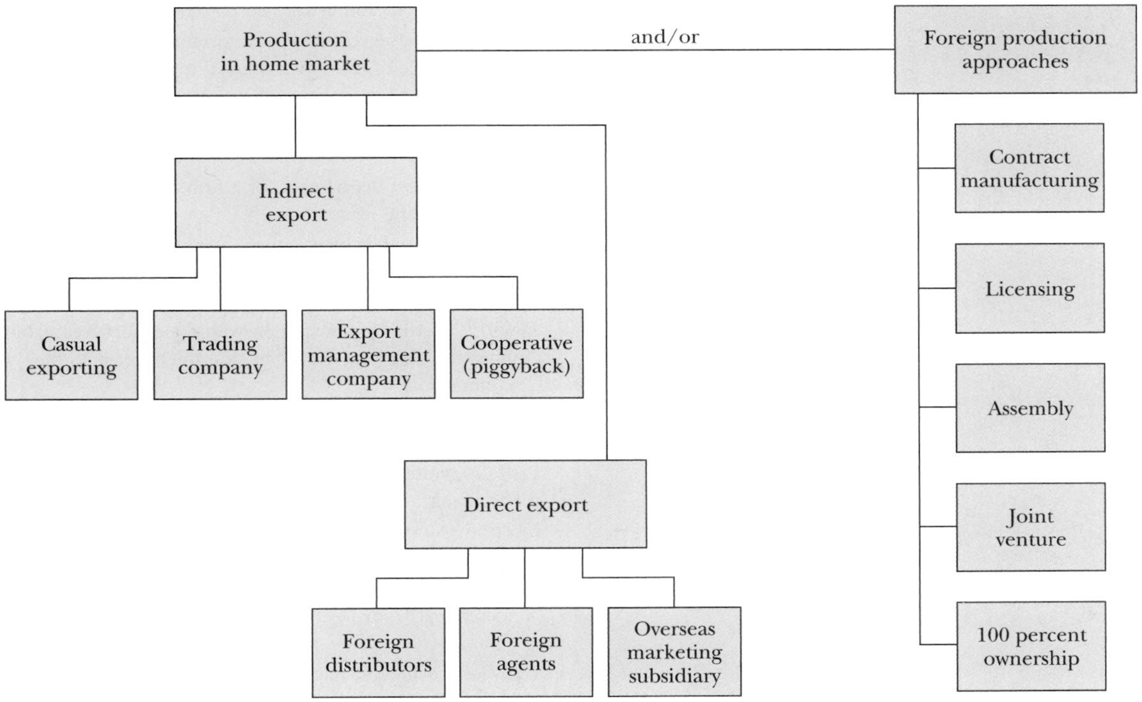

Source: Adapted from International Marketing, 3rd ed., by Vern Terpstra (Hinsdale, Ill.: Dryden Press, 1983), 320. Copyright 1983 by Vern Terpstra. Reproduced by permission from the author.

for a significant part of this type of exporting. At this level of exporting, little thought tends to be given to other international channel alternatives.

Trading Companies   Foreign trading companies are typically large, powerful international organizations for conducting worldwide trade. Some of the largest, such as Mitsubishi, are based in Japan, but a number of major trading companies are also located in Europe.[25]

Because the trading companies are large and have access to many world markets, they can provide the U.S. firm with a rapid entry into foreign countries. But because the trading companies are so large and powerful, the U.S. firm can do little to influence how its products are sold by the trading company. Hence this is also very much an arm's-length approach to international marketing.

Trade Intermediaries   These firms, sometimes referred to as **export management companies**, are essentially domestically based wholesalers, manufacturers' representatives, agents, or brokers who specialize in overseas sales. Table 18.1 provides a list of some of the more common types of trade intermediaries that participate in international channels.

It is estimated that some 2,000 to 2,500 of these intermediaries exist in the United States and account for as much as 10 percent of all U.S. exports. As shown in the table,

TABLE 18.1 COMMON TYPES OF TRADE INTERMEDIARIES PARTICIPATING IN INTERNATIONAL CHANNELS

TYPE OF INTERMEDIARY	PRIMARY ROLE/DESCRIPTION IN CHANNEL
Traditional Merchant Wholesaler with Global Operations	Full service, wholesale distributors who follow clients to foreign markets and establish global operations
Foreign Agents	Independent businesses which do not take title to the products they represent and usually do not take physical possession
	They are, however, capable of performing or arranging for the performance of most international marketing tasks
Foreign Distributors	Buy and sell on their own behalf and take title and ownership risk
Export Merchant	Buy and sell on their own account, but typically export as well as import, thus, with facilities across many national markets
Export Management Company	Act as an export department for a firm, representing multiple noncompeting firms
Manufacturer's Export Agent	Similar to an export management company, but often offering more limited functions and operating in its own name rather than that of the manufacturer
Export Commission House	Low-risk alternative to exporter, with the export commission house representing the buyer, and the buyer pays the commission
Resident Buyer	Basically, an export commission house with long-term continuous contact
Confirming House	Provides limited functions for an exporter, primarily related to financing
Export Desk Jobber	Buy and sell, typically raw materials, never taking physical possession
Freight Forwarder	Primarily arrange transportation and documentation, and increasingly moving into additional distribution channel functions
Third-Party Logistic Provider	Logistics provider, increasingly providing extensive distribution functions for global companies

Source: Bert Rosenbloom and Trina Larsen Andras, "Wholesalers as Global Marketers," *Journal of Marketing Channels*, Vol. 15, No. 4 (2008): 242. Copyright © 2008 by Taylor & Francis Group. Reprinted by permission of the publisher, http://www.informaworld.com

some are merchant wholesalers who take title to and actually handle the merchandise. Others are agents who do not take title and usually do not physically take possession of the merchandise, but handle the sales and technical aspects of overseas marketing; many handle credit arrangements as well. For the firm that seeks a higher level of involvement in international marketing than that provided by casual exporting or trading companies, but wants to stop short of establishing an in-house exporting department, trade intermediaries can offer an attractive alternative.

Cooperative or Piggybacking Arrangements Another approach to entering overseas markets is through a cooperative effort by two or more firms. Under the Webb-Pomerene Export Trade Act, U.S. firms are permitted to join together for purposes of competing in foreign markets without being subject to the anticollusion provisions of the Sherman and Clayton acts (see Chapter 3), which apply in domestic marketing. Though this provision has existed since the passage of the act in 1918, Webb-Pomerene associations have never really caught on. Currently, they account for less than 2 percent of U.S. export sales.

Piggybacking is the term used to describe a special type of cooperative arrangement between two firms for entering foreign markets. The **carrier** is the firm already involved in exporting and the **rider** is the firm that uses the international expertise and capabilities of the carrier to enter foreign markets. Such piggybacking arrangements, if well conceived, can offer the rider an opportunity to gain entry into foreign markets with little capital outlay, while the carrier can obtain a desirable product to sell.

Direct Exporting

The term **direct exporting**, as used in the international marketing literature, means that the manufacturer itself gets directly involved in exporting rather than delegating all of the tasks to others. Thus, under direct exporting, such tasks as making market contacts, performing market research, handling physical distribution, preparing export documentation, pricing, and many other tasks will be undertaken mainly by the manufacturer's own export department.[26] Table 18.2 outlines elements in the export marketing mix.

Even though the manufacturer is heavily involved in performing the international marketing tasks as shown in Table 18.2, it may still call on foreign distributors and/or agents to assist its in-house export department. Further, even if the manufacturer has set up its own overseas marketing subsidiary, it may still use distributors and agents to help meet its foreign distribution objectives.[27]

Foreign Distributors Like many domestic distributors, foreign distributors are independently owned businesses that usually take title to the products they handle. As such, just as in the domestic setting, they may want to do things their way rather than the manufacturer's way. Thus the manufacturer's ability to exercise control over how its products are marketed by distributors is a crucial issue in both domestic and international marketing. But the greater distances and, in many cases, the cultural and communications differences involved when dealing with foreign distributors make the difficulties involved in exercising control over them even more challenging in the international setting.[28]

On the other hand, modern technology, especially the Internet, email, cell phones, and even "old-fashioned" fax machines have made it much easier and cheaper for U.S. manufacturers to communicate with foreign distributors all over the world. The availability of such low-cost technology coupled with the capabilities of foreign distributors have led to substantial increases in exports by U.S. manufacturers. During the eight year period from 2000 to 2008, exports by U.S. producers and manufacturers grew from $782 billion to almost $1.3 trillion, an increase of almost 65 percent.[29]

Foreign Agents   Overseas or foreign agents are also independent businesses, but they do not take title to the products they represent and usually do not take physical possession. They are, however, capable of performing or arranging for the performance of most international marketing tasks listed in Table 18.2.

TABLE 18.2 EXAMPLES OF ELEMENTS INCLUDED IN THE EXPORT MARKETING MIX

A. Promotional Support
1. Local advertising
2. Umbrella advertising
3. Direct-mail advertising
4. Descriptive literature
5. Trade shows
6. Demonstration items
7. Printing

B. Direct Selling
8. Direct selling to customers
9. Maintenance of sales force
10. Commissions to sales agents

C. Marketing Service and Sales Service Support
11. Market research
12. Annual catalog of products
13. Sales budget by product
14. Prompt quote requests
15. Technical sales assistance
16. In-store service
17. Information for selling agents in advance of new products and discontinued products
18. Training agents' sales staff
19. General customer service
20. Claims and adjustments
21. Warranty services
22. Service to foreign subsidiaries arranged through U.S. parents
23. Periodic sales reports
24. General competitive intelligence

D. Pricing Support
25. Establishment of prices
26. Distribution of price lists and charges
27. Pricing information concerning competitive items

E. Inventory Support
28. Maintenance of inventories
29. Rotation of inventory to avoid obsolescence
30. Warehousing

F. Product Management Support
31. Development of new products for export market

32. Selecting correct products for each market
33. Determination of which producing location will provide product to which market
34. General product management

G. Financial Support
35. Planning and scheduling budget data and reports
36. Floor plan financing
37. Rental operations for heavy equipment
38. Billing and collecting invoices
39. Credit authorizations
40. Auditing
41. General financing of sales

H. Technical Support
42. Manufacturing specifications
43. Machine designs for special markets
44. Quality control
45. Product testing
46. Parts supply
47. Training service personnel

I. Packaging Support
48. Export packaging
49. Provision of a variety of packaging and sizes in each product line to be more competitive
50. Export labels

J. Shipping Support
51. Adequate traffic and distribution support
52. Processing of orders
53. Export preparation
54. Inland freight
55. Shipping overseas
56. Landing expenses

K. Other Support
57. Data processing
58. System design
59. Insurance
60. Legal services
61. Tax analysis
62. Translations
63. Metric conversion of operating data

Source: James R. Basche, Jr., *Export Marketing Services and Costs* (New York: The Conference Board, 1971), 4.

Overseas Marketing Subsidiary When the manufacturer establishes its own foreign sales branch overseas and it can perform most or all of the international marketing tasks shown in Table 18.2, it has a full-fledged overseas marketing subsidiary. This approach requires a substantially greater commitment and investment in international marketing than the use of distributors or agents, but because the subsidiary is owned by the manufacturer, the degree of control is greater.

Choosing the Appropriate Structure

Deciding which alternative is best for distributing in foreign markets is analogous to Phases 5 and 6 in the channel design paradigm (see Chapter 6). The channel manager must evaluate all of the relevant variables (Phase 5) and then use some procedure to make the actual choice (Phase 6).

Although the six basic categories of variables to consider (market, product, company, intermediary, environmental, and behavioral) are the same for domestic and international channel strategy, the *specific* variables considered and the circumstances may be quite different. For example, as we pointed out earlier in the chapter, environmental and behavioral variables differ substantially from country to country.[30] The category of intermediary variables provides another example. In the United States, the set of wholesalers, retailers, or various agent intermediaries that the manufacturer may be considering will be quite different from the set of intermediaries (foreign distributors) it will consider if it wants to market in England, France, Japan, Australia or other countries. In short, it is impossible to generalize about all of the specific variables and sets of circumstances that should be considered when evaluating alternative international channel structures. Such an evaluation can only be made on a case-by-case basis.

The actual choice of channel structure for international marketing (Phase 6) can also be made on a case-by-case basis, but any of the approaches discussed in Chapter 6 can help in this process. In practice, judgmental-heuristic approaches are the most commonly used for choosing international channels, just as they are for selecting domestic channels.

Finally, the seventh and last phase of channel design, selection of channel members, also applies to the international setting if foreign distributors are to be used.[31] The three-step process of finding prospective distributors, applying selection criteria to determine their suitability, and securing the prospective distributors as actual channel members differs only in terms of the specifics involved. For example, the American firm seeking prospective channel members in the United States may have to look no further than its own field sales force, or even a telephone book. But if it is looking for prospective distributors in, say, the newly opened markets in Eastern European countries such as Hungary, the Czech Republic, Poland, or Russia in the former Soviet Union as well as China,[32] much more effort will be needed to locate and select these foreign channel members. (Table 18.3 lists some helpful sources for locating prospective distributors in foreign markets.)

There is no universally applicable list of selection criteria for choosing domestic distributors, and the same holds true for international distributors. Thus criteria will vary from country to country and situation to situation. The generalized lists of criteria presented in Chapter 7, however, can be used as an overall guide to developing more specialized lists of selection criteria for both domestic and overseas distributors.

Finally, securing prospective channel members as actual channel members, whether domestic or foreign, is based on the same principles of mutual benefit even though the details and nuances of establishing the relationship will be different for domestic versus

---

TABLE 18.3 SOURCES FOR FINDING FOREIGN DISTRIBUTORS

I. Government Sources
  A. U.S. Department of Commerce programs
    1. Export mailing list, data tape service
    2. Trade lists
      a. Business firms and state trading organizations.
      b. Global market survey trade lists
    3. Agent/distributor service.
    4. U.S. trade centers.
  B. State agencies overseas
  C. U.S. embassies and consulates
  D. Foreign embassies and consulates in the United States
 	
II. Institutional Contacts
  A. Banks
    1. Your commercial bank
    2. Foreign resident banks
  B. Attorneys
  C. Advertising agencies
  D. Accounting firms
 	
III. Private Trade Lists
  A. Dun & Bradstreet
  B. Blytmann International (P.O. Box 10700, Bainbridge, WA 98110)
  C. Local phone books.
  D. *American Firms, Subsidiaries and Affiliates Operating in Foreign Countries*
	IV. Transportation Industry
	  A. Foreign forwarders
	  B. Airlines
	  C. Shipping agents
	
	V. Chambers of Commerce and Trade Associations
	  A. Foreign Chambers in the (*world* years Commerce)
	  B. U.S. Chambers
	  C. Foreign chambers
	  D. World trade
	  E. Trade Direction
	
	VI. Miscellaneous
	  A. Related country
	  B. Personal/business contacts region
	  C. Mailing lists from association

Source: From Multinational Distribution: Channel, Tax, and Legal Strategies, by R. Duane Hall and Ralph J. Gilbert, 21–22. Copyright 1985. Reproduced with permission of ABC-CLIO INC. via Copyright Clearance Center.

foreign companies. In Poland, for example, prospective retailers expect to be coddled by suppliers until they learn the basics of retail merchandising and operations.[33]

Motivating International Channel Members

In Chapter 9 we defined motivation as the actions taken by the manufacturer to foster channel member cooperation in implementing the manufacturer's distribution objectives. We discussed three basic facets of motivation management: (1) finding out the needs and problems of channel members, (2) offering support to the channel members that is consistent with their needs and problems, and (3) providing leadership through the effective use of power.

This approach to motivation management applies equally in an international context.[34] The American firm seeking to accomplish its distribution objectives through overseas channel members needs to know what their needs and problems are, the kind of support that can be offered to meet their needs and problems, and how power can be used effectively to exercise control and leadership. So, in principle, the motivation of channel members is the same in both domestic and international settings, but with significant differences in *how* the approach is implemented in the different environments and with greater difficulties involved in attempting to motivate overseas channel members.[35]

Finding Out Needs and Problems of Foreign Channel Members

The domestic manufacturer that feels it has a "good handle" on the needs and problems of its domestic channel members can be in for a rude awakening when it ventures into foreign markets. Depending upon the country, the needs and problems of foreign channel members at the wholesale and retail levels can be significantly different from those of the domestic channel members the manufacturer is accustomed to dealing with.[36]

One of the most common differences is in the size of foreign channel members. Many foreign wholesalers and retailers are quite small by U.S. standards. This is particularly true in the less-developed countries but also holds for highly developed countries such as Japan and Italy.[37] The problems of goal differences and communications difficulties experienced by large U.S. manufacturers dealing with relatively small channel members (see Chapter 4) are magnified greatly in the international setting where cultural differences are already so great.[38] For example, many small foreign wholesalers and retailers have little desire to grow larger. Thus, they are not diligent and aggressive in promoting a foreign manufacturer's products. From the American manufacturer's standpoint, such channel members may be viewed as lazy when in fact they are simply operating according to *their* objectives, which do not place a high priority on aggressive efforts to grow.

Many foreign channel members at the wholesale and retail levels may be underfinanced to a much greater degree than is typical in the United States. They may be able to stock only limited assortments of products and may expect consignment arrangements and very long credit terms of up to ten months or even one year, as is common in Japan. Therefore, instead of providing financing *for* the overseas manufacturer, many foreign channel members actually may be in *need* of substantial financial assistance *from* the foreign manufacturer.

On the other hand, in a number of European countries virtually the opposite situation may prevail. Retailers, particularly those dealing in fashion merchandise, stock substantial inventories financed on their own. These retailers often want an arm's-length relationship with foreign manufacturers.[39] They are far less amenable to partnerships or strategic alliances based on just-in-time (JIT) merchandise deliveries and electronic data interchange (EDI) technology, which have become increasingly common in the United States.

Another problem with many foreign wholesalers and retailers is their high cost structure. High costs may be a result of small-scale operations, high labor costs because of government-mandated minimum wage laws (as is the case in countries such as Australia and New Zealand), and/or inefficient operating management. In order to cover their costs, they may seek very high margins—sometimes as high as 200 percent. The need for such high margins can seriously affect the competitive position of the manufacturer's products.

Still another problem faced by foreign wholesalers and retailers is that they may be at the mercy of particular governments that happen to be in power. This is a significant problem, for example, in some Latin American countries. Distributors or retailers in such a situation may lose many of their privileges to conduct business if there is a change in government.

The foregoing are but a few of the many different needs and problems of overseas channel members that the American manufacturer may encounter when dealing with them. So, the channel manager must be especially careful and thorough when addressing these issues.[40] In addition to all of the methods for learning about channel members' needs and problems discussed in Chapter 9, regular personal visits by key executives to major foreign distributors should also be considered so that they can see firsthand the needs and problems faced by the firm's foreign channel members.

Supporting Foreign Channel Members

The approaches for providing support for domestic channel members discussed in Chapter 9 were presented in terms of three levels of comprehensiveness. The cooperative approach is the least comprehensive and most distant relationship between manufacturer and channel members. Partnerships or strategic alliances are more comprehensive and involve fairly close relationships based on mutual commitments between manufacturer and channel members.[41] Distribution programming is the most comprehensive and closely knit arrangement, with specific and detailed direction of channel members by the manufacturer. Except for the case of business format franchising as practiced by McDonald's, Pizza Hut, and others in the fast-food business and some of the major hotel chains such as Hilton and Hyatt in international channels, close relationships at the distribution programming level are less common than in the United States. Much more common is the cooperative approach, with some relationships at the partnership (or strategic alliance) stage.[42] Separations of distance and cultural environments make it difficult to attain distribution programming with a channel structure consisting of a U.S.-based manufacturer distributing through independent foreign distributors. Arrangements similar to distribution programming do exist, however, in licensing and joint venture structures (see Figure 18.1), but these are beyond the scope of our discussion.

Although the specific support program provided by the manufacturer to foreign channel members should be based on a careful analysis of the foreign distributors' or dealers' needs and problems,[43] leading authorities in international marketing stress the following factors as crucial in many countries around the world: (1) adequacy of margins, (2) territorial protection, (3) advertising support, (4) financial assistance, (5) sales and service training, (6) business advice, (7) market research, and (8) missionary selling.[44]

The need to provide adequate margins has a familiar ring in dealing with channel members in the domestic setting.[45] But, as we mentioned earlier, in light of the cost structures faced by many small foreign distributors, the need to provide them with good margin potentials on the products they handle is even more important. Doing so, however, requires U.S. manufacturers to change their frame of reference as to what constitutes a "fair" or "reasonable" margin for foreign distributors. A wholesale margin of 20 to 30 percent, which the manufacturer may view as being more than generous for U.S. distributors, may be totally inadequate for many foreign distributors' standards.

Territorial protection, or even the guarantee of exclusive territories sought by many distributors in the domestic market, can be even more desirable in foreign markets. An overseas distributor, most of whom have quite limited financial resources, will not want to assume the risk of handling and promoting the manufacturer's product line if other distributors will be competing in the same territory for the same customers.

Advertising support for foreign distributors and dealers is another vital form of assistance. A large U.S-based company can actually have an advantage over indigenous firms in providing advertising support because of its greater financial resources and experience in the use of advertising. The massive and sophisticated advertising employed by such U.S. giants as Whirlpool Corporation for its major appliances, Estee Lauder Inc. for cosmetics, and Levi Strauss for its jeans have provided tremendous advantages to foreign channel members who sell these products.

As mentioned earlier, many foreign distributors have very limited financial resources and some are seriously underfinanced by U.S. standards. Thus the offer of financial assistance, especially in the form of extended credit, is almost always welcome. In many countries credit terms that would be considered extended in the United States, such as

60 or 90 days, may actually be considerably *less* than the normal credit terms in those countries. American firms, believing that the credit terms they offer are generous, must be careful to use the frame of reference of the country in question when making this determination.

Sales and service training, business advice, and market research can all be used by firms, especially large multinational corporations, for building foreign distributor cooperation. As Terpstra points out:

> *The size and experience of multinational companies gives them an advantage in other avenues of obtaining distributor cooperation, such as training of sales or service personnel, business advisory service, and market research assistance. A firm with operations in several countries can draw on its experience in helping distributors in any one market. It can gain economies of scale in developing qualified training personnel, and perhaps in operating a centralized training center for distributor personnel from several countries. Most national [indigenous] firms cannot match these advantages.*[46]

Finally, missionary selling (see Chapter 12) provides a way to maintain contact with foreign channel members and to help them sell the product more effectively. As an example, Terpstra cites Wrigley's use of missionary selling in Europe to offset lower-priced European competition. Missionary salespeople were used to convince retailers that they could make greater profits by concentrating on the well-established Wrigley brand rather than the lower-priced but lesser-known European brands.[47]

Leading Foreign Marketing Channels

Leadership in the sense of providing direction and gaining at least some degree of control over channel members is necessary in both domestic and international channels.[48] It is, however, more difficult to exercise such leadership in the international arena than in the domestic one.[49] As we have pointed out frequently in this chapter, environment, culture, distance, and many other factors make international channel management more complex than domestic channel management. This applies especially to leadership of foreign channel members. Foreign distributors and dealers are independent businesses just as their U.S. counterparts are.[50] But foreign distributors and dealers are operating in *their* country based on *their* business traditions, customs, cultural norms,[51] and legal systems. Thus, exercising control over the actions of foreign channel members can be fraught with difficulties.[52] Take, for example, the knotty problem of foreign channel members who transship the manufacturer's products, which were supposed to be sold in foreign markets, back to the United States for sale in the **gray market** (see Chapter 11). One of the most potent remedies for dealing with channel members who engage in such gray market practices, according to Weigand, is to terminate them from the channel. But as Weigand goes on to point out, the manufacturer's freedom to do so varies widely in different countries:

> *Manufacturers must exercise far more caution in some countries than others in selecting distributors and policing their sales; terminating a perfidious middleman can be so costly that it is nearly a useless strategy. Puerto Rico's legislation is so notoriously protective of local dealers that many manufacturers prefer to sell directly into the Commonwealth; on the other hand, termination in many Asian countries is rather simple.*[53]

In some countries, wholesalers, retailers, and various types of agents and brokers may have been operating in a particular fashion for hundreds, or even thousands, of years. Attempts by an "upstart" U.S. firm to lead them in a new direction may at best be ignored and at worst be highly resented. Hence, any attempts by U.S. manufacturers to exercise control over foreign distributors must take such factors into account.

The constraints just mentioned do not mean that the U.S.-based manufacturer selling through foreign distributors cannot exercise any leadership. On the contrary, effective leadership is possible, but the approach may have to be quite different from that taken in domestic channels. Impersonal, business-to-business relationships, so common in the United States between large manufacturers and relatively smaller distributors or dealers, are usually far less effective in other countries that expect more personal, participative types of relationships.[54] One study of manufacturer and foreign distributor relationships, for example, found that the best arrangements had the following characteristics:

- *The roles and routines of foreign distributors were not rigidly set by the overseas manufacturer, but were adapted by the distributor to changing circumstances in the market.*
- *Marketing strategy decisions were made jointly by the manufacturer and distributors rather than being imposed on the distributors by the manufacturer.*
- *A high degree of personal contact between manufacturer and foreign distributors was maintained through personal visits, phone calls and letters.*[55]

Though such factors are not universally applicable or a "formula for success" in dealing with foreign distributors, they do at least suggest that the American firm seeking to influence the behavior of foreign distributors cannot simply transplant into foreign settings the same approaches used domestically.[56] Instead, more attention must be paid to the traditions and customs that underlie channel relationships in the country (or countries) in question.[57] As Stern and El-Ansary point out in referring to countries in the Middle East:

> *Agents and distributors in the Middle East are influenced by thousands of years of bazaar trading. Marketing to them means to "sit on the product" and wait for the customer to come to them. A common attitude among merchants is that they do not sell, but people buy. The "carrot and stick" philosophy of motivating agents and distributors in the United States and Europe fails in the Middle East. Financial incentives may not motivate them to push the product aggressively if the process is complex and long. If they are making money today, they are not particularly motivated by making more.*[58]

As these comments suggest, a firm attempting to exercise leadership over distributors in the Middle East must be sensitive to their way of doing business. Getting them to engage in aggressive promotion to "drum up" sales for the manufacturer's products through monetary incentives is not likely to work. Rather, whether in the Middle East or indeed any other region around the globe, the manufacturer would be much better off putting some effort into learning about the customs and traditions that affect the behavior of foreign channel members. From such an understanding, insights about what kinds of leadership practices *will* be effective are more likely to emerge.

Summary

In today's world of global markets and global competition, more and more U.S. firms will need to consider prospects in international marketing. Channel strategy, as one of the key components of the marketing mix, will therefore need to focus increasingly on the international dimension of channel management.

The environment within which international channels operate is more complex than the domestic environment because so many different countries and cultures are involved. To develop and manage channels successfully in foreign environments, the channel manager needs to be aware of and sensitive to the differences in the countries involved and how these differences affect channel strategy. This applies to all of the major categories of environmental variables, such as economic conditions, competitive factors, sociocultural forces, technological developments, and legal/political constraints in foreign environments.

An understanding of behavioral processes in marketing channels is just as important in the international setting as it is in the domestic one. Indeed, the behavioral side of channel systems can be even more important in foreign channels because cultural patterns in a number of countries often place more emphasis on person-to-person relationships than is typical in the United States. Hence, an understanding of how to avoid channel conflicts, how power operates in foreign channels, and how to promote effective channel communications processes is crucial for successful overseas distribution.

The design of international channels follows the same seven-phase paradigm as the design of domestic channels discussed in Chapters 6 and 7. Phase 4 (the development of alternative channel structures) is different, however, because of the different overseas channel structure alternatives involved. If the firm's channel structure is based on indirect exporting, where it does not have any special division within its organization for international marketing, the channel alternatives are

casual exporting, trading companies, export management companies, or cooperative/piggybacking arrangements. If the firm chooses to use direct exporting, where it gets directly involved in exporting rather than delegating most of the international marketing tasks to others, the major channel alternatives are to use foreign distributors, foreign agents, an overseas marketing subsidiary, or a combination of the three.

If the firm does decide to use foreign distributors, agents, or dealers, it is faced with the challenge of motivating them to do an effective job of selling its products. While this is a difficult job in the domestic setting, it is even more difficult in the international arena because of the greater separation between the manufacturer and foreign channel members, in terms of both distance and culture. This makes it especially important for the manufacturer to go out of its way to find out the needs and problems facing channel members, to provide appropriate support, and to exercise leadership based on an understanding of the customs and traditions under which foreign channel members operate.

Review Questions

1. Discuss some of the major factors that have made growing numbers of U.S. firms seriously consider international marketing.

2. The basic concepts and approaches to channel management all change drastically when the firm ventures into foreign markets. Do you agree or disagree? Explain.

3. Nobody, and especially executives involved in channel management, could be expected to know everything about the foreign environments into which their firms' channels extend. If this is true, what *can* they be expected to know about foreign environments?

4. Economic, competitive, sociocultural, technological, and legal/political environmental variables operate throughout the world. Provide examples in terms of changes for any *three* of these categories in any country (or countries) other than the United States.

5. "Business and social relationships don't mix very well." How does this statement hold up outside of the U.S. environment? Discuss.

6. "Getting right down to business and getting things done quickly and efficiently are universal virtues." Discuss this statement in terms of some other cultures around the world.

7. Briefly discuss the channel design paradigm presented in Chapter 6 in terms of its application to the design of international marketing channels.

8. Explain the difference between indirect exporting and direct exporting.

9. The motivation of foreign channel members can proceed in essentially the same way as in the domestic setting. Analyze this statement in terms of basic approaches versus actual methods and procedures.

10. Why is it typically more difficult to exercise leadership in foreign channels than in domestic ones?

Channel Issues for Discussion

1. Dunkin Donuts first entered the Russian market in 1996 using Russian franchisees. But after three years of sustaining heavy losses, Dunkin Donuts left Russia in 1999. One of the main problems was Dunkin Donuts' inability to control its franchisees. One franchise, for example, sold

meat pies and liquor along with donuts and coffee! But by the spring of 2010, Dunkin Donuts embarked on another attempt to crack the Russian market by again using franchise channels. Twenty franchise stores were opened in Moscow. After its failed attempt to exercise control of its Russian franchisees in its previous attempt to penetrate the Russian market, Dunkin Donuts believes it has learned an important lesson: *pay attention to the franchisees who know what Russians want.* American style donuts are not high on their list. In fact, most Russians hardly know what a donut is. They prefer products such as scalded cream raspberry jam pastries and other special baked goods. So, to succeed in the Russian market, even though Dunkin Donuts needs to control the franchisees in terms of assuring quality and consistency, when it comes to product development, Dunkin Donuts needs to listen closely to what the franchisees have to say.

Do you think it is possible for Dunkin Donuts to "walk this fine line" of exercising strong control of its Russian franchisees while deferring to them when it comes to product development?

2. Dell Inc. in an attempt to gain penetration in the Chinese market decided to augment its direct sales channel model with indirect retail store channels. Two desk tops and two laptops both low-priced and specially designed for emerging markets will be sold through 2700 Gome and Suning consumer electronics stores not only in Beijing and Shanghai and other large cities but in smaller cities as well. Dell believes that the Chinese market is growing so fast that its traditional direct sales channel structure would not be able to keep up with the rapidly growing demand for personal computers in China. By relying on Chinese retailers, Dell hopes to provide many more touch points for Chinese consumers to gain access to Dell computers.

Do you agree with Dell's strategy? Why or why not? What pitfalls might this strategy encounter?

3. Ethan Allen Interiors Inc., one of the leading U.S. furniture manufacturers, is restructuring its Japanese marketing channels. Originally, Ethan Allen sold its products in department stores and they, in turn, bought the furniture from local Japanese distributors. The department stores allocated very

little space for Ethan Allen furniture and charged high prices because of the extra margins going to the local distributors and the high operating overhead in department stores. With the new marketing channel, Ethan Allen will sell directly to a large Japanese specialty retailer—Otsuka Kagu Ltd.—that will devote as much as 12,000 square feet of space to Ethan Allen furniture. This is triple the space it had in a typical Japanese department store. Moreover, this space will be set up to create a clear identity for Ethan Allen furniture in a kind of "store within a store" concept. Ethan Allen has had to invest more capital and devote more effort to this new channel, but it hopes it will pay off in the long run.

Discuss Ethan Allen's new marketing channel for gaining more access to the Japanese market in light of frequent complaints by U.S. firms that Japanese markets are virtually closed and the Japanese response that U.S. firms too often take a short-term view and are not willing to invest the time and money needed to sell their products in Japan.

4. Coca-Cola Co. has not done so well in establishing strong marketing channels in India. Its flagship product, Coke, has only about 15 percent of the market compared to Pepsi's almost 25 percent. Coca-Cola is usually accustomed to dominating any foreign market it enters, but India has been a major exception. The potential is certainly there with over one billion consumers, a large middle class, and a hot climate. But several problems confronted Coca-Cola. First, it imported too much of the raw materials, which had high import duties and hence made Coke too expensive relative to the competition. Second, outdated bottling plants reduced efficiency and quality consistency. Finally, the company had not invested in the distribution network, including advertising and promotional support, to secure strong cooperation from both large and small distributors throughout the vast country.

Why do you suppose a company of Coca-Cola's stature and extraordinary marketing capabilities could stumble so badly in establishing a strong distribution channel for Coke in a developing country such as India? Discuss.

5. "We need to expand our market base," argued the vice president of marketing for a major American beer brewery during a strategic

planning conference presentation. "Our sales growth in the United States has been decreasing over the past five years. Maybe we need to look to international markets to sustain our sales growth."

"I don't know," replied the president of the company. "We are really good at marketing in the United States—we know most of the ins and outs of the operation here. If we were to go overseas, we would need to learn a whole new bag of marketing tricks."

What does the president mean by his statement about having to learn a whole new bag of tricks? Explain.

6. Procter & Gamble, the world's largest producer of consumer packaged goods, has been very aggressive in its attempts to market its products in the international arena. But even this marketing colossus with all of its vast resources has run into trouble developing international distribution for its products. In Mexico, for example, Procter & Gamble's growth in the detergent market was limited by local laws that required the company to build detergent plants in Mexico and sell a majority stake in them to Mexican companies.

Discuss this situation in terms of possible limitations on firms seeking to manufacture their products in the United States and then simply sell them overseas.

7. Overseas Private Investment Corp. (OPIC.gov). globalEDGE (globalEDGE.msu.edu), and CountryWatch (CountryWatch.com) are three Web sites that can potentially provide valuable information relevant to designing and managing international marketing channels. OPIC.gov, is a U.S. government agency that is especially focused on helping U.S. companies enter emerging markets. The globalEDGE Web site is provided by Michigan State University's International Business Center. It provides a wide range of country statistics, training modules, and a blog on international business topics. The CountryWatch Web site was developed by Houston-based CountryWatch Inc. It offers country profiles as well as economic and political data at no charge. But more specific and detailed information is available on a fee basis.

Visit these three Web sites and briefly describe how the information provided could be of value in the design and/or management of international marketing channels.

References

1. Elisabeth A. Sullivan, "The International Advantage," *Marketing News* (April 15, 2009): 9; Eugene H. Fram and Riad A. Ajami, "International Distributors and the Role of U.S. Top Management," *Journal of Business and Industrial Marketing* 9, 4 (1994): 33–41.

2. Steve Hamm, "The Back Roads to IT Growth," *Business Week* (August 6, 2007): 78; see, for example, Aviv Shoham, Gregory M. Rose, and Fredric Kroff, "International Channels of Distribution and the Role of Centralization," *Journal of Global Marketing* 13, 1 (1999): 87–103; James Wills, A. Coskun Samli, and Laurence Jacobs, "Developing Global Products and Marketing Strategies: A Construct and Research Agenda," *Journal of the Academy of Marketing Science* (Winter 1991): 1–10.

3. Michael R. Czinkota and Ilkka A. Ronkainen, *International Marketing*, 5th ed. (Fort Worth, Tex: Dryden Press, 1999); Vern Terpstra and Ravi Sarathy, *International Marketing*, 6th ed. (Fort Worth, Tex: Dryden Press, 1994); Warren J. Keegan, *Global Marketing Management*, 5th ed. (Englewood Cliffs, N.J.: Prentice-Hall 1995).

4. Peter Child, "Lessons from a Global Retailer: An Interview with the President of Carrefour China," *McKinsey Quarterly* Special Edition (2006): 70–81; Bert Rosenbloom, Trina Larsen, and Rajiv Mehta, "Global Marketing Channels and the Standardization Controversy," *Journal of Global Marketing* 11, 1 (1997): 49–64.

5. For a related discussion see: Aviv Shoham, Maja Makovec, Vesna Virant, and Ayalla Ruvio, "International Standardization of Channel Management and Its Behavioral and Performance Outcomes," *Journal of International Marketing* Vol. 16, No. 2, (2008): 120–151; see, for example, David Arnold, "Seven Rules of International Distribution," *Harvard Business Review* (November-December 2000): 131–137.

6. See for example: Emanuel Yujuico and Betsy D. Gelb, "Better Marketing to Developing Countries: Why and How," *Business Horizons* Vol. 53 (2010): 501–509; Saul Klein, Gary L. Frazier, and Victor J. Roth, "A Transaction Cost Analysis Model of Channel Integration in International Markets," *Journal of Marketing Research* (May 1990): 195–208.

7. See for example: Dexter Roberts, "Behind Caterpillar's Big Scoop in China," *Business Week* (December 22, 2008): 58.

8. For a related discussion, see Luis V. Dominguez and Walter Zinn, "International Supplier Characteristics Associated with Successful Long-Term Buyer/Seller Relationships," *Journal of Business Logistics* 15, 2 (1994): 63–87.

9. See, for example, Jeanne Whalen, "Russian Market Is Looking Friendlier to Retailers Making Moves into Moscow," *Wall Street Journal* (August 13, 2001): A B7.

10. See, for example, Ahmed A. Ahmed and Ahmed A. Al-Motawa, "Communication and Related Channel Phenomena in International Markets: The Saudi Car-Market," *Journal of Global Marketing* 10, 3 (1997): 67–81; Robert E. Weigand, "Daitenhol Japan's Clogged Distribution System," *Asian Wall Street Journal* (November 2, 1989): 10.

11. See for example: Carlos Niezen and Julio Rodriguez "Distribution Lessons from Mom and Pop," *Harvard Business Review* (April 2008): 23–24.

12. For a related discussion, see Aviv Shoham, Gregory M. Rose, and Fredric Kroff, "Conflict in International Channels of Distribution," *Journal of Global Marketing* 11, 2 (1997): 5–22.

13. A. Coskun Samli, James R. Wills, Jr. and Paul Herbig, "The Information Superhighway Goes International: Implications for Industrial Sales Transactions," *Industrial Marketing Management* 26 (1997): 51–58.

14. For an excellent background article on Japan's distribution system, see Arich Goldman, "Japan's Distribution System: Institutional Structure, Internal Political Economy, and Modernization," *Journal of Retailing* (Summer 1991): 154–183.

15. Jacob M. Schlesinger, "A Slot-Machine Maker Trying to Sell in Japan Hits Countless Barriers," *Wall Street Journal* (May 11, 1993): A1, A8.

16. For two excellent related articles, see Michael R. Czinkota, "Distribution in Japan: Problems and Changes," *Columbia Journal of World Business* (Fall 1985): 65–71; and Robert H. Hacker, "Avoiding Export Failure in Japan," *Journal of Business Strategy* (Spring 1985): 31–34.

17. For an article that did *not* find evidence of discrimination against foreign products in Japan, see Norm Borin, Cynthia Van Vranken, and Paul W. Farris, "A Pilot Test of Discrimination in the Japanese Distribution System," *Journal of Retailing* (Spring 1991): 93–106.

18. Gregory M. Rose and Aviv Shoham, "Interorganizational Task and Emotional Conflict with International Channels of Distribution," *Journal of Business Research* Vol.

57 (2004): 942–958; Jean L. Johnson and Peter V. Raven, "Relationship, Quality, Satisfaction, and Performance in Export Marketing Channels," *Journal of Marketing Channels* 5, 3/4 (1996): 19–48; Peter Raven, Patriya Tansuhaj, and Jim McCullough, "Effects of Power in Export Channels," *Journal of Global Marketing* 7, 2 (1993): 97–116.

19. See for example: Nicola Calicchio, Tracy Francis, and Alastair Ramsay, "How Big Retailers Can Serve Brazil's Mass-Market Shoppers," *McKinsey Quarterly* Special Edition (2007): 51–57; Meeyoung Song, "How to Sell in Korea? Marketers Count the Ways," *Wall Street Journal* (August 24, 2001): A6.

20. For a related discussion, see Daniel C. Bello, Li Zhang, and Harash J. Sachdev, "The Quasi-Integrated Export Marketing Channel," *Journal of Marketing Channels* 5, 1 (1996): 59–90.

21. For an excellent article that discusses the importance of marketing channels in gaining success for products in foreign markets, see S. Tamer Cavusgil and V.H. Kirpalani, "Introducing Products into Export Markets: Success Factors," *Journal of Business Research* 27 (1993): 1–15.

22. Pankoj Ghemawat, "Distance Still Matters: The Hard Reality of Global Expansion," *Harvard Business Review* (September 2001): 137–147.

23. See for example: Kathy Sandler, "Apple Adds Second iPhone Seller in U.K.," *Wall Street Journal* (September 2, 2009): B8.

24. Saeed Samiee and Peter G. P. Walters, "Segmenting Corporate Exporting Activities: Sporadic versus Regular Exporters," *Journal of the Academy of Marketing Science* (Spring 1991): 93–104.

25. V.H. Kirpalani, *International Marketing* (New York: Random House, 1985), 78–79.

26. Mary Anne Raymond, Jonghoon Kim, and Alan T. Shao, "Export Strategy and Performance: Comparison of Exports in a Developing Market and an Emerging Market," *Journal of Global Marketing* 15, 2 (2001): 5–27.

27. See for example: Ellen Byron, "P&G's Global Target: Shelves of Tiny Stores," *Wall Street Journal* (July 16, 2007): A1, A10.

28. Ahmed A. Ahmed, "Channel Control in International Markets," *European Journal of Marketing* (1977): 327–334.

29. *Statistical Abstract of the United States 2010*, 129th edition, Washington, D.C., U.S. Census Bureau: 786.

30. See, for example, Ghozi M. Habib and John J. Burnett, "An Assessment of Channel Behavior in an Alternative Structural Arrangement: The International Joint Venture," *International Marketing Review* 6 (1989): 7–21.

31. Andre Beaujanot Q., Larry Lockshin, and Pascale Quester, "Distribution Business Characteristics, Buyer/Seller Relationship and Market Orientation: An Empirical Study of the Australian Wine Export Industry," *Journal of Marketing Channels* Vol. 12, No.1 (2004): 79–100; S. Tamar Cavusgil, Poh-Lin Yeoh, and Michel Mitri, "Selecting Foreign Distributors: An Export Systems Approach," *Industrial Marketing Management* 24 (1995): 297–304.

32. David Murphy and David Lague, "As China's Car Market Takes Off the Party Grows a Bit Crowded," *Wall Street Journal* (July 3, 2002): A9.

33. For a related discussion see: Alejandro Diaz, Jorge A. Lacayo, and Luis Salcedo, "Selling to Mom-and-Pop Stores in Latin America," *McKinsey Quarterly* Special Edition (2007): 71–81.

34. Bert Rosenbloom, "Motivating Your International Channel Partner," *Business Horizons* (March-April 1990): 53–57.

35. For an in-depth analysis and empirical study of this proposition as it applies to an industrial product channel in India, see Gary L. Frazier, James D. Gill, and Sudhir H. Kale, "Dealer Dependence Levels and Reciprocal Actions in a Channel of Distribution in a Developing Country," *Journal of Marketing* (January 1989): 50–69.

36. For a discussion of how this might apply in Australia, see B. Ramaseshan and Leyland F. Pitt, "Major Industrial Distribution Issues Facing Managers in Australia," *Industrial Marketing Management* 19 (1990): 225–234.

37. See for example: William J. Holstein, "Why Wall-Mart Can't Find Happiness in Japan," *Fortune* (August 6, 2007): 73–78; Rustan Kosenko and Don Rathz, "The Japanese Channels of Distribution: Difficult but Not Insurmountable," in *Proceedings of the Annual Educators' Conference of the American Marketing Association*, eds. Gary Frazier et al. (Chicago: American Marketing Association, 1988), 233–236.

38. See, for example, Soumava Banbdyopadhyay and Robert H. Robicheaux, "Dealer Satisfaction Through Relationship Marketing Across Cultures," *Journal of Marketing Channels* 6, 2 (1997): 35–55.

39. For a related discussion see: Michael Arndt, "Urban Outfitters' Grow-Slow Strategy," *Bloomberg Business Week* (March 1, 2010): 56.

40. Dionysis Skarmeas, Constantine S. Katsikeas, Stavroula Spyropoulou, and Esmail Salehi-Sangari, "Market and Supplier Characteristics Driving Distributor Relationship Quality in International Marketing Channels of Industrial Products," *Industrial Marketing Management* Vol. 57 (2008): 23–36.

41. Rajiv Mehta, Trina Larsen, Bert Rosenbloom, and Joseph Ganitsky, "The Impact of Cultural Differences in U.S. Business-to-Business Export Marketing Channel Strategic Alliances," *Industrial Marketing Management* (February 2006): 156–165.

42. Dogan Eroglu and Ugar Yavas, "Determinants of Satisfaction with Partnership in International Joint Ventures: A Channels Perspective," *Journal of Marketing Channels* 5, 2 (1996): 63–80; James R. Lowry, "A Partnering Approach to Mass Merchandising in Russia," *Business Horizons* (July-August 1995): 28–31.

43. See, for example, Saul Klein and Victor J. Roth, "Satisfaction with International Marketing Channels," *Journal of the Academy of Marketing Science* (Winter 1993): 39–44.

44. Terpstra and Sarathy, *International Marketing*, 6th ed., 388–391.

45. Bert Rosenbloom and Trina L. Larsen, "How Foreign Firms View Their U.S. Distributors," *Industrial Marketing Management* 21 (1992): 93–101.

46. Terpstra and Sarathy, *International Marketing*, 6th ed., 390.

47. Terpstra and Sarathy, *International Marketing*, 6th ed., 391.

48. Bert Rosenbloom, Rajiv Mehta, Trina Larsen, and Michael Pearson, " Leadership Styles, Culture and Cooperation in Global Marketing Channels," *Journal of Shopping Center Research* (Fall 1997): 95–116.

49. For a discussion related to how this issue might affect international franchised channels, see Gordon Storholm and Sreedhar Kavi, "Impediments to International Franchising in the Business Format Sector," *Journal of Marketing Channels* (1992): 81–95.

50. Carl Arthur Solberg, "Product Complexity and Cultural Distance Effects on Managing International Distributor Relationships: A Contingency Approach," *Journal of International Marketing*, Vol. 16, No. 3, (2008): 57–83.

51. See, for example, Douglass G. Norvell and Robert Morey, "Ethnodomination in the Channels of Distribution of Third World Nations," *Journal of the Academy of Marketing Science* (Summer 1983): 204–215.

52. Rajiv Mehta, Trina Larsen, and Bert Rosenbloom, "The Influence of Leadership Styles on Co-operation in Channels of Distribution," *International Journal of Physical Distribution & Logistics Management* 26, 6 (1996): 32–59.

53. Robert E. Weigand, "Parallel Import Channels—Options for Preserving Territorial Integrity," *Columbia Journal of World Business* (Spring 1991): 59.

54. Bert Rosenbloom and Trina L. Larsen, "Communications in International Business-to-Business Marketing

Channels," *Industrial Marketing Management* (April 2003): 1–7.

55. Philip J. Rosson and I. David Ford, "Manufacturer-Distributor Relations and Export Performance," Paper presented at the Academy of International Business, New Orleans, October 1980.

56. See, for example, Daniel C. Bello and David I. Gilliland, "The Effect of Output Controls, Process Controls, and Flexibility on Export Channel Performance," *Journal of Marketing* (January 1997): 22–38.

57. Boryana Dimatrova and Bert Rosenbloom, "Standardization Versus Adaptation in Global Markets: Is Channel Strategy Different?," *Journal of Marketing Channels* (April-June 2010): 157–176; Bert Rosenbloom and Trina L. Larsen, "International Channels of Distribution and the Role of Comparative Marketing Analysis," *Journal of Global Marketing* 4 (1991): 39–54.

58. Louis W. Stern and Adel I. Al-Ansary, *Marketing Channels*, 2nd ed. (Englewood Cliffs, N.J.: Prentice-Hall, 1982), 537.

PART 5

Cases

CASE NUMBER	CASE	CHAPTER																	
		1	2	3	4	5	6	7	8	9	10	11	12	13	14	15	16	17	18
1	JCPenny	X		X		X	X	X	X							X		X	X
2	Microsoft Retail Stores		X	X		X	X	X	X		X			X		X		X	
3	Clark's Flower Shop	X	X			X	X	X			X				X				X
4	Precision Electronics Corporation		X			X	X	X							X				X
5	Hyde-Phillip Chemical Corporation	X	X	X	X	X	X	X					X		X				
6	Plattsburgh Motor-Service		X			X	X	X	X			X							
7	Motorsports			X	X	X	X	X	X								X	X	
8	Hassler & Howard Inc.		X		X					X			X	X			X		
9	Barnes & Nobles College Bookstores				X				X	X	X					X			
10	Snap-on Tools Corporation			X		X	X	X			X		X	X		X			X
11	Star Chemical Company	X	X	X	X		X												
12	Innovative Toys Inc.	X	X	X	X		X	X	X						X				
13	Best Buy		X	X	X	X			X			X				X			X
14	American Olean Tile Company				X					X			X			X			
15	ALDI		X			X	X	X			X			X					X
16	Dunkin' Donuts Inc.	X	X	X	X	X					X		X		X		X		
17	Ben & Jerry's			X	X	X	X	X	X	X	X			X		X			X
18	Saturn Motor Corporation	X		X		X	X	X	X		X	X					X		
19	Nespresso					X	X	X	X		X	X				X			X
20	Bristol-Meyers Squibb			X					X	X			X					X	X
21	General Electric Company				X						X			X		X			
22	GENCO	X	X	X										X	X	X			X
23	Koehring Company	X	X	X	X														
24	SESAC			X		X	X	X	X	X					X		X	X	
25	TESCO	X	X	X		X								X	X				X

CASE 1

JCPenney
Facebook as a Marketing Channel

Social media, especially such popular sites as Facebook, Twitter, MySpace, and LinkedIn, have enjoyed explosive growth in the last few years. By the end of the first decade of the twenty-first century it was estimated that over 600 million people were registered on Facebook alone and among younger Americans, age 18–33, almost 75 percent were registered on Facebook and/or MySpace (see Exhibit 1).

For the most part, especially for users in the youngest age bracket, social media participants have used social networking sites as a high-tech communication medium to conveniently interact with friends and family, to share photographs, play games, access entertainment and engage in a variety of other activities (see Exhibit 2).

Even though the activity of shopping at 18 percent ranks in 8th place compared with the 1st place activity of photo sharing at 89 percent, the fact that younger people are already using social networks for shopping means that social networking sites are beginning to emerge as marketing channels for shopping. Already a number of well-known companies have recognized the potential.[1] For example, 193-year-old retailer Brooks Brothers has established an e-commerce capability on its Facebook page that enables Facebook users to order a wide variety of products direct from the Brooks Brothers Facebook page without having to leave the site (see Exhibit 3).

Other early adopters of social media as a full-fledged online marketing channel include 1-800 Flowers (see Exhibit 4) and Delta Airlines, which refers to its online

EXHIBIT 1 Social Network Use by Age

Age	Percent Having a Facebook or MySpace Account
18–33	74
34–44	47
45–54	41
55 and older	24

Source: Compiled from *DMA 2010 Statistical Fact Book*. New York: Direct Marketing Association 2010.

---

[1] http://econsultancy.com/us/blog/7540-101-f-commerce-examples

EXHIBIT 2 Ranking of Social Media Activities for 18–24 Year Olds

Activities	Percent
Photos (sharing)	89
Games	53
Entertainment	51
News	32
Weather	29
Travel	27
Sports	22
Shopping	18
Food	14
Others	53

Source: Compiled from *DMA 2010 Statistical Fact Book.* New York. Direct Marketing Association 2010: p. 111.

Facebook channel as the Delta Ticket Counter (see Exhibit 5).[2] But by far the most ambitious and comprehensive effort to use social media as a marketing channel is that undertaken by the venerable national department store chain JCPenney.[3]

JCPenney's Facebook Marketing Channel

JCPenney has been around for over a century. Although a highly respected retailer, the firm has not generally been regarded as a high-tech leader in the mold of an Amazon.com. This perception may soon change because JCPenney has become the first major retailer to offer its entire catalog of merchandise on Facebook. All products that customers can buy on JCPenney's regular Web site can now be bought directly from its Facebook page without the customer having to leave the Facebook page to go to the JCPenney Web site (see Exhibit 6). Moreover, JCPenney Facebook page users can also post recommendations and comments about their purchases to their friends and family on the Facebook network. With 1.3 million fans already on JCPenney's Facebook network, and substantial growth expected, the new JCPenney e-commerce Facebook-based marketing channel could become a major revenue producer for JCPenney.[4]

Tom Nelson, who heads JCPenney's digital initiatives, believes that the firm's new social networking channel will do more than provide just another source of sales. Nelson believes that the firm's Facebook E-commerce channel will "encourage social integration and user contribution as our customers shop."[5] In other words, the type of communication, sharing and dialog associated with social networking will accrue to JCPenney creating a closer customer bond with the retailer.

[2] http://www.tnooz.com/2010/08/12/news/delta-beats-easyjet-as-first-airline-to-offer-bookin…
[3] http://mashable.com/2010/12/14/jcpenney-sets-up-shop-on-facebook/
[4] http://www.practicalecommerce.com/blogs/post/788-J-C-Penney-Moves-Entire-Product-C…
[5] http://www.ft.com/intl/cms/s/0/ff2a0eb2-0713-11e0-94fl-00144feabdc0.html

EXHIBIT 3 Brooks Brothers' Online Facebook Marketing Channel Site

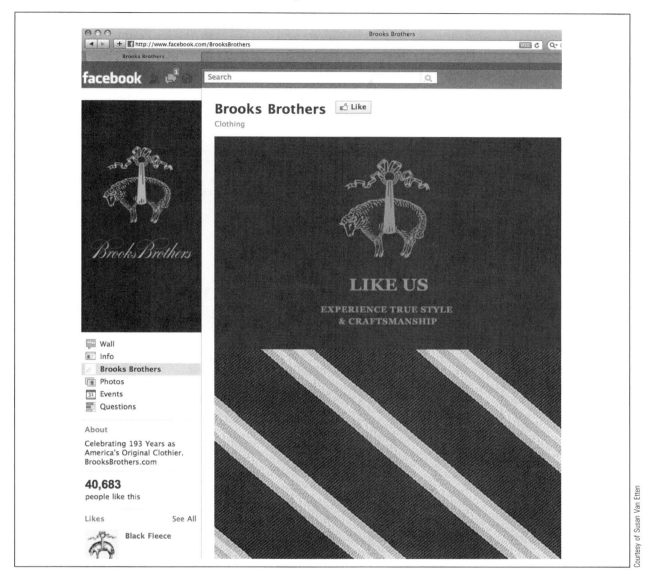

Courtesy of Susan Van Etten

Implications of Social Network Marketing Channels

The emergence of JCPenney as an innovator and major force in what is likely to become a "parade" of other firms that will establish online marketing channels on social networking sites raises several implications that could affect not only the future development of online marketing channels on social networks, but other channels and the overall distribution landscape as well.[6] These implications are discussed below.

---

[6] http://finance. yahoo.com/news/Penneys-shopping-experience-apf-4160026686.html?x=0

EXHIBIT 4 1–800 Flowers Online Facebook Marketing Channel Site

Are Social Network Marketing Channels Different?

Having the ability to make online purchases from social networking sites without having to leave the site provides shoppers not only with the obvious convenience of not having to log on to another site to make an online purchase, but might also provide a different shopping context. When consumers visit a regular online shopping Web site, they do so for the express purpose of making a purchase. In contrast, visitors to social media sites, such as Facebook, visit these sites for a wide variety of purposes other than shopping (see Exhibit 1). Consequently, the context as well as the social networking site user's frame of mind and mood may be different. E-commerce, which for almost two decades has been used to describe online shopping from purely commercial Web sites, could be augmented by S-commerce (Social shopping) or F-commerce (Facebook shopping) whereby shopping becomes a "byproduct" associated with other activities engaged in by users of

EXHIBIT 5 Delta
Airlines Online
Facebook Marketing
Channel Site (Ticket
Counter)

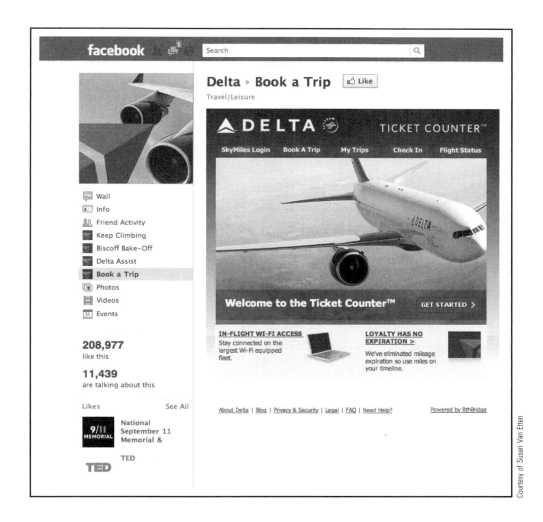

Courtesy of Susan Van Etten

social networks. This different context might affect how consumers perceive and relate to the products they purchase and the firm selling those products on the social networking site.

Will Consumers Embrace Marketing Channels on Social Networks?

The social networking phenomenon of recent years has enabled millions of people all over the globe to stay in touch and interact on a literally 24/7 basis. As the word "social" suggests, most of the interaction via Facebook, Twitter, MySpace, Linked In and others sites has stressed social rather than commercial or economic interaction among users. Even the social networking sites of large and small businesses used to interact with customers and potential customers have tried to convey a social rather than commercial tone. So, will the widespread introduction of unabashedly commercial online channels imbedded in social networking sites be perceived by significant segments of consumers as a perversion of social media rather than a positive development?

EXHIBIT 6 JCPenney's Online Facebook Marketing Channel Site

Courtesy of Susan Van Etten

Will "Everybody" Be Doing It?

Embedding full-fledged online marketing channels on social networking sites is still a novel marketing channel strategy. But the technology that enables firms to develop this capability is widely available and the cost is likely to decrease in the future. Thus, the distinct possibility exists that virtually every firm with a social networking site, which already includes the majority of firms, will also have an online shopping channel embedded in their social networking sites. Once such channels have become "run-of-the-mill," because virtually everyone will have this capability, will the strategic benefit be lost because social network users will expect to have an S-commerce or F-commerce option available on the social networking sites of each and every business they visit?

Discussion Questions

1. Is the emergence of full-fledged marketing channels on social networks sites by most major retailers inevitable? Why or why not?

2. Will social media sites be viewed by many manufacturers as a channel to sell their products directly to consumers?

3. Do you think shopping from a firm's online channel embedded in a social networking site is somehow different from shopping on the firm's regular Web site? Explain.

CASE **2**

Microsoft Retail Stores
Recognizing the Need for New Channel Strategy

Microsoft History

Microsoft was founded by Bill Gates and Paul Allen in 1975. The company is best known for its Windows operating system supporting personal computers (PCs), Microsoft Office, and software server products. During the 1980s, Microsoft worked closely with IBM to create an operating system (OS) compatible with the first IBM PC. Until 1990, the company was mainly a supplier of programming languages and operating systems for hardware manufacturers. After 1990, Microsoft put more emphasis on selling its system software to corporate users and individual consumers. Today this segment accounts for a significant portion of Microsoft sales—for the last two quarters of 2009, the segment accounted for over 43 percent of the company's total revenue[1] Prior to 2009, Microsoft software products to individual consumers were distributed only through independent retailers such as BestBuy and CompUSA. In its desire to grow and diversify its businesses, Microsoft has also expanded into new industries. After forming a joint venture with NBC in 1996, the company created MSNBC, a 24/7 cable news station. During the early 2000s, the company also penetrated the video game console market by introducing the first version of the Xbox.

Microsoft has become one of the leading companies in the high-tech industry and the world's largest software company. Its key focus now is on innovation and creativity that will lead not only to the enhancement of its existing products, but also to the introduction of new products that "better serve its customers and accelerate new technologies."[2]

The Need for a Change

Despite Microsoft's dominance in the OS market, the company has faced growing competition from rival Apple over the past few years as Mac's OS market share increased by 37 percent between 2008 and 2009 while Windows' market share decreased by 3.1 percent over the same time period[3] (see Exhibits 1 and 2). As a result, Microsoft has seen a decrease in its total revenue and gross profit in 2009 compared to 2008 whereas Apple has enjoyed a substantial revenue and profit increase in 2009 (see Exhibit 3).

---

[1] http://www.microsoft.com/msft/IC/FinancialStatements.aspx?table=SegmentRevenues

[2] http://www.microsoft.com/about/companyinformation/ourbusinesses/business.mspx

[3] http://www.tuaw.com/2009/02/02/apple-market-share-continues-to-climb-windows-drops/http://news.cnet.com/8301-1023_3-10426369-93.html

EXHIBIT 1 Windows
Market Share: January
2008–December 2009

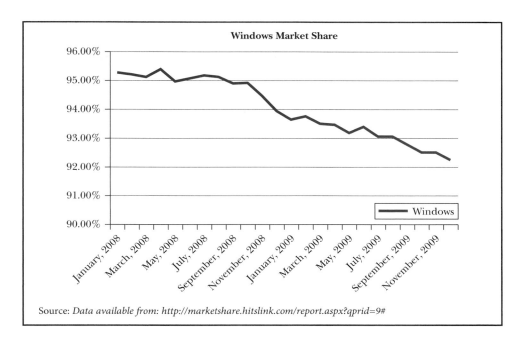

Source: *Data available from: http://marketshare.hitslink.com/report.aspx?qprid=9#*

EXHIBIT 2 Mac
Market Share: January
2008–December 2009

Source: *Data available from: http://marketshare.hitslink.com/report.aspx?qprid=9#*

Although Apple has not generally been considered to be a serious competitor capable of undermining Microsoft's OS market position, this view is changing. Microsoft executives believe that Apple is now emerging as a real competitor in the OS market. Moreover, the unprecedented success of Apple retail stores has been one of the major factors contributing to Apple's recent market share increase. In fact, in 2008, Apple stores generated sales of approximately $4,700 per square foot[4]—the highest revenue

---

[4] http://www.nytimes.com/2009/10/13/business/media/13disney.html?_r=1&pagewanted=print

EXHIBIT 3 Microsoft Corporation and Apple Inc. Revenue and Gross Profit: 2008–2009

	Microsoft Corporation		Apple, Inc.	
	June-09	June-08	June-09	June-08
Revenue (mill. $)	58,437	60,420	36,537	32,479
Cost of goods sold (mill. $)	12,155	11,598	23,397	21,334
Gross profit (mill. $)	46,282	48,822	13,140	11,145

Source: Data available from: http://www.hoovers.com/company

per square foot in retailing. Through its retail stores, Apple has not only created an alternative channel for its products but has also provided its customers with a memorable store atmosphere and exceptional in-store experience and customer service. This, in turn, has led many PC users looking for better customer and tech support to consider switching to Apple's Macbook because Microsoft has failed to deliver a comparable level of service.

In an attempt to counteract Windows' declining market share, Microsoft executives have sought to devise a strategy that will enable the company to maintain and expand its existing customer base. Kevin Turner, Microsoft's Chief Operating Officer (COO), pointed out that Microsoft strives to establish a long-term relationship with its customers, "truly connect with their needs and help illuminate the magic of software and the value of the technology."[5] The Microsoft management team has thus decided that one way to, similar to Apple, "create a deeper engagement with consumers and continue to learn firsthand about what they want and how they buy"[6] is by opening company-owned retail stores. Microsoft believes that, by doing this, it can gain better control over how new and existing products are marketed to its customers.

So, in February 2009 Microsoft hired David Porter, a former Wal-Mart Stores Inc. executive, and appointed him as corporate vice president of Microsoft Retail.[7] Mr. Porter has since been in charge of building a strong team of professionals who can help the company attain its long-term retail sales objectives. Commenting on Microsoft's new channel strategy, Mr. Porter stated:

> Our customers told us they want choice, better value and great service when shopping for technology, and that is what we will deliver through our Microsoft stores.... We want to showcase what's possible with the full Microsoft brand.[8]

The stores

The first two Microsoft stores were opened at the end of October 2009 in Scottsdale, AZ and Mission Viejo, CA[9] During the first half of 2010 Microsoft opened two more stores—one in San Diego, CA and one in Lone Tree, CO.[10] In July 2010,

[5] http://www.foxnews.com/story/0,2933,569264,00.html

[6] Nick Wingfield. (2009, February 13). "Microsoft to Open Stores, Hires Retail Hand." *Wall Street Journal* (Eastern Edition), p. B.4.

[7] Nick Wingfield. (2009, October 15). "Microsoft Seeks to Take a Bite Out of Apple With New Stores." *Wall Street Journal* (Eastern Edition), p. B.1.

[8] http://www.microsoft.com/presspass/features/2009/oct09/10-22retailopens.mspx

[9] http://www.microsoft.com/presspass/features/2009/oct09/10-22retailopens.mspx

[10] http://www.microsoft.com/presspass/presskits/retailstores/

Microsoft COO Kevin Turner said that Microsoft is planning on building at least a dozen more retail stores because "[Microsoft stores] are an incredible learning vehicle for us."[11]

The Microsoft store layout is such that each store consists of four "zones." This allows consumers to experience different types of technology. In addition, the stores feature stylish PCs set up with Zunes, Xbox consoles, headphones, and widescreen displays. Huge LCD screens line the store walls. Toward the back of the store, consumers can find laptop bags and a variety of Microsoft software products. Consumers who purchase software products can use a kiosk to select and pay for the selected items after being provided with a virtual card and a software disc. The disc cover and software manual are created almost instantaneously. Xbox fans are able to enjoy a gaming zone with a 94-inch widescreen, seating, and numerous controllers to play with. Store visitors can also custom-tailor their computers, Xbox consoles, and Zunes with external "skins" thanks to a partnership between Microsoft and a company called Skinit.[12] According to Microsoft's Scottsdale store manager Cheryl Hibbard:

> *The Microsoft Stores…celebrate personal choice and preference, and so the service offerings in the store let people express their individual style through technology—inside and out.[13]*

Microsoft is committed to providing exceptional sales assistance in its stores by creating a friendly store environment in which its customers can learn about Microsoft products as well as receive professional advice on product usage and features.

---

[11] http://www.crn.com/software/225900095

[12] http://www.microsoft.com/presspass/features/2009/oct09/10-22retailopens.mspx

[13] http://www.microsoft.com/presspass/features/2009/oct09/10-22retailopens.mspx

What's Ahead?

Microsoft has been the leader in the OS market for quite some time, but it does not know much about retailing. Thus, the opening of company-owned retail stores in an attempt to counteract Apple's channel strategy success is indeed a bold step on the part of the OS giant. Is Microsoft going to be able to do it? One could argue that Microsoft lacks the type of innovative flare that Apple has built its business around and that has played a crucial role in the successful implementation of Apple's retail strategy. Microsoft executives do recognize the numerous challenges associated with the opening of their own retail stores, but they are determined to carefully plan, develop, and improve the company's retail strategy in order to deliver higher levels of customer service and tech support to its existing and future customers. As David Porter noted:

> *Retail is an interesting business. In retail you are never finished. There's always a new item. There's always a better way. We can always improve our service. So let's get better tomorrow. That's what Microsoft retail will be. It will be better tomorrow than it is today, and it will steadily make progress every single day.*[14]

Despite the optimistic expectations about the future of Microsoft retail among company executives, Microsoft stores have been criticized for being mere copies of Apple stores. It has even been alleged that Microsoft recruited Apple store employees and store managers and that, by doing so, Microsoft would "rub off" on the Apple stores.[15] In short, Microsoft has been accused of "imitating" Apple's channel strategy instead of devising its own. Further, by opening company-owned retail stores, Microsoft is hoping to enhance its channel strategy, which has until now relied on consumer electronics superstores such as BestBuy and CompUSA for the distribution of Microsoft products to consumers.[16] The crucial question then is: Will Microsoft be able to enhance its channel strategy without alienating its independent retailers?

Discussion Questions

1. Why do you think Microsoft decided to change its long-established channel strategy by opening its own retail stores?

2. Will the opening and operation of company-owned retail stores allow Microsoft to deliver the level of customer service and experience that its customers have been looking for over the years? Why or why not?

3. Do you think that by opening its own retail stores, Microsoft has employed a "me too" strategy in order to imitate Apple? Or are there sound reasons behind Microsoft's decision to open its own retail stores? Explain.

---

[14] http://www.microsoft.com/presspass/features/2009/oct09/10-22retailopens.mspx

[15] http://www.loopinsight.com/2009/09/21/microsoft-pouching-apple-store-managers-and-sales-staff/

[16] Nick Wingfield. (2009, October 15). "Microsoft Seeks to Take a Bite Out of Apple With New Stores." *Wall Street Journal* (Eastern Edition), p. B.1.

CASE **3**

Clark's Flower Shops

Will Disintermediation Occur in the Channel?

Marketing Channels for Flowers

Twenty years ago the local grocery store, the discount store, and the mass marketer were not recognized as major sellers of floral products. Flowers were not an everyday part of people's lives. Consumers purchased flowers mainly from their local retail florist. National wire services, such as Florists' Transworld Delivery Association (FTD), also played an important role in the retail floral community by facilitating purchases and deliveries of flowers throughout the world. Credit cards were not as widely used as they are today. As a result, individuals used their local florists to arrange for delivery of flowers to other areas. Most consumers perceived flowers as something for special occasions.

Today, mass-market retailing and the promotion of flowers for everyday use permit consumers to help themselves through cash-and-carry merchandising. Moreover, consumers can use the Internet to contact florists worldwide directly and place an order through the individual florist's Web site. Alternatively, consumers can access a dot-com wire service, transmission clearinghouse, or even a grower to have fresh flowers delivered locally, nationally, or internationally.

History of Clark's Flower Shops

Clark's Flower Shops is an eleven-year-old cut-flower retailer located in rural upstate New York. Clark's, founded and owned by Bob and Dee Clark, represents their vision to put fresh flowers in everyone's home. The Clarks have been in the flower business since 1976. The company has grown from a home-based greenhouse business to a regional grower and wholesaler of potted plants with three full-service flower shops, a garden center, and two retail "bucket shops." Clark's offers fresh, affordable flowers to the consumer using a cash-and-carry business model. Roses are the number-one selling flower, and Valentine's Day is the number-one holiday for the business. Refrigeration in the building is minimal and the flowers are marketed European-style in buckets and vases displayed around the store.

Historically, Bob and Dee have purchased primarily from regional wholesalers located in Albany, New York; in Burlington, Vermont; and throughout Quebec Province, Canada. Always open to new ideas, they have also sourced flowers from the flower auction in Montreal, buying direct from growers, and on the Internet, by using an online broker and auction service, FlowerBuyer.com.

Flowers come from all around the world: bulb and corm flowers such as tulips, lilies, and irises from Holland; roses from Colombia and Ecuador; tropical flowers such as anthurium and heliconia from Hawaii; protea from South Africa; and potted plants

537

from Canada. Because the pricing strategy of the market is based on volume sales, Clark's purchases the majority of its flowers in box lots, not individual bunches. This enables Clark's to price competitively with mass marketers and grocery chains. Purchase price is extremely important to the profitability of the flower business, and pennies saved on the "cost per stem" and costs savings resulting from more efficient methods of shipping have a strong impact on the bottom line.

The Industry

E-commerce and the opportunity to buy directly from the grower or online suppliers, possibly disintermediating the regional wholesaler, have placed floral retailers such as Clark's in an enviable position. Traditional channels of distribution are experiencing competition from technology-oriented direct sellers, offering a change in traditional purchasing methods.

Twenty years ago cut flowers were distributed to rural upstate New York by wholesaler truck and Greyhound bus, and by rail before that. Typically, the flowers were either grown in the United States and transported overland to a regional wholesaler, or imported via broker to a receiving port such as Miami, Florida, and then shipped via truck to a regional wholesale distributor. Interstate haulers transported flowers in refrigerated trucks, and then regional distributors "spider-webbed" with panel trucks and vans to reach local retailers. Traditional channels of distribution in the floral industry have been from grower to wholesaler, to retailer, to ultimate consumer (see Exhibit 1). Wholesaler trucks still transport floral products; however, Federal Express (FedEx) and United Parcel Service (UPS) have also emerged as strong competitors in moving flowers to the retailer and the consumer.

Although the methods of communication and transportation have changed, retail florists still distribute the majority of floral products; nontraditional retailers such as

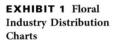

EXHIBIT 1 Floral Industry Distribution Charts

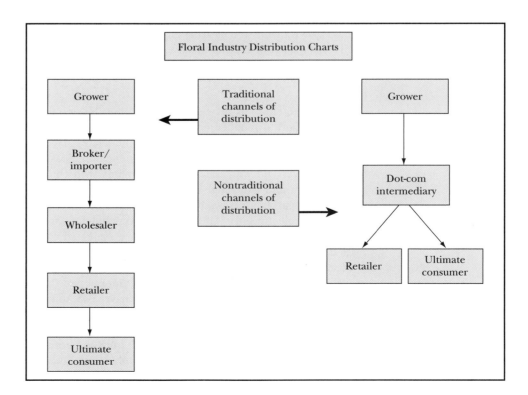

supermarkets, discount stores, and street vendors account for the rest. Customers still buy about half of their flowers for special occasions, such as Valentine's Day. But distribution channels are evolving in new directions in the twenty-first century. Retailers and consumers can purchase directly from growers via phone or through a broker via an Internet dot-com or other intermediary reseller. These options were previously not available.

The Wholesaler's Role

Some retailers like to personally select the flowers they resell. If that is not possible, then they must have confidence in the wholesaler's ability to make selections, so having a trusted wholesaler nearby is very useful. Many small floral businesses, such as Clark's Flower Shops, do not sell large quantities of certain flower varieties. However, consumers often demand a wide variety of products. Consequently, retail florists need quick and reliable access to broad inventories of flowers to operate a viable business. Here again, traditional wholesalers have been a valuable resource for providing such product availability for retail florists.

Flowers are traditionally shipped in box lots, not bunches, to the wholesaler. The traditional wholesaler can then repackage the product and provide the needed assortments and sizes. The small retailer confronts the dilemma of variety versus quantity versus perishability, especially during peak demand periods when it is difficult to stock the required inventory given needed lead times.

Discussion Questions

1. What factors underlie the traditional wholesaler's role in the marketing channels for floral products?

2. Have these factors changed significantly in the twenty-first century?

3. Do you think the traditional wholesaler will or should be largely disintermediated from floral marketing channels? Explain your rationale for disintermediation of the wholesaler or the need for the wholesaler to remain in the channel.

Precision Electronics Corporation

Manufacturer's Representatives versus Industrial Distributors

Background

Seimitu Denki Kogyo Ltd. (SDK) Japan developed the world's thinnest sealed polarized electromechanical relay in the early 1970s. This represented a technological breakthrough for at least three features of such relay devices: First, it was miniaturized, especially with regard to height (for electronic devices, reducing the height of components that are mounted on printed circuit boards is critical). Second, it was resistant to adverse atmospheric conditions due to its plastic enclosure construction filled with dry nitrogen gas. Third, it could be used for memory functions and other logic circuits because of its polarity.

SDK wanted to sell this new relay in the huge U.S. market, but lacked its own industrial marketing organization. So instead of attempting to sell the relay as an identified branded component part, SDK tried to market the relays through two U.S. manufacturing firms under their own OEM brands. However, SDK achieved little success doing so. The first firm, a manufacturer of industrial equipment, lacked experience in the component business; hence it was not able to reach the appropriate target markets. The exclusive sales agreement SDK had negotiated with the firm was therefore terminated within a year. The second manufacturer, a famous maker of military and aviation-related components, relegated SDK relays to a minor supplementary role in its product line rather than that of a featured product that would receive intensive sales effort. After two years of such neglect, sales were much lower than had been projected.

Having attained little success marketing its new relay component through manufacturers that paid little attention to the product, SDK decided to become much more heavily involved in marketing the relays by establishing its own industrial marketing organization in the United States.

Establishment of Precision Electronics Corporation and Its Distribution Goals

Precision Electronics Corporation (PEC) was established in Morristown, New Jersey, on October 1, 1974, as a wholly owned subsidiary of SDK, Japan. PEC began its marketing activity for relays with seven employees consisting of four Americans (executive VP, national sales manager, secretary, and clerk) and three Japanese (planning manager, accounting manager, and product control supervisor).

PEC's distribution goal for the relays was to penetrate the U.S. market and attain a sales volume of $50 million (a 10 percent market share) through its own distribution network within ten years.

The Channel Decision

Management at both SDK and PEC discussed whether the distribution structure of the new corporation should be composed entirely of its own salespeople or should use outside sales forces such as manufacturer's representatives.

To arrive at a decision, management made some basic calculations: First, PEC wanted to determine how many of its own salespeople it could afford. To do this, PEC decided to use typical commission rates that would have to be paid to manufacturers' representatives to achieve the sales goal as a benchmark and then work backward from there. Thus, if a 5 percent commission were paid on the projected $50 million in sales, this would amount to $2.5 million. Assuming each company salesperson would be paid $75,000, PEC could employ 33 salespeople to match what it would be paying in commissions to manufacturers' representatives ($2,500,000/$75,000). Given the huge U.S. market, PEC had serious doubts about whether 33 salespeople would be sufficient to cover the market. And, of course, this calculation was made based on achieving $50 million in sales, which was not expected to occur until the tenth year. Obviously, the number of salespeople that PEC could afford in the earlier years would be much lower and hence even less sufficient to cover the giant U.S. market.

PEC decided to do some further calculations to determine the coverage that might be provided by manufacturers' representatives at the same level of the projected ten-year sales target of $50 million. After checking with industry sources, PEC estimated that each manufacturer's representative could, on average, provide market coverage equal to five company salespeople. If this estimate were accurate, PEC could get sales coverage equivalent to 33 company salespeople by using only six or seven manufacturers' representatives (33/5 = 6.6). Further, by using 18 to 20 manufacturers' representatives, PEC could get the equivalent of between 90 and 100 company salespeople ($18 \times 5 = 90$; $20 \times 5 = 100$).

Yet management did not want to make such an important channel design decision based only on some rough calculations of ten-year sales projections. They believed that other qualitative factors also needed to be considered. It was decided that management should hold a retreat to brainstorm about some of the issues involved in choosing an appropriate channel structure for distributing the relay in the U.S. market.

At the retreat, which was held at a hotel in nearby New Brunswick, New Jersey, a freewheeling discussion ensued among the executive vice president (EVP) John Slager, national sales manager Bob Weinburger, and planning manager Tetsuo Yamaguchi. Slager pointed out, for instance, that the manufacturer's own salespeople can be very productive because they are available anytime exclusively for the manufacturer and can devote themselves exclusively to its particular products and policies. But offsetting this advantage, argued Bob Weinburger, is the fact that the manufacturer must pay its own salespeople regular compensation, which becomes a virtual fixed expense, regardless of whether there is sufficient sales volume to cover the compensation and provide a profit. In contrast, by using manufacturers' representatives, a manufacturer needs to pay commission to the reps only when they produce sales, so the costs are variable rather than fixed. Therefore, he continued, reps can be the ideal sales channel for a company such as PEC that seeks to enter the national market in a short time span without making a huge investment in setting up its own distribution network.

Tetsuo Yamaguchi finally entered the discussion by arguing that manufacturers' representatives often have good technical knowledge and complementary product lines that can be very helpful to the manufacturer. The debate over the merits of the manufacturer's own sales force versus manufacturers' representatives continued for another hour or so until John Slager put his hand on his head in a gesture suggestive of "How can we all be so dumb?" "Why are we only debating the merits of our own salespeople versus manufacturers' representatives?" he practically screamed. "We are missing another very important and possibly highly feasible alternative for distributing our relay in the U.S. market—industrial distributors." The other executives in the room, with noticeable embarrassment at their apparent oversight, nodded their heads in agreement. The discussion then moved to include industrial distributors.

Tetsuo Yamaguchi, who had experience working with U.S. industrial distributors in a previous job, led off the discussion by pointing out some key advantages of using this type of intermediary: First, they offer complete sales and distribution operations to the manufacturer by purchasing their stock in bulk quantities, taking title from manufacturers, and reselling to many different kinds of customers because of their broad market coverage. Also, their external sales forces often have strong knowledge of local markets, which can be very helpful to distant manufacturers. The full range of services provided by industrial distributors and their substantial market knowledge can also be invaluable for the manufacturer seeking to increase its customer base and penetrate the market without being burdened by order processing, credit checking, and other functions needed to service many new and often small accounts. Of course, there are also disadvantages to using industrial distributors that were pointed out by Yamaguchi. The most serious drawback he referred to is the fact that most industrial distributors carry directly competitive products, so PEC's products might not get the full attention of the distributors or could even get completely lost in the shuffle. Furthermore, industrial distributors demand high margins, often two or three times higher than reps, and the quality of their salespeople, especially with regard to their technical expertise, may not be as high as the reps who focus on fewer types of products.

The discussion/debate continued for about an hour until John Slager suddenly began waving his arms to get the group's attention. When all eyes were focused on him, he said in a polite but forceful manner: "I'll tell you what, I'm getting a little tired of this debate. It's too unstructured so we are wasting a lot of time. What we need is a more systematic

EXHIBIT 1 Comparative Analysis of Manufacturers' Representatives versus Industrial Distributors

Criteria	Manufacturers' Representatives	Industrial Distributors
Salespeople		
Academic background	High	Low
Technical knowledge	High	Low
Income level	High	Low
Professional status	High	Low
Functional Performance Capabilities		
Inventory stocking	No	Yes
Credit and collections	No	Yes
Technical sales	Yes	No
Value-added service	No	Yes
Territorial coverage	Clear	Mixed
Title	No	Yes
Products carried	8–12	Many
Customer relations	Good	Good
Compensation	Commission	Sales margins

comparison of alternatives. But let's limit it to a comparison between manufacturers' representatives and industrial distributors, because it is now pretty obvious to all of us that using our own sales force would be out of the question from the standpoint of costs." The other executives again nodded in agreement and decided to adjourn, return to the office, and spend the next several weeks doing some research, talking with consultants, and reviewing the minutes of the retreat to develop a comparative analysis. John Slager agreed but with one stipulation: He did not want a long report. Instead, he asked the executives to prepare a simple and succinct comparison chart that would focus on key criteria and rate manufacturers' representatives and industrial distributors on those criteria. The results of the group's efforts are shown in Exhibit 1.

Discussion Questions

1. Do you agree with John Slager's statement that "it is now pretty obvious to all of us that using our own sales force would be out of the question from the standpoint of costs"?

2. Develop an argument for the use of manufacturers' representatives to distribute the relay.

Develop an argument for the use of industrial distributors.

3. Could a combination of manufacturers' representatives and industrial distributors be used in the channel design?

Hyde-Phillip Chemical Company

Alternative Forms of Sales Representation

Michael Claxton, a recent marketing graduate of a well-known college, has been assigned the task of evaluating Hyde-Phillip Chemical Company's methods of selling the firm's products. Hyde-Phillip currently utilizes a mix of salespersons to present its products to current and potential users: (1) company sales force, (2) industrial distributors, and (3) manufacturers' agents. While this mix of channels is somewhat unusual in this industry, it reflects the orientation of management over time as to the relative values of alternative forms of sales representation. Claxton's challenge is to review the data that have been gathered on the three types of channels, determine if additional information is needed, and make recommendations as to what changes, if any, should be made in the firm's approach to sales representation.

Information on the Company

Hyde-Phillip was formed in the early 1960s through the merger of Hyde Industrial Chemicals and Phillip Laboratories. Both firms had a broad range of experience in the development and production of certain types of chemicals and related supplies for a variety of industrial users. While the two firms had a few overlapping product lines, each brought to the merger some exclusive product offerings. The resulting combination of the two firms yielded a new organization capable of marketing a complete line of chemicals for industrial use.

Prior to the merger, Hyde Industrial Chemicals had utilized a group of industrial distributors (merchant wholesalers) to market its products. Phillip Laboratories, on the other hand, had several manufacturers' agents (agent wholesalers) who sold its product offering. The new firm, after the merger, retained some of the industrial distributors and some of the manufacturing agents and then began to develop its own sales force.

Today, Hyde-Phillip serves 30 sales territories in states east of the Mississippi through its own sales force of 50 individuals (6 women and 44 men), 9 industrial distributors, and 9 manufacturers' agents. The 50 salespeople are about evenly allocated across 12 of the sales territories. Each of the industrial distributors and manufacturers' agents has exclusive selling rights in one of the 18 remaining sales territories. Individual distributors and agents have from 5 to 30 people working for them and many represent other noncompeting manufacturers. The 30 sales territories were originally established to represent areas of approximately equal sales potential for Hyde-Phillip's products.

Many types of sales support are made available to each sales territory by the company. Individual managers of the territories have the option of using or not using each type of sales support. Sales support items currently available include (1) a variety of descriptive brochures to supplement the information given in the firm's product catalog, (2) study programs with DVDs and online access to Hyde-Phillip's Web site to enable sales representatives to be more familiar with the firm's products as well as current market situations and developments,

(3) a program to provide generous product samples to potential customers for test purposes, and (4) direct-mail and e-mail blast promotions aimed at prospective customers to solicit inquiries for descriptive materials and product samples.

Data on Sales Territories

As a first step in beginning his analysis, Claxton asked his assistant to compile the available information on each of the 30 sales territories. This information is presented in coded form in Exhibit 1.

EXHIBIT 1 Available Data on Sales Territories

Territory Number	Level of Sales	Type of Representation	Use of Sales Support	Geographic Location
1	2	1	2	3
2	3	1	3	3
3	2	2	1	1
4	1	1	1	1
5	2	3	1	1
6	2	1	2	1
7	3	3	2	3
8	1	2	1	1
9	2	1	2	2
10	2	1	2	3
11	1	2	1	1
12	1	1	1	2
13	2	2	2	2
14	2	3	2	1
15	1	1	2	3
16	2	3	2	2
17	2	1	3	1
18	1	2	1	2
19	2	3	2	2
20	3	1	3	2
21	1	3	1	3
22	2	2	1	3
23	3	3	1	1
24	3	1	3	2
25	3	2	3	1
26	1	2	1	2
27	2	1	2	2
28	1	2	1	3
29	2	3	3	3
30	2	3	2	3

Codes: Level of sales: 1 = over $2 million; 2 = $1–$2 million; 3 = under $1 million
Type of representation: 1 = company sales force; 2 = industrial distributor; 3 = manufacturers' agent
Use of sales support: 1 = extensive user; 2 = moderate user; 3 = light user
Geographic location: 1 = Northern; 2 = Southern; 3 = Eastern

In terms of level of sales, 9 territories have annual sales in excess of $2 million, 15 have sales between $1 and $2 million, and 6 have sales less than $1 million. As already indicated, in 12 of the territories the firm is represented by its own sales force, and industrial distributors and manufacturers' agents each represent the company in 9 territories.

Based on estimates provided by the sales support department, 12 of the territories make extensive use of the available sales support programs, 12 are moderate users, and 6 are light users. Each of the firm's sales territories is also divided into one of three geographic divisions: Northern, Southern, or Eastern. As indicated in Exhibit 1, each of these geographic locations includes 10 sales territories.

Initial Analysis

Using the information in Exhibit 1, Claxton constructed the cross-tabulation of sales versus type of representation shown in Exhibit 2. He first set up the cross-tabulation using raw numbers and then calculated the conditional probabilities for each row and column.

As seen in part (B) of Exhibit 2, 55.6 percent of Hyde-Phillip's territories with sales over $2 million were served by industrial distributors. Only 11.1 percent of the largest sales territories were represented by manufacturers' agents, and 33.3 percent were served by the company's sales force. Stated differently, as shown in part (C) of Exhibit 2,

EXHIBIT 2
Cross-Tabulation of Level of Sales versus Type of Representation

		Company Sales Force (1)	Industrial Distributor (2)	Manufacturers' Agent (3)	Totals (A)
Level of Sales	Over $2 million	3	5	1	9
	$1–2 million	6	3	6	15
	Under $1 million	3	1	2	6
	Totals	12	9	9	30

		Company Sales Force (1)	Industrial Distributor (2)	Manufacturers' Agent (3)	Totals (B)
Level of Sales	Over $2 million	33.3	55.6	11.1	100.0
	$1–2 million	40.0	20.0	40.0	100.0
	Under $1 million	50.0	16.7	33.3	100.0
	Totals	40.0	30.0	30.0	100.0%

		Company Sales Force (1)	Industrial Distributor (2)	Manufacturers' Agent (3)	Totals (C)
Level of Sales	Over $2 million	25.0	55.6	11.1	30.0
	$1–2 million	50.0	33.3	66.7	50.0
	Under $1 million	25.0	11.1	22.2	20.0
	Totals	100.0	100.0	100.0	100.0%

Notes: (A) 5 Raw numbers
   (B) 5 Row conditional probabilities
   (C) 5 Column conditional probabilities

25.0 percent of territories served by the company's sales force had sales over $2 million, while 55.6 percent of the industrial distributors and 11.1 percent of the manufacturers' agents served territories with sales over $2 million.

Claxton's initial reaction was that the firm should consider replacing part of its own sales force and the manufacturers' agents with more industrial distributors. He was concerned, however, with what other variables should be taken into account to more fully analyze and evaluate Hyde-Phillip's current approach to sales representation.

Discussion Question

1. What changes, if any, should Hyde-Phillip Chemical Company make in its approach to sales representation?

Plattsburgh Motor Service

*Adapting Channel Strategy to
a Changing Environment*

Plattsburgh Motor Service (PMS) is a distributor of automotive replacement parts and accessories. Located in the northeastern corner of New York State, it is a family-owned business established in 1924 by Walter H. Church, Sr. The business is currently being managed by a third generation of the Church family.

The Industry and Its Traditional Distribution Channel

PMS is a member of the traditional distribution channel in the automotive aftermarket industry. The traditional automotive aftermarket channel begins with the auto parts manufacturer, moves to warehouse distributors, then to jobbers, to dealers, and finally to consumers (see Exhibit 1).

Warehouse distributors must demonstrate to the manufacturer that they are capable of moving large amounts of product through the distribution channel. In return, they earn an additional discount off jobber prices. Warehouse distributors sell primarily to jobbers. These jobbers are known to most of the public as auto parts stores. Other customers of the warehouse distributor include firms with large fleets of vehicles and high-volume dealers, whose volume places them in a preferred customer category.

The jobber's customers include (1) the dealer group and (2) the do-it-yourself customer group. The dealer group is composed mostly of service stations buying automotive parts to be used in maintaining or repairing consumers' vehicles. The do-it-yourself customer group may comprise up to 50 percent of a jobber's sales.

PMS has six locations in five different localities. Its largest location has warehouse distributor status, with its five other stores having jobber status. The five PMS jobber stores buy from the firm's warehouse distributor store. These jobber stores are known as captive stores because PMS's warehouse distributor store is assured of sales to these five stores. However, most jobbers in the automotive aftermarket industry purchase from independent warehouse distributors. Hence PMS is in the enviable position of not having to "drum up" business from independent jobbers.

The Current State of the Industry

The automotive aftermarket industry has grown steadily over the years and was once considered to be a recession-proof industry. During recessions, when new car sales decline, consumers are more likely to keep and fix their older cars than to buy new automobiles. However, during the recession of 2007–2008, the traditional automotive aftermarket experienced a downturn. The automotive aftermarket industry is now considered to be a mature industry characterized by slow growth.

EXHIBIT 1 Distribution Channels in the Automotive Aftermarket Industry

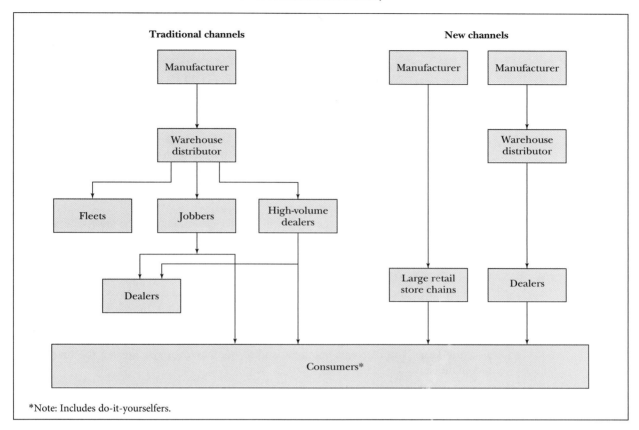

*Note: Includes do-it-yourselfers.

Several factors may account for the sales decline in the traditional automotive after-market industry. First, during the last recession consumers were neither buying new cars in substantial numbers nor having their older cars fixed as frequently. Those in the industry feel that consumers were ignoring the minor rattles and malfunctions in their cars and were waiting until a major breakdown occurred or was imminent to get their vehicles fixed.

Second, more consumers have begun to perform minor maintenance or repair jobs on their cars. The reasons are an increasing number of self-service gas stations, a decreasing number of gas stations that perform service on automobiles, and an increase in labor costs for automobile maintenance or repairs.

Third, manufacturers of automotive replacement parts have begun to use a multiple-channel distribution strategy. In addition to using the traditional auto parts channel (manufacturer to warehouse distributor to jobber to dealer to consumer), manufacturers have more aggressively marketed their products directly to large retail chains. Consumers can find automotive replacement parts and accessories (such as oil, spark plugs, air filters, and batteries) in national mass merchandising chains, discount department stores, supermarkets, and even drugstores. Advertising of branded auto parts by manufacturers has become more common. Furthermore, the consumer often finds these products being used as loss leaders by retail stores.

Finally, technological improvements in auto parts design, manufacture, and materials have led to a longer life for some products. Hence new forms of competition from outside the traditional channel as well as increased competition within the traditional channel have created new pressures in the automotive aftermarket industry.

Industry Pricing and Inventory Practices

Pricing Practices

Manufacturers of automotive parts customarily provide members of their distribution channels with price sheets. These price sheets are printed on different colored stock, and the color indicates the member(s) of the distribution channel for which the price is intended.

For example, *yellow* price sheets show three prices:

- *List price:* the highest price, but rarely charged
- *User/net price:* the price charged to nondealer customers such as do-it-yourselfers
- *Dealer price:* the lowest price on the yellow sheet

Green price sheets show list price and stocking dealer price. Stocking dealers earn a larger discount than regular dealers because they carry larger amounts of inventory. The *blue* price sheet is used by warehouse distributors for two purposes. First, they use it to "price out" sales made to their jobber customers. Second, the warehouse distributor buys merchandise at a discount off the blue price sheet (jobber prices). As is the case in most distribution channel relationships, the greater the intermediary's responsibility and risk, the larger the discount on merchandise purchased or the greater the markup on merchandise sold.

Inventory Practices

In addition to providing distribution channel members with price sheets, manufacturers use standardized national rankings, which indicate how popular certain auto parts are. Automotive parts are ranked A, B, C, D, or W.

Parts ranked A are extremely popular and are the fastest-moving parts industrywide. They should be stocked by all members of the traditional distribution channel. Parts ranked B are not as popular as those ranked A, but should also be stocked by all levels of the traditional aftermarket channel. Parts ranked C are less popular. They should be carried by warehouse distributors and jobbers, but it is suggested that dealers stock these parts with caution. Parts ranked D should be stocked by warehouse distributors, while jobbers should stock them with caution. Finally, parts ranked W are suggested for warehouse distributors' stock only.

These letters (A, B, C, D, and W) signify only *which* level(s) of the distribution channel should carry *which* automotive parts. The letters are not related to, and have nothing to do with, the pricing practices for each type of part. For example, the jobber would charge the same markup percentage on a fast-moving A part as on a slower-moving C part.

Inventory Investment Requirements

Inventory investment requirements in the traditional automotive aftermarket industry have grown at a very rapid rate in recent years due to the problem of "parts proliferation." The number of automotive parts being made has proliferated as a result of (1) a larger number of different automobile models (both American and foreign) being produced for highly segmented markets and (2) government-mandated safety and

EXHIBIT 2 Comparison of Sales by Letter Ranking

Part Letter	2005 Sales	2010 Sales
A	$1,800,000	$1,500,000
B	1,080,000	825,000
C	324,000	675,000
D	252,000	450,000
W	144,000	300,000
	$3,600,000	$3,750,000

emission control equipment. Government regulations have created entirely new categories of automotive parts. And because many people are keeping their automobiles longer, auto parts distributors not only are forced to stock a larger number of parts for each model year, but they must also carry a larger number of model years in inventory.

When a firm must increase its investment in inventory, this increases overhead and reduces profitability. However, not all sellers of automobile replacement parts have increased their investment in inventory. Some have found their niche by selling only the most popular and fastest-moving parts. By stocking only parts with high turnover, these distributors can afford to sell them at prices lower than those suggested by the manufacturer.

The Major Problem at Plattsburgh

The top-level executives at PMS were concerned because their sales had been somewhat stagnant over a period of two to three years while total industry volume had increased modestly. More important, PMS profits had declined slightly over the same period. A comparison of company sales for 2005 and 2010 and a breakdown of total sales by letter ranking are presented in Exhibit 2.

Discussion Questions

1. Identify the possible sources of Plattsburgh Motor Service's dual problem of stagnant sales and declining profits.

2. Evaluate the current industry and company inventory and pricing practices.

3. Develop alternative marketing mix strategies to present to PMS management that might solve their current problems.

Motorsports

Legal Issues in an Entertainment Services Channel

Background

As tourism director for a major metropolitan city in the United States, Linda Swader was exploring the possibility of hosting a motorsports race in the downtown streets of the city. Typically, a street race represents the culminating event of a festival week celebrating a city and its people and has an estimated economic impact of $50–75 million.[1] Other cities such as St. Petersburg, Florida; Denver, Colorado; Houston, Texas and San Jose, California were recent race venues involving open-wheel leagues such as the *IndyCar Series* and the *Champ Car World Series*. Arguably, the most famous race in the world, the Grand Prix of Monoco, has hosted *Formula 1* open-wheel cars in the streets of Monte Carlo for over sixty-five years. Swader would soon initiate discussions with representatives from each of the three open-wheel series to determine the level of interest on each of their parts in terms of holding a race in her city.

Swader was also a member of the economic development commission for the city. The commission members met recently with a group of local entrepreneurs who plan to build a permanent racetrack on the outskirts of the city limits. The entrepreneurs were seeking some degree of taxpayer-financing to complete the project. The track, a mile and a half oval, would be primarily designed to host stockcar races from leagues such as *NASCAR* and the *ARCA Series*, as well as possible open-wheel events. *NASCAR* and its affiliated stockcar racing series, with its 75 million fans is rivaled only by the National Football League in terms of leadership among spectator sports in the United States.[2] Hosting a *NASCAR Nextel Cup* race virtually assures financial success for any racetrack community fortunate enough to be selected as a venue. For example, the Las Vegas Convention and Visitors Authority estimates that its *Nextel Cup* race brings $106 million in non-gaming revenue to the city each year.[3] As an aside, *NASCAR* had no interest in running street races in the United States in terms of its top two stockcar leagues, the *Nextel Cup Series* and the *Busch Series*. A lesser *NASCAR* created series, the *Rolex Sports Car Series* had participated as a support event for the Grand Prix of Long Beach, California open wheel *Champ Car* street race in recent years.

---

[1]Tybur, Bill (2006). "PIR Attempting to Sink Potential Phoenix Street Race," *RacingPress.com*. Retrieved September 6, 2006, from: http://www.racingpress.com/btpirstreet060106.shtml, (June 1).

[2]Anonymous (2006). "What is NASCAR?" *The Irish Times*. (July 21).

[3]Wolfe, Jeff (2006). "NASCAR WEEKEND: Another Sip From the Cup?" *ReviewJournal.com*. Retrieved September 6, 2006, from: http://www.reviewjournal.com/lvrj_home/2006/Mar-12-Sun-2006/news/6126281.html, (May 12).

Last month, at a national convention for tourism directors, Swader met with colleagues from Miami, Florida; Cincinnati, Ohio; and Phoenix, Arizona. She discussed her city's interest in pursuing motorsports entertainment as an economic development engine in terms of tourism and employment opportunities for her community. Each of her colleagues had prior experience with motorsports venues in their cities and briefly discussed challenges they encountered in recent years. To a person, each recommended that Swader do her homework in terms of *NASCAR* and its influence on the sport. Swader left the convention with notes in hand and plans to familiarize herself with the business of *NASCAR*.

Swader Does Some Research on Motorsports

Upon returning home, Swader quickly completed her background research. She discovered numerous publications that provided information about *NASCAR* and motorsports in general. Two types of motorsports have dominated the American landscape over the last century: open-wheel racing with its heritage closely tied to the Indianapolis Motor Speedway in Indiana and stockcar racing with its roots in the south and Daytona, Florida.

NASCAR and the International Speedway Corporation (ISC) with interlocking boards of directors are both controlled by members of the France family—whose patriarch, Bill France, started *NASCAR* in the 1950s.[4] ISC is the track-ownership affiliate of *NASCAR*, the sanctioning body. Racetracks owned or operated by ISC host 20 of 38 *Nextel Cup* series races each year. Though ISC is a publicly traded company on the Nasdaq Stock Exchange, the France family owns controlling interest in the corporation. *NASCAR*, however, remains a privately owned organization. In total, ISC owns 12 racetracks in the United States with all but one being oval tracks. Upon reviewing the list of tracks, Swader located five ISC-owned or affiliated racetracks that host *Nextel Cup* races all within a six-hour drive of her city, with one of the four only 80 miles away.

The Indianapolis Motor Speedway (IMS) and the *IndyCar* series are both privately owned endeavors of the Hulman-George family—whose patriarch Anton "Tony" Hulman, Jr., purchased the historic track in 1945 and brought it back to life after the war years.[5] In 2007, the *IndyCar* series, which predominately races on oval tracks, is comprised of 17 events. Of the 17 races, 6 will be held at ISC-owned tracks with 2 others held on *NASCAR Nextel Cup* affiliated tracks in Texas and California. In recent years, the *IndyCar* series has struggled to put together an optimal race schedule for its league. With its use of ISC racetracks, *IndyCar* seldom, if ever, receives priority over *Nextel Cup* events at these venues. For the 2007 season, however, ISC had agreed to three date changes that provided *IndyCar* its best schedule to date.

Open wheel racing has witnessed the demise of its historically strong fan base since the breakup of the original series in 1995. Today, the existence of two competing series, comprised of the *IndyCar Series* and the *Champ Car World Series*, which races entirely on permanent road courses and temporary street circuits, mostly hinders growth prospects for American open wheel racing in terms of driver talent, sponsorship dollars and media exposure. Almost simultaneously in the mid 1990s, *NASCAR* made its debut at the Indianapolis Motor Speedway and has dominated the nation's motorsports landscape ever since.

---

[4]Musgrave, Beth and Alicia Wincze (2005). "Kentucky Speedway Sues NASCAR." *The Lexington Herald-Leader*, (July 14).

[5]www.indianapolismotorspeedway.com.

Swader also found numerous newspaper articles that documented the experiences of her tourism colleagues. In 2002, the city of Miami, Florida and two local entrepreneurs presented an open-wheel *CART,* now known as *Champ Car,* race in the streets of downtown Miami. In the days and months leading up to the race, ISC and its Homestead-Miami Speedway filed suit to stop the race, and asked for the opportunity to bid on a downtown race itself.[6] Though the event was not stopped, the race was not considered a financial success and continued for only two more years.[7] More recently, in 2006, ISC and its Phoenix International Raceway (PIR) lobbied the Arizona state legislature to institute an urban noise ordinance that would effectively ban racing from city streets.[8] The City of Phoenix planned to hold a festival race weekend with the *Champ Car* series in 2007 within weeks of a scheduled *NASCAR Nextel Cup* race at PIR. Eventually, the City and *Champ Car* agreed to move the street race to later in the year and as a result, ISC lost interest in pushing for the new legislation. On a more encouraging note, Swader learned that the *IndyCar* series encountered no interference when it added a new street race for 2007 in Detroit, Michigan on Labor Day weekend even though it and *NASCAR* race on separate weekends in August at the ISC-owned Michigan International Speedway located 90 miles west of Detroit.[9]

In 2005, the independently owned Kentucky Speedway, located just south of Cincinnati, Ohio, filed a $400 million lawsuit against *NASCAR* and ISC.[10] The track wants a *Nextel Cup* race and without one, its financial future is questionable. The Kentucky Speedway hosts *NASCAR Busch* series, *NASCAR Craftsman Truck* series, and *IndyCar* series races. Speedway Motorsports Incorporated (SMI), alleging ISC received preferential treatment from *NASCAR* in soliciting race dates, filed a similar suit in 2002.[11] SMI owns several oval racetracks throughout the United States. In addition, SMI had an oral agreement from *NASCAR* that promised a second *Nextel Cup* race at its Texas track. *NASCAR* settled the SMI lawsuit out of court by awarding the SMI-owned Texas Motor Speedway a second *Nextel Cup* race by relocating an existing North Carolina race to the track. As a result, however, Texas Motor Speedway dropped the season ending *IndyCar* race from its fall schedule to focus on its new *Nextel Cup* race.[12]

Without *Nextel Cup* races, the Homestead-Miami Speedway and the Pikes Peak International Speedway (PPIR), located south of Denver, Colorado, faced similar financial hardships as the Kentucky Speedway prior to their purchase by ISC. Under ISC-ownership, *NASCAR* immediately awarded the Homestead track a *Nextel Cup race.* Upon the purchase of PPIR, ISC permanently closed the track at season-end to pursue plans for building a larger track closer to the Denver metropolitan area that would host a *Nextel Cup* race. PPIR was an annual stop on the *IndyCar* series as well. The Kentucky Speedway lawsuit seeks the creation of a competitive bidding process for *Nextel Cup* events. *NASCAR* has stated that at no time in the Speedway's brief five-year history was it promised a *Nextel Cup* race and insists that a bidding process for awarding races

[6]Corral, Oscar (2002). "Legal Fight over Miami Auto Race Sees No Finish Line in Sight," *The Miami Herald,* (September 30).

[7]Anonymous (2003). "CART Eliminates Miami Road Race," *Chicago Sun-Times,* (December 19).

[8]Cipolloni, Mark (2006). "NASCAR/ISC Gets Dirty in Phoenix, Out to Destroy Open Wheel Racing?" *AutoRacing1.com.* Retrieved September 6, 2006, from: http://www.autoracing1.com/MarkC/2006/0527Phoenix-Lies.asp, (May 27).

[9]Josar, David (2006). "Detroit Resumes Racing," *The Detroit News,* (September 30).

[10]Musgrave, Beth (2005). "NASCAR Requests Dismissal of Lawsuit," *The Lexington Herald-Leader,* (September 14).

[11]Hodges, Jane (2004). "Daytona Beach, Fla.-Based Racetrack Developer Settles Suit with Rival." *The Seattle Times,* (May 15).

[12]Blount, Terry (2004). "Second Cup Date will Cost TMS." *The Dallas Morning News"* (April 22).

would hurt the sport. Since 1999, *NASCAR* has created only three additional *Nextel Cup* races, all on ISC-owned tracks.[13] With no *Nextel Cup* event at the Kentucky Speedway, the $170 million facility with 70,000 seats may be sold. Industry insiders believe, however, that without a *Nextel Cup* race to headline, the owners may not even get $50 million for the racetrack.[14] Yet, smaller racetracks not dependent upon *Nextel Cup* racing continue to be constructed. With the opening of the 25,000 seat, $70 million Iowa Speedway in 2006, the *IndyCar* series gains a new oval track for the 2007 season.[15]

Swader's Recommendations?

After completing her research, Swader was ready to meet once again with city officials to discuss the future of motorsports in her city. What once seemed to be an exciting growth opportunity for this major metropolitan city instead may represent a complicated legal quagmire that no one had anticipated. At the very least, she has concluded that motorsports is very much a business and not simply a day at the races.

Discussion Questions

1. Diagram the typical channel of distribution for motorsports. What entity would be considered the "manufacturer"? What entity would be considered the "retailer"?

2. What legal issues in marketing channels appear to be involved here? Discuss.

3. What channel strategy might you recommend to the director of the *IndyCar* series in terms of selecting venues for its races? Discuss.

4. What course of action do you recommend for Swader? Should she pursue a street race or should she recommend that the city focus on a permanent racetrack? Discuss.

---

[13]Musgrave, Beth and Alicia Wincze (2005). "Kentucky Speedway Sues NASCAR." *The Lexington Herald-Leader*, (July 14).

[14]May, Lucy (2005). "Owners Might Sell KY Speedway." *Cincinnati Business Courier*, (May 16).

[15]Cavin, Curt (2006). "Why Here? Iowa Speedway Opens for Business." *Autoweek*, (September 25).

Hassler & Howard Inc.: Manufacturers' Representatives

Dealing with Channel Conflict

Company History

Hassler & Howard Inc. was founded in 1975 by Bob Hassler and Brad Howard. Previously, they had worked as manufacturers' representatives of Grey Associates, a small sole proprietorship selling electronic components. Both Hassler and Howard were key salespeople, but after the firm's owner died suddenly in late 1974 (with a home-drawn will), his family and employees could not settle the estate and resorted to the courts.

By law, the contracts that Grey's principals had signed with the firm ceased to exist upon the owner's death. Several of Grey's principals (led by Eastern Technologies, Grey's largest principal) did not want to wait for the courts to settle the estate. They approached Hassler and Howard and offered them their contracts and the opportunity to start their own rep company. Both salespeople accepted and formed a partnership, Hassler & Howard Inc.

The firm maintained a steady level of commission income over the first seven years of its existence. In 1982, however, Hassler died in an automobile accident. His wife Jeanne—who had previously worked for Hassler & Howard as a bookkeeper—replaced him, in accord with a legal agreement, as a partner in the firm. Jeanne Hassler learned the ropes of the business and began to expand the firm's operations. Hassler & Howard broadened its customer base over the next decade and accepted several new principals, as shown in Exhibit 1. Hassler also added four salespeople to accommodate the firm's increasing business needs, as shown in Exhibit 2. During this period of expansion, Hassler & Howard became incorporated and achieved a profitable financial status, as shown in Exhibits 3 and 4.

Emergence of Conflict

Jeanne Hassler arrived in her office early on Monday morning. By Friday, she would have to make a key decision that would significantly impact Hassler & Howard's future growth. On her desk was a file for Hassler & Howard's largest principal, Consolidated Computer Components, an eight-year client of Hassler & Howard's. Brad Howard described the principal:

Consolidated is a real go-getter. When they want something, they are not afraid to ask. They are always trying to sell their reps on new ideas for promoting Consolidated products to the industry. Sell, hard and fast—that's their rule. When they launch a new product, it's like a storm hitting port. There is an all-out onslaught of promotion to the trade. They sponsor seminars for training our salespeople in addition to supplying useful support materials. Consolidated knows what they want and goes out and gets it.

EXHIBIT 1
Commission
Percentages from
Hassler & Howard
Principals

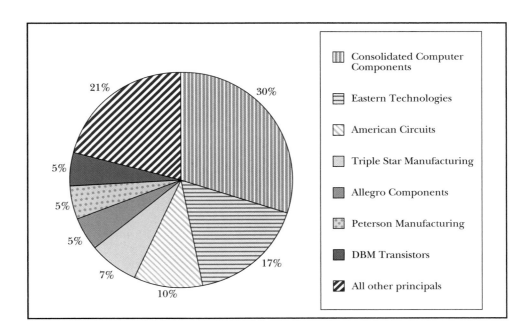

EXHIBIT 2 Hassler & Howard Inc. Salespeople

Jack Olsen

Jack Olsen, who covers the sales territory of northeast Philadelphia, joined Hassler & Howard in 1984. Previously, he was employed by Summers Inc., an electronic distribution firm, as a salesperson and ultimately as the Philadelphia regional sales manager. While in his position with Summers Inc., he gained product knowledge and established relationships with many of Hassler & Howard's principals. After he joined Hassler & Howard, Olsen further developed many of his existing principal relationships and attracted several new principals and customers. Due to Olsen's performance, Hassler & Howard was considering making him a stockholder. Olsen received his bachelor of science degree in engineering from Temple University. He is pursuing his master's degree in business administration from Rutgers University.

John Perril

John Perril, whose sales territory is the Philadelphia suburbs, joined Hassler & Howard in 1982. Before joining the firm, he worked as a purchasing agent for Texas Instruments. At Texas Instruments, Perril gained the technical background necessary in the representative business. Perril received his bachelor of arts degree in English from Villanova University.

Tom Kirsh

Tom Kirsh, whose sales territory is southwest Philadelphia, received his degree in electrical engineering from Drexel University in 1985. From 1985 to 1988 he worked in the Consumer Products Division of General Electric. His technical knowledge assisted him in acquiring many highly specialized OEM (original equipment manufacturer) accounts. Kirsh is currently attending the evening program at Drexel to receive his master's degree in business administration.

Chris Thomas

Chris Thomas joined Hassler & Howard in 1988 as a junior member of the sales team. After his graduation from Pace University, a large business school in New York City, Thomas worked for his uncle's Boston-based manufacturer's representative firm, Electron Inc. In 1988 Thomas decided to relocate to Philadelphia and joined Hassler & Howard.

Support Personnel

In addition to its five outside salespeople (Howard, Olsen, Perril, Kirsh, and Thomas), Hassler & Howard has four support personnel: Hassler; an inside sales/customer service representative; and two secretarial/clerical/bookkeeping employees. Hassler believed the firm's financial performance to be typical for this level of personnel.

EXHIBIT 3 Hassler & Howard Inc. Profit and Loss Statement for Year Ending December 31, 2010

Profit and Loss Data		
Commission income		$1,095,194.00
Other income		+$22,976.00
Total income		$1,118,170.00
Total expense		−$1,097,148.00
Net profit		$21,022.00
% Net profit		1.88%
Major Expense Items		
Salaries		$632,506.00
Officers (2)	$245,700.00	
Other outside sales (4)	289,566.00	
Office and inside sales (4)	97,240.00	
Travel and sales expense		$56,394.00
Automobile expense		59,904.00
Advertising		5,596.00
Meetings		23,150.00
Communications		63,306.00
Postage and freight		12,288.00
Occupancy		48,494.00
Insurance		44,434.00
Taxes*		38,840.00
Office supplies		50,798.00
Professional services		11,850.00
Retirement		26,002.00
Miscellaneous		23,586.00

*Note: Includes corporate income taxes.

Hassler agreed that Consolidated Computer was a powerful principal that supplied its reps with information and constant support. She thought back on Hassler & Howard's relationship with the principal:

Every time Consolidated makes a request of us they expect immediate compliance, and we provide it. Our salespeople often suggest more effective alternatives, but once Consolidated has made a decision it is never reversed. Now, we simply agree to their requests. We spend a large proportion of our time working with their products.

Unfortunately, Consolidated had confronted Hassler with a pressing problem. Last Friday, Bill Sawyers, eastern regional manager for Consolidated, had called Hassler on the telephone. Hassler and Sawyers had engaged in the following heated conversation:

Sawyers: "Jeanne, I'm having some trouble and I think you should know about it. I don't like the way Jack Olsen is representing my company. His style is too laid-back. This is the fourth consecutive month that he hasn't sent in an activity report."

Hassler: "Bill, I'll talk with him about the activity reports. I had no idea that he wasn't completing them."

EXHIBIT 4 Hassler & Howard Inc. Balance Sheet—December 31, 2010

Assets		
Current Assets		
Cash	$110,122.00	
Investments	16,456.00	
Receivables	43,264.00	
Inventories	4,240.00	
Prepayments	1,478.00	
Other	2,878.00	
Total current assets		$178,438.00
Fixed Assets		
Office equipment (net)	$65,896.00	
Leasehold improvements (net)	1,094.00	
Autos (net)	62,486.00	
Total fixed assets		129,476.00
Other Assets		
Cash surrender value life insurance		85,652.00
Total assets		$393,566.00
Liabilities		
Current Liabilities		
Payables	$6,812.00	
Taxes	6,774.00	
Notes payable (current)	11,640.00	
Total current liabilities		$25,226.00
Long-Term Liabilities		
Notes payable	$23,486.00	
Insurance policy loans	73,586.00	
Total long-term liabilities		97,072.00
Total liabilities		$122,298.00
Stockholders' Equity		
Capital stock	$40,000.00	
Retained earnings	231,268.00	
Total stockholders' equity		$271,268.00
Total liabilities and stockholders' equity		$393,566.00

Sawyers: "That's not the whole story, Jeanne. Yesterday, at our sales meeting, Jack disagreed with me about product sales policy in front of my entire executive staff."

Hassler: "Let's meet and talk this over, Bill."

Sawyers: "I don't think you see what I'm getting at. I've given Olsen enough chances. I don't want to deal with him anymore."

Hassler: "What are you suggesting?"

Sawyers: "Look, you've got to get rid of that guy. He contradicted my authority in front of my own employees."

Hassler: "Let's not judge him without a hearing."

Sawyers: "No! There is no way I would feel comfortable having a company work for me that had that man on the payroll. Why, I couldn't command the respect of my people if I did."

Hassler: "Bill—"

Sawyers: "Either you get rid of Olsen or I'll find myself a new rep. You have until next Friday to make a decision."

Hassler took out Olsen's personnel file. She had not reviewed it recently, since Olsen seemed to be performing well. In the file she found the following comments:

His sales figures are great. He never completes activity reports, but his sales more than compensate for his lack of documentation. (Triple Star Manufacturing)

We never see him. He doesn't do call reports. (Allegro Components)

He's a great guy. Always knows how to handle our customers. Gives us helpful product suggestions. (Peterson Manufacturing)

Just recently, Hassler had had lunch with Rick Taylor, vice president of purchasing for the Laythem Corporation, Hassler & Howard's largest customer. Taylor commented on Olsen's performance:

Jack is the greatest salesman I've ever seen. He could sell me anything. You know, we've been purchasing more of your products due to his outstanding performance. He couldn't be doing a better job.

Hassler sat at her desk considering all of the information. She thought:

I had no idea that Bill had problems with Jack's performance. His sales for Consolidated were more than adequate for his area. His overall sales performance has always been above average. Jack has been with us for ten years. The customers like him. But Consolidated represents a major portion of our commissions, at least 30 percent. Without Consolidated we would be on the rocks financially. I don't know if we could survive.

Discussion Questions

1. What do you think is the cause of the emerging conflict between Consolidated Computer Components and Hassler & Howard?

2. How would you resolve the conflict?

3. What actions would you recommend to Hassler & Howard to help avoid such conflicts in the future?

CASE 9

Barnes & Noble College Bookstores

Power Struggle and Conflict in the Textbook Channel

Amberly Knight, a senior marketing major, had been working as an intern in the university's Office of Business Affairs for only two weeks when she was presented with quite a challenging assignment. She had just returned from a meeting with the vice president for business affairs in which she learned of a potential conflict between the B&N College bookstore and McGraw-Hill publishing. The vice president asked Amberly to prepare an analysis of the conflict and propose a possible solution.

B&N College (a unit of Barnes & Noble, the world's largest bookseller) operates the only official bookstore for the university and is contractually obligated to stock all course textbooks and materials. Consequently, professors are required to submit all textbook requests to the bookstore. The conflict began last month when McGraw-Hill implemented a new return policy. McGraw-Hill would now assess a fee for all new, unsold textbooks returned by college bookstores. Referred to as a "restocking fee" in the publishing industry, the 5 percent fee was to be assessed against only those bookstores that failed to keep their returns below an established level of 15 percent. Prior to this time, McGraw-Hill allowed retailers such as B&N College to return all new, unsold textbooks without penalty.

The campus bookstore, troubled by the seemingly abrupt change in policy, promptly sent a letter to each of the university's professors. The letter, in effect, urged professors not to select textbooks published by McGraw-Hill for use in their courses and attempted to explain why McGraw-Hill's new policy was not only unjustified, but ultimately burdened the students. The bookstore suggested that McGraw-Hill already factors the cost of returns into the prices of its textbooks. Thus the restocking fee would simply be an incremental charge added to the already bloated prices of college textbooks. Citing circumstances beyond its control, the bookstore also felt it could not possibly predict textbook demand with any real accuracy. In addition, the bookstore's policy is to place textbook orders early enough to ensure having the textbooks on the shelf for the first day of class instead of waiting just weeks before the first day of classes when enrollment figures are most stable. Thus, according to the bookstore, substantial returns will always exist.

McGraw-Hill immediately rebutted by sending its own letter to professors explaining why its new policy was, indeed, justified. The publisher claimed that B&N College failed to manage inventories adequately. According to McGraw-Hill's own statistics, the majority of bookstores in its distribution channel have return levels below 20 percent. The B&N College chain, on the other hand, has an average return rate of 34 percent, with the most recent academic year return rate a whopping 51 percent at Amberly's university. The concept of the "restocking fee" was also apparently not a new revelation. McGraw-Hill claims it allowed the bookstores several years to solve their inventory problems before actually implementing the revised return policy.

McGraw-Hill was unsympathetic to the bookstore's alleged difficulty of estimating inventory needs. The publisher virtually guarantees delivery of textbooks to stores in just five working days upon receipt of an order. Thus, in McGraw-Hill's opinion, there is no need to carry such large inventories at the retail level, especially since an estimated 5 to 10 percent of publishers' operating costs arise directly from processing returned books. From McGraw-Hill's perspective, B&N College bookstores, in general, order large quantities of new textbooks simply as "insurance" to have plenty on hand in case not enough used books are available.

Amberly was determined to write a thorough analysis and to find an acceptable solution to the conflict; however, she was not quite sure she fully understood the situation. Amberly intuitively felt the issue was a distribution channel conflict and decided she needed to examine the textbook industry to gain an understanding of the industry's typical channel structure. That evening, armed with her marketing channels textbook, Amberly walked to the library to begin her research.

The College Textbook Industry

Total publishers' net sales of college textbooks were over $4.5 billion in 2010, representing approximately 19 percent of all book sales.[1] According to the Association of American Publishers and the National Association of College Stores, 66 percent of every dollar spent by a college student on a textbook is received by the publisher. The university professor who authors the textbook normally receives 10 percent of sales as royalty, while the freight and shipping companies who move the books to the campus bookstores command an average of 3 percent of every sales dollar. For an on-campus bookstore, an additional 6 percent is given to the college or university for use in either academic programs or student activities. The remaining 15 percent belongs to the bookstore with the majority going for employee salaries and benefits. A typical allocation of the retail price of a new college textbook is illustrated in Exhibit 1.

Unlike the fragmented U.S. trade and mass market publishing sectors, college educational publishing has remained concentrated in the hands of a few large publishers as a result of several factors unique to educational publishing. The volume of college textbooks produced is substantially smaller than trade and mass-market books. While the per-unit cost of a book decreases with increased print run size, only the largest and best established publishers are able to shoulder the burden of small volume per-unit costs associated with most textbook runs.

Cost of production, however, is not the only barrier to entry in the college textbook market. According to the Association of American Publishers, the college sector experiences one of the highest return rates in the publishing industry—bookstores typically return to the publishers approximately 23 percent of all new textbooks for full refund.[2] Once again, only the largest publishers are able to sustain the subsequent price reductions necessary to sell the returned textbooks in the secondary marketplace.

Textbook returns are primarily caused by inaccuracies in predicting college enrollment levels, a task made more difficult over the past decade by two demographic-related factors. Enrollments at many U.S. colleges and universities have been declining in recent years, with the college-age population falling about 2 percent per year.[3] Although enrollments are predicted to grow again in the near future, accurately predicting the number of students needing textbooks from year to year and semester to

---

[1] Association of American Publishers.

[2] Ibid.

[3] Ibid.

EXHIBIT 1 Breakdown of the Price of a New $180 Textbook*

New $180.00 Textbook	Dollars	Percent
1. Publisher	118.80	66
2. Author	18.00	10
3. Freight company	5.40	3
4. Revenue given to college or university for academic programs, student activities, and/or reduction of school operating expenses	10.80	6
5. Bookstore		
a. Employee salaries and benefits	18.00	10
b. Earning and other direct expenses including taxes, equipment, maintenance repairs, supplies, etc.	9.00	5
Total	$180.00	100%

*Note: Based on statistics provided by the Association of American Publishers and the National Association of College Stores.

semester still remains open to substantial error. For example, the recent trend of greater numbers of nontraditional students in college is compounding the problem. The enrollment of nontraditional students is highly dependent upon economic conditions, as either the unemployed return to school to acquire new skills, or individuals with extra money return part-time to complete their old degree or begin a new one.

The traditionally high prices of college textbooks, combined with changing economic conditions, have engendered a strong market for the sale and purchase of used textbooks. Bookstores typically repurchase used textbooks from students at the close of each semester for prices substantially lower than those at which the textbooks were originally sold. The bookstore then resells the textbooks at an average discount of 25 percent off the retail prices of identical new textbooks. Even with the discount, bookstores make a substantial profit, typically much higher than the profit earned on the sale of a new textbook. Not only are bookstores repurchasing used textbooks, but independent used-book wholesalers buy used textbooks directly from students, then resell them to college bookstores. Currently, sales of used textbooks account for 20 to 40 percent of total college textbook sales and can virtually eliminate the demand for a textbook edition within two to three years of its first publication.[4] Used-book wholesalers, however, do not accept any returns of unsold books from bookstores.

The Textbook Channel

With the knowledge she gained from her research, Amberly was able to sketch the relevant channel of distribution for textbooks for the university. McGraw-Hill and other publishers sit at the top of channel and sell new textbooks directly to the university's B&N College bookstore, as well as to other independent college bookstores that have recently opened near the campus. Professors play a somewhat facilitating role in the channel's operation by determining which textbooks will be selected for a course. In addition, since one of the retail outlets is a campus bookstore, the university's Office of Business Affairs has some input into the management of the channel. At the retail level, the bookstores then sell the books directly to students. For used books, the used-book wholesalers,

[4]Ibid.

along with the bookstores and student-to-student sales, comprise the secondary channel structure for textbooks.

Amberly felt satisfied with her depiction of the channel structure until she remembered that B&N College operates its own used-book wholesaling division. In addition, she recalled a recent trend at many colleges and universities to outsource the bookstore function to retailers such as B&N College instead of running the bookstore in-house.

Discussion Questions

1. What environmental factors are contributing to the conflict between B&N College and McGraw-Hill?

2. Discuss the balance of power in the channel. Who has the advantage?

3. What causes of channel conflict can you identify within the channel?

4. What solution might you recommend to Amberly as a potential avenue for consideration?

CASE **10**

Snap-on Tools Corporation
Differential Advantage through
Channel Strategy

Snap-on Tools is the world's largest manufacturer and distributor of tools and related service items for professional mechanics. Its principal products are hand tools, including wrenches, screwdrivers, hammers, and similar products, as well as pneumatic impact wrenches and chisels, power-assisted drills, tool cabinets, and electronic automotive diagnostic equipment. In all, 12,000 different products are manufactured by Snap-on. These products are used primarily for automotive service and maintenance, but they are also used in manufacturing and other repair and maintenance activities.

The products are sold through 4,800 independent dealers throughout the world. Each dealer operates out of a walk-in display van or similar vehicle that carries an extensive inventory of products and parts directly to customers. Total 2010 sales for Snap-on were over $2.6 billion. Exhibit 1 provides additional sales data for the company.

Company History

The history of Snap-on Tools begins in 1919. The nation was recovering from World War I and many factories were attempting to shift from military to civilian production. One of these factories, Milwaukee-based American Grinder Manufacturing Company, had just promoted an employee to manager of the socket division. This division was in the business of making one-piece wrenches (see Exhibit 2).

The employee's name was Joe Johnson, and he had just turned 25. Joe was promoted because of his manufacturing knowledge as well as his marketing skills. After a few months, Joe recognized a flaw in the product. He asked, "Why buy a handle in order to use the socket?" His idea was that instead of buying a socket and handle for each size, buy only *one* handle and many different sizes of sockets that would all fit on the same handle (see Exhibit 3). This idea would significantly reduce the cost of wrenches and would require less storage space. Joe presented his idea to the management of American Grinder and it was immediately refused. "We sell tools, not toys," said management.

Undaunted, Joe quit American Grinder, found a partner, hired two salesmen, and began producing the new wrenches himself. Using the slogan, "Five do the work of fifty," he was able to sell 500 C.O.D. orders in the remainder of that year alone. In 1920, Snap-on Wrench Company was legally incorporated.

The company grew tremendously during the next few years, and by 1929 Snap-on had spread to 26 branches and employed more than 300 salesmen. In 1930, Snap-on Wrench Company merged with Blue Point Tools to form a new tool-making giant. In 1931, Snap-on took its first corporate step on international territory by establishing a Canadian subsidiary. The sales orders were increasing faster than the plants could fill them, and profits were increasing every year. But then the Great Depression swept over the nation.

EXHIBIT 1 Snap-on
Tools Corporation
Sales Results, 2010

Net Sales	Sales (millions of dollars)	Percent of Total
Commercial & Industrial Group	$913.0	34.86
Snap-on Tools Group	945.0	36.08
Repair Systems & Information Group	761.2	29.06
Total	$2,619.2	100%

EXHIBIT 2
One-Piece Wrenches,
the Only Kind
Available before 1919

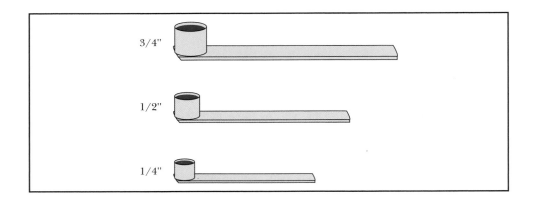

EXHIBIT 3
Joe Johnson's
Interchangeable
Sockets, 1919

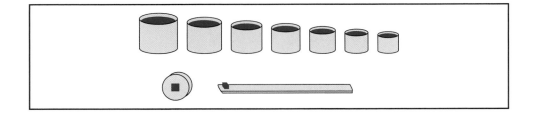

During the depression, Snap-on salesmen introduced two new sales strategies that kept them (and the company) from sinking. The first idea, still rather novel at that time, was referred to as time payment selling—that is, extending credit and accepting monthly payments. The second idea was so successful that Snap-on Tools adopted it and turned it into a competitive advantage. The idea was to "pre-sell" tools to customers for future use. The salesmen would place orders but would not ship the tools or charge customers until the economic situation improved. These presale orders were a big hit and were eventually referred to as "dream lists."

The depression had eased by 1937, so Snap-on Tools opened its second manufacturing plant in Illinois. By 1939, the company had fully recovered from the depression and declared its first dividend payments to stockholders.

The next major event that affected the history of Snap-on Tools was World War II. During this period, government demand was very high. Tanks, jeeps, boats, aircraft, and other war equipment had to be repaired. Snap-on Tools signed a contract making it a major supplier of industrial tools to the government during the war. But although the manufacturing plants ran at full capacity, the many civilian customers could not get their orders filled at all. Management's answer to this problem was to release any excess stock to the salesmen. Because the excess tools were shipped to the individual salesmen rather than to customers, it soon became common to see Snap-on salesmen with cars loaded with tools and mechanical accessories. In effect, their cars and trucks became both mini-warehouses and display floors for the Snap-on tools they were selling. Although this did not completely solve the demand problem, it soon became the normal way of selling Snap-on tools for several reasons: (1) it reduced the inventory carrying costs of the company; (2) it met some of the civilian demand; (3) it was a strong sign of goodwill toward civilian customers; and, most important, (4) it added to the earnings of the Snap-on salesmen. In fact, this new distribution strategy became so effective that the logical next step was to let each salesman operate as an individual business with Snap-on franchising rights and an assigned territory.

After World War II, with an innovative and strong independent dealer distribution system in place, the key emphasis at Snap-on was on marketing. The company developed and planned effective advertising campaigns, coupled with a strong commitment to providing customers with the tools and equipment they asked for. This marketing focus continued into the 1950s with Snap-on diversifying into new markets primarily through acquisitions, both national and international.

The 1960s were a period of increased technology and innovations in the automobile market. Cars were becoming more complex, stimulating a need for electronic diagnostic and tune-up equipment. Snap-on satisfied this need by matching manufacturing with marketing—developing a myriad of new and innovative products and marketing them aggressively through its dealers. As market share and profits grew, Snap-on was one of the first U.S. companies to own its own mainframe computer for order processing and inventory management. With this strong grounding in manufacturing, marketing, and distribution, Snap-on was well prepared for the 1970s, and the next ten years would show the biggest growth in the company's history. Between 1969 and 1973 sales doubled; between 1973 and 1979 sales doubled again to $373 million.

In the early 1980s a recession led to a significant decrease in demand for new tools and, hence, sales growth slowed during the first few years of the decade. Then in the mid-1980s sales picked up so that, by 1989, sales had more than doubled over the 1980 level. Strong sales growth continued through the 1990s and through the first decade of the twenty first century (See Exhibit 1).

Channel Strategy and Structure

The Snap-on Tools channel structure stresses a very strong and well-supported effort on the part of its independent mobile dealers to provide an extraordinary standard of customer service that is unique in the industry. The dealers bring a wide assortment of products directly to the mechanics in their places of business, whenever needed, and provide product information and servicing. In effect, the entire range of resources of Snap-on Tools Corporation is brought right to customers' doors through the mobile van dealer.

Exhibit 4 provides an overview of the channel structure for Snap-on Tools.

The independent dealers replenish their inventories, usually weekly, from the branch inventories. Because dealers' territories are generally close to a branch, the combined inventories ensure that the vast majority of customer product needs can be filled by their dealers quickly, if not immediately.

The most direct and important connection between the independent dealers and Snap-on Tools is the field manager. The field manager is an employee and former successful dealer who works closely with a small dealer group. Field managers undergo extensive training in product knowledge, sales techniques, inventory management, tool

EXHIBIT 4 The
Snap-on Tools Channel
Structure

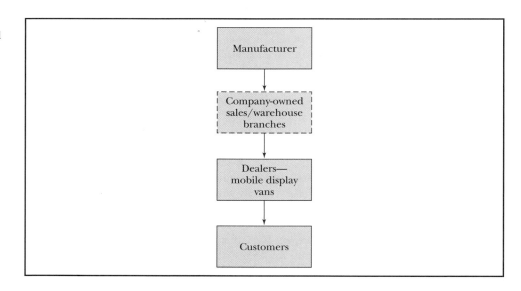

displays, and overall dealer business operations. They in turn transfer the benefits of this training to individual dealers by demonstrating and helping dealers to sell new tools and more sophisticated diagnostic equipment. Field managers also provide a critical communications channel to Snap-on Tools regarding shifts in customer demand, reaction to new products, and the effectiveness of the company's marketing programs.

In addition to the marketing and service support for the individual dealer provided by the field managers, Snap-on provides a variety of other types of support for its dealers. For example, dealers are able to offer customers fast and reliable repair service for air tools, tune-up equipment, and other items through one of six regional centers. To mechanics, who depend on tools and equipment for their livelihood, prompt repair service is of immeasurable value.

Mechanics have similarly grown to rely on the fast replacement of parts and other needed items not normally carried by dealers. A national parts distribution center, operating out of Kenosha, Wisconsin, provides such a service. Parts are routinely shipped within 24 hours of receipt of the order. Because most dealers provide loaners for the short time that a customer waits for a repaired tool or needed part, the customer is still equipped with tools and equipment to perform any automotive repair. These services demonstrate to the customer that his dealer has a thorough understanding of the demanding nature of an auto mechanic's business and a commitment to satisfy those demands.

Several other elements play a key role in the Snap-on Tools channel strategy. First, Snap-on assigns territories to each of its dealers. They are expected to cultivate the assigned territory extensively but not venture outside of the territory in search of additional business. Second, the company operates on an exclusive arrangement with its dealers. They are required to sell only Snap-on products and no other competitive or even complementary products. Third, Snap-on expects dealers to carry a full assortment of Snap-on products in their mobile vans so that customers have high levels of selection in tools and equipment. Finally, Snap-on supplies much of the inventory to its dealers on a consignment basis whereby the dealers do not have to pay for an item until it is sold. Snap-on believes that this strategy plays a vital role in sustaining its dealer network because it reduces dealers' capital requirements and the cost of dealer start-up, while improving dealer cash flow. These benefits are especially important during adverse economic conditions. Snap-on also feels that its consignment strategy helps the company to recruit the most highly qualified and motivated dealers.

Discussion Questions

1. What do you see as the most valuable benefits that Snap-on Tools offers to its customers? On what are they based? Discuss.

2. Discuss the rationale underlying the main features of the Snap-on Tools channel structure and strategy.

Star Chemical Company
Choosing Alternative Channel Structures

The Star Chemical Company is an old-line manufacturer of chemicals with annual sales of $500 million. In recent years it has experienced a profit slump, mainly because of excess capacity and severe price competition. Industrial buyers choose their chemical suppliers chiefly on price. They pay some attention to delivery reliability and service, but generally they show little loyalty. Star had been more profitable in the past because of superior production efficiency, but competitors had built newer plants and were enjoying equal or lower costs than Star.

A number of stockholders were critical of Star's management for not getting into consumer products. Other chemical companies had integrated forward into making and branding some of the final products that were sold to consumers, thereby capturing the value added and sheltering these products from strict price competition. Star Chemical had not done this, primarily because of its lack of experience in consumer marketing and the absence of any specific product opportunities.

Star's research and development department recently formulated a new line of chlorinated organic chemicals that function as bleaches, germicides, and oxidants. Ralph Hemstead, the R&D director, suggested that one of the uses of the line could be a germicidal chemical for the swimming pool market. He believed that the new chemical would have qualities superior to those of existing swimming pool chemicals. Top management was interested because this offered an opportunity to enter the consumer market on a small scale and gain experience.

A new products committee consisting of the research director, sales manager, marketing research manager, and advertising manager met to discuss what to do with this new consumer product opportunity. They knew that there were a great number of swimming pools in the United States (residential pools, motel pools, public pools, school pools, etc.). Most of the private residential pools were found in states with warmer climates, although some were located in all big cities. Pools required periodic chemical treatment to keep them safe to use. Pool owners and managers bought their supplies through department stores, hardware stores, garden supply stores, pool specialty supply houses, pool service firms, and so on.

Star Chemical's sales force had no experience selling to wholesale or retail firms in the consumer area. However, the sales manager felt that the sales force should be given a chance to sell the new product to the appropriate channels of distribution. Otherwise the company's salespeople would feel bypassed and demoralized by losing a chance to make commissions on the new product. The other managers, however, felt that the company's sales force should not be diverted from its regular job and that a new sales force or distributor could handle the new task more efficiently.

The new product committee faced some additional decisions. It had to decide whether to brand the product to sell it in bulk form for private labeling. It had to decide whether to cover a large number of distribution channels and markets or concentrate on certain channels and markets. It had to decide whether to push the brand through with good sales force effort or pull the brand through with heavy advertising.

The members of the new product committee realized that there were many alternative approaches to the marketing of this germicidal chemical. They recognized the need for clear criteria to make a choice among distribution alternatives. The members agreed to judge alternative proposals against the following criteria (percentages show the criterion's rated importance):

1. Effectiveness in reaching swimming pool owners (15 percent)
2. Amount of profit if this alternative works well (25 percent)
3. Experience company will gain in consumer marketing (10 percent)
4. Amount of investment involved (lower investment considered preferable) (30 percent)
5. Ability of company to cut short its losses (20 percent)

Discussion Question

1. Star Chemical has called you in to consult on this problem. Management would like to receive a clear picture of its major distribution alternatives. It would also like you to propose a method for evaluating the major distribution alternatives on a quantitative basis.

Innovative Toys Inc.

Consumer Shopping Behavior and Channel Design

By 2009, Innovative Toys Inc. developed a new toy line consisting of six high-quality toys for infants, ranging in price from $3.79 to $5.99. Because of the fierce competition for shelf space in the major retail channels for infant toys (mass merchandisers, discount toy stores, and discount department stores), Innovative was considering the possibility of selling the new infant toy line through supermarkets.

To appraise the feasibility of using supermarkets to distribute the infant toy line, Donald Morrison, vice president of marketing, hired an outside marketing research firm to study the question. The research report follows.

Marketing Research Firm's Report

Supermarkets have not played a large role in the distribution of infant toys or other classes of toys. In fact, it is estimated that only about 3 percent of total industry toy volume is accounted for by supermarkets. But in the next several years, substantial changes may be in store for the distribution of toys through supermarkets. The underlying factor responsible for this change is the heavy push by the supermarket industry to put more emphasis on the sale of nonfoods, particularly general merchandise, because of the higher margins available. Toys, particularly infant toys, might play a prominent role in this overall trend toward more emphasis on general merchandise (GM) by supermarkets.

Two basic factors must be present, however, in order to market toys successfully through supermarket channels: (1) supermarket buyers must be favorably disposed toward toys as an important and profitable GM category, and (2) consumers must be willing to purchase toys from supermarkets. An analysis of each of these factors follows.

Disposition of Supermarket Executives toward Toys as a General Merchandise Category

Several studies show a generally favorable attitude by supermarket executives toward toys as an important GM category. For example, a study of a nationwide panel of supermarket executives reported in *Progressive Grocer* yielded the results shown in Exhibit 1. No ratings were less than good, while 54 percent of the supermarket executives rated toys as either very good or excellent as a GM category.

Another study conducted by the research division of *Progressive Grocer* developed a comparative rating scale to show how toys are rated by supermarket executives among 30 GM categories. This is shown in Exhibit 2. As indicated, toys do reasonably well, scoring 79 (peg) and 67 (boxed) out of a possible 100. While toys are not rated as highly as light bulbs, disposable lighters, motor oil, and other GM categories, peg toys rated ahead of such items as basic soft goods, batteries, and sunglasses; and boxed toys are rated higher than glassware, photo finishing, hardware, and other items.

EXHIBIT 1 Sales and Profit Ratings of Toys by a Representative Panel of Supermarket Executives

	Rating (%)
Excellent	8
Very good	46
Good	46
Fair/poor	0

EXHIBIT 2 How Supermarket Executives Rate 30 General Merchandise Product Groups

Product	Score
1. Light bulbs	100
2. Disposable lighters	96
3. Pet supplies	91
4. Pantyhose	88
5. School supplies, stationery	88
6. Gloves	87
7. Magazines	86
8. Motor oil	85
9. Housewares	84
10. Photo supplies	80
11. Paperbacks	79
12. Toys (peg)	79
13. Soft goods, basics	78
14. Soft goods, kitchen	76
15. Batteries	75
16. Greeting cards	74
17. Sunglasses	73
18. Soft goods, accessories	73
19. Baby goods	70
20. Toys (boxed)	67
21. Glassware	66
22. Children's books	65
23. Footwear	62
24. Yarn	61
25. Photo finishing	61
26. Party goods	59
27. Hardware, paint supplies	58
28. Sewing notions	58
29. Auto accessories	55
30. Small appliances	51

Index: Highest score = 100

Median score = 75

It would appear, then, that toys in general are viewed quite favorably by supermarkets as a potentially important GM category.

With respect to supermarket executives' attitudes toward the more specialized category of infant toys, and particularly Innovative Toys' line of infant toys, no survey data exist. Nevertheless, it is possible at this point to appraise probable supermarket executive attitudes toward Innovative's infant toy line by comparing the line against certain basic criteria commonly used by supermarket buyers when selecting a new GM item. The most important of these criteria are the following:

1. Margin potential
2. Frequency of sale or repeat factor (turnover)
3. Impulse buying potential
4. Size
5. Degree to which purchased by women
6. Stability

Each of these will be discussed in terms of how well Innovative's infant toy line is likely to rate on each criterion.

Margin Potential

Deteriorating margins on food products and rapidly increasing operating expenses have made supermarket operators highly sensitive to the margin potentials of prospective new GM products. They want margins that are much better than the average 20 to 21 percent of sales for all products sold by independent and chain supermarkets. While there is no definite minimum margin requirement for a GM item, if the item is capable of yielding a margin approximately 50 percent higher than the 20 to 21 percent average (i.e., at least 30 percent), it is more likely to be acceptable in terms of margin requirements. Exhibit 3 shows how Innovative's infant toys rate in terms of potential margins. If these toys could be sold at the prices in column 3, the margins generated would be attractive and competitive with many other GM items.

Turnover

With respect to frequency of sales, the product should be one that can be sold frequently, and to a large percentage of the consumers who shop in supermarkets. Even though supermarkets have high traffic, the shoppers are essentially the same week after week. So, if the product is to be sold over and over again to yield a high turnover, it must be consumed fairly rapidly. It should be pointed out, however, that the turnover figure on

EXHIBIT 3 Margin Potentials for Innovative Toys' Infant Toys, Using Estimated Retail Selling Prices

Toy	Cost	Selling Price	Markup	Margin on Selling Price
Infant Ball	$2.47	$3.79	$1.32	34.8%
Little Teether	2.63	3.99	1.36	34.1
Feel and Look	2.76	4.29	1.53	35.7
Fun Rings	3.04	4.49	1.45	32.3
Look and Find	3.34	4.99	1.65	33.1
Johnny Teething	4.19	5.99	1.80	30.0
			Average	33.3%

GM need not be as high as the 12 to 14 average stockturns for grocery products. A turnover rate between 6 and 7 is quite acceptable for a GM product yielding a margin of 30 to 35 percent. If Innovative Toys could achieve an annual turnover rate of not less than 6 per year, it would meet the turnover criteria of many supermarkets.

Impulse Buying

A good GM product must lend itself to impulse buying. Packaging, price, and quality must be such that the customer does not have to comparison shop other stores. The customer should be able to decide on its purchase within a few moments of contact with the product at the point of sale. Innovative's infant toy line appears to meet this criterion quite well. Packaging, quality, and price are geared to promote impulse purchasing.

Size

Display space is limited, even in the modern supermarkets of 50,000 to 75,000 square feet, and, of course, in the smaller supermarkets of 30,000 square feet and under space is even tighter. A good GM product, therefore, must not be overly bulky. On the other hand, given the theft and pilferage problem that exists today, very small items can also pose concerns. Innovative's infant toy line appears to present no particular problems on this criterion. But care will have to be given in the future to developing even more effective yet compact prepack displays.

Women Shoppers

About 80 percent of supermarket customers are women. Accordingly, a GM product must be one normally purchased by women. There is no problem here with Innovative's infant toy line because these toys normally would be bought by women.

Stableness

A desirable GM product should be relatively stable in the sense that variations in colors, sizes, and styles should be at a minimum. Supermarkets do not have the space to offer wide selections and they are very reluctant to handle style or fashion merchandise except for brief in-and-out promotions. Innovative's infant toy line scores well on this criterion. The selection is limited and it is not subject to rapid fashion changes.

Consumer Willingness to Purchase Toys in Supermarkets

Even though supermarket operators have a generally favorable disposition toward toys as a GM category and Innovative's infant toy line should rate highly in terms of meeting basic supermarket purchasing criteria for GM, the ultimate determinant of whether the line will sell successfully in supermarkets lies in the area of consumer shopping habits and patterns. In short, are consumers likely to buy more toys (and, particularly, Innovative's infant toys) from supermarkets?

In order to deal with this question, a general profile of supermarket shopping behavior will be discussed in terms of how this shopping behavior is likely to facilitate or inhibit toy sales in supermarkets. Second, a preliminary survey was conducted dealing specifically with consumer attitudes toward the purchase of infant toys in supermarkets.

Supermarket Shopping Behavior and the Purchase of Toys

Customers shop in supermarkets quite frequently. The latest studies show about 2.4 trips per week. Most of these customers are women (about 80 percent), although there is a growing tendency for men to participate more frequently. Children are present on about

	Make a List	Read Newspapers	Read Advertising Circulars	Consult Other Family Members
Almost always	65	64	52	20
Frequently	16	14	18	25
Occasionally	13	16	19	33
Almost never	6	6	11	22
	100	100	100	100

17 percent of the trips. In general, during their trips to the supermarket, customers are in a buying mood. Most buy more than they had planned to purchase before visiting the supermarket. With the continuing stigma of the recession, however, careful planning by the shopper is becoming more common as a way of staying within the budget. A recent study conducted by the Home Testing Institute yielded the findings shown in Exhibit 4.

Because much of the success of supermarket GM marketing stems from frequent shopping and impulse buying, any indication of a decline in shopping frequency and impulse buying could have negative implications for GM sales, whether for toys or other GM products. Fortunately, this does not appear to be the case. Shopping frequency has remained relatively stable over the past five years, and although consumers are becoming more *careful and sharper* shoppers, they are not turning away from impulse buying. They will, however, exercise more care and judgment about which impulse items they buy at the supermarket. More attention will be given to the quality and value of the GM products they buy. Impulse buying in the more extreme sense (haphazardly grabbing a GM item off the shelf and tossing it into the shopping cart) will be replaced by what might be called "point-of-purchase judgment shopping." New GM products (and new food products, for that matter) will be more carefully scrutinized at the point of purchase. If the product passes this more careful scrutiny, then the basic advantages of having a desirable GM item available in the supermarket will prevail. Customers will be happy to take advantage of the one-stop shopping offered by the supermarket because they will be able to take care of more requirements without making additional stops at the drugstore, hardware store, discount department store, toy store, or other retail outlets.

In summary, while becoming more planned and careful, consumers will still be quite amenable to impulse purchases of GM products of all types, including toys, if these products appear to offer *good value* as well as the *convenience* of buying them in supermarkets.

Survey of Consumer Attitudes toward the Purchase of Infant Toys in Supermarkets

In order to appraise the attitudes and behavior of consumers dealing *specifically* with the purchases of infant toys from supermarkets, a survey of 500 mothers with infant children was conducted. About 460 usable questionnaires were obtained. The findings are shown in Exhibits 5 to 13. Analysis of the findings follows.

Exhibit 5 shows that for the sample group of consumers, the overwhelming choice of retail outlet for purchasing infant toys currently is the discount toy store. Only 8 (1.7 percent) mentioned supermarkets. This is not surprising, however, especially in light of consumer perceptions of low quality of infant toys presently sold in supermarkets, as shown in Exhibit 6. Hence, at present, it is very rare to find consumers who look to supermarkets as their most likely choice for buying infant toys.

EXHIBIT 5 Types of Retail Outlets from Which Consumers Buy Infant Toys Most Often

	Number	Percent
Discount toy stores	350	76.1
Discount department stores	40	8.8
Department stores	20	4.3
Variety stores	20	4.3
Supermarkets	8	1.7
Drug stores	12	2.6
Other	10	2.2
Total	460	100.0

EXHIBIT 6 Consumer Ratings of Quality of Infant Toys Sold in Supermarkets

	Number	Percent
Very high quality	0	0.0
Good quality	60	13.0
Mediocre quality	100	21.8
Poor quality	180	39.1
Very low quality	120	26.1
Total	460	100.0

EXHIBIT 7 Extent to Which Consumers Plan for the Purchase of Infant Toys Before Shopping

	Number	Percent
Almost always	160	34.8
Frequently	140	30.4
Usually	80	17.4
Seldom	20	4.4
Almost never	60	13.0
Total	460	100.0

Exhibit 7 shows that the overwhelming majority of consumers plan their purchases of infant toys before shopping. This suggests that consumers are not *at present* heavily inclined toward impulse purchasing when it comes to buying infant toys. This does not mean, however, that they could not become more amenable to impulse buying if quality infant toys were more readily available in highly convenient retail outlets such as supermarkets. This is implied by the findings shown in Exhibits 8 and 9. Exhibit 8 shows 65.2 percent of the respondents expressed at least some likelihood of buying infant toys from supermarkets if good quality and competitive prices were to become available. Exhibit 9 shows that, for those who would be likely to buy from supermarkets, the most important reasons for doing so are the greater convenience offered by supermarkets (73.3 percent) and the savings in time (20 percent). Thus, the heavy trend toward one-stop shopping, which fosters impulse buying, is evident here.

Exhibit 10 shows the other side of the coin. For those consumers who expressed no likelihood of buying infant toys in the supermarket (34.8 percent), the reasons offered were perception of lower quality (25 percent), poor selection (37.5 percent), and the

EXHIBIT 8 Likelihood of Consumers Buying Infant Toys in Supermarkets in the Future If Such Toys Were of High Quality and Competitively Priced

	Number	Percent
Extremely likely	80	17.4
Very likely	100	21.7
Somewhat likely	120	26.1
Unlikely	137	29.8
Very unlikely	23	5.0
Total	460	100.0

EXHIBIT 9 Reasons Given for Purchasing Infant Toys in Supermarkets by Those Consumers Expressing Any Degree of Likelihood* of Buying Infant Toys from Supermarkets

	Number	Percent
Greater convenience of supermarkets	220	73.3
Lower prices	17	5.7
Better selection	0	0.0
Savings in time	60	20.0
Other	3	1.0
Total	300	100.0

*Note: Somewhat likely, very likely, extremely likely

EXHIBIT 10 Reasons Given for *Not* Purchasing Infant Toys in Supermarkets by Those Consumers Expressing No Likelihood* of Buying Infant Toys from Supermarkets

	Number	Percent
Lower quality of toys sold in supermarkets	40	25.0
Higher prices charged	0	0.0
Poor selection offered	60	37.5
Need for planning infant toy purchases	20	12.5
Other	40	25.0
Total	160	100.0

*Note: Unlikely, very unlikely

need for planning (12.5 percent). A reasonable inference that may be drawn from Exhibit 10, though, is that if quality and selection of infant toys in supermarkets were improved, a significant portion of the "unlikely to purchase" group might move into the "likely to purchase" group.

Thus, on balance, the data presented in Exhibits 5 to 10 suggest that from the standpoint of consumer propensities to shop for infant toys in the supermarkets, the prospects are promising.

Exhibits 11 to 13 summarize other information relevant to the marketing of infant toys through supermarkets. Exhibit 11 shows the maximum amounts that consumers said they would be willing to spend on unplanned purchases of infant toys in supermarkets. The $9 amount appears to be the upper limit. No consumers expressed a willingness to spend more than that amount on an unplanned infant toy purchase.

Exhibit 12 shows that the highest percentage of consumers (60.9 percent) purchased infant toys about twice per year. The next highest percentage (21.7 percent) made purchases about once per month. It should be pointed out, though, that this frequency of

EXHIBIT 11 Maximum
Amount Consumers Are
Willing to Spend on
Unplanned Purchases of
Infant Toys in
Supermarkets

	Number	Percent
Under $2	47	10.2
$2–3.49	44	9.6
$3.50–4.99	142	30.9
$5–6.99	151	32.8
$7–8.99	76	16.5
$9–10.99	0	0.0
Total	460	100.0

EXHIBIT 12 Frequency
of Infant Toy Purchases

	Number	Percent
Every 6 months	280	60.9
Every 3 months	40	8.7
Once per month	100	21.7
Every 2 weeks	40	8.7
Total	460	100.0

EXHIBIT 13 Section of
the Supermarket in Which
Consumers Expect to
Find Infant Toys

	Number	Percent
Baby department	420	91.3
Section where other toys are sold	36	7.8
Household items section	1	0.2
Checkout counter	3	0.7
Others	0	0.0
Total	460	100.0

purchase pattern reflects consumer shopping behaviors associated with the types of retail outlets *currently patronized* for infant toy purchases. If quality infant toys were more readily available in supermarkets, these patterns could change significantly.

Finally, Exhibit 13 shows the section of the supermarket in which consumers would expect to find infant toys displayed. The overwhelming majority (91.3 percent) expects to find them in the baby department.

Discussion Questions

1. Based on the findings from the market research study, do you think Innovative should attempt to market the infant toy line through supermarkets?

2. What are some of the major obstacles Innovative might face if it does attempt to sell the infant toy line through supermarkets?

3. What other kinds of retail outlets might be appropriate for the infant toy line?

CASE 13

Best Buy
Dealing with Intertype Competition

Best Buy was founded in 1966 as Sound of Music and changed its name in 1983 to Best Buy. Today, Best Buy is a Fortune 500 company and is the world's largest specialty retailer of consumer electronics products, accounting for approximately 20 percent of sales of these products in the United States. Sales for 2010 were in excess of $50 billion, and the employee headcount was over 180,000. Best Buy operates several subsidiaries, including Future Shop, Geek Squad, Magnolia, Napster, Pacific Sales, and Speakeasy, but is best known for its chain of more than 1,100 "big-box" stores, ranging in size from 20,000 to 58,000 square feet (see Exhibit 1). In recent years, Best Buy has expanded internationally with stores located in Canada, Mexico, Europe, and China and is in the process of adding several hundred much smaller retail stores called Best Buy Express, which will focus mainly on mobile phones.[1]

EXHIBIT 1
Typical Best Buy "big-box" store

Eliza Snow/iStockphoto.com

---

[1] http://www.webhostingreport.com/learn/bestbuy.html

For several decades, Best Buy has been the dominant player as a destination place for consumers to go to buy a huge range of consumer electronics such as flat-screen televisions, stereo equipment, laptop computers, iPods, GPS systems, and in more recent years, musical instruments. With the demise of Circuit City, the second largest consumer electronics retailer in 2009, it looked like Best Buy would become even more dominant. But by mid-2010, Best Buy's growth trajectory did not continue on its upward path. In fact, sales decreased for five straight quarters, and in the third quarter of 2011, net profits had also plunged by 30 percent. Gross margin on sales also decreased from 25.8 percent to 25.3 percent for the same quarter of the previous year.[2]

The Competitive Challenge from Online Channels

Best Buy's vast network of "brick-and-mortar," big-box stores as well as its smaller and more specialized stores provide millions of consumers who visit the stores with a shopping experience that is not available to online shoppers.[3] This is, of course, the ability to see the actual products, touch them, try them out, compare them directly to competitive products, get on-the-spot information and advice from salespeople, and take possession of the products immediately after purchase. Online electronic marketing channels, even the most sophisticated and state-of-the-art, such as Amazon.com, cannot provide these features. So, it would appear that each channel alternative has its own distinct advantages and disadvantages. Physical retail store channels enable customers to have direct access to products and take possession immediately. But, consumers do not have the convenience of shopping from a laptop, iPod, or smartphone without even having to leave home, office, or wherever they may be. Online shopping provides great convenience and better product selection than even the largest retail stores; however, there is no direct contact with actual products, and consumers must wait for delivery, which can take at least 12 hours, even with expedited shipping.

But what if the core features of each channel option are combined so that the best features of each are made available via a multichannel platform? This is precisely what more and more consumers have been doing in recent years as they "channel surf" to obtain an optimum channel mix. Increasingly, consumers are using big-box retailers such as Best Buy as a showroom where they can see and try out products that they might have identified online. Then, after visiting a Best Buy (or another retailer), instead of buying the products at the store, they return to their home or office computers—or better yet, while still in the store, pull out their smartphones—search for the lowest price, and purchase the product online while standing in the same aisle as the product display! Here is how one such shopper described his own experience in combining Best Buy's retail store channel with online channels to optimize the buying process:

> *For people like me, getting more comfortable with online purchasing, I simply don't know what would stop me from using Best Buy as a research center. I can go to the store, check out a new camcorder or surround sound system, and then decide if it's*

---

[2] Miguel Bustillo, Ann Zimmerman, and Donna Mattioli, "Holiday Fear Mixed in with Cheer," *Wall Street Journal* (November 21, 2011: B1, B8).

[3] http://pr.bby.com/phoenix.zhtml?c=244152&p=irol-factsheet_pf

something I want. If it is, I'll ask the manager if they can match Amazon's deeply discounted price. If it can, I'll buy it at Best Buy. If not, I'll go home and order online.[4]

The option of using the physical retail channel as a "research center" to gain direct access to products and then buying online if lower prices can be found is further enhanced by several other key advantages associated with online shopping:

- *No sales tax*
- *Very common free shipping offers*
- *At your door delivery*

Who Wins and Who Loses?

Best Buy, as a mainly land-based retailer, has invested many billions of dollars in the course of building and maintaining a vast physical infrastructure of stores and incurs the continuing expenses of operating and managing those stores with tens of thousands of employees. In addition, huge quantities of inventory spread across more than 1,100 stores must be held to provide for store displays and backup stock to allow for immediate availability of products to customers. Further, Best Buy must collect, keep track of, and forward sales taxes in the various states and foreign countries in which it operates. In addition to its store operations, Best Buy also operates its own online sales channel to provide customers with a Best Buy option for online shopping. But maintaining its own dual channel platform of stores and online operations increases Best Buy's cost structure.

In contrast, pure-play (online only) retailers such as Amazon.com do not provide any retail stores for consumers to visit or any sales employees to deal with consumers on a face-to-face basis. Instead, all of their physical facilities and most of their employees are focused on back-office, order-fulfillment tasks, and to some extent on providing follow-up customer service when needed. Moreover, for the most part, online retailers do not have to collect sales taxes except in the few states in which their physical facilities are located.[5]

So which parties (consumers, store-based retailer, online retailer) win and which parties lose in this form of intertype competition where a conventional retailer sells consumer electronics products predominantly via its retail store channel versus the retailer selling consumer electronics products through the online channel?

The Consumer: Winner or Loser? The existence of the conventional retail channel offered by Best Buy and the competitive online channel offered by Amazon and other online retailers would appear to provide the consumer with the best of both worlds. Millions of consumers all over the United States and several foreign countries can visit a Best Buy store to see, touch, feel, try out, and get information and advice on a wide selection of products. And, if they choose to buy an item at Best Buy, they get immediate availability. But, consumers also have the option of simply using the facilities at Best Buy as a consumer electronics research center, to reduce their risk and uncertainty about the products they are considering. Then, when they use their laptops, iPods, or smartphones to find the lowest price from a competitive online seller, thanks to Best

---

[4] http://ledfrog.com/blog/2011/04/the-future-of-big-box-retailers/

[5] Stu Woo, "Amazon Primes Pump for Loyalty," *Wall Street Journal* (November 14, 2011: B1, B2).

Buy, they have already had the advantage of seeing the product "in the flesh" before making a purchase.

Thus, the availability of the conventional retail store channel in competition with the online channel would appear to make the consumer, who is taking advantage of using both channels, a winner—at least in the short run. However, in the longer run, such intertype competition could be problematic. Why? Because if Best Buy is not "rewarded" for the extra services it is providing to consumers, it, and other land-based retailers, may disappear from the scene, leaving only online retailers to sell consumer electronics. Consumers would no longer have the opportunity to actually see, try, and immediately take delivery of products, because only online retailers would exist.

Online Retailer: Winner or Loser?   The existence of a giant, land-based consumer electronics retailer such as Best Buy essentially creates a tremendous resource for online retailers such as Amazon.com. Amazon.com has an innovative and sophisticated online customer interface and state-of-the-art order-fulfillment capabilities; however, prior to purchase, Amazon.com can only show pictures of products to consumers, not the products themselves. But this seemingly huge shortcoming can be largely eliminated if consumers use Best Buy's stores as a substitute "showroom" for Amazon.com. Thus, with Best Buy's store channel and Amazon's online channel available to consumers, the opportunity to pick and choose from each channel to get the best deal is the most attractive option for consumers. If many or most consumers pursue this "best of each channel" option, Amazon.com, in effect, gets a "free ride" from Best Buy. That is, Amazon.com does not have to pay the price of establishing its own physical store showrooms where consumers could see and try out products. Instead, Amazon.com gets this resource for "free" when consumers use Best Buy's massive retail store facilities for this purpose. So in this scenario (sometimes refer to as *showromming*), Amazon.com and other online-only retailers are the winners.

Best Buy: Winner or Loser?   The core of Best Buy's channel strategy has been based on providing millions of consumers with big-box retail stores carrying a wide assortment of consumer electronics products. Further, although not renowned for the excellence of its sales help, Best Buy still has staffed its stores with salespeople who could explain the features of products, provide information, and, at least to some extent, offer some product advice as well.

Best Buy believed that its strategy of providing consumers with a wide selection of consumer electronics products available for immediate delivery, in massive displays, with a friendly and helpful sales staff on the floor, all housed in one giant store, would be rewarded by consumers. And for several decades, consumers did respond with rewards in the form of tens of billions of dollars in sales, rapid growth, and store expansion, as well as solid profits.

But more recently, and particularly by the end of the first decade of the twenty-first century, intertype competition in the form of online channels, particularly from Amazon.com, began to seriously challenge Best Buy's channel strategy. Although Best Buy developed its own online channel option, it was no match for Amazon.com's online capabilities. More and more consumers began behaving opportunistically by "cherry picking" from the best features of store channels and online channels. In short, consumers used Best Buy as a place *to see the product*, but Amazon.com (or another online retailer) as the place *to buy the product*. The result? Best Buy becomes the loser. Best Buy's huge investment in its land-based retail channel effectively accrues to the benefit of online retailers such as Amazon.com, which gets to enjoy the benefit of this massive retail infrastructure without having to pay for it.

Discussion Questions

1. Are consumers behaving rationally when they take advantage of the best features provided by physical store channels and online channels? Explain.

2. Is intertype competition, whereby store-based retailers such as Best Buy compete with online retailers such as Amazon.com in the sale of consumer electronics, a "good thing" for customers? Discuss.

3. What do you think Best Buy can do to overcome the problem of showrooming whereby store showrooms serve as "research centers" for consumers who, after gathering first-hand product information at Best Buy retail stores, actually make their product purchases from online retailers such as Amazon.com?

CASE **14**

American Olean Tile Company

Motivating Independent Distributor Salespeople

Getting the attention of distributor salespeople in the floor-covering business, as in many industries, can be a daunting challenge. For American Olean Tile Company, relatively new in distributor sales, the challenge yielded to a well-conceived sales incentive plan that brought major increases in volume and many new retail accounts.

The firm's Bright Choices campaign to motivate distributor sales personnel earned an Incentive Showcase Award from National Premium Sales Executives.

American Olean Tile Company of Lansdale, Pennsylvania, maker of ceramic wall and floor tiles, has relied heavily on distributors in recent years, according to Ron Autenrieth, marketing manager for glazed wall products. Although the company has been known in the trade primarily for wall tile products, the incentive program focused on the floor tile lines to increase awareness of and sales effort for them, and "to reposition our glazed floor offerings in the minds of the distributor salespeople," he said.

American Olean's six-month campaign offered tile distributor salespeople a variety of merchandise awards ranging in value from about $100 to $1,000. Awards were individually chosen to fit the target audience—overwhelmingly male, 25 to 34, college-educated, with income over $50,000. Items were hand-selected, Autenrieth points out, for appeal to the special audience and high quality. "A building materials manufacturer cannot just go to an incentive house and say, 'I want to sell more; create a program for me.'" This was a custom program developed in a collaborative process by the manufacturer, the advertising agency (Dudnyk Company, Horsham, Pennsylvania), and Don Jagoda Associates, a consulting firm specializing in the development of incentive programs.

Autenrieth wrote the rules, which tied the awards to sales of six brands of ceramic floor tile and colored grout. Incentives were priced in points and sales were credited in the same language. Fifty points were given for every 1,000 square feet increments of product sold to a ceramic tile contractor, floor-covering dealer, or other customer. Salespeople also earned 20, 30, or 50 points on the sale of display units to dealers, and 10 points for a product-panel carrying case used by tile contractors to present the floor tiles.

Monthly reporting of each salesperson's sales was requested, using a specially designed Product Sales Sheet accompanied by copies of invoices showing shipping dates. An extra 10 points were given for reporting on a monthly basis to spread the administrative burden over the time period of the program.

Low-end awards, from 100 to 300 points, could bring the participant such items as an espresso/cappuccino maker, cordless phone, or a food processor. Reaching 1,000 points was worth such items as a personal copier, roll-top desk, video camera, or computer.

Salespeople were required to register for the program by returning a postcard with information including home address and Social Security number. This provided an element of control, and the opportunity for targeted follow-up promotion. "We spent some extra money," Ron Autenrieth notes, "to create a monthly report that listed each rep by distributor, by sales region, and the points earned. This was crucial to the execution of the program by American Olean salespeople and instrumental in its success."

The sellers showed they were paying attention. Fifty percent of the target salespeople participated, all selling the priority floor tile and grout. In all, 264 awards were given, valued at more than $150,000.

Distributors signed 244 new retail and contractor accounts during the promotion, Autenrieth reports. Moreover, major distributors delivered sharply improved performance: The five key accounts increased sales of the targeted products an average of 82 percent over the previous period, and two of them more than doubled their volume of American Olean floor tile.

Overall, Autenrieth says, the program "achieved a level of selling effort significantly greater than we have ever had before." The distributor salespeople recognized American Olean floor products as a viable line.

American Olean had previously used incentives "from time to time," but this was called "a step up from what we have done before. Our distributor network has grown to the extent that we could strategically think about focusing distributor support. We didn't depend on distributors so much till the last three years."

Discussion Question

1. The American Olean Tile Company's distributor incentive program was apparently very successful in motivating the distributors' field salespeople to push its ceramic floor tiles and grout, which had previously been neglected. Which element or elements of the incentive program do you think were most important in securing such a strong response from the distributors' salespeople?

ALDI

Superior Consumer Value through Strategic Channel Alliances

ALDI is an international grocery discount retailer specializing in private-label, high-quality products. ALDI, which opened its first stores in Germany more than 40 years ago, now operates in 8 countries with over 8,500 stores (see Exhibit 1 for a view of a typical ALDI store). It is ranked number 10 out of the top 30 food retailers worldwide and was selected as "Germany's top brand" in the year 2000. What separates ALDI from the wide range of other discount retailers is its core competency embedded in its unique approach to buying: ALDI buys only a relatively small number of different products but in huge quantities at the lowest possible prices. Moreover, virtually all of these products are sold under private label.

The Limited Assortment Concept

What makes this strategy work is ALDI's limited assortment concept. ALDI's product line includes no more than 700 to 1,500 items (retailers like Wal-Mart offer more than 25,000 different items). The range is strictly focused on the products most needed and frequently used in the average home. These basic product categories are enriched by weekly "special buys" where customers can find anything from DVD players to clothing to kitchenware. This strict "no-frills" strategy eliminates virtually all of the "extras" found at other grocery stores. For example, ALDI uses no baggers, fancy displays, check cashing, or preferred-customer savings programs. Further, at ALDI the consumer shops from open carton displays that are easy to replenish (see Exhibit 2) and pays only cash to avoid delays associated with credit card verification. The customer even has to use a coin to obtain a shopping cart from ALDI's "cart rental system." When the consumer returns the cart, the coin deposit is returned. This minimized the need for staff to collect shopping carts. Wherever one looks at ALDI, ruthless cost control is the leading philosophy. Indeed, it is not unusual to mistake the store manager for a "blue-collar" guy wheeling a pallet of canned vegetables to the sales floor. One of the founders of ALDI, Theodor Albrecht, is said to be so thrifty that the first thing he does when entering a room is to turn off the lights and heat!

Operational Efficiencies at ALDI

The combination of low overhead, high volume, and heavy use of private goods is what enables ALDI to underprice other chains. This differential advantage is further reinforced by ALDI's superior relationship with suppliers as well as its outstanding logistics capabilities. What makes it so difficult for competitors to catch up with ALDI is that the company is able to offer high-quality products that match or exceed the quality of leading national brands for a significantly lower price. By focusing on a streamlined product assortment that remains relatively stable over time, ALDI and its vendors are able to allocate resources efficiently.

EXHIBIT 1 View of a Typical ALDI Store

An added benefit of ALDI's "bare-bones" approach to inventory acquisition, control, merchandising, and logistics is that it is much easier for ALDI to plan and order far in advance. Vendors can rely on ALDI's dependable and substantial cash reserves and the mostly long-term agreements that ALDI negotiates with them.

Customers hardly ever find empty trays at ALDI, and products are always fresh because the product turnover is so high. In fact, merchandise turnover is so rapid that, on average, the entire inventory of a store is completely renewed after only two weeks. Yet ALDI's stores receive deliveries of new goods daily from decentralized regional logistics centers. These depots are in constant contact with vendors, creating a super-efficient replenishment system that competitors find hard to imitate. For instance, ALDI has used cross-docking in its warehouses for more than 30 years now, well before Wal-Mart became famous for using this system. In addition to all of these operational efficiencies, from its earliest days in business ALDI has also encouraged and worked with its suppliers to develop packages that are easy to handle for logistics providers as well as store staff on the sales floor and stockroom. So, instead of store staff having to open boxes and place items on shelves, consumers can grab products from a pallet that has already been stacked by the supplier.

The Private-Label Advantage

Although private branding is often associated with lesser quality than famous national brands, this is not the case at ALDI. Indeed, the opposite is true. ALDI's private-label

EXHIBIT 2 ALDI's Open Carton Displays

© Susan Van Etten

product quality meets or exceeds national name-brand standards. "Meeting brand standards" is more than a slogan, as many of the products manufactured for ALDI are especially modified for ALDI to significantly upgrade quality. A vendor is accepted to deal with ALDI only if it can provide products with consistent quality, guaranteed to meet or surpass those of its competitors but at a lower price. Designing quality specifications that equal or surpass government standards is also a frequent criterion for ALDI's private retail brands, as quality defects within only a few products can endanger the quality positioning of the whole company. Consequently, only suppliers that use the best ingredients and excellent processing are admitted into the highly select circle of ALDI vendors.

Relationship Marketing at ALDI

ALDI's approach to relationship marketing focuses much more on its vendors than its customers. ALDI does not use data mining methods to profile its customers and does not provide them with rebates or bonus cards. ALDI believes that customers will stick with ALDI as long as it is able to provide high-quality goods at the lowest possible prices. Thus, ALDI constantly works at perfecting its supplier-retailer relationships to assure that the quality of products, low prices, and flawless delivery that keep bringing consumers back to ALDI's stores will continue in the future.

ALDI's strategic alliance with a bread supplier in the company's homeland, Germany, illustrates how strong cooperation between ALDI and its vendors creates better value for consumers. As mentioned earlier, ALDI tries to stock a core assortment of food products. One of these products is fresh bread. All over the world bread is one of the items to be found in nearly every shopping cart. But offering fresh bread (instead of preserved packaged bread, which has a relatively long shelf life) of high quality at a low price is a challenging proposition. To meet this challenge, ALDI has established a special relationship with its bread supplier. ALDI is able to get bread delivered fresh and crispy every day from a German bakery at a price that is 40 percent lower than what consumers would pay for a product of the same quality at a local bakery. How can ALDI and its vendor do this? ALDI contracted to buy fresh bread over a five-year period exclusively from this particular bakery (as long as the quality is stable) and at a certain minimum price guaranteed by ALDI. This created a win-win situation for both companies. ALDI gets a quality product for a significantly lower price than its competitors, and the bakery can focus and allocate its resources because it has the certainty of a long-term (five-year) strategic alliance with ALDI. Although such single or exclusive sourcing is often viewed as risky because it can lead to a one-sided dependency, this approach has worked very successfully for ALDI, not only for fresh bread, but for numerous other product categories as well.

From Bread to Consumer Electronics

Although ALDI's "bread and butter" is its core assortment of staple products that its customers buy day in and day out, its weekly specials provide another dimension of excitement and value for ALDI shoppers. But how does ALDI, with its highly concentrated focus on the everyday grocery needs of consumers, manage to also be a value leader in such products as PCs and consumer electronics? ALDI does this by again relying on its ability to create strategic alliances with its vendors and other "upstream" channel partners. For the merchandise used in the weekly specials, ALDI relies on Medion, a full-service marketing support vendor publicly listed on the German stock exchange. Medion's service package covers the complete management process needed to support ALDI's aggressive weekly special promotions, including market research, product design, production oversight, quality control, logistics, and after-sale service. By partnering with Medion, ALDI, which is essentially a grocery retailer, can offer high-quality electronic products from well-known manufacturers at prices that are often lower than those charged by consumer electronics discount retailers.

Here again, ALDI has created a win-win situation through a strategic alliance with a channel partner. ALDI's huge market power and close contact with its loyal customers provide Medion with a tremendous opportunity to profitably utilize its expertise in marketing management. At the same time, Medion's efforts free ALDI from having to manage complex product development, marketing, and promotional activities that are not part of its core competency.

Discussion Questions

1. Do you think ALDI could pursue its business model without developing strategic alliances with channel members? Discuss.

2. Discuss the concept of win-win in the context of strategic alliances in marketing channels.

Dunkin' Donuts Inc.
Channel Member Training

Dunkin' Donuts Inc., a fast-food franchisor with an annual sales volume of $6 billion worldwide in 2010, opened its first doughnut and coffee shop in 1950. Today the company has more than 9,700 locations in North America and 31 foreign countries. The majority of its shops are operated by independent franchisees, all of whom have undergone intensive training at "Dunkin' Donuts University," which the company maintains at Quincy, Massachusetts.

The six-week training program consists of a five-week formal course, broken up into six-day work weeks, and a final week spent on the job in a local doughnut shop. Approximately half of the program deals with technical production techniques used in the manufacture of doughnuts and similar products. The other half is concerned with financial, personnel, and management practices to be followed by owner–managers of the retail stores.

The training schedule for each franchisee and the instructional materials for each of the 30 days in training are precisely programmed. Exhibit 1 illustrates a typical daily schedule.

As the trainees proceed through the program, they are tested with a series of exams. These measure both their retention of the material covered and their aptitude in performing the various manual tasks associated with doughnut production. The trainees are given uniforms, operating manuals, and all the other items required for the course.

During the two and a half weeks they spend on doughnut production, the trainees study subjects ranging from the fermentation process occurring in yeast doughnuts to the correct selection of frying oils, the maintenance of equipment, batch planning, and so on. Trainees are required to achieve a certain level of proficiency in doughnut production before they can move on to the management training portion of the program.

During this management training phase, the company attempts to convert what are often blue-collar employees into professional managers. Franchisees are introduced to techniques used in interviewing and selecting employees, rating their job performances, and carrying out many other managerial tasks. They also learn how to train employees in the use of supplies and selling techniques.

A record is kept of each trainee's progress in the program. Exhibit 2 illustrates a weekly training report. Copies of such reports are made available to the district manager in whose assigned area the franchisee is to be located.

The faculty of Dunkin' Donuts University consists of a director of training and two assistants, augmented by technical, financial, and marketing executives from the nearby corporate headquarters. A local company-owned outlet is used for on-the-job training. Training does not end with graduation from Dunkin' Donuts University. Each franchisee is expected to participate later in a continuing series of regional and national training seminars scheduled by the company.

EXHIBIT 1
Franchisee Daily Training
and Classroom Schedule
(Dunkin' Donuts Inc.)

Place/Time	Instructor	Subject
(Week 1 Day 1)		
Classroom		**Orientation**
8:00 A.M. 9:30 A.M.	Staff	1. Introduction and background information on members of the training staff a. University Organizational Chart
		2. Distribution and review of detailed training schedule and associated manuals
		3. Discussion of the training school's requirements, rules, and regulations
9:30 A.M.	Director of Management Development	4. Review of the objectives, purpose, and scope of the 5-week training and classroom schedule
		5. Discussion of the evaluation of franchise owners and other operating personnel during the 5-week training and classroom schedule
Classroom		**Introduction to Cake Donut Production**
10:00 A.M. 10:30 A.M.	Staff	1. Distribution and review of the cake donut production training manual
Work Area		
10:30 A.M. 11:00 A.M.	Staff	2. Introduction to cake donut production equipment and related tools
11:00 A.M. 12:30 P.M.	Staff	3. Demonstration of how to produce and prepare cake donuts
Lunch		
12:30 P.M. 1:30 P.M.		(Not to exceed one hour)

EXHIBIT 2
Franchisee Weekly
Training Report
(Dunkin' Donuts Inc.)

Week Ending _____

Trainee _____   Capacity of Trainee _____

Location _____   Est. Completion Date _____

Area of Training   **Number of Hours**

Donut production   _____

Sales and finishing   _____

Financial management   _____

On-the-job training   _____

Dunkin' Donuts University classes   _____

  Total training hours   _____

Examination   **Working Donut Examination**

Subject _____   Date taken _____

Date taken _____   Score _____

Score _____

Comments on Training

_____

_____

_____

_____

_____

_____

_____

Progress

Below Average _____ Average _____ Above Average _____ Outstanding _____

Trainer _____ Date _____

_____

A number of Dunkin' Donuts University graduates have gone on to become owners of multiple franchise units. The company, which reports that it has had relatively few franchisee failures, attributes this in large part to the preparation its franchisees receive during the training program.

Discussion Questions

1. Evaluate this training program.

2. What suggestions do you have for improvements?

CASE **17**

Ben & Jerry's
Strategic Alliances for Profit and Social Good

Ben & Jerry's manufactures superpremium ice cream products. Approaching business in an unconventional manner, Ben & Jerry's believes that it is running a unique experiment: proving that business can be democratic, compassionate, politically principled, and profitable all at the same time. Headquartered in Waterbury, Vermont, Ben & Jerry's mission is to give consumers a good, high-quality ice cream product, while designating a portion of the profits to support social and environmental issues.

Company Background

Ben & Jerry's was founded in 1977 by two friends, Ben Cohen and Jerry Greenfield. The company features superpremium ice cream, frozen yogurt, and sorbet created from natural ingredients. The first Ben & Jerry's retail store opened in a renovated gas station in Burlington, Vermont; the first factory was not opened until 1984. By 1985, sales had reached almost $10 million and by 2010 had soared to almost $500 million. The products are sold in the U.S. and 29 other countries around the world.

Ben & Jerry's interest in social causes is not just an interesting beginning to a lucrative business or a marketing gimmick—Ben & Jerry's "walks the talk." In 1985, the company established the Ben & Jerry's Foundation, which donates 7.5 percent of company pretax profits to an ever-changing list of charities. By 2008, this 7.5 percent had amounted to over $2.1 million per year. Yves Couette, the company's CEO, has continued this vision of "caring capitalism." He said: "As Ben & Jerry's goes on a tour of the world, we will never forget where we've come from, who our friends and family are, and what we stand for."

Ben & Jerry's success has not been without its ups and downs. One of the downs occurred when Ben & Jerry's entered the lucrative novelty ice cream market with its Peace Pops (an alternative to Dove Bars and Jell-O Pudding Pops). After six months, sales were 50 percent short of projections, mainly because the product flopped in supermarkets. Apparently consumers were not willing to pay for a superpremium product in supermarket channels. However, when the product was shifted to convenience store channels, sales increased by 60 percent.

On the up side, Ben & Jerry's has been able to capitalize on its customers' loyalty, based on its reputation as a concerned corporate citizen. For instance, the company marshaled grassroots support to counteract Pillsbury's efforts to prevent distributors that carried its Häagen-Dazs ice cream from selling Ben & Jerry's ice cream products. Ben & Jerry's efforts included a bumper sticker campaign, an 800 number, and a media kit containing a complaint letter to Pillsbury and a letter to the state attorney general. Ben & Jerry's low-budget, high-social-consciousness campaign resulted in considerable media hype, painting Pillsbury as the "bad guy" and Ben & Jerry's as the underdog that represented everyman's interest. This positive media attention set the stage for future innovative marketing approaches.

In August of 2000, Ben & Jerry's agreed to a unique and groundbreaking combination in which Ben & Jerry's was bought out by Unilever and became a wholly owned subsidiary of this multinational consumer products company. This union was expected to create an even more dynamic, socially positive ice cream business with global reach. In commenting on the transaction, cofounders Cohen and Greenfield said:

> *Neither of us could have anticipated, twenty years ago, that a major multinational would some day sign on, enthusiastically, to pursue and expand the social mission that continues to be an essential part of Ben & Jerry's and a driving force behind our many successes. But today, Unilever has done just that. While we and others certainly would have preferred to pursue our mission as an independent enterprise, we hope that, as part of Unilever, Ben & Jerry's will continue to expand its role in society.*

Products

In addition to pint ice cream, Ben & Jerry's expanded product line includes frozen yogurt, sorbets, and novelty items such as Peace Pops and Brownie Bars. The company also has a line of Conscious Concoctions, specialty ice cream products whose manufacture promotes quality of life and social responsibility in a specific community.

For instance, one flavor of Conscious Concoctions is Chocolate Fudge Brownie ice cream and frozen yogurt, produced in the Greyston community in Yonkers, New York. At this plant, previously unemployed and underskilled people produce more than 2,000 pounds of brownies per day. The Greyston Community Network uses the profit for such programs as housing and job training.

Rainforest Crunch ice cream and Peace Pops use cashews and nuts from Brazilian rainforests. As an alternative to destroying these resources, profits from the ice cream are reinvested in the people who harvest the nuts. The money is used to develop factories cooperatively owned and operated by the rainforest people.

Maine's Passamaquoddy Indian tribe sells its blueberry crop to Ben & Jerry's to make Wild Maine Blueberry ice cream. There is a message about First Group, the nonprofit organization that supports Native American life, on every container of this product. The profits support the Indians' economic development and way of life.

Another flavor of Conscious Concoctions is Fresh Georgia Peach Light. Ben & Jerry's buys all the peaches from a family farm in Georgia as a way to support the endangered livelihood of the family farmer.

Marketing Strategy

Ben & Jerry's has a reputation for producing gourmet quality natural ice cream and for creating innovative lighthearted promotions. Most of Ben & Jerry's marketing revolves around sponsoring peace, music, and art festivals all over the country. During these events, the company draws attention to many social causes as it promotes its products. Ben & Jerry's uses a mere 6 percent of its earnings to advertise, and most of this is used to fund music festivals. The primary goal is to use advertising dollars to return something to the consumer and promote consumer activism.

With a low marketing budget, Ben & Jerry's relies heavily on free publicity to generate product awareness. Says one industry analyst, "Ben & Jerry's does not spend much on advertising, but they are very good at marketing." By supporting a variety of social causes, it is able to stay in the news often enough to make this strategy pay off.

The company also relies on sample promotions. At all company-sponsored events, it distributes ice cream, sometimes free of charge. Ben & Jerry's also promotes its products through the renowned "circusmobile." This unique vehicle travels from city to city performing free vaudeville shows and giving out samples. In keeping with the company's social consciousness, the "circusmobile" bus uses solar energy to supply the power needed for the shows. Another promotional strategy is to provide free ice cream to any legitimate charitable group that asks for it.

In 1995, Ben & Jerry's became an early user of the Internet to provide company information, from flavor lists to "whens" and "wheres" of the social awareness events. The company has also creatively used the packaging of some of its products, such as Peace Pops, to invite customers to learn about these social causes on its Web site and Facebook page.

Even though Ben & Jerry's is still committed to its social mission, Unilever has introduced a more disciplined, focused approach to the company's marketing strategy. This initiative involved the establishment of companywide goals that included two very broad social mission programs: combating global warming and publicizing abuses of West African children who are conscripted into the production of cocoa. Introduced publicly in 2002, the campaign was designed to educate consumers, change personal habits, and alter public policy in support of the goal of reducing carbon dioxide emissions and slowing the impact of global warming.

Distribution Strategy

Ben & Jerry's markets its ice cream, frozen yogurt, sorbet, and novelty items at the retail level primarily through supermarkets, grocery stores, and convenience stores. The company also markets ice cream and frozen yogurt in 2½-gallon bulk containers through franchised (called Scoop Shops) and company-owned ice cream shops and through restaurants. Mail-order and online channels are also used, and licensing arrangements have been developed for international sales. Exhibit 1 provides a diagram of Ben & Jerry's distribution channel structure.

Supermarket Distribution

Ben & Jerry's concentrates heavily on national distribution through supermarkets. Supermarkets are a growing business, accounting for much of the company's sales growth. Most of these supermarkets are reached through wholesalers selected by Ben & Jerry's.

The company's distribution strategy is different from that of other superpremium ice cream companies. Ben & Jerry's is much more selective about who sells its products. First, wholesalers must have adequate access to retail outlets as well as trucks and facilities to handle the ice cream at proper temperature ranges. Second, wholesalers must demonstrate that they operate socially conscious businesses. As one executive stated, "We have an opportunity not only to create alliances with businesses that share our social vision, we also seek to influence and encourage other businesses to use their resources to address social concerns that are part of their own experience."

Ben & Jerry's ice cream is distributed throughout the U.S. by independent regional ice cream distributors. Outside of North America, Ben & Jerry's products are marketed and distributed by affiliated companies within Unilever, and a third-party licensee in Israel.

The company believes its relationship with distributors is generally good. With the buyout by Unilever, Ben & Jerry's believes it has more access to additional established Unilever supplier relationships as well.

EXHIBIT 1
Distribution Channel Structure for Ben & Jerry's

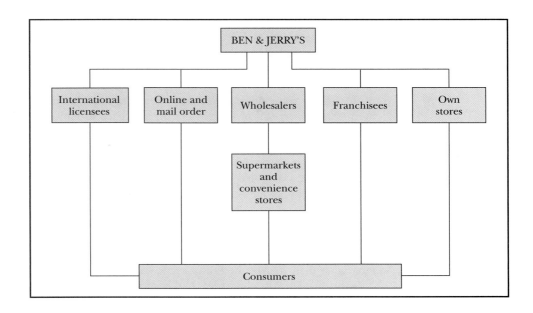

Franchising

As of December 2010, Ben & Jerry's had 750 franchise Scoop Shops worldwide.

Ben & Jerry's supports franchisees with a special interest or social focus. For example, it waived the franchise fee for a Baltimore shop owned by People Encouraging People, a nonprofit organization that hires and trains people with psychiatric disabilities.

Most of the company's franchise agreements are for a ten-year term with the option to renew for another ten years. The franchise is granted an exclusive area, and it must purchase all its ice cream and other specified items from the designated local distributor. Each must pay an initial franchise fee of $37,000 per store as well as a 3 percent royalty on gross sales. The franchisee also pays an advertising fee equal to 4 percent of its total gross sales, which Ben & Jerry's uses for regional and local advertising.

In addition, the company has entered into several exclusive area franchise agreements by which the franchisee agrees to pay a specified franchise fee in installments and to open a specified number of stores in a particular territory according to a specified schedule. The franchisee is given exclusive franchise rights in the territory.

Mail Order and Online Sales

One distribution strategy that Ben & Jerry's uses is quite different from other superpremium ice cream companies: The company offers customers the option of buying ice cream online or by mail. Ben & Jerry's packs its ice cream and frozen yogurt in dry ice and ships it anywhere in the United States. Customers can choose from a wide variety of flavors.

International Licensing

Since 1987, when Ben & Jerry's began to expand internationally, the company has granted international licensees the right to establish new franchisees to sell Ben & Jerry's ice cream and can also sublicense the manufacture of the ice cream. The licensee must pay an initial fee, plus royalties on the franchises. The agreement is for a ten-year period with the option to renew. Ben & Jerry's has a different renewal policy for each country, and the company reserves the right to terminate an agreement if the licensee does not abide by the terms.

In 1990, Ben & Jerry's entered into a joint venture agreement, called Iceverk, in what was then the Soviet Union, to establish a Ben & Jerry's ice cream parlor in the state of Karelia. The goal was to provide a model of a small-scale private enterprise while fostering international cooperation and global understanding, with profits from the joint venture to be used for cultural student exchanges. Most of the raw materials were purchased in Russia, but some dairy ingredients were purchased in Finland. Twenty-five percent of the finished ice cream products were shipped back to Finland for resale.

However, Ben & Jerry's came across some distribution obstacles in these emerging Russian markets. Russia still lacks a developed wholesale distribution system that will deliver products to stores on time, consistently, and in good condition. Also, distribution in Russia is often controlled by a monopoly with links to organized crime, creating expensive substandard conditions. The company also encountered the lack of customer service to which the Western-style customer has become so accustomed. Ben & Jerry's has made an avid effort to mitigate these hurdles in Russia by creating its own diverse distribution system.

However, by 1996, the business climate in Russia was changing so rapidly that Ben & Jerry's felt their management of Iceverk was becoming less effective. They began to understand that their local partners had become better equipped to manage Iceverk. Therefore, they decided to donate the manufacturing equipment to Iceverk and donate the equity in Iceverk to the local partners. The agreement with Iceverk was officially terminated in 1997.

With the creation of an international expansion team to develop the company's growth overseas, Ben & Jerry's has gained increasing momentum on the international scene (Already in 29 foreign countries and more are expected to be added in the future).

Discussion Questions

1. Do you think Ben & Jerry's strategic alliances with wholesalers, franchisees, and international licensees are viable in the long run, given that Ben & Jerry's expects more from its partners than simply earning profits?

2. Given the multichannel arrangements used to distribute Ben & Jerry's products, do you see a potential for channel conflict developing despite Ben & Jerry's noble intentions?

3. Do you think Ben & Jerry's existing channel structure is an ideal one, given the kinds of social objectives the company is pursuing? Explain.

Saturn Motor Corporation

Channel Strategy vs. Product Strategy:
A Postmortem

Saturn Motor Corporation, a subsidiary of General Motors, was a car company with an innovative approach. The company's mission was to market quality vehicles that maintained low cost and high customer satisfaction through the integration of people, technology, and business systems—all within the United States.

History of Saturn

In early 1982, "Project Saturn" was established by GM's vice president of Advanced Product and Manufacturing Engineering Staff, Robert Eaton. Along with the other members of his department, he set out to reexamine the auto-making industry and come up with new methods for manufacturing high-quality, lower-cost vehicles to compete specifically with foreign manufacturers. The "No-Year Car" (as it was known at this point) had no particular target date. Then, on January 7, 1985, GM's board of directors changed the future of the "No-Year Car" by approving the creation of a separate wholly owned subsidiary to assume all operational responsibility in a self-contained unit. Thus, Saturn Corporation was born, with the intention of creating a compact American-designed and manufactured car that could surpass its Japanese competition. In July of that same year, General Motors authorized a separate labor contract for the Saturn division that had been developed by a joint United Auto Workers (UAW)–GM task force. General Motors also authorized a new dealer franchise system that would be serviced by a separate organization designed to sell Saturn vehicles. Saturn utilized its labor arrangement to incorporate the union's ideas into its planning and operation, design of the work unit, recruitment and selection, orientation and training, and worker and management relations. The company believed that what was learned through this partnership would have a positive effect on the competitiveness of the entire organization.

It took several more years for the first Saturns to roll off the assembly line at the plant in Spring Hill, Tennessee, and make it to the new Saturn showrooms on October 25, 1990.

Marketing Strategy

From its roots in 1982, Saturn set out to do things differently from other automakers—and its marketing strategy was no exception. The strategy focused on building the brand through a single-minded focus on how customers related to the product and the company behind it, reflected in innovations like the "no-haggle" pricing policy and an advertising campaign that centered more on the employees and buyers than on the car itself.

Saturn wanted to deviate from the traditional automobile commercial that stressed only the vehicle, instead concentrating its efforts on images, perceptions, purchasing, shopping, and owning. A pivotal portion of this advertising campaign was a 26-minute film called "Spring, in Spring Hill," which documented the Saturn story and used Saturn team members to explain the project's history from a very personal perspective. This film was later used as a presentation tool for Saturn dealerships when attempting to obtain bank loans and zoning variances.

Saturn's overall marketing strategy was to create a high level of awareness about the company's products and services among its main target of 18- to 49-year-old college graduates and white-collar workers who earned more than $35,000 a year. But Saturn also deviated from this target market by featuring some advertisements that showed older women using their new Saturns to pick up their friends to play bingo. The media support involved a mix of national and regional magazines (including ethnic publications) as well as television spots, outdoor billboards, regional newspapers, and regional radio.

Saturn's Channel Strategy

The team at Saturn studied all existing auto dealer organizations before designing its own. The result was a dealer organization based on a strict set of standards to which Saturn expected its dealers or retailers (as they were referred to by Saturn Motor Corporation) to conform. Everything, right down to the width of the canopy in front of the retailer, was specified by Saturn. Another characteristic that set Saturn retailers apart from other car dealerships was that the owner's name could not appear in the name of the dealership. Each Saturn dealership was referred to only as "Saturn of [name of the city]," so that brand loyalty could be enhanced.

Saturn retailers utilized what the company referred to as the Market Area Approach (MAA), whereby each of the 433 retailers was assigned exclusive rights to operate and cultivate the market within one or more specified geographic areas. Although there was only one Saturn retailer for each designated area, retailers could communicate with other areas using an IBM AS/400 system coupled with a 24-hour satellite, for two-way data and video information exchanges, so that the customer was better served.

Saturn retailers played an important role in formulating the company's overall channel strategy by having input into all key decisions that affected them as well as consumers. They helped create a set of uniform performance standards against which all dealers were judged, as well as a mediation and arbitration process to settle disputes internally instead of resorting to the courts for settlements. Although Saturn was highly standardized across all of its dealerships, in most aspects of its channel strategy, retailers were empowered to devise their own customer convenience systems and monthly order allotments based on their individual sales and seasonality requirements.

Perhaps the most unique aspect of Saturn's channel strategy was its "no haggle" pricing policy, by which automobile prices were set at one base figure and salespeople worked on a flat commission rate. This approach eliminated the traditional and often unpopular style of bargaining or haggling for the "best" price. Saturn believed this new method enhanced the image of its dealers and helped to prevent the potential car buyer from going from one dealer to another looking for the best deal.

The "Saturnization" process, in which all Saturn employees had to go to the Spring Hill plant for four days to learn about organizational behavior, conflict resolution, assertive listening, and transactional leadership, was also instrumental in building a superior dealer organization because the program helped employees to focus more intensely on customer satisfaction.

How successful was this innovative approach to channel strategy in the automobile industry? According to the respected J. D. Powers Customer Satisfaction Index, it was very successful. Saturn retailers were rated second, behind only Infiniti, in overall dealership customer satisfaction and finished first in dealer relations. The pricing policy, as well as the deliberate policy to treat prospective buyers as "honored guests" rather than just customers, also received high marks in the survey.

The Saturn Dream Is Shattered

In October 2009, General Motors announced that it would discontinue its Saturn brand. Eleventh-hour attempts were made to save the brand by selling it to Penske Automotive Group, the second largest chain of automobile dealers in the United States. The plan was to have Saturn cars manufactured by Renault/Nissan and sold under the Saturn name through dealers in the Penske chain. But this fell through when Penske could not get the financials to work. On October 30, 2010, almost two decades to the day after the first Saturn cars were sold in October 1990, the Saturn brand was officially discontinued.

So, although the Saturn division of General Motors was launched with high hopes as a "different kind of car company" (and in which GM had invested over $5 billion), sales never reached projected goals, and costs were much higher than anticipated. Some industry experts estimated that GM lost as much as $3,000 on each Saturn sold. The end of Saturn resulted in 350 Saturn dealers closing and 13,000 people being laid off.

What Went Wrong at Saturn?

Auto industry analysts have offered numerous explanations for Saturn's demise. But most of these explanations relate to failures in Saturn's product strategy, *not* its channel strategy. The core focus of GM's vision for Saturn, years before the first Saturn cars were produced or any dealerships were opened, was to create an entirely different and superior customer experience in the automobile buying process. Saturn dealers would provide a user-friendly channel not available at other auto dealerships. When consumers visited a Saturn dealership, they were not stepping into a "pressure cooker" environment, where selling cars through aggressive sales tactics and price haggling was the prevailing culture. Instead, the environment and interaction with Saturn dealer employees were focused on putting the customer at ease and developing a relationship that would foster trust.

Saturn *did* attain these goals. Dealer ratings on customer satisfaction were higher than for any other auto dealers (except Infiniti) and were on a trajectory to surpass even this luxury brand. But a channel strategy, even an innovative and well-implemented one that results in great dealer ratings and highly satisfied customers, needs to be supported by products that meet customer needs and that can be manufactured at a cost that allows for a profit.

Unfortunately, in the area of product strategy, industry observers did not give Saturn very high marks. In fact, Saturn's product strategy was seriously flawed in several ways.

First, as already alluded to, Saturn cars cost too much to produce. As a separate division of GM, Saturn did attain a distinctive image. But, it also did not reap the benefits of economies of scale in production that would have resulted in lower costs. For example, many parts used in Saturn vehicles were engineered and developed just for Saturn, rather than "off the shelf" parts from other GM divisions.

A second product shortcoming involved quality. While Saturns were not "bad" cars, most objective auto industry observers ranked Saturn well below the world-class, similarly priced cars produced by Japanese automakers Toyota, Honda, and Nissan.

A third product strategy problem for Saturn was an inadequate product line. From 1990 to 1999, Saturn had essentially just three products to offer: a coupe, a sedan, and a wagon—all of which were small cars built on the same platform as the S-Series. Yet during this decade, large segments of consumers were shifting into not only larger cars, but increasingly into SUVs and minivans. Saturn offered no products in those categories. It was not until 1999 that Saturn offered the larger L-Series wagon, and not until the mid-2000s when Saturn introduced an SUV called the Vue.

A fourth and related product line strategy shortcoming was Saturn's failure to offer products that met consumers' trade-up needs. When satisfied consumers who had bought Saturn cars in the early years were ready to trade up, Saturn had no products to offer them. So instead, they turned to such cars as the Honda Accord and the Toyota Camry.

Finally, by the beginning of the second decade of Saturn's existence, GM seemed to lose some of its commitment to treat Saturn as a "different animal" from its other divisions and instead viewed Saturn as just another of its then other five GM car divisions. In this new environment, Saturn cars increasingly competed with cars from other GM divisions and therefore lost some of their distinctiveness.

Discussion Questions

1. Was Saturn's demise in spite of its innovative and successful channel strategy inevitable, given the product strategy shortcomings at Saturn?

2. Do you think that the "founding fathers" of Saturn gave sufficient consideration to the channel management/product management interface?

3. Are there situations where an innovative and superior channel strategy can overcome shortcomings in product strategy? Discuss.

Nespresso

Direct Channel Strategy and Brand Equity

Nespresso manufactures espresso machines and dedicated capsules (pods), each of which produces a single serving of espresso or a larger cup of coffee referred to as "lungo" (see Exhibits 1 and 2). Nespresso prides itself on being the quality leader in the rapidly growing market for single-serve coffee. The Nespresso machines and Nespresso pods produce a perfect cup of espresso or lungo coffee with outstanding crema (the hallmark of great espresso), excellent aroma, and robust taste equal to or better than coffee served in the finest coffee shops in Europe. But actually making this superior coffee with the Nespresso machine and pods is simple and foolproof. One need only turn on the machine, select a pod (pods are color coded and come in a wide variety of strengths and flavors), place it in the machine, and then press one button. In about thirty seconds, a cup of world-class espresso or lungo coffee is ready to enjoy. Although many single cup machines have appeared on the market in recent years, none has come close to Nespresso's superior quality and ease of use. The world's finest coffee can be made by anyone literally by pushing a single button.

History of Nespresso

Nespresso was established in 1986 as a fully autonomous subsidiary of Nestle SA, the world's largest food company headquartered in Switzerland. The first patent application for the process of extracting coffee from capsules of finely ground coffee dates to 1976 but it was not until 1988 that the process began to gain a foothold in consumer markets, first in Europe and then around the world.

During the 1990s and continuing through the first decade of the 21st century, Nespresso has enjoyed spectacular growth estimated to be as high as 30 percent year over year since 2000. Millions of coffee machines and over 20 billion pods have been sold in over fifty countries around the globe. By 2010, sales were estimated to be in excess of $2.8 billion with Nespresso being by far the fastest growing of any of Nestle SA's subsidiaries.

Nespresso has become a widely recognized global brand associated with superb coffee and excellence in the quality and design of its coffee machines. Nespresso is well aware of its leadership position in the premium single portion coffee market and has developed its policies and strategies to maintain and enhance brand equity.

Distribution Strategy

From the beginning of its emergence as an innovator in the coffee industry, Nespresso has jealously guarded its products and brand to maintain its premier position as the un-disputed quality leader. Nespresso holds over 1,700 patents to protect its proprietary

EXHIBIT 1 Examples of Nespresso Coffee Machine

EXHIBIT 2 Nespresso Coffee Pods

methods of producing coffee machines and coffee pods, which can only be used in coffee machines manufactured by Nespresso. The brand equity enjoyed by Nespresso enables the firm to charge as much as three times the price charged by some of the other thirty-one single-serve coffee makers. The price for a typical Nespresso coffee pod which produces a single serving of coffee is about 55 cents in the U.S.

The distribution of Nespresso coffee pods is tightly controlled by Nespresso. They are available through only three channels all of which are owned and operated by Nespresso (see Exhibit 3). The first is through Nespresso's Web site where customers place orders online and can expect to receive the pods at their doorstep within 48 hours. The second channel is via phone. Here highly knowledgeable and trained call center representatives take the order, and again customers can expect at-their-door delivery within 48 hours of placing the telephone order. Finally, the third channel consists of over 200 company owned stores referred to as Nespresso boutiques located around the globe in some of the world's most glamorous cities such as Paris, Geneva, and Miami. These Nespresso boutiques are decidedly upscale and avant garde in design to create a sophisticated store atmosphere. The botiques carry not only the full range of Nespresso coffee pods, but also display and demonstrate Nespresso coffee machines. Customers who have purchased a Nespresso machine automatically become a member of what Nespresso refers to as its Coffee Club. Coffee Club members entering a Nespresso store anywhere in the world are offered a free cup of coffee that might be the Coffee Club member's favorite flavor or a new one that Nespresso has recently introduced. Nespresso currently has over eight million Coffee Club members and the number keeps growing.

The only exception to Nespresso's selling its products only through its three company-owned direct channels is for its coffee machines, which are also sold through independent, upscale cookware and gourmet retailers all over the world.

Analysts who have examined Nespresso's business model liken it to the classic razor/razorblade or printer/print cartridge model where the real money is made on the razor blades and print cartridges rather than the razors and printers. But they have also observed that Nespresso has taken this business model to the next level. Nespresso is both the only company that manufacturers the pods that will work in the coffee machines and the only firm that provides the marketing channels through which the pods are sold. So, Nespresso's direct channel strategy has provided the firm with total control over how, when, and where its coffee pods are sold as well as the price consumers pay for them.

EXHIBIT 3 Nespresso Channel Structure

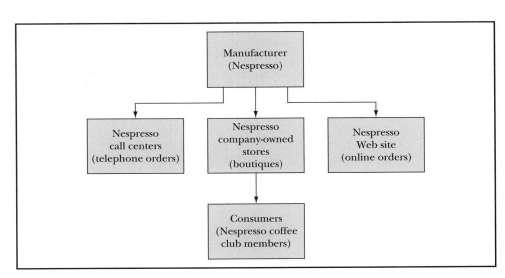

As of the end of 2009, there were no competitive coffee pods available from any other manufacturer or marketing channel. Nespresso firmly believes that its tightly controlled direct multi-channel strategy is absolutely essential to preserve the brand equity that in turn supports Nespresso's premium prices.

Nespresso Faces a Competitive Challenge

In early 2010, Jean-Paul Gaillard, who had headed Nestle's Nespresso subsidiary from 1988 through 1999, planned to introduce a less expensive coffee pod that would fit Nespresso machines. The pods would also be more environmentally friendly because they would be made of an organic composite material that is more biodegradable than Nespresso's aluminum pods. The name planned for the new company manufacturing the pods would be the Ethical Coffee Company. By the early spring of 2010, several major French and Swiss supermarkets had already agreed to sell the new coffee pods at about 20 percent less than the price of Nespresso pods.

About one month after the launch of the Ethical Coffee Company pods, Food giant Sara Lee also introduced a coffee pod that could be used in Nespresso coffee machines. The Sara Lee coffee pods were to be sold under the well-known French coffee brand, Maison de Café's L'Or. Within weeks, these pods were available in about 2,000 French supermarkets at a price approximately 10 percent lower than Nespresso pods.

Soon after the appearance of the rival coffee pods, Nespresso, claiming that the Ethical Coffee Company and Sara Lee had infringed on a number of Nespressos patents, took legal action to prevent these competitors from producing and distributing the rival coffee pods.

Discussion Questions

1. Do you think that Nespresso's direct distribution system plays a cricial role in maintaining the quality and brand equity associated with Nespresso coffee? Might other channel strategies work just as well? Explain.

2. Do you think Nespresso is missing opportunities to sell more of its coffee pods by not making its products available through indirect marketing channels? Explain.

3. Will the closed channel structure used by Nespresso help or hinder competitors from challenging Nespresso with alternative coffee pods? Explain.

CASE **20**

Bristol-Myers Squibb

Pull versus Push Promotion in the Channel

Company History

Clinton Pharmaceutical was a failing drug manufacturing firm located in Clinton, New York, when William McLaren Bristol and John Ripley Myers invested $5,000 in the company in 1887. The company remained Clinton Pharmaceuticals until May of 1898 when it was renamed Bristol, Myers Company and then, following the death of Myers in 1899, became Bristol-Myers Corporation. Prior to Myers's death, the two partners worked diligently to expand the business, which eventually proved profitable when they shifted their focus from prescription pharmaceuticals to over-the-counter health care products for the consumer market. In the 1890s the company introduced its first nationally recognized product, Sal Hepatica, a laxative mineral salt. The product sold modestly for eight years until there was a sudden surge in sales from 1903 to 1905. During this time Bristol-Myers also had great success with another consumer product, Ipana toothpaste, which was the first toothpaste to be formulated with a disinfectant to protect against the effects of bleeding gums. Having entered the consumer products market, Bristol-Myers began advertising its products directly to the public. The success of Sal Hepatica and Ipana helped catapult and transform Bristol-Myers from a regional company into a national and ultimately an international company.

The company returned its attention to prescription pharmaceuticals in 1943 with the acquisition of Cheplin Laboratories in Syracuse, New York. Cheplin mass-produced penicillin for the allied armed forces during World War II. After the war, Bristol-Myers realized the enormous opportunity penicillin and other antibiotics offered. In order to enter into this market, it acquired Cheplin and renamed the facility Bristol Laboratories.

In 1989 Bristol-Myers merged with Squibb Corporation, a worldwide pharmaceutical manufacturing company dedicated to the production of consistently pure medicines. In 1944 Squibb opened the world's largest penicillin manufacturing plant. The merger, which combined Squibb's manufacturing capabilities with Bristol-Myers's strength in product marketing, resulted in the formation of Bristol-Myers Squibb (BMS), a global leader in the health care industry and the world's second-largest pharmaceutical company. Then, in 1994, BMS signed a licensing agreement with Merck Sante SAS (formerly known as Lipha) and acquired Glucophage®, a new oral medication for Type II diabetes.[1]

---

[1]http://www.bms.com/aboutbms/history.

History of Glucophage

Glucophage, a unique advancement for lowering blood sugar in the treatment of Type II diabetes patients, was discovered and introduced in 1958 by a French pharmacist, Jan Aron. In 1960 Aron began to market Glucophage to doctors throughout France. Glucophage enjoyed positive results and a good reputation that spread rapidly throughout Europe. By the mid 1980s, Glucophage's popularity was worldwide, but it had yet to be introduced into the United States. During this time, a company by the name of Merck Sante SAS became responsible for the production and distribution of Glucophage and began the process of obtaining approval for the sale of the product in the United States.

Merck Sante SAS began looking for a U.S. distribution partner with a focus on sales and marketing strength because Glucophage had only five years of Hatch-Waxman exclusivity. (Hatch-Waxman, formally known as the Drug Price Competition and Patent Term Restoration Act of 1984, grants a five-year period of exclusivity to new drug applications for products containing chemical entities never previously approved by the Food and Drug Administration [FDA], either alone or in combination.) They selected and signed a licensing agreement with BMS. According to the BMS Web site, "The appeal of Bristol-Myers Squibb for Merck Sante was not that we had other anti-diabetic medications—for we did not. It was rather that we had the potential to make an impact on the market quickly."

In March 1995, following eight years of clinical trials and registration procedures, Glucophage was approved by the FDA for marketing in the United States. The launch of Glucophage far exceeded original sales forecasts and it soon became the most prescribed diabetes pill in the United States. (See the Glucophage timeline in Exhibit 1.)

Direct-to-Consumer Marketing

The advent of direct-to-consumer (DTC) marketing for prescription drugs is a relatively new marketing strategy in the pharmaceutical industry. Prior to 1997, prescription medications were promoted only through health care professionals such as doctors, nurses, and pharmacists. Drug companies used the health care professionals as intermediaries in order to communicate and push their products to patients (the final consumers). However, pharmaceutical companies felt they were being denied access to the end consumer, and in the 1990s drug companies began using DTC marketing by promoting

EXHIBIT 1
Glucophage Timeline

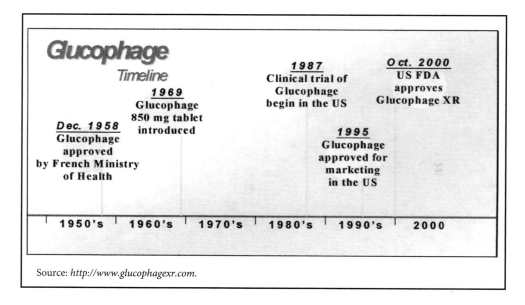

Source: *http://www.glucophagexr.com.*

their products through print and TV advertisements under strict FDA regulation. In 1997, the FDA relaxed their regulations governing DTC advertising, and as a result promotional expenditures by drug companies on DTC advertising skyrocketed, from $220 million in 1996 to a record $4.2 billion in 2005.[2, 3]

DTC marketing is a sensitive and controversial subject among the three major players involved: patients, health care professionals, and pharmaceutical companies, all of whom have their own specific concerns.

Patients: With increased accessibility to information through DTC advertising and the Internet, consumers are taking a more active role over decisions involving their health care than ever before. Consumers demand information that is not only accurate but also balanced and complete. A survey conducted by Insight-Express, an online market research firm, found that one in three adults had asked their doctor about a medication they saw in a TV commercial.[4] According to a Harris Interactive poll, the number of people going online for information about health topics in the United States grew from 54 million in 1998 to 175 million in 2010, and 39 percent of online health information seekers report they rely on physician verification before accepting the information.

Health Care Professionals: Because consumers still rely heavily on physician verification regarding health care information and because doctors must order prescription medications, health care professionals still play a crucial role in the distribution of prescription drugs. Although DTC advertising does equip consumers with information and creates dialogue regarding health concerns, a majority of doctors feel that DTC advertisements complicate patient-doctor relations and often present patients with misleading views on drugs. An online study conducted by IMS Health Consulting Firm revealed that, regardless of the doctors' views on DTC advertising, there was a strong belief that pharmaceutical companies should provide advance notice of DTC campaigns to physicians and managed care organizations. According to the study, an average of 74 percent of the respondents said they were more likely to prescribe brand-name medication based on a patient request when they had a sample available to give the patient.

Pharmaceutical Companies: Patents extended to pharmaceutical companies are allotted for 18 years, but companies must perform extensive clinical trials to test the safety and efficacy of their drugs, as required by the FDA. By the time a product reaches the market, a company typically has only 11 years before generic versions can be introduced. Generic drugs are identical to, or the bioequivalent of, brand-name drugs in dosage, safety, strength, route of administration, quality, performance characteristics, and intended use. Although generic drugs are chemically identical, they are often sold at substantial discounts because the companies providing generic drugs do not incur any of the research and development costs associated with the brand-name drugs. Typically, a brand-name drug has an 80 percent decrease in sales when a generic substitute becomes available. As a result, pharmaceutical companies are making extensive efforts to create brand loyalty via DTC advertising to gain from the advantage of having their product on the market first.

Public interest in DTC advertising has been growing, especially with regard to the rising cost of prescription drugs. Spending on mass media for prescription drug advertisements

---

[2]Susan Warner, "Coupons Are Part of Marketing Blitz by Drug Companies," *Philadelphia Inquirer* (May 31, 2001).

[3]"DTC Advertising Continues to Grow," *Standard & Poor Healthcare: Pharmaceuticals Industry Survey* (June 27, 2002): 9.

[4]Marketing Health Services, "Survey Says," (Summer 2002): 4.

EXHIBIT 2
Ad Expenditures by
Media for Drugs and
Remedies, First
Quarter 2002

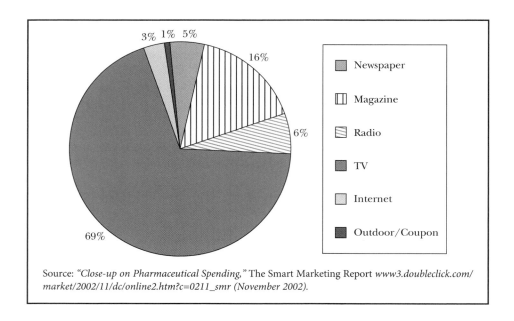

Source: *"Close-up on Pharmaceutical Spending,"* The Smart Marketing Report *www3.doubleclick.com/ market/2002/11/dc/online2.htm?c=0211_smr (November 2002).*

has grown between 13 and 20 percent per year since 1995 and is now the fastest growing health care expense.[5] (See Exhibit 2 for the breakdown of ad expenditures by media.)

A link between DTC advertising and the escalating cost of prescription drugs has been suggested. Those opposed to DTC advertising address the correlation between the soaring cost of prescription drugs and pharmaceutical companies' exorbitant promotional expenditures on DTC advertising. They feel the rising cost of drugs threatens the affordability of health care. Amanda McCloskey, the director of health policy analysis for Family USA, a nonprofit health care organization based in Washington, D.C., said, "Direct-to-consumer advertising drives demand for certain products which are the most expensive and patent-protected, without considering other alternatives." She also added that retirees who have switched from employer insurance to Medicare are especially hard hit.

On the other hand, proponents for DTC advertising argue that the ads equip consumers with knowledge and awareness of their options, educate them about side effects, and inform them of new treatments. According to Alan F. Holmer, president of Pharmaceutical Researchers and Manufacturers, a trade organization based in Washington, D.C., "Six million people don't know they have diabetes, a third of the people with depression don't seek treatment, nor do millions with high blood pressure. Direct-to-consumer advertising empowers patients with information so they can have more informed conversations with their doctors about new cures and treatments.[6]"

In an attempt to address the effectiveness of DTC ad campaigns, Tuck School of Business marketing professor J. Rapp conducted a study to determine the return on investment (ROI) for DTC advertising.[7] Focusing on a five-year for ads for products that brought in over $200 million, it was determined that the ROI for DTC ads was significantly below the ROI for other forms of marketing for prescription drugs, such as medical events and trade shows, medical journals, and detail efforts when pharmaceutical sales representatives promote products by visiting doctor's offices, informing them about

[5]Steven Findlay, "Do Ads Really Drive Pharmaceutical Sales?" *Marketing Health Services* (Spring 2002): 20–25.
[6]"DTC Advertising Continues to Grow."
[7]M. Vanelli, S. Adler, J. Vermilyea, "Reconfiguring DTC with Patient Behavior in Mind," In Vivo: The Business and Medicine Report (October 2002): 71–76.

products, and providing free samples for doctors to give to patients. The evidence suggests that DTC advertising can be effective for short-term product use, such as driving new-product use, and in creating brand awareness, but DTC doesn't seem to promote long-term patient use, which is ultimately the greatest estimate of product value. However, pharmaceutical companies find pushing new products through trade channels to be more difficult than having their products pulled through by patient and physician demand. Recent surveys by the FDA and *Prevention* magazine confirm that DTC ads have significant influence on consumer behavior and that consumers are very aware of drug advertisements. A study from the National Center for Health Statistics and Centers for Disease Control and Prevention found that the drugs most heavily prescribed by doctors were those that were most heavily advertised.[8]

In the midst of all the controversy surrounding DTC advertising, yet another new development has come about—the use of coupons to promote prescription drugs. Coupons, which offer a one-month free supply of a drug (with a valid doctor's prescription), are yet another example of attempts by pharmaceutical companies to implement a "pull" marketing strategy to entice patient awareness of their products and to encourage brand preference and loyalty. The strategy is a combination of DTC advertising with the more traditional free-sampling method that is done through doctors' offices. Coupons give pharmaceutical companies the opportunity to give samples to consumers whose doctors don't see pharmaceutical sales representatives. Coupons are intended to make patients pull for specific drugs by putting pressure on their doctors because patients receive the discounts only if physicians prescribe the drug the coupon is for. Many doctors disagree with the use of coupons for prescription drugs, arguing it is medically unsound to replace one drug for another simply because it is cheaper. According to Dr. Phillip Kennedy, a family practitioner in Augusta, Georgia, "You end up spending your time talking about the medicine they had a coupon for, that might not be right for them, instead of talking about the best way to treat their disease. It undermines what we are trying to do." Arguably the most successful coupon campaign to date was launched by BMS to persuade patients using Glucophage to switch to Glucophage® XR (a modified version of Glucophage that had to be taken only once a day compared to twice daily with the original Glucophage).

BMS Introduces Glucophage XR

Glucophage has been an extremely successful product for BMS. Sales grew steadily after its introduction in 1995, and by 2000, Glucophage was the leading branded oral medication for Type II diabetes (see Exhibit 3 for Glucophage sales, 1995–2001). With $1.732 billion in sales in 2000, Glucophage represented 9 percent of BMS's total sales and had captured 33.4 percent of the market share.[9]

With Glucophage approaching the end of its five-year exclusivity and facing the threat of generic competition for one of their top-selling products, BMS and Merck Sante SAS worked to develop Glucophage XR. In October 2000, the FDA approved Glucophage XR for sale in the United States and allotted a three-year exclusivity right. (Under the Hatch-Waxman Act, a three-year period of exclusivity is granted for a drug product that is a modified version of a drug previously approved by the FDA.)

BMS spent close to $81 million in 2001 on an ad campaign that included coupons for Glucophage XR. The coupon campaign, which was managed by the Princeton marketing firm Pharmaceutical Partners Group, was a part of BMS's overall marketing

---

[8]Steven Findlay, "Do Ads Really Drive Pharmaceutical Sales?" *Marketing Health Services* (Spring 2002): 22.

[9]Bristol-Myers Squibb Company, 2001 Annual Report: 29.

EXHIBIT 3
Glucophage Sales,
1995–2001

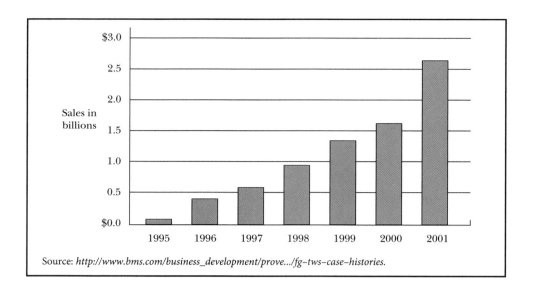

Source: *http://www.bms.com/business_development/prove.../fg–tws–case–histories.*

approach to encourage brand loyalty and entice consumers to switch to the upgraded Glucophage XR, which BMS contends is an improvement over upcoming generic alternatives and is worth the brand-name price. BMS sent coupons via mail and e-mail and printed them in newspapers and magazines, including the *New York Times,* the *Wall Street Journal,* and *Health Magazine.* Coupons were also made available online at http://www.glucophagexr.com under introductory offer (see this coupon in Exhibit 4). The site also offers diabetes management tools such as refill reminders, diet and exercise plans, and lifestyle management. The coupons offer 30 days of XR free with a valid prescription. The launch of Glucophage XR, along with the coupon campaign, was extremely successful, and according to Direct Marketing Dynamics consulting firm, Glucophage XR produced the greatest coupon activity among the prescription drugs that offered coupons.

Introductory sales of Glucophage XR in 2000 were $160 million. According to BMS's 2001 annual report, the Glucophage family of products was number one of the company's top 10 products with a total of $2.68 billion in sales. Of that $2.682 billion, Glucophage still represented the majority of sales with $2.049 billion in sales, followed by Glucophage XR and Glucovance with a combined $633 million in sales.[10] In January 2002, a generic form of Glucophage became available in the United States, which had a dramatic impact on 2002 sales. At the end of the first quarter of 2002, sales for the Glucophage family of products had decreased by 71 percent compared to the first quarter of 2001, resulting from an 88 percent decrease in Glucophage sales. Although sales of Glucophage XR increased over 200 percent ($14 million in 2001 to $62 million in 2002), sales were not enough to compensate for the drastic decline in Glucophage sales (see Exhibit 5 for Glucophage sales for the first quarter 2002).[11]

BMS is approaching the end of its exclusivity rights for Glucophage XR. Under the Hatch-Waxman data protection, exclusivity for Glucophage XR ends in October 2003. Generic competition with Glucophage XR would further dilute profits in the Glucophage franchise of products, which is currently one of BMS's best-selling product lines. With

---

[10]Wendy L. Bonifazi, "Hard Sell: Drug Makers Are Spending Billions on 'Direct-to-Consumer' Ads; How Effective Are the Products?" Wall Street Journal (March 25): R8.

[11]*http://www.bms.com/news/press/data/fg_press_release_2436.html.*

EXHIBIT 4 Online Coupon for Glucophage® XR

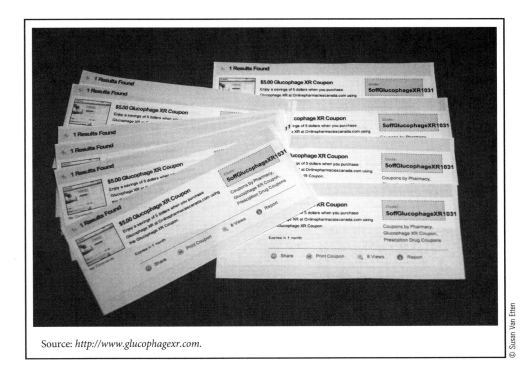

Source: *http://www.glucophagexr.com.*

© Susan Van Etten

EXHIBIT 5

Glucophage U.S. Sales, First Quarter 2001 and 2002 ($ million)

	2002	2001	% Growth
Total company sales	$2,769	$3,255	–15%
Metabolics			
Glucophage Franchise	158	551	–71%
Glucophage	64	513	–88%
Glucophage XR	62	14	443%
Glucovance	32	24	33%

Source: *www.bms.com/investors/financial–reports.*

the threat of increased competition from generic manufacturers on the horizon, on October 22, 2002, BMS announced that the FDA had approved Metaglip™, another variation of Glucophage. Metaglip was shown in clinical trials to be more effective at lowering blood sugar levels than other medications currently offered in the market. According to Peter R. Dolan, CEO and chairman of BMS, "As a leader in the field of type 2 diabetes, Bristol-Myers Squibb continues to work to develop new treatment options for the more than 17 million people in the United States with this condition. Metaglip represents an important new therapeutic choice for the management of type 2 diabetes and is a significant addition to our company's portfolio of oral anti-diabetic products, which also includes Glucovance and Glucophage XR."[12] (See Exhibit 6 for the Metaglip Web site.)

---

[12]*http://www.bms.com/news/press/data/fg_press_release_3220.html.*

EXHIBIT 6   Metaglip

Source: *http://www.bms.com.*

Discussion Questions

1. Do you think BMS's use of DTC advertising and coupon campaigns as pull strategies to promote Glucophage XR were successful? Should BMS implement another coupon program for Metaglip? Why or why not?

2. Do you think BMS's use of pull promotional strategies affected brand recognition and customer loyalty?

3. Do you think Glucophage XR sales will increase enough to offset sales lost from generic competition with Glucophage? With exclusivity on Glucophage XR running out, do you think BMS can effectively market Metaglip to offset sales lost to generic competition?

4. What is your view of DTC advertising for prescription drugs? Do you feel it is an effective means of marketing prescription drugs as compared to more traditional push strategies, such as detailing and trade show promotions? Why or why not?

5. What effects do pull strategies for prescription drugs have on the distribution channel for pharmceutical companies? How do they affect the channel relationship between health care professionals and pharmaceutical companies?

CASE 21

General Electric Company

Promotion for Gaining Distributor Selling Support

Anybody can replace a light bulb, but it takes a motivated sales rep to market the benefits of upgraded quality lighting. And that's where the growth and profits lie for General Electric Company and its lamp distributors.

To focus attention on its upscale products, GE created a pair of incentive campaigns for distributor salespeople, featuring fun themes of ups and downs: first, "Scale Mt. Sellmore ..." and then "Run the Sellmore Rapids." Distributor salespeople handle approximately 50 lines in most cases, so the campaign's goal was to catch their attention and hold a share of their minds for GE's upscale lighting products. They had five months to reach the "summit" and then a July breather before starting down the "rapids." The combination brought GE a 40 percent increase in sales of the featured products.

The twin promotions ran under the banner of "GE Lamp and Ballast Upsell Expedition." Each segment offered merchandise prizes on three plateaus to provide target sales levels for distributor reps. The salesperson could claim a prize at each level or continue climbing to reach greater value up the mountain.

At the summit, the winner's name was entered in a "The Sky's the Limit!" sweepstakes offering 50 trips to a choice of five destinations. These champion climbers also received a Mt. Sellmore brass paperweight inscribed "I Reached the Top."

At the end of the year, those who made the rapids finish line also had a chance to win vacation trips, including a Virgin Islands windjammer cruise and a Grand Canyon white-water expedition.

The promotion began in January, when Mt. Sellmore announcements, catalogs, and other materials were mailed to distributors. GE's own sales force of 300 visited distributors to pitch the program, put up posters, and hold sales meetings.

The distributor signed up its people, and they were given a sales log and claim form to order any of 12 incentive items where they qualified. To reach the first level of Mt. Sellmore, the sales rep had to sell 10 cases of the featured products. Level 2 was reached at 20 cases, and the level 3 goal was 30 cases. Backing the sales effort, sales reps had a "Try-A-Case" form to start customers on the Watt-Miser or other upscale lines.

To keep the salespeople concentrating on selling, with a minimum of paperwork, they had only to fill out the claim form listing the customer's name, invoice number, product code, and number of cases. This was verified by the GE sales rep, and no invoice copies or other records were required.

Each rep could claim up to three awards during the five-month campaign. Thus, when a salesperson sold 10 cases, he or she had to decide whether to take the incentive immediately, or continue to the next level.

Five choices were offered at level 1: a poplin jacket, knife set, binoculars, electric drill, or cordless phone. At the next plateau, the sales rep could earn a disc camera, four-piece luggage set, or a fishing kit. At the summit, a salesperson could select a wristwatch, TV, or stereo equipment.

Every time the sales rep earned a summit-level award by selling 30 cases of lamps, one sweepstakes chance was entered. Ten trips were awarded by drawings in each of five sales regions. Trips were individual, rather than in groups, and each winner could choose between Colorado, New Orleans, Las Vegas, Orlando and Disney World, or the Bahamas. Each trip was for four days and three nights, with $200 spending money thrown in.

The Mt. Sellmore climb ended on June 30, and in July the Sellmore Rapids campaign materials were in the field, ready for an August 1 start. The concept was the same, with three plateaus of merchandise prizes and a sweepstakes for a choice of adventure trips. Merchandise items were similar, and level 3 jumped to 40 cases in sales to provide bigger rewards. And now winners could earn up to five prizes instead of three, including an extra award if they completed all three rapids levels before September 12.

In both campaigns, the sales objective emphasized increased movement of the upgraded lighting products and promoted relighting, not just replacing lamps. Convincing commercial and industrial buyers that "The time is right to relight" requires creative selling by the distributor rep.

Approximately 15,000 reps were in the field, and more than 14,000 registered to participate in GE's campaign. Of this number, 3,706 of them earned awards, with many earning more than one—for a total of more than 6,200 incentives given.

GE's upscale products covered by the incentive program offered improved lighting quality and energy savings. These products were more profitable, and they accounted for about 35 percent of total sales. During the campaign, however, sales for GE's upscale lines increased on average by 40 percent over the previous year, despite heavy price competition and import pressure. More than 2.5 million of these upscale lamps were sold, while sales of standard products were flat.

The GE Lamp and Ballast Upsell Expedition was a big hit with distributors and their salespeople from the start. All the way up the mountain and down the rapids, exciting incentives kept the reps' attention on the sales objective and on the finish line.

Discussion Questions

1. What do you think accounted for the dramatic success of GE's promotion program in gaining distributor selling support? Discuss.

2. Do you think that "fun and games" are really necessary in promoting a "serious" product such as industrial lighting? Why or why not?

GENCO Supply Chain Solutions

3PL Leads in High-Tech Logistics

Background

GENCO Supply Chain Solutions is the second largest third-party logistics provider (3PL) in North America and is among the top fifty 3PLs in the world. GENCO provides a full range of logistical services to over 150 customers, including many Fortune 500 manufacturers, retailers, and U.S. government agencies. The company manages over 37 million square feet of customer warehouse space, employs over 10,000 workers, and has total revenues in excess of $1.5 billion.

GENCO has become a leader among 3PLs in the application of technology to solve its customers' logistics problems and improve efficiency. A case in point is GENCO's use of Sky-Trax's high-tech warehouse management system (WMS).

Sky-Trax Overview

Sky-Trax, founded in 2004 by three former DuPont executives, is a technology solutions provider with a unique application for streamlining warehouse operations. Its "Total-Trax®" system uses a combination of forklift-mounted hardware, warehouse location and product barcodes, and software to manage pallet picking, put away, and inventory replenishment in warehouses. Instead of traditional RF (radio frequency) scanners, digital cameras (sensors) are mounted on the top and front of a forklift truck (see Exhibit 1). The top camera is pointed up and takes pictures of barcodes mounted on the ceiling of a warehouse (optical position markers) to identify the forklift's warehouse location (see Exhibit 2). The front-mounted forklift camera (or two cameras for warehouses with a lot of double-stacked pallets) reads the product barcode on each pallet. This warehouse location and product information are then used by Sky-Trax's "OpsMan®", a visibility tool for tracking vehicles and inventory in real time, to relay information to the forklift truck drivers to ensure that the right product is being picked from or put away in the right warehouse location. The Total-Trax system provides users with the ability to have WMS-directed tasks performed without having forklift drivers' workflows interrupted by having to manually scan locations or products. Tasks are performed in a much more efficient manner with less waste because the forklift driver simply follows the onscreen commands. Since the forklift and its driver are tracked throughout the work day and in all warehouse locations, the system captures a large amount of data and produces reports that can be used for process improvement events to increase productivity, improve

EXHIBIT 1
Forklift with Sensors

Source: *Reprinted with permission of Evan Armstrong. http://www.3plogistics.com/Sky-Trax_9-2010.htm.*

inventory accuracy, and optimize operational performance. Total-Trax has been integrated with multiple WMSs and has a growing customer list (including GENCO Supply Chain Solutions).

How GENCO Uses Total-Trax

GENCO Supply Chain Solutions has been especially successful using the Total-Trax system to help manage its 200,000-square-foot Pinnacle Foods Northeast Distribution Center operation in Lemoyne, Pennsylvania. The operation runs five days a week with 12 warehouse workers split between two shifts. Approximately 20 to 25 inbound and outbound truckloads of products are processed each day. All products are palletized, and approximately 60 percent are stored in bulk floor warehouse locations; the remaining product is stored in two-high, conventional-rack storage units.

The Total-Trax system is being used on each forklift, and its OpsMan® operating system is integrated with GENCO's "D-Log PLUS" proprietary WMS.

EXHIBIT 2
Warehouse Ceiling
Position Barcodes
(Markers)

Source: *Reprinted with permission of Evan Armstrong. http://www.3plogistics.com/Sky-Trax_9-2010.htm.*

According to GENCO's Matt Stoner, who manages the operation, his forklift operators are very happy with the Total-Trax system because they no longer have to stop to scan locations and products for the WMS. Sky-Trax proactively notifies them if they are picking the wrong product or putting products away in the wrong location, so operational failures are avoided.

After deploying the Total-Trax system, Stoner saw a direct productivity increase of over 5 percent, a 12-percent increase in throughput, and was able to reduce his employee headcount by one. In 2009, the Lemoyne, Pennsylvania, warehousing operation won GENCO's Contract Logistics Facility of the Year Award.

GENCO has also been utilizing the Total-Trax system at an Atlanta reverse logistics warehouse. In the Atlanta operation, GENCO realized an 18-percent gain in pallets moved per hour after the first two days of implementing the Total-Trax system. Using current operations as a benchmark, the Atlanta operation has achieved a 47-percent productivity gain and has accomplished a 61-percent labor reduction in three main operational areas. In addition, the operation is currently running at 100-percent pallet and location inventory accuracy.

Total-Trax Technology Summary

GENCO's highly positive experience with Total-Trax has shown that this technology offers an excellent solution for applications involving high-volume, pallet-in/pallet-out warehousing operations. The fact that GENCO, as one of the world's leading 3PLs, has adopted and successfully implemented Sky-Trax's technology demonstrates that the use of high-tech systems such as Total-Trax for improving the operational efficiency of WMSs is practical and viable.

Discussion Questions

1. Why do 3PLs need to be on the leading edge in applying technology to logistics?

2. Should 3PLs be expected to develop all or most of the technology needed to improve the logistical effectiveness and efficiency of their clients?

CASE **23**

Koehring Company
Evaluating Channel Member Performance

The Koehring Company of Milwaukee manufactures and sells a broad range of construction machinery and other heavy equipment, including industrial machinery and specialty oil well hardware items. The company has 11 domestic operating divisions, each of which is responsible for its own sales, service, and product research and development.

The number of the company's divisions and its annual sales have grown in recent years, and so has the number of distributors selling Koehring products. Complicating the Koehring distribution setup is the fact that some distributors handle several of the company's construction equipment lines, while others carry only one or two lines of company manufacture.

Several years ago, the company reviewed its methods of distributor evaluation, which at the time were "subjective, irregular, and fragmentary." Routine appraisals were not a part of company procedures, and when management asked field salespeople about the performance of an individual distributor, the answer elicited often ran, "Well, they're doing all right," "They could be better," or something equally vague.

Finding this approach to distributor evaluation unsatisfactory, management decided the company needed a better and more comprehensive reporting system—namely, one that would give both the divisions and corporate headquarters better knowledge and control of distributor operations without having to wade through volumes of disorganized, subjective information. One problem of particular concern emanated from the uneven performance of many distributors: they might be doing an excellent job on certain Koehring lines, but a poor one on others. How could intelligence about such performance be effectively communicated to corporate headquarters and between divisions?

In short, an efficient evaluation procedure was called for, one that would uniformly measure distributor performance.

The Dealer Rating Form

The corporate marketing staff hit upon an answer—the "Koehring Dealer Rating Form," which provides the basis for an annual evaluation system. Exhibit 1 illustrates the form.

The key to the rating system is found in the lower half of the form and is known as the "Penetration Index." This index is computed, as the instruction sheet explains, by dividing the annual dollar value of the dealer equipment sales by the annual equipment sales quota that was assigned to the dealer at the beginning of the year. (Annual quotas assigned to dealers for each Koehring product line they carry are fixed with their advice and consent.) The penetration index is then converted into the dealer rating. (Exhibit 2 is the instruction sheet.)

To take a hypothetical example: If a dealer's annual equipment sales amount to $100,000 and an equipment sales quota was set at $110,000, then $100,000 divided by

EXHIBIT 1 Koehring
Company Dealer
Rating Form

KOEHRING COMPANY DEALER RATING FORM

Division: .... Fiscal Year: ....

Dealer Name: .... Dlr. Code No. ....

MAIN OFFICE AND BRANCHES (List main office first) State, City	Number of employees	Number of salesmen	Service facilities rating	Number of Servicemen	Quality of service rendered ratg.	Parts stock rating	Equipment stock ratg.	All product promotion rating
Total, All Branches								

Type of sales contract or products under sales franchise

Products	Exclusive	Non exclusive

Koehring Company Representation

Koeh. Div. .... Kwik-Mix ....
Schield .... Johnson ....
Parsons .... KO-CAL ....
Buf. Spr. ....

Other major accounts handled: ....

Regional representative (Name) .... Region or area no. ....
Credit rating: ....

Dealer sales, (All accounts)　　　　　**Profit**　　　　　**Net Worth**

1962 _____
1963 _____
1964 _____
1965 _____

Division Dealer Volume

	Equipment A	Parts	Total	$ Volume quota (Equipment) B	Total division dem. sales	Potential U.S. sales	Penetration Index *
					Dealer percentages		
1961							
1962							
1963							
1964							
1965							

Performance rating:

1961	1962	1963	1964	1965

Action in 1966 _____
_____
_____
_____

*Penetration Index = $\dfrac{\text{Dealer equipment sales (Column A)}}{\text{Dealer equipment sales quota (Column B)}}$

EXHIBIT 2

Instruction Sheet for Koehring Annual Dealer Rating

Theoretically, each dealer should be rated annually on his overall performance in terms of sales volume, penetration, efforts, financing, parts, services, etc. However, in actual practice such ratings tend to become subjective, thereby reducing the comparability and consistency necessary for a continuing program of distributor analysis and review. The following is a guide for making more reliable and valid objective judgments:

Method for Computing Rating

1. Fill in the required information for each dealer on the Dealer Rating Forms.

2. Compute the Penetration Index. (Divide the dollar value of column A by the dollar value of column B.)

Formula:

$$\frac{\text{Dealer Equipment Sales (Col. A)}}{\text{Dealer Equipment Sales Quota (Col. B)}}$$

An index of 1.0 indicates the dealer's attainment of his equipment dollar quota. An index value above 1.0 signifies that the dealer has exceeded his quota and any index value below 1.0 expresses the degree to which he has fallen short of his quota.

3. Assign a tentative Performance Rating to each dealer based on his Penetration Index (refer to columns I and II in the table).

4. Evaluate this rating in terms of the dealer's total performance indicated by his accomplishments of the items listed under the description for that rating in column III.

5. Adjust the rating accordingly if warranted by your evaluation of his total performance.

6. Analyze the situation and record the suggested necessary action for improving his penetration for next year.

I Penetration Index Range	II Dealer Rating Code	III Description
1.5 and over	1	Excellent—Performance in sales, penetration, efforts, financing, parts, service, etc.
1.2 to 1.4	2	Good—Performance above average in sales, penetration, efforts, financing, parts, service, etc.
0.9 to 1.1	3	Average—Performance satisfactory or average in sales, penetration, efforts, financing, parts, service, etc.
0.6 to 0.8	4	Fair—Performance below average, weak in all or most of the areas of sales, penetration, efforts, financing, parts, service, etc. and needs improvement.
0.5 or less	5	Poor—Performance unsatisfactory, requiring definite corrective action. Should be considered for cancellation.

$110,000 equals 0.909, which falls in the penetration index range of 0.9 to 1.1. A penetration figure in this range equals a dealer rating of 3, which is considered "average." Dealer ratings range from 1 (excellent) to 5 (poor).

The performance rating developed in this manner is not necessarily the final rating the distributor receives. As described in steps 4 and 5 on the instruction sheet, the computed rating is next evaluated "in terms of the dealer's total performance," so that the rating can be further adjusted if warranted.

An independent rating is prepared on each distributor for every Koehring product line represented. If two or more company lines are carried, the distributor receives independent ratings for each line; no overall rating, combining performance ratings on each line, is computed.

Ratings and Potentials

A supplementary check on the company's distributor organization is made by matching the dealer's rating with that state's construction-potential classification.

The classification by state and its use are described in an instruction sheet, as follows:

To help in reviewing and evaluating the annual dealer performance ratings on a more objective basis, each state has been classified according to its annual potential. The potential for each state is based on dollar volume expressed as a percent of the total U.S. contract awards for engineered construction projects relevant to each Koehring division.

Alphabetical potential classifications are as signed to each state based on the dollar volume awards expressed as a percentage of total U.S. construction awards for each division's category. The following key shows the range of percentages comprising each potential class:

Potential Classification	*Range of the Percent of Total U.S. Awards per Class:*
A	6% and over
B	5.0–5.9%
C	4.0–4.9
D	3.0–3.9
E	2.0–2.9
F	1.0–1.9
G	0.0–0.9

Thus, a state classified as having "A" potential would account for 6 percent or more of the dollar awards made in the country for projects most likely requiring a particular division's equipment.

Management believes that, while excellent dealers everywhere are of course desirable, states with the heaviest concentration of business should have dealers with superior performance ratings. Thus, a dealer in an "A" or "B" state achieving a performance rating of 4 or 5 would indicate that a great deal of business in that state remains untapped or, at any rate, is not falling to the company.

Ratings of distributors are carried out by district sales representatives, in conjunction with their sales managers, at least once per year.

Performance Reports

While a number of company reports are drawn, to a greater or lesser extent, from the annual dealer rating process, two are reported to be especially useful to management: U.S. Construction Equipment Dealers Performance Ratings and a summary report, Annual Dealer Ratings by Divisions.

The first report gives the performance rating for every domestic and Canadian distributor for every division in the company (Exhibit 3). The entire annual performance for any distributor may be ascertained at once; and, since the data are arranged by states and provinces, the distributor may also be measured against all colleagues in the same area. Also, the quality of any division's representation in any area is immediately apparent. The report is, in effect, a composite of all ratings of all dealers through which the products of Koehring's divisions are sold. Also shown are the two most recent years' ratings for each division on each of its distributors, giving a further quick comparison of distributor performances.

EXHIBIT 3 Koehring Company Construction Equipment Dealers' Performance Ratings

State and Dealer	B-S Road equip.	Flaherty products	Johnson products	KO-CAL products	Parsons trenchers	Parsons dumptors	Parsons loader-hoe	PCM M&MH	PCM KA-MO	Koehring products	Schield products	Thew CR. & excav.	Thew loaders
Alabama													
.... Equip. Co.	3				3	1	3		2	4			
.... Service								4	3				
.... Equip. Co.											2	2	
.... Mach. Co.						3					3	3	3
.... Tr. Co.		3 3	2 4										
Alaska													
.... Equip. Co.								3					
.... Equipment		1 2											
.... Equip.							5	5					
.... Equip. Co.			5					5	3		5	4	5
Arizona													
....		2 2											
.... Constr. Co.			*										
.... Equip. Co.											5		
..............Co.				3 3						4 5			
...........Equip. Co.							5	5 5	5				
...Machinery Co.	3 3												
.........Machy. Co.				*	*	*						2	
Arkansas													
.... Equip. Co.											4 3		
..............Machy.		3 2										4	
.......Equip.	4 4		3 3	*		4		5	1	4 4			
...........Supp.								5	4				

The second report on annual dealer ratings by divisions, in bar chart form, shows the composite quality of each division's distributor representation during the year (Exhibit 4). Of 79 dealers rated by the Schield Bantam division, the chart indicates that 5 percent of this division's dealers earned Rating 1 (excellent); 23 percent, Rating 2 (good); 40 percent, Rating 3 (average); 23 percent, Rating 4 (fair); and 9 percent, Rating 5 (poor).

The dealer ratings form the basis for supplementary reports that receive limited distribution and are for special internal use. In addition, the ratings are helpful in discussions of problem areas and problem distributors at companywide sales meetings.

The corporate marketing staff, which is responsible for all statistics, market research, and market analyses, including the annual dealer ratings, acts as a clearinghouse for divisional marketing intelligence and prepares the consolidated reports for management.

According to the company, cooperation of the sales force in filling out and sending in dealer ratings has been excellent, and the field sales force is solidly in favor of the dealer rating system.

Commenting on the pros and cons of the approach, a Koehring marketing executive points out:

There are too many variables, of course, to evaluate our distributors completely and with absolute accuracy by this mathematical method. The human element of judgment cannot be eliminated—nor should it be. We do feel, however, that we are on the right track by evaluating in this manner, in that a common denominator is achieved for all distributors by rating them all on the same basis.

EXHIBIT 4
Annual Dealer Rating Summary for the Schield Bantam Division

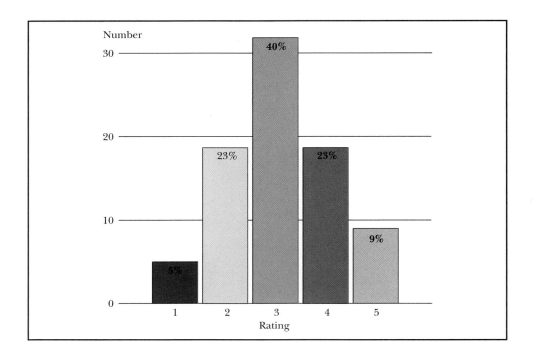

Then, and only then, may the refinements, modifications, and exceptions be noted and taken into account. In this way, the 'by gosh and by golly' sort of approach is eliminated. In general, we are most pleased with our evaluation procedures.

Discussion Question

1. Evaluate Koehring's approach to measuring channel member performance.

SESAC

Channel Design Strategy for an Intangible Service

Natasha Lee opened the market share report and she didn't like what she saw. As VP of Sales and Marketing at SESAC (pronounced see'sak) she was responsible for generating profitable revenue. But the data showed her company losing ground in the general licensing category across the United States, with market share slipping relative to industry competitors. She had heard from her chief executive that some of SESAC's best known artists and publishers were becoming uneasy with the pace of growth on the collections side. There were whispers that some might even be considering defecting to ASCAP, the largest of the industry's three performing rights organizations (PROs). It was time to take a serious look at the sales and distribution strategy for SESAC's service.

Natasha had one week to prepare an analysis of the situation for the CEO, and make a recommendation for growing the general licensing category (e.g., function halls, nightclubs, restaurants, etc.). Specifically, Natasha needed to decide whether SESAC should keep the call center that it had used for the previous 20 years, or change its channel strategy, perhaps by hiring a sales force.

Performing Rights Organizations

PROs have existed in the United States since the early 20th century. Emulating similar organizations in Europe, musicians organized an effort in the United States to protect their compositions from businesses that sold their material at a profit, giving the artist neither recognition nor reimbursement.[1] The first PRO in America was established in New York City on February 13, 1914 primarily to protect the copyrighted musical compositions of Tin Pan Alley musicians. The American Society of Composers, Authors, and Publishers (ASCAP), as it was called, counted Irving Berlin and John Philip Sousa as some of its initial members.

Today, there are three PROs operating in the United States: ASCAP, BMI, and SESAC. The PRO business model is essentially the same. The PRO collects royalties from broadcasters and venues that play music, and then distributes the money to a pool of copyright owners that have signed to its roster (see Exhibit 1).

Royalties are negotiated with each user of the copyrighted material on an individual basis. Payments are then made to affiliates (i.e., copyright owners) based on the number of plays and audience size for each song registered in the PROs library; these calculations are generally made from nationwide sampling of radio plays.

---

[1]Broadcasting & Cable (1999). It all begins with a song. 10/25/99, Vol. 129 (44), pp. 42–47.

EXHIBIT 1 Business Model of Performing Rights Organizations

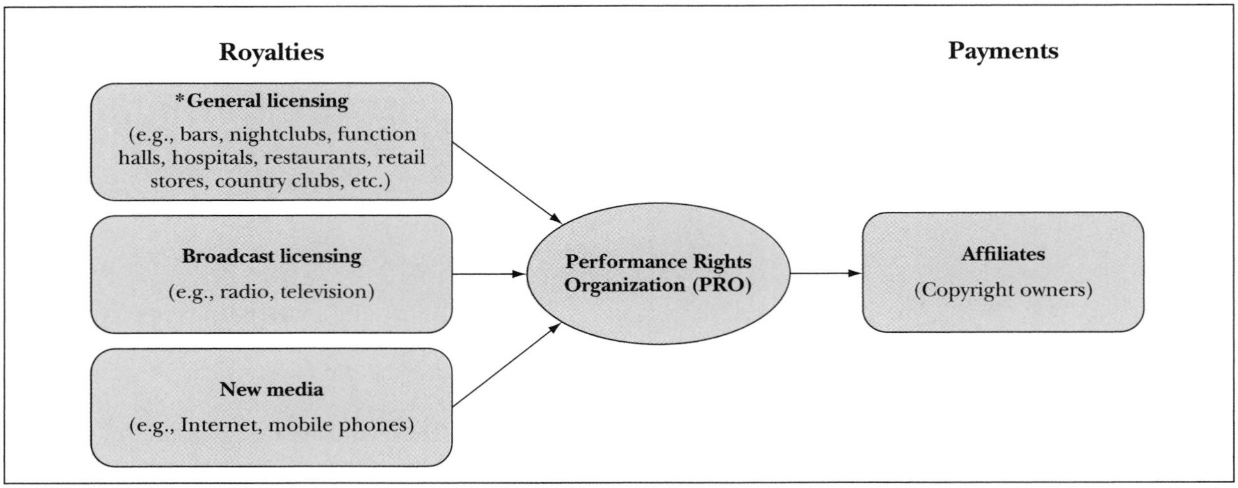

Artists must commit exclusively to one of the three PROs, but each PRO can sign as many artists, publishers, and other copyright owners as it wishes. PROs must maintain a delicate balance between expanding their roster of artists and signing venues and broadcasters. If there are too many affiliated artists, the royalties pie is split too many ways, which is unattractive to artists. But if there are too few artists, then organizations that pay royalties are reluctant to sign up, thinking that chances are slim that they are actually playing the PROs' music.

Traditionally, royalties were generated by sales of sheet music, record album sales, and radio play, but the new frontier appears to be in live performance and other nontraditional channels. It is estimated that between 50 and 75 percent of songwriters' compensation now comes from channels other than radio. For example, radio provides 35% of ASCAP's total royalties, with the majority coming from television and performance venues. At BMI, general licensing and new media licensing had grown by almost 15% since 2000, while radio royalties had fallen by almost 20% over the same period.

All individuals and businesses that play live or recorded copyrighted music are required by law to pay royalties to the copyright holder, either directly or through a PRO. Violators face penalties of up to $20,000 per infraction. Special exemptions apply to organizations such as non-profit institutions that have no admission charge, record stores, movie houses, religious organizations (during worship only), and government bodies (state and federal).

The Company

SESAC, originally called Society of European Stage Authors & Composers, is based in Nashville, Tennessee. Founded in 1930 to support European music artists in the US market, it is the smallest of the three performing rights organizations in the United States (see Exhibit 2). SESAC is a privately held enterprise that operates as a for-profit business, and it retains an undisclosed amount of performance royalty income as profit.

EXHIBIT 2 US-Based Performing Rights Organizations[2]

	Revenues (2007)	Affiliates (i.e., artists)	Employees	Web site
ASCAP	$599 million	235,000	800	www.ascap.com
BMI	$611 million	300,000	550	www.bmi.com
SESAC	$52 million	9,000	110	www.sesac.com

The company has three primary divisions which are independently responsible for generating revenues for the company: General licensing, Broadcast licensing, and New Media licensing:

- *General licensing: Sales receipts in the general licensing segment are primarily collected from entertainment venues such as restaurants, pubs, nightclubs, hospitals, and function halls. Any establishment at which patrons are charged, and music is a substantial part of the experience is legally required to pay royalties. Fees for venues are based on an algorithm that includes variables such as type of establishment, square footage, amount of live music played, and number of seats; the calculation is meant to estimate the number of people who hear music during a given week. Licensing fees can range from as little as $200 to thousands of dollars per year. Approximately one third of SESAC revenues come from the general licensing category.[3]*
- *Broadcast licensing: Music played on the airwaves is monitored primarily by a sophisticated digital tracking service called BDS (Broadcast Data Systems). SESAC generates revenues from every facet of public performance, including mainstream radio, college radio, satellite radio, Internet radio, and television.*
- *New media licensing: This division covers non-traditional channels such as Internet radio, satellite radio transmissions, and ringtones. While new media currently represents a relatively small proportion of SESAC revenue, this division is growing quickly.*

Despite SESAC's small size, company executives believe that its for-profit status affords it a competitive advantage in the industry. ASCAP and BMI are not-for-profit organizations, so they are required to accept all qualified copyright holders that apply for membership and to distribute all royalties to their affiliates (less an administrative fee). In contrast, SESAC's has fewer operating restrictions. It enticed headliners such as Neil Diamond, Bob Dylan and Bryan-Michael Cox by tailoring agreements to the needs of those artists. The same flexibility is possible when signing general licensing venues. Thus, the company's plan is not to challenge BMI and ASCAP head-to-head; rather it is to provide the best value to affiliates and licensees by being selective about the markets and segments it enters.[4]

[2]Noam, Eli M. (2009) Media Ownership and Concentration in America, Oxford University Press: New York; Krasilovsky, M. William and Sidney Schemel (2007) *This Business of Music: the Definitive Guide to the Music Industry*, 10th ed. Billboard Books: New York, NY.; Op cit., Broadcasting & Cable (1999); Stark, Phillis (2004) *Changing of the guard at SESAC*, Billboard, 6/12/2004, Vol. 116 (24).

[3]Op cit., Krasilovsky and Schemel (2007) *This Business of Music.*

[4]Stooksbury, Cindy (1995) SESAC third player in music licensing. *Amusement Business*, 9/11/1995, Vol. 107, Issue 37.

EXHIBIT 3 Number of Establishments in United States for Select Categories[5]

Category	Number of Establishments (designated as taxable by US census)
Full-service restaurants	195,659
Drinking places (pubs, taverns, nightclubs)	48,856
Hotels & motels (except casino hotels)	46,295
Colleges & universities	38,299
Health & fitness centers	17,866
Golf courses & country clubs	8,546
Bowling centers	5,590
Theater companies, & dinner theaters	1,600
Skiing facilities	379

General Licensing

The general licensing division of SESAC has a wide array of licensees. The size of SESAC's library is the smallest of the industry; nonetheless, it has a sufficient number so that it would be difficult for an establishment that played music frequently to avoid hitting SESAC material. In practical terms, this means that nearly every venue in America could be a paying customer. Jazz, Latin, and Christian music venues are even more likely to play SESAC music. Exhibit 3 shows the number of establishments in key potential business segments.

SESAC typically charges between $400–$1000 per year for unlimited use of all SESAC material at a single location; the average price of a SESAC general license is just under $600. Some businesses (e.g., retail stores) play background music in a way that is barely noticeable, while others (e.g., dance clubs) feature music as their raison d'être. SESAC tries to reflect these sorts of differences in their calculations. The company believes strongly that if an establishment profits from the use of copyrighted materials, it should be responsible for paying music copyright fees. However, SESAC prides itself on eschewing the adversarial "pay-us-or-we'll-sue-you" position that ASCAP had been accused of taking in the past. SESAC wants to build a relationship with licensees—a relationship built on mutual benefit. A reasonable fee can be worked out when licensees understand the value that SESAC songs can bring them.

Two Options for Channel Structure

Call Center Channel

For the past 20 years, SESAC has operated a call center in order to develop the general licensing program. There are currently 35 full-time employees working in the center. The system is simple. Leads are generated by purchasing lists of establishments in entertainment related industries, such as pubs. Leads can be inputted automatically into the database and set on "active" status. This means that a direct mail piece is generated automatically and sent to the establishment telling the prospect that a representative will be calling to answer questions and arrange for payment of money owed based on

---

[5]US Census, 2002, www.census.gov.

the characteristics of each establishment. In order for a lead to become active it has to be assigned to a call center member. Each caller is given 500 accounts to work on at any one time. When a customer account is successfully contracted as a licensee, the next lead in the queue is assigned to whoever closes the account, and the corresponding direct mail piece is sent out. The caller's database automatically alerts him or her that the mailing needs to be followed-up with a call in a timely fashion. In the event that a caller finds it impossible to secure an agreement from an establishment, he or she can terminate an account with the approval of a supervisor. This is a source of numerous disputes between callers and supervisors since it is quite difficult to secure a sale and callers are always eager for fresh leads.

Many of SESAC's affiliates are artists that are concerned with their reputation. SESAC takes its responsibility as a representative of affiliates very seriously. A sales manager is assigned to control quality for all calls. Calls are recorded at random and monitored to ensure that callers act with courtesy and professionalism. Scripts are used in order to guide callers through conversations with prospects. These scripts have phrases of introduction, answers to frequently asked questions, and suggestions on ways to close a sale.

Each quarter, the call center manages to sign 8% of all open leads on average, although rates of individual callers vary considerably. It generally takes about 3 months from the moment that a lead is assigned to the time that a contract is signed. There are three reasons why it is difficult to close sales.

- *Managers at establishments that play music are exceedingly difficult to reach. Many primarily use their cellular phone which may not be registered and others are protected by gatekeepers who keep undesirable callers from getting through. Moreover, some managers view royalties as a non-revenue generating expense and avoid calls from SESAC call center.*
- *The service is difficult to explain to managers. It may require a phone conversation and several letters just to assure prospects that SESAC is a legitimate business representing artists that are entitled to royalties. Establishments that are already paying ASCAP and BMI may think that this absolves them from contracting with SESAC as well (most establishments must sign with all three PROs to get full coverage).*
- *Suing establishments is not a credible threat. Although SESAC is legally entitled to file suit against establishments that infringe on copyright laws, the company tries to avoid this path at all costs. SESAC does not want to be seen as attempting to strong-arm small businesses since it could result in a public backlash against SESAC and its affiliates.*

Most callers have some experience in other telemarketing jobs, but very few have college degrees or experience in the recording or hospitality industries. Employees working in the call center are paid just under $15 per hour and usually work an eight hour shift from 11:00am-7:00pm. Each employee is expected to make at least fifteen calls per hour.

Sales Force Channel

The call center channel had operated of for years and Natasha was hesitant to propose a change that might mean a significant investment in time and money for SESAC. Nevertheless, she wondered whether sales might pick up with a decentralized sales force in local markets. An arrangement like this would give individuals more freedom to contact whomever they wished without the burden of scripts or monitoring. She thought that a more professional sales force might have greater success with the difficult clients that are found in the hospitality business. Her calculations suggest that with a portfolio of around 500 leads a professional sales person could probably convert about 15% each quarter. This translated to 75 accounts per quarter per sales rep on average.

Of course, sales people would have to be compensated at a considerably higher rate than call center employees, eroding margins. Professional sales people demanded a salary of between $60,000 and $150,000 depending on experience. A 50% commission on first year revenues of newly acquired customers would be consistent with norms for sales people compensation.

Hiring sales consultants on a commission basis might actually lower SESAC's overhead. For field-based sales consultants, $150,000 per quarter would cover an experienced sales manager and training of new field-agents. In contrast, fixed costs for the call center reached $250,000 (not including wages) per quarter; this includes renting the space, maintain the telephone system, and paying managers to monitor callers. All othe costs were comparable for either scenario.

The Decision

General licensing presented a substantial opportunity for revenue growth, but SESAC's coverage of venues was still quite spotty. It was essential to increase the base of licensed clients in order to balance the steady growth of affiliates. A good decision could put SESAC in an enviable position as successful company in an industry with strong cash flows. The wrong decision could do irreparable harm to the company's standing as respectable player in the industry.

Natasha's needed to decide:

- *Should SESAC keep the centralized call center channel or move to a field-based sales force channel model?*
- *What are the benefits and risks of remaining with the call center channel?*
- *What are the benefits and risks of moving to a sales force channel model?*

Discussion Questions

1. What other channel strategies might be appropriate here besides a direct field sales force channel structure or the call center channel structure?

2. Given the intangible nature of the service provided by a PRO such as SESAC, are there any channel strategies or tactics that might help to tangibilize the service?

CASE 25

TESCO

Channel Design for a New Market

Background

TESCO, a British grocery and general merchandise retailer, is the fourth largest retailer in the world in terms of sales, after U.S.-based Wal-Mart, French-based Carrefour, and German-based Metro. TESCO currently has operations in 14 countries in Europe, Asia, and North America. For the fiscal year ending February 2011, TESCO had sales of over $105.6 billion, generated a profit of almost $6 billion (before tax), had 103.6 million sq. ft. of retail space, and 5,380 stores. More than two-thirds of TESCO's profits come from markets outside the United Kingdom.

TESCO operates several store formats that are designed to cater to the needs of different consumer segments: (1) TESCO Extra: large, out-of-town hypermarkets selling both food and non-food items (the stores often have a café); (2) TESCO Supercenters: large supermarkets selling both food and non-food items; (3) TESCO Metro: stores located mainly in city centers and the inner city; (4) TESCO Express: neighborhood convenience shops selling primarily food items (these stores are located in city centers as well as small residential areas and small towns); (5) One-stop, convenience stores, the smallest TESCO stores with an average area of 1,500 sq. ft. (142 sq. m.); and (6) TESCO Homeplus: warehouse-style stores that sell a variety of non-food items.

TESCO, as a multi-channel retailer, also seeks to expand its online retail business in order to make shopping more convenient for consumers. According to TESCO's 2011 Annual Report, the firm's key strategic priorities are: (1) grow its U.K. business, (2) be an outstanding international retailer in stores and online, and (3) grow retail services in all their markets. TESCO's core mission is to "create value for customers to earn their lifetime loyalty."[1]

TESCO has penetrated a large number of countries in its desire to be among the world's leading retail powers. In most countries where it operates, TESCO tailors its stores to local conditions by taking into consideration local consumption habits, tastes, and preferences. TESCO believes that in order to provide superior value to its customers, it should use advice and insights provided by its local management teams regarding such factors as store design, merchandise selection, product pricing, and in-store promotions.[2] For example, in its South Korean stores, TESCO sells fresh food as well as home appliances, clothes, toys, books, and golf items to fit local consumers' expectations.

---

[1]http://ar2011.tescoplc.com/

[2]Ibid.

EXHIBIT 1 Exterior of TESCO Fresh & Easy

Source: *ZUMA Wire Service/Alamy*

In addition, in TESCO's Seoul stores, customers can buy a pet iguana, pick an octopus from a tank of live seafood, and even take ballet lessons.[3]

TESCO's Initial U.S. Entry

Prior to entering the U.S. market, TESCO spent considerable time learning about U.S. consumption behavior. The British retailer collected data on many aspects of American life. TESCO not only conducted focus groups and surveys, but also sent some of its executives to live with American families in order to better understand the American way of life. The "observers poked around in [consumers'] kitchen cupboards" and watched people cook and shop.[4] After its extensive market research, TESCO decided against opening large store formats such as hypermarkets and supermarkets that were already prevalent in the United States. Instead, TESCO decided to open smaller stores called Fresh & Easy neighborhood markets (the exterior of the TESCO Fresh & Easy stores can be seen in Exhibit 1). In 2007, TESCO opened its first Fresh & Easy convenience stores in three western states: Arizona, Nevada, and California.[5] By 2011, there were approximately 200 Fresh & Easy stores in the United States. The stores offer lower prices than supermarkets (the Fresh & Easy stores promise everyday low prices) and sell locally sourced fruits and vegetables that are wrapped in plastic trays or separated in bags (see Exhibit 2), but the product assortment in the Fresh & Easy stores is somewhat limited because the stores sell only about 3,500 SKUs vs. 60,000 in a typical supermarket. In addition, Fresh & Easy stores are 10,000 sq. ft., compared to around 60,000 sq. ft. of a

---

[3]Coe, N. M. & Y.-S. Lee, (2006). The Strategic Localization of Transnational Retailers: The Case of Samsung-Tesco in South Korea, *Economic Geography*, 82 (1), 61–88.

[4]http://www.economist.com/node/9358986

[5]http://www.csdecisions.com/2011/08/04/fresh-easy-express-to-hit-california/

EXHIBIT 2 TESCO Fresh & Easy Fresh Fruits and Vegetables Assortment

Source: *ZUMA Wire Service/Alamy*

regular supermarket. The Fresh & Easy stores also offer a wide variety of cooked meals and natural products. Fresh & Easy's private label products do not contain preservatives, artificial flavors, or trans fats. The eggs sold in the stores are from cage-free chickens, and milk does not contain the growth hormone rbST. TESCO Fresh & Easy stores also work with an accredited master of wine who partners with local vineyards to develop 60 specially selected wines. These wines are sold exclusively at Fresh & Easy stores.[6]

In terms of store layout, the shelves in the Fresh & Easy stores are low, so customers can see from one end of the store to the other. The aisles in the stores are wide enough to fit three carts passing at the same time. There are no cashiers in the stores; all lanes are self-checkout. Additionally, consumers cannot redeem manufacturer coupons in Fresh & Easy stores. Finally, Fresh & Easy stores operate mainly in markets underserved by regular supermarkets and target consumers of a variety of income groups.[7] For example, in Phoenix, Arizona, TESCO opened stores in some of the poorest parts of the city where the median annual household income is just a little over $37,000 (compared to median annual household income of $44,000 in the United States). On the other hand, in Chandler, Arizona, the British retailer opened stores in neighborhoods where the median annual household income is $93,000.[8] TESCO Fresh & Easy does not advertise on TV or in newspapers. When a new Fresh & Easy store opens in a given neighborhood, $5 coupons are mailed to residents living in the area.[9]

---

[6]http://www.reuters.com/article/2008/03/03/idUS230112+03-Mar-2008+PRN20080303

[7]http://www.reuters.com/article/2009/05/20/us-tesco-idUSTRE54J44S20090520

[8]http://www.economist.com/node/9358986

[9]http://www.usatoday.com/money/industries/food/2008-04-06-tesco-fresh-easy_N.htm

TESCO's U.S. Performance

Fresh & Easy stores have not performed as well as TESCO had hoped. In fact, TESCO has experienced significant losses in the United States. During the 2010–2011 fiscal year alone, TESCO lost about $303 million. TESCO attributed a large portion of this loss to the purchase of two fresh-food suppliers in the United States, but the retailer is still struggling to appeal to U.S. consumers. Consumers who have shopped in Fresh & Easy stores actually admit that they "just don't get this place." One Fresh & Easy customer even pointed out that:

> *It's like the place was designed by a bunch of Dilberts. … It's as if the place purports to solve all kinds of vexing marketing "problems" while failing to address the most basic of real world problem(sic). Namely, why would anyone even want to come here to begin with?*[10]

It seems that TESCO's desire to change the way people shop was not well accepted by American consumers and that consumers were somewhat skeptical about shopping in a new (for them) store format. So, in a sense, Fresh & Easy stores are "fresh, but far from easy," at least in the eyes of American consumers.[11]

Despite the disappointing results in the United States, TESCO believes that it will be able to revive its U.S. operations. In a financial statement released to the public in April 2011, TESCO noted that "… our clear objective now is to accelerate strong growth in customer numbers.…"[12] As a result, TESCO has decided to improve the atmospherics in its Fresh & Easy stores by placing wooden flooring and flower stands at entrances and by better displaying fresh products.[13] It also launched a "clip-strip" cross-merchandising program in its stores by offering general merchandise products such as kitchen gadgets and cookware on plastic "clips" next to grocery shelf strips throughout the stores. Clip-strips, long plastic or metal strips with clips, are used for product display in retail stores. The purpose of a clip-strip is to stimulate impulse sales by cross-merchandising related items and to increase the dollar amount spent by consumers on each trip to the store.[14]

TESCO also plans to implement its Clubcard loyalty scheme, which allows customers to earn a point for every dollar spent in the stores. Once customers become members of TESCO's Clubcard, they will also receive personalized email and coupons.[15]

TESCO's Next Step

In a desire to find a "winning formula" for its U.S. operations, TESCO has decided to open smaller convenience stores called Fresh & Easy Express.[16] Although TESCO is planning on keeping its primary focus on its Fresh & Easy stores, it has decided to add the Fresh & Easy Express stores as a secondary format.[17] The first Fresh & Easy Express store was opened in Los Angeles, California, in November 2011. The Fresh & Easy Express stores are about 4,000 sq. ft. TESCO hopes to expand its customer base by reaching neighborhoods where the opening of its standard Fresh & Easy 10,000-sq.-ft.

---

[10]http://www.hartman-group.com/hartbeat/tesco-fresh-easy-finally-comes-clean

[11]http://www.economist.com/node/9358986

[12]http://fastfood.ocregister.com/2011/04/19/fresh-easy-continues-to-lose-millions/93135/

[13]http://www.guardian.co.uk/business/2011/aug/03/tesco-fresh-and-easy-us-chain-to-trial-express-format/

[14]http://freshneasybuzz.blogspot.com/2011/05/tesco-fresh-easy-neighborhood-market_03.html

[15]http://www.usatoday.com/money/industries/food/2008-04-06-tesco-fresh-easy_N.htm

[16]http://www.guardian.co.uk/business/2011/aug/03/tesco-fresh-and-easy-us-chain-to-trial-express-format/

[17]http://freshneasybuzz.blogspot.com/2011/07/first-4000-square-foot-fresh-easy.html

stores is not possible. Brendan Winnacott, a spokesperson for Fresh & Easy Neighborhood Market, notes that:

We are always looking to serve more neighborhoods and in order to open stores in more communities we are going to be trialing a handful of small stores called Fresh & Easy Express.[18]

TESCO has used its smaller TESCO Express format in the United Kingdom as well as other European countries and has decided that it can implement some of the TESCO Express store features in its Fresh & Easy Express stores in the United States. The stores will sell groceries and alcohol.[19] According to Mr. Winnacott, the Fresh & Easy Express stores "will have all the things that our customers have come to love ... in a smaller format."[20]

TESCO has struggled with its U.S. operations even though it conducted extensive market research prior to entering the country. The British retailer's new Fresh & Easy marketing channel so far does not seem to be meeting the needs and expectations of U.S. consumers. So, despite TESCO's experience in doing business internationally and its proven ability to adjust its store formats to local markets, TESCO has been unable to replicate this success in the U.S. market. Hence, retail analysts keep asking the question: "What is tripping TESCO in the United States?" TESCO executives are also trying to answer this question in order to improve the retailer's U.S. performance.

Discussion Questions

1. Why do you think TESCO's Fresh & Easy stores have not been successful in the United States?

2. What should the British retailer have done to improve its U.S. operations prior to opening the Fresh & Easy Express stores?

3. Do you think that by opening the Fresh & Easy Express stores, TESCO will finally be able to appeal to U.S. consumers? Why or why not?

[18]http://www.ft.com/intl/cms/s/0/c2834256-bdd6-11e0-babc-00144feabdc0.html#axzzla2DbH4KA

[19]http://www.ft.com/intl/cms/s/0/c2834256-bdd6-11e0-babc-00144feabdc0.html#axzzla2DbH4KA; http://freshneasybuzz.blogspot.com/2011/07/first-4000-square-foot-fresh-easy.html

[20]http://articles.coastlinepilot.com/2011-09-19/news/tn-cpt-0923-freshandeasy-20110919_1_laguna-niguel-brendan-wonnacott-crown-valley-parkway

Acknowledgments

Case 1.   This case was written by Bert Rosenbloom, Rauth Professor of Marketing Management, LeBow College of Business, Drexel University. Reproduced by permission.

Case 2.   This case was prepared by Boryana Dimitrova, Doctoral Candidate in Marketing, LeBow College of Business, Drexel University. Reproduced by permission.

Case 3.   This case was prepared by Dee Clark, Director, Small Business Development Center, State University of New York at Plattsburgh. Reproduced by permission.

Case 4.   This case was prepared by Professor Yasuo Doi, Hannan University, Osaka, Japan. Reproduced by permission.

Case 5.   From Talarzyk. Cases for Analysis in Marketing, 2e, pp. 91–95. Copyright 1981 South-Western, a part of Cengage Learning, Inc. Reproduced by permission. www.cengage.com/permissions

Case 6.   This case was prepared by Nancy J. Church, Distinguished Service Professor of Marketing, State University of New York at Plattsburgh. Reproduced by permission.

Case 7.   This case was written by Joyce A. Young, Ph.D., Professor of Marketing, College of Business, Indiana State University. Reproduced by permission

Case 8.   This case was prepared by Laura A. Peraccio and Jeanne A. Kierman under the direction of Erin M. Anderson, Professor of Marketing at INSEAD (Fontaine-bleu, France). Reproduced by permission.

Case 9.   This case was prepared by Dennis J. Low, graduate assistant, and Joyce A. Young, Associate Professor of Marketing, Indiana State University. Reproduced by permission.

Case 10.   This case was prepared by Dave Birgham, Gerry Boccuti, Shawn Buchanan, Mark Chando, Denise Gabinski, and Mike Tate, students at Drexel University, in cooperation with Bert Rosenbloom, Professor of Marketing, Drexel University. Reproduced by permission.

Case 11.   Philip Kotler, Marketing Management: Analysis, Planning and Control, 3rd ed., pp. 507–508. Copyright © 1976. Printed and electronically reproduced by permission of Pearson Education, Inc. Upper Saddle River, New Jersey.

Case 12.   This case was prepared by Dr. Bert Rosenbloom, Professor of Marketing, Drexel University.

Case 13.   This case was written by Bert Rosenbloom, Rauth Professor of Marketing Management, LeBow College of Business, Drexel University.

Case 14.   This case was adapted from "American Olean Spurs Tile Sales with Incentives," in Incentive Casebook (Union, NJ: National Premium sales executives Inc. 1989).

Case 15.   This case was prepared by Prof. Dr. Thomas Rudolph, Director, Gottlieb Duttweiler Chair of International Retail Management, Institute of Marketing and Retailing, University of St. Gallen, Switzerland. Reproduced by permission.

Case 16.   Reprinted with permission from Franchised Distribution by E. Patrick McGuire, Conference Board Report No. 523 (New York: The Conference Board). © 2010, The Conference Board, Inc. Reproduced by permission.

Case 17.   This case updated and revised by Robyn Rosenbloom. Previously prepared by Heather Frey, Belinda Goldshine, Kimberly C. Rangniro, Patricia Jasmin, T. Ryan Schish, and Joe Morgan, students at Drexel University, in cooperation with Bert Rosenbloom, Professor of Marketing.

Case 18.   This case was written by Bert Rosenbloom, Rauth Professor of Marketing Management, LeBow College of Business, Drexel University.

Case 19.   This case was written by Bert Rosenbloom, Rauth Chair Professor of Marketing, LeBow College of Business, Drexel University.

Case 20.   This case was prepared by Nicole Erard-Coupe, MBA student at Drexel University, Research Assistant for Dr. Bert Rosenbloom.

Case 21.   This case was adapted from "GE Promotes Relighting with Sales Incentive Offer," in Incentive Casebook (Union, NJ: National Premium Sales Executives Inc., 1989), S1b. Reproduced by permission.

Case 22.   This case is based on Armstrong & Associates Inc. case study "3PLs Increase Productivity with Sky-Trax New Castle, DE, Lemoyne, PA", by Evan Armstrong, President of Armstrong Associates.

Case 23.   Reproduced with permission from Selecting and Evaluating Distributors, by Roger M. Pegram, Business Policy Study No. 116 (New York: The Conference Board, 1965). © 2010, The Conference Board, Inc. Reproduced by permission.

Case 24.   This case was written by Daniel Korschun, Assistant Professor of Marketing, LeBow College of Business, Drexel University. Reproduced by permission.

Case 25.   This case was written by Boryana Dimitrova, Doctoral Candidate in Marketing, LeBow College of Business, Drexel University.

Name Index

Hulman, A. Jr., 553
Hult, A. M., 262n15, 378
Hult, G. T., 377n34
Hult, T. M., 262n15
Hulu, 5, 236, 245, 251
Hunt, K. A., 116n21, 119n23, 133n70, 261n13
Hunt, S. D., 112n5, 132n65
Hussain, D., 449n7
Hutchinson, W. M., 380n37
Hutt, M. D., 180n3
Hy-Vee, 58
Hyatt Legal Services, 496, 514
Hyde Athletic Industries, 297–298
Hyde Industrial Chemicals, 544
Hyde-Phillip Chemical Company, 524, 544–547

I

IBM (International Business Machines), 37, 94, 102, 199, 438, 503, 532, 600
Iglesias, V., 225n26
Ignacio, L., 225n26
Ihlwan, M., 269n43
IKEA, 61, 87
IMS Health Consulting Firm, 609
Independent Grocers' Alliance (IGA), 83
Infiniti, 601
Ingene, C. A., 319n2
Ingles Markets, 60
Inlow, N. S., 99, 99n60
Innovative Toys Inc., 524, 572–579
INSEAD, 642
Insight-Express, 609
Inter Continental Hotels Group PLC, 412
Intermerc, Inc., 524
International Association of Plastics Distributors, 217
International Game Technologies (IGT), 505
International Speedway Corporation (ISC), 553–555
Iocobucci, D., 344n15
Ireland, L. C., 438n45
Irwin, R. D., 151n2
Ishida, C., 461n34
Ivie, R. M., 376n30
Iyer, G., 319n2

J

J. C. Penney Company, Inc., 56, 63, 89, 302, 525–531
Jackson, A., 220n14, 461n35
Jackson, D. M., 43, 43n12
Jackson, D. W. Jr., 11n23, 16n30, 123n34, 183n10, 196n41, 266n30, 266n33
Jacobs, L., 502n2
Jacobson Companies, 70
Jaguar Cars Ltd., 298, 389
Janakiraman, R., 437n43
Janiszewski, C., 433n30

Jannarone, J., 83n21, 258
Jargon, J., 78n8, 303n32, 307n39
Jasmin, P., 643
J.D. Power & Associates, Inc., 153, 156, 164, 298, 601
Jefferson Industries, 141
Jenkins, H. W. Jr., 490n13
Jennings, M. M., 98n58
Jenny Craig International, 448
Jensen, S., 30
Jeter, D., 351
J.H. Collectibles, 358
Jobs, S., 155, 337
John, G., 166n38, 200n52
John Paul Mitchell Systems, Inc., 231
Johnson, D. S., 419n3
Johnson, J. C., 375n28
Johnson, J. L., 105, 133n72, 166n36, 269n42, 505n18, 565
Johnson, R., 84n25, 112n3, 130n53, 448n5, 459n30
Johnson & Johnson (J&J), 314
Johnston, L., 141
Jones, G. W., 342n7
Jones Apparel Group Inc., 129, 174, 231, 331
Jones New York, 302
Josar, D., 554n9
Joshi, A. W., 201n54, 269n40
Jussaume, R. A. Jr., 229n31

K

Kabadayi, S., 8n12, 182n7
Kahn, B. F., 245n17
Kale, S. H., 513n35
Kallyanam, K., 437n43
Kalwani, M. U., 396n6
Kalyanam, K., 281n64
Kamar, V., 75n1
Kamen, J., 329n20
Kamins, M. A., 293n8
Kanaley, R., 161n25
Kane, Y. I., 98n56, 155n12
Kannam, P. K., 293n7, 437n43
Kaplan, A. M., 430n25
Kapoor, A., 296n17
Kasualis, J. J., 132n62, 344n15, 354n37
Katsikeas, C. S., 513n40
Kaufmann, P. J., 100n62, 114n13, 196n44, 449n7, 453n20, 495n24
Kavi, S., 515n49
Kay's Kloset, 100
Keegan, W. J., 502n3
Keen, C., 486n6
Keenan, F., 274n51
Keith, J. E., 11n23, 123n34, 183n10, 266n30, 266n33
Keller, S. B., 377n35, 396n5
Kelley, S. W., 112n7, 259n3
Kellogg Company, 343
Kelly, C., 196n41

Kelly, E. J., 197n46, 198
Kelly, J. P., 486n4
Kelly, J. S., 122n32, 248n34
Kelly, L., 236n4
Kelly, M., 93
Kendall, B., 101n64
Kenderdine, J. M., 299n24, 344n15, 354n37
Kennedy, A., 100
Kennedy, K., 33
Kennedy, P., 611
Kentucky Fried Chicken (KFC), 237
Kenyon, G., 367n8
Kerin, R. A., 342n7
Kesmodel, D., 180n2, 326n12–13, 332n27, 343n11
Ketchen, D. J. Jr., 377n34, 378
Kharif, O., 419n4, 432n29
Kierman, J. A., 642
Kim, J., 509n26
Kim, K., 131n57, 133n74, 277n57
Kim, N., 342n2
Kim, S. Y., 342n3
Kimberly-Clark Corporation, 248
King, R. L., 85n28, 168n43, 397n12
Kingshott, R. P. J., 112n7, 229n31
Kinney Shoe Corporation, 103
Kirpalani, V. H., 506n21, 508n25
Kirsh, T., 557
Kistner, L. J., 151n3
Kiwi, 303
Klein, D. M., 42n8, 396n5
Klein, S., 200n52, 502n6, 514n43
Kleinberg, E. M., 262n18
Knapp, J., 85n30
Knight, A., 561–562
Kocas, C., 319n2
Kochan, T. A., 113n11
Koder, P., 204
Koehring Company, 524, 621–626
Kohl's Corporation, 56, 64, 247, 302
Konica Minolta Business Solutions, 11–12
Kopp, R. J., 344n15
Korshun, D., 643
Kosenko, R., 513n37
Kotler, P., 151n1, 203n64–65, 249n41, 367n1, 367n3, 407n27, 642
Kovar, J. F., 262n17
Kraft Foods Inc., 187, 258, 295, 343, 352
Krantz, J., 353
Krapfel, R. E. Jr., 132n61, 376, 376n32
Krasilovsky, M. W., 629n2–3
Kreindler, P., 6n9
Kroff, F., 502n2, 504n12
Kroger Co., 55, 115, 295
Kroll, K. M., 433n31
Kumar, N., 124n40, 124n43
Kumar, S., 367n8
Kumar, V., 5n6, 85n28, 151n3, 428n23
Kung, M., 420n7
Kurtz, D. L., 12n24, 299n25, 367n5

Subject Index